The Almanac
of American
Education
2019

The Almanac of American Education

2019

11th Edition
Edited by Hannah Anderson Krog

Bernan Press

Lanham, MD

Published in the United States of America
by Bernan Press, a wholly owned subsidiary of
The Rowman & Littlefield Publishing Group, Inc.
4501 Forbes Boulevard, Suite 200
Lanham, Maryland 20706

Bernan Press
800-462-6420
www.rowman.com

ISBN: 978-1-64143-363-1
E-ISBN: 978-1-64143-364-8

∞™ The paper used in this publication meets the minimum requirements of American National
Standard for Information Sciences—Permanence of Paper for Printed Library Materials,
ANSI/NISO Z39.48-1992.

Manufactured in the United States of America.

Contents

Tables

PART A—NATIONAL EDUCATION STATISTICS

ENROLLMENT TABLES

HISTORICAL ENROLLMENT TABLES

ATTAINMENT TABLES

PART C—COUNTY EDUCATION STATISTICS

Figures

PART C—COUNTY EDUCATION STATISTICS

Preface

The Almanac of American Education serves as a guide to understanding and comparing the quality of education at the national, state, and county levels. Compiled from sources such as the U.S. Census Bureau and the National Center for Education Statistics (NCES), *The Almanac* contains historical and current data, insightful analysis, and useful graphics that paint a compelling picture of the state of education in the United States.

The 11th edition of the *Almanac* includes tables updated from the 10th edition alongside several new tables and figures.

The Almanac is organized into three sections: Part A—National Education Statistics; Part B—Region and State Education Statistics; and Part C—County Education Statistics. Most of the data presented in Part A are no longer available in print form from the Census Bureau. Additional tables in Part A are excerpted from the *Digest of Education Statistics* from the NCES, providing an overview of higher education in the United States. The data in Parts B and C have been specially tabulated for this publication from data obtained from the NCES, the Census Bureau, and other sources.

The Almanac's content allows users to ask—and answer—important questions about historic and current trends in U.S. education, including:

- What are the nationwide trends in earnings by educational attainment level?

- Is the earnings gap between high-school graduates and college graduates growing or shrinking?
- Which states have the highest and lowest high school dropout rates?
- Is there a relationship between childhood poverty rates and state-level expenditures per student?
- Which states have the largest county-to-county variation in high-school graduation rates?

The data in this volume meet the publication standards of the federal statistical agencies from which they were obtained. Every effort has been made to select accurate, meaningful, and useful data. All statistical data are subject to error arising from sampling variability, reporting errors, incomplete coverage, imputation, and other causes. The responsibility of the editors and publisher of this volume is limited to reasonable care in the reproduction and presentation of data obtained from established sources.

Hannah Anderson Krog has edited several previous titles for Bernan Press including *State Profiles: The Population and Economy of Each U.S. State* and *Patterns of Economic Change.* She earned her bachelor of arts in journalism from the University of Maryland.

Much appreciation is due to the federal agency personnel who prepared the original data and generously responded to our requests for assistance.

PART A
NATIONAL EDUCATION STATISTICS

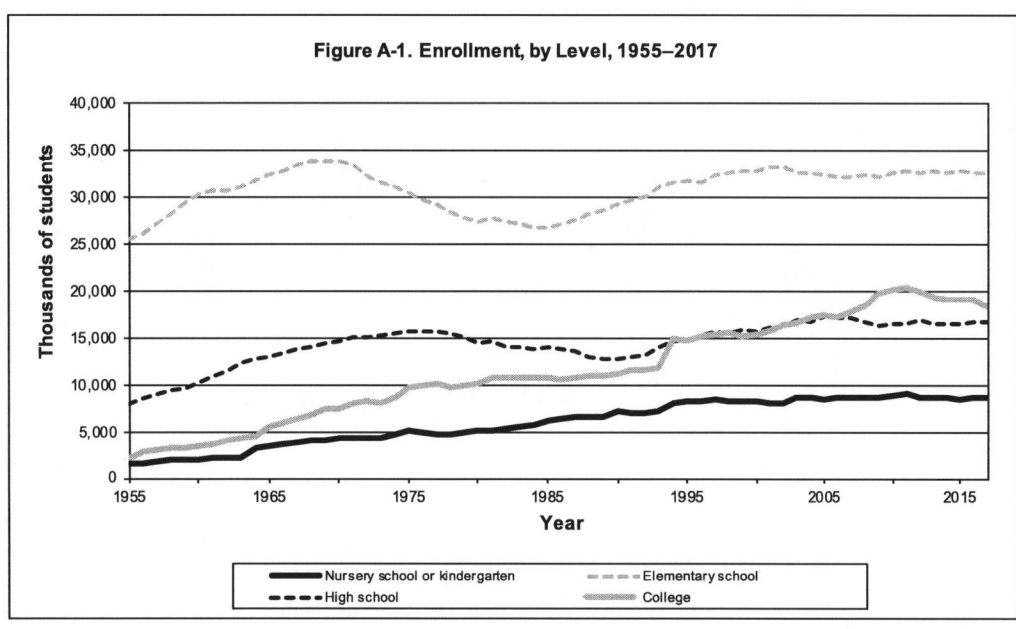

Figure A-1. Enrollment, by Level, 1955–2017

More than 76 million people were enrolled in school in 2017. Total school enrollment decreased in the late 1970s and early 1980s, but it began to rise again by 1985. Enrollment peaked in 2011, with more than 79 million students enrolled in school. Enrollment has declined since then, a trend that continued in 2017. College enrollment decreased in 2017 after a small increase in 2016, which had followed four years of decreased enrollment. Elementary school enrollment has remained between 32.0 and 33.2 million since 1997, similar to the baby boom levels of the 1960s but never quite reaching the 33.9 million elementary school enrollees of 1970. High-school enrollment in 2017 saw a slight increase for the second year in a row, with 173,000 more students enrolled than in 2016. College enrollment decreased by 798,000 students from 2016 to 2017, with private colleges experiencing a greater decrease than public colleges (633,000 fewer students and 165,000 fewer students, respectively). (Table A-10)

In 2017, 24.7 percent of people age 3 years and over were enrolled in school. For the population 3 to 4 years old, 53.8 percent were enrolled in nursery school or kindergarten, and 46.2 percent were not enrolled in school. Among the population 18 to 24 years old, 47.0 percent were enrolled in school (40.4 percent enrolled in college), as were 12.1 percent of 25 to 29 year olds. The proportion of 30 to 44 year olds enrolled in school was 4.3 percent. (Table A-1)

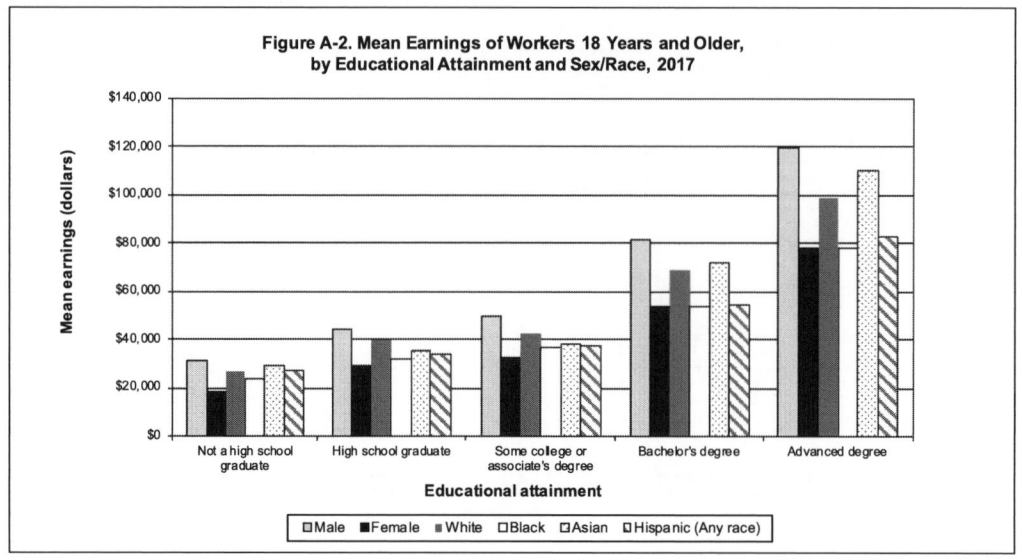

Figure A-2. Mean Earnings of Workers 18 Years and Older, by Educational Attainment and Sex/Race, 2017

In 2017, the wage gap between males and females age 18 years and older was seen for all levels of educational attainment. The largest gap was between males and females without a high-school diploma: the mean earnings of females without a high-school diploma were 40.4 percent less than the mean earnings of males without a high-school diploma ($18,885 versus $31,688). (Table A-34)

In 2017, the median annual earnings for men 25 years old and over was $45,256; for women it was $27,709, with half of the men or women earning more than this amount and half earning less. For those who attended but did not finish high school, the median annual earnings were $24,085 for men, $13,801 for women. For high school graduates, including GED, median earnings were $35,276 for men and $20,199 for women. Men with bachelor's degrees had median earnings of $65,325 while women with bachelor's degrees had median earnings of $41,827. Workers with a professional degree had the highest median earnings, $110,651 for men and $77,090 for women. Men continued to earn at least 30 percent more than women at all levels of educational attainment, except for the doctorate degree level, where the median earnings for women was 24.1 percent less than for men. (Table A-35)

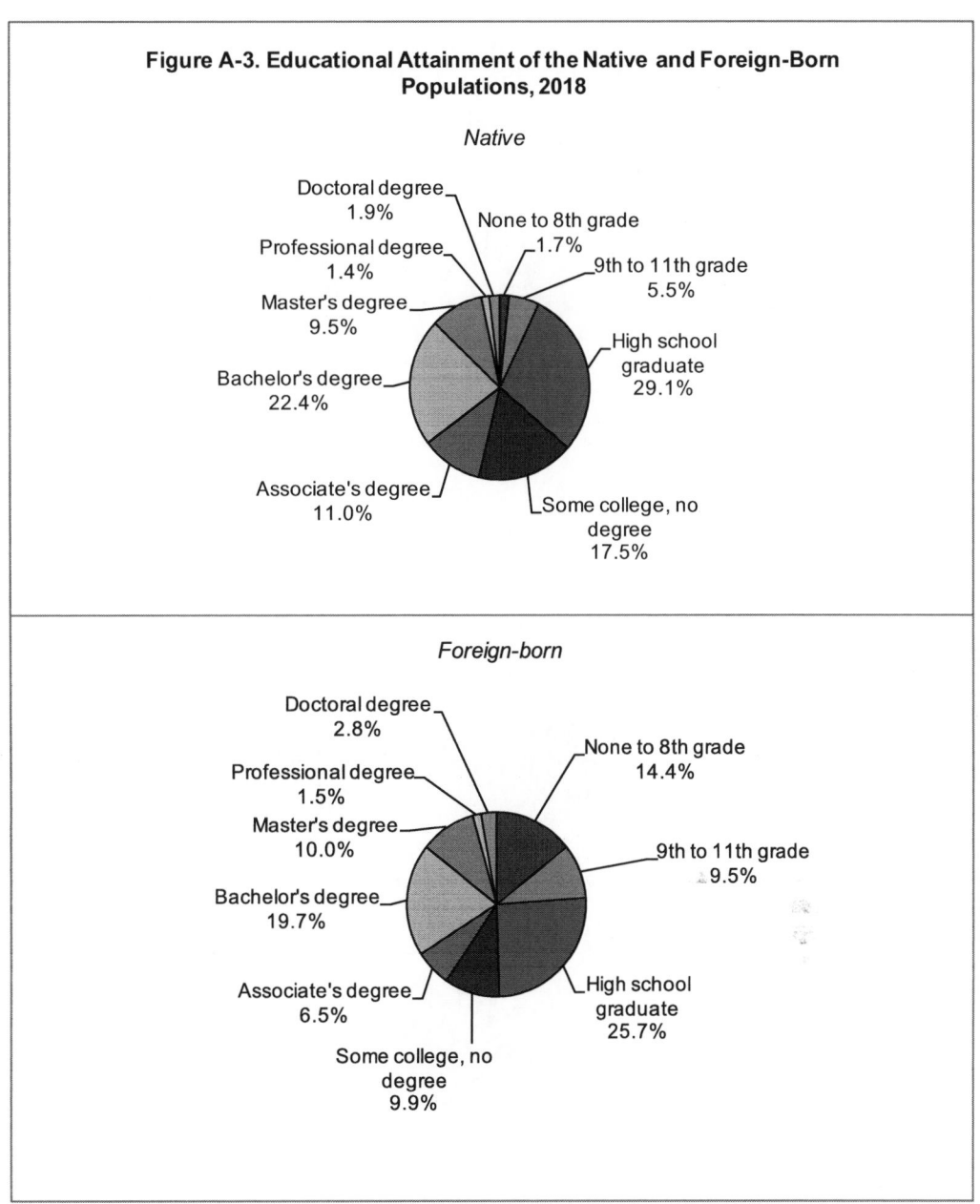

Figure A-3. Educational Attainment of the Native and Foreign-Born Populations, 2018

Native

Doctoral degree 1.9%
Professional degree 1.4%
Master's degree 9.5%
Bachelor's degree 22.4%
Associate's degree 11.0%
None to 8th grade 1.7%
9th to 11th grade 5.5%
High school graduate 29.1%
Some college, no degree 17.5%

Foreign-born

Doctoral degree 2.8%
Professional degree 1.5%
Master's degree 10.0%
Bachelor's degree 19.7%
Associate's degree 6.5%
None to 8th grade 14.4%
9th to 11th grade 9.5%
High school graduate 25.7%
Some college, no degree 9.9%

In 2018, 81.9 percent of the population age 25 years and older in the United States was native-born, and 18.1 percent of the population was foreign-born. The foreign-born population had a much larger proportion of people with less than a 9th-grade education, with 14.4 percent of the foreign-born population was in this category, compared to 1.7 percent of the native population. However, the foreign-born population also had a higher percent of people with doctoral degrees than the native population (2.8 percent, compared to 1.9 percent of natives). (Table A-30)

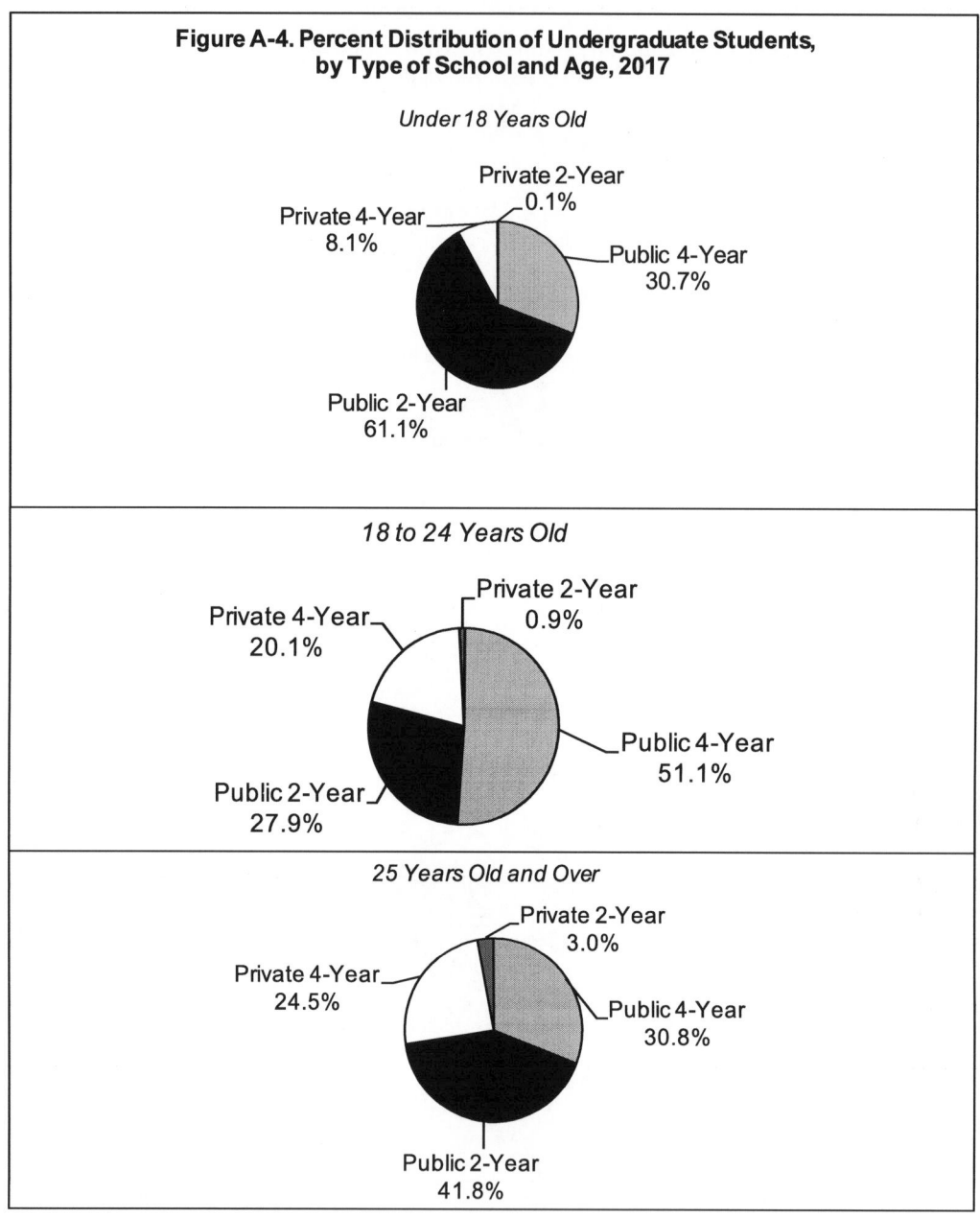

Figure A-4. Percent Distribution of Undergraduate Students, by Type of School and Age, 2017

Under 18 Years Old

Private 2-Year 0.1%
Private 4-Year 8.1%
Public 4-Year 30.7%
Public 2-Year 61.1%

18 to 24 Years Old

Private 2-Year 0.9%
Private 4-Year 20.1%
Public 4-Year 51.1%
Public 2-Year 27.9%

25 Years Old and Over

Private 2-Year 3.0%
Private 4-Year 24.5%
Public 4-Year 30.8%
Public 2-Year 41.8%

In 2017, more than 18 million students 15 years old and over were enrolled in colleges and universities. More than 14.5 million of them were undergraduates. A higher percent of under-graduates attending four-year colleges were full-time students (83.8 percent) compared to those attending two-year colleges (62.9 percent full-time). The proportion of full-time to part-time college students decreased as age increased. Among students 15 to 19 years old, 91.4 percent were full-time students, followed by 84.0 percent of 20- to 24-year-olds, 57.0 percent of 25- to 34-year-olds, and 36.5 percent of students age 35 years and older. Among graduate students, 59.6 percent were full-time students in 2017. Since 2008 there have been more full-time graduate students than part-time, but prior to 2008 the reverse was usually true: part-time students outnumbered full-time in graduate programs most years. (Table A-5 and A-17)

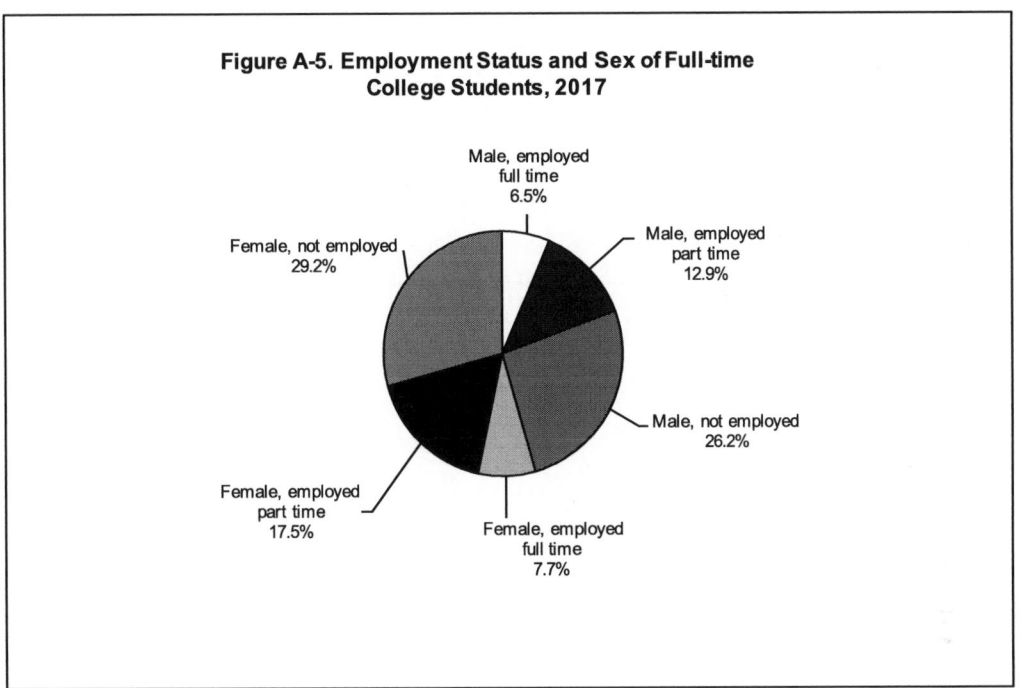

Figure A-5. Employment Status and Sex of Full-time
College Students, 2017

In 2017, women made up 54.9 percent of all undergraduate students. In contrast, only 42.2 percent of all undergraduate students in 1970 were women. By the end of the 1970s, the proportions of men and women were more equal; since then, women's share has steadily increased, staying above 55 percent in most years since the early 1990s and reaching its highest levels of 56.9 percent in 2005 and 56.8 percent in 2012. (Table A-17)

In 2016, 62.9 percent of college students who identified as Black were female. Among Hispanic college students, 58.0 percent were female, and females comprised 53.2 percent of the Asian post-secondary student population. Among graduate students, women accounted for 58.9 percent of enrollment in 2016. (Table A-22)

In 2017, 44.6 percent of full-time college students were employed—either full- or part-time—and 83.6 percent of part-time college students were employed. Among those who were enrolled in vocational courses, 72.8 percent were employed, either full-time or part-time. (Tables A–5 and A-6)

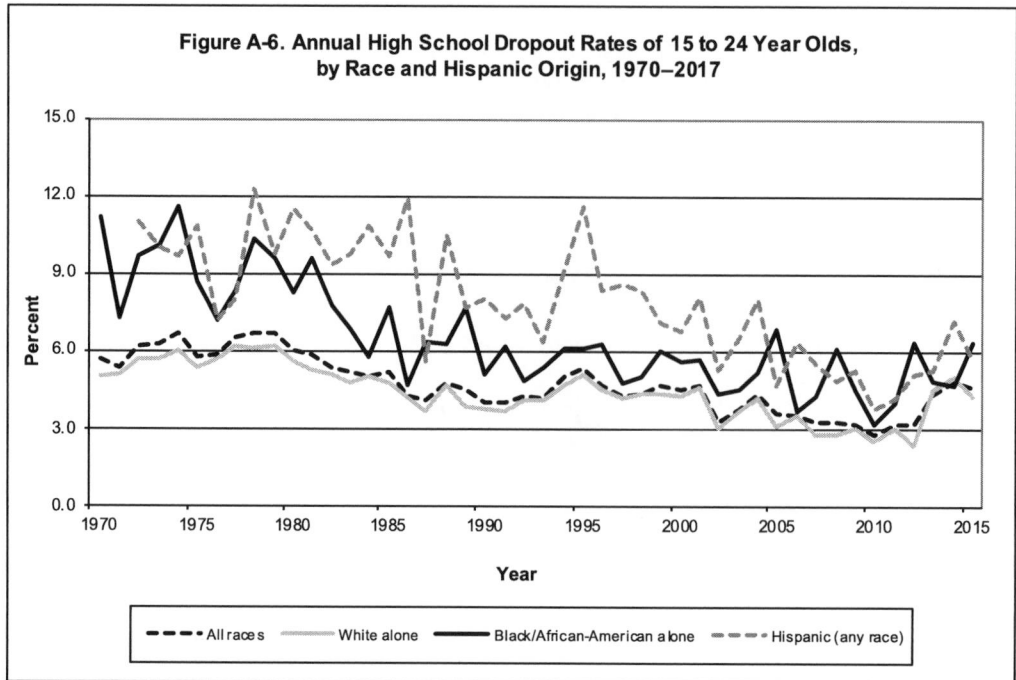

Figure A-6. Annual High School Dropout Rates of 15 to 24 Year Olds, by Race and Hispanic Origin, 1970–2017

The annual high school dropout rate for all students in grades 10 through 12 was 4.5 percent in 2017. The percent of dropouts increased with grade level: 1.0 percent of students dropped out during 10th grade; 3.0 percent of students dropped out during 11th grade; and 10.6 percent of students dropped out during 12th grade. The annual dropout rate was higher for students who identified as Black and/or Hispanic, with 5.0 percent of Black students in grades 10 through 12 dropping out, and 6.1 percent of Hispanic students in grades 10 though 12 dropping out (students of Hispanic origin can be of any race). (Table A-13)

In 1940, only one in four Americans had completed high school. By 1966, the ratio had only increased to 1 in 2 – 49.9 percent of the U.S. population 25 years old and older had completed high school. As of 2018, 89.8 percent of Americans age 25 years and over were high-school graduates. (Table A-32)

The percentage of college graduates, which constituted just 4.6 percent of the population in 1940, had risen to 9.8 percent by 1966. In 2018, college graduates constituted 35.0 percent of the population 25 years old and over. There are more women than men who have graduated from college. In 2018, 34.6 percent of males and 35.3 percent of females age 25 and over were college graduates. (Table A-32)

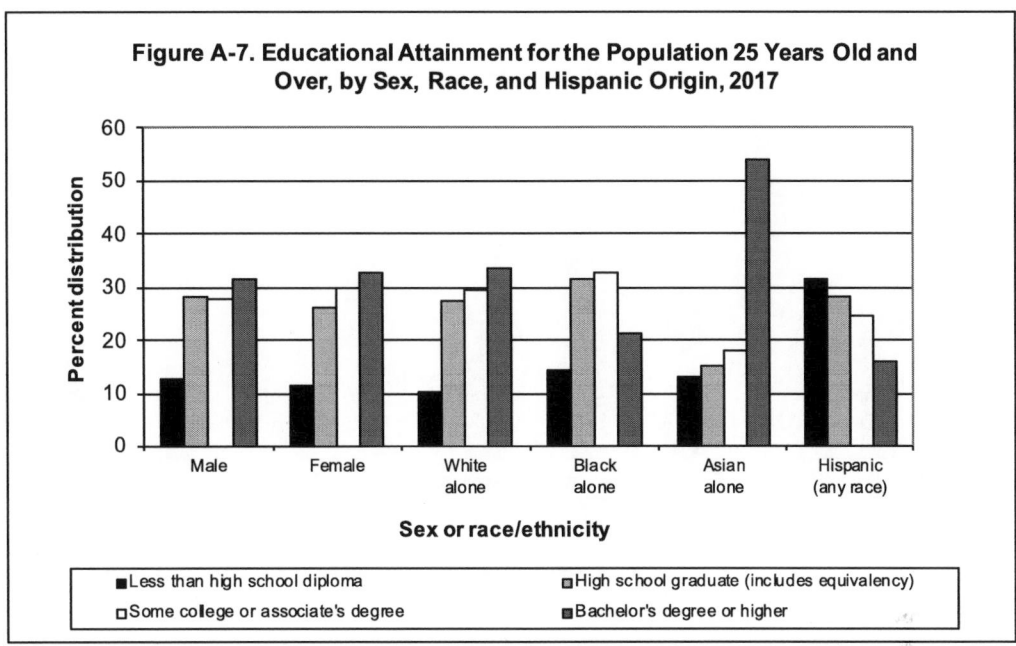

Figure A-7. Educational Attainment for the Population 25 Years Old and Over, by Sex, Race, and Hispanic Origin, 2017

In 2018, 89.8 percent of Americans 25 years old and over had completed high school, and 35.0 percent held completed college. For people age 25 to 29 years, 92.9 percent had completed high school and 37.0 percent had completed college. Women 25 years of age and older had slightly higher rates of high school attainment and college attainment, at 94.0 percent and 40.8 percent, respectively. Among race and ethnic groups (age 25 and older) in 2018, those who identified as Asian had the highest high school completion rate (90.5 percent), followed by White (90.2 percent), Black (87.9 percent), and Hispanic (71.6 percent) individuals. More than half (56.5 percent) of those identified as Asian had completed college, followed by those who identified as White (35.2 percent), Black (25.2 percent), and Hispanic (18.3 percent). (Tables A-32)

In 2018, 40.7 percent of civilians over 25 years of age in the labor force held a bachelor's degree or more. About 7.2 percent of the labor force had not graduated from high school, compared to 10.2 percent of all civilians (in or out of the labor force) over 25 years of age. (Table A-27)

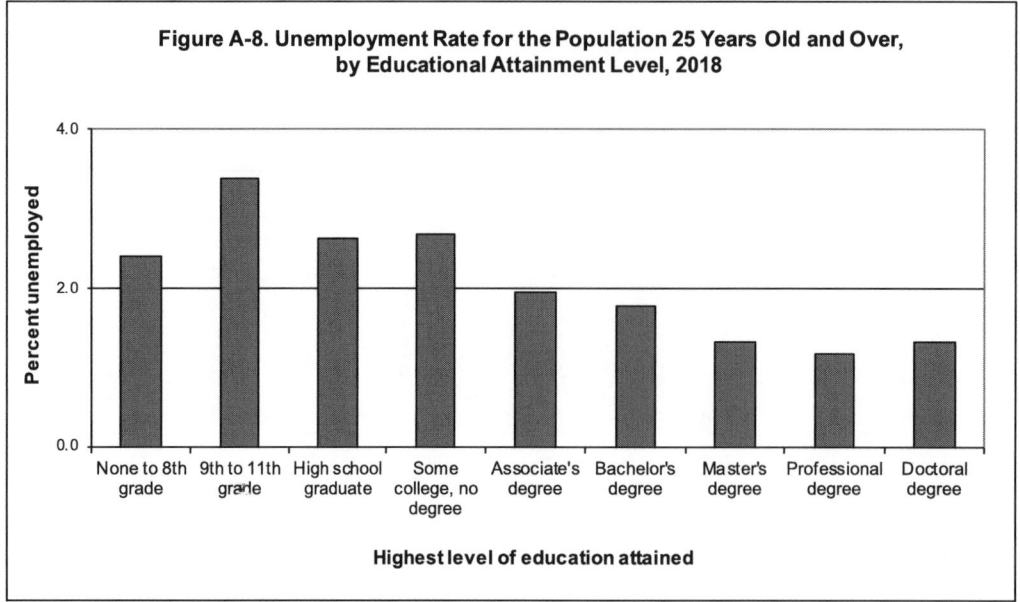

Figure A-8. Unemployment Rate for the Population 25 Years Old and Over, by Educational Attainment Level, 2018

Unemployment data for 2018 show once again that the more education a person has obtained, the less likely he or she will be unemployed. The unemployment rate for the population age 25 and over with a 9th to 11th grade education was 3.4 percent in 2018. For high-school graduates, the rate of unemployment was 2.6 percent; for civilians with a bachelor's degree, it was 1.8 percent. With a doctoral degree, this percentage dropped to 1.3; and the lowest unemployment rate was for those with a professional degree (1.2 percent). The overall unemployment rate in 2018 was 2.2 percent. The unemployment rate for men (2.6 percent) was higher than that for women (1.9 percent). However, there were fewer women than men in the work force. In 2018, the labor force participation rate was 70.9 percent for men, and 57.7 percent for women. (Table A-27)

For persons 25 years old and over, professional and related occupations provided the most jobs in 2018. This category includes teachers, lawyers, scientists, artists, doctors, nurses, and other healthcare professionals. Of individuals employed in professional and related occupations, 73.9 percent held a bachelor's degree or more. In contrast, 11.0 percent of those employed in farming, forestry and fishing, construction, maintenance, production, and transportation occupations had a bachelor's degree or more. Farming, forestry, and fishing employed the greatest percent of people without a high-school diploma (40.8 percent), and service occupations employed the highest number of people without a high-school diploma (3.3 million). (Table A-28)

The educational and health services industry was the largest employer in the United States and employed more than 32.4 million people in 2018. More than half (56.8 percent) of the population in the education and health services industry held a bachelor's degree or higher, and 29.4 percent of workers in this field had a master's degree or higher. Mining was the smallest industry in terms of employment, with 690,000 workers, of whom 203,000 (29.4 percent) held a bachelor's degree or higher. (Table A-29)

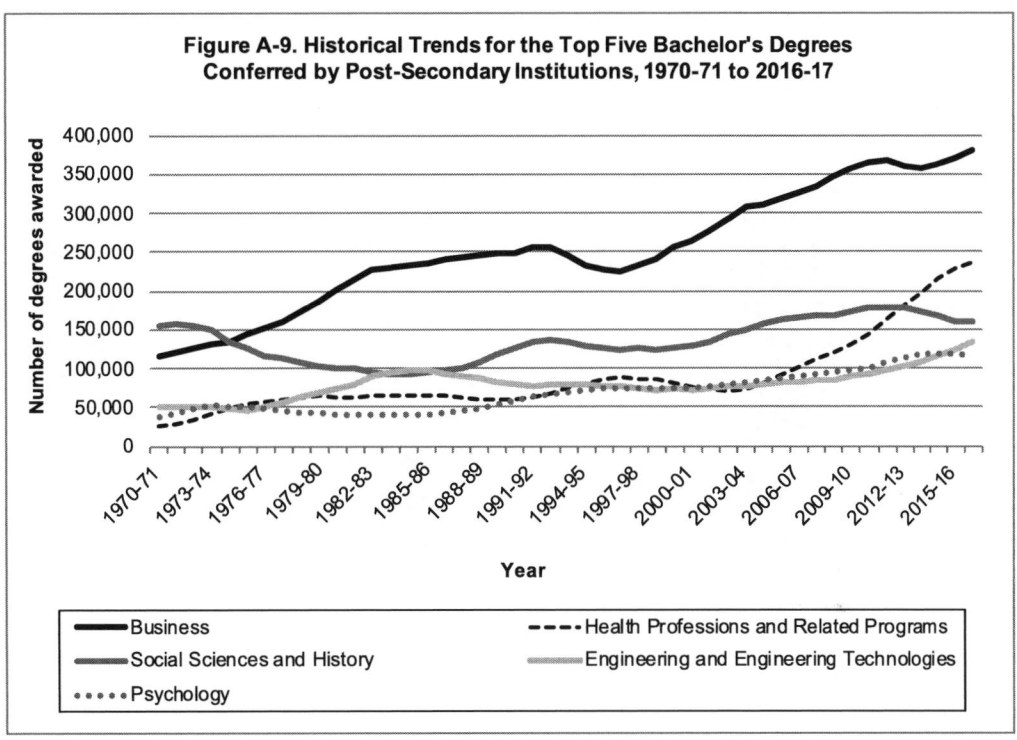

Figure A-9. Historical Trends for the Top Five Bachelor's Degrees Conferred by Post-Secondary Institutions, 1970-71 to 2016-17

The top five bachelor's degrees conferred by post-secondary institutions in the United States during the 2016-2017 school year were: business (381,353 bachelor's degrees conferred), health professions and related programs (238,014 bachelor's degrees), social sciences and history (159,099 bachelor's degrees), engineering and engineering technologies (133,761 bachelor's degrees), and psychology (116,861 bachelor's degrees). The top three master's degrees granted in 2016-2017 were in: business (187,404 master's degrees conferred), education (145,680 master's degrees conferred), and health professions and related programs (119,273 master's degrees conferred). (Table A-37)

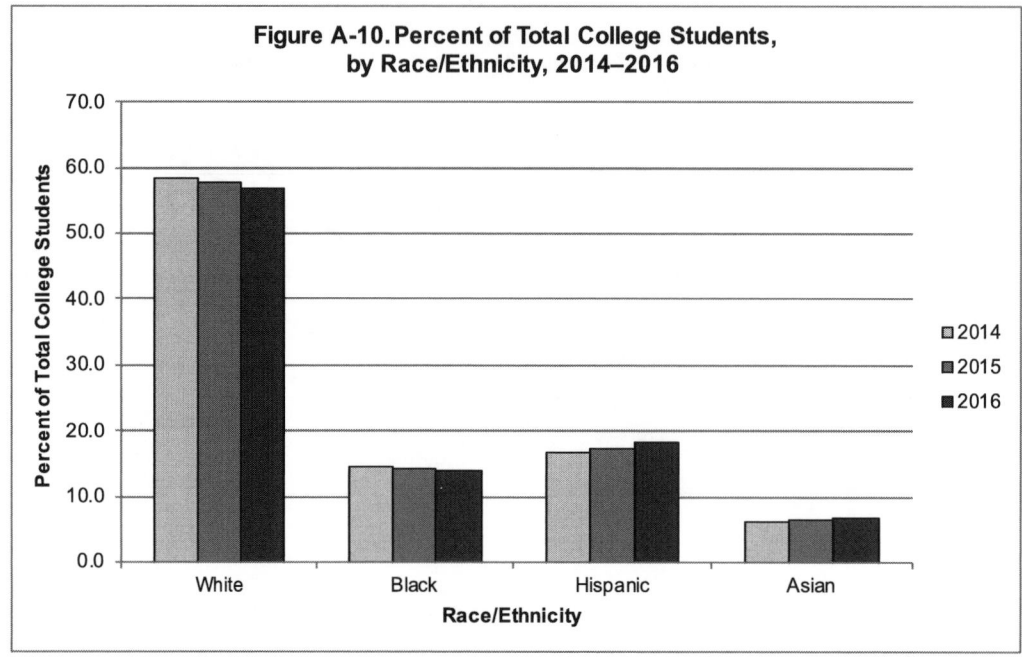

The past three years saw an increase in the percent of Hispanic and Asian college students, and a decrease in the percent of college students who identified as White or Black. In 2014, 58.3 percent of college students identified as White, 14.5 percent identified as Black, 16.5 percent identified as Hispanic, and 6.5 percent identified as Asian. In 2016, the proportions were 56.9 percent White, 13.7 percent Black, 18.2 percent Hispanic, and 6.7 percent Asian. (Table A-23)

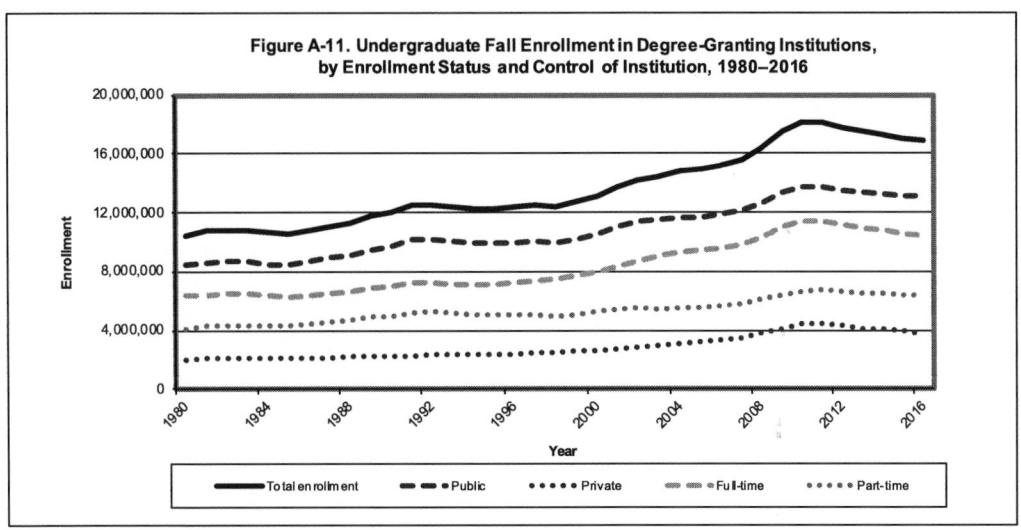

Figure A-11. Undergraduate Fall Enrollment in Degree-Granting Institutions, by Enrollment Status and Control of Institution, 1980–2016

College enrollment increased 37.3 percent between 2000 and 2010, but it has decreased each year since 2010. In 2016, 19.8 million students were enrolled in college, with almost 14.6 million of them enrolled in public institutions. Enrollment in private colleges peaked at nearly 5.9 million students in 2011, but enrollment has decreased each year since then. There were less than 5.3 million students enrolled in private colleges in 2016. Public 4-year colleges continued to enroll the most students, with 8.7 million students enrolled in 2016. Both public and private 2-year colleges saw a decrease in enrollment from 2015 to 2016, with 383,000 fewer students enrolled in public, 2-year schools and 26,000 fewer students enrolled in private, 2-year colleges. There have been more females than males enrolled in college since 1978, with women comprising 56.5 percent of college students in 2016. The percentage of females reached its peak of 57.4 percent in 2005. (Tables A-18 and A-19)

PART A

NATIONAL EDUCATION STATISTICS

■ **Enrollment Tables**

Table A-1. Enrollment Status of the Population 3 Years Old and Over, by Sex, Age, Race, Hispanic Origin, Foreign Born, and Foreign-Born Parentage, October 2017

(Numbers in thousands; percent; civilian noninstitutionalized population.)

Age, sex, race, Hispanic origin, and nativity	Population Number	Enrolled in school							
		Total		Nursery or kindergarten		Elementary		High school	
		Number	Percent	Number	Percent	Number	Percent	Number	Percent
ALL RACES									
Both Sexes									
Total..................................	308,935	76,409	24.7	8,640	2.8	32,530	10.5	16,841	5.5
3 and 4 years old	8,030	4,319	53.8	4,319	53.8	*	*	*	*
5 and 6 years old	8,039	7,516	93.5	4,283	53.3	3,234	40.2	*	*
7 to 9 years old	12,238	11,879	97.1	38	0.3	11,840	96.8	*	*
10 to 13 years old	16,634	16,273	97.8	*	*	15,984	96.1	289	1.7
14 and 15 years old	8,228	8,082	98.2	*	*	1,359	16.5	6,688	81.3
16 and 17 years old	8,541	7,933	92.9	*	*	32	0.4	7,701	90.2
18 and 19 years old	8,222	5,606	68.2	*	*	9	0.1	1,654	20.1
20 and 21 years old	8,311	4,570	55.0	*	*	2	*	201	2.4
22 to 24 years old	13,005	3,696	28.4	*	*	5	*	64	0.5
25 to 29 years old	22,731	2,758	12.1	*	*	9	*	75	0.3
30 to 34 years old	21,359	1,251	5.9	*	*	15	0.1	29	0.1
35 to 44 years old	40,101	1,403	3.5	*	*	18	*	65	0.2
45 to 54 years old	41,649	699	1.7	*	*	12	*	38	0.1
55 years old and over..........	91,847	424	0.5	*	*	10	*	37	*
Male									
Total..................................	150,775	37,779	25.1	4,403	2.9	16,710	11.1	8,554	5.7
3 and 4 years old	4,132	2,208	53.4	2,208	53.4	*	*	*	*
5 and 6 years old	4,113	3,817	92.8	2,180	53.0	1,637	39.8	*	*
7 to 9 years old	6,239	6,057	97.1	15	0.2	6,042	96.8	*	*
10 to 13 years old	8,486	8,304	97.8	*	*	8,179	96.4	125	1.5
14 and 15 years old	4,188	4,111	98.2	*	*	777	18.6	3,312	79.1
16 and 17 years old	4,344	4,008	92.3	*	*	28	0.7	3,917	90.2
18 and 19 years old	4,153	2,704	65.1	*	*	7	0.2	951	22.9
20 and 21 years old	4,202	2,136	50.8	*	*	2	0.1	108	2.6
22 to 24 years old	6,478	1,738	26.8	*	*	3	0.1	47	0.7
25 to 29 years old	11,327	1,233	10.9	*	*	4	*	41	0.4
30 to 34 years old	10,570	545	5.2	*	*	7	0.1	12	0.1
35 to 44 years old	19,675	506	2.6	*	*	5	*	19	0.1
45 to 54 years old	20,362	262	1.3	*	*	11	0.1	13	0.1
55 years old and over..........	42,505	149	0.4	*	*	6	*	10	*
Female									
Total..................................	158,159	38,630	24.4	4,236	2.7	15,820	10.0	8,287	5.2
3 and 4 years old	3,897	2,110	54.1	2,110	54.1	*	*	*	*
5 and 6 years old	3,926	3,699	94.2	2,103	53.6	1,596	40.7	*	*
7 to 9 years old	5,999	5,822	97.0	23	0.4	5,798	96.7	*	*
10 to 13 years old	8,148	7,969	97.8	*	*	7,806	95.8	164	2.0
14 and 15 years old	4,040	3,971	98.3	*	*	582	14.4	3,375	83.5
16 and 17 years old	4,197	3,925	93.5	*	*	3	0.1	3,784	90.2
18 and 19 years old	4,070	2,902	71.3	*	*	2	*	703	17.3
20 and 21 years old	4,109	2,434	59.2	*	*	*	*	93	2.3
22 to 24 years old	6,526	1,958	30.0	*	*	2	*	17	0.3
25 to 29 years old	11,405	1,525	13.4	*	*	5	*	34	0.3
30 to 34 years old	10,789	706	6.5	*	*	8	0.1	17	0.2
35 to 44 years old	20,425	897	4.4	*	*	12	0.1	46	0.2
45 to 54 years old	21,287	437	2.1	*	*	1	*	25	0.1
55 years old and over..........	49,341	275	0.6	*	*	4	*	27	0.1
WHITE ALONE OR IN COMBINATION									
Both Sexes									
Total..................................	244,574	58,381	23.9	6,713	2.7	25,040	10.2	12,926	5.3
3 and 4 years old	6,169	3,280	53.2	3,280	53.2	*	*	*	*
5 and 6 years old	6,210	5,817	93.7	3,417	55.0	2,400	38.7	*	*
7 to 9 years old	9,426	9,143	97.0	16	0.2	9,126	96.8	*	*
10 to 13 years old	12,930	12,617	97.6	*	*	12,404	95.9	214	1.7
14 and 15 years old	6,338	6,238	98.4	*	*	1,010	15.9	5,213	82.3
16 and 17 years old	6,540	6,101	93.3	*	*	32	0.5	5,916	90.5
18 and 19 years old	6,408	4,362	68.1	*	*	6	0.1	1,235	19.3
20 and 21 years old	6,265	3,423	54.6	*	*	2	*	115	1.8
22 to 24 years old	9,979	2,678	26.8	*	*	5	*	52	0.5

* = Quantity equals zero or rounds to zero.

Table A-1. Enrollment Status of the Population 3 Years Old and Over, by Sex, Age, Race, Hispanic Origin, Foreign Born, and Foreign-Born Parentage, October 2017—*Continued*

(Numbers in thousands; percent; civilian noninstitutionalized population.)

Age, sex, race, Hispanic origin, and nativity	Population	Enrolled in school		Not enrolled in school					
		College undergraduate or graduate		Total		High school graduate		Not high school graduate	
	Number	Number	Percent	Number	Percent	Number	Percent	Number	Percent
ALL RACES									
Both Sexes									
Total	308,935	18,398	6	232,526	75.3	203,148	65.8	29,378	9.5
3 and 4 years old	8,030	*	*	3,711	46.2	*	*	3,711	46.2
5 and 6 years old	8,039	*	*	522	6.5	*	*	522	6.5
7 to 9 years old	12,238	*	*	359	2.9	*	*	359	2.9
10 to 13 years old	16,634	*	*	361	2.2	*	*	361	2.2
14 and 15 years old	8,228	35	0.4	146	1.8	*	*	146	1.8
16 and 17 years old	8,541	201	2.3	608	7.1	181	2.1	426	5.0
18 and 19 years old	8,222	3,943	48	2,617	31.8	2,049	24.9	568	6.9
20 and 21 years old	8,311	4,367	52.5	3,741	45.0	3,284	39.5	457	5.5
22 to 24 years old	13,005	3,627	27.9	9,308	71.6	8,562	65.8	747	5.7
25 to 29 years old	22,731	2,674	11.8	19,973	87.9	18,445	81.1	1,528	6.7
30 to 34 years old	21,359	1,207	5.6	20,109	94.1	18,237	85.4	1,872	8.8
35 to 44 years old	40,101	1,320	3.3	38,698	96.5	34,917	87.1	3,781	9.4
45 to 54 years old	41,649	649	1.6	40,950	98.3	36,938	88.7	4,012	9.6
55 years old and over..........	91,847	377	0.4	91,422	99.5	80,536	87.7	10,886	11.9
Male									
Total	150,775	8,112	5.4	112,997	74.9	98,177	65.1	14,820	9.8
3 and 4 years old	4,132	*	*	1,924	46.6	*	*	1,924	46.6
5 and 6 years old	4,113	*	*	296	7.2	*	*	296	7.2
7 to 9 years old	6,239	*	*	182	2.9	*	*	182	2.9
10 to 13 years old	8,486	*	*	182	2.2	*	*	182	2.2
14 and 15 years old	4,188	21	0.5	77	1.8	*	*	77	1.8
16 and 17 years old	4,344	63	1.5	335	7.7	92	2.1	244	5.6
18 and 19 years old	4,153	1,746	42.1	1,449	34.9	1,103	26.6	346	8.3
20 and 21 years old	4,202	2,025	48.2	2,067	49.2	1,777	42.3	290	6.9
22 to 24 years old	6,478	1,688	26.1	4,740	73.2	4,358	67.3	382	5.9
25 to 29 years old	11,327	1,188	10.5	10,094	89.1	9,270	81.8	824	7.3
30 to 34 years old	10,570	526	5	10,025	94.8	9,017	85.3	1,008	9.5
35 to 44 years old	19,675	482	2.4	19,169	97.4	17,175	87.3	1,994	10.1
45 to 54 years old	20,362	238	1.2	20,100	98.7	17,987	88.3	2,113	10.4
55 years old and over..........	42,505	134	0.3	42,356	99.6	37,399	88	4,957	11.7
Female									
Total	158,159	10,287	6.5	119,529	75.6	104,972	66.4	14,558	9.2
3 and 4 years old	3,897	*	*	1,787	45.9	*	*	1,787	45.9
5 and 6 years old	3,926	*	*	226	5.8	*	*	226	5.8
7 to 9 years old	5,999	*	*	177	3.0	*	*	177	3.0
10 to 13 years old	8,148	*	*	179	2.2	*	*	179	2.2
14 and 15 years old	4,040	14	0.3	69	1.7	*	*	69	1.7
16 and 17 years old	4,197	137	3.3	272	6.5	90	2.1	182	4.3
18 and 19 years old	4,070	2,197	54	1,168	28.7	946	23.2	222	5.5
20 and 21 years old	4,109	2,341	57	1,675	40.8	1,507	36.7	167	4.1
22 to 24 years old	6,526	1,939	29.7	4,568	70.0	4,204	64.4	364	5.6
25 to 29 years old	11,405	1,486	13	9,880	86.6	9,176	80.5	704	6.2
30 to 34 years old	10,789	681	6.3	10,083	93.5	9,220	85.5	863	8.0
35 to 44 years old	20,425	839	4.1	19,529	95.6	17,742	86.9	1,787	8.7
45 to 54 years old	21,287	410	1.9	20,850	97.9	18,951	89	1,899	8.9
55 years old and over..........	49,341	243	0.5	49,067	99.4	43,137	87.4	5,930	12.0
WHITE ALONE OR IN COMBINATION									
Both Sexes									
Total	244,574	13,703	5.6	186,193	76.1	163,183	66.7	23,010	9.4
3 and 4 years old	6,169	*	*	2,889	46.8	*	*	2,889	46.8
5 and 6 years old	6,210	*	*	393	6.3	*	*	393	6.3
7 to 9 years old	9,426	*	*	283	3.0	*	*	283	3.0
10 to 13 years old	12,930	*	*	313	2.4	*	*	313	2.4
14 and 15 years old	6,338	15	0.2	100	1.6	*	*	100	1.6
16 and 17 years old	6,540	153	2.3	439	6.7	131	2.0	308	4.7
18 and 19 years old	6,408	3,121	48.7	2,046	31.9	1,585	24.7	461	7.2
20 and 21 years old	6,265	3,306	52.8	2,842	45.4	2,492	39.8	350	5.6
22 to 24 years old	9,979	2,621	26.3	7,301	73.2	6,722	67.4	579	5.8

* = Quantity equals zero or rounds to zero.

Table A-1. Enrollment Status of the Population 3 Years Old and Over, by Sex, Age, Race, Hispanic Origin, Foreign Born, and Foreign-Born Parentage, October 2017—*Continued*

(Numbers in thousands; percent; civilian noninstitutionalized population.)

Age, sex, race, Hispanic origin, and nativity	Population	Enrolled in school								
		Total		Nursery or kindergarten		Elementary		High school		
	Number	Number	Percent	Number	Percent	Number	Percent	Number	Percent	
25 to 29 years old	17,176	1,973	11.5	*	*	8.0	*	62	0.4	
30 to 34 years old	16,420	923	5.6	*	*	15	0.1	22	0.1	
35 to 44 years old	30,987	988	3.2	*	*	16	0.1	38	0.1	
45 to 54 years old	32,979	501	1.5	*	*	12	*	26	0.1	
55 years old and over..........	76,747	336	0.4	*	*	3	*	31	*	
Male										
Total.......................................	120,356	28,955	24.1	3,360	2.8	12,901	10.7	6,635	5.5	
3 and 4 years old	3,137	1,636	52.2	1,636	52.2	*	*	*	*	
5 and 6 years old	3,144	2,929	93.2	1,719	54.7	1,210	38.5	*	*	
7 to 9 years old	4,816	4,683	97.2	5	0.1	4,678	97.1	*	*	
10 to 13 years old	6,625	6,473	97.7	*	*	6,374	96.2	100	1.5	
14 and 15 years old	3,226	3,177	98.5	*	*	571	17.7	2,595	80.4	
16 and 17 years old	3,344	3,106	92.9	*	*	28	0.8	3,025	90.5	
18 and 19 years old	3,233	2,118	65.5	*	*	4	0.1	744	23.0	
20 and 21 years old	3,174	1,602	50.5	*	*	2	0.1	67	2.1	
22 to 24 years old	5,017	1,255	25.0	*	*	3	0.1	39	0.8	
25 to 29 years old	8,635	882	10.2	*	*	4	*	31	0.4	
30 to 34 years old	8,227	421	5.1	*	*	7	0.1	5	0.1	
35 to 44 years old	15,483	362	2.3	*	*	5	*	11	0.1	
45 to 54 years old	16,366	189	1.2	*	*	11	0.1	9	0.1	
55 years old and over..........	35,928	121	0.3	*	*	3	*	10	*	
Female										
Total.......................................	124,218	29,426	23.7	3,353	2.7	12,139	9.8	6,291	5.1	
3 and 4 years old	3,033	1,644	54.2	1,644	54.2	*	*	*	*	
5 and 6 years old	3,065	2,888	94.2	1,698	55.4	1,190	38.8	*	*	
7 to 9 years old	4,611	4,460	96.7	11	0.2	4,449	96.5	*	*	
10 to 13 years old	6,305	6,144	97.4	*	*	6,030	95.6	114	1.8	
14 and 15 years old	3,112	3,061	98.4	*	*	439	14.1	2,619	84.2	
16 and 17 years old	3,196	2,995	93.7	*	*	3	0.1	2,891	90.5	
18 and 19 years old	3,174	2,244	70.7	*	*	2	0.1	492	15.5	
20 and 21 years old	3,091	1,821	58.9	*	*	*	*	49	1.6	
22 to 24 years old	4,962	1,423	28.7	*	*	1	*	13	0.3	
25 to 29 years old	8,541	1,091	12.8	*	*	4.0	*	31	0.4	
30 to 34 years old	8,193	501	6.1	*	*	8	0.1	17	0.2	
35 to 44 years old	15,504	626	4.0	*	*	11	0.1	27	0.2	
45 to 54 years old	16,612	312	1.9	*	*	1	*	17	0.1	
55 years old and over..........	40,819	215	0.5	*	*	1	*	21	0	
BLACK ALONE OR IN COMBINATION										
Both Sexes										
Total.......................................	43,988	13,598	30.9	1,560	3.5	6,087	13.8	2,884	6.6	
3 and 4 years old	1,506	853	56.7	853	56.7	*	*	*	*	
5 and 6 years old	1,479	1,363	92.1	692	46.8	670	45.3	*	*	
7 to 9 years old	2,335	2,266	97.1	14	0.6	2,252	96.4	*	*	
10 to 13 years old	2,965	2,929	98.8	*	*	2,872	96.9	56	1.9	
14 and 15 years old	1,370	1,325	96.8	*	*	288	21.0	1,021	74.6	
16 and 17 years old	1,496	1,367	91.4	*	*	*	*	1,336	89.3	
18 and 19 years old	1,414	946	66.9	*	*	2	0.2	347	24.5	
20 and 21 years old	1,392	667	47.9	*	*	*	*	61	4.4	
22 to 24 years old	2,128	588	27.6	*	*	*	*	9	0.4	
25 to 29 years old	3,725	507	13.6	*	*	*	*	14	0.4	
30 to 34 years old	3,107	228	7.3	*	*	*	*	3	0.1	
35 to 44 years old	5,637	327	5.8	*	*	1	*	23	0.4	
45 to 54 years old	5,534	169	3.1	*	*	*	*	8	0.1	
55 years old and over..........	9,899	62	0.6	*	*	*	*	7	0.1	
Male										
Total.......................................	20,545	6,529	31.8	813	4.0	3,052	14.9	1,391	6.8	
3 and 4 years old	781	456	58.3	456	58.3	*	*	*	*	
5 and 6 years old	754	687	91.2	353	46.8	335	44.4	*	*	
7 to 9 years old	1,153	1,107	96.0	5	0.4	1,102	95.6	*	*	
10 to 13 years old	1,487	1,469	98.8	*	*	1,448	97.4	21	1.4	
14 and 15 years old	678	650	95.9	*	*	165	24.3	476	70.2	

* = Quantity equals zero or rounds to zero.

Table A-1. Enrollment Status of the Population 3 Years Old and Over, by Sex, Age, Race, Hispanic Origin, Foreign Born, and Foreign-Born Parentage, October 2017—*Continued*

(Numbers in thousands; percent; civilian noninstitutionalized population.)

| Age, sex, race, Hispanic origin, and nativity | Population | Enrolled in school | | Not enrolled in school | | | | | |
| | | College undergraduate or graduate | | Total | | High school graduate | | Not high school graduate | |
	Number	Number	Percent	Number	Percent	Number	Percent	Number	Percent
25 to 29 years old	17,176	1,904	11.1	15,203	88.5	13,998	81.5	1,205	7.0
30 to 34 years old	16,420	885	5.4	15,497	94.4	13,948	84.9	1,550	9.4
35 to 44 years old	30,987	933	3.0	29,999	96.8	26,905	86.8	3,094	10.0
45 to 54 years old	32,979	462	1.4	32,478	98.5	29,334	88.9	3,144	9.5
55 years old and over	76,747	302	0.4	76,411	99.6	68,069	88.7	8,342	10.9
Male									
Total	120,356	6,059	5.0	91,401	75.9	79,528	66.1	11,873	9.9
3 and 4 years old	3,137	*	*	1,500	47.8	*	*	1,500	47.8
5 and 6 years old	3,144	*	*	215	6.8	*	*	215	6.8
7 to 9 years old	4,816	*	*	133	2.8	*	*	133	2.8
10 to 13 years old	6,625	*	*	152	2.3	*	*	152	2.3
14 and 15 years old	3,226	12	0.4	48	1.5	*	*	48	1.5
16 and 17 years old	3,344	53	1.6	238	7.1	64	1.9	174	5.2
18 and 19 years old	3,233	1,370	42.4	1,116	34.5	839	26.0	276	8.5
20 and 21 years old	3,174	1,533	48.3	1,572	49.5	1,350	42.5	222	7.0
22 to 24 years old	5,017	1,212	24.2	3,762	75.0	3,464	69.1	298	5.9
25 to 29 years old	8,635	847	9.8	7,753	89.8	7,069	81.9	685	7.9
30 to 34 years old	8,227	409	5.0	7,806	94.9	6,975	84.8	831	10.1
35 to 44 years old	15,483	345	2.2	15,122	97.7	13,455	86.9	1,667	10.8
45 to 54 years old	16,366	169	1.0	16,177	98.8	14,431	88.2	1,746	10.7
55 years old and over	35,928	108	0.3	35,807	99.7	31,882	88.7	3,925	10.9
Female									
Total	124,218	7,644	6.2	94,792	76.3	83,655	67.3	11,137	9.0
3 and 4 years old	3,033	*	*	1,389	45.8	*	*	1,389	45.8
5 and 6 years old	3,065	*	*	177	5.8	*	*	177	5.8
7 to 9 years old	4,611	*	*	151	3.3	*	*	151	3.3
10 to 13 years old	6,305	*	*	161	2.6	*	*	161	2.6
14 and 15 years old	3,112	3	0.1	51	1.6	*	*	51	1.6
16 and 17 years old	3,196	100	3.1	201	6.3	67	2.1	134	4.2
18 and 19 years old	3,174	1,751	55.1	930	29.3	745	23.5	185	5.8
20 and 21 years old	3,091	1,772	57.3	1,270	41.1	1,142	36.9	128	4.1
22 to 24 years old	4,962	1,408	28.4	3,539	71.3	3,258	65.7	281	5.7
25 to 29 years old	8,541	1,057	12.4	7,450	87.2	6,930	81.1	520	6.1
30 to 34 years old	8,193	476	5.8	7,691	93.9	6,973	85.1	719	8.8
35 to 44 years old	15,504	588	3.8	14,877	96.0	13,450	86.8	1,427	9.2
45 to 54 years old	16,612	294	1.8	16,301	98.1	14,903	89.7	1,398	8.4
55 years old and over	40,819	194	0.5	40,604	99.5	36,187	88.7	4,417	10.8
BLACK ALONE OR IN COMBINATION									
Both Sexes									
Total	43,988	3,068	7.0	30,389	69.1	25,911	58.9	4,478	10.2
3 and 4 years old	1,506	*	*	653	43.3	*	*	653	43.3
5 and 6 years old	1,479	*	*	116	7.9	*	*	116	7.9
7 to 9 years old	2,335	*	*	69	2.9	*	*	69	2.9
10 to 13 years old	2,965	*	*	37	1.2	*	*	37	1.2
14 and 15 years old	1,370	16	1.2	44	3.2	*	*	44	3.2
16 and 17 years old	1,496	31	2.1	129	8.6	48	3.2	81	5.4
18 and 19 years old	1,414	597	42.2	469	33.1	391	27.6	78	5.5
20 and 21 years old	1,392	606	43.6	725	52.1	634	45.6	91	6.5
22 to 24 years old	2,128	579	27.2	1,540	72.4	1,413	66.4	128	6.0
25 to 29 years old	3,725	493	13.2	3,218	86.4	2,957	79.4	262	7.0
30 to 34 years old	3,107	225	7.3	2,878	92.7	2,639	84.9	240	7.7
35 to 44 years old	5,637	303	5.4	5,309	94.2	4,856	86.2	453	8.0
45 to 54 years old	5,534	161	2.9	5,365	96.9	4,819	87.1	546	9.9
55 years old and over	9,899	56	0.6	9,837	99.4	8,155	82.4	1,682	17.0
Male									
Total	20,545	1,273	6.2	14,016	68.2	11,894	57.9	2,122	10.3
3 and 4 years old	781	*	*	326	41.7	*	*	326	41.7
5 and 6 years old	754	*	*	66	8.8	*	*	66	8.8
7 to 9 years old	1,153	*	*	46	4.0	*	*	46	4.0
10 to 13 years old	1,487	*	*	17	1.2	*	*	17	1.2
14 and 15 years old	678	9	1.4	28	4.1	*	*	28	4.1

* = Quantity equals zero or rounds to zero.

Table A-1. Enrollment Status of the Population 3 Years Old and Over, by Sex, Age, Race, Hispanic Origin, Foreign Born, and Foreign-Born Parentage, October 2017—*Continued*

(Numbers in thousands; percent; civilian noninstitutionalized population.)

| Age, sex, race, Hispanic origin, and nativity | Population | Enrolled in school | | | | | | | | |
| | | Total | | Nursery or kindergarten | | Elementary | | High school | |
	Number	Number	Percent	Number	Percent	Number	Percent	Number	Percent
16 and 17 years old	753	683	90.7	*	*	*	*	679	90.1
18 and 19 years old	701	440	62.8	*	*	2	0.3	169	24.2
20 and 21 years old	706	292	41.4	*	*	*	*	25	3.5
22 to 24 years old	1,006	239	23.8	*	*	*	*	8	0.8
25 to 29 years old	1,798	217	12.1	*	*	*	*	10	0.5
30 to 34 years old	1,410	84	6.0	*	*	*	*	3	0.2
35 to 44 years old	2,544	120	4.7	*	*	*	*	*	*
45 to 54 years old	2,504	66	2.6	*	*	*	*	*	*
55 years old and over	4,271	17	0.4	*	*	*	*	*	*
Female									
Total	23,443	7,069	30.2	746	3.2	3,035	12.9	1,493	6.4
3 and 4 years old	725	398	54.9	398	54.9	*	*	*	*
5 and 6 years old	725	675	93.1	339	46.8	336	46.3	*	*
7 to 9 years old	1,182	1,159	98.1	9	0.8	1,150	97.3	*	*
10 to 13 years old	1,478	1,459	98.7	*	*	1,424	96.3	35	2.3
14 and 15 years old	692	675	97.6	*	*	123	17.8	545	78.8
16 and 17 years old	743	684	92.1	*	*	*	*	657	88.5
18 and 19 years old	713	505	70.9	*	*	*	*	177	24.9
20 and 21 years old	686	375	54.6	*	*	*	*	36	5.2
22 to 24 years old	1,123	349	31.1	*	*	*	*	1	0.1
25 to 29 years old	1,928	290	15.0	*	*	*	*	4	0.2
30 to 34 years old	1,697	144	8.5	*	*	*	*	*	*
35 to 44 years old	3,093	207	6.7	*	*	1	*	23	0.8
45 to 54 years old	3,030	104	3.4	*	*	*	*	8	0.3
55 years old and over	5,628	45	0.8	*	*	*	*	7	0.1
ASIAN ALONE OR IN COMBINATION									
Both Sexes									
Total	20,064	5,708	28.5	662	3.3	2,165	10.8	1132	5.6
3 and 4 years old	571	314	54.9	314	54.9	*	*	*	*
5 and 6 years old	610	585	96.0	342	56.1	243	39.8	*	*
7 to 9 years old	781	767	98.1	6	0.7	761	97.4	*	*
10 to 13 years old	1,118	1102	98.6	*	*	1082	96.8	20	1.8
14 and 15 years old	547	547	100.0	*	*	67	12.3	476	86.9
16 and 17 years old	602	569	94.5	*	*	*	*	541	89.9
18 and 19 years old	433	360	83.1	*	*	1	0.1	62	14.3
20 and 21 years old	653	503	77.0	*	*	*	*	15	2.3
22 to 24 years old	904	442	49.0	*	*	1	0.2	3	0.3
25 to 29 years old	1,734	287	16.6	*	*	1	0.1	*	*
30 to 34 years old	1,744	107	6.1	*	*	2	0.1	4	0.2
35 to 44 years old	3,161	81	2.6	*	*	*	*	7	0.2
45 to 54 years old	2,758	24	0.9	*	*	*	*	4	0.1
55 years old and over	4,449	20	0.4	*	*	7	0.2	*	*
Male									
Total	9,564	2,845	29.8	316	3.3	1,123	11.7	584	6.1
3 and 4 years old	282	152	53.7	152	53.7	*	*	*	*
5 and 6 years old	298	282	94.7	160	53.9	122	40.8	*	*
7 to 9 years old	411	404	98.3	4	0.9	400	97.3	*	*
10 to 13 years old	574	564	98.2	*	*	557	97.0	7	1.3
14 and 15 years old	274	274	100.0	*	*	38	14.0	235	85.8
16 and 17 years old	297	281	94.7	*	*	*	*	275	92.6
18 and 19 years old	220	176	80.0	*	*	1	0.3	42	19.1
20 and 21 years old	325	247	76.0	*	*	*	*	11	3.3
22 to 24 years old	458	243	53.0	*	*	*	*	*	*
25 to 29 years old	839	131	15.6	*	*	*	*	*	*
30 to 34 years old	829	47	5.6	*	*	2	0.3	4	0.5
35 to 44 years old	1,485	27	1.8	*	*	*	*	7	0.5
45 to 54 years old	1,313	9	0.7	*	*	*	*	4	0.3
55 years old and over	1,959	10	0.5	*	*	3	0.2	*	*
Female									
Total	10,500	2,863	27.3	346	3.3	1,042	9.9	547	5.2
3 and 4 years old	289	162	56.1	162	56.1	*	*	*	*

* = Quantity equals zero or rounds to zero.

Table A-1. Enrollment Status of the Population 3 Years Old and Over, by Sex, Age, Race, Hispanic Origin, Foreign Born, and Foreign-Born Parentage, October 2017—*Continued*

(Numbers in thousands; percent; civilian noninstitutionalized population.)

| Age, sex, race, Hispanic origin, and nativity | Population | Enrolled in school | | Not enrolled in school | | | | | |
| | | College undergraduate or graduate | | Total | | High school graduate | | Not high school graduate | |
	Number	Number	Percent	Number	Percent	Number	Percent	Number	Percent
16 and 17 years old	753	4	0.6	70	9.3	23	3.0	47	6.3
18 and 19 years old	701	269	38.3	261	37.2	208	29.7	53	7.5
20 and 21 years old	706	267	37.9	413	58.6	360	51.1	53	7.5
22 to 24 years old	1,006	231	23.0	767	76.2	696	69.2	70	7.0
25 to 29 years old	1,798	208	11.6	1,580	87.9	1,448	80.6	132	7.3
30 to 34 years old	1,410	82	5.8	1,326	94.0	1,205	85.5	121	8.6
35 to 44 years old	2,544	120	4.7	2,424	95.3	2,199	86.5	224	8.8
45 to 54 years old	2,504	66	2.6	2,438	97.4	2,206	88.1	232	9.3
55 years old and over..........	4,271	17	0.4	4,254	99.6	3,548	83.1	706	16.5
Female									
Total................................	23,443	1,794	7.7	16,373	69.8	14,017	59.8	2,356	10.0
3 and 4 years old	725	*	*	327	45.1	*	*	327	45.1
5 and 6 years old	725	*	*	50	6.9	*	*	50	6.9
7 to 9 years old	1,182	*	*	22	1.9	*	*	22	1.9
10 to 13 years old	1,478	*	*	19	1.3	*	*	19	1.3
14 and 15 years old	692	7	1.0	16	2.4	*	*	16	2.4
16 and 17 years old	743	27	3.6	59	7.9	25	3.4	33	4.5
18 and 19 years old	713	328	46.0	208	29.1	182	25.6	25	3.5
20 and 21 years old	686	339	49.4	312	45.4	274	39.9	38	5.5
22 to 24 years old	1,123	347	31.0	774	68.9	716	63.8	57	5.1
25 to 29 years old	1,928	286	14.8	1,638	85.0	1,508	78.2	130	6.7
30 to 34 years old	1,697	144	8.5	1,553	91.5	1,434	84.5	119	7.0
35 to 44 years old	3,093	183	5.9	2,886	93.3	2,657	85.9	229	7.4
45 to 54 years old	3,030	96	3.2	2,926	96.6	2,613	86.2	314	10.4
55 years old and over..........	5,628	38	0.7	5,583	99.2	4,608	81.9	976	17.3
ASIAN ALONE OR IN COMBINATION									
Both Sexes									
Total................................	20,064	1,750	8.7	14,355	71.5	12,822	63.9	1,533	7.6
3 and 4 years old	571	*	*	257	45.1	*	*	257	45.1
5 and 6 years old	610	*	*	25	4.0	*	*	25	4.0
7 to 9 years old	781	*	*	15	1.9	*	*	15	1.9
10 to 13 years old	1,118	*	*	16	1.4	*	*	16	1.4
14 and 15 years old	547	4	0.8	*	*	*	*	*	*
16 and 17 years old	602	28	4.7	33	5.5	3	0.5	30	4.9
18 and 19 years old	433	297	68.7	73	16.9	62	14.3	11	2.6
20 and 21 years old	653	488	74.7	150	23.0	140	21.4	10	1.6
22 to 24 years old	904	438	48.5	461	51.0	450	49.8	11	1.2
25 to 29 years old	1,734	286	16.5	1,447	83.4	1,407	81.2	39	2.3
30 to 34 years old	1,744	101	5.8	1,638	93.9	1,564	89.7	73	4.2
35 to 44 years old	3,161	74	2.4	3,079	97.4	2,954	93.5	125	3.9
45 to 54 years old	2,758	21	0.7	2,733	99.1	2,486	90.1	247	9.0
55 years old and over..........	4,449	13	0.3	4,429	99.6	3,755	84.4	674	15.1
Male									
Total................................	9,564	822	8.6	6,718	70.2	6,109	63.9	609	6.4
3 and 4 years old	282	*	*	131	46.3	*	*	131	46.3
5 and 6 years old	298	*	*	16	5.3	*	*	16	5.3
7 to 9 years old	411	*	*	7	1.7	*	*	7	1.7
10 to 13 years old	574	*	*	10	1.8	*	*	10	1.8
14 and 15 years old	274	1	0.2	*	*	*	*	*	*
16 and 17 years old	297	6	2.1	16	5.3	1	0.2	15	5.1
18 and 19 years old	220	133	60.6	44	20.0	41	18.7	3	1.3
20 and 21 years old	325	236	72.7	78	24.0	67	20.8	10	3.2
22 to 24 years old	458	243	53.0	215	47.0	213	46.4	3	0.6
25 to 29 years old	839	131	15.6	708	84.4	703	83.7	6	0.7
30 to 34 years old	829	40	4.9	782	94.4	757	91.3	25	3.1
35 to 44 years old	1,485	20	1.4	1,458	98.2	1,408	94.8	50	3.4
45 to 54 years old	1,313	5	0.4	1,304	99.3	1,208	92.0	96	7.3
55 years old and over..........	1,959	7	0.3	1,949	99.5	1,712	87.4	237	12.1
Female									
Total................................	10,500	928	8.8	7,637	72.7	6,713	63.9	924	8.8
3 and 4 years old	289	*	*	127	43.9	*	*	127	43.9

* = Quantity equals zero or rounds to zero.

Table A-1. Enrollment Status of the Population 3 Years Old and Over, by Sex, Age, Race, Hispanic Origin, Foreign Born, and Foreign-Born Parentage, October 2017—*Continued*

(Numbers in thousands; percent; civilian noninstitutionalized population.)

| Age, sex, race, Hispanic origin, and nativity | Population | Enrolled in school | | | | | | | | |
| | | Total | | Nursery or kindergarten | | Elementary | | High school | |
	Number	Number	Percent	Number	Percent	Number	Percent	Number	Percent
5 and 6 years old	312	303	97.2	182	58.3	121	38.9	*	*
7 to 9 years old	370	363	98.0	2	0.6	361	97.4	*	*
10 to 13 years old	543	538	98.9	*	*	525	96.5	13	2.4
14 and 15 years old	273	273	100.0	*	*	29	10.6	241	88.1
16 and 17 years old	305	288	94.4	*	*	*	*	266	87.3
18 and 19 years old	213	184	86.4	*	*	*	*	20	9.4
20 and 21 years old	328	256	78.0	*	*	*	*	4	1.3
22 to 24 years old	445	199	44.8	*	*	1	0.3	3	0.6
25 to 29 years old	895	156	17.5	*	*	1	0.1	*	*
30 to 34 years old	915	60	6.6	*	*	*	*	*	*
35 to 44 years old	1,675	54	3.2	*	*	*	*	*	*
45 to 54 years old	1,445	15	1.1	*	*	*	*	*	*
55 years old and over	2,490	10	0.4	*	*	4	0.2	*	*
HISPANIC (OF ANY RACE)									
Both Sexes									
Total	55,207	17,974	32.6	2,123	3.8	8,340	15.1	3,936	7.1
3 and 4 years old	2,117	1015	47.9	1015	47.9	*	*	*	*
5 and 6 years old	2,064	1,960	95.0	1,100	53.3	861	41.7	*	*
7 to 9 years old	3,193	3,098	97.0	9	0.3	3,089	96.7	*	*
10 to 13 years old	4,226	4,113	97.3	*	*	4,029	95.3	84	2.0
14 and 15 years old	1,927	1,896	98.4	*	*	309	16.1	1,587	82.3
16 and 17 years old	1,915	1,774	92.7	*	*	10	0.5	1,685	88.0
18 and 19 years old	1,965	1,321	67.2	*	*	*	*	390	19.9
20 and 21 years old	1,819	837	46.0	*	*	2	0.1	66	3.6
22 to 24 years old	2,869	744	25.9	*	*	3	0.1	31	1.1
25 to 29 years old	4,651	571	12.3	*	*	8	0.2	32	0.7
30 to 34 years old	4,373	210	4.8	*	*	8	0.2	15	0.3
35 to 44 years old	8,310	286	3.4	*	*	6	0.1	23	0.3
45 to 54 years old	6,849	96	1.4	*	*	11	0.2	12	0.2
55 years old and over	8,928	52	0.6	*	*	3	*	11	0.1
Male									
Total	27,605	8,873	32.1	1,060	3.8	4,306	15.6	1,977	7.2
3 and 4 years old	1,077	507	47.1	507	47.1	*	*	*	*
5 and 6 years old	1,058	1000	94.6	548	51.8	452	42.8	*	*
7 to 9 years old	1,618	1,578	97.5	5	0.3	1,573	97.2	*	*
10 to 13 years old	2,157	2,101	97.4	*	*	2,058	95.4	43	2.0
14 and 15 years old	970	952	98.2	*	*	184	19.0	768	79.2
16 and 17 years old	982	901	91.7	*	*	7	0.7	865	88.0
18 and 19 years old	982	622	63.3	*	*	*	*	209	21.3
20 and 21 years old	868	355	40.9	*	*	2	0.2	41	4.7
22 to 24 years old	1,505	347	23.0	*	*	3	0.2	23	1.5
25 to 29 years old	2,379	236	9.9	*	*	4	0.2	13	0.6
30 to 34 years old	2,254	114	5.0	*	*	5	0.2	5	0.2
35 to 44 years old	4,210	110	2.6	*	*	4	0.1	4	0.1
45 to 54 years old	3,428	37	1.1	*	*	11	0.3	4	0.1
55 years old and over	4,116	13	0.3	*	*	3	0.1	3	0.1
Female									
Total	27,603	9,101	33.0	1,063	3.9	4,034	14.6	1,959	7.1
3 and 4 years old	1,041	507	48.8	507	48.8	*	*	*	*
5 and 6 years old	1,006	960	95.5	552	54.9	408	40.6	*	*
7 to 9 years old	1,575	1,520	96.5	4	0.3	1,516	96.3	*	*
10 to 13 years old	2,069	2,012	97.3	*	*	1,971	95.3	41	2.0
14 and 15 years old	957	944	98.6	*	*	125	13.1	818	85.5
16 and 17 years old	932	873	93.6	*	*	3	0.3	820	88.0
18 and 19 years old	983	699	71.1	*	*	*	*	181	18.4
20 and 21 years old	952	482	50.7	*	*	*	*	25	2.6
22 to 24 years old	1,363	398	29.2	*	*	*	*	8	0.6
25 to 29 years old	2,272	334	14.7	*	*	4	0.2	19	0.8
30 to 34 years old	2,119	96	4.6	*	*	4	0.2	10	0.5
35 to 44 years old	4,100	176	4.3	*	*	2	*	19	0.5
45 to 54 years old	3,422	59	1.7	*	*	*	*	9	0.3
55 years old and over	4,812	39	0.8	*	*	1	*	8	0.2

* = Quantity equals zero or rounds to zero.

Table A-1. Enrollment Status of the Population 3 Years Old and Over, by Sex, Age, Race, Hispanic Origin, Foreign Born, and Foreign-Born Parentage, October 2017—*Continued*

(Numbers in thousands; percent; civilian noninstitutionalized population.)

Age, sex, race, Hispanic origin, and nativity	Population	Enrolled in school — College undergraduate or graduate		Not enrolled in school — Total		Not enrolled in school — High school graduate		Not enrolled in school — Not high school graduate	
	Number	Number	Percent	Number	Percent	Number	Percent	Number	Percent
5 and 6 years old	312	*	*	9	2.8	*	*	9	2.8
7 to 9 years old	370	*	*	7	2.0	*	*	7	2.0
10 to 13 years old	543	*	*	6	1.1	*	*	6	1.1
14 and 15 years old	273	4	1.3	*	*	*	*	*	*
16 and 17 years old	305	22	7.1	17	5.6	3	0.9	14	4.7
18 and 19 years old	213	164	77.1	29	13.6	21	9.7	8	3.9
20 and 21 years old	328	252	76.7	72	22.0	72	22.0	*	*
22 to 24 years old	445	195	43.8	246	55.2	238	53.4	8	1.8
25 to 29 years old	895	155	17.4	738	82.5	705	78.8	33	3.7
30 to 34 years old	915	60	6.6	855	93.4	807	88.2	48	5.2
35 to 44 years old	1,675	54	3.2	1,621	96.8	1,546	92.3	75	4.5
45 to 54 years old	1,445	15	1.1	1,430	98.9	1,278	88.5	152	10.5
55 years old and over	2,490	6	0.2	2,480	99.6	2,043	82.0	437	17.6
HISPANIC (OF ANY RACE)									
Both Sexes									
Total	55,207	3,574	6.5	37,234	67.4	25,307	45.8	11,926	21.6
3 and 4 years old	2,117	*	*	1,103	52.1	*	*	1,103	52.1
5 and 6 years old	2,064	*	*	103	5.0	*	*	103	5.0
7 to 9 years old	3,193	*	*	95	3.0	*	*	95	3.0
10 to 13 years old	4,226	*	*	113	2.7	*	*	113	2.7
14 and 15 years old	1,927	*	*	31	1.6	*	*	31	1.6
16 and 17 years old	1,915	80	4.2	141	7.3	34	1.8	107	5.6
18 and 19 years old	1,965	931	47.4	644	32.8	463	23.6	181	9.2
20 and 21 years old	1,819	769	42.3	982	54.0	797	43.8	185	10.2
22 to 24 years old	2,869	710	24.8	2,125	74.1	1,787	62.3	337	11.8
25 to 29 years old	4,651	530	11.4	4,081	87.7	3,321	71.4	760	16.3
30 to 34 years old	4,373	187	4.3	4,163	95.2	3,068	70.1	1,096	25.1
35 to 44 years old	8,310	258	3.1	8,024	96.6	5,632	67.8	2,391	28.8
45 to 54 years old	6,849	72	1.1	6,753	98.6	4,707	68.7	2,046	29.9
55 years old and over	8,928	38	0.4	8,877	99.4	5,498	61.6	3,379	37.8
Male									
Total	27,605	1,529	5.5	18,732	67.9	12,522	45.4	6,210	22.5
3 and 4 years old	1,077	*	*	570	52.9	*	*	570	52.9
5 and 6 years old	1,058	*	*	58	5.4	*	*	58	5.4
7 to 9 years old	1,618	*	*	40	2.5	*	*	40	2.5
10 to 13 years old	2,157	*	*	56	2.6	*	*	56	2.6
14 and 15 years old	970	*	*	18	1.8	*	*	18	1.8
16 and 17 years old	982	30	3.0	81	8.3	13	1.3	69	7.0
18 and 19 years old	982	413	42.0	360	36.7	247	25.1	113	11.5
20 and 21 years old	868	311	35.9	513	59.1	391	45.0	123	14.1
22 to 24 years old	1,505	321	21.3	1,159	77.0	965	64.1	193	12.9
25 to 29 years old	2,379	219	9.2	2,143	90.1	1,703	71.6	440	18.5
30 to 34 years old	2,254	104	4.6	2,140	95.0	1,533	68.0	607	26.9
35 to 44 years old	4,210	103	2.4	4,099	97.4	2,819	67.0	1,280	30.4
45 to 54 years old	3,428	22	0.6	3,391	98.9	2,325	67.8	1,066	31.1
55 years old and over	4,116	7	0.2	4,104	99.7	2,527	61.4	1,577	38.3
Female									
Total	27,603	2,045	7.4	18,502	67.0	12,785	46.3	5,717	20.7
3 and 4 years old	1,041	*	*	533	51.2	*	*	533	51.2
5 and 6 years old	1,006	*	*	46	4.5	*	*	46	4.5
7 to 9 years old	1,575	*	*	55	3.5	*	*	55	3.5
10 to 13 years old	2,069	*	*	56	2.7	*	*	56	2.7
14 and 15 years old	957	*	*	13	1.4	*	*	13	1.4
16 and 17 years old	932	50	5.3	59	6.4	21	2.3	38	4.1
18 and 19 years old	983	518	52.7	284	28.9	216	22.0	67	6.9
20 and 21 years old	952	457	48.1	469	49.3	407	42.7	63	6.6
22 to 24 years old	1,363	390	28.6	966	70.8	822	60.3	144	10.5
25 to 29 years old	2,272	312	13.7	1,938	85.3	1,618	71.2	320	14.1
30 to 34 years old	2,119	83	3.9	2,023	95.4	1,534	72.4	488	23.0
35 to 44 years old	4,100	155	3.8	3,924	95.7	2,814	68.6	1,111	27.1
45 to 54 years old	3,422	50	1.5	3,362	98.3	2,382	69.6	980	28.7
55 years old and over	4,812	30	0.6	4,773	99.2	2,971	61.7	1,802	37.4

* = Quantity equals zero or rounds to zero.

Table A-1. Enrollment Status of the Population 3 Years Old and Over, by Sex, Age, Race, Hispanic Origin, Foreign Born, and Foreign-Born Parentage, October 2017—*Continued*

(Numbers in thousands; percent; civilian noninstitutionalized population.)

| Age, sex, race, Hispanic origin, and nativity | Population | Enrolled in school | | | | | | | | |
| | | Total | | Nursery or kindergarten | | Elementary | | High school | |
	Number	Number	Percent	Number	Percent	Number	Percent	Number	Percent
FOREIGN–BORN									
Both Sexes									
Total	43,377	4,498	10.4	222	0.5	1,072	2.5	956	2.2
3 and 4 years old	192	96	50.3	96	50.3	*	*	*	*
5 and 6 years old	254	239	94.3	123	48.6	116	45.7	*	*
7 to 9 years old	393	381	97.1	2	0.5	379	96.6	*	*
10 to 13 years old	550	521	94.8	*	*	503	91.5	18	3.3
14 and 15 years old	350	336	96.0	*	*	45	12.9	291	83.1
16 and 17 years old	466	407	87.4	*	*	*	*	398	85.5
18 and 19 years old	670	437	65.2	*	*	*	*	142	21.1
20 and 21 years old	790	392	49.7	*	*	*	*	17	2.1
22 to 24 years old	1,529	466	30.5	*	*	*	*	4	0.3
25 to 29 years old	3,426	507	14.8	*	*	5	0.2	27	0.8
30 to 34 years old	4,379	211	4.8	*	*	4	0.1	15	0.4
35 to 44 years old	9,164	302	3.3	*	*	4	*	26	0.3
45 to 54 years old	8,559	133	1.6	*	*	7	0.1	10	0.1
55 years old and over..........	12,657	68	0.5	*	*	8	0.1	8	0.1
Male									
Total	21,034	2,169	10.3	101	0.5	568	2.7	483	2.3
3 and 4 years old	102	52	51.1	52	51.1	*	*	*	*
5 and 6 years old	92	92	100.0	49	52.9	43	47.1	*	*
7 to 9 years old	234	233	99.9	*	*	233	99.9	*	*
10 to 13 years old	272	248	91.4	*	*	241	88.6	8	2.8
14 and 15 years old	167	167	100.0	*	*	32	19.2	135	80.8
16 and 17 years old	247	210	85.0	*	*	*	*	204	82.7
18 and 19 years old	365	218	59.6	*	*	*	*	85	23.3
20 and 21 years old	407	188	46.1	*	*	*	*	3	0.7
22 to 24 years old	777	217	27.9	*	*	*	*	4	0.6
25 to 29 years old	1,765	267	15.1	*	*	4	0.2	18	1.0
30 to 34 years old	2,141	79	3.7	*	*	*	*	12	0.6
35 to 44 years old	4,495	116	2.6	*	*	4	0.1	11	0.2
45 to 54 years old	4,228	56	1.3	*	*	7	0.2	4	0.1
55 years old and over..........	5,745	26	0.5	*	*	3	0.1	*	*
Female									
Total	22,343	2,329	10.4	121	0.5	504	2.3	473	2.1
3 and 4 years old	90	44	49.3	44	49.3	*	*	*	*
5 and 6 years old	162	147	91.0	75	46.1	73	44.9	*	*
7 to 9 years old	159	148	93.0	2	1.3	146	91.8	*	*
10 to 13 years old	278	273	98.1	*	*	263	94.3	10	3.7
14 and 15 years old	183	169	92.3	*	*	13	7.1	156	85.3
16 and 17 years old	219	197	90.0	*	*	*	*	194	88.6
18 and 19 years old	304	219	72.0	*	*	*	*	56	18.5
20 and 21 years old	382	205	53.5	*	*	*	*	14	3.7
22 to 24 years old	752	249	33.1	*	*	*	*	*	*
25 to 29 years old	1,661	240	14.4	*	*	1	0.1	9	0.5
30 to 34 years old	2,239	132	5.9	*	*	4	0.2	4	0.2
35 to 44 years old	4,669	186	4.0	*	*	*	*	16	0.3
45 to 54 years old	4,332	77	1.8	*	*	*	*	6	0.1
55 years old and over..........	6,912	42	0.6	*	*	4	0.1	8	0.1
CHILDREN OF FOREIGN–BORN PARENTS									
Both Sexes									
Total	79,046	20,624	26.1	2,194	2.8	8,566	10.8	4,333	5.5
3 and 4 years old	2,018	1,047	51.9	1,047	51.9	*	*	*	*
5 and 6 years old	2,177	2,056	94.4	1,129	51.9	927	42.6	*	*
7 to 9 years old	3,114	3,014	96.8	18	0.6	2,997	96.2	*	*
10 to 13 years old	4,481	4,372	97.6	*	*	4,285	95.6	86	1.9
14 and 15 years old	2,115	2,072	98.0	*	*	315	14.9	1,753	82.9
16 and 17 years old	2,169	2,013	92.8	*	*	3	0.2	1,914	88.2
18 and 19 years old	2,134	1,555	72.9	*	*	*	*	402	18.9
20 and 21 years old	2,200	1,244	56.5	*	*	2	0.1	53	2.4
22 to 24 years old	3,569	1,208	33.8	*	*	*	*	15	0.4

* = Quantity equals zero or rounds to zero.

Table A-1. Enrollment Status of the Population 3 Years Old and Over, by Sex, Age, Race, Hispanic Origin, Foreign Born, and Foreign-Born Parentage, October 2017—*Continued*

(Numbers in thousands; percent; civilian noninstitutionalized population.)

| Age, sex, race, Hispanic origin, and nativity | Population | Enrolled in school | | Not enrolled in school | | | | | |
| | | College undergraduate or graduate | | Total | | High school graduate | | Not high school graduate | |
	Number	Number	Percent	Number	Percent	Number	Percent	Number	Percent
FOREIGN–BORN									
Both Sexes									
Total...	43,377	2,248	5.2	38,879	89.6	28,906	66.6	9,974	23.0
3 and 4 years old	192	*	*	95	49.7	*	*	95	49.7
5 and 6 years old	254	*	*	15	5.7	*	*	15	5.7
7 to 9 years old	393	*	*	11	2.9	*	*	11	2.9
10 to 13 years old	550	*	*	29	5.2	*	*	29	5.2
14 and 15 years old	350	*	*	14	4.0	*	*	14	4.0
16 and 17 years old	466	9	1.8	59	12.6	26	5.5	33	7.2
18 and 19 years old	670	295	44.1	233	34.8	154	23.1	78	11.7
20 and 21 years old	790	376	47.6	397	50.3	308	39.0	89	11.3
22 to 24 years old	1,529	461	30.2	1,063	69.5	852	55.7	211	13.8
25 to 29 years old	3,426	475	13.9	2,919	85.2	2,343	68.4	576	16.8
30 to 34 years old	4,379	192	4.4	4,168	95.2	3,184	72.7	984	22.5
35 to 44 years old	9,164	271	3.0	8,862	96.7	6,644	72.5	2,218	24.2
45 to 54 years old	8,559	116	1.4	8,426	98.4	6,321	73.8	2,105	24.6
55 years old and over..........	12,657	52	0.4	12,589	99.5	9,075	71.7	3,513	27.8
Male									
Total...	21,034	1,018	4.8	18,865	89.7	13,939	66.3	4,926	23.4
3 and 4 years old	102	*	*	50	48.9	*	*	50	48.9
5 and 6 years old	92	*	*	*	*	*	*	*	*
7 to 9 years old	234	*	*	*	0.1	*	*	*	0.1
10 to 13 years old	272	*	*	23	8.6	*	*	23	8.6
14 and 15 years old	167	*	*	*	*	*	*	*	*
16 and 17 years old	247	6	2.3	37	15.0	11	4.6	25	10.3
18 and 19 years old	365	132	36.3	148	40.4	96	26.3	52	14.1
20 and 21 years old	407	185	45.4	220	53.9	165	40.5	55	13.4
22 to 24 years old	777	213	27.4	560	72.1	440	56.7	120	15.4
25 to 29 years old	1,765	245	13.9	1,498	84.9	1,163	65.9	335	19.0
30 to 34 years old	2,141	67	3.2	2,061	96.3	1,556	72.7	506	23.6
35 to 44 years old	4,495	102	2.3	4,379	97.4	3,226	71.8	1,152	25.6
45 to 54 years old	4,228	45	1.1	4,171	98.7	3,119	73.8	1,052	24.9
55 years old and over..........	5,745	23	0.4	5,719	99.5	4,163	72.5	1,556	27.1
Female									
Total...	22,343	1,231	5.5	20,014	89.6	14,967	67.0	5,048	22.6
3 and 4 years old	90	*	*	46	50.7	*	*	46	50.7
5 and 6 years old	162	*	*	15	9.0	*	*	15	9.0
7 to 9 years old	159	*	*	11	7.0	*	*	11	7.0
10 to 13 years old	278	*	*	5	1.9	*	*	5	1.9
14 and 15 years old	183	*	*	14	7.7	*	*	14	7.7
16 and 17 years old	219	3	1.4	22	10.0	14	6.4	8	3.6
18 and 19 years old	304	163	53.5	85	28.0	58	19.2	27	8.8
20 and 21 years old	382	191	49.9	178	46.5	143	37.4	35	9.1
22 to 24 years old	752	249	33.1	503	66.9	412	54.7	92	12.2
25 to 29 years old	1,661	230	13.8	1,421	85.6	1,180	71.0	241	14.5
30 to 34 years old	2,239	125	5.6	2,107	94.1	1,628	72.7	479	21.4
35 to 44 years old	4,669	170	3.6	4,483	96.0	3,418	73.2	1,066	22.8
45 to 54 years old	4,332	71	1.6	4,255	98.2	3,202	73.9	1,053	24.3
55 years old and over..........	6,912	30	0.4	6,870	99.4	4,912	71.1	1,957	28.3
CHILDREN OF FOREIGN– BORN PARENTS									
Both Sexes									
Total...	79,046	5,531	7.0	58,422	73.9	45,634	57.7	12,787	16.2
3 and 4 years old	2,018	*	*	971	48.1	*	*	971	48.1
5 and 6 years old	2,177	*	*	121	5.6	*	*	121	5.6
7 to 9 years old	3,114	*	*	99	3.2	*	*	99	3.2
10 to 13 years old	4,481	*	*	110	2.4	*	*	110	2.4
14 and 15 years old	2,115	4	0.2	43	2.0	*	*	43	2.0
16 and 17 years old	2,169	95	4.4	156	7.2	47	2.2	110	5.1
18 and 19 years old	2,134	1,153	54.0	579	27.1	440	20.6	139	6.5
20 and 21 years old	2,200	1,188	54.0	957	43.5	794	36.1	162	7.4
22 to 24 years old	3,569	1,194	33.4	2,361	66.2	2,031	56.9	330	9.2

* = Quantity equals zero or rounds to zero.

Table A-1. Enrollment Status of the Population 3 Years Old and Over, by Sex, Age, Race, Hispanic Origin, Foreign Born, and Foreign-Born Parentage, October 2017—*Continued*

(Numbers in thousands; percent; civilian noninstitutionalized population.)

Age, sex, race, Hispanic origin, and nativity	Population	Enrolled in school								
		Total		Nursery or kindergarten		Elementary		High school	
	Number	Number	Percent	Number	Percent	Number	Percent	Number	Percent
25 to 29 years old	6,544	961	14.7	*	*	5	0.1	37	0.6
30 to 34 years old	6,565	370	5.6	*	*	10	0.2	15	0.2
35 to 44 years old	12,381	453	3.7	*	*	6	*	34	0.3
45 to 54 years old	11,139	178	1.6	*	*	7	0.1	16	0.1
55 years old and over	18,439	81	0.4	*	*	8	*	8	*
Male									
Total	38,534	10,104	26.2	1,077	2.8	4,381	11.4	2,186	5.7
3 and 4 years old	987	506	51.3	506	51.3	*	*	*	*
5 and 6 years old	1079	1018	94.3	559	51.8	459	42.6	*	*
7 to 9 years old	1,569	1,531	97.6	12	0.7	1,519	96.8	*	*
10 to 13 years old	2,285	2,229	97.6	*	*	2,188	95.8	41	1.8
14 and 15 years old	1063	1046	98.4	*	*	183	17.2	863	81.1
16 and 17 years old	1,088	1004	92.3	*	*	3	0.3	966	88.8
18 and 19 years old	1,063	743	69.8	*	*	*	*	226	21.2
20 and 21 years old	1,100	556	50.5	*	*	2	0.2	24	2.2
22 to 24 years old	1,856	586	31.6	*	*	*	*	15	0.8
25 to 29 years old	3,282	432	13.2	*	*	4	0.1	18	0.5
30 to 34 years old	3,229	181	5.6	*	*	7	0.2	12	0.4
35 to 44 years old	6,091	170	2.8	*	*	4	0.1	14	0.2
45 to 54 years old	5,502	71	1.3	*	*	7	0.1	7	0.1
55 years old and over	8,338	30	0.4	*	*	3	*	*	*
Female									
Total	40,512	10,521	26.0	1,117	2.8	4,185	10.3	2,148	5.3
3 and 4 years old	1031	540	52.4	540	52.4	*	*	*	*
5 and 6 years old	1098	1038	94.6	570	52.0	468	42.6	*	*
7 to 9 years old	1,545	1,483	96.0	6	0.4	1,477	95.6	*	*
10 to 13 years old	2,196	2,142	97.6	*	*	2,097	95.5	45	2.1
14 and 15 years old	1,052	1,026	97.5	*	*	132	12.6	890	84.6
16 and 17 years old	1,081	1,008	93.3	*	*	*	*	948	87.7
18 and 19 years old	1,071	813	75.9	*	*	*	*	177	16.5
20 and 21 years old	1,101	688	62.5	*	*	*	*	29	2.7
22 to 24 years old	1,713	622	36.3	*	*	*	*	*	*
25 to 29 years old	3,262	529	16.2	*	*	1	*	19	0.6
30 to 34 years old	3,336	189	5.7	*	*	4	0.1	4	0.1
35 to 44 years old	6,289	283	4.5	*	*	2	*	20	0.3
45 to 54 years old	5,637	107	1.9	*	*	*	*	9	0.2
55 years old and over	10,100	51	0.5	*	*	4	*	8	0.1

* = Quantity equals zero or rounds to zero.

Table A-1. Enrollment Status of the Population 3 Years Old and Over, by Sex, Age, Race, Hispanic Origin, Foreign Born, and Foreign-Born Parentage, October 2017—*Continued*

(Numbers in thousands; percent; civilian noninstitutionalized population.)

Age, sex, race, Hispanic origin, and nativity	Population	Enrolled in school		Not enrolled in school					
		College undergraduate or graduate		Total		High school graduate		Not high school graduate	
	Number	Number	Percent	Number	Percent	Number	Percent	Number	Percent
25 to 29 years old	6,544	919	14.0	5,583	85.3	4,843	74.0	740	11.3
30 to 34 years old	6,565	344	5.2	6,195	94.4	5,072	77.3	1,123	17.1
35 to 44 years old	12,381	413	3.3	11,927	96.3	9,539	77.0	2,388	19.3
45 to 54 years old	11,139	155	1.4	10,961	98.4	8,705	78.1	2,256	20.3
55 years old and over	18,439	65	0.4	18,358	99.6	14,163	76.8	4,195	22.7
Male									
Total	38,534	2,460	6.4	28,430	73.8	22,058	57.2	6,372	16.5
3 and 4 years old	987	*	*	480	48.7	*	*	480	48.7
5 and 6 years old	1079	*	*	61	5.7	*	*	61	5.7
7 to 9 years old	1,569	*	*	38	2.4	*	*	38	2.4
10 to 13 years old	2,285	*	*	56	2.4	*	*	56	2.4
14 and 15 years old	1063	1	*	17	1.6	*	*	17	1.6
16 and 17 years old	1,088	35	3.2	83	7.7	20	1.9	63	5.8
18 and 19 years old	1,063	517	48.6	321	30.2	227	21.3	94	8.8
20 and 21 years old	1,100	530	48.2	544	49.5	435	39.5	109	9.9
22 to 24 years old	1,856	572	30.8	1,270	68.4	1,079	58.1	191	10.3
25 to 29 years old	3,282	410	12.5	2,850	86.8	2,424	73.9	426	13.0
30 to 34 years old	3,229	162	5.0	3,049	94.4	2,455	76.0	594	18.4
35 to 44 years old	6,091	152	2.5	5,921	97.2	4,687	76.9	1,234	20.3
45 to 54 years old	5,502	56	1.0	5,431	98.7	4,288	77.9	1,143	20.8
55 years old and over	8,338	26	0.3	8,309	99.6	6,444	77.3	1,865	22.4
Female									
Total	40,512	3,071	7.6	29,991	74.0	23,576	58.2	6,415	15.8
3 and 4 years old	1031	*	*	491	47.6	*	*	491	47.6
5 and 6 years old	1098	*	*	60	5.4	*	*	60	5.4
7 to 9 years old	1,545	*	*	61	4.0	*	*	61	4.0
10 to 13 years old	2,196	*	*	54	2.4	*	*	54	2.4
14 and 15 years old	1,052	4	0.3	26	2.5	*	*	26	2.5
16 and 17 years old	1,081	61	5.6	73	6.7	26	2.4	47	4.3
18 and 19 years old	1,071	636	59.4	258	24.1	213	19.9	45	4.2
20 and 21 years old	1,101	659	59.9	413	37.5	360	32.7	53	4.8
22 to 24 years old	1,713	622	36.3	1,091	63.7	953	55.6	139	8.1
25 to 29 years old	3,262	509	15.6	2,734	83.8	2,419	74.2	314	9.6
30 to 34 years old	3,336	182	5.5	3,146	94.3	2,617	78.5	529	15.9
35 to 44 years old	6,289	261	4.2	6,006	95.5	4,852	77.1	1,154	18.3
45 to 54 years old	5,637	98	1.7	5,530	98.1	4,417	78.4	1,113	19.7
55 years old and over	10,100	39	0.4	10,049	99.5	7,719	76.4	2,330	23.1

* = Quantity equals zero or rounds to zero.

Table A-2. Single Grade of Enrollment and High School Graduation Status for Population 3 Years Old and Over, by Sex, Age (Single Years for 3 to 24 Years), Race, and Hispanic Origin, October 2017

(Numbers in thousands; percent; civilian noninstitutionalized population.)

Age, sex, race, and Hispanic origin	Population	Enrolled		Enrolled		Elementary grades							
		Number	Percent	Nursery	Kinder-garten	1	2	3	4	5	6	7	8
ALL RACES													
Both Sexes													
Total	308,935	76,409	24.7	4,676	3,964	4,100	3,905	4,281	3,900	4,098	4,174	4,176	3,894
3 years old	4,086	1,641	40.2	1,577	64	*	*	*	*	*	*	*	*
4 years old	3,943	2,678	67.9	2,389	289	*	*	*	*	*	*	*	*
5 years old	3,972	3,576	90.0	654	2,744	150	28	*	*	*	*	*	*
6 years old	4,067	3,940	96.9	56	829	2,871	151	33	*	*	*	*	*
7 years old	4,065	3,912	96.2	*	38	991	2,681	183	19	*	*	*	*
8 years old	4,064	3,958	97.4	*	*	71	927	2,750	180	30	*	*	*
9 years old	4,108	4,009	97.6	*	*	16	86	1,182	2,495	198	32	*	*
10 years old	4,099	4,002	97.6	*	*	*	32	117	1,041	2,627	154	30	*
11 years old	4,255	4,160	97.8	*	*	*	16	134	1,055	2,682	244	29	
12 years old	4,229	4,145	98.0	*	*	*	*	*	32	160	1,086	2,698	134
13 years old	4,051	3,965	97.9	*	*	*	*	*	*	29	138	1,021	2,525
14 years old	4,083	3,972	97.3	*	*	*	*	*	*	*	35	122	1,018
15 years old	4,146	4,111	99.2	*	*	*	*	*	*	*	3	21	160
16 years old	4,184	3,942	94.2	*	*	*	*	*	*	*	2	4	19
17 years old	4,357	3,991	91.6	*	*	*	*	*	*	*	*	6	*
18 years old	4,155	3,064	73.7	*	*	*	*	*	*	*	*	6	
19 years old	4,067	2,542	62.5	*	*	*	*	*	*	*	*	2	
20 years old	4,085	2,416	59.2	*	*	*	*	*	*	*	2	*	
21 years old	4,226	2,154	51.0	*	*	*	*	*	*	*	*	*	
22 years old	4,262	1,553	36.4	*	*	*	*	*	*	*	*	3	
23 years old	4,278	1,138	26.6	*	*	*	*	*	*	*	*	2	
24 years old	4,465	1005	22.5	*	*	*	*	*	*	*	*	*	
25 to 29 years old	22,731	2,758	12.1	*	*	*	*	*	*	*	5	4	
30 to 34 years old	21,359	1,251	5.9	*	*	*	*	*	*	*	13	2	*
35 to 39 years old	20,836	836	4.0	*	*	*	*	*	*	*	*	*	10
40 to 44 years old	19,265	567	2.9	*	*	*	*	*	*	*	4	4	*
45 to 49 years old	20,606	448	2.2	*	*	*	*	*	*	*	9	*	
50 to 54 years old	21,043	251	1.2	*	*	*	*	*	*	*	*	4	
55 to 59 years old	21,707	227	1.0	*	*	*	*	*	*	*	*	*	
60 to 64 years old	20,113	117	0.6	*	*	*	*	*	*	*	4	*	
65 years and over	50,027	80	0.2	*	*	*	*	*	*	*	4	3	*
Male													
Total	150,775	37,779	25.1	2,377	2,027	2,113	1,981	2,257	1,891	2,030	2,233	2,182	2,023
3 years old	2,091	830	39.7	788	43	*	*	*	*	*	*	*	*
4 years old	2,041	1,378	67.5	1,227	151	*	*	*	*	*	*	*	*
5 years old	2,030	1,794	88.4	334	1,368	77	15	*	*	*	*	*	*
6 years old	2,083	2,023	97.1	28	450	1,468	69	8	*	*	*	*	*
7 years old	2,071	1,984	95.8	*	15	523	1,350	85	10	*	*	*	*
8 years old	2,091	2,038	97.5	*	*	37	492	1,429	64	17	*	*	*
9 years old	2,077	2,035	98.0	*	*	8	41	662	1,190	122	13	*	*
10 years old	2,019	1,970	97.6	*	*	*	15	59	540	1,243	89	24	*
11 years old	2,245	2,204	98.2	*	*	*	*	15	66	560	1,399	144	21
12 years old	2,167	2,125	98.0	*	*	*	*	*	20	73	594	1,357	61
13 years old	2,055	2,005	97.5	*	*	*	*	*	*	15	83	556	1,245
14 years old	2,072	2,018	97.4	*	*	*	*	*	*	*	24	56	570
15 years old	2,116	2,093	98.9	*	*	*	*	*	*	*	3	14	111
16 years old	2,116	1,988	94.0	*	*	*	*	*	*	*	2	4	15
17 years old	2,228	2,020	90.7	*	*	*	*	*	*	*	*	6	*
18 years old	2,136	1,513	70.8	*	*	*	*	*	*	*	*	4	*
19 years old	2,016	1,191	59.0	*	*	*	*	*	*	*	*	2	*
20 years old	2,139	1,199	56.1	*	*	*	*	*	*	*	2	*	
21 years old	2,063	936	45.4	*	*	*	*	*	*	*	*	*	
22 years old	2,151	776	36.1	*	*	*	*	*	*	*	*	3	
23 years old	2,124	512	24.1	*	*	*	*	*	*	*	*	*	
24 years old	2,204	450	20.4	*	*	*	*	*	*	*	*	*	
25 to 29 years old	11,327	1,233	10.9	*	*	*	*	*	*	*	4	*	*
30 to 34 years old	10,570	545	5.2	*	*	*	*	*	*	*	7	*	*
35 to 39 years old	10,249	287	2.8	*	*	*	*	*	*	*	*	*	*
40 to 44 years old	9,427	219	2.3	*	*	*	*	*	*	*	2	4	*
45 to 49 years old	10,090	186	1.8	*	*	*	*	*	*	*	8	*	*
50 to 54 years old	10,273	76	0.7	*	*	*	*	*	*	*	*	4	*
55 to 59 years old	10,485	77	0.7	*	*	*	*	*	*	*	*	*	*

* = Quantity zero or rounds to zero.

Table A-2. Single Grade of Enrollment and High School Graduation Status for Population 3 Years Old and Over, by Sex, Age (Single Years for 3 to 24 Years), Race, and Hispanic Origin, October 2017—Continued

(Numbers in thousands; percent; civilian noninstitutionalized population.)

Age, sex, race, and Hispanic origin	Enrolled										Not enrolled		Not enrolled	
	High school				Undergraduate college				Graduate school		H.S. grad	Not grad	Number	Percent
	9	10	11	12	1	2	3	4	1	2+				
ALL RACES														
Both Sexes														
Total	4,279	3,967	4,057	4,537	4,192	4,147	3,518	2,733	1,364	2,445	203,148	29,378	232,526	75.3
3 years old	*	*	*	*	*	*	*	*	*	*	*	2,445	2,445	59.8
4 years old	*	*	*	*	*	*	*	*	*	*	*	1,266	1,266	32.1
5 years old	*	*	*	*	*	*	*	*	*	*	*	396	396	10.0
6 years old	*	*	*	*	*	*	*	*	*	*	*	127	127	3.1
7 years old	*	*	*	*	*	*	*	*	*	*	*	153	153	3.8
8 years old	*	*	*	*	*	*	*	*	*	*	*	106	106	2.6
9 years old	*	*	*	*	*	*	*	*	*	*	*	100	100	2.4
10 years old	*	*	*	*	*	*	*	*	*	*	*	97	97	2.4
11 years old	*	*	*	*	*	*	*	*	*	*	*	95	95	2.2
12 years old	35	*	*	*	*	*	*	*	*	*	*	84	84	2.0
13 years old	232	22	*	*	*	*	*	*	*	*	*	86	86	2.1
14 years old	2,574	199	24	*	*	*	*	*	*	*	*	111	111	2.7
15 years old	1,196	2,307	314	75	22	*	*	*	9	3	*	35	35	0.8
16 years old	191	1,113	2,325	242	40	*	5	*	*	*	58	183	242	5.8
17 years old	20	203	1,111	2,496	119	13	6	*	16	*	123	243	366	8.4
18 years old	2	31	162	1,198	1,514	108	24	*	20	*	776	315	1,091	26.3
19 years old	7	3	42	209	891	1,158	188	37	4	*	1,273	253	1,526	37.5
20 years old	11	4	9	100	428	819	961	74	8	*	1,468	200	1,669	40.8
21 years old	4	15	5	52	123	465	629	763	38	59	1,816	257	2,073	49.0
22 years old	*	*	7	15	100	269	364	517	143	135	2,496	213	2,709	63.6
23 years old	1	*	4	9	127	184	180	273	149	207	2,879	261	3,140	73.4
24 years old	*	3	10	14	112	136	173	178	151	227	3,188	272	3,460	77.5
25 to 29 years old	*	20	17	38	253	472	422	446	361	720	18,445	1,528	19,973	87.9
30 to 34 years old	*	4	4	22	163	189	208	142	134	371	18,237	1,872	20,109	94.1
35 to 39 years old	3	12	7	15	112	115	153	114	92	203	18,043	1,957	20,000	96.0
40 to 44 years old	*	15	5	7	62	77	94	64	79	155	16,874	1,824	18,698	97.1
45 to 49 years old	*	4	3	14	38	91	34	57	64	134	18,159	1,999	20,158	97.8
50 to 54 years old	4	5	6	3	39	33	25	11	43	79	18,779	2,014	20,792	98.8
55 to 59 years old	*	4	2	16	14	11	30	37	35	77	19,271	2,209	21,480	99.0
60 to 64 years old	*	*	*	3	22	4	16	13	7	48	18,061	1,934	19,995	99.4
65 years and over	*	3	*	10	11	4	3	7	10	26	43,204	6,743	49,947	99.8
Male														
Total	2,134	1,948	2,173	2,299	1,824	1,934	1,616	1,206	513	1,017	98,177	14,820	112,997	74.9
3 years old	*	*	*	*	*	*	*	*	*	*	*	1,261	1,261	60.3
4 years old	*	*	*	*	*	*	*	*	*	*	*	663	663	32.5
5 years old	*	*	*	*	*	*	*	*	*	*	*	236	236	11.6
6 years old	*	*	*	*	*	*	*	*	*	*	*	60	60	2.9
7 years old	*	*	*	*	*	*	*	*	*	*	*	87	87	4.2
8 years old	*	*	*	*	*	*	*	*	*	*	*	53	53	2.5
9 years old	*	*	*	*	*	*	*	*	*	*	*	42	42	2.0
10 years old	*	*	*	*	*	*	*	*	*	*	*	49	49	2.4
11 years old	*	*	*	*	*	*	*	*	*	*	*	41	41	1.8
12 years old	19	*	*	*	*	*	*	*	*	*	*	42	42	2.0
13 years old	94	12	*	*	*	*	*	*	*	*	*	50	50	2.5
14 years old	1,261	92	16	*	*	*	*	*	*	*	*	55	55	2.6
15 years old	631	1,095	162	57	15	*	*	*	5	*	*	22	22	1.1
16 years old	105	581	1,154	114	10	*	3	*	*	*	34	94	128	6.0
17 years old	9	98	668	1,189	40	*	4	*	6	*	58	149	207	9.3
18 years old	1	17	114	668	626	52	14	*	17	*	441	182	623	29.2
19 years old	7	3	29	112	457	489	75	17	*	*	662	164	826	41.0
20 years old	4	*	5	62	224	399	463	32	7	*	812	128	940	43.9
21 years old	*	11	*	25	56	225	285	296	12	27	964	162	1,127	54.6
22 years old	*	*	7	12	45	187	165	250	52	55	1,258	117	1,375	63.9
23 years old	*	*	4	4	55	82	71	142	65	88	1,480	132	1,612	75.9
24 years old	*	3	7	9	36	59	80	90	62	105	1,620	134	1,754	79.6
25 to 29 years old	*	12	4	24	101	228	219	178	157	305	9,270	824	10,094	89.1
30 to 34 years old	*	4	*	8	73	81	104	65	34	170	9,017	1,008	10,025	94.8
35 to 39 years old	*	7	3	*	33	44	48	41	28	83	8,954	1,008	9,962	97.2
40 to 44 years old	*	1	*	7	30	21	34	32	28	61	8,221	987	9,208	97.7
45 to 49 years old	*	4	1	3	12	51	13	35	15	46	8,836	1,067	9,903	98.2
50 to 54 years old	4	1	*	*	1	12	10	1	11	32	9,151	1,046	10,197	99.3
55 to 59 years old	*	4	*	3	*	5	18	15	10	21	9,229	1,179	10,408	99.3

* = Quantity zero or rounds to zero.

Table A-2. Single Grade of Enrollment and High School Graduation Status for Population 3 Years Old and Over, by Sex, Age (Single Years for 3 to 24 Years), Race, and Hispanic Origin, October 2017—*Continued*

(Numbers in thousands; percent; civilian noninstitutionalized population.)

| Age, sex, race, and Hispanic origin | Population | Enrolled | | Nursery | Kinder-garten | Enrolled | | | | | | | | |
| | | | | | | Elementary grades | | | | | | | | |
		Number	Percent			1	2	3	4	5	6	7	8
60 to 64 years old	9,633	38	0.4	*	*	*	*	*	*	*	*	*	*
65 years and over	22,387	35	0.2	*	*	*	*	*	*	*	3	3	*
Female													
Total	158,159	38,630	24.4	2,300	1,937	1,986	1,925	2,024	2,009	2,068	1,942	1,995	1,872
3 years old	1,995	810	40.6	789	21	*	*	*	*	*	*	*	*
4 years old	1,902	1,300	68.3	1,162	137	*	*	*	*	*	*	*	*
5 years old	1,941	1,782	91.8	320	1,376	73	13	*	*	*	*	*	*
6 years old	1,984	1,917	96.6	28	379	1,403	82	25	*	*	*	*	*
7 years old	1,994	1,928	96.7	*	23	467	1,331	98	8	*	*	*	*
8 years old	1,973	1,920	97.3	*	*	34	436	1,321	116	13	*	*	*
9 years old	2,031	1,973	97.2	*	*	8	45	520	1,305	76	19	*	*
10 years old	2,080	2,032	97.7	*	*	*	18	58	501	1,384	66	6	*
11 years old	2,010	1,956	97.3	*	*	*	*	1	68	495	1,284	101	8
12 years old	2,062	2,021	98.0	*	*	*	*	*	11	87	493	1,340	73
13 years old	1,996	1,960	98.2	*	*	*	*	*	*	14	55	464	1,280
14 years old	2,010	1,954	97.2	*	*	*	*	*	*	*	11	67	449
15 years old	2,030	2,017	99.4	*	*	*	*	*	*	*	*	7	49
16 years old	2,068	1,954	94.5	*	*	*	*	*	*	*	*	*	3
17 years old	2,129	1,970	92.6	*	*	*	*	*	*	*	*	*	*
18 years old	2,019	1,551	76.8	*	*	*	*	*	*	*	*	2	*
19 years old	2,051	1,351	65.9	*	*	*	*	*	*	*	*	*	*
20 years old	1,946	1,217	62.5	*	*	*	*	*	*	*	*	*	*
21 years old	2,163	1,217	56.3	*	*	*	*	*	*	*	*	*	*
22 years old	2,112	778	36.8	*	*	*	*	*	*	*	*	*	*
23 years old	2,154	626	29.1	*	*	*	*	*	*	*	*	2	*
24 years old	2,260	555	24.5	*	*	*	*	*	*	*	*	*	*
25 to 29 years old	11,405	1,525	13.4	*	*	*	*	*	*	*	1	4	*
30 to 34 years old	10,789	706	6.5	*	*	*	*	*	*	*	6	2	*
35 to 39 years old	10,587	549	5.2	*	*	*	*	*	*	*	*	*	10
40 to 44 years old	9,838	348	3.5	*	*	*	*	*	*	*	3	*	*
45 to 49 years old	10,517	262	2.5	*	*	*	*	*	*	*	1	*	*
50 to 54 years old	10,770	174	1.6	*	*	*	*	*	*	*	*	*	*
55 to 59 years old	11,222	150	1.3	*	*	*	*	*	*	*	*	*	*
60 to 64 years old	10,480	80	0.8	*	*	*	*	*	*	*	4	*	*
65 years and over	27,640	45	0.2	*	*	*	*	*	*	*	1	*	*
WHITE ALONE NON-HISPANIC													
Both Sexes	189,026	39,649	21.0	2,461	1,955	1,922	1,889	2,176	1,897	2,100	2,052	2,171	2,065
Total	1,973	903	45.7	880	23	*	*	*	*	*	*	*	*
3 years old	1,942	1288	66.3	1,191	97	*	*	*	*	*	*	*	*
4 years old	1,970	1,770	89.9	366	1,337	54	14	*	*	*	*	*	*
5 years old	1,989	1,911	96.1	24	491	1,319	66	11	*	*	*	*	*
6 years old	1,988	1,911	96.1	*	8	507	1,310	74	13	*	*	*	*
7 years old	1,991	1,938	97.4	*	*	33	452	1,373	59	21	*	*	*
8 years old	2,056	2,006	97.6	*	*	9	26	658	1,214	88	11	*	*
9 years old	2,031	1,992	98.1	*	*	*	21	57	526	1,311	70	8	*
10 years old	2,204	2,142	97.2	*	*	*	*	4	82	579	1,386	78	14
11 years old	2,197	2,153	98.0	*	*	*	*	*	3	95	520	1,475	37
12 years old	2,119	2,071	97.8	*	*	*	*	*	*	6	48	541	1,372
13 years old	2,181	2,136	97.9	*	*	*	*	*	*	*	8	40	546
14 years old	2,183	2,163	99.1	*	*	*	*	*	*	*	*	12	81
15 years old	2,263	2,133	94.2	*	*	*	*	*	*	*	2	4	10
16 years old	2,294	2,118	92.3	*	*	*	*	*	*	*	*	6	*
17 years old	2,252	1,660	73.7	*	*	*	*	*	*	*	*	6	*
18 years old	2,147	1,322	61.6	*	*	*	*	*	*	*	*	*	*
19 years old	2,183	1,380	63.2	*	*	*	*	*	*	*	*	*	*
20 years old	2,249	1,196	53.2	*	*	*	*	*	*	*	*	*	*
21 years old	2,255	838	37.1	*	*	*	*	*	*	*	*	*	*
22 years old	2,412	611	25.3	*	*	*	*	*	*	*	*	*	*
23 years old	2,446	484	19.8	*	*	*	*	*	*	*	*	*	*
24 years old	12,487	1409	11.3	*	*	*	*	*	*	*	*	*	*
25 to 29 years old	12,058	703	5.8	*	*	*	*	*	*	*	3	2	*
30 to 34 years old	11,843	405	3.4	*	*	*	*	*	*	*	*	*	6
35 to 39 years old	11,040	308	2.8	*	*	*	*	*	*	*	4	*	*

* = Quantity zero or rounds to zero.

Table A-2. Single Grade of Enrollment and High School Graduation Status for Population 3 Years Old and Over, by Sex, Age (Single Years for 3 to 24 Years), Race, and Hispanic Origin, October 2017—*Continued*

(Numbers in thousands; percent; civilian noninstitutionalized population.)

Age, sex, race, and Hispanic origin	Enrolled										Not enrolled		Not enrolled	
	High school				Undergraduate college				Graduate school		H.S. grad	Not grad	Number	Percent
	9	10	11	12	1	2	3	4	1	2+				
60 to 64 years old	*	*	*	*	5	1	10	10	3	8	8,675	920	9,595	99.6
65 years and over	*	3	*	*	5	*	*	3	*	18	19,495	2,858	22,353	99.8
Female														
Total	2,145	2,019	1,884	2,238	2,367	2,212	1,902	1,527	851	1,428	104,972	14,558	119,529	75.6
3 years old	*	*	*	*	*	*	*	*	*	*	*	1,185	1,185	59.4
4 years old	*	*	*	*	*	*	*	*	*	*	*	603	603	31.7
5 years old	*	*	*	*	*	*	*	*	*	*	*	159	159	8.2
6 years old	*	*	*	*	*	*	*	*	*	*	*	67	67	3.4
7 years old	*	*	*	*	*	*	*	*	*	*	*	66	66	3.3
8 years old	*	*	*	*	*	*	*	*	*	*	*	53	53	2.7
9 years old	*	*	*	*	*	*	*	*	*	*	*	58	58	2.8
10 years old	*	*	*	*	*	*	*	*	*	*	*	48	48	2.3
11 years old	*	*	*	*	*	*	*	*	*	*	*	54	54	2.7
12 years old	17	*	*	*	*	*	*	*	*	*	*	41	41	2.0
13 years old	137	10	*	*	*	*	*	*	*	*	*	35	35	1.8
14 years old	1,312	107	8	*	*	*	*	*	*	*	*	56	56	2.8
15 years old	565	1,212	152	18	7	*	*	*	3	3	*	12	12	0.6
16 years old	85	532	1,171	129	31	*	2	*	*	*	25	89	114	5.5
17 years old	12	105	443	1,307	79	13	2	*	10	*	65	93	158	7.4
18 years old	1	14	48	530	888	56	10	*	3	*	335	133	468	23.2
19 years old	*	*	13	97	435	669	113	20	4	*	611	89	700	34.1
20 years old	7	4	4	38	204	420	498	42	1	*	656	72	729	37.5
21 years old	4	5	5	27	67	240	344	467	26	32	851	95	946	43.7
22 years old	*	*	*	3	56	82	200	267	90	80	1,238	96	1,334	63.2
23 years old	1	*	*	4	72	103	110	131	84	119	1,399	129	1,528	70.9
24 years old	*	*	3	5	76	77	94	88	89	122	1,567	138	1,706	75.5
25 to 29 years old	*	8	13	14	151	244	203	268	204	415	9,176	704	9,880	86.6
30 to 34 years old	*	*	4	14	90	108	104	78	100	201	9,220	863	10,083	93.5
35 to 39 years old	3	5	4	15	80	71	105	74	64	120	9,089	949	10,038	94.8
40 to 44 years old	*	14	5	*	32	56	59	33	51	95	8,653	837	9,490	96.5
45 to 49 years old	*	*	3	11	26	40	22	23	49	88	9,323	932	10,255	97.5
50 to 54 years old	*	3	6	3	37	21	15	11	31	47	9,628	968	10,595	98.4
55 to 59 years old	*	*	2	13	14	6	12	21	25	57	10,041	1,031	11,072	98.7
60 to 64 years old	*	*	*	3	17	3	6	2	4	41	9,386	1,014	10,400	99.2
65 years and over	*	*	*	10	6	4	3	3	10	8	23,709	3,885	27,594	99.8
WHITE ALONE NON-HISPANIC														
Both Sexes	2,278	2,101	2,161	2,364	2,180	2,098	1,911	1,536	786	1,543	137,837	11,541	149,377	79.0
Total	*	*	*	*	*	*	*	*	*	*	*	1,071	1,071	54.3
3 years old	*	*	*	*	*	*	*	*	*	*	*	653	653	33.7
4 years old	*	*	*	*	*	*	*	*	*	*	*	200	200	10.1
5 years old	*	*	*	*	*	*	*	*	*	*	*	78	78	3.9
6 years old	*	*	*	*	*	*	*	*	*	*	*	77	77	3.9
7 years old	*	*	*	*	*	*	*	*	*	*	*	52	52	2.6
8 years old	*	*	*	*	*	*	*	*	*	*	*	50	50	2.4
9 years old	*	*	*	*	*	*	*	*	*	*	*	38	38	1.9
10 years old	*	*	*	*	*	*	*	*	*	*	*	62	62	2.8
11 years old	23	*	*	*	*	*	*	*	*	*	*	44	44	2.0
12 years old	89	15	*	*	*	*	*	*	*	*	*	48	48	2.2
13 years old	1,435	92	16	*	*	*	*	*	*	*	*	45	45	2.1
14 years old	645	1,233	140	37	14	*	*	*	*	*	*	20	20	0.9
15 years old	73	643	1,266	113	16	*	5	*	*	*	41	90	130	5.8
16 years old	2	77	592	1,388	39	10	4	*	*	*	61	115	176	7.7
17 years old	2	13	82	635	842	58	12	*	10	*	407	185	592	26.3
18 years old	4	*	27	85	467	643	77	16	4	*	717	108	825	38.4
19 years old	5	*	5	21	232	440	632	37	8	*	735	68	803	36.8
20 years old	*	5	*	29	40	223	334	486	26	53	953	100	1,053	46.8
21 years old	*	*	4	5	63	117	177	294	120	56	1,332	86	1,418	62.9
22 years old	*	*	3	4	52	101	94	128	91	138	1,697	104	1,801	74.7
23 years old	*	*	10	1	69	55	76	81	54	138	1,867	95	1,962	80.2
24 years old	*	8	8	13	135	203	177	238	196	430	10,600	478	11,078	88.7
25 to 29 years old	*	*	*	7	77	77	116	89	64	267	10,865	490	11,355	94.2
30 to 34 years old	*	*	3	*	49	45	80	59	55	106	10,972	466	11,438	96.6
35 to 39 years old	*	7	2	4	26	42	59	28	38	96	10,329	404	10,732	97.2

* = Quantity zero or rounds to zero.

Table A-2. Single Grade of Enrollment and High School Graduation Status for Population 3 Years Old and Over, by Sex, Age (Single Years for 3 to 24 Years), Race, and Hispanic Origin, October 2017—*Continued*

(Numbers in thousands; percent; civilian noninstitutionalized population.)

| Age, sex, race, and Hispanic origin | Population | Enrolled | | Enrolled | | | | | | | | | | |
| | | Number | Percent | Nursery | Kinder-garten | Elementary grades | | | | | | | | |
						1	2	3	4	5	6	7	8
40 to 44 years old	12,678	250	2.0	*	*	*	*	*	*	*	1	*	*
45 to 49 years old	13,663	160	1.2	*	*	*	*	*	*	*	*	*	*
50 to 54 years old	15,156	143	0.9	*	*	*	*	*	*	*	*	*	*
55 to 59 years old	14,428	83	0.6	*	*	*	*	*	*	*	*	*	*
60 to 64 years old	38,348	63	0.2	*	*	*	*	*	*	*	*	*	*
65 years and over													
Male	92,715	19,749	21.3	1,249	994	1,008	959	1,163	913	1,031	1,133	1,148	1,037
Total	1,021	453	44.4	439	15	*	*	*	*	*	*	*	*
3 years old	998	642	64.4	599	43	*	*	*	*	*	*	*	*
4 years old	1,013	892	88.1	199	662	24	7	*	*	*	*	*	*
5 years old	1,022	990	96.9	11	274	671	30	4	*	*	*	*	*
6 years old	1,019	981	96.3	*	1	294	646	33	8	*	*	*	*
7 years old	1,023	1,002	97.9	*	*	18	258	699	12	15	*	*	*
8 years old	1,059	1,031	97.4	*	*	1	11	390	572	52	6	*	*
9 years old	998	980	98.3	*	*	*	7	35	280	605	48	5	*
10 years old	1,169	1,139	97.5	*	*	*	*	2	40	323	723	41	10
11 years old	1,156	1,131	97.8	*	*	*	*	*	2	35	320	749	13
12 years old	1,053	1,033	98.1	*	*	*	*	*	*	1	27	306	660
13 years old	1,114	1,095	98.3	*	*	*	*	*	*	*	5	29	292
14 years old	1,114	1,102	99.0	*	*	*	*	*	*	*	*	6	53
15 years old	1,141	1,080	94.7	*	*	*	*	*	*	*	2	4	9
16 years old	1,192	1,084	91.0	*	*	*	*	*	*	*	*	6	*
17 years old	1,147	833	72.6	*	*	*	*	*	*	*	*	4	*
18 years old	1,115	647	58.0	*	*	*	*	*	*	*	*	*	*
19 years old	1,147	698	60.9	*	*	*	*	*	*	*	*	*	*
20 years old	1,137	549	48.3	*	*	*	*	*	*	*	*	*	*
21 years old	1,147	391	34.1	*	*	*	*	*	*	*	*	*	*
22 years old	1,163	291	25.0	*	*	*	*	*	*	*	*	*	*
23 years old	1,240	238	19.2	*	*	*	*	*	*	*	*	*	*
24 years old	6,232	655	10.5	*	*	*	*	*	*	*	*	*	*
25 to 29 years old	6,026	304	5.0	*	*	*	*	*	*	*	*	*	*
30 to 34 years old	5,915	153	2.6	*	*	*	*	*	*	*	*	*	*
35 to 39 years old	5,475	97	1.8	*	*	*	*	*	*	*	2	*	*
40 to 44 years old	6,254	95	1.5	*	*	*	*	*	*	*	*	*	*
45 to 49 years old	6,734	56	0.8	*	*	*	*	*	*	*	*	*	*
50 to 54 years old	7,450	53	0.7	*	*	*	*	*	*	*	*	*	*
55 to 59 years old	6,987	31	0.4	*	*	*	*	*	*	*	*	*	*
60 to 64 years old	17,454	23	0.1	*	*	*	*	*	*	*	*	*	*
65 years and over													
Female	96,311	19,899	20.7	1,213	961	914	930	1,013	983	1,070	919	1,023	1,028
Total	953	449	47.2	441	8	*	*	*	*	*	*	*	*
3 years old	943	646	68.4	592	54	*	*	*	*	*	*	*	*
4 years old	957	878	91.7	167	675	30	6	*	*	*	*	*	*
5 years old	967	921	95.2	13	217	649	36	6	*	*	*	*	*
6 years old	970	930	95.9	*	7	213	664	41	5	*	*	*	*
7 years old	968	937	96.8	*	*	15	194	674	47	7	*	*	*
8 years old	998	976	97.8	*	*	8	16	269	642	36	5	*	*
9 years old	1,033	1,012	97.9	*	*	*	14	22	245	706	22	3	*
10 years old	1,035	1,003	96.9	*	*	*	*	1	42	255	663	37	4
11 years old	1,041	1,022	98.2	*	*	*	*	*	1	60	200	726	24
12 years old	1,065	1,038	97.4	*	*	*	*	*	*	6	21	235	713
13 years old	1,067	1,041	97.5	*	*	*	*	*	*	*	2	11	254
14 years old	1,069	1,060	99.2	*	*	*	*	*	*	*	*	6	28
15 years old	1,122	1,052	93.8	*	*	*	*	*	*	*	*	*	*
16 years old	1,102	1,034	93.8	*	*	*	*	*	*	*	*	*	*
17 years old	1,105	827	74.8	*	*	*	*	*	*	*	*	2	*
18 years old	1,033	676	65.4	*	*	*	*	*	*	*	*	*	*
19 years old	1,036	682	65.8	*	*	*	*	*	*	*	*	*	*
20 years old	1,111	646	58.1	*	*	*	*	*	*	*	*	*	*
21 years old	1,109	447	40.3	*	*	*	*	*	*	*	*	*	*
22 years old	1,249	321	25.7	*	*	*	*	*	*	*	*	*	*
23 years old	1,206	246	20.4	*	*	*	*	*	*	*	*	*	*
24 years old	6,254	754	12.1	*	*	*	*	*	*	*	*	*	*
25 to 29 years old	6,032	399	6.6	*	*	*	*	*	*	*	3	2	*
30 to 34 years old	5,928	252	4.3	*	*	*	*	*	*	*	*	*	6

* = Quantity zero or rounds to zero.

Table A-2. Single Grade of Enrollment and High School Graduation Status for Population 3 Years Old and Over, by Sex, Age (Single Years for 3 to 24 Years), Race, and Hispanic Origin, October 2017—*Continued*

(Numbers in thousands; percent; civilian noninstitutionalized population.)

Age, sex, race, and Hispanic origin	Enrolled										Not enrolled		Not enrolled	
	High school				Undergraduate college				Graduate school		H.S. grad	Not grad	Number	Percent
	9	10	11	12	1	2	3	4	1	2+				
40 to 44 years old	*	*	1	3	14	40	19	37	40	96	11,843	585	12,428	98.0
45 to 49 years old	*	5	3	3	14	27	15	10	36	48	12,880	622	13,502	98.8
50 to 54 years old	*	4	*	9	10	7	23	13	26	50	14,130	883	15,013	99.1
55 to 59 years old	*	*	*	*	10	4	8	13	6	43	13,508	837	14,345	99.4
60 to 64 years old	*	*	*	7	10	4	3	7	10	22	34,901	3,384	38,285	99.8
65 years and over														
Male	1,154	1,049	1,148	1,246	981	1,000	939	672	276	650	67,041	5,924	72,966	78.7
Total	*	*	*	*	*	*	*	*	*	*	*	567	567	55.6
3 years old	*	*	*	*	*	*	*	*	*	*	*	356	356	35.6
4 years old	*	*	*	*	*	*	*	*	*	*	*	121	121	11.9
5 years old	*	*	*	*	*	*	*	*	*	*	*	32	32	3.1
6 years old	*	*	*	*	*	*	*	*	*	*	*	37	37	3.7
7 years old	*	*	*	*	*	*	*	*	*	*	*	22	22	2.1
8 years old	*	*	*	*	*	*	*	*	*	*	*	28	28	2.6
9 years old	*	*	*	*	*	*	*	*	*	*	*	17	17	1.7
10 years old	*	*	*	*	*	*	*	*	*	*	*	30	30	2.5
11 years old	13	*	*	*	*	*	*	*	*	*	*	25	25	2.2
12 years old	33	8	*	*	*	*	*	*	*	*	*	20	20	1.9
13 years old	712	45	12	*	*	*	*	*	*	*	*	19	19	1.7
14 years old	351	596	57	28	11	*	*	*	*	*	*	12	12	1.0
15 years old	39	345	619	52	7	*	3	*	*	*	23	37	61	5.3
16 years old	2	33	356	674	9	*	4	*	*	*	32	76	108	9.0
17 years old	1	8	58	375	343	30	7	*	7	*	217	98	314	27.4
18 years old	4	*	20	58	254	275	28	8	*	*	392	76	468	42.0
19 years old	*	*	5	16	124	219	312	15	7	*	416	33	449	39.1
20 years old	*	*	*	20	25	98	180	195	5	27	513	75	588	51.7
21 years old	*	*	4	5	25	87	86	133	39	11	708	47	756	65.9
22 years old	*	*	3	*	28	56	35	74	40	55	839	33	872	75.0
23 years old	*	*	7	1	26	28	49	38	17	73	955	47	1,002	80.8
24 years old	*	8	4	5	66	106	95	95	88	187	5,317	261	5,578	89.5
25 to 29 years old	*	*	*	*	26	31	69	39	16	123	5,463	260	5,723	95.0
30 to 34 years old	*	*	3	*	15	24	23	21	13	53	5,529	233	5,762	97.4
35 to 39 years old	*	*	*	4	10	10	17	11	14	29	5,143	236	5,379	98.2
40 to 44 years old	*	*	1	3	4	21	7	20	8	31	5,809	349	6,159	98.5
45 to 49 years old	*	1	*	*	*	10	8	*	11	25	6,307	371	6,678	99.2
50 to 54 years old	*	4	*	3	*	5	11	9	6	15	6,915	482	7,397	99.3
55 to 59 years old	*	*	*	*	4	1	4	10	3	8	6,540	416	6,956	99.6
60 to 64 years old	*	*	*	*	5	*	*	3	*	14	15,924	1,507	17,431	99.9
65 years and over														
Female	1,124	1,053	1,013	1,118	1,199	1,099	971	864	511	893	70,795	5,617	76,412	79.3
Total	*	*	*	*	*	*	*	*	*	*	*	503	503	52.8
3 years old	*	*	*	*	*	*	*	*	*	*	*	298	298	31.6
4 years old	*	*	*	*	*	*	*	*	*	*	*	79	79	8.3
5 years old	*	*	*	*	*	*	*	*	*	*	*	46	46	4.8
6 years old	*	*	*	*	*	*	*	*	*	*	*	40	40	4.1
7 years old	*	*	*	*	*	*	*	*	*	*	*	31	31	3.2
8 years old	*	*	*	*	*	*	*	*	*	*	*	22	22	2.2
9 years old	*	*	*	*	*	*	*	*	*	*	*	21	21	2.1
10 years old	*	*	*	*	*	*	*	*	*	*	*	32	32	3.1
11 years old	11	*	*	*	*	*	*	*	*	*	*	19	19	1.8
12 years old	56	7	*	*	*	*	*	*	*	*	*	28	28	2.6
13 years old	722	47	4	*	*	*	*	*	*	*	*	26	26	2.5
14 years old	294	637	83	8	3	*	*	*	*	*	*	8	8	0.8
15 years old	34	298	647	61	9	*	2	*	*	*	18	52	70	6.2
16 years old	*	44	236	713	30	10	*	*	*	*	29	40	68	6.2
17 years old	1	5	24	259	499	29	5	*	3	*	190	88	278	25.2
18 years old	*	*	7	27	214	368	49	7	4	*	325	32	357	34.6
19 years old	5	*	*	5	108	221	320	22	1	*	319	35	354	34.2
20 years old	*	5	*	9	15	125	154	291	21	26	440	26	465	41.9
21 years old	*	*	*	*	38	30	91	161	81	46	624	38	662	59.7
22 years old	*	*	*	4	24	45	59	54	51	83	858	71	929	74.3
23 years old	*	*	3	*	44	27	28	42	37	65	912	48	960	79.6
24 years old	*	*	4	8	70	98	82	144	107	242	5,283	218	5,500	87.9
25 to 29 years old	*	*	*	7	51	46	47	50	48	144	5,402	231	5,633	93.4
30 to 34 years old	*	*	*	*	34	21	57	38	42	53	5,443	232	5,676	95.7

* = Quantity zero or rounds to zero.

Table A-2. Single Grade of Enrollment and High School Graduation Status for Population 3 Years Old and Over, by Sex, Age (Single Years for 3 to 24 Years), Race, and Hispanic Origin, October 2017—*Continued*

(Numbers in thousands; percent; civilian noninstitutionalized population.)

Age, sex, race, and Hispanic origin	Population	Enrolled			Kinder-garten	Enrolled								
						Elementary grades								
		Number	Percent	Nursery		1	2	3	4	5	6	7	8
35 to 39 years old	5,565	211	3.8	*	*	*	*	*	*	*	3	*	*
40 to 44 years old	6,424	155	2.4	*	*	*	*	*	*	*	1	*	*
45 to 49 years old	6,929	105	1.5	*	*	*	*	*	*	*	*	*	*
50 to 54 years old	7,706	90	1.2	*	*	*	*	*	*	*	*	*	*
55 to 59 years old	7,441	52	0.7	*	*	*	*	*	*	*	*	*	*
60 to 64 years old	20,894	40	0.2	*	*	*	*	*	*	*	*	*	*
65 years and over													
BLACK ALONE													
Both Sexes													
Total	40,380	11,609	28.7	754	507	677	657	652	587	576	599	741	558
3 years old	629	260	41.3	254	6	*	*	*	*	*	*	*	*
4 years old	615	458	74.4	398	60	*	*	*	*	*	*	*	*
5 years old	564	476	84.5	97	336	38	5	*	*	*	*	*	*
6 years old	625	611	97.8	5	91	464	40	12	*	*	*	*	*
7 years old	646	612	94.9	*	14	146	420	29	3	*	*	*	*
8 years old	691	676	97.9	*	*	25	171	419	56	4	*	*	*
9 years old	554	541	97.8	*	*	3	18	162	321	35	3	*	*
10 years old	619	607	98.1	*	*	*	4	18	195	355	31	4	*
11 years old	642	642	100.0	*	*	*	*	12	11	163	377	64	13
12 years old	648	635	97.9	*	*	*	*	*	*	14	131	478	12
13 years old	570	567	99.5	*	*	*	*	*	*	5	42	155	318
14 years old	600	566	94.3	*	*	*	*	*	*	*	15	33	183
15 years old	608	601	98.8	*	*	*	*	*	*	*	*	4	30
16 years old	574	526	91.7	*	*	*	*	*	*	*	*	*	*
17 years old	690	621	90.0	*	*	*	*	*	*	*	*	*	*
18 years old	674	477	70.7	*	*	*	*	*	*	*	*	*	*
19 years old	571	358	62.7	*	*	*	*	*	*	*	*	2	*
20 years old	649	344	53.0	*	*	*	*	*	*	*	*	*	*
21 years old	628	263	41.9	*	*	*	*	*	*	*	*	*	*
22 years old	686	208	30.3	*	*	*	*	*	*	*	*	*	*
23 years old	607	162	26.7	*	*	*	*	*	*	*	*	*	*
24 years old	642	163	25.5	*	*	*	*	*	*	*	*	*	*
25 to 29 years old	3,459	468	13.5	*	*	*	*	*	*	*	*	*	*
30 to 34 years old	2,897	222	7.7	*	*	*	*	*	*	*	*	*	*
35 to 39 years old	2,799	199	7.1	*	*	*	*	*	*	*	*	*	1
40 to 44 years old	2,532	115	4.5	*	*	*	*	*	*	*	*	*	1
45 to 49 years old	2,646	122	4.6	*	*	*	*	*	*	*	*	*	*
50 to 54 years old	2,689	46	1.7	*	*	*	*	*	*	*	*	*	*
55 to 59 years old	2,557	40	1.6	*	*	*	*	*	*	*	*	*	*
60 to 64 years old	2,408	18	0.8	*	*	*	*	*	*	*	*	*	*
65 years and over	4,660	4	0.1	*	*	*	*	*	*	*	*	*	*
Male													
Total	18,860	5,601	29.7	412	278	327	328	339	268	284	326	380	290
3 years old	345	169	49.0	163	6	*	*	*	*	*	*	*	*
4 years old	317	227	71.4	192	34	*	*	*	*	*	*	*	*
5 years old	302	246	81.7	52	179	15	*	*	*	*	*	*	*
6 years old	327	319	97.6	5	54	237	23	*	*	*	*	*	*
7 years old	303	281	92.7	*	5	61	206	10	*	*	*	*	*
8 years old	360	352	97.9	*	*	11	92	228	19	2	*	*	*
9 years old	270	261	96.9	*	*	3	7	77	152	22	*	*	*
10 years old	288	286	99.2	*	*	*	*	12	92	167	11	4	*
11 years old	350	350	100.0	*	*	*	*	12	5	76	206	42	9
12 years old	351	342	97.2	*	*	*	*	*	*	14	77	243	8
13 years old	265	262	98.8	*	*	*	*	*	*	3	22	77	142
14 years old	303	279	92.1	*	*	*	*	*	*	*	10	8	106
15 years old	306	302	98.7	*	*	*	*	*	*	*	*	4	25
16 years old	267	235	87.9	*	*	*	*	*	*	*	*	*	*
17 years old	366	329	89.8	*	*	*	*	*	*	*	*	*	*
18 years old	365	236	64.7	*	*	*	*	*	*	*	*	*	*
19 years old	250	153	61.1	*	*	*	*	*	*	*	*	2	*
20 years old	355	168	47.4	*	*	*	*	*	*	*	*	*	*
21 years old	293	108	36.9	*	*	*	*	*	*	*	*	*	*
22 years old	324	96	29.5	*	*	*	*	*	*	*	*	*	*
23 years old	295	68	23.1	*	*	*	*	*	*	*	*	*	*

* = Quantity zero or rounds to zero.

Table A-2. Single Grade of Enrollment and High School Graduation Status for Population 3 Years Old and Over, by Sex, Age (Single Years for 3 to 24 Years), Race, and Hispanic Origin, October 2017—*Continued*

(Numbers in thousands; percent; civilian noninstitutionalized population.)

Age, sex, race, and Hispanic origin	Enrolled High school 9	10	11	12	Undergraduate college 1	2	3	4	Graduate school 1	2+	Not enrolled H.S. grad	Not grad	Not enrolled Number	Percent
35 to 39 years old	*	7	2	*	16	32	42	17	24	68	5,186	168	5,354	96.2
40 to 44 years old	*	*	*	*	9	19	11	17	32	65	6,034	236	6,270	97.6
45 to 49 years old	*	3	3	3	14	17	7	10	25	23	6,574	251	6,824	98.5
50 to 54 years old	*	*	*	6	10	3	12	4	20	35	7,215	401	7,616	98.8
55 to 59 years old	*	*	*	*	6	2	3	2	3	35	6,968	421	7,389	99.3
60 to 64 years old	*	*	*	7	5	4	3	3	10	8	18,977	1,877	20,854	99.8
65 years and over														
BLACK ALONE														
Both Sexes														
Total	531	629	576	751	719	664	608	324	200	298	24,662	4,110	28,772	71.3
3 years old	*	*	*	*	*	*	*	*	*	*	*	369	369	58.7
4 years old	*	*	*	*	*	*	*	*	*	*	*	157	157	25.6
5 years old	*	*	*	*	*	*	*	*	*	*	*	87	87	15.5
6 years old	*	*	*	*	*	*	*	*	*	*	*	14	14	2.2
7 years old	*	*	*	*	*	*	*	*	*	*	*	33	33	5.1
8 years old	*	*	*	*	*	*	*	*	*	*	*	15	15	2.1
9 years old	*	*	*	*	*	*	*	*	*	*	*	12	12	2.2
10 years old	*	*	*	*	*	*	*	*	*	*	*	12	12	1.9
11 years old	*	*	*	*	*	*	*	*	*	*	*	*	*	*
12 years old	*	*	*	*	*	*	*	*	*	*	*	14	14	2.1
13 years old	46	*	*	*	*	*	*	*	*	*	*	3	3	0.5
14 years old	295	40	*	*	*	*	*	*	*	*	*	34	34	5.7
15 years old	150	335	62	4	4	*	*	*	9	3	*	7	7	1.2
16 years old	32	178	266	46	5	*	*	*	*	*	5	43	48	8.3
17 years old	6	67	187	347	14	*	*	*	*	*	38	31	69	10.0
18 years old	*	4	47	194	224	7	*	*	*	*	164	34	198	29.3
19 years old	2	*	*	59	114	128	44	7	*	*	183	31	213	37.3
20 years old	*	*	4	38	59	137	88	17	*	*	267	38	305	47.0
21 years old	*	*	5	14	30	41	91	76	4	2	321	44	365	58.1
22 years old	*	*	*	*	17	27	62	57	14	30	437	42	478	69.7
23 years old	1	*	*	4	39	29	28	46	5	10	399	46	445	73.3
24 years old	*	*	*	4	15	39	41	20	24	21	442	36	478	74.5
25 to 29 years old	*	4	*	10	69	110	116	36	64	61	2,757	233	2,991	86.5
30 to 34 years old	*	*	*	3	46	40	55	23	25	29	2,482	193	2,675	92.3
35 to 39 years old	*	*	4	15	31	47	33	14	17	36	2,369	232	2,601	92.9
40 to 44 years old	*	*	*	*	10	24	18	9	17	36	2,235	183	2,418	95.5
45 to 49 years old	*	*	*	8	20	32	9	7	15	31	2,324	200	2,525	95.4
50 to 54 years old	*	*	*	*	10	3	11	*	*	23	2,319	324	2,643	98.3
55 to 59 years old	*	*	*	3	3	*	5	11	7	11	2,234	283	2,517	98.4
60 to 64 years old	*	*	*	*	8	*	6	*	*	4	2,072	318	2,390	99.2
65 years and over	*	*	*	3	*	*	*	*	*	*	3,616	1,040	4,656	99.9
Male														
Total	257	292	301	343	298	322	246	104	69	135	11,301	1,957	13,259	70.3
3 years old	*	*	*	*	*	*	*	*	*	*	*	176	176	51.0
4 years old	*	*	*	*	*	*	*	*	*	*	*	91	91	28.6
5 years old	*	*	*	*	*	*	*	*	*	*	*	55	55	18.3
6 years old	*	*	*	*	*	*	*	*	*	*	*	8	8	2.4
7 years old	*	*	*	*	*	*	*	*	*	*	*	22	22	7.3
8 years old	*	*	*	*	*	*	*	*	*	*	*	8	8	2.1
9 years old	*	*	*	*	*	*	*	*	*	*	*	8	8	3.1
10 years old	*	*	*	*	*	*	*	*	*	*	*	2	2	0.8
11 years old	*	*	*	*	*	*	*	*	*	*	*	*	*	*
12 years old	*	*	*	*	*	*	*	*	*	*	*	10	10	2.8
13 years old	18	*	*	*	*	*	*	*	*	*	*	3	3	1.2
14 years old	136	19	*	*	*	*	*	*	*	*	*	24	24	7.9
15 years old	79	145	37	2	4	*	*	*	5	*	*	4	4	1.3
16 years old	18	89	117	11	*	*	*	*	*	*	5	28	32	12.1
17 years old	4	35	118	167	4	*	*	*	*	*	18	19	37	10.2
18 years old	*	4	29	93	106	5	*	*	*	*	104	25	129	35.3
19 years old	2	*	*	25	52	48	20	4	*	*	77	20	97	38.9
20 years old	*	*	*	24	31	70	41	1	*	*	156	31	187	52.6
21 years old	*	*	*	*	12	30	46	16	4	*	167	18	185	63.1
22 years old	*	*	*	*	7	16	23	16	5	29	199	30	228	70.5
23 years old	*	*	*	4	21	11	6	16	1	10	196	30	227	76.9

* = Quantity zero or rounds to zero.

Table A-2. Single Grade of Enrollment and High School Graduation Status for Population 3 Years Old and Over, by Sex, Age (Single Years for 3 to 24 Years), Race, and Hispanic Origin, October 2017—*Continued*

(Numbers in thousands; percent; civilian noninstitutionalized population.)

Age, sex, race, and Hispanic origin	Population	Enrolled Number	Enrolled Percent	Nursery	Kinder-garten	1	2	3	4	5	6	7	8
24 years old	291	54	18.6	*	*	*	*	*	*	*	*	*	*
25 to 29 years old	1,656	203	12.3	*	*	*	*	*	*	*	*	*	*
30 to 34 years old	1,336	83	6.2	*	*	*	*	*	*	*	*	*	*
35 to 39 years old	1,274	51	4.0	*	*	*	*	*	*	*	*	*	*
40 to 44 years old	1,139	61	5.3	*	*	*	*	*	*	*	*	*	*
45 to 49 years old	1,198	52	4.3	*	*	*	*	*	*	*	*	*	*
50 to 54 years old	1,229	12	1.0	*	*	*	*	*	*	*	*	*	*
55 to 59 years old	1,148	12	1.0	*	*	*	*	*	*	*	*	*	*
60 to 64 years old	1101	6	0.5	*	*	*	*	*	*	*	*	*	*
65 years and over	1,887	-	-	*	*	*	*	*	*	*	*	*	*
Female													
Total	21,520	6,007	27.9	342	229	350	329	312	320	293	273	361	268
3 years old	284	91	32.0	91	*	*	*	*	*	*	*	*	*
4 years old	298	232	77.7	206	25	*	*	*	*	*	*	*	*
5 years old	262	230	87.7	45	157	24	5	*	*	*	*	*	*
6 years old	298	292	97.9	*	37	227	16	11	*	*	*	*	*
7 years old	343	331	96.7	*	9	85	214	19	3	*	*	*	*
8 years old	331	324	97.9	*	*	14	79	191	37	2	*	*	*
9 years old	284	280	98.6	*	*	*	11	85	169	13	3	*	*
10 years old	330	321	97.2	*	*	*	4	6	104	188	20	*	*
11 years old	292	292	100.0	*	*	*	*	*	7	87	171	23	4
12 years old	297	293	98.7	*	*	*	*	*	*	*	54	235	4
13 years old	305	305	100.0	*	*	*	*	*	*	2	20	78	176
14 years old	297	287	96.6	*	*	*	*	*	*	*	5	26	77
15 years old	302	299	98.9	*	*	*	*	*	*	*	*	*	4
16 years old	307	292	94.9	*	*	*	*	*	*	*	*	*	*
17 years old	324	292	90.2	*	*	*	*	*	*	*	*	*	*
18 years old	309	240	77.8	*	*	*	*	*	*	*	*	*	*
19 years old	322	206	63.9	*	*	*	*	*	*	*	*	*	*
20 years old	294	176	59.7	*	*	*	*	*	*	*	*	*	*
21 years old	335	155	46.3	*	*	*	*	*	*	*	*	*	*
22 years old	362	112	30.9	*	*	*	*	*	*	*	*	*	*
23 years old	312	94	30.1	*	*	*	*	*	*	*	*	*	*
24 years old	351	109	31.1	*	*	*	*	*	*	*	*	*	*
25 to 29 years old	1,803	265	14.7	*	*	*	*	*	*	*	*	*	*
30 to 34 years old	1,560	138	8.9	*	*	*	*	*	*	*	*	*	*
35 to 39 years old	1,526	148	9.7	*	*	*	*	*	*	*	*	*	1
40 to 44 years old	1,393	54	3.9	*	*	*	*	*	*	*	*	*	*
45 to 49 years old	1,448	70	4.8	*	*	*	*	*	*	*	*	*	*
50 to 54 years old	1,460	34	2.3	*	*	*	*	*	*	*	*	*	*
55 to 59 years old	1,409	29	2.0	*	*	*	*	*	*	*	*	*	*
60 to 64 years old	1,307	13	1.0	*	*	*	*	*	*	*	*	*	*
65 years and over	2,772	4	0.1	*	*	*	*	*	*	*	*	*	*
ASIAN ALONE													
Both Sexes													
Total	18,232	4,636	25.4	253	239	222	187	211	196	244	185	193	194
3 years old	225	98	43.5	95	3	*	*	*	*	*	*	*	*
4 years old	180	131	72.8	115	16	*	*	*	*	*	*	*	*
5 years old	232	214	92.1	36	171	6	*	*	*	*	*	*	*
6 years old	230	224	97.4	7	44	170	3	*	*	*	*	*	*
7 years old	217	207	95.4	*	5	42	155	6	*	*	*	*	*
8 years old	154	153	99.6	*	*	4	17	123	10	*	*	*	*
9 years old	228	228	99.9	*	*	*	9	67	141	7	4	*	*
10 years old	232	227	97.9	*	*	*	4	15	41	160	5	3	*
11 years old	205	204	99.5	*	*	*	*	*	4	58	131	11	*
12 years old	188	187	99.5	*	*	*	*	*	*	11	31	134	10
13 years old	207	201	97.3	*	*	*	*	*	7	7	38	129	
14 years old	237	237	100.0	*	*	*	*	*	*	*	*	7	41
15 years old	227	227	100.0	*	*	*	*	*	*	*	*	*	15
16 years old	224	213	95.0	*	*	*	*	*	*	*	*	*	*
17 years old	266	247	92.8	*	*	*	*	*	*	*	*	*	*
18 years old	187	160	86.0	*	*	*	*	*	*	*	*	1	*
19 years old	189	149	78.8	*	*	*	*	*	*	*	*	*	*
20 years old	240	190	79.2	*	*	*	*	*	*	*	*	*	*

* = Quantity zero or rounds to zero.

Table A-2. Single Grade of Enrollment and High School Graduation Status for Population 3 Years Old and Over, by Sex, Age (Single Years for 3 to 24 Years), Race, and Hispanic Origin, October 2017—*Continued*

(Numbers in thousands; percent; civilian noninstitutionalized population.)

Age, sex, race, and Hispanic origin	Enrolled — High school				Enrolled — Undergraduate college				Enrolled — Graduate school		Not enrolled H.S. grad	Not enrolled Not grad	Not enrolled Number	Not enrolled Percent
	9	10	11	12	1	2	3	4	1	2+				
24 years old	*	*	*	4	5	15	11	11	5	3	227	9	236	81.4
25 to 29 years old	*	*	*	10	14	62	52	13	24	28	1,336	118	1,453	87.7
30 to 34 years old	*	*	*	3	21	19	13	9	5	15	1,145	108	1,253	93.8
35 to 39 years old	*	*	*	*	8	21	4	8	8	2	1,100	123	1,223	96.0
40 to 44 years old	*	*	*	*	6	7	13	6	5	24	1,000	78	1,078	94.7
45 to 49 years old	*	*	*	*	7	17	4	5	4	15	1,054	92	1,146	95.7
50 to 54 years old	*	*	*	*	1	2	2	*	*	6	1,080	137	1,217	99.0
55 to 59 years old	*	*	*	*	*	*	5	*	4	3	991	146	1,136	99.0
60 to 64 years old	*	*	*	*	*	*	6	*	*	*	949	146	1,096	99.5
65 years and over	*	*	*	*	*	*	*	*	*	*	1,498	390	1,887	100.0
Female														
Total	274	337	275	408	421	341	362	220	131	163	13,360	2,152	15,513	72.1
3 years old	*	*	*	*	*	*	*	*	*	*	*	193	193	68.0
4 years old	*	*	*	*	*	*	*	*	*	*	*	67	67	22.3
5 years old	*	*	*	*	*	*	*	*	*	*	*	32	32	12.3
6 years old	*	*	*	*	*	*	*	*	*	*	*	6	6	2.1
7 years old	*	*	*	*	*	*	*	*	*	*	*	11	11	3.3
8 years old	*	*	*	*	*	*	*	*	*	*	*	7	7	2.1
9 years old	*	*	*	*	*	*	*	*	*	*	*	4	4	1.4
10 years old	*	*	*	*	*	*	*	*	*	*	*	9	9	2.8
11 years old	*	*	*	*	*	*	*	*	*	*	*	*	*	*
12 years old	*	*	*	*	*	*	*	*	*	*	*	4	4	1.3
13 years old	28	*	*	*	*	*	*	*	*	*	*	*	*	*
14 years old	158	21	*	*	*	*	*	*	*	*	*	10	10	3.4
15 years old	71	190	25	2	*	*	*	*	3	3	*	3	3	1.1
16 years old	14	90	149	34	5	*	*	*	*	*	*	16	16	5.1
17 years old	2	32	69	179	10	*	*	*	*	*	20	12	32	9.8
18 years old	*	*	19	101	119	2	*	*	*	*	59	9	69	22.2
19 years old	*	*	*	35	62	80	25	4	*	*	106	10	116	36.1
20 years old	*	*	4	13	28	67	47	16	*	2	111	7	119	40.3
21 years old	*	*	5	14	18	11	45	61	*	2	154	26	180	53.7
22 years old	*	*	*	*	11	11	38	42	9	1	238	12	250	69.1
23 years old	1	*	*	*	18	18	22	29	4	*	203	16	218	69.9
24 years old	*	*	*	*	10	24	30	9	19	17	215	27	242	68.9
25 to 29 years old	*	4	*	*	55	48	63	23	40	33	1,422	115	1,537	85.3
30 to 34 years old	*	*	*	*	25	21	42	15	20	14	1,337	85	1,422	91.1
35 to 39 years old	*	*	4	15	23	27	29	6	8	35	1,268	109	1,378	90.3
40 to 44 years old	*	*	*	*	5	17	6	3	11	12	1,234	105	1,339	96.1
45 to 49 years old	*	*	*	8	13	16	5	2	11	16	1,270	109	1,379	95.2
50 to 54 years old	*	*	*	*	8	1	8	*	*	16	1,239	187	1,426	97.7
55 to 59 years old	*	*	*	3	3	*	*	11	4	8	1,243	137	1,380	98.0
60 to 64 years old	*	*	*	*	8	*	*	*	*	4	1,123	172	1,294	99.0
65 years and over	*	*	*	3	*	*	*	*	*	*	2,118	650	2,768	99.9
ASIAN ALONE														
Both Sexes														
Total	254	215	241	220	227	315	272	316	171	280	12,178	1,418	13,596	74.6
3 years old	*	*	*	*	*	*	*	*	*	*	*	127	127	56.5
4 years old	*	*	*	*	*	*	*	*	*	*	*	49	49	27.2
5 years old	*	*	*	*	*	*	*	*	*	*	*	18	18	7.9
6 years old	*	*	*	*	*	*	*	*	*	*	*	6	6	2.6
7 years old	*	*	*	*	*	*	*	*	*	*	*	10	10	4.6
8 years old	*	*	*	*	*	*	*	*	*	*	*	1	1	0.4
9 years old	*	*	*	*	*	*	*	*	*	*	*	*	*	0.1
10 years old	*	*	*	*	*	*	*	*	*	*	*	5	5	2.1
11 years old	*	*	*	*	*	*	*	*	*	*	*	1	1	0.5
12 years old	*	*	*	*	*	*	*	*	*	*	*	1	1	0.5
13 years old	20	*	*	*	*	*	*	*	*	*	*	6	6	2.7
14 years old	177	12	*	*	*	*	*	*	*	*	*	*	*	*
15 years old	46	133	22	7	4	*	*	*	*	*	*	*	*	*
16 years old	6	37	147	22	*	*	*	*	*	*	3	8	11	5.0
17 years old	*	11	69	139	16	3	*	*	9	*	*	19	19	7.2
18 years old	*	3	3	38	99	10	*	*	6	*	23	3	26	14.0
19 years old	1	*	*	3	51	76	15	3	*	*	32	8	40	21.2
20 years old	*	*	*	4	17	91	64	14	*	*	44	6	50	20.8

* = Quantity zero or rounds to zero.

Table A-2. Single Grade of Enrollment and High School Graduation Status for Population 3 Years Old and Over, by Sex, Age (Single Years for 3 to 24 Years), Race, and Hispanic Origin, October 2017—*Continued*

(Numbers in thousands; percent; civilian noninstitutionalized population.)

Age, sex, race, and Hispanic origin	Population	Enrolled Number	Enrolled Percent	Nursery	Kinder-garten	1	2	3	4	5	6	7	8
21 years old	318	254	80.0	*	*	*	*	*	*	*	*	*	*
22 years old	261	165	63.3	*	*	*	*	*	*	*	*	*	*
23 years old	239	110	46.1	*	*	*	*	*	*	*	*	*	*
24 years old	320	139	43.3	*	*	*	*	*	*	*	*	*	*
25 to 29 years old	1,580	263	16.7	*	*	*	*	*	*	*	1	*	*
30 to 34 years old	1,619	94	5.8	*	*	*	*	*	*	*	*	*	*
35 to 39 years old	1,553	45	2.9	*	*	*	*	*	*	*	*	*	*
40 to 44 years old	1,425	24	1.7	*	*	*	*	*	*	*	*	*	*
45 to 49 years old	1,356	10	0.8	*	*	*	*	*	*	*	*	*	*
50 to 54 years old	1,306	14	1.0	*	*	*	*	*	*	*	*	*	*
55 to 59 years old	1,086	9	0.8	*	*	*	*	*	*	*	*	*	*
60 to 64 years old	983	4	0.4	*	*	*	*	*	*	*	4	*	*
65 years and over	2,318	6	0.3	*	*	*	*	*	*	*	3	*	*
Male													
Total	8,666	2,313	26.7	119	126	113	83	113	103	120	92	104	113
3 years old	111	27	24.5	27	*	*	*	*	*	*	*	*	*
4 years old	95	84	87.9	72	11	*	*	*	*	*	*	*	*
5 years old	121	108	89.1	14	88	6	*	*	*	*	*	*	*
6 years old	116	113	97.7	5	24	81	3	*	*	*	*	*	*
7 years old	94	87	92.7	*	3	22	60	3	*	*	*	*	*
8 years old	87	87	100.0	*	*	4	13	67	3	*	*	*	*
9 years old	127	127	99.8	*	*	*	3	39	81	4	*	*	*
10 years old	109	105	96.3	*	*	*	4	4	17	75	3	3	*
11 years old	117	116	99.5	*	*	*	*	*	2	33	74	8	*
12 years old	87	86	98.8	*	*	*	*	*	*	4	8	68	6
13 years old	114	111	97.5	*	*	*	*	*	*	3	3	18	78
14 years old	117	117	100.0	*	*	*	*	*	*	*	*	7	23
15 years old	119	119	100.0	*	*	*	*	*	*	*	*	*	6
16 years old	131	128	97.4	*	*	*	*	*	*	*	*	*	*
17 years old	105	96	90.8	*	*	*	*	*	*	*	*	*	*
18 years old	97	79	80.8	*	*	*	*	*	*	*	*	1	*
19 years old	97	73	75.7	*	*	*	*	*	*	*	*	*	*
20 years old	123	89	72.9	*	*	*	*	*	*	*	*	*	*
21 years old	162	134	82.8	*	*	*	*	*	*	*	*	*	*
22 years old	137	87	63.8	*	*	*	*	*	*	*	*	*	*
23 years old	132	64	48.8	*	*	*	*	*	*	*	*	*	*
24 years old	148	75	51.0	*	*	*	*	*	*	*	*	*	*
25 to 29 years old	779	127	16.3	*	*	*	*	*	*	*	*	*	*
30 to 34 years old	771	34	4.4	*	*	*	*	*	*	*	*	*	*
35 to 39 years old	737	10	1.3	*	*	*	*	*	*	*	*	*	*
40 to 44 years old	641	10	1.6	*	*	*	*	*	*	*	*	*	*
45 to 49 years old	673	5	0.8	*	*	*	*	*	*	*	*	*	*
50 to 54 years old	590	4	0.6	*	*	*	*	*	*	*	*	*	*
55 to 59 years old	487	3	0.7	*	*	*	*	*	*	*	*	*	*
60 to 64 years old	449	-	-	*	*	*	*	*	*	*	*	*	*
65 years and over	993	6	0.6	*	*	*	*	*	*	*	3	*	*
Female													
Total	9,566	2,323	24.3	135	113	109	105	98	93	123	93	89	81
3 years old	114	70	62.0	67	3	*	*	*	*	*	*	*	*
4 years old	85	47	55.8	43	5	*	*	*	*	*	*	*	*
5 years old	111	106	95.4	22	84	*	*	*	*	*	*	*	*
6 years old	114	111	97.1	2	20	89	*	*	*	*	*	*	*
7 years old	123	120	97.4	*	2	20	95	3	*	*	*	*	*
8 years old	67	66	99.0	*	*	*	4	56	6	*	*	*	*
9 years old	100	100	100.0	*	*	*	6	28	61	3	4	*	*
10 years old	122	121	99.3	*	*	*	*	11	24	84	2	*	*
11 years old	88	88	99.4	*	*	*	*	*	3	25	57	3	*
12 years old	101	101	100.0	*	*	*	*	*	*	7	23	66	4
13 years old	93	90	97.0	*	*	*	*	*	*	4	3	20	51
14 years old	120	120	100.0	*	*	*	*	*	*	*	*	*	18
15 years old	108	108	100.0	*	*	*	*	*	*	*	*	*	8
16 years old	93	85	91.7	*	*	*	*	*	*	*	*	*	*
17 years old	161	152	94.2	*	*	*	*	*	*	*	*	*	*
18 years old	89	82	91.6	*	*	*	*	*	*	*	*	*	*
19 years old	92	76	82.1	*	*	*	*	*	*	*	*	*	*

* = Quantity zero or rounds to zero.

Table A-2. Single Grade of Enrollment and High School Graduation Status for Population 3 Years Old and Over, by Sex, Age (Single Years for 3 to 24 Years), Race, and Hispanic Origin, October 2017—*Continued*

(Numbers in thousands; percent; civilian noninstitutionalized population.)

Age, sex, race, and Hispanic origin	Enrolled										Not enrolled		Not enrolled	
	High school				Undergraduate college				Graduate school					
	9	10	11	12	1	2	3	4	1	2+	H.S. grad	Not grad	Number	Percent
21 years old	*	11	*	*	9	77	79	75	4	*	63	*	63	20.0
22 years old	*	*	*	3	1	21	41	69	4	26	93	2	96	36.7
23 years old	*	*	*	*	1	2	9	37	41	21	129	*	129	53.9
24 years old	*	*	*	*	4	11	16	36	29	42	173	8	182	56.7
25 to 29 years old	*	*	*	*	5	12	30	57	49	108	1,280	37	1,317	83.3
30 to 34 years old	*	4	*	*	6	8	14	3	12	47	1,453	72	1,525	94.2
35 to 39 years old	*	4	*	*	11	5	*	13	1	12	1,466	42	1,507	97.1
40 to 44 years old	*	*	*	3	*	*	1	*	6	14	1,320	81	1,401	98.3
45 to 49 years old	*	*	*	*	*	*	3	5	3	*	1,230	116	1,346	99.2
50 to 54 years old	4	*	*	*	3	*	*	*	6	*	1,169	124	1,293	99.0
55 to 59 years old	*	*	*	*	*	*	*	3	*	6	966	111	1,077	99.2
60 to 64 years old	*	*	*	*	*	*	*	*	*	1	880	98	979	99.6
65 years and over	*	*	*	*	*	*	*	*	*	3	1,854	457	2,311	99.7
Male														
Total	128	119	123	108	89	151	144	163	95	107	5,794	559	6,353	73.3
3 years old	*	*	*	*	*	*	*	*	*	*	*	84	84	75.5
4 years old	*	*	*	*	*	*	*	*	*	*	*	12	12	12.1
5 years old	*	*	*	*	*	*	*	*	*	*	*	13	13	10.9
6 years old	*	*	*	*	*	*	*	*	*	*	*	3	3	2.3
7 years old	*	*	*	*	*	*	*	*	*	*	*	7	7	7.3
8 years old	*	*	*	*	*	*	*	*	*	*	*	*	*	*
9 years old	*	*	*	*	*	*	*	*	*	*	*	*	*	0.2
10 years old	*	*	*	*	*	*	*	*	*	*	*	4	4	3.7
11 years old	*	*	*	*	*	*	*	*	*	*	*	1	1	0.5
12 years old	*	*	*	*	*	*	*	*	*	*	*	1	1	1.2
13 years old	7	*	*	*	*	*	*	*	*	*	*	3	3	2.5
14 years old	81	6	*	*	*	*	*	*	*	*	*	*	*	*
15 years old	29	66	10	7	1	*	*	*	*	*	*	*	*	*
16 years old	6	29	75	17	*	*	*	*	*	*	1	3	3	2.6
17 years old	*	1	34	54	3	*	*	*	3	*	*	10	10	9.2
18 years old	*	*	3	22	40	6	*	*	6	*	16	3	19	19.2
19 years old	1	*	*	3	21	40	8	*	*	*	24	*	24	24.3
20 years old	*	*	*	*	9	34	36	10	*	*	27	6	33	27.1
21 years old	*	11	*	*	7	41	36	36	4	*	28	*	28	17.2
22 years old	*	*	*	*	*	17	18	37	4	11	48	2	50	36.2
23 years old	*	*	*	*	*	*	6	25	24	9	67	*	67	51.2
24 years old	*	*	*	*	4	6	7	22	20	16	71	1	72	49.0
25 to 29 years old	*	*	*	*	4	3	24	18	26	51	646	6	652	83.7
30 to 34 years old	*	4	*	*	*	3	7	3	3	14	712	25	737	95.6
35 to 39 years old	*	4	*	*	*	*	*	4	1	1	717	10	727	98.7
40 to 44 years old	*	*	*	3	*	*	1	*	3	3	591	40	631	98.4
45 to 49 years old	*	*	*	*	*	*	1	5	*	*	619	49	668	99.2
50 to 54 years old	4	*	*	*	*	*	*	*	*	*	542	44	586	99.4
55 to 59 years old	*	*	*	*	*	*	*	3	*	*	440	43	484	99.3
60 to 64 years old	*	*	*	*	*	*	*	*	*	*	422	26	449	100.0
65 years and over	*	*	*	*	*	*	*	*	*	3	822	164	987	99.4
Female														
Total	126	96	118	113	138	164	127	153	76	174	6,385	858	7,243	75.7
3 years old	*	*	*	*	*	*	*	*	*	*	*	43	43	38.0
4 years old	*	*	*	*	*	*	*	*	*	*	*	38	38	44.2
5 years old	*	*	*	*	*	*	*	*	*	*	*	5	5	4.6
6 years old	*	*	*	*	*	*	*	*	*	*	*	3	3	2.9
7 years old	*	*	*	*	*	*	*	*	*	*	*	3	3	2.6
8 years old	*	*	*	*	*	*	*	*	*	*	*	1	1	1.0
9 years old	*	*	*	*	*	*	*	*	*	*	*	*	*	*
10 years old	*	*	*	*	*	*	*	*	*	*	*	1	1	0.7
11 years old	*	*	*	*	*	*	*	*	*	*	*	1	1	0.6
12 years old	*	*	*	*	*	*	*	*	*	*	*	*	*	*
13 years old	13	*	*	*	*	*	*	*	*	*	*	3	3	3.0
14 years old	96	6	*	*	*	*	*	*	*	*	*	*	*	*
15 years old	17	67	12	*	4	*	*	*	*	*	*	*	*	*
16 years old	*	9	72	5	*	*	*	*	*	*	3	5	8	8.3
17 years old	*	10	35	85	13	3	*	*	6	*	*	9	9	5.8
18 years old	*	3	*	16	59	4	*	*	*	*	7	1	8	8.4
19 years old	*	*	*	*	30	36	6	3	*	*	9	8	17	17.9

* = Quantity zero or rounds to zero.

Table A-2. Single Grade of Enrollment and High School Graduation Status for Population 3 Years Old and Over, by Sex, Age (Single Years for 3 to 24 Years), Race, and Hispanic Origin, October 2017—*Continued*

(Numbers in thousands; percent; civilian noninstitutionalized population.)

Age, sex, race, and Hispanic origin	Population	Enrolled		Enrolled										
		Number	Percent	Nursery	Kinder-garten	Elementary grades							
						1	2	3	4	5	6	7	8
20 years old	118	101	85.8	*	*	*	*	*	*	*	*	*	*
21 years old	156	120	77.1	*	*	*	*	*	*	*	*	*	*
22 years old	124	78	62.8	*	*	*	*	*	*	*	*	*	*
23 years old	107	46	43.0	*	*	*	*	*	*	*	*	*	*
24 years old	172	63	36.6	*	*	*	*	*	*	*	*	*	*
25 to 29 years old	801	136	17.0	*	*	*	*	*	*	*	1	*	*
30 to 34 years old	848	60	7.1	*	*	*	*	*	*	*	*	*	*
35 to 39 years old	816	36	4.4	*	*	*	*	*	*	*	*	*	*
40 to 44 years old	784	14	1.8	*	*	*	*	*	*	*	*	*	*
45 to 49 years old	683	5	0.7	*	*	*	*	*	*	*	*	*	*
50 to 54 years old	717	10	1.4	*	*	*	*	*	*	*	*	*	*
55 to 59 years old	599	6	0.9	*	*	*	*	*	*	*	*	*	*
60 to 64 years old	534	4	0.8	*	*	*	*	*	*	*	4	*	*
65 years and over	1,325	-	-	*	*	*	*	*	*	*	*	*	*
HISPANIC (OF ANY RACE)													
Both Sexes													
Total	55,207	17,974	32.6	1,007	1,116	1,052	1,053	1,056	1,028	1,050	1,187	956	959
3 years old	1,077	332	30.9	297	35	*	*	*	*	*	*	*	*
4 years old	1,040	682	65.6	573	109	*	*	*	*	*	*	*	*
5 years old	1,033	957	92.7	116	789	44	8	*	*	*	*	*	*
6 years old	1,030	1003	97.4	21	173	753	41	15	*	*	*	*	*
7 years old	1,071	1,041	97.3	*	9	251	720	59	3	*	*	*	*
8 years old	1,063	1,034	97.2	*	*	*	250	715	70	*	*	*	*
9 years old	1,059	1,023	96.6	*	*	4	31	238	677	60	12	*	*
10 years old	1,065	1,025	96.2	*	*	*	4	28	226	716	46	5	*
11 years old	1,091	1061	97.3	*	*	*	*	*	35	231	689	105	1
12 years old	1029	1009	98.0	*	*	*	*	*	19	33	364	509	71
13 years old	1041	1018	97.9	*	*	*	*	*	*	10	37	271	628
14 years old	929	904	97.3	*	*	*	*	*	*	*	12	43	213
15 years old	999	993	99.4	*	*	*	*	*	*	*	3	5	34
16 years old	955	910	95.3	*	*	*	*	*	*	*	*	1	9
17 years old	960	864	90.0	*	*	*	*	*	*	*	*	1	*
18 years old	944	687	72.8	*	*	*	*	*	*	*	*	*	*
19 years old	1021	634	62.0	*	*	*	*	*	*	*	*	*	*
20 years old	918	457	49.8	*	*	*	*	*	*	*	2	*	*
21 years old	902	380	42.1	*	*	*	*	*	*	*	*	*	*
22 years old	925	300	32.4	*	*	*	*	*	*	*	*	3	*
23 years old	975	235	24.1	*	*	*	*	*	*	*	*	*	*
24 years old	969	209	21.6	*	*	*	*	*	*	*	*	*	*
25 to 29 years old	4,651	571	12.3	*	*	*	*	*	*	*	4	4	*
30 to 34 years old	4,373	210	4.8	*	*	*	*	*	*	*	8	*	*
35 to 39 years old	4,321	177	4.1	*	*	*	*	*	*	*	*	*	2
40 to 44 years old	3,989	109	2.7	*	*	*	*	*	*	*	*	4	*
45 to 49 years old	3,662	60	1.6	*	*	*	*	*	*	*	8	*	*
50 to 54 years old	3,187	36	1.1	*	*	*	*	*	*	*	*	4	*
55 to 59 years old	2,670	35	1.3	*	*	*	*	*	*	*	*	*	*
60 to 64 years old	2,056	11	0.5	*	*	*	*	*	*	*	*	*	*
65 years and over	4,202	6	0.1	*	*	*	*	*	*	*	1	3	*
Male													
Total	27,605	8,873	32.1	496	564	559	551	530	517	523	605	497	525
3 years old	544	142	26.2	117	25	*	*	*	*	*	*	*	*
4 years old	533	365	68.5	309	56	*	*	*	*	*	*	*	*
5 years old	521	480	92.2	58	388	26	8	*	*	*	*	*	*
6 years old	537	520	96.9	13	90	403	12	3	*	*	*	*	*
7 years old	565	546	96.7	*	5	125	381	32	3	*	*	*	*
8 years old	538	522	97.0	*	*	*	127	360	35	*	*	*	*
9 years old	515	509	99.0	*	*	4	19	127	320	38	2	*	*
10 years old	541	516	95.4	*	*	*	4	7	130	343	26	5	*
11 years old	549	540	98.3	*	*	*	*	*	19	116	342	61	1
12 years old	505	501	99.1	*	*	*	*	*	11	19	183	247	34
13 years old	562	545	96.9	*	*	*	*	*	*	7	27	151	323
14 years old	491	479	97.6	*	*	*	*	*	*	*	3	14	134
15 years old	479	473	98.7	*	*	*	*	*	*	*	3	4	25

* = Quantity zero or rounds to zero.

Table A-2. Single Grade of Enrollment and High School Graduation Status for Population 3 Years Old and Over, by Sex, Age (Single Years for 3 to 24 Years), Race, and Hispanic Origin, October 2017—*Continued*

(Numbers in thousands; percent; civilian noninstitutionalized population.)

Age, sex, race, and Hispanic origin	Enrolled										Not enrolled		Not enrolled	
	High school				Undergraduate college				Graduate school		H.S. grad	Not grad	Number	Percent
	9	10	11	12	1	2	3	4	1	2+				
20 years old	*	*	*	4	8	57	28	4	*	*	17	*	17	14.2
21 years old	*	*	*	*	2	36	44	39	*	*	36	*	36	22.9
22 years old	*	*	*	3	1	4	22	32	*	15	45	1	46	37.2
23 years old	*	*	*	*	1	2	2	12	17	12	61	*	61	57.0
24 years old	*	*	*	*	*	4	9	14	9	27	102	7	109	63.4
25 to 29 years old	*	*	*	*	1	9	6	39	23	58	634	31	665	83.0
30 to 34 years old	*	*	*	*	6	4	7	*	9	34	741	47	788	92.9
35 to 39 years old	*	*	*	*	11	5	*	9	*	11	749	31	780	95.6
40 to 44 years old	*	*	*	*	*	*	*	*	2	11	729	41	770	98.2
45 to 49 years old	*	*	*	*	*	*	2	*	3	*	610	68	678	99.3
50 to 54 years old	*	*	*	*	3	*	*	*	6	*	627	80	707	98.6
55 to 59 years old	*	*	*	*	*	*	*	*	*	6	526	67	593	99.1
60 to 64 years old	*	*	*	*	*	*	*	*	*	1	458	72	530	99.2
65 years and over	*	*	*	*	*	*	*	*	*	*	1,032	293	1,325	100.0

HISPANIC (OF ANY RACE)

Both Sexes

Age, sex, race, and Hispanic origin	9	10	11	12	1	2	3	4	1	2+	H.S. grad	Not grad	Number	Percent
Total	1,030	956	880	1,070	968	935	660	492	208	311	25,307	11,926	37,234	67.4
3 years old	*	*	*	*	*	*	*	*	*	*	*	745	745	69.1
4 years old	*	*	*	*	*	*	*	*	*	*	*	358	358	34.4
5 years old	*	*	*	*	*	*	*	*	*	*	*	76	76	7.3
6 years old	*	*	*	*	*	*	*	*	*	*	*	27	27	2.6
7 years old	*	*	*	*	*	*	*	*	*	*	*	29	29	2.7
8 years old	*	*	*	*	*	*	*	*	*	*	*	29	29	2.8
9 years old	*	*	*	*	*	*	*	*	*	*	*	36	36	3.4
10 years old	*	*	*	*	*	*	*	*	*	*	*	40	40	3.8
11 years old	*	*	*	*	*	*	*	*	*	*	*	30	30	2.7
12 years old	12	*	*	*	*	*	*	*	*	*	*	20	20	2.0
13 years old	71	1	*	*	*	*	*	*	*	*	*	22	22	2.1
14 years old	564	64	8	*	*	*	*	*	*	*	*	25	25	2.7
15 years old	289	557	78	27	*	*	*	*	*	*	*	6	6	0.6
16 years old	71	231	511	63	24	*	*	*	*	*	9	36	45	4.7
17 years old	13	49	226	521	47	*	2	*	7	*	24	71	96	10.0
18 years old	*	10	22	290	317	32	12	*	4	*	171	86	257	27.2
19 years old	*	*	7	62	241	274	45	5	*	*	292	95	388	38.0
20 years old	2	4	*	41	110	132	154	11	*	*	382	79	460	50.2
21 years old	4	6	*	8	38	104	114	98	4	4	415	107	522	57.9
22 years old	*	*	3	10	10	96	70	78	4	26	550	75	625	67.6
23 years old	*	*	1	*	24	48	51	57	14	39	605	134	740	75.9
24 years old	*	3	*	13	8	32	36	42	48	26	632	128	760	78.4
25 to 29 years old	*	8	9	16	43	127	100	114	48	99	3,321	760	4,081	87.7
30 to 34 years old	*	*	4	12	38	44	21	20	38	26	3,068	1,096	4,163	95.2
35 to 39 years old	3	8	*	*	20	17	38	23	16	50	2,922	1,222	4,144	95.9
40 to 44 years old	*	8	3	*	25	10	9	26	17	8	2,710	1,169	3,880	97.3
45 to 49 years old	*	4	3	3	2	15	3	8	7	7	2,483	1,119	3,602	98.4
50 to 54 years old	*	*	3	*	16	*	*	*	*	13	2,224	927	3,151	98.9
55 to 59 years old	*	*	2	3	1	4	3	9	*	14	1,717	918	2,635	98.7
60 to 64 years old	*	*	*	3	4	*	2	*	1	*	1,391	654	2,045	99.5
65 years and over	*	3	*	*	*	*	*	*	*	*	2,390	1,807	4,196	99.9

Male

Age, sex, race, and Hispanic origin	9	10	11	12	1	2	3	4	1	2+	H.S. grad	Not grad	Number	Percent
Total	507	448	480	542	448	407	252	229	79	114	12,522	6,210	18,732	67.9
3 years old	*	*	*	*	*	*	*	*	*	*	*	401	401	73.8
4 years old	*	*	*	*	*	*	*	*	*	*	*	168	168	31.5
5 years old	*	*	*	*	*	*	*	*	*	*	*	41	41	7.8
6 years old	*	*	*	*	*	*	*	*	*	*	*	17	17	3.1
7 years old	*	*	*	*	*	*	*	*	*	*	*	19	19	3.3
8 years old	*	*	*	*	*	*	*	*	*	*	*	16	16	3.0
9 years old	*	*	*	*	*	*	*	*	*	*	*	5	5	1.0
10 years old	*	*	*	*	*	*	*	*	*	*	*	25	25	4.6
11 years old	*	*	*	*	*	*	*	*	*	*	*	9	9	1.7
12 years old	6	*	*	*	*	*	*	*	*	*	*	4	4	0.9
13 years old	36	*	*	*	*	*	*	*	*	*	*	18	18	3.1
14 years old	295	30	4	*	*	*	*	*	*	*	*	12	12	2.4
15 years old	129	246	47	19	*	*	*	*	*	*	*	6	6	1.3

* = Quantity zero or rounds to zero.

Table A-2. Single Grade of Enrollment and High School Graduation Status for Population 3 Years Old and Over, by Sex, Age (Single Years for 3 to 24 Years), Race, and Hispanic Origin, October 2017—*Continued*

(Numbers in thousands; percent; civilian noninstitutionalized population.)

Age, sex, race, and Hispanic origin	Population	Enrolled Number	Enrolled Percent	Nursery	Kinder-garten	1	2	3	4	5	6	7	8
16 years old	485	456	94.0	*	*	*	*	*	*	*	*	1	6
17 years old	498	445	89.5	*	*	*	*	*	*	*	*	*	*
18 years old	498	335	67.3	*	*	*	*	*	*	*	*	*	*
19 years old	484	287	59.2	*	*	*	*	*	*	*	*	*	*
20 years old	450	223	49.6	*	*	*	*	*	*	*	2	*	*
21 years old	418	132	31.5	*	*	*	*	*	*	*	*	*	*
22 years old	494	172	34.9	*	*	*	*	*	*	*	*	3	*
23 years old	538	87	16.2	*	*	*	*	*	*	*	*	*	*
24 years old	473	88	18.5	*	*	*	*	*	*	*	*	*	*
25 to 29 years old	2,379	236	9.9	*	*	*	*	*	*	*	4	*	*
30 to 34 years old	2,254	114	5.0	*	*	*	*	*	*	*	5	*	*
35 to 39 years old	2,205	66	3.0	*	*	*	*	*	*	*	*	*	*
40 to 44 years old	2,004	44	2.2	*	*	*	*	*	*	*	*	4	*
45 to 49 years old	1,835	32	1.7	*	*	*	*	*	*	*	8	*	*
50 to 54 years old	1,593	5	0.3	*	*	*	*	*	*	*	*	4	*
55 to 59 years old	1,297	6	0.5	*	*	*	*	*	*	*	*	*	*
60 to 64 years old	993	1	0.1	*	*	*	*	*	*	*	*	*	*
65 years and over	1,827	5	0.3	*	*	*	*	*	*	*	*	3	*
Female													
Total	27,603	9,101	33.0	511	552	493	502	526	511	527	582	459	434
3 years old	534	190	35.6	180	10	*	*	*	*	*	*	*	*
4 years old	507	317	62.6	264	53	*	*	*	*	*	*	*	*
5 years old	513	477	93.1	58	401	18	*	*	*	*	*	*	*
6 years old	493	483	97.9	9	84	350	28	12	*	*	*	*	*
7 years old	505	495	97.9	*	4	125	339	27	*	*	*	*	*
8 years old	525	512	97.4	*	*	*	123	355	35	*	*	*	*
9 years old	544	514	94.3	*	*	*	12	112	357	23	10	*	*
10 years old	524	509	97.1	*	*	*	*	21	96	372	20	*	*
11 years old	542	521	96.2	*	*	*	*	*	16	114	348	44	*
12 years old	524	508	97.0	*	*	*	*	*	8	15	181	262	37
13 years old	478	474	99.0	*	*	*	*	*	*	3	10	120	305
14 years old	438	424	96.9	*	*	*	*	*	*	*	8	30	79
15 years old	520	520	100.0	*	*	*	*	*	*	*	*	1	8
16 years old	470	454	96.6	*	*	*	*	*	*	*	*	*	3
17 years old	462	419	90.6	*	*	*	*	*	*	*	*	*	*
18 years old	446	352	79.0	*	*	*	*	*	*	*	*	*	*
19 years old	537	347	64.6	*	*	*	*	*	*	*	*	*	*
20 years old	468	234	50.0	*	*	*	*	*	*	*	*	*	*
21 years old	484	248	51.3	*	*	*	*	*	*	*	*	*	*
22 years old	431	128	29.6	*	*	*	*	*	*	*	*	*	*
23 years old	437	148	33.9	*	*	*	*	*	*	*	*	*	*
24 years old	496	122	24.5	*	*	*	*	*	*	*	*	*	*
25 to 29 years old	2,272	334	14.7	*	*	*	*	*	*	*	*	4	*
30 to 34 years old	2,119	96	4.6	*	*	*	*	*	*	*	4	*	*
35 to 39 years old	2,116	111	5.2	*	*	*	*	*	*	*	*	*	2
40 to 44 years old	1,984	65	3.3	*	*	*	*	*	*	*	*	*	*
45 to 49 years old	1,827	28	1.5	*	*	*	*	*	*	*	*	*	*
50 to 54 years old	1,595	31	1.9	*	*	*	*	*	*	*	*	*	*
55 to 59 years old	1,374	29	2.1	*	*	*	*	*	*	*	*	*	*
60 to 64 years old	1063	9	0.9	*	*	*	*	*	*	*	*	*	*
65 years and over	2,376	1	-	*	*	*	*	*	*	*	1	*	*

* = Quantity zero or rounds to zero.

Table A-2. Single Grade of Enrollment and High School Graduation Status for Population 3 Years Old and Over, by Sex, Age (Single Years for 3 to 24 Years), Race, and Hispanic Origin, October 2017—*Continued*

(Numbers in thousands; percent; civilian noninstitutionalized population.)

Age, sex, race, and Hispanic origin	Enrolled										Not enrolled		Not enrolled	
	High school				Undergraduate college				Graduate school		H.S. grad	Not grad	Number	Percent
	9	10	11	12	1	2	3	4	1	2+				
16 years old	38	109	268	30	3	*	*	*	*	*	5	24	29	6.0
17 years old	3	34	131	251	24	*	*	*	3	*	7	45	52	10.5
18 years old	*	5	21	153	133	11	7	*	4	*	109	54	163	32.7
19 years old	*	*	5	25	128	113	16	*	*	*	138	59	197	40.8
20 years old	*	*	*	30	59	68	58	5	*	*	174	53	227	50.4
21 years old	*	6	*	4	15	43	20	43	*	*	217	70	287	68.5
22 years old	*	*	3	7	8	58	28	50	4	9	281	41	322	65.1
23 years old	*	*	1	*	4	15	29	22	1	15	364	87	451	83.8
24 years old	*	3	*	8	*	10	8	20	25	13	320	66	386	81.5
25 to 29 years old	*	4	*	9	17	52	49	50	18	33	1,703	440	2,143	90.1
30 to 34 years old	*	*	*	5	31	22	14	9	10	18	1,533	607	2,140	95.0
35 to 39 years old	*	4	*	*	8	*	20	7	6	21	1,495	644	2,139	97.0
40 to 44 years old	*	*	*	*	14	4	*	14	5	4	1,323	637	1,960	97.8
45 to 49 years old	*	4	*	*	1	12	*	5	3	*	1,217	587	1,803	98.3
50 to 54 years old	*	*	*	*	*	*	*	*	*	1	1,109	479	1,588	99.7
55 to 59 years old	*	*	*	*	*	*	3	3	*	*	789	502	1,291	99.5
60 to 64 years old	*	*	*	*	1	*	*	*	*	*	674	317	992	99.9
65 years and over	*	3	*	*	*	*	*	*	*	*	1,064	758	1,821	99.7
Female														
Total	522	508	400	528	519	528	408	263	129	197	12,785	5,717	18,502	67.0
3 years old	*	*	*	*	*	*	*	*	*	*	*	344	344	64.4
4 years old	*	*	*	*	*	*	*	*	*	*	*	190	190	37.4
5 years old	*	*	*	*	*	*	*	*	*	*	*	35	35	6.9
6 years old	*	*	*	*	*	*	*	*	*	*	*	10	10	2.1
7 years old	*	*	*	*	*	*	*	*	*	*	*	10	10	2.1
8 years old	*	*	*	*	*	*	*	*	*	*	*	13	13	2.6
9 years old	*	*	*	*	*	*	*	*	*	*	*	31	31	5.7
10 years old	*	*	*	*	*	*	*	*	*	*	*	15	15	2.9
11 years old	*	*	*	*	*	*	*	*	*	*	*	21	21	3.8
12 years old	6	*	*	*	*	*	*	*	*	*	*	16	16	3.0
13 years old	35	1	*	*	*	*	*	*	*	*	*	5	5	1.0
14 years old	269	34	4	*	*	*	*	*	*	*	*	13	13	3.1
15 years old	160	312	31	7	*	*	*	*	*	*	*	*	*	*
16 years old	32	122	243	32	21	*	*	*	*	*	4	12	16	3.4
17 years old	10	15	95	270	22	*	2	*	4	*	17	26	43	9.4
18 years old	*	4	1	137	184	21	5	*	*	*	62	32	93	21.0
19 years old	*	*	2	37	113	161	29	5	*	*	155	36	190	35.4
20 years old	2	4	*	11	51	65	96	6	*	*	208	26	234	50.0
21 years old	4	*	*	4	22	61	94	55	4	4	198	37	235	48.7
22 years old	*	*	*	3	2	37	42	28	*	16	269	34	303	70.4
23 years old	*	*	*	*	20	34	21	36	14	24	241	47	288	66.1
24 years old	*	*	*	5	8	23	27	23	23	13	312	62	374	75.5
25 to 29 years old	*	4	9	6	26	75	51	64	29	67	1,618	320	1,938	85.3
30 to 34 years old	*	*	4	7	7	21	7	11	28	8	1,534	488	2,023	95.4
35 to 39 years old	3	5	*	*	11	17	18	16	10	30	1,426	578	2,005	94.8
40 to 44 years old	*	8	3	*	10	7	9	12	12	4	1,387	533	1,920	96.7
45 to 49 years old	*	*	3	3	1	4	3	3	4	7	1,267	532	1,799	98.5
50 to 54 years old	*	*	3	*	16	*	*	*	*	12	1,115	448	1,563	98.1
55 to 59 years old	*	*	2	3	1	4	*	6	*	14	929	416	1,345	97.9
60 to 64 years old	*	*	*	3	3	*	2	*	1	*	716	337	1,053	99.1
65 years and over	*	*	*	*	*	*	*	*	*	*	1,326	1,049	2,375	100.0

* = Quantity zero or rounds to zero.

Table A-3. Nursery and Primary School Enrollment of Population 3 to 6 Years Old, by Control of School, Attendance Status, Age, Race, Hispanic Origin, Mother's Labor Force Status and Education, and Family Income, October 2017

(Numbers in thousands; civilian noninstitutionalized population.)

Characteristic	Total	Not enrolled	Enrolled in nursery school								
			Total			Public			Private		
			Total	Part-day	Full-day	Total	Part-day	Full-day	Total	Part-day	Full-day
3 TO 6 YEARS OLD											
Total	16,068	4,233	4,676	2,057	2,619	2,782	1,272	1,510	1,894	785	1,109
Race and Hispanic origin											
White alone	11,491	3,039	3,315	1,620	1,694	1,885	988	897	1,430	633	797
White alone non-Hispanic	7,874	2,002	2,461	1,170	1,291	1,211	612	600	1,250	559	692
Black alone	2,433	628	754	189	565	576	147	428	178	42	137
Asian alone	868	201	253	113	140	123	67	56	130	46	84
Hispanic (of any race)	4,181	1,206	1007	500	508	751	398	352	257	101	155
Labor force status of mother											
Children not living with mother	1,683	443	460	183	277	344	146	198	116	37	79
Mother employed part-time	2,278	547	746	425	320	400	251	149	346	175	171
Mother employed full-time	6,640	1,547	1,953	675	1,278	1,079	397	682	874	278	596
Mother unemployed	422	112	120	27	92	79	25	55	40	3	38
Mother not in the labor force	5,046	1,584	1,398	747	650	880	454	426	518	293	225
Education of mother											
Children not living with mother	1,683	443	460	183	277	344	146	198	116	37	79
Elementary: 0 to 8 years	494	202	74	56	18	54	44	10	20	12	8
High school: 9 to 11 years	1,028	316	257	139	118	223	119	104	34	20	14
High school graduate	3,210	937	843	368	476	662	285	377	182	83	99
Some college or associate's degree	4,292	1,238	1,170	508	662	704	298	406	465	210	256
Bachelor's degree or more	5,363	1,097	1,872	804	1068	795	380	415	1,077	425	653
Family income											
Less than $20,000	1,758	533	445	184	261	375	148	227	70	36	34
$20,000 to $29,999	1,078	283	319	153	166	267	136	131	52	17	35
$30,000 to $39,999	1,347	422	329	170	159	211	119	91	118	51	67
$40,000 to $49,999	1,025	281	254	115	139	176	81	95	78	34	44
$50,000 to $74,999	2,394	648	734	335	399	452	196	256	282	139	143
$75,000 and over	5,385	1048	1,800	792	1008	775	385	390	1,025	407	618
Not reported	3,082	1018	794	307	487	525	206	319	270	101	168
3 AND 4 YEARS OLD											
Total	8,030	3,711	3,966	1,742	2,223	2,333	1,084	1,249	1,633	659	974
Race and Hispanic origin											
White alone	5,716	2,664	2,818	1,387	1,431	1,593	849	744	1,224	537	687
White alone non-Hispanic	3,915	1,724	2,071	982	1,090	1003	512	492	1,068	470	598
Black alone	1,245	527	652	158	495	489	132	358	163	26	137
Asian alone	405	176	210	89	121	100	55	45	110	34	75
Hispanic (of any race)	2,117	1,103	870	443	427	649	354	295	221	90	132
Labor force status of mother											
Children not living with mother	800	378	384	161	223	271	124	147	113	37	76
Mother employed part-time	1,161	488	631	368	263	335	218	117	295	150	146
Mother employed full-time	3,174	1,363	1,678	565	1112	932	347	585	746	219	527
Mother unemployed	228	104	110	21	89	70	19	51	40	3	38
Mother not in the labor force	2,666	1,377	1,163	627	537	725	376	349	438	251	187
Education of mother											
Children not living with mother	800	378	384	161	223	271	124	147	113	37	76
Elementary: 0 to 8 years	240	176	55	44	11	39	32	7	16	12	5
High school: 9 to 11 years	525	260	238	133	105	204	113	91	34	20	14
High school graduate	1,611	823	702	305	397	568	245	323	134	60	74
Some college or associate's degree	2,176	1098	984	413	570	585	241	344	399	172	227
Bachelor's degree or more	2,676	976	1,602	686	916	665	328	338	936	358	578
Family income											
Less than $20,000	905	493	368	142	226	318	121	197	50	21	29
$20,000 to $29,999	534	252	254	140	114	211	127	84	44	13	30
$30,000 to $39,999	677	363	289	159	130	182	108	73	107	51	57
$40,000 to $49,999	493	250	216	99	117	148	69	79	67	30	37
$50,000 to $74,999	1,285	594	630	274	356	384	153	231	246	121	125
$75,000 and over	2,559	924	1,533	672	862	655	334	320	879	337	541
Not reported	1,576	835	676	257	419	436	172	264	240	85	155
5 YEARS OLD											
Total	3,972	396	654	293	361	405	175	231	249	119	130
Race and Hispanic origin											
White alone	2,862	269	457	220	237	258	128	130	199	92	106
White alone non-Hispanic	1,970	200	366	183	184	191	97	94	175	86	89
Black alone	564	87	97	31	66	82	16	66	16	16	*

* = Quantity zero or rounds to zero.

Table A-3. Nursery and Primary School Enrollment of Population 3 to 6 Years Old, by Control of School, Attendance Status, Age, Race, Hispanic Origin, Mother's Labor Force Status and Education, and Family Income, October 2017—*Continued*

(Numbers in thousands; civilian noninstitutionalized population.)

Characteristic	Enrolled in kindergarten									Enrolled in elementary school		
	Total			Public			Private					
	Total	Part-day	Full-day	Total	Part-day	Full-day	Total	Part-day	Full-day	Total	Public	Private
3 TO 6 YEARS OLD												
Total.........................	3,925	801	3,124	3,504	720	2,783	422	81	341	3,234	2,981	252
Race and Hispanic origin												
White alone.........................	2,902	608	2,294	2,564	547	2,018	338	62	276	2,235	2,032	203
White alone non-Hispanic	1,947	380	1,567	1,692	339	1,353	256	41	215	1,463	1,309	153
Black alone.........................	493	75	418	463	64	399	30	11	19	559	538	20
Asian alone	234	49	185	199	43	156	35	7	28	180	160	19
Hispanic (of any race)	1,107	272	835	1023	251	772	83	21	63	861	805	56
Labor force status of mother.........................												
Children not living with mother	419	73	345	402	69	333	16	4	12	361	345	15
Mother employed part-time	573	157	416	508	142	366	65	15	50	412	366	46
Mother employed full-time	1,735	309	1,426	1,515	272	1,243	220	37	183	1,405	1,324	81
Mother unemployed.........................	80	12	68	79	12	67	2	*	2	110	106	4
Mother not in the labor force	1,118	250	868	999	225	774	119	25	95	946	840	106
Education of mother.........................												
Children not living with mother	419	73	345	402	69	333	16	4	12	361	345	15
Elementary: 0 to 8 years	114	23	91	114	23	91	*	*	*	104	91	13
High school: 9 to 11 years	240	53	187	232	49	183	8	4	4	214	207	7
High school graduate.........................	763	137	626	699	124	575	65	13	51	666	644	22
Some college or associate's degree	1,008	218	790	938	202	736	69	16	53	877	813	64
Bachelor's degree or more	1,382	296	1,086	1,118	253	866	263	43	220	1,012	881	131
Family income.........................												
Less than $20,000	403	67	336	392	63	329	11	4	7	376	368	8
$20,000 to $29,999	237	39	197	219	39	180	18	1	17	239	224	15
$30,000 to $39,999	347	57	289	320	54	266	27	4	24	249	240	9
$40,000 to $49,999	280	73	207	251	63	188	29	11	19	210	188	21
$50,000 to $74,999	579	123	455	512	104	409	67	20	47	434	398	36
$75,000 and over.........................	1,403	298	1105	1,177	260	917	226	38	187	1134	1016	117
Not reported.........................	677	142	535	633	138	495	44	4	40	593	546	46
3 AND 4 YEARS OLD												
Total.........................	353	137	216	297	112	185	56	25	31	*	*	*
Race and Hispanic origin												
White alone.........................	235	100	135	186	79	108	48	21	27	*	*	*
White alone non-Hispanic	120	52	68	89	42	47	31	9	21	*	*	*
Black alone.........................	66	28	38	62	24	38	4	4	*	*	*	*
Asian alone	19	*	19	19	*	19	*	*	*	*	*	*
Hispanic (of any race)	144	66	79	127	54	73	18	12	6	*	*	*
Labor force status of mother.........................												
Children not living with mother	38	5	33	38	5	33	*	*	*	*	*	*
Mother employed part-time	42	26	16	38	23	15	4	4	1	*	*	*
Mother employed full-time	133	53	79	106	41	65	27	12	15	*	*	*
Mother unemployed.........................	14	4	10	14	4	10	*	*	*	*	*	*
Mother not in the labor force	126	48	77	101	39	62	25	9	16	*	*	*
Education of mother.........................												
Children not living with mother	38	5	33	38	5	33	*	*	*	*	*	*
Elementary: 0 to 8 years	9	*	9	9	*	9	*	*	*	*	*	*
High school: 9 to 11 years	27	13	13	27	13	13	*	*	*	*	*	*
High school graduate.........................	86	30	56	75	25	49	11	4	7	*	*	*
Some college or associate's degree	95	39	56	80	28	52	15	11	4	*	*	*
Bachelor's degree or more	98	50	49	69	41	29	29	9	20	*	*	*
Family income.........................												
Less than $20,000	44	19	25	42	19	22	2	*	2	*	*	*
$20,000 to $29,999	28	4	25	28	4	25	*	*	*	*	*	*
$30,000 to $39,999	25	9	16	20	8	12	5	1	4	*	*	*
$40,000 to $49,999	27	22	6	23	17	6	4	4	*	*	*	*
$50,000 to $74,999	61	28	33	45	20	25	16	8	8	*	*	*
$75,000 and over.........................	101	35	66	78	27	51	23	8	15	*	*	*
Not reported.........................	65	20	45	60	16	44	5	4	2	*	*	*
5 YEARS OLD												
Total.........................	2,744	522	2,222	2,466	477	1,989	278	45	233	179	169	10
Race and Hispanic origin												
White alone.........................	2,017	400	1,616	1,798	370	1,427	219	30	189	119	109	10
White alone non-Hispanic	1,337	251	1,085	1,158	226	932	178	25	153	67	57	10
Black alone.........................	336	33	303	320	27	294	16	7	9	43	43	*

* = Quantity zero or rounds to zero.

Table A-3. Nursery and Primary School Enrollment of Population 3 to 6 Years Old, by Control of School, Attendance Status, Age, Race, Hispanic Origin, Mother's Labor Force Status and Education, and Family Income, October 2017—*Continued*

(Numbers in thousands; civilian noninstitutionalized population.)

Characteristic	Total	Not enrolled	Enrolled in nursery school								
			Total			Public			Private		
			Total	Part-day	Full-day	Total	Part-day	Full-day	Total	Part-day	Full-day
Asian alone	232	18	36	17	19	20	10	10	16	7	9
Hispanic (of any race)	1,033	76	116	44	72	86	37	48	30	7	24
Labor force status of mother											
Children not living with mother	455	56	67	18	49	65	18	46	3	*	3
Mother employed part-time	560	41	109	56	53	60	32	27	49	24	25
Mother employed full-time	1,696	150	256	96	160	133	42	91	123	54	69
Mother unemployed	83	8	10	6	4	10	6	4	*	*	*
Mother not in the labor force	1,177	140	212	117	96	138	76	62	74	41	33
Education of mother											
Children not living with mother	455	56	67	18	49	65	18	46	3	*	3
Elementary: 0 to 8 years	145	24	16	10	6	13	10	3	3	*	3
High school: 9 to 11 years	220	46	15	6	9	15	6	9	*	*	*
High school graduate	786	83	127	56	70	84	39	45	43	18	25
Some college or associate's degree	1,019	95	176	92	84	110	55	55	67	38	29
Bachelor's degree or more	1,346	92	252	110	142	119	47	72	134	63	70
Family income											
Less than $20,000	408	33	72	40	32	53	25	27	20	15	5
$20,000 to $29,999	222	19	54	14	40	45	10	36	8	4	5
$30,000 to $39,999	357	48	40	11	29	29	11	18	11	*	11
$40,000 to $49,999	291	24	38	16	22	27	12	15	10	4	6
$50,000 to $74,999	581	39	102	59	42	66	41	25	35	18	18
$75,000 and over	1,325	88	243	107	136	109	46	63	134	62	72
Not reported	787	144	106	46	60	76	30	46	30	16	14
6 YEARS OLD											
Total	4,067	127	56	22	35	44	14	30	12	8	4
Race and Hispanic origin											
White alone	2,913	106	40	13	27	33	10	22	7	3	4
White alone non-Hispanic	1,989	78	24	6	18	17	3	14	7	3	4
Black alone	625	14	5	*	5	5	*	5	*	*	*
Asian alone	230	6	7	7	*	2	2	*	5	5	*
Hispanic (of any race)	1,030	27	21	12	9	16	7	9	5	5	*
Labor force status of mother											
Children not living with mother	427	9	9	3	6	9	3	6	*	*	*
Mother employed part-time	557	18	6	1	5	5	*	5	1	1	*
Mother employed full-time	1,770	34	20	13	6	15	8	6	5	5	*
Mother unemployed	110	*	*	*	*	*	*	*	*	*	*
Mother not in the labor force	1,202	66	22	4	18	16	2	14	6	2	4
Education of mother											
Children not living with mother	427	9	9	3	6	9	3	6	*	*	*
Elementary: 0 to 8 years	108	2	2	2	*	2	2	*	*	*	*
High school: 9 to 11 years	282	10	4	*	4	4	*	4	*	*	*
High school graduate	812	32	14	6	8	9	1	8	5	5	*
Some college or associate's degree	1,097	45	10	2	7	10	2	7	*	*	*
Bachelor's degree or more	1,341	29	18	8	10	11	5	6	7	3	4
Family income											
Less than $20,000	445	7	5	2	3	5	2	3	*	*	*
$20,000 to $29,999	321	13	12	*	12	12	*	12	*	*	*
$30,000 to $39,999	313	11	*	*	*	*	*	*	*	*	*
$40,000 to $49,999	241	7	1	*	1	1	*	1	*	*	*
$50,000 to $74,999	528	15	2	2	*	2	2	*	*	*	*
$75,000 and over	1,501	36	24	13	11	12	5	6	12	8	4
Not reported	719	39	13	4	8	13	4	8	*	*	*

* = Quantity zero or rounds to zero.

Table A-3. Nursery and Primary School Enrollment of Population 3 to 6 Years Old, by Control of School, Attendance Status, Age, Race, Hispanic Origin, Mother's Labor Force Status and Education, and Family Income, October 2017—*Continued*

(Numbers in thousands; civilian noninstitutionalized population.)

Characteristic	Enrolled in kindergarten									Enrolled in elementary school		
	Total			Public			Private					
	Total	Part-day	Full-day	Total	Part-day	Full-day	Total	Part-day	Full-day	Total	Public	Private
Asian alone	171	42	129	143	36	108	28	7	21	6	6	*
Hispanic (of any race)	789	174	615	749	169	579	41	5	36	52	52	*
Labor force status of mother												
Children not living with mother	297	64	233	283	61	222	14	4	11	35	32	3
Mother employed part-time	404	104	300	350	92	258	54	11	42	6	3	3
Mother employed full-time	1,229	202	1027	1,093	182	911	136	21	116	61	61	*
Mother unemployed	56	8	48	54	8	46	2	*	2	10	10	*
Mother not in the labor force	758	144	614	686	135	551	72	9	63	67	62	4
Education of mother												
Children not living with mother	297	64	233	283	61	222	14	4	11	35	32	3
Elementary: 0 to 8 years	92	18	74	92	18	74	*	*	*	13	9	4
High school: 9 to 11 years	152	27	125	148	23	125	4	4	*	7	7	*
High school graduate	534	90	443	493	84	409	41	6	35	42	42	*
Some college or associate's degree	697	139	558	656	138	518	41	1	40	50	49	1
Bachelor's degree or more	972	183	789	795	153	642	177	31	147	30	29	1
Family income												
Less than $20,000	273	37	236	269	33	236	4	4	*	29	29	*
$20,000 to $29,999	142	26	116	128	26	101	15	*	15	8	8	*
$30,000 to $39,999	256	45	211	240	43	197	16	3	14	13	13	*
$40,000 to $49,999	212	44	168	190	41	149	21	3	19	17	17	*
$50,000 to $74,999	409	81	328	370	73	297	39	8	31	31	31	*
$75,000 and over	954	197	757	808	170	638	147	28	119	40	35	4
Not reported	497	91	406	461	91	370	36	*	36	41	35	5
6 YEARS OLD												
Total	829	142	686	741	132	609	88	11	78	3,055	2,812	243
Race and Hispanic origin												
White alone	651	108	543	580	98	483	71	11	60	2,116	1,923	193
White alone non-Hispanic	491	77	414	444	71	373	47	6	40	1,396	1,252	144
Black alone	91	14	77	81	14	67	10	*	10	516	495	20
Asian alone	44	7	37	36	7	30	7	*	7	173	154	19
Hispanic (of any race)	173	32	142	148	27	121	25	4	21	809	753	56
Labor force status of mother												
Children not living with mother	84	5	79	82	4	78	2	1	2	325	313	12
Mother employed part-time	127	27	100	120	27	93	7	*	7	407	363	43
Mother employed full-time	373	53	320	316	49	267	56	4	53	1,344	1,263	81
Mother unemployed	10	*	10	10	*	10	*	*	*	100	96	4
Mother not in the labor force	235	58	177	212	51	161	23	6	16	879	777	102
Education of mother												
Children not living with mother	84	5	79	82	4	78	2	1	2	325	313	12
Elementary: 0 to 8 years	13	5	8	13	5	8	*	*	*	91	82	9
High school: 9 to 11 years	62	13	48	58	13	44	4	*	4	207	199	7
High school graduate	144	17	126	131	14	117	13	3	9	623	601	22
Some college or associate's degree	215	39	176	202	36	167	13	4	9	827	764	63
Bachelor's degree or more	311	63	248	255	60	195	56	3	53	982	852	130
Family income												
Less than $20,000	86	11	75	81	11	70	5	*	5	347	339	8
$20,000 to $29,999	66	9	57	63	9	54	3	1	3	231	216	15
$30,000 to $39,999	66	3	62	60	3	56	6	*	6	236	228	9
$40,000 to $49,999	41	8	33	37	4	33	4	4	*	192	171	21
$50,000 to $74,999	108	14	94	96	11	86	12	4	8	403	367	36
$75,000 and over	347	65	281	291	63	228	56	3	53	1094	981	113
Not reported	115	32	84	113	32	81	3	*	3	552	511	41

* = Quantity zero or rounds to zero.

Table A-4. Current Grade for People 15 to 24 Years Old Enrolled in School, and Highest Grade Completed for People with Selected Enrollment and Completion Status, by Sex, Age, Race, and Hispanic Origin, October 2017

(Numbers in thousands; civilian noninstitutionalized population.)

Age, sex, race, and Hispanic origin	Total	Enrolled — Current grade							Not enrolled — Enrolled last year — Highest grade completed						Not enrolled last year
		Less than 9th grade	9th grade	10th grade	11th grade	12th grade	College (graduated this year)	Other college	Less than 9th grade	9th grade	10th grade	11th or 12th, no diploma	New HS graduate	Other[1]	
ALL RACES															
Both Sexes															
Total	42,225	232	1,432	3,681	3,990	4,409	1,930	10,242	19	41	137	344	955	2,385	12,427
15 years old	4,146	184	1,196	2,307	314	75	15	20	2	1	7	2	*	*	23
16 years old	4,184	26	191	1,113	2,325	242	25	21	3	26	60	43	7	10	94
17 years old	4,357	6	20	203	1,111	2,496	77	78	7	2	39	114	45	12	147
18 years old	4,155	6	2	31	162	1,198	1,179	486	2	1	22	127	464	98	377
19 years old	4,067	2	7	3	42	209	483	1,794	*	6	*	50	251	266	952
20 to 24 years old	21,315	8	16	23	36	190	150	7,843	4	6	9	8	189	2,000	10,834
Male															
Total	21,293	169	756	1,808	2,150	2,252	831	4,713	12	35	86	186	523	1,180	6,592
15 years old	2,116	128	631	1,095	162	57	9	13	*	1	3	2	*	*	17
16 years old	2,116	22	105	581	1,154	114	10	3	3	19	29	27	3	3	44
17 years old	2,228	6	9	98	668	1,189	15	35	3	2	28	67	17	7	84
18 years old	2,136	4	1	17	114	668	487	222	2	1	17	71	256	53	223
19 years old	2,016	2	7	3	29	112	243	794	*	6	*	19	129	116	556
20 to 24 years old	10,681	6	4	14	23	113	67	3,646	4	6	9	*	119	1,002	5,667
Female															
Total	20,932	63	675	1,872	1,840	2,157	1,099	5,529	7	6	51	158	432	1,205	5,836
15 years old	2,030	56	565	1,212	152	18	7	7	2	*	4	*	*	*	7
16 years old	2,068	3	85	532	1,171	129	16	18	*	6	31	16	4	7	50
17 years old	2,129	*	12	105	443	1,307	61	43	4	*	11	47	28	5	63
18 years old	2,019	2	1	14	48	530	692	264	1	*	5	56	207	45	154
19 years old	2,051	*	*	*	13	97	241	1,000	*	*	*	31	123	150	396
20 to 24 years old	10,635	2	12	9	12	77	83	4,197	*	*	*	8	70	998	5,167
WHITE ALONE															
Total	30,999	175	1,055	2,671	2,841	3,222	1,444	7,402	19	29	95	245	705	1,735	9,362
15 years old	3,026	132	899	1,683	212	59	7	7	2	*	7	*	*	*	17
16 years old	3,064	26	124	836	1,700	170	25	8	3	21	41	18	4	9	79
17 years old	3,120	6	15	117	764	1,858	49	60	7	1	26	82	26	7	102
18 years old	3,089	6	2	23	104	885	892	365	2	*	13	107	335	72	282
19 years old	3,063	*	4	*	33	135	366	1,358	*	6	*	32	198	186	745
20 to 24 years old	15,636	6	11	12	26	114	104	5,604	4	*	9	7	142	1,460	8,137
WHITE ALONE NON-HISPANIC															
Total	22,684	121	731	1,971	2,129	2,318	1,113	5,520	15	24	47	164	495	1,365	6,671
15 years old	2,183	93	645	1,233	140	37	7	7	2	*	4	*	*	*	14
16 years old	2,263	16	73	643	1,266	113	16	6	3	21	21	12	4	9	59
17 years old	2,294	6	2	77	592	1,388	26	28	3	1	13	54	16	7	81
18 years old	2,252	6	2	13	82	635	705	218	2	*	9	81	262	44	194
19 years old	2,147	*	4	*	27	85	284	922	*	1	*	11	138	139	536
20 to 24 years old	11,545	*	5	5	22	61	76	4,340	4	*	*	5	75	1,165	5,788
BLACK ALONE															
Total	6,331	37	190	585	572	709	254	1,376	*	5	27	56	171	379	1,969
15 years old	608	34	150	335	62	4	4	12	*	*	*	2	*	*	5
16 years old	574	*	32	178	266	46	*	5	*	4	12	22	2	*	8
17 years old	690	*	6	67	187	347	5	9	*	*	6	11	14	4	34
18 years old	674	*	*	4	47	194	159	72	*	*	10	10	93	19	66
19 years old	571	2	2	*	*	59	66	228	*	*	*	11	37	64	101
20 to 24 years old	3,212	*	1	*	9	59	20	1,050	*	*	*	*	26	291	1,755

[1]Other includes people whose response to questions on educational attainment did not fall into one of the listed categories (e.g., completed high school (not last year), but enrolled in college or some other type of school last year).
* = Quantity zero or rounds to zero.

Table A-4. Current Grade for People 15 to 24 Years Old Enrolled in School, and Highest Grade Completed for People with Selected Enrollment and Completion Status, by Sex, Age, Race, and Hispanic Origin, October 2017—*Continued*

(Numbers in thousands; civilian noninstitutionalized population.)

Age, sex, race, and Hispanic origin	Total	Enrolled — Current grade							Not enrolled — Enrolled last year — Highest grade completed						Not enrolled last year
		Less than 9th grade	9th grade	10th grade	11th grade	12th grade	College (graduated this year)	Other college	Less than 9th grade	9th grade	10th grade	11th or 12th, no diploma	New HS graduate	Other[1]	
ASIAN ALONE															
Total..........................	2,471	15	53	195	241	217	141	992	*	6	12	24	29	182	363
15 years old	227	15	46	133	22	7	4	*	*	*	*	*	*	*	*
16 years old	224	*	6	37	147	22	*	*	*	*	5	3	1	*	3
17 years old	266	*	*	11	69	139	19	9	*	*	7	10	*	*	3
18 years old	187	1	*	3	3	38	80	35	*	*	*	3	11	7	5
19 years old	189	*	1	*	*	3	27	118	*	*	*	7	9	10	14
20 to 24 years old	1,378	*	*	11	*	7	11	830	*	6	*	1	7	165	339
HISPANIC (OF ANY RACE)															
Total..........................	9,567	57	379	861	849	1,034	364	2,125	4	11	59	92	233	440	3,060
15 years old	999	41	289	557	78	27	*	*	*	*	3	*	*	*	3
16 years old	955	10	71	231	511	63	9	15	*	*	20	5	*	*	20
17 years old	960	*	13	49	226	521	23	32	4	*	19	31	10	*	31
18 years old	944	*	*	10	22	290	203	162	*	*	8	32	86	28	103
19 years old	1,021	*	*	*	7	62	85	480	*	4	*	21	64	52	247
20 to 24 years old	4,688	6	6	14	4	72	44	1,435	*	6	9	2	74	360	2,656

[1]Other includes people whose response to questions on educational attainment did not fall into one of the listed categories (e.g., completed high school (not last year), but enrolled in college or some other type of school last year).
* = Quantity zero or rounds to zero.

Table A-5. Type of College and Year Enrolled for College Students 15 Years Old and Over, by Age, Sex, Race, Attendance Status, Control of School, Disability Status, and Enrollment Status, October 2017

(Numbers in thousands; civilian noninstitutionalized population.)

Characteristic	Total enrolled	Undergraduate college — All colleges 1st year	2nd year	3rd year	4th year	Two-year college 1st year	2nd or higher	Four-year college 1st year	2nd or higher	Graduate school 1st year	2nd or higher
BOTH SEXES	18,398	4,192	4,147	3,518	2,733	1,809	2,463	2,383	7,935	1,364	2,445
Full-Time Students											
Total	13,606	3,329	3,142	2,752	2,112	1,188	1,500	2,141	6,505	834	1,437
Age											
15–19 years old	3,821	2,343	1,187	201	37	703	336	1,640	1,089	50	3
20–24 years old	6,716	657	1,464	2,055	1,619	304	818	352	4,319	411	511
25–34 years old	2,214	221	364	358	325	134	271	88	776	261	685
35 years old and over	856	108	127	138	132	47	76	61	321	113	238
Race											
White alone	9,623	2,414	2,202	1,932	1,524	863	997	1,550	4,660	545	1,006
White alone non-Hispanic	7,404	1,746	1,609	1,538	1,235	557	684	1,189	3,698	443	832
Black alone	2,034	546	478	479	238	216	297	330	898	124	169
Asian alone	1,330	196	275	231	266	53	106	143	666	150	212
Hispanic (of any race)	2,510	763	660	452	315	326	357	437	1,069	118	202
Employment Status											
Full time	1,930	268	370	380	341	106	272	162	819	202	368
Part time	4,135	877	983	954	696	448	516	429	2,117	213	412
Not employed	7,541	2,183	1,788	1,417	1,075	634	712	1,549	3,570	419	657
Control of School											
Public	10,864	2,887	2,690	2,199	1,572	1,148	1,374	1,739	5,086	569	947
Private	2,742	441	452	553	540	40	126	401	1,419	265	490
Disability Status											
No disability	13,276	3,265	3,062	2,690	2,062	1,157	1,452	2,108	6,361	801	1,397
Any disability	330	64	80	62	50	31	48	33	144	34	40
Part-Time Students											
Total	4,792	863	1,005	766	621	621	962	242	1,430	530	1008
Age											
15–19 years old	358	244	91	23	*	189	64	55	50	*	*
20–24 years old	1,278	234	409	253	187	152	325	82	523	78	117
25–34 years old	1,667	194	297	272	263	145	339	49	494	234	407
35 years old and over	1,490	191	208	217	171	135	234	56	363	219	484
Race											
White alone	3,601	616	732	559	466	446	709	171	1,048	427	801
White alone non-Hispanic	2,651	434	489	373	301	310	469	124	694	343	711
Black alone	778	172	185	129	85	127	155	45	245	76	129
Asian alone	251	31	40	41	49	20	47	11	83	21	69
Hispanic (of any race)	1,064	204	275	208	177	153	270	51	390	90	109
Employment Status											
Full time	2,821	358	462	469	348	241	467	116	812	401	783
Part time	1,187	268	377	164	171	195	323	73	389	80	126
Not employed	785	237	165	133	103	184	172	52	229	49	98
Control of School											
Public	3,942	789	920	663	517	572	885	217	1,214	384	671
Private	850	74	85	103	105	49	78	25	215	146	337
Disability Status											
No disability	4,571	796	961	742	597	569	914	227	1,386	507	968
Any disability	222	67	44	24	24	52	49	15	43	23	40
MALE	8,112	1,824	1,934	1,616	1,206	846	1,142	979	3,615	513	1,017
Full-Time Students											
Total	6,203	1,459	1,506	1,299	945	576	741	883	3,009	350	644
Age											
15–19 years old	1,685	1,048	503	89	17	384	169	663	440	28	*
20–24 years old	3,167	294	748	966	743	136	413	158	2,045	182	233
25–34 years old	1,035	80	196	186	136	37	127	43	391	117	320
35 years old and over	316	38	60	57	49	19	32	19	133	22	91
Race											
White alone	4,415	1,071	1,046	940	699	430	496	641	2,189	217	441
White alone non-Hispanic	3,447	776	797	780	549	273	366	503	1,760	175	371
Black alone	897	258	242	205	61	105	143	154	365	38	92
Asian alone	639	82	124	111	141	28	44	54	333	89	92
Hispanic (of any race)	1,101	339	294	175	157	166	155	173	470	54	83
Employment Status											
Full time	878	132	202	177	119	47	137	84	361	80	169

* = Quantity zero or rounds to zero.

Table A-5. Type of College and Year Enrolled for College Students 15 Years Old and Over, by Age, Sex, Race, Attendance Status, Control of School, Disability Status, and Enrollment Status, October 2017—Continued

(Numbers in thousands; civilian noninstitutionalized population.)

Characteristic	Total enrolled	Undergraduate college				Two-year college		Four-year college		Graduate school	
		All colleges									
		1st year	2nd year	3rd year	4th year	1st year	2nd or higher	1st year	2nd or higher	1st year	2nd or higher
Part time	1,760	346	420	410	317	188	213	158	934	75	192
Not employed	3,565	982	884	712	509	340	391	641	1,715	195	283
Control of School											
Public	5,095	1,313	1,341	1,038	723	553	703	760	2,399	272	408
Private	1,108	146	166	261	222	23	38	123	611	78	236
Disability Status											
No disability	6,051	1,431	1,468	1,253	920	562	716	869	2,926	341	638
Any disability	152	28	39	46	25	14	26	14	84	9	6
Part-Time Students											
Total	1,908	365	428	317	261	270	401	96	605	163	374
Age											
15–19 years old	146	101	38	7	*	89	20	11	25	*	*
20–24 years old	547	122	203	96	67	83	160	39	207	17	42
25–34 years old	679	94	113	136	106	60	126	34	229	74	155
35 years old and over	537	49	74	77	87	38	95	11	144	73	177
Race											
White alone	1,449	303	301	225	183	228	293	75	416	126	310
White alone non-Hispanic	1,071	205	203	159	123	145	197	60	288	101	279
Black alone	277	40	80	41	43	30	70	9	94	31	43
Asian alone	111	8	27	34	22	4	19	4	63	6	15
Hispanic (of any race)	428	109	113	78	72	94	109	14	153	25	31
Employment Status											
Full time	1,212	155	225	226	152	93	217	62	386	133	322
Part time	439	121	147	54	68	101	122	20	147	22	27
Not employed	258	89	57	37	41	76	62	14	73	8	25
Control of School											
Public	1,604	332	395	271	220	251	381	80	505	124	262
Private	304	34	33	46	41	18	20	15	100	39	111
Disability Status											
No disability	1,805	336	404	306	244	244	371	91	583	159	356
Any disability	104	30	24	11	17	26	29	4	22	4	18
FEMALE	10,287	2,367	2,212	1,902	1,527	963	1,321	1,404	4,320	851	1,428
Full-Time Students											
Total	7,403	1,870	1,635	1,453	1,167	612	759	1,257	3,496	484	794
Age											
15–19 years old	2,136	1,296	685	111	20	319	167	976	649	21	3
20–24 years old	3,549	363	715	1,088	876	169	405	194	2,274	229	278
25–34 years old	1,178	141	168	172	188	97	144	44	385	144	365
35 years old and over	540	70	67	81	83	28	44	42	188	90	148
Race											
White alone	5,207	1,342	1,155	991	825	433	501	910	2,471	327	565
White alone non-Hispanic	3,957	970	812	758	686	284	318	686	1,939	268	462
Black alone	1,137	288	236	273	177	111	153	177	533	86	76
Asian alone	691	114	151	120	125	25	62	89	334	61	120
Hispanic (of any race)	1,409	424	366	278	158	160	202	264	599	65	120
Employment Status											
Full time	1,051	136	168	203	222	59	135	77	458	122	200
Part time	2,375	531	564	544	378	260	304	272	1,183	138	219
Not employed	3,976	1,202	904	705	566	294	321	908	1,855	225	374
Control of School											
Public	5,769	1,574	1,349	1,161	849	595	671	979	2,688	297	539
Private	1,634	295	286	293	318	17	89	278	808	187	255
Disability Status											
No disability	7,225	1,834	1,594	1,437	1,141	595	737	1,239	3,435	460	759
Any disability	178	36	42	16	25	17	22	19	61	25	35
Part-Time Students											
Total	2,884	498	577	449	360	351	562	147	825	366	634
Age											
15–19 years old	212	143	53	16	*	99	44	44	24	*	*
20–24 years old	731	112	206	157	119	70	166	43	316	61	76
25–34 years old	988	100	184	136	157	85	212	15	264	160	251
35 years old and over	953	142	134	141	84	97	139	45	219	145	307

* = Quantity zero or rounds to zero.

Table A-5. Type of College and Year Enrolled for College Students 15 Years Old and Over, by Age, Sex, Race, Attendance Status, Control of School, Disability Status, and Enrollment Status, October 2017—*Continued*

(Numbers in thousands; civilian noninstitutionalized population.)

Characteristic	Total enrolled	Undergraduate college								Graduate school	
		All colleges				Two-year college		Four-year college			
		1st year	2nd year	3rd year	4th year	1st year	2nd or higher	1st year	2nd or higher	1st year	2nd or higher
Race...											
White alone...............................	2,153	313	431	334	283	218	416	96	632	301	490
White alone non-Hispanic......	1,581	229	286	213	178	165	272	64	406	242	432
Black alone...............................	500	133	105	88	42	97	85	36	151	45	86
Asian alone	140	24	13	7	28	17	28	7	20	15	53
Hispanic (of any race)...............	636	95	163	130	105	59	161	37	237	65	78
Employment Status......................											
Full time.....................................	1,609	203	238	243	196	148	250	55	426	268	462
Part time.....................................	748	147	231	110	103	94	202	53	242	58	99
Not employed.............................	527	147	109	96	61	109	110	39	156	40	73
Control of School..........................											
Public...	2,338	458	525	391	297	321	504	137	709	259	408
Private..	546	40	52	58	64	30	58	10	115	107	226
Disability Status											
No disability	2,766	461	557	436	353	324	542	136	804	348	612
Any disability.............................	118	37	20	13	7	26	19	10	21	19	22

Table A-6. Employment Status and Enrollment in Vocational Courses for the Population 15 Years Old and Over, by Sex, Age, Educational Attainment, and College Enrollment, October 2017[1]

(Numbers in thousands; percent; civilian noninstitutionalized population.)

Characteristic	Total	Total Enrolled in vocational courses Number	Total Enrolled in vocational courses Percent	Employed full-time Total	Employed full-time Enrolled in vocational courses Number	Employed full-time Enrolled in vocational courses Percent	Employed part-time Total	Employed part-time Enrolled in vocational courses Number	Employed part-time Enrolled in vocational courses Percent	Not employed Total	Not employed Enrolled in vocational courses Number	Not employed Enrolled in vocational courses Percent
BOTH SEXES												
Total..	259,912	3,495	1.3	127,350	1,864	1.5	27,530	679	2.5	105,032	953	0.9
Age..												
15 to 19 years old	20,909	275	1.3	1,432	38	2.6	3,754	113	3.0	15,723	124	0.8
20 to 24 years old	21,315	653	3.1	9,324	217	2.3	4,938	212	4.3	7,054	224	3.2
25 to 34 years old	44,091	879	2.0	30,225	527	1.7	4,395	135	3.1	9,471	218	2.3
35 to 44 years old	40,101	612	1.5	28,800	445	1.5	3,475	55	1.6	7,826	112	1.4
45 to 64 years old	83,468	853	1.0	51,708	562	1.1	7,315	121	1.7	24,445	170	0.7
65 years and over	50,027	223	0.4	5,860	76	1.3	3,653	43	1.2	40,514	104	0.3
Educational attainment................................												
Not a high school graduate	38,065	139	0.4	8,901	49	0.6	3,743	46	1.2	25,421	44	0.2
High school graduate only	72,277	684	0.9	33,473	334	1.0	6,883	122	1.8	31,921	227	0.7
Some college or associate's degree	70,237	1,394	2.0	34,562	595	1.7	9,557	351	3.7	26,117	447	1.7
Bachelor's degree or more	79,334	1,278	1.6	50,414	885	1.8	7,347	159	2.2	21,573	234	1.1
College enrollment												
Enrolled in college..................................	18,398	1,181	6.4	4,751	406	8.5	5,322	356	6.7	8,326	420	5.0
Not enrolled in college	241,513	2,314	1.0	122,599	1,458	1.2	22,208	323	1.5	96,706	533	0.6
MALE												
Total..	125,733	1,626	1.3	72,108	985	1.4	10,056	269	2.7	43,568	372	0.9
Age..												
15 to 19 years old	10,612	167	1.6	844	31	3.7	1,720	67	3.9	8,049	69	0.9
20 to 24 years old	10,681	322	3.0	5,094	116	2.3	2,191	78	3.6	3,395	127	3.8
25 to 34 years old	21,897	382	1.7	17,263	287	1.7	1,393	42	3.0	3,240	53	1.6
35 to 44 years old	19,675	280	1.4	16,479	237	1.4	871	14	1.6	2,326	29	1.2
45 to 64 years old	40,480	383	0.9	28,884	279	1.0	2,160	47	2.2	9,437	57	0.6
65 years and over	22,387	92	0.4	3,545	35	1.0	1,721	19	1.1	17,122	38	0.2
Educational attainment................................												
Not a high school graduate	19,332	73	0.4	6,118	27	0.4	1,624	22	1.3	11,591	25	0.2
High school graduate only	36,140	348	1.0	20,752	201	1.0	2,576	55	2.1	12,813	93	0.7
Some college or associate's degree	32,534	629	1.9	18,675	315	1.7	3,452	137	4.0	10,407	177	1.7
Bachelor's degree or more	37,727	575	1.5	26,564	443	1.7	2,405	55	2.3	8,758	77	0.9
College enrollment												
Enrolled in college..................................	8,112	517	6.4	2,090	165	7.9	2,199	156	7.1	3,822	195	5.1
Not enrolled in college	117,621	1,109	0.9	70,018	820	1.2	7,858	112	1.4	39,745	177	0.4
FEMALE												
Total..	134,179	1,869	1.4	55,241	879	1.6	17,474	410	2.3	61,464	580	0.9
Age..												
15 to 19 years old	10,297	108	1.0	589	7	1.1	2,034	46	2.3	7,674	56	0.7
20 to 24 years old	10,635	331	3.1	4,230	101	2.4	2,747	134	4.9	3,659	97	2.6
25 to 34 years old	22,194	497	2.2	12,962	240	1.8	3,001	93	3.1	6,231	165	2.6
35 to 44 years old	20,425	332	1.6	12,321	208	1.7	2,604	41	1.6	5,500	83	1.5
45 to 64 years old	42,988	470	1.1	22,825	282	1.2	5,155	74	1.4	15,008	114	0.8
65 years and over	27,640	131	0.5	2,316	41	1.8	1,932	24	1.2	23,392	66	0.3
Educational attainment................................												
Not a high school graduate	18,733	66	0.4	2,783	23	0.8	2,119	24	1.1	13,830	19	0.1
High school graduate only	36,137	336	0.9	12,721	134	1.1	4,308	68	1.6	19,109	134	0.7
Some college or associate's degree	37,703	765	2.0	15,887	280	1.8	6,105	215	3.5	15,710	270	1.7
Bachelor's degree or more	41,607	703	1.7	23,850	442	1.9	4,941	104	2.1	12,815	157	1.2
College enrollment												
Enrolled in college..................................	10,287	665	6.5	2,660	241	9.0	3,123	200	6.4	4,503	224	5.0
Not enrolled in college	123,893	1,205	1.0	52,581	638	1.2	14,350	211	1.5	56,961	356	0.6

[1]People enrolled in vocational courses are not considered to be enrolled in school for all tables. People enrolled in regular school below the college level are not asked about vocational enrollment in the CPS. They are counted in this table as not enrolled in vocational courses.

Table A-7. Enrollment Status of High School Graduates 15 to 24 Years Old, by Type of School, Attendance Status, and Sex, October 2017

(Numbers in thousands; civilian noninstitutionalized population.)

Characteristic	Total	Enrolled in college or vocational school						Not enrolled	
		2-year college		4-year college		Graduate school	Vocational school	Employed	Not employed
		Full-time	Part-time	Full-time	Part-time				
ALL RACES									
Both sexes	26,175	2,145	721	7,367	696	1,170	222	10,556	3,297
Graduated this year............................	2,885	540	116	1,236	34	3	11	532	412
Graduated earlier................................	23,290	1,604	604	6,131	663	1,167	211	10,024	2,885
Male...	12,841	1,089	352	3,292	278	502	125	5,680	1,524
Graduated this year............................	1,354	278	52	484	17	*	4	298	221
Graduated earlier................................	11,488	811	300	2,808	261	502	121	5,382	1,303
Female	13,333	1,055	369	4,075	419	668	97	4,876	1,773
Graduated this year............................	1,531	262	64	752	17	3	6	234	192
Graduated earlier................................	11,802	793	305	3,323	402	665	91	4,642	1,581
WHITE ALONE									
Both sexes	19,291	1,518	565	5,345	513	846	163	8,071	2,271
Graduated this year............................	2,149	389	85	954	16	1	9	393	302
Graduated earlier................................	17,142	1,129	480	4,391	497	845	153	7,678	1,968
Male...	9,514	771	298	2,422	189	334	90	4,407	1,002
Graduated this year............................	1,029	211	49	380	12	*	4	227	145
Graduated earlier................................	8,485	560	249	2,042	177	334	86	4,180	857
Female	9,777	747	267	2,923	323	512	73	3,664	1,268
Graduated this year............................	1,120	177	36	574	4	1	6	166	157
Graduated earlier................................	8,657	569	231	2,349	320	512	67	3,498	1,111
WHITE ALONE, NON-HISPANIC									
Both sexes	14,403	1,023	356	4,203	316	698	112	6,151	1,545
Graduated this year............................	1,608	283	52	761	16	1	9	287	198
Graduated earlier................................	12,795	739	304	3,441	300	697	103	5,864	1,347
Male...	7,169	547	178	1,952	116	280	66	3,320	709
Graduated this year............................	764	157	27	311	12	*	4	151	102
Graduated earlier................................	6,405	390	151	1,641	104	280	63	3,169	607
Female	7,234	476	177	2,250	200	418	46	2,831	836
Graduated this year............................	845	127	25	451	4	1	6	136	96
Graduated earlier................................	6,390	349	153	1,800	196	418	40	2,695	740
BLACK ALONE									
Both sexes	3,871	361	85	946	102	122	22	1,565	669
Graduated this year............................	425	79	17	143	14	*	*	94	77
Graduated earlier................................	3,446	282	68	803	88	122	22	1,471	592
Male...	1,848	198	26	378	36	62	19	772	358
Graduated this year............................	207	44	*	59	5	*	*	48	52
Graduated earlier................................	1,641	154	26	319	31	62	19	724	306
Female	2,023	163	59	568	66	60	3	793	311
Graduated this year............................	218	35	17	84	10	*	*	46	25
Graduated earlier................................	1,805	127	42	484	57	60	3	746	286
ASIAN ALONE									
Both sexes	1,694	139	30	726	55	183	23	391	146
Graduated this year............................	169	36	11	90	4	*	1	18	10
Graduated earlier................................	1,524	103	19	636	51	183	23	374	135
Male...	849	70	10	354	37	97	12	209	60
Graduated this year............................	77	15	3	37	*	*	*	11	10
Graduated earlier................................	773	55	7	317	37	97	12	198	50
Female	844	70	20	372	17	86	12	182	85
Graduated this year............................	93	21	8	53	4	*	1	6	*
Graduated earlier................................	751	48	12	319	14	86	11	176	85
HISPANIC (OF ANY RACE)									
Both sexes	5,546	542	231	1,300	214	177	56	2,196	829
Graduated this year............................	597	111	33	218	*	3	*	122	111
Graduated earlier................................	4,948	431	198	1,082	214	174	56	2,075	718
Male...	2,686	248	127	536	85	75	23	1,261	330
Graduated this year............................	295	55	22	81	*	*	*	88	49
Graduated earlier................................	2,391	192	106	455	85	75	23	1,174	281
Female	2,860	294	104	764	129	102	32	935	499
Graduated this year............................	302	55	11	137	*	3	*	34	62
Graduated earlier................................	2,558	239	93	627	129	99	32	901	437

* = Quantity zero or rounds to zero.

Table A-8. Enrollment Status for Families with Children 5 to 24 Years Old, by Control of School, Race, Type of Family, and Family Income, October 2017

(Numbers in thousands; civilian noninstitutionalized population.)

Characteristic	Total	Families with no dependents 5 to 24 years old[1]	Families with dependents 5 to 24 years old[2]						
			Kindergarten, elementary, and high school enrollment status				College enrollment status		
			None enrolled in elementary or high school	Public only	Public and private	Private only	None enrolled in college	One enrolled in college	Two or more enrolled in college
ALL RACES									
All Families	83,361	44,285	8,038	28,189	617	2,233	32,718	5,432	926
Less than $20,000	6,663	2,969	612	2,952	42	88	3,371	290	32
$20,000 to $74,999	29,530	15,762	2,629	10,322	168	649	11,862	1,703	203
$75,000 and over	27,920	14,283	2,898	9,336	262	1,142	10,894	2,283	460
Not reported	19,248	11,270	1,898	5,579	145	355	6,591	1,155	231
Married-couple families	60,990	35,999	4,819	17,961	455	1,756	20,591	3,652	747
Less than $20,000	2,609	1,644	136	790	12	27	874	78	13
$20,000 to $74,999	19,968	12,428	1,291	5,714	109	427	6,464	918	158
$75,000 and over	24,470	12,913	2,344	7,946	232	1,035	9,243	1,924	389
Not reported	13,943	9,014	1,049	3,511	101	268	4,009	732	188
Unmarried householder[3]	22,371	8,285	3,219	10,228	162	477	12,127	1,780	179
Less than $20,000	4,053	1,325	476	2,162	30	61	2,497	212	19
$20,000 to $74,999	9,562	3,334	1,339	4,608	58	222	5,397	785	45
$75,000 and over	3,450	1,369	555	1,390	29	107	1,650	360	71
Not reported	5,305	2,257	849	2,069	44	87	2,582	423	44
WHITE ALONE									
All Families	65,793	36,269	6,085	21,188	473	1,779	24,730	4,096	698
Less than $20,000	4,245	1,949	398	1,811	29	59	2,100	180	17
$20,000 to $74,999	23,289	13,059	1,962	7,640	141	486	8,837	1,242	151
$75,000 and over	23,393	12,168	2,384	7,689	198	954	8,972	1,869	383
Not reported	14,865	9,092	1,340	4,048	105	280	4,820	805	148
Married-couple families	50,917	30,712	3,863	14,546	341	1,455	16,715	2,920	570
Less than $20,000	1,918	1,220	97	570	4	27	636	57	5
$20,000 to $74,999	16,780	10,711	1,007	4,633	89	339	5,245	710	113
$75,000 and over	20,772	11,170	1,954	6,608	173	867	7,673	1,597	332
Not reported	11,447	7,611	805	2,735	75	222	3,160	556	121
Unmarried householder[3]	14,876	5,557	2,221	6,642	132	324	8,015	1,176	128
Less than $20,000	2,328	729	301	1,241	25	32	1,464	123	12
$20,000 to $74,999	6,509	2,348	955	3,007	52	147	3,592	532	38
$75,000 and over	2,621	998	430	1,081	24	87	1,299	272	51
Not reported	3,418	1,482	535	1,312	30	59	1,660	249	27
WHITE ALONE NON-HISPANIC									
All Families	53,883	31,954	4,647	15,378	390	1,514	18,419	2,984	527
Less than $20,000	2,631	1,378	242	934	21	57	1,162	86	5
$20,000 to $74,999	17,822	11,145	1,316	4,863	108	391	5,871	726	79
$75,000 and over	21,229	11,410	2,128	6,703	169	819	7,896	1,585	338
Not reported	12,201	8,021	961	2,879	93	248	3,489	586	104
Married-couple families	43,182	27,673	3,087	10,905	280	1,238	12,863	2,208	438
Less than $20,000	1,203	858	61	259	*	26	315	29	2
$20,000 to $74,999	13,149	9,353	652	2,803	64	276	3,374	374	48
$75,000 and over	19,034	10,573	1,768	5,801	149	743	6,784	1,378	298
Not reported	9,796	6,889	606	2,042	66	193	2,390	427	90
Unmarried householder[3]	10,701	4,281	1,560	4,474	111	276	5,555	776	89
Less than $20,000	1,427	520	182	675	21	30	847	57	3
$20,000 to $74,999	4,673	1,792	664	2,059	43	115	2,497	352	31
$75,000 and over	2,195	837	360	902	20	76	1,112	207	40
Not reported	2,405	1,132	354	837	27	55	1,099	159	15
BLACK ALONE									
All Families	10,264	4,665	1,159	4,142	59	238	4,782	729	88
Less than $20,000	1,769	690	177	872	4	25	980	91	7
$20,000 to $74,999	3,855	1,672	409	1,662	13	99	1,932	245	6

* = Quantity zero or rounds to zero.
[1]Unmarried (or married with spouse absent) child, grandchild, brother/sister or other relative.
[2]No spouse present.
[3]May be of any race.

Table A-8. Enrollment Status for Families with Children 5 to 24 Years Old, by Control of School, Race, Type of Family, and Family Income, October 2017—*Continued*

(Numbers in thousands; civilian noninstitutionalized population.)

Characteristic	Total	Families with no dependents 5 to 24 years old[1]	Families with dependents 5 to 24 years old[2]						
			Kindergarten, elementary, and high school enrollment status				College enrollment status		
			None enrolled in elementary or high school	Public only	Public and private	Private only	None enrolled in college	One enrolled in college	Two or more enrolled in college
$75,000 and over	1,876	910	249	622	18	77	721	215	30
Not reported	2,764	1,393	324	986	24	37	1,148	178	45
Married-couple families	4,720	2,711	431	1,428	33	118	1,652	306	51
Less than $20,000	355	214	19	121	*	*	128	13	*
$20,000 to $74,999	1,592	980	119	441	9	43	543	64	5
$75,000 and over	1,446	707	175	492	13	59	563	159	17
Not reported	1,327	809	118	374	11	16	419	71	28
Unmarried householder[3]	5,544	1,954	728	2,715	26	120	3,129	423	38
Less than $20,000	1,414	476	157	751	4	25	853	78	7
$20,000 to $74,999	2,263	692	290	1,221	4	56	1,390	180	1
$75,000 and over	430	203	75	130	4	18	158	56	13
Not reported	1,437	584	206	613	13	21	729	108	17
ASIAN ALONE									
All Families	4,775	2,347	511	1,709	61	147	1,892	425	110
Less than $20,000	289	182	23	80	3	*	88	10	8
$20,000 to $74,999	1,335	634	141	531	4	24	527	137	36
$75,000 and over	1,999	933	198	737	37	93	864	164	37
Not reported	1,153	597	148	360	17	30	413	113	29
Married-couple families	3,871	1,921	374	1,380	60	136	1,526	324	100
Less than $20,000	203	145	14	40	3	*	45	5	8
$20,000 to $74,999	1,004	492	105	383	4	19	370	111	31
$75,000 and over	1,756	809	158	662	37	91	779	136	32
Not reported	909	476	97	294	16	26	332	73	29
Unmarried householder[3]	903	425	138	329	1	11	367	101	11
Less than $20,000	86	37	9	40	*	*	43	6	*
$20,000 to $74,999	331	142	36	148	*	5	157	27	5
$75,000 and over	242	124	41	75	1	2	85	28	5
Not reported	244	122	52	66	1	4	81	41	*
HISPANIC[3]									
All Families	13,386	4,853	1,626	6,536	83	288	7,117	1,219	196
Less than $20,000	1,824	651	176	986	9	2	1,059	102	12
$20,000 to $74,999	6,130	2,127	720	3,140	34	109	3,353	573	77
$75,000 and over	2,470	898	291	1,118	28	135	1,233	294	45
Not reported	2,962	1,176	439	1,293	12	42	1,472	251	63
Married-couple families	8,515	3,362	862	3,999	61	232	4,231	770	152
Less than $20,000	772	401	37	329	4	1	336	32	3
$20,000 to $74,999	3,964	1,475	380	2,017	25	67	2,060	359	70
$75,000 and over	1,994	718	220	907	24	125	1,013	229	34
Not reported	1,785	767	225	746	8	39	822	150	46
Unmarried householder[3]	4,871	1,491	764	2,537	21	57	2,886	450	44
Less than $20,000	1,052	249	140	657	5	1	723	71	9
$20,000 to $74,999	2,166	653	340	1,123	9	42	1,293	213	7
$75,000 and over	476	180	71	211	4	11	220	65	11
Not reported	1,177	409	214	547	4	3	650	101	17

* = Quantity zero or rounds to zero.
[1]Unmarried (or married with spouse absent) child, grandchild, brother/sister or other relative.
[2]No spouse present.
[3]May be of any race.

Table A-9. Total Fall Enrollment in Degree-Granting Postsecondary Institutions, by Level of Enrollment, Control and Type of Institution, Age, and Attendance Status of Student, 2017

(Number; percent.)

Age of student and attendance status	Undergraduate													
	Total	Percent	Public						Private, nonprofit					
			Total	Percent	4-year	Percent	2-year	Percent	Total	Percent	4-year	Percent	2-year	Percent
All students	16,760,331	100.0	13,100,953	100.0	7,394,275	100.0	5,706,678	100.0	2,817,017	100.0	2,768,627	100.0	48,390	100.0
Under 18.......	1,230,274	7.3	1,128,680	8.6	377,282	5.1	751,398	13.2	96,905	3.4	96,246	3.5	659	1.4
18 and 19......	4,444,557	26.5	3,526,056	26.9	2,172,387	29.4	1,353,669	23.7	859,887	30.5	852,686	30.8	7,201	14.9
20 and 21......	4,060,204	24.2	3,132,761	23.9	2,172,028	29.4	960,733	16.8	846,904	30.1	841,486	30.4	5,418	11.2
22 to 24	2,542,471	15.2	2,063,678	15.8	1,295,451	17.5	768,227	13.5	362,734	12.9	355,690	12.8	7,044	14.6
25 to 29	1,729,875	10.3	1,336,473	10.2	630,442	8.5	706,031	12.4	209,884	7.5	200,225	7.2	9,659	20.0
30 to 34	944,490	5.6	672,970	5.1	282,854	3.8	390,116	6.8	134,719	4.8	128,676	4.6	6,043	12.5
35 to 39	633,621	3.8	431,135	3.3	172,504	2.3	258,631	4.5	103,076	3.7	98,888	3.6	4,188	8.7
40 to 49	725,529	4.3	485,482	3.7	185,088	2.5	300,394	5.3	128,763	4.6	123,616	4.5	5,147	10.6
50 to 64	371,156	2.2	261,608	2.0	88,680	1.2	172,928	3.0	62,437	2.2	59,709	2.2	2,728	5.6
65 and over....	53,499	0.3	47,262	0.4	13,342	0.2	33,920	0.6	4,426	0.2	4,211	0.2	215	0.4
Age unknown.	24,655	0.1	14,848	0.1	4,217	0.1	10,631	0.2	7,282	0.3	7,194	0.3	88	0.2
Full-time	10,370,665	100.0	7,516,055	100.0	5,498,470	100.0	2,017,585	100.0	2,299,345	100.0	2,258,255	100.0	41,090	100.0
Under 18.......	220,568	2.1	184,668	2.5	103,439	1.9	81,229	4.0	33,761	1.5	33,495	1.5	266	0.6
18 and 19......	3,693,798	35.6	2,811,170	37.4	1,981,161	36.0	830,009	41.1	830,031	36.1	823,198	36.5	6,833	16.6
20 and 21......	3,234,486	31.2	2,355,461	31.3	1,921,933	35.0	433,528	21.5	813,321	35.4	808,612	35.8	4,709	11.5
22 to 24	1,539,873	14.8	1,163,070	15.5	926,697	16.9	236,373	11.7	293,606	12.8	287,792	12.7	5,814	14.1
25 to 29	761,146	7.3	515,230	6.9	320,767	5.8	194,463	9.6	124,780	5.4	116,648	5.2	8,132	19.8
30 to 34	361,656	3.5	208,214	2.8	112,576	2.0	95,638	4.7	69,388	3.0	64,320	2.8	5,068	12.3
35 to 39	221,706	2.1	114,384	1.5	57,328	1.0	57,056	2.8	48,999	2.1	45,511	2.0	3,488	8.5
40 to 49	228,966	2.2	109,930	1.5	51,968	0.9	57,962	2.9	57,122	2.5	52,825	2.3	4,297	10.5
50 to 64	91,789	0.9	44,192	0.6	18,734	0.3	25,458	1.3	23,804	1.0	21,547	1.0	2,257	5.5
65 and over....	5,176	*	3,296	*	1,022	*	2,274	0.1	954	*	776	*	178	0.4
Age unknown.	11,501	0.1	6,440	0.1	2,845	0.1	3,595	0.2	3,579	0.2	3,531	0.2	48	0.1
Part-time	6,389,666	100.0	5,584,898	100.0	1,895,805	100.0	3,689,093	100.0	517,672	100.0	510,372	100.0	7,300	100.0
Under 18.......	1,009,706	15.8	944,012	16.9	273,843	14.4	670,169	18.2	63,144	12.2	62,751	12.3	393	5.4
18 and 19......	750,759	11.7	714,886	12.8	191,226	10.1	523,660	14.2	29,856	5.8	29,488	5.8	368	5.0
20 and 21......	825,718	12.9	777,300	13.9	250,095	13.2	527,205	14.3	33,583	6.5	32,874	6.4	709	9.7
22 to 24	1,002,598	15.7	900,608	16.1	368,754	19.5	531,854	14.4	69,128	13.4	67,898	13.3	1,230	16.8
25 to 29	968,729	15.2	821,243	14.7	309,675	16.3	511,568	13.9	85,104	16.4	83,577	16.4	1,527	20.9
30 to 34	582,834	9.1	464,756	8.3	170,278	9.0	294,478	8.0	65,331	12.6	64,356	12.6	975	13.4
35 to 39	411,915	6.4	316,751	5.7	115,176	6.1	201,575	5.5	54,077	10.4	53,377	10.5	700	9.6
40 to 49	496,563	7.8	375,552	6.7	133,120	7.0	242,432	6.6	71,641	13.8	70,791	13.9	850	11.6
50 to 64	279,367	4.4	217,416	3.9	69,946	3.7	147,470	4.0	38,633	7.5	38,162	7.5	471	6.5
65 and over....	48,323	0.8	43,966	0.8	12,320	0.6	31,646	0.9	3,472	0.7	3,435	0.7	37	0.5
Age unknown.	13,154	0.2	8,408	0.2	1,372	0.1	7,036	0.2	3,703	0.7	3,663	0.7	40	0.5

Note: Degree-granting institutions grant associate's or higher degrees and participate in Title IV federal financial aid programs. Details may not sum to totals because of rounding.

* = Quantity zero or equals zero

Table A-9. Total Fall Enrollment in Degree-Granting Postsecondary Institutions, by Level of Enrollment, Control and Type of Institution, Age, and Attendance Status of Student, 2017—*Continued*

(Number; percent.)

Age of student and attendance status	Undergraduate						Postbaccalaureate							
			Private, for-profit											
	Total	Percent	4-year	Percent	2-year	Percent	Total	Percent	Public	Percent	Private, non-profit	Percent	Private, for- profit	Percent
All students	842,361	100.0	655,471	100.0	186,890	100.0	3,005,267	100.0	1,459,202	100.0	1,289,460	100.0	256,605	100.0
Under 18........	4,689	0.6	3,577	0.5	1,112	0.6	145	*	42	*	100	*	3	*
18 and 19.......	58,614	7.0	36,724	5.6	21,890	11.7	998	*	448	*	522	*	28	*
20 and 21.......	80,539	9.6	54,176	8.3	26,363	14.1	36,312	1.2	19,738	1.4	16,113	1.2	461	0.2
22 to 24	116,059	13.8	83,076	12.7	32,983	17.6	660,801	22.0	358,850	24.6	289,071	22.4	12,880	5.0
25 to 29	183,518	21.8	143,558	21.9	39,960	21.4	962,511	32.0	492,268	33.7	423,618	32.9	46,625	18.2
30 to 34	136,801	16.2	113,317	17.3	23,484	12.6	475,932	15.8	234,930	16.1	196,011	15.2	44,991	17.5
35 to 39	99,410	11.8	83,806	12.8	15,604	8.3	298,710	9.9	134,919	9.2	121,428	9.4	42,363	16.5
40 to 49	111,284	13.2	94,468	14.4	16,816	9.0	362,647	12.1	146,384	10.0	150,379	11.7	65,884	25.7
50 to 64	47,111	5.6	39,701	6.1	7,410	4.0	188,000	6.3	66,195	4.5	81,772	6.3	40,033	15.6
65 and over....	1,811	0.2	1,465	0.2	346	0.2	13,538	0.5	5,013	0.3	5,720	0.4	2,805	1.1
Age unknown ..	2,525	0.3	1,603	0.2	922	0.5	5,673	0.2	415	*	4,726	0.4	532	0.2
Full-time	555,265	100.0	385,963	100.0	169,302	100.0	1,706,639	100.0	812,018	100.0	782,941	100.0	111,680	100.0
Under 18........	2,139	0.4	1,052	0.3	1,087	0.6	47	*	18	*	28	*	1	*
18 and 19.......	52,597	9.5	31,598	8.2	20,999	12.4	827	*	404	*	405	0.1	18	*
20 and 21.......	65,704	11.8	41,208	10.7	24,496	14.5	32,762	1.9	17,969	2.2	14,457	1.8	336	0.3
22 to 24	83,197	15.0	53,351	13.8	29,846	17.6	529,068	31.0	285,767	35.2	235,523	30.1	7,778	7.0
25 to 29	121,136	21.8	85,274	22.1	35,862	21.2	612,001	35.9	302,645	37.3	286,497	36.6	22,859	20.5
30 to 34	84,054	15.1	63,177	16.4	20,877	12.3	230,371	13.5	107,172	13.2	103,883	13.3	19,316	17.3
35 to 39	58,323	10.5	44,432	11.5	13,891	8.2	117,236	6.9	46,241	5.7	53,207	6.8	17,788	15.9
40 to 49	61,914	11.2	47,086	12.2	14,828	8.8	121,675	7.1	37,517	4.6	57,618	7.4	26,540	23.8
50 to 64	23,793	4.3	17,549	4.5	6,244	3.7	57,021	3.3	13,449	1.7	27,963	3.6	15,609	14.0
65 and over....	926	0.2	623	0.2	303	0.2	3,803	0.2	752	0.1	1,909	0.2	1,142	1.0
Age unknown ..	1,482	0.3	613	0.2	869	0.5	1,828	0.1	84	0.0	1,451	0.2	293	0.3
Part-time	287,096	100.0	269,508	100.0	17,588	100.0	1,298,628	100.0	647,184	100.0	506,519	100.0	144,925	100.0
Under 18........	2,550	0.9	2,525	0.9	25	0.1	98	*	24	*	72	*	2	*
18 and 19.......	6,017	2.1	5,126	1.9	891	5.1	171	*	44	*	117	*	10	*
20 and 21.......	14,835	5.2	12,968	4.8	1,867	10.6	3,550	0.3	1,769	0.3	1,656	0.3	125	0.1
22 to 24	32,862	11.4	29,725	11.0	3,137	17.8	131,733	10.1	73,083	11.3	53,548	10.6	5,102	3.5
25 to 29	62,382	21.7	58,284	21.6	4,098	23.3	350,510	27.0	189,623	29.3	137,121	27.1	23,766	16.4
30 to 34	52,747	18.4	50,140	18.6	2,607	14.8	245,561	18.9	127,758	19.7	92,128	18.2	25,675	17.7
35 to 39	41,087	14.3	39,374	14.6	1,713	9.7	181,474	14.0	88,678	13.7	68,221	13.5	24,575	17.0
40 to 49	49,370	17.2	47,382	17.6	1,988	11.3	240,972	18.6	108,867	16.8	92,761	18.3	39,344	27.1
50 to 64	23,318	8.1	22,152	8.2	1,166	6.6	130,979	10.1	52,746	8.2	53,809	10.6	24,424	16.9
65 and over.....	885	0.3	842	0.3	43	0.2	9,735	0.7	4,261	0.7	3,811	0.8	1,663	1.1
Age unknown ..	1,043	0.4	990	0.4	53	0.3	3,845	0.3	331	0.1	3,275	0.6	239	0.2

Note: Degree-granting institutions grant associate's or higher degrees and participate in Title IV federal financial aid programs. Details may not sum to totals because of rounding.

* = Quantity zero or equals zero

PART A

NATIONAL EDUCATION STATISTICS

- ■ **Historical Enrollment Tables**

Table A-10. School Enrollment of the Population 3 Years Old and Over, by Level and Control of School, Selected Race, and Hispanic Origin, October 1955–2017

(Numbers in thousands; civilian noninstitutionalized population.)

Year, race, and Hispanic origin	Total enrolled	Nursery school			Kindergarten			Elementary school		
		Total	Public	Private	Total	Public	Private	Total	Public	Private
ALL RACES										
2017	76,409	4,676	2,782	1,894	3,964	3,542	422	32,530	29,873	2,656
2016	77,232	4,746	2,806	1,941	4,017	3,654	364	32,604	29,978	2,627
2015	77,066	4,532	2,610	1,922	4,073	3,644	428	32,826	30,173	2,653
2014	77,214	4,694	2,693	2,001	4,069	3,617	453	32,622	29,805	2,817
2013	77,772	4,682	2,558	2,124	4,150	3,725	425	32,873	30,171	2,702
2012	78,426	4,628	2,732	1,896	4,138	3,684	454	32,683	29,865	2,818
2011	79,043	4,946	2,904	2,042	4,214	3,732	482	32,872	29,965	2,907
2010	78,519	4,835	2,776	2,059	4,172	3,764	408	32,663	29,841	2,822
2009	77,288	4,708	2,744	1,964	4,132	3,767	365	32,238	29,365	2,874
2008	76,353	4,614	2,632	1,982	4,047	3,578	469	32,344	29,162	3,182
2007	75,967	4,628	2,570	2,058	4,132	3,656	476	32,169	29,052	3,117
2006	75,197	4,688	2,519	2,169	4,039	3,552	487	32,089	28,975	3,113
2005	75,780	4,603	2,480	2,123	3,912	3,349	563	32,438	29,072	3,366
2004	75,461	4,739	2,487	2,252	3,992	3,417	575	32,556	29,166	3,389
2003	74,911	4,928	2,567	2,361	3,719	3,098	622	32,565	29,204	3,361
2002	74,046	4,471	2,246	2,225	3,571	2,976	594	33,132	29,658	3,474
2001	73,124	4,289	2,161	2,128	3,737	3,145	591	33,166	29,800	3,366
2000	72,214	4,401	2,217	2,184	3,832	3,173	659	32,898	29,378	3,520
1999	72,395	4,578	2,269	2,309	3,825	3,167	658	32,873	29,264	3,609
1998	72,109	4,577	2,265	2,313	3,828	3,128	700	32,573	29,124	3,449
1997	72,031	4,500	2,254	2,246	3,933	3,271	663	32,369	29,308	3,061
1996	70,297	4,212	1,868	2,344	4,034	3,353	681	31,515	28,153	3,362
1995	69,769	4,399	2,012	2,387	3,877	3,174	704	31,815	28,384	3,431
1994[1]	69,272	4,259	1,940	2,319	3,863	3,278	585	31,512	28,131	3,381
1993r	64,414	3,032	1,258	1,774	4,275	3,589	686	31,219	28,278	2,941
1993	62,730	3,018	1,230	1,788	4,180	3,499	681	30,604	27,688	2,914
1992	62,082	2,899	1,098	1,801	4,130	3,507	623	30,165	27,066	3,102
1991	61,276	2,933	1,094	1,839	4,152	3,531	621	29,591	26,632	2,958
1990	60,588	3,401	1,212	2,188	3,899	3,332	567	29,265	26,591	2,674
1989	59,236	2,877	971	1,906	3,868	3,293	575	28,637	25,897	2,740
1988	58,847	2,639	838	1,770	3,958	3,420	538	28,223	25,443	2,778
1987	58,691	2,587	848	1,739	4,018	3,423	595	27,524	24,760	2,765
1986	58,153	2,554	835	1,719	3,961	3,328	633	27,121	24,163	2,958
1985	58,014	2,491	854	1,637	3,815	3,221	594	26,866	23,803	3,063
1984	57,313	2,354	761	1,593	3,484	2,953	531	26,838	24,120	2,718
1983	57,745	2,350	809	1,541	3,361	2,706	656	27,198	24,203	2,994
1982	57,905	2,153	729	1,423	3,299	2,746	553	27,412	24,381	3,031
1981	58,390	2,058	663	1,396	3,161	2,616	545	27,795	24,758	3,037
1980	57,348	1,987	633	1,354	3,176	2,690	486	27,449	24,398	3,051
1979	57,854	1,869	636	1,233	3,025	2,593	432	27,865	24,756	3,109
1978	58,616	1,824	587	1,237	2,989	2,493	496	28,490	25,252	3,238
1977	60,013	1,618	562	1,056	3,191	2,665	526	29,234	25,983	3,251
1976	60,482	1,526	476	1,050	3,490	2,962	528	29,774	26,698	3,075
1975	60,969	1,748	574	1,174	3,393	2,851	542	30,446	27,166	3,279
1974	60,259	1,607	423	1,184	3,252	2,726	526	31,126	27,956	3,169
1973	59,392	1,324	400	924	3,074	2,582	493	31,469	28,201	3,268
1972	60,142	1,283	402	881	3,135	2,636	499	32,242	28,693	3,549
1971	61,106	1,066	317	749	3,263	2,689	574	33,507	29,829	3,678
1970	60,357	1,096	333	763	3,183	2,647	536	33,950	30,001	3,949
1969	59,913	860	245	615	3,276	2,682	594	33,788	29,825	3,964
1968	58,791	816	262	554	3,268	2,709	559	33,761	29,527	4,234
1967	57,656	713	230	484	3,312	2,678	635	33,440	28,877	4,562
1966	56,167	688	215	473	3,115	2,527	588	32,916	28,208	4,706
1965	54,701	520	127	393	3,057	2,439	618	32,474	27,596	4,878
1964	52,490	471	91	380	2,830	2,349	481	31,734	26,811	4,923
1963	50,356	NA	NA	NA	2,340	1,936	404	31,245	26,502	4,742
1962	48,704	NA	NA	NA	2,319	1,914	405	30,661	26,148	4,513
1961	47,708	NA	NA	NA	2,299	1,926	373	30,718	26,221	4,497
1960	46,260	NA	NA	NA	2,092	1,691	401	30,349	25,814	4,535
1959	44,370	NA	NA	NA	2,032	1,678	354	29,382	24,680	4,702
1958	42,900	NA	NA	NA	1,991	1,569	422	28,184	23,800	4,385
1957	41,166	NA	NA	NA	1,824	1,471	353	27,248	23,076	4,172
1956	39,353	NA	NA	NA	1,758	1,566	192	26,169	22,474	3,695
1955	37,426	NA	NA	NA	1,628	1,365	263	25,458	22,078	3,379
WHITE ALONE										
2017	55,148	3,315	1,885	1,430	2,918	2,580	338	23,411	21,385	2,026
2016	56,007	3,445	1,984	1,461	2,859	2,578	281	23,732	21,786	1,946
2015	56,056	3,230	1,778	1,452	2,970	2,630	340	23,863	21,776	2,088

Note: Data shown for 1955 to 1966 for the Black population are for Black and Other races.

NA = Not available.

r = Revised, controlled to 1990 census based population estimates; previous 1993 data controlled to 1980 census based population estimates.

[1] Prior to 1994, total enrolled does not include the 35 and over population.

Table A-10. School Enrollment of the Population 3 Years Old and Over, by Level and Control of School, Selected Race, and Hispanic Origin, October 1955–2017—*Continued*

(Numbers in thousands; civilian noninstitutionalized population.)

Year, race, and Hispanic origin	High school			College			
	Total	Public	Private	Total	Public	Private	Full-time
ALL RACES							
2017	16,841	15,546	1,295	18,398	14,806	3,592	13,606
2016	16,668	15,330	1,338	19,196	14,971	4,225	14,421
2015	16,535	15,358	1,177	19,101	15,175	3,926	14,236
2014	16,654	15,379	1,275	19,175	15,325	3,850	14,400
2013	16,601	15,468	1,133	19,467	15,514	3,953	14,228
2012	17,047	15,704	1,343	19,930	15,778	4,152	14,602
2011	16,613	15,426	1,187	20,397	16,134	4,263	14,903
2010	16,574	15,338	1,236	20,275	16,153	4,122	14,600
2009	16,445	15,269	1,177	19,764	15,722	4,042	14,364
2008	16,715	15,397	1,319	18,632	14,739	3,893	13,245
2007	17,082	15,804	1,278	17,956	14,072	3,884	12,656
2006	17,149	15,617	1,532	17,232	13,466	3,766	12,070
2005	17,354	15,934	1,420	17,472	13,435	4,037	12,237
2004	16,791	15,498	1,293	17,383	13,652	3,731	11,990
2003	17,062	15,785	1,276	16,638	13,109	3,529	11,490
2002	16,374	15,064	1,310	16,497	12,834	3,664	11,141
2001	16,059	14,830	1,230	15,873	12,421	3,452	10,404
2000	15,770	14,431	1,339	15,314	12,008	3,305	10,159
1999	15,916	14,638	1,278	15,203	11,659	3,544	10,112
1998	15,584	14,299	1,285	15,547	11,984	3,563	10,184
1997	15,793	14,634	1,159	15,436	12,091	3,345	10,236
1996	15,309	14,113	1,197	15,226	12,014	3,212	9,839
1995	14,963	13,750	1,213	14,715	11,372	3,343	9,544
1994[1]	14,616	13,539	1,077	15,022	11,694	3,329	9,573
1993r	13,989	12,985	1,004	11,901	9,440	2,461	8,706
1993	13,522	12,542	977	11,409	9,031	2,374	8,308
1992	13,219	12,268	952	11,671	9,282	2,386	8,503
1991	13,010	12,069	945	11,589	9,078	2,511	8,461
1990	12,719	11,818	903	11,306	8,889	2,417	8,154
1989	12,786	11,980	806	11,066	8,576	2,490	7,905
1988	13,093	12,095	998	10,937	8,663	2,278	7,771
1987	13,647	12,577	1,070	10,915	8,556	2,361	7,560
1986	13,912	12,746	1,166	10,605	8,153	2,452	7,507
1985	13,979	12,764	1,215	10,863	8,379	2,483	7,720
1984	13,777	12,721	1,057	10,859	8,467	2,392	7,822
1983	14,010	12,792	1,218	10,825	8,185	2,640	7,711
1982	14,123	13,004	1,118	10,919	8,354	2,565	7,736
1981	14,642	13,523	1,119	10,734	8,159	2,576	7,569
1980	14,556	NA	NA	10,180	NA	NA	7,147
1979	15,116	13,994	1,122	9,978	7,699	2,280	7,010
1978	15,475	14,231	1,244	9,838	7,427	2,410	6,979
1977	15,753	14,505	1,248	10,217	7,925	2,292	7,196
1976	15,742	14,541	1,201	9,950	7,739	2,211	7,176
1975	15,683	14,503	1,180	9,697	7,704	1,994	7,105
1974	15,447	14,275	1,172	8,827	6,905	1,922	6,351
1973	15,347	14,162	1,184	8,179	6,224	1,955	6,089
1972	15,169	14,015	1,155	8,313	6,337	1,976	6,314
1971	15,183	14,057	1,126	8,087	6,271	1,816	6,204
1970	14,715	13,545	1,170	7,413	5,699	1,714	5,763
1969	14,553	13,400	1,153	7,435	5,439	1,995	5,810
1968	14,145	12,793	1,352	6,801	4,948	1,854	5,357
1967	13,790	12,498	1,292	6,401	4,540	1,861	4,976
1966	13,364	11,985	1,377	6,085	4,178	1,908	4,847
1965	12,975	11,517	1,457	5,675	3,840	1,835	4,414
1964	12,812	11,403	1,410	4,643	3,025	1,618	3,556
1963	12,438	11,186	1,251	4,336	2,897	1,439	3,260
1962	11,516	10,431	1,085	4,208	2,820	1,388	3,237
1961	10,959	9,817	1,141	3,731	2,376	1,354	2,902
1960	10,249	9,215	1,033	3,570	2,307	1,262	2,681
1959	9,616	8,571	1,045	3,340	2,120	1,220	2,464
1958	9,482	8,485	998	3,242	2,088	1,155	NA
1957	8,956	8,059	897	3,138	2,054	1,084	NA
1956	8,543	7,668	875	2,883	1,824	1,059	NA
1955	7,961	7,181	780	2,379	1,515	864	NA
WHITE ALONE							
2017	12,281	11,306	975	13,224	10,524	2,700	9,623
2016	12,071	11,017	1,053	13,901	10,846	3,054	10,373
2015	12,133	11,199	934	13,859	11,039	2,821	10,254

Note: Data shown for 1955 to 1966 for the Black population are for Black and Other races.
NA = Not available.
r = Revised, controlled to 1990 census based population estimates; previous 1993 data controlled to 1980 census based population estimates.
[1]Prior to 1994, total enrolled does not include the 35 and over population.

Table A-10. School Enrollment of the Population 3 Years Old and Over, by Level and Control of School, Selected Race, and Hispanic Origin, October 1955–2017—*Continued*

(Numbers in thousands; civilian noninstitutionalized population.)

Year, race, and Hispanic origin	Total enrolled	Nursery school			Kindergarten			Elementary school		
		Total	Public	Private	Total	Public	Private	Total	Public	Private
2014	56,343	3,354	1,814	1,540	2,866	2,557	309	23,886	21,677	2,209
2013	56,914	3,346	1,740	1,606	2,933	2,588	345	24,238	22,090	2,148
2012	57,702	3,393	1,925	1,468	2,940	2,584	355	24,187	21,928	2,260
2011	59,647	3,624	1,997	1,627	3,198	2,806	393	24,864	22,419	2,445
2010	59,236	3,659	1,992	1,668	3,069	2,745	324	24,680	22,395	2,284
2009	58,586	3,404	1,832	1,572	3,154	2,860	293	24,575	22,257	2,319
2008	58,244	3,479	1,830	1,649	3,121	2,748	373	24,552	21,986	2,565
2007	58,021	3,545	1,880	1,665	3,223	2,836	387	24,431	21,869	2,562
2006	57,419	3,624	1,815	1,809	3,084	2,701	382	24,472	21,923	2,549
2005	58,013	3,542	1,767	1,775	3,056	2,611	445	24,652	21,858	2,795
2004	57,585	3,566	1,703	1,863	3,043	2,571	472	24,773	21,889	2,883
2003[2]	57,391	3,909	1,918	1,990	2,866	2,367	499	24,711	21,893	2,818
2002	57,501	3,473	1,613	1,860	2,760	2,240	520	25,625	22,703	2,922
2001	56,649	3,278	1,484	1,794	2,893	2,394	499	25,729	22,848	2,881
2000	56,344	3,392	1,539	1,853	2,998	2,453	545	25,562	22,538	3,024
1999	56,713	3,590	1,571	2,019	2,956	2,422	534	25,628	22,552	3,076
1998	56,515	3,549	1,598	1,951	2,933	2,356	577	25,489	22,547	2,942
1997	56,587	3,489	1,572	1,917	3,078	2,532	546	25,289	22,679	2,610
1996	55,378	3,284	1,314	1,970	3,163	2,596	567	24,692	21,785	2,907
1995	55,186	3,553	1,435	2,118	3,032	2,440	592	24,963	22,010	2,954
1994[1]	54,823	3,376	1,330	2,046	3,010	2,505	505	24,786	21,903	2,883
1993r	51,034	2,434	851	1,583	3,323	2,730	593	24,637	22,078	2,559
1993	49,985	2,447	843	1,604	3,273	2,681	592	24,249	21,714	2,535
1992	49,713	2,387	785	1,602	3,256	2,727	529	23,932	21,213	2,718
1991	49,156	2,447	810	1,637	3,274	2,766	508	23,547	20,948	2,599
1990	48,897	2,830	869	1,961	3,081	2,609	472	23,343	20,984	2,359
1989	47,923	2,393	712	1,681	3,118	2,611	506	22,867	20,468	2,399
1988	47,672	2,234	651	1,583	3,192	2,722	471	22,541	20,086	2,455
1987	47,471	2,204	630	1,574	3,120	2,591	529	22,037	19,538	2,498
1986	47,267	2,144	601	1,543	3,161	2,589	572	21,761	19,090	2,671
1985	47,452	2,087	617	1,470	3,060	2,545	515	21,593	18,817	2,776
1984	46,941	1,915	543	1,372	2,788	2,319	469	21,730	19,282	2,449
1983	47,423	1,932	563	1,369	2,769	2,181	588	22,054	19,340	2,714
1982	47,662	1,783	504	1,279	2,677	2,189	489	22,297	19,583	2,713
1981	48,169	1,685	447	1,238	2,597	2,130	467	22,663	19,924	2,739
1980	47,673	1,637	432	1,205	2,595	2,172	423	22,510	19,743	2,768
1979	48,225	1,537	428	1,110	2,437	2,069	368	22,959	20,174	2,785
1978	48,843	1,456	351	1,105	2,452	2,009	444	23,524	20,551	2,973
1977	50,151	1,314	372	942	2,611	2,153	458	24,262	21,312	2,950
1976	50,761	1,246	318	929	2,881	2,423	457	24,776	21,947	2,829
1975	51,430	1,432	392	1,040	2,845	2,363	483	25,412	22,351	3,059
1974	50,992	1,340	293	1,048	2,745	2,268	477	26,051	23,063	2,990
1973	50,617	1,087	242	845	2,584	2,139	445	26,531	23,506	3,025
1972	51,314	1,079	285	794	2,633	2,185	448	27,185	23,869	3,316
1971	52,081	888	225	664	2,735	2,207	527	28,187	24,720	3,466
1970	51,719	893	198	695	2,706	2,233	473	28,638	24,923	3,715
1969	51,465	676	136	539	2,803	2,289	515	28,572	24,803	3,768
1968	50,608	664	163	501	2,775	2,272	504	28,634	24,580	4,054
1967	49,721	564	134	429	2,840	2,254	587	28,415	24,044	4,371
1966	48,620	564	127	437	2,693	2,163	530	28,012	23,469	4,542
1965	47,451	451	93	358	2,648	2,086	562	27,679	22,976	4,703
1964	44,850	NA	NA	NA	2,157	1,795	362	27,099	22,381	4,718
1963	43,815	NA	NA	NA	2,064	1,699	365	26,709	22,181	4,527
1962	42,501	NA	NA	NA	2,025	1,667	358	26,272	21,922	4,350
1961	42,498	NA	NA	NA	1,968	1,618	350	26,294	22,014	4,281
1960	40,348	NA	NA	NA	1,849	1,485	364	26,035	21,6__	4,339
1959	38,857	NA	NA	NA	1,758	1,434	324	25,395	20,854	4,541
1958	37,662	NA	NA	NA	1,769	1,383	336	24,380	20,178	4,203
1957	36,132	NA	NA	NA	1,595	1,258	337	23,610	19,595	4,015
1956	34,641	NA	NA	NA	1,544	1,364	180	22,740	19,186	3,554
1955	32,929	NA	NA	NA	1,484	1,244	240	22,185	18,947	3,238
WHITE ALONE NON-HISPANIC										
2017	39,649	2,461	1,211	1,250	1,955	1,699	256	16,272	14,594	1,679
2016	40,606	2,499	1,275	1,224	1,956	1,697	259	16,640	14,939	1,701
2015	41,145	2,410	1,143	1,268	2,022	1,748	273	16,879	15,095	1,783
2014	41,456	2,477	1,159	1,317	1,990	1,726	264	16,904	15,008	1,897

Note: Data shown for 1955 to 1966 for the Black population are for Black and Other races.
NA = Not available.
r = Revised, controlled to 1990 census based population estimates; previous 1993 data controlled to 1980 census based population estimates.
[1]Prior to 1994, total enrolled does not include the 35 and over population.
[2]Starting in 2003 respondents could identify more than one race. Except as noted, the race data in this table from 2003 onward represent those respondents who indicated only one race category.

Table A-10. School Enrollment of the Population 3 Years Old and Over, by Level and Control of School, Selected Race, and Hispanic Origin, October 1955–2017—*Continued*

(Numbers in thousands; civilian noninstitutionalized population.)

Year, race, and Hispanic origin	High school			College			
	Total	Public	Private	Total	Public	Private	Full-time
2014...	12,283	11,315	969	13,953	11,227	2,727	10,506
2013...	12,157	11,270	887	14,240	11,378	2,862	10,281
2012...	12,554	11,494	1,060	14,628	11,530	3,098	10,694
2011...	12,548	11,542	1,007	15,412	12,161	3,251	11,205
2010...	12,570	11,525	1,045	15,258	12,179	3,079	10,818
2009...	12,425	11,419	1,006	15,027	11,948	3,079	10,847
2008...	12,687	11,585	1,103	14,405	11,432	2,973	10,256
2007...	12,986	11,886	1,100	13,835	10,855	2,979	9,696
2006...	12,966	11,694	1,273	13,273	10,338	2,936	9,236
2005...	13,296	12,109	1,187	13,466	10,303	3,163	9,392
2004...	12,823	11,684	1,138	13,381	10,478	2,904	9,257
2003[2]	13,036	11,939	1,097	12,870	10,101	2,769	8,855
2002...	12,862	11,730	1,132	12,781	9,774	3,007	8,613
2001...	12,540	11,473	1,067	12,208	9,503	2,705	7,909
2000...	12,392	11,259	1,133	11,999	9,364	2,636	7,945
1999...	12,487	11,374	1,113	12,053	9,185	2,868	7,886
1998...	12,142	11,013	1,130	12,401	9,518	2,883	8,012
1997...	12,290	11,287	1,003	12,442	9,713	2,729	8,127
1996...	12,052	10,999	1,053	12,188	9,567	2,622	7,849
1995...	11,617	10,574	1,042	12,021	9,311	2,711	7,773
1994[1]	11,430	10,514	916	12,222	9,472	2,751	7,722
1993r...	10,960	10,124	836	9,685	7,695	1,990	6,996
1993...	10,651	9,834	819	9,366	7,428	1,940	6,739
1992...	10,480	9,648	833	9,658	7,653	2,001	6,985
1991...	10,309	9,467	841	9,579	7,464	2,118	6,919
1990...	10,177	9,370	807	9,466	7,411	2,056	6,776
1989...	10,172	9,443	730	9,374	7,219	2,158	6,658
1988...	10,462	9,571	890	9,245	7,302	1,940	6,488
1987...	10,967	10,019	947	9,143	7,113	2,034	6,275
1986...	11,259	10,229	1,030	8,943	6,821	2,122	6,253
1985...	11,378	10,258	1,120	9,334	7,131	2,203	6,597
1984...	11,240	10,266	974	9,269	7,163	2,105	6,672
1983...	11,425	10,339	1,086	9,242	6,949	2,293	6,532
1982...	11,577	10,541	1,036	9,328	7,102	2,227	6,579
1981...	12,062	11,035	1,027	9,162	6,906	2,256	6,452
1980...	12,056	NA	NA	8,875	NA	NA	6,212
1979...	12,583	11,549	1,033	8,709	6,672	2,037	6,058
1978...	12,897	11,741	1,156	8,514	6,368	2,145	5,974
1977...	13,152	11,980	1,172	8,812	6,743	2,069	6,165
1976...	13,214	12,093	1,121	8,644	6,657	1,987	6,170
1975...	13,224	12,112	1,112	8,516	6,724	1,792	6,183
1974...	13,073	11,966	1,107	7,781	6,049	1,732	5,575
1973...	13,091	11,967	1,124	7,324	5,550	1,773	5,408
1972...	12,959	11,876	1,083	7,458	5,644	1,814	5,678
1971...	12,998	11,937	1,061	7,273	5,624	1,650	5,560
1970...	12,723	11,599	1,124	6,759	5,168	1,591	5,221
1969...	12,588	11,502	1,085	6,827	4,967	1,860	5,307
1968...	12,280	11,007	1,272	6,255	4,501	1,753	4,919
1967...	11,997	10,769	1,228	5,905	4,155	1,750	4,604
1966...	11,643	10,312	1,329	5,708	3,914	1,795	4,556
1965...	11,356	9,961	1,395	5,317	3,568	1,749	4,111
1964...	11,257	9,898	1,359	4,338	2,798	1,540	NA
1963...	10,994	9,782	1,212	4,050	2,680	1,370	NA
1962...	10,270	9,217	1,053	3,934	2,620	1,314	NA
1961...	9,737	8,635	1,102	3,498	2,205	1,293	NA
1960...	9,122	8,124	999	3,342	2,126	1,215	NA
1959...	8,586	7,572	1,014	3,118	1,960	1,158	NA
1958...	8,484	7,501	982	3,030	1,928	1,101	NA
1957...	7,995	7,121	874	2,932	1,924	1,006	NA
1956...	7,670	6,825	845	2,687	1,704	983	NA
1955...	7,036	6,303	733	2,224	1,429	795	NA
WHITE ALONE NON-HISPANIC							
2017...	8,905	8,051	854	10,055	7,736	2,319	7,404
2016...	8,760	7,839	921	10,749	8,219	2,530	8,135
2015...	8,931	8,087	843	10,904	8,526	2,377	8,226
2014...	9,018	8,155	862	11,068	8,775	2,292	8,456

Note: Data shown for 1955 to 1966 for the Black population are for Black and Other races.
NA = Not available.
r = Revised, controlled to 1990 census based population estimates; previous 1993 data controlled to 1980 census based population estimates.
[1]Prior to 1994, total enrolled does not include the 35 and over population.
[2]Starting in 2003 respondents could identify more than one race. Except as noted, the race data in this table from 2003 onward represent those respondents who indicated only one race category.

Table A-10. School Enrollment of the Population 3 Years Old and Over, by Level and Control of School, Selected Race, and Hispanic Origin, October 1955–2017—*Continued*

(Numbers in thousands; civilian noninstitutionalized population.)

Year, race, and Hispanic origin	Total enrolled	Nursery school			Kindergarten			Elementary school		
		Total	Public	Private	Total	Public	Private	Total	Public	Private
2013	42,025	2,531	1,089	1,442	1,968	1,691	277	17,309	15,379	1,930
2012	42,776	2,509	1,227	1,283	2,011	1,691	320	17,413	15,401	2,012
2011	44,951	2,743	1,332	1,411	2,238	1,903	335	17,830	15,670	2,160
2010	44,968	2,766	1,274	1,492	2,120	1,842	278	17,942	15,960	1,981
2009	45,470	2,575	1,188	1,387	2,252	1,990	262	18,244	16,198	2,046
2008	45,373	2,710	1,213	1,497	2,206	1,884	323	18,349	16,029	2,320
2007	45,334	2,711	1,225	1,486	2,279	1,929	351	18,306	15,998	2,307
2006	45,386	2,769	1,152	1,616	2,288	1,940	348	18,622	16,322	2,301
2005	46,338	2,810	1,211	1,599	2,308	1,936	372	18,858	16,335	2,523
2004	46,095	2,840	1,153	1,687	2,325	1,917	408	19,093	16,447	2,646
2003[2]	46,440	3,184	1,382	1,802	2,245	1,804	440	19,252	16,735	2,517
2002	46,725	2,881	1,172	1,709	2,065	1,585	480	20,124	17,495	2,628
2001	46,110	2,725	1,054	1,671	2,203	1,781	422	20,298	17,693	2,605
2000	46,660	2,854	1,149	1,705	2,346	1,846	500	20,574	17,747	2,827
1999	47,292	3,044	1,146	1,898	2,307	1,839	468	20,779	17,960	2,819
1998	47,386	2,964	1,136	1,828	2,336	1,790	547	20,806	18,107	2,699
1997	47,776	2,956	1,143	1,813	2,456	1,970	486	20,839	18,426	2,413
1996	46,947	2,767	922	1,845	2,590	2,081	509	20,447	17,808	2,639
1995	48,019	3,104	1,129	1,975	2,551	2,047	504	21,256	18,518	2,738
1994[1]	47,679	3,024	1,090	1,934	2,522	2,059	462	21,170	18,555	2,615
1993	43,827	2,277	720	1,557	2,779	2,239	540	20,961	18,617	2,344
BLACK ALONE										
2017	11,609	754	576	178	507	477	30	5,048	4,739	309
2016	11,684	620	457	163	668	631	37	4,855	4,522	333
2015	11,544	703	501	202	618	596	23	4,883	4,647	236
2014	11,796	746	557	189	690	605	86	4,844	4,587	257
2013	11,824	683	465	218	736	691	46	4,848	4,625	224
2012	11,918	708	516	193	646	598	48	4,856	4,583	273
2011	12,037	794	562	232	559	503	56	4,902	4,658	245
2010	11,969	698	522	175	736	682	54	4,795	4,498	298
2009	11,748	811	640	171	619	578	41	4,749	4,424	325
2008	11,421	706	548	158	601	545	56	4,993	4,665	329
2007	11,475	700	485	215	605	548	56	4,926	4,572	353
2006	11,400	715	513	202	608	536	71	4,952	4,608	344
2005	11,384	719	542	177	538	486	52	5,106	4,747	359
2004	11,540	825	600	224	596	535	61	5,159	4,905	254
2003[2]	11,408	697	484	212	558	495	63	5,245	4,942	302
2002	11,703	725	503	221	598	543	55	5,545	5,210	335
2001	11,630	787	537	250	605	536	69	5,478	5,160	318
2000	11,503	726	531	195	629	547	82	5,481	5,133	347
1999	11,282	729	569	160	632	558	74	5,388	5,002	386
1998	11,411	761	528	233	689	592	97	5,332	5,031	301
1997	11,270	796	582	214	632	571	61	5,332	5,049	284
1996	10,851	702	459	243	634	545	89	5,171	4,846	325
1995	10,753	663	478	185	653	564	89	5,185	4,845	340
1994[1]	10,702	721	513	208	662	603	59	5,086	4,709	378
1993r	9,786	433	320	113	721	649	72	5,009	4,733	276
1993	9,470	414	307	107	687	618	69	4,865	4,599	266
1992	9,150	374	250	124	688	625	63	4,730	4,494	234
1991	9,031	360	244	117	676	598	79	4,672	4,445	229
1990	8,854	431	283	148	636	574	62	4,627	4,428	199
1989	8,707	366	216	150	601	557	44	4,528	4,296	232
1988	8,609	286	168	118	591	547	44	4,538	4,289	250
1987	8,712	277	164	113	699	658	41	4,402	4,206	194
1986	8,556	315	200	115	647	600	47	4,326	4,134	193
1985	8,444	332	212	120	625	562	63	4,307	4,131	175
1984	8,226	340	179	161	563	513	51	4,123	3,947	177
1983	8,199	326	215	111	476	427	48	4,153	3,964	189
1982	8,262	305	192	113	508	463	45	4,194	3,974	220
1981	8,350	284	182	102	474	412	62	4,291	4,087	204
1980	8,251	294	180	115	490	440	50	4,259	4,058	202
1979	8,317	278	185	95	497	443	54	4,296	4,053	243
1978	8,416	312	210	102	451	414	38	4,356	4,154	202
1977	8,564	250	171	78	496	447	50	4,387	4,166	221
1976	8,518	226	146	80	542	482	60	4,430	4,256	175
1975	8,400	276	171	105	468	426	42	4,509	4,344	165

Note: Data shown for 1955 to 1966 for the Black population are for Black and Other races.
r = Revised, controlled to 1990 census based population estimates; previous 1993 data controlled to 1980 census based population estimates.
[1]Prior to 1994, total enrolled does not include the 35 and over population.
[2]Starting in 2003 respondents could identify more than one race. Except as noted, the race data in this table from 2003 onward represent those respondents who indicated only one race category.

Table A-10. School Enrollment of the Population 3 Years Old and Over, by Level and Control of School, Selected Race, and Hispanic Origin, October 1955–2017—*Continued*

(Numbers in thousands; civilian noninstitutionalized population.)

Year, race, and Hispanic origin	High school			College			
	Total	Public	Private	Total	Public	Private	Full-time
2013..	8,869	8,109	760	11,348	8,889	2,459	8,362
2012..	9,193	8,252	941	11,650	8,977	2,672	8,604
2011..	9,437	8,535	902	12,703	9,842	2,861	9,333
2010..	9,528	8,598	930	12,613	9,900	2,713	9,122
2009..	9,573	8,655	919	12,826	10,022	2,803	9,368
2008..	9,783	8,798	986	12,324	9,630	2,694	8,925
2007..	10,171	9,204	966	11,867	9,141	2,726	8,379
2006..	10,222	9,072	1,150	11,485	8,821	2,664	8,105
2005..	10,647	9,566	1,081	11,715	8,852	2,863	8,246
2004..	10,266	9,221	1,044	11,571	8,928	2,643	8,082
2003[2]..	10,463	9,473	990	11,295	8,742	2,553	7,810
2002..	10,419	9,388	1,031	11,236	8,488	2,749	7,673
2001..	10,281	9,331	950	10,602	8,133	2,469	6,980
2000..	10,250	9,222	1,029	10,636	8,202	2,434	7,105
1999..	10,344	9,314	1,030	10,818	8,158	2,660	7,162
1998..	10,170	9,131	1,039	11,109	8,435	2,674	7,251
1997..	10,280	9,358	922	11,245	8,688	2,558	7,378
1996..	10,107	9,148	959	11,034	8,584	2,450	7,178
1995..	10,084	9,094	991	11,024	8,439	2,585	7,194
1994[1]..	9,786	8,951	835	11,178	8,568	2,610	7,152
1993..	9,216	8,449	767	8,594	6,772	1,822	6,247
BLACK ALONE							
2017..	2,488	2,366	122	2,812	2,414	398	2,034
2016..	2,656	2,556	100	2,885	2,271	614	2,064
2015..	2,515	2,420	95	2,826	2,260	566	2,045
2014..	2,581	2,451	130	2,934	2,284	650	2,055
2013..	2,699	2,588	111	2,857	2,340	517	2,092
2012..	2,669	2,528	141	3,038	2,507	531	2,168
2011..	2,635	2,545	91	3,146	2,541	605	2,279
2010..	2,657	2,552	105	3,083	2,495	587	2,223
2009..	2,680	2,592	89	2,889	2,322	567	2,061
2008..	2,639	2,524	115	2,481	1,975	506	1,690
2007..	2,743	2,627	116	2,501	1,968	533	1,683
2006..	2,792	2,628	165	2,334	1,816	518	1,628
2005..	2,723	2,592	131	2,298	1,800	498	1,526
2004..	2,660	2,584	76	2,301	1,831	470	1,504
2003[2]..	2,765	2,691	74	2,144	1,773	371	1,416
2002..	2,558	2,451	107	2,278	1,868	410	1,468
2001..	2,531	2,412	119	2,230	1,766	463	1,475
2000..	2,502	2,350	152	2,164	1,721	443	1,351
1999..	2,536	2,427	109	1,998	1,587	411	1,372
1998..	2,614	2,515	99	2,016	1,595	421	1,284
1997..	2,605	2,516	89	1,903	1,546	357	1,280
1996..	2,443	2,338	105	1,901	1,519	381	1,179
1995..	2,481	2,370	111	1,772	1,353	419	1,117
1994[1]..	2,434	2,313	121	1,800	1,439	361	1,147
1993r..	2,317	2,197	120	1,305	1,006	299	951
1993..	2,244	2,128	115	1,261	973	288	914
1992..	2,152	2,072	72	1,217	980	237	904
1991..	2,100	2,044	56	1,220	1,004	217	900
1990..	1,975	1,909	65	1,188	963	227	869
1989..	2,069	2,027	42	1,139	932	208	833
1988..	2,079	2,016	62	1,114	894	220	801
1987..	2,140	2,056	84	1,193	977	218	852
1986..	2,130	2,040	91	1,138	896	242	859
1985..	2,131	2,068	63	1,049	860	190	767
1984..	2,061	2,002	59	1,138	918	220	810
1983..	2,143	2,057	86	1,102	858	245	806
1982..	2,128	2,073	55	1,127	865	263	800
1981..	2,168	2,102	65	1,133	898	235	815
1980..	2,200	NA	NA	1,007	NA	NA	723
1979..	2,245	2,171	74	1,002	814	188	748
1978..	2,276	2,211	65	1,020	822	199	753
1977..	2,327	2,269	59	1,103	916	187	803
1976..	2,258	2,187	71	1,062	887	175	817
1975..	2,199	2,140	59	948	782	166	742

Note: Data shown for 1955 to 1966 for the Black population are for Black and Other races.
NA = Not available.
r = Revised, controlled to 1990 census based population estimates; previous 1993 data controlled to 1980 census based population estimates.
[1]Prior to 1994, total enrolled does not include the 35 and over population.
[2]Starting in 2003 respondents could identify more than one race. Except as noted, the race data in this table from 2003 onward represent those respondents who indicated only one race category.

Table A-10. School Enrollment of the Population 3 Years Old and Over, by Level and Control of School, Selected Race, and Hispanic Origin, October 1955–2017—*Continued*

(Numbers in thousands; civilian noninstitutionalized population.)

Year, race, and Hispanic origin	Total enrolled	Nursery school			Kindergarten			Elementary school		
		Total	Public	Private	Total	Public	Private	Total	Public	Private
1974	8,215	227	121	106	463	416	47	4,585	4,455	131
1973	7,834	210	146	64	423	391	32	4,473	4,277	196
1972	7,959	185	113	72	448	402	46	4,573	4,382	191
1971	8,179	151	90	61	464	422	42	4,877	4,712	165
1970	7,829	178	129	49	426	374	53	4,868	4,668	200
1969	7,680	170	102	68	425	361	64	4,785	4,633	151
1968	7,448	132	89	43	448	397	51	4,716	4,569	146
1967	7,196	140	92	47	418	375	44	4,618	4,444	173
1966	7,547	125	88	37	420	364	56	4,904	4,739	165
1965	7,252	72	37	35	407	353	54	4,796	4,620	176
1964	6,807	NA	NA	NA	312	275	37	4,634	4,430	205
1963	6,541	NA	NA	NA	276	237	39	4,536	4,321	215
1962	6,203	NA	NA	NA	294	247	47	4,389	4,226	163
1961	6,210	NA	NA	NA	331	308	23	4,424	4,207	216
1960	5,910	NA	NA	NA	243	206	37	4,313	4,118	195
1959	5,513	NA	NA	NA	274	244	30	3,987	3,826	161
1958	5,238	NA	NA	NA	222	186	36	3,804	3,621	182
1957	5,034	NA	NA	NA	229	213	16	3,638	3,483	155
1956	4,712	NA	NA	NA	214	202	12	3,429	3,287	142
1955	4,498	NA	NA	NA	144	121	23	3,273	3,131	142
ASIAN ALONE[3]										
2017	4,636	253	123	130	239	204	35	1,632	1,478	154
2016	4,720	304	138	166	214	188	26	1,781	1,658	123
2015	4,567	244	102	142	215	188	27	1,704	1,552	152
2014	4,449	257	105	152	179	147	32	1,643	1,476	167
2013	4,375	242	113	129	165	149	16	1,576	1,402	174
2012	4,275	208	90	118	224	196	28	1,540	1,388	152
2011	3,779	212	120	92	209	189	21	1,469	1,336	133
2010	3,815	223	97	127	196	181	15	1,488	1,358	130
2009	3,515	239	107	132	167	146	21	1,296	1,170	125
2008	3,545	205	110	95	144	119	24	1,356	1,168	188
2007	3,470	171	77	94	137	112	25	1,421	1,305	115
2006	3,287	143	65	78	162	149	13	1,235	1,105	130
2005	3,377	185	80	105	138	99	39	1,228	1,137	91
2004	3,409	165	72	93	164	152	12	1,239	1,153	86
2003[2]	3,312	138	56	82	122	93	29	1,258	1,122	136
2002	3,787	217	85	132	157	137	20	1,431	1,237	195
2001	3,803	161	91	70	181	161	20	1,409	1,263	146
2000	3,442	222	91	132	152	124	28	1,350	1,257	93
1999	3,621	205	96	109	195	148	47	1,461	1,343	118
1998	3,386	196	77	118	145	120	25	1,380	1,190	189
1997	3,261	168	59	108	161	110	51	1,329	1,186	144
1996	3,258	183	63	120	177	158	19	1,255	1,144	111
1995	1,863	76	28	47	75	62	13	697	622	74
1994[1]	2,057	76	27	50	74	60	14	785	707	78
1993	2,321	100	38	62	139	125	14	1,012	930	82
HISPANIC (OF ANY RACE)										
2017	17,974	1,007	751	257	1,116	1,032	83	8,340	7,924	416
2016	17,865	1,079	791	287	1,034	1,008	26	8,148	7,835	313
2015	17,362	933	735	198	1,090	1,020	70	8,187	7,824	364
2014	17,122	1,016	769	248	1,044	991	54	8,085	7,699	386
2013	16,971	991	781	210	1,090	1,018	73	7,942	7,680	262
2012	17,043	988	781	206	1,050	1,009	41	7,841	7,566	275
2011	16,131	1,010	766	244	1,042	984	58	7,716	7,401	315
2010	15,670	994	794	200	1,050	1,002	49	7,403	7,052	351
2009	14,528	930	717	213	965	933	32	7,058	6,716	342
2008	13,967	844	668	177	961	910	51	6,742	6,450	292
2007	13,708	905	711	194	990	954	37	6,582	6,299	284
2006	13,111	911	707	205	846	798	48	6,394	6,109	285
2005	12,809	797	601	196	804	725	79	6,330	5,991	339
2004	12,509	787	591	196	769	699	70	6,184	5,895	290
2003	11,929	768	561	206	694	633	61	5,974	5,651	322
2002	11,544	637	476	161	727	688	39	5,909	5,585	324
2001	11,163	593	452	141	728	641	87	5,779	5,478	301
2000	10,163	574	419	154	687	639	48	5,224	5,012	213

Note: Data shown for 1955 to 1966 for the Black population are for Black and Other races.
NA = Not available.
[1]Prior to 1994, total enrolled does not include the 35 and over population.
[2]Starting in 2003 respondents could identify more than one race. Except as noted, the race data in this table from 2003 onward represent those respondents who indicated only one race category.
[3]The data shown prior to 2003 consists of those identifying themselves as "Asian or Pacific Islanders."

Table A-10. School Enrollment of the Population 3 Years Old and Over, by Level and Control of School, Selected Race, and Hispanic Origin, October 1955–2017—*Continued*

(Numbers in thousands; civilian noninstitutionalized population.)

Year, race, and Hispanic origin	High school			College			
	Total	Public	Private	Total	Public	Private	Full-time
1974..	2,125	2,072	54	814	659	155	589
1973..	2,044	1,988	56	685	537	147	536
1972..	2,025	1,971	54	727	582	145	525
1971..	2,006	1,951	55	680	532	148	534
1970..	1,834	1,794	41	522	422	100	427
1969..	1,808	1,751	57	492	372	120	401
1968..	1,718	1,656	62	434	359	75	338
1967..	1,651	1,605	46	370	280	90	271
1966..	1,721	1,673	48	282	NA	NA	210
1965..	1,619	1,556	62	358	272	86	218
1964..	1,556	1,505	51	306	227	78	NA
1963..	1,444	1,404	39	286	217	69	NA
1962..	1,246	1,214	32	274	200	74	NA
1961..	1,222	1,182	39	233	171	61	NA
1960..	1,127	1,092	34	227	180	46	NA
1959..	1,030	999	31	222	160	62	NA
1958..	998	981	17	212	160	53	NA
1957..	961	939	22	206	132	74	NA
1956..	873	843	30	196	120	76	NA
1955..	926	878	48	155	86	69	NA
ASIAN ALONE[3]							
2017..	931	853	78	1,581	1,219	362	1,330
2016..	837	776	62	1,585	1,163	421	1,349
2015..	787	727	60	1,616	1,232	384	1,340
2014..	827	766	61	1,543	1,202	341	1,247
2013..	817	741	76	1,576	1,144	432	1,260
2012..	857	778	79	1,447	1,078	369	1,175
2011..	685	635	50	1,204	936	268	963
2010..	586	542	43	1,322	969	353	1,090
2009..	582	530	53	1,231	950	282	972
2008..	620	564	56	1,220	918	301	917
2007..	638	616	23	1,103	841	261	896
2006..	663	611	51	1,084	862	223	866
2005..	642	596	46	1,184	904	279	948
2004..	650	619	31	1,191	928	263	881
2003[2]..	632	585	47	1,162	833	328	901
2002..	723	664	59	1,258	1,040	218	951
2001..	771	736	35	1,280	1,026	254	921
2000..	668	622	46	1,049	831	218	792
1999..	719	666	53	1,041	779	261	787
1998..	650	599	51	1,016	783	233	821
1997..	656	600	57	947	712	235	721
1996..	644	606	38	999	816	183	710
1995..	399	375	24	617	470	147	456
1994[1]..	399	365	34	723	548	174	530
1993..	428	390	37	641	519	122	542
HISPANIC (OF ANY RACE)							
2017..	3,936	3,769	167	3,574	3,133	442	2,510
2016..	3,943	3,787	156	3,661	3,050	612	2,571
2015..	3,777	3,658	120	3,374	2,861	514	2,343
2014..	3,681	3,545	136	3,295	2,799	496	2,352
2013..	3,729	3,596	133	3,219	2,768	452	2,179
2012..	3,765	3,633	131	3,400	2,948	451	2,397
2011..	3,410	3,294	116	2,953	2,515	438	2,041
2010..	3,344	3,219	125	2,879	2,478	401	1,868
2009..	3,142	3,052	90	2,434	2,122	312	1,651
2008..	3,192	3,066	126	2,227	1,919	308	1,434
2007..	3,058	2,902	156	2,172	1,888	284	1,459
2006..	2,990	2,856	134	1,968	1,664	304	1,246
2005..	2,937	2,824	113	1,942	1,625	316	1,255
2004..	2,793	2,685	108	1,975	1,676	299	1,276
2003..	2,779	2,667	112	1,714	1,480	235	1,139
2002..	2,614	2,513	101	1,656	1,374	283	1,004
2001..	2,363	2,246	117	1,700	1,445	255	1,005
2000..	2,253	2,144	108	1,426	1,219	207	873

Note: Data shown for 1955 to 1966 for the Black population are for Black and Other races.
NA = Not available.
[1]Prior to 1994, total enrolled does not include the 35 and over population.
[2]Starting in 2003 respondents could identify more than one race. Except as noted, the race data in this table from 2003 onward represent those respondents who indicated only one race category.
[3]The data shown prior to 2003 consists of those identifying themselves as "Asian or Pacific Islanders."

Table A-10. School Enrollment of the Population 3 Years Old and Over, by Level and Control of School, Selected Race, and Hispanic Origin, October 1955–2017—*Continued*

(Numbers in thousands; civilian noninstitutionalized population.)

Year, race, and Hispanic origin	Total enrolled	Nursery school			Kindergarten			Elementary school		
		Total	Public	Private	Total	Public	Private	Total	Public	Private
1999	9,936	585	458	127	666	594	73	5,088	4,829	259
1998	9,528	618	492	126	639	608	31	4,831	4,568	262
1997	9,220	548	436	112	648	589	59	4,644	4,427	217
1996	8,818	533	403	130	602	539	63	4,443	4,162	281
1995	8,563	510	350	160	558	465	93	4,434	4,165	269
1994[1]	8,183	400	278	122	559	516	43	4,162	3,848	314
1993r	7,651	231	169	62	639	576	63	4,027	3,779	248
1993	6,689	194	142	52	538	484	53	3,534	3,317	217
1992	6,598	209	139	70	554	493	60	3,525	3,271	252
1991	6,306	215	146	69	552	525	27	3,461	3,240	221
1990	6,072	242	153	88	475	446	29	3,301	3,107	197
1989	5,722	181	95	86	404	382	21	3,219	3,031	188
1988	5,588	151	111	40	461	445	16	3,160	2,954	207
1987	5,619	226	138	88	439	399	39	3,048	2,861	187
1986	5,513	179	114	65	465	421	44	2,995	2,787	208
1985	5,070	168	105	63	364	315	49	2,803	2,607	196
1984	4,284	117	78	39	293	267	26	2,384	2,218	166
1983	4,618	108	60	48	335	285	50	2,548	2,323	225
1982	4,478	83	46	37	329	291	37	2,501	2,276	225
1981	4,551	131	68	63	306	282	24	2,474	2,239	235
1980	4,263	146	70	75	263	234	30	2,363	2,134	228
1979	3,608	89	50	39	226	210	16	1,934	1,745	189
1978	3,455	87	47	39	231	198	33	1,893	1,704	188
1977	3,516	75	30	46	220	206	14	1,874	1,654	220
1976	3,623	68	38	30	262	242	20	1,934	1,768	165
1975	3,741	85	47	39	235	218	17	2,062	1,858	204
1974	3,620	85	37	48	225	207	18	2,040	1,780	260
1973	3,171	68	41	27	171	165	6	1,884	1,712	172
1972	3,257	61	43	18	241	227	14	1,879	1,705	173
WHITE ALONE OR IN COMBINATION										
2017	58,381	3,576	2,022	1,554	3,137	2,780	356	25,040	22,895	2,145
2016	58,973	3,695	2,119	1,576	3,046	2,746	300	25,148	23,034	2,114
2015	59,162	3436	1890	1546	3133	2762	371	25,493	23,271	2223
2014	59,281	3,575	1,942	1,634	3,125	2,791	334	25,391	23,054	2,337
2013	60,066	3,650	1,896	1,754	3,166	2,813	353	25,776	23,510	2,266
2012	60,618	3601	2058	1543	3177	2799	378	25,613	23,244	2369
2011	61,979	3,833	2,132	1,702	3,393	2,988	405	25,989	23,474	2,516
2010	61,498	3,880	2,130	1,749	3,188	2,848	339	25,844	23,469	2,375
2009	60,778	3,582	1,931	1,651	3,271	2,974	298	25,629	23,238	2,391
2008	60,309	3,642	1,927	1,715	3,247	2,863	385	25,498	22,849	2,649
2007	59,896	3,689	1,959	1,730	3,339	2,946	393	25,321	22,689	2,632
2006	59,391	3,765	1,895	1,871	3,213	2,820	393	25,424	22,809	2,615
2005	60,035	3,642	1,819	1,823	3,179	2,715	463	25,682	22,794	2,888
2004	59,427	3,682	1,762	1,920	3,169	2,670	498	25,691	22,682	3,009
2003	59,184	4,039	1,989	2,050	3,002	2,477	525	25,581	22,686	2,895
BLACK ALONE OR IN COMBINATION										
2017	13,598	909	663	246	651	615	36	6,087	5,695	391
2016	13,507	792	561	231	797	749	48	5,749	5,332	417
2015	13,248	820	594	226	710	680	29	5,883	5,598	285
2014	13,387	840	624	216	830	739	91	5,720	5,409	312
2013	13,517	852	560	291	855	804	51	5,637	5,378	259
2012	13,534	834	613	221	799	744	55	5,603	5,299	305
2011	13,288	904	649	255	696	628	68	5,524	5,253	271
2010	13,105	798	589	210	809	743	66	5,402	5,069	333
2009	12,825	894	687	206	674	632	42	5,295	4,942	353
2008	12,542	776	589	187	668	609	59	5,593	5,225	368
2007	12,401	788	546	242	673	617	57	5,395	5,030	365
2006	12,261	801	568	234	678	607	71	5,365	5,002	363
2005	12,118	763	563	200	593	531	62	5,504	5,122	382
2004	12,303	864	622	242	676	606	70	5,540	5,251	289
2003	12,144	787	526	262	637	559	78	5,604	5,276	327

Note: Data shown for 1955 to 1966 for the Black population are for Black and Other races.
NA = Not available.
r = Revised, controlled to 1990 census based population estimates; previous 1993 data controlled to 1980 census based population estimates.
[1]Prior to 1994, total enrolled does not include the 35 and over population.

Table A-10. School Enrollment of the Population 3 Years Old and Over, by Level and Control of School, Selected Race, and Hispanic Origin, October 1955–2017—*Continued*

(Numbers in thousands; civilian noninstitutionalized population.)

Year, race, and Hispanic origin	High school			College			
	Total	Public	Private	Total	Public	Private	Full-time
1999..	2,290	2,200	91	1,307	1,093	214	765
1998..	2,077	1,978	98	1,363	1,137	226	801
1997..	2,119	2,035	84	1,260	1,079	181	797
1996..	2,018	1,922	96	1,223	1,031	192	708
1995[1]..	1,854	1,772	83	1,207	1,037	170	709
1994[1]..	1,874	1,781	92	1,187	1,019	169	640
1993r..	1,722	1,653	69	1,029	872	157	686
1993..	1,556	1,496	60	867	731	134	573
1992..	1,494	1,435	59	813	710	104	487
1991..	1,357	1,299	61	721	607	115	481
1990..	1,437	1,374	64	617	515	100	380
1989..	1,278	1,231	48	642	557	82	416
1988..	1,163	1,113	49	654	592	60	414
1987..	1,239	1,160	80	668	551	115	414
1986..	1,197	1,116	81	677	540	137	418
1985..	1,156	1,090	167	579	464	116	381
1984..	966	909	57	524	433	91	356
1983..	1,104	1,027	77	523	441	82	335
1982..	1,072	995	77	493	398	96	312
1981..	1,130	1,056	74	510	398	112	343
1980..	1,048	NA	NA	443	NA	NA	294
1979..	920	875	45	440	365	75	314
1978..	868	825	43	377	315	62	231
1977..	928	836	92	418	357	60	287
1976..	932	867	65	427	354	73	297
1975..	948	886	61	411	358	53	287
1974..	916	858	59	354	297	57	247
1973..	758	707	51	290	247	43	201
1972..	834	784	50	242	213	29	178
WHITE ALONE OR IN COMBINATION							
2017..	12,926	11,869	1,056	13,703	10,897	2,805	10,029
2016..	12,728	11,627	1,102	14,355	11,223	3,132	10,731
2015..	12,805	11,813	992	14,295	11,365	2930	10,581
2014..	12,879	11,824	1,055	14,310	11,503	2,807	10,778
2013..	12,732	11,803	929	14,743	11,768	2,975	10,647
2012..	13,110	12,010	1101	15,117	11,919	3198	11,038
2011..	12,979	11,952	1,027	15,785	12,449	3,336	11,476
2010..	13,001	11,924	1,077	15,586	12,460	3,127	11,062
2009..	12,905	11,877	1,029	15,391	12,236	3,155	11,150
2008..	13,184	12,050	1,133	14,738	11,692	3,046	10,511
2007..	13,433	12,302	1,131	14,114	11,058	3,056	9,912
2006..	13,425	12,115	1,309	13,564	10,569	2,995	9,433
2005..	13,741	12,516	1,225	13,791	10,561	3,230	9,618
2004..	13,218	12,047	1,170	13,668	10,711	2,957	9,468
2003..	13,398	12,267	1,131	13,164	10,366	2,798	9,048
BLACK ALONE OR IN COMBINATION							
2017..	2,884	2,727	157	3,068	2,609	459	2,261
2016..	3,090	2,959	131	3,079	2,435	644	2,219
2015..	2,850	2,730	120	2,985	2,364	621	2,163
2014..	2,898	2,730	168	3,099	2,405	694	2,185
2013..	3,055	2,921	134	3,118	2,542	577	2,297
2012..	2,962	2,816	146	3,335	2,752	583	2,373
2011..	2,847	2,752	95	3,317	2,676	641	2,401
2010..	2,846	2,724	122	3,250	2,641	610	2,354
2009..	2,932	2,836	97	3,030	2,434	596	2,178
2008..	2,886	2,769	118	2,619	2,065	554	1,779
2007..	2,915	2,792	122	2,630	2,059	571	1,774
2006..	2,971	2,798	174	2,444	1,907	537	1,702
2005..	2,870	2,729	141	2,387	1,866	521	1,585
2004..	2,811	2,726	85	2,412	1,922	490	1,591
2003..	2,889	2,800	89	2,227	1,846	381	1,482

Note: Data shown for 1955 to 1966 for the Black population are for Black and Other races.
NA = Not available.
r = Revised, controlled to 1990 census based population estimates; previous 1993 data controlled to 1980 census based population estimates.
[1]Prior to 1994, total enrolled does not include the 35 and over population.

Table A-10. School Enrollment of the Population 3 Years Old and Over, by Level and Control of School, Selected Race, and Hispanic Origin, October 1955–2017—*Continued*

(Numbers in thousands; civilian noninstitutionalized population.)

Year, race, and Hispanic origin	Total enrolled	Nursery school			Kindergarten			Elementary school		
		Total	Public	Private	Total	Public	Private	Total	Public	Private
ASIAN ALONE OR IN COMBINATION										
2017	5,708	356	172	184	305	257	48	2,165	1,952	213
2016	5,669	402	170	232	266	233	34	2,207	1,990	217
2015	5,417	334	125	209	256	211	44	2,047	1,830	217
2014	5,353	320	122	198	255	214	41	2,078	1,857	221
2013	5,399	367	157	210	240	214	26	2,026	1,780	246
2012	5,154	268	118	150	270	232	38	1,939	1,733	206
2011	4,571	273	139	134	257	235	22	1,860	1,686	173
2010	4,591	297	132	165	230	212	18	1,876	1,696	180
2009	4,117	316	140	175	195	170	25	1,571	1,410	160
2008	4,122	267	143	123	188	156	32	1,570	1,351	219
2007	4,025	219	94	125	179	151	28	1,664	1,513	151
2006	3,849	189	78	111	203	181	22	1,497	1,331	166
2005	3,964	220	94	126	159	118	41	1,495	1,362	133
2004	3,943	208	82	127	191	169	21	1,497	1,350	148
2003	3,817	164	73	90	148	111	38	1,507	1,346	161

Note: Data shown for 1955 to 1966 for the Black population are for Black and Other races.

Table A-10. School Enrollment of the Population 3 Years Old and Over, by Level and Control of School, Selected Race, and Hispanic Origin, October 1955–2017—*Continued*

(Numbers in thousands; civilian noninstitutionalized population.)

Year, race, and Hispanic origin	High school			College			
	Total	Public	Private	Total	Public	Private	Full-time
ASIAN ALONE OR IN COMBINATION							
2017	1,132	1,015	117	1,750	1,356	394	1,460
2016	1,014	922	92	1,780	1,324	455	1,512
2015	960	879	81	1,821	1,385	436	1,501
2014	988	893	96	1,712	1,337	375	1,392
2013	1,000	909	91	1,766	1,295	471	1,412
2012	1,060	949	111	1,617	1,201	415	1,300
2011	825	757	68	1,356	1,053	302	1,063
2010	722	668	54	1,467	1,089	378	1,205
2009	701	636	65	1,334	1,033	301	1,061
2008	758	690	68	1,340	1,009	331	1,009
2007	760	718	42	1,204	917	287	988
2006	806	743	63	1,154	918	235	900
2005	792	726	67	1,297	993	305	1,036
2004	786	743	43	1,260	980	281	936
2003	736	674	62	1,262	925	337	965

Note: Data shown for 1955 to 1966 for the Black population are for Black and Other races.

Table A-11. Percentage of the Population 3 Years Old and Over Enrolled in School, by Age, Sex, Race, and Hispanic Origin, October 1947–2017

(Percent; civilian noninstitutionalized population.)

Year, sex, race, and Hispanic origin	Total enrolled 3 to 34 years old	Total enrolled 3 years old and over	Age											
			3 and 4	5 and 6	7 to 9	10 to 13	14 and 15	16 and 17	18 and 19	20 and 21	22 to 24	25 to 29	30 to 34	35 and over
ALL RACES														
Both Sexes														
2017	54.6	24.7	53.8	93.5	97.1	97.8	98.2	92.9	68.2	55.0	28.4	12.1	5.9	1.5
2016	55.2	25.1	53.8	93.3	97.8	98.5	98.0	93.0	69.5	55.5	28.8	13.2	6.4	1.5
2015	55.2	25.3	52.7	94.2	97.3	98.0	98.0	93.7	68.5	53.3	28.8	13.2	6.6	1.6
2014	55.2	25.6	54.5	93.4	97.7	97.5	97.8	92.9	68.4	51.4	29.6	13.1	6.4	1.8
2013	55.8	25.9	54.9	93.8	97.9	98.2	98.4	93.7	67.1	52.8	29.7	13.3	6.7	1.8
2012	56.6	26.4	53.5	93.2	98.0	98.0	98.2	95.8	69.0	54.0	30.7	14.0	7.5	1.9
2011	56.8	26.9	52.4	95.1	98.0	98.5	98.6	95.7	71.1	52.7	31.1	14.8	7.7	2.0
2010	56.5	26.9	53.2	94.5	97.7	98.2	98.1	96.1	69.2	52.4	28.9	14.6	8.3	2.1
2009	56.5	26.7	52.4	94.1	97.7	98.5	98.0	94.6	68.9	51.7	30.4	13.5	8.1	2.1
2008	56.2	26.6	52.8	93.8	98.3	98.9	98.6	95.2	66.0	50.1	28.2	13.2	7.3	2.0
2007	56.1	26.6	54.5	94.7	98.1	98.6	98.7	94.3	66.8	48.4	27.3	12.4	7.2	1.9
2006	56.2	26.7	55.7	94.6	98.2	98.3	98.3	94.5	65.5	47.5	26.7	11.7	7.2	1.9
2005	56.5	27.1	53.6	95.4	98.6	98.6	98.0	95.1	67.6	48.7	27.3	11.9	6.9	2.0
2004	56.2	27.2	54.0	95.4	98.1	98.6	98.5	94.5	64.4	48.9	26.3	13.0	6.6	2.0
2003	56.2	27.2	55.1	94.5	98.1	98.4	97.5	94.9	64.5	48.3	27.8	11.8	6.8	1.9
2002	56.1	27.3	54.5	95.2	98.0	98.5	98.4	94.3	63.3	47.8	25.6	12.1	6.6	2.1
2001	55.7	27.2	52.2	95.3	98.2	98.4	98.1	93.4	61.0	45.5	25.1	11.7	6.8	2.0
2000	55.9	27.5	52.1	95.6	98.1	98.3	98.7	92.8	61.2	44.1	24.6	11.4	6.7	1.9
1999	56.0	27.7	54.2	96.0	98.5	98.8	98.2	93.6	60.6	45.3	24.5	11.1	6.2	2.1
1998	55.8	27.9	52.1	95.6	98.8	99.0	98.4	93.9	62.2	44.8	24.9	11.9	6.6	2.1
1997	55.6	28.3	52.6	96.6	98.8	99.3	98.9	94.3	61.5	45.9	26.4	11.8	5.7	2.3
1996	54.1	27.8	48.3	94.0	97.2	98.1	98.0	92.8	61.5	44.4	24.8	11.9	6.1	2.3
1995	53.7	27.8	48.7	96.0	98.7	99.1	98.9	93.6	59.4	44.9	23.2	11.6	6.0	2.2
1994	53.3	27.9	47.3	96.7	99.3	99.4	98.8	94.4	60.2	44.9	24.1	10.8	6.7	2.3
1993r	51.9	NA	40.1	95.3	99.5	99.5	98.9	93.9	61.4	42.6	23.5	10.2	5.9	NA
1993	51.8	26.9	40.4	95.4	99.5	99.5	98.9	94.0	61.6	42.7	23.6	10.2	5.9	2.2
1992	51.4	26.9	39.7	95.5	99.4	99.4	99.1	94.1	61.4	44.0	23.7	9.8	6.1	2.1
1991	50.7	26.9	40.5	95.4	99.6	99.7	98.8	93.3	59.6	42.0	22.2	10.2	6.2	2.2
1990	50.2	26.8	44.4	96.5	99.7	99.6	99.0	92.5	57.3	39.7	21.0	9.7	5.8	2.1
1989	49.1	26.4	39.1	95.2	99.2	99.4	98.8	92.7	56.0	38.5	19.9	9.3	5.7	2.0
1988	48.7	26.5	38.2	96.0	99.6	99.7	98.9	91.6	55.7	39.1	18.3	8.3	5.9	2.1
1987	48.6	26.6	38.3	95.1	99.6	99.5	98.6	91.7	55.6	38.7	17.5	9.0	5.9	1.8
1986	48.2	26.6	39.0	95.3	99.3	99.1	97.6	92.3	54.6	33.0	17.9	8.8	6.0	1.8
1985	48.3	26.8	38.9	96.1	99.1	99.3	98.1	91.7	51.6	35.3	16.9	9.2	6.1	1.7
1984	47.9	26.6	36.3	94.5	99.0	99.4	97.8	91.5	50.1	33.9	17.3	9.1	6.3	1.5
1983	48.4	27.1	37.6	95.4	98.9	99.4	98.3	91.7	50.4	32.5	16.6	9.6	6.4	1.7
1982	48.6	27.4	36.4	95.0	99.2	99.1	98.5	90.6	47.8	34.0	16.8	9.6	6.3	1.6
1981	48.9	27.9	36.0	94.0	99.2	99.3	98.0	90.6	49.0	31.6	16.5	9.0	6.9	1.7
1980	49.7	28.2	36.7	95.7	99.1	99.4	98.2	89.0	46.4	31.0	16.3	9.3	6.5	1.6
1979	50.3	28.7	35.1	95.8	99.2	99.1	98.1	89.2	45.0	30.2	15.8	9.6	6.4	1.7
1978	51.2	29.3	34.2	95.3	99.3	99.0	98.4	89.1	45.4	29.5	16.3	9.4	6.4	1.6
1977	52.5	NA	32.0	95.8	99.5	99.4	98.5	88.9	46.2	31.8	16.5	10.8	6.9	NA
1976	53.1	31.7	31.3	95.5	99.2	99.2	98.2	89.1	46.2	32.0	17.1	10.0	6.0	3.9
1975	53.7	NA	31.5	94.7	99.3	99.3	98.2	89.0	46.9	31.2	16.2	10.1	6.6	NA
1974	53.6	NA	28.8	94.2	99.1	99.5	97.9	87.9	43.1	30.2	15.1	9.6	5.7	NA
1973	53.5	NA	24.2	92.5	99.1	99.2	97.5	88.3	42.9	30.1	14.5	8.5	4.5	NA
1972	54.9	NA	24.4	91.9	99.0	99.3	97.6	88.9	46.3	31.4	14.8	8.6	4.6	NA
1971	56.2	NA	21.2	91.6	99.1	99.2	98.6	90.2	49.2	32.2	15.4	8.0	4.9	NA
1970	56.4	NA	20.5	89.5	99.3	99.2	98.1	90.0	47.7	31.9	14.9	7.5	4.2	NA
1969	57.0	NA	16.1	88.4	99.3	99.1	98.1	89.7	50.2	34.1	15.4	7.9	4.8	NA
1968	56.7	NA	15.7	87.6	99.1	99.1	98.0	90.2	50.4	31.2	13.8	7.0	3.9	NA
1967	56.6	NA	14.2	87.4	99.4	99.1	98.2	88.8	47.6	33.3	13.6	6.6	4.0	NA
1966	56.1	NA	12.5	85.1	99.3	99.3	98.6	88.5	47.2	29.9	13.2	6.5	2.7	NA
1965	55.5	NA	10.6	84.4	99.3	99.4	98.9	87.4	46.3	27.6	13.2	6.1	3.2	NA
1964	54.5	NA	9.5	83.3	99.0	99.0	98.6	87.7	41.6	26.3	9.9	5.2	2.6	NA
1963	58.5	NA	NA	82.7	99.4	99.3	98.4	87.1	40.9	25.0	11.4	4.9	2.5	NA
1962	57.8	NA	NA	82.2	99.2	99.3	98.0	84.3	41.8	23.0	10.3	5.0	2.6	NA
1961	56.8	NA	NA	81.7	99.4	99.3	97.6	83.6	38.0	21.5	8.4	4.4	2.0	NA
1960	56.4	NA	NA	80.7	99.6	99.5	97.8	82.6	38.4	19.4	8.7	4.9	2.4	NA
1959	55.5	NA	NA	80.0	99.4	99.4	97.5	82.9	36.8	18.8	8.6	5.1	2.2	NA
1958	54.8	NA	NA	80.4	99.5	99.5	96.9	80.6	37.6	------13.4------		5.7	2.2	NA
1957	53.6	NA	NA	78.6	99.5	99.5	97.1	80.5	34.9	------14.0------		5.5	1.8	NA
1956	52.3	NA	NA	77.6	99.4	99.2	96.9	78.4	35.4	------12.8------		5.1	1.9	NA

Note: Data shown for 1947 to 1966 for the Black population are for Black and other races. Data for 1947 to 1963 exclude kindergarten. Nursery school was first collected in 1964.
NA = Not available.
r = Revised, controlled to 1990 census based population estimates; previous 1993 data controlled to 1980 census based population estimates.

Table A-11. Percentage of the Population 3 Years Old and Over Enrolled in School, by Age, Sex, Race, and Hispanic Origin, October 1947–2017—*Continued*

(Percent; civilian noninstitutionalized population.)

Year, sex, race, and Hispanic origin	Total enrolled 3 to 34 years old	Total enrolled 3 years old and over	3 and 4	5 and 6	7 to 9	10 to 13	14 and 15	16 and 17	18 and 19	20 and 21	22 to 24	25 to 29	30 to 34	35 and over
1955	50.8	NA	NA	78.1	99.2	99.2	95.9	77.4	31.5	------11.1------		4.2	1.6	NA
1954	50.0	NA	NA	77.3	99.2	99.5	95.8	78.0	32.4	------11.2------		4.1	1.5	NA
1953	48.8	NA	NA	55.7	99.4	99.4	96.5	74.7	31.2	------11.1------		2.9	1.7	NA
1952	46.8	NA	NA	54.7	98.7	98.9	96.2	73.4	28.7	-------9.5------		2.6	1.1	NA
1951	45.4	NA	NA	54.5	99.0	99.2	94.8	75.1	26.3	-------8.3------		2.5	NA	NA
1950	44.2	NA	NA	58.2	98.9	98.6	94.7	71.3	29.4	-------9.0------		3.0	NA	NA
1949	43.9	NA	NA	59.3	98.5	98.7	93.5	69.5	25.3	-------9.2------		3.8	1.1	NA
1948	43.1	NA	NA	56.0	98.3	98.0	92.7	71.2	26.9	-------9.7------		2.6	0.9	NA
1947	42.3	NA	NA	58.0	98.4	98.6	91.6	67.6	24.3	------10.2------		3.0	1.0	NA
Male														
2017	54.0	25.1	53.4	92.8	97.1	97.8	98.2	92.3	65.1	50.8	26.8	10.9	5.2	1.1
2016	54.8	25.6	54.1	92.7	97.5	98.3	98.7	92.7	68.2	51.4	27.6	11.8	5.5	1.2
2015	54.9	25.7	53.6	93.5	97.5	98.3	97.9	93.1	65.7	50.2	27.5	11.7	5.5	1.2
2014	54.8	25.9	53.5	94.0	97.5	96.9	97.5	92.1	64.9	49.1	28.1	12.2	5.3	1.4
2013	55.2	26.2	53.2	93.8	97.9	98.1	98.2	93.3	65.1	48.5	27.6	12.2	5.3	1.4
2012	55.9	26.6	52.7	93.2	97.7	98.2	98.3	95.7	65.8	49.5	29.4	11.9	5.8	1.3
2011	56.2	27.2	52.8	95.1	98.1	98.6	98.4	95.4	68.8	49.2	30.3	12.9	6.4	1.5
2010	55.9	27.1	53.0	93.7	97.6	97.9	98.0	94.9	66.9	49.2	27.0	13.5	6.7	1.6
2009	55.7	26.9	51.6	93.9	97.6	98.6	97.6	94.5	65.0	48.7	29.0	11.7	6.9	1.5
2008	55.6	26.9	52.3	93.8	98.0	98.7	99.0	94.9	64.0	47.4	26.3	12.1	6.3	1.4
2007	55.4	26.9	54.4	94.0	98.1	98.4	98.4	94.4	66.3	43.7	25.4	10.2	6.4	1.5
2006	55.5	27.0	56.0	94.4	98.1	98.2	98.2	94.1	63.6	44.0	25.0	10.4	5.9	1.5
2005	55.8	27.4	52.8	94.8	98.2	98.4	97.5	95.1	66.5	45.3	25.2	9.6	5.9	1.5
2004	55.0	27.6	54.7	95.5	97.8	98.5	98.7	94.9	60.3	46.6	24.1	11.5	5.6	1.6
2003	55.9	27.8	55.9	94.7	97.9	98.3	97.5	95.0	62.4	43.4	26.1	10.8	6.3	1.5
2002	55.8	27.9	54.6	95.3	98.1	98.3	98.4	94.0	61.8	44.8	23.8	10.7	5.5	1.7
2001	55.4	27.8	51.6	95.2	98.5	98.1	98.1	93.0	58.9	44.0	23.8	10.3	5.7	1.5
2000	55.8	28.0	50.8	95.1	98.0	98.3	98.7	92.7	58.3	41.0	23.9	10.0	5.6	1.5
1999	56.6	28.6	53.3	95.9	98.3	98.7	98.0	93.7	60.3	44.7	23.6	10.7	5.8	1.6
1998	55.9	28.6	53.3	95.2	98.7	99.0	98.3	93.5	60.1	42.7	24.6	10.9	5.5	1.6
1997	55.8	28.8	51.9	96.7	98.6	99.4	99.1	94.2	60.6	44.4	25.4	11.7	4.7	1.6
1996	54.4	28.5	46.9	93.8	97.2	98.0	98.5	93.2	60.8	43.9	25.2	11.4	4.9	1.8
1995	54.3	28.7	49.4	95.3	98.9	99.1	99.0	94.5	59.5	44.7	22.8	11.0	5.4	1.8
1994	53.7	28.7	47.6	97.0	99.2	99.4	98.8	94.3	60.4	42.7	24.2	10.5	5.9	1.7
1993r	52.6	NA	41.1	95.5	99.5	99.6	99.0	94.9	61.1	42.3	25.3	9.6	5.2	NA
1993	52.6	27.9	41.5	95.5	99.5	99.6	99.0	95.0	61.6	42.6	25.5	9.6	5.2	1.6
1992	51.9	27.7	40.3	95.7	99.5	99.5	99.2	95.4	61.6	41.7	23.8	9.1	5.2	1.5
1991	51.5	27.9	39.9	95.0	99.7	99.8	99.1	93.7	59.8	41.8	24.0	10.6	5.6	1.6
1990	50.9	27.7	43.9	96.5	99.7	99.6	99.1	92.7	58.2	40.3	22.3	9.2	4.8	1.5
1989	49.7	27.3	38.8	95.1	99.3	99.2	99.2	93.2	56.6	37.3	20.4	9.3	5.0	1.4
1988	49.6	27.6	38.3	95.9	99.6	99.7	98.9	92.1	56.2	39.0	20.5	8.1	5.5	1.5
1987	49.9	27.9	40.0	95.7	99.7	99.7	98.7	92.3	57.9	41.2	18.7	9.1	5.0	1.3
1986	49.3	27.8	38.8	96.0	99.4	98.9	97.6	92.3	57.1	33.4	19.0	9.4	5.6	1.3
1985	49.2	27.9	36.8	95.3	99.1	99.2	98.3	92.4	52.2	36.5	18.8	9.4	5.4	1.3
1984	49.1	28.0	35.9	94.0	98.8	99.3	97.5	91.8	52.4	36.2	20.1	9.6	5.8	1.1
1983	49.7	28.6	38.1	95.1	98.8	99.3	98.4	91.8	50.4	35.2	19.4	10.7	5.8	1.2
1982	49.7	28.8	36.4	94.7	99.2	99.0	98.7	91.3	48.9	35.2	18.5	10.1	5.6	1.2
1981	50.2	29.3	36.8	94.2	98.9	99.2	98.2	90.7	50.5	32.1	19.2	9.6	6.2	1.2
1980	50.9	29.6	37.8	95.0	99.0	99.4	98.7	89.1	47.0	32.6	17.8	9.8	5.9	1.2
1979	51.8	30.2	34.6	96.3	99.0	98.9	98.3	90.8	46.6	31.6	17.6	10.4	6.0	1.3
1978	52.9	31.0	34.0	95.1	99.1	98.8	98.4	89.5	47.8	31.7	19.1	10.9	6.5	1.3
1977	54.3	NA	32.1	94.7	99.5	99.2	98.7	90.0	48.4	34.6	19.7	12.6	7.1	NA
1976	55.1	33.6	30.9	95.6	98.9	99.1	98.6	90.5	48.2	33.6	20.7	13.0	6.8	3.6
1975	56.0	NA	30.6	94.3	99.2	98.9	98.4	90.7	49.9	35.3	20.0	13.1	7.7	NA
1974	56.0	NA	28.1	94.4	99.1	99.3	98.0	88.6	45.8	34.8	19.4	12.7	6.7	NA
1973	56.1	NA	24.5	92.2	99.0	99.2	97.9	89.4	47.9	34.4	19.1	11.8	5.6	NA
1972	57.8	NA	24.4	91.7	98.9	99.3	97.7	90.2	51.2	37.3	21.3	12.1	5.8	NA
1971	59.3	NA	20.0	90.9	99.0	98.8	98.7	91.7	55.4	38.9	23.3	11.9	6.3	NA
1970	59.7	NA	21.2	88.9	99.3	98.8	98.2	91.3	54.4	42.7	21.2	11.0	5.3	NA
1969	60.5	NA	15.5	87.7	99.0	98.9	98.1	91.6	59.4	46.5	22.9	11.4	5.9	NA
1968	60.4	NA	15.4	87.3	98.9	98.9	98.2	91.7	60.4	45.0	20.5	10.8	5.0	NA
1967	60.0	NA	14.2	86.6	99.4	98.9	98.3	91.0	56.3	44.3	21.0	9.9	5.4	NA
1966	59.7	NA	12.3	84.5	99.2	99.1	98.7	89.9	57.8	41.4	21.3	9.6	3.8	NA
1965	58.8	NA	10.2	84.4	99.3	99.3	99.0	88.0	55.6	37.6	21.1	9.4	4.5	NA
1964	57.5	NA	8.9	83.4	98.7	98.9	99.0	89.8	50.9	34.4	16.1	8.1	3.6	NA

Note: Data shown for 1947 to 1966 for the Black population are for Black and other races. Data for 1947 to 1963 exclude kindergarten. Nursery school was first collected in 1964.

NA = Not available.

r = Revised, controlled to 1990 census based population estimates; previous 1993 data controlled to 1980 census based population estimates.

Table A-11. Percentage of the Population 3 Years Old and Over Enrolled in School, by Age, Sex, Race, and Hispanic Origin, October 1947–2017—Continued

(Percent; civilian noninstitutionalized population.)

Year, sex, race, and Hispanic origin	Total enrolled 3 to 34 years old	Total enrolled 3 years old and over	3 and 4	5 and 6	7 to 9	10 to 13	14 and 15	16 and 17	18 and 19	20 and 21	22 to 24	25 to 29	30 to 34	35 and over
1963	62.3	NA	NA	82.7	99.2	99.0	98.7	89.4	51.0	33.6	19.5	7.8	3.7	NA
1962	61.7	NA	NA	82.6	99.1	99.2	98.7	87.1	51.2	31.3	17.7	8.5	3.9	NA
1961	60.4	NA	NA	82.0	99.5	99.2	98.1	84.7	48.6	29.5	13.9	7.1	2.9	NA
1960	60.0	NA	NA	80.8	99.6	99.4	97.9	84.5	47.8	27.1	15.0	8.4	3.7	NA
1959	59.1	NA	NA	79.5	99.2	99.4	97.8	84.8	45.6	28.3	13.7	8.9	3.3	NA
1958	58.7	NA	NA	80.6	99.6	99.4	96.9	83.8	47.5	------21.0------		9.5	2.9	NA
1957	57.5	NA	NA	78.3	99.4	99.6	98.0	82.8	43.3	------21.3------		9.5	2.6	NA
1956	56.3	NA	NA	77.1	99.2	99.1	97.1	79.9	45.1	--------20.6------		8.9	2.7	NA
1955	54.9	NA	NA	78.1	99.1	99.4	95.7	81.1	42.5	------18.1------		7.0	2.1	NA
1954	54.0	NA	NA	76.3	99.0	99.4	96.1	80.9	40.6	------19.1------		6.7	1.9	NA
1953	50.2	NA	NA	55.0	99.3	99.1	96.4	76.5	37.7	------18.5------		5.5	2.0	NA
1952	49.4	NA	NA	54.8	98.6	98.9	96.2	73.9	37.2	------16.9------		4.7	1.7	NA
1951	56.8	NA	NA	55.1	99.1	99.1	95.1	74.3	32.4	------14.3------		4.2	NA	NA
1950	54.8	NA	NA	56.8	98.8	98.7	95.2	72.8	35.7	------14.3------		5.9	NA	NA
1949	45.8	NA	NA	60.1	98.5	98.6	93.9	70.8	31.6	------15.4------		6.8	1.9	NA
1948	44.8	NA	NA	55.1	99.5	98.1	92.0	72.1	34.3	------16.5------		5.1	1.5	NA
1947	44.3	NA	NA	57.4	98.5	98.7	90.3	67.6	31.4	------17.0------		5.8	1.7	NA
Female														
2017	55.2	24.4	54.1	94.2	97.0	97.8	98.3	93.5	71.3	59.2	30.0	13.4	6.5	1.8
2016	55.6	24.7	53.5	93.8	98.1	98.7	97.3	93.3	70.7	59.7	30.0	14.7	7.2	1.7
2015	55.6	24.9	51.8	94.9	97.2	97.6	98.1	94.4	71.4	56.5	30.1	14.6	7.7	1.9
2014	55.7	25.2	55.5	92.8	97.9	98.1	98.2	93.8	72.1	53.9	31.0	14.0	7.4	2.1
2013	56.4	25.7	56.7	93.7	97.9	98.2	98.6	94.1	69.2	57.3	31.7	14.4	8.1	2.3
2012	57.4	26.2	54.4	93.3	98.4	97.8	98.2	95.9	72.3	58.3	32.1	16.0	9.2	2.3
2011	57.4	26.5	52.1	95.2	97.9	98.4	98.9	96.0	73.5	56.4	32.0	16.8	8.9	2.4
2010	57.4	26.7	53.4	95.3	98.0	98.6	98.3	97.3	71.5	56.0	30.8	15.8	9.9	2.6
2009	57.3	26.6	53.2	94.4	97.9	98.4	98.5	94.7	72.9	54.9	31.8	15.3	9.3	2.7
2008	56.7	26.3	53.3	93.7	98.7	99.2	98.2	95.4	68.1	53.0	30.1	14.3	8.3	2.5
2007	56.8	26.3	54.7	95.3	98.1	98.7	99.0	94.1	67.2	53.3	29.2	14.7	7.9	2.4
2006	56.6	26.3	55.4	94.8	98.3	98.4	98.4	95.0	67.4	51.1	28.5	13.0	8.5	2.3
2005	57.2	26.8	54.4	96.1	99.0	98.9	98.4	95.1	68.8	52.3	29.2	14.2	7.9	2.4
2004	56.5	26.8	53.2	95.3	98.5	98.7	98.3	94.1	68.5	51.3	28.4	14.4	7.7	2.5
2003	56.4	26.6	54.1	94.4	98.3	98.6	97.5	94.8	66.6	52.9	29.5	12.8	7.3	2.2
2002	56.4	26.8	54.4	95.1	97.9	98.7	98.5	94.7	65.0	50.9	27.3	13.5	7.7	2.5
2001	55.9	26.7	52.9	95.4	97.8	98.8	98.2	93.8	63.2	46.9	26.5	13.0	7.9	2.5
2000	56.0	26.9	53.4	96.1	98.2	98.3	98.6	92.9	64.2	47.3	25.3	12.7	7.7	2.3
1999	55.5	27.0	55.2	96.1	98.7	98.9	98.3	93.5	60.9	45.8	25.4	11.4	6.6	2.4
1998	55.6	27.3	50.9	95.9	98.8	99.1	98.5	94.3	64.4	47.2	25.2	12.9	7.7	2.6
1997	55.4	27.6	53.2	96.4	99.1	99.3	98.7	94.4	62.4	47.4	27.4	11.9	6.6	2.9
1996	53.8	27.1	49.8	94.3	97.3	98.2	97.5	92.4	62.2	44.8	24.5	12.5	7.3	2.8
1995	53.2	27.0	48.1	96.8	98.5	99.1	98.8	92.6	59.2	45.1	23.6	12.2	6.5	2.7
1994	52.9	27.2	46.9	96.4	99.5	99.4	98.7	94.4	60.0	47.0	23.9	11.1	7.5	2.8
1993r	51.1	NA	39.0	95.2	99.4	99.5	98.7	92.8	61.7	42.8	21.7	10.8	6.6	NA
1993	51.0	25.9	39.3	95.2	99.4	99.5	98.7	92.9	61.7	42.9	21.8	10.8	6.6	2.6
1992	51.0	26.1	39.1	95.2	99.2	99.2	99.1	92.7	61.2	46.1	23.6	10.5	7.0	2.6
1991	49.9	26.0	41.1	95.8	99.5	99.6	98.4	92.8	59.4	42.2	20.4	9.8	6.8	2.8
1990	49.5	25.9	44.9	96.4	99.6	99.7	98.9	92.4	56.3	39.2	19.9	10.2	6.9	2.7
1989	48.4	25.5	39.5	95.2	99.2	99.6	98.4	92.2	55.5	39.7	19.5	9.3	6.4	2.5
1988	47.7	25.5	38.1	96.0	99.6	99.7	98.8	91.2	55.2	39.1	16.2	8.6	6.4	2.6
1987	47.4	25.3	36.6	94.5	99.5	99.2	98.4	91.1	53.4	36.4	16.5	9.0	6.7	2.2
1986	47.1	25.4	39.0	94.6	99.2	99.3	97.5	92.3	52.1	32.7	16.8	8.2	6.4	2.2
1985	47.4	25.7	41.2	97.0	99.2	99.4	97.9	90.9	51.0	34.1	15.1	9.1	6.8	2.1
1984	46.6	25.3	36.7	95.1	99.3	99.4	98.2	91.2	48.0	31.7	14.6	8.6	6.7	1.9
1983	47.0	25.7	36.9	95.8	99.0	99.5	98.2	91.6	50.3	29.9	13.9	8.5	7.0	2.0
1982	47.5	26.1	36.4	95.3	99.2	99.3	98.3	89.9	46.8	32.9	15.1	9.0	6.9	1.9
1981	47.7	26.6	35.2	93.8	99.5	99.4	97.7	90.5	47.5	31.2	13.9	8.4	7.5	2.0
1980	48.5	26.9	35.5	96.4	99.2	99.4	97.7	88.8	45.8	29.5	14.9	8.8	7.0	1.9
1979	49.0	27.3	35.6	95.2	99.4	99.4	97.9	87.6	43.4	28.9	14.1	8.8	6.7	2.0
1978	49.5	27.8	34.5	95.5	99.5	99.2	98.4	88.8	43.0	27.5	13.6	7.9	6.2	2.0
1977	50.7	NA	32.0	96.9	99.5	99.6	98.3	87.7	44.0	29.1	13.6	9.1	6.7	NA
1976	51.0	29.8	31.6	95.5	99.4	99.3	97.8	87.7	44.4	30.6	13.8	7.3	5.2	4.2
1975	51.5	NA	32.4	95.2	99.5	99.6	98.0	87.2	44.2	27.4	12.6	7.2	5.6	NA
1974	51.3	NA	29.5	93.9	99.2	99.7	97.9	87.1	40.7	26.0	11.1	6.7	4.6	NA
1973	50.9	NA	23.8	92.9	99.3	99.2	97.1	87.2	38.2	26.3	10.2	5.4	3.6	NA
1972	52.0	NA	24.4	92.2	99.1	99.4	97.5	87.6	41.8	26.3	8.9	5.3	3.6	NA

Note: Data shown for 1947 to 1966 for the Black population are for Black and other races. Data for 1947 to 1963 exclude kindergarten. Nursery school was first collected in 1964.

NA = Not available.

r = Revised, controlled to 1990 census based population estimates; previous 1993 data controlled to 1980 census based population estimates.

Table A-11. Percentage of the Population 3 Years Old and Over Enrolled in School, by Age, Sex, Race, and Hispanic Origin, October 1947–2017—*Continued*

(Percent; civilian noninstitutionalized population.)

Year, sex, race, and Hispanic origin	Total enrolled 3 to 34 years old	Total enrolled 3 years old and over	3 and 4	5 and 6	7 to 9	10 to 13	14 and 15	16 and 17	18 and 19	20 and 21	22 to 24	25 to 29	30 to 34	35 and over
1971	53.2	NA	22.4	92.3	99.2	99.5	98.5	88.7	43.4	26.8	8.4	4.4	3.6	NA
1970	53.2	NA	19.8	90.2	99.3	99.5	98.0	88.6	41.6	23.6	9.4	4.3	3.1	NA
1969	53.6	NA	16.8	89.1	99.6	99.4	98.2	87.7	41.8	25.3	9.1	4.6	3.8	NA
1968	53.2	NA	16.1	88.0	99.3	99.3	97.8	88.7	41.3	21.5	8.3	3.4	2.9	NA
1967	53.3	NA	14.1	88.2	99.5	99.3	98.2	86.7	40.3	24.9	7.4	3.6	2.8	NA
1966	52.7	NA	12.7	85.7	99.4	99.5	98.4	87.1	37.7	20.9	6.6	3.6	1.7	NA
1965	52.3	NA	10.9	84.4	99.3	99.5	98.7	86.9	37.7	19.5	6.5	3.1	2.1	NA
1964	51.5	NA	10.2	83.2	99.3	99.2	98.2	85.6	33.7	19.5	4.4	2.6	1.6	NA
1963	54.9	NA	NA	82.6	99.6	99.6	98.0	84.8	32.3	17.8	4.4	2.4	1.5	NA
1962	54.0	NA	NA	81.7	99.3	99.4	97.3	81.5	33.7	16.1	3.9	1.8	1.4	NA
1961	53.4	NA	NA	81.4	99.3	99.4	97.2	82.4	28.6	14.9	3.7	1.9	1.2	NA
1960	52.8	NA	NA	80.6	99.6	99.5	97.6	80.6	30.0	13.1	3.4	1.8	1.2	NA
1959	52.0	NA	NA	80.5	99.6	99.5	97.1	81.0	29.2	11.1	4.4	1.7	1.3	NA
1958	51.0	NA	NA	80.2	99.4	99.5	96.9	77.3	29.4	------7.3------		2.2	1.5	NA
1957	50.0	NA	NA	79.0	99.6	99.5	96.2	78.1	28.1	------8.2------		1.9	1.1	NA
1956	48.7	NA	NA	78.2	99.5	99.4	96.8	76.9	27.4	------6.8------		1.7	1.2	NA
1955	47.0	NA	NA	78.1	99.3	99.0	96.1	73.8	22.5	------6.1------		1.8	1.1	NA
1954	46.3	NA	NA	78.3	99.5	99.7	95.4	75.2	25.4	------6.0------		1.7	1.1	NA
1953	43.0	NA	NA	56.6	99.5	99.7	96.6	72.9	25.9	------6.4------		0.5	1.4	NA
1952	41.9	NA	NA	54.6	98.9	98.9	96.6	72.9	22.1	------4.9------		0.6	0.7	NA
1951	49.1	NA	NA	54.0	98.9	99.3	94.5	75.4	21.3	------4.3------		1.0	NA	NA
1950	48.4	NA	NA	59.5	99.0	98.4	94.3	69.8	24.3	------4.6------		0.4	NA	NA
1949	39.2	NA	NA	58.4	98.5	98.8	93.1	68.2	19.9	------3.7------		1.1	0.4	NA
1948	38.4	NA	NA	56.8	98.2	97.8	93.5	70.3	20.3	------3.4------		0.4	0.4	NA
1947	38.0	NA	NA	58.7	98.4	98.5	92.8	67.5	18.5	------3.9------		0.4	0.3	NA
WHITE ALONE														
Both Sexes														
2017	53.9	23.2	53.4	93.5	96.9	97.5	98.4	93.1	67.8	54.7	26.9	11.5	5.6	1.3
2016	54.7	23.6	53.7	93.8	98.0	98.4	98.4	92.4	69.4	56.2	27.5	12.7	5.9	1.3
2015	54.6	23.8	52.2	94.1	97.5	97.8	97.8	93.8	68.6	53.8	27.7	12.8	6.1	1.4
2014	54.6	24.0	53.6	93.6	97.6	97.5	97.7	93.5	68.3	53.0	28.6	12.4	5.9	1.5
2013	55.0	24.3	54.0	93.9	98.1	98.2	98.4	93.6	67.6	52.2	28.9	12.2	6.4	1.6
2012	55.8	24.8	54.0	93.3	98.2	97.7	98.3	96.0	68.7	54.4	29.5	13.4	6.5	1.6
2011	56.2	25.5	51.4	95.7	98.2	98.6	98.6	95.5	70.3	53.8	30.9	14.0	6.9	1.7
2010	55.8	25.4	52.1	94.2	97.7	98.1	98.0	96.2	70.0	51.6	28.1	13.9	7.8	1.9
2009	55.7	25.3	51.1	94.0	97.9	98.7	98.7	94.4	68.7	52.6	28.9	12.9	7.3	1.9
2008	55.5	25.3	52.0	94.0	98.2	98.9	98.7	95.4	67.1	51.2	28.1	12.3	6.2	1.8
2007	55.5	25.3	54.1	94.8	98.0	98.7	98.7	94.6	67.1	50.1	26.3	11.5	6.6	1.8
2006	55.5	25.3	55.6	95.0	98.4	98.4	98.4	95.0	64.9	48.2	25.5	11.3	6.7	1.7
2005	55.9	25.7	54.2	95.3	98.6	98.7	98.3	95.4	68.0	49.3	26.0	11.3	6.2	1.8
2004	55.5	25.7	52.8	95.5	98.1	98.3	98.5	94.2	64.9	49.3	25.3	12.2	6.4	1.8
2003[1]	55.4	25.8	55.3	94.7	98.0	98.4	97.3	95.0	64.4	48.2	26.7	11.0	6.2	1.8
2002	55.4	26.0	53.9	95.1	98.0	98.5	98.5	94.6	63.8	47.4	24.6	11.4	5.9	2.0
2001	54.8	25.8	51.7	94.8	98.3	98.7	98.2	93.5	60.4	45.9	23.3	10.7	6.0	1.8
2000	55.1	26.1	50.2	95.3	98.2	98.3	98.4	92.8	61.3	44.9	23.7	10.4	6.0	1.8
1999	55.2	26.4	53.7	95.6	98.5	98.8	98.2	93.5	60.5	45.6	24.1	10.5	5.8	1.9
1998	55.0	26.6	50.7	95.4	98.8	99.1	98.6	94.1	61.9	44.8	24.1	11.0	6.2	2.0
1997	54.8	26.8	50.9	96.8	98.8	99.3	98.8	94.5	61.5	46.4	25.8	11.3	5.4	2.2
1996	53.4	26.4	47.9	94.8	97.1	98.2	98.0	92.8	62.5	44.9	24.6	11.3	5.7	2.2
1995	53.2	26.6	49.6	96.2	98.9	99.0	98.8	93.7	59.3	46.2	23.1	11.5	5.5	2.1
1994	52.6	26.6	47.0	96.6	99.2	99.3	98.7	94.3	60.9	46.2	23.5	10.4	6.6	2.2
1993r	51.2	NA	40.4	95.4	99.5	99.5	98.9	93.9	61.4	43.7	23.1	9.7	5.9	NA
1993	51.1	25.7	40.8	95.5	99.5	99.5	98.9	94.1	61.7	44.0	23.3	9.8	5.9	2.1
1992	50.7	NA	40.1	95.4	99.4	99.3	99.2	94.2	61.7	45.3	23.3	9.6	6.0	NA
1991	50.0	NA	41.3	95.3	99.6	99.7	98.7	93.3	59.7	43.2	21.7	9.9	6.0	NA
1990	49.5	NA	44.9	96.5	99.7	99.6	99.1	92.5	57.1	41.0	20.2	9.9	5.9	NA
1989	48.4	NA	39.4	95.2	99.2	99.4	98.8	92.3	56.4	39.5	20.0	9.4	5.6	NA
1988	48.0	NA	38.9	96.1	99.7	99.7	98.8	91.4	55.8	40.2	18.6	8.2	5.9	NA
1987	47.7	NA	38.2	94.8	99.6	99.4	98.5	91.8	55.3	39.6	17.3	8.7	5.7	NA
1986	47.7	NA	39.1	95.3	99.3	97.8	99.0	92.2	55.3	33.9	17.7	9.1	6.2	NA
1985	47.8	NA	38.6	96.4	99.3	99.3	98.1	91.6	52.4	36.1	17.0	9.2	5.9	NA
1984	47.3	NA	36.0	94.6	99.0	99.4	97.8	91.2	51.1	34.3	17.2	9.1	6.2	NA

Note: Data shown for 1947 to 1966 for the Black population are for Black and other races. Data for 1947 to 1963 exclude kindergarten. Nursery school was first collected in 1964.

NA = Not available.

r = Revised, controlled to 1990 census based population estimates; previous 1993 data controlled to 1980 census based population estimates.

[1]Starting in 2003, respondents could identify more than one race. Except as noted, the race data in this table from 2003 onward represent those respondents who indicated only one race category.

Table A-11. Percentage of the Population 3 Years Old and Over Enrolled in School, by Age, Sex, Race, and Hispanic Origin, October 1947–2017—*Continued*

(Percent; civilian noninstitutionalized population.)

Year, sex, race, and Hispanic origin	Total enrolled 3 to 34 years old	Total enrolled 3 years old and over	Age 3 and 4	5 and 6	7 to 9	10 to 13	14 and 15	16 and 17	18 and 19	20 and 21	22 to 24	25 to 29	30 to 34	35 and over
1983	47.7	NA	37.6	95.7	98.9	99.3	98.4	91.4	50.9	33.4	16.4	9.4	6.1	NA
1982	47.9	NA	35.9	94.9	99.2	99.2	98.6	90.3	47.9	35.1	16.2	9.6	6.2	NA
1981	48.2	NA	35.6	93.9	99.3	99.3	98.1	90.4	48.5	32.6	16.2	8.5	6.1	NA
1980	48.9	NA	36.3	95.8	99.0	99.4	98.3	88.6	46.3	31.9	16.4	9.2	6.3	NA
1979	49.6	NA	33.9	95.8	99.2	99.2	98.2	89.0	44.5	31.1	15.7	9.7	6.3	NA
1978	50.3	NA	32.7	95.4	99.3	99.0	98.4	88.7	44.9	29.6	16.1	9.4	6.2	NA
1977	51.6	NA	31.1	95.6	99.5	99.4	98.5	88.5	45.5	31.8	16.3	10.6	6.6	NA
1976	52.3	NA	30.4	95.8	99.1	99.2	98.1	89.1	45.4	32.5	17.0	10.0	5.7	NA
1975	53.1	NA	30.9	94.8	99.4	99.3	98.3	89.3	46.5	31.8	16.8	10.0	6.6	NA
1974	53.0	NA	28.6	94.4	99.2	99.4	98.1	87.9	42.6	30.7	15.2	9.6	5.5	NA
1973	53.1	NA	23.2	93.0	99.1	99.3	97.6	88.3	43.4	31.3	14.6	8.7	4.5	NA
1972	54.4	NA	23.8	92.2	99.1	99.3	97.6	88.9	46.6	32.6	15.0	8.7	4.5	NA
1971	55.8	NA	20.9	91.9	99.1	99.2	98.7	90.5	49.4	32.7	15.9	8.1	4.8	NA
1970	56.2	NA	19.9	90.3	99.3	99.1	98.2	90.6	48.7	33.1	15.7	7.7	4.2	NA
1969	56.8	NA	15.1	89.2	99.4	99.2	98.2	90.2	50.9	35.4	16.2	8.2	5.0	NA
1968	56.6	NA	15.0	88.5	99.1	99.1	98.1	90.8	50.9	32.8	14.5	7.4	3.9	NA
1967	56.5	NA	13.3	88.2	99.5	99.2	98.5	89.5	48.4	34.7	14.1	6.7	4.1	NA
1966	56.1	NA	12.3	85.7	99.3	99.3	98.8	89.0	48.2	32.2	14.0	6.9	2.7	NA
1965	55.5	NA	10.3	85.3	99.4	99.4	99.0	87.8	47.1	29.4	14.1	6.5	3.2	NA
1964	54.4	NA	9.3	84.0	99.0	99.0	98.8	88.3	42.3	27.8	10.6	5.4	2.6	NA
1963	58.4	NA	NA	83.7	99.5	99.3	98.5	87.8	41.0	26.2	12.2	5.2	2.6	NA
1962	57.9	NA	NA	83.2	99.3	99.4	98.2	85.9	43.0	24.1	10.9	5.2	2.7	NA
1961	56.9	NA	NA	82.2	99.6	99.5	98.0	84.5	39.0	22.4	9.0	4.6	2.1	NA
1960	56.4	NA	NA	82.0	99.7	99.5	98.1	83.3	38.9	20.6	9.3	5.2	2.6	NA
1959	55.5	NA	NA	81.0	99.5	99.5	97.9	83.8	37.3	19.9	8.9	5.4	2.3	NA
1958	54.9	NA	NA	81.4	-----99.6-----		-------90.0------		38.1	------14.1------		5.9	2.3	NA
1957	53.7	NA	NA	79.3	-----99.7-----		-------90.1------		34.6	------14.7------		5.7	1.9	NA
1956	52.5	NA	NA	78.4	-----99.4-----		-------89.2------		35.9	------13.4------		5.4	2.1	NA
1955	50.8	NA	NA	79.2	-----99.3-----		-------87.5------		32.1	------11.6------		4.2	1.6	NA
1954	50.2	NA	NA	78.6	-----99.6-----		-------88.3------		33.6	------12.0------		4.0	1.5	NA
1953	46.6	NA	NA	67.1	-----99.7-----		-------86.4------		31.7	------11.9------		3.1	1.8	NA
1952	45.4	NA	NA	54.8	-----99.1-----		-------86.1------		28.9	-------9.8------		2.7	1.2	NA
1951	52.8	NA	NA	54.5	-----99.3-----		-------86.3------		26.9	-------8.8------		2.8	NA	NA
1950	51.6	NA	NA	----------89.0--------			-------84.4------		30.5	-------9.5------		3.0	NA	NA
1949	42.6	NA	NA	----------88.8----------			-------83.0------		25.9	-------9.6------		4.0	1.2	NA
1948	41.8	NA	NA	----------87.8----------			-------83.9------		27.3	------10.0------		2.8	0.9	NA
1947	41.2	NA	NA	----------88.7--------			-------80.2------		24.8	------10.5------		3.0	1.1	NA
Male														
2017	53.2	23.4	52.1	92.9	97.3	97.6	98.4	92.6	65.1	50.8	25.1	10.3	5.1	1.0
2016	54.0	23.9	55.6	93.8	97.9	98.2	98.8	92.2	67.9	51.2	25.8	10.9	4.9	1.0
2015	53.9	24.0	53.0	93.5	97.5	98.0	97.5	92.9	65.1	50.8	25.7	11.5	5.3	1.1
2014	53.9	24.2	52.3	93.7	97.2	96.8	97.3	92.5	64.8	50.4	26.8	11.6	5.0	1.2
2013	54.1	24.4	52.2	93.7	98.0	98.2	98.3	92.8	66.0	47.2	26.1	11.1	5.3	1.2
2012	54.9	24.9	52.9	93.1	98.0	98.0	98.3	95.8	66.0	48.5	28.3	11.6	5.5	1.2
2011	55.5	25.8	52.0	95.5	98.4	98.6	98.5	95.5	67.6	50.3	30.1	12.3	6.0	1.4
2010	54.9	25.5	51.8	93.2	97.3	97.6	98.0	95.0	67.5	48.2	25.9	13.0	6.5	1.5
2009	54.8	25.4	50.0	93.7	97.7	98.9	97.9	94.1	64.6	48.8	28.3	11.2	6.4	1.4
2008	54.8	25.5	51.8	93.8	97.9	98.7	99.0	94.9	64.3	48.4	26.5	11.5	5.5	1.3
2007	54.4	25.4	52.9	94.1	97.9	98.6	98.3	94.5	66.4	44.6	24.2	9.6	5.7	1.4
2006	54.6	25.5	55.9	94.8	98.3	98.4	98.2	94.7	62.7	43.8	24.0	10.2	5.5	1.3
2005	54.9	25.9	53.1	94.6	98.2	98.6	98.3	95.1	66.1	45.1	24.4	8.9	5.5	1.4
2004	54.8	26.0	53.4	95.8	97.9	98.2	98.8	94.5	60.0	46.0	23.3	11.2	5.5	1.4
2003[1]	54.8	26.2	56.2	95.0	97.6	98.2	97.2	95.3	61.7	43.2	25.6	9.9	5.6	1.4
2002	54.9	26.5	54.0	95.0	98.0	98.3	98.4	94.2	62.5	44.1	23.5	10.2	5.0	1.6
2001	54.3	26.2	51.8	94.7	98.6	98.4	98.0	92.8	58.2	43.6	21.5	9.8	5.0	1.4
2000	54.8	26.5	49.1	94.8	97.8	98.3	98.4	93.1	58.5	41.8	23.2	9.5	4.9	1.4
1999	55.5	27.1	53.5	95.4	98.5	98.6	98.2	93.1	60.0	44.5	23.7	10.3	5.4	1.5
1998	54.9	27.1	52.4	94.9	98.8	99.1	98.7	93.3	59.7	42.1	24.5	10.2	5.2	1.6
1997	54.7	27.3	50.4	97.4	98.5	99.4	99.1	94.2	60.0	45.0	24.9	10.8	4.3	1.5
1996	53.3	27.0	46.5	94.6	96.9	98.0	98.6	93.0	60.9	43.6	25.4	10.6	4.3	1.7
1995	53.5	27.3	49.6	95.5	99.0	99.0	98.8	94.2	59.4	46.3	22.7	11.3	5.0	1.7
1994	52.7	27.2	46.2	97.0	99.1	99.3	98.7	94.3	61.3	43.4	23.6	9.9	5.8	1.7
1993r	51.6	NA	41.2	95.1	99.5	99.5	98.9	95.0	60.1	44.4	24.5	9.1	5.2	NA

Note: Data shown for 1947 to 1966 for the Black population are for Black and other races. Data for 1947 to 1963 exclude kindergarten. Nursery school was first collected in 1964.

NA = Not available.

r = Revised, controlled to 1990 census based population estimates; previous 1993 data controlled to 1980 census based population estimates.

[1]Starting in 2003, respondents could identify more than one race. Except as noted, the race data in this table from 2003 onward represent those respondents who indicated only one race category.

Table A-11. Percentage of the Population 3 Years Old and Over Enrolled in School, by Age, Sex, Race, and Hispanic Origin, October 1947–2017—*Continued*

(Percent; civilian noninstitutionalized population.)

Year, sex, race, and Hispanic origin	Total enrolled 3 to 34 years old	Total enrolled 3 years old and over	3 and 4	5 and 6	7 to 9	10 to 13	14 and 15	16 and 17	18 and 19	20 and 21	22 to 24	25 to 29	30 to 34	35 and over
1993	51.6	26.4	41.7	95.2	99.5	99.5	99.0	95.1	60.6	44.8	24.9	9.1	5.2	1.5
1992	50.8	NA	39.8	95.1	99.5	99.5	99.0	99.5	60.7	44.0	23.6	8.6	5.2	NA
1991	50.4	NA	40.6	94.9	99.7	99.8	98.9	94.2	58.4	42.4	23.3	10.0	5.4	NA
1990	50.0	NA	44.9	96.7	99.7	99.6	99.2	92.3	57.3	41.2	21.8	9.4	4.9	NA
1989	48.9	NA	38.7	95.4	99.3	99.2	99.3	92.6	57.3	39.3	20.4	9.3	5.0	NA
1988	48.7	NA	39.0	96.1	99.7	99.6	98.9	91.6	56.5	40.9	20.7	7.8	5.4	NA
1987	48.8	NA	39.8	95.2	99.6	99.7	98.8	92.5	57.3	42.1	18.4	8.6	5.0	NA
1986	48.6	NA	39.3	95.6	99.4	99.0	99.1	92.1	57.5	34.2	19.2	9.6	5.7	NA
1985	48.5	NA	37.3	95.7	99.3	99.2	98.2	92.5	51.9	37.2	19.0	9.5	5.4	NA
1984	48.3	NA	35.8	94.1	98.7	99.3	97.6	91.5	52.6	36.3	20.2	9.2	5.4	NA
1983	48.9	NA	38.2	95.1	98.8	99.3	98.3	91.6	50.7	36.6	19.2	10.4	5.6	NA
1982	48.9	NA	36.3	94.8	99.2	99.1	98.8	91.0	48.5	36.5	18.0	10.2	5.4	NA
1981	49.2	NA	36.8	94.3	99.1	99.2	98.3	90.5	49.2	33.3	19.1	9.1	5.5	NA
1980	50.0	NA	38.0	95.2	98.8	99.4	98.7	88.8	47.5	33.7	18.2	9.6	5.6	NA
1979	50.7	NA	33.5	96.3	99.0	99.0	98.3	90.3	46.1	32.2	17.6	10.5	5.9	NA
1978	51.9	NA	33.1	95.3	99.2	98.9	98.3	88.9	47.2	32.0	19.2	10.9	6.4	NA
1977	53.3	NA	31.7	94.3	99.6	99.3	98.7	89.5	47.7	34.7	19.4	12.6	6.8	NA
1976	54.2	NA	29.9	95.8	98.8	99.1	98.5	90.6	46.9	34.2	20.4	12.9	6.5	NA
1975	55.4	NA	30.8	94.3	99.2	99.0	98.5	91.0	49.6	36.3	20.5	13.1	7.5	NA
1974	55.2	NA	27.7	94.8	99.1	99.2	98.2	88.2	45.5	35.0	19.2	12.8	6.4	NA
1973	55.6	NA	23.5	92.7	99.0	99.3	98.0	89.4	48.4	35.7	19.6	12.1	5.4	NA
1972	57.3	NA	23.4	91.7	98.9	99.2	97.7	90.4	51.5	38.4	21.6	12.5	5.8	NA
1971	59.0	NA	20.1	91.2	99.0	98.9	98.9	92.0	55.9	39.7	24.6	12.1	6.2	NA
1970	59.6	NA	20.7	89.7	99.3	98.8	98.3	92.2	56.0	45.0	22.6	11.2	5.4	NA
1969	60.5	NA	14.5	88.5	99.1	98.9	98.2	92.2	60.9	48.9	24.2	12.2	6.2	NA
1968	60.4	NA	14.8	87.9	99.0	99.0	98.2	92.1	61.5	47.8	21.9	11.4	5.0	NA
1967	60.0	NA	13.6	87.5	99.5	99.0	98.5	91.4	57.2	46.9	22.0	10.5	5.4	NA
1966	59.8	NA	12.2	85.0	99.2	99.1	98.8	90.3	59.0	44.9	23.0	10.3	3.8	NA
1965	59.0	NA	10.4	84.8	99.3	99.3	99.1	88.6	56.6	39.9	23.3	10.0	4.5	NA
1964	57.6	NA	8.8	84.0	98.8	98.9	99.0	90.4	52.4	36.6	17.7	8.3	3.6	NA
1963	62.3	NA	NA	84.1	99.4	99.0	98.8	89.8	51.6	35.2	21.1	8.2	3.8	NA
1962	61.9	NA	NA	83.9	99.1	99.3	98.7	88.5	52.7	33.7	18.8	8.9	4.2	NA
1961	60.4	NA	NA	82.6	99.7	99.4	98.3	85.5	49.6	31.1	15.0	7.5	3.1	NA
1960	60.3	NA	NA	82.3	99.7	99.5	98.1	85.2	49.5	29.2	16.3	8.9	4.0	NA
1959	59.2	NA	NA	80.1	99.3	99.4	98.1	85.9	47.1	30.8	14.1	9.5	3.4	NA
1958	58.8	NA	NA	81.5	------99.6------		-------91.1------		48.1	------22.3------		9.9	3.0	NA
1957	57.7	NA	NA	79.1	------99.7------		-------91.9------		44.0	------22.9------		9.9	2.7	NA
1956	56.5	NA	NA	78.2	------99.4------		-------90.1------		46.4	------21.8------		9.3	2.9	NA
1955	54.9	NA	NA	79.0	------99.4------		-------89.1------		43.9	------19.3------		7.1	2.2	NA
1954	54.3	NA	NA	78.0	------99.4------		-------89.6------		43.3	------20.5------		6.5	1.9	NA
1953	50.5	NA	NA	56.8	------99.4------		-------87.9------		38.1	------20.3------		5.7	2.2	NA
1952	49.4	NA	NA	55.2	------99.1------		-------87.0------		38.3	------17.8------		5.0	1.6	NA
1951	56.8	NA	NA	55.4	------99.3------		-------86.6------		33.8	------14.9------		4.2	NA	NA
1950	54.7	NA	NA	----------88.6----------			-------85.0------		37.3	------14.6------		5.9	NA	NA
1949	45.9	NA	NA	----------89.1----------			-------84.1------		32.1	------15.7------		7.1	2.0	NA
1948	45.3	NA	NA	----------87.6----------			-------84.4------		35.9	------17.2------		5.3	1.5	NA
1947	44.4	NA	NA	----------88.6----------			-------79.6------		32.6	------17.4------		5.9	1.8	NA
Female														
2017	54.6	23.0	54.8	94.2	96.6	97.5	98.4	93.7	70.7	58.6	28.7	12.8	6.2	1.6
2016	55.3	23.4	51.7	93.7	98.0	98.7	97.9	92.7	71.0	61.3	29.3	14.6	7.0	1.5
2015	55.2	23.5	51.4	94.9	97.4	97.5	98.0	94.8	72.2	56.9	29.8	14.1	6.8	1.7
2014	55.4	23.8	55.0	93.6	97.9	98.3	98.1	94.5	72.0	56.1	30.3	13.2	6.9	1.8
2013	55.9	24.3	55.8	94.0	98.1	98.2	98.5	94.5	69.2	57.5	31.6	13.3	7.5	2.0
2012	56.7	24.7	55.1	93.6	98.3	97.4	98.4	96.1	71.6	60.1	30.7	15.2	7.5	2.0
2011	56.9	25.2	50.8	96.0	97.9	98.5	98.8	95.6	73.2	57.5	31.7	15.8	7.9	2.0
2010	56.8	25.3	52.5	95.1	98.0	98.5	98.1	97.4	72.5	55.5	30.2	14.9	9.0	2.2
2009	56.7	25.2	52.2	94.3	98.1	98.4	98.4	94.8	73.0	56.6	29.5	14.7	8.3	2.4
2008	56.3	25.1	52.3	94.2	98.6	99.1	98.5	95.9	69.9	54.3	29.8	13.1	6.9	2.3
2007	56.7	25.2	55.4	95.6	98.1	98.8	99.2	94.7	67.8	55.7	28.5	13.6	7.6	2.2
2006	56.3	25.1	55.3	95.2	98.5	98.5	98.7	95.3	67.2	52.6	27.1	12.4	8.0	2.1
2005	57.0	25.6	55.4	96.0	98.9	98.8	98.4	95.7	70.1	53.8	27.7	13.8	7.0	2.2
2004	56.2	25.4	52.0	95.2	98.4	98.5	98.2	93.9	69.8	52.6	27.4	13.3	7.2	2.2
2003[1]	55.9	25.4	54.3	94.4	98.4	98.6	97.4	94.8	67.3	53.1	27.8	12.1	6.8	2.1

Note: Data shown for 1947 to 1966 for the Black population are for Black and other races. Data for 1947 to 1963 exclude kindergarten. Nursery school was first collected in 1964.

NA = Not available.

[1] Starting in 2003, respondents could identify more than one race. Except as noted, the race data in this table from 2003 onward represent those respondents who indicated only one race category.

Table A-11. Percentage of the Population 3 Years Old and Over Enrolled in School, by Age, Sex, Race, and Hispanic Origin, October 1947–2017—*Continued*

(Percent; civilian noninstitutionalized population.)

Year, sex, race, and Hispanic origin	Total enrolled 3 to 34 years old	Total enrolled 3 years old and over	3 and 4	5 and 6	7 to 9	10 to 13	14 and 15	16 and 17	18 and 19	20 and 21	22 to 24	25 to 29	30 to 34	35 and over
2002	55.8	25.6	53.7	95.1	98.0	98.7	98.5	95.0	65.1	50.8	25.7	12.7	6.9	2.3
2001	55.3	25.4	51.5	94.9	97.9	98.9	98.4	94.3	62.7	48.2	25.1	11.7	7.0	2.2
2000	55.4	25.7	51.4	95.8	98.5	98.4	98.3	92.5	64.2	48.2	24.2	11.3	7.1	2.2
1999	55.0	25.8	53.9	95.8	98.7	98.9	98.3	93.8	60.9	46.8	24.5	10.7	6.3	2.3
1998	55.0	26.0	49.0	96.0	98.8	99.2	98.5	94.9	64.2	47.9	23.8	11.9	7.2	2.4
1997	54.9	26.3	51.3	96.2	99.1	99.2	98.6	94.8	63.1	47.9	26.7	11.8	6.4	2.8
1996	53.5	25.9	49.3	95.0	97.4	98.3	97.3	92.7	64.1	46.1	23.6	12.0	7.1	2.6
1995	52.9	25.8	49.6	96.9	98.8	99.1	98.8	93.3	59.2	46.0	23.6	11.7	6.0	2.6
1994	52.6	26.0	47.9	96.1	99.4	99.4	98.8	94.4	60.5	49.0	23.5	11.0	7.4	2.7
1993r	50.7	NA	39.5	95.7	99.5	99.5	98.9	92.8	62.8	43.0	21.7	10.4	6.5	NA
1993	50.6	24.9	39.9	95.8	99.5	99.5	98.9	93.0	62.9	43.3	21.8	10.4	6.5	2.6
1992	50.5	NA	40.4	95.7	99.2	99.1	99.4	92.8	62.7	46.6	22.9	10.6	6.7	NA
1991	49.5	NA	42.0	95.7	99.5	99.6	98.5	92.5	60.9	43.9	20.2	9.7	6.7	NA
1990	49.0	NA	44.8	96.4	99.7	99.7	98.9	92.8	57.0	40.9	18.7	10.4	6.9	NA
1989	47.8	NA	40.2	94.9	99.2	99.6	98.1	92.1	55.6	39.7	19.6	9.6	6.3	NA
1988	47.2	NA	38.8	96.1	99.6	99.8	98.8	91.1	55.1	39.6	16.5	8.6	6.3	NA
1987	46.7	NA	36.4	94.4	99.5	99.2	98.3	91.0	53.3	37.3	16.2	8.7	6.4	NA
1986	46.8	NA	39.0	94.9	99.1	99.3	98.8	92.2	53.0	33.7	16.2	8.7	6.7	NA
1985	47.0	NA	39.9	97.1	99.3	99.3	97.9	90.8	52.9	35.0	15.0	9.0	6.4	NA
1984	46.3	NA	36.1	95.2	99.3	99.4	98.0	91.0	49.6	32.3	14.2	8.9	6.9	NA
1983	46.6	NA	36.0	96.5	99.0	99.4	98.4	91.2	51.1	30.5	13.6	8.5	6.7	NA
1982	46.9	NA	35.5	95.0	99.2	99.4	98.4	89.6	47.4	33.7	14.5	9.0	6.9	NA
1981	47.1	NA	34.3	93.5	99.5	99.4	97.8	90.4	47.8	31.9	13.4	7.9	6.7	NA
1980	47.9	NA	34.6	96.4	99.2	99.4	97.8	88.4	45.1	30.2	14.8	8.9	7.0	NA
1979	48.4	NA	34.4	95.3	99.5	99.5	98.1	87.7	43.0	30.0	13.9	9.0	6.7	NA
1978	48.7	NA	32.2	95.6	99.5	99.2	98.5	88.4	42.7	27.4	13.0	7.9	6.0	NA
1977	49.9	NA	30.5	96.9	99.5	99.6	98.4	87.4	43.4	29.0	13.3	8.8	6.3	NA
1976	50.4	NA	31.0	95.8	99.5	99.3	97.6	87.7	44.0	30.9	13.7	7.1	4.8	NA
1975	50.9	NA	30.9	95.3	99.5	99.6	98.1	87.5	43.5	27.5	12.2	7.0	5.7	NA
1974	50.9	NA	29.5	94.0	99.3	99.7	97.9	87.6	39.9	26.6	11.4	6.5	4.6	NA
1973	50.5	NA	22.9	93.2	99.3	99.3	97.1	87.3	38.7	27.4	9.9	5.4	3.6	NA
1972	51.5	NA	24.4	92.7	99.2	99.4	97.5	87.3	41.9	27.5	8.9	5.1	3.2	NA
1971	52.6	NA	21.7	92.6	99.3	99.5	98.4	88.9	43.2	27.0	8.1	4.3	3.5	NA
1970	52.9	NA	19.1	90.9	99.3	99.5	98.1	89.0	41.8	24.1	9.7	4.4	3.1	NA
1969	53.2	NA	15.8	89.8	99.6	99.5	98.2	88.2	41.8	25.8	9.4	4.5	3.7	NA
1968	52.9	NA	15.2	89.0	99.3	99.3	98.0	89.4	41.3	22.3	8.2	3.7	2.8	NA
1967	53.0	NA	13.1	89.0	99.6	99.4	98.5	87.4	41.0	25.6	7.5	3.3	2.9	NA
1966	52.5	NA	12.4	86.4	99.5	99.5	98.7	87.6	38.6	22.3	6.6	3.9	1.7	NA
1965	52.2	NA	10.3	85.7	99.4	99.5	98.9	87.0	38.3	20.9	6.3	3.2	2.0	NA
1964	51.3	NA	9.9	83.9	99.2	99.1	98.6	86.1	33.7	20.3	4.5	2.6	1.6	NA
1963	54.7	NA	NA	83.8	99.7	99.5	98.2	85.7	32.1	18.6	4.4	2.4	1.5	NA
1962	54.0	NA	NA	82.4	99.5	99.5	97.6	83.3	34.6	16.3	4.1	1.8	1.4	NA
1961	53.4	NA	NA	81.7	99.5	99.5	97.7	83.5	29.7	15.3	3.8	2.1	1.3	NA
1960	52.7	NA	NA	81.6	99.7	99.6	98.1	81.4	29.7	13.5	3.5	1.8	1.2	NA
1959	52.0	NA	NA	81.9	99.7	99.6	97.7	81.6	28.8	11.1	4.6	1.7	1.3	NA
1958	51.1	NA	NA	81.2	99.6		88.9		29.9	7.5		2.2	1.6	NA
1957	49.8	NA	NA	79.5	99.7		88.2		27.0	8.3		1.7	1.1	NA
1956	48.6	NA	NA	78.6	99.5		88.2		27.3	7.0		1.8	1.3	NA
1955	46.9	NA	NA	79.5	99.3		85.9		22.4	6.2		1.5	1.0	NA
1954	46.4	NA	NA	79.1	99.8		87.0		25.3	6.4		1.7	1.1	NA
1953	42.9	NA	NA	57.4	99.9		84.9		26.5	6.5		0.6	1.5	NA
1952	41.7	NA	NA	54.3	99.1		85.3		21.1	4.3		0.6	0.7	NA
1951	49.0	NA	NA	53.6	99.4		86.0		21.7	4.3		0.9	NA	NA
1950	48.6	NA	NA	89.4			83.7		24.2	4.8		0.4	NA	NA
1949	39.4	NA	NA	88.6			81.9		20.5	3.8		1.2	0.4	NA
1948	38.4	NA	NA	87.9			83.4		19.7	3.5		0.4	0.4	NA
1947	38.1	NA	NA	88.9			80.8		18.3	4.1		0.4	0.4	NA
WHITE ALONE NON-HISPANIC														
Both Sexes														
2017	53.2	21.0	56.0	93.0	97.0	97.8	98.5	93.3	67.8	58.1	27.2	11.3	5.8	1.2
2016	54.1	21.5	55.5	93.9	98.0	98.5	98.7	92.2	70.4	57.3	27.7	13.3	6.6	1.2
2015	54.4	21.8	56.0	94.1	97.5	98.1	98.3	94.4	70.1	55.5	28.9	13.1	6.5	1.3
2014	54.4	21.9	57.6	93.4	97.3	97.5	97.8	93.4	69.3	56.1	29.9	12.9	6.3	1.4

Note: Data shown for 1947 to 1966 for the Black population are for Black and other races. Data for 1947 to 1963 exclude kindergarten. Nursery school was first collected in 1964.
NA = Not available.
r = Revised, controlled to 1990 census based population estimates; previous 1993 data controlled to 1980 census based population estimates.

Table A-11. Percentage of the Population 3 Years Old and Over Enrolled in School, by Age, Sex, Race, and Hispanic Origin, October 1947–2017—*Continued*

(Percent; civilian noninstitutionalized population.)

Year, sex, race, and Hispanic origin	Total enrolled 3 to 34 years old	Total enrolled 3 years old and over	Age											
			3 and 4	5 and 6	7 to 9	10 to 13	14 and 15	16 and 17	18 and 19	20 and 21	22 to 24	25 to 29	30 to 34	35 and over
2013	54.7	22.3	57.4	93.6	97.9	98.5	98.4	93.6	69.6	55.2	29.1	12.9	6.5	1.6
2012	55.6	22.7	56.5	93.8	98.1	97.5	98.2	96.4	68.8	55.9	30.2	14.6	6.6	1.6
2011	56.4	23.6	56.2	95.8	98.2	98.5	98.9	95.9	72.1	56.2	32.9	15.2	7.8	1.7
2010	56.1	23.6	56.1	94.2	97.4	98.3	98.0	96.2	71.0	55.5	29.1	14.6	8.5	1.8
2009	56.8	23.9	55.5	94.1	98.4	98.9	98.3	95.0	72.4	56.4	31.1	14.0	8.1	1.9
2008	56.7	23.9	56.0	94.9	98.8	98.9	98.8	95.9	70.0	55.8	30.3	13.3	6.9	1.8
2007	56.6	23.9	56.3	95.0	98.6	98.6	98.8	95.6	69.7	54.5	28.4	12.5	7.4	1.8
2006	56.8	24.0	58.2	95.6	98.5	98.6	98.4	95.9	67.9	52.9	27.4	12.5	7.4	1.7
2005	57.6	24.6	58.5	95.9	99.0	99.0	98.6	96.1	71.6	54.4	27.8	12.5	6.9	1.8
2004	56.9	24.5	56.0	96.2	98.3	98.6	98.5	95.1	68.1	54.0	27.0	13.5	6.7	1.8
2003[1]	57.0	24.7	58.8	95.8	98.2	98.5	97.5	95.6	67.9	51.8	29.4	12.5	6.8	1.8
2002	56.8	24.9	57.8	95.3	98.1	98.6	98.6	95.3	67.1	53.1	27.3	12.2	6.3	1.9
2001	56.2	24.7	55.1	95.3	98.5	98.8	98.2	94.6	64.2	50.8	25.5	11.7	6.4	1.8
2000	56.0	25.0	54.6	95.5	98.4	98.5	98.9	94.0	63.9	49.2	24.9	11.1	6.1	1.8
1999	56.2	25.4	58.6	96.0	98.5	98.9	98.4	94.5	64.1	50.0	26.3	10.9	5.9	1.9
1998	55.9	25.6	54.0	96.1	98.8	99.2	98.9	95.1	66.6	49.2	26.1	11.5	6.3	2.0
1997	55.6	25.9	54.9	96.9	98.9	99.2	98.9	95.1	64.1	49.9	27.8	12.2	5.6	2.2
1996	54.0	25.5	50.3	96.1	97.3	98.3	98.2	93.6	65.5	48.9	25.9	11.8	5.8	2.2
1995	53.8	25.9	52.3	96.6	99.0	99.0	98.8	94.4	61.8	49.7	24.4	12.3	5.7	2.1
1994	54.5	25.9	50.1	96.7	99.2	99.3	99.2	95.1	62.6	50.1	24.9	10.8	6.7	2.2
1993	51.4	25.0	43.1	95.7	99.5	99.5	99.1	95.0	63.6	46.1	24.9	10.2	6.0	2.1
Male														
2017	52.8	21.3	54.3	92.5	97.2	97.9	98.6	92.8	65.4	54.6	25.9	10.5	5.0	0.9
2016	53.8	21.9	56.6	94.2	98.0	98.3	98.8	91.9	69.4	52.8	26.8	11.7	5.5	1.0
2015	54.1	22.1	57.1	93.2	97.8	98.3	98.3	93.8	67.2	53.3	26.9	12.3	5.9	1.0
2014	54.1	22.3	56.5	93.7	96.9	96.8	97.1	92.7	66.0	55.3	28.3	12.1	5.8	1.1
2013	54.1	22.4	55.2	93.7	97.8	98.4	98.4	92.8	68.6	51.0	26.2	11.4	5.6	1.1
2012	55.0	22.9	55.6	93.6	97.7	97.7	97.9	96.0	65.4	49.7	29.6	13.0	6.1	1.2
2011	56.1	23.9	56.4	95.5	98.3	98.5	98.4	95.8	69.9	53.0	33.1	13.2	7.0	1.3
2010	55.5	23.9	55.9	93.3	97.1	97.7	98.0	94.7	67.8	52.1	27.8	13.8	7.2	1.4
2009	56.2	24.2	54.9	93.3	98.2	99.0	97.9	94.7	68.4	53.2	30.8	12.4	7.1	1.4
2008	56.5	24.3	57.2	94.7	98.5	98.7	99.1	95.5	66.8	52.4	29.1	12.6	6.2	1.3
2007	56.0	24.2	53.8	94.0	98.5	98.5	98.3	95.2	69.3	49.9	26.9	10.6	6.7	1.3
2006	56.4	24.4	58.3	95.9	98.5	98.6	97.9	95.5	65.4	49.2	26.2	11.9	6.3	1.3
2005	57.1	24.9	56.8	95.4	98.9	99.1	98.4	95.9	69.8	50.5	26.4	10.2	6.5	1.3
2004	56.7	25.0	57.2	96.2	98.2	98.4	98.7	95.6	63.8	50.6	25.1	12.7	6.2	1.4
2003[1]	57.1	25.4	60.6	96.2	97.7	98.2	97.4	96.1	65.4	47.9	28.9	11.7	6.3	1.4
2002	56.8	25.5	57.8	94.9	98.1	98.5	98.5	95.2	66.3	49.2	27.6	11.1	5.5	1.6
2001	56.0	25.2	54.4	94.8	98.8	98.4	97.8	94.0	62.7	49.1	23.7	10.8	5.3	1.3
2000	55.8	25.5	54.1	94.5	98.1	98.2	98.8	94.7	61.2	45.8	25.0	10.5	4.7	1.4
1999	56.7	26.2	59.2	96.1	98.4	98.7	98.2	94.3	63.7	48.9	26.8	10.7	5.8	1.5
1998	55.7	26.3	54.8	95.5	98.8	99.0	99.0	94.4	65.2	46.4	27.4	10.9	5.3	1.6
1997	55.9	26.5	54.9	97.4	98.8	99.3	99.0	94.5	63.3	48.5	27.5	12.0	4.6	1.5
1996	54.2	26.1	48.0	95.5	97.2	98.1	98.8	93.5	63.7	48.7	27.3	11.4	4.3	1.6
1995	54.2	26.6	51.1	95.9	99.0	99.0	98.9	95.0	61.9	50.0	24.1	12.2	5.0	1.6
1994	53.5	26.6	49.0	97.1	99.2	99.4	99.4	95.4	62.5	47.6	25.5	10.3	6.0	1.6
1993	52.2	25.9	44.1	95.4	99.5	99.6	99.3	96.2	62.5	47.0	26.7	9.9	5.2	1.5
Female														
2017	53.6	20.7	57.8	93.5	96.8	97.6	98.4	93.8	70.3	61.8	28.4	12.1	6.6	1.5
2016	54.4	21.1	54.3	93.5	97.9	98.8	98.6	92.5	71.6	62.0	28.5	14.9	7.8	1.4
2015	54.6	21.4	54.8	95.1	97.2	97.9	98.4	95.0	73.1	57.7	30.9	14.0	7.1	1.6
2014	54.7	21.6	58.8	93.1	97.7	98.1	98.5	94.1	72.9	57.0	31.4	13.6	6.9	1.7
2013	55.4	22.1	59.7	93.5	98.0	98.5	98.4	94.5	70.8	59.6	31.9	14.3	7.4	2.0
2012	56.2	22.5	57.4	94.0	98.5	97.3	98.4	96.8	72.3	61.7	30.8	16.2	7.1	2.0
2011	56.8	23.3	56.1	96.1	98.1	98.5	99.3	95.9	74.3	59.5	32.7	17.3	8.5	2.0
2010	56.7	23.4	56.3	95.2	97.7	98.9	98.1	97.8	74.3	59.2	30.4	15.4	9.8	2.2
2009	57.4	23.7	56.2	95.0	98.7	98.7	98.7	95.4	76.5	59.8	31.4	15.6	9.0	2.4
2008	57.0	23.5	54.8	95.0	99.1	99.2	98.4	96.3	73.4	59.5	31.5	14.0	7.6	2.2
2007	57.3	23.7	58.9	96.0	98.8	98.7	99.2	96.0	70.1	59.2	29.9	14.4	8.0	2.2
2006	57.1	23.7	58.1	95.3	98.6	98.5	99.0	96.2	70.5	56.5	28.7	13.2	8.5	2.1
2005	58.0	24.3	60.3	96.3	99.0	98.8	98.7	96.3	73.5	58.5	29.1	14.7	7.4	2.2
2004	57.1	24.1	54.7	96.2	98.5	98.7	98.3	94.5	72.5	57.4	28.8	14.4	7.2	2.1
2003[1]	57.0	24.1	56.9	95.3	98.6	98.8	97.6	95.1	70.3	55.6	29.9	13.2	7.3	2.1

Note: Data shown for 1947 to 1966 for the Black population are for Black and other races. Data for 1947 to 1963 exclude kindergarten. Nursery school was first collected in 1964.

[1] Starting in 2003, respondents could identify more than one race. Except as noted, the race data in this table from 2003 onward represent those respondents who indicated only one race category.

Table A-11. Percentage of the Population 3 Years Old and Over Enrolled in School, by Age, Sex, Race, and Hispanic Origin, October 1947–2017—*Continued*

(Percent; civilian noninstitutionalized population.)

Year, sex, race, and Hispanic origin	Total enrolled 3 to 34 years old	Total enrolled 3 years old and over	3 and 4	5 and 6	7 to 9	10 to 13	14 and 15	16 and 17	18 and 19	20 and 21	22 to 24	25 to 29	30 to 34	35 and over
2002	56.8	24.3	57.7	95.6	98.0	98.6	98.6	95.5	67.9	57.0	27.0	13.4	7.2	2.2
2001	56.4	24.2	55.9	95.9	98.3	99.1	98.6	95.3	65.8	52.4	27.3	12.5	7.4	2.2
2000	56.1	24.6	55.2	96.4	98.6	98.8	99.0	93.3	66.7	52.7	24.8	11.8	7.4	2.1
1999	55.7	24.7	57.9	96.0	98.5	99.1	98.6	94.8	64.6	51.1	25.7	11.0	6.1	2.3
1998	55.7	25.0	53.1	96.7	98.7	99.3	98.8	95.7	68.0	52.2	24.8	12.1	7.3	2.4
1997	55.2	25.4	55.0	96.4	99.0	99.1	98.8	95.7	64.9	51.3	28.1	12.4	6.6	2.9
1996	53.8	25.0	52.9	96.7	97.3	98.6	97.7	93.7	67.3	49.0	24.5	12.1	7.3	2.6
1995	53.4	25.1	53.5	97.4	98.9	99.0	98.7	93.8	61.8	49.3	24.8	12.3	6.3	2.5
1994	52.9	25.3	51.3	96.3	99.3	99.3	98.9	94.8	62.7	52.4	24.3	11.4	7.3	2.7
1993	50.6	24.3	42.0	96.0	99.5	99.5	98.9	93.7	64.8	45.2	23.1	10.5	6.7	2.6

BLACK ALONE

Both Sexes

Year, sex, race, and Hispanic origin	Total enrolled 3 to 34 years old	Total enrolled 3 years old and over	3 and 4	5 and 6	7 to 9	10 to 13	14 and 15	16 and 17	18 and 19	20 and 21	22 to 24	25 to 29	30 to 34	35 and over
2017	55.1	28.7	57.7	91.5	96.8	98.9	96.6	90.7	67.0	47.5	27.5	13.5	7.7	2.7
2016	55.4	29.2	50.8	93.5	97.4	98.6	96.1	94.9	67.2	48.2	28.0	12.7	8.7	2.9
2015	55.3	29.2	52.7	93.7	95.4	98.3	98.7	94.4	64.5	43.7	27.5	13.1	8.2	2.8
2014	56.0	30.2	57.5	94.5	98.8	97.7	98.9	91.8	65.2	41.1	24.5	14.6	9.1	3.8
2013	57.2	30.7	57.2	94.4	96.7	97.8	98.7	92.8	64.2	47.9	27.0	16.7	8.6	3.1
2012	58.3	31.4	53.1	91.5	97.2	98.9	97.3	94.2	68.6	49.4	27.9	16.1	12.2	3.2
2011	58.4	32.3	55.2	92.0	97.1	98.5	98.5	95.7	74.1	41.1	31.2	18.1	11.4	3.8
2010	58.4	32.5	56.2	94.3	97.1	98.6	98.5	95.5	62.7	50.2	29.0	16.0	10.9	4.0
2009	58.5	32.4	57.7	93.6	97.4	98.6	97.8	94.1	65.2	44.7	31.9	14.6	11.0	3.7
2008	57.8	31.7	54.6	93.1	98.9	99.0	97.9	94.2	59.2	40.3	24.9	14.7	11.5	2.8
2007	58.4	32.2	58.5	94.0	98.2	97.9	99.0	93.4	61.7	38.7	28.0	15.0	9.4	3.0
2006	58.1	32.3	59.2	92.6	97.1	97.2	97.5	93.3	64.7	39.1	27.2	11.8	8.6	3.1
2005	58.4	32.7	52.2	95.9	98.6	98.6	95.8	93.1	62.8	37.6	28.0	11.7	10.0	3.1
2004	59.0	33.4	59.6	94.1	97.5	99.4	99.0	95.7	59.2	40.0	25.1	14.3	7.2	3.3
2003[1]	59.2	33.4	55.5	94.4	98.3	98.2	97.9	94.3	61.9	41.4	27.4	12.2	8.6	2.8
2002	59.6	34.1	57.5	95.7	98.1	98.1	98.2	93.3	57.7	43.5	23.5	13.6	9.8	3.1
2001	59.5	34.3	58.8	96.0	97.8	97.0	97.6	92.1	59.6	37.2	26.0	12.2	11.5	3.2
2000	59.0	34.0	59.9	96.3	97.5	98.4	99.6	91.4	57.2	36.6	24.2	14.3	9.6	2.6
1999	58.1	33.7	56.3	97.5	98.2	98.7	98.2	93.3	57.4	39.4	21.7	10.4	7.8	2.5
1998	58.9	34.6	58.5	95.3	98.7	98.6	98.9	92.9	60.2	39.2	21.5	13.6	8.5	2.6
1997	58.4	34.6	60.0	95.8	99.2	99.4	99.2	93.4	58.2	35.9	25.4	10.7	6.5	2.8
1996	56.2	33.8	49.9	90.5	97.4	97.4	98.9	92.1	52.8	37.0	21.0	13.7	7.1	3.0
1995	56.1	33.9	47.5	95.5	97.7	99.2	99.0	92.9	57.4	37.4	19.9	10.0	7.8	2.7
1994	56.4	34.4	51.9	97.2	99.7	99.6	99.2	95.4	54.0	34.9	22.6	10.5	7.2	2.9
1993r	53.8	NA	39.8	94.5	99.0	99.8	98.5	94.8	57.6	30.1	18.0	10.4	5.5	NA
1993	53.6	32.4	39.8	94.6	99.0	99.8	98.5	94.7	57.7	30.0	18.1	10.4	5.5	2.6
1992	53.0	NA	38.6	95.9	99.4	99.7	99.4	93.0	56.2	33.3	20.3	7.9	5.3	NA
1991	52.5	NA	37.2	95.8	99.6	100.0	99.1	91.7	55.6	30.0	18.2	8.7	6.5	NA
1990	51.9	NA	41.6	96.3	99.9	99.9	99.2	91.7	55.2	28.4	20.0	6.1	4.4	NA
1989	51.3	NA	38.9	94.9	99.0	99.4	99.4	93.7	50.2	30.7	17.2	6.4	4.9	NA
1988	50.6	NA	33.4	95.5	99.7	99.7	98.9	91.5	50.3	28.1	13.2	7.2	5.6	NA
1987	51.7	NA	36.8	95.8	99.7	99.8	98.3	91.5	53.2	28.7	15.0	9.3	6.0	NA
1986	51.6	NA	38.6	95.4	99.8	99.0	98.3	93.9	50.7	25.6	17.1	8.0	6.2	NA
1985	50.9	NA	42.7	95.7	98.4	99.5	97.9	91.7	44.1	27.7	13.7	7.5	5.9	NA
1984	50.1	NA	38.2	94.1	99.5	99.3	97.9	92.4	44.3	27.7	15.7	7.4	5.1	NA
1983	50.8	NA	36.2	94.7	99.1	99.7	97.8	92.6	46.1	23.4	15.6	7.4	6.5	NA
1982	51.6	NA	38.6	95.4	99.2	98.9	98.1	91.6	43.6	24.3	17.0	7.8	7.6	NA
1981	52.5	NA	36.7	94.5	98.8	99.4	97.1	91.3	48.2	23.4	14.7	8.4	7.0	NA
1980	53.9	NA	38.2	95.4	99.4	99.4	97.9	90.6	45.7	23.4	13.6	8.8	6.8	NA
1979	55.0	NA	40.8	96.0	99.4	98.7	97.4	90.8	46.6	23.7	15.0	7.9	6.8	NA
1978	56.3	NA	41.3	93.9	99.5	98.9	98.5	91.2	46.2	25.6	15.0	8.7	7.9	NA
1977	57.7	NA	35.2	96.5	99.3	99.0	98.8	90.8	48.3	29.5	15.2	11.3	9.0	NA
1976	57.9	NA	34.5	94.0	99.3	98.8	99.0	89.0	50.4	28.2	16.4	9.4	8.1	NA
1975	57.7	NA	33.5	94.3	99.3	99.2	97.4	86.9	47.1	27.1	14.2	9.4	7.1	NA
1974	57.3	NA	29.1	92.8	99.2	99.8	97.0	87.1	44.0	23.4	12.1	8.9	6.9	NA
1973	55.8	NA	28.9	89.9	99.2	99.0	96.7	87.7	37.8	20.5	12.4	6.1	5.0	NA
1972	57.8	NA	28.3	90.0	98.7	99.3	97.4	89.5	42.8	22.0	13.1	6.5	5.9	NA
1971	58.6	NA	21.5	89.8	99.0	98.8	98.4	89.2	46.6	27.3	11.4	6.2	5.2	NA
1970	57.4	NA	22.7	84.9	99.3	99.3	97.6	85.7	40.1	22.8	8.0	4.8	3.4	NA
1969	57.8	NA	21.2	84.1	98.8	99.1	97.9	85.8	44.5	23.3	8.6	4.3	3.4	NA

Note: Data shown for 1947 to 1966 for the Black population are for Black and other races. Data for 1947 to 1963 exclude kindergarten. Nursery school was first collected in 1964.
NA = Not available.
r = Revised, controlled to 1990 census based population estimates; previous 1993 data controlled to 1980 census based population estimates.
[1]Starting in 2003, respondents could identify more than one race. Except as noted, the race data in this table from 2003 onward represent those respondents who indicated only one race category.

Table A-11. Percentage of the Population 3 Years Old and Over Enrolled in School, by Age, Sex, Race, and Hispanic Origin, October 1947–2017—*Continued*

(Percent; civilian noninstitutionalized population.)

Year, sex, race, and Hispanic origin	Total enrolled 3 to 34 years old	Total enrolled 3 years old and over	3 and 4	5 and 6	7 to 9	10 to 13	14 and 15	16 and 17	18 and 19	20 and 21	22 to 24	25 to 29	30 to 34	35 and over
1968	57.4	NA	18.7	82.7	99.2	99.0	97.7	86.4	45.4	18.2	7.9	3.1	3.3	NA
1967	56.8	NA	17.7	82.2	99.1	98.7	86.1	84.1	40.7	21.2	7.2	5.0	2.4	NA
1966	55.5	NA	13.7	80.8	99.2	99.2	97.4	85.2	37.7	11.6	6.1	2.3	2.3	NA
1965	55.6	NA	11.8	79.1	98.9	99.3	98.1	83.9	39.6	12.8	6.2	2.1	2.4	NA
1964	54.5	NA	10.5	80.3	99.0	99.0	96.9	82.4	35.6	14.0	3.8	3.1	2.9	NA
1963	58.8	NA	NA	76.6	98.5	99.5	97.6	82.0	39.8	16.2	5.5	3.3	2.0	NA
1962	57.1	NA	NA	76.0	98.6	98.8	97.1	73.2	33.4	14.9	6.1	3.8	1.5	NA
1961	56.8	NA	NA	79.1	98.0	98.3	95.1	76.8	30.6	15.9	4.3	2.4	1.1	NA
1960	55.9	NA	NA	73.3	99.3	99.0	95.9	76.9	34.6	11.9	4.4	2.9	1.0	NA
1959	55.1	NA	NA	74.3	98.9	99.1	93.9	76.3	33.6	11.6	6.3	2.8	1.3	NA
1958	54.0	NA	NA	73.9	------98.8------		------82.8------		34.3	-------8.7------		3.9	1.3	NA
1957	53.5	NA	NA	74.3	------98.2------		------84.8------		36.7	-------8.8------		4.6	1.2	NA
1956	51.5	NA	NA	72.8	------98.4------		------81.2------		31.8	-------8.7------		3.1	0.7	NA
1955	50.7	NA	NA	71.1	------98.2------		-----82.8-----		27.6	-------7.2------		4.9	1.8	NA
1954	48.6	NA	NA	68.8	------98.0------		-----78.8-----		24.0	-------5.8------		4.8	1.4	NA
1953	45.5	NA	NA	46.3	------97.3------		-----82.3-----		27.6	-----5.4------		1.7	0.8	NA
1952	46.4	NA	NA	54.0	------96.4------		-----77.3-----		------6.3--------					NA
1951	53.4	NA	NA	54.9	------97.3------		------77.1-----		20.8	-------6.2------		2.7	NA	NA
1950	51.2	NA	NA	--------------86.8----------			-----75.5-----		23.3	-------6.3------		3.0	NA	NA
1949	40.9	NA	NA	--------------83.7----------			-----69.5-----		20.0	-------6.2------		1.8	0.5	NA
1948	39.2	NA	NA	--------------80.1----------			-----66.8-----		24.6	-------6.3------		1.5	0.6	NA
1947	41.0	NA	NA	--------------84.8----------			-----71.9-----		20.2	-------6.9------		2.5	0.5	NA
Male														
2017	54.7	29.7	59.7	90.0	96.0	98.8	95.4	89.0	63.2	42.6	24.0	12.3	6.2	2.1
2016	56.0	30.5	46.6	91.2	96.1	98.6	98.9	95.7	66.6	46.2	26.8	12.9	7.4	2.3
2015	55.6	30.3	51.0	92.1	95.8	99.2	99.5	94.7	63.3	39.6	30.4	10.1	4.5	1.8
2014	56.2	31.2	58.0	96.1	98.6	97.3	98.7	92.6	60.3	41.8	22.2	11.6	7.0	2.7
2013	56.8	31.5	54.1	94.4	96.5	97.8	98.8	94.3	59.9	43.2	25.2	13.1	5.2	2.4
2012	58.1	31.9	51.1	92.1	97.0	98.9	98.5	95.5	60.5	48.8	26.8	11.5	7.3	1.9
2011	57.9	33.0	53.4	92.4	97.5	98.5	97.8	94.0	72.6	38.0	29.8	14.2	7.5	2.7
2010	57.9	33.1	55.5	93.7	97.5	98.4	97.7	93.5	60.8	44.5	28.5	13.2	6.5	2.7
2009	58.0	32.9	56.3	93.7	96.8	98.5	96.4	95.2	60.5	42.2	26.6	11.7	7.9	2.2
2008	58.0	32.7	53.3	95.5	98.5	98.5	98.9	94.0	57.9	37.8	23.2	10.6	8.5	1.5
2007	59.5	33.9	59.6	93.9	98.3	97.2	99.2	95.2	61.9	37.8	28.0	10.4	9.4	2.0
2006	58.7	33.7	56.6	93.5	97.2	96.8	97.7	91.8	63.9	38.0	24.2	9.3	6.9	2.5
2005	58.9	34.0	54.0	94.8	97.7	97.7	93.6	93.6	67.2	35.1	23.4	9.3	6.3	2.4
2004	59.2	34.6	61.1	94.7	96.7	99.2	98.8	96.5	58.1	37.8	20.2	8.7	4.0	2.2
2003[1]	60.0	34.9	56.5	92.4	98.8	98.1	98.3	94.0	61.5	34.3	23.5	9.7	7.4	1.9
2002	60.2	35.4	57.5	96.2	99.1	97.9	97.6	92.9	54.9	39.5	16.6	10.1	7.5	2.1
2001	60.1	35.7	55.4	95.6	98.3	96.0	99.0	93.2	57.3	36.2	22.7	8.2	8.3	2.3
2000	59.5	35.3	57.6	95.8	98.3	98.7	99.6	89.1	52.4	30.5	21.8	11.3	8.3	2.2
1999	59.9	35.8	53.0	98.4	97.7	99.0	97.9	94.4	60.3	42.3	16.1	9.0	6.5	2.0
1998	60.1	36.2	57.8	95.0	98.5	98.6	97.7	93.9	58.2	40.7	15.1	12.6	5.6	1.8
1997	59.5	36.2	57.3	94.2	98.7	99.1	99.6	93.9	56.7	34.1	21.5	10.5	5.6	2.0
1996	57.8	35.7	47.0	90.1	98.1	97.2	98.1	93.7	55.2	39.0	18.6	12.8	5.4	2.4
1995	58.3	36.2	51.5	94.7	98.2	99.5	99.6	95.2	59.1	36.1	20.3	6.1	6.7	2.3
1994	58.4	36.5	56.8	97.1	99.6	99.5	99.7	95.3	53.4	33.7	21.3	10.8	5.7	2.1
1993r	56.0	NA	41.6	96.8	99.3	100.0	99.0	96.1	63.4	23.7	19.6	10.4	3.1	NA
1993	55.8	34.8	41.7	96.9	99.3	100.0	99.0	96.0	63.6	23.9	19.6	10.3	3.1	2.0
1992	54.8	NA	41.3	97.6	99.9	99.7	99.9	94.5	60.7	27.1	18.7	7.6	3.3	NA
1991	54.5	NA	35.2	95.4	99.8	100.0	100.0	90.4	62.2	30.1	19.3	8.6	4.8	NA
1990	53.9	NA	38.3	96.1	99.9	99.9	99.7	93.2	60.7	31.1	20.0	4.6	2.3	NA
1989	52.6	NA	40.2	92.9	98.9	98.8	99.3	95.6	51.0	23.2	15.5	5.5	3.2	NA
1988	52.4	NA	34.5	96.0	99.6	100.0	99.1	93.2	49.7	20.7	14.7	6.3	4.1	NA
1987	54.0	NA	39.0	97.4	100.0	99.8	98.1	91.8	58.7	30.3	15.5	8.4	3.4	NA
1986	53.8	NA	38.7	97.1	99.6	98.8	98.4	94.7	54.1	25.4	17.3	7.1	5.9	NA
1985	52.6	NA	34.6	94.6	98.2	99.1	98.2	91.8	49.5	29.7	13.2	6.9	5.7	NA
1984	52.6	NA	37.2	92.8	99.5	99.1	96.9	93.2	48.6	29.7	17.5	5.7	3.9	NA
1983	52.9	NA	37.1	95.8	98.9	99.4	98.4	91.8	46.6	23.5	17.2	9.1	6.6	NA
1982	53.2	NA	37.4	93.9	99.3	98.4	97.8	92.2	46.5	20.9	17.4	8.5	7.1	NA
1981	54.5	NA	34.8	94.5	98.5	99.2	97.3	92.1	51.9	20.6	14.7	8.4	5.6	NA
1980	56.1	NA	36.6	94.1	99.5	99.4	98.5	90.8	42.8	23.0	13.3	10.6	7.3	NA
1979	57.8	NA	40.4	96.6	99.0	98.4	98.5	94.6	48.0	26.9	14.6	8.1	6.3	NA

Note: Data shown for 1947 to 1966 for the Black population are for Black and other races. Data for 1947 to 1963 exclude kindergarten. Nursery school was first collected in 1964.

NA = Not available.

r = Revised, controlled to 1990 census based population estimates; previous 1993 data controlled to 1980 census based population estimates.

[1]Starting in 2003, respondents could identify more than one race. Except as noted, the race data in this table from 2003 onward represent those respondents who indicated only one race category.

Table A-11. Percentage of the Population 3 Years Old and Over Enrolled in School, by Age, Sex, Race, and Hispanic Origin, October 1947–2017—*Continued*

(Percent; civilian noninstitutionalized population.)

Year, sex, race, and Hispanic origin	Total enrolled 3 to 34 years old	Total enrolled 3 years old and over	3 and 4	5 and 6	7 to 9	10 to 13	14 and 15	16 and 17	18 and 19	20 and 21	22 to 24	25 to 29	30 to 34	35 and over
1978	58.7	NA	37.9	93.2	99.4	98.8	99.0	92.8	50.5	25.2	14.7	9.5	7.8	NA
1977	60.3	NA	32.4	96.0	99.1	98.6	99.0	92.5	50.5	31.0	18.5	12.1	9.2	NA
1976	61.1	NA	36.3	94.4	99.5	98.8	99.5	90.9	54.9	28.0	18.7	11.0	8.8	NA
1975	60.3	NA	29.5	94.6	99.3	99.0	97.6	88.2	49.9	28.7	14.7	11.8	8.6	NA
1974	60.7	NA	30.3	91.8	99.5	99.6	96.1	90.1	46.1	27.7	16.0	10.4	9.7	NA
1973	58.6	NA	29.2	89.0	99.2	99.1	96.9	89.0	43.5	24.5	13.9	6.9	6.5	NA
1972	60.9	NA	32.1	90.8	98.4	99.4	97.6	88.9	47.7	27.1	18.4	7.3	5.2	NA
1971	60.4	NA	19.0	88.7	99.1	98.1	97.7	90.0	50.7	31.3	12.9	8.5	6.4	NA
1970	59.5	NA	22.3	84.2	99.2	99.1	98.0	85.4	41.3	27.8	9.6	6.1	3.6	NA
1969	60.0	NA	21.3	83.1	98.3	98.9	98.0	87.4	49.5	28.4	10.7	2.8	2.9	NA
1968	60.0	NA	16.9	84.1	98.8	98.4	98.5	88.5	53.1	23.4	7.5	5.2	3.4	NA
1967	59.2	NA	17.0	81.0	99.0	98.3	96.5	86.7	48.6	24.5	9.0	3.5	3.5	NA
1966	58.1	NA	12.7	80.0	99.1	99.0	98.2	87.4	46.3	14.4	9.1	2.6	2.7	NA
1965	57.7	NA	9.5	81.0	99.3	99.4	98.7	82.2	47.5	18.5	4.3	2.6	2.3	NA
1964	56.8	NA	9.4	80.7	98.2	98.7	98.8	84.3	39.9	14.2	3.8	3.5	4.0	NA
1963	61.9	NA	NA	74.3	97.7	99.2	98.2	85.9	46.5	21.7	7.1	4.7	2.7	NA
1962	60.4	NA	NA	74.5	98.9	98.6	99.1	77.1	40.3	15.0	10.1	5.8	1.7	NA
1961	60.0	NA	NA	78.7	98.4	97.6	96.6	78.6	41.7	19.9	6.1	4.0	1.9	NA
1960	58.3	NA	NA	71.8	99.4	98.7	97.0	79.1	36.9	13.7	6.3	3.9	1.0	NA
1959	58.0	NA	NA	76.0	98.7	99.1	95.8|	76.3	35.5	12.5|	10.6	4.5	1.8	NA
1958	58.0	NA	NA	74.2	------98.8-----		------87.6------		43.4	-------11.8-----		6.3	2.4	NA
1957	55.9	NA	NA	73.1	------98.2-----		------84.7------		38.5	-------10.3-----		6.0	1.2	NA
1956	54.3	NA	NA	70.4	------97.6-----		------81.3------		36.8	-------12.5-----		5.3	0.9	NA
1955	54.4	NA	NA	72.8	------98.2-----		------85.2------		32.9	-------9.8------		6.2	1.9	NA
1954	52.0	NA	NA	64.7	------97.5-----		------82.8------		21.6	-------10.1-----		7.9	1.9	NA
1953	47.8	NA	NA	41.6	------97.1-----		------79.1------		34.6|	-------5.8------		3.3|	0.9	NA
1952	49.7	NA	NA	51.4	------96.0-----		------72.5------		--------------------6.0--------------------					NA
1951	56.9	NA	NA	52.8	------98.0-----		------74.9------		23.6	-------9.0-------		4.3	NA	NA
1950	56.0	NA	NA	-----------87.0---------			------79.3------		19.9	-------11.1-----		6.1	NA	NA
1949	45.0	NA	NA	-----------83.1----------			------68.8------		26.1	-------11.8-----		3.3	1.1	NA
1948	40.4	NA	NA	-----------78.9----------			------63.9------		24.0	-------10.5-----		2.5	1.4	NA
1947	45.1	NA	NA	-----------84.6----------			------72.6------		20.7	-------12.3-----		5.1	0.8	NA
Female														
2017	55.4	27.9	55.4	93.1	97.7	98.9	97.8	92.5	70.7	52.5	30.7	14.7	8.9	3.1
2016	54.9	28.0	55.1	95.9	98.7	98.6	93.2	94.0	67.8	50.3	29.0	12.5	9.8	3.4
2015	55.0	28.3	54.6	95.3	94.9	97.4	97.8	94.1	65.6	47.7	24.8	15.7	11.2	3.6
2014	55.7	29.4	57.0	92.9	98.9	98.0	99.1	91.0	70.1	40.5	26.8	17.2	10.8	4.6
2013	57.6	30.0	60.2	94.4	96.8	97.8	98.6	91.3	68.3	52.1	28.7	19.8	11.5	3.6
2012	58.6	30.9	55.1	90.9	97.3	98.9	96.1	92.8	76.6	50.0	28.9	20.0	16.1	4.2
2011	58.9	31.7	57.1	91.5	96.8	98.6	99.3	97.3	75.6	44.6	32.2	21.7	14.7	4.8
2010	58.8	31.9	56.8	95.0	96.8	98.8	99.3	97.5	64.5	55.4	29.6	18.5	14.6	4.9
2009	58.9	31.9	59.0	93.6	98.0	98.8	99.3	92.9	69.7	47.3	36.2	17.2	13.5	4.8
2008	57.6	30.9	55.8	90.8	99.4	99.4	96.9	94.4	60.5	42.6	26.3	18.3	13.8	3.8
2007	57.4	30.8	57.3	94.2	98.1	98.6	98.8	91.7	61.6	39.5	27.9	18.9	9.4	3.8
2006	57.6	31.1	61.5	91.7	96.9	97.6	97.2	94.7	65.4	40.2	30.0	14.0	9.9	3.6
2005	57.9	31.5	50.6	97.1	99.5	99.5	98.0	92.5	58.5	40.1	31.8	13.8	13.0	3.6
2004	58.7	32.3	57.7	94.5	98.2	99.6	99.1	94.8	60.2	41.9	29.5	19.0	9.8	4.2
2003¹	58.4	32.1	54.5	96.4	97.7	98.3	97.5	94.6	62.2	47.4	30.8	14.2	9.6	3.5
2002	59.1	33.0	57.4	95.2	97.2	98.3	98.8	93.7	60.6	47.1	28.8	16.3	11.7	3.8
2001	58.9	33.1	62.1	96.5	97.2	98.1	96.2	91.0	62.0	37.9	29.0	15.3	14.0	3.9
2000	58.7	32.9	62.3	96.8	96.8	98.2	99.6	93.8	61.5	41.3	26.4	16.5	10.7	2.9
1999	56.5	32.0	59.1	96.5	98.7	98.6	98.5	92.1	54.7	36.9	25.9	11.5	8.9	2.9
1998	57.8	33.2	59.1	95.6	98.9	98.7	100.0	91.8	62.2	37.8	26.2	14.4	10.9	3.2
1997	57.4	33.3	62.9	97.2	99.8	99.7	98.9	92.9	59.6	37.3	28.7	10.8	7.2	3.5
1996	54.7	32.2	52.6	90.8	96.7	97.6	99.6	90.4	50.5	35.5	23.2	14.4	8.6	3.5
1995	54.1	31.9	43.6	96.3	97.2	99.0	98.3	90.4	55.9	38.5	19.5	13.0	8.7	3.0
1994	54.4	32.5	47.0	97.2	99.7	99.7	98.6	95.5	54.6	35.9	23.6	10.3	8.5	3.4
1993r	51.6	NA	37.9	92.0	98.7	99.7	97.9	93.4	52.0	35.3	16.6	10.5	7.4	NA
1993	51.6	30.4	37.8	92.1	98.7	99.7	97.9	93.4	51.9	35.1	16.7	10.5	7.5	3.0
1992	51.3	NA	35.8	94.1	98.9	99.6	98.8	91.5	51.8	38.6	21.6	8.2	6.9	NA
1991	50.6	NA	39.5	96.1	99.5	100.0	98.2	93.1	49.4	29.9	17.3	8.8	7.9	NA
1990	50.1	NA	45.0	96.5	99.8	99.8	98.7	90.2	50.0	26.0	20.1	7.3	6.2	NA
1989	50.1	NA	37.6	97.1	99.2	99.9	99.5	91.7	49.4	37.3	18.6	7.1	6.3	NA

Note: Data shown for 1947 to 1966 for the Black population are for Black and other races. Data for 1947 to 1963 exclude kindergarten. Nursery school was first collected in 1964.
NA = Not available.
r = Revised, controlled to 1990 census based population estimates; previous 1993 data controlled to 1980 census based population estimates.
¹Starting in 2003, respondents could identify more than one race. Except as noted, the race data in this table from 2003 onward represent those respondents who indicated only one race category.

Table A-11. Percentage of the Population 3 Years Old and Over Enrolled in School, by Age, Sex, Race, and Hispanic Origin, October 1947–2017—*Continued*

(Percent; civilian noninstitutionalized population.)

Year, sex, race, and Hispanic origin	Total enrolled 3 to 34 years old	Total enrolled 3 years old and over	Age											
			3 and 4	5 and 6	7 to 9	10 to 13	14 and 15	16 and 17	18 and 19	20 and 21	22 to 24	25 to 29	30 to 34	35 and over
1988	49.0	NA	32.3	94.9	99.8	99.3	98.6	89.8	50.9	34.3	11.9	7.9	6.9	NA
1987	49.6	NA	34.4	94.1	99.3	99.7	98.6	91.2	48.2	27.4	14.6	10.0	8.1	NA
1986	49.5	NA	38.6	93.7	100.0	99.3	98.2	93.1	47.6	25.7	16.9	8.6	6.5	NA
1985	49.4	NA	50.2	97.1	98.7	99.9	97.6	91.6	39.0	26.0	14.1	7.9	6.1	NA
1984	47.8	NA	39.2	95.3	99.5	99.4	99.0	91.7	40.3	25.9	14.1	8.8	6.2	NA
1983	48.8	NA	35.2	93.6	99.3	100.0	97.1	93.4	45.7	23.3	14.2	6.0	6.5	NA
1982	50.2	NA	39.8	97.0	99.1	99.5	98.3	91.0	41.0	27.2	16.6	7.2	8.0	NA
1981	50.6	NA	38.7	94.4	99.1	99.6	97.0	90.5	44.9	25.7	14.7	8.4	8.1	NA
1980	52.0	NA	39.7	96.7	99.3	99.3	97.4	90.4	48.2	23.7	13.9	7.4	6.5	NA
1979	52.5	NA	41.2	95.5	99.7	99.0	96.4	87.1	45.4	21.1	15.3	7.7	7.3	NA
1978	54.1	NA	44.8	94.7	99.6	99.1	98.0	89.6	42.4	26.0	15.2	8.1	8.0	NA
1977	55.4	NA	38.1	97.0	99.4	99.4	98.5	89.1	46.3	28.2	12.6	10.7	8.9	NA
1976	55.0	NA	32.6	93.6	99.1	98.8	98.4	87.0	46.4	28.4	14.5	8.1	7.6	NA
1975	55.3	NA	37.6	93.9	99.3	99.4	97.2	85.6	44.7	25.8	13.8	7.5	5.9	NA
1974	54.2	NA	28.0	93.8	98.9	100.0	97.9	84.2	42.1	20.1	9.0	7.7	4.8	NA
1973	53.3	NA	28.5	90.9	99.2	98.9	96.5	86.4	32.8	17.3	11.1	5.5	3.8	NA
1972	54.9	NA	24.5	89.1	99.0	99.3	97.3	90.1	38.7	17.9	8.5	5.9	6.5	NA
1971	56.9	NA	24.1	90.9	98.9	99.4	99.0	88.4	43.1	24.1	10.1	4.2	4.2	NA
1970	55.5	NA	23.2	85.7	99.5	99.5	97.2	85.9	38.9	18.9	6.7	3.6	3.3	NA
1969	55.8	NA	21.1	85.0	99.4	99.2	97.7	84.3	40.1	19.6	6.9	5.5	3.7	NA
1968	54.9	NA	20.5	81.3	99.7	99.5	96.9	84.3	38.6	14.5	8.3	1.5	3.2	NA
1967	54.6	NA	18.5	83.4	99.2	99.0	95.8	81.6	34.0	18.5	5.6	6.1	1.5	NA
1966	53.2	NA	14.7	81.6	99.3	99.4	96.5	83.1	30.3	9.3	3.6	2.0	2.0	NA
1965	53.6	NA	14.1	77.3	98.6	99.2	97.6	85.6	32.5	8.0	7.8	1.7	2.4	NA
1964	52.5	NA	11.7	79.9	99.9	99.3	95.0	80.6	31.7	13.7	3.8	2.8	2.0	NA
1963	56.0	NA	NA	79.0	99.2	99.8	96.9	78.2	33.9	11.5	4.3	2.2	1.5	NA
1962	54.1	NA	NA	77.5	98.3	99.1	95.2	69.5	27.3	14.9	3.0	2.2	1.3	NA
1961	53.8	NA	NA	79.5	97.6	99.0	93.5	75.1	20.6	12.4	2.7	1.0	0.4	NA
1960	53.7	NA	NA	74.9	99.1	99.3	94.8	74.7	32.2	10.4	2.8	2.1	1.0	NA
1959	52.4	NA	NA	72.5	99.2	99.1	92.0	76.4	31.9	10.8	2.7	1.4	1.0	NA
1958	50.3	NA	NA	73.7	------98.7------		------78.1------		26.4	------6.0------		1.9	0.4	NA
1957	51.3	NA	NA	75.6	------98.2------		------85.0------		35.1	------7.6------		3.5	1.1	NA
1956	49.0	NA	NA	75.2	------99.1------		------81.1------		27.5	------5.7------		1.3	0.6	NA
1955	47.4	NA	NA	69.4	------98.1------		------80.5------		23.1	------5.5------		3.8	1.7	NA
1954	45.6	NA	NA	73.0	------98.6------		------74.7------		25.7	------2.9------		2.3	0.9	NA
1953	43.5	NA	NA	51.1	------97.6------		------85.5------		21.6	------5.0------		0.3	0.7	NA
1952	43.6	NA	NA	56.3	------97.0------		------82.3------		----------------6.4----------------					NA
1951	50.3	NA	NA	57.1	------96.5------		------79.2------		17.9	------4.3------		1.5	NA	NA
1950	47.0	NA	NA	----------86.5----------			------71.9------		25.7	------3.0------		0.6	NA	NA
1949	37.3	NA	NA	----------84.5----------			------70.0------		14.5	------1.9------		0.7	*	NA
1948	38.2	NA	NA	----------81.3----------			------69.6------		25.2	------2.7------		0.6	*	NA
1947	37.3	NA	NA	----------84.9----------			------71.3------		19.9	------2.5------		0.3	0.3	NA
ASIAN[2]														
Both Sexes														
2017	55.1	25.4	56.5	94.8	98.2	98.5	100.0	93.8	82.4	79.7	50.5	16.7	5.8	1.1
2016	54.7	25.9	62.8	89.5	97.8	98.5	97.9	94.2	77.1	75.6	46.5	21.0	6.4	1.4
2015	56.4	26.6	56.2	95.4	97.4	98.3	99.7	86.8	83.7	83.8	49.7	20.2	8.6	1.5
2014	55.8	26.9	53.9	90.5	96.3	97.5	95.5	94.5	88.1	75.8	56.5	19.2	5.4	1.9
2013	56.6	27.4	57.5	91.7	96.9	98.8	98.8	96.8	83.8	81.7	47.3	18.9	8.0	2.1
2012	57.2	27.6	54.1	93.5	99.9	98.3	98.7	97.3	81.0	74.6	53.0	18.8	8.6	1.8
2011	56.8	26.9	51.8	96.7	97.4	96.7	97.9	97.2	84.5	79.0	42.6	16.4	8.3	2.0
2010	58.6	27.9	61.8	96.5	98.5	98.4	97.6	95.3	82.3	80.2	46.5	20.9	10.3	1.8
2009	57.8	26.9	52.4	94.7	96.4	95.4	96.2	96.6	94.1	73.0	56.7	19.3	10.8	2.0
2008	57.3	27.4	55.8	90.8	98.0	99.5	98.7	92.4	85.4	81.1	43.1	23.4	11.5	2.4
2007	55.6	26.9	53.4	94.3	98.2	99.2	99.8	92.6	86.5	66.5	47.4	19.0	9.9	1.7
2006	54.7	26.9	48.3	96.7	99.1	99.2	99.5	92.2	83.0	74.7	44.8	17.8	8.7	2.2
2005	55.6	28.2	55.0	94.7	99.5	97.6	98.8	98.3	88.3	80.5	42.7	21.0	9.3	2.2
2004	56.8	29.3	58.3	97.2	99.9	99.1	97.5	98.6	82.6	79.7	46.8	21.5	9.5	2.6
2003[1]	56.8	29.3	54.5	89.4	99.0	99.3	99.0	97.6	87.3	79.8	48.1	22.5	9.2	2.2
2002	57.3	30.8	56.1	95.6	96.9	98.8	98.4	94.9	78.9	72.8	49.5	18.3	8.3	2.4
2001	57.7	31.7	41.9	99.4	96.3	99.6	98.4	95.7	84.0	72.6	50.8	22.6	7.8	2.2

Note: Data shown for 1947 to 1966 for the Black population are for Black and other races. Data for 1947 to 1963 exclude kindergarten. Nursery school was first collected in 1964.
* = Quantity zero or rounds to zero.
NA = Not available.
[1]Starting in 2003, respondents could identify more than one race. Except as noted, the race data in this table from 2003 onward represent those respondents who indicated only one race category.
[2]The data shown prior to 2003 consists of those identifying themselves as "Asian or Pacific Islanders."

Table A-11. Percentage of the Population 3 Years Old and Over Enrolled in School, by Age, Sex, Race, and Hispanic Origin, October 1947–2017—*Continued*

(Percent; civilian noninstitutionalized population.)

Year, sex, race, and Hispanic origin	Total enrolled 3 to 34 years old	Total enrolled 3 years old and over	3 and 4	5 and 6	7 to 9	10 to 13	14 and 15	16 and 17	18 and 19	20 and 21	22 to 24	25 to 29	30 to 34	35 and over
2000	58.3	32.6	56.0	97.6	97.8	97.6	99.6	98.4	78.8	66.2	45.3	18.7	8.9	2.8
1999	60.9	34.3	55.8	98.9	99.6	100.0	95.8	97.3	78.5	61.7	45.6	20.3	7.8	3.0
1998	59.9	34.2	53.4	97.9	97.9	98.1	95.3	95.6	83.3	70.6	49.0	21.3	8.7	2.6
1997	60.6	34.6	60.2	94.0	97.7	100.0	99.4	94.7	80.2	73.2	41.8	24.2	9.6	2.7
1996	58.6	35.0	50.4	95.7	98.9	99.3	96.8	94.3	78.3	65.8	39.5	18.6	9.9	3.6
1995	57.3	32.5	42.1	95.9	99.5	99.8	100.0	95.9	83.1	63.4	46.7	21.2	11.1	3.2
1994	60.9	33.1	42.3	97.8	99.5	99.7	100.0	97.3	81.8	67.4	53.5	23.8	8.4	2.7
1993	62.2	34.7	39.6	97.1	99.7	100.0	99.9	91.1	82.5	76.1	55.3	21.0	8.6	3.4
Male														
2017	55.5	26.7	53.7	93.3	97.7	98.0	100.0	94.4	78.2	78.6	54.5	16.3	4.4	0.8
2016	56.2	27.8	60.5	86.4	98.0	98.8	98.8	91.7	75.1	77.6	51.4	22.3	7.0	1.7
2015	57.1	27.6	60.4	97.8	97.6	98.4	99.7	85.3	80.5	81.8	47.2	20.2	8.4	1.1
2014	57.4	28.7	53.9	91.2	97.8	97.2	94.7	93.3	87.5	74.0	62.2	22.0	3.7	1.8
2013	58.4	29.0	60.1	94.5	97.7	99.0	98.0	95.2	83.0	86.6	48.4	22.3	6.1	1.7
2012	57.9	28.8	48.7	93.0	99.7	97.9	97.5	97.4	83.1	74.8	52.8	19.9	7.0	1.5
2011	57.7	28.0	51.6	96.9	96.8	98.2	98.4	96.5	89.2	80.5	39.4	15.8	8.1	1.3
2010	59.8	29.4	63.2	97.5	98.8	97.8	97.1	96.0	77.6	82.9	42.7	22.8	10.8	1.8
2009	58.0	28.2	51.9	94.2	95.6	94.5	97.3	95.1	92.6	71.8	56.9	19.6	9.5	2.3
2008	57.1	27.9	54.2	91.1	96.8	99.1	100.0	96.0	89.0	74.1	38.0	25.2	10.3	1.9
2007	57.2	28.6	56.7	96.9	99.0	99.0	99.7	93.5	91.8	67.6	46.0	18.1	10.3	1.9
2006	55.5	28.3	56.7	96.8	98.3	98.8	99.4	91.0	79.7	76.1	42.2	16.3	8.5	2.4
2005	56.9	29.7	53.2	96.8	99.8	96.9	97.8	97.8	85.2	84.0	42.6	21.1	10.3	2.0
2004	59.3	31.9	58.3	96.0	99.7	99.8	96.5	99.0	85.9	84.2	49.8	24.1	11.4	2.9
2003[1]	59.6	31.8	53.3	90.8	97.9	99.9	97.8	100.0	90.4	77.0	47.8	28.9	11.9	2.3
2002	58.7	32.3	54.1	97.7	95.6	98.4	99.5	94.3	80.0	70.2	50.1	20.6	9.5	2.4
2001	59.1	33.6	35.9	99.6	96.0	100.0	97.1	94.5	83.3	74.9	58.9	22.9	10.6	1.7
2000	60.5	35.0	56.0	96.8	99.5	97.0	99.3	97.8	75.5	67.2	49.1	16.0	10.2	2.7
1999	62.0	35.8	53.5	97.9	99.2	100.0	93.7	98.7	74.4	59.6	50.5	21.4	10.6	3.1
1998	60.8	35.2	51.5	100.0	97.9	98.5	95.0	96.8	74.8	68.0	51.3	21.4	11.1	2.2
1997	63.4	36.6	61.3	89.7	99.4	100.0	98.6	95.5	88.2	71.6	46.9	31.0	10.6	2.5
1996	62.1	38.0	51.0	94.0	99.0	99.6	97.9	93.7	81.0	70.7	37.3	24.4	14.4	3.6
1995	60.0	35.6	38.0	94.5	98.9	99.6	100.0	96.9	81.9	60.3	47.8	24.8	15.7	3.5
1994	64.7	35.8	45.5	98.2	99.0	100.0	100.0	96.9	81.5	70.9	57.0	31.3	10.7	2.1
1993	65.9	37.9	43.0	95.9	99.8	99.9	100.0	93.4	79.4	78.5	65.4	21.0	11.2	3.4
Female														
2017	54.7	24.3	59.4	96.3	98.7	99.0	100.0	93.3	86.8	80.8	46.4	17.0	7.1	1.4
2016	53.3	24.2	65.4	92.8	97.5	98.2	97.1	96.3	79.3	73.7	41.2	19.5	5.9	1.2
2015	55.7	25.7	51.9	92.6	97.1	98.2	99.7	88.2	86.9	85.6	52.5	20.1	8.9	1.9
2014	54.2	25.4	53.8	89.8	94.9	97.8	96.3	95.5	88.7	77.8	50.7	16.7	7.0	2.0
2013	54.9	26.0	54.6	88.8	96.2	98.5	99.6	98.0	84.6	76.3	46.0	15.7	9.6	2.5
2012	56.5	26.6	59.0	94.0	100.0	98.6	100.0	97.3	78.7	74.4	53.3	17.7	10.0	2.1
2011	55.9	25.9	52.0	96.5	98.0	95.3	97.3	98.0	79.2	77.5	46.0	17.0	8.5	2.5
2010	57.3	26.5	60.5	95.6	98.2	99.0	98.1	94.3	87.2	77.8	50.3	19.1	9.9	1.8
2009	57.5	25.8	53.1	95.3	97.3	96.2	94.5	98.3	95.8	74.1	56.5	19.1	12.0	1.8
2008	57.4	26.8	57.8	90.4	99.0	100.0	97.5	88.7	81.8	89.5	47.5	21.7	12.7	2.9
2007	54.0	25.3	49.1	91.9	97.3	99.5	100.0	91.7	81.0	65.4	48.5	19.8	9.6	1.5
2006	53.8	25.6	39.1	96.5	100.0	99.5	99.0	93.3	87.3	72.9	47.0	19.1	8.9	2.0
2005	54.4	26.8	56.8	92.3	99.3	98.3	100.0	98.8	91.7	75.9	42.9	20.9	8.4	2.4
2004	54.1	26.9	58.4	99.1	100.0	98.2	98.5	98.1	79.0	74.7	43.9	19.1	7.6	2.4
2003[1]	54.0	27.1	55.8	87.4	100.0	98.4	100.0	94.9	84.6	82.5	48.3	16.6	6.7	2.1
2002	56.1	29.5	58.1	93.4	97.9	99.2	97.5	95.5	77.9	75.8	48.9	16.1	7.2	2.3
2001	56.2	29.9	47.7	99.1	96.6	99.2	100.0	97.2	84.6	70.0	42.5	22.3	5.1	2.6
2000	56.0	30.4	55.9	98.6	[illegible]	98.2	100.0	99.1	82.0	65.1	41.7	20.6	7.5	2.9
1999	59.8	32.9	57.8	100.0	100.0	100.0	97.6	95.8	82.0	63.7	42.2	19.4	5.2	2.9
1998	59.0	33.2	55.0	95.6	97.8	97.7	95.6	94.4	91.5	73.6	46.6	21.2	6.5	3.0
1997	57.9	32.7	59.5	98.4	95.5	100.0	100.0	93.8	71.6	74.3	36.5	17.4	8.8	2.9
1996	54.9	32.0	49.5	97.9	98.8	99.0	95.5	95.0	75.4	80.8	42.2	13.5	6.1	3.7
1995	54.5	29.6	46.0	98.1	100.0	100.0	100.0	94.8	84.4	67.0	46.2	17.8	6.8	3.1
1994	57.3	30.6	39.0	97.4	100.0	99.4	100.0	97.7	81.9	64.2	49.3	16.9	6.7	3.2
1993	58.6	31.9	36.1	98.5	99.6	100.0	99.8	88.7	87.0	74.5	43.4	20.9	6.3	3.4

Note: Data shown for 1947 to 1966 for the Black population are for Black and other races. Data for 1947 to 1963 exclude kindergarten. Nursery school was first collected in 1964.
[1]Starting in 2003, respondents could identify more than one race. Except as noted, the race data in this table from 2003 onward represent those respondents who indicated only one race category.

Table A-11. Percentage of the Population 3 Years Old and Over Enrolled in School, by Age, Sex, Race, and Hispanic Origin, October 1947–2017—*Continued*

(Percent; civilian noninstitutionalized population.)

Year, sex, race, and Hispanic origin	Total enrolled 3 to 34 years old	Total enrolled 3 years old and over	Age											
			3 and 4	5 and 6	7 to 9	10 to 13	14 and 15	16 and 17	18 and 19	20 and 21	22 to 24	25 to 29	30 to 34	35 and over
HISPANIC (OF ANY RACE)														
Both Sexes														
2017	56.4	32.6	47.9	95.0	97.0	97.3	98.4	92.7	67.2	46.0	25.9	12.3	4.8	1.8
2016	56.8	32.9	49.5	93.0	97.0	98.4	97.6	93.6	68.4	51.7	26.7	11.3	4.7	1.6
2015	55.8	32.7	44.1	93.7	97.9	97.1	96.7	92.6	65.2	48.8	25.2	11.2	4.6	1.7
2014	55.4	33.1	45.5	94.4	98.2	97.3	97.1	92.2	64.7	44.7	24.0	10.7	5.3	1.9
2013	55.5	33.4	45.4	93.9	98.4	97.7	98.3	93.9	59.3	43.9	26.7	10.4	5.7	2.0
2012	56.4	34.2	46.3	92.1	98.1	98.3	98.5	94.8	68.1	49.5	27.1	9.4	6.2	1.8
2011	55.6	34.0	41.6	95.6	98.2	98.5	98.2	94.6	65.2	45.7	23.6	10.5	4.5	1.6
2010	55.1	33.8	44.2	94.3	98.5	97.3	97.9	96.0	66.2	37.0	23.8	11.4	5.7	2.3
2009	52.8	32.3	41.9	93.7	96.5	98.0	97.9	92.6	57.1	37.2	20.4	9.5	5.6	2.2
2008	51.9	31.9	43.6	91.8	97.1	98.6	98.7	93.8	55.1	32.1	19.8	9.2	4.2	2.2
2007	51.7	32.1	48.2	94.3	96.3	99.0	98.4	90.6	57.2	32.3	18.8	8.3	4.5	2.1
2006	51.3	31.9	48.8	93.4	98.1	98.2	98.4	91.1	53.4	30.6	17.9	7.3	5.3	1.8
2005	50.9	32.1	43.0	93.8	97.4	97.9	97.3	92.6	54.3	30.0	19.5	7.8	4.2	2.0
2004	50.7	32.4	43.9	93.9	97.2	97.5	99.0	89.2	43.9	30.6	17.2	6.7	3.3	1.5
2003	49.6	31.6	43.7	91.6	97.5	98.3	96.7	92.1	50.5	33.7	16.1	6.2	4.6	1.8
2002	49.9	32.3	41.0	94.4	97.9	98.1	98.1	90.9	50.6	24.6	15.3	8.4	4.4	2.4
2001	49.5	32.4	39.7	93.6	97.4	98.3	97.8	88.2	45.5	27.9	15.5	7.7	4.4	2.5
2000	51.3	32.6	35.9	94.3	97.5	97.4	96.2	87.0	49.5	26.1	18.2	7.4	5.6	2.0
1999	51.1	32.9	36.9	93.9	99.0	98.3	97.6	88.1	44.5	22.6	15.0	9.1	5.6	2.3
1998	50.4	32.6	36.7	98.2	98.8	99.1	96.8	89.1	40.3	25.6	16.3	8.7	5.5	2.3
1997	50.8	32.7	36.6	96.6	98.6	99.6	98.4	91.1	49.4	28.9	16.4	7.3	3.7	1.8
1996	50.3	32.8	38.1	89.5	96.6	97.6	96.6	88.7	47.0	25.3	17.6	8.6	5.0	2.5
1995	49.7	32.9	36.9	93.9	98.5	99.2	98.9	88.2	46.1	27.1	15.6	7.1	4.7	2.7
1994	49.0	32.6	30.8	96.1	99.2	99.4	96.1	88.3	51.4	24.9	15.1	8.1	5.7	2.7
1993r	48.6	NA	26.8	93.6	99.6	99.2	97.6	88.1	50.0	31.8	13.8	7.7	5.1	NA
1993	48.9	31.6	26.8	93.8	99.6	99.2	97.6	88.3	50.0	31.8	13.7	7.7	5.1	1.9
1992	49.2	NA	28.8	96.0	99.5	99.1	98.8	87.2	53.7	30.1	14.5	6.7	6.0	NA
1991	47.9	NA	30.6	92.4	99.9	99.4	97.2	82.6	47.9	26.4	11.6	6.9	5.9	NA
1990	47.4	NA	29.8	94.8	99.6	99.2	99.0	85.4	44.1	27.2	9.9	6.3	3.1	NA
1989	45.8	NA	23.8	92.8	98.0	99.3	96.5	86.4	44.6	18.8	12.0	6.6	3.5	NA
1988	46.0	NA	24.5	95.7	99.6	99.8	98.8	78.8	44.1	16.7	12.1	5.8	6.2	NA
1987	47.2	NA	30.7	93.0	99.2	99.4	97.6	87.1	39.1	26.5	12.3	7.5	4.9	NA
1986	48.2	NA	28.8	93.7	99.4	99.3	97.2	84.0	46.0	21.4	13.7	9.2	5.6	NA
1985	47.7	NA	27.0	94.5	98.4	99.4	96.1	84.5	41.8	24.0	11.6	8.6	5.6	NA
1984	47.7	NA	24.2	93.9	98.7	99.4	94.9	85.7	39.9	28.1	11.3	6.6	7.5	NA
1983	49.3	NA	23.5	95.1	98.5	99.7	96.0	88.6	44.3	24.0	12.5	7.1	5.7	NA
1982	49.4	NA	21.8	92.2	98.7	98.8	96.9	85.5	39.2	22.7	10.4	8.2	4.4	NA
1981	49.0	NA	24.5	90.4	99.2	99.1	94.0	82.8	37.8	20.6	12.3	8.0	4.7	NA
1980	49.8	NA	28.5	94.5	98.4	99.7	94.3	81.8	37.8	19.5	11.7	6.9	4.1	NA
1979	48.6	NA	22.5	92.5	98.7	99.0	96.3	82.3	39.9	22.6	10.0	7.8	7.1	NA
1978	48.3	NA	22.5	91.4	99.5	98.0	95.2	83.0	35.7	16.8	11.8	8.0	4.1	NA
1977	50.8	NA	19.5	93.7	99.0	99.3	97.6	83.6	40.6	23.1	10.8	9.3	5.6	NA
1976	51.8	NA	22.2	95.0	97.5	99.1	95.4	81.3	45.2	24.0	14.8	7.9	2.7	NA
1975	54.8	NA	27.3	92.1	99.6	99.2	95.6	86.2	44.0	27.5	14.1	8.3	4.1	NA
1974	54.3	NA	25.3	92.1	98.8	99.2	96.1	78.3	45.2	23.2	11.3	6.7	2.2	NA
1973	52.8	NA	18.8	90.7	98.7	99.1	94.4	80.2	39.2	21.5	10.0	6.8	1.3	NA
1972	53.0	NA	20.5	90.0	98.7	99.1	96.7	83.9	41.4	17.0	9.9	5.2	3.5	NA
Male														
2017	55.0	32.1	47.1	94.6	97.5	97.4	98.2	91.7	63.3	40.9	23.0	9.9	5.0	1.4
2016	55.4	32.6	50.7	91.8	96.3	98.1	98.4	93.4	66.3	46.0	23.4	9.3	3.6	1.3
2015	54.4	32.4	44.3	93.6	97.5	97.3	96.0	91.7	59.9	44.4	24.2	9.2	3.3	1.6
2014	53.6	32.6	43.1	94.6	97.8	96.7	97.8	89.3	61.6	37.4	21.5	10.0	3.2	1.9
2013	54.0	33.1	44.2	93.6	98.6	97.7	97.9	93.5	55.4	38.0	24.4	10.8	3.9	1.6
2012	54.7	33.9	45.4	92.2	98.2	98.6	98.9	95.1	65.7	44.4	24.7	7.4	3.3	1.8
2011	54.1	33.9	43.6	95.9	98.8	98.8	98.7	94.6	61.0	43.1	21.0	9.9	3.4	1.6
2010	52.9	32.8	43.3	93.4	98.1	96.9	97.5	96.0	64.9	34.0	18.6	9.6	4.9	1.9

Note: Data shown for 1947 to 1966 for the Black population are for Black and other races. Data for 1947 to 1963 exclude kindergarten. Nursery school was first collected in 1964.
NA = Not available.
r = Revised, controlled to 1990 census based population estimates; previous 1993 data controlled to 1980 census based population estimates.

Table A-11. Percentage of the Population 3 Years Old and Over Enrolled in School, by Age, Sex, Race, and Hispanic Origin, October 1947–2017—*Continued*

(Percent; civilian noninstitutionalized population.)

Year, sex, race, and Hispanic origin	Total enrolled 3 to 34 years old	Total enrolled 3 years old and over	Age 3 and 4	5 and 6	7 to 9	10 to 13	14 and 15	16 and 17	18 and 19	20 and 21	22 to 24	25 to 29	30 to 34	35 and over
2009	50.9	31.3	39.4	94.1	96.2	98.8	98.1	92.5	51.8	32.1	18.6	7.8	5.2	1.6
2008	50.0	31.1	40.5	91.0	96.7	98.6	98.6	93.1	54.7	30.8	16.6	8.2	4.1	1.6
2007	49.4	31.1	50.7	94.1	96.4	99.0	97.8	91.1	55.2	24.6	14.4	6.7	3.1	1.8
2006	49.0	30.9	49.1	91.7	97.7	97.9	99.0	91.7	51.5	24.1	16.0	5.4	3.5	1.2
2005	48.4	31.0	43.0	92.4	96.0	97.2	97.8	92.5	51.8	25.2	17.5	5.6	2.6	1.6
2004	48.5	31.5	43.8	93.9	97.2	97.5	99.0	89.2	43.9	30.6	17.2	6.7	3.3	1.5
2003	47.3	30.8	42.9	91.3	97.5	98.4	96.7	90.4	47.0	27.2	13.3	4.9	3.8	1.3
2002	48.1	31.9	41.7	95.1	97.8	97.6	98.2	88.8	48.4	24.5	11.5	7.0	3.1	2.2
2001	48.4	32.2	42.9	94.9	97.9	98.6	98.4	87.8	40.0	24.4	14.6	6.5	3.5	2.2
2000	50.5	32.5	31.9	95.4	96.6	98.4	96.9	85.7	48.0	24.2	15.2	5.1	5.7	1.4
1999	50.3	32.9	33.5	92.8	98.8	98.5	98.1	87.9	45.3	21.5	11.2	8.6	3.9	2.0
1998	49.0	32.4	44.9	92.8	98.8	99.3	97.0	88.0	33.7	24.6	12.9	6.9	4.7	1.8
1997	49.0	32.3	35.5	97.7	97.7	99.8	99.5	92.5	45.4	27.6	14.0	5.9	2.7	1.6
1996	49.2	33.0	39.6	91.0	95.4	97.9	98.0	90.4	46.8	19.5	16.2	6.8	4.3	2.6
1995	49.1	33.1	40.8	93.6	98.8	98.8	98.4	88.4	47.4	24.8	14.8	5.6	4.5	2.1
1994	48.0	32.5	32.6	96.5	98.6	99.3	94.6	86.6	54.2	23.7	14.0	7.1	4.2	2.3
1993r	46.6	NA	26.9	93.4	99.8	98.8	96.9	88.7	47.8	31.6	13.0	5.5	5.4	NA
1993	47.4	31.5	27.0	93.6	99.8	98.8	96.9	89.1	47.7	31.6	12.8	5.5	5.4	1.5
1992	47.9	NA	24.9	96.5	100.0	99.2	98.1	89.2	52.6	24.3	13.8	5.3	3.5	NA
1991	46.4	NA	30.7	92.3	99.8	99.7	97.8	83.6	42.1	20.8	9.9	6.8	3.3	NA
1990	47.1	NA	27.3	95.6	99.5	99.0	99.1	85.5	40.7	21.7	11.2	4.6	4.0	NA
1989	45.8	NA	21.3	92.5	97.7	98.6	98.0	88.7	44.2	17.1	12.2	7.3	4.1	NA
1988	46.2	NA	27.9	96.7	99.2	100.0	98.1	80.9	44.7	21.6	12.5	4.5	5.0	NA
1987	47.8	NA	30.5	92.8	99.7	100.0	98.1	90.9	42.3	30.1	11.4	7.8	5.1	NA
1986	47.3	NA	29.4	93.0	100.0	99.4	96.8	85.0	45.8	19.2	13.0	9.1	4.4	NA
1985	47.5	NA	26.4	95.3	98.9	99.1	96.2	88.9	38.6	20.3	12.6	8.7	3.8	NA
1984	48.6	NA	20.0	93.6	98.2	100.0	95.7	85.1	38.8	27.5	12.3	8.2	4.0	NA
1983	50.7	NA	25.0	91.9	98.8	99.6	97.8	88.2	40.4	26.2	15.1	6.9	4.6	NA
1982	50.4	NA	25.2	90.3	99.6	98.4	96.8	87.8	39.7	21.6	11.2	10.8	3.1	NA
1981	49.6	NA	25.5	89.6	98.8	99.0	92.3	84.5	36.0	24.4	11.4	8.3	4.3	NA
1980	49.9	NA	30.1	94.0	97.7	99.4	96.7	81.5	36.9	21.4	10.7	6.8	6.2	NA
1979	51.0	NA	22.8	93.8	98.7	99.0	96.6	85.1	42.6	24.0	12.4	8.7	6.1	NA
1978	50.5	NA	22.6	93.2	99.1	97.8	94.0	80.4	40.0	18.1	13.6	9.5	4.4	NA
1977	54.2	NA	23.2	91.4	100.0	98.7	99.1	89.4	43.1	22.8	16.0	13.1	6.4	NA
1976	55.0	NA	22.1	94.6	97.4	98.5	97.3	85.5	46.3	27.1	18.6	11.4	5.6	NA
1975	58.1	NA	26.7	89.7	99.6	98.8	97.4	88.3	51.9	31.3	15.9	11.9	7.2	NA
1974	56.0	NA	23.5	93.1	98.3	98.5	97.9	78.6	46.8	22.3	14.5	8.4	7.4	NA
1973	55.5	NA	23.1	92.4	99.1	99.1	96.5	86.6	45.8	23.8	10.8	9.9	6.7	NA
1972	54.7	NA	20.4	90.3	98.8	99.1	98.1	87.8	40.5	20.0	13.9	5.8	2.5	NA
Female														
2017	57.8	33.0	48.8	95.5	96.5	97.3	98.6	93.6	71.1	50.7	29.2	14.7	4.6	2.2
2016	58.3	33.2	48.2	94.2	97.6	98.8	96.8	93.9	70.5	57.5	30.2	13.3	5.9	1.9
2015	55.7	32.9	44.0	93.9	98.4	96.9	97.4	93.7	70.1	53.2	26.3	13.2	5.9	1.8
2014	57.4	33.6	47.8	94.2	98.6	97.9	96.4	95.3	67.8	53.8	26.3	11.5	7.6	2.0
2013	57.0	33.7	46.7	94.1	98.2	97.7	98.8	94.3	63.2	50.6	29.1	10.0	7.6	2.3
2012	58.2	34.5	47.1	92.1	98.1	98.0	98.1	94.5	70.7	55.0	29.7	11.5	9.3	1.9
2011	57.2	34.1	39.6	95.3	97.6	98.2	97.6	94.6	70.3	48.8	26.6	11.2	5.8	1.6
2010	57.4	34.8	45.0	95.2	98.9	97.7	98.3	96.0	67.6	40.5	29.2	13.6	6.6	2.7
2009	55.0	33.3	44.4	93.2	96.7	97.2	97.6	92.6	62.5	43.1	22.2	11.6	6.0	2.8
2008	53.9	32.8	46.9	92.6	97.4	98.7	98.8	94.5	55.5	33.5	23.4	10.4	4.4	2.7
2007	54.3	33.1	45.6	94.5	96.2	99.0	99.1	90.0	59.2	41.0	23.7	10.3	6.1	2.3
2006	53.9	33.1	48.5	95.3	98.5	98.6	97.7	90.4	55.4	37.5	20.1	9.7	7.3	2.3
2005	58.0	33.3	43.0	95.3	98.8	98.6	96.7	92.6	57.2	35.3	21.8	10.4	6.1	2.4
2004	53.1	33.3	44.0	92.2	97.9	97.5	97.5	91.3	56.9	34.0	22.0	9.7	7.5	2.8
2003	52.2	32.5	44.7	92.0	97.5	98.2	96.8	93.8	54.4	41.1	19.4	7.9	5.6	2.2
2002	51.8	32.8	40.3	93.8	98.1	98.7	97.9	92.8	53.2	24.6	20.2	9.9	6.0	2.7
2001	50.6	32.6	36.3	92.4	96.9	98.1	97.2	88.7	51.1	31.6	16.7	9.1	5.3	2.8
2000	52.2	32.8	40.0	93.1	98.4	96.4	95.4	88.3	51.1	28.1	21.6	9.5	5.5	2.6
1999	52.1	32.8	40.5	95.0	99.3	98.0	96.9	88.3	43.6	23.6	19.2	9.5	7.3	2.7
1998	51.9	32.8	34.3	93.7	98.8	98.9	96.7	90.5	46.8	26.8	20.0	10.6	6.5	2.8
1997	52.7	33.0	37.7	95.7	99.6	99.5	97.3	89.6	53.9	30.4	19.2	8.8	4.9	2.0
1996	51.4	32.7	36.8	87.8	97.9	97.4	95.0	86.9	47.2	31.1	19.3	10.5	5.7	2.5
1995	50.3	32.7	32.7	94.3	98.2	99.6	99.4	88.0	44.8	29.2	16.6	8.7	4.9	3.2
1994	50.2	32.7	28.9	95.7	99.8	99.4	97.6	90.2	48.6	26.4	16.5	9.1	7.3	3.0
1993r	50.7	NA	26.7	93.9	99.4	99.6	98.2	87.3	51.9	31.9	14.7	10.2	4.7	NA

Note: Data shown for 1947 to 1966 for the Black population are for Black and other races. Data for 1947 to 1963 exclude kindergarten. Nursery school was first collected in 1964.
NA = Not available.
r = Revised, controlled to 1990 census based population estimates; previous 1993 data controlled to 1980 census based population estimates.

Table A-11. Percentage of the Population 3 Years Old and Over Enrolled in School, by Age, Sex, Race, and Hispanic Origin, October 1947–2017—Continued

(Percent; civilian noninstitutionalized population.)

Year, sex, race, and Hispanic origin	Total enrolled 3 to 34 years old	Total enrolled 3 years old and over	Age											
			3 and 4	5 and 6	7 to 9	10 to 13	14 and 15	16 and 17	18 and 19	20 and 21	22 to 24	25 to 29	30 to 34	35 and over
1993	50.6	31.6	26.7	93.9	99.4	99.6	98.2	87.4	51.9	32.0	14.5	10.2	4.8	2.2
1992	50.6	NA	32.7	95.4	99.0	99.1	99.6	85.0	54.9	35.6	15.4	8.2	6.0	NA
1991	49.5	NA	30.5	92.6	100.0	99.2	96.6	81.5	53.7	32.0	13.6	7.0	5.9	NA
1990	47.7	NA	32.3	93.9	99.7	99.4	98.8	85.3	47.2	33.1	8.4	8.1	3.1	NA
1989	45.9	NA	26.5	93.3	98.3	100.0	95.1	83.7	45.0	20.8	11.9	5.8	3.5	NA
1988	45.8	NA	20.7	94.6	100.0	99.6	99.6	76.6	43.5	11.2	11.5	7.2	6.2	NA
1987	46.5	NA	30.8	93.2	98.7	98.9	97.1	82.6	36.2	22.0	13.2	7.3	4.9	NA
1986	49.0	NA	28.2	94.4	98.7	99.2	97.5	83.0	46.2	23.7	14.5	9.2	5.6	NA
1985	47.9	NA	27.7	93.7	98.0	99.7	96.0	80.0	44.7	27.4	10.4	8.6	5.6	NA
1984	46.8	NA	28.2	94.2	99.2	98.7	94.0	86.3	40.8	28.7	10.4	4.9	7.5	NA
1983	48.0	NA	22.0	98.3	99.8	99.4	94.1	89.1	47.6	21.7	10.1	7.4	5.7	NA
1982	48.4	NA	16.3	93.9	97.8	99.2	97.1	82.8	38.7	23.7	9.7	5.7	4.4	NA
1981	48.4	NA	23.4	91.3	99.6	99.3	95.7	80.8	39.4	16.8	13.1	7.7	4.7	NA
1980	49.8	NA	26.6	94.9	99.0	99.9	92.1	82.2	38.8	17.6	12.6	6.9	4.1	NA
1979	46.3	NA	22.3	91.1	98.7	98.9	95.9	79.5	37.1	21.5	7.8	7.0	7.1	NA
1978	46.2	NA	22.5	89.4	100.0	98.2	96.6	86.2	31.9	15.7	10.1	6.5	4.1	NA
1977	47.6	NA	15.8	96.3	97.9	99.9	95.9	77.4	38.5	23.4	6.2	5.9	5.6	NA
1976	48.8	NA	22.3	95.5	97.6	99.7	93.6	77.6	44.2	21.4	12.1	4.8	2.7	NA
1975	51.7	NA	27.9	94.4	99.5	99.7	93.8	84.0	37.1	24.3	12.5	5.3	4.1	NA
1974	52.5	NA	27.4	91.1	99.2	100.0	94.1	77.9	43.7	23.9	8.4	4.9	2.2	NA
1973	50.1	NA	14.0	88.9	98.3	99.1	92.5	74.9	32.9	19.4	9.2	3.9	1.3	NA
1972	51.4	NA	20.5	89.7	98.5	99.0	95.4	80.0	42.4	14.6	6.8	4.7	3.5	NA

WHITE ALONE OR IN COMBINATION

Both Sexes

Year, sex, race, and Hispanic origin	Total enrolled 3 to 34 years old	Total enrolled 3 years old and over	3 and 4	5 and 6	7 to 9	10 to 13	14 and 15	16 and 17	18 and 19	20 and 21	22 to 24	25 to 29	30 to 34	35 and over
2017	54.5	23.9	53.2	93.7	97.0	97.6	98.4	93.3	68.1	54.6	26.8	11.5	5.6	1.3
2016	55.2	24.2	53.8	93.7	98.5	98.4	92.6	69.7	56.0	27.4	12.7	5.9	1.3
2015	55.2	24.4	52.1	94.2	97.6	97.9	97.9	94.0	68.5	53.4	27.7	12.7	6.1	1.4
2014	55.1	24.6	54.0	93.4	97.7	97.5	97.7	93.4	68.1	52.3	28.6	12.3	5.9	1.5
2013	55.5	25.0	54.4	93.9	98.2	98.2	98.5	93.7	67.0	52.3	29.1	12.2	6.3	1.6
2012	56.2	25.4	53.6	93.7	98.1	97.8	98.3	96.1	68.4	54.0	29.5	13.3	6.7	1.7
2011	56.5	25.9	51.6	95.6	98.2	98.6	98.7	95.7	70.2	53.7	30.8	14.1	7.0	1.7
2010	56.1	25.8	52.3	94.3	97.8	98.1	98.1	96.2	70.0	51.4	28.0	14.0	7.7	1.9
2009	56.0	25.7	51.3	94.2	98.0	98.7	98.1	94.6	68.4	52.5	28.8	13.0	7.4	1.9
2008	55.9	25.7	52.4	94.0	98.2	98.9	98.7	95.5	67.0	51.0	28.1	12.4	6.3	1.8
2007	55.7	25.7	54.0	94.8	98.0	98.7	98.7	94.6	67.1	49.7	26.2	16.2	9.4	1.8
2006	55.8	25.7	55.5	94.8	98.4	98.5	98.4	94.9	65.0	47.9	25.6	11.4	6.8	1.7
2005	56.2	26.1	53.9	95.3	98.6	98.7	98.3	95.3	67.7	49.3	26.2	11.3	6.2	1.8
2004	55.7	26.1	52.7	95.5	98.2	98.4	98.5	94.0	64.8	49.4	25.2	12.2	6.4	1.8
2003	55.6	26.1	55.2	94.8	98.0	98.4	97.4	95.0	64.2	48.3	26.8	11.0	6.3	1.7

Male

Year, sex, race, and Hispanic origin	Total enrolled 3 to 34 years old	Total enrolled 3 years old and over	3 and 4	5 and 6	7 to 9	10 to 13	14 and 15	16 and 17	18 and 19	20 and 21	22 to 24	25 to 29	30 to 34	35 and over
2017	53.8	24.1	52.2	93.2	97.2	97.7	98.5	92.9	65.5	50.5	25.0	10.2	5.1	1.0
2016	54.5	24.5	55.3	93.7	97.9	98.2	98.7	92.2	68.4	51.0	25.7	10.7	4.9	1.0
2015	54.6	24.7	53.4	93.4	97.7	98.1	97.6	93.2	65.3	50.6	25.4	11.5	5.3	1.1
2014	54.4	24.9	52.6	93.8	97.4	96.8	97.3	92.4	64.6	49.4	26.7	11.5	5.1	1.2
2013	54.7	25.1	52.7	93.9	98.1	98.2	98.4	93.0	65.4	47.4	26.6	11.2	5.2	1.2
2012	55.3	25.5	52.8	93.6	97.8	98.1	98.2	95.9	65.6	48.2	28.2	11.5	5.6	1.3
2011	55.9	26.3	52.5	95.6	98.4	98.7	98.5	95.6	67.4	50.3	30.1	12.5	6.2	1.4
2010	55.2	26.0	52.2	93.4	97.4	97.7	98.1	95.0	67.5	48.2	25.9	13.1	6.4	1.5
2009	55.1	25.8	50.5	93.8	97.8	98.9	97.8	94.3	64.3	49.2	27.9	11.3	6.5	1.4
2008	55.2	25.9	52.1	93.6	97.9	98.7	99.0	95.0	64.4	48.1	26.4	11.6	5.7	1.3
2007	54.6	25.8	53.2	94.0	97.9	98.6	98.3	94.4	66.4	44.1	24.0	12.9	9.4	1.4
2006	54.9	25.9	56.0	94.5	98.3	98.4	98.2	94.7	62.7	43.5	24.1	10.3	5.6	1.3
2005	55.2	26.2	52.6	94.7	98.2	98.6	98.3	95.2	65.7	45.1	24.6	8.9	5.4	1.4
2004	55.0	26.3	53.4	95.8	98.0	98.2	98.8	94.3	59.9	46.5	23.2	11.1	5.5	1.4
2003	55.0	26.5	55.9	95.2	97.7	98.2	97.3	95.1	61.6	43.4	25.5	9.8	5.7	1.4

Female

Year, sex, race, and Hispanic origin	Total enrolled 3 to 34 years old	Total enrolled 3 years old and over	3 and 4	5 and 6	7 to 9	10 to 13	14 and 15	16 and 17	18 and 19	20 and 21	22 to 24	25 to 29	30 to 34	35 and over
2017	55.1	23.7	54.2	94.2	96.7	97.4	98.4	93.7	70.7	58.9	28.7	12.8	6.1	1.6
2016	55.9	24.0	52.3	93.7	98.2	98.8	98.0	93.0	71.0	61.2	29.0	14.8	6.9	1.5
2015	55.7	24.2	50.9	95.1	97.6	97.6	98.1	94.8	71.8	56.2	30.0	14.0	6.9	1.7
2014	55.8	24.3	55.4	92.9	98.0	98.2	98.1	94.4	71.7	55.7	30.3	13.1	6.8	1.8
2013	56.4	24.9	56.1	94.0	98.3	98.3	98.6	94.5	68.8	57.6	31.7	13.2	7.4	2.0

Note: Data shown for 1947 to 1966 for the Black population are for Black and other races. Data for 1947 to 1963 exclude kindergarten. Nursery school was first collected in 1964.
NA = Not available.

Table A-11. Percentage of the Population 3 Years Old and Over Enrolled in School, by Age, Sex, Race, and Hispanic Origin, October 1947–2017—*Continued*

(Percent; civilian noninstitutionalized population.)

Year, sex, race, and Hispanic origin	Total enrolled 3 to 34 years old	Total enrolled 3 years old and over	Age											
			3 and 4	5 and 6	7 to 9	10 to 13	14 and 15	16 and 17	18 and 19	20 and 21	22 to 24	25 to 29	30 to 34	35 and over
2012................................	57.2	25.3	54.5	93.8	98.4	97.5	98.5	96.3	71.4	59.6	31.0	15.1	7.8	2.0
2011................................	57.2	25.6	50.7	95.7	98.0	98.5	98.8	95.7	73.1	57.4	31.6	15.9	7.9	2.0
2010................................	57.1	25.7	52.5	95.2	98.1	98.5	98.1	97.4	72.5	55.0	30.1	15.0	9.1	2.3
2009................................	57.0	25.7	52.1	94.5	98.1	98.4	98.4	94.8	72.7	56.0	29.7	14.8	8.3	2.4
2008................................	56.6	25.5	52.7	94.4	98.6	99.1	98.5	96.0	69.7	54.0	29.8	13.2	7.0	2.3
2007................................	56.9	25.6	54.9	95.6	98.1	98.7	99.2	94.9	67.9	55.5	28.4	19.2	9.4	2.2
2006................................	56.6	25.5	55.0	95.2	98.5	98.5	98.6	95.2	67.3	52.4	27.1	12.4	8.1	2.1
2005................................	57.4	26.0	55.3	96.0	98.9	98.8	98.4	95.5	70.0	53.8	27.9	13.8	7.1	2.3
2004................................	56.5	25.8	51.9	95.3	98.4	98.5	98.2	93.8	69.7	52.4	27.1	13.4	7.3	2.2
2003................................	56.3	25.7	54.4	94.5	98.3	98.7	97.5	94.9	66.8	53.1	28.1	12.2	7.0	2.1
BLACK ALONE OR IN COMBINATION														
Both Sexes														
2017................................	56.9	30.9	56.7	92.1	97.1	98.8	96.8	91.4	66.9	47.9	27.6	13.6	7.3	2.7
2016................................	57.1	31.1	52.4	93.2	97.7	98.8	96.3	95.0	67.2	47.6	27.2	12.6	8.7	2.9
2015................................	56.6	31.0	51.2	93.7	96.2	98.5	98.3	95	64.7	42.4	26.8	12.6	8.3	2.8
2014................................	57.1	31.8	56.9	94.6	98.8	97.8	98.7	91.7	64.8	39.7	24.7	14.2	9.0	3.7
2013................................	58.5	32.5	58.4	94.3	97.1	98.0	98.7	92.9	64.0	49.1	27.4	16.7	8.2	3.0
2012................................	59.5	33.2	51.8	92.4	96.7	99.0	97.6	94.6	68.7	49.6	29.3	15.7	12.2	3.3
2011................................	59.3	33.6	53.9	92.1	97.3	98.5	98.7	96.0	74.1	41.8	31.0	18.1	11.3	3.8
2010................................	59.2	33.6	55.8	94.8	97.5	98.7	98.6	95.7	63.2	49.9	28.9	16.0	10.8	3.9
2009................................	59.4	33.5	57.1	93.8	97.4	98.6	97.7	94.4	64.7	44.2	31.6	14.7	11.1	3.7
2008................................	58.8	33.0	54.5	92.9	98.8	99.1	98.1	94.5	59.7	40.4	24.8	15.1	11.4	2.8
2007................................	59.0	33.2	58.2	94.2	98.2	98.0	99.1	93.7	62.0	38.1	27.3	15.3	9.6	3.0
2006................................	58.8	33.3	59.0	92.4	96.9	97.2	97.4	93.2	64.9	38.9	27.8	11.9	8.9	3.2
2005................................	59.0	33.5	51.3	96.1	98.5	98.6	95.9	92.9	62.5	38.1	27.8	11.7	9.9	3.1
2004................................	59.6	34.3	58.6	94.5	97.4	99.4	98.6	95.3	59.7	40.8	25.3	14.8	7.0	3.3
2003................................	59.8	34.2	56.5	94.6	98.1	98.3	98.0	94.2	60.9	42.1	27.2	12.4	8.4	2.8
Male														
2017................................	56.3	31.8	58.3	91.2	96.0	98.8	95.9	90.7	62.8	41.4	23.8	12.1	6.0	2.2
2016................................	57.4	32.4	48.1	90.8	96.6	98.8	98.5	95.4	66.9	44.2	25.8	12.3	7.3	2.2
2015................................	57.2	32.2	50.6	92.4	96.5	99.3	99.1	95.2	64.6	39.4	29.3	9.7	4.6	1.8
2014................................	57.4	32.8	56.4	95.7	98.8	97.8	98.4	91.7	61.1	39.2	21.9	11.6	7.2	2.6
2013................................	58.5	33.5	55.4	94.6	97.0	97.8	98.6	95.0	59.4	44.6	26.2	13.7	4.9	2.4
2012................................	59.0	33.7	48.8	93.5	95.8	99.1	98.7	95.6	61.4	49.4	27.2	11.1	7.2	2.1
2011................................	59.0	34.5	52.8	92.8	97.5	98.6	97.9	94.5	71.6	38.9	30.0	14.1	7.7	2.7
2010................................	58.8	34.4	55.0	94.2	97.7	98.6	97.8	93.8	62.0	44.9	28.0	12.9	6.3	2.7
2009................................	58.9	34.0	57.4	93.8	97.2	98.3	95.9	95.6	60.4	42.3	25.7	11.5	8.1	2.2
2008................................	58.8	34.0	53.1	94.0	98.3	98.7	99.0	94.3	58.0	38.1	22.7	11.0	8.6	1.6
2007................................	60.1	35.0	60.5	93.9	98.1	97.5	99.2	95.2	61.5	37.8	27.8	10.7	9.7	2.0
2006................................	59.5	34.8	57.0	92.5	97.0	97.1	97.8	91.9	64.1	38.8	25.6	9.5	7.0	2.5
2005................................	59.2	34.6	52.5	95.1	97.5	97.9	93.8	93.8	66.2	34.9	23.9	9.3	6.1	2.3
2004................................	59.7	35.3	59.9	93.9	96.8	99.2	98.8	96.3	57.9	38.2	21.0	9.3	3.9	2.2
2003................................	60.6	35.7	57.6	93.2	98.8	98.2	98.3	93.8	61.1	35.6	23.4	9.4	7.2	1.9
Female														
2017................................	57.4	30.2	54.9	93.1	98.1	98.7	97.6	92.1	70.9	54.6	31.1	15.0	8.5	3.0
2016................................	56.8	29.9	56.6	95.6	98.9	98.8	93.9	94.6	67.6	51.1	28.5	12.8	9.9	3.4
2015................................	56.1	29.9	51.9	94.9	95.8	97.6	97.6	94.8	64.8	45.2	24.6	15.1	11.5	3.6
2014................................	56.8	31.0	57.4	93.6	98.9	97.9	99.1	91.6	68.4	40.1	27.5	16.4	10.5	4.5
2013................................	58.6	31.7	61.2	94.0	97.3	98.1	98.8	91.0	68.4	53.1	28.6	19.1	10.9	3.5
2012................................	59.9	32.7	54.7	91.3	97.7	99.0	96.5	93.7	76.4	49.7	31.2	19.6	16.3	4.3
2011................................	59.5	32.8	55.0	91.3	97.2	98.4	99.4	97.5	76.5	45.0	31.7	21.7	14.4	4.7
2010................................	59.6	33.0	56.7	95.4	97.2	98.8	99.4	97.6	64.3	54.2	29.7	18.7	14.5	4.9
2009................................	59.8	33.0	56.?	93.9	97.6	98.9	99.4	93.1	68.9	46.1	36.5	17.5	13.5	4.8
2008................................	58.8	32.1	55.7	91.7	99.4	99.5	97.2	94.7	61.3	42.5	26.6	18.6	13.8	3.8
2007................................	57.9	31.7	55.7	94.5	98.2	98.4	98.9	92.2	62.6	38.5	26.8	19.4	9.5	3.8
2006................................	58.2	32.0	60.9	92.3	96.9	97.4	97.0	94.6	65.6	39.0	29.8	14.0	10.5	3.6
2005................................	58.8	32.4	50.0	97.1	99.4	99.3	97.8	92.0	59.1	41.3	31.1	13.8	12.8	3.7
2004................................	59.6	33.4	57.0	95.0	98.1	99.6	98.4	94.2	61.3	43.1	29.3	19.3	9.5	4.2
2003................................	59.1	32.9	55.3	95.9	97.3	98.4	97.6	94.5	60.7	47.5	30.7	14.7	9.4	3.5

Note: Data shown for 1947 to 1966 for the Black population are for Black and other races. Data for 1947 to 1963 exclude kindergarten. Nursery school was first collected in 1964.

Table A-11. Percentage of the Population 3 Years Old and Over Enrolled in School, by Age, Sex, Race, and Hispanic Origin, October 1947–2017—*Continued*

(Percent; civilian noninstitutionalized population.)

Year, sex, race, and Hispanic origin	Total enrolled 3 to 34 years old	Total enrolled 3 years old and over	Age											
			3 and 4	5 and 6	7 to 9	10 to 13	14 and 15	16 and 17	18 and 19	20 and 21	22 to 24	25 to 29	30 to 34	35 and over
ASIAN ALONE OR IN COMBINATION														
Both Sexes														
2017	57.6	28.5	54.9	96.0	98.1	98.6	100.0	94.5	83.1	77.0	49.0	16.6	6.1	1.2
2016	57.0	28.6	63.2	90.7	98.1	98.8	98.2	94.0	78.4	73.7	46.7	20.6	6.4	1.4
2015	58.0	28.8	59.9	95.6	97.8	98.2	98.2	88.1	83.3	83.1	48.4	19.8	9.0	1.5
2014	57.4	29.4	54.2	89.3	97.0	97.7	96.3	93.8	85.9	73.7	53.9	19.5	5.6	2.0
2013	58.7	30.3	57.4	92.5	97.7	98.5	99.0	97.4	83.0	80.3	46.2	18.1	7.8	2.2
2012	59.1	30.1	56.7	93.9	99.9	98.6	99.0	97.8	79.4	72.8	52.2	18.5	8.4	1.8
2011	58.8	29.7	55.4	96.6	97.9	97.4	98.2	97.6	80.4	77.1	41.4	17.2	9.1	2.1
2010	60.5	30.6	62.4	96.7	98.9	98.4	98.0	96.1	81.9	76.9	46.5	21.3	10.1	1.8
2009	59.3	29.0	55.3	95.6	97.2	95.8	96.8	97.0	90.1	73.6	53.5	18.7	10.8	2.1
2008	59.2	29.5	57.4	92.6	98.3	99.6	98.8	93.5	85.9	79.4	43.0	23.0	11.9	2.5
2007	57.0	28.8	54.1	93.9	98.4	99.3	99.7	93.4	86.3	64.3	45.9	19.6	9.5	1.8
2006	56.3	29.0	51.5	94.6	99.0	99.3	99.6	92.0	82.3	72.2	43.1	17.3	8.8	2.2
2005	57.6	30.5	54.4	95.5	99.6	97.5	98.7	98.2	86.2	77.1	44.4	20.9	9.4	2.3
2004	58.5	31.4	57.7	97.6	99.9	99.2	98.0	97.1	79.9	77.7	46.2	20.8	9.3	2.7
2003	58.2	31.3	51.4	89.3	99.2	99.4	99.1	95.7	87.1	77.0	48.1	21.6	9.4	2.2
Male														
2017	58.2	29.8	53.7	94.7	98.3	98.2	100.0	94.7	80.0	76.0	53.0	15.6	5.6	1.0
2016	58.7	30.6	60.1	87.5	98.2	98.9	99.0	91.1	76.3	76.9	52.1	21.4	7.2	1.6
2015	58.5	29.8	65.2	96.6	98.0	98.6	97.9	87.5	81.4	82.3	44.7	19.8	8.4	1.1
2014	59.0	31.1	55.3	92.0	98.3	97.7	95.6	94.0	85.2	71.3	59.2	21.6	4.1	1.9
2013	59.6	31.3	57.8	94.1	98.2	98.3	98.3	96.1	82.4	84.2	47.9	20.4	5.6	1.6
2012	59.5	31.2	57.8	94.2	99.8	98.3	98.0	97.8	82.3	72.6	49.4	19.6	6.3	1.5
2011	59.4	30.7	55.9	97.4	97.3	98.6	98.6	96.9	83.3	79.5	39.1	17.0	9.5	1.4
2010	61.5	32.2	63.1	97.4	97.9	99.0	98.0	97.6	78.1	80.7	43.1	23.5	10.3	1.7
2009	59.5	30.5	54.9	95.3	96.6	95.3	97.8	96.1	91.4	74.3	51.5	17.9	9.7	2.3
2008	59.4	30.2	56.1	92.8	97.3	99.2	100.0	96.4	89.7	74.2	39.0	24.5	11.3	2.0
2007	58.6	30.4	58.9	95.4	99.1	99.1	99.7	93.5	90.6	62.7	47.0	19.5	9.8	2.1
2006	57.0	30.2	60.4	94.7	98.2	99.0	100.0	90.1	78.1	74.6	43.0	14.9	8.5	2.4
2005	58.3	31.7	51.1	97.4	99.7	96.5	98.0	97.3	83.6	82.1	42.2	20.2	9.9	2.0
2004	60.8	33.9	57.2	96.5	99.8	99.9	99.9	97.1	96.9	83.5	83.6	49.6	23.0	10.9	2.9
2003	60.2	33.4	49.3	91.9	98.2	99.9	98.2	95.9	89.6	74.0	47.3	27.9	12.1	2.4
Female														
2017	56.9	27.3	56.1	97.2	98.0	98.9	100.0	94.4	86.4	78.0	44.8	17.5	6.6	1.4
2016	55.3	26.8	66.4	94.0	98.0	98.6	97.6	96.7	80.4	70.6	40.4	19.7	5.8	1.2
2015	57.4	28.0	54.4	94.4	97.5	97.8	98.5	88.7	85.2	83.8	52.5	19.8	9.6	1.9
2014	55.8	27.9	53.2	86.4	95.6	97.8	97.1	93.6	86.5	76.2	48.6	17.6	7.0	2.0
2013	57.8	29.4	57.0	90.5	97.2	98.7	99.7	98.4	83.6	76.0	44.4	15.8	9.6	2.7
2012	58.7	29.2	55.5	93.7	100.0	98.8	100.0	97.9	76.3	72.9	55.3	17.5	10.2	2.1
2011	58.3	28.7	54.9	95.7	98.5	96.2	97.9	98.3	77.1	74.8	44.0	17.4	8.7	2.6
2010	59.4	29.1	61.7	95.5	98.7	98.9	98.4	95.7	86.2	73.1	50.0	19.1	9.9	2.0
2009	59.2	27.7	55.8	95.9	97.8	96.3	95.2	98.1	88.8	73.0	55.6	19.5	11.9	1.9
2008	58.9	28.8	59.1	92.3	99.2	100.0	97.5	90.8	82.4	85.7	46.8	21.7	12.5	2.9
2007	55.5	27.4	48.3	92.5	97.6	99.5	99.7	93.2	82.2	66.1	45.0	19.7	9.2	1.5
2006	55.7	27.9	41.4	94.5	100.0	99.6	99.1	93.6	87.8	69.4	43.2	19.4	9.0	2.1
2005	57.0	29.3	57.5	93.2	99.5	98.5	99.7	99.1	89.2	71.2	46.2	21.6	8.9	2.5
2004	56.1	29.0	58.4	99.2	99.9	98.5	98.9	97.2	76.3	71.5	42.9	18.8	7.8	2.5
2003	56.2	29.3	54.2	86.0	100.0	98.7	100.0	95.4	85.1	79.7	48.8	15.8	6.9	2.1

Note: Data shown for 1947 to 1966 for the Black population are for Black and other races. Data for 1947 to 1963 exclude kindergarten. Nursery school was first collected in 1964.

Table A-12. Population 6 to 17 Years Old Enrolled Below Modal Grade, 1971–2017

(Numbers in thousands; percent; civilian noninstitutionalized population.)

Year, sex, race, and Hispanic origin	Percent below modal grade				Dropout rate, 15 to 17 years	Population in age group			
	6 to 8 years	9 to 11 years	12 to 14 years	15 to 17 years		6 to 8 years	9 to 11 years	12 to 14 years	15 to 17 years
ALL RACES									
Both Sexes									
2017	23.9	29.5	29.5	31.9	3.6	12,196	12,463	12,363	12,687
2016	23.9	29.6	29.6	30.2	3.8	12,152	12,497	12,326	12,663
2015	23.3	29.1	30.3	30.5	3.2	12,182	12,520	12,361	12,663
2014	22.6	28.0	29.9	31.0	4.1	12,320	12,286	12,433	12,502
2013	22.4	26.0	30.4	31.5	3.7	12,405	12,246	12,448	12,422
2012	23.5	27.6	30.2	33.3	2.4	12,185	12,236	12,435	12,554
2011	22.4	28.3	29.4	31.4	2.3	12,643	12,408	11,834	12,282
2010	18.2	24.6	28.6	28.9	2.2	12,618	12,190	11,963	12,273
2009	18.9	26.3	29.7	29.5	3.0	12,305	11,819	12,030	12,391
2008	19.8	27.0	31.0	30.5	2.7	12,104	11,793	12,128	12,746
2007	20.1	26.2	27.9	30.0	2.9	12,011	11,805	12,398	12,857
2006	20.1	26.1	27.9	30.5	3.0	11,776	11,902	12,473	12,926
2005	20.7	25.4	28.3	30.6	2.8	11,784	11,998	12,689	13,204
2004	21.7	25.4	28.2	32.0	3.5	11,799	12,034	12,870	12,766
2003	21.3	28.1	28.8	30.6	3.2	11,866	12,124	12,951	12,753
2002	18.0	25.5	27.1	30.1	3.3	12,029	12,421	12,592	12,187
2001	18.6	23.7	25.9	29.7	3.8	11,972	12,738	12,357	12,031
2000	19.2	24.0	27.8	30.2	4.3	12,079	12,713	12,003	11,933
1999	17.4	25.3	26.5	30.8	4.0	12,159	12,537	11,921	12,048
1998	19.0	23.8	26.7	31.9	3.8	12,165	11,960	11,600	11,314
1997	18.6	24.2	28.5	32.1	3.6	12,325	11,866	11,650	11,953
1996	17.9	23.3	28.8	31.0	4.8	12,191	11,845	11,653	11,617
1995	17.5	25.6	30.8	32.8	4.1	11,728	11,812	11,582	11,401
1994	18.9	26.2	31.3	30.9	3.8	11,601	11,528	11,462	10,560
1993r	18.7	28.1	31.0	32.3	3.8	11,363	11,283	10,981	10,247
1993	18.7	28.0	30.8	32.0	3.7	11,363	11,283	10,981	10,247
1992	19.4	28.4	30.9	30.5	3.6	11,260	11,183	10,723	10,114
1991	21.2	26.9	29.6	30.0	4.6	11,120	11,099	10,440	9,923
1990	21.5	27.6	31.0	30.1	4.7	11,015	10,914	10,152	9,912
1989	21.4	29.0	31.8	28.0	4.5	11,007	10,673	9,928	10,020
1988	20.4	28.4	28.7	26.2	5.1	10,906	10,350	9,869	10,379
1987	20.9	26.7	27.6	24.8	5.1	10,702	10,053	9,795	10,944
1986	19.2	26.5	27.3	25.8	4.9	10,389	9,959	9,908	11,149
1985	17.9	24.9	25.7	25.5	5.1	10,076	9,673	10,442	11,024
1984	16.6	23.9	27.0	24.6	5.3	9,707	9,594	10,858	10,711
1983	15.4	24.4	24.8	23.7	5.2	9,605	9,730	11,123	10,768
1982	16.6	22.8	23.9	23.0	5.4	9,492	10,169	10,989	11,131
1981	14.4	23.3	23.0	23.8	6.1	9,519	10,657	10,712	11,757
1980	14.3	20.3	22.6	22.5	6.6	9,350	10,681	10,537	11,835
1979	13.0	20.2	20.3	21.6	6.5	9,804	10,545	10,886	12,190
1978	12.4	19.5	19.2	21.8	6.5	10,246	10,448	11,391	12,346
1977	10.7	18.9	18.9	21.2	6.4	10,449	10,537	11,826	12,472
1976	10.6	18.1	19.8	22.2	6.3	10,334	10,872	12,137	12,550
1975	11.1	17.4	21.3	22.5	6.4	10,256	11,343	12,372	12,531
1974	10.3	17.8	21.7	21.6	7.1	10,343	11,789	12,415	12,566
1973	10.7	18.4	21.5	21.3	7.1	10,614	11,946	12,542	12,309
1972	10.7	19.6	21.9	22.3	6.6	11,119	12,152	12,451	12,283
1971	11.1	19.7	22.0	22.5	5.7	11,938	12,648	12,429	11,906
Male									
2017	24.7	31.0	31.6	34.8	4.1	6,244	6,341	6,295	6,460
2016	25.1	30.8	33.0	33.5	4.1	6,197	6,358	6,296	6,413
2015	24.0	30.6	30.8	33.8	3.3	6,201	6,398	6,302	6,464
2014	24.1	29.5	32.1	33.5	4.7	6,269	6,316	6,346	6,375
2013	23.7	29.5	33.2	35.2	3.9	6,264	6,272	6,347	6,328
2012	25.8	30.4	34.3	37.1	2.6	6,252	5,251	6,347	6,423
2011	24.6	31.9	32.1	35.8	2.4	6,478	6,326	6,067	6,256
2010	20.0	27.4	30.7	31.5	2.4	6,451	6,213	6,104	6,300
2009	20.0	29.7	32.4	33.2	3.2	6,260	6,058	6,144	6,334
2008	22.0	28.3	34.0	33.3	2.8	6,174	6,005	6,220	6,502
2007	23.0	28.1	29.8	33.7	2.9	6,159	6,031	6,310	6,572
2006	21.7	28.2	31.1	35.0	3.3	5,991	6,115	6,374	6,574
2005	23.2	28.6	30.7	34.3	3.0	6,014	6,126	6,523	6,645
2004	23.9	28.2	31.7	36.8	3.5	6,075	6,120	6,685	6,395
2003	23.9	32.0	31.8	35.1	3.4	6,198	6,331	6,426	6,569
2002	20.3	29.2	31.0	35.6	3.5	6,156	6,349	6,436	6,210
2001	22.1	26.1	28.7	34.0	4.3	6,147	6,540	6,311	6,182
2000	22.1	27.2	31.3	34.3	4.5	6,181	6,504	6,148	6,136

r = Revised, controlled to 1990 census based population estimates; previous 1993 data controlled to 1980 census based population estimates.

Table A-12. Population 6 to 17 Years Old Enrolled Below Modal Grade, 1971–2017—*Continued*

(Numbers in thousands; percent; civilian noninstitutionalized population.)

Year, sex, race, and Hispanic origin	Percent below modal grade				Dropout rate, 15 to 17 years	Population in age group			
	6 to 8 years	9 to 11 years	12 to 14 years	15 to 17 years		6 to 8 years	9 to 11 years	12 to 14 years	15 to 17 years
1999	18.8	28.9	30.2	36.2	3.9	6,211	6,471	6,048	6,195
1998	21.4	26.6	30.4	37.4	4.1	6,234	6,125	5,897	5,791
1997	21.9	27.7	33.4	37.8	3.7	6,295	6,112	5,932	6,126
1996	20.7	26.0	33.9	36.9	4.5	6,268	6,043	5,934	5,985
1995	20.2	28.0	35.2	38.5	3.5	5,999	6,027	5,930	5,840
1994	21.1	28.0	35.6	35.7	3.9	5,894	6,026	5,874	5,640
1993r	21.2	32.1	35.4	40.3	3.3	5,837	5,736	5,629	5,262
1993	21.1	32.0	35.0	38.7	3.1	5,837	5,736	5,629	5,262
1992	21.6	32.6	37.0	35.2	2.7	5,738	5,742	5,502	5,166
1991	24.0	30.7	34.7	35.5	4.3	5,674	5,704	5,343	5,085
1990	23.9	32.0	36.2	35.3	4.6	5,629	5,603	5,200	5,078
1989	25.1	32.9	36.7	33.4	4.3	5,632	5,472	5,088	5,151
1988	23.5	33.2	33.7	30.6	4.8	5,580	5,298	5,065	5,286
1987	23.7	31.8	31.8	29.2	4.6	5,496	5,147	5,036	5,535
1986	22.9	30.4	32.2	30.2	4.9	5,311	5,113	5,066	5,697
1985	20.6	28.3	29.0	30.2	4.9	5,159	4,946	5,340	5,623
1984	18.8	27.7	31.1	30.2	5.5	4,963	4,905	5,521	5,469
1983	17.8	28.7	30.3	28.5	5.3	4,913	4,974	5,690	5,463
1982	19.2	26.4	28.0	27.9	5.2	4,852	5,198	5,566	5,688
1981	17.2	27.9	25.6	28.1	6.2	4,866	5,447	5,510	5,914
1980	16.4	23.4	27.3	26.8	6.4	4,774	5,453	5,282	6,067
1979	15.5	23.4	24.1	27.4	5.9	5,004	5,379	5,555	6,174
1978	14.7	22.9	22.9	26.2	6.7	5,227	5,326	5,797	6,265
1977	12.5	22.4	22.6	25.3	6.1	5,327	5,371	6,044	6,297
1976	12.5	20.9	23.4	27.5	5.7	5,265	5,540	6,185	6,356
1975	12.6	21.2	25.8	26.8	5.7	5,223	5,782	6,336	6,309
1974	12.2	21.2	25.9	26.3	7.0	5,267	6,011	6,329	6,352
1973	12.8	20.8	25.2	26.4	6.8	5,403	6,082	6,397	6,215
1972	12.5	23.3	26.8	26.8	6.2	5,662	6,188	6,322	6,232
1971	13.5	22.8	26.1	27.2	5.0	6,088	6,440	6,293	6,019
Female									
2017	23.0	28.0	27.2	28.9	3.1	5,952	6,122	6,068	6,227
2016	22.6	28.3	26.1	26.7	3.5	5,955	6,140	6,030	6,250
2015	22.5	27.6	29.9	27.0	3.0	5,981	6,123	6,060	6,199
2014	21.1	26.4	27.6	28.4	3.4	6,050	5,970	6,087	6,126
2013	21.1	22.3	27.6	27.5	3.4	6,141	5,974	6,100	6,095
2012	21.0	24.6	25.8	29.3	2.1	5,933	5,985	6,087	6,132
2011	20.0	24.7	26.6	26.9	2.1	6,165	6,082	5,767	6,026
2010	16.4	21.7	26.4	26.1	1.5	6,166	5,977	5,860	5,973
2009	17.8	22.8	26.9	25.6	2.8	6,046	5,761	5,886	6,057
2008	17.5	25.6	27.7	27.7	2.4	5,930	5,787	5,908	6,244
2007	17.2	24.1	25.9	26.2	2.9	5,852	5,773	6,088	6,285
2006	18.4	23.9	24.6	25.9	2.6	5,785	5,787	6,099	6,352
2005	18.2	22.0	25.8	26.8	2.6	5,769	5,872	6,167	6,559
2004	19.4	22.5	24.4	27.1	3.5	5,724	5,914	6,185	6,371
2003	18.5	23.8	25.8	25.8	3.0	5,668	5,793	6,524	6,184
2002	15.6	21.7	23.0	24.4	3.1	5,872	6,072	6,156	5,977
2001	14.9	21.3	23.0	25.2	3.3	5,825	6,197	6,046	5,849
2000	16.1	20.6	24.2	25.8	4.2	5,897	6,209	5,855	5,797
1999	16.1	21.6	22.7	25.1	4.2	5,948	6,066	5,872	5,852
1998	16.5	20.9	22.8	26.2	3.5	5,931	5,835	5,703	5,523
1997	15.1	20.4	23.3	26.1	3.5	6,030	5,754	5,718	5,827
1996	14.9	20.4	23.4	24.7	5.3	5,923	5,802	5,719	5,632
1995	14.6	23.1	26.0	26.7	4.4	5,728	5,786	5,653	5,552
1994	16.5	24.2	26.7	24.8	3.6	5,705	5,644	5,666	5,384
1993r	16.3	24.0	26.4	26.4	4.4	5,526	5,545	5,353	4,984
1993	16.1	23.9	26.2	24.9	4.3	5,526	5,545	5,353	4,984
1992	17.1	23.5	24.6	25.6	4.5	5,523	5,441	5,220	4,947
1991	18.2	22.8	24.6	24.2	5.1	5,445	5,395	5,098	4,838
1990	19.1	23.2	25.7	24.7	4.7	5,387	5,312	4,951	4,834
1989	18.1	22.6	26.6	22.3	4.6	5,375	5,201	4,840	4,869
1988	17.3	23.6	23.4	21.7	5.4	5,327	5,052	4,803	5,093
1987	17.8	21.5	23.2	20.2	5.6	5,206	4,906	4,759	5,408
1986	15.2	22.4	22.1	21.1	4.9	5,078	4,846	4,842	5,452
1985	15.1	21.4	22.1	20.6	5.5	4,917	4,727	5,102	5,401
1984	14.2	19.8	22.9	18.7	5.1	4,744	4,689	5,337	5,242
1983	12.9	19.9	19.1	18.6	5.2	4,692	4,756	5,433	5,305
1982	13.8	19.0	19.7	17.9	5.7	4,640	4,971	5,423	5,443
1981	11.6	18.4	20.1	19.6	6.1	4,653	5,210	5,202	5,843
1980	12.1	17.0	17.8	18.0	6.7	4,576	5,228	5,255	5,768

r = Revised, controlled to 1990 census based population estimates; previous 1993 data controlled to 1980 census based population estimates.

Table A-12. Population 6 to 17 Years Old Enrolled Below Modal Grade, 1971–2017—*Continued*

(Numbers in thousands; percent; civilian noninstitutionalized population.)

Year, sex, race, and Hispanic origin	Percent below modal grade				Dropout rate, 15 to 17 years	Population in age group			
	6 to 8 years	9 to 11 years	12 to 14 years	15 to 17 years		6 to 8 years	9 to 11 years	12 to 14 years	15 to 17 years
1979	10.4	16.9	16.4	15.6	7.1	4,800	5,166	5,331	6,016
1978	10.1	16.0	15.3	17.2	6.4	5,019	5,122	5,594	6,081
1977	8.9	15.2	15.0	17.1	6.6	5,122	5,166	5,782	6,175
1976	8.6	15.1	16.0	16.8	7.0	5,069	5,332	5,952	6,194
1975	9.4	13.5	16.7	18.2	7.2	5,033	5,561	6,036	6,222
1974	8.3	14.4	17.4	16.8	7.1	5,076	5,778	6,086	6,214
1973	8.7	15.8	16.5	16.1	7.4	5,211	5,864	6,145	6,094
1972	8.9	15.7	17.0	17.7	7.1	5,457	5,964	6,129	6,051
1971	8.7	12.3	17.8	17.6	6.5	5,850	6,208	6,136	5,887
WHITE ALONE									
Both Sexes									
2017	24.6	29.2	29.6	31.7	3.6	8,720	9,036	9,077	9,210
2016	24.5	29.7	30.1	30.4	4.1	8,772	9,060	9,073	9,267
2015	23.9	29.5	30.6	30.5	3.2	8,865	9,038	9,095	9,271
2014	23.2	27.7	29.1	30.3	3.9	8,983	9,035	9,181	9,220
2013	22.7	26.6	31.1	31.8	3.7	9,014	9,034	9,236	9,228
2012	23.9	27.7	30.7	32.7	2.4	9,006	9,067	9,247	9,291
2011	23.1	28.3	30.2	31.4	2.2	9,488	9,401	9,020	9,337
2010	19.1	24.7	28.3	28.5	2.3	9,455	9,276	9,110	9,344
2009	19.1	26.2	29.0	28.6	3.3	9,377	9,006	9,167	9,495
2008	20.3	27.1	29.4	29.7	2.6	9,288	8,967	9,250	9,658
2007	21.3	26.2	27.6	28.3	2.8	9,118	9,021	9,432	9,834
2006	20.6	25.5	26.8	29.9	3.0	8,981	9,074	9,542	9,813
2005	21.4	23.8	28.0	29.5	2.6	8,929	9,194	9,680	10,131
2004	22.4	25.6	27.6	30.7	3.8	9,051	9,173	9,853	9,784
2003[1]	21.5	27.6	28.3	29.4	3.2	9,102	9,112	9,875	9,889
2002	18.1	25.7	26.2	29.6	3.1	9,230	9,682	9,832	9,520
2001	19.2	22.7	25.2	28.9	3.8	9,330	9,826	9,651	9,480
2000	19.4	23.7	26.3	29.7	4.5	9,404	9,937	9,368	9,449
1999	18.3	24.6	25.8	30.0	4.2	9,539	9,768	9,323	9,428
1998	19.5	23.5	25.8	30.5	3.8	9,481	9,413	9,130	8,926
1997	18.8	24.0	27.9	30.3	3.5	9,555	9,390	9,167	9,352
1996	18.1	22.6	27.6	30.1	4.9	9,458	9,420	9,184	9,135
1995	17.7	24.9	29.2	31.0	3.9	9,221	9,340	9,130	8,933
1994	19.4	25.8	30.1	29.6	3.7	9,087	9,261	9,121	8,668
1993r	18.8	27.3	29.4	31.2	3.9	9,018	8,967	8,728	8,160
1993	18.7	27.2	29.2	29.7	3.6	9,074	9,017	8,783	8,159
1992	19.5	27.5	29.6	28.1	3.5	8,956	8,996	8,520	8,031
1991	21.3	25.7	27.7	27.2	4.7	8,874	8,840	8,328	7,903
1990	21.9	26.8	28.4	27.3	4.6	8,860	8,752	8,140	7,909
1989	22.4	26.8	29.9	25.7	4.6	8,858	8,527	7,994	8,026
1988	21.0	27.6	27.2	23.9	5.4	8,758	8,323	7,929	8,353
1987	21.1	25.9	26.0	22.7	5.1	8,606	8,117	7,846	8,887
1986	19.1	25.1	25.3	23.7	5.0	8,395	8,000	8,054	9,037
1985	18.0	23.3	23.3	23.0	5.3	8,136	7,840	8,429	9,045
1984	16.3	22.1	24.7	22.7	5.6	7,915	7,781	8,827	8,853
1983	15.5	22.4	23.1	21.1	5.4	7,821	7,906	9,152	8,831
1982	16.4	21.8	22.1	21.1	5.6	7,729	8,294	9,035	9,184
1981	14.7	22.2	21.0	21.6	6.1	7,782	8,741	8,813	9,762
1980	14.1	19.0	21.1	19.3	6.7	7,635	8,823	8,739	10,132
1979	12.9	18.4	18.5	19.4	6.5	8,041	8,747	9,026	10,239
1978	12.4	18.0	17.9	19.3	6.8	8,460	8,686	9,522	10,358
1977	10.6	17.7	17.5	19.3	6.6	8,675	8,771	9,918	10,510
1976	10.5	17.2	18.7	19.7	6.3	8,612	9,066	10,187	10,622
1975	11.0	16.0	20.0	20.4	6.3	8,566	9,486	10,466	10,583
1974	10.2	16.5	19.7	19.4	6.9	8,656	9,912	10,508	10,678
1973	10.6	17.3	19.9	19.1	7.0	8,929	10,117	10,704	10,481
1972	10.3	18.2	20.1	20.0	6.6	9,359	10,313	10,606	10,506
1971	10.5	18.3	20.4	19.9	5.5	9,988	10,692	10,682	10,231
Male									
2017	26.1	31.9	32.0	33.8	4.0	4,460	4,622	4,643	4,704
2016	26.4	30.6	32.9	34.6	4.3	4,486	4,637	4,639	4,737
2015	25.5	31.0	31.3	33.8	3.6	4,535	4,628	4,650	4,742
2014	24.7	29.3	31.1	33.2	4.5	4,600	4,629	4,703	4,721
2013	25.1	30.1	33.9	35.3	4.2	4,618	4,626	4,733	4,726
2012	25.6	30.3	35.4	36.9	2.8	4,615	4,642	4,741	4,764

r = Revised, controlled to 1990 census based population estimates; previous 1993 data controlled to 1980 census based population estimates.
[1]Starting in 2003, respondents could identify more than one race. Except as noted, the race data in this table from 2003 onward represent those respondents who indicated only one race category.

Table A-12. Population 6 to 17 Years Old Enrolled Below Modal Grade, 1971–2017—*Continued*

(Numbers in thousands; percent; civilian noninstitutionalized population.)

Year, sex, race, and Hispanic origin	Percent below modal grade				Dropout rate, 15 to 17 years	Population in age group			
	6 to 8 years	9 to 11 years	12 to 14 years	15 to 17 years		6 to 8 years	9 to 11 years	12 to 14 years	15 to 17 years
2011	25.7	31.6	32.9	36.5	2.2	4,861	4,816	4,626	4,809
2010	21.3	27.2	30.3	31.2	3.0	4,825	4,746	4,666	4,805
2009	20.4	29.5	31.7	31.9	3.5	4,816	4,611	4,697	4,866
2008	22.5	29.3	32.6	32.9	2.7	4,764	4,568	4,748	4,966
2007	24.3	28.4	29.5	31.8	2.9	4,671	4,620	4,851	5,022
2006	22.5	27.0	29.8	34.2	3.3	4,596	4,652	4,900	5,011
2005	24.3	27.4	31.0	33.2	2.7	4,576	4,715	4,995	5,116
2004	24.9	28.0	31.4	35.2	3.8	4,706	4,647	5,168	4,905
2003[1]	24.4	31.6	31.2	34.0	3.4	4,785	4,795	4,961	5,026
2002	21.7	29.5	30.4	34.7	3.2	4,737	4,965	5,044	4,875
2001	22.7	25.3	28.3	32.8	4.4	4,789	5,040	4,949	4,862
2000	22.5	27.6	29.6	34.0	4.4	4,815	5,094	4,798	4,861
1999	19.9	28.2	29.7	35.8	4.2	4,883	5,009	4,777	4,851
1998	21.9	26.4	30.2	36.2	4.4	4,851	4,823	4,686	4,571
1997	22.3	27.8	32.7	37.0	3.8	4,897	4,819	4,702	4,821
1996	20.8	25.9	32.3	36.5	4.5	4,849	4,836	4,706	4,694
1995	20.5	28.0	33.4	36.5	3.8	4,727	4,797	4,680	4,592
1994	22.0	27.9	34.4	35.2	4.0	4,659	4,758	4,679	4,457
1993r	21.4	31.8	33.8	37.6	3.2	4,625	4,601	4,476	4,178
1993	21.4	31.6	33.6	36.1	3.1	4,662	4,614	4,485	4,178
1992	21.5	31.8	35.8	32.4	2.8	4,602	4,607	4,359	4,115
1991	24.4	29.1	32.5	32.5	4.2	4,556	4,568	4,270	4,047
1990	24.6	31.3	33.3	32.6	4.8	4,555	4,482	4,186	4,054
1989	26.0	32.1	35.0	30.8	4.6	4,544	4,378	4,112	4,107
1988	24.7	32.8	32.2	28.8	5.1	4,493	4,272	4,062	4,281
1987	24.6	30.5	30.4	26.6	4.5	4,415	4,167	4,069	4,504
1986	22.9	28.9	30.1	27.9	5.2	4,307	4,108	4,125	4,624
1985	21.1	26.5	26.7	28.0	4.9	4,175	4,024	4,307	4,634
1984	18.1	25.8	28.7	28.1	5.8	4,061	3,994	4,501	4,542
1983	18.1	26.3	28.0	26.3	5.6	4,002	4,054	4,697	4,481
1982	19.3	26.2	26.2	26.1	5.3	3,956	4,260	4,591	4,711
1981	17.3	26.9	24.2	25.4	6.3	3,990	4,480	4,556	4,937
1980	16.3	21.9	25.7	23.9	6.7	3,907	4,517	4,399	5,066
1979	15.4	20.8	22.3	24.8	6.2	4,114	4,475	4,616	5,201
1978	14.7	21.2	22.0	23.1	7.2	4,328	4,441	4,843	5,287
1977	12.5	21.1	21.2	23.5	6.3	4,436	4,484	5,079	5,325
1976	12.6	20.2	22.1	24.8	5.6	4,402	4,632	5,200	5,398
1975	12.9	19.7	24.7	24.7	5.4	4,376	4,848	5,385	5,332
1974	12.1	19.5	23.7	23.8	7.0	4,422	5,066	5,383	5,402
1973	12.5	19.6	23.1	24.0	6.6	4,559	5,165	5,469	5,319
1972	12.2	21.9	24.6	24.3	6.1	4,778	5,266	5,410	5,340
1971	12.6	21.6	23.9	24.4	4.6	5,106	5,461	5,455	5,185
Female									
2017	23.0	26.4	27.0	29.5	3.1	4,260	4,414	4,434	4,506
2016	22.5	28.8	27.1	26.0	3.9	4,286	4,423	4,434	4,530
2015	22.1	27.8	29.9	27.0	2.7	4,330	4,410	4,445	4,529
2014	21.7	26.0	27.0	27.3	3.4	4,383	4,406	4,479	4,500
2013	20.2	23.0	28.2	28.0	3.1	4,397	4,408	4,502	4,502
2012	22.0	24.9	25.7	28.2	2.0	4,392	4,425	4,506	4,527
2011	20.4	24.8	27.4	26.1	2.2	4,627	4,585	4,394	4,528
2010	16.9	22.1	26.1	25.7	1.4	4,630	4,530	4,444	4,539
2009	17.8	22.8	26.2	25.1	3.0	4,561	4,394	4,470	4,629
2008	18.0	24.8	26.0	26.3	2.4	4,524	4,398	4,502	4,692
2007	18.2	23.9	25.7	24.6	2.7	4,447	4,401	4,582	4,812
2006	18.6	24.0	23.8	25.5	2.6	4,385	4,422	4,643	4,801
2005	18.3	20.1	24.8	25.8	2.5	4,353	4,479	4,685	5,015
2004	19.7	23.3	23.4	26.1	3.8	4,345	4,527	4,686	4,878
2003[1]	18.3	23.1	25.3	24.7	3.0	4,317	4,317	4,914	4,863
2002	14.4	21.7	21.9	24.3	3.0	4,493	4,717	4,788	4,645
2001	15.5	20.0	21.8	24.9	3.1	4,541	4,786	4,701	4,618
2000	16.1	19.7	22.9	25.2	4.5	4,587	4,843	4,570	4,588
1999	16.7	20.7	21.8	23.9	4.1	4,655	4,579	4,546	4,578
1998	16.9	20.5	21.2	24.4	3.2	4,629	4,589	4,444	4,355
1997	15.1	20.0	22.7	23.2	3.3	4,658	4,571	4,464	4,530
1996	15.3	19.2	22.7	23.2	5.3	4,609	4,583	4,477	4,441
1995	14.7	21.6	24.8	25.0	4.1	4,494	4,543	4,449	4,342
1994	16.7	23.5	25.7	23.6	3.4	4,427	4,504	4,443	4,212
1993r	15.9	22.6	24.8	24.4	4.3	4,393	4,366	4,252	3,982

r = Revised, controlled to 1990 census based population estimates; previous 1993 data controlled to 1980 census based population estimates.
[1]Starting in 2003, respondents could identify more than one race. Except as noted, the race data in this table from 2003 onward represent those respondents who indicated only one race category.

Table A-12. Population 6 to 17 Years Old Enrolled Below Modal Grade, 1971–2017—*Continued*

(Numbers in thousands; percent; civilian noninstitutionalized population.)

Year, sex, race, and Hispanic origin	Percent below modal grade				Dropout rate, 15 to 17 years	Population in age group			
	6 to 8 years	9 to 11 years	12 to 14 years	15 to 17 years		6 to 8 years	9 to 11 years	12 to 14 years	15 to 17 years
1993	15.8	22.5	24.6	23.1	4.2	4,412	4,404	4,298	3,982
1992	17.3	22.9	23.2	23.6	4.3	4,354	4,389	4,161	3,916
1991	18.1	22.1	22.6	21.5	5.2	4,318	4,272	4,058	3,856
1990	19.0	22.2	23.2	21.8	4.5	4,305	4,270	3,954	3,855
1989	18.6	21.3	24.5	20.3	4.7	4,314	4,149	3,882	3,919
1988	17.1	22.2	21.9	18.8	5.6	4,265	4,051	3,867	4,072
1987	17.3	21.0	21.3	18.7	5.8	4,191	3,950	3,777	4,383
1986	15.0	21.1	20.2	19.3	4.8	4,088	3,892	3,929	4,413
1985	14.8	19.9	19.7	17.6	5.7	3,961	3,816	4,122	4,411
1984	14.3	18.3	20.5	17.0	5.4	3,854	3,787	4,326	4,311
1983	12.7	18.3	17.9	15.8	5.2	3,819	3,852	4,455	4,350
1982	13.4	17.2	17.8	15.8	6.0	3,773	4,034	4,444	4,473
1981	11.9	17.3	17.6	17.6	5.9	3,792	4,261	4,257	4,825
1980	11.7	16.0	16.5	14.7	6.6	3,728	4,306	4,340	5,066
1979	10.3	15.8	14.5	13.8	6.9	3,927	4,272	4,410	5,038
1978	10.0	14.7	13.7	15.2	6.4	4,132	4,245	4,679	5,071
1977	8.5	14.1	13.7	14.9	6.8	4,239	4,287	4,839	5,185
1976	8.4	14.1	15.1	14.5	6.9	4,210	4,434	4,987	5,224
1975	9.1	12.2	15.1	16.0	7.1	4,190	4,638	5,081	5,251
1974	8.2	13.4	15.5	15.0	6.7	4,234	4,846	5,125	5,276
1973	8.5	14.8	16.5	14.0	7.4	4,370	4,952	5,235	5,162
1972	8.3	14.2	15.4	15.5	7.2	4,581	5,047	5,196	5,166
1971	8.4	14.9	16.6	15.2	6.3	4,882	5,231	5,227	5,046
WHITE ALONE NON-HISPANIC									
Both Sexes									
2017	25.4	31.2	27.8	31.9	3.3	5,968	6,291	6,497	6,739
2016	24.9	29.3	30.4	29.6	4.4	6,038	6,340	6,533	6,757
2015	24.9	29.4	30.2	29.5	2.7	6,185	6,411	6,574	6,806
2014	23.9	28.0	28.7	29.2	4.0	6,300	6,443	6,656	6,829
2013	22.7	25.4	30.4	30.7	3.6	6,287	6,489	6,752	6,865
2012	24.6	27.4	30.8	31.4	2.2	6,366	6,552	6,812	6,916
2011	24.5	28.5	30.6	29.9	1.8	6,648	6,765	6,750	7,033
2010	20.3	24.7	28.0	26.8	2.2	6,707	6,836	6,821	7,243
2009	19.4	26.3	29.3	27.8	2.8	6,768	6,755	6,989	7,437
2008	21.2	27.7	29.4	28.4	2.2	6,798	6,768	7,008	7,534
2007	21.3	25.3	26.5	26.8	2.1	6,763	6,783	7,182	7,784
2006	20.5	24.5	25.1	28.6	2.3	6,748	6,887	7,368	7,827
2005	22.4	23.2	26.3	29.0	2.1	6,728	7,052	7,584	8,150
2004	22.7	25.1	27.0	29.8	3.3	6,878	7,090	7,768	7,892
2003[1]	21.8	27.1	27.3	28.7	2.8	7,006	7,102	7,889	7,980
2002	18.9	24.9	25.8	28.1	2.5	7,118	7,627	7,913	7,803
2001	19.9	23.1	25.3	28.1	3.1	7,325	7,726	7,773	7,829
2000	19.4	23.7	26.1	28.8	3.5	7,418	8,045	7,727	7,852
1999	18.9	24.2	25.3	28.9	3.6	7,717	7,938	7,669	7,879
1998	20.5	23.7	26.0	28.9	3.0	7,755	7,794	7,697	7,859
1997	19.7	24.6	27.3	28.4	3.2	7,729	7,775	7,789	7,866
1996	18.8	22.7	26.2	28.6	4.2	7,803	7,792	7,731	7,716
1995	18.2	24.5	28.0	29.2	3.4	7,853	8,000	7,872	7,795
1994	19.8	25.6	30.0	28.0	3.1	7,779	7,864	7,845	7,490
1993	18.8	27.2	28.8	29.5	3.0	7,736	7,802	7,600	7,022
Male									
2017	27.9	33.8	30.6	35.0	3.6	3,064	3,225	3,323	3,447
2016	27.5	31.3	32.8	32.9	4.9	3,086	3,251	3,360	3,467
2015	27.6	31.8	30.7	32.7	2.9	3,150	3,289	3,390	3,479
2014	25.0	28.9	31.1	31.5	4.6	3,218	3,303	3,412	3,487
2013	25.0	28.4	33.0	34.9	4.2	3,232	3,320	3,474	3,515
2012	25.9	30.8	31.4	32.5	2.2	3,264	3,371	3,518	3,545
2011	28.1	32.4	33.8	35.8	1.9	3,394	3,473	3,472	3,619
2010	23.3	27.7	30.6	30.5	3.1	3,414	3,498	3,487	3,728
2009	21.8	30.1	31.9	32.0	3.1	3,489	3,453	3,593	3,793
2008	24.4	29.9	33.2	31.8	2.4	3,485	3,459	3,599	3,862
2007	24.1	28.4	28.1	30.3	2.2	3,457	3,473	3,715	3,970
2006	23.1	26.0	27.6	32.4	2.9	3,449	3,537	3,775	3,984
2005	25.4	26.8	28.2	32.5	2.2	3,450	3,618	3,902	4,136
2004	25.0	27.9	30.6	35.0	3.4	3,548	3,605	4,054	3,994
2003[1]	24.6	31.7	30.7	33.4	2.9	3,668	3,725	3,960	4,101
2002	22.7	29.0	30.7	33.6	2.4	3,667	3,969	4,005	4,038

[1]Starting in 2003, respondents could identify more than one race. Except as noted, the race data in this table from 2003 onward represent those respondents who indicated only one race category.

Table A-12. Population 6 to 17 Years Old Enrolled Below Modal Grade, 1971–2017—*Continued*

(Numbers in thousands; percent; civilian noninstitutionalized population.)

Year, sex, race, and Hispanic origin	Percent below modal grade				Dropout rate, 15 to 17 years	Population in age group			
	6 to 8 years	9 to 11 years	12 to 14 years	15 to 17 years		6 to 8 years	9 to 11 years	12 to 14 years	15 to 17 years
2001	23.1	26.2	28.5	31.6	3.7	3,808	3,971	3,920	4,020
2000	22.5	27.7	30.0	33.4	3.4	3,795	4,135	3,970	4,034
1999	20.3	27.7	29.7	35.1	3.5	3,955	4,076	3,913	4,058
1998	23.1	26.5	30.8	34.3	3.6	4,016	4,003	3,894	3,981
1997	24.1	29.0	32.5	35.3	3.8	3,977	3,971	3,996	4,020
1996	22.5	25.9	30.8	35.1	4.1	3,964	4,035	3,957	3,959
1995	22.1	27.3	31.9	34.9	3.1	4,038	4,094	4,017	4,010
1994	22.8	28.0	34.3	33.6	2.9	3,993	4,010	4,030	3,866
1993	22.0	31.5	33.2	35.6	2.4	3,952	4,021	3,889	3,578
Female									
2017	22.7	28.5	24.9	28.6	3.0	2,904	3,066	3,173	3,293
2016	22.3	27.3	27.9	26.1	3.9	2,952	3,089	3,173	3,290
2015	22.2	26.7	29.6	26.1	2.6	3,035	3,122	3,184	3,327
2014	22.7	27.0	26.2	26.8	3.3	3,082	3,141	3,245	3,342
2013	20.3	22.1	27.6	26.2	3.0	3,055	3,169	3,279	3,350
2012	23.3	23.8	25.0	26.2	2.8	3,102	3,181	3,295	3,371
2011	20.8	24.4	27.3	23.6	1.7	3,254	3,292	3,278	3,414
2010	17.2	21.5	25.3	23.0	1.3	3,294	3,338	3,334	3,515
2009	16.9	22.4	26.6	23.5	2.4	3,280	3,301	3,396	3,644
2008	18.0	25.3	25.4	24.9	2.1	3,313	3,309	3,408	3,673
2007	18.4	22.0	24.7	23.1	2.0	3,306	3,310	3,467	3,814
2006	17.6	22.8	22.6	24.6	1.8	3,299	3,350	3,593	3,843
2005	19.2	19.4	24.2	25.3	2.0	3,277	3,434	3,682	4,014
2004	20.3	22.2	23.1	24.5	3.3	3,330	3,485	3,714	3,898
2003[1]	18.6	22.2	24.0	23.7	2.6	3,337	3,377	3,929	3,878
2002	14.8	20.4	20.9	22.2	2.6	3,451	3,658	3,908	3,765
2001	16.4	19.8	22.0	24.4	2.6	3,517	3,755	3,853	3,809
2000	16.2	19.6	21.9	23.9	3.7	3,623	3,910	3,757	3,818
1999	17.4	20.5	20.8	22.3	3.6	3,761	3,864	3,757	3,840
1998	17.6	20.8	21.2	23.5	2.5	3,740	3,791	3,803	3,878
1997	15.0	19.9	21.8	21.3	2.6	3,752	3,804	3,793	3,846
1996	15.0	19.3	21.3	21.7	4.3	3,839	3,757	3,773	3,757
1995	14.1	21.5	23.8	23.1	3.8	3,815	3,906	3,854	3,784
1994	16.6	23.1	25.5	22.1	3.2	3,786	3,854	3,814	3,624
1993	15.4	22.6	24.2	23.1	3.6	3,784	3,782	3,710	3,444
BLACK ALONE									
Both Sexes									
2017	23.0	32.3	31.8	34.9	4.4	1,962	1,814	1,818	1,873
2016	23.5	33.0	30.6	31.4	2.8	1,877	1,878	1,817	1,895
2015	21.2	28.2	31.7	34.1	3.1	1,794	1,913	1,831	1,899
2014	21.8	31.5	34.8	35.8	5.2	1,772	1,822	1,871	1,869
2013	23.9	27.4	31.5	34.1	4.6	1,885	1,781	1,892	1,865
2012	24.5	28.0	34.9	36.6	2.6	1,719	1,828	1,897	1,879
2011	20.2	30.0	28.9	32.4	2.7	1,882	1,831	1,773	1,855
2010	16.7	26.3	33.0	31.5	2.2	1,871	1,710	1,809	1,911
2009	20.1	30.7	32.7	34.8	2.7	1,692	1,814	1,801	1,943
2008	18.6	27.3	40.9	37.8	3.1	1,781	1,797	1,851	1,994
2007	17.7	28.1	33.0	39.2	3.0	1,797	1,770	1,937	2,021
2006	19.1	29.9	35.7	35.7	3.1	1,813	1,811	1,960	2,059
2005	20.8	35.6	34.1	38.8	4.2	1,806	1,826	2,011	2,085
2004	19.8	27.4	34.1	40.1	2.3	1,775	1,906	2,034	1,992
2003[1]	22.7	34.2	33.9	37.4	3.7	1,760	2,043	2,110	1,950
2002	19.6	28.6	32.8	36.2	3.9	2,017	2,048	2,036	1,943
2001	17.3	29.7	31.1	35.6	4.0	1,937	2,144	1,998	1,823
2000	19.6	26.9	37.8	34.6	4.7	1,976	2,082	1,961	1,852
1999	16.1	30.2	31.7	34.8	3.5	1,948	2,108	1,912	1,911
1998	18.3	26.6	31.4	38.4	3.6	2,019	1,934	1,840	1,801
1997	18.4	26.1	33.5	40.0	3.8	2,061	1,908	1,845	1,938
1996	18.4	29.2	36.8	36.9	4.8	2,054	1,847	1,839	1,858
1995	16.8	31.1	38.3	41.3	4.1	1,909	1,890	1,822	1,851
1994	18.4	35.1	36.1	37.7	3.3	1,912	1,795	1,835	1,809
1993r	20.0	33.6	34.8	45.1	3.6	1,767	1,763	1,747	1,641
1993	19.9	33.4	38.8	43.3	3.6	1,709	1,710	1,695	1,642
1992	20.6	28.7	38.0	40.6	4.2	1,761	1,635	1,686	1,621
1991	21.0	34.3	40.7	43.4	5.3	1,674	1,701	1,643	1,574
1990	21.9	33.1	46.1	42.9	5.2	1,645	1,712	1,574	1,571

r = Revised, controlled to 1990 census based population estimates; previous 1993 data controlled to 1980 census based population estimates.
[1]Starting in 2003, respondents could identify more than one race. Except as noted, the race data in this table from 2003 onward represent those respondents who indicated only one race category.

Table A-12. Population 6 to 17 Years Old Enrolled Below Modal Grade, 1971–2017—*Continued*

(Numbers in thousands; percent; civilian noninstitutionalized population.)

Year, sex, race, and Hispanic origin	Percent below modal grade				Dropout rate, 15 to 17 years	Population in age group			
	6 to 8 years	9 to 11 years	12 to 14 years	15 to 17 years		6 to 8 years	9 to 11 years	12 to 14 years	15 to 17 years
1989	19.6	34.0	41.3	39.3	3.9	1,642	1,682	1,554	1,618
1988	18.6	33.1	37.6	38.4	4.7	1,680	1,629	1,545	1,637
1987	19.8	33.1	35.6	35.3	5.1	1,679	1,554	1,552	1,654
1986	12.7	34.6	38.5	38.3	4.6	1,611	1,542	1,530	1,692
1985	18.0	33.9	37.9	37.7	4.6	1,568	1,498	1,635	1,627
1984	17.9	32.3	38.1	34.6	4.1	1,445	1,442	1,652	1,536
1983	15.3	34.9	34.4	35.8	4.7	1,429	1,450	1,601	1,617
1982	17.2	27.1	32.5	32.6	4.6	1,765	1,874	1,953	1,947
1981	13.9	26.2	33.7	36.1	6.3	1,437	1,594	1,615	1,679
1980	14.9	27.8	30.5	37.6	5.1	1,460	1,606	1,568	1,728
1979	12.5	29.5	29.2	34.3	6.4	1,515	1,576	1,636	1,722
1978	12.6	27.8	26.6	35.4	5.7	1,557	1,523	1,664	1,764
1977	11.3	24.9	26.3	32.2	5.4	1,552	1,558	1,698	1,754
1976	10.5	23.2	26.1	35.6	6.7	1,493	1,633	1,724	1,726
1975	11.9	26.1	29.2	34.9	8.0	1,489	1,656	1,720	1,760
1974	11.6	26.2	33.2	34.4	8.2	1,509	1,684	1,750	1,682
1973	12.0	25.8	31.7	35.4	8.2	1,525	1,650	1,671	1,671
1972	13.2	30.5	33.1	37.3	6.6	1,585	1,638	1,691	1,636
1971	14.2	27.9	34.7	40.2	7.0	1,794	1,787	1,638	1,533
Male									
2017	22.9	31.3	34.5	39.6	5.4	990	908	919	939
2016	21.1	35.2	36.4	30.0	2.4	962	931	918	952
2015	17.9	29.6	33.4	38.0	2.2	903	971	927	954
2014	23.0	33.4	37.2	38.0	4.6	883	959	948	939
2013	21.2	29.9	35.7	40.3	3.8	921	905	961	936
2012	28.5	33.1	36.9	39.1	1.4	918	911	963	943
2011	20.9	35.2	32.2	34.5	4.1	977	902	898	927
2010	16.8	30.9	34.7	35.0	3.0	954	856	912	961
2009	19.2	34.6	34.4	42.3	2.6	805	954	911	980
2008	19.4	26.2	46.3	41.3	3.4	917	908	934	992
2007	22.7	31.6	35.4	43.5	2.2	946	886	964	1,027
2006	20.3	35.1	40.3	43.9	3.3	929	920	991	1,032
2005	22.6	37.9	35.8	43.0	5.2	912	913	1,011	1,041
2004	21.0	31.4	37.8	46.5	2.0	885	992	1,012	1,009
2003[1]	23.6	36.8	38.7	43.4	3.9	927	1,059	975	1,047
2002	17.5	32.5	37.0	44.7	5.0	1,044	1,036	1,012	973
2001	21.1	31.1	33.3	42.8	3.5	978	1,108	1,010	924
2000	20.8	27.5	43.3	37.0	6.4	1,003	1,057	994	941
1999	15.9	34.2	36.3	37.6	3.0	964	1,085	969	992
1998	20.9	29.3	33.3	41.9	3.0	1,027	973	926	928
1997	21.3	29.3	39.4	43.8	3.1	1,019	994	934	979
1996	21.3	30.4	45.1	43.2	4.5	1,054	925	931	943
1995	18.8	31.2	45.0	47.5	2.9	982	944	922	952
1994	19.4	30.3	39.9	39.8	3.2	951	928	928	898
1993r	21.8	36.5	44.3	53.0	2.5	903	884	891	832
1993	21.6	36.5	44.2	51.8	2.5	864	857	867	832
1992	24.5	28.7	44.5	47.0	2.8	864	862	860	813
1991	22.9	39.6	46.2	50.6	5.4	846	878	839	798
1990	23.2	37.3	52.7	49.1	4.3	828	877	791	795
1989	21.7	38.8	44.8	46.7	2.8	831	858	785	828
1988	18.9	37.2	43.7	41.4	4.1	851	828	780	828
1987	21.6	41.1	39.7	42.3	4.9	861	779	802	818
1986	15.0	39.0	45.2	45.9	4.0	806	792	770	855
1985	19.5	38.2	41.4	40.3	5.4	778	775	830	816
1984	24.1	38.1	42.5	42.8	4.2	729	727	832	769
1983	16.8	42.0	43.1	40.6	4.4	721	723	808	799
1982	18.8	27.5	36.2	36.9	4.8	898	937	975	977
1981	17.7	34.2	33.3	42.4	5.4	723	811	814	832
1980	16.8	31.8	36.2	43.3	4.9	736	807	770	876
1979	14.7	37.3	33.8	43.6	4.0	762	796	828	853
1978	15.4	33.0	30.3	43.1	4.1	774	767	847	870
1977	12.1	29.8	31.1	35.3	4.8	776	782	858	868
1976	11.5	26.1	30.9	43.3	5.7	755	816	870	855
1975	12.8	30.7	32.5	40.2	7.6	743	849	845	879
1974	13.5	31.0	40.9	41.1	7.2	747	858	861	849
1973	14.1	29.5	38.0	42.0	8.5	752	831	837	824
1972	14.5	36.8	41.3	43.8	6.6	787	828	836	818
1971	18.1	30.9	38.5	47.6	7.4	890	900	810	757

r = Revised, controlled to 1990 census based population estimates; previous 1993 data controlled to 1980 census based population estimates.
[1]Starting in 2003, respondents could identify more than one race. Except as noted, the race data in this table from 2003 onward represent those respondents who indicated only one race category.

Table A-12. Population 6 to 17 Years Old Enrolled Below Modal Grade, 1971–2017—*Continued*

(Numbers in thousands; percent; civilian noninstitutionalized population.)

Year, sex, race, and Hispanic origin	Percent below modal grade				Dropout rate, 15 to 17 years	Population in age group			
	6 to 8 years	9 to 11 years	12 to 14 years	15 to 17 years		6 to 8 years	9 to 11 years	12 to 14 years	15 to 17 years
Female									
2017	23.2	33.4	29.1	30.2	3.3	972	906	899	933
2016	26.0	31.0	24.7	32.9	3.3	915	947	899	943
2015	24.4	26.8	30.0	30.2	3.9	891	942	905	945
2014	20.6	29.5	32.5	33.7	5.8	890	863	923	930
2013	26.4	24.8	27.2	27.9	5.4	964	877	931	929
2012	20.0	22.8	32.8	34.0	3.9	801	917	934	935
2011	19.5	25.0	25.4	30.4	1.4	905	930	875	928
2010	16.5	21.6	31.4	28.0	1.4	917	853	897	951
2009	20.9	26.4	30.9	27.1	2.8	887	860	891	963
2008	17.7	28.4	35.5	34.2	2.9	864	889	917	1,003
2007	12.2	24.7	30.5	34.5	3.9	851	885	972	993
2006	17.7	24.7	31.0	27.5	2.8	884	891	968	1,027
2005	19.0	33.3	32.4	34.7	3.3	893	913	999	1,044
2004	18.6	23.1	30.5	33.4	2.6	890	914	1,022	983
2003[1]	21.7	31.5	39.8	30.3	3.4	833	983	1,135	903
2002	22.0	24.7	28.7	27.8	2.8	973	1,012	1,024	970
2001	13.3	28.2	29.0	27.9	4.5	959	1,036	988	900
2000	18.2	26.4	32.0	32.3	2.9	974	1,025	968	911
1999	16.3	25.8	27.0	31.6	4.0	984	1,022	944	919
1998	15.6	23.8	29.6	34.6	4.3	992	960	914	873
1997	15.9	22.8	27.4	36.0	4.5	1,041	915	911	959
1996	13.4	28.1	28.4	30.3	4.9	1,000	922	909	915
1995	14.8	23.6	30.9	34.6	5.3	928	946	901	898
1994	17.5	29.1	32.3	35.4	3.6	961	867	908	911
1993r	18.0	30.8	33.1	36.6	4.7	864	879	856	809
1993	18.1	30.3	33.2	34.6	4.7	844	854	828	809
1992	16.7	28.7	31.2	34.2	5.6	897	773	826	808
1991	19.0	28.6	35.0	36.0	5.2	828	823	804	776
1990	20.7	28.7	39.3	36.6	6.1	817	835	783	776
1989	17.5	29.0	37.7	31.5	5.1	811	824	769	790
1988	18.2	28.8	31.4	35.2	5.3	829	801	765	809
1987	18.0	25.2	31.3	28.5	5.3	818	775	750	836
1985	16.6	29.3	34.2	35.1	3.8	790	723	805	811
1984	11.5	26.4	33.5	26.3	4.0	716	715	820	767
1983	13.8	27.8	25.5	31.2	5.0	708	727	793	818
1982	15.5	26.7	28.7	28.1	4.3	867	937	978	970
1981	10.1	17.9	34.2	29.9	7.1	714	783	801	847
1980	12.8	23.8	25.1	31.7	5.3	724	799	798	852
1979	10.4	21.5	24.5	25.2	8.7	753	780	808	869
1978	9.8	22.6	22.6	27.9	7.2	783	756	817	894
1977	10.6	20.0	21.3	29.1	6.0	776	776	840	886
1976	9.5	20.3	21.2	28.1	7.7	738	817	854	871
1975	11.0	21.3	25.9	29.6	8.3	746	807	875	881
1974	9.7	21.3	25.8	27.5	9.2	762	826	889	833
1973	10.0	22.1	25.4	28.9	7.9	773	819	834	847
1972	11.9	24.1	25.1	30.9	6.6	798	810	855	818
1971	10.4	24.9	31.0	33.1	6.7	904	887	828	776
ASIAN ALONE[2]									
Both Sexes									
2017	19.7	29.7	22.4	25.7	3.8	602	664	632	717
2016	21.0	22.2	22.7	26.0	2.9	642	700	628	681
2015	24.5	21.8	22.3	23.2	4.8	605	691	619	644
2014	12.5	24.3	25.7	26.9	1.4	618	611	625	650
2013	14.5	14.7	20.9	18.4	1.2	606	630	542	615
2012	16.8	18.9	17.3	29.7	1.6	590	560	591	624
2011	16.8	23.1	24.3	25.6	2.4	602	582	481	536
2010	8.9	20.3	22.3	18.9	3.1	618	575	495	424
2009	8.8	11.7	25.5	20.0	1.5	522	491	448	421
2008	17.2	22.7	26.7	18.8	4.4	491	517	482	507
2007	11.3	21.9	17.0	24.2	3.7	545	534	497	463
2006	15.2	19.7	20.9	23.0	3.2	425	472	490	476
2005	12.8	12.2	16.3	19.1	1.2	502	429	486	457
2004	12.1	11.4	20.9	23.6	1.7	417	468	490	491
2003[1]	7.5	13.6	19.7	24.5	1.6	486	453	459	458
2002	11.1	12.3	20.4	18.6	2.7	602	490	530	553

r = Revised, controlled to 1990 census based population estimates; previous 1993 data controlled to 1980 census based population estimates.
[1]Starting in 2003, respondents could identify more than one race. Except as noted, the race data in this table from 2003 onward represent those respondents who indicated only one race category.
[2]The data shown prior to 2003 consists of those identifying themselves as "Asian or Pacific Islanders."

Table A-12. Population 6 to 17 Years Old Enrolled Below Modal Grade, 1971–2017—*Continued*

(Numbers in thousands; percent; civilian noninstitutionalized population.)

Year, sex, race, and Hispanic origin	Percent below modal grade				Dropout rate, 15 to 17 years	Population in age group			
	6 to 8 years	9 to 11 years	12 to 14 years	15 to 17 years		6 to 8 years	9 to 11 years	12 to 14 years	15 to 17 years
2001	11.9	17.9	20.3	21.0	2.8	503	565	523	565
2000	10.7	15.5	17.5	22.2	0.6	524	490	490	475
1999	7.5	16.5	17.9	25.5	3.2	533	496	560	555
Male									
2017	23.8	28.6	21.0	29.7	3.5	298	353	318	356
2016	23.2	27.9	24.9	27.5	3.3	337	360	313	307
2015	21.8	20.5	17.0	23.6	4.9	299	352	285	327
2014	18.0	24.6	30.1	28.9	2.9	316	306	323	303
2013	12.7	17.9	23.6	20.9	1.4	297	298	281	287
2012	18.7	19.3	16.6	29.2	2.4	300	259	307	327
2011	16.5	25.3	24.9	28.6	2.3	324	293	249	266
2010	8.0	20.0	24.1	20.7	2.6	327	296	247	237
2009	9.2	12.7	25.2	21.3	0.7	272	232	227	233
2008	23.8	20.4	24.3	17.4	2.4	227	257	249	253
2007	7.6	20.5	18.2	26.0	4.0	278	272	240	246
2006	14.3	18.4	23.5	21.7	3.3	206	256	264	227
2005	12.3	13.8	13.2	18.1	1.6	261	202	265	228
2004	10.9	16.0	20.9	23.5	2.4	220	216	282	231
2003[1]	7.3	15.9	20.3	19.3	-	226	223	261	231
2002	9.6	12.4	23.3	18.9	1.7	274	239	267	287
2001	15.2	16.6	19.0	22.2	4.9	265	294	256	313
2000	14.7	14.2	16.1	30.3	1.0	286	243	267	261
1999	8.4	16.4	17.6	30.3	2.2	277	269	246	276
Female									
2017	15.7	31.0	23.9	21.8	4.0	304	311	314	362
2016	18.5	16.2	20.5	24.7	2.5	305	340	315	374
2015	27.0	23.1	26.8	22.8	4.8	305	339	334	318
2014	6.7	24.0	21.0	25.1	0.1	302	306	302	346
2013	16.2	11.9	18.1	16.1	1.0	309	332	262	327
2012	14.9	18.7	18.1	30.3	0.7	290	301	284	296
2011	17.1	20.9	23.7	22.7	2.6	278	289	232	270
2010	10.0	20.6	20.6	16.6	3.7	290	279	248	187
2009	8.5	10.9	25.9	18.5	2.4	251	259	220	188
2008	11.5	25.0	29.3	20.3	6.5	264	260	233	254
2007	15.2	23.5	15.8	22.2	3.4	268	263	257	217
2006	16.1	21.2	17.9	24.2	3.1	218	216	226	249
2005	13.4	10.8	20.0	20.1	0.9	241	227	221	229
2004	13.5	7.3	20.8	23.7	1.1	196	253	208	260
2003[1]	7.6	11.3	18.8	29.9	3.2	259	230	198	227
2002	12.4	12.2	17.5	18.2	3.7	327	251	263	266
2001	8.3	19.3	21.4	19.6	0.2	238	270	268	252
2000	5.9	16.7	19.2	12.3	0.1	239	247	224	215
1999	6.6	16.7	18.5	20.6	4.0	256	227	314	278
HISPANIC (OF ANY RACE)									
Both Sexes									
2017	22.2	24.8	33.4	31.9	3.9	3,164	3,215	2,999	2,913
2016	23.1	29.2	28.3	32.8	3.0	3,104	3,173	2,956	2,978
2015	20.7	30.3	30.3	32.4	4.0	3,134	3,165	2,909	2,871
2014	21.4	26.9	29.5	32.4	4.5	3,159	2,967	2,901	2,703
2013	22.0	29.3	32.2	34.3	3.6	3,117	2,926	2,868	2,662
2012	22.4	28.0	28.6	36.7	3.0	3,025	2,954	2,791	2,661
2011	19.8	28.0	28.6	36.1	3.3	3,161	2,847	2,496	2,502
2010	15.6	23.4	27.9	34.3	2.5	3,046	2,681	2,494	2,307
2009	18.1	26.0	28.3	32.1	4.7	2,893	2,524	2,418	2,254
2008	17.8	25.2	29.1	34.2	3.5	2,690	2,402	2,422	2,321
2007	20.9	28.9	31.1	34.0	5.7	2,541	2,414	2,418	2,211
2006	20.6	29.2	32.6	35.3	5.7	2,441	2,382	2,361	2,165
2005	18.1	26.2	33.2	32.1	4.9	2,390	2,317	2,322	2,202
2004	21.5	28.1	30.0	34.6	6.1	2,382	2,250	2,283	2,072
2003	20.2	28.7	31.3	32.7	5.2	2,280	2,221	2,167	2,063
2002	15.5	28.4	27.9	35.6	5.9	2,258	2,204	2,079	1,841
2001	16.7	22.1	25.0	34.6	6.9	2,143	2,198	2,011	1,733
2000	19.4	23.2	27.3	34.4	8.8	2,067	1,965	1,744	1,671
1999	15.7	25.9	27.9	36.5	7.3	1,902	1,922	1,734	1,653
1998	15.4	23.2	24.6	33.8	7.6	1,903	1,740	1,542	1,424
1997	15.2	21.5	31.0	41.4	5.5	1,909	1,666	1,444	1,575

[1]Starting in 2003, respondents could identify more than one race. Except as noted, the race data in this table from 2003 onward represent those respondents who indicated only one race category.

Table A-12. Population 6 to 17 Years Old Enrolled Below Modal Grade, 1971–2017—*Continued*

(Numbers in thousands; percent; civilian noninstitutionalized population.)

Year, sex, race, and Hispanic origin	Percent below modal grade				Dropout rate, 15 to 17 years	Population in age group			
	6 to 8 years	9 to 11 years	12 to 14 years	15 to 17 years		6 to 8 years	9 to 11 years	12 to 14 years	15 to 17 years
1996	14.9	22.9	35.5	39.0	8.4	1,711	1,680	1,550	1,478
1995	14.4	26.1	38.5	43.6	7.4	1,597	1,628	1,496	1,373
1994	16.8	28.4	32.3	39.9	8.8	1,526	1,593	1,442	1,347
1993r	18.9	29.2	33.2	42.2	8.2	1,390	1,255	1,204	1,225
1993	18.9	29.2	32.7	38.3	7.9	1,455	1,295	1,243	1,226
1992	16.2	25.3	34.3	39.9	8.1	1,272	1,371	1,141	1,110
1991	21.8	30.7	35.8	38.4	11.3	1,290	1,356	1,088	1,023
1990	21.5	34.8	37.7	39.8	9.0	1,270	1,230	1,095	1,062
1989	21.9	33.8	39.9	39.5	10.6	1,257	1,154	1,079	1,001
1988	23.2	37.0	45.0	36.8	13.7	1,248	1,107	1,052	953
1987	16.9	31.2	38.9	37.3	9.1	1,181	1,054	1,063	981
1986	19.1	33.3	42.5	35.5	11.0	1,067	1,119	1,025	1,018
1985	18.7	32.4	35.8	35.7	11.3	1,035	1,047	957	946
1984	20.2	32.7	34.7	38.5	10.7	901	829	806	816
1983	20.2	32.7	39.5	38.0	8.3	903	909	949	860
1982	21.9	32.6	37.3	37.0	10.9	923	875	924	883
1981	17.9	34.7	34.9	34.9	13.3	882	939	866	963
1980	20.8	26.1	34.8	35.8	12.6	881	949	863	889
1979	18.2	33.6	33.0	30.3	10.9	729	712	697	755
1978	19.8	29.1	33.6	37.8	12.3	723	684	666	751
1977	13.0	24.1	25.1	35.2	11.0	676	693	662	773
Male									
2017	21.9	26.6	35.3	33.1	5.1	1,641	1,604	1,559	1,461
2016	24.2	27.9	31.5	39.2	2.7	1,570	1,620	1,507	1,530
2015	20.1	30.7	30.6	35.0	4.6	1,595	1,608	1,492	1,512
2014	23.2	30.3	30.5	35.4	5.5	1,594	1,510	1,481	1,402
2013	24.0	34.2	34.3	36.5	4.0	1,579	1,507	1,458	1,373
2012	26.1	29.0	31.7	39.1	2.7	1,571	1,513	1,408	1,382
2011	29.3	20.7	30.5	30.0	3.0	1,605	1,465	1,290	1,294
2010	16.3	24.2	28.4	33.6	3.1	1,544	1,381	1,290	1,178
2009	16.4	27.7	31.8	32.5	4.9	1,458	1,322	1,216	1,165
2008	17.8	26.6	30.9	36.3	3.7	1,377	1,218	1,233	1,198
2007	24.3	28.5	34.1	37.4	5.9	1,302	1,252	1,217	1,130
2006	20.0	31.0	37.7	40.6	4.9	1,251	1,214	1,208	1,111
2005	20.5	29.2	39.2	37.0	4.7	1,219	1,192	1,202	1,087
2004	25.2	28.8	34.3	36.6	6.4	1,247	1,142	1,202	1,001
2003	23.0	31.2	32.3	35.9	6.2	1,205	1,178	1,081	1,020
2002	17.4	31.6	28.7	38.5	7.4	1,140	1,090	1,137	911
2001	21.2	23.4	27.8	40.8	7.7	1,065	1,128	1,093	895
2000	23.1	26.7	27.7	36.9	9.0	1,048	993	875	872
1999	17.9	29.5	29.7	38.9	7.6	973	990	893	854
1998	16.8	26.6	26.9	44.9	8.1	933	887	841	792
1997	15.3	22.3	33.7	45.8	3.7	969	863	735	836
1996	13.5	25.8	40.5	45.1	6.8	914	808	798	764
1995	11.4	31.1	42.4	47.6	7.5	794	839	776	697
1994	16.4	27.5	36.3	45.1	11.4	778	845	721	676
1993r	19.1	35.1	37.2	50.4	7.6	722	612	618	658
1993	19.1	34.3	36.9	46.0	7.3	778	637	648	658
1992	15.6	27.2	42.5	46.2	6.8	636	687	602	576
1991	22.7	31.5	43.9	42.6	10.7	651	691	544	521
1990	22.2	36.4	40.2	43.8	9.0	676	616	590	564
1989	23.7	36.1	40.0	45.2	7.8	642	584	560	511
1988	26.9	42.0	53.8	40.5	12.4	676	566	470	523
1987	19.8	31.7	44.8	38.7	6.4	600	524	569	517
1986	22.2	38.0	49.3	37.8	10.8	544	555	535	471
1985	16.7	36.8	38.4	43.4	7.8	521	527	502	449
1984	18.3	35.7	33.1	42.8	10.0	443	420	423	432
1983	22.2	38.8	45.7	41.8	8.2	445	479	479	428
1982	23.1	36.4	39.1	43.4	10.1	428	426	466	477
1981	19.9	39.8	38.0	40.0	14.3	438	480	439	495
1980	22.5	29.9	40.5	40.7	13.5	418	481	415	445
1979	19.0	34.6	36.4	31.3	8.8	368	358	349	386
1978	23.5	29.9	33.9	37.3	13.6	388	335	339	413
1977	11.5	31.4	23.3	38.4	6.7	365	325	330	406
Female									
2017	22.6	23.0	31.4	30.8	2.6	1,524	1,611	1,440	1,452
2016	22.1	30.6	24.9	26.0	3.3	1,534	1,553	1,449	1,448
2015	21.3	29.8	29.9	29.6	3.4	1,539	1,556	1,417	1,359
2014	19.7	23.4	28.4	29.2	3.5	1,565	1,457	1,420	1,301

r = Revised, controlled to 1990 census based population estimates; previous 1993 data controlled to 1980 census based population estimates.

Table A-12. Population 6 to 17 Years Old Enrolled Below Modal Grade, 1971–2017—*Continued*

(Numbers in thousands; percent; civilian noninstitutionalized population.)

Year, sex, race, and Hispanic origin	Percent below modal grade				Dropout rate, 15 to 17 years	Population in age group			
	6 to 8 years	9 to 11 years	12 to 14 years	15 to 17 years		6 to 8 years	9 to 11 years	12 to 14 years	15 to 17 years
2013	20.0	24.0	30.0	32.0	3.0	1,539	1,420	1,410	1,289
2012	18.4	27.0	25.4	34.1	3.3	1,454	1,441	1,382	1,279
2011	19.0	25.3	27.1	34.2	3.7	1,556	1,382	1,206	1,209
2010	15.0	22.6	27.3	35.1	2.0	1,502	1,301	1,204	1,129
2009	19.9	24.0	24.8	31.6	4.6	1,435	1,202	1,202	1,089
2008	17.8	23.7	27.2	32.1	3.2	1,313	1,184	1,189	1,123
2007	17.3	29.4	28.2	30.5	5.4	1,239	1,162	1,202	1,080
2006	21.3	27.4	27.3	29.5	6.5	1,190	1,168	1,153	1,054
2005	15.6	23.0	26.7	27.3	5.1	1,171	1,126	1,119	1,115
2004	17.6	27.3	25.1	32.8	5.7	1,135	1,108	1,080	1,070
2003	17.1	25.7	30.3	29.7	4.3	1,075	1,043	1,086	1,042
2002	13.6	25.3	27.0	32.7	4.5	1,118	1,115	942	930
2001	12.2	20.8	21.6	28.0	6.0	1,078	1,070	918	838
2000	15.7	19.7	26.9	31.8	8.6	1,020	974	869	800
1999	13.5	22.0	26.1	33.8	6.9	930	932	841	800
1998	14.1	19.7	21.8	31.1	7.0	970	853	701	632
1997	15.0	20.4	28.8	36.1	7.4	939	803	710	739
1996	16.6	20.3	30.4	32.4	10.4	798	871	753	712
1995	17.5	20.6	34.5	39.5	7.2	802	789	721	677
1994	17.2	29.2	28.5	34.9	6.1	748	747	722	671
1993r	18.9	24.2	29.0	32.3	8.7	667	643	586	567
1993	18.7	24.3	28.3	29.3	8.6	678	658	597	567
1992	16.8	23.4	25.0	33.1	9.6	636	684	539	534
1991	20.8	29.8	27.6	34.1	12.0	639	665	544	502
1990	20.7	33.2	34.9	35.3	9.0	594	614	505	498
1989	20.0	31.4	39.7	33.5	13.5	615	570	519	490
1988	18.7	31.8	37.8	32.3	15.3	572	541	582	430
1987	13.8	30.8	32.2	35.8	12.1	581	530	494	464
1986	15.9	28.7	35.1	33.5	11.2	523	564	490	547
1985	20.8	27.9	33.0	28.8	14.5	514	520	455	497
1984	22.1	29.6	36.6	33.6	11.5	458	409	383	384
1983	18.1	25.8	33.2	34.3	8.3	458	430	470	432
1982	20.8	29.0	35.6	29.6	11.8	495	449	458	406
1981	16.0	29.4	31.6	29.5	12.2	444	459	427	468
1980	19.2	22.2	29.5	30.9	11.7	463	468	448	444
1979	17.5	32.5	29.6	29.3	13.0	361	354	348	369
1978	15.5	28.4	33.3	38.5	10.7	335	349	327	338
1977	14.8	17.7	26.8	31.6	15.8	311	368	332	367
WHITE ALONE OR IN COMBINATION									
Both Sexes									
2017	24.3	28.9	29.7	31.7	3.4	9,320	9,694	9,618	9,720
2016	24.2	29.4	30.0	30.3	4.0	9,274	9,615	9,586	9,779
2015	23.8	29.7	30.5	30.4	3.1	9,492	9,632	9,658	9,802
2014	23.5	27.6	29.0	30.5	3.9	9,623	9,586	9,679	9,679
2013	22.7	26.8	30.7	31.6	3.6	9,664	9,574	9,754	9,681
2012	23.8	27.8	30.2	32.5	2.4	9,607	9,630	9,685	9,740
2011	23.1	28.4	30.0	31.5	2.1	9,956	9,824	9,378	9,652
2010	19.0	24.7	28.1	28.5	2.2	9,935	9,712	9,435	9,699
2009	19.2	26.3	29.2	28.7	3.2	9,887	9,345	9,515	9,832
2008	20.2	27.1	29.2	29.6	2.5	9,680	9,298	9,577	10,043
2007	21.1	26.1	27.4	28.5	2.8	9,502	9,326	9,734	10,169
2006	20.6	25.6	26.7	29.9	3.0	9,346	9,444	9,850	10,175
2005	21.1	23.9	27.9	29.4	2.6	9,314	9,588	10,026	10,479
2004	22.4	25.6	27.4	30.5	3.9	9,422	9,506	10,175	10,079
2003	21.7	27.4	28.1	29.4	3.2	9,447	9,446	10,194	10,151
Male									
2017	25.5	31.1	31.8	33.9	3.9	4,758	4,943	4,921	4,968
2016	26.0	30.3	32.9	34.4	4.3	4,731	4,923	4,922	4,998
2015	25.4	31.4	31.1	33.9	3.4	4,855	4,935	4,968	5,003
2014	24.8	29.0	31.1	33.4	4.6	4,945	4,931	4,960	4,948
2013	25.1	30.5	33.2	35.0	4.1	4,911	4,940	4,965	4,951
2012	25.9	30.4	35.0	36.6	2.8	4,898	4,966	4,935	4,979
2011	25.8	31.6	32.6	36.4	2.1	5,089	5,042	4,820	4,956
2010	21.2	27.3	30.1	31.0	3.0	5,039	4,970	4,824	4,996
2009	20.6	29.5	32.3	31.8	3.4	5,072	4,776	4,866	5,039
2008	22.3	29.1	32.3	32.4	2.7	4,963	4,744	4,934	5,163
2007	24.0	28.2	29.1	32.0	2.9	4,857	4,770	4,997	5,203
2006	22.4	27.2	29.6	34.1	3.4	4,769	4,842	5,042	5,193

r = Revised, controlled to 1990 census based population estimates; previous 1993 data controlled to 1980 census based population estimates.

Table A-12. Population 6 to 17 Years Old Enrolled Below Modal Grade, 1971–2017—*Continued*

(Numbers in thousands; percent; civilian noninstitutionalized population.)

Year, sex, race, and Hispanic origin	Percent below modal grade				Dropout rate, 15 to 17 years	Population in age group			
	6 to 8 years	9 to 11 years	12 to 14 years	15 to 17 years		6 to 8 years	9 to 11 years	12 to 14 years	15 to 17 years
2005	23.9	27.3	30.9	33.1	2.7	4,751	4,925	5,151	5,268
2004	24.9	28.1	31.2	35.1	3.9	4,876	4,823	5,318	5,043
2003	24.5	31.6	31.0	33.8	3.4	4,965	4,946	5,108	5,172
Female									
2017	23.1	26.7	27.4	29.4	3.0	4,562	4,750	4,697	4,753
2016	22.3	28.4	26.9	26.0	3.7	4,543	4,692	4,664	4,782
2015	22.1	28.0	29.9	26.8	2.8	4,636	4,697	4,690	4,799
2014	22.2	26.1	26.9	27.6	3.2	4,678	4,655	4,718	4,731
2013	20.2	22.9	28.0	28.1	3.1	4,753	4,633	4,789	4,729
2012	21.7	25.1	25.2	28.3	1.9	4,709	4,664	4,751	4,761
2011	20.4	25.0	27.2	26.4	2.2	4,867	4,782	4,558	4,696
2010	16.8	21.9	26.0	25.9	1.4	4,896	4,743	4,610	4,703
2009	17.7	22.9	26.0	25.4	2.9	4,815	4,569	4,649	4,792
2008	17.9	25.0	26.0	26.6	2.4	4,717	4,554	4,643	4,880
2007	18.1	23.9	25.5	24.7	2.7	4,646	4,555	4,737	4,966
2006	18.7	23.8	23.6	25.5	2.6	4,577	4,602	4,808	4,982
2005	18.2	20.2	24.7	25.7	2.6	4,563	4,663	4,875	5,211
2004	19.6	23.0	23.2	25.9	3.9	4,545	4,683	4,857	5,037
2003	18.6	22.7	25.2	24.8	3.0	4,482	4,500	5,086	4,979
BLACK ALONE OR IN COMBINATION									
Both Sexes									
2017	22.3	31.3	31.7	34.6	4.0	2,395	2,245	2,098	2,187
2016	23.5	32.7	30.3	31.1	2.8	2,217	2,212	2,130	2,238
2015	21.4	29.8	31.7	34.3	2.7	2,146	2,321	2,148	2,144
2014	22.6	31.1	34.5	35.6	5.2	2,157	2,130	2,131	2,133
2013	23.5	27.6	30.2	33.9	4.5	2,235	2,055	2,163	2,145
2012	25.1	28.2	33.2	36.6	2.4	2,066	2,094	2,139	2,113
2011	21.0	30.1	28.1	33.1	2.5	2,186	2,061	1,945	2,003
2010	16.9	25.9	32.4	31.6	2.1	2,122	1,938	1,971	2,067
2009	20.7	30.2	32.6	34.8	2.5	1,939	2,006	2,001	2,116
2008	18.3	26.8	39.4	37.1	3.0	2,026	2,002	2,036	2,179
2007	17.6	27.3	32.1	38.8	2.8	1,998	1,950	2,071	2,146
2006	18.9	28.3	34.8	35.0	3.1	1,982	1,988	2,074	2,202
2005	20.3	34.8	33.4	37.9	4.4	1,970	1,982	2,137	2,194
2004	20.3	27.0	33.2	39.1	2.5	1,950	2,022	2,174	2,107
2003	23.2	33.5	33.4	36.8	3.8	1,921	2,183	2,220	2,034
Male									
2017	20.4	28.9	33.0	39.4	4.7	1,210	1,115	1,049	1,090
2016	21.4	35.2	35.2	30.6	2.7	1,138	1,093	1,083	1,135
2015	19.4	30.5	32.8	38.1	2.0	1,058	1,187	1,105	1,075
2014	22.4	33.1	37.4	37.7	5.3	1,055	1,122	1,097	1,053
2013	21.2	31.0	34.2	38.6	3.3	1,088	1,050	1,100	1,061
2012	30.1	31.6	35.5	38.3	1.4	1,095	1,061	1,085	1,047
2011	22.9	35.0	31.6	35.1	3.8	1,135	1,017	991	994
2010	16.7	30.4	34.1	34.2	3.0	1,085	961	978	1,041
2009	21.2	33.0	35.9	41.5	2.4	934	1,042	1,006	1,059
2008	19.8	25.6	44.8	39.7	3.3	1,026	1,020	1,032	1,090
2007	21.7	29.9	34.4	42.6	2.1	1,053	983	1,034	1,086
2006	20.0	33.5	39.0	42.8	3.5	1,013	1,018	1,050	1,094
2005	22.1	37.0	35.5	41.8	5.0	981	999	1,061	1,082
2004	21.1	30.6	37.3	45.3	1.9	966	1,042	1,065	1,056
2003	24.2	36.6	38.5	42.9	4.0	1,014	1,116	1,033	1,083
Female									
2017	24.3	33.7	30.4	29.9	3.4	1,184	1,130	1,050	1,097
2016	25.7	30.2	25.2	31.5	2.8	1,079	1,119	1,047	1,103
2015	23.4	29.1	30.5	30.4	3.5	1,088	1,134	1,044	1,069
2014	22.9	28.9	31.4	33.6	5.1	1,102	1,008	1,033	1,080
2013	25.7	24.0	26.1	29.4	5.6	1,147	1,005	1,063	1,085
2012	19.6	24.6	30.8	34.9	3.4	971	1,032	1,054	1,066
2011	18.8	25.4	24.4	31.2	1.3	1,051	1,044	954	1,009
2010	17.0	21.4	30.7	28.9	1.3	1,037	977	993	1,026
2009	20.3	27.1	29.3	28.1	2.5	1,004	965	995	1,058
2008	16.8	28.1	34.0	34.5	2.7	1,000	982	1,004	1,089
2007	13.2	24.6	29.9	34.8	3.6	945	967	1,037	1,061
2006	17.8	23.0	30.6	27.3	2.7	969	969	1,024	1,108
2005	18.6	32.6	31.4	34.1	3.7	990	983	1,076	1,112

Table A-12. Population 6 to 17 Years Old Enrolled Below Modal Grade, 1971–2017—*Continued*

(Numbers in thousands; percent; civilian noninstitutionalized population.)

Year, sex, race, and Hispanic origin	Percent below modal grade				Dropout rate, 15 to 17 years	Population in age group			
	6 to 8 years	9 to 11 years	12 to 14 years	15 to 17 years		6 to 8 years	9 to 11 years	12 to 14 years	15 to 17 years
2004	17.8	23.0	30.6	27.3	2.7	969	969	1,024	1,108
2003	22.0	30.4	29.0	29.8	3.4	907	1,067	1,187	951
ASIAN ALONE OR IN COMBINATION									
Both Sexes									
2017	19.3	26.6	22.7	24.3	3.4	802	866	817	869
2016	22.6	21.0	22.3	24.0	3.0	784	890	761	813
2015	25.5	23.3	21.6	22.1	4.5	761	793	765	772
2014	15.0	23.2	24.7	26.8	1.3	801	783	756	760
2013	16.6	16.2	21.0	18.5	1.0	825	772	693	734
2012	16.8	19.1	17.5	30.2	1.3	751	707	738	768
2011	16.9	22.1	25.2	27.1	2.0	744	718	614	650
2010	10.6	19.6	22.2	19.1	2.5	779	728	603	532
2009	9.2	13.2	25.7	19.3	1.2	690	563	513	508
2008	16.4	23.5	24.7	19.7	3.9	599	587	558	603
2007	11.4	20.6	15.6	25.3	3.6	650	613	600	548
2006	15.0	19.9	19.2	22.2	3.2	528	574	574	603
2005	13.0	12.3	16.5	18.4	1.2	600	531	576	581
2004	13.9	12.4	20.3	24.6	2.6	494	576	585	599
2003	8.8	14.9	18.4	23.5	2.4	579	548	552	543
Male									
2017	21.4	25.9	23.6	27.3	3.5	411	444	414	437
2016	24.0	26.4	24.6	24.3	3.9	411	460	389	382
2015	23.5	21.9	16.9	23.0	4.1	377	402	358	388
2014	19.9	20.8	28.7	30.1	2.5	414	395	373	348
2013	15.9	19.0	22.0	20.6	1.2	383	373	339	343
2012	18.5	20.5	17.2	32.0	2.0	376	341	368	397
2011	17.0	22.6	26.7	29.9	2.0	380	368	324	300
2010	9.5	19.3	24.9	20.9	2.1	397	385	309	291
2009	10.1	16.4	25.6	20.1	0.6	363	269	271	285
2008	21.3	22.6	20.4	15.5	2.1	285	291	299	289
2007	8.4	20.2	16.7	28.4	4.3	316	307	287	289
2006	15.4	15.4	15.4	15.4	4.1	259	311	291	285
2005	12.5	13.2	14.5	16.5	1.6	318	254	307	286
2004	12.4	16.2	19.3	22.3	3.6	254	278	324	286
2003	9.3	19.8	19.4	19.2	1.8	263	268	299	277
Female									
2017	17.0	27.3	21.8	21.3	3.3	391	422	403	432
2016	21.0	15.2	19.9	23.8	2.2	373	430	372	432
2015	27.5	24.6	25.7	21.1	4.9	383	392	407	384
2014	9.7	25.6	20.8	24.0	0.3	388	389	383	411
2013	17.2	13.6	20.0	16.6	0.8	442	400	354	391
2012	15.0	17.8	17.9	28.3	0.5	376	366	370	371
2011	16.9	21.5	23.6	24.7	2.0	364	350	290	350
2010	11.8	19.9	19.3	16.9	2.0	382	344	294	242
2009	8.2	10.2	25.9	18.3	2.1	326	293	242	223
2008	12.0	24.3	29.6	23.6	5.5	314	295	259	314
2007	14.3	21.1	14.6	21.8	2.9	334	306	314	259
2006	14.6	20.6	15.4	22.2	2.4	269	263	283	318
2005	13.7	11.5	18.8	20.2	0.9	282	276	269	295
2004	15.5	8.8	21.6	26.7	1.6	241	298	261	313
2003	8.4	10.3	17.2	28.0	3.1	316	280	253	266

Table A-13. Annual High School Dropout Rates of 15 to 24 Year Olds by Sex, Race, Grade, and Hispanic Origin, October 1967–2017

(Numbers in thousands; percent; civilian noninstitutionalized population.)

Year, grade, race, and Hispanic origin	Total[1]			Male			Female		
	Total students	Dropouts	Dropout rate	Total students	Dropouts	Dropout rate	Total students	Dropouts	Dropout rate
ALL RACES									
Grades 10–12									
2017	11,719	523	4.5	5,971	307	5.1	5,748	215	3.7
2016	11,807	532	4.5	5,939	305	5.1	5,868	227	3.9
2015	11,646	535	4.6	5,894	283	4.8	5,752	252	4.4
2014	11,634	567	4.9	5,932	300	5.1	5,702	267	4.7
2013	11,495	508	4.4	5,844	267	4.6	5,651	241	4.3
2012	11,962	386	3.2	5,997	201	3.4	5,965	184	3.1
2011	11,726	375	3.2	6,010	206	3.4	5,716	169	2.9
2010	11,647	326	2.8	6,006	172	2.9	5,641	154	2.7
2009	11,651	373	3.2	5,798	189	3.3	5,853	184	3.1
2008	11,750	390	3.3	5,999	174	2.9	5,751	216	3.8
2007	11,584	383	3.3	5,879	206	3.5	5,705	177	3.1
2006	11,604	407	3.5	5,932	227	3.8	5,672	180	3.2
2005	11,494	414	3.6	5,843	233	4.0	5,651	181	3.2
2004	11,166	486	4.4	5,624	266	4.7	5,542	220	4.0
2003	11,378	429	3.8	5,705	225	4.0	5,674	203	3.6
2002	10,989	367	3.3	5,504	193	3.5	5,484	174	3.2
2001	10,777	507	4.7	5,534	293	5.3	5,243	214	4.1
2000	10,773	488	4.5	5,417	280	5.2	5,356	208	3.9
1999	11,067	520	4.7	5,659	243	4.3	5,411	277	5.1
1998	10,791	479	4.4	5,486	237	4.3	5,305	243	4.6
1997	10,645	454	4.3	5,330	251	4.7	5,313	203	3.8
1996	10,249	485	4.7	5,175	240	4.6	5,072	244	4.8
1995	10,106	544	5.4	5,161	297	5.8	4,946	247	5.0
1994	9,922	497	5.0	5,048	249	4.9	4,873	247	5.1
1993r	9,430	404	4.3	4,787	211	4.4	4,640	192	4.1
1993	9,021	382	4.2	4,570	199	4.4	4,452	183	4.1
1992	8,939	384	4.3	4,580	175	3.8	4,357	207	4.8
1991	8,612	348	4.0	4,380	167	3.8	4,231	180	4.3
1990	8,679	347	4.0	4,356	177	4.1	4,323	170	3.9
1989	8,974	404	4.5	4,519	203	4.5	4,453	199	4.5
1988	9,590	461	4.8	4,960	256	5.2	4,628	206	4.5
1987	9,802	403	4.1	4,921	215	4.4	4,879	187	3.8
1986	9,829	421	4.3	4,910	213	4.3	4,917	208	4.2
1985	9,704	504	5.2	4,831	259	5.4	4,874	245	5.0
1984	10,041	507	5.0	4,986	268	5.4	5,054	238	4.7
1983	10,331	535	5.2	5,130	294	5.7	5,200	241	4.6
1982	10,611	577	5.4	5,310	305	5.7	5,301	271	5.1
1981	10,868	639	5.9	5,379	322	6.0	5,487	316	5.8
1980	10,891	658	6.0	5,445	362	6.6	5,448	296	5.4
1979	11,136	744	6.7	5,479	369	6.7	5,658	377	6.7
1978	11,116	743	6.7	5,558	415	7.5	5,558	328	5.9
1977	11,300	734	6.5	5,657	392	6.9	5,643	342	6.1
1976	10,996	644	5.9	5,534	360	6.5	5,463	285	5.2
1975	11,033	639	5.8	5,485	296	5.4	5,548	343	6.2
1974	11,026	742	6.7	5,421	402	7.4	5,605	340	6.1
1973	10,851	683	6.3	5,407	370	6.8	5,444	313	5.7
1972	10,664	659	6.2	5,305	317	6.0	5,358	341	6.4
1971	10,451	562	5.4	5,193	297	5.7	5,258	266	5.1
1970	10,281	588	5.7	5,145	288	5.6	5,138	302	5.9
1969	10,212	551	5.4	5,069	273	5.4	5,142	278	5.4
1968	9,814	506	5.2	4,831	247	5.1	4,983	259	5.2
1967	9,350	486	5.2	4,605	237	5.1	4,745	249	5.2
Grade 10									
2017	3,975	41	1.0	2,153	35	1.6	1,822	6	0.3
2016	3,985	69	1.7	2,013	36	1.8	1,972	33	1.7
2015	3,994	61	1.5	2,016	24	1.2	1,979	37	1.9
2014	4,026	73	1.8	2,095	58	2.8	1,931	16	0.8
2013	3,971	35	0.9	1,996	19	0.9	1,976	16	0.8
2012	4,226	34	0.8	2,104	20	1.0	2,122	14	0.7
2011	3,998	48	1.2	2,009	26	1.3	1,989	22	1.1
2010	3,983	27	0.7	2,008	17	0.8	1,976	10	0.5
2009	3,983	50	1.2	1,993	28	1.4	1,989	22	1.1
2008	4,154	56	1.4	2,104	25	1.2	2,050	31	1.5

r = Revised, controlled to 1990 census based population estimates; previous 1993 data controlled to 1980 census based population estimates.
[1] Starting in 2003 respondents could identify more than one race. Except as noted, the race data in this table from 2003 onward represent those respondents who indicated only one race category.

Table A-13. Annual High School Dropout Rates of 15 to 24 Year Olds by Sex, Race, Grade, and Hispanic Origin, October 1967–2017—*Continued*

(Numbers in thousands; percent; civilian noninstitutionalized population.)

Year, grade, race, and Hispanic origin	Total[1]			Male			Female		
	Total students	Dropouts	Dropout rate	Total students	Dropouts	Dropout rate	Total students	Dropouts	Dropout rate
2007	4,064	63	1.6	2,027	32	1.6	2,037	31	1.5
2006	4,179	31	0.7	2,053	19	0.9	2,126	12	0.5
2005	4,483	72	1.6	2,244	49	2.2	2,239	23	1.0
2004	4,028	99	2.5	2,096	56	2.7	1,931	42	2.2
2003	4,107	64	1.6	2,111	26	1.2	1,995	37	1.9
2002	3,896	55	1.4	1,963	36	1.8	1,934	19	1.0
2001	3,900	90	2.3	1,988	50	2.5	1,913	41	2.1
2000	3,957	77	1.9	2,036	48	2.4	1,920	28	1.5
1999	3,910	104	2.7	2,036	54	2.7	1,875	50	2.7
1998	3,883	90	2.3	1,971	36	1.8	1,911	54	2.8
1997	3,738	79	2.1	1,894	44	2.3	1,843	35	1.9
1996	3,691	94	2.5	1,906	50	2.6	1,784	43	2.4
1995	3,552	88	2.5	1,823	40	2.2	1,728	47	2.7
1994	3,474	76	2.2	1,793	45	2.5	1,681	31	1.8
1993r	3,265	86	2.6	1,696	52	3.1	1,567	33	2.1
1993	3,139	81	2.6	1,627	50	3.1	1,513	31	2.0
1992	3,197	81	2.5	1,657	37	2.2	1,539	43	2.8
1991	3,132	105	3.4	1,571	46	2.9	1,561	59	3.8
1990	3,215	90	2.8	1,660	43	2.6	1,555	47	3.0
1989	3,071	99	3.2	1,567	56	3.6	1,504	43	2.9
1988	3,308	112	3.4	1,716	63	3.7	1,592	49	3.1
1987	3,492	106	3.0	1,818	45	2.5	1,674	61	3.6
1986	3,555	119	3.3	1,820	56	3.1	1,734	63	3.6
1985	3,491	143	4.1	1,797	74	4.1	1,695	69	4.1
1984	3,415	135	4.0	1,735	76	4.4	1,680	59	3.5
1983	3,468	129	3.7	1,755	70	4.0	1,713	59	3.4
1982	3,540	144	4.1	1,792	69	3.9	1,747	74	4.2
1981	3,735	144	3.9	1,816	65	3.6	1,918	78	4.1
1980	3,817	166	4.3	1,957	95	4.9	1,861	71	3.8
1979	3,920	217	5.5	1,985	102	5.1	1,934	114	5.9
1978	3,878	185	4.8	1,943	96	4.9	1,935	89	4.6
1977	3,970	177	4.5	2,021	96	4.8	1,949	81	4.2
1976	3,914	145	3.7	1,960	79	4.0	1,955	67	3.4
1975	3,983	183	4.6	2,017	87	4.3	1,967	97	4.9
1974	3,901	223	5.7	1,951	122	6.3	1,949	101	5.2
1973	3,899	210	5.4	1,930	112	5.8	1,969	98	5.0
1972	3,868	203	5.2	1,940	106	5.5	1,928	97	5.0
1971	3,762	174	4.6	1,925	95	4.9	1,838	79	4.3
1970	3,686	186	5.0	1,865	90	4.8	1,822	97	5.3
1969	3,485	159	4.6	1,756	84	4.8	1,729	75	4.3
1968	3,615	151	4.2	1,849	75	4.1	1,767	76	4.3
1967	3,370	129	3.8	1,726	64	3.7	1,644	65	4.0
Grade 11									
2017	4,510	137	3.0	2,327	86	3.7	2,183	51	2.3
2016	4,261	126	3.0	2,191	78	3.6	2,070	48	2.3
2015	4,338	137	3.2	2,198	63	2.9	2,140	74	3.4
2014	4,274	151	3.5	2,189	89	4.1	2,085	63	3.0
2013	4,232	149	3.5	2,172	89	4.1	2,060	60	2.9
2012	4,378	66	1.5	2,228	28	1.2	2,150	39	1.8
2011	4,358	84	1.9	2,234	52	2.3	2,124	32	1.5
2010	4,247	84	2.0	2,201	50	2.3	2,046	34	1.7
2009	4,444	106	2.4	2,226	51	2.3	2,218	55	2.5
2008	4,186	96	2.3	2,113	60	2.9	2,073	36	1.7
2007	4,388	118	2.7	2,280	64	2.8	2,108	55	2.6
2006	4,212	112	2.6	2,271	62	2.7	2,004	50	2.4
2005	4,080	72	1.8	2,184	46	2.1	1,896	26	1.4
2004	4,010	141	3.5	2,012	76	3.8	1,998	65	3.3
2003	4,327	117	2.7	2,158	68	3.2	2,169	49	2.3
2002	4,137	99	2.4	2,111	54	2.6	2,026	45	2.2
2001	4,114	139	3.4	2,134	72	3.4	1,979	67	3.4
2000	3,833	170	4.4	1,933	78	4.0	1,901	93	4.9
1999	4,036	150	3.7	2,052	69	3.4	1,984	81	4.0
1998	3,735	110	2.9	1,902	55	2.9	1,833	55	3.0
1997	3,882	142	3.7	1,957	71	3.6	1,925	71	3.7
1996	3,606	138	3.8	1,828	76	4.2	1,778	62	3.5
1995	3,568	159	4.5	1,846	89	4.8	1,724	71	4.1
1994	3,587	132	3.7	1,864	61	3.3	1,722	70	4.1

r = Revised, controlled to 1990 census based population estimates; previous 1993 data controlled to 1980 census based population estimates.
[1] Starting in 2003 respondents could identify more than one race. Except as noted, the race data in this table from 2003 onward represent those respondents who indicated only one race category.

Table A-13. Annual High School Dropout Rates of 15 to 24 Year Olds by Sex, Race, Grade, and Hispanic Origin, October 1967–2017—*Continued*

(Numbers in thousands; percent; civilian noninstitutionalized population.)

Year, grade, race, and Hispanic origin	Total[1]			Male			Female		
	Total students	Dropouts	Dropout rate	Total students	Dropouts	Dropout rate	Total students	Dropouts	Dropout rate
1993r	3,375	106	3.1	1,725	43	2.5	1,650	63	3.8
1993	3,218	100	3.1	1,643	40	2.4	1,575	60	3.8
1992	3,213	120	3.7	1,642	52	3.2	1,570	67	4.3
1991	3,083	101	3.3	1,598	42	2.6	1,484	58	3.9
1990	2,976	98	3.3	1,462	57	3.9	1,514	41	2.7
1989	3,302	125	3.8	1,683	67	4.0	1,618	57	3.5
1988	3,447	161	4.7	1,819	89	4.9	1,627	72	4.4
1987	3,566	122	3.4	1,766	71	4.0	1,800	51	2.8
1986	3,433	116	3.4	1,700	51	3.0	1,733	65	3.8
1985	3,274	139	4.2	1,618	70	4.3	1,656	69	4.2
1984	3,328	163	4.9	1,682	87	5.2	1,646	76	4.6
1983	3,601	162	4.5	1,825	87	4.8	1,775	75	4.2
1982	3,694	218	5.9	1,872	122	6.5	1,822	96	5.3
1981	3,787	262	6.9	1,937	144	7.4	1,850	118	6.4
1980	3,670	225	6.1	1,832	120	6.6	1,839	105	5.7
1979	3,718	229	6.2	1,840	102	5.5	1,879	128	6.8
1978	3,708	230	6.2	1,905	113	5.9	1,803	117	6.5
1977	3,832	244	6.4	1,964	133	6.8	1,867	110	5.9
1976	3,786	227	6.0	1,955	123	6.3	1,831	104	5.7
1975	3,596	230	6.4	1,828	103	5.6	1,767	126	7.1
1974	3,721	237	6.4	1,819	123	6.8	1,902	114	6.0
1973	3,631	237	6.5	1,877	126	6.7	1,754	111	6.3
1972	3,581	241	6.7	1,825	107	5.9	1,756	134	7.6
1971	3,585	185	5.2	1,772	82	4.6	1,811	103	5.7
1970	3,456	198	5.7	1,750	96	5.5	1,706	102	6.0
1969	3,489	190	5.4	1,779	100	5.6	1,710	90	5.3
1968	3,255	179	5.5	1,640	91	5.5	1,614	88	5.5
1967	3,068	169	5.5	1,557	76	4.9	1,511	93	6.2
Grade 12									
2017	3,234	344	10.6	1,491	186	12.5	1,744	158	9.1
2016	3,561	337	9.5	1,735	191	11.0	1,826	146	8.0
2015	3,315	337	10.2	1,680	196	11.7	1,634	141	8.6
2014	3,334	343	10.3	1,648	154	9.3	1,686	189	11.2
2013	3,291	325	9.9	1,675	159	9.5	1,615	166	10.3
2012	3,358	285	8.5	1,665	154	9.2	1,693	131	7.7
2011	3,370	243	7.2	1,767	129	7.3	1,603	114	7.1
2010	3,417	215	6.3	1,798	106	5.9	1,620	110	6.8
2009	3,224	217	6.7	1,578	109	6.9	1,646	108	6.5
2008	3,409	237	7.0	1,781	89	5.0	1,628	149	9.1
2007	3,133	202	6.4	1,572	111	7.0	1,561	91	5.8
2006	3,101	265	8.5	1,608	146	9.1	1,492	119	8.0
2005	2,931	270	9.2	1,415	138	9.7	1,516	132	8.7
2004	3,130	247	7.9	1,516	133	8.8	1,614	114	7.1
2003	2,945	248	8.4	1,435	131	9.1	1,510	117	7.7
2002	2,956	214	7.2	1,432	104	7.3	1,524	110	7.2
2001	2,762	277	10.0	1,411	171	12.1	1,351	106	7.8
2000	2,983	241	8.1	1,447	154	10.6	1,535	87	5.7
1999	3,121	266	8.5	1,571	120	7.6	1,552	146	9.4
1998	3,173	279	8.8	1,613	146	9.0	1,560	133	8.5
1997	3,025	233	7.7	1,479	136	9.2	1,545	97	6.3
1996	2,952	253	8.6	1,441	114	7.9	1,510	139	9.2
1995	2,986	297	9.9	1,492	168	11.3	1,494	129	8.6
1994	2,861	289	10.1	1,391	143	10.3	1,470	146	9.9
1993r	2,790	212	7.6	1,366	116	8.5	1,423	96	6.7
1993	2,664	201	7.5	1,300	109	8.4	1,364	92	6.7
1992	2,529	183	7.2	1,281	86	6.7	1,248	97	7.8
1991	2,397	142	5.9	1,211	79	6.5	1,186	63	5.3
1990	2,488	159	6.4	1,234	77	6.2	1,254	82	6.5
1989	2,601	180	6.9	1,269	80	6.3	1,331	99	7.4
1988	2,835	188	6.6	1,425	104	7.3	1,409	85	6.0
1987	2,744	175	6.4	1,337	99	7.4	1,405	75	5.3
1986	2,841	186	6.5	1,390	106	7.6	1,450	80	5.5
1985	2,939	222	7.6	1,416	115	8.1	1,523	107	7.0
1984	3,298	209	6.3	1,569	105	6.7	1,728	103	6.0
1983	3,262	244	7.5	1,550	137	8.8	1,712	107	6.3
1982	3,377	215	6.4	1,646	114	6.9	1,732	101	5.8
1981	3,346	233	7.0	1,626	113	6.9	1,719	120	7.0

r = Revised, controlled to 1990 census based population estimates; previous 1993 data controlled to 1980 census based population estimates.
[1] Starting in 2003 respondents could identify more than one race. Except as noted, the race data in this table from 2003 onward represent those respondents who indicated only one race category.

Table A-13. Annual High School Dropout Rates of 15 to 24 Year Olds by Sex, Race, Grade, and Hispanic Origin, October 1967–2017—*Continued*

(Numbers in thousands; percent; civilian noninstitutionalized population.)

Year, grade, race, and Hispanic origin	Total[1]			Male			Female		
	Total students	Dropouts	Dropout rate	Total students	Dropouts	Dropout rate	Total students	Dropouts	Dropout rate
1980	3,404	267	7.8	1,656	147	8.9	1,748	120	6.9
1979	3,498	298	8.5	1,654	164	9.9	1,845	135	7.3
1978	3,530	328	9.3	1,710	206	12.0	1,820	122	6.7
1977	3,498	313	8.9	1,672	163	9.7	1,827	151	8.3
1976	3,296	272	8.3	1,619	158	9.8	1,677	114	6.8
1975	3,454	226	6.5	1,640	106	6.5	1,814	120	6.6
1974	3,404	282	8.3	1,651	157	9.5	1,754	125	7.1
1973	3,321	236	7.1	1,600	132	8.3	1,721	104	6.0
1972	3,215	215	6.7	1,540	104	6.8	1,674	110	6.6
1971	3,104	203	6.5	1,496	120	8.0	1,609	84	5.2
1970	3,139	204	6.5	1,530	102	6.7	1,610	103	6.4
1969	3,238	202	6.2	1,534	89	5.8	1,703	113	6.6
1968	2,944	176	6.0	1,342	81	6.0	1,602	95	5.9
1967	2,912	188	6.5	1,322	97	7.3	1,590	91	5.7
WHITE ALONE									
Grades 10–12									
2017	8,528	369	4.3	4,401	209	4.8	4,126	159	3.9
2016	8,541	371	4.3	4,303	211	4.9	4,238	159	3.8
2015	8,605	369	4.3	4,382	213	4.9	4,223	156	3.7
2014	8,594	434	5.0	4,379	218	5.0	4,215	216	5.1
2013	8,501	386	4.5	4,391	216	4.9	4,110	171	4.2
2012	8,767	207	2.4	4,479	126	2.8	4,288	81	1.9
2011	8,815	261	3.0	4,559	145	3.2	4,256	116	2.7
2010	8,793	221	2.5	4,592	127	2.8	4,201	94	2.2
2009	8,886	269	3.0	4,459	146	3.3	4,427	123	2.8
2008	8,942	246	2.8	4,588	123	2.7	4,353	123	2.8
2007	8,927	246	2.8	4,518	126	2.8	4,409	120	2.7
2006	8,924	311	3.5	4,568	177	3.9	4,355	133	3.1
2005	8,855	271	3.1	4,472	151	3.4	4,382	120	2.7
2004	8,585	359	4.2	4,344	211	4.9	4,241	148	3.5
2003[1]	8,781	321	3.7	4,434	172	3.9	4,347	148	3.4
2002	8,636	259	3.0	4,371	133	3.0	4,265	126	3.0
2001	8,490	388	4.6	4,363	230	5.3	4,126	158	3.8
2000	8,540	371	4.3	4,368	204	4.7	4,172	167	4.0
1999	8,665	380	4.4	4,426	180	4.1	4,238	198	4.7
1998	8,487	371	4.4	4,306	188	4.4	4,181	183	4.4
1997	8,402	355	4.2	4,220	208	4.9	4,180	145	3.5
1996	8,005	361	4.5	4,077	198	4.8	3,928	163	4.1
1995	7,926	402	5.1	4,079	220	5.4	3,849	183	4.8
1994	7,862	371	4.7	4,014	184	4.6	3,848	188	4.9
1993r	7,442	306	4.1	3,790	157	4.1	3,654	150	4.1
1993	7,152	290	4.1	3,623	147	4.1	3,530	143	4.1
1992	7,077	292	4.1	3,646	140	3.8	3,430	151	4.4
1991	6,856	254	3.7	3,514	127	3.6	3,343	128	3.8
1990	6,984	266	3.8	3,522	144	4.1	3,462	122	3.5
1989	7,243	286	3.9	3,653	149	4.1	3,589	136	3.8
1988	7,727	362	4.7	4,016	203	5.1	3,712	161	4.3
1987	7,979	299	3.7	4,023	163	4.1	3,953	135	3.4
1986	8,011	333	4.2	4,007	168	4.2	4,007	166	4.1
1985	7,967	384	4.8	3,963	195	4.9	4,003	188	4.7
1984	8,221	410	5.0	4,119	220	5.3	4,101	190	4.6
1983	8,531	410	4.8	4,264	232	5.4	4,264	177	4.2
1982	8,769	444	5.1	4,381	231	5.3	4,390	214	4.9
1981	9,067	478	5.3	4,532	254	5.6	4,536	224	4.9
1980	9,177	517	5.6	4,624	294	6.4	4,554	224	4.9
1979	9,437	588	6.2	4,694	311	6.6	4,742	277	5.8
1978	9,360	574	6.1	4,747	329	6.9	4,611	244	5.3
1977	9,536	594	6.2	4,766	327	6.9	4,770	267	5.6
1976	9,362	532	5.7	4,708	297	6.3	4,654	235	5.0
1975	9,440	507	5.4	4,709	234	5.0	4,732	274	5.8
1974	9,403	566	6.0	4,650	326	7.0	4,754	241	5.1
1973	9,359	537	5.7	4,708	288	6.1	4,649	248	5.3
1972	9,173	520	5.7	4,588	247	5.4	4,583	272	5.9
1971	9,140	470	5.1	4,577	244	5.3	4,562	226	5.0
1970	8,959	449	5.0	4,496	212	4.7	4,462	237	5.3

r = Revised, controlled to 1990 census based population estimates; previous 1993 data controlled to 1980 census based population estimates.
[1] Starting in 2003 respondents could identify more than one race. Except as noted, the race data in this table from 2003 onward represent those respondents who indicated only one race category.

Table A-13. Annual High School Dropout Rates of 15 to 24 Year Olds by Sex, Race, Grade, and Hispanic Origin, October 1967–2017—*Continued*

(Numbers in thousands; percent; civilian noninstitutionalized population.)

Year, grade, race, and Hispanic origin	Total[1]			Male			Female		
	Total students	Dropouts	Dropout rate	Total students	Dropouts	Dropout rate	Total students	Dropouts	Dropout rate
1969	8,878	429	4.8	4,438	208	4.7	4,439	221	5.0
1968	8,580	387	4.5	4,246	190	4.5	4,331	196	4.5
1967	8,186	379	4.6	4,060	189	4.7	4,126	190	4.6
WHITE ALONE, NON-HISPANIC									
Grades 10–12									
2017	6,224	235	3.8	3,231	132	4.1	2,993	103	3.4
2016	6,230	273	4.4	3,234	164	5.1	2,996	109	3.6
2015	6,382	233	3.6	3,289	145	4.4	3,092	87	2.8
2014	6,397	285	4.5	3,288	154	4.7	3,109	131	4.2
2013	6,268	256	4.1	3,236	144	4.5	3,031	112	3.7
2012	6,436	95	1.5	3,257	61	1.9	3,179	34	1.1
2011	6,647	171	2.6	3,404	89	2.6	3,243	82	2.5
2010	6,851	150	2.2	3,568	97	2.7	3,284	53	1.6
2009	6,944	160	2.3	3,491	91	2.6	3,453	68	2.0
2008	7,079	156	2.2	3,638	83	2.3	3,441	73	2.1
2007	7,274	155	2.1	3,684	82	2.2	3,590	73	2.0
2006	7,171	200	2.8	3,693	120	3.2	3,478	80	2.3
2005	7,227	196	2.7	3,652	103	2.8	3,575	93	2.6
2004	7,015	245	3.5	3,582	130	3.6	3,434	115	3.4
2003[1]	7,139	214	3.0	3,665	116	3.2	3,474	98	2.8
2002	7,124	173	2.4	3,620	84	2.3	3,504	89	2.6
2001	7,070	272	3.8	3,647	173	4.7	3,423	98	2.9
2000	7,159	276	3.9	3,648	150	4.1	3,511	126	3.6
1999	7,265	274	3.8	3,744	130	3.5	3,523	145	4.1
1998	7,174	266	3.7	3,605	130	3.6	3,570	137	3.8
1997	7,090	242	3.4	3,533	140	4.0	3,558	103	2.9
1996	6,850	267	3.9	3,511	145	4.1	3,337	121	3.6
1995	6,905	296	4.3	3,564	164	4.6	3,341	131	3.9
1994	6,839	274	4.0	3,496	137	3.9	3,343	137	4.1
1993	6,277	237	3.8	3,229	128	4.0	3,047	108	3.5
BLACK ALONE									
Grades 10–12									
2017	1,784	88	5.0	879	58	6.6	905	31	3.4
2016	1,815	98	5.4	919	49	5.3	897	49	5.5
2015	1,735	112	6.4	842	49	5.8	893	63	7.0
2014	1,757	83	4.7	905	44	4.9	852	39	4.5
2013	1,791	88	4.9	859	37	4.3	931	51	5.5
2012	1,949	124	6.4	897	49	5.5	1,052	75	7.1
2011	1,944	78	4.0	965	54	5.6	978	24	2.4
2010	1,898	62	3.2	946	36	3.8	952	26	2.7
2009	1,797	81	4.5	870	38	4.4	927	42	4.6
2008	1,868	114	6.1	925	42	4.6	943	72	7.6
2007	1,781	76	4.3	914	45	4.9	867	31	3.6
2006	1,767	65	3.7	902	29	3.2	864	37	4.3
2005	1,763	122	6.9	943	71	7.5	820	51	6.2
2004	1,716	90	5.2	833	40	4.8	883	50	5.7
2003[1]	1,698	76	4.5	812	33	4.1	886	43	4.9
2002	1,664	73	4.4	782	40	5.1	882	33	3.8
2001	1,655	95	5.7	828	51	6.2	827	45	5.4
2000	1,706	96	5.6	819	62	7.6	888	34	3.8
1999	1,794	107	6.0	925	48	5.2	870	59	6.8
1998	1,759	88	5.0	918	42	4.6	841	46	5.5
1997	1,678	80	4.8	813	33	4.1	866	49	5.7
1996	1,704	107	6.3	803	37	4.6	901	70	7.8
1995	1,598	97	6.1	797	63	7.9	802	35	4.4
1994	1,559	96	6.1	763	50	6.5	795	45	5.7
1993r	1,499	80	5.3	740	43	5.8	758	37	4.9
1993	1,447	78	5.4	724	41	5.7	722	36	5.0
1992	1,422	70	4.9	702	23	3.3	720	48	6.7
1991	1,366	85	6.2	685	38	5.5	683	48	7.0
1990	1,303	66	5.1	636	26	4.1	666	40	6.0
1989	1,384	106	7.7	684	47	6.9	701	60	8.6
1988	1,468	93	6.3	751	50	6.7	717	43	6.0

r = Revised, controlled to 1990 census based population estimates; previous 1993 data controlled to 1980 census based population estimates.
[1] Starting in 2003 respondents could identify more than one race. Except as noted, the race data in this table from 2003 onward represent those respondents who indicated only one race category.

Table A-13. Annual High School Dropout Rates of 15 to 24 Year Olds by Sex, Race, Grade, and Hispanic Origin, October 1967–2017—*Continued*

(Numbers in thousands; percent; civilian noninstitutionalized population.)

Year, grade, race, and Hispanic origin	Total[1]			Male			Female		
	Total students	Dropouts	Dropout rate	Total students	Dropouts	Dropout rate	Total students	Dropouts	Dropout rate
1987	1,463	93	6.4	730	45	6.2	732	47	6.4
1986	1,449	68	4.7	711	34	4.8	737	34	4.6
1985	1,422	110	7.7	703	58	8.3	719	52	7.2
1984	1,524	88	5.8	711	44	6.2	813	43	5.3
1983	1,498	103	6.9	687	48	7.0	810	55	6.8
1982	1,553	121	7.8	786	71	9.0	767	50	6.5
1981	1,516	146	9.6	704	66	9.4	815	83	10.2
1980	1,496	124	8.3	714	57	8.0	781	66	8.5
1979	1,479	142	9.6	679	51	7.5	802	92	11.5
1978	1,542	160	10.4	706	78	11.0	835	81	9.7
1977	1,588	133	8.4	746	62	8.3	789	71	9.0
1976	1,449	105	7.2	729	62	8.5	721	45	6.2
1975	1,416	123	8.7	673	56	8.3	743	67	9.0
1974	1,441	167	11.6	679	73	10.8	761	93	12.2
1973	1,372	138	10.1	650	78	12.0	725	61	8.4
1972	1,373	133	9.7	644	65	10.1	756	68	9.0
1971	1,195	87	7.3	552	51	9.2	643	37	5.8
1970	1,192	133	11.2	587	74	12.6	606	60	9.9
1969	1,209	113	9.3	562	58	10.3	646	55	8.5
1968	1,123	113	10.1	523	52	9.9	600	61	10.2
1967	1,066	106	9.9	485	47	9.7	578	58	10.0
ASIAN[2]									
Grades 10–12									
2017	657	42	6.3	323	22	6.8	334	20	5.9
2016	594	20	3.3	281	11	3.9	313	9	2.8
2015	552	34	6.2	263	20	7.5	288	14	5.0
2014	566	5	0.9	259	3	1.2	307	2	0.6
2013	604	10	1.7	279	4	1.5	324	6	1.8
2012	592	19	3.2	331	9	2.7	261	10	3.8
2011	495	17	3.5	272	4	1.5	223	13	6.0
2010	419	12	2.8	220	6	2.9	199	5	2.6
2009	426	7	1.7	215	2	0.8	210	5	2.6
2008	429	17	3.9	219	*	0.2	210	16	7.8
2007	404	30	7.5	202	13	6.6	202	17	8.3
2006	445	19	4.2	237	11	4.5	208	8	3.7
2005	425	6	1.5	219	5	2.4	206	1	0.5
2004	452	4	0.9	233	*	*	219	4	1.9
2003[1]	457	11	2.4	237	3	1.4	221	7	3.4
2002	515	12	2.3	266	8	3.0	249	4	1.6
2001	470	10	2.1	274	9	3.3	197	1	0.5
2000	399	13	3.3	178	12	6.7	221	1	0.5
1999	523	25	4.8	269	13	4.8	253	12	4.7
HISPANIC ORIGIN (OF ANY RACE)									
Grades 10–12									
2017	2,650	161	6.1	1,357	104	7.7	1,293	56	4.4
2016	2,747	118	4.3	1,331	67	5.1	1,416	51	3.6
2015	2,599	148	5.7	1,314	67	5.1	1,285	80	6.3
2014	2,490	179	7.2	1,254	86	6.8	1,236	93	7.5
2013	2,509	132	5.3	1,291	71	5.5	1,218	61	5.0
2012	2,671	136	5.1	1,377	76	5.5	1,294	60	4.6
2011	2,376	100	4.2	1,260	56	4.4	1,116	44	4.0
2010	2,130	80	3.8	1,113	30	2.7	1,018	51	5.0
2009	2,129	114	5.3	1,039	55	5.3	1,090	59	5.4
2008	2,062	101	4.9	1,052	44	4.2	1,011	57	5.6
2007	1,785	99	5.5	904	49	5.5	882	49	5.6
2006	1,923	124	6.4	958	61	6.3	965	63	6.6
2005	1,814	86	4.7	910	51	5.6	904	35	3.9
2004	1,723	138	8.0	842	97	11.5	881	40	4.6
2003	1,792	116	6.5	846	65	7.7	945	51	5.4
2002	1,614	86	5.3	801	50	6.2	814	36	4.4
2001	1,487	121	8.1	755	57	7.5	732	64	8.7
2000	1,465	100	6.8	761	54	7.1	704	46	6.5
1999	1,482	105	7.1	729	50	6.9	751	55	7.3

* = Quantity zero or rounds to zero.
[1] Starting in 2003 respondents could identify more than one race. Except as noted, the race data in this table from 2003 onward represent those respondents who indicated only one race category.
[2] The data shown prior to 2003 consists of those identifying themselves as "Asian or Pacific Islanders."

Table A-13. Annual High School Dropout Rates of 15 to 24 Year Olds by Sex, Race, Grade, and Hispanic Origin, October 1967–2017—*Continued*

(Numbers in thousands; percent; civilian noninstitutionalized population.)

Year, grade, race, and Hispanic origin	Total[1] Total students	Dropouts	Dropout rate	Male Total students	Dropouts	Dropout rate	Female Total students	Dropouts	Dropout rate
1998	1,368	115	8.4	731	63	8.6	637	52	8.2
1997	1,377	119	8.6	710	74	10.4	668	45	6.7
1996	1,195	100	8.4	588	54	9.2	608	46	7.6
1995	1,251	145	11.6	644	70	10.9	608	76	12.5
1994	1,179	109	9.2	607	51	8.4	572	58	10.1
1993r	1,061	69	6.5	488	25	5.1	573	44	7.5
1993	943	60	6.4	436	21	4.8	508	39	7.7
1992	917	72	7.9	468	27	5.8	441	38	8.6
1991	809	59	7.3	396	41	10.4	417	20	4.8
1990	811	65	8.0	379	33	8.7	428	31	7.2
1989	762	59	7.7	394	30	7.6	366	28	7.7
1988	730	77	10.5	398	49	12.3	333	28	8.4
1987	769	43	5.6	380	19	5.0	389	24	6.2
1986	764	91	11.9	376	44	11.7	388	48	12.4
1985	729	71	9.7	333	31	9.3	396	39	9.8
1984	706	77	10.9	311	38	12.2	396	40	10.1
1983	691	68	9.8	351	48	13.7	340	21	6.2
1982	692	65	9.4	370	35	9.5	321	29	9.0
1981	717	77	10.7	350	37	10.6	367	40	10.9
1980	646	74	11.5	295	50	16.9	350	24	6.9
1979	593	58	9.8	295	30	10.2	298	27	9.1
1978	567	70	12.3	295	46	15.6	271	23	8.5
1977	627	50	8.0	341	35	10.3	287	15	5.2
1976	638	46	7.2	300	22	7.3	336	23	6.8
1975	614	67	10.9	317	32	10.1	294	34	11.6
1974	547	53	9.7	271	34	12.5	278	20	7.2
1973	499	50	10.0	240	19	7.9	259	31	12.0
1972	498	55	11.0	253	28	11.1	247	27	10.9
WHITE ALONE OR IN COMBINATION									
Grades 10–12									
2017	8,968	375	4.2	4,619	212	4.6	4,348	163	3.7
2016	9,054	385	4.3	4,566	224	4.9	4,488	161	3.6
2015	9,037	378	4.2	4,610	213	4.6	4,427	165	3.7
2014	9,005	446	5.0	4,580	229	5.0	4,424	217	4.9
2013	8,854	404	4.6	4,577	226	4.9	4,276	178	4.2
2012	9,101	220	2.4	4,629	137	3.0	4,473	83	1.9
2011	9,087	272	3.0	4,696	145	3.1	4,391	127	2.9
2010	9,112	242	2.7	4,764	130	2.7	4,348	112	2.6
2009	9,216	280	3.0	4,610	148	3.2	4,606	132	2.9
2008	9,277	257	2.8	4,766	129	2.7	4,511	128	2.8
2007	9,199	251	2.7	4,664	131	2.8	4,535	120	2.7
2006	9,212	320	3.5	4,695	185	3.9	4,517	136	3.0
2005	9,158	281	3.1	4,610	155	3.4	4,548	126	2.8
2004	8,821	382	4.3	4,464	222	5.0	4,357	160	3.7
2003	9,045	335	3.7	4,573	183	4.0	4,471	151	3.4
BLACK ALONE OR IN COMBINATION									
Grades 10–12									
2017	2,084	95	4.6	1,022	58	5.7	1,062	37	3.4
2016	2,142	106	4.9	1,077	56	5.2	1,066	49	4.6
2015	1,950	112	5.7	951	49	5.1	999	63	6.3
2014	2,012	95	4.7	1,019	55	5.4	993	40	4.0
2013	1,989	98	4.9	962	42	4.3	1,027	56	5.4
2012	2,124	129	6.1	976	52	5.3	1,148	77	6.7
2011	2,051	82	4.0	1,024	54	5.3	1,027	28	2.8
2010	2,038	76	3.7	1,021	38	3.7	1,017	39	3.8
2009	1,985	86	4.3	958	40	4.2	1,026	46	4.5
2008	2,033	121	5.9	1,012	46	4.5	1,021	75	7.3
2007	1,900	78	4.1	977	47	4.8	923	31	3.4
2006	1,891	66	3.5	952	29	3.0	939	38	4.0
2005	1,870	129	6.9	979	71	7.3	890	58	6.5
2004	1,797	99	5.5	869	40	4.6	928	59	6.3
2003	1,808	79	4.4	853	36	4.2	955	43	4.5

r = Revised, controlled to 1990 census based population estimates; previous 1993 data controlled to 1980 census based population estimates.
[1] Starting in 2003 respondents could identify more than one race. Except as noted, the race data in this table from 2003 onward represent those respondents who indicated only one race category.

Table A-13. Annual High School Dropout Rates of 15 to 24 Year Olds by Sex, Race, Grade, and Hispanic Origin, October 1967–2017—*Continued*

(Numbers in thousands; percent; civilian noninstitutionalized population.)

Year, grade, race, and Hispanic origin	Total[1]			Male			Female		
	Total students	Dropouts	Dropout rate	Total students	Dropouts	Dropout rate	Total students	Dropouts	Dropout rate
ASIAN ALONE OR IN COMBINATION									
Grades 10–12									
2017...	796	44	5.5	397	24	6.2	398	20	4.9
2016...	731	25	3.4	353	16	4.4	378	9	2.3
2015...	661	38	5.7	312	20	6.3	349	18	5.2
2014...	660	5	0.8	300	3	1.0	361	2	0.5
2013...	744	10	1.4	339	4	1.2	405	6	1.5
2012...	696	19	2.7	368	9	2.5	328	10	3.1
2011...	579	17	3.0	303	4	1.3	275	13	4.9
2010...	520	16	3.2	270	6	2.4	250	10	4.0
2009...	525	8	1.4	255	2	0.8	270	5	2.0
2008...	511	17	3.3	256	*	0.2	255	16	6.4
2007...	483	30	6.2	233	13	5.8	250	17	6.7
2006...	542	23	4.2	279	15	5.4	263	8	3.0
2005...	525	8	1.5	270	6	2.3	255	2	0.6
2004...	516	8	1.6	273	3	1.2	243	5	2.1
2003...	533	17	3.1	278	8	3.0	254	8	3.3

* = Quantity zero or rounds to zero.
[1] Starting in 2003 respondents could identify more than one race. Except as noted, the race data in this table from 2003 onward represent those respondents who indicated only one race category.

Table A-14. Population 14 to 24 Years Old, by High School Graduate Status, College Enrollment, Attainment, Sex, Race, and Hispanic Origin, October 1967–2017

(Numbers in thousands; percent; civilian noninstitutionalized population.)

Year, race, and Hispanic origin	Population 18 to 24 years old								High school graduates, 14 to 24 years old		
		High school graduates		Percent			High school dropouts			Percent	
	Total	Total	Enrolled in college	High school graduates	Enrolled in college	High school graduate enrolled in college	Number	Percent	All graduates	Enrolled in college	Enrolled or completed some college
ALL RACES											
Both Sexes											
2017	29,538	25,831	11,937	87.5	40.4	46.2	1,772	6.0	26,248	46.4	72.0
2016	29,893	26,123	12,320	87.4	41.2	47.2	1,911	6.4	26,571	47.3	72.3
2015	30,037	26,248	12,152	87.4	40.5	46.3	1,917	6.4	26,673	46.4	72.2
2014	30,304	26,311	12,132	86.8	40.0	46.1	2,090	6.9	26,700	46.3	72.0
2013	30,556	26,317	12,202	86.1	39.9	46.4	2,215	7.3	26,734	46.8	71.8
2012	30,377	25,866	12,456	85.1	41.0	48.2	2,319	7.6	26,255	48.5	72.9
2011	29,943	25,435	12,570	84.9	42.0	49.4	2,481	8.3	25,765	49.6	73.1
2010	29,659	25,224	12,213	85.0	41.2	48.4	2,590	8.7	25,564	48.7	72.6
2009	29,223	24,647	12,073	84.3	41.3	49.0	2,733	9.4	25,015	49.1	72.0
2008	28,950	24,568	11,466	84.9	39.6	46.7	2,702	9.3	24,922	47.0	70.6
2007	28,778	24,146	11,161	83.9	38.8	46.2	2,937	10.2	24,491	46.3	69.7
2006	28,372	23,430	10,586	82.6	37.3	45.2	3,128	11.0	23,800	45.4	69.3
2005	27,855	23,103	10,834	82.9	38.9	46.9	3,154	11.3	23,445	47.0	69.8
2004	27,948	23,086	10,611	82.6	38.0	46.0	3,836	12.1	23,379	46.2	69.0
2003	27,404	22,603	10,364	82.5	37.8	45.9	3,228	11.8	22,898	45.9	68.8
2002	27,367	22,319	10,033	81.6	36.7	45.0	3,375	12.3	22,639	45.2	67.6
2001	26,965	21,836	9,629	81.0	35.7	44.1	3,519	13.0	22,136	44.1	66.7
2000	26,658	21,822	9,452	81.9	35.5	43.3	3,315	12.4	22,080	43.5	66.7
1999	26,041	21,127	9,259	81.1	35.6	43.8	3,413	13.1	21,390	44.0	67.2
1998	25,507	20,567	9,322	80.6	36.6	45.3	3,544	13.9	20,775	45.5	68.0
1997	24,973	20,338	9,204	81.4	36.9	45.2	3,236	13.0	20,577	45.6	67.3
1996	24,671	20,131	8,767	81.6	35.5	43.5	3,147	12.8	20,465	44.0	67.2
1995	24,900	20,125	8,539	80.8	34.3	42.4	3,471	13.9	20,359	42.7	67.1
1994	25,254	20,581	8,729	81.5	34.6	42.4	3,365	13.3	20,779	42.7	66.9
1993r	25,522	20,844	8,630	81.7	33.8	41.4	3,349	13.1	21,060	41.6	65.3
1993	24,100	19,772	8,193	82.0	34.0	41.4	3,070	12.7	19,979	41.6	65.4
1992	24,278	19,921	8,343	82.1	34.4	41.9	3,083	12.7	20,194	42.3	65.6
1991	24,572	19,883	8,172	80.9	33.3	41.1	3,486	14.2	20,065	41.4	60.7
1990	24,852	20,311	7,964	82.3	32.0	39.1	3,379	13.6	20,571	39.6	58.9
1989	25,261	20,461	7,804	81.0	30.9	38.1	3,644	14.4	20,749	38.5	57.9
1988	25,733	20,900	7,791	81.2	30.3	37.3	3,749	14.6	21,204	37.6	57.4
1987	25,950	21,118	7,693	81.4	29.6	36.4	3,751	14.5	21,477	36.9	56.2
1986	26,512	21,768	7,477	82.1	28.2	34.3	3,687	13.9	22,086	34.8	55.0
1985	27,122	22,349	7,537	82.4	27.8	33.7	3,687	13.9	22,722	34.3	54.3
1984	28,031	22,870	7,591	81.6	27.1	33.2	4,142	14.8	23,252	33.7	53.0
1983	28,580	22,988	7,477	80.4	26.2	32.5	4,410	15.4	23,359	33.1	52.8
1982	28,846	23,291	7,678	80.7	26.6	33.0	4,500	15.6	23,708	33.5	52.7
1981	28,965	23,343	7,575	80.6	26.2	32.5	4,520	15.6	23,705	32.9	51.7
1980	28,957	23,413	7,400	80.9	25.6	31.6	4,515	15.6	23,856	32.1	51.1
1979	27,974	22,421	6,991	80.1	25.0	31.2	4,560	16.3	22,911	31.9	51.6
1978	27,647	22,309	6,995	80.7	25.3	31.4	4,388	15.9	22,759	31.9	51.4
1977	27,331	22,008	7,142	80.5	26.1	32.5	4,313	15.8	22,499	33.0	52.0
1976	26,919	21,677	7,181	80.5	26.7	33.1	4,276	15.9	22,158	33.7	53.4
1975	26,387	21,326	6,935	80.8	26.3	32.5	4,110	15.6	21,824	33.1	52.5
1974	25,670	20,725	6,316	80.7	24.6	30.5	4,070	15.9	21,267	31.2	50.7
1973	25,237	20,377	6,055	80.7	24.0	29.7	3,973	15.7	20,895	30.4	50.7
1972	24,579	19,618	6,257	79.8	25.5	31.9	4,068	16.6	20,107	32.6	52.9
1971	23,668	18,691	6,210	79.0	26.2	33.2	4,025	17.0	19,130	33.9	53.1
1970	22,552	17,768	5,805	78.8	25.7	32.7	3,908	17.3	18,218	33.5	52.3
1969	21,362	16,703	5,840	78.2	27.3	35.0	3,769	17.6	17,152	35.7	52.5
1968	20,562	15,683	5,356	76.3	26.0	34.2	3,929	19.1	16,165	35.2	51.5
1967	20,009	15,114	5,100	75.5	25.5	33.7	3,967	19.8	15,642	34.9	50.5
Male											
2017	14,833	12,697	5,460	85.6	36.8	43.0	1,019	6.9	12,873	43.1	67.8
2016	15,042	12,851	5,800	85.4	38.6	45.1	1,134	7.5	13,014	45.2	68.1
2015	15,074	13,031	5,694	86.5	37.8	43.7	1,034	6.9	13,256	43.8	68.0

r = Revised, controlled to 1990 census based population estimates; previous 1993 data controlled to 1980 census based population estimates.
Note: The change in the educational attainment question and the college completion categories from "4 or more years of college" to "at least some college," in 1992 caused an increase in the proportion of 14-to-24-year-old high school graduates enrolled in college or completed some college, of approximately 5 percentage points. High school graduates are people who have completed 4 years of high school or more, for 1967 to 1991. Beginning in 1992, they were people whose highest degree was a high school diploma (including equivalency) or higher.

Table A-14. Population 14 to 24 Years Old, by High School Graduate Status, College Enrollment, Attainment, Sex, Race, and Hispanic Origin, October 1967–2017—*Continued*

(Numbers in thousands; percent; civilian noninstitutionalized population.)

| Year, race, and Hispanic origin | Population 18 to 24 years old | | | | | | | | High school graduates, 14 to 24 years old | | |
| | Total | High school graduates | | Percent | | | High school dropouts | | | Percent | |
		Total	Enrolled in college	High school graduates	Enrolled in college	High school graduate enrolled in college	Number	Percent	All graduates	Enrolled in college	Enrolled or completed some college
2014	15,234	13,019	5,676	85.5	37.3	43.6	1,132	7.4	13,225	43.9	67.7
2013	15,379	13,051	5,630	84.9	36.6	43.1	1,183	7.7	13,254	43.6	67.0
2012	15,252	12,753	5,731	83.6	37.6	44.9	1,300	8.5	12,940	45.3	68.4
2011	15,211	12,659	5,953	83.2	39.1	47.0	1,374	9.0	12,834	47.2	69.0
2010	14,887	12,371	5,698	83.1	38.3	46.1	1,473	9.9	12,540	46.2	68.4
2009	14,677	12,111	5,640	82.5	38.4	46.6	1,568	10.7	12,277	46.7	68.5
2008	14,559	12,181	5,383	83.7	37.0	44.2	1,445	9.9	12,374	44.6	66.7
2007	14,515	11,825	5,156	81.5	35.5	43.6	1,680	11.6	11,972	43.7	66.0
2006	14,300	11,508	4,874	80.5	34.1	42.4	1,741	12.2	11,659	42.5	65.1
2005	14,077	11,182	4,973	79.4	35.3	44.5	1,852	13.2	11,330	44.4	65.9
2004	14,018	11,258	4,865	80.3	34.7	43.2	1,942	13.9	11,364	43.5	65.0
2003	13,681	10,919	4,697	79.8	34.3	43.0	1,875	13.7	11,040	43.1	65.0
2002	13,744	10,823	4,629	78.7	33.7	42.8	1,925	14.0	10,975	42.9	64.6
2001	13,434	10,461	4,437	77.9	33.0	42.4	2,028	15.1	10,587	42.4	63.9
2000	13,338	10,622	4,343	79.6	32.6	40.9	1,837	13.8	10,736	41.0	63.1
1999	12,905	10,201	4,396	79.1	34.0	43.1	1,818	14.9	10,331	43.3	64.5
1998	12,764	9,915	4,403	77.7	34.5	44.4	2,018	15.8	10,006	44.5	64.9
1997	12,513	9,933	4,374	79.4	35.0	44.0	1,765	14.1	10,025	44.2	64.9
1996	12,285	9,815	4,187	80.0	34.1	42.6	1,628	13.2	9,960	43.0	65.6
1995	12,351	9,789	4,089	79.3	33.1	41.8	1,791	14.5	9,884	42.1	64.2
1994	12,557	9,970	4,152	79.4	33.1	41.6	1,804	14.4	10,051	41.9	64.9
1993r	12,712	10,142	4,237	79.8	33.3	41.8	1,745	13.7	10,229	42.0	63.9
1993	11,898	9,541	3,994	80.2	33.6	41.9	1,575	13.2	9,625	42.0	64.1
1992	11,965	9,576	3,912	80.0	32.7	40.9	1,617	13.5	9,706	41.3	64.1
1991	12,036	9,493	3,954	78.9	32.9	41.7	1,810	15.0	9,564	41.9	59.2
1990	12,134	9,778	3,922	80.6	32.3	40.1	1,689	13.9	9,894	40.5	58.0
1989	12,325	9,700	3,717	78.7	30.2	38.3	1,941	15.7	9,810	38.6	57.2
1988	12,491	9,832	3,770	78.7	30.2	38.3	1,950	15.6	9,947	38.5	56.5
1987	12,626	10,030	3,867	79.4	30.6	38.6	1,948	15.4	10,207	39.0	56.0
1986	12,921	10,338	3,702	80.0	28.7	35.8	1,924	14.9	10,465	36.2	54.4
1985	13,199	10,614	3,749	80.4	28.4	35.3	2,015	15.3	10,784	36.0	54.6
1984	13,744	10,914	3,929	79.4	28.6	36.0	2,184	15.9	11,052	36.4	53.6
1983	14,003	10,906	3,820	77.9	27.3	35.0	2,379	17.0	10,959	35.5	52.7
1982	14,083	11,120	3,837	79.0	27.2	34.5	2,329	16.5	11,295	35.0	53.0
1981	14,127	11,052	3,833	78.2	27.1	34.7	2,424	17.2	11,203	35.1	52.1
1980	14,107	11,125	3,717	78.9	26.3	33.4	2,390	16.9	11,309	33.7	51.4
1979	13,571	10,657	3,508	78.5	25.8	32.9	2,320	17.1	10,838	33.6	52.4
1978	13,385	10,614	3,621	79.3	27.1	34.1	2,200	16.4	10,789	34.5	52.6
1977	13,218	10,440	3,712	79.0	28.1	35.6	2,170	16.4	10,626	36.0	54.2
1976	13,012	10,312	3,673	79.2	28.2	35.6	2,109	16.2	10,492	36.0	55.7
1975	12,724	10,214	3,693	80.3	29.0	36.2	1,928	15.2	10,415	36.7	56.1
1974	12,315	9,835	3,411	79.9	27.7	34.7	1,958	15.9	10,073	35.3	55.6
1973	12,111	9,716	3,360	80.2	27.7	34.6	1,853	15.3	9,908	35.1	55.4
1972	11,712	9,247	3,534	79.0	30.2	38.2	1,898	16.2	9,461	38.8	59.0
1971	11,092	8,669	3,599	78.2	32.4	41.5	1,865	16.8	8,855	42.1	60.1
1970	10,385	8,087	3,331	77.9	32.1	41.2	1,746	16.8	8,279	41.8	59.2
1969	9,649	7,445	3,392	77.2	35.2	45.6	1,640	17.0	7,609	46.2	61.2
1968	9,251	6,864	3,152	74.2	34.1	45.9	1,777	19.2	8,038	46.7	61.1
1967	8,999	6,678	2,982	74.2	33.1	44.7	1,804	20.0	6,829	45.1	58.8
Female											
2017	14,705	13,134	6,477	89.3	44.0	49.3	754	5.1	13,375	49.6	76.1
2016	14,851	13,273	6,521	89.4	43.9	49.1	778	5.2	13,557	49.3	76.4
2015	14,963	13,217	6,459	88.3	43.2	48.9	883	5.9	13,418	49.0	76.3
2014	15,070	13,293	6,456	88.2	42.8	48.6	958	6.4	13,475	48.7	76.3
2013	15,177	13,266	6,573	87.4	43.3	49.5	1,033	6.8	13,480	49.9	76.6
2012	15,125	13,113	6,725	86.7	44.5	51.3	1,019	6.7	13,316	51.6	77.2
2011	14,732	12,776	6,617	86.7	44.9	51.8	1,107	7.5	12,930	51.9	77.2
2010	14,772	12,854	6,515	87.0	44.1	50.7	1,116	7.6	13,024	51.1	76.7
2009	14,546	12,536	6,432	86.2	44.2	51.3	1,165	8.0	12,738	51.4	75.5

r = Revised, controlled to 1990 census based population estimates; previous 1993 data controlled to 1980 census based population estimates.
Note: The change in the educational attainment question and the college completion categories from "4 or more years of college" to "at least some college," in 1992 caused an increase in the proportion of 14-to-24-year-old high school graduates enrolled in college or completed some college, of approximately 5 percentage points. High school graduates are people who have completed 4 years of high school or more, for 1967 to 1991. Beginning in 1992, they were people whose highest degree was a high school diploma (including equivalency) or higher.

Table A-14. Population 14 to 24 Years Old, by High School Graduate Status, College Enrollment, Attainment, Sex, Race, and Hispanic Origin, October 1967–2017—_Continued_

(Numbers in thousands; percent; civilian noninstitutionalized population.)

Year, race, and Hispanic origin	Population 18 to 24 years old								High school graduates, 14 to 24 years old		
		High school graduates		Percent			High school dropouts			Percent	
	Total	Total	Enrolled in college	High school graduates	Enrolled in college	High school graduate enrolled in college	Number	Percent	All graduates	Enrolled in college	Enrolled or completed some college
2008..................	14,391	12,387	6,083	86.1	42.3	49.1	1,257	8.7	12,548	49.3	74.5
2007..................	14,263	12,321	6,005	86.4	42.1	48.7	1,256	8.8	12,519	48.8	73.3
2006..................	14,073	11,922	5,712	84.7	40.6	47.9	1,387	9.9	12,141	48.1	73.3
2005..................	13,778	11,921	5,861	86.5	42.5	49.2	1,302	9.5	12,115	49.4	73.4
2004..................	13,930	11,828	5,746	84.9	41.2	48.6	1,444	10.4	12,015	48.8	72.8
2003..................	13,724	11,684	5,667	85.1	41.3	48.5	1,354	9.9	11,858	48.5	72.2
2002..................	13,623	11,496	5,404	84.4	39.7	47.0	1,450	10.6	11,664	47.3	70.3
2001..................	13,531	11,375	5,192	84.1	38.4	45.7	1,491	11.0	11,549	45.7	69.4
2000..................	13,319	11,200	5,109	84.1	38.4	45.6	1,478	11.1	11,344	45.8	70.1
1999..................	13,136	10,926	4,863	83.2	37.0	44.5	1,594	12.1	11,058	44.6	69.8
1998..................	12,743	10,651	4,919	83.6	38.6	46.2	1,526	12.0	10,768	46.4	70.7
1997..................	12,460	10,403	4,829	83.5	38.8	46.4	1,471	11.8	10,549	46.8	69.6
1996..................	12,386	10,317	4,582	83.3	37.0	44.4	1,519	12.3	10,507	44.9	68.6
1995..................	12,548	10,338	4,452	82.4	35.5	43.1	1,679	13.4	10,477	43.4	69.8
1994..................	12,696	10,611	4,576	83.6	36.0	43.1	1,561	12.3	10,729	43.4	68.7
1993r................	12,810	10,702	4,393	83.5	34.3	41.0	1,604	12.5	10,831	41.3	66.6
1993..................	12,202	10,232	4,199	83.9	34.4	41.0	1,494	12.2	10,355	41.2	66.7
1992..................	12,313	10,344	4,429	84.0	36.0	42.8	1,466	11.9	10,486	43.3	66.9
1991..................	12,536	10,391	4,218	82.9	33.6	40.6	1,676	13.4	10,502	41.0	62.1
1990..................	12,718	10,533	4,042	82.8	31.8	38.4	1,690	13.3	10,676	38.7	59.8
1989..................	12,936	10,758	4,085	83.2	31.6	38.0	1,702	13.2	10,936	38.4	58.6
1988..................	13,242	11,068	4,021	83.6	30.4	36.3	1,799	13.5	11,257	36.8	58.2
1987..................	13,324	11,086	3,826	83.2	28.7	34.5	1,803	13.5	11,268	35.0	56.4
1986..................	13,591	11,430	3,775	84.1	27.8	33.0	1,751	12.9	11,623	33.5	55.5
1985..................	13,923	11,736	3,788	84.3	27.2	32.3	1,804	13.0	11,937	32.8	54.0
1984..................	14,287	11,956	3,662	83.7	25.6	30.6	1,958	13.7	12,199	31.3	52.4
1983..................	14,577	12,082	3,657	82.9	25.1	30.3	2,031	13.9	12,294	31.0	52.8
1982..................	14,763	12,171	3,841	82.4	26.0	31.6	2,171	14.7	12,411	32.1	52.4
1981..................	14,838	12,290	3,741	82.8	25.2	30.4	2,097	14.1	12,503	31.0	51.3
1980..................	14,851	12,287	3,682	82.7	24.8	30.0	2,124	14.3	12,547	30.6	50.8
1979..................	14,403	11,763	3,482	81.7	24.2	29.6	2,240	15.6	12,074	30.4	50.8
1978..................	14,262	11,694	3,373	82.0	23.7	28.8	2,188	15.3	11,969	29.6	50.3
1977..................	14,113	11,569	3,431	82.0	24.3	29.7	2,143	15.2	11,875	30.3	50.0
1976..................	13,907	11,365	3,508	81.7	25.2	30.9	2,168	15.6	11,666	31.6	51.4
1975..................	13,663	11,113	3,243	81.3	23.7	29.2	2,181	16.0	11,407	29.9	49.2
1974..................	13,355	10,889	2,905	81.5	21.8	26.7	2,112	15.8	11,194	27.4	47.5
1973..................	13,126	10,663	2,696	81.2	20.5	25.3	2,119	16.1	10,986	26.1	46.5
1972..................	12,867	10,371	2,724	80.6	21.2	26.3	2,170	16.9	10,644	27.0	47.4
1971..................	12,576	10,020	2,610	79.7	20.8	26.0	2,159	17.2	10,272	26.9	47.1
1970..................	12,167	9,680	2,474	79.6	20.3	25.6	2,163	17.8	9,908	26.3	46.6
1969..................	11,713	9,259	2,448	79.0	20.9	26.4	2,128	18.2	9,499	27.1	45.7
1968..................	11,311	8,820	2,205	78.0	19.5	25.0	2,150	19.0	9,072	25.9	44.4
1967..................	11,011	8,436	2,117	76.6	19.2	25.1	2,162	19.6	8,694	26.0	44.7
WHITE ALONE											
Both Sexes											
2017..................	21,789	19,069	8,690	87.5	39.9	45.6	1,358	6.2	19,351	45.7	72.1
2016..................	22,018	19,373	9,106	88.0	41.4	47.0	1,381	6.3	19,673	47.1	72.7
2015..................	22,244	19,451	8,969	87.4	40.3	46.1	1,430	6.4	19,747	46.2	72.6
2014..................	22,507	19,541	9,077	86.8	40.3	46.4	1,599	7.1	19,786	46.6	72.1
2013..................	22,658	19,660	9,049	86.8	39.9	46.0	1,599	7.1	19,985	46.5	72.1
2012..................	22,712	19,555	9,302	86.1	41.0	47.6	1,641	7.2	19,831	47.9	73.5
2011..................	23,089	19,760	9,813	85.6	42.5	49.7	1,885	8.2	20,007	49.8	74.0
2010..................	22,851	19,517	9,325	85.4	40.8	47.8	1,941	8.5	19,741	48.0	73.0
2009..................	22,606	19,241	9,327	85.1	41.3	48.5	2,059	9.1	19,512	48.6	72.1
2008..................	22,530	19,334	9,141	85.8	40.6	47.3	1,991	8.8	19,586	47.5	71.6
2007..................	22,392	18,913	8,780	84.5	39.2	46.4	2,248	10.0	19,170	46.5	70.3
2006..................	22,169	18,489	8,298	83.4	37.4	44.9	2,399	10.8	18,751	45.1	69.9
2005..................	21,777	18,130	8,498	83.3	39.0	46.9	2,466	11.3	18,352	46.9	70.0

r = Revised, controlled to 1990 census based population estimates; previous 1993 data controlled to 1980 census based population estimates.
Note: The change in the educational attainment question and the college completion categories from "4 or more years of college" to "at least some college," in 1992 caused an increase in the proportion of 14-to-24-year-old high school graduates enrolled in college or completed some college, of approximately 5 percentage points. High school graduates are people who have completed 4 years of high school or more, for 1967 to 1991. Beginning in 1992, they were people whose highest degree was a high school diploma (including equivalency) or higher.

Table A-14. Population 14 to 24 Years Old, by High School Graduate Status, College Enrollment, Attainment, Sex, Race, and Hispanic Origin, October 1967–2017—*Continued*

(Numbers in thousands; percent; civilian noninstitutionalized population.)

Year, race, and Hispanic origin	Population 18 to 24 years old								High school graduates, 14 to 24 years old		
		High school graduates		Percent			High school dropouts				Percent
	Total	Total	Enrolled in college	High school graduates	Enrolled in college	High school graduate enrolled in college	Number	Percent	All graduates	Enrolled in college	Enrolled or completed some college
2004	21,896	18,213	8,351	82.6	38.0	45.9	2,599	11.9	18,414	46.1	69.1
2003[1]	21,502	17,901	8,150	83.3	37.9	45.5	2,489	11.6	18,123	45.5	69.1
2002	21,704	17,793	7,921	82.0	36.5	44.5	2,641	12.2	17,995	44.6	67.5
2001	21,372	17,348	7,548	81.2	35.3	43.5	2,865	13.4	17,547	43.5	67.0
2000	21,257	17,512	7,566	82.4	35.6	43.2	2,598	12.2	17,714	43.4	66.9
1999	20,866	17,052	7,447	81.7	35.7	43.7	2,680	12.8	17,220	43.8	67.5
1998	20,465	16,701	7,541	81.6	36.9	45.2	2,810	13.7	16,855	45.3	68.3
1997	20,020	16,557	7,495	82.7	37.4	45.3	2,476	12.4	16,733	45.6	67.7
1996	19,676	16,199	7,123	82.3	36.2	44.0	2,458	12.5	16,436	44.3	68.4
1995	19,866	16,269	7,011	81.9	35.3	43.1	2,711	13.6	16,439	43.4	68.3
1994	20,171	16,670	7,118	82.6	35.3	42.7	2,553	12.7	16,814	42.9	67.6
1993r	20,493	16,989	7,074	82.9	34.5	41.6	2,595	12.7	17,161	41.8	66.5
1993	19,430	16,196	6,763	83.4	34.8	41.8	2,369	12.2	16,361	41.9	66.7
1992	19,671	16,379	6,916	83.3	35.2	42.2	2,398	12.2	16,586	42.7	67.0
1991	19,980	16,324	6,813	81.7	34.1	41.7	2,845	14.2	16,467	42.0	62.3
1990	20,393	16,823	6,635	82.5	32.5	39.4	2,751	13.5	17,022	39.8	60.1
1989	20,825	17,089	6,631	82.1	31.8	38.8	2,926	14.1	17,329	39.1	58.9
1988	21,261	17,491	6,659	82.3	31.3	38.1	3,012	14.2	17,720	38.4	58.5
1987	21,493	17,689	6,483	82.3	30.2	36.6	3,042	14.2	17,982	37.1	56.8
1986	22,020	18,291	6,307	83.1	28.6	34.5	2,961	13.4	18,554	34.9	55.5
1985	22,632	18,916	6,500	83.6	28.7	34.4	3,050	13.5	19,229	35.0	55.3
1984	23,347	19,373	6,256	83.0	28.0	33.7	3,281	14.1	19,686	34.2	53.8
1983	23,899	19,643	6,463	82.2	27.0	32.9	3,428	14.3	19,948	33.5	53.4
1982	24,206	19,944	6,694	82.4	27.2	33.1	3,523	14.6	20,292	33.6	53.1
1981	24,486	20,123	6,549	82.2	26.7	32.5	3,590	14.7	20,439	33.0	52.1
1980	24,482	20,214	6,423	82.6	26.2	31.8	3,525	14.4	20,583	32.3	51.4
1979	23,895	19,616	6,120	82.1	25.6	31.2	3,571	14.9	20,033	31.8	51.7
1978	23,650	19,526	6,077	82.6	25.7	31.1	3,464	14.6	19,911	31.7	51.3
1977	23,430	19,291	6,209	82.3	26.5	32.2	3,445	14.7	19,712	32.6	52.1
1976	23,119	19,045	6,276	82.4	27.1	33.0	3,407	14.7	19,462	33.5	53.5
1975	22,703	18,883	6,116	83.2	26.9	32.4	3,149	13.9	19,298	33.0	52.7
1974	22,141	18,318	5,589	82.7	25.2	30.5	3,212	14.5	18,794	31.2	51.7
1973	21,766	18,023	5,438	82.8	25.0	30.2	3,085	14.2	18,470	30.8	51.6
1972	21,315	17,410	5,624	81.7	26.4	32.3	3,241	15.2	17,838	33.0	53.9
1971	20,533	16,593	5,594	81.3	27.2	33.5	3,156	15.4	17,087	34.2	54.1
1970	19,608	15,960	5,305	81.4	27.1	33.2	2,974	15.2	16,334	33.9	53.4
1969	18,606	15,031	5,347	80.8	28.7	35.6	2,915	15.7	15,383	36.2	53.5
1968	17,951	14,127	4,929	78.7	27.5	34.9	3,107	17.3	14,506	35.7	52.5
1967	17,500	13,657	4,708	78.0	26.9	34.5	3,141	17.9	14,022	35.2	51.4
Male											
2017	11,012	9,408	3,973	85.4	36.1	42.2	780	7.1	9,536	42.3	67.6
2016	11,139	9,614	4,267	86.3	38.3	44.4	818	7.3	9,734	44.4	67.7
2015	11,251	9,714	4,189	86.3	37.2	43.1	791	7.0	9,875	43.2	67.6
2014	11,397	9,781	4,296	85.8	37.7	43.9	866	7.6	9,904	44.1	67.4
2013	11,475	9,792	4,131	85.3	36.0	42.2	855	7.5	9,956	42.6	66.7
2012	11,499	9,692	4,261	84.3	37.1	44.0	937	8.1	9,810	44.3	68.0
2011	11,850	9,928	4,685	83.8	39.5	47.2	1,077	9.1	10,061	47.3	70.0
2010	11,579	9,651	4,369	83.3	37.7	45.3	1,124	9.7	9,754	45.4	68.6
2009	11,449	9,535	4,404	83.3	38.5	46.2	1,201	10.5	9,662	46.4	68.3
2008	11,432	9,646	4,340	84.4	38.0	45.0	1,122	9.8	9,784	45.2	67.8
2007	11,387	9,311	4,040	81.8	35.5	43.4	1,333	11.7	9,430	43.5	66.0
2006	11,264	9,139	3,842	81.1	34.1	42.0	1,396	12.4	9,237	42.2	66.0
2005	11,116	8,885	3,924	79.9	35.3	44.1	1,469	13.2	8,986	44.1	65.9
2004	11,107	9,001	3,855	81.0	34.7	42.8	1,524	13.7	9,067	43.1	64.4
2003[1]	10,885	8,763	3,726	80.5	34.2	42.5	1,452	13.3	8,862	42.6	65.1
2002	10,986	8,717	3,701	79.4	33.7	42.5	1,506	13.7	8,833	42.5	64.6
2001	10,817	8,490	3,521	78.5	32.6	41.5	1,659	15.3	8,582	41.5	64.0

r = Revised, controlled to 1990 census based population estimates; previous 1993 data controlled to 1980 census based population estimates.
Note: The change in the educational attainment question and the college completion categories from "4 or more years of college" to "at least some college," in 1992 caused an increase in the proportion of 14-to-24-year-old high school graduates enrolled in college or completed some college, of approximately 5 percentage points. High school graduates are people who have completed 4 years of high school or more, for 1967 to 1991. Beginning in 1992, they were people whose highest degree was a high school diploma (including equivalency) or higher.
[1] Starting in 2003 respondents could identify more than one race. Except as noted, the race data in this table from 2003 onward represent those respondents who indicated only one race category.

Table A-14. Population 14 to 24 Years Old, by High School Graduate Status, College Enrollment, Attainment, Sex, Race, and Hispanic Origin, October 1967–2017—*Continued*

(Numbers in thousands; percent; civilian noninstitutionalized population.)

Year, race, and Hispanic origin	Population 18 to 24 years old								High school graduates, 14 to 24 years old		
	Total	High school graduates		Percent			High school dropouts			Percent	
		Total	Enrolled in college	High school graduates	Enrolled in college	High school graduate enrolled in college	Number	Percent	All graduates	Enrolled in college	Enrolled or completed some college
2000	10,739	8,603	3,522	80.1	32.8	40.9	1,450	13.5	8,690	41.1	63.5
1999	10,532	8,382	3,585	79.6	34.0	42.7	1,462	13.9	8,457	42.8	64.8
1998	10,400	8,194	3,634	78.8	34.9	44.3	1,628	15.7	8,256	44.4	65.5
1997	10,173	8,204	3,633	80.6	35.7	44.3	1,406	13.8	8,274	44.5	65.3
1996	9,897	8,000	3,419	80.8	34.5	42.7	1,275	12.9	8,104	43.0	66.0
1995	9,980	8,001	3,398	80.2	34.0	42.5	1,430	14.3	8,067	42.7	65.3
1994	10,123	8,168	3,406	80.7	33.6	41.7	1,377	13.6	8,227	41.9	65.4
1993r	10,294	8,338	3,498	81.0	34.0	42.0	1,388	13.5	8,411	42.1	65.1
1993	9,641	7,857	3,313	81.5	34.4	42.2	1,379	12.9	7,926	42.3	65.4
1992	9,744	7,911	3,291	81.2	33.8	41.6	1,300	13.3	8,016	42.1	65.8
1991	9,896	7,843	3,270	79.3	33.0	41.7	1,520	15.4	7,899	41.9	59.9
1990	10,053	8,157	3,292	81.1	32.7	40.3	1,430	14.2	8,246	40.7	58.8
1989	10,240	8,177	3,223	79.9	31.5	39.4	1,572	15.4	8,271	39.7	58.5
1988	10,380	8,268	3,260	79.7	31.4	39.4	1,594	15.4	8,365	39.6	57.8
1987	10,549	8,498	3,289	80.6	31.2	38.7	1,593	15.1	8,647	39.2	56.4
1986	10,814	8,780	3,168	81.2	29.3	36.1	1,575	14.6	8,886	36.4	55.1
1985	11,108	9,077	3,254	81.7	29.3	35.8	1,637	14.7	9,229	36.6	55.5
1984	11,521	9,348	3,406	81.1	29.6	36.4	1,744	15.1	9,459	36.8	54.2
1983	11,787	9,411	3,335	79.8	28.3	35.4	1,865	15.8	9,534	35.9	53.5
1982	11,874	9,611	3,308	80.9	27.9	34.4	1,810	15.2	9,761	34.9	53.2
1981	12,040	9,619	3,340	79.9	27.7	34.7	1,960	16.3	9,754	35.1	52.8
1980	12,011	9,686	3,275	80.6	27.3	33.8	1,883	15.7	9,838	34.1	51.8
1979	11,721	9,457	3,104	80.7	26.5	32.8	1,830	15.6	9,615	33.4	52.7
1978	11,572	9,438	3,195	81.6	27.6	33.9	1,722	14.9	9,582	34.3	52.5
1977	11,445	9,263	3,286	80.9	28.7	35.5	1,779	15.5	9,422	35.8	54.5
1976	11,279	9,186	3,250	81.4	28.8	35.4	1,691	15.0	9,340	35.7	55.9
1975	11,050	9,139	3,326	82.7	30.1	36.4	1,490	13.5	9,310	36.9	56.6
1974	10,722	8,768	3,035	81.8	28.3	34.6	1,579	14.7	8,980	35.2	55.9
1973	10,511	8,637	3,032	82.2	28.8	35.1	1,453	13.8	8,817	35.6	56.5
1972	10,212	8,278	3,195	81.1	31.3	38.6	1,506	14.7	8,462	39.2	60.1
1971	9,653	7,807	3,284	80.9	34.0	42.1	1,429	14.8	7,978	42.6	61.4
1970	9,053	7,324	3,096	80.9	34.2	42.3	1,297	14.3	7,496	42.9	60.9
1969	8,420	6,740	3,146	80.0	37.4	46.7	1,248	14.8	6,882	47.3	62.8
1968	8,084	6,221	2,949	77.0	36.5	47.4	1,401	17.3	6,372	48.1	62.7
1967	7,864	6,073	2,761	77.2	35.1	45.5	1,391	17.7	6,210	45.9	60.0
Female											
2017	10,777	9,661	4,717	89.6	43.8	48.8	578	5.4	9,814	49.0	76.4
2016	10,879	9,759	4,839	89.7	44.5	49.6	563	5.2	9,939	49.8	77.5
2015	10,993	9,736	4,780	88.6	43.5	49.1	639	5.8	9,872	49.1	77.5
2014	11,110	9,760	4,780	87.9	43.0	49.0	733	6.6	9,882	49.2	76.8
2013	11,183	9,868	4,919	88.2	44.0	49.8	744	6.7	10,029	50.2	77.5
2012	11,214	9,863	5,041	88.0	45.0	51.1	704	6.3	10,021	51.5	78.8
2011	11,238	9,832	5,128	87.5	45.6	51.8	808	7.2	9,946	52.2	78.0
2010	11,271	9,867	4,956	87.5	44.0	50.2	817	7.2	9,987	50.6	77.3
2009	11,157	9,706	4,923	87.0	44.1	50.7	858	7.7	9,850	50.8	75.8
2008	11,098	9,688	4,801	87.3	43.3	49.6	869	7.8	9,802	49.9	75.4
2007	11,005	9,603	4,741	87.3	43.1	49.4	915	8.3	9,741	49.5	74.4
2006	10,905	9,350	4,456	85.7	40.9	47.7	1,003	9.2	9,513	47.9	73.7
2005	10,661	9,245	4,574	86.7	42.9	49.5	997	9.4	9,366	49.7	73.9
2004	10,789	9,212	4,496	85.4	41.7	48.8	1,075	10.0	9,347	49.0	73.5
2003[1]	10,617	9,138	4,424	86.1	41.7	48.4	1,037	9.8	9,260	48.3	72.9
2002	10,718	9,075	4,220	84.7	39.4	46.5	1,135	10.6	9,162	46.6	70.4
2001	10,555	8,859	4,027	83.9	38.1	45.5	1,206	11.4	8,965	45.5	69.8
2000	10,517	8,909	4,044	84.7	38.5	45.4	1,148	10.9	9,024	45.6	70.2
1999	10,334	8,671	3,862	83.9	37.4	44.5	1,218	11.8	8,763	44.7	70.1
1998	10,065	8,507	3,907	84.5	38.8	45.9	1,181	11.7	8,599	46.2	71.0

r = Revised, controlled to 1990 census based population estimates; previous 1993 data controlled to 1980 census based population estimates.
Note: The change in the educational attainment question and the college completion categories from "4 or more years of college" to "at least some college," in 1992 caused an increase in the proportion of 14-to-24-year-old high school graduates enrolled in college or completed some college, of approximately 5 percentage points. High school graduates are people who have completed 4 years of high school or more, for 1967 to 1991. Beginning in 1992, they were people whose highest degree was a high school diploma (including equivalency) or higher.
[1] Starting in 2003 respondents could identify more than one race. Except as noted, the race data in this table from 2003 onward represent those respondents who indicated only one race category.

Table A-14. Population 14 to 24 Years Old, by High School Graduate Status, College Enrollment, Attainment, Sex, Race, and Hispanic Origin, October 1967–2017—*Continued*

(Numbers in thousands; percent; civilian noninstitutionalized population.)

Year, race, and Hispanic origin	Population 18 to 24 years old								High school graduates, 14 to 24 years old		
		High school graduates		Percent			High school dropouts			Percent	
	Total	Total	Enrolled in college	High school graduates	Enrolled in college	High school graduate enrolled in college	Number	Percent	All graduates	Enrolled in college	Enrolled or completed some college
1997..................	9,847	8,352	3,863	84.8	39.2	46.3	1,072	10.9	8,458	46.6	70.1
1996..................	9,778	8,200	3,705	83.9	37.9	45.2	1,182	12.1	8,333	45.6	70.7
1995..................	9,886	8,271	3,615	83.7	36.6	43.7	1,281	13.0	8,376	44.0	71.3
1994..................	10,048	8,503	3,714	84.6	37.0	43.7	1,175	11.7	8,588	43.9	69.7
1993r................	10,199	8,651	3,576	84.8	35.1	41.3	1,207	11.8	8,750	41.5	67.9
1993..................	9,790	8,339	3,450	85.2	35.2	41.4	1,125	11.5	8,435	41.6	68.0
1992..................	9,928	8,468	3,625	85.3	36.5	42.8	1,098	11.1	8,569	43.2	68.1
1991..................	10,119	8,481	3,544	83.8	35.0	41.8	1,324	13.1	8,568	42.1	64.5
1990..................	10,340	8,666	3,344	83.8	32.3	38.6	1,322	12.8	8,775	38.9	61.4
1989..................	10,586	8,913	3,409	84.2	32.2	38.2	1,354	12.8	9,059	38.6	59.2
1988..................	10,881	9,223	3,399	84.8	31.2	36.9	1,418	13.0	9,355	37.3	59.1
1987..................	10,944	9,189	3,192	84.0	29.2	34.7	1,449	13.2	9,334	36.2	57.2
1986..................	11,205	9,509	3,139	84.9	28.0	33.0	1,388	12.4	9,667	33.6	55.8
1985..................	11,524	9,840	3,247	85.4	28.2	33.0	1,413	12.3	10,001	33.6	55.2
1984..................	11,826	10,026	3,120	84.8	26.4	31.1	1,535	13.0	10,089	31.8	53.4
1983..................	12,112	10,233	3,129	84.5	25.8	30.6	1,563	12.9	10,233	31.3	53.4
1982..................	12,332	10,333	3,285	83.8	26.6	31.8	1,713	13.0	10,530	32.3	52.9
1981..................	12,446	10,504	3,208	84.4	25.8	30.5	1,629	13.1	10,687	31.1	51.6
1980..................	12,471	10,528	3,147	84.4	25.2	29.9	1,642	13.2	10,749	30.6	50.9
1979..................	12,174	10,157	3,015	83.4	24.8	29.7	1,741	14.3	10,417	30.3	50.8
1978..................	12,078	10,088	2,882	83.5	23.9	28.6	1,742	14.4	10,327	29.3	50.3
1977..................	11,985	10,029	2,923	83.7	24.4	29.1	1,666	13.9	10,292	29.7	50.0
1976..................	11,840	9,860	3,026	83.3	25.6	30.7	1,717	14.5	10,118	31.4	51.3
1975..................	11,653	9,743	2,790	83.6	23.9	28.6	1,658	14.2	9,986	29.4	49.1
1974..................	11,419	9,551	2,555	83.6	22.4	26.8	1,633	14.3	9,811	27.5	47.8
1973..................	11,255	9,387	2,406	83.4	21.4	25.6	1,632	14.5	9,653	26.4	47.1
1972..................	11,103	9,132	2,428	82.2	21.9	26.6	1,735	15.6	9,377	27.4	48.3
1971..................	10,880	8,887	2,310	81.7	21.2	26.0	1,726	15.9	9,107	26.8	47.7
1970..................	10,555	8,634	2,209	81.8	20.9	25.6	1,675	15.9	8,837	26.3	47.2
1969..................	10,186	8,291	2,200	81.4	21.6	26.5	1,668	16.4	8,501	27.2	46.3
1968..................	9,866	7,906	1,980	80.1	20.1	25.0	1,706	17.3	8,135	26.0	45.1
1967..................	9,637	7,586	1,949	78.7	20.2	25.7	1,750	18.2	7,815	26.6	45.7
WHITE ALONE NON-HISPANIC											
Both Sexes											
2017..................	15,945	14,251	6,544	89.4	41.0	45.9	747	4.7	14,442	45.9	74.3
2016..................	16,363	14,641	6,895	89.5	42.1	47.1	822	5.0	14,816	47.1	74.6
2015..................	16,615	14,812	6,938	89.1	41.8	46.8	816	4.9	15,025	46.9	74.6
2014..................	16,723	14,877	7,054	89.0	42.2	47.4	890	5.3	15,066	47.6	74.9
2013..................	16,962	15,135	7,065	89.2	41.6	46.7	876	5.2	15,394	47.1	75.0
2012..................	17,072	15,216	7,189	89.1	42.1	47.2	819	4.8	15,421	47.6	75.0
2011..................	17,627	15,565	7,882	88.3	44.7	50.6	1,002	5.7	15,752	50.7	76.2
2010..................	17,693	15,761	7,663	89.1	43.3	48.6	1,003	5.7	15,927	48.8	75.4
2009..................	17,750	15,839	7,983	89.2	45.0	50.4	1,029	5.8	16,051	50.5	75.2
2008..................	17,839	16,038	7,894	89.9	44.2	49.2	960	5.4	16,224	49.4	74.2
2007..................	17,669	15,727	7,533	89.0	42.6	47.9	1,064	6.0	15,921	48.0	72.9
2006..................	17,565	15,452	7,200	88.0	41.0	46.6	1,189	6.8	15,642	46.8	72.5
2005..................	17,293	15,187	7,393	87.8	42.8	48.7	1,216	7.0	15,368	48.7	72.6
2004..................	17,326	15,224	7,228	87.9	41.7	47.5	1,313	7.6	15,382	47.7	71.8
2003[1]...............	17,158	15,070	7,129	87.8	41.6	47.3	1,267	7.4	15,255	47.3	71.5
2002..................	17,131	14,910	7,004	87.0	40.9	47.0	1,289	7.5	15,089	47.1	70.4
2001..................	16,721	14,480	6,565	86.6	39.3	45.3	1,390	8.3	14,646	45.3	69.7
2000..................	17,327	15,187	6,709	87.7	38.7	44.2	1,316	7.6	15,344	44.3	69.0
1999..................	17,080	14,812	6,735	86.7	39.4	45.5	1,404	8.2	14,952	45.6	70.2
1998..................	16,634	14,402	6,757	86.6	40.6	46.9	1,491	9.0	14,542	47.0	70.6
1997..................	16,575	14,414	6,728	87.0	40.6	46.7	1,432	8.6	14,527	46.9	70.0

r = Revised, controlled to 1990 census based population estimates; previous 1993 data controlled to 1980 census based population estimates.
Note: The change in the educational attainment question and the college completion categories from "4 or more years of college" to "at least some college," in 1992 caused an increase in the proportion of 14-to-24-year-old high school graduates enrolled in college or completed some college, of approximately 5 percentage points. High school graduates are people who have completed 4 years of high school or more, for 1967 to 1991. Beginning in 1992, they were people whose highest degree was a high school diploma (including equivalency) or higher.
[1] Starting in 2003 respondents could identify more than one race. Except as noted, the race data in this table from 2003 onward represent those respondents who indicated only one race category.

Table A-14. Population 14 to 24 Years Old, by High School Graduate Status, College Enrollment, Attainment, Sex, Race, and Hispanic Origin, October 1967–2017—*Continued*

(Numbers in thousands; percent; civilian noninstitutionalized population.)

Year, race, and Hispanic origin	Total	Population 18 to 24 years old							High school graduates, 14 to 24 years old		
		High school graduates		Percent			High school dropouts				Percent
		Total	Enrolled in college	High school graduates	Enrolled in college	High school graduate enrolled in college	Number	Percent	All graduates	Enrolled in college	Enrolled or completed some college
1996................................	16,339	14,288	6,447	87.5	39.5	45.1	1,303	8.0	14,501	45.5	70.7
1995................................	16,867	14,523	6,393	86.1	37.9	44.0	1,647	9.8	14,672	44.3	70.2
1994................................	17,114	14,916	6,521	87.2	38.1	43.7	1,505	8.8	15,049	44.0	69.2
1993................................	16,895	14,665	6,221	86.8	36.8	42.4	1,524	9.0	14,801	42.6	68.1
Male											
2017................................	8,096	7,098	3,057	87.7	37.8	43.1	409	5.1	7,187	43.0	69.8
2016................................	8,259	7,279	3,288	88.1	39.8	45.2	463	5.6	7,348	45.2	69.6
2015................................	8,401	7,396	3,284	88.0	39.1	44.4	451	5.4	7,512	44.4	69.7
2014................................	8,446	7,426	3,391	87.9	40.2	45.7	485	5.7	7,526	45.8	70.5
2013................................	8,562	7,526	3,260	87.9	38.1	43.3	462	5.4	7,658	43.8	70.2
2012................................	8,598	7,552	3,290	87.8	38.3	43.6	455	5.3	7,637	43.9	69.5
2011................................	8,864	7,697	3,754	86.8	42.4	48.8	554	6.2	7,794	48.9	72.7
2010................................	8,919	7,808	3,617	87.5	40.6	46.3	569	6.4	7,884	46.4	70.9
2009................................	8,957	7,818	3,787	87.3	42.3	48.4	632	7.1	7,915	48.5	71.9
2008................................	9,032	8,028	3,766	88.9	41.7	46.9	546	6.0	8,126	47.1	70.4
2007................................	8,940	7,786	3,541	87.1	39.6	45.5	622	7.0	7,883	45.5	68.8
2006................................	8,842	7,660	3,354	86.6	37.9	43.8	647	7.3	7,734	43.9	68.4
2005................................	8,700	7,443	3,429	85.5	39.4	46.1	685	7.9	7,526	46.0	68.6
2004	8,644	7,527	3,322	87.1	38.4	44.1	691	8.0	7,576	44.4	66.7
2003²	8,538	7,325	3,291	85.8	38.5	44.9	721	8.4	7,401	45.0	68.5
2002................................	8,453	7,244	3,287	85.7	38.9	45.4	668	7.9	7,352	45.5	67.9
2001................................	8,343	7,112	3,094	85.3	37.1	43.4	741	8.9	7,191	43.4	67.1
2000................................	8,670	7,493	3,136	86.4	36.2	41.9	677	7.8	7,556	42.0	65.4
1999................................	8,580	7,301	3,284	85.1	38.3	45.0	753	8.8	7,369	45.0	67.7
1998................................	8,380	7,094	3,300	84.7	39.4	46.5	826	9.9	7,151	46.6	68.2
1997................................	8,326	7,112	3,276	85.4	39.3	46.1	797	9.6	7,154	46.3	68.1
1996................................	8,168	7,050	3,130	86.3	38.3	44.4	651	8.0	7,143	44.7	68.6
1995................................	8,399	7,089	3,105	84.4	37.0	43.8	883	10.5	7,147	44.0	67.3
1994................................	8,457	7,261	3,126	85.9	37.0	43.1	777	9.2	7,317	43.3	67.0
1993................................	8,403	7,138	3,071	84.9	36.6	43.0	811	9.7	7,191	43.2	67.1
Female											
2017................................	7,849	7,154	3,487	91.1	44.4	48.7	338	4.3	7,255	48.8	78.8
2016................................	8,104	7,362	3,606	90.8	44.5	49.0	360	4.4	7,468	49.0	79.5
2015................................	8,215	7,416	3,654	90.3	44.5	49.3	365	4.4	7,513	49.3	79.5
2014................................	8,278	7,451	3,663	90.0	44.2	49.2	404	4.9	7,541	49.3	79.3
2013................................	8,400	7,609	3,804	90.6	45.3	50.0	414	4.9	7,736	50.4	79.8
2012................................	8,474	7,664	3,899	90.4	46.0	50.9	364	4.3	7,784	51.2	80.5
2011................................	8,763	7,868	4,128	89.8	47.1	52.5	448	5.1	7,958	52.5	79.6
2010................................	8,774	7,953	4,046	90.6	46.1	50.9	434	4.9	8,044	51.2	79.8
2009................................	8,793	8,021	4,195	91.2	47.7	52.3	398	4.5	8,136	52.4	78.3
2008................................	8,808	8,010	4,127	90.9	46.9	51.5	414	4.7	8,099	51.7	78.0
2007................................	8,728	7,941	3,992	91.0	45.7	50.3	442	5.1	8,039	50.4	76.9
2006................................	8,724	7,791	3,846	89.3	44.1	49.4	542	6.2	7,908	49.5	76.4
2005................................	8,593	7,744	3,964	90.1	46.1	51.2	531	6.2	7,842	51.4	76.4
2004	8,628	7,697	3,906	89.2	45.3	50.7	622	7.2	7,805	50.9	76.8
2003¹	8,620	7,745	3,838	89.9	44.5	49.6	546	6.3	7,854	49.5	74.4
2002................................	8,678	7,666	3,717	88.3	42.8	48.5	621	7.2	7,736	48.6	72.8
2001................................	8,378	7,368	3,471	87.9	41.4	47.2	648	7.7	7,455	47.2	72.3
2000................................	8,657	7,693	3,573	88.9	41.3	46.4	638	7.4	7,789	46.6	72.5
1999................................	8,500	7,510	3,451	88.4	40.6	46.0	651	7.7	7,583	46.2	72.5
1998................................	8,254	7,308	3,457	88.5	41.9	47.3	665	8.1	7,391	47.5	73.0
1997................................	8,249	7,302	3,452	88.5	41.9	47.3	636	7.7	7,373	47.5	71.9
1996................................	8,171	7,238	3,317	88.6	40.6	45.8	652	8.0	7,358	46.3	72.8
1995................................	8,467	7,433	3,288	87.8	38.8	44.2	764	9.0	7,525	44.6	73.1
1994................................	8,657	7,655	3,395	88.4	39.2	44.4	728	8.4	7,732	44.6	71.3
1993................................	8,492	7,527	3,150	88.6	37.1	41.9	714	8.4	7,610	42.0	69.1

Note: The change in the educational attainment question and the college completion categories from "4 or more years of college" to "at least some college," in 1992 caused an increase in the proportion of 14-to-24-year-old high school graduates enrolled in college or completed some college, of approximately 5 percentage points. High school graduates are people who have completed 4 years of high school or more, for 1967 to 1991. Beginning in 1992, they were people whose highest degree was a high school diploma (including equivalency) or higher.
¹ Starting in 2003 respondents could identify more than one race. Except as noted, the race data in this table from 2003 onward represent those respondents who indicated only one race category.
² The data shown prior to 2003 consists of those identifying themselves as "Asian or Pacific Islanders."

Table A-14. Population 14 to 24 Years Old, by High School Graduate Status, College Enrollment, Attainment, Sex, Race, and Hispanic Origin, October 1967–2017—*Continued*

(Numbers in thousands; percent; civilian noninstitutionalized population.)

Year, race, and Hispanic origin	Population 18 to 24 years old								High school graduates, 14 to 24 years old		
		High school graduates		Percent			High school dropouts				
	Total	Total	Enrolled in college	High school graduates	Enrolled in college	High school graduate enrolled in college	Number	Percent	All graduates	Enrolled in college	Percent Enrolled or completed some college
BLACK ALONE											
Both Sexes											
2017.................................	4,458	3,807	1,595	85.4	35.8	41.9	270	6.1	3,885	41.9	65.4
2016.................................	4,551	3,857	1,644	84.7	36.1	42.6	314	6.9	3,937	42.5	65.6
2015.................................	4,635	3,971	1,636	85.7	35.3	41.2	347	7.5	4,019	41.3	64.5
2014.................................	4,704	3,993	1,528	84.9	32.5	38.3	345	7.3	4,061	39.0	65.9
2013.................................	4,746	3,885	1,600	81.9	33.7	41.2	393	8.3	3,929	41.5	65.7
2012.................................	4,714	3,754	1,689	79.6	35.8	45.0	467	9.9	3,816	45.0	66.6
2011.................................	4,503	3,649	1,639	81.0	36.4	44.9	399	8.9	3,702	45.3	66.3
2010.................................	4,457	3,669	1,692	82.3	38.0	46.1	450	10.1	3,731	46.2	66.2
2009.................................	4,346	3,458	1,604	79.6	36.9	46.4	505	11.6	3,532	46.4	67.5
2008.................................	4,265	3,387	1,349	79.4	31.6	40.0	548	12.1	3,445	40.2	60.7
2007.................................	4,182	3,423	1,396	81.8	33.4	40.8	425	10.2	3,483	40.9	61.4
2006.................................	4,085	3,156	1,321	77.3	32.3	41.9	532	13.0	3,224	41.9	60.8
2005.................................	3,964	3,137	1,297	79.1	32.7	41.3	512	12.9	3,212	41.3	63.5
2004	3,940	3,050	1,238	77.4	31.4	40.6	596	15.1	3,112	41.1	63.2
2003[1]	3,837	2,948	1,225	76.8	31.9	41.6	545	14.2	2,997	41.8	62.5
2002.................................	3,924	3,040	1,226	77.5	31.3	40.3	571	14.5	3,117	41.1	61.2
2001.................................	3,916	3,016	1,206	77.0	30.8	40.0	540	13.8	3,095	40.0	59.0
2000.................................	4,013	3,090	1,216	77.0	30.3	39.4	615	15.3	3,129	39.5	61.0
1999.................................	3,827	2,911	1,145	76.1	29.9	39.4	613	16.0	2,985	39.9	60.4
1998.................................	3,745	2,747	1,116	73.4	29.8	40.6	642	17.1	2,790	40.8	61.8
1997.................................	3,650	2,725	1,085	74.7	29.7	39.8	611	16.7	2,762	40.2	60.0
1996.................................	3,637	2,738	983	75.3	27.0	35.9	581	16.0	2,805	36.6	54.6
1995.................................	3,625	2,788	988	76.9	27.3	35.4	522	14.4	2,828	35.8	58.0
1994.................................	3,661	2,818	1,001	77.0	27.3	35.5	568	15.5	2,859	36.3	59.2
1993r.................................	3,666	2,747	897	74.9	24.5	32.7	600	16.4	2,771	32.8	54.0
1993.................................	3,516	2,629	861	74.8	24.5	32.8	578	16.4	2,653	32.9	53.9
1992.................................	3,521	2,625	886	74.6	25.2	33.8	575	16.3	2,668	34.3	53.3
1991.................................	3,504	2,630	828	75.1	23.6	31.5	545	15.6	2,658	31.8	46.0
1990.................................	3,520	2,710	894	77.0	25.4	33.0	530	15.1	2,759	33.7	48.0
1989.................................	3,559	2,708	835	76.1	23.5	30.8	583	16.4	2,750	31.5	49.2
1988.................................	3,568	2,680	752	75.1	21.1	28.1	631	17.7	2,741	28.6	46.3
1987.................................	3,603	2,739	823	76.0	22.8	30.0	611	17.0	2,790	30.6	48.1
1986.................................	3,653	2,795	812	76.5	22.2	29.1	617	16.8	2,837	29.3	47.8
1985.................................	3,716	2,810	734	75.6	19.8	26.1	655	17.6	2,848	26.5	43.8
1984.................................	3,862	2,885	786	74.7	20.4	27.2	712	18.4	2,950	28.0	45.2
1983.................................	3,865	2,740	741	70.9	19.2	27.0	832	21.5	2,790	27.7	45.0
1982.................................	3,872	2,744	767	70.9	19.8	28.0	851	22.0	2,793	28.2	45.5
1981.................................	3,778	2,678	750	70.9	19.9	28.0	821	21.7	2,718	28.7	44.8
1980.................................	3,721	2,592	715	69.7	19.2	27.6	876	23.5	2,656	28.1	45.9
1979.................................	3,510	2,356	696	67.1	19.8	29.5	895	25.5	2,415	30.6	48.4
1978.................................	3,452	2,340	694	67.8	20.1	29.7	850	24.6	2,396	30.6	47.8
1977.................................	3,387	2,286	721	67.5	21.3	31.5	808	23.9	2,342	32.4	46.9
1976.................................	3,315	2,239	749	67.5	22.6	33.5	803	24.2	2,291	34.2	50.4
1975.................................	3,213	2,081	665	64.8	20.7	32.0	877	27.3	2,149	32.6	48.1
1974.................................	3,105	2,083	555	67.1	17.9	26.6	780	25.1	2,145	27.5	44.8
1973.................................	3,114	2,079	498	66.8	16.0	24.0	826	26.5	2,139	25.0	41.6
1972.................................	2,986	1,992	540	66.7	18.1	27.1	782	26.2	2,044	28.0	42.0
1971.................................	2,866	1,789	522	62.4	18.2	29.2	825	28.8	1,833	30.0	42.3
1970.................................	2,692	1,602	416	59.5	15.5	26.0	897	33.3	1,635	26.7	39.4
1969.................................	2,542	1,497	407	58.9	16.0	27.2	828	32.6	1,547	27.5	40.1
1968.................................	2,421	1,399	352	57.8	14.5	25.2	799	33.0	1,432	26.0	38.1
1967.................................	2,283	1,276	297	55.9	13.0	23.3	788	34.5	1,316	23.7	35.0

r = Revised, controlled to 1990 census based population estimates; previous 1993 data controlled to 1980 census based population estimates.
Note: The change in the educational attainment question and the college completion categories from "4 or more years of college" to "at least some college," in 1992 caused an increase in the proportion of 14-to-24-year-old high school graduates enrolled in college or completed some college, of approximately 5 percentage points. High school graduates are people who have completed 4 years of high school or more, for 1967 to 1991. Beginning in 1992, they were people whose highest degree was a high school diploma (including equivalency) or higher.
[1] Starting in 2003 respondents could identify more than one race. Except as noted, the race data in this table from 2003 onward represent those respondents who indicated only one race category.

Table A-14. Population 14 to 24 Years Old, by High School Graduate Status, College Enrollment, Attainment, Sex, Race, and Hispanic Origin, October 1967–2017—*Continued*

(Numbers in thousands; percent; civilian noninstitutionalized population.)

| Year, race, and Hispanic origin | Population 18 to 24 years old | | | | | | | | High school graduates, 14 to 24 years old | | |
| | | High school graduates | | Percent | | | High school dropouts | | | Percent | |
	Total	Total	Enrolled in college	High school graduates	Enrolled in college	High school graduate enrolled in college	Number	Percent	All graduates	Enrolled in college	Enrolled or completed some college
Male											
2017	2,172	1,821	695	83.8	32.0	38.2	163	7.5	1,857	38.1	60.4
2016	2,218	1,774	728	80.0	32.8	41.0	204	9.2	1,795	41.2	61.4
2015	2,257	1,923	779	85.2	34.5	40.5	165	7.3	1,947	40.6	63.3
2014	2,289	1,889	633	82.5	27.6	33.5	166	7.3	1,934	34.7	61.1
2013	2,303	1,847	690	80.2	30.0	37.4	221	9.6	1,865	38.0	61.7
2012	2,278	1,787	760	78.4	33.4	42.5	258	11.3	1,820	42.7	63.8
2011	2,165	1,701	717	78.6	33.1	42.2	205	9.5	1,732	42.7	60.9
2010	2,140	1,692	734	79.1	34.3	43.4	258	12.1	1,730	43.2	61.4
2009	2,082	1,592	673	76.5	32.3	42.3	289	13.9	1,617	42.0	63.5
2008	2,045	1,641	595	80.2	29.1	36.3	210	10.2	1,668	36.9	54.8
2007	2,011	1,622	649	80.6	32.3	40.0	202	10.0	1,642	40.1	59.3
2006	1,959	1,488	541	76.0	27.6	36.4	219	11.2	1,519	36.3	53.4
2005	1,897	1,393	530	73.4	27.9	38.0	280	14.8	1,420	37.9	58.4
2004	1,852	1,341	479	72.4	25.9	35.7	331	17.9	1,363	36.1	60.9
2003[1]	1,801	1,331	499	73.9	27.7	37.5	300	16.7	1,346	37.8	57.1
2002	1,843	1,354	475	73.5	25.8	35.1	311	16.9	1,372	35.6	56.1
2001	1,818	1,287	470	70.8	25.8	36.4	308	16.9	1,310	36.4	53.1
2000	1,885	1,389	470	73.7	24.9	33.8	329	17.4	1,409	34.1	53.5
1999	1,747	1,292	501	73.9	28.7	38.8	285	16.3	1,336	40.2	57.7
1998	1,724	1,163	445	67.5	25.8	38.2	354	20.5	1,186	38.5	57.5
1997	1,701	1,214	425	71.4	25.0	35.0	297	17.5	1,232	35.1	56.3
1996	1,682	1,199	422	71.3	25.1	35.2	292	17.4	1,225	35.8	53.7
1995	1,660	1,247	430	75.1	25.9	34.4	235	14.2	1,262	35.1	56.2
1994	1,733	1,277	440	73.7	25.4	34.5	303	17.5	1,293	35.3	57.9
1993r	1,703	1,240	387	72.8	22.7	31.2	266	15.6	1,247	31.4	50.1
1993	1,659	1,207	379	72.8	22.8	31.4	258	15.6	1,214	31.5	50.0
1992	1,676	1,211	356	72.3	21.2	29.4	259	15.5	1,226	29.7	49.4
1991	1,635	1,174	378	71.8	23.1	32.2	252	15.4	1,188	32.4	47.0
1990	1,634	1,240	426	75.9	26.1	34.4	223	13.6	1,260	35.1	48.8
1989	1,654	1,195	324	72.2	19.6	27.1	307	18.6	1,207	27.5	45.8
1988	1,653	1,189	297	71.9	18.0	25.0	312	18.9	1,205	25.1	42.5
1987	1,666	1,188	377	71.3	22.6	31.7	312	18.7	1,209	32.3	48.0
1986	1,687	1,220	349	72.3	20.7	28.6	300	17.8	1,239	29.1	44.4
1985	1,720	1,244	345	72.3	20.1	27.7	323	18.8	1,258	28.2	43.6
1984	1,811	1,272	367	70.2	20.3	28.9	362	20.2	1,295	29.6	45.2
1983	1,807	1,202	331	66.5	18.3	27.5	435	24.1	1,228	27.9	43.6
1982	1,786	1,171	331	65.6	18.5	28.3	458	25.6	1,188	28.6	44.5
1981	1,730	1,154	325	66.7	18.8	28.2	419	24.2	1,165	28.5	42.3
1980	1,690	1,115	293	66.0	17.3	26.3	440	26.0	1,141	26.9	44.1
1979	1,577	973	304	61.7	19.3	31.2	457	29.0	988	32.0	46.7
1978	1,554	956	305	61.5	19.6	31.9	451	29.0	981	32.4	49.3
1977	1,528	970	309	63.5	20.2	31.9	369	24.1	991	33.0	47.6
1976	1,503	936	331	62.3	22.0	35.4	393	26.1	952	35.9	50.3
1975	1,451	897	294	61.8	20.3	32.8	404	27.8	923	33.4	50.5
1974	1,396	919	280	65.8	20.1	30.5	346	24.8	941	31.1	47.3
1973	1,434	952	266	66.4	18.5	27.9	371	25.9	962	28.4	44.2
1972	1,373	870	287	63.4	20.9	33.0	373	27.2	897	34.0	47.4
1971	1,318	769	262	58.3	19.9	34.1	416	31.6	783	34.9	45.8
1970	1,220	668	192	54.8	15.7	28.7	436	35.7	684	29.5	41.4
1969	1,141	631	202	55.3	17.7	32.0	383	33.6	653	32.5	44.6
1968	1,087	582	170	53.5	15.6	29.2	370	34.0	600	30.3	43.2
1967	1,032	525	167	50.9	16.2	31.8	397	38.5	539	32.3	41.6

r = Revised, controlled to 1990 census based population estimates; previous 1993 data controlled to 1980 census based population estimates.
Note: The change in the educational attainment question and the college completion categories from "4 or more years of college" to "at least some college," in 1992 caused an increase in the proportion of 14-to-24-year-old high school graduates enrolled in college or completed some college, of approximately 5 percentage points. High school graduates are people who have completed 4 years of high school or more, for 1967 to 1991. Beginning in 1992, they were people whose highest degree was a high school diploma (including equivalency) or higher.
[1] Starting in 2003 respondents could identify more than one race. Except as noted, the race data in this table from 2003 onward represent those respondents who indicated only one race category.

Table A-14. Population 14 to 24 Years Old, by High School Graduate Status, College Enrollment, Attainment, Sex, Race, and Hispanic Origin, October 1967–2017—*Continued*

(Numbers in thousands; percent; civilian noninstitutionalized population.)

Year, race, and Hispanic origin	Total	Population 18 to 24 years old							High school graduates, 14 to 24 years old		
		High school graduates		Percent			High school dropouts			Percent	
		Total	Enrolled in college	High school graduates	Enrolled in college	High school graduate enrolled in college	Number	Percent	All graduates	Enrolled in college	Enrolled or completed some college
Female											
2017	2,286	1,986	900	86.9	39.3	45.3	107	4.7	2,028	45.4	70.1
2016	2,333	2,083	916	89.3	39.3	44.0	111	4.7	2,142	43.6	69.1
2015	2,378	2,048	857	86.1	36.1	41.9	182	7.7	2,071	42.0	65.6
2014	2,415	2,104	895	87.2	37.1	42.5	179	7.4	2,128	42.9	70.2
2013	2,442	2,038	909	83.4	37.2	44.6	173	7.1	2,064	44.7	69.3
2012	2,436	1,967	929	80.8	38.1	47.2	209	8.6	1,996	47.0	69.2
2011	2,339	1,949	921	83.3	39.4	47.3	194	8.3	1,970	47.6	71.0
2010	2,317	1,977	958	85.3	41.3	48.4	192	8.3	2,001	48.8	70.4
2009	2,263	1,865	931	82.4	41.1	49.9	216	9.5	1,915	50.1	70.9
2008	2,220	1,746	754	78.7	34.0	43.2	304	13.7	1,777	43.3	66.2
2007	2,171	1,801	747	82.9	34.4	41.5	223	10.3	1,841	41.5	63.3
2006	2,126	1,668	780	78.5	36.7	46.7	313	14.7	1,705	46.9	67.3
2005	2,067	1,745	767	84.4	37.1	44.0	232	11.2	1,793	44.0	67.5
2004	2,088	1,709	759	81.8	36.3	44.4	266	12.7	1,749	44.9	65.0
2003[1]	2,035	1,618	726	79.5	35.7	44.9	245	12.0	1,652	45.1	66.8
2002	2,081	1,686	751	81.0	36.1	44.5	260	12.5	1,745	45.5	65.2
2001	2,098	1,729	736	82.4	35.1	42.7	232	11.0	1,785	42.7	63.3
2000	2,128	1,700	747	79.9	35.1	43.9	287	13.5	1,720	43.9	67.1
1999	2,080	1,619	644	77.9	31.0	39.8	327	15.7	1,650	39.6	62.6
1998	2,021	1,584	671	78.4	33.2	42.4	288	14.3	1,604	42.4	65.0
1997	1,949	1,511	659	77.5	33.8	43.6	314	16.1	1,529	43.1	63.0
1996	1,956	1,539	561	78.7	28.7	36.4	288	14.7	1,580	37.3	55.3
1995	1,965	1,541	558	78.4	28.4	36.2	287	14.6	1,566	36.3	59.5
1994	1,928	1,542	561	80.0	29.1	36.4	265	13.7	1,567	37.1	60.3
1993r	1,965	1,508	511	76.7	26.0	33.9	337	17.2	1,526	34.1	57.2
1993	1,857	1,425	484	76.7	26.1	34.0	319	17.2	1,441	34.1	57.1
1992	1,845	1,417	531	76.8	28.8	37.5	315	17.1	1,446	38.2	56.6
1991	1,869	1,455	450	77.8	24.1	30.9	296	15.8	1,468	31.4	45.2
1990	1,886	1,468	467	77.8	24.8	31.8	306	16.2	1,498	32.4	47.3
1989	1,905	1,511	511	79.3	26.8	33.8	277	14.5	1,541	34.7	51.8
1988	1,915	1,492	455	77.9	23.8	30.5	318	16.6	1,538	31.3	49.2
1987	1,937	1,550	445	80.0	23.0	28.7	298	15.4	1,579	29.4	48.9
1986	1,966	1,574	462	80.1	23.5	29.4	306	15.6	1,598	29.3	50.4
1985	1,996	1,565	389	78.4	19.5	24.9	332	16.6	1,592	25.1	44.0
1984	2,052	1,613	419	78.6	20.4	26.0	349	17.0	1,655	26.8	45.1
1983	2,058	1,539	411	74.8	20.0	26.7	398	19.3	1,561	27.5	46.3
1982	2,086	1,572	436	75.4	20.9	27.7	393	18.8	1,604	27.9	46.3
1981	2,049	1,526	424	74.5	20.7	27.8	402	19.6	1,554	28.8	46.6
1980	2,031	1,475	422	72.6	20.8	28.6	436	21.5	1,511	29.1	47.4
1979	1,934	1,383	392	71.5	20.3	28.3	439	22.7	1,426	29.7	49.8
1978	1,897	1,384	390	73.0	20.6	28.2	398	21.0	1,415	29.3	46.7
1977	1,859	1,317	413	70.8	22.2	31.4	439	23.6	1,354	31.9	46.2
1976	1,813	1,302	417	71.8	23.0	32.0	410	22.6	1,338	32.9	50.3
1975	1,761	1,182	372	67.1	21.1	31.5	473	26.9	1,224	32.0	46.4
1974	1,709	1,167	277	68.3	16.2	23.7	434	25.4	1,207	24.8	42.9
1973	1,681	1,125	231	66.9	13.7	20.5	456	27.1	1,177	22.2	39.4
1972	1,613	1,123	253	69.6	15.7	22.5	408	25.3	1,150	23.2	37.9
1971	1,547	1,019	259	65.9	16.7	25.4	409	26.4	1,049	26.4	39.8
1970	1,471	935	225	63.6	15.3	24.1	461	31.3	955	24.7	39.3
1969	1,402	867	206	61.8	14.7	23.8	444	31.7	896	24.0	38.6
1968	1,334	819	183	61.4	13.7	22.3	430	32.2	834	22.9	35.9
1967	1,249	751	130	60.1	10.4	17.3	391	31.3	778	17.9	33.2
ASIAN ALONE[2]											
Both Sexes											
2017	1,753	1,658	1,101	94.6	62.8	66.4	28	1.6	1,694	66.9	90.6

r = Revised, controlled to 1990 census based population estimates; previous 1993 data controlled to 1980 census based population estimates.
Note: The change in the educational attainment question and the college completion categories from "4 or more years of college" to "at least some college," in 1992 caused an increase in the proportion of 14-to-24-year-old high school graduates enrolled in college or completed some college, of approximately 5 percentage points. High school graduates are people who have completed 4 years of high school or more, for 1967 to 1991. Beginning in 1992, they were people whose highest degree was a high school diploma (including equivalency) or higher.
[1] Starting in 2003 respondents could identify more than one race. Except as noted, the race data in this table from 2003 onward represent those respondents who indicated only one race category.
[2] The data shown prior to 2003 consists of those identifying themselves as "Asian or Pacific Islanders."

Table A-14. Population 14 to 24 Years Old, by High School Graduate Status, College Enrollment, Attainment, Sex, Race, and Hispanic Origin, October 1967–2017—*Continued*

(Numbers in thousands; percent; civilian noninstitutionalized population.)

Year, race, and Hispanic origin	Population 18 to 24 years old								High school graduates, 14 to 24 years old		
		High school graduates		Percent			High school dropouts			Percent	
	Total	Total	Enrolled in college	High school graduates	Enrolled in college	High school graduate enrolled in college	Number	Percent	All graduates	Enrolled in college	Enrolled or completed some college
2016	1,768	1,628	1,003	92.1	56.7	61.6	53	3.0	1,661	61.5	87.7
2015	1,634	1,514	1,026	92.6	62.8	67.8	38	2.3	1,560	67.1	91.9
2014	1,590	1,504	1,023	94.6	64.3	68.0	17	1.1	1,541	67.6	91.7
2013	1,639	1,495	1,001	91.2	61.1	66.9	61	3.7	1,530	67.4	86.8
2012	1,537	1,385	915	90.1	59.5	66.0	54	3.5	1,418	66.3	84.9
2011	1,252	1,123	748	89.8	59.7	66.5	65	5.2	1,149	66.9	88.1
2010	1,303	1,193	811	91.5	62.2	68.0	64	4.9	1,232	68.4	89.8
2009	1,181	1,080	768	91.4	65.0	71.1	26	2.2	1,096	71.0	91.8
2008	1,113	1,021	655	91.8	58.9	64.1	42	3.8	1,056	64.6	90.4
2007	1,165	1,010	658	86.7	56.4	65.1	86	7.4	1,026	65.1	91.6
2006	1,148	1,046	661	91.1	57.6	63.2	46	4.0	1,064	63.0	87.0
2005	1,145	1,072	693	93.6	60.5	64.6	34	3.0	1,098	65.1	87.0
2004	1,152	1,066	695	92.5	60.3	65.2	49	4.3	1,090	65.7	89.1
2003¹	1,144	1,030	693	90.1	60.6	67.3	56	4.9	1,046	67.7	88.2
2002	1,339	1,230	803	91.8	60.0	65.3	57	4.2	1,265	65.7	86.9
2001	1,312	1,197	794	91.2	60.5	66.5	47	3.6	1,218	66.5	87.6
2000	1,143	1,038	639	90.8	55.9	61.6	52	4.6	1,053	61.8	83.9
1999	1,130	1,019	626	90.2	55.4	61.4	58	5.1	1,035	62.0	85.5
Male											
2017	895	842	561	94.1	62.7	66.7	12	1.3	849	66.9	89.4
2016	914	842	533	92.1	58.3	63.3	21	2.3	854	63.0	87.1
2015	819	758	493	92.6	60.2	65.0	24	2.9	783	64.2	90.0
2014	809	771	549	95.3	67.9	71.2	13	1.6	793	71.0	91.1
2013	859	795	534	92.5	62.2	67.2	18	2.1	806	67.2	86.1
2012	776	695	455	89.6	58.6	65.4	21	2.6	713	65.9	84.7
2011	639	573	379	89.6	59.3	66.2	30	4.7	582	66.1	87.6
2010	651	597	390	91.7	59.9	65.3	29	4.5	619	65.7	87.5
2009	590	546	383	92.4	64.9	70.2	7	1.2	559	69.9	90.1
2008	547	487	295	89.1	53.9	60.5	21	3.9	510	62.0	89.9
2007	560	481	318	85.8	56.9	66.3	38	6.8	483	66.4	91.8
2006	591	525	338	88.8	57.2	64.4	34	5.8	536	64.0	84.0
2005	590	552	366	93.5	62.0	66.3	17	2.9	565	66.4	88.2
2004	586	549	373	93.7	63.6	67.9	15	2.5	561	68.4	88.2
2003¹	543	483	337	88.9	62.0	69.8	43	7.8	486	69.9	90.0
2002	707	637	417	90.0	59.0	65.5	38	5.4	652	65.3	86.7
2001	661	583	417	88.1	63.1	72.0	35	5.3	594	72.0	88.9
2000	571	521	337	91.1	58.9	64.7	34	6.0	527	64.7	85.6
1999	505	443	284	87.8	56.2	64.0	39	7.7	454	64.9	82.5
Female											
2017	859	816	540	95.0	62.8	66.1	17	1.9	844	66.9	91.9
2016	854	787	469	92.2	55.0	59.7	32	3.8	808	60.0	88.3
2015	816	756	533	92.6	65.4	70.6	14	1.7	776	70.0	93.8
2014	780	732	473	93.9	60.6	64.6	4	0.5	748	63.9	92.3
2013	780	700	467	89.8	59.8	66.6	43	5.5	723	67.5	87.5
2012	761	690	460	90.7	60.4	66.6	33	4.3	704	66.8	85.1
2011	612	551	369	89.9	60.2	66.9	35	5.8	567	67.8	88.7
2010	653	596	422	91.3	64.6	70.7	35	5.3	614	71.2	92.1
2009	591	534	384	90.4	65.1	72.0	19	3.3	538	72.2	93.7
2008	566	534	360	94.4	63.7	67.5	21	3.6	546	67.0	90.9
2007	605	529	339	87.4	56.0	64.1	48	7.9	543	63.9	91.5
2006	557	521	324	93.6	58.1	62.2	11	2.1	528	61.9	90.0
2005	555	521	327	93.8	58.9	62.8	17	3.0	533	63.7	85.8
2004	567	517	323	91.3	56.9	62.4	35	6.1	529	62.8	90.0
2003¹	601	547	356	91.2	59.3	65.1	13	2.2	561	65.9	86.7
2002	632	593	386	93.8	61.0	65.1	19	2.9	613	66.1	87.2
2001	651	614	377	94.3	57.9	61.3	12	1.8	625	61.3	86.3

Note: The change in the educational attainment question and the college completion categories from "4 or more years of college" to "at least some college," in 1992 caused an increase in the proportion of 14-to-24-year-old high school graduates enrolled in college or completed some college, of approximately 5 percentage points. High school graduates are people who have completed 4 years of high school or more, for 1967 to 1991. Beginning in 1992, they were people whose highest degree was a high school diploma (including equivalency) or higher.

¹ Starting in 2003 respondents could identify more than one race. Except as noted, the race data in this table from 2003 onward represent those respondents who indicated only one race category.

Table A-14. Population 14 to 24 Years Old, by High School Graduate Status, College Enrollment, Attainment, Sex, Race, and Hispanic Origin, October 1967–2017—*Continued*

(Numbers in thousands; percent; civilian noninstitutionalized population.)

Year, race, and Hispanic origin	Population 18 to 24 years old								High school graduates, 14 to 24 years old		
		High school graduates		Percent			High school dropouts			Percent	
	Total	Total	Enrolled in college	High school graduates	Enrolled in college	High school graduate enrolled in college	Number	Percent	All graduates	Enrolled in college	Enrolled or completed some college
2000	572	517	302	90.4	52.9	58.5	18	3.1	526	58.9	82.3
1999	626	576	342	92.1	54.7	59.4	19	3.1	582	59.7	87.8

HISPANIC (OF ANY RACE)

Both Sexes

2017	6,653	5,457	2,410	82.0	36.2	44.2	703	10.6	5,571	44.7	65.9
2016	6,539	5,477	2,565	83.8	39.2	46.8	648	9.9	5,608	47.3	67.2
2015	6,464	5,366	2,368	83.0	36.6	44.1	669	10.3	5,460	44.2	66.6
2014	6,568	5,324	2,282	81.1	34.7	42.9	777	11.8	5,409	43.1	62.8
2013	6,489	5,118	2,193	78.9	33.8	42.8	889	13.7	5,190	43.1	62.3
2012	6,416	4,902	2,403	76.4	37.5	49.0	972	15.1	4,987	49.4	68.1
2011	5,974	4,569	2,079	76.5	34.8	45.5	975	16.3	4,630	45.7	65.4
2010	5,685	4,138	1,814	72.8	31.9	43.8	1,050	18.5	4,199	44.2	63.2
2009	5,332	3,747	1,465	70.3	27.5	39.1	1,112	20.8	3,813	39.6	57.8
2008	5,176	3,618	1,338	69.9	25.8	37.0	1,155	22.3	3,691	37.7	58.7
2007	5,175	3,487	1,375	67.4	26.6	39.4	1,310	25.3	3,553	39.9	58.0
2006	5,006	3,301	1,182	65.9	23.6	35.8	1,313	26.2	3,379	36.6	57.2
2005	4,898	3,230	1,215	66.0	24.8	37.6	1,335	27.3	3,280	38.0	57.3
2004	4,941	3,244	1,221	65.6	24.7	37.7	1,386	28.0	3,287	37.9	55.9
2003	4,754	3,096	1,115	65.1	23.5	36.0	1,353	28.4	3,135	36.0	56.5
2002	4,918	3,078	979	62.6	19.9	31.8	1,479	30.1	3,109	32.0	53.1
2001	4,892	3,031	1,035	62.0	21.1	34.2	1,548	31.7	3,068	34.2	52.8
2000	4,134	2,462	899	59.6	21.7	36.5	1,335	32.3	2,509	36.8	53.1
1999	3,953	2,325	739	58.8	18.7	31.8	1,340	33.9	2,359	31.7	49.6
1998	4,014	2,403	820	59.8	20.4	34.1	1,383	34.4	2,419	34.3	53.2
1997	3,606	2,236	806	62.0	22.4	36.0	1,103	30.6	2,302	37.1	54.3
1996	3,510	2,019	706	57.5	20.1	35.0	1,210	34.5	2,046	34.5	52.5
1995	3,603	2,112	745	58.6	20.7	35.3	1,250	34.7	2,142	35.7	55.8
1994	3,523	1,995	662	56.6	18.8	33.2	1,224	34.7	2,009	33.4	54.3
1993r	3,363	2,049	728	60.9	21.6	35.5	1,103	32.8	2,081	35.8	55.6
1993	2,772	1,682	602	60.7	21.7	35.8	907	32.7	1,712	36.0	55.8
1992	2,754	1,579	586	57.3	21.3	37.1	936	33.9	1,603	37.6	55.0
1991	2,874	1,498	516	52.1	18.0	34.4	1,139	39.6	1,519	34.6	47.6
1990	2,749	1,498	435	54.5	15.8	29.0	1,025	37.3	1,523	29.4	44.7
1989	2,818	1,576	453	55.9	16.1	28.7	1,062	37.7	1,600	29.4	43.6
1988	2,642	1,458	450	55.2	17.0	30.9	1,046	39.6	1,481	31.3	47.0
1987	2,592	1,597	455	61.6	17.6	28.5	849	32.8	1,612	28.7	44.0
1986	2,514	1,507	458	59.9	18.2	30.4	864	34.4	1,535	30.9	45.6
1985	2,221	1,396	375	62.9	16.9	26.9	700	31.5	1,419	27.6	46.7
1984	2,018	1,212	362	60.1	17.9	29.9	691	34.2	1,223	30.0	46.0
1983	2,025	1,110	349	54.8	17.2	31.4	759	37.5	1,134	32.3	48.4
1982	2,001	1,153	337	57.6	16.8	29.2	740	37.0	1,173	30.0	47.3
1981	2,052	1,144	342	55.8	16.7	29.9	790	38.5	1,166	30.5	45.8
1980	2,033	1,099	327	54.1	16.1	29.8	820	40.3	1,117	30.1	47.3
1979	1,754	968	292	55.2	16.6	30.2	687	39.2	1,001	31.2	45.7
1978	1,672	935	254	55.9	15.2	27.2	656	39.2	965	28.0	43.2
1977	1,609	880	277	54.7	17.2	31.5	622	38.7	900	32.4	43.8
1976	1,551	862	309	55.6	19.9	35.8	566	36.5	891	36.3	48.9
1975	1,446	832	295	57.5	20.4	35.5	505	34.9	849	36.5	50.8
1974	1,506	842	272	55.9	18.1	32.3	558	37.1	858	33.1	47.8
1973	1,285	709	206	55.2	16.0	29.1	500	38.9	732	30.3	43.0
1972	1,338	694	179	51.9	13.4	25.8	541	40.4	709	27.2	36.7

Male

2017	3,355	2,648	1,045	78.9	31.1	39.5	429	12.8	2,690	40.0	62.1
2016	3,291	2,674	1,148	81.3	34.9	42.9	395	12.0	2,729	43.1	63.0
2015	3,246	2,661	1,063	82.0	32.8	40.0	360	11.1	2,711	40.1	61.3
2014	3,354	2,667	1,016	79.5	30.3	38.1	429	12.8	2,700	38.1	57.7

r = Revised, controlled to 1990 census based population estimates; previous 1993 data controlled to 1980 census based population estimates.
Note: The change in the educational attainment question and the college completion categories from "4 or more years of college" to "at least some college," in 1992 caused an increase in the proportion of 14-to-24-year-old high school graduates enrolled in college or completed some college, of approximately 5 percentage points. High school graduates are people who have completed 4 years of high school or more, for 1967 to 1991. Beginning in 1992, they were people whose highest degree was a high school diploma (including equivalency) or higher.

Table A-14. Population 14 to 24 Years Old, by High School Graduate Status, College Enrollment, Attainment, Sex, Race, and Hispanic Origin, October 1967–2017—*Continued*

(Numbers in thousands; percent; civilian noninstitutionalized population.)

Year, race, and Hispanic origin	Total	High school graduates — Total	High school graduates — Enrolled in college	Percent — High school graduates	Percent — Enrolled in college	Percent — High school graduate enrolled in college	High school dropouts — Number	High school dropouts — Percent	High school graduates, 14 to 24 years old — All graduates	Percent — Enrolled in college	Percent — Enrolled or completed some college
2013	3,329	2,564	968	77.0	29.1	37.7	491	14.7	2,597	38.0	55.7
2012	3,311	2,455	1,109	74.1	33.5	45.2	560	16.9	2,496	45.5	63.2
2011	3,250	2,421	1,006	74.5	31.0	41.6	568	17.5	2,458	41.9	60.2
2010	2,930	2,034	819	69.4	27.9	40.2	623	21.3	2,065	40.6	58.5
2009	2,741	1,894	663	69.1	24.2	35.0	616	22.5	1,925	35.6	51.3
2008	2,675	1,797	615	67.2	23.0	34.2	649	24.3	1,841	35.1	54.4
2007	2,706	1,689	560	62.4	20.7	33.1	790	29.2	1,711	33.6	52.2
2006	2,618	1,600	523	61.1	20.0	32.7	812	31.0	1,628	33.2	53.2
2005	2,613	1,569	540	60.1	20.7	34.4	838	32.1	1,589	34.6	52.4
2004	2,648	1,597	574	60.3	21.7	36.0	888	33.5	1,614	35.9	53.0
2003	2,541	1,548	465	60.9	18.3	30.0	805	31.7	1,571	30.0	48.7
2002	2,707	1,562	439	57.7	16.2	28.1	914	33.8	1,572	28.1	48.4
2001	2,596	1,455	449	56.1	17.3	31.0	962	37.1	1,468	31.0	48.1
2000	2,171	1,172	401	54.0	18.5	34.2	800	36.8	1,197	34.5	50.8
1999	2,045	1,122	322	54.9	15.8	28.7	746	36.4	1,131	28.7	45.7
1998	2,109	1,146	346	54.3	16.4	30.2	838	39.7	1,153	30.0	47.2
1997	1,937	1,140	371	58.9	19.2	32.5	643	33.2	1,168	33.0	49.2
1996	1,815	994	300	54.8	16.5	30.2	657	36.2	1,005	30.6	48.8
1995	1,907	1,106	356	58.0	18.7	32.2	653	34.2	1,022	36.2	52.3
1994	1,896	1,021	312	53.8	16.5	30.6	685	36.1	1,026	30.7	52.7
1993r	1,710	1,005	338	58.8	19.8	33.6	591	34.6	1,023	33.7	51.2
1993	1,354	786	266	58.1	19.6	33.8	470	34.7	803	33.9	51.1
1992	1,384	720	247	52.0	17.8	34.3	531	38.4	736	34.8	52.2
1991	1,503	719	211	47.8	14.0	29.3	668	44.4	728	29.7	42.2
1990	1,403	753	214	53.7	15.3	28.4	559	39.8	770	29.4	46.5
1989	1,439	756	211	52.5	14.7	27.9	580	40.3	767	28.2	42.7
1988	1,375	724	228	52.7	16.6	31.5	553	40.2	736	32.2	48.3
1987	1,337	795	247	59.5	18.5	31.1	461	34.5	803	31.1	45.1
1986	1,339	769	233	57.4	17.4	30.3	499	37.3	776	30.5	44.4
1985	1,132	659	168	58.2	14.8	25.5	405	35.8	675	26.4	44.9
1984	956	549	154	57.4	16.1	28.1	338	35.4	554	28.2	45.7
1983	968	476	152	49.2	15.7	31.9	396	40.9	489	33.1	47.4
1982	944	519	141	55.0	14.9	27.2	347	36.8	525	28.0	44.8
1981	988	498	164	50.4	16.6	32.9	428	43.3	506	33.6	48.6
1980	1,012	518	160	51.2	15.8	30.9	431	42.6	521	31.1	49.5
1979	837	454	153	54.2	18.3	33.7	328	39.2	469	34.3	49.5
1978	781	420	126	53.8	16.1	30.0	313	40.1	438	30.4	46.3
1977	754	396	139	52.5	18.4	35.1	295	39.1	404	35.9	46.5
1976	701	378	150	53.9	21.4	39.7	253	36.1	403	39.8	51.8
1975	678	383	145	56.5	21.4	37.9	221	32.6	390	37.9	55.4
1974	720	390	141	54.2	19.6	36.2	279	38.8	401	36.7	51.4
1973	625	348	105	55.7	16.8	30.2	228	36.5	361	32.1	45.4
1972	609	301	92	49.4	15.1	30.6	253	41.5	309	32.0	44.3
Female											
2017	3,298	2,810	1,365	85.2	41.4	48.6	274	8.3	2,881	49.1	69.4
2016	3,248	2,803	1,417	86.3	43.6	50.6	253	7.8	2,879	51.3	71.2
2015	3,218	2,704	1,305	84.0	40.5	48.2	309	9.6	2,750	48.2	71.9
2014	3,214	2,657	1,265	82.7	39.4	47.6	348	10.8	2,709	48.2	67.9
2013	3,160	2,554	1,225	80.8	38.8	48.0	398	12.6	2,593	48.1	69.0
2012	3,105	2,447	1,294	78.8	41.7	52.9	411	13.2	2,491	53.3	72.9
2011	2,724	2,147	1,073	78.8	39.4	50.0	407	15.0	2,173	50.0	71.4
2010	2,755	2,104	995	76.4	36.1	47.3	426	15.5	2,134	47.7	67.8
2009	2,591	1,853	803	71.5	31.0	43.3	496	19.1	1,888	43.6	64.5
2008	2,501	1,821	723	72.8	28.9	39.7	506	20.2	1,850	40.3	63.1
2007	2,469	1,798	816	72.8	33.0	45.4	520	21.1	1,842	45.6	63.4
2006	2,388	1,701	660	71.2	27.6	38.8	501	21.0	1,751	39.7	61.0
2005	2,285	1,661	675	72.7	29.5	40.6	498	21.8	1,691	41.2	62.0
2004	2,293	1,647	647	71.8	28.2	39.3	498	21.7	1,673	39.8	58.6
2003	2,213	1,548	651	69.9	29.4	42.1	548	24.7	1,563	41.9	64.4

r = Revised, controlled to 1990 census based population estimates; previous 1993 data controlled to 1980 census based population estimates.
Note: The change in the educational attainment question and the college completion categories from "4 or more years of college" to "at least some college," in 1992 caused an increase in the proportion of 14-to-24-year-old high school graduates enrolled in college or completed some college, of approximately 5 percentage points. High school graduates are people who have completed 4 years of high school or more, for 1967 to 1991. Beginning in 1992, they were people whose highest degree was a high school diploma (including equivalency) or higher.

Table A-14. Population 14 to 24 Years Old, by High School Graduate Status, College Enrollment, Attainment, Sex, Race, and Hispanic Origin, October 1967–2017—*Continued*

(Numbers in thousands; percent; civilian noninstitutionalized population.)

Year, race, and Hispanic origin	Population 18 to 24 years old								High school graduates, 14 to 24 years old		
	Total	High school graduates		Percent			High school dropouts			Percent	
		Total	Enrolled in college	High school graduates	Enrolled in college	High school graduate enrolled in college	Number	Percent	All graduates	Enrolled in college	Enrolled or completed some college
2002	2,211	1,516	540	68.6	24.4	35.6	565	25.6	1,537	35.9	57.9
2001	2,296	1,576	585	68.6	25.5	37.1	586	25.5	1,600	37.1	57.0
2000	1,963	1,290	498	65.7	25.4	38.6	535	27.3	1,312	38.9	55.2
1999	1,908	1,203	417	63.0	21.8	34.7	593	31.1	1,228	34.4	53.3
1998	1,906	1,257	474	66.0	24.9	37.7	545	28.6	1,266	38.2	58.7
1997	1,669	1,097	436	65.7	26.1	39.7	460	27.6	1,135	41.4	59.6
1996	1,694	1,026	406	60.6	24.0	39.6	554	32.7	1,043	40.4	56.0
1995	1,696	1,011	389	59.6	22.9	38.4	598	35.4	1,022	38.6	59.6
1994	1,628	973	350	59.8	21.5	36.0	539	33.1	983	36.2	55.9
1993r	1,652	1,045	390	63.3	23.6	37.3	510	30.9	1,059	37.8	60.1
1993	1,418	895	336	63.1	23.7	37.5	439	31.0	907	38.0	60.4
1992	1,369	860	339	62.8	24.8	39.4	405	29.6	867	39.9	57.4
1991	1,372	780	305	56.9	22.2	39.1	473	34.5	791	39.2	52.5
1990	1,346	745	221	55.3	16.4	29.7	465	34.5	753	29.5	43.0
1989	1,377	823	244	59.8	17.7	29.6	482	35.0	836	30.5	44.5
1988	1,267	736	224	58.1	17.7	30.4	492	38.8	747	30.5	45.8
1987	1,256	801	208	63.8	16.6	26.0	387	30.8	808	26.4	43.2
1986	1,175	739	226	62.9	19.2	30.6	365	31.1	759	31.4	46.8
1985	1,091	734	205	67.3	18.8	27.9	295	27.0	743	28.4	48.0
1984	1,061	661	207	62.3	19.5	31.3	353	33.2	667	31.5	46.6
1983	1,057	634	198	60.0	18.7	31.2	363	34.3	644	31.8	49.7
1982	1,056	634	196	60.0	18.6	30.9	393	37.2	648	31.8	49.2
1981	1,064	646	178	60.7	16.7	27.6	362	34.0	662	28.2	43.4
1980	1,021	579	165	56.7	16.2	28.5	389	38.1	595	29.1	45.4
1979	917	516	140	56.3	15.3	27.1	358	39.0	534	28.1	42.3
1978	891	516	128	57.9	14.4	24.8	343	38.5	528	25.8	40.0
1977	855	483	139	56.5	16.3	28.8	326	38.1	495	29.7	41.6
1976	850	483	160	56.8	18.8	33.1	313	36.8	489	33.5	46.5
1975	769	449	150	58.4	19.5	33.4	283	36.8	460	34.8	46.7
1974	786	451	129	57.4	16.4	28.6	280	35.6	459	29.2	43.4
1973	658	362	102	55.0	15.5	28.2	272	41.3	372	28.8	41.1
1972	728	394	88	54.1	12.1	22.3	288	39.6	402	23.6	31.1
WHITE ALONE OR IN COMBINATION											
Both Sexes											
2017	22,651	19,846	9,048	87.6	39.9	45.6	1,390	6.1	20,145	45.7	72.0
2016	22,830	20,100	9,446	88.0	41.4	47.0	1,419	6.2	20,416	47.2	72.6
2015	23,067	20,193	9,268	87.5	40.2	45.9	1,464	6.3	20,507	46.0	72.5
2014	23,327	20,258	9,329	86.8	40.0	46.1	1,638	7.0	20,520	46.2	72.0
2013	23,539	20,436	9,422	86.8	40.0	46.1	1,679	7.1	20,773	46.5	72.1
2012	23,516	20,257	9,614	86.1	40.9	47.5	1,710	7.3	20,546	47.8	73.4
2011	23,679	20,256	10,043	85.5	42.4	49.6	1,941	8.2	20,504	49.7	73.9
2010	23,381	19,949	9,524	85.3	40.7	47.7	2,013	8.6	20,180	48.0	72.9
2009	23,256	19,784	9,562	85.1	41.1	48.3	2,127	9.1	20,060	48.5	72.0
2008	23,120	19,810	9,360	85.7	40.5	47.2	2,072	9.0	20,067	47.5	71.6
2007	22,928	19,330	8,958	84.3	39.1	46.3	2,338	10.2	19,595	46.5	70.3
2006	22,670	18,882	8,465	83.3	37.3	44.8	2,458	10.8	19,153	45.1	69.9
2005	22,345	18,583	8,721	83.2	39.0	47.1	2,539	11.4	18,818	47.0	70.0
2004	22,411	18,663	8,544	83.3	38.1	45.8	2,639	11.8	18,868	46.0	69.0
2003	22,029	18,335	8,358	83.2	37.9	45.6	2,558	11.6	18,565	45.6	69.0
Male											
2017	11,424	9,769	4,116	85.5	36.0	42.1	796	7.0	9,898	42.2	67.5
2016	11,534	9,967	4,432	86.4	38.4	44.5	845	7.3	10,093	44.5	67.9
2015	11,635	10,059	4,319	86.5	37.1	42.9	812	7.0	10,224	43.0	67.6
2014	11,801	10,108	4,397	85.7	37.3	43.5	900	7.6	10,237	43.7	67.4
2013	11,921	10,185	4,323	85.4	36.3	42.4	896	7.5	10,357	42.9	66.7
2012	11,925	10,045	4,399	84.2	36.9	43.8	991	8.3	10,174	44.2	68.1

r = Revised, controlled to 1990 census based population estimates; previous 1993 data controlled to 1980 census based population estimates.
Note: The change in the educational attainment question and the college completion categories from "4 or more years of college" to "at least some college," in 1992 caused an increase in the proportion of 14-to-24-year-old high school graduates enrolled in college or completed some college, of approximately 5 percentage points. High school graduates are people who have completed 4 years of high school or more, for 1967 to 1991. Beginning in 1992, they were people whose highest degree was a high school diploma (including equivalency) or higher.

Table A-14. Population 14 to 24 Years Old, by High School Graduate Status, College Enrollment, Attainment, Sex, Race, and Hispanic Origin, October 1967–2017—*Continued*

(Numbers in thousands; percent; civilian noninstitutionalized population.)

Year, race, and Hispanic origin	Population 18 to 24 years old								High school graduates, 14 to 24 years old		
	Total	High school graduates		Percent			High school dropouts			Percent	
		Total	Enrolled in college	High school graduates	Enrolled in college	High school graduate enrolled in college	Number	Percent	All graduates	Enrolled in college	Enrolled or completed some college
2011	12,153	10,175	4,789	83.7	39.4	47.1	1,105	9.1	10,308	47.2	69.7
2010	11,832	9,869	4,472	83.4	37.8	45.3	1,152	9.7	9,976	45.4	68.5
2009	11,774	9,824	4,513	83.4	38.3	45.9	1,224	10.4	9,952	46.1	68.3
2008	11,738	9,891	4,444	84.3	37.9	44.9	1,165	9.9	10,031	45.2	67.8
2007	11,670	9,511	4,116	81.5	35.3	43.3	1,397	12.0	9,634	43.4	66.0
2006	11,502	9,331	3,923	81.1	34.1	42.0	1,427	12.4	9,435	42.2	66.1
2005	11,394	9,086	4,018	79.7	35.3	43.5	1,519	13.3	9,193	44.2	60.0
2004	11,371	9,227	3,956	81.1	34.8	42.9	1,548	13.6	9,296	43.1	64.4
2003	11,147	8,967	3,815	80.4	34.2	42.5	1,493	13.4	9,070	42.6	65.1
Female											
2017	11,228	10,077	4,931	89.8	43.9	48.9	593	5.3	10,248	49.1	76.4
2016	11,296	10,133	5,014	89.7	44.4	49.5	574	5.1	10,323	49.7	77.3
2015	11,433	10,134	4,949	88.6	43.3	48.8	653	5.7	10,283	48.9	77.4
2014	11,526	10,151	4,932	88.1	42.8	48.6	739	6.4	10,283	48.8	76.5
2013	11,617	10,251	5,099	88.2	43.9	49.7	783	6.7	10,415	50.1	77.4
2012	11,590	10,212	5,215	88.1	45.0	51.1	719	6.2	10,372	51.4	78.5
2011	11,525	10,081	5,254	87.5	45.6	52.1	836	7.3	10,196	52.1	78.1
2010	11,549	10,080	5,052	87.3	43.7	50.1	861	7.5	10,204	50.5	77.1
2009	11,482	9,960	5,049	86.7	44.0	50.7	903	7.9	10,108	50.8	75.6
2008	11,381	9,919	4,916	87.2	43.2	49.6	908	8.0	10,036	49.9	75.4
2007	11,258	9,820	4,842	87.2	43.0	49.3	941	8.4	9,960	49.4	74.4
2006	11,168	9,551	4,542	85.5	40.7	47.6	1,032	9.2	9,718	47.8	73.6
2005	10,952	9,497	4,702	86.7	42.9	49.4	1,020	9.3	9,625	49.7	73.9
2004	11,040	9,436	4,588	85.5	41.6	48.6	1,091	9.9	9,572	48.8	73.5
2003	10,882	9,367	4,543	86.1	41.7	48.5	1,065	9.8	9,495	48.5	72.7
BLACK ALONE OR IN COMBINATION											
Both Sexes											
2017	4,935	4,219	1,782	85.5	36.1	42.2	296	6.0	4,314	42.4	65.7
2016	4,978	4,216	1,782	84.7	35.8	42.3	342	6.9	4,305	42.2	65.5
2015	5,032	4,316	1,741	85.8	34.6	40.3	359	7.1	4,367	40.5	64.2
2014	5,121	4,352	1,645	85.0	32.1	37.8	366	7.1	4,426	38.4	65.7
2013	5,199	4,297	1,806	82.7	34.7	42.0	422	8.1	4,345	42.4	66.4
2012	5,142	4,119	1,891	80.1	36.8	45.9	500	9.7	4,187	45.9	67.2
2011	4,793	3,902	1,759	81.4	36.7	45.1	424	8.8	3,955	45.5	67.3
2010	4,745	3,898	1,808	82.1	38.1	46.4	493	10.4	3,965	46.6	66.7
2009	4,623	3,688	1,699	79.8	36.8	46.1	532	11.5	3,766	46.0	67.2
2008	4,531	3,588	1,435	79.2	31.7	40.0	548	12.1	3,646	40.3	60.9
2007	4,425	3,603	1,468	81.4	33.2	40.7	477	10.8	3,671	40.9	61.8
2006	4,264	3,287	1,387	77.1	32.5	42.2	560	13.1	3,359	42.2	61.1
2005	4,158	3,303	1,371	79.4	33.0	31.7	530	12.7	3,378	41.5	63.5
2004	4,115	3,190	1,318	77.5	32.0	41.3	620	15.1	3,253	41.8	63.5
2003	4,016	3,091	1,285	77.0	32.0	41.6	563	14.0	3,141	41.9	62.0
Male											
2017	2,413	2,032	767	84.2	31.8	37.8	176	7.3	2,068	37.7	60.2
2016	2,407	1,924	777	79.9	32.3	40.4	226	9.4	1,948	40.6	61.2
2015	2,421	2,067	833	85.4	34.4	40.3	172	7.1	2,094	40.5	63.2
2014	2,451	2,008	660	81.9	26.9	32.8	183	7.4	2,055	34.0	60.6
2013	2,491	2,020	780	81.1	31.3	38.6	230	9.2	2,042	39.3	62.5
2012	2,500	1,972	859	78.9	34.4	43.6	279	11.2	2,009	43.8	65.0
2011	2,289	1,800	762	78.6	33.3	42.4	218	9.5	1,831	42.9	61.4
2010	2,250	1,781	779	79.2	34.6	43.7	269	11.9	1,823	43.7	61.9
2009	2,211	1,702	712	76.9	32.2	41.9	301	13.6	1,726	41.6	63.7
2008	2,190	1,743	633	79.6	28.9	36.3	235	10.7	1,770	36.9	54.9
2007	2,132	1,703	686	79.9	32.2	40.3	234	11.0	1,728	40.4	59.6
2006	2,032	1,545	577	76.0	28.4	37.3	225	11.0	1,576	37.2	54.5

Note: The change in the educational attainment question and the college completion categories from "4 or more years of college" to "at least some college," in 1992 caused an increase in the proportion of 14-to-24-year-old high school graduates enrolled in college or completed some college, of approximately 5 percentage points. High school graduates are people who completed 4 years of high school or more, for 1967 to 1991. Beginning in 1992, they were people whose highest degree was a high school diploma (including equivalency) or higher.

Table A-14. Population 14 to 24 Years Old, by High School Graduate Status, College Enrollment, Attainment, Sex, Race, and Hispanic Origin, October 1967–2017—*Continued*

(Numbers in thousands; percent; civilian noninstitutionalized population.)

Year, race, and Hispanic origin	Population 18 to 24 years old								High school graduates, 14 to 24 years old		
		High school graduates		Percent			High school dropouts			Percent	
	Total	Total	Enrolled in college	High school graduates	Enrolled in college	High school graduate enrolled in college	Number	Percent	All graduates	Enrolled in college	Enrolled or completed some college
2005................................	1,988	1,466	557	73.7	28.0	42.5	290	14.6	1,492	37.9	58.2
2004................................	1,951	1,418	521	72.7	26.7	36.7	347	17.8	1,442	37.0	61.3
2003................................	1,868	1,382	525	74.0	28.1	38.0	311	16.6	1,397	38.3	57.4
Female											
2017................................	2,522	2,187	1,014	86.7	40.2	46.4	120	4.8	2,246	46.7	70.7
2016................................	2,571	2,292	1,004	89.1	39.1	43.8	116	4.5	2,357	43.5	69.1
2015................................	2,612	2,249	908	86.1	34.8	40.4	188	7.2	2,273	40.6	65.2
2014................................	2,670	2,344	985	87.8	36.9	42.0	183	6.9	2,371	42.3	70.1
2013................................	2,708	2,277	1,026	84.1	37.9	45.0	192	7.1	2,303	45.1	69.9
2012................................	2,642	2,147	1,032	81.3	39.1	48.1	221	8.4	2,178	47.9	69.4
2011................................	2,504	2,102	997	84.0	39.8	47.4	206	8.2	2,124	47.7	72.3
2010................................	2,495	2,117	1,029	84.8	41.3	48.6	224	9.0	2,142	49.0	70.7
2009................................	2,411	1,987	987	82.4	40.9	49.7	231	9.6	2,040	49.8	70.1
2008................................	2,341	1,845	802	78.8	34.2	43.5	313	13.4	1,876	43.5	66.5
2007................................	2,293	1,900	782	82.9	34.1	41.2	243	10.6	1,942	41.3	63.7
2006................................	2,232	1,742	810	78.1	36.3	46.5	335	15.0	1,783	46.5	66.8
2005................................	2,170	1,837	814	84.7	37.5	21.2	240	11.1	1,885	44.3	67.7
2004................................	2,164	1,772	797	81.9	36.8	45.0	272	12.6	1,811	45.5	65.3
2003................................	2,148	1,708	760	79.5	35.4	44.5	252	11.7	1,744	44.7	65.7
ASIAN ALONE OR IN COMBINATION											
Both Sexes											
2017................................	1,989	1,875	1,223	94.2	61.5	65.2	33	1.6	1,910	65.7	90.1
2016................................	2,025	1,867	1,161	92.2	57.3	62.2	61	3.0	1,903	62.1	87.3
2015................................	1,889	1,747	1,182	92.5	62.6	67.7	52	2.8	1,795	67.0	91.5
2014................................	1,844	1,737	1,132	94.2	61.4	65.2	17	0.9	1,781	64.6	90.2
2013................................	1,947	1,765	1,156	90.6	59.4	65.5	70	3.6	1,801	65.9	86.5
2012................................	1,780	1,610	1,043	90.5	58.6	64.8	61	3.4	1,650	65.2	85.2
2011................................	1,435	1,295	833	90.2	58.0	64.3	67	4.6	1,149	66.9	88.1
2010................................	1,465	1,338	904	91.3	61.7	67.6	80	5.5	1,382	68.0	88.9
2009................................	1,345	1,231	844	91.5	62.8	68.5	29	2.1	1,249	68.5	90.8
2008................................	1,251	1,153	738	92.1	59.0	64.0	42	3.4	1,188	64.4	89.7
2007................................	1,293	1,126	720	87.1	55.7	63.9	94	7.3	1,143	63.9	90.3
2006................................	1,270	1,158	705	91.2	55.5	60.9	49	3.9	1,180	60.6	86.1
2005................................	1,299	1,214	773	93.5	59.5	63.7	38	2.9	1,243	64.2	86.0
2004................................	1,263	1,167	750	92.5	59.4	64.3	53	4.2	1,191	64.6	87.6
2003................................	1,280	1,162	774	90.8	60.5	66.6	56	4.4	1,184	66.9	87.8
Male											
2017................................	1,003	934	613	93.1	61.1	65.6	16	1.6	941	65.8	89.3
2016................................	1,045	969	624	92.7	59.7	64.4	25	2.3	984	64.1	87.3
2015................................	937	869	561	92.8	59.9	64.6	30	3.2	896	63.9	89.2
2014................................	932	882	600	94.6	64.3	68.0	13	1.4	904	67.9	89.8
2013................................	1,009	927	612	91.9	60.7	66.1	22	2.2	939	66.1	84.8
2012................................	900	807	510	89.7	56.7	63.2	28	3.1	832	63.9	84.5
2011................................	747	673	429	90.1	57.4	63.7	31	4.2	582	66.1	87.6
2010................................	750	685	453	91.4	60.4	66.1	40	5.3	711	66.5	87.4
2009................................	673	624	418	92.8	62.2	67.0	7	1.1	637	66.8	89.8
2008................................	626	560	340	89.4	54.4	60.8	22	3.4	582	62.2	89.2
2007................................	560	481	318	85.8	56.9	66.3	38	6.8	483	66.4	91.8
2006................................	649	578	362	89.1	55.8	62.7	34	5.3	591	62.3	83.8
2005................................	653	603	392	92.4	59.9	65.0	20	3.1	621	65.1	86.3
2004................................	634	588	398	92.8	62.7	67.7	18	2.9	601	68.0	87.8
2003................................	609	545	370	89.5	60.8	67.9	43	7.1	551	67.7	88.7
Female											
2017................................	986	941	611	95.4	61.9	64.9	17	1.7	969	65.6	90.9
2016................................	980	898	536	91.6	54.7	59.7	36	3.7	919	60.0	87.3

Note: The change in the educational attainment question and the college completion categories from "4 or more years of college" to "at least some college," in 1992 caused an increase in the proportion of 14-to-24-year-old high school graduates enrolled in college or completed some college, of approximately 5 percentage points. High school graduates are people who have completed 4 years of high school or more, for 1967 to 1991. Beginning in 1992, they were people whose highest degree was a high school diploma (including equivalency) or higher.

Table A-14. Population 14 to 24 Years Old, by High School Graduate Status, College Enrollment, Attainment, Sex, Race, and Hispanic Origin, October 1967–2017—*Continued*

(Numbers in thousands; percent; civilian noninstitutionalized population.)

Year, race, and Hispanic origin	Population 18 to 24 years old								High school graduates, 14 to 24 years old		
		High school graduates		Percent			High school dropouts				Percent
	Total	Total	Enrolled in college	High school graduates	Enrolled in college	High school graduate enrolled in college	Number	Percent	All graduates	Enrolled in college	Enrolled or completed some college
2015	952	878	621	92.2	65.2	70.7	22	2.3	899	70.2	93.8
2014	911	855	533	93.8	58.5	62.3	4	0.5	877	61.3	90.6
2013	938	838	544	89.3	58.0	64.9	48	5.1	861	65.7	88.4
2012	880	803	533	91.2	60.6	66.4	33	3.7	817	66.5	85.8
2011	688	622	403	90.4	58.7	64.9	35	5.1	567	67.8	88.7
2010	715	652	451	91.2	63.1	69.1	41	5.7	671	69.7	90.4
2009	673	607	426	90.3	63.3	70.1	21	3.2	611	70.2	91.8
2008	625	593	397	94.9	63.6	67.0	21	3.3	605	66.5	90.3
2007	605	529	339	87.4	56.0	64.1	48	7.9	543	63.9	91.5
2006	621	580	343	93.4	55.3	59.2	14	2.3	589	58.8	88.5
2005	645	610	381	94.6	59.1	62.5	17	2.7	622	63.3	85.8
2004	628	579	352	92.1	56.0	60.8	35	5.5	591	61.2	87.5
2003	671	617	404	92.0	60.2	65.5	13	1.9	633	66.3	87.0

Note: The change in the educational attainment question and the college completion categories from "4 or more years of college" to "at least some college," in 1992 caused an increase in the proportion of 14-to-24-year-old high school graduates enrolled in college or completed some college, of approximately 5 percentage points. High school graduates are people who have completed 4 years of high school or more, for 1967 to 1991. Beginning in 1992, they were people whose highest degree was a high school diploma (including equivalency) or higher.

Table A-15. Population 18 and 19 Years Old, by School Enrollment Status, Sex, Race, and Hispanic Origin, October 1967–2017

(Numbers in thousands; percent; civilian noninstitutionalized population.)

| Year, race, and Hispanic origin | Total | Population 18 and 19 years old | | | | | | | |
		Still in high school	Percent	Dropped out	Percent	High school graduate only	Percent	In college	Percent
ALL RACES									
Both Sexes									
2017	8,222	1,663	20.2	568	6.9	2,049	24.9	3,943	48.0
2016	8,266	1,570	19.0	532	6.4	1,993	24.1	4,171	50.5
2015	8,158	1,613	19.8	611	7.5	1,957	24.0	3,978	48.8
2014	8,261	1,618	19.6	588	7.1	2,019	24.4	4,036	48.9
2013	8,473	1,736	20.5	529	6.2	2,257	26.6	3,951	46.6
2012	8,484	1,840	21.7	605	7.1	2,025	23.9	4,015	47.3
2011	8,465	1,775	21.0	545	6.4	1,903	22.5	4,242	50.1
2010	8,529	1,540	18.1	622	7.3	2,003	23.5	4,364	51.2
2009	8,615	1,645	19.1	736	8.5	1,944	22.6	4,289	49.8
2008	8,492	1,481	17.4	750	8.8	2,134	25.1	4,126	48.6
2007	8,338	1,491	17.9	675	8.1	2,097	25.2	4,075	48.9
2006	8,102	1,560	19.3	743	9.2	2,053	25.3	3,746	46.2
2005	7,559	1,372	18.1	661	8.7	1,694	22.4	3,832	50.7
2004	7,701	1,266	16.4	840	10.9	1,910	24.8	3,685	47.8
2003	7,533	1,345	17.9	817	10.8	1,859	24.7	3,512	46.6
2002	7,907	1,427	18.0	884	11.2	2,015	25.5	3,581	45.3
2001	7,985	1,394	17.5	1,034	12.9	2,079	26.0	3,478	43.6
2000	8,045	1,327	16.5	1,012	12.6	2,107	26.2	3,599	44.7
1999	7,991	1,321	16.5	1,047	13.1	2,103	26.3	3,520	44.0
1998	7,902	1,244	15.7	1,104	14.0	1,884	23.8	3,670	46.4
1997	7,510	1,256	16.7	1,038	13.8	1,854	24.7	3,362	44.8
1996	7,376	1,230	16.7	940	12.7	1,897	25.7	3,309	44.9
1995	7,198	1,173	16.3	1,051	14.6	1,873	26.0	3,101	43.1
1994	6,946	1,129	16.3	929	13.4	1,837	26.4	3,051	43.9
1993	6,594	1,137	17.2	778	11.8	1,753	26.6	2,926	44.4
1992	6,535	1,121	17.2	780	11.9	1,742	26.7	2,892	44.3
1991	6,664	1,040	15.6	889	13.3	1,806	27.1	2,929	44.0
1990	7,064	1,024	14.5	1,003	14.2	2,018	28.6	3,019	42.7
1989	7,361	1,058	14.4	1,033	14.0	2,204	29.9	3,066	41.7
1988	7,294	1,013	13.9	1,063	14.6	2,172	29.8	3,046	41.8
1987	7,160	937	13.1	954	13.3	2,224	31.1	3,045	42.5
1986	7,095	930	13.1	872	12.3	2,351	33.1	2,942	41.5
1985	7,204	809	11.2	1,031	14.3	2,457	34.1	2,907	40.4
1984	7,428	857	11.5	1,129	15.2	2,575	34.7	2,867	38.6
1983	7,819	999	12.8	1,132	14.5	2,748	35.1	2,940	37.6
1982	8,023	908	11.3	1,336	16.7	2,850	35.5	2,929	36.5
1981	8,115	932	11.5	1,299	16.0	2,840	35.0	3,044	37.5
1980	8,160	855	10.5	1,284	15.7	3,088	37.8	2,933	35.9
1979	8,214	849	10.3	1,382	16.8	3,139	38.2	2,844	34.6
1978	8,153	801	9.8	1,361	16.7	3,092	37.9	2,899	35.6
1977	8,151	849	10.4	1,355	16.6	3,034	37.2	2,913	35.7
1976	8,148	831	10.2	1,355	16.6	3,025	37.1	2,937	36.0
1975	8,024	822	10.2	1,286	16.0	2,973	37.1	2,943	36.7
1974	7,822	777	9.9	1,302	16.6	3,146	40.2	2,597	33.2
1973	7,649	766	10.0	1,228	16.1	3,138	41.0	2,517	32.9
1972	7,462	778	10.4	1,100	14.7	2,904	38.9	2,680	35.9
1971	7,231	830	11.5	1,108	15.3	2,567	35.5	2,726	37.7
1970	6,958	728	10.5	1,125	16.2	2,511	36.1	2,594	37.3
1969	6,677	749	11.2	1,007	15.1	2,320	34.7	2,601	39.0
1968	6,587	816	12.4	1,033	15.7	2,237	34.0	2,501	38.0
1967	6,358	741	11.7	1,086	17.1	2,245	35.3	2,286	36.0
Male									
2017	4,153	957	23.1	346	8.3	1,103	26.6	1,746	42.1
2016	4,192	916	21.9	303	7.2	1,028	24.5	1,944	46.4
2015	4,106	860	20.9	359	8.7	1,050	25.6	1,838	44.7
2014	4,183	935	22.4	323	7.7	1,146	27.4	1,779	42.5
2013	4,319	1,004	23.2	272	6.3	1,235	28.6	1,809	41.9
2012	4,310	1,033	23.7	359	8.3	1,114	25.9	1,803	41.8
2011	4,341	1,038	23.9	293	6.8	1,060	24.4	1,949	44.9
2010	4,296	867	20.2	347	8.1	1,073	25.0	2,009	46.8
2009	4,352	899	20.7	410	9.4	1,114	25.6	1,928	44.3
2008	4,289	834	19.5	376	8.8	1,169	27.3	1,909	44.5
2007	4,222	895	21.2	354	8.4	1,070	25.3	1,903	45.1
2006	4,103	907	22.1	414	10.1	1,079	26.3	1,703	41.5
2005	3,880	899	23.2	392	10.1	914	23.6	1,675	43.2

Note: High school graduates are people who have completed 4 years of high school or more, for 1967 to 1991. Beginning in 1992, they were people whose highest degree was a high school diploma (including equivalency) or higher.

Table A-15. Population 18 and 19 Years Old, by School Enrollment Status, Sex, Race, and Hispanic Origin, October 1967–2017—*Continued*

(Numbers in thousands; percent; civilian noninstitutionalized population.)

Year, race, and Hispanic origin	Total	Population 18 and 19 years old							
		Still in high school	Percent	Dropped out	Percent	High school graduate only	Percent	In college	Percent
2004	3,861	714	18.5	522	13.5	1,015	26.3	1,610	41.7
2003	3,764	781	20.7	480	12.8	935	24.8	1,568	41.7
2002	4,042	862	21.3	523	12.9	1,022	25.3	1,635	40.5
2001	4,027	801	19.9	614	15.2	1,042	25.9	1,570	39.0
2000	4,037	783	19.4	571	14.1	1,113	27.6	1,570	38.9
1999	4,026	780	19.4	550	13.7	1,048	26.0	1,648	40.9
1998	3,994	732	18.3	611	15.3	984	24.6	1,667	41.7
1997	3,816	750	19.7	585	15.3	920	24.1	1,561	40.9
1996	3,711	769	20.7	488	13.2	965	26.0	1,489	40.1
1995	3,611	719	19.9	532	14.7	929	25.7	1,431	39.6
1994	3,485	688	19.7	499	14.3	882	25.3	1,416	40.6
1993	3,329	712	21.4	403	12.1	877	26.3	1,337	40.2
1992	3,275	694	21.2	400	12.2	856	26.1	1,325	40.5
1991	3,307	650	19.7	453	13.7	878	26.5	1,326	40.1
1990	3,503	595	17.0	512	14.6	953	27.2	1,443	41.2
1989	3,640	640	17.6	531	14.6	1,047	28.8	1,422	39.1
1988	3,618	666	18.4	566	15.6	1,021	28.2	1,365	37.7
1987	3,537	564	15.9	493	13.9	997	28.2	1,483	41.9
1986	3,502	594	17.0	459	13.1	1,045	29.8	1,404	40.1
1985	3,550	503	14.2	580	16.3	1,118	31.5	1,349	38.0
1984	3,674	551	15.0	594	16.2	1,156	31.5	1,373	37.4
1983	3,877	616	15.9	630	16.2	1,291	33.3	1,340	34.6
1982	3,961	562	14.2	709	17.9	1,314	33.2	1,376	34.7
1981	3,996	567	14.2	706	17.7	1,273	31.9	1,450	36.3
1980	3,993	510	12.8	673	16.9	1,441	36.1	1,369	34.3
1979	4,023	533	13.2	739	18.4	1,410	35.0	1,341	33.3
1978	3,975	511	12.9	692	17.4	1,381	34.7	1,391	35.0
1977	3,961	522	13.2	702	17.7	1,341	33.9	1,396	35.2
1976	3,957	516	13.0	684	17.3	1,366	34.5	1,391	35.2
1975	3,891	514	13.2	603	15.5	1,348	34.6	1,426	36.6
1974	3,782	469	12.4	706	18.7	1,345	35.6	1,262	33.4
1973	3,720	490	13.2	589	15.8	1,348	36.2	1,293	34.8
1972	3,630	492	13.6	555	15.3	1,217	33.5	1,366	37.6
1971	3,503	496	14.2	551	15.7	1,012	28.9	1,444	41.2
1970	3,349	485	14.5	537	16.0	981	29.3	1,346	40.2
1969	3,173	489	15.4	473	14.9	814	25.7	1,397	44.0
1968	3,133	535	17.1	485	15.5	756	24.1	1,357	43.3
1967	2,908	438	15.1	500	17.2	772	26.5	1,198	41.2
Female									
2017	4,070	705	17.3	222	5.5	946	23.2	2,197	54.0
2016	4,075	654	16.0	229	5.6	965	23.7	2,227	54.7
2015	4,052	752	18.6	252	6.2	907	22.4	2,141	52.8
2014	4,079	683	16.7	265	6.5	873	21.4	2,257	55.3
2013	4,154	732	17.6	257	6.2	1,022	24.6	2,142	51.6
2012	4,174	807	18.9	245	5.9	911	21.8	2,212	53.0
2011	4,124	737	17.9	252	6.1	843	20.4	2,293	55.6
2010	4,233	673	15.9	275	6.5	930	22.0	2,355	55.6
2009	4,263	746	17.5	325	7.6	830	19.5	2,361	55.4
2008	4,203	647	15.4	374	8.9	965	23.0	2,217	52.7
2007	4,116	595	14.5	321	7.8	1,027	25.0	2,172	52.8
2006	3,999	654	16.3	328	8.2	974	24.4	2,043	51.1
2005	3,679	472	12.8	269	7.3	886	24.1	2,052	55.8
2004	3,840	553	14.4	318	8.3	895	23.3	2,074	54.0
2003	3,769	565	15.0	337	8.9	923	24.5	1,944	51.6
2002	3,865	565	14.6	361	9.3	993	25.7	1,946	50.3
2001	3,958	594	15.0	420	10.6	1,037	26.2	1,907	48.2
2000	4,008	544	13.6	440	11.0	995	24.8	2,029	50.6
1999	3,965	540	13.6	497	12.5	1,056	26.6	1,872	47.2
1998	3,908	513	13.1	492	12.6	900	23.0	2,003	51.3
1997	3,694	506	13.7	453	12.3	934	25.3	1,801	48.8
1996	3,665	460	12.6	452	12.3	932	25.4	1,821	49.7
1995	3,587	453	12.6	519	14.5	944	26.3	1,671	46.6
1994	3,461	440	12.7	430	12.4	956	27.6	1,635	47.2
1993	3,265	425	13.0	375	11.5	877	26.9	1,588	48.6
1992	3,260	428	13.1	380	11.7	886	27.2	1,566	48.0
1991	3,357	389	11.6	436	13.0	929	27.7	1,603	47.8
1990	3,561	429	12.0	491	13.8	1,065	29.9	1,576	44.3
1989	3,721	421	11.3	501	13.5	1,156	31.1	1,643	44.2

Note: High school graduates are people who have completed 4 years of high school or more, for 1967 to 1991. Beginning in 1992, they were people whose highest degree was a high school diploma (including equivalency) or higher.

Table A-15. Population 18 and 19 Years Old, by School Enrollment Status, Sex, Race, and Hispanic Origin, October 1967–2017—*Continued*

(Numbers in thousands; percent; civilian noninstitutionalized population.)

Year, race, and Hispanic origin	Total	Population 18 and 19 years old							
		Still in high school	Percent	Dropped out	Percent	High school graduate only	Percent	In college	Percent
1988	3,676	346	9.4	497	13.5	1,151	31.3	1,682	45.8
1987	3,623	374	10.3	461	12.7	1,226	33.8	1,562	43.1
1986	3,593	337	9.4	413	11.5	1,306	36.3	1,537	42.8
1985	3,654	304	8.3	451	12.3	1,340	36.7	1,559	42.7
1984	3,754	306	8.2	535	14.3	1,419	37.8	1,494	39.8
1983	3,942	383	9.7	502	12.7	1,457	37.0	1,600	40.6
1982	4,062	346	8.5	627	15.4	1,536	37.8	1,553	38.2
1981	4,119	364	8.8	594	14.4	1,567	38.0	1,594	38.7
1980	4,167	345	8.3	611	14.7	1,646	39.5	1,565	37.6
1979	4,191	317	7.6	643	15.3	1,728	41.2	1,503	35.9
1978	4,178	291	7.0	669	16.0	1,711	41.0	1,507	36.1
1977	4,190	326	7.8	654	15.6	1,693	40.4	1,517	36.2
1976	4,191	314	7.5	672	16.0	1,659	39.6	1,546	36.9
1975	4,133	308	7.5	683	16.5	1,625	39.3	1,517	36.7
1974	4,040	309	7.6	596	14.8	1,800	44.6	1,335	33.0
1973	3,929	276	7.0	638	16.2	1,791	45.6	1,224	31.2
1972	3,832	287	7.5	545	14.2	1,686	44.0	1,314	34.3
1971	3,728	337	9.0	556	14.9	1,554	41.7	1,281	34.4
1970	3,609	253	7.0	589	16.3	1,519	42.1	1,248	34.6
1969	3,504	260	7.4	534	15.2	1,506	43.0	1,204	34.4
1968	3,454	281	8.1	548	15.9	1,481	42.9	1,144	33.1
1967	3,450	302	8.8	586	17.0	1,474	42.7	1,088	31.5
WHITE									
Both Sexes									
2017	6,153	1,192	19.4	450	7.3	1,529	24.8	2,982	48.5
2016	6,144	1,097	17.9	370	6.0	1,506	24.5	3,170	51.6
2015	6,147	1,159	18.9	474	7.7	1,456	23.7	3,057	49.7
2014	6,213	1,182	19.0	451	7.3	1,517	24.4	3,064	49.3
2013	6,294	1,219	19.4	390	6.2	1,652	26.2	3,033	48.2
2012	6,372	1,303	20.1	418	6.6	1,575	24.7	3,077	48.3
2011	6,501	1,274	19.6	449	6.9	1,480	22.8	3,298	50.7
2010	6,523	1,168	17.9	435	6.7	1,522	23.3	3,398	52.1
2009	6,594	1,194	18.1	526	8.0	1,536	23.3	3,337	50.6
2008	6,589	1,067	16.2	558	8.5	1,611	24.4	3,353	50.9
2007	6,446	1,083	16.8	517	8.0	1,605	24.9	3,242	50.3
2006	6,321	1,121	17.7	600	9.5	1,619	25.6	2,982	47.2
2005	5,893	1,023	17.4	515	8.7	1,383	23.5	2,972	50.4
2004	6,043	963	15.9	634	10.5	1,500	24.8	2,946	48.8
2003[1]	5,915	979	16.6	659	11.1	1,444	24.4	2,833	47.9
2002	6,252	1,096	17.5	663	10.6	1,602	25.6	2,891	46.2
2001	6,254	1,022	16.3	843	13.5	1,634	26.1	2,755	44.1
2000	6,399	1,010	15.8	795	12.4	1,680	26.3	2,914	45.5
1999	6,383	1,009	15.8	810	12.7	1,715	26.9	2,849	44.6
1998	6,266	884	14.1	848	13.5	1,540	24.6	2,994	47.8
1997	5,995	896	14.9	816	13.6	1,491	24.9	2,792	46.6
1996	5,833	914	15.7	735	12.6	1,453	24.9	2,731	46.8
1995	5,698	803	14.1	809	14.2	1,509	26.5	2,577	45.2
1994	5,559	817	14.7	681	12.3	1,493	26.9	2,568	46.2
1993	5,252	786	15.0	628	12.0	1,382	26.3	2,456	46.8
1992	5,203	793	15.2	582	11.2	1,409	27.1	2,419	46.5
1991	5,358	709	13.2	722	13.5	1,440	26.9	2,487	46.4
1990	5,725	724	12.6	799	14.0	1,654	28.9	2,548	44.5
1989	6,013	744	12.4	819	13.6	1,802	30.0	2,648	44.0
1988	5,981	699	11.7	855	14.3	1,788	29.9	2,639	44.1
1987	5,845	667	11.4	762	13.0	1,852	31.7	2,564	43.9
1986	5,825	669	11.5	693	11.9	1,940	33.3	2,523	43.3
1985	5,922	566	9.6	815	13.8	2,002	33.8	2,539	42.9
1984	6,139	594	9.7	913	14.9	2,091	34.1	2,541	41.4
1983	6,452	688	10.7	884	13.7	2,283	35.4	2,597	40.3
1982	6,666	647	9.7	1,051	15.8	2,419	36.3	2,549	38.2
1981	6,794	656	9.7	1,054	15.5	2,445	36.0	2,639	38.8
1980	6,913	621	9.0	1,032	14.9	2,682	38.8	2,578	37.3
1979	6,980	607	8.7	1,115	16.0	2,760	39.5	2,498	35.8
1978	6,933	560	8.1	1,082	15.6	2,738	39.5	2,553	36.8

Note: High school graduates are people who have completed 4 years of high school or more, for 1967 to 1991. Beginning in 1992, they were people whose highest degree was a high school diploma (including equivalency) or higher.
[1] Starting in 2003 respondents could identify more than one race. Except as noted, the race data in this table from 2003 onward represent those respondents who indicated only one race category.

Table A-15. Population 18 and 19 Years Old, by School Enrollment Status, Sex, Race, and Hispanic Origin, October 1967–2017—*Continued*

(Numbers in thousands; percent; civilian noninstitutionalized population.)

Year, race, and Hispanic origin	Total	Population 18 and 19 years old							
		Still in high school	Percent	Dropped out	Percent	High school graduate only	Percent	In college	Percent
1977..	6,944	581	8.4	1,103	15.9	2,681	38.6	2,579	37.1
1976..	6,951	581	8.4	1,131	16.3	2,662	38.3	2,577	37.1
1975..	6,855	572	8.3	1,005	14.7	2,665	38.9	2,613	38.1
1974..	6,707	551	8.2	1,045	15.6	2,803	41.8	2,308	34.4
1973..	6,559	568	8.7	962	14.7	2,748	41.9	2,281	34.8
1972..	6,424	582	9.1	857	13.3	2,574	40.1	2,411	37.5
1971..	6,243	596	9.5	875	14.0	2,287	36.6	2,485	39.8
1970..	6,009	563	9.4	845	14.1	2,240	37.3	2,361	39.3
1969..	5,762	557	9.7	772	13.4	2,056	35.7	2,377	41.3
1968..	5,692	614	10.8	822	14.4	1,972	34.6	2,284	40.1
1967..	5,506	558	10.1	875	15.9	1,968	35.7	2,105	38.2
Male									
2017..	3,123	717	22.9	273	8.7	816	26.1	1,317	42.2
2016..	3,119	649	20.8	202	6.5	798	25.6	1,470	47.1
2015..	3,123	621	19.9	282	9.0	806	25.8	1,414	45.3
2014..	3,165	653	20.6	236	7.5	879	27.8	1,397	44.1
2013..	3,212	732	22.8	196	6.1	898	27.9	1,386	43.2
2012..	3,259	763	23.1	237	7.3	872	26.8	1,387	42.6
2011..	3,352	748	22.3	240	7.2	845	25.2	1,520	45.3
2010..	3,316	667	20.1	246	7.4	830	25.0	1,573	47.4
2009..	3,349	652	19.5	291	8.7	894	26.7	1,511	45.1
2008..	3,350	589	17.6	299	8.9	896	26.7	1,566	46.7
2007..	3,277	668	20.4	281	8.6	819	25.0	1,508	46.0
2006..	3,211	645	20.1	351	10.9	848	26.4	1,367	42.6
2005..	3,049	665	21.8	304	10.0	737	24.2	1,343	44.1
2004..	3,062	524	17.1	406	13.3	824	26.9	1,308	42.7
2003[1]..	3,003	594	19.8	381	12.7	770	25.6	1,258	41.9
2002..	3,186	661	20.7	366	11.5	830	26.1	1,329	41.7
2001..	3,192	585	18.3	494	15.5	840	26.3	1,273	39.9
2000..	3,248	612	18.8	447	13.8	900	27.7	1,289	39.7
1999..	3,242	609	18.8	423	13.0	874	27.0	1,336	41.2
1998..	3,197	533	16.7	472	14.8	816	25.5	1,376	43.0
1997..	3,060	523	17.1	473	15.5	750	24.5	1,314	42.9
1996..	2,953	575	19.5	382	12.9	773	26.2	1,223	41.4
1995..	2,886	519	18.0	408	14.1	764	26.5	1,195	41.4
1994..	2,813	512	18.2	355	12.6	734	26.1	1,212	43.1
1993..	2,641	497	18.8	338	12.8	703	26.6	1,103	41.8
1992..	2,608	482	18.5	304	11.7	720	27.6	1,102	42.3
1991..	2,677	451	16.8	381	14.2	733	27.4	1,112	41.5
1990..	2,852	416	14.6	421	14.8	797	27.9	1,218	42.7
1989..	2,997	463	15.4	433	14.4	848	28.3	1,253	41.8
1988..	2,976	487	16.4	461	15.5	834	28.0	1,194	40.1
1987..	2,906	404	13.9	400	13.8	842	29.0	1,260	43.4
1986..	2,888	411	14.2	370	12.8	866	30.0	1,241	43.0
1985..	2,937	349	11.9	478	16.3	934	31.8	1,176	40.0
1984..	3,047	378	12.4	480	15.8	965	31.7	1,224	40.2
1983..	3,216	434	13.5	500	15.5	1,085	33.7	1,197	37.2
1982..	3,301	412	12.5	549	16.6	1,151	34.9	1,189	36.0
1981..	3,356	394	11.7	599	17.8	1,104	32.9	1,259	37.5
1980..	3,407	385	11.3	549	16.1	1,241	36.4	1,232	36.2
1979..	3,445	395	11.5	610	17.7	1,248	36.2	1,192	34.6
1978..	3,405	368	10.8	554	16.3	1,244	36.5	1,239	36.4
1977..	3,396	348	10.2	577	17.0	1,199	35.3	1,272	37.5
1976..	3,393	348	10.3	582	17.2	1,219	35.9	1,244	36.7
1975..	3,343	374	11.2	458	13.7	1,228	36.7	1,283	38.4
1974..	3,265	343	10.5	568	17.4	1,211	37.1	1,143	35.0
1973..	3,208	375	11.7	454	14.2	1,202	37.5	1,177	36.7
1972..	3,137	374	11.9	423	13.5	1,098	35.0	1,242	39.6
1971..	3,035	367	12.1	432	14.2	908	29.9	1,328	43.8
1970..	2,901	374	12.9	384	13.2	892	30.7	1,251	43.1
1969..	2,745	374	13.6	345	12.6	728	26.5	1,298	47.3
1968..	2,710	403	14.9	387	14.3	658	24.3	1,262	46.6
1967..	2,511	340	13.5	386	15.4	688	27.4	1,097	43.7

Note: High school graduates are people who have completed 4 years of high school or more, for 1967 to 1991. Beginning in 1992, they were people whose highest degree was a high school diploma (including equivalency) or higher.
[1] Starting in 2003 respondents could identify more than one race. Except as noted, the race data in this table from 2003 onward represent those respondents who indicated only one race category.

Table A-15. Population 18 and 19 Years Old, by School Enrollment Status, Sex, Race, and Hispanic Origin, October 1967–2017—*Continued*

(Numbers in thousands; percent; civilian noninstitutionalized population.)

Year, race, and Hispanic origin	Total	Population 18 and 19 years old							
		Still in high school	Percent	Dropped out	Percent	High school graduate only	Percent	In college	Percent
Female									
2017	3,029	476	15.7	177	5.8	712	23.5	1,665	54.9
2016	3,025	448	14.8	168	5.6	709	23.4	1,700	56.2
2015	3,024	538	17.8	192	6.3	650	21.5	1,644	54.4
2014	3,049	529	17.4	215	7.1	638	20.9	1,667	54.7
2013	3,083	487	15.8	195	6.3	754	24.5	1,646	53.4
2012	3,113	540	16.9	181	5.8	702	22.6	1,690	54.3
2011	3,148	526	16.7	209	6.6	635	20.2	1,779	56.5
2010	3,206	501	15.6	188	5.9	692	21.6	1,825	56.9
2009	3,245	542	16.7	235	7.2	642	19.8	1,826	56.3
2008	3,239	478	14.8	259	8.0	715	22.1	1,787	55.2
2007	3,169	414	13.1	235	7.4	785	24.8	1,734	54.7
2006	3,111	476	15.3	249	8.0	771	24.8	1,615	51.9
2005	2,844	358	12.6	210	7.4	647	22.7	1,629	57.3
2004	2,980	440	14.7	227	7.6	675	22.7	1,638	55.0
2003[1]	2,913	385	13.2	279	9.6	674	23.1	1,575	54.1
2002	3,066	435	14.2	297	9.7	772	25.2	1,562	50.9
2001	3,062	438	14.3	349	11.4	794	25.9	1,481	48.4
2000	3,151	397	12.6	348	11.0	781	24.8	1,625	51.6
1999	3,141	400	12.7	387	12.3	841	26.8	1,513	48.2
1998	3,069	351	11.4	376	12.3	724	23.6	1,618	52.7
1997	2,934	371	12.6	344	11.7	740	25.2	1,479	50.4
1996	2,879	338	11.7	353	12.3	680	23.6	1,508	52.4
1995	2,812	283	10.1	401	14.3	745	26.5	1,383	49.2
1994	2,746	305	11.1	325	11.8	759	27.6	1,357	49.4
1993	2,611	289	11.1	290	11.1	679	26.0	1,353	51.8
1992	2,595	311	12.0	278	10.7	689	26.6	1,317	50.8
1991	2,681	259	9.7	341	12.7	706	26.3	1,375	51.3
1990	2,873	307	10.7	378	13.2	857	29.8	1,331	46.3
1989	3,016	281	9.3	386	12.8	954	31.6	1,395	46.3
1988	3,005	212	7.1	394	13.1	954	31.7	1,445	48.1
1987	2,939	263	8.9	362	12.3	1,010	34.4	1,304	44.4
1986	2,937	257	8.8	323	11.0	1,074	36.6	1,283	43.7
1985	2,985	217	7.3	337	11.3	1,068	35.8	1,363	45.7
1984	3,092	216	7.0	432	14.0	1,127	36.4	1,317	42.6
1983	3,236	255	7.9	383	11.8	1,198	37.0	1,400	43.3
1982	3,365	234	7.0	502	14.9	1,269	37.7	1,360	40.4
1981	3,438	262	7.6	454	13.2	1,342	39.0	1,380	40.1
1980	3,506	237	6.8	483	13.8	1,440	41.1	1,346	38.4
1979	3,535	213	6.0	505	14.3	1,511	42.7	1,306	36.9
1978	3,528	193	5.5	528	15.0	1,493	42.3	1,314	37.2
1977	3,548	232	6.5	526	14.8	1,483	41.8	1,307	36.8
1976	3,558	230	6.5	550	15.5	1,444	40.6	1,334	37.5
1975	3,512	199	5.7	547	15.6	1,436	40.9	1,330	37.9
1974	3,442	207	6.0	477	13.9	1,592	46.3	1,166	33.9
1973	3,351	192	5.7	508	15.2	1,547	46.2	1,104	32.9
1972	3,287	208	6.3	434	13.2	1,476	44.9	1,169	35.6
1971	3,208	229	7.1	442	13.8	1,380	43.0	1,157	36.1
1970	3,108	190	6.1	460	14.8	1,348	43.4	1,110	35.7
1969	3,017	183	6.1	427	14.2	1,328	44.0	1,079	35.8
1968	2,981	210	7.0	435	14.6	1,314	44.1	1,022	34.3
1967	2,996	218	7.3	489	16.3	1,280	42.7	1,009	33.7
WHITE NON-HISPANIC									
Both Sexes									
2017	4,400	853	19.4	294	6.7	1,124	25.5	2,129	48.4
2016	4,563	775	17.0	242	5.3	1,106	24.2	2,439	53.5
2015	4,575	839	18.3	305	6.7	1,063	23.2	2,368	51.8
2014	4,555	860	18.9	290	6.4	1,106	24.3	2,299	50.5
2013	4,645	856	18.4	248	5.3	1,162	25.0	2,379	51.2
2012	4,748	905	18.6	249	5.2	1,232	26.0	2,363	49.8
2011	4,889	937	19.2	291	5.9	1,074	22.0	2,588	52.9
2010	4,935	804	16.3	277	5.6	1,156	23.4	2,699	54.7
2009	5,068	826	16.3	288	5.7	1,112	21.9	2,842	56.1
2008	5,185	780	15.0	296	5.7	1,258	24.3	2,850	55.0

Note: High school graduates are people who have completed 4 years of high school or more, for 1967 to 1991. Beginning in 1992, they were people whose highest degree was a high school diploma (including equivalency) or higher.
[1] Starting in 2003 respondents could identify more than one race. Except as noted, the race data in this table from 2003 onward represent those respondents who indicated only one race category.

Table A-15. Population 18 and 19 Years Old, by School Enrollment Status, Sex, Race, and Hispanic Origin, October 1967–2017—*Continued*

(Numbers in thousands; percent; civilian noninstitutionalized population.)

Year, race, and Hispanic origin	Total	Population 18 and 19 years old							
		Still in high school	Percent	Dropped out	Percent	High school graduate only	Percent	In college	Percent
2007	5,067	793	15.7	283	5.6	1,252	24.7	2,739	54.1
2006	5,018	843	16.8	361	7.2	1,251	24.9	2,564	51.1
2005	4,770	790	16.6	297	6.2	1,065	22.3	2,618	54.9
2004	4,885	731	15.0	363	7.4	1,195	24.5	2,596	53.1
2003[1]	4,780	758	15.9	379	7.9	1,157	24.2	2,486	52.0
2002	5,016	817	16.3	369	7.4	1,281	25.5	2,549	50.8
2001	4,928	780	15.8	467	9.5	1,298	26.3	2,383	48.4
2000	5,221	757	14.5	500	9.6	1,384	26.5	2,580	49.4
1999	5,228	779	14.9	491	9.4	1,384	26.5	2,574	49.2
1998	5,080	691	13.6	475	9.4	1,211	23.8	2,703	53.2
Male									
2017	2,262	528	23.4	174	7.7	608	26.9	952	42.1
2016	2,351	463	19.7	123	5.2	597	25.4	1,168	49.7
2015	2,350	460	19.6	181	7.7	589	25.1	1,121	47.7
2014	2,334	490	21.0	147	6.3	646	27.7	1,050	45.0
2013	2,392	516	21.6	123	5.2	629	26.3	1,124	47.0
2012	2,412	527	21.4	124	5.1	710	29.4	1,051	43.6
2011	2,470	543	22.0	145	5.9	599	24.2	1,184	47.9
2010	2,516	470	18.7	166	6.6	645	25.6	1,236	49.1
2009	2,573	473	18.4	173	6.7	641	24.9	1,286	50.0
2008	2,649	423	16.0	170	6.4	709	26.8	1,346	50.8
2007	2,587	496	19.2	150	5.8	643	24.9	1,298	50.2
2006	2,553	501	19.6	204	8.0	679	26.6	1,168	45.7
2005	2,449	515	21.0	168	6.9	573	23.4	1,193	48.7
2004	2,443	408	16.7	204	8.4	681	27.9	1,150	47.1
2003[1]	2,407	460	19.1	230	9.6	602	25.0	1,115	46.3
2002	2,502	481	19.2	182	7.3	660	26.4	1,179	47.1
2001	2,526	453	17.9	257	10.2	685	27.1	1,131	44.8
2000	2,628	471	17.9	274	10.4	745	28.3	1,138	43.3
1999	2,648	473	17.9	255	9.6	706	26.7	1,214	45.8
1998	2,613	432	16.5	254	9.7	653	25.0	1,274	48.8
Female									
2017	2,138	325	15.2	120	5.6	515	24.1	1,178	55.1
2016	2,212	312	14.1	119	5.4	510	23.1	1,271	57.5
2015	2,225	379	17.1	124	5.6	474	21.3	1,248	56.1
2014	2,222	370	16.6	143	6.4	460	20.7	1,249	56.2
2013	2,253	340	15.1	125	5.5	533	23.7	1,254	55.7
2012	2,336	377	15.7	125	5.3	522	22.3	1,312	56.2
2011	2,470	543	22.0	145	5.9	599	24.2	1,184	47.9
2010	2,419	334	13.8	111	4.6	511	21.1	1,463	60.5
2009	2,495	353	14.1	115	4.6	471	18.9	1,556	62.4
2008	2,536	357	14.1	126	5.0	549	21.7	1,504	59.3
2007	2,480	298	12.0	132	5.3	609	24.6	1,441	58.1
2006	2,466	341	13.8	157	6.4	571	23.2	1,396	56.6
2005	2,321	275	11.9	129	5.6	491	21.2	1,425	61.4
2004	2,441	323	13.2	159	6.5	513	21.0	1,446	59.2
2003[1]	2,373	298	12.6	149	6.3	555	23.4	1,371	57.8
2002	2,514	336	13.4	187	7.4	621	24.7	1,370	54.5
2001	2,402	328	13.7	209	8.7	613	25.5	1,252	52.1
2000	2,593	286	11.0	225	8.7	639	24.6	1,443	55.6
1999	2,580	307	11.9	236	9.1	677	26.2	1,360	52.7
1998	2,467	259	10.5	221	9.0	558	22.6	1,429	57.9
BLACK									
Both Sexes									
2017	1,246	310	24.9	64	5.2	346	27.8	525	42.1
2016	1,244	305	24.5	87	7.0	321	25.8	530	42.6
2015	1,233	286	23.2	84	6.8	354	28.7	509	41.3
2014	1,251	307	24.5	94	7.5	341	27.3	510	40.7
2013	1,305	386	29.6	92	7.1	375	28.8	451	34.6
2012	1,356	400	29.2	110	8.1	315	23.2	531	39.1
2011	1,316	396	30.1	60	4.5	281	21.3	580	44.0
2010	1,336	271	20.3	144	10.8	355	26.5	567	42.4

Note: High school graduates are people who have completed 4 years of high school or more, for 1967 to 1991. Beginning in 1992, they were people whose highest degree was a high school diploma (including equivalency) or higher.
[1] Starting in 2003 respondents could identify more than one race. Except as noted, the race data in this table from 2003 onward represent those respondents who indicated only one race category.

Table A-15. Population 18 and 19 Years Old, by School Enrollment Status, Sex, Race, and Hispanic Origin, October 1967–2017—*Continued*

(Numbers in thousands; percent; civilian noninstitutionalized population.)

Year, race, and Hispanic origin	Total	Population 18 and 19 years old							
		Still in high school	Percent	Dropped out	Percent	High school graduate only	Percent	In college	Percent
2009	1,346	319	23.7	180	13.4	288	21.4	559	41.5
2008	1,335	311	23.3	145	10.8	400	30.0	479	35.9
2007	1,284	300	23.4	112	8.7	380	29.6	492	38.3
2006	1,230	332	27.0	103	8.3	332	27.0	464	37.7
2005	1,126	256	22.7	110	9.8	309	27.4	451	40.0
2004	1,112	218	19.6	162	14.5	292	26.3	440	39.6
2003[1]	1,052	277	26.3	128	12.2	273	26.0	374	35.6
2002	1,181	251	21.3	180	15.2	320	27.1	430	36.4
2001	1,246	299	24.0	152	12.2	351	28.2	444	35.6
2000	1,251	262	20.9	187	14.9	348	27.8	454	36.3
1999	1,199	259	21.6	190	15.8	320	26.7	430	35.9
1998	1,246	290	23.3	224	18.0	271	21.7	461	37.0
1997	1,133	278	24.5	172	15.2	302	26.7	381	33.6
1996	1,161	268	23.1	175	15.1	373	32.1	345	29.7
1995	1,099	287	26.1	177	16.1	291	26.5	344	31.3
1994	1,017	239	23.5	199	19.6	269	26.5	310	30.5
1993	1,040	290	27.9	133	12.8	306	29.4	311	29.9
1992	1,007	275	27.3	166	16.5	275	27.3	291	28.9
1991	1,041	276	26.5	146	14.0	316	30.4	303	29.1
1990	1,079	246	22.8	178	16.5	306	28.4	349	32.3
1989	1,078	239	22.2	194	18.0	343	31.8	302	28.0
1988	1,057	251	23.7	189	17.9	336	31.8	281	26.6
1987	1,043	213	20.4	166	15.9	323	31.0	341	32.7
1986	1,048	212	20.2	156	14.9	374	35.7	306	29.2
1985	1,072	213	19.9	186	17.4	414	38.6	259	24.2
1984	1,092	218	20.0	186	17.0	423	38.7	265	24.3
1983	1,134	265	23.4	199	17.5	412	36.3	258	22.8
1982	1,146	226	19.7	253	22.1	393	34.3	274	23.9
1981	1,128	238	21.1	218	19.3	366	32.4	306	27.1
1980	1,081	211	19.5	229	21.2	358	33.1	283	26.2
1979	1,072	221	20.6	246	22.9	326	30.4	279	26.0
1978	1,065	221	20.8	258	24.2	316	29.7	270	25.4
1977	1,072	249	23.2	235	21.9	319	29.8	269	25.1
1976	1,055	230	21.8	211	20.0	312	29.6	302	28.6
1975	1,030	225	21.8	262	25.4	283	27.5	260	25.2
1974	1,004	209	20.8	235	23.4	327	32.6	233	23.2
1973	997	182	18.3	252	25.3	369	37.0	194	19.5
1972	958	181	18.9	229	23.9	319	33.3	229	23.9
1971	908	219	24.1	219	24.1	266	29.3	204	22.5
1970	878	161	18.3	274	31.2	252	28.7	191	21.8
1969	837	179	21.4	227	27.1	238	28.4	193	23.1
1968	830	195	23.5	202	24.3	251	30.2	182	21.9
1967	780	175	22.4	203	26.0	261	33.5	141	18.1
Male									
2017	615	155	25.3	45	7.4	181	29.4	234	38.0
2016	612	193	31.5	56	9.2	148	24.2	215	35.1
2015	606	155	25.5	49	8.0	173	28.6	229	37.8
2014	617	197	31.9	56	9.1	189	30.6	175	28.4
2013	646	201	31.1	58	8.9	201	31.1	186	28.9
2012	673	201	29.9	87	12.9	179	26.6	206	30.6
2011	645	226	35.0	39	6.0	138	21.4	242	37.6
2010	654	159	24.4	83	12.6	174	26.5	238	36.4
2009	659	174	26.4	102	15.5	158	24.0	225	34.1
2008	653	173	26.5	53	8.1	222	34.0	205	31.4
2007	628	161	25.7	54	8.6	186	29.6	227	36.2
2006	600	210	35.0	42	7.0	174	29.0	174	28.9
2005	552	178	32.2	60	10.9	121	21.9	193	35.0
2004	519	137	26.4	91	17.6	126	24.3	165	31.7
2003[1]	502	143	28.5	77	15.3	116	23.1	166	33.1
2002	608	155	25.5	123	20.2	151	24.8	179	29.4
2001	624	179	28.7	97	15.5	169	27.1	179	28.7
2000	593	148	25.0	105	17.7	177	29.8	163	27.5
1999	586	144	24.6	97	16.6	136	23.2	209	35.7
1998	613	163	26.6	128	20.9	128	20.9	194	31.6
1997	554	172	31.0	90	16.2	150	27.1	142	25.6

Note: High school graduates are people who have completed 4 years of high school or more, for 1967 to 1991. Beginning in 1992, they were people whose highest degree was a high school diploma (including equivalency) or higher.
[1] Starting in 2003 respondents could identify more than one race. Except as noted, the race data in this table from 2003 onward represent those respondents who indicated only one race category.

Table A-15. Population 18 and 19 Years Old, by School Enrollment Status, Sex, Race, and Hispanic Origin, October 1967–2017—*Continued*

(Numbers in thousands; percent; civilian noninstitutionalized population.)

Year, race, and Hispanic origin	Total	Still in high school	Percent	Dropped out	Percent	High school graduate only	Percent	In college	Percent
						Population 18 and 19 years old			
1996	564	167	29.6	90	16.0	162	28.7	145	25.7
1995	519	162	31.2	94	18.1	118	22.7	145	27.9
1994	497	134	27.0	116	23.3	115	23.1	132	26.6
1993	517	181	35.0	53	10.3	135	26.1	148	28.6
1992	499	180	36.1	82	16.4	114	22.8	123	24.6
1991	504	176	34.9	62	12.3	129	25.6	137	27.2
1990	520	152	29.2	80	15.4	124	23.8	164	31.5
1989	516	137	26.6	90	17.4	163	31.6	126	24.4
1988	510	145	28.4	92	18.0	165	32.4	108	21.2
1987	501	140	27.9	80	16.0	127	25.3	154	30.7
1986	506	149	29.4	74	14.6	165	32.6	118	23.3
1985	518	135	26.1	92	17.8	170	32.8	121	23.4
1984	524	143	27.3	103	19.7	166	31.7	112	21.4
1983	539	158	29.3	106	19.7	182	33.8	93	17.3
1982	549	132	24.0	145	26.4	148	27.0	124	22.6
1981	538	145	27.0	102	19.0	158	29.4	133	24.7
1980	503	118	23.5	114	22.7	173	34.4	98	19.5
1979	497	128	25.8	122	24.5	137	27.6	110	22.1
1978	493	135	27.4	127	25.8	117	23.7	114	23.1
1977	496	161	32.5	118	23.8	127	25.6	90	18.1
1976	499	153	30.7	96	19.2	129	25.9	121	24.2
1975	476	127	26.7	132	27.7	106	22.3	111	23.3
1974	474	116	24.5	128	27.0	128	27.0	102	21.5
1973	467	106	22.7	130	27.8	135	28.9	96	20.6
1972	445	110	24.7	121	27.2	112	25.2	102	22.9
1971	423	120	28.4	110	26.0	99	23.4	94	22.2
1970	414	98	23.7	151	36.5	92	22.2	73	17.6
1969	394	109	27.7	124	31.5	75	19.0	86	21.8
1968	390	124	31.8	93	23.8	90	23.1	83	21.3
1967	356	95	26.7	109	30.6	74	20.8	78	21.9
Female									
2017	631	155	24.6	19	3.1	165	26.2	291	46.1
2016	631	112	17.8	31	4.9	173	27.4	316	50.0
2015	627	131	20.9	36	5.7	180	28.8	280	44.6
2014	635	110	17.4	38	6.0	152	24.0	334	52.7
2013	659	186	28.2	35	5.2	174	26.4	265	40.1
2012	683	198	28.5	23	3.4	136	20.0	325	47.6
2011	671	170	25.4	21	3.1	143	21.3	337	50.3
2010	682	111	16.3	61	9.0	181	26.5	329	48.2
2009	687	145	21.1	78	11.3	130	19.0	334	48.6
2008	681	138	20.3	92	13.5	178	26.1	274	40.2
2007	655	139	21.2	58	8.8	194	29.6	265	40.4
2006	631	122	19.3	60	9.6	158	25.0	291	46.1
2005	574	78	13.6	49	8.6	189	32.9	258	44.9
2004	593	81	13.7	70	11.9	167	28.2	275	46.5
2003[1]	550	133	24.2	51	9.3	157	28.5	209	38.0
2002	574	97	16.9	57	9.9	169	29.4	251	43.7
2001	623	122	19.6	54	8.7	182	29.2	265	42.5
2000	658	113	17.2	82	12.5	172	26.1	291	44.2
1999	613	114	18.6	94	15.3	184	30.0	221	36.1
1998	633	127	20.1	96	15.2	143	22.6	267	42.2
1997	579	107	18.5	82	14.2	152	26.3	238	41.1
1996	597	102	17.1	85	14.2	211	35.3	199	33.3
1995	581	126	21.7	83	14.3	173	29.8	199	34.3
1994	520	105	20.2	83	16.0	154	29.6	178	34.2
1993	523	108	20.7	80	15.3	172	32.9	163	31.2
1992	508	95	18.7	84	16.5	161	31.7	168	33.1
1991	537	99	18.4	85	15.8	187	34.8	166	30.9
1990	559	95	17.0	98	17.5	181	32.4	185	33.1
1989	562	102	18.1	104	18.5	180	32.0	176	31.3
1988	547	105	19.2	97	17.7	172	31.4	173	31.6
1987	542	75	13.8	85	15.7	196	36.2	186	34.3
1986	542	62	11.4	83	15.3	209	38.6	188	34.7
1985	554	78	14.1	94	17.0	244	44.0	138	24.9
1984	568	76	13.4	82	14.4	257	45.2	153	26.9

Note: High school graduates are people who have completed 4 years of high school or more, for 1967 to 1991. Beginning in 1992, they were people whose highest degree was a high school diploma (including equivalency) or higher.
[1] Starting in 2003 respondents could identify more than one race. Except as noted, the race data in this table from 2003 onward represent those respondents who indicated only one race category.

Table A-15. Population 18 and 19 Years Old, by School Enrollment Status, Sex, Race, and Hispanic Origin, October 1967–2017—*Continued*

(Numbers in thousands; percent; civilian noninstitutionalized population.)

| Year, race, and Hispanic origin | Total | Population 18 and 19 years old | | | | | | | |
		Still in high school	Percent	Dropped out	Percent	High school graduate only	Percent	In college	Percent
1983	595	108	18.2	93	15.6	230	38.7	164	27.6
1982	597	95	15.9	108	18.1	244	40.9	150	25.1
1981	590	93	15.8	116	19.7	209	35.4	172	29.2
1980	578	93	16.1	115	19.9	185	32.0	185	32.0
1979	576	93	16.1	125	21.7	189	32.8	169	29.3
1978	572	88	15.4	130	22.7	199	34.8	155	27.1
1977	576	88	15.3	117	20.3	192	33.3	179	31.1
1976	556	77	13.8	115	20.7	183	32.9	181	32.6
1975	553	97	17.5	130	23.5	176	31.8	150	27.1
1974	530	92	17.4	107	20.2	200	37.7	131	24.7
1973	530	77	14.5	122	23.0	234	44.2	97	18.3
1972	513	71	13.8	108	21.1	207	40.4	127	24.8
1971	485	100	20.6	109	22.5	167	34.4	109	22.5
1970	464	62	13.4	124	26.7	160	34.5	118	25.4
1969	443	70	15.8	102	23.0	163	36.8	108	24.4
1968	439	69	15.7	109	24.8	161	36.7	100	22.8
1967	424	81	19.1	93	21.9	187	44.1	63	14.9
ASIAN ALONE[2]									
Both Sexes									
2017	376	49	13.1	11	3.0	55	14.6	260	69.3
2016	405	57	14.1	16	4.1	76	18.9	255	63.0
2015	358	65	18.1	17	4.7	41	11.5	235	65.6
2014	352	40	11.3	*	*	42	11.9	270	76.8
2013	442	68	15.5	4	0.9	68	15.3	302	68.3
2012	388	61	15.7	23	5.8	51	13.1	253	65.3
2011	337	44	13.2	13	3.7	40	11.8	240	71.3
2010	331	38	11.5	12	3.7	46	14.0	234	70.8
2009	327	64	19.7	2	0.7	17	5.2	243	74.4
2008	259	49	19.0	7	2.7	31	12.0	172	66.4
2007	296	55	18.4	12	4.2	27	9.3	201	68.1
2006	297	43	14.4	9	3.0	41	14.0	204	68.6
2005	251	34	13.4	4	1.5	25	10.0	188	74.9
2004	257	31	11.9	10	3.8	34	13.2	182	70.7
2003[1]	286	41	14.3	3	1.0	33	11.5	209	73.1
2002	353	42	11.9	14	4.0	61	17.3	236	66.9
2001	353	50	14.2	18	5.1	38	10.8	247	70.0
2000	326	45	13.8	17	5.2	52	16.0	212	65.0
1999	339	43	12.7	22	6.5	51	15.0	223	65.8
Male									
2017	194	30	15.5	3	1.5	39	20.2	122	62.7
2016	215	27	12.6	10	4.4	44	20.5	135	62.5
2015	178	31	17.4	14	8.0	20	11.5	112	63.1
2014	177	19	11.0	*	*	22	12.5	136	76.5
2013	230	37	16.2	1	0.3	38	16.7	154	66.9
2012	200	37	18.7	14	7.1	20	9.7	129	64.5
2011	178	28	15.4	*	*	19	10.8	131	73.7
2010	170	16	9.6	8	5.0	30	17.4	116	68.1
2009	178	31	17.6	*	*	13	7.4	134	75.0
2008	128	39	30.2	6	5.1	8	5.9	75	58.9
2007	150	33	22.1	2	1.1	11	7.1	104	69.7
2006	167	20	12.2	8	4.7	26	15.7	113	67.5
2005	131	21	16.3	3	2.0	17	13.0	90	68.9
2004	133	22	16.7	1	0.7	18	13.5	92	69.3
2003[1]	129	14	10.9	3	2.3	9	7.0	103	79.8
2002	179	22	12.3	10	5.6	26	14.5	121	67.6
2001	168	27	16.1	14	8.3	14	8.3	113	67.3
2000	162	14	8.6	14	8.6	26	16.0	108	66.7
1999	156	23	14.7	17	10.9	23	14.7	93	59.6
Female									
2017	182	19	10.5	8	4.6	16	8.7	138	76.3
2016	189	30	15.7	7	3.6	32	17.0	120	63.6

Note: High school graduates are people who have completed 4 years of high school or more, for 1967 to 1991. Beginning in 1992, they were people whose highest degree was a high school diploma (including equivalency) or higher.
[1] Starting in 2003 respondents could identify more than one race. Except as noted, the race data in this table from 2003 onward represent those respondents who indicated only one race category.
[2] The data shown prior to 2003 consists of those identifying themselves as "Asian or Pacific Islanders."

Table A-15. Population 18 and 19 Years Old, by School Enrollment Status, Sex, Race, and Hispanic Origin, October 1967–2017—Continued

(Numbers in thousands; percent; civilian noninstitutionalized population.)

Year, race, and Hispanic origin	Total	Population 18 and 19 years old							
		Still in high school	Percent	Dropped out	Percent	High school graduate only	Percent	In college	Percent
2015	180	34	18.7	3	1.5	21	11.6	123	68.2
2014	175	20	11.6	*	*	20	11.3	134	77.0
2013	212	31	14.8	3	1.6	29	13.8	148	69.8
2012	188	24	12.6	8	4.5	32	16.8	124	66.2
2011	158	17	10.7	13	7.9	20	12.8	109	68.6
2010	161	22	13.6	4	2.4	17	10.4	118	73.6
2009	149	33	22.2	2	1.6	4	2.7	109	73.6
2008	132	11	8.0	*	0.4	24	17.9	97	73.7
2007	146	21	14.6	11	7.5	17	11.5	97	66.4
2006	130	23	17.3	1	0.9	15	11.8	91	70.0
2005	120	12	10.3	1	0.9	9	7.5	98	81.4
2004	124	8	6.8	9	7.1	18	14.5	89	72.2
2003[1]	157	26	16.6	*	*	24	15.3	107	68.2
2002	173	20	11.6	3	1.7	35	20.2	115	66.5
2001	185	23	12.4	4	2.2	24	13.0	134	72.4
2000	164	30	18.3	4	2.4	26	15.9	104	63.4
1999	183	20	10.9	5	2.7	28	15.3	130	71.0

HISPANIC (OF ANY RACE)

Both Sexes

Year, race, and Hispanic origin	Total	Still in high school	Percent	Dropped out	Percent	High school graduate only	Percent	In college	Percent
2017	1,965	390	19.9	181	9.2	463	23.6	931	47.4
2016	1,825	364	19.9	146	8.0	430	23.6	884	48.5
2015	1,760	372	21.1	181	10.3	432	24.5	776	44.1
2014	1,908	377	19.8	183	9.6	491	25.7	857	44.9
2013	1,889	393	20.8	184	9.7	585	31.0	727	38.5
2012	1,871	449	23.8	222	11.9	374	20.0	827	44.2
2011	1,743	371	21.3	166	9.5	441	25.3	765	43.9
2010	1,768	389	22.0	179	10.1	418	23.6	783	44.3
2009	1,680	409	24.3	261	15.5	460	27.4	550	32.7
2008	1,539	320	20.8	296	19.3	395	25.7	528	34.3
2007	1,523	311	20.4	254	16.7	399	26.2	559	36.7
2006	1,406	307	21.8	253	18.0	402	28.6	444	31.6
2005	1,253	272	21.7	227	18.1	348	27.8	406	32.4
2004	1,270	244	19.2	296	23.3	346	27.2	384	30.2
2003	1,214	229	18.9	291	24.0	315	25.9	379	31.2
2002	1,309	303	23.1	310	23.7	336	25.7	360	27.5
2001	1,391	246	17.7	399	28.7	359	25.8	387	27.8
2000	1,248	268	21.5	311	24.9	320	25.6	349	28.0
1999	1,220	246	20.2	337	27.6	340	27.9	297	24.3
1998	1,209	199	16.5	402	33.3	320	26.5	288	23.8
1997	1,087	221	20.3	274	25.2	276	25.4	316	29.1
1996	1,000	229	22.9	295	29.5	236	23.6	240	24.0
1995	1,012	203	20.1	312	30.8	233	23.0	264	26.1
1994	925	250	27.0	237	25.6	213	23.0	225	24.3
1993	710	159	22.4	201	28.3	155	21.8	195	27.5
1992	778	188	24.2	197	25.3	163	21.0	230	29.6
1991	823	206	25.0	269	32.7	160	19.4	188	22.8
1990	746	181	24.3	255	34.2	162	21.7	148	19.8
1989	733	150	20.5	205	28.0	201	27.4	177	24.1
1988	734	121	16.5	229	31.2	181	24.7	203	27.7
1987	699	121	17.3	195	27.9	231	33.0	152	21.7
1986	614	114	18.6	164	26.7	171	27.9	165	26.9
1985	570	111	19.5	175	30.7	157	27.5	127	22.3
1984	561	88	15.7	146	26.0	191	34.0	136	24.2
1983	573	119	20.8	166	29.0	154	26.9	134	23.4
1982	600	92	15.3	198	33.0	167	27.8	143	23.8
1981	606	100	16.5	220	36.3	157	25.9	129	21.3
1980	597	89	14.9	233	39.0	138	23.1	137	22.9
1979	507	78	15.4	157	31.0	148	29.2	124	24.5
1978	478	61	12.8	183	38.3	125	26.2	109	22.8
1977	515	86	16.7	168	32.6	138	26.8	123	23.9
1976	534	98	18.4	164	30.7	129	24.2	143	26.8
1975	489	97	19.8	147	30.1	127	26.0	118	24.1
1974	467	99	21.2	139	29.8	117	25.1	112	24.0
1973	387	70	18.1	142	36.7	93	24.0	82	21.2
1972	381	88	23.1	117	30.7	106	27.8	70	18.4

* = Quantity zero or rounds to zero.
Note: High school graduates are people who have completed 4 years of high school or more, for 1967 to 1991. Beginning in 1992, they were people whose highest degree was a high school diploma (including equivalency) or higher.
[1] Starting in 2003 respondents could identify more than one race. Except as noted, the race data in this table from 2003 onward represent those respondents who indicated only one race category.

Table A-15. Population 18 and 19 Years Old, by School Enrollment Status, Sex, Race, and Hispanic Origin, October 1967–2017—*Continued*

(Numbers in thousands; percent; civilian noninstitutionalized population.)

Year, race, and Hispanic origin	Total	Population 18 and 19 years old							
		Still in high school	Percent	Dropped out	Percent	High school graduate only	Percent	In college	Percent
Male									
2017	982	209	21.3	113	11.5	247	25.1	413	42.0
2016	894	210	23.4	90	10.0	212	23.7	383	42.8
2015	849	194	22.8	108	12.8	232	27.3	315	37.1
2014	958	206	21.5	105	10.9	263	27.4	385	40.2
2013	953	233	24.4	98	10.3	326	34.2	295	31.0
2012	950	252	26.5	143	15.1	183	19.2	372	39.2
2011	952	229	24.1	102	10.7	269	28.3	351	36.9
2010	896	201	22.4	97	10.9	217	24.2	381	42.5
2009	853	200	23.4	129	15.2	282	33.0	242	28.4
2008	779	190	24.4	141	18.1	212	27.2	236	30.3
2007	780	185	23.7	145	18.5	205	26.3	246	31.5
2006	708	152	21.4	150	21.2	193	27.3	213	30.1
2005	663	166	25.1	144	21.7	180	27.1	173	26.2
2004	668	117	17.5	214	32.0	166	24.9	171	25.6
2003	635	142	22.4	161	25.4	179	28.2	153	24.1
2002	716	191	26.7	200	27.9	169	23.6	156	21.8
2001	701	131	18.7	254	36.2	167	23.8	149	21.3
2000	656	154	23.5	183	27.9	159	24.2	160	24.4
1999	642	148	23.1	180	28.0	171	26.6	143	22.3
1998	598	104	17.4	234	39.1	163	27.3	97	16.2
1997	579	130	22.5	162	28.0	154	26.6	133	23.0
1996	506	139	27.5	154	30.4	115	22.7	98	19.4
1995	535	132	24.7	145	27.1	137	25.6	121	22.6
1994	454	157	34.6	118	26.0	90	19.8	89	19.6
1993	325	86	26.5	105	32.3	65	20.0	69	21.2
1992	385	110	28.6	99	25.7	83	21.6	93	24.2
1991	416	107	25.7	161	38.7	80	19.2	68	16.3
1990	358	76	21.2	141	39.4	71	19.8	70	19.6
1989	371	89	24.0	96	25.9	111	29.9	75	20.2
1988	364	88	24.2	128	35.2	73	20.1	75	20.6
1987	333	66	19.8	105	31.5	86	25.8	76	22.8
1986	326	58	17.8	95	29.1	86	26.4	87	26.7
1985	275	62	22.5	116	42.2	53	19.3	44	16.0
1984	249	55	22.1	65	26.1	87	34.9	42	16.9
1983	266	66	24.8	87	32.7	72	27.1	41	15.4
1982	304	69	22.7	106	34.9	77	25.3	52	17.1
1981	288	47	16.3	127	44.1	57	19.8	57	19.8
1980	310	46	14.8	134	43.2	62	20.0	68	21.9
1979	256	42	16.4	89	34.8	58	22.7	67	26.2
1978	221	35	15.8	81	36.7	52	23.5	53	24.0
1977	238	49	20.6	80	33.6	55	23.1	54	22.7
1976	258	51	19.8	82	31.8	56	21.7	69	26.7
1975	229	66	28.8	60	26.2	50	21.8	53	23.1
1974	222	49	22.1	78	35.1	40	18.0	55	24.8
1973	190	48	25.3	62	32.6	41	21.6	39	20.5
1972	190	49	25.8	67	35.3	46	24.2	28	14.7
Female									
2017	983	181	18.4	67	6.9	216	22.0	518	52.7
2016	930	154	16.6	56	6.1	218	23.5	501	53.9
2015	912	179	19.6	72	7.9	200	21.9	461	50.5
2014	950	172	18.1	78	8.2	228	24.0	472	49.7
2013	936	160	17.1	86	9.1	259	27.6	432	46.2
2012	921	197	21.0	79	8.6	191	20.7	454	49.3
2011	791	142	17.9	64	8.1	172	21.7	414	52.4
2010	872	188	21.5	82	9.4	201	23.0	402	46.1
2009	827	209	25.3	132	15.9	179	21.6	308	37.2
2008	760	130	17.1	156	20.5	183	24.0	292	38.4
2007	743	126	17.0	109	14.7	193	26.1	313	42.2
2006	698	156	22.3	102	14.7	209	30.0	231	33.1
2005	591	105	17.8	83	14.0	171	28.9	232	39.3
2004	602	127	21.1	82	13.6	180	29.9	213	35.4
2003	579	87	15.0	130	22.5	136	23.5	226	39.0
2002	593	112	18.9	110	18.5	167	28.2	204	34.4
2001	691	116	16.8	145	21.0	192	27.8	238	34.4
2000	591	114	19.3	128	21.7	161	27.2	188	31.8
1999	577	99	17.2	157	27.2	168	29.1	153	26.5

Note: High school graduates are people who have completed 4 years of high school or more, for 1967 to 1991. Beginning in 1992, they were people whose highest degree was a high school diploma (including equivalency) or higher.

Table A-15. Population 18 and 19 Years Old, by School Enrollment Status, Sex, Race, and Hispanic Origin, October 1967–2017—*Continued*

(Numbers in thousands; percent; civilian noninstitutionalized population.)

Year, race, and Hispanic origin	Total	Still in high school	Percent	Dropped out	Percent	High school graduate only	Percent	In college	Percent
		Population 18 and 19 years old							
1998	611	95	15.5	169	27.7	156	25.5	191	31.3
1997	508	91	17.9	112	22.0	122	24.0	183	36.0
1996	494	91	18.4	140	28.3	121	24.5	142	28.7
1995	478	71	14.9	167	34.9	97	20.3	143	29.9
1994	471	93	19.7	119	25.3	123	26.1	136	28.9
1993	385	74	19.2	96	24.9	89	23.1	126	32.7
1992	393	78	19.8	98	24.9	80	20.4	137	34.9
1991	407	98	24.1	109	26.8	80	19.7	120	29.5
1990	388	105	27.1	114	29.4	91	23.5	78	20.1
1989	362	60	16.6	108	29.8	91	25.1	103	28.5
1988	370	32	8.6	101	27.3	108	29.2	129	34.9
1987	367	58	15.8	89	24.3	144	39.2	76	20.7
1986	288	54	18.8	69	24.0	86	29.9	79	27.4
1985	296	51	17.2	59	19.9	104	35.1	82	27.7
1984	311	33	10.6	81	26.0	103	33.1	94	30.2
1983	307	53	17.3	79	25.7	82	26.7	93	30.3
1982	296	23	7.8	92	31.1	90	30.4	91	30.7
1981	318	53	16.7	93	29.2	100	31.4	72	22.6
1980	287	44	15.3	99	34.5	76	26.5	68	23.7
1979	251	35	13.9	68	27.1	90	35.9	58	23.1
1978	257	26	10.1	102	39.7	73	28.4	56	21.8
1977	277	37	13.4	88	31.8	82	29.6	70	25.3
1976	276	49	17.8	81	29.3	72	26.1	74	26.8
1975	261	32	12.3	87	33.3	77	29.5	65	24.9
1974	245	50	20.4	62	25.3	77	31.4	56	22.9
1973	197	21	10.7	80	40.6	52	26.4	44	22.3
1972	191	37	19.4	50	26.2	61	31.9	43	22.5
WHITE ALONE OR IN COMBINATION									
Both Sexes									
2017	6,408	1,241	19.4	461	7.2	1,585	24.7	3,121	48.7
2016	6,392	1,139	17.8	383	6.0	1,554	24.3	3,316	51.9
2015	6,376	1,204	18.9	489	7.7	1,519	23.8	3,163	49.6
2014	6,450	1,238	19.2	467	7.2	1,592	24.7	3,154	48.9
2013	6,502	1,235	19.0	414	6.4	1,728	26.6	3,124	48.0
2012	6,539	1,331	20.0	437	6.7	1,627	24.9	3,144	48.1
2011	6,686	1,309	19.6	455	6.8	1,540	23.0	3,381	50.6
2010	6,679	1,195	17.9	450	6.7	1,556	23.3	3,478	52.1
2009	6,780	1,227	18.1	538	7.9	1,601	23.6	3,414	50.3
2008	6,762	1,093	16.2	581	8.6	1,647	24.4	3,440	50.9
2007	6,595	1,108	16.8	525	8.0	1,644	24.9	3,318	50.3
2006	6,466	1,160	17.9	615	9.5	1,648	25.5	3,043	47.1
2005	6,078	1,064	17.5	537	8.8	1,442	23.7	3,035	49.9
2004	6,191	988	16.0	643	10.4	1,548	25.0	3,012	48.7
2003	6,093	994	16.3	675	11.1	1,519	24.9	2,905	47.7
Male									
2017	3,233	747	23.1	276	8.5	839	26.0	1,370	42.4
2016	3,233	664	20.5	209	6.5	813	25.1	1,547	47.8
2015	3,232	639	19.8	289	8.9	832	25.7	1,472	45.5
2014	3,292	694	21.1	252	7.7	913	27.7	1,433	43.5
2013	3,327	743	22.3	209	6.3	943	28.3	1,433	43.1
2012	3,364	779	22.9	254	7.5	902	26.8	1,429	42.5
2011	3,457	776	22.4	247	7.1	881	25.5	1,554	44.9
2010	3,396	674	19.8	251	7.4	852	25.1	1,620	47.7
2009	3,422	665	19.4	297	8.7	925	27.0	1,535	44.9
2008	3,435	605	17.6	305	8.9	917	26.7	1,607	46.8
2007	3,350	684	20.4	284	8.5	842	25.1	1,540	46.0
2006	3,278	657	20.0	357	10.9	864	26.4	1,399	42.7
2005	3,149	692	22.0	321	10.2	358	11.4	1,778	56.5
2004	3,129	538	17.2	415	13.3	845	27.0	1,331	42.5
2003	3,078	604	19.6	390	12.7	801	26.0	1,283	41.7
Female									
2017	3,174	494	15.6	185	5.8	745	23.5	1,751	55.1
2016	3,159	475	15.0	174	5.5	741	23.5	1,770	56.0

Note: High school graduates are people who have completed 4 years of high school or more, for 1967 to 1991. Beginning in 1992, they were people whose highest degree was a high school diploma (including equivalency) or higher.

Table A-15. Population 18 and 19 Years Old, by School Enrollment Status, Sex, Race, and Hispanic Origin, October 1967–2017—*Continued*

(Numbers in thousands; percent; civilian noninstitutionalized population.)

Year, race, and Hispanic origin	Total	Population 18 and 19 years old							
		Still in high school	Percent	Dropped out	Percent	High school graduate only	Percent	In college	Percent
2015...............................	3,144	565	18.0	200	6.4	687	21.9	1,691	53.8
2014...............................	3,159	544	17.2	215	6.8	679	21.5	1,720	54.5
2013...............................	3,174	492	15.5	206	6.5	786	24.7	1,691	53.3
2012...............................	3,175	552	16.9	183	5.8	725	22.8	1,715	54.0
2011...............................	3,228	533	16.5	209	6.5	659	20.4	1,828	56.6
2010...............................	3,282	521	15.9	200	6.1	704	21.4	1,858	56.6
2009...............................	3,358	562	16.7	242	7.2	676	20.1	1,879	55.9
2008...............................	3,328	488	14.7	277	8.3	730	21.9	1,833	55.1
2007...............................	3,245	424	13.1	241	7.4	801	24.7	1,779	54.8
2006...............................	3,188	503	15.8	258	8.1	784	24.6	1,643	51.5
2005...............................	2,929	372	12.7	216	7.4	669	22.8	1,672	57.1
2004...............................	3,062	450	14.7	228	7.4	702	22.9	1,682	54.9
2003...............................	3,015	390	12.9	284	9.4	719	23.8	1,622	53.8
BLACK ALONE OR IN COMBINATION									
Both Sexes									
2017...............................	1,414	349	24.7	78	5.5	391	27.6	597	42.2
2016...............................	1,399	338	24.2	99	7.1	360	25.7	602	43.1
2015...............................	1,370	326	23.8	90	6.5	394	28.8	560	40.8
2014...............................	1,384	345	24.9	106	7.7	380	27.5	553	39.9
2013...............................	1,420	399	28.1	101	7.1	411	29.0	509	35.9
2012...............................	1,461	426	28.9	117	8.0	340	23.3	579	39.6
2011...............................	1,381	409	29.6	65	4.7	292	21.2	615	44.5
2010...............................	1,439	287	20.0	158	11.0	371	25.8	622	43.2
2009...............................	1,450	335	23.1	191	13.1	321	22.1	604	41.7
2008...............................	1,431	339	23.7	155	10.8	422	29.5	515	36.0
2007...............................	1,347	306	22.7	116	8.6	395	29.3	530	39.3
2006...............................	1,287	343	26.6	111	8.6	341	26.5	492	38.2
2005...............................	1,195	266	22.3	112	9.4	336	28.1	481	40.2
2004...............................	1,163	229	19.7	163	14.0	305	26.2	466	40.1
2003...............................	1,129	288	25.5	131	11.6	310	27.5	400	35.4
Male									
2017...............................	701	172	24.5	53	7.5	208	29.7	269	38.3
2016...............................	686	208	30.4	64	9.3	163	23.8	250	36.5
2015...............................	661	167	25.3	49	7.4	186	28.1	259	39.2
2014...............................	679	222	32.8	66	9.7	198	29.2	192	28.4
2013...............................	700	206	29.4	62	8.9	222	31.7	210	30.0
2012...............................	744	213	28.6	94	12.6	194	26.0	244	32.7
2011...............................	681	238	35.0	44	6.5	149	21.9	250	36.6
2010...............................	700	170	24.3	86	12.3	180	25.7	264	37.7
2009...............................	708	182	25.8	110	15.5	171	24.1	245	34.6
2008...............................	706	191	27.0	58	8.3	238	33.7	219	31.1
2007...............................	657	164	25.0	56	8.5	197	30.0	240	36.5
2006...............................	623	213	34.3	45	7.3	178	28.6	186	29.8
2005...............................	586	187	31.8	62	10.7	136	23.2	201	34.3
2004...............................	549	142	25.9	93	17.0	139	25.3	175	31.9
2003...............................	525	146	27.8	81	15.4	123	23.4	175	33.3
Female									
2017...............................	713	177	24.9	25	3.5	182	25.6	328	46.0
2016...............................	713	130	18.2	35	4.9	197	27.6	352	49.3
2015...............................	709	159	22.4	41	5.8	209	29.5	300	42.3
2014...............................	705	122	17.3	41	5.7	182	25.8	360	51.1
2013...............................	720	193	26.8	38	5.3	189	26.3	299	41.6
2012...............................	717	213	29.1	23	3.2	146	20.4	335	46.7
2011...............................	699	170	24.3	21	3.0	143	20.5	365	52.2
2010...............................	739	117	15.9	72	9.8	192	25.9	358	48.4
2009...............................	742	152	20.5	81	11.3	150	20.2	359	48.4
2008...............................	724	148	20.5	96	13.3	184	25.4	296	40.8
2007...............................	690	142	20.6	61	8.8	198	28.6	290	42.0
2006...............................	665	130	19.5	66	9.9	163	24.5	307	46.1
2005...............................	609	80	13.1	49	8.1	200	32.8	280	45.9
2004...............................	615	86	14.0	70	11.4	169	27.5	290	47.2
2003...............................	604	142	23.5	51	8.4	186	30.8	225	37.3

Note: High school graduates are people who have completed 4 years of high school or more, for 1967 to 1991. Beginning in 1992, they were people whose highest degree was a high school diploma (including equivalency) or higher.

Table A-15. Population 18 and 19 Years Old, by School Enrollment Status, Sex, Race, and Hispanic Origin, October 1967–2017—*Continued*

(Numbers in thousands; percent; civilian noninstitutionalized population.)

Year, race, and Hispanic origin	Total	Population 18 and 19 years old								
		Still in high school	Percent	Dropped out	Percent	High school graduate only	Percent	In college	Percent
ASIAN ALONE OR IN COMBINATION									
Both Sexes									
2017	433	63	14.5	11	2.6	62	14.3	297	68.7
2016	487	69	14.2	17	3.6	88	18.1	313	64.2
2015	430	71	16.5	24	5.6	48	11.1	287	66.8
2014	407	53	13.0	*	*	58	14.1	296	72.8
2013	529	89	16.7	9	1.7	81	15.4	350	66.2
2012	436	71	16.4	23	5.2	67	15.4	274	63.0
2011	399	55	13.6	13	3.1	66	16.4	267	66.8
2010	369	39	10.5	13	3.6	53	14.4	264	71.5
2009	384	74	19.3	3	0.9	35	9.0	271	70.8
2008	309	52	16.8	7	2.3	37	11.8	214	69.1
2007	336	58	17.2	12	3.7	34	10.0	232	69.1
2006	318	47	14.8	9	2.8	47	14.9	215	67.5
2005	286	42	14.7	4	1.3	36	12.6	204	71.5
2004	299	36	12.0	14	4.5	46	15.4	203	67.9
2003	320	43	13.4	3	1.1	38	11.9	236	73.8
Male									
2017	220	43	19.4	3	1.3	41	18.7	133	60.6
2016	244	27	11.2	10	3.9	48	19.8	159	65.2
2015	213	32	15.1	18	8.3	22	10.3	141	66.3
2014	206	29	14.3	*	*	30	14.8	146	71.0
2013	265	48	18.0	1	0.2	46	17.3	171	64.5
2012	225	42	18.6	14	6.3	26	11.4	143	63.7
2011	214	33	15.5	*	*	36	16.7	145	67.9
2010	196	17	8.6	9	4.6	34	17.2	136	69.5
2009	188	34	18.3	1	0.3	16	8.3	138	73.2
2008	150	41	27.6	6	4.3	9	6.0	93	62.1
2007	161	33	20.7	2	1.0	14	8.4	113	69.9
2006	179	22	12.4	8	4.3	31	17.5	118	65.8
2005	152	30	19.5	3	1.7	22	14.5	97	64.1
2004	149	27	18.1	5	3.2	20	13.4	97	65.1
2003	144	17	11.8	3	2.3	12	8.3	112	77.8
Female									
2017	213	20	9.4	8	3.9	21	9.7	164	77.1
2016	243	42	17.2	8	3.2	40	16.3	153	63.3
2015	217	39	18.0	6	2.9	26	11.9	146	67.3
2014	201	24	11.8	*	*	27	13.5	150	74.7
2013	263	41	15.5	8	3.1	35	13.4	179	68.0
2012	210	30	14.1	8	4.0	41	19.7	131	62.2
2011	186	21	11.6	13	6.8	30	16.1	122	65.6
2010	174	22	12.6	4	2.5	20	11.3	128	73.7
2009	196	40	20.4	3	1.5	19	9.7	134	68.4
2008	159	11	6.6	*	0.3	28	17.3	121	75.8
2007	174	24	13.9	11	6.3	20	11.5	119	68.3
2006	139	25	18.0	1	0.8	16	11.4	97	69.7
2005	134	12	9.2	1	0.9	14	10.4	107	80.0
2004	150	8	5.3	9	5.9	27	18.0	106	70.7
2003	176	25	14.2	*	*	27	15.3	124	70.5

* = Quantity zero or rounds to zero.
Note: High school graduates are people who have completed 4 years of high school or more, for 1967 to 1991. Beginning in 1992, they were people whose highest degree was a high school diploma (including equivalency) or higher.

Table A-16. Age Distribution of College Students 14 Years Old and Over, by Sex, October 1947–2017

(Numbers in thousands; civilian noninstitutionalized population.)

Year, sex, race, and Hispanic origin	All students								Male							
	Total	14 to 17 years	18 and 19 years	20 and 21 years	22 to 24 years	25 to 29 years	30 to 34 years	35 years and over	Total	14 to 17 years	18 and 19 years	20 and 21 years	22 to 24 years	25 to 29 years	30 to 34 years	35 years and over
ALL RACES																
2017	18,398	236	3,943	4,367	3,627	2,674	1,207	2,346	8,112	85	1,746	2,025	1,688	1,188	526	853
2016	19,196	241	4,171	4,417	3,733	2,882	1,336	2,417	8,644	80	1,944	2,085	1,771	1,264	574	927
2015	19,101	222	3,978	4,505	3,669	2,805	1,370	2,551	8,484	108	1,838	2,113	1,743	1,238	565	878
2014	19,175	234	4,036	4,218	3,878	2,722	1,267	2,820	8,629	126	1,779	2,090	1,808	1,283	509	1,036
2013	19,467	308	3,951	4,326	3,925	2,715	1,351	2,891	8,536	148	1,809	2,001	1,819	1,253	522	983
2012	19,930	269	4,015	4,562	3,879	2,817	1,516	2,871	8,602	130	1,803	2,049	1,878	1,194	576	972
2011	20,397	203	4,242	4,459	3,869	3,066	1,551	3,007	9,132	108	1,949	2,127	1,877	1,343	643	1,084
2010	20,275	229	4,364	4,348	3,501	2,992	1,632	3,210	9,007	94	2,009	2,108	1,580	1,396	659	1,160
2009	19,764	206	4,289	4,034	3,749	2,769	1,524	3,193	8,642	89	1,928	1,943	1,770	1,194	649	1,069
2008	18,632	241	3,920	3,420	2,657	1,356	2,911		8,311	133	1,909	1,908	1,566	1,229	577	989
2007	17,956	186	4,075	3,794	3,292	2,496	1,342	2,772	7,826	76	1,903	1,729	1,524	1,029	596	968
2006	17,232	212	3,746	3,675	3,166	2,312	1,346	2,776	7,506	79	1,703	1,682	1,489	1,033	537	982
2005	17,472	181	3,727	3,945	3,162	2,291	1,309	2,857	7,539	62	1,675	1,878	1,420	923	562	1,019
2004	17,383	198	3,685	3,777	3,149	2,403	1,287	2,884	7,575	75	1,610	1,811	1,444	1,068	533	1,033
2003[1]	16,638	150	3,512	3,533	3,320	2,164	1,330	2,630	7,318	61	1,568	1,551	1,578	982	607	970
2002	16,497	195	3,581	3,525	2,927	2,093	1,308	2,867	7,240	80	1,635	1,640	1,354	918	542	1,071
2001	15,873	138	3,478	3,421	2,731	2,084	1,337	2,685	6,875	54	1,570	1,579	1,287	917	559	908
2000	15,314	149	3,599	3,169	2,683	1,962	1,244	2,507	6,682	61	1,570	1,472	1,300	844	517	918
1999	15,203	151	3,520	3,120	2,620	1,940	1,155	2,697	6,956	78	1,648	1,525	1,224	911	547	1,023
1998	15,546	123	3,670	3,092	2,561	2,148	1,266	2,685	6,905	48	1,667	1,517	1,219	979	521	953
1997	15,436	171	3,362	3,143	2,699	2,154	1,116	2,791	6,843	59	1,561	1,521	1,292	1,052	457	899
1996	15,226	237	3,309	2,907	2,551	2,215	1,228	2,778	6,820	97	1,489	1,379	1,319	1,038	485	1,013
1995	14,715	158	3,101	2,940	2,498	2,143	1,206	2,669	6,703	68	1,431	1,423	1,235	1,008	553	985
1994[2]	15,022	150	3,051	3,028	2,650	2,026	1,393	2,725	6,764	65	1,416	1,414	1,322	972	617	958
1993r	14,394	130	3,070	2,892	2,668	1,914	1,226	2,493	6,599	55	1,407	1,405	1,425	892	534	880
1993	13,898	123	2,926	2,734	2,533	1,867	1,227	2,488	6,324	52	1,337	1,312	1,345	872	534	873
1992	14,035	205	2,892	2,938	2,512	1,829	1,296	2,364	6,192	97	1,325	1,344	1,243	845	547	789
1991	14,057	132	2,929	2,939	2,304	1,983	1,302	2,468	6,439	49	1,326	1,390	1,238	1,018	587	832
1990	13,621	178	3,019	2,767	2,178	1,927	1,235	2,319	6,192	86	1,443	1,364	1,115	910	502	772
1989	13,180	183	3,066	2,570	2,168	1,889	1,192	2,112	5,950	73	1,422	1,228	1,067	926	517	716
1988	13,116	182	3,046	2,681	2,064	1,915	1,228	2,179	5,950	58	1,365	1,295	1,110	835	560	727
1987	12,719	239	3,045	2,642	2,006	1,826	1,159	1,802	6,030	116	1,483	1,350	1,034	921	500	625
1986	12,651	201	2,967	2,374	2,136	1,860	1,245	1,867	5,957	82	1,421	1,161	1,120	968	577	628
1985	12,524	262	2,907	2,616	2,014	1,884	1,180	1,661	5,906	131	1,349	1,313	1,087	942	522	561
1984	12,304	253	2,867	2,597	2,127	1,857	1,158	1,445	5,989	91	1,373	1,337	1,219	965	527	476
1983	12,320	260	2,940	2,495	2,042	1,921	1,167	1,495	6,010	108	1,340	1,310	1,170	1,055	521	506
1982	12,308	254	2,929	2,689	2,060	1,859	1,129	1,389	5,899	112	1,376	1,346	1,115	968	492	490
1981	12,127	232	3,044	2,545	1,986	1,717	1,211	1,393	5,825	96	1,450	1,239	1,144	909	533	453
1980	11,387	249	2,933	2,423	1,870	1,641	1,062	1,207	5,430	96	1,369	1,246	989	853	472	405
1979	11,380	311	2,844	2,353	1,794	1,691	996	1,402	5,480	129	1,341	1,192	975	893	463	487
1978	11,141	274	2,899	2,298	1,798	1,619	950	1,303	5,580	106	1,391	1,202	1,028	922	474	457
1977	11,546	274	2,913	2,430	1,799	1,809	992	1,329	5,889	112	1,396	1,280	1,036	1,035	511	520
1976	11,139	281	2,937	2,398	1,846	1,686	803	1,189	5,785	105	1,391	1,209	1,073	1,067	451	489
1975	10,880	293	2,943	2,313	1,679	1,616	853	1,183	5,911	128	1,426	1,256	1,011	1,025	496	569
1974	9,852	309	2,597	2,192	1,527	1,482	720	1,025	5,402	145	1,262	1,206	943	951	420	476
1973	8,966	295	2,517	2,073	1,465	1,278	551	787	5,048	121	1,293	1,130	937	867	329	371
1972	9,096	295	2,680	2,116	1,461	1,229	531	783	5,218	141	1,366	1,170	998	848	330	365
1971	8,087	284	2,726	1,997	1,487	1,067	527	NA	4,850	129	1,444	1,090	1,065	787	334	NA
1970	7,413	260	2,594	1,857	1,354	939	410	NA	4,401	130	1,346	1,083	902	684	256	NA
1969	7,435	242	2,601	1,945	1,294	918	435	NA	4,448	120	1,397	1,112	883	671	265	NA
1968	6,801	281	2,501	1,826	1,029	790	373	NA	4,124	134	1,357	1,093	702	603	236	NA
1967	6,401	239	2,286	1,816	998	707	356	NA	3,841	96	1,198	1,066	718	524	239	NA
1966	6,085	254	2,440	1,472	987	679	254	NA	3,749	105	1,355	899	722	494	174	NA
1965	5,675	264	2,215	1,326	940	616	314	NA	3,503	113	1,218	804	699	458	211	NA
1964	4,643	291	1,616	1,287	670	523	256	NA	2,888	165	866	769	510	396	182	NA
1963	4,336	180	1,504	1,212	717	482	241	NA	2,742	99	796	734	574	365	174	NA
1962	4,208	233	1,612	996	630	486	251	NA	2,742	125	891	617	508	406	195	NA
1961	3,731	213	1,470	892	507	437	212	NA	2,356	84	834	554	393	337	154	NA
1960	3,570	222	1,299	790	509	491	259	NA	2,339	99	734	503	411	399	193	NA
1959	3,340	210	1,175	739	489	503	224	NA	2,187	92	651	501	355	422	166	NA
1958	3,242	167	1,114	-----1,221----		534	206	NA	2,129	73	621	----850----		439	146	NA
1957	3,138	176	989	-----1,236----		553	184	NA	2,028	77	538	----827----		459	127	NA

NA = Not available

r = Revised, controlled to 1990 census based population estimates; previous 1993 data controlled to 1980 census based population estimates.

[1] Starting in 2003, respondents could identify more than one race. Except as noted, the race data in this table from 2003 onward represent those respondents who indicated only one race category.

[2] Before 1994, total enrolled does not include the 35 and over population.

Table A-16. Age Distribution of College Students 14 Years Old and Over, by Sex, October 1947–2017—*Continued*

(Numbers in thousands; civilian noninstitutionalized population.)

Year, sex, race, and Hispanic origin	Total	14 to 17 years	18 and 19 years	20 and 21 years	22 to 24 years	25 to 29 years	30 to 34 years	35 years and over
			Female					
ALL RACES								
2017	10,287	151	2,197	2,341	1,939	1,486	681	1,492
2016	10,551	161	2,227	2,331	1,962	1,618	762	1,490
2015	10,617	113	2,141	2,392	1,927	1,567	805	1,673
2014	10,546	108	2,257	2,128	2,070	1,439	758	1,784
2013	10,931	159	2,142	2,325	2,105	1,462	829	1,908
2012	11,327	139	2,212	2,513	2,001	1,623	940	1,900
2011	11,266	95	2,293	2,333	1,992	1,722	908	1,923
2010	11,268	135	2,355	2,240	1,920	1,596	973	2,049
2009	11,123	116	2,361	2,091	1,980	1,575	875	2,124
2008	10,321	108	2,217	2,013	1,854	1,428	779	1,922
2007	10,130	109	2,172	2,065	1,768	1,466	746	1,804
2006	9,726	133	2,043	1,993	1,677	1,278	809	1,793
2005	9,934	119	2,052	2,067	1,742	1,368	747	1,838
2004	9,808	123	2,074	1,966	1,705	1,335	753	1,850
2003[1]	9,319	89	1,944	1,982	1,742	1,181	723	1,660
2002	9,258	116	1,946	1,885	1,573	1,175	766	1,797
2001	8,998	84	1,907	1,841	1,444	1,167	778	1,776
2000	8,631	88	2,029	1,697	1,383	1,118	728	1,589
1999	8,247	73	1,872	1,595	1,396	1,029	608	1,674
1998	8,641	74	2,003	1,574	1,342	1,170	745	1,732
1997	8,593	112	1,801	1,622	1,406	1,102	658	1,892
1996	8,406	140	1,821	1,528	1,233	1,177	743	1,765
1995	8,013	90	1,671	1,518	1,263	1,135	653	1,684
1994[2]	8,258	85	1,635	1,613	1,328	1,054	776	1,766
1993r	7,795	75	1,663	1,487	1,243	1,022	692	1,613
1993	7,574	71	1,588	1,422	1,189	995	693	1,616
1992	7,844	107	1,566	1,594	1,269	984	748	1,575
1991	7,618	83	1,603	1,549	1,066	965	715	1,636
1990	7,429	91	1,576	1,403	1,063	1,017	732	1,546
1989	7,231	110	1,643	1,342	1,100	964	675	1,396
1988	7,166	124	1,682	1,386	953	900	668	1,452
1987	6,689	123	1,562	1,292	972	905	659	1,176
1986	6,694	120	1,546	1,213	1,016	892	667	1,240
1985	6,618	129	1,559	1,303	926	941	658	1,100
1984	6,315	161	1,494	1,260	908	892	630	970
1983	6,310	153	1,600	1,185	872	865	645	989
1982	6,410	141	1,553	1,343	945	891	637	900
1981	6,303	136	1,594	1,305	842	808	677	940
1980	5,957	153	1,565	1,178	882	788	590	802
1979	5,900	183	1,503	1,161	818	786	533	914
1978	5,559	168	1,507	1,096	770	697	476	845
1977	5,657	162	1,517	1,151	763	774	481	809
1976	5,354	176	1,546	1,189	773	619	352	700
1975	4,969	164	1,517	1,058	668	590	357	614
1974	4,449	165	1,335	986	584	531	300	548
1973	3,918	174	1,224	944	528	411	222	416
1972	3,877	153	1,314	946	464	381	200	418
1971	3,236	154	1,281	906	423	280	192	NA
1970	3,013	130	1,248	774	452	255	154	NA
1969	2,987	122	1,204	833	411	247	171	NA
1968	2,677	147	1,144	733	328	187	138	NA
1967	2,560	143	1,088	749	280	183	117	NA
1966	2,337	149	1,085	573	265	185	80	NA
1965	2,172	151	997	522	241	156	105	NA
1964	1,755	126	750	518	160	127	74	NA
1963	1,594	81	708	478	143	117	67	NA
1962	1,466	108	721	379	122	80	56	NA
1961	1,375	129	636	338	114	100	58	NA
1960	1,231	123	565	287	98	92	66	NA
1959	1,153	118	524	238	134	81	58	NA
1958	1,113	94	493	----371----		95	60	NA
1957	1,110	99	451	----409----		94	57	NA

NA = Not available

r = Revised, controlled to 1990 census based population estimates; previous 1993 data controlled to 1980 census based population estimates.

[1] Starting in 2003, respondents could identify more than one race. Except as noted, the race data in this table from 2003 onward represent those respondents who indicated only one race category.

[2] Before 1994, total enrolled does not include the 35 and over population.

Table A-16. Age Distribution of College Students 14 Years Old and Over, by Sex, October 1947–2017—*Continued*

(Numbers in thousands; civilian noninstitutionalized population.)

Year, sex, race, and Hispanic origin	All students								Male							
	Total	14 to 17 years	18 and 19 years	20 and 21 years	22 to 24 years	25 to 29 years	30 to 34 years	35 years and over	Total	14 to 17 years	18 and 19 years	20 and 21 years	22 to 24 years	25 to 29 years	30 to 34 years	35 years and over
1956	2,883	167	934	----1,105----		494	183	NA	1,932	77	512	----781----		429	133	NA
1955	2,379	147	745	-------931------		406	150	NA	1,579	57	432	----647----		337	107	NA
1950	2,175	180	733	-----939----		324	NA	NA	1,474	74	395	-----692----		314	NA	NA
1947	2,311	188	620	-----1,088----		321	94	NA	1,687	87	343	-----872----		301	84	NA
WHITE ALONE																
2017	13,224	156	2,982	3,178	2,530	1,845	861	1,672	5,864	64	1,317	1,484	1,172	825	396	606
2016	13,901	166	3,170	3,289	2,647	2,041	925	1,663	6,222	55	1,470	1,549	1,247	872	385	644
2015	13,859	149	3,057	3,308	2,604	2,021	945	1,776	6,253	78	1,414	1,586	1,189	920	415	651
2014	13,953	148	3,064	3,232	2,781	1,942	888	1,898	6,398	67	1,397	1,621	1,278	927	374	733
2013	14,240	234	3,033	3,160	2,857	1,879	970	2,107	6,241	115	1,386	1,452	1,292	867	406	721
2012	14,628	204	3,077	3,427	2,798	2,048	1,002	2,072	6,392	87	1,387	1,497	1,377	892	428	725
2011	15,412	141	3,298	3,545	2,970	2,254	1,085	2,120	7,054	78	1,520	1,679	1,486	1,013	470	808
2010	15,258	154	3,398	3,297	2,629	2,217	1,197	2,366	6,883	59	1,573	1,624	1,172	1,051	511	893
2009	15,027	160	3,337	3,205	2,784	2,066	1,097	2,377	6,681	77	1,511	1,533	1,360	904	483	814
2008	14,405	171	3,353	3,119	2,669	1,952	907	2,234	6,570	85	1,566	1,524	1,250	938	413	794
2007	13,835	141	3,242	3,053	2,485	1,817	952	2,144	6,050	62	1,508	1,359	1,172	770	413	766
2006	13,273	161	2,982	2,958	2,358	1,740	985	2,090	5,829	57	1,367	1,344	1,131	799	396	734
2005	13,466	116	2,972	3,176	2,350	1,708	939	2,205	5,843	38	1,343	1,488	1,092	685	420	777
2004	13,381	134	2,946	3,016	2,389	1,776	974	2,146	5,944	49	1,308	1,437	1,110	837	421	782
2003[1]	12,870	100	2,833	2,796	2,521	1,585	960	2,075	5,714	48	1,258	1,236	1,232	723	435	783
2002	12,781	109	2,891	2,810	2,220	1,582	933	2,236	5,719	57	1,329	1,306	1,066	712	394	855
2001	12,208	88	2,755	2,774	2,019	1,514	956	2,103	5,383	36	1,273	1,305	943	693	401	731
2000	11,999	117	2,914	2,590	2,062	1,433	906	1,978	5,311	47	1,289	1,225	1,008	662	367	713
1999	12,053	87	2,849	2,520	2,077	1,475	870	2,174	5,562	33	1,336	1,226	1,024	715	414	816
1998	12,401	93	2,994	2,537	2,011	1,604	964	2,199	5,602	30	1,376	1,256	1,002	746	396	795
1997	12,442	127	2,792	2,602	2,101	1,666	856	2,298	5,552	48	1,314	1,289	1,030	802	345	725
1996	12,189	167	2,731	2,362	2,030	1,704	940	2,254	5,453	70	1,223	1,117	1,079	797	357	811
1995	12,021	116	2,577	2,437	1,997	1,745	941	2,208	5,535	44	1,195	1,201	1,002	857	432	804
1994[2]	12,222	101	2,568	2,459	2,091	1,592	1,143	2,267	5,524	44	1,212	1,140	1,054	749	512	815
1993r	11,735	103	2,566	2,356	2,152	1,507	1,003	2,049	5,403	44	1,157	1,196	1,145	705	451	705
1993	11,434	98	2,456	2,243	2,064	1,490	1,015	2,068	5,222	41	1,103	1,120	1,090	699	457	711
1992	11,710	158	2,419	2,466	2,031	1,512	1,070	2,053	5,210	82	1,102	1,162	1,027	689	471	678
1991	11,686	104	2,487	2,449	1,877	1,598	1,063	2,107	5,304	41	1,112	1,146	1,012	809	480	703
1990	11,488	132	2,548	2,341	1,746	1,638	1,060	2,023	5,235	63	1,218	1,151	923	782	434	665
1989	11,243	147	2,648	2,170	1,813	1,611	986	1,868	5,136	63	1,253	1,070	900	789	438	623
1988	11,140	137	2,639	2,270	1,750	1,425	1,023	1,896	5,078	50	1,194	1,114	952	685	470	613
1987	10,731	194	2,564	2,254	1,665	1,483	985	1,584	5,104	97	1,260	1,156	873	740	436	541
1986	10,707	173	2,549	2,015	1,743	1,580	1,037	1,609	5,074	69	1,254	982	932	835	475	528
1985	10,781	229	2,539	2,257	1,704	1,590	1,014	1,448	5,103	120	1,176	1,137	941	812	449	468
1984	10,520	209	2,541	2,206	1,779	1,566	967	1,252	5,111	73	1,224	1,143	1,039	796	434	402
1983	10,565	214	2,597	2,161	1,705	1,603	961	1,324	5,162	87	1,197	1,149	989	875	421	444
1982	10,551	216	2,549	2,348	1,697	1,581	938	1,222	5,077	95	1,189	1,188	931	831	415	428
1981	10,353	197	2,639	2,239	1,671	1,390	1,027	1,190	5,010	86	1,259	1,104	977	745	448	391
1980	9,925	212	2,578	2,131	1,625	1,413	915	1,051	4,804	79	1,232	1,114	878	735	400	366
1979	9,956	256	2,498	2,079	1,543	1,474	859	1,247	4,823	110	1,192	1,058	854	788	398	423
1978	9,661	229	2,553	1,993	1,531	1,399	808	1,148	4,913	90	1,239	1,056	900	810	413	405
1977	9,962	227	2,579	2,099	1,531	1,550	827	1,149	5,156	91	1,272	1,124	890	907	433	439
1976	9,679	237	2,577	2,108	1,591	1,458	673	1,035	5,084	89	1,244	1,073	933	936	382	427
1975	9,546	252	2,613	2,042	1,461	1,410	737	1,031	5,263	111	1,283	1,134	909	911	426	489
1974	8,689	271	2,308	1,940	1,341	1,308	613	908	4,782	128	1,143	1,067	825	855	350	414
1973	8,014	253	2,281	1,865	1,292	1,152	481	690	4,218	111	1,177	1,017	838	789	286	NA
1972	7,458	259	2,411	1,917	1,296	1,119	456	NA	4,395	120	1,242	1,062	891	784	296	NA
1971	7,273	251	2,485	1,758	1,351	965	463	NA	4,407	117	1,328	964	992	712	293	NA
1970	6,759	230	2,361	1,684	1,260	853	371	NA	4,066	117	1,251	995	850	622	231	NA
1969	6,827	222	2,377	1,762	1,208	855	404	NA	4,146	110	1,298	1,021	827	637	252	NA
1968	6,255	251	2,284	1,691	954	741	333	NA	3,843	117	1,262	1,021	666	564	213	NA
1967	5,905	220	2,105	1,688	915	646	329	NA	3,560	88	1,097	998	666	494	217	NA
1966	5,708	233	2,293	----2,313----		----869----		NA	3,536	93	1,281	----1,541----		----621----		NA
1965	5,317	233	2,074	----2,139----		----871----		NA	3,326	104	1,152	----1,441----		----629----		NA
1964	4,337	257	1,519	----1,850----		----711----		NA	2,720	147	823	----1,226----		----524----		NA
1963	4,050	171	1,391	----1,817----		----671----		NA	2,593	94	746	----1,246----		----507----		NA
1962	3,934	217	1,509	----1,517----		----691----		NA	2,586	120	836	----1,066----		----564----		NA

NA = Not available

r = Revised, controlled to 1990 census based population estimates; previous 1993 data controlled to 1980 census based population estimates.

[1]Starting in 2003, respondents could identify more than one race. Except as noted, the race data in this table from 2003 onward represent those respondents who indicated only one race category.

[2]Before 1994, total enrolled does not include the 35 and over population.

Table A-16. Age Distribution of College Students 14 Years Old and Over, by Sex, October 1947–2017—*Continued*

(Numbers in thousands; civilian noninstitutionalized population.)

Year, sex, race, and Hispanic origin	Female							
	Total	14 to 17 years	18 and 19 years	20 and 21 years	22 to 24 years	25 to 29 years	30 to 34 years	35 years and over
1956	951	90	422	----324----		65	50	NA
1955	800	90	313	----285----		69	43	NA
1950	701	106	338	----247----		10	NA	NA
1947	624	101	277	----216----		20	10	NA
WHITE ALONE								
2017	7,360	92	1,665	1,695	1,358	1,020	465	1,066
2016	7,678	112	1,700	1,740	1,400	1,169	540	1,019
2015	7,607	71	1,644	1,721	1,415	1,101	530	1,124
2014	7,555	81	1,667	1,611	1,502	1,015	514	1,165
2013	7,999	119	1,646	1,707	1,565	1,011	564	1,386
2012	8,236	117	1,690	1,930	1,421	1,156	574	1,347
2011	8,358	63	1,779	1,866	1,484	1,241	615	1,311
2010	8,375	95	1,825	1,673	1,458	1,166	686	1,472
2009	8,346	84	1,826	1,672	1,424	1,162	614	1,564
2008	7,835	85	1,787	1,595	1,419	1,014	493	1,440
2007	7,785	80	1,734	1,694	1,313	1,047	539	1,378
2006	7,445	104	1,615	1,613	1,227	941	588	1,355
2005	7,624	79	1,629	1,688	1,258	1,024	519	1,428
2004	7,438	86	1,638	1,579	1,279	939	553	1,364
2003[1]	7,155	53	1,575	1,560	1,289	862	525	1,291
2002	7,062	52	1,562	1,504	1,154	870	539	1,381
2001	6,826	52	1,481	1,468	1,077	820	555	1,372
2000	6,689	70	1,625	1,365	1,054	770	539	1,266
1999	6,491	55	1,513	1,296	1,053	760	455	1,359
1998	6,799	63	1,618	1,281	1,008	858	567	1,405
1997	6,890	79	1,479	1,313	1,071	864	511	1,573
1996	6,735	97	1,508	1,246	951	906	583	1,443
1995	6,486	72	1,383	1,237	995	887	508	1,404
1994[2]	6,698	57	1,357	1,320	1,037	844	631	1,453
1993r	6,331	59	1,409	1,160	1,007	802	552	1,344
1993	6,212	57	1,353	1,123	974	791	558	1,357
1992	6,499	76	1,317	1,303	1,005	823	599	1,376
1991	6,382	63	1,375	1,304	865	789	583	1,404
1990	6,253	69	1,331	1,190	823	856	627	1,358
1989	6,107	84	1,395	1,101	913	822	548	1,245
1988	6,063	87	1,445	1,156	798	740	554	1,283
1987	5,627	97	1,304	1,097	791	743	550	1,044
1986	5,632	105	1,295	1,033	811	745	562	1,081
1985	5,679	110	1,363	1,120	764	778	565	979
1984	5,410	136	1,317	1,063	740	770	533	851
1983	5,404	127	1,400	1,012	717	728	540	880
1982	5,472	120	1,360	1,159	766	749	523	795
1981	5,342	111	1,380	1,134	694	646	578	799
1980	5,121	133	1,346	1,017	747	678	514	686
1979	5,131	146	1,306	1,021	688	686	461	823
1978	4,748	139	1,314	937	631	590	395	742
1977	4,806	135	1,307	975	641	643	394	711
1976	4,593	147	1,334	1,034	658	521	291	608
1975	4,284	141	1,330	908	552	500	311	542
1974	3,907	143	1,166	873	516	453	263	493
1973	3,107	142	1,104	848	454	363	196	NA
1972	3,061	138	1,169	855	404	334	160	NA
1971	2,867	134	1,157	794	359	252	170	NA
1970	2,693	113	1,110	689	410	231	140	NA
1969	2,681	112	1,079	741	380	218	151	NA
1968	2,412	134	1,022	670	288	177	120	NA
1967	2,345	133	1,009	690	250	152	112	NA
1966	2,172	140	1,012	----772----		----248----		NA
1965	1,991	129	922	----698----		----242----		NA
1964	1,617	110	696	----624----		----187----		NA
1963	1,457	77	645	----571----		----164----		NA
1962	1,348	97	673	----451----		----127----		NA

NA = Not available

r = Revised, controlled to 1990 census based population estimates; previous 1993 data controlled to 1980 census based population estimates.

[1] Starting in 2003, respondents could identify more than one race. Except as noted, the race data in this table from 2003 onward represent those respondents who indicated only one race category.

[2] Before 1994, total enrolled does not include the 35 and over population.

Table A-16. Age Distribution of College Students 14 Years Old and Over, by Sex, October 1947–2017—*Continued*

(Numbers in thousands; civilian noninstitutionalized population.)

Year, sex, race, and Hispanic origin	All students Total	14 to 17 years	18 and 19 years	20 and 21 years	22 to 24 years	25 to 29 years	30 to 34 years	35 years and over	Male Total	14 to 17 years	18 and 19 years	20 and 21 years	22 to 24 years	25 to 29 years	30 to 34 years	35 years and over
1961	3,498	204	1,388	----1,296-----		-----610-----		NA	2,208	79	786	------883----		------460----		NA
1960	3,342	214	1,211	----1,209-----		-----709-----		NA	2,214	97	691	------859----		------567----		NA
1959	3,118	193	1,101	----1,134-----		-----690-----		NA	2,067	88	620	------798----		------561----		NA
1958	3,030	155	1,044	----1,136-----		-----695-----		NA	1,999	68	577	------802----		------552----		NA
1957	2,932	161	921	----1,165-----		-----685-----		NA	1,938	68	510	------797----		------563----		NA
1956	2,687	152	869	----1,025-----		-----641-----		NA	1,808	68	474	-------733----		------533----		NA
1955	2,224	125	715	------880-----		-----504-----		NA	1,495	47	418	------621----		------409----		NA

WHITE ALONE NON-HISPANIC

Year, sex, race, and Hispanic origin	All students Total	14 to 17 years	18 and 19 years	20 and 21 years	22 to 24 years	25 to 29 years	30 to 34 years	35 years and over	Male Total	14 to 17 years	18 and 19 years	20 and 21 years	22 to 24 years	25 to 29 years	30 to 34 years	35 years and over
2017	10,055	89	2,129	2,510	1,905	1,379	691	1,351	4,518	34	952	1,206	899	637	304	486
2016	10,749	82	2,439	2,465	1,990	1,615	789	1,368	4,879	30	1,168	1,168	952	702	327	531
2015	10,904	106	2,368	2,517	2,053	1,593	777	1,489	4,970	54	1,121	1,234	930	744	353	534
2014	11,068	113	2,299	2,545	2,209	1,545	742	1,613	5,115	58	1,050	1,310	1,031	728	337	600
2013	11,348	193	2,379	2,456	2,230	1,529	764	1,798	4,944	97	1,124	1,135	1,001	668	322	597
2012	11,650	150	2,363	2,620	2,207	1,734	778	1,799	5,074	61	1,051	1,126	1,113	761	356	606
2011	12,703	105	2,588	2,867	2,427	1,892	936	1,888	5,731	55	1,184	1,349	1,221	817	417	689
2010	12,613	114	2,699	2,813	2,152	1,818	996	2,022	5,673	39	1,236	1,395	986	854	416	747
2009	12,826	120	2,842	2,755	2,385	1,736	913	2,074	5,709	54	1,286	1,327	1,174	765	397	706
2008	12,324	121	2,850	2,734	2,309	1,625	779	1,906	5,602	58	1,346	1,322	1,098	766	347	664
2007	11,867	104	2,739	2,677	2,117	1,509	816	1,904	5,269	45	1,298	1,223	1,021	639	370	674
2006	11,485	114	2,564	2,606	2,030	1,494	830	1,848	5,085	41	1,168	1,208	979	702	347	640
2005	11,715	93	2,618	2,769	2,006	1,445	806	1,977	5,114	30	1,193	1,308	928	590	373	692
2004	11,571	111	2,596	2,618	2,014	1,513	814	1,905	5,146	44	1,150	1,242	930	710	372	698
2003[1]	11,295	90	2,486	2,419	2,225	1,371	832	1,872	5,067	41	1,115	1,082	1,094	639	386	710
2002	11,236	97	2,549	2,525	1,931	1,317	812	2,007	5,060	57	1,179	1,162	947	596	350	770
2001	10,602	74	2,383	2,450	1,732	1,283	827	1,854	4,691	30	1,131	1,170	794	587	348	632
2000	10,636	92	2,580	2,333	1,796	1,275	770	1,790	4,716	35	1,138	1,109	890	603	296	646
1999	10,818	80	2,574	2,324	1,837	1,283	755	1,965	5,033	30	1,214	1,141	929	627	368	722
1998	11,109	84	2,715	2,281	1,760	1,408	840	2,020	5,084	30	1,280	1,123	897	668	348	738
1997	11,246	81	2,491	2,361	1,876	1,504	779	2,153	5,024	33	1,184	1,161	930	732	314	669
1996	11,034	147	2,504	2,156	1,788	1,514	834	2,091	4,961	61	1,136	1,039	955	727	303	740
1995	11,024	103	2,372	2,226	1,796	1,618	859	2,051	5,068	36	1,111	1,103	892	799	380	749
1994[2]	11,178	93	2,362	2,255	1,904	1,444	1,018	2,101	5,053	41	1,132	1,039	955	689	457	741
1993	10,554	83	2,270	2,026	1,924	1,367	923	1,960	4,838	36	1,038	1,016	1,017	663	399	670

BLACK

Year, sex, race, and Hispanic origin	All students Total	14 to 17 years	18 and 19 years	20 and 21 years	22 to 24 years	25 to 29 years	30 to 34 years	35 years and over	Male Total	14 to 17 years	18 and 19 years	20 and 21 years	22 to 24 years	25 to 29 years	30 to 34 years	35 years and over
2017	2,812	35	525	546	524	455	219	509	1,175	13	234	251	210	193	81	192
2016	2,885	30	530	572	542	405	247	559	1,217	12	215	276	237	192	97	188
2015	2,826	25	509	575	553	404	223	537	1,147	12	229	252	298	145	57	154
2014	2,934	54	510	537	482	414	242	695	1,132	38	175	244	214	162	79	220
2013	2,857	32	451	633	515	461	225	539	1,116	18	186	268	236	172	54	182
2012	3,038	27	531	636	522	443	326	553	1,152	18	206	316	238	142	85	148
2011	3,146	38	580	489	570	511	307	651	1,212	23	242	243	232	189	92	191
2010	3,083	33	567	622	503	438	277	643	1,185	14	238	262	234	180	77	180
2009	2,889	34	559	495	550	410	253	587	1,058	5	225	237	212	151	81	147
2008	2,481	36	479	463	408	377	269	451	919	21	205	217	174	115	82	106
2007	2,501	27	492	436	468	400	229	449	1,016	10	227	213	209	126	102	130
2006	2,334	30	464	416	441	303	199	480	896	10	174	182	186	112	70	163
2005	2,217	28	431	393	435	282	217	430	832	6	182	178	153	99	64	150
2004	2,301	40	440	398	400	352	170	501	776	13	165	169	146	92	41	151
2003[1]	2,144	28	374	415	435	289	214	388	798	10	166	153	180	100	84	105
2002	2,278	56	430	418	379	301	241	454	802	14	179	175	121	97	83	133
2001	2,230	33	444	383	379	283	279	429	781	7	179	137	153	88	90	126
2000	2,164	19	454	375	387	325	242	361	815	10	163	137	169	110	92	133
1999	1,998	45	430	389	325	254	199	354	833	34	210	193	98	93	79	123
1998	2,016	22	461	354	300	328	211	340	770	12	194	162	88	140	67	105
1997	1,903	24	381	321	383	258	165	372	723	7	142	137	146	110	65	117
1996	1,901	45	345	346	292	337	182	354	764	17	145	155	122	142	64	120
1995	1,772	24	344	339	305	233	193	334	710	13	145	142	143	65	80	122

NA = Not available

[1]Starting in 2003, respondents could identify more than one race. Except as noted, the race data in this table from 2003 onward represent those respondents who indicated only one race category.

[2]Before 1994, total enrolled does not include the 35 and over population.

Table A-16. Age Distribution of College Students 14 Years Old and Over, by Sex, October 1947–2017—*Continued*

(Numbers in thousands; civilian noninstitutionalized population.)

Year, sex, race, and Hispanic origin	Female							
	Total	14 to 17 years	18 and 19 years	20 and 21 years	22 to 24 years	25 to 29 years	30 to 34 years	35 years and over
1961	1,290	125	602	-----413-----		-----150-----		NA
1960	1,128	117	520	-----350-----		-----142-----		NA
1959	1,051	105	481	-----336-----		-----129-----		NA
1958	1,031	87	467	-----334-----		-----143-----		NA
1957	994	93	411	-----368-----		-----122-----		NA
1956	879	84	395	-----292-----		-----108-----		NA
1955	729	78	297	-----259-----		-----95-----		NA
WHITE ALONE NON-HISPANIC								
2017	5,537	55	1,178	1,304	1,006	742	387	865
2016	5,870	52	1,271	1,297	1,038	913	463	837
2015	5,934	52	1,248	1,283	1,123	849	424	954
2014	5,953	55	1,249	1,235	1,179	817	405	1,013
2013	6,404	95	1,254	1,321	1,229	861	442	1,201
2012	6,575	88	1,312	1,494	1,094	973	422	1,193
2011	6,972	50	1,404	1,517	1,206	1,075	519	1,199
2010	6,940	75	1,463	1,417	1,166	964	581	1,275
2009	7,116	66	1,556	1,429	1,211	971	516	1,368
2008	6,722	63	1,504	1,412	1,211	859	432	1,242
2007	6,598	59	1,441	1,455	1,096	870	447	1,230
2006	6,400	73	1,396	1,398	1,051	792	483	1,208
2005	6,601	63	1,425	1,461	1,078	855	433	1,285
2004	6,425	67	1,446	1,375	1,085	803	442	1,207
2003[1]	6,228	49	1,371	1,337	1,130	732	446	1,163
2002	6,177	40	1,370	1,364	984	721	462	1,237
2001	5,912	44	1,252	1,280	938	695	479	1,222
2000	5,921	57	1,443	1,224	906	672	474	1,145
1999	5,785	49	1,360	1,183	908	656	387	1,241
1998	6,025	54	1,435	1,158	863	740	493	1,282
1997	6,222	48	1,307	1,200	946	771	465	1,485
1996	6,073	86	1,367	1,117	833	787	531	1,352
1995	5,956	67	1,261	1,123	904	819	479	1,302
1994[2]	6,124	53	1,229	1,216	950	755	561	1,361
1993	5,715	48	1,232	1,010	907	704	524	1,290
BLACK								
2017	1,637	22	291	295	314	262	138	316
2016	1,669	18	316	296	305	212	151	372
2015	1,679	13	280	323	255	259	166	383
2014	1,802	17	334	293	268	252	164	475
2013	1,740	14	265	365	280	289	171	357
2012	1,886	10	325	320	284	301	241	406
2011	1,934	16	337	246	338	322	215	460
2010	1,898	20	329	360	269	258	199	463
2009	1,831	29	334	258	338	259	172	441
2008	1,562	15	274	246	234	261	188	345
2007	1,485	18	265	223	259	274	127	320
2006	1,438	20	291	234	255	191	130	318
2005	1,385	22	249	215	282	183	153	281
2004	1,525	27	275	229	254	259	130	350
2003[1]	1,346	19	209	262	255	188	130	283
2002	1,476	42	251	243	257	204	158	321
2001	1,449	26	265	245	226	195	190	302
2000	1,349	9	291	238	218	215	150	228
1999	1,164	10	221	196	227	161	120	229
1998	1,247	9	267	192	212	188	144	234
1997	1,180	17	238	184	237	149	100	255
1996	1,136	28	199	192	170	195	119	234
1995	1,062	11	199	197	162	168	113	212

NA = Not available
[1]Starting in 2003, respondents could identify more than one race. Except as noted, the race data in this table from 2003 onward represent those respondents who indicated only one race category.
[2]Before 1994, total enrolled does not include the 35 and over population.

Table A-16. Age Distribution of College Students 14 Years Old and Over, by Sex, October 1947–2017—Continued

(Numbers in thousands; civilian noninstitutionalized population.)

Year, sex, race, and Hispanic origin	All students								Male							
	Total	14 to 17 years	18 and 19 years	20 and 21 years	22 to 24 years	25 to 29 years	30 to 34 years	35 years and over	Total	14 to 17 years	18 and 19 years	20 and 21 years	22 to 24 years	25 to 29 years	30 to 34 years	35 years and over
1994	1,800	36	310	347	344	256	184	323	745	16	132	161	147	118	72	99
1993r	1,599	13	322	311	264	253	143	293	652	4	151	109	127	118	36	107
1993	1,545	13	311	297	253	245	141	284	636	4	148	107	124	116	36	102
1992	1,424	28	291	316	279	170	132	208	527	8	123	114	119	73	37	54
1991	1,477	18	303	302	223	216	157	257	629	7	137	138	103	99	55	90
1990	1,393	35	349	287	258	150	108	207	587	16	164	151	111	52	26	65
1989	1,287	32	302	290	243	156	119	146	480	8	126	104	94	65	37	47
1988	1,321	33	281	273	198	188	142	206	494	6	108	90	99	75	48	68
1987	1,351	32	341	264	218	220	121	155	587	13	154	124	99	99	37	62
1986	1,359	19	308	242	262	187	143	198	580	12	120	111	118	81	64	74
1985	1,263	21	259	274	201	183	112	213	552	10	121	140	84	64	40	93
1984	1,332	40	265	274	247	182	131	193	618	16	112	129	126	99	62	74
1983	1,273	31	258	242	241	179	151	171	560	12	93	112	126	91	64	62
1982	1,294	22	274	242	251	196	142	167	544	9	124	92	115	91	51	62
1981	1,335	31	306	232	212	219	132	203	566	7	133	92	100	115	57	62
1980	1,163	30	283	225	180	176	113	156	476	14	98	101	79	92	53	39
1979	1,156	43	279	224	193	150	112	155	498	12	110	110	84	71	47	64
1978	1,175	38	270	238	186	167	121	155	504	13	114	106	85	82	52	52
1977	1,284	37	269	262	190	210	136	180	571	18	90	115	104	101	62	81
1976	1,217	34	302	252	195	171	109	154	551	11	121	113	97	90	57	62
1975	1,099	34	260	237	168	151	97	152	523	14	111	107	76	82	53	80
1974	930	34	233	190	132	136	88	117	485	13	102	100	78	70	60	62
1973	781	37	194	164	140	89	60	97	358	7	96	93	77	49	36	NA
1972	727	32	229	168	143	87	68	NA	384	18	102	91	94	49	30	NA
1971	680	29	204	199	119	79	50	NA	363	11	94	106	62	58	31	NA
1970	522	21	191	152	73	54	31	NA	253	10	73	81	38	33	19	NA
1969	492	19	193	149	65	39	26	NA	236	10	86	75	41	15	10	NA
1968	434	20	182	112	58	33	29	NA	221	12	83	61	26	27	13	NA
1967	370	16	141	105	51	42	15	NA	199	7	78	57	32	15	11	NA
1966	282	17	112	-----112-----		-----41-----		NA	154	10	47	-----72-----		-----25-----		NA
1965	274	30	111	-----99-----		-----34-----		NA	126	8	52	-----47-----		-----19-----		NA
1964	234	30	78	-----79-----		-----47-----		NA	120	16	35	-----36-----		-----33-----		NA
1963	286	9	113	-----112-----		-----52-----		NA	149	5	50	-----62-----		-----32-----		NA
1962	274	16	103	-----109-----		-----46-----		NA	156	5	55	-----59-----		-----37-----		NA
1961	233	9	82	-----103-----		-----39-----		NA	148	5	48	-----64-----		-----31-----		NA
1960	227	8	88	-----90-----		-----41-----		NA	125	2	43	-----55-----		-----25-----		NA
1959	222	17	74	-----94-----		-----37-----		NA	120	4	31	-----58-----		-----27-----		NA
1958	212	12	70	-----85-----		-----45-----		NA	130	5	44	-----48-----		-----33-----		NA
1957	206	15	68	-----71-----		-----52-----		NA	90	9	28	-----30-----		-----23-----		NA
1956	196	15	65	-----80-----		-----36-----		NA	124	9	38	-----48-----		-----29-----		NA
1955	155	21	31	-----51-----		-----52-----		NA	84	9	15	-----25-----		-----35-----		NA
BLACK ALONE NON-HISPANIC[3]																
2005	2,217	28	431	393	435	282	217	430	832	6	182	178	153	99	64	150
2004	2,231	40	430	392	379	344	163	483	760	13	161	166	143	92	38	147
2003[1]	2,090	28	368	399	423	282	205	385	773	10	166	145	177	93	80	102
2002	2,217	56	428	410	358	293	233	439	782	14	177	174	113	95	83	126
2001	2,173	33	430	373	375	263	275	423	759	7	174	137	150	78	90	123
2000	2,119	19	439	373	370	321	242	355	798	10	154	137	164	110	92	130
1999	1,952	45	413	390	320	250	192	342	811	35	192	193	99	91	76	125
1998	1,971	22	453	351	282	322	211	331	752	12	194	159	83	134	67	102
1997	1,868	21	371	314	378	253	161	369	712	7	138	137	143	105	65	117
1996	1,863	41	342	342	281	329	176	350	750	17	142	155	122	134	64	117
1995	1,745	24	332	337	302	231	189	330	699	13	136	142	143	65	80	120
1994	1,783	36	308	347	342	253	182	314	734	16	131	161	145	116	72	93
1993	1,505	13	310	291	246	232	134	279	615	4	149	105	121	104	33	100
ASIAN[4]																
2017	1,581	32	260	430	411	262	90	95	750	7	122	213	227	127	30	25
2016	1,585	19	255	358	390	328	108	127	835	4	135	177	222	177	53	68

NA = Not available
r = Revised, controlled to 1990 census based population estimates; previous 1993 data controlled to 1980 census based population estimates.
[1]Starting in 2003, respondents could identify more than one race. Except as noted, the race data in this table from 2003 onward represent those respondents who indicated only one race category.
[3]This series was discontinued in 2006.
[4]The data shown before 2003 consists of those identifying themselves as "Asian or Pacific Islanders."

Table A-16. Age Distribution of College Students 14 Years Old and Over, by Sex, October 1947–2017—*Continued*

(Numbers in thousands; civilian noninstitutionalized population.)

Year, sex, race, and Hispanic origin	Female							
	Total	14 to 17 years	18 and 19 years	20 and 21 years	22 to 24 years	25 to 29 years	30 to 34 years	35 years and over
1994	1,054	21	178	186	197	138	112	224
1993r	947	9	172	202	137	135	107	186
1993	909	8	163	191	130	129	106	182
1992	897	21	168	202	161	97	95	154
1991	848	11	166	164	120	118	102	167
1990	807	19	185	136	146	98	82	141
1989	807	24	176	186	149	91	82	99
1988	827	27	173	183	99	113	94	138
1987	764	19	186	140	119	121	84	93
1986	779	7	187	131	144	106	79	124
1985	712	11	138	134	117	119	72	121
1984	714	24	153	145	121	83	69	119
1983	714	19	164	131	116	88	87	109
1982	750	12	150	150	136	105	92	105
1981	769	24	172	140	112	105	75	141
1980	686	16	185	124	101	84	60	116
1979	659	31	169	114	109	79	66	91
1978	671	25	155	133	102	85	68	103
1977	712	19	179	147	87	108	74	98
1976	665	23	181	139	97	81	52	92
1975	577	20	150	130	92	69	44	72
1974	448	22	131	91	55	66	28	55
1973	325	30	97	71	63	40	24	NA
1972	343	14	127	77	49	38	38	NA
1971	317	18	109	93	57	21	19	NA
1970	269	11	118	71	36	22	11	NA
1969	256	9	108	74	24	25	17	NA
1968	213	8	100	51	32	7	15	NA
1967	171	9	63	48	19	27	4	NA
1966	128	7	65	-----40-----		-----16-----		NA
1965	148	22	59	-----52-----		-----15-----		NA
1964	114	14	43	-----43-----		-----14-----		NA
1963	137	4	63	-----50-----		-----20-----		NA
1962	118	11	48	-----50-----		------9-----		NA
1961	85	4	34	-----39-----		------8-----		NA
1960	102	6	45	-----35-----		-----16-----		NA
1959	102	13	43	-----36-----		-----10-----		NA
1958	82	7	26	-----37-----		-----12-----		NA
1957	116	6	40	-----41-----		-----29-----		NA
1956	72	6	27	-----32-----		------7-----		NA
1955	71	12	16	-----26-----		-----17-----		NA
BLACK ALONE NON-HISPANIC[3]								
2005	1,385	22	249	215	282	183	153	281
2004	1,471	27	268	227	237	251	125	336
2003[1]	1,317	19	202	254	246	188	125	283
2002	1,435	42	251	237	244	198	150	313
2001	1,414	26	256	236	226	186	185	300
2000	1,321	9	285	235	206	211	150	225
1999	1,141	10	221	196	221	159	117	218
1998	1,219	9	259	192	199	188	144	229
1997	1,156	14	233	177	235	149	96	252
1996	1,113	25	199	188	160	195	113	234
1995	1,046	11	196	195	159	167	109	210
1994	1,049	21	178	186	197	138	109	221
1993	890	8	161	186	125	128	102	179
ASIAN[4]								
2017	831	25	138	217	184	135	60	71
2016	749	15	120	181	168	151	55	59

NA = Not available

r = Revised, controlled to 1990 census based population estimates; previous 1993 data controlled to 1980 census based population estimates.

[1]Starting in 2003, respondents could identify more than one race. Except as noted, the race data in this table from 2003 onward represent those respondents who indicated only one race category.

[3]This series was discontinued in 2006.

[4]The data shown before 2003 consists of those identifying themselves as "Asian or Pacific Islanders."

Table A-16. Age Distribution of College Students 14 Years Old and Over, by Sex, October 1947–2017—*Continued*

(Numbers in thousands; civilian noninstitutionalized population.)

Year, sex, race, and Hispanic origin	All students								Male							
	Total	14 to 17 years	18 and 19 years	20 and 21 years	22 to 24 years	25 to 29 years	30 to 34 years	35 years and over	Total	14 to 17 years	18 and 19 years	20 and 21 years	22 to 24 years	25 to 29 years	30 to 34 years	35 years and over
2015	1,616	20	235	421	370	291	135	143	752	10	112	193	188	138	61	49
2014	1,543	19	270	305	447	273	80	148	797	14	136	158	255	149	26	59
2013	1,576	30	302	340	359	261	111	174	789	8	154	188	193	151	38	58
2012	1,447	26	253	289	372	247	116	143	700	15	129	140	185	131	44	55
2011	1,204	21	240	281	227	189	99	147	567	6	131	141	107	92	45	45
2010	1,322	32	234	308	269	237	117	126	647	17	116	150	124	126	58	57
2009	1,231	11	243	216	308	197	114	141	613	8	134	97	153	96	53	73
2008	1,220	27	172	247	236	245	137	156	567	22	75	123	96	132	61	58
2007	1,103	10	201	204	252	206	123	105	533	2	104	106	108	98	60	54
2006	1,084	8	204	215	242	187	103	125	535	5	113	121	104	80	51	61
2005	1,184	22	188	272	234	226	114	129	605	10	90	163	113	110	61	58
2004	1,191	20	182	245	269	217	113	146	636	11	92	135	145	116	65	71
2003[1]	1,162	16	209	219	264	228	108	116	606	3	103	104	130	141	67	59
2002	1,258	28	236	269	299	182	105	140	649	8	121	137	160	101	56	67
2001	1,280	17	247	245	302	265	90	115	664	10	113	127	177	134	63	40
2000	1,049	12	212	200	227	188	81	130	517	4	108	109	120	66	51	60
1999	1,041	16	223	192	211	187	71	142	506	11	93	95	96	97	47	67
HISPANIC (OF ANY RACE)																
2017	3,574	80	931	769	710	530	187	368	1,529	30	413	311	321	219	104	132
2016	3,661	89	884	948	732	491	191	326	1,582	28	383	437	327	210	76	120
2015	3,374	43	776	930	663	459	189	315	1,484	23	315	421	327	192	69	136
2014	3,295	52	857	797	628	441	189	332	1,441	11	385	356	275	222	47	144
2013	3,219	43	727	773	692	417	222	345	1,438	19	295	352	321	237	84	130
2012	3,400	61	827	912	664	365	257	313	1,510	26	372	421	316	155	72	148
2011	2,953	36	765	740	574	407	175	256	1,438	23	351	376	279	212	67	130
2010	2,879	41	783	517	514	424	228	373	1,302	19	381	242	196	197	108	159
2009	2,434	43	550	482	433	373	217	336	1,080	23	242	221	200	159	108	127
2008	2,227	53	528	407	402	359	141	337	1,042	31	236	210	169	186	76	135
2007	2,172	41	559	412	404	332	155	269	880	16	246	154	160	145	57	102
2006	1,968	54	444	386	353	271	190	271	808	19	213	146	164	109	64	94
2005	1,942	31	406	420	389	288	150	257	804	10	173	183	183	111	52	92
2004	1,975	23	384	431	407	280	179	271	852	5	171	212	191	131	53	89
2003	1,714	12	379	407	329	224	156	207	703	7	153	167	145	93	61	77
2002	1,656	15	360	303	316	274	140	249	705	3	156	151	132	118	49	97
2001	1,700	14	387	342	306	255	136	260	731	6	149	145	156	116	57	102
2000	1,426	24	349	268	282	167	142	194	619	12	160	118	123	61	75	70
1999	1,307	7	297	197	247	207	127	225	568	2	143	84	96	94	54	95
1998	1,363	9	288	263	269	206	130	198	550	—	97	139	110	86	54	64
1997	1,260	49	316	254	236	174	80	151	555	15	133	132	106	78	31	60
1996	1,223	22	240	213	253	198	112	184	529	8	98	78	124	79	54	90
1995	1,207	20	264	245	236	153	97	193	568	14	121	111	124	71	55	73
1994[2]	1,187	9	225	230	207	180	132	205	529	3	89	115	108	73	55	86
1993r	1,169	17	222	299	207	178	106	139	539	7	81	154	103	71	67	56
1993	995	15	195	241	166	149	100	129	442	6	69	118	79	57	63	51
1992	918	17	230	200	156	124	90	102	388	9	93	80	74	57	35	40
1991	830	10	188	203	125	124	72	109	347	5	68	79	64	64	30	37
1990	748	13	148	188	99	109	59	130	364	12	70	80	64	39	30	67
1989	754	17	177	134	142	112	58	114	353	5	75	66	70	63	31	42
1988	747	13	203	110	137	118	73	93	355	9	75	76	77	48	29	43
1987	739	8	152	155	148	137	67	73	390	3	76	100	71	77	42	21
1986	794	16	171	146	141	164	67	89	377	4	92	67	74	80	26	34
1985	580	16	127	128	120	111	78	NA	279	10	44	53	71	72	29	NA
1984	524	5	136	133	93	100	57	NA	231	2	42	63	49	49	26	NA
1983	521	17	134	124	91	114	41	NA	253	10	41	61	50	74	17	NA
1982	494	16	143	104	90	94	47	NA	216	6	52	47	42	49	20	NA
1981	510	15	129	123	90	103	50	NA	258	6	57	68	39	55	33	NA
1980	443	10	137	94	84	69	49	NA	222	2	68	52	34	36	30	NA
1979	439	18	124	95	73	73	56	NA	225	8	67	43	43	39	25	NA
1978	377	15	109	68	77	78	30	NA	196	7	53	30	43	49	14	NA
1977	417	14	123	95	59	81	45	NA	224	6	54	45	40	56	23	NA
1976	426	13	143	83	83	73	31	NA	223	3	69	39	42	50	20	NA

NA = Not available

r = Revised, controlled to 1990 census based population estimates; previous 1993 data controlled to 1980 census based population estimates.

[1]Starting in 2003, respondents could identify more than one race. Except as noted, the race data in this table from 2003 onward represent those respondents who indicated only one race category.

[2]Before 1994, total enrolled does not include the 35 and over population.

Table A-16. Age Distribution of College Students 14 Years Old and Over, by Sex, October 1947–2017—*Continued*

(Numbers in thousands; civilian noninstitutionalized population.)

Year, sex, race, and Hispanic origin	Female							
	Total	14 to 17 years	18 and 19 years	20 and 21 years	22 to 24 years	25 to 29 years	30 to 34 years	35 years and over
2015..............................	864	10	123	229	182	153	74	94
2014..............................	746	5	134	147	192	124	55	89
2013..............................	787	22	148	152	166	110	73	116
2012..............................	747	11	124	148	187	116	72	88
2011..............................	637	16	109	140	120	97	54	101
2010..............................	676	15	118	158	145	111	59	69
2009..............................	619	4	109	120	155	101	61	68
2008..............................	653	5	97	123	140	113	76	98
2007..............................	569	8	97	98	144	108	63	51
2006..............................	549	3	91	94	139	107	52	64
2005..............................	579	12	98	109	120	116	53	71
2004..............................	556	9	89	110	124	101	48	75
2003[1].........................	556	13	107	115	134	88	42	57
2002..............................	609	19	115	132	139	82	49	73
2001..............................	616	6	134	118	125	131	27	75
2000..............................	532	8	104	91	107	122	30	69
1999..............................	534	5	130	97	115	89	24	74
HISPANIC (OF ANY RACE)								
2017..............................	2,045	50	518	457	390	312	83	236
2016..............................	2,079	60	501	511	405	281	115	206
2015..............................	1,890	20	461	508	336	267	120	179
2014..............................	1,855	40	472	441	352	219	142	188
2013..............................	1,781	24	432	421	371	180	138	215
2012..............................	1,890	35	454	491	348	211	185	166
2011..............................	1,515	13	414	364	294	196	108	126
2010..............................	1,576	21	402	275	319	227	119	213
2009..............................	1,354	20	308	261	234	214	108	209
2008..............................	1,185	23	292	197	233	173	65	202
2007..............................	1,292	25	313	258	244	187	98	167
2006..............................	1,161	36	231	240	189	162	126	177
2005..............................	1,137	21	232	237	206	178	98	165
2004..............................	1,123	19	213	219	216	150	126	182
2003..............................	1,011	5	226	240	185	131	95	130
2002..............................	951	12	204	152	184	156	92	152
2001..............................	969	8	238	197	150	139	80	157
2000..............................	807	13	188	150	160	106	67	124
1999..............................	739	5	154	113	151	113	73	130
1998..............................	814	9	191	124	159	120	77	134
1997..............................	704	34	183	123	130	96	49	91
1996..............................	693	15	142	136	128	119	59	95
1995..............................	639	6	143	134	112	82	42	120
1994[2].........................	659	6	136	115	99	106	78	119
1993r............................	630	10	141	145	104	107	40	83
1993..............................	553	9	126	123	87	93	38	78
1992..............................	530	7	137	120	82	67	55	62
1991..............................	483	5	120	124	61	59	42	72
1990..............................	384	1	78	108	35	70	29	63
1989..............................	401	11	103	69	72	49	27	71
1988..............................	391	4	129	35	60	70	43	51
1987..............................	349	5	76	56	76	60	25	51
1986..............................	417	12	79	80	67	84	41	54
1985..............................	299	6	82	75	48	39	49	NA
1984..............................	292	3	94	70	43	51	31	NA
1983..............................	270	7	93	64	41	40	25	NA
1982..............................	278	10	91	57	48	45	27	NA
1981..............................	252	9	72	55	51	48	17	NA
1980..............................	221	8	63	42	50	33	20	NA
1979..............................	215	10	58	52	30	34	31	NA
1978..............................	181	8	56	38	34	29	16	NA
1977..............................	194	8	70	50	19	25	22	NA
1976..............................	203	9	74	45	41	23	11	NA

NA = Not available
r = Revised, controlled to 1990 census based population estimates; previous 1993 data controlled to 1980 census based population estimates.
[1]Starting in 2003, respondents could identify more than one race. Except as noted, the race data in this table from 2003 onward represent those respondents who indicated only one race category.
[2]Before 1994, total enrolled does not include the 35 and over population.

Table A-16. Age Distribution of College Students 14 Years Old and Over, by Sex, October 1947–2017—*Continued*

(Numbers in thousands; civilian noninstitutionalized population.)

Year, sex, race, and Hispanic origin	All students								Male							
	Total	14 to 17 years	18 and 19 years	20 and 21 years	22 to 24 years	25 to 29 years	30 to 34 years	35 years and over	Total	14 to 17 years	18 and 19 years	20 and 21 years	22 to 24 years	25 to 29 years	30 to 34 years	35 years and over
1975	411	13	118	101	76	68	35	NA	218	3	53	52	40	45	25	NA
1974	354	11	112	96	64	39	32	NA	195	6	55	44	42	24	24	NA
1973	289	15	82	69	55	45	23	NA	168	11	39	37	29	32	20	NA
1972	242	14	70	60	49	34	15	NA	126	7	28	35	29	20	7	NA
WHITE ALONE OR IN COMBINATION																
2017	13,703	168	3,121	3,306	2,621	1,904	885	1,698	6,059	64	1,370	1,533	1,212	847	409	623
2016	14,355	180	3,316	3,418	2,712	2,099	942	1,687	6,415	60	1,547	1,602	1,284	876	396	651
2015	14,295	165	3,163	3,416	2,689	2,072	972	1,818	6,425	81	1,472	1,627	1,220	942	423	658
2014	14,310	154	3,154	3,299	2,877	1,982	910	1,935	6,549	73	1,433	1,646	1,318	947	385	748
2013	14,743	246	3,124	3,292	3,005	1,942	988	2,145	6,500	123	1,433	1,521	1,369	905	411	738
2012	15,117	216	3,144	3,574	2,897	2,099	1,058	2,130	6,612	98	1,429	1,547	1,423	915	442	759
2011	15,785	141	3,381	3,631	3,031	2,316	1,124	2,160	7,239	78	1,554	1,719	1,517	1,046	496	830
2010	15,586	157	3,478	3,359	2,687	2,287	1,220	2,399	7,030	60	1,620	1,656	1,196	1,080	516	902
2009	15,391	160	3,414	3,289	2,859	2,125	1,133	2,411	6,848	77	1,535	1,591	1,387	930	501	826
2008	14,738	175	3,440	3,181	2,738	2,003	936	2,264	6,730	87	1,607	1,550	1,286	966	426	807
2007	14,114	147	3,318	3,111	2,529	1,857	978	2,174	6,169	64	1,540	1,390	1,186	789	425	774
2006	13,564	166	3,043	3,006	2,416	1,791	1,016	2,125	5,966	61	1,399	1,363	1,161	827	411	744
2005	13,791	125	3,043	3,244	2,433	1,740	954	2,251	5,978	43	1,371	1,519	1,128	696	424	796
2004	13,668	135	3,012	3,106	2,425	1,807	989	2,192	6,068	49	1,331	1,494	1,131	847	425	792
2003	13,164	106	2,905	2,868	2,584	1,613	989	2,099	5,837	48	1,283	1,274	1,257	730	446	798
BLACK ALONE OR IN COMBINATION																
2017	3,068	47	597	606	579	493	225	520	1,273	13	269	267	231	208	82	203
2016	3,079	35	602	607	572	430	261	572	1,283	14	250	280	247	195	102	194
2015	2,985	28	560	602	580	421	244	551	1,216	14	259	269	305	150	63	156
2014	3,099	56	553	562	530	432	259	707	1,181	40	192	244	223	173	88	220
2013	3,118	36	509	716	581	499	228	550	1,238	22	210	306	263	192	54	190
2012	3,335	33	579	721	592	465	348	598	1,292	22	244	353	263	149	89	174
2011	3,317	39	615	540	605	533	321	665	1,279	23	250	264	249	196	100	198
2010	3,250	38	622	653	533	463	286	655	1,241	19	264	271	244	186	78	180
2009	3,030	34	604	520	574	428	268	601	1,109	5	245	250	217	155	88	149
2008	2,619	36	515	490	429	400	278	470	983	21	219	229	184	127	85	116
2007	2,630	33	530	459	479	432	243	455	1,077	12	240	229	217	139	110	130
2006	2,444	30	492	423	471	318	217	493	951	10	186	186	206	120	74	170
2005	2,387	31	481	428	462	299	229	458	895	9	201	189	167	109	66	154
2004	2,412	40	466	436	416	371	170	512	827	13	175	187	159	100	41	153
2003	2,227	30	400	440	445	303	214	395	826	10	175	165	186	100	84	107
ASIAN ALONE OR IN COMBINATION																
2017	1,750	32	297	488	438	286	101	108	822	7	133	236	243	131	40	32
2016	1,780	22	313	421	427	346	118	133	937	7	159	211	254	178	59	70
2015	1,821	21	287	488	407	315	156	147	840	11	141	218	202	151	67	49
2014	1,712	19	296	347	490	310	90	161	878	14	146	175	278	166	30	68
2013	1,766	31	350	394	412	274	117	188	872	8	171	221	221	153	38	60
2012	1,617	33	274	348	421	266	124	151	774	21	143	165	202	140	44	58
2011	1,356	21	267	323	243	220	121	161	658	6	145	162	123	110	60	53
2010	1,467	37	264	343	298	268	125	133	740	20	136	177	141	149	61	57
2009	1,334	11	271	242	330	207	122	150	656	8	138	115	165	98	57	76
2008	1,340	27	214	265	259	260	149	167	632	22	93	134	113	135	70	65
2007	1,204	11	232	220	268	232	126	116	592	2	113	116	123	113	61	64
2006	1,154	9	215	227	263	198	110	131	566	6	118	122	122	81	55	62
2005	1,297	25	204	292	277	240	122	137	640	13	97	170	124	113	63	60
2003	1,262	19	236	248	290	232	117	121	649	3	112	115	143	142	72	61

NA = Not available

Table A-16. Age Distribution of College Students 14 Years Old and Over, by Sex, October 1947–2017—*Continued*

(Numbers in thousands; civilian noninstitutionalized population.)

Year, sex, race, and Hispanic origin	Female							
	Total	14 to 17 years	18 and 19 years	20 and 21 years	22 to 24 years	25 to 29 years	30 to 34 years	35 years and over
1975..............................	193	10	65	49	36	23	10	NA
1974..............................	157	5	56	51	22	15	8	NA
1973..............................	123	5	44	33	25	13	3	NA
1972..............................	117	7	43	25	20	14	8	NA
WHITE ALONE OR IN COMBINATION								
2017..............................	7,644	104	1,751	1,772	1,408	1,057	476	1,076
2016..............................	7,940	121	1,770	1,816	1,428	1,224	546	1,036
2015..............................	7,870	84	1,691	1,789	1,469	1,129	548	1,160
2014..............................	7,761	81	1,720	1,653	1,559	1,036	525	1,187
2013..............................	8,243	123	1,691	1,771	1,637	1,037	577	1,407
2012..............................	8,505	119	1,715	2,027	1,473	1,184	615	1,372
2011..............................	8,545	63	1,828	1,912	1,514	1,270	627	1,330
2010..............................	8,556	97	1,858	1,702	1,491	1,207	703	1,497
2009..............................	8,544	84	1,879	1,698	1,473	1,195	631	1,585
2008..............................	8,008	88	1,833	1,631	1,452	1,037	510	1,457
2007..............................	7,945	82	1,779	1,721	1,343	1,068	553	1,400
2006..............................	7,598	105	1,643	1,643	1,255	964	605	1,382
2005..............................	7,813	82	1,672	1,725	1,305	1,044	530	1,454
2004..............................	7,600	86	1,682	1,612	1,295	960	564	1,401
2003..............................	7,328	57	1,622	1,594	1,327	883	543	1,302
BLACK ALONE OR IN COMBINATION								
2017..............................	1,794	34	328	339	347	286	144	317
2016..............................	1,797	21	352	328	325	234	159	378
2015..............................	1,770	14	300	332	275	271	181	396
2014..............................	1,919	17	360	318	307	259	171	486
2013..............................	1,880	14	299	409	317	306	174	360
2012..............................	2,043	11	335	368	329	316	259	424
2011..............................	2,037	16	365	276	356	337	221	467
2010..............................	2,009	20	358	383	289	277	208	474
2009..............................	1,921	29	359	270	357	274	180	451
2008..............................	1,636	15	296	261	245	272	193	354
2007..............................	1,553	20	290	230	263	292	133	325
2006..............................	1,493	20	307	238	265	198	143	323
2005..............................	1,493	22	280	239	295	190	164	303
2004..............................	1,584	27	290	249	258	271	130	359
2003..............................	1,401	20	225	275	260	203	130	288
ASIAN ALONE OR IN COMBINATION								
2017..............................	928	25	164	252	195	155	60	76
2016..............................	843	15	153	209	174	169	60	63
2015..............................	981	10	146	270	205	164	88	98
2014..............................	834	5	150	171	212	145	60	92
2013..............................	894	22	179	173	191	121	78	128
2012..............................	843	11	131	183	219	126	80	94
2011..............................	697	16	122	161	121	110	61	108
2010..............................	727	17	128	166	157	119	63	76
2009..............................	678	4	134	127	165	109	65	74
2008..............................	708	5	121	131	146	125	79	102
2007..............................	612	9	119	104	145	118	65	52
2006..............................	588	3	97	105	141	117	55	69
2005..............................	657	12	107	122	153	128	59	77
2003..............................	613	16	124	133	147	89	44	60

NA = Not available

Table A-17. College Enrollment of Students 14 Years Old and Over, by Type of College, Attendance Status, Age, and Sex, October 1970–2017

(Numbers in thousands; civilian noninstitutionalized population.)

Year and type of college	All students								Male		
	Total	14 to 19 years	20 to 21 years	22 to 24 years	25 to 34 years	35 years and over	Public	Private	Total	Full-time	Part-time
ALL UNDERGRADUATES											
2017	14,589	4,126	4,261	2,615	2,295	1,293	12,236	2,353	6,581	5,210	1,371
2016	15,497	4,369	4,295	2,916	2,489	1,427	12,523	2,974	7,075	5,630	1,445
2015	15,433	4,165	4,371	2,774	2,570	1,553	12,762	2,671	7,002	5,477	1,525
2014	15,498	4,249	4,075	2,978	2,438	1,759	12,877	2,620	7,071	5,713	1,358
2013	15,738	4,202	4,159	3,052	2,598	1,727	13,129	2,609	7,097	5,606	1,492
2012	16,170	4,236	4,420	3,025	2,783	1,706	13,451	2,719	7,107	5,603	1,505
2011	16,625	4,435	4,368	3,000	3,019	1,802	13,816	2,809	7,515	5,830	1,685
2010	16,354	4,546	4,225	2,671	2,912	2,000	13,701	2,653	7,300	5,582	1,718
2009	16,012	4,463	3,965	2,849	2,737	1,999	13,356	2,656	7,121	5,632	1,488
2008	14,955	4,347	3,862	2,600	2,430	1,716	12,340	2,616	6,737	5,220	1,517
2007	14,365	4,237	3,732	2,513	2,277	1,605	11,811	2,554	6,405	5,053	1,353
2006	13,854	3,940	3,591	2,437	2,178	1,709	11,269	2,585	6,135	4,686	1,450
2005	14,169	3,901	3,847	2,588	2,142	1,690	11,292	2,876	6,189	4,799	1,391
2004	14,004	3,863	3,700	2,431	2,257	1,753	11,384	2,620	6,156	4,714	1,442
2003	13,370	3,633	3,449	2,687	2,094	1,506	10,980	2,389	5,902	4,476	1,425
2002	13,426	3,743	3,457	2,355	2,106	1,764	10,830	2,595	5,929	4,462	1,467
2001	12,552	3,568	3,329	2,136	1,979	1,540	10,188	2,364	5,522	4,057	1,464
2000	12,401	3,710	3,093	2,113	1,988	1,498	10,044	2,357	5,520	4,059	1,461
1999	12,046	3,625	3,043	2,000	1,885	1,493	9,689	2,357	5,554	4,143	1,411
1998	12,509	3,749	3,019	2,025	2,101	1,616	10,100	2,410	5,621	4,051	1,570
1997	12,409	3,504	3,080	2,137	1,970	1,718	10,074	2,335	5,539	4,165	1,375
1996	12,305	3,526	2,856	2,017	2,226	1,680	10,121	2,183	5,533	4,032	1,502
1995	11,966	3,251	2,881	2,033	2,151	1,651	9,570	2,396	5,413	3,911	1,501
1994	12,410	3,192	3,006	2,099	2,281	1,832	9,983	2,427	5,526	3,969	1,557
1993r	11,959	3,197	2,879	2,131	2,118	1,634	9,706	2,253	5,442	4,020	1,422
1993	11,507	3,045	2,721	2,020	2,088	1,633	9,330	2,176	5,194	3,812	1,382
1992	11,643	3,097	2,902	2,004	2,090	1,550	9,519	2,124	5,091	3,724	1,365
1991	11,374	3,061	2,902	1,757	2,120	1,534	9,257	2,117	5,120	3,724	1,395
1990	11,108	3,194	2,740	1,681	2,067	1,425	9,031	2,076	5,030	3,628	1,402
1989	10,661	3,250	2,529	1,658	1,921	1,304	8,633	2,027	4,730	3,436	1,295
1988	10,605	3,229	2,645	1,600	1,865	1,266	8,617	1,988	4,763	3,441	1,322
1987	10,304	3,283	2,585	1,512	1,848	1,076	8,306	1,998	4,878	3,476	1,403
1986	10,036	3,158	2,298	1,583	1,932	1,065	7,955	2,081	4,663	3,350	1,312
1985	10,097	3,169	2,586	1,475	1,884	984	8,042	2,055	4,667	3,454	1,213
1984	9,910	3,120	2,564	1,547	1,826	852	7,944	1,966	4,725	3,573	1,152
1983	9,925	3,200	2,464	1,475	1,873	914	7,808	2,117	4,759	3,472	1,287
1982	9,952	3,183	2,657	1,526	1,745	843	7,908	2,044	4,703	3,485	1,218
1981	9,969	3,276	2,511	1,458	1,808	916	7,789	2,180	4,724	3,452	1,273
1980	9,279	3,182	2,393	1,316	1,598	791	NA	NA	4,353	3,247	1,105
1979	9,193	3,156	2,308	1,297	1,526	905	7,331	1,861	4,387	3,219	1,168
1978	8,947	3,173	2,246	1,233	1,505	790	7,008	1,939	4,445	3,269	1,176
1977[1]	8,408	3,184	2,376	1,206	1,640	NA	6,683	1,724	4,372	3,304	1,068
1976	8,988	3,216	2,358	1,224	1,472	718	7,196	1,787	4,569	3,353	1,213
1975	8,108	3,237	2,255	1,072	1,546	NA	6,598	1,510	4,393	3,394	999
1974	7,338	2,906	2,131	1,028	1,272	NA	5,843	1,494	4,030	3,128	902
1973	6,794	2,812	2,031	924	1,028	NA	5,279	1,516	3,791	3,035	756
1972	6,992	2,974	2,065	944	1,011	NA	5,460	1,532	3,982	3,231	751
1971	6,895	3,008	1,936	1,019	931	NA	5,472	1,423	4,017	3,240	777
1970	6,274	2,854	1,803	866	750	NA	4,910	1,363	3,627	3,045	582
TWO-YEAR COLLEGE STUDENTS											
2017	4,272	1,292	956	644	888	491	3,979	293	1,988	1,317	671
2016	4,346	1,363	876	692	903	512	4,054	293	2,040	1,350	690
2015	4,717	1,433	1,104	632	912	637	4,344	373	2,124	1,379	745
2014	4,841	1,432	989	734	973	714	4,410	431	2,056	1,363	693
2013	5,270	1,502	1,052	938	1,008	770	4,920	350	2,390	1,617	772
2012	5,830	1,624	1,307	892	1,205	802	5,377	453	2,509	1,665	844
2011	5,705	1,596	1,187	845	1,237	840	5,265	440	2,453	1,664	790
2010	5,904	1,754	1,230	836	1,170	915	5,450	454	2,693	1,803	890
2009	5,551	1,636	960	813	1,221	920	5,095	456	2,363	1,573	790
2008	5,345	1,731	1,001	726	1,095	792	5,006	339	2,331	1,487	844
2007	4,814	1,496	856	774	963	725	4,418	396	2,061	1,322	739

NA = Not available.
r = Revised, controlled to 1990 census based population estimates; previous 1993 data controlled to 1980 census based population estimates.
[1]Data for 1970–1975 and 1977 do not include people ages 35 and over.

Table A-17. College Enrollment of Students 14 Years Old and Over, by Type of College, Attendance Status, Age, and Sex, October 1970–2017—*Continued*

(Numbers in thousands; civilian noninstitutionalized population.)

Year and type of college	Female			Full time	Part time					
	Total	Full-time	Part-time	Total	Total	14 to 19 years	20 to 21 years	22 to 24 years	25 to 34 years	35 years and over
ALL UNDERGRADUATES										
2017	8,008	6,125	1,884	11,334	3,255	358	429	654	1,027	788
2016	8,422	6,486	1,936	12,116	3,381	359	539	602	1,091	790
2015	8,431	6,438	1,992	11,915	3,518	414	523	604	1,146	831
2014	8,427	6,524	1,903	12,237	3,260	306	455	640	895	964
2013	8,641	6,507	2,133	12,113	3,625	379	532	802	990	922
2012	9,063	6,789	2,274	12,391	3,779	416	616	655	1,109	983
2011	9,110	6,908	2,202	12,738	3,887	376	514	766	1,261	970
2010	9,054	6,773	2,282	12,354	4,000	514	572	599	1,237	1,077
2009	8,891	6,686	2,205	12,318	3,694	335	431	573	1,189	1,165
2008	8,218	6,158	2,060	11,378	3,577	347	417	583	1,190	1,040
2007	7,959	5,813	2,146	10,866	3,499	358	450	656	992	1,043
2006	7,719	5,695	2,024	10,380	3,474	373	441	627	936	1,097
2005	7,979	5,852	2,127	10,651	3,518	360	479	611	1,003	1,065
2004	7,848	5,704	2,144	10,418	3,586	330	449	595	1,107	1,105
2003	7,468	5,391	2,077	9,868	3,502	334	457	739	1,013	959
2002	7,497	5,273	2,223	9,735	3,690	387	399	619	1,033	1,253
2001	7,030	4,949	2,082	9,006	3,546	378	489	612	1,003	1,064
2000	6,881	4,832	2,049	8,891	3,510	342	435	633	1,058	1,041
1999	6,492	4,548	1,945	8,691	3,355	345	418	514	997	1,081
1998	6,888	4,765	2,123	8,816	3,693	421	400	563	1,145	1,164
1997	6,870	4,752	2,118	8,917	3,492	360	376	560	1,010	1,186
1996	6,772	4,502	2,269	8,534	3,771	394	396	501	1,236	1,243
1995	6,554	4,433	2,121	8,344	3,622	349	419	589	1,147	1,118
1994	6,883	4,480	2,404	8,449	3,961	350	421	644	1,300	1,245
1993r	6,517	4,346	2,171	8,366	3,593	332	366	619	1,176	1,102
1993	6,313	4,182	2,130	7,994	3,513	314	342	590	1,161	1,106
1992	6,553	4,338	2,214	8,063	3,580	259	396	578	1,255	1,092
1991	6,254	4,145	2,109	7,869	3,505	252	368	509	1,242	1,134
1990	6,077	3,967	2,109	7,597	3,511	282	408	515	1,244	1,062
1989	5,931	3,880	2,051	7,314	3,346	260	321	536	1,266	963
1988	5,842	3,816	2,026	7,257	3,348	303	371	521	1,173	981
1987	5,426	3,445	1,981	6,920	3,384	391	406	507	1,238	841
1986	5,373	3,474	1,899	6,825	3,212	278	324	528	1,254	828
1985	5,430	3,578	1,852	7,033	3,065	269	349	457	1,184	806
1984	5,185	3,419	1,766	6,992	2,918	274	344	480	1,139	683
1983	5,166	3,424	1,742	6,896	3,029	305	340	482	1,153	748
1982	5,249	3,480	1,769	6,965	2,987	302	372	547	1,083	684
1981	5,245	3,490	1,755	6,942	3,027	293	353	471	1,195	715
1980	4,927	3,210	1,717	6,457	2,822	283	287	505	1,098	649
1979	4,805	3,163	1,642	6,383	2,810	264	314	482	1,003	748
1978	4,502	3,031	1,471	6,300	2,647	302	328	412	947	658
1977[1]	4,027	3,002	1,025	6,304	2,104	329	301	431	1,042	NA
1976	4,419	3,166	1,253	6,519	2,466	253	325	403	909	577
1975	3,715	2,902	813	6,296	1,812	250	297	376	891	NA
1974	3,307	2,561	746	5,689	1,649	245	289	331	784	NA
1973	3,004	2,423	581	5,460	1,334	183	230	294	630	NA
1972	3,010	2,445	565	5,678	1,314	177	220	320	599	NA
1971	2,878	2,348	530	5,588	1,307	207	207	319	574	NA
1970	2,646	2,164	482	5,208	1,066	169	175	275	449	NA
TWO-YEAR COLLEGE STUDENTS										
2017	2,284	1,372	912	2,689	1,583	253	225	253	483	369
2016	2,306	1,432	875	2,782	1,565	238	290	276	457	304
2015	2,593	1,669	924	3,048	1,669	291	312	229	454	383
2014	2,786	1,839	946	3,202	1,639	207	324	259	415	434
2013	2,881	1,865	1,016	3,482	1,788	249	305	367	472	396
2012	3,321	2,119	1,201	3,784	2,046	312	369	324	574	466
2011	3,252	2,053	1,199	3,716	1,989	255	306	387	564	477
2010	3,211	2,066	1,144	3,870	2,034	332	362	282	516	542
2009	3,188	2,060	1,128	3,633	1,918	227	271	274	580	566
2008	3,014	1,910	1,104	3,397	1,948	281	239	271	628	529
2007	2,753	1,666	1,087	2,988	1,826	221	230	349	520	506

NA = Not available.

r = Revised, controlled to 1990 census based population estimates; previous 1993 data controlled to 1980 census based population estimates.

[1]Data for 1970–1975 and 1977 do not include people ages 35 and over.

Table A-17. College Enrollment of Students 14 Years Old and Over, by Type of College, Attendance Status, Age, and Sex, October 1970–2017—*Continued*

(Numbers in thousands; civilian noninstitutionalized population.)

Year and type of college	Total	14 to 19 years	20 to 21 years	22 to 24 years	25 to 34 years	35 years and over	Public	Private	Total	Full-time	Part-time
									Male		
2006	4,294	1,367	788	573	836	731	3,878	416	1,788	1,169	620
2005	4,327	1,259	833	603	882	751	3,890	437	1,866	1,197	669
2004	4,340	1,243	802	568	898	829	3,939	401	1,756	1,141	615
2003	4,384	1,178	746	843	834	784	3,999	385	1,782	1,055	726
2002	4,378	1,227	777	656	880	838	3,948	431	1,884	1,102	783
2001	4,159	1,200	776	605	832	746	3,749	410	1,802	1,057	745
2000	3,881	1,232	710	525	673	741	3,590	291	1,655	969	686
1999	3,794	1,187	715	460	683	749	3,482	312	1,637	949	688
1998	4,234	1,301	701	619	839	774	3,865	369	1,845	1,049	796
1997	4,078	1,178	760	528	806	807	3,780	298	1,663	983	680
1996	4,174	1,223	669	515	922	845	3,890	284	1,752	974	778
1995	3,882	1,028	608	593	892	761	3,553	330	1,626	898	728
1994	4,208	1,063	623	621	1,011	890	3,846	362	1,704	937	766
1993r	4,345	1,131	745	648	978	843	4,024	321	1,825	1,061	764
1993	4,196	1,077	696	614	965	844	3,884	311	1,748	1,006	742
1992	4,239	1,084	789	581	988	797	3,937	302	1,688	936	751
1991	4,277	1,120	732	560	1,084	781	4,025	252	1,798	973	825
1990	3,965	1,059	689	475	967	775	3,689	276	1,624	849	775
1989	3,627	1,048	557	467	880	676	3,382	245	1,464	777	688
1988	3,837	1,134	665	497	879	662	3,609	228	1,542	847	695
1987	3,648	1,111	624	457	851	605	3,405	243	1,522	780	742
1986	3,391	1,023	506	427	875	559	3,089	302	1,466	752	714
1985	3,289	959	558	403	851	518	3,009	281	1,336	702	634
1984	3,172	994	525	442	795	417	2,875	298	1,436	834	601
1983	3,416	1,050	595	405	882	485	3,136	280	1,498	807	691
1982	3,448	1,088	604	494	826	437	3,164	283	1,477	854	623
1981	3,347	1,144	566	414	768	455	3,091	255	1,475	837	638
1980	3,107	1,079	450	417	721	441	NA	NA	1,331	768	563
1979	2,897	933	403	407	664	490	2,710	187	1,251	684	567
1978	2,904	966	427	391	670	451	2,686	218	1,368	698	669
1977[1]	2,510	933	455	380	741	NA	2,362	148	1,253	681	572
1976	2,854	907	444	367	718	419	2,688	165	1,400	760	640
1975	2,561	1,024	431	354	752	NA	2,437	123	1,412	850	562
1974	2,072	834	369	305	565	NA	1,917	154	1,172	709	463
1973	1,797	816	278	254	449	NA	1,669	128	1,012	629	383
1972	1,910	883	334	267	426	NA	1,816	94	1,125	770	355
1971	1,830	928	307	263	331	NA	1,726	105	1,087	726	361
1970	1,692	895	281	234	283	NA	1,559	133	1,001	726	275
GRADUATE STUDENTS											
2017	3,809	53	105	1,012	1,586	1,053	2,570	1,239	1,531	994	537
2016	3,699	42	121	817	1,729	990	2,448	1,251	1,569	1,071	498
2015	3,668	35	134	895	1,605	998	2,413	1,255	1,482	1,043	439
2014	3,677	22	143	900	1,551	1,061	2,447	1,230	1,559	957	602
2013	3,729	57	168	873	1,468	1,164	2,385	1,344	1,439	933	506
2012	3,760	48	142	854	1,550	1,165	2,327	1,433	1,495	910	585
2011	3,773	11	91	868	1,598	1,205	2,318	1,454	1,617	905	712
2010	3,921	47	123	830	1,712	1,209	2,453	1,468	1,708	1,050	658
2009	3,752	32	70	901	1,556	1,194	2,366	1,386	1,521	852	669
2008	3,676	20	58	819	1,583	1,195	2,399	1,277	1,574	880	694
2007	3,591	24	62	779	1,560	1,166	2,261	1,330	1,420	819	601
2006	3,378	18	84	729	1,480	1,067	2,197	1,181	1,371	692	678
2005	3,304	7	98	574	1,458	1,167	2,143	1,161	1,349	711	638
2004	3,378	20	77	718	1,433	1,131	2,267	1,111	1,419	726	693
2003	3,268	29	84	632	1,399	1,123	2,129	1,139	1,416	774	643
2002	3,072	33	68	572	1,296	1,104	2,003	1,068	1,311	632	679
2001	3,321	48	91	595	1,442	1,145	2,233	1,088	1,353	614	739
2000	2,913	38	77	571	1,218	1,009	1,965	948	1,162	546	616
1999	3,157	45	77	620	1,211	1,205	1,970	1,188	1,403	699	703
1998	3,037	45	73	536	1,313	1,070	1,884	1,153	1,284	614	669
1997	3,027	30	63	562	1,299	1,073	2,016	1,010	1,304	651	653
1996	2,922	21	52	534	1,217	1,098	1,893	1,029	1,288	650	638
1995	2,749	8	60	465	1,198	1,018	1,802	947	1,290	646	644
1994	2,613	9	21	551	1,138	893	1,710	902	1,238	619	619
1993r	2,435	3	14	537	1,022	859	1,611	824	1,156	601	555

NA = Not available.

r = Revised, controlled to 1990 census based population estimates; previous 1993 data controlled to 1980 census based population estimates.

[1]Data for 1970–1975 and 1977 do not include people ages 35 and over.

Table A-17. College Enrollment of Students 14 Years Old and Over, by Type of College, Attendance Status, Age, and Sex, October 1970–2017—*Continued*

(Numbers in thousands; civilian noninstitutionalized population.)

| Year and type of college | Female | | | Full time | Part time | | | | | |
	Total	Full-time	Part-time	Total	Total	14 to 19 years	20 to 21 years	22 to 24 years	25 to 34 years	35 years and over
2006	2,506	1,531	975	2,699	1,595	221	188	261	435	490
2005	2,462	1,436	1,026	2,632	1,695	228	228	230	489	520
2004	2,584	1,461	1,123	2,602	1,738	216	249	241	472	560
2003	2,603	1,507	1,095	2,563	1,822	205	230	457	404	526
2002	2,494	1,363	1,131	2,464	1,914	252	206	312	506	638
2001	2,357	1,252	1,105	2,310	1,850	250	247	304	524	525
2000	2,226	1,224	1,002	2,193	1,688	239	202	247	444	557
1999	2,157	1,157	1,000	2,105	1,688	231	217	199	453	588
1998	2,389	1,287	1,103	2,336	1,899	277	206	288	537	591
1997	2,415	1,307	1,108	2,290	1,788	231	238	245	479	595
1996	2,423	1,235	1,187	2,209	1,965	227	212	244	607	674
1995	2,256	1,124	1,132	2,022	1,860	218	211	295	571	565
1994	2,504	1,234	1,270	2,172	2,036	215	216	302	669	634
1993r	2,520	1,317	1,203	2,378	1,967	240	230	300	613	585
1993	2,448	1,268	1,179	2,274	1,922	227	213	288	605	588
1992	2,551	1,268	1,283	2,205	2,034	187	261	294	683	609
1991	2,479	1,239	1,239	2,212	2,065	205	256	291	723	589
1990	2,340	1,103	1,237	1,953	2,012	212	281	247	657	615
1989	2,163	949	1,214	1,725	1,902	188	189	307	669	548
1988	2,295	1,054	1,241	1,901	1,936	207	256	288	651	534
1987	2,127	937	1,190	1,716	1,932	272	256	264	639	500
1986	1,924	856	1,068	1,608	1,783	209	210	257	652	454
1985	1,954	914	1,040	1,615	1,674	180	217	229	607	440
1984	1,738	829	909	1,663	1,509	182	195	252	548	333
1983	1,919	897	1,022	1,703	1,713	195	221	245	631	420
1982	1,971	961	1,011	1,814	1,634	205	223	280	566	356
1981	1,872	909	963	1,745	1,601	217	209	243	579	353
1980	1,777	798	979	1,566	1,542	195	163	256	554	374
1979	1,646	725	921	1,408	1,489	184	152	251	480	423
1978	1,537	701	835	1,400	1,505	190	184	234	503	394
1977[1]	1,256	691	565	1,372	1,138	216	172	218	533	NA
1976	1,454	743	711	1,503	1,351	143	183	190	490	346
1975	1,148	717	431	1,567	994	159	157	199	478	NA
1974	899	528	371	1,237	835	132	136	154	413	NA
1973	785	471	314	1,100	697	114	113	133	338	NA
1972	785	484	301	1,255	655	111	111	133	300	NA
1971	743	473	270	1,199	631	131	98	139	261	NA
1970	691	452	239	1,177	515	109	84	120	203	NA
GRADUATE STUDENTS										
2017	2,278	1,278	1,000	2,272	1,537	*	20	175	640	702
2016	2,130	1,234	896	2,305	1,394	*	26	123	627	618
2015	2,186	1,278	908	2,321	1,347	*	29	146	555	617
2014	2,119	1,205	913	2,163	1,515	*	32	161	640	682
2013	2,291	1,182	1,108	2,115	1,614	18	25	171	602	798
2012	2,265	1,301	964	2,211	1,549	3	21	155	625	745
2011	2,156	1,261	895	2,165	1,607	5	14	185	643	761
2010	2,214	1,196	1,017	2,246	1,675	12	4	133	685	842
2009	2,232	1,194	1,038	2,046	1,707	6	20	197	641	843
2008	2,103	987	1,116	1,867	1,810	*	5	173	732	899
2007	2,171	971	1,200	1,790	1,801	1	4	210	745	842
2006	2,007	998	1,009	1,690	1,688	3	14	187	671	813
2005	1,955	875	1,079	1,587	1,717	3	*	150	691	873
2004	1,959	845	1,114	1,571	1,807	*	1	170	757	878
2003	1,852	849	1,003	1,622	1,646	3	8	153	662	820
2002	1,761	774	987	1,406	1,666	2	6	140	666	852
2001	1,968	784	1,184	1,398	1,923	10	14	139	812	947
2000	1,750	722	1,028	1,268	1,645	6	10	156	674	798
1999	1,755	722	1,033	1,421	1,736	8	6	133	672	918
1998	1,753	758	995	1,372	1,665	*	15	107	734	808
1997	1,723	668	1,055	1,319	1,708	3	6	160	694	844
1996	1,634	655	979	1,305	1,617	3	9	114	647	844
1995	1,459	554	905	1,199	1,550	*	17	112	627	793
1994	1,375	505	870	1,124	1,489	*	2	174	594	718
1993r	1,278	458	820	1,059	1,376	*	3	161	540	673

* = Quantity zero or rounds to zero.
NA = Not available.
r = Revised, controlled to 1990 census based population estimates; previous 1993 data controlled to 1980 census based population estimates.
[1]Data for 1970–1975 and 1977 do not include people ages 35 and over.

Table A-17. College Enrollment of Students 14 Years Old and Over, by Type of College, Attendance Status, Age, and Sex, October 1970–2017—*Continued*

(Numbers in thousands; civilian noninstitutionalized population.)

Year and type of college	All students								Male		
	Total	14 to 19 years	20 to 21 years	22 to 24 years	25 to 34 years	35 years and over	Public	Private	Total	Full-time	Part-time
1993	2,391	3	13	514	1,006	856	1,580	812	1,130	579	551
1992	2,392	*	36	508	1,035	814	1,546	846	1,102	606	496
1991	2,683	*	37	547	1,165	934	1,824	859	1,320	688	631
1990	2,514	2	27	497	1,095	893	1,722	792	1,162	569	593
1989	2,520	*	40	509	1,161	809	1,662	857	1,219	626	594
1988	2,511	*	36	464	1,098	913	1,716	795	1,187	522	666
1987	2,415	1	57	494	1,137	725	1,655	760	1,152	579	573
1986	2,365	*	44	530	1,057	732	1,624	741	1,184	596	589
1985	2,427	*	31	540	1,179	678	1,652	775	1,239	607	632
1984	2,395	*	32	580	1,190	594	1,648	747	1,263	654	610
1983	2,442	*	32	568	1,214	629	1,614	829	1,279	665	614
1982	2,393	1	31	534	1,244	584	1,587	806	1,216	626	590
1981	2,205	*	34	528	1,120	523	1,478	726	1,127	546	581
1980	2,173	2	31	554	1,104	481	NA	NA	1,106	526	581
1979	2,214	*	45	497	1,149	523	1,537	678	1,105	503	602
1978	2,217	*	51	565	1,064	536	1,454	762	1,149	516	633
1977[1]	1,810	2	53	593	1,161	NA	1,241	568	995	548	447
1976	2,152	*	40	622	1,017	472	1,516	634	1,216	576	638
1975	1,590	*	59	607	923	NA	1,105	484	949	542	407
1974	1,490	*	61	499	930	NA	1,061	428	897	457	440
1973	1,385	*	42	541	801	NA	945	439	887	467	420
1972	1,320	1	52	517	749	NA	877	443	872	481	391
1971	1,192	1	60	468	663	NA	799	393	833	480	353
1970	1,140	*	54	488	599	NA	789	351	774	432	342

* = Quantity zero or rounds to zero.
NA = Not available.
[1]Data for 1970–1975 and 1977 do not include people ages 35 and over.

Table A-17. College Enrollment of Students 14 Years Old and Over, by Type of College, Attendance Status, Age, and Sex, October 1970–2017—*Continued*

(Numbers in thousands; civilian noninstitutionalized population.)

Year and type of college	Female			Full time	Part time					
	Total	Full-time	Part-time	Total	Total	14 to 19 years	20 to 21 years	22 to 24 years	25 to 34 years	35 years and over
1993.........	1,261	446	815	1,025	1,366	*	3	156	536	672
1992.........	1,291	521	770	1,126	1,266	*	3	120	557	586
1991.........	1,364	491	872	1,180	1,504	*	8	124	626	746
1990.........	1,352	531	820	1,100	1,413	*	2	121	577	714
1989.........	1,300	515	786	1,140	1,380	*	7	135	637	601
1988.........	1,324	435	889	956	1,555	*	5	160	634	756
1987.........	1,263	462	801	1,041	1,374	*	5	151	660	558
1986.........	1,181	479	702	1,074	1,291	*	4	120	593	575
1985.........	1,188	395	793	1,002	1,424	*	4	155	728	537
1984.........	1,132	440	692	1,093	1,302	*	6	153	644	498
1983.........	1,163	438	725	1,103	1,339	*	*	148	685	507
1982.........	1,178	421	756	1,047	1,346	1	4	153	721	467
1981.........	1,078	347	731	893	1,312	*	6	173	673	459
1980.........	1,066	372	694	898	1,275	*	6	152	702	415
1979.........	1,109	355	754	858	1,356	*	14	140	752	451
1978.........	1,068	366	702	882	1,335	*	14	169	688	465
1977[1].........	813	338	475	886	922	*	10	211	702	NA
1976.........	937	292	644	869	1,282	*	5	217	662	398
1975.........	640	267	373	809	780	*	16	225	537	NA
1974.........	593	205	388	662	828	*	20	210	600	NA
1973.........	498	163	335	630	755	*	9	191	553	NA
1972.........	450	155	295	636	686	*	8	185	487	NA
1971.........	359	136	223	616	576	*	3	169	402	NA
1970.........	366	123	243	555	585	*	12	184	387	NA

* = Quantity zero or rounds to zero.
NA = Not available.
[1]Data for 1970–1975 and 1977 do not include people ages 35 and over.

Table A-18. Total Fall Enrollment in Degree-Granting Institutions, by Attendance Status, Sex of Student, and Control of Institution, Selected Years, 1947–2016

(Number; percent.)

Year	Total enrolled	Attendance status			Sex of student			Control of institution			
		Full-time	Part-time	Percent part-time	Male	Female	Percent Female	Public	Private		
									Total	Not-for-profit	For-profit
2016............	19,841,014	12,126,325	7,714,689	38.9	8,635,699	11,205,315	56.5	14,582,972	5,258,042	4,077,797	1,180,245
2015............	19,988,204	12,287,512	7,700,692	38.5	8,723,819	11,264,385	56.4	14,572,843	5,415,361	4,065,891	1,349,470
2014............	20,209,092	12,454,464	7,754,628	38.4	8,797,530	11,411,562	56.5	14,654,660	5,554,432	3,997,249	1,557,183
2013............	20,376,677	12,596,610	7,780,067	38.2	8,861,197	11,515,480	56.5	14,746,848	5,629,829	3,971,390	1,658,439
2012............	20,644,478	12,734,404	7,910,074	38.3	8,919,006	11,725,472	56.8	14,884,667	5,759,811	3,951,388	1,808,423
2011............	21,010,590	13,002,531	8,008,059	38.1	9,034,256	11,976,334	57.0	15,116,303	5,894,287	3,926,819	1,967,468
2010............	21,019,438	13,087,182	7,932,256	37.7	9,045,759	11,973,679	57.0	15,142,171	5,877,267	3,854,482	2,022,785
2009............	20,313,594	12,605,355	7,708,239	37.9	8,732,953	11,580,641	57.0	14,810,768	5,502,826	3,767,672	1,735,154
2008............	19,102,814	11,747,743	7,355,071	38.5	8,188,895	10,913,919	57.1	13,972,153	5,130,661	3,661,519	1,469,142
2007............	18,248,128	11,269,892	6,978,236	38.2	7,815,914	10,432,214	57.2	13,490,780	4,757,348	3,571,150	1,186,198
2006............	17,758,870	10,957,305	6,801,565	38.3	7,574,815	10,184,055	57.3	13,180,133	4,578,737	3,512,866	1,065,871
2005............	17,487,475	10,797,011	6,690,464	38.3	7,455,925	10,031,550	57.4	13,021,834	4,465,641	3,454,692	1,010,949
2004............	17,272,044	10,610,177	6,661,867	38.6	7,387,262	9,884,782	57.2	12,980,112	4,291,932	3,411,685	880,247
2003............	16,911,481	10,326,133	6,585,348	38.9	7,260,264	9,651,217	57.1	12,858,698	4,052,783	3,341,048	711,735
2002............	16,611,711	9,946,359	6,665,352	40.1	7,202,116	9,409,595	56.6	12,751,993	3,859,718	3,265,476	594,242
2001............	15,927,987	9,447,502	6,480,485	40.7	6,960,815	8,967,172	56.3	12,233,156	3,694,831	3,167,330	527,501
2000............	15,312,289	9,009,600	6,302,689	41.2	6,721,769	8,590,520	56.1	11,752,786	3,559,503	3,109,419	450,084
1999............	14,849,691	8,803,139	6,046,552	40.7	6,515,164	8,334,527	56.1	11,375,739	3,473,952	3,055,029	418,923
1998............	14,506,967	8,563,338	5,943,629	41.0	6,369,265	8,137,702	56.1	11,137,769	3,369,198	3,004,925	364,273
1997............	14,502,334	8,438,062	6,064,272	41.8	6,396,028	8,106,306	55.9	11,196,119	3,306,215	2,977,614	328,601
1996............	14,367,520	8,302,953	6,064,567	42.2	6,352,825	8,014,695	55.8	11,120,499	3,247,021	2,942,556	304,465
1995............	14,261,781	8,128,802	6,132,979	43.0	6,342,539	7,919,242	55.5	11,092,374	3,169,407	2,929,044	240,363
1994............	14,278,790	8,137,776	6,141,014	43.0	6,371,898	7,906,892	55.4	11,133,680	3,145,110	2,910,107	235,003
1993............	14,304,803	8,127,618	6,177,185	43.2	6,427,450	7,877,353	55.1	11,189,088	3,115,715	2,888,897	226,818
1992............	14,487,359	8,162,118	6,325,241	43.7	6,523,989	7,963,370	55.0	11,384,567	3,102,792	2,872,523	230,269
1991............	14,358,953	8,115,329	6,243,624	43.5	6,501,844	7,857,109	54.7	11,309,563	3,049,390	2,819,041	230,349
1990............	13,818,637	7,820,985	5,997,652	43.4	6,283,909	7,534,728	54.5	10,844,717	2,973,920	2,760,227	213,693
1989............	13,538,560	7,660,950	5,877,610	43.4	6,190,015	7,348,545	54.3	10,577,963	2,960,597	2,731,174	229,423
1988............	13,055,337	7,436,768	5,618,569	43.0	6,001,896	7,053,441	54.0	10,161,388	2,893,949	2,673,567	220,382
1987............	12,766,642	7,231,085	5,535,557	43.4	5,932,056	6,834,586	53.5	9,973,254	2,793,388	2,602,350	191,038[3]
1986............	12,503,511	7,119,550	5,383,961	43.1	5,884,515	6,618,996	52.9	9,713,893	2,789,618	2,572,479	217,139[3]
1985............	12,247,055	7,075,221	5,171,834	42.2	5,818,450	6,428,605	52.5	9,479,273	2,767,782	2,571,791	195,991
1984............	12,241,940	7,098,388	5,143,552	42.0	5,863,574	6,378,366	52.1	9,477,370	2,764,570	2,574,419	190,151
1983............	12,464,661	7,261,050	5,203,611	41.7	6,023,725	6,440,936	51.7	9,682,734	2,781,927	2,589,187	192,740
1982............	12,425,780	7,220,618	5,205,162	41.9	6,031,384	6,394,396	51.5	9,696,087	2,729,693	2,552,739	176,954[2]
1981............	12,371,672	7,181,250	5,190,422	42.0	5,975,056	6,396,616	51.7	9,647,032	2,724,640	2,572,405	152,235[2]
1980............	12,096,895	7,097,958	4,998,937	41.3	5,874,374	6,222,521	51.4	9,457,394	2,639,501	2,527,787	152,235[2]
1979............	11,569,899	6,794,039	4,775,860	41.3	5,682,877	5,887,022	50.9	9,036,822	2,533,077	2,461,773	71,304
1978............	11,260,092	6,667,657	4,592,435	40.8	5,640,998	5,619,094	49.9	8,785,893	2,474,199	2,408,331	65,868
1977............	11,285,787	6,792,925	4,492,862	39.8	5,789,016	5,496,771	48.7	8,846,993	2,438,794	2,386,652	52,142
1976............	11,012,137	6,717,058	4,295,079	39.0	5,810,828	5,201,309	47.2	8,653,477	2,358,660	2,314,298	44,362
1975............	11,184,859	6,841,334	4,343,525	38.8	6,148,997	5,035,862	45.0	8,834,508	2,350,351	2,311,448	38,903
1974............	10,223,729	6,370,273	3,853,456	37.7	5,622,429	4,601,300	45.0	7,988,500	2,235,229	2,200,963	34,266
1973............	9,602,123	6,189,493	3,412,630	35.5	5,371,052	4,231,071	44.1	7,419,516	2,182,607	2,148,784	33,823
1972............	9,214,860	6,072,389	3,142,471	34.1	5,238,757	3,976,103	43.1	7,070,635	2,144,225	2,123,245	20,980
1971............	8,948,644	6,077,232	2,871,412	32.1	5,207,004	3,741,640	41.8	6,804,309	2,144,335	2,121,913	22,422
1970............	8,580,887	5,816,290	2,764,597	32.2	5,043,642	3,537,245	41.2	6,428,134	2,152,753	2,134,420	18,333
1969............	8,004,660	5,498,883	2,505,777	31.3	4,746,201	3,258,459	40.7	5,896,868	2,107,792	2,087,653	20,139
1968............	7,513,091	5,210,155	2,302,936	30.7	4,477,649	3,035,442	40.4	5,430,652	2,082,439	2,061,211	21,228
1967[1]	6,911,748	4,793,128	2,118,620	30.7	4,132,800	2,778,948	40.2	4,816,028	2,095,720	2,074,041	21,679
1966[1]	6,389,872	4,438,606	1,951,266	30.5	3,856,216	2,533,656	39.7	4,348,917	2,040,955	NA	NA
1965[1]	5,920,864	4,095,728	1,825,136	30.8	3,630,020	2,290,844	38.7	3,969,596	1,951,268	NA	NA
1964[1]	5,280,020	3,573,238	1,706,782	32.3	3,248,713	2,031,307	38.5	3,467,708	1,812,312	NA	NA
1963[1]	4,779,609	3,183,833	1,595,776	33.4	2,961,540	1,818,069	38.0	3,081,279	1,698,330	NA	NA
1961[1]	4,145,065	2,785,133	1,359,932	32.8	2,585,821	1,559,244	37.6	2,561,447	1,583,618	NA	NA

Note: Data through 1995 are for institutions of higher education, while later data are for degree-granting institutions. Degree-granting institutions grant associate's or higher degrees and participate in Title IV federal financial aid programs. The degree-granting classification is very similar to the earlier higher education classification, but it includes more 2-year colleges and excludes a few higher education institutions that did not grant degrees. Some data have been revised from previously published figures.
NA = Not available.
[1]Includes part-time resident students and all extension students (students attending courses at sites separate from the primary reporting campus).

Table A-18. Total Fall Enrollment in Degree-Granting Institutions, by Attendance Status, Sex of Student, and Control of Institution, Selected Years, 1947–2016—*Continued*

(Number; percent.)

Year	Total enrolled	Attendance status			Sex of student			Control of institution			
		Full-time	Part-time	Percent part-time	Male	Female	Percent Female	Public	Private Total	Not-for-profit	For-profit
1959[1]	3,639,847	2,421,016	1,218,831	33.5	2,332,617	1,307,230	35.9	2,180,982	1,458,865	NA	NA
1957............	3,323,783	NA	NA	NA	2,170,765	1,153,018	34.7	1,972,673	1,351,110	NA	NA
1956[2]	2,918,212	NA	NA	NA	1,911,458	1,006,754	34.5	1,656,402	1,261,810	NA	NA
1955[2]	2,653,034	NA	NA	NA	1,733,184	919,850	34.7	1,476,282	1,176,752	NA	NA
1954[2]	2,446,693	NA	NA	NA	1,563,382	883,311	36.1	1,353,531	1,093,162	NA	NA
1953[2]	2,231,054	NA	NA	NA	1,422,598	808,456	36.2	1,185,876	1,045,178	NA	NA
1952[2]	2,134,242	NA	NA	NA	1,380,357	753,885	35.3	1,101,240	1,033,002	NA	NA
1951[2]	2,101,962	NA	NA	NA	1,390,740	711,222	33.8	1,037,938	1,064,024	NA	NA
1950[2]	2,281,298	NA	NA	NA	1,560,392	720,906	31.6	1,139,699	1,141,599	NA	NA
1949[2]	2,444,900	NA	NA	NA	1,721,572	723,328	29.6	1,207,151	1,237,749	NA	NA
1948[2]	2,403,396	NA	NA	NA	1,709,367	694,029	28.9	1,185,588	1,217,808	NA	NA
1947[2]	2,338,226	NA	NA	NA	1,659,249	678,977	29.0	1,152,377	1,185,849	NA	NA

Note: Data through 1995 are for institutions of higher education, while later data are for degree-granting institutions. Degree-granting institutions grant associate's or higher degrees and participate in Title IV federal financial aid programs. The degree-granting classification is very similar to the earlier higher education classification, but it includes more 2-year colleges and excludes a few higher education institutions that did not grant degrees. Some data have been revised from previously published figures.

NA = Not available.

[1] Includes part-time resident students and all extension students (students attending courses at sites separate from the primary reporting campus).

[2] Degree-credit enrollment only.

Table A-19. Total Fall Enrollment in Degree-Granting Institutions, by Control and Type of Institution, 1970–2016

(Numbers in thousands.)

Year	All institutions			Public institutions			Private institutions		
	Total	4-year	2-year	Total	4-year	2-year	Total	4-year	2-year
2016..............	19,841	13,751	6,090	14,583	8,742	5,841	5,258	5,009	249
2015..............	19,988	13,489	6,499	14,573	8,349	6,224	5,415	5,140	275
2014..............	20,209	13,494	6,715	14,655	8,257	6,398	5,554	5,237	317
2013..............	20,377	13,406	6,971	14,747	8,120	6,626	5,630	5,286	344
2012..............	20,644	13,477	7,168	14,885	8,093	6,792	5,760	5,384	376
2011..............	21,011	13,499	7,511	15,116	8,048	7,068	5,894	5,451	443
2010..............	21,019	13,336	7,684	15,142	7,924	7,218	5,877	5,412	466
2009..............	20,314	12,791	7,523	14,811	7,709	7,102	5,503	5,082	421
2008..............	19,103	12,131	6,971	13,972	7,332	6,640	5,131	4,800	331
2007..............	18,248	11,630	6,618	13,491	7,167	6,324	4,757	4,464	294
2006..............	17,759	11,240	6,519	13,180	6,955	6,225	4,579	4,285	293
2005..............	17,487	10,999	6,488	13,022	6,838	6,184	4,466	4,162	304
2004..............	17,272	10,726	6,546	12,980	6,737	6,244	4,292	3,990	302
2003..............	16,911	10,417	6,494	12,859	6,649	6,209	4,053	3,768	285
2002..............	16,612	10,082	6,529	12,752	6,482	6,270	3,860	3,601	259
2001..............	15,928	9,677	6,251	12,233	6,236	5,997	3,695	3,441	254
2000..............	15,312	9,364	5,948	11,753	6,055	5,697	3,560	3,308	251
1999..............	14,850	9,196	5,654	11,376	5,978	5,398	3,474	3,218	255
1998..............	14,507	9,018	5,489	11,138	5,892	5,246	3,369	3,126	243
1997..............	14,502	8,897	5,606	11,196	5,835	5,361	3,306	3,061	245
1996..............	14,368	8,804	5,563	11,120	5,806	5,314	3,247	2,998	249
1995..............	14,262	8,769	5,493	11,092	5,815	5,278	3,169	2,955	215
1994..............	14,279	8,749	5,530	11,134	5,825	5,308	3,145	2,924	221
1993..............	14,305	8,739	5,566	11,189	5,852	5,337	3,116	2,887	229
1992..............	14,487	8,765	5,722	11,385	5,900	5,485	3,103	2,865	238
1991..............	14,359	8,707	5,652	11,310	5,905	5,405	3,049	2,802	247
1990..............	13,819	8,579	5,240	10,845	5,848	4,996	2,974	2,730	244
1989..............	13,539	8,388	5,151	10,578	5,694	4,884	2,961	2,693	267
1988..............	13,055	8,180	4,875	10,161	5,546	4,615	2,894	2,634	260
1987..............	12,767	7,990	4,776	9,973	5,432	4,541	2,793	2,558	235[2]
1986..............	12,504	7,824	4,680	9,714	5,300	4,414	2,790	2,524	265[2]
1985..............	12,247	7,716	4,531	9,479	5,210	4,270	2,768	2,506	261
1984..............	12,242	7,711	4,531	9,477	5,198	4,279	2,765	2,513	252
1983..............	12,465	7,741	4,723	9,683	5,223	4,459	2,782	2,518	264
1982..............	12,426	7,654	4,772	9,696	5,176	4,520	2,730	2,478	264[1]
1981..............	12,372	7,655	4,716	9,647	5,166	4,481	2,725	2,489	264[1]
1980..............	12,097	7,571	4,526	9,457	5,129	4,329	2,640	2,442	264[1]
1979..............	11,570	7,353	4,217	9,037	4,980	4,057	2,533	2,373	160
1978..............	11,260	7,232	4,028	8,786	4,912	3,874	2,474	2,319	155
1977..............	11,286	7,243	4,043	8,847	4,945	3,902	2,439	2,298	141
1976..............	11,012	7,129	3,883	8,653	4,902	3,752	2,359	2,227	132
1975..............	11,185	7,215	3,970	8,835	4,998	3,836	2,350	2,217	134
1974..............	10,224	6,820	3,404	7,989	4,703	3,285	2,235	2,117	119
1973..............	9,602	6,590	3,012	7,420	4,530	2,890	2,183	2,060	122
1972..............	9,215	6,459	2,756	7,071	4,430	2,641	2,144	2,029	115
1971..............	8,949	6,369	2,579	6,804	4,347	2,457	2,144	2,022	122
1970..............	8,581	6,262	2,319	6,428	4,233	2,195	2,153	2,029	124

Note: Data through 1995 are for institutions of higher education, while later data are for degree-granting institutions. Degree-granting institutions grant associate's or higher degrees and participate in Title IV federal financial aid programs. The degree-granting classification is very similar to the earlier higher education classification, but it includes more 2-year colleges and excludes a few higher education institutions that did not grant degrees. A university is an institution of higher education consisting of a liberal arts college, a diverse graduate program, and usually two or more professional schools or faculties. It is empowered to confer degrees in various fields of study; for purposes of maintaining trend data in this publication, the selection of university institutions has not been revised since 1982. Some data have been revised from previously published figures.

This page is intentionally left blank

Table A-20. Total Undergraduate Fall Enrollment in Degree-Granting Institutions, by Attendance Status, Sex of Student, and Control of Institution, Selected Years 1970–2016

(Number.)

Year	Total	Full-time	Part-time	Males	Females	Males	
						Full-time	Part-time
2016	16,869,212	10,430,542	6,438,670	7,414,312	9,454,900	4,725,638	2,688,674
2015	17,046,673	10,603,030	6,443,643	7,502,254	9,544,419	4,809,098	2,693,156
2014	17,294,136	10,784,392	6,509,744	7,586,299	9,707,837	4,877,531	2,708,768
2013	17,476,304	10,939,276	6,537,028	7,660,140	9,816,164	4,950,210	2,709,930
2012	17,735,638	11,097,092	6,638,546	7,714,938	10,020,700	4,984,389	2,730,549
2011	18,077,303	11,365,175	6,712,128	7,822,992	10,254,311	5,070,553	2,752,439
2010	18,082,427	11,457,040	6,625,387	7,836,282	10,246,145	5,118,975	2,717,307
2009	17,464,179	11,038,275	6,425,904	7,563,176	9,901,003	4,942,120	2,621,056
2008	16,365,738	10,254,930	6,110,808	7,066,623	9,299,115	4,577,431	2,489,192
2007	15,603,771	9,840,978	5,762,793	6,727,600	8,876,171	4,396,868	2,330,732
2006	15,184,302	9,571,079	5,613,223	6,513,756	8,670,546	4,264,606	2,249,150
2005	14,963,964	9,446,430	5,517,534	6,408,871	8,555,093	4,200,863	2,208,008
2004	14,780,630	9,284,336	5,496,294	6,340,048	8,440,582	4,140,628	2,199,420
2003	14,480,364	9,045,253	5,435,111	6,227,372	8,252,992	4,048,682	2,178,690
2002	14,257,077	8,734,252	5,522,825	6,192,390	8,064,687	3,934,168	2,258,222
2001	13,715,610	8,327,640	5,387,970	6,004,431	7,711,179	3,768,630	2,235,801
2000	13,155,393	7,922,926	5,232,467	5,778,268	7,377,125	3,588,246	2,190,022
1999	12,739,445	7,753,548	4,985,897	5,584,234	7,155,211	3,524,586	2,059,648
1998	12,436,937	7,538,711	4,898,226	5,446,133	6,990,804	3,428,161	2,017,972
1997	12,450,587	7,418,598	5,031,989	5,468,532	6,982,055	3,379,597	2,088,935
1996	12,326,948	7,298,839	5,028,109	5,420,672	6,906,276	3,339,108	2,081,564
1995	12,231,719	7,145,268	5,086,451	5,401,130	6,830,589	3,296,610	2,104,520
1994	12,262,608	7,168,706	5,093,902	5,422,113	6,840,495	3,341,591	2,080,522
1993	12,323,959	7,179,482	5,144,477	5,483,682	6,840,277	3,381,997	2,101,685
1992	12,537,700	7,244,442	5,293,258	5,582,936	6,954,764	3,424,739	2,158,197
1991	12,439,287	7,221,412	5,217,875	5,571,003	6,868,284	3,435,526	2,135,477
1990	11,959,106	6,976,030	4,983,076	5,379,759	6,579,347	3,336,535	2,043,224
1989	11,742,531	6,840,696	4,901,835	5,310,990	6,431,541	3,278,647	2,032,343
1988	11,316,548	6,642,428	4,674,120	5,137,644	6,178,904	3,206,442	1,931,202
1987	11,046,235	6,462,549	4,583,686	5,068,457	5,977,778	3,163,676	1,904,781
1986	10,797,975	6,352,073	4,445,902	5,017,505	5,780,470	3,146,330	1,871,175
1985	10,596,674	6,319,592	4,277,082	4,962,080	5,634,594	3,156,446	1,805,634
1984	10,618,071	6,347,653	4,270,418	5,006,813	5,611,258	3,194,930	1,811,883
1983	10,845,995	6,514,034	4,331,961	5,158,300	5,687,695	3,304,247	1,854,053
1982	10,825,062	6,483,805	4,341,257	5,170,494	5,654,568	3,299,436	1,871,058
1981	10,754,522	6,449,068	4,305,454	5,108,271	5,646,251	3,260,473	1,847,798
1980	10,475,055	6,361,744	4,113,311	5,000,177	5,474,878	3,226,857	1,773,320
1975	9,679,455	6,168,396	3,511,059	5,257,005	4,422,450	3,459,328	1,797,677
1970	7,368,644	5,280,064	2,088,580	4,249,702	3,118,942	3,096,371	1,153,331

Note: Data include unclassified undergraduate students. Data through 1995 are for institutions of higher education, while later data are for degree-granting institutions. Degree-granting institutions grant associate's or higher degrees and participate in Title IV federal financial aid programs. The degree-granting classification is very similar to the earlier higher education classification, but it includes more 2-year colleges and excludes a few higher education institutions that did not grant degrees. Some data have been revised from previously published figures. Details may not sum to totals because of rounding.

Table A-20. Total Undergraduate Fall Enrollment in Degree-Granting Institutions, by Attendance Status, Sex of Student, and Control of Institution, Selected Years 1970–2016—*Continued*

(Number.)

Year	Females		Public	Private		
	Full-time	Part-time		Total	Nonprofit	For-profit
2016	5,704,904	3,749,996	13,141,086	3,728,126	2,812,769	915,357
2015	5,793,932	3,750,487	13,150,823	3,895,850	2,822,122	1,073,728
2014	5,906,861	3,800,976	13,244,533	4,049,603	2,772,065	1,277,538
2013	5,989,066	3,827,098	13,348,292	4,128,012	2,755,463	1,372,549
2012	6,112,703	3,907,997	13,478,100	4,257,538	2,744,400	1,513,138
2011	6,294,622	3,959,689	13,694,899	4,382,404	2,718,923	1,663,481
2010	6,338,065	3,908,080	13,703,000	4,379,427	2,652,993	1,726,434
2009	6,096,155	3,804,848	13,386,375	4,077,804	2,595,171	1,482,633
2008	5,677,499	3,621,616	12,591,217	3,774,521	2,536,532	1,237,989
2007	5,444,110	3,432,061	12,137,583	3,466,188	2,470,327	995,861
2006	5,306,473	3,364,073	11,847,426	3,336,876	2,448,240	888,636
2005	5,245,567	3,309,526	11,697,730	3,266,234	2,418,368	847,866
2004	5,143,708	3,296,874	11,650,580	3,130,050	2,389,366	740,684
2003	4,996,571	3,256,421	11,523,103	2,957,261	2,346,673	610,588
2002	4,800,084	3,264,603	11,432,855	2,824,222	2,306,091	518,131
2001	4,559,010	3,152,169	10,985,871	2,729,739	2,257,718	472,021
2000	4,334,680	3,042,445	10,539,322	2,616,071	2,213,180	402,891
1999	4,228,962	2,926,249	10,174,228	2,565,217	2,185,290	379,927
1998	4,110,550	2,880,254	9,950,212	2,486,725	2,152,655	334,070
1997	4,039,001	2,943,054	10,007,479	2,443,108	2,139,824	303,284
1996	3,959,731	2,946,545	9,935,283	2,391,665	2,112,318	279,347
1995	3,848,658	2,981,931	9,903,626	2,328,093	2,104,693	223,400
1994	3,827,115	3,013,380	9,945,128	2,317,480	2,100,465	217,015
1993	3,797,485	3,042,792	10,011,787	2,312,172	2,099,197	212,975
1992	3,819,703	3,135,061	10,216,297	2,321,403	2,101,721	219,682
1991	3,785,886	3,082,398	10,147,957	2,291,330	2,072,354	218,976
1990	3,639,495	2,939,852	9,709,596	2,249,510	2,043,407	206,103
1989	3,562,049	2,869,492	9,487,742	2,254,789	NA	NA
1988	3,435,986	2,742,918	9,103,146	2,213,402	NA	NA
1987	3,298,873	2,678,905	8,918,589	2,127,646	1,939,942	187,704
1986	3,205,743	2,574,727	8,660,716	2,137,259	1,928,294	208,965
1985	3,163,146	2,471,448	8,477,125	2,119,549	1,928,996	190,553
1984	3,152,723	2,458,535	8,493,491	2,124,580	1,940,310	184,270
1983	3,209,787	2,477,908	8,697,118	2,148,877	1,961,076	187,801
1982	3,184,369	2,470,199	8,713,073	2,111,989	1,939,389	172,600
1981	3,188,595	2,457,656	8,648,363	2,106,159	1,958,848	147,311
1980	3,134,887	2,339,991	8,441,955	2,033,100	1,926,703	106,397
1975	2,709,068	1,713,382	7,826,032	1,853,423	1,814,844	38,579
1970	2,183,693	935,249	5,620,255	1,748,389	1,730,133	18,256

NA = Not available.

Note: Data include unclassified undergraduate students. Data through 1995 are for institutions of higher education, while later data are for degree-granting institutions. Degree-granting institutions grant associate's or higher degrees and participate in Title IV federal financial aid programs. The degree-granting classification is very similar to the earlier higher education classification, but it includes more 2-year colleges and excludes a few higher education institutions that did not grant degrees. Some data have been revised from previously published figures. Details may not sum to totals because of rounding.

Table A-21. Total Postbaccalaureate Fall Enrollment in Degree-Granting Institutions, by Attendance Status, Sex of Student, and Control of Institution, 1967–2016

(Number.)

Year	Total	Full-time	Part-time	Males	Females	Males Full-time	Males Part-time
2016	2,971,802	1,695,783	1,276,019	1,221,387	1,750,415	747,531	473,856
2015	2,941,531	1,684,482	1,257,049	1,221,565	1,719,966	749,349	472,216
2014	2,914,956	1,670,072	1,244,884	1,211,231	1,703,725	742,247	468,984
2013	2,900,373	1,657,334	1,243,039	1,201,057	1,699,316	732,112	468,945
2012	2,908,840	1,637,312	1,271,528	1,204,068	1,704,772	724,017	480,051
2011	2,933,287	1,637,356	1,295,931	1,211,264	1,722,023	722,265	488,999
2010	2,937,011	1,630,142	1,306,869	1,209,477	1,727,534	719,408	490,069
2009	2,849,415	1,567,080	1,282,335	1,169,777	1,679,638	689,977	479,800
2008	2,737,076	1,492,813	1,244,263	1,122,272	1,614,804	656,926	465,346
2007	2,644,357	1,428,914	1,215,443	1,088,314	1,556,043	632,576	455,738
2006	2,574,568	1,386,226	1,188,342	1,061,059	1,513,509	614,709	446,350
2005	2,523,511	1,350,581	1,172,930	1,047,054	1,476,457	602,525	444,529
2004	2,491,414	1,325,841	1,165,573	1,047,214	1,444,200	598,727	448,487
2003	2,431,117	1,280,880	1,150,237	1,032,892	1,398,225	589,190	443,702
2002	2,354,634	1,212,107	1,142,527	1,009,726	1,344,908	566,930	442,796
2001	2,212,377	1,119,862	1,092,515	956,384	1,255,993	531,260	425,124
2000	2,156,896	1,086,674	1,070,222	943,501	1,213,395	522,847	420,654
1999	2,110,246	1,049,591	1,060,655	930,930	1,179,316	508,930	422,000
1998	2,070,030	1,024,627	1,045,403	923,132	1,146,898	505,492	417,640
1997	2,051,747	1,019,464	1,032,283	927,496	1,124,251	510,845	416,651
1996	2,040,572	1,004,114	1,036,458	932,153	1,108,419	512,100	420,053
1995	2,030,062	983,534	1,046,528	941,409	1,088,653	510,782	430,627
1994	2,016,182	969,070	1,047,112	949,785	1,066,397	513,592	436,193
1993	1,980,844	948,136	1,032,708	943,768	1,037,076	508,574	435,194
1992	1,949,659	917,676	1,031,983	941,053	1,008,606	502,166	438,887
1991	1,919,666	893,917	1,025,749	930,841	988,825	493,849	436,992
1990	1,859,531	844,955	1,014,576	904,150	955,381	471,217	432,933
1989	1,796,029	820,254	975,775	879,025	917,004	461,596	417,429
1988	1,738,789	794,340	944,449	864,252	874,537	455,337	408,915
1987	1,720,407	768,536	951,871	863,599	856,808	447,212	416,387
1986	1,705,536	767,477	938,059	867,010	838,526	452,717	414,293
1985	1,650,381	755,629	894,752	856,370	794,011	451,274	405,096
1984	1,623,869	750,735	873,134	856,761	767,108	452,579	404,182
1983	1,618,666	747,016	871,650	865,425	753,241	455,540	409,885
1982	1,600,718	736,813	863,905	860,890	739,828	453,519	407,371
1981	1,617,150	732,182	884,968	866,785	750,365	452,364	414,421
1980	1,621,840	736,214	885,626	874,197	747,643	462,387	411,810
1979	1,571,922	714,624	857,298	862,754	709,168	456,197	406,557
1978	1,575,693	704,831	870,862	879,931	695,762	458,865	421,066
1977	1,569,084	698,902	870,182	891,819	677,265	462,038	429,781
1976	1,577,546	683,825	893,721	904,551	672,995	459,286	445,265
1975	1,505,404	672,938	832,466	891,992	613,412	467,425	424,567
1974	1,425,001	643,927	781,074	856,847	568,154	454,706	402,141
1973	1,342,452	610,935	731,517	833,453	508,999	444,219	389,234
1972	1,272,421	583,299	689,122	810,164	462,257	436,533	373,631
1971	1,204,390	564,236	640,154	789,131	415,259	428,167	360,964
1970	1,212,243	536,226	676,017	793,940	418,303	407,724	386,216
1969	1,120,175	506,833	613,342	738,673	381,502	383,630	355,043
1968	1,037,377	469,747	567,630	696,649	340,728	358,686	337,963
1967	896,065	448,238	447,827	630,701	265,364	354,628	276,073

Note: Data include unclassified graduate students. Data through 1995 are for institutions of higher education, while later data are for degree-granting institutions. Degree-granting institutions grant associate's or higher degrees and participate in Title IV federal financial aid programs. The degree-granting classification is very similar to the earlier higher education classification, but it includes more 2-year colleges and excludes a few higher education institutions that did not grant degrees. Some data have been revised from previously published figures.

Table A-21. Total Postbaccalaureate Fall Enrollment in Degree-Granting Institutions, by Attendance Status, Sex of Student, and Control of Institution, 1967–2016—*Continued*

(Number.)

| Year | Females | | Public | Private | | |
	Full-time	Part-time		Total	Nonprofit	For-profit
2016	948,252	802,163	1,441,886	1,529,916	1,265,028	264,888
2015	935,133	784,833	1,422,020	1,519,511	1,243,769	275,742
2014	927,825	775,900	1,410,127	1,504,829	1,225,184	279,645
2013	925,222	774,094	1,398,556	1,501,817	1,215,927	285,890
2012	913,295	791,477	1,406,567	1,502,273	1,206,988	295,285
2011	915,091	806,932	1,421,404	1,511,883	1,207,896	303,987
2010	910,734	816,800	1,439,171	1,497,840	1,201,489	296,351
2009	877,103	802,535	1,424,393	1,425,022	1,172,501	252,521
2008	835,887	778,917	1,380,936	1,356,140	1,124,987	231,153
2007	796,338	759,705	1,353,197	1,291,160	1,100,823	190,337
2006	771,517	741,992	1,332,707	1,241,861	1,064,626	177,235
2005	748,056	728,401	1,324,104	1,199,407	1,036,324	163,083
2004	727,114	717,086	1,329,532	1,161,882	1,022,319	139,563
2003	691,690	706,535	1,335,595	1,095,522	994,375	101,147
2002	645,177	699,731	1,319,138	1,035,496	959,385	76,111
2001	588,602	667,391	1,247,285	965,092	909,612	55,480
2000	563,827	649,568	1,213,464	943,432	896,239	47,193
1999	540,661	638,655	1,201,511	908,735	869,739	38,996
1998	519,135	627,763	1,187,557	882,473	852,270	30,203
1997	508,619	615,632	1,188,640	863,107	837,790	25,317
1996	492,014	616,405	1,185,216	855,356	830,238	25,118
1995	472,752	615,901	1,188,748	841,314	824,351	16,963
1994	455,478	610,919	1,188,552	827,630	809,642	17,988
1993	439,562	597,514	1,177,301	803,543	789,700	13,843
1992	415,510	593,096	1,168,270	781,389	770,802	10,587
1991	400,068	588,757	1,161,606	758,060	746,687	11,373
1990	373,738	581,643	1,135,121	724,410	716,820	7,590
1989	358,658	558,346	1,090,221	705,808	NA	NA
1988	339,003	535,534	1,058,242	680,547	NA	NA
1987	321,324	535,484	1,054,665	665,742	662,408	3,334
1986	314,760	523,766	1,053,177	652,359	644,185	8,174
1985	304,355	489,656	1,002,148	648,233	642,795	5,438
1984	298,156	468,952	983,879	639,990	634,109	5,881
1983	291,476	461,765	985,616	633,050	628,111	4,939
1982	283,294	456,534	983,014	617,704	613,350	4,354
1981	279,818	470,547	998,669	618,481	613,557	4,924
1980	273,827	473,816	1,015,439	606,401	601,084	5,317
1979	258,427	450,741	989,991	581,931	578,425	3,506
1978	245,966	449,796	998,608	577,085	573,563	3,522
1977	236,864	440,401	1,004,013	565,071	561,384	3,687
1976	224,539	448,456	1,033,115	544,431	541,064	3,367
1975	205,513	407,899	1,008,476	496,928	496,604	324
1974	189,221	378,933	956,770	468,231	467,950	281
1973	166,716	342,283	897,104	445,348	445,205	143
1972	146,766	315,491	848,031	424,390	424,278	112
1971	136,069	279,190	796,516	407,874	407,804	70
1970	128,502	289,801	807,879	404,364	404,287	77
1969	123,203	258,299	738,551	381,624	381,558	66
1968	111,061	229,667	648,657	388,720	388,681	39
1967	93,610	171,754	522,623	373,442	373,336	106

NA = Not available.

Note: Data include unclassified graduate students. Data through 1995 are for institutions of higher education, while later data are for degree-granting institutions. Degree-granting institutions grant associate's or higher degrees and participate in Title IV federal financial aid programs. The degree-granting classification is very similar to the earlier higher education classification, but it includes more 2-year colleges and excludes a few higher education institutions that did not grant degrees. Some data have been revised from previously published figures.

Table A-22. Total Fall Enrollment in Degree-Granting Institutions, by Race/Ethnicity, Sex, Attendance Status, and Level of Student: Selected Years, 1976–2016

(Numbers in thousands; percent.)

Race/ethnicity, sex, attendance status, and level of student	1976 Number	1976 Percent	1990 Number	1990 Percent	2000 Number	2000 Percent	2010 Number	2010 Percent
All students, total	10,985.6	100.0	13,818.6	100.0	15,312.3	100.0	21,019.4	100.0
White	9,076.1	84.3	10,722.5	79.9	10,462.1	70.8	12,720.8	62.6
Black	1,033.0	9.6	1,247.0	9.3	1,730.3	11.7	3,039.0	15.0
Hispanic	383.8	3.6	782.4	5.8	1,461.8	9.9	2,748.8	13.5
Asian/Pacific Islander	197.9	1.8	572.4	4.3	978.2	6.6	1,281.6	6.3
Asian	NA	NA	NA	NA	NA	NA	1,217.6	6.0
Pacific Islander	NA	NA	NA	NA	NA	NA	64.0	0.3
American Indian/Alaska Native	76.1	0.7	102.8	0.8	151.2	1.0	196.2	1.0
Two or more races	NA	NA	NA	NA	NA	NA	325.4	1.6
Nonresident alien	218.7	X	391.5	X	528.7	X	707.7	X
Male	5,794.4	100.0	6,283.9	100.0	6,721.8	100.0	9,045.8	100.0
White	4,813.7	85.3	4,861.0	80.5	4,634.6	72.1	5,605.8	64.7
Black	469.9	8.3	484.7	8.0	635.3	9.9	1,089.0	12.6
Hispanic	209.7	3.7	353.9	5.9	627.1	9.8	1,157.6	13.4
Asian/Pacific Islander	108.4	1.9	294.9	4.9	465.9	7.3	600.6	6.9
Asian	NA	NA	NA	NA	NA	NA	572.1	6.6
Pacific Islander	NA	NA	NA	NA	NA	NA	28.5	0.3
American Indian/Alaska Native	38.5	0.7	43.1	0.7	61.4	1.0	78.7	0.9
Two or more races	NA	NA	NA	NA	NA	NA	134.4	1.6
Nonresident alien	154.1	X	246.3	X	297.3	X	379.6	X
Female	5,191.2	100.0	7,534.7	100.0	8,590.5	100.0	11,973.7	100.0
White	4,262.4	83.1	5,861.5	79.3	5,827.5	69.7	7,115.0	61.1
Black	563.1	11.0	762.3	10.3	1,095.0	13.1	1,949.9	16.7
Hispanic	174.1	3.4	428.5	5.8	834.7	10.0	1,591.2	13.7
Asian/Pacific Islander	89.4	1.7	277.5	3.8	512.3	6.1	681.0	5.8
Asian	NA	NA	NA	NA	NA	NA	645.5	5.5
Pacific Islander	NA	NA	NA	NA	NA	NA	35.5	0.3
American Indian/Alaska Native	37.6	0.7	59.7	0.8	89.7	1.1	117.5	1.0
Two or more races	NA	NA	NA	NA	NA	NA	191.0	1.6
Nonresident alien	64.6	X	145.2	X	231.4	X	328.0	X
Full-time	6,703.6	100.0	7,821.0	100.0	9,009.6	100.0	13,087.2	100.0
White	5,512.6	84.2	6,016.5	79.9	6,231.1	72.5	8,053.5	64.3
Black	659.2	10.1	718.3	9.5	982.6	11.4	1,811.3	14.5
Hispanic	211.1	3.2	394.7	5.2	710.3	8.3	1,501.0	12.0
Asian/Pacific Islander	117.7	1.8	347.4	4.6	591.2	6.9	820.8	6.6
Asian	NA	NA	NA	NA	NA	NA	783.0	6.3
Pacific Islander	NA	NA	NA	NA	NA	NA	37.8	0.3
American Indian/Alaska Native	43.0	0.7	54.4	0.7	84.4	1.0	118.3	0.9
Two or more races	NA	NA	NA	NA	NA	NA	217.2	1.7
Nonresident alien	160.0	X	289.6	X	410.0	X	565.2	X
Part-time	4,282.1	100.0	5,997.7	100.0	6,302.7	100.0	7,932.3	100.0
White	3,563.5	84.4	4,706.0	79.8	4,231.0	68.4	4,667.3	59.9
Black	373.8	8.9	528.7	9.0	747.7	12.1	1,227.7	15.8
Hispanic	172.7	4.1	387.7	6.6	751.5	12.2	1,247.9	16.0
Asian/Pacific Islander	80.2	1.9	225.1	3.8	387.1	6.3	460.8	5.9
Asian	NA	NA	NA	NA	NA	NA	434.6	5.6
Pacific Islander	NA	NA	NA	NA	NA	NA	26.2	0.3
American Indian/Alaska Native	33.1	0.8	48.4	0.8	66.8	1.1	78.0	1.0
Two or more races	NA	NA	NA	NA	NA	NA	108.2	1.4
Nonresident alien	58.7	X	101.8	X	118.7	X	142.5	X
Undergraduate, total	9,419.0	100.0	11,959.1	100.0	13,155.4	100.0	18,082.4	100.0
White	7,740.5	83.4	9,272.6	79.0	8,983.5	69.8	10,895.9	61.6
Black	943.4	10.2	1,147.2	9.8	1,548.9	12.0	2,677.1	15.1
Hispanic	352.9	3.8	724.6	6.2	1,351.0	10.5	2,551.0	14.4
Asian/Pacific Islander	169.3	1.8	500.5	4.3	845.5	6.6	1,087.3	6.1
Asian	NA	NA	NA	NA	NA	NA	1,029.8	5.8
Pacific Islander	NA	NA	NA	NA	NA	NA	57.5	0.3

NA = Not available.
X = Not applicable.
Note: Race categories exclude persons of Hispanic ethnicity. Because of underreporting and nonreporting of racial/ethnic data, some figures are slightly lower than corresponding data in other tables. Data through 1990 are for institutions of higher education, while later data are for degree-granting institutions. Degree-granting institutions grant associate's or higher degrees and participate in Title IV federal financial aid programs. The degree-granting classification is very similar to the earlier higher education classification, but it includes more 2-year colleges and excludes a few higher education institutions that did not grant degrees. Some data have been revised from previously published figures. Detail may not sum to totals because of rounding.

Table A-22. Total Fall Enrollment in Degree-Granting Institutions, by Race/Ethnicity, Sex, Attendance Status, and Level of Student: Selected Years, 1976–2016—*Continued*

(Numbers in thousands; percent.)

Race/ethnicity, sex, attendance status, and level of student	2013 Number	2013 Percent	2014 Number	2014 Percent	2015 Number	2015 Percent	2016 Number	2016 Percent
All students, total	20,376.7	100.0	20,209.1	100.0	19,988.2	100.0	19,841.0	100.0
White	11,589.4	59.3	11,239.3	58.3	10,939.2	57.6	10,712.9	56.9
Black	2,872.0	14.7	2,792.8	14.5	2,681.0	14.1	2,588.2	13.7
Hispanic	3,093.2	15.8	3,191.9	16.5	3,297.7	17.4	3,426.8	18.2
Asian/Pacific Islander	1,259.7	6.4	1,272.2	6.6	1,284.3	6.8	1,306.5	6.9
Asian	1,198.7	6.1	1,213.8	6.3	1,229.0	6.5	1,253.3	6.7
Pacific Islander	61.0	0.3	58.5	0.3	55.3	0.3	53.2	0.3
American Indian/Alaska Native	162.2	0.8	152.9	0.8	146.1	0.8	142.3	0.8
Two or more races	560.0	2.9	642.2	3.3	657.6	3.5	666.4	3.5
Nonresident alien	840.2	X	917.8	X	982.3	X	998.0	X
Male	8,861.2	100.0	8,797.5	100.0	8,723.8	100.0	8,635.7	100.0
White	5,132.4	61.1	4,974.3	60.0	4,848.5	59.3	4,734.4	58.6
Black	1,064.9	12.7	1,035.1	12.5	998.9	12.2	959.0	11.9
Hispanic	1,307.7	15.6	1,348.2	16.3	1,389.2	17.0	1,438.7	17.8
Asian/Pacific Islander	594.3	7.1	599.1	7.2	602.9	7.4	610.0	7.5
Asian	567.1	6.8	573.0	6.9	577.8	7.1	586.3	7.3
Pacific Islander	27.2	0.3	26.1	0.3	25.1	0.3	23.7	0.3
American Indian/Alaska Native	64.7	0.8	61.3	0.7	58.2	0.7	56.3	0.7
Two or more races	237.1	2.8	269.7	3.3	277.6	3.4	281.9	3.5
Nonresident alien	460.1	X	509.9	X	548.6	X	555.5	X
Female	11,515.5	100.0	11,411.6	100.0	11,264.4	100.0	11,205.3	100.0
White	6,457.0	58.0	6,265.0	56.9	6,090.7	56.2	5,978.6	55.5
Black	1,807.1	16.2	1,757.7	16.0	1,682.1	15.5	1,629.2	15.1
Hispanic	1,785.5	16.0	1,843.7	16.8	1,908.5	17.6	1,988.0	18.5
Asian/Pacific Islander	665.4	6.0	673.1	6.1	681.5	6.3	696.5	6.5
Asian	631.6	5.7	640.7	5.8	651.3	6.0	667.0	6.2
Pacific Islander	33.7	0.3	32.4	0.3	30.2	0.3	29.5	0.3
American Indian/Alaska Native	97.5	0.9	91.6	0.8	88.0	0.8	86.0	0.8
Two or more races	322.9	2.9	372.5	3.4	379.9	3.5	384.5	3.6
Nonresident alien	380.1	X	407.9	X	433.7	X	442.5	X
Full-time	12,596.6	100.0	12,454.5	100.0	12,287.5	100.0	12,126.3	100.0
White	7,237.7	60.8	6,983.3	59.7	6,784.0	59.1	6,611.1	58.5
Black	1,669.0	14.0	1,600.4	13.7	1,537.3	13.4	1,470.1	13.0
Hispanic	1,701.8	14.3	1,747.9	14.9	1,786.2	15.6	1,843.6	16.3
Asian/Pacific Islander	821.2	6.9	832.1	7.1	843.8	7.4	857.3	7.6
Asian	785.5	6.6	798.1	6.8	812.2	7.1	826.8	7.3
Pacific Islander	35.7	0.3	34.0	0.3	31.6	0.3	30.4	0.3
American Indian/Alaska Native	94.2	0.8	88.0	0.8	82.8	0.7	80.5	0.7
Two or more races	377.5	3.2	440.3	3.8	440.2	3.8	435.9	3.9
Nonresident alien	695.2	X	762.6	X	813.2	X	827.9	X
Part-time	7,780.1	100.0	7,754.6	100.0	7,700.7	100.0	7,714.7	100.0
White	4,351.7	57.0	4,256.0	56.0	4,155.1	55.2	4,101.8	54.4
Black	1,203.0	15.8	1,192.5	15.7	1,143.7	15.2	1,118.1	14.8
Hispanic	1,391.4	18.2	1,444.0	19.0	1,511.5	20.1	1,583.2	21.0
Asian/Pacific Islander	438.5	5.7	440.2	5.8	440.5	5.8	449.2	6.0
Asian	413.2	5.4	415.7	5.5	416.9	5.5	426.4	5.7
Pacific Islander	25.3	0.3	24.4	0.3	23.6	0.3	22.7	0.3
American Indian/Alaska Native	68.0	0.9	64.9	0.9	63.3	0.8	61.8	0.8
Two or more races	182.5	2.4	201.9	2.7	217.4	2.9	230.5	3.1
Nonresident alien	145.0	X	155.2	X	169.1	X	170.1	X
Undergraduate, total	17,476.3	100.0	17,294.1	100.0	17,046.7	100.0	16,869.2	100.0
White	9,898.1	58.2	9,582.5	57.2	9,303.8	56.4	9,082.1	55.7
Black	2,504.7	14.7	2,426.7	14.5	2,316.5	14.1	2,225.3	13.7
Hispanic	2,872.2	16.9	2,962.4	17.7	3,055.0	18.5	3,167.2	19.4
Asian/Pacific Islander	1,064.5	6.3	1,074.9	6.4	1,084.0	6.6	1,100.1	6.7
Asian	1,010.3	5.9	1,022.9	6.1	1,034.8	6.3	1,053.0	6.5
Pacific Islander	54.1	0.3	52.1	0.3	49.2	0.3	47.1	0.3

X = Not applicable.

Note: Race categories exclude persons of Hispanic ethnicity. Because of underreporting and nonreporting of racial/ethnic data, some figures are slightly lower than corresponding data in other tables. Data through 1990 are for institutions of higher education, while later data are for degree-granting institutions. Degree-granting institutions grant associate's or higher degrees and participate in Title IV federal financial aid programs. The degree-granting classification is very similar to the earlier higher education classification, but it includes more 2-year colleges and excludes a few higher education institutions that did not grant degrees. Some data have been revised from previously published figures. Detail may not sum to totals because of rounding.

170 THE ALMANAC OF AMERICAN EDUCATION (BERNAN PRESS)

Table A-22. Total Fall Enrollment in Degree-Granting Institutions, by Race/Ethnicity, Sex, Attendance Status, and Level of Student: Selected Years, 1976–2016—*Continued*

(Numbers in thousands; percent.)

Race/ethnicity, sex, attendance status, and level of student	1976 Number	1976 Percent	1990 Number	1990 Percent	2000 Number	2000 Percent	2010 Number	2010 Percent
American Indian/Alaska Native	69.7	0.8	95.5	0.8	138.5	1.1	179.1	1.0
Two or more races	NA	NA	NA	NA	NA	NA	293.7	1.7
Nonresident alien	143.2	X	218.7	X	288.0	X	398.4	X
Undergraduate, male	4,896.8	100.0	5,379.8	100.0	5,778.3	100.0	7,836.3	100.0
White	4,052.2	84.4	4,184.4	79.6	4,010.1	71.3	4,861.0	63.7
Black	430.7	9.0	448.0	8.5	577.0	10.3	982.9	12.9
Hispanic	191.7	4.0	326.9	6.2	582.6	10.4	1,082.9	14.2
Asian/Pacific Islander	91.1	1.9	254.5	4.8	401.9	7.1	513.4	6.7
Asian	NA	NA	NA	NA	NA	NA	487.4	6.4
Pacific Islander	NA	NA	NA	NA	NA	NA	26.0	0.3
American Indian/Alaska Native	34.8	0.7	39.9	0.8	56.4	1.0	72.3	0.9
Two or more races	NA	NA	NA	NA	NA	NA	122.3	1.6
Nonresident alien	96.4	X	126.1	X	150.2	X	201.5	X
Undergraduate, female	4,522.1	100.0	6,579.3	100.0	7,377.1	100.0	10,246.1	100.0
White	3,688.3	82.4	5,088.2	78.4	4,973.3	68.7	6,035.0	60.1
Black	512.7	11.5	699.2	10.8	971.9	13.4	1,694.2	16.9
Hispanic	161.2	3.6	397.6	6.1	768.4	10.6	1,468.1	14.6
Asian/Pacific Islander	78.2	1.7	246.0	3.8	443.6	6.1	573.9	5.7
Asian	NA	NA	NA	NA	NA	NA	542.4	5.4
Pacific Islander	NA	NA	NA	NA	NA	NA	31.5	0.3
American Indian/Alaska Native	34.9	0.8	55.5	0.9	82.1	1.1	106.8	1.1
Two or more races	NA	NA	NA	NA	NA	NA	171.3	1.7
Nonresident alien	46.8	X	92.6	X	137.8	X	196.9	X
Postbaccalaureate, total	1,566.6	100.0	1,859.5	100.0	2,156.9	100.0	2,937.0	100.0
White	1,335.6	89.6	1,449.8	86.0	1,478.6	77.2	1,824.9	69.4
Black	89.7	6.0	99.8	5.9	181.4	9.5	361.9	13.8
Hispanic	30.9	2.1	57.9	3.4	110.8	5.8	197.8	7.5
Asian/Pacific Islander	28.6	1.9	72.0	4.3	132.7	6.9	194.3	7.4
Asian	NA	NA	NA	NA	NA	NA	187.8	7.1
Pacific Islander	NA	NA	NA	NA	NA	NA	6.5	0.2
American Indian/Alaska Native	6.4	0.4	7.3	0.4	12.6	0.7	17.1	0.7
Two or more races	NA	NA	NA	NA	NA	NA	31.7	1.2
Nonresident alien	75.5	X	172.7	X	240.7	X	309.3	X
Postbaccalaureate, male	897.6	100.0	904.2	100.0	943.5	100.0	1,209.5	100.0
White	761.6	90.7	676.6	86.3	624.5	78.4	744.9	72.2
Black	39.2	4.7	36.7	4.7	58.3	7.3	106.1	10.3
Hispanic	18.1	2.2	27.0	3.4	44.5	5.6	74.7	7.2
Asian/Pacific Islander	17.4	2.1	40.4	5.2	64.0	8.0	87.2	8.5
Asian	NA	NA	NA	NA	NA	NA	84.7	8.2
Pacific Islander	NA	NA	NA	NA	NA	NA	2.5	0.2
American Indian/Alaska Native	3.7	0.4	3.2	0.4	5.0	0.6	6.4	0.6
Two or more races	NA	NA	NA	NA	NA	NA	12.0	1.2
Nonresident alien	57.7	X	120.2	X	147.1	X	178.2	X
Postbaccalaureate, female	669.1	100.0	955.4	100.0	1,213.4	100.0	1,727.5	100.0
White	574.1	88.1	773.2	85.6	854.1	76.3	1,080.0	67.7
Black	50.5	7.7	63.1	7.0	123.1	11.0	255.8	16.0
Hispanic	12.8	2.0	30.9	3.4	66.3	5.9	123.1	7.7
Asian/Pacific Islander	11.2	1.7	31.5	3.5	68.7	6.1	107.0	6.7
Asian	NA	NA	NA	NA	NA	NA	103.1	6.5
Pacific Islander	NA	NA	NA	NA	NA	NA	3.9	0.2
American Indian/Alaska Native	2.7	0.4	4.1	0.5	7.6	0.7	10.7	0.7
Two or more races	NA	NA	NA	NA	NA	NA	19.7	1.2
Nonresident alien	17.8	X	52.5	X	93.6	X	131.1	X

NA = Not available.
X = Not applicable.
Note: Race categories exclude persons of Hispanic ethnicity. Because of underreporting and nonreporting of racial/ethnic data, some figures are slightly lower than corresponding data in other tables. Data through 1990 are for institutions of higher education, while later data are for degree-granting institutions. Degree-granting institutions grant associate's or higher degrees and participate in Title IV federal financial aid programs. The degree-granting classification is very similar to the earlier higher education classification, but it includes more 2-year colleges and excludes a few higher education institutions that did not grant degrees. Some data have been revised from previously published figures. Detail may not sum to totals because of rounding.

Table A-22. Total Fall Enrollment in Degree-Granting Institutions, by Race/Ethnicity, Sex, Attendance Status, and Level of Student: Selected Years, 1976–2016—*Continued*

(Numbers in thousands; percent.)

Race/ethnicity, sex, attendance status, and level of student	2013 Number	2013 Percent	2014 Number	2014 Percent	2015 Number	2015 Percent	2016 Number	2016 Percent
American Indian/Alaska Native	147.4	0.9	138.6	0.8	132.2	0.8	128.6	0.8
Two or more races	505.8	3.0	579.6	3.5	590.1	3.6	595.7	3.7
Nonresident alien	483.6	X	529.3	X	565.1	X	570.3	X
Undergraduate, male	7,660.1	100.0	7,586.3	100.0	7,502.3	100.0	7,414.3	100.0
White	4,438.9	60.0	4,299.0	58.9	4,188.1	58.2	4,085.4	57.5
Black	955.3	12.9	924.9	12.7	888.4	12.3	849.0	12.0
Hispanic	1,224.1	16.5	1,261.8	17.3	1,298.3	18.0	1,343.0	18.9
Asian/Pacific Islander	507.5	6.9	511.7	7.0	515.0	7.2	520.5	7.3
Asian	482.9	6.5	488.1	6.7	492.3	6.8	499.1	7.0
Pacific Islander	24.5	0.3	23.5	0.3	22.7	0.3	21.4	0.3
American Indian/Alaska Native	59.4	0.8	56.1	0.8	53.2	0.7	51.5	0.7
Two or more races	216.6	2.9	245.9	3.4	252.1	3.5	255.3	3.6
Nonresident alien	258.5	X	286.8	X	307.2	X	309.6	X
Undergraduate, female	9,816.2	100.0	9,707.8	100.0	9,544.4	100.0	9,454.9	100.0
White	5,459.2	56.9	5,283.5	55.8	5,115.7	55.1	4,996.7	54.3
Black	1,549.4	16.2	1,501.7	15.9	1,428.2	15.4	1,376.3	15.0
Hispanic	1,648.1	17.2	1,700.6	18.0	1,756.7	18.9	1,824.2	19.8
Asian/Pacific Islander	557.0	5.8	563.2	6.0	569.0	6.1	579.6	6.3
Asian	527.4	5.5	534.7	5.6	542.5	5.8	553.9	6.0
Pacific Islander	29.6	0.3	28.5	0.3	26.5	0.3	25.7	0.3
American Indian/Alaska Native	88.0	0.9	82.6	0.9	79.1	0.9	77.1	0.8
Two or more races	289.2	3.0	333.7	3.5	337.9	3.6	340.4	3.7
Nonresident alien	225.1	X	242.5	X	257.9	X	260.7	X
Postbaccalaureate, total	2,900.4	100.0	2,915.0	100.0	2,941.5	100.0	2,971.8	100.0
White	1,691.3	66.5	1,656.7	65.6	1,635.4	64.8	1,630.8	64.1
Black	367.3	14.4	366.2	14.5	364.5	14.4	362.9	14.3
Hispanic	221.0	8.7	229.4	9.1	242.7	9.6	259.6	10.2
Asian/Pacific Islander	195.2	7.7	197.3	7.8	200.3	7.9	206.3	8.1
Asian	188.4	7.4	190.9	7.6	194.3	7.7	200.2	7.9
Pacific Islander	6.8	0.3	6.4	0.3	6.1	0.2	6.1	0.2
American Indian/Alaska Native	14.8	0.6	14.3	0.6	13.9	0.6	13.7	0.5
Two or more races	54.2	2.1	62.6	2.5	67.5	2.7	70.7	2.8
Nonresident alien	356.5	X	388.5	X	417.2	X	427.8	X
Postbaccalaureate, male	1,201.1	100.0	1,211.2	100.0	1,221.6	100.0	1,221.4	100.0
White	693.5	69.4	675.2	68.3	660.3	67.4	649.0	66.5
Black	109.6	11.0	110.2	11.1	110.5	11.3	110.0	11.3
Hispanic	83.6	8.4	86.4	8.7	90.9	9.3	95.8	9.8
Asian/Pacific Islander	86.9	8.7	87.4	8.8	87.8	9.0	89.4	9.2
Asian	84.2	8.4	84.9	8.6	85.5	8.7	87.2	8.9
Pacific Islander	2.7	0.3	2.5	0.3	2.3	0.2	2.3	0.2
American Indian/Alaska Native	5.3	0.5	5.3	0.5	5.0	0.5	4.8	0.5
Two or more races	20.6	2.1	23.7	2.4	25.5	2.6	26.6	2.7
Nonresident alien	201.6	X	223.0	X	241.4	X	245.9	X
Postbaccalaureate, female	1,699.3	100.0	1,703.7	100.0	1,720.0	100.0	1,750.4	100.0
White	997.8	64.6	981.5	63.8	975.0	63.1	981.8	62.6
Black	257.7	16.7	256.0	16.6	254.0	16.4	253.0	16.1
Hispanic	137.4	8.9	143.1	9.3	151.8	9.8	163.8	10.4
Asian/Pacific Islander	108.3	7.0	109.9	7.1	112.5	7.3	116.9	7.5
Asian	104.2	6.7	106.0	6.9	108.8	7.0	113.1	7.2
Pacific Islander	4.1	0.3	3.9	0.3	3.7	0.2	3.8	0.2
American Indian/Alaska Native	9.5	0.6	9.0	0.6	8.9	0.6	8.9	0.6
Two or more races	33.6	2.2	38.8	2.5	42.0	2.7	44.1	2.8
Nonresident alien	155.0	X	165.5	X	175.8	X	181.9	X

X = Not applicable.
Note: Race categories exclude persons of Hispanic ethnicity. Because of underreporting and nonreporting of racial/ethnic data, some figures are slightly lower than corresponding data in other tables. Data through 1990 are for institutions of higher education, while later data are for degree-granting institutions. Degree-granting institutions grant associate's or higher degrees and participate in Title IV federal financial aid programs. The degree-granting classification is very similar to the earlier higher education classification, but it includes more 2-year colleges and excludes a few higher education institutions that did not grant degrees. Some data have been revised from previously published figures. Detail may not sum to totals because of rounding.

Table A-23. Total Fall Enrollment in Degree-Granting Institutions, by Race/Ethnicity of Student and Type and Control of Institution, Selected Years, 1976–2016

(Numbers in thousands; percent.)

Race/ethnicity of student and type and control of institution	1976 Number	1976 Percent	1990 Number	1990 Percent	2000 Number	2000 Percent	2010 Number	2010 Percent
All students, total	10,986	100.0	13,819	100.0	15,312	100.0	21,019	100.0
White	9,076	84.3	10,722	79.9	10,462	70.8	12,721	62.6
Black	1,033	9.6	1,247	9.3	1,730	11.7	3,039	15.0
Hispanic	384	3.6	782	5.8	1,462	9.9	2,749	13.5
Asian/Pacific Islander	198	1.8	572	4.3	978	6.6	1,282	6.3
Asian	NA	NA	NA	NA	NA	NA	1,218	6.0
Pacific Islander	NA	NA	NA	NA	NA	NA	64	0.3
American Indian/Alaska Native	76	0.7	103	0.8	151	1.0	196	1.0
Two or more races	NA	NA	NA	NA	NA	NA	325	1.6
Nonresident alien	219	X	391	X	529	X	708	X
Public	8,641	78.7	10,845	78.5	11,753	76.8	15,142	72.0
White	7,095	83.5	8,385	79.2	7,963	69.8	9,182	62.5
Black	831	9.8	976	9.2	1,319	11.6	1,989	13.5
Hispanic	337	4.0	671	6.3	1,229	10.8	2,164	14.7
Asian/Pacific Islander	166	2.0	461	4.4	771	6.8	969	6.6
Asian	NA	NA	NA	NA	NA	NA	925	6.3
Pacific Islander	NA	NA	NA	NA	NA	NA	44	0.3
American Indian/Alaska Native	68	0.8	90	0.9	127	1.1	151	1.0
Two or more races	NA	NA	NA	NA	NA	NA	235	1.6
Nonresident alien	145	X	260	X	343	X	453	X
Private	2,345	21.3	2,974	21.5	3,560	23.2	5,877	28.0
White	1,982	87.3	2,337	82.2	2,499	74.1	3,539	62.9
Black	202	8.9	271	9.5	411	12.2	1,050	18.7
Hispanic	47	2.1	111	3.9	233	6.9	585	10.4
Asian/Pacific Islander	32	1.4	111	3.9	208	6.2	313	5.6
Asian	NA	NA	NA	NA	NA	NA	293	5.2
Pacific Islander	NA	NA	NA	NA	NA	NA	20	0.4
American Indian/Alaska Native	9	0.4	12	0.4	24	0.7	45	0.8
Two or more races	NA	NA	NA	NA	NA	NA	90	1.6
Nonresident alien	73	X	131	X	186	X	255	X
4-year, total	7,107	64.7	8,579	62.1	9,364	61.2	13,336	63.4
White	5,999	86.6	6,768	82.0	6,658	74.6	8,400	66.0
Black	604	8.7	723	8.8	995	11.2	1,840	14.5
Hispanic	174	2.5	358	4.3	618	6.9	1,356	10.7
Asian/Pacific Islander	119	1.7	357	4.3	576	6.5	818	6.4
Asian	NA	NA	NA	NA	NA	NA	782	6.1
Pacific Islander	NA	NA	NA	NA	NA	NA	36	0.3
American Indian/Alaska Native	35	0.5	48	0.6	76	0.9	109	0.9
Two or more races	NA	NA	NA	NA	NA	NA	205	1.6
Nonresident alien	177	X	324	X	440	X	608	X
Public	4,893	68.9	5,848	68.2	6,055	64.7	7,924	59.4
White	4,120	86.1	4,606	81.5	4,311	74.4	5,070	67.0
Black	422	8.8	495	8.8	628	10.8	913	12.1
Hispanic	129	2.7	263	4.6	420	7.2	870	11.5
Asian/Pacific Islander	87	1.8	251	4.4	381	6.6	523	6.9
Asian	NA	NA	NA	NA	NA	NA	505	6.7
Pacific Islander	NA	NA	NA	NA	NA	NA	18	0.2
American Indian/Alaska Native	28	0.6	38	0.7	57	1.0	69	0.9
Two or more races	NA	NA	NA	NA	NA	NA	122	1.6
Nonresident alien	106	X	196	X	258	X	358	X
Private	2,214	31.1	2,730	31.8	3,308	35.3	5,412	40.6
White	1,879	87.7	2,163	83.1	2,347	75.1	3,330	64.5
Black	182	8.5	228	8.7	368	11.8	927	18.0
Hispanic	44	2.1	96	3.7	198	6.3	486	9.4
Asian/Pacific Islander	31	1.5	107	4.1	195	6.2	296	5.7

NA = Not available.
X = Not applicable.
Note: Race categories exclude persons of Hispanic ethnicity. Because of underreporting and nonreporting of racial/ethnic data, some figures are slightly lower than corresponding data in other tables. Data through 1990 are for institutions of higher education, while later data are for degree-granting institutions. Degree-granting institutions grant associate's or higher degrees and participate in Title IV federal financial aid programs. The degree-granting classification is very similar to the earlier higher education classification, but it includes more 2-year colleges and excludes a few higher education institutions that did not grant degrees. Some data have been revised from previously published figures. Detail may not sum to totals because of rounding.

Table A-23. Total Fall Enrollment in Degree-Granting Institutions, by Race/Ethnicity of Student and Type and Control of Institution, Selected Years, 1976–2016—*Continued*

(Numbers in thousands; percent.)

Race/ethnicity of student and type and control of institution	2013 Number	2013 Percent	2014 Number	2014 Percent	2015 Number	2015 Percent	2016 Number	2016 Percent
All students, total	20,376	100.0	20,209	100.0	19,988	100.0	19,841	100.0
White	11,591	59.3	11,239	58.3	10,939	57.6	10,713	56.9
Black	2,872	14.7	2,793	14.5	2,681	14.1	2,588	13.7
Hispanic	3,091	15.8	3,192	16.5	3,298	17.4	3,427	18.2
Asian/Pacific Islander	1,260	6.4	1,272	6.6	1,284	6.8	1,306	6.9
Asian	1,199	6.1	1,214	6.3	1,229	6.5	1,253	6.7
Pacific Islander	61	0.3	58	0.3	55	0.3	53	0.3
American Indian/Alaska Native	163	0.8	153	0.8	146	0.8	142	0.8
Two or more races	559	2.9	642	3.3	658	3.5	666	3.5
Nonresident alien	840	X	918	X	982	X	998	X
Public	14,746	72.4	14,655	100.0	14,573	100.0	14,583	100.0
White	8,364	58.9	8,120	57.7	7,911	56.7	7,786	55.8
Black	1,887	13.3	1,840	13.1	1,775	12.7	1,740	12.5
Hispanic	2,477	17.4	2,580	18.3	2,695	19.3	2,819	20.2
Asian/Pacific Islander	945	6.6	956	6.8	970	7.0	990	7.1
Asian	906	6.4	918	6.5	934	6.7	956	6.9
Pacific Islander	39	0.3	37	0.3	36	0.3	35	0.2
American Indian/Alaska Native	125	0.9	118	0.8	114	0.8	111	0.8
Two or more races	413	2.9	453	3.2	482	3.5	505	3.6
Nonresident alien	534	X	588	X	627	X	634	X
Private	5,630	27.6	5,554	100.0	5,415	100.0	5,258	100.0
White	3,227	60.6	3,120	59.7	3,029	59.9	2,927	59.8
Black	985	18.5	953	18.2	906	17.9	849	17.3
Hispanic	614	11.5	611	11.7	603	11.9	608	12.4
Asian/Pacific Islander	315	5.9	316	6.1	314	6.2	316	6.5
Asian	293	5.5	295	5.7	295	5.8	297	6.1
Pacific Islander	22	0.4	21	0.4	19	0.4	19	0.4
American Indian/Alaska Native	38	0.7	35	0.7	32	0.6	32	0.6
Two or more races	146	2.7	189	3.6	176	3.5	162	3.3
Nonresident alien	306	X	330	X	355	X	365	X
4-year, total	13,407	65.8	13,494	100.0	13,489	100.0	13,751	100.0
White	7,955	62.8	7,829	61.8	7,713	61.2	7,712	60.0
Black	1,799	14.2	1,779	14.0	1,741	13.8	1,723	13.4
Hispanic	1,600	12.6	1,671	13.2	1,742	13.8	1,932	15.0
Asian/Pacific Islander	844	6.7	865	6.8	882	7.0	929	7.2
Asian	806	6.4	827	6.5	847	6.7	894	7.0
Pacific Islander	38	0.3	37	0.3	35	0.3	36	0.3
American Indian/Alaska Native	92	0.7	87	0.7	83	0.7	84	0.7
Two or more races	370	2.9	442	3.5	449	3.6	467	3.6
Nonresident alien	748	X	822	X	878	X	904	X
Public	8,120	60.6	8,257	100.0	8,349	100.0	8,742	100.0
White	4,867	63.4	4,834	62.3	4,790	61.2	4,879	59.5
Black	909	11.8	915	11.8	916	11.7	951	11.6
Hispanic	1,064	13.9	1,133	14.6	1,199	15.3	1,379	16.8
Asian/Pacific Islander	545	7.1	563	7.3	579	7.4	624	7.6
Asian	526	6.9	544	7.0	562	7.2	605	7.4
Pacific Islander	19	0.2	19	0.2	17	0.2	18	0.2
American Indian/Alaska Native	58	0.8	56	0.7	55	0.7	55	0.7
Two or more races	233	3.0	262	3.4	283	3.6	312	3.8
Nonresident alien	445	X	495	X	526	X	543	X
Private	5,287	39.4	5,237	100.0	5,140	100.0	5,009	100.0
White	3,088	62.0	2,995	61.0	2,923	61.1	2,834	61.0
Black	890	17.9	864	17.6	824	17.2	772	16.6
Hispanic	536	10.8	538	11.0	543	11.3	553	11.9
Asian/Pacific Islander	299	6.0	302	6.1	303	6.3	306	6.6

X = Not applicable.

Note: Race categories exclude persons of Hispanic ethnicity. Because of underreporting and nonreporting of racial/ethnic data, some figures are slightly lower than corresponding data in other tables. Data through 1990 are for institutions of higher education, while later data are for degree-granting institutions. Degree-granting institutions grant associate's or higher degrees and participate in Title IV federal financial aid programs. The degree-granting classification is very similar to the earlier higher education classification, but it includes more 2-year colleges and excludes a few higher education institutions that did not grant degrees. Some data have been revised from previously published figures. Detail may not sum to totals because of rounding.

Table A-23. Total Fall Enrollment in Degree-Granting Institutions, by Race/Ethnicity of Student and Type and Control of Institution, Selected Years, 1976–2016—*Continued*

(Numbers in thousands; percent.)

Race/ethnicity of student and type and control of institution	1976		1990		2000		2010	
	Number	Percent	Number	Percent	Number	Percent	Number	Percent
Asian	NA	NA	NA	NA	NA	NA	278	5.4
Pacific Islander	NA	NA	NA	NA	NA	NA	18	0.3
American Indian/Alaska Native	7	0.3	10	0.4	19	0.6	40	0.8
Two or more races	NA	NA	NA	NA	NA	NA	82	1.6
Nonresident alien	70	X	128	X	182	X	251	X
2-year, total	3,879	35.3	5,240	37.9	5,948	38.8	7,684	36.6
White	3,077	80.2	3,954	76.4	3,804	64.9	4,321	57.0
Black	429	11.2	524	10.1	735	12.5	1,199	15.8
Hispanic	210	5.5	424	8.2	844	14.4	1,393	18.4
Asian/Pacific Islander	79	2.1	215	4.2	402	6.9	463	6.1
Asian	NA	NA	NA	NA	NA	NA	435	5.7
Pacific Islander	NA	NA	NA	NA	NA	NA	28	0.4
American Indian/Alaska Native	41	1.1	55	1.1	75	1.3	87	1.1
Two or more races	NA	NA	NA	NA	NA	NA	121	1.6
Nonresident alien	42	X	67	X	89	X	99	X
Public	3,748	96.6	4,996	95.4	5,697	95.8	7,218	93.9
White	2,974	80.2	3,780	76.6	3,652	65.1	4,113	57.7
Black	409	11.0	481	9.8	691	12.3	1,076	15.1
Hispanic	208	5.6	409	8.3	809	14.4	1,294	18.2
Asian/Pacific Islander	78	2.1	210	4.3	389	6.9	446	6.3
Asian	NA	NA	NA	NA	NA	NA	420	5.9
Pacific Islander	NA	NA	NA	NA	NA	NA	26	0.4
American Indian/Alaska Native	39	1.1	52	1.1	70	1.2	81	1.1
Two or more races	NA	NA	NA	NA	NA	NA	113	1.6
Nonresident alien	39	X	64	X	85	X	95	X
Private	131	3.4	244	4.6	251	4.2	466	6.1
White	103	80.3	174	72.7	152	61.4	209	45.2
Black	20	15.5	43	17.9	44	17.6	123	26.6
Hispanic	3	2.1	15	6.4	35	14.0	99	21.4
Asian/Pacific Islander	1	0.7	5	2.0	13	5.1	17	3.7
Asian	NA	NA	NA	NA	NA	NA	15	3.2
Pacific Islander	NA	NA	NA	NA	NA	NA	2	0.5
American Indian/Alaska Native	2	1.4	3	1.1	5	1.8	6	1.3
Two or more races	NA	NA	NA	NA	NA	NA	8	1.8
Nonresident alien	3	X	3	X	4	X	4	X

NA = Not available.
X = Not applicable.
Note: Race categories exclude persons of Hispanic ethnicity. Because of underreporting and nonreporting of racial/ethnic data, some figures are slightly lower than corresponding data in other tables. Data through 1990 are for institutions of higher education, while later data are for degree-granting institutions. Degree-granting institutions grant associate's or higher degrees and participate in Title IV federal financial aid programs. The degree-granting classification is very similar to the earlier higher education classification, but it includes more 2-year colleges and excludes a few higher education institutions that did not grant degrees. Some data have been revised from previously published figures. Detail may not sum to totals because of rounding.

Table A-23. Total Fall Enrollment in Degree-Granting Institutions, by Race/Ethnicity of Student and Type and Control of Institution, Selected Years, 1976–2016—*Continued*

(Numbers in thousands; percent.)

Race/ethnicity of student and type and control of institution	2013 Number	2013 Percent	2014 Number	2014 Percent	2015 Number	2015 Percent	2016 Number	2016 Percent
Asian	280	5.6	283	5.8	285	6.0	289	6.2
Pacific Islander	19	0.4	19	0.4	18	0.4	17	0.4
American Indian/Alaska Native	33	0.7	31	0.6	29	0.6	28	0.6
Two or more races	136	2.7	180	3.7	166	3.5	155	3.3
Nonresident alien	303	X	328	X	353	X	361	X
2-year, total	6,969	34.2	6,715	100.0	6,499	100.0	6,090	100.0
White	3,636	52.9	3,410	51.5	3,226	50.4	3,000	50.0
Black	1,073	15.6	1,014	15.3	941	14.7	865	14.4
Hispanic	1,491	21.7	1,521	23.0	1,556	24.3	1,495	24.9
Asian/Pacific Islander	416	6.0	407	6.2	402	6.3	377	6.3
Asian	392	5.7	386	5.8	382	6.0	360	6.0
Pacific Islander	23	0.3	21	0.3	20	0.3	17	0.3
American Indian/Alaska Native	71	1.0	66	1.0	63	1.0	59	1.0
Two or more races	190	2.8	201	3.0	209	3.3	200	3.3
Nonresident alien	92	X	95	X	104	X	94	X
Public	6,625	95.1	6,398	100.0	6,224	100.0	5,841	100.0
White	3,497	53.5	3,286	52.1	3,120	51.0	2,907	50.6
Black	978	15.0	925	14.7	859	14.0	789	13.7
Hispanic	1,414	21.6	1,447	23.0	1,495	24.4	1,439	25.0
Asian/Pacific Islander	400	6.1	393	6.2	391	6.4	367	6.4
Asian	379	5.8	374	5.9	372	6.1	351	6.1
Pacific Islander	21	0.3	19	0.3	18	0.3	16	0.3
American Indian/Alaska Native	66	1.0	62	1.0	59	1.0	55	1.0
Two or more races	180	2.8	191	3.0	199	3.2	193	3.4
Nonresident alien	90	X	93	X	101	X	91	X
Private	344	4.9	317	100.0	275	100.0	249	100.0
White	139	40.7	125	39.6	105	38.7	93	38.0
Black	95	27.9	89	28.2	82	29.9	77	31.2
Hispanic	77	22.7	74	23.4	61	22.2	55	22.5
Asian/Pacific Islander	16	4.6	15	4.7	11	4.1	10	4.2
Asian	13	3.8	12	3.9	10	3.5	9	3.6
Pacific Islander	3	0.8	3	0.8	2	0.6	1	0.6
American Indian/Alaska Native	4	1.3	4	1.3	4	1.4	3	1.4
Two or more races	10	2.8	9	2.9	10	3.7	7	2.8
Nonresident alien	2	X	2	X	3	X	3	X

X = Not applicable.
Note: Race categories exclude persons of Hispanic ethnicity. Because of underreporting and nonreporting of racial/ethnic data, some figures are slightly lower than corresponding data in other tables. Data through 1990 are for institutions of higher education, while later data are for degree-granting institutions. Degree-granting institutions grant associate's or higher degrees and participate in Title IV federal financial aid programs. The degree-granting classification is very similar to the earlier higher education classification, but it includes more 2-year colleges and excludes a few higher education institutions that did not grant degrees. Some data have been revised from previously published figures. Detail may not sum to totals because of rounding.

PART A

NATIONAL EDUCATION STATISTICS

■ **Attainment Tables**

Table A-24. Educational Attainment of the Population 18 Years Old and Over, by Age, Sex, Race, and Hispanic Origin, 2018

(Numbers in thousands; civilian noninstitutionalized population.[1])

Age, sex, race, and Hispanic origin	Total	None	1st to 4th grade	5th to 6th grade	7th to 8th grade	9th grade	10th grade	11th grade[2]	High school graduate
ALL RACES									
Both Sexes									
18 years old and over	249,193	824	1,445	3,173	3,669	3,415	4,070	10,577	71,368
18 to 24 years old	29,363	76	65	91	151	189	522	3,670	8,683
25 years old and over	219,830	748	1,381	3,082	3,518	3,227	3,548	6,907	62,685
25 to 29 years old	23,160	41	23	128	204	251	307	679	6,162
30 to 34 years old	21,695	38	79	210	234	294	277	626	5,297
35 to 39 years old	21,269	60	109	320	251	361	263	705	5,049
40 to 44 years old	19,391	61	122	304	250	288	265	525	4,870
45 to 49 years old	20,638	76	93	282	289	317	289	671	5,547
50 to 54 years old	20,899	45	123	328	265	285	343	662	6,215
55 to 59 years old	21,622	66	127	292	324	276	323	811	6,807
60 to 64 years old	20,078	82	129	325	265	247	277	594	6,137
65 to 69 years old	17,007	63	132	260	277	239	277	489	4,895
70 to 74 years old	13,359	64	111	216	294	223	273	367	4,114
75 years old and over	20,713	152	332	417	864	447	653	777	7,592
Male									
18 years old and over	120,705	347	678	1,590	1,838	1,688	2,055	5,563	36,274
18 to 24 years old	14,844	19	33	56	88	107	323	1,937	4,949
25 years old and over	105,862	328	645	1,534	1,750	1,581	1,732	3,626	31,325
25 to 29 years old	11,674	20	13	88	112	143	168	401	3,529
30 to 34 years old	10,816	24	39	129	103	175	160	384	3,001
35 to 39 years old	10,567	36	58	170	130	177	143	403	2,849
40 to 44 years old	9,504	36	63	157	136	125	153	296	2,622
45 to 49 years old	10,123	32	61	119	152	140	144	357	3,025
50 to 54 years old	10,217	20	49	166	154	151	192	375	3,256
55 to 59 years old	10,503	34	74	174	190	133	174	405	3,464
60 to 64 years old	9,399	31	51	144	127	117	119	295	2,877
65 to 69 years old	8,047	21	51	126	135	109	113	251	2,169
70 to 74 years old	6,294	21	35	89	126	118	118	159	1,785
75 years old and over	8,719	53	150	173	386	192	246	301	2,747
Female									
18 years old and over	128,488	477	767	1,583	1,831	1,727	2,015	5,014	35,094
18 to 24 years old	14,519	57	31	35	63	82	199	1,733	3,733
25 years old and over	113,969	420	736	1,548	1,768	1,646	1,816	3,281	31,360
25 to 29 years old	11,486	22	10	40	92	108	139	279	2,633
30 to 34 years old	10,878	14	40	80	131	119	117	242	2,297
35 to 39 years old	10,701	24	51	150	121	184	120	301	2,200
40 to 44 years old	9,887	25	59	147	115	163	112	230	2,247
45 to 49 years old	10,515	44	32	164	137	176	145	315	2,521
50 to 54 years old	10,682	25	74	162	111	134	151	287	2,959
55 to 59 years old	11,120	32	53	118	134	142	149	406	3,343
60 to 64 years old	10,679	51	78	181	138	130	158	299	3,260
65 to 69 years old	8,961	41	81	134	142	130	163	239	2,726
70 to 74 years old	7,066	43	76	127	168	105	155	208	2,329
75 years old and over	11,994	99	182	244	478	255	407	476	4,845
WHITE ALONE									
Both Sexes									
18 years old and over	194,250	556	1,113	2,531	2,938	2,698	2,988	7,550	55,649
18 to 24 years old	21,565	58	49	72	124	131	374	2,692	6,330
25 years old and over	172,685	498	1,064	2,459	2,814	2,567	2,613	4,857	49,319
25 to 29 years old	16,927	35	23	109	158	193	215	470	4,413
30 to 34 years old	16,167	31	59	187	195	234	183	468	3,986
35 to 39 years old	16,023	45	82	272	224	302	211	495	3,755
40 to 44 years old	14,628	50	95	266	218	253	218	380	3,734
45 to 49 years old	15,905	50	81	234	244	250	205	442	4,247
50 to 54 years old	16,438	33	102	286	214	232	246	426	4,850
55 to 59 years old	17,494	37	105	230	240	211	244	588	5,455
60 to 64 years old	16,112	44	110	270	196	190	184	382	4,882

[1]Civilian noninstitutionalized population, plus armed forces living off post or with their families on post.
[2]Population who attained the 12th grade but received no diploma are included in this category.

Table A-24. Educational Attainment of the Population 18 Years Old and Over, by Age, Sex, Race, and Hispanic Origin, 2018—*Continued*

(Numbers in thousands; civilian noninstitutionalized population.[1])

Age, sex, race, and Hispanic origin	Educational attainment						
	Some college, no degree	Associate's degree, occupational	Associate's degree, academic	Bachelor's degree	Master's degree	Professional degree	Doctoral degree
ALL RACES							
Both Sexes							
18 years old and over	46,175	10,341	13,761	51,406	21,280	3,202	4,487
18 to 24 years old	10,734	695	1039	3,170	232	29	18
25 years old and over	35,442	9,647	12,722	48,235	21,048	3,172	4,468
25 to 29 years old	4,543	924	1,331	6,478	1,618	209	259
30 to 34 years old	3,312	1044	1,346	5,893	2,210	314	520
35 to 39 years old	3,295	964	1,282	5,308	2,494	317	492
40 to 44 years old	2,837	920	1,161	4,725	2,353	279	430
45 to 49 years old	3,110	909	1,338	4,658	2,256	369	435
50 to 54 years old	3,208	954	1,362	4,465	1,944	297	402
55 to 59 years old	3,437	1,060	1,303	4,352	1,787	297	359
60 to 64 years old	3,399	967	1,211	3,920	1,788	300	435
65 to 69 years old	2,820	790	989	3,293	1,826	260	398
70 to 74 years old	2,251	487	632	2,423	1312	244	348
75 years old and over	3,229	628	766	2,719	1,459	287	390
Male							
18 years old and over	22,096	4,830	5,659	24,379	9,294	1,800	2,614
18 to 24 years old	5,115	357	445	1,299	76	21	18
25 years old and over	16,981	4,474	5,213	23,080	9,217	1,780	2,597
25 to 29 years old	2,298	479	551	3,021	639	105	107
30 to 34 years old	1,651	485	583	2,813	848	144	277
35 to 39 years old	1,595	448	545	2,529	1094	146	244
40 to 44 years old	1,435	452	504	2,184	988	129	223
45 to 49 years old	1,547	453	528	2,122	1026	189	229
50 to 54 years old	1,535	441	507	2,076	888	150	254
55 to 59 years old	1,600	507	550	2,062	741	181	211
60 to 64 years old	1,603	418	447	1,892	830	197	250
65 to 69 years old	1381	356	413	1699	801	163	260
70 to 74 years old	1,030	220	280	1,274	616	176	248
75 years old and over	1,306	214	305	1,408	745	200	293
Female							
18 years old and over	24,079	5,511	8,102	27,027	11,987	1,401	1,872
18 to 24 years old	5,619	338	593	1,871	156	8	1
25 years old and over	18,461	5,173	7,508	25,155	11,831	1,393	1,872
25 to 29 years old	2,245	446	780	3,457	979	104	151
30 to 34 years old	1,661	559	763	3,080	1,362	170	243
35 to 39 years old	1,700	516	737	2,778	1,400	171	248
40 to 44 years old	1,402	468	656	2,541	1,365	150	207
45 to 49 years old	1,564	455	810	2,536	1,230	180	206
50 to 54 years old	1,673	513	855	2,389	1,056	146	148
55 to 59 years old	1,837	552	753	2,289	1046	116	148
60 to 64 years old	1,797	549	764	2,029	958	103	185
65 to 69 years old	1,439	435	577	1,594	1025	97	138
70 to 74 years old	1,221	267	352	1149	696	68	100
75 years old and over	1,923	413	461	1,312	714	88	97
WHITE ALONE							
Both Sexes							
18 years old and over	35,542	8,384	10,922	40,818	16,560	2,599	3,403
18 to 24 years old	7,840	537	802	2,376	143	23	12
25 years old and over	27,701	7,847	10,120	38,442	16,417	2,576	3,390
25 to 29 years old	3,205	682	1,010	4,978	1,077	148	210
30 to 34 years old	2,427	800	1,005	4,433	1,578	242	339
35 to 39 years old	2,395	754	987	4,120	1,808	240	333
40 to 44 years old	2,108	738	860	3,563	1,665	202	279
45 to 49 years old	2,351	751	1,051	3,684	1,719	285	310
50 to 54 years old	2,504	784	1,073	3,666	1,487	238	297
55 to 59 years old	2,787	874	1,070	3,606	1,516	246	286
60 to 64 years old	2,745	806	980	3,201	1,506	275	343

[1] Civilian noninstitutionalized population, plus armed forces living off post or with their families on post.

Table A-24. Educational Attainment of the Population 18 Years Old and Over, by Age, Sex, Race, and Hispanic Origin, 2018—*Continued*

(Numbers in thousands; civilian noninstitutionalized population.[1])

Age, sex, race, and Hispanic origin	Total	None	1st to 4th grade	5th to 6th grade	7th to 8th grade	9th grade	10th grade	11th grade[2]	High school graduate
65 to 69 years old	14,034	46	88	183	213	174	195	343	3,978
70 to 74 years old	11,279	38	87	142	219	189	204	252	3,473
75 years old and over	17,678	90	232	279	694	338	508	612	6,546
Male									
18 years old and over	95,229	272	536	1,322	1,513	1,388	1,562	4,047	28,396
18 to 24 years old	10,953	19	30	45	70	83	241	1,425	3,683
25 years old and over	84,276	253	506	1,277	1,443	1,305	1,322	2,622	24,713
25 to 29 years old	8,651	19	13	77	89	122	110	286	2,603
30 to 34 years old	8,197	19	32	114	92	136	110	288	2,287
35 to 39 years old	8,131	26	44	141	112	154	120	283	2,203
40 to 44 years old	7,296	33	48	137	126	115	125	205	2,045
45 to 49 years old	7,940	20	54	107	121	111	118	257	2,337
50 to 54 years old	8,170	19	45	145	130	127	145	247	2,535
55 to 59 years old	8,583	24	61	142	149	117	129	297	2,785
60 to 64 years old	7,662	21	39	130	103	86	81	217	2,303
65 to 69 years old	6,729	13	36	94	102	82	87	177	1,762
70 to 74 years old	5,386	16	33	69	90	105	100	118	1,485
75 years old and over	7,530	42	101	122	329	150	196	248	2,367
Female									
18 years old and over	99,021	284	578	1,209	1,424	1,310	1,426	3,503	27,253
18 to 24 years old	10,612	39	19	27	53	48	134	1,268	2,647
25 years old and over	88,409	245	558	1,182	1,371	1,262	1,292	2,235	24,606
25 to 29 years old	8,276	16	10	32	69	72	105	184	1,811
30 to 34 years old	7,970	11	27	74	103	98	73	180	1,698
35 to 39 years old	7,891	19	39	131	112	149	90	212	1,552
40 to 44 years old	7,331	17	47	128	92	138	93	174	1,689
45 to 49 years old	7,965	30	27	127	122	139	87	185	1,909
50 to 54 years old	8,268	14	58	141	84	105	101	179	2,315
55 to 59 years old	8,910	13	44	89	91	94	115	291	2,670
60 to 64 years old	8,450	23	71	140	93	103	103	165	2,579
65 to 69 years old	7,306	33	52	89	111	92	108	166	2,216
70 to 74 years old	5,894	22	54	73	129	85	105	134	1,988
75 years old and over	10,147	48	131	158	366	188	313	364	4,179
BLACK ALONE									
Both Sexes									
18 years old and over	31,483	94	137	195	410	391	761	2,045	10,410
18 to 24 years old	4,435	13	10	10	17	29	92	599	1,568
25 years old and over	27,047	80	128	185	393	362	669	1,446	8,842
25 to 29 years old	3,529	6	*	9	19	45	63	142	1200
30 to 34 years old	2,977	7	12	5	17	22	60	115	855
35 to 39 years old	2,848	5	8	20	19	29	39	147	834
40 to 44 years old	2,563	2	10	8	10	21	28	92	769
45 to 49 years old	2,669	11	8	9	30	13	59	127	819
50 to 54 years old	2,682	5	3	10	27	24	61	176	944
55 to 59 years old	2,539	10	6	15	45	38	53	157	920
60 to 64 years old	2,406	12	4	14	36	38	61	165	834
65 to 69 years old	1,797	2	14	17	40	33	61	114	581
70 to 74 years old	1231	7	12	31	49	27	54	87	386
75 years old and over	1,806	12	51	47	101	70	129	123	698
Male									
18 years old and over	14,383	27	62	93	183	168	328	1,032	5,311
18 to 24 years old	2,187	*	2	8	9	13	43	322	843
25 years old and over	12,196	27	60	85	174	155	285	710	4,469
25 to 29 years old	1,697	1	*	7	13	19	37	80	639
30 to 34 years old	1,392	5	1	1	4	11	35	72	465
35 to 39 years old	1,304	5	4	13	11	17	19	88	423
40 to 44 years old	1,156	*	4	3	*	7	15	59	385
45 to 49 years old	1,215	6	5	3	20	6	18	64	457
50 to 54 years old	1,228	1	*	7	17	8	27	96	529

[1]Civilian noninstitutionalized population, plus armed forces living off post or with their families on post.
[2]Population who attained the 12th grade but received no diploma are included in this category.

Table A-24. Educational Attainment of the Population 18 Years Old and Over, by Age, Sex, Race, and Hispanic Origin, 2018—*Continued*

(Numbers in thousands; civilian noninstitutionalized population.[1])

Age, sex, race, and Hispanic origin	Educational attainment						
	Some college, no degree	Associate's degree, occupational	Associate's degree, academic	Bachelor's degree	Master's degree	Professional degree	Doctoral degree
65 to 69 years old	2,366	669	852	2,718	1624	233	352
70 to 74 years old	1,957	422	522	2,096	1,169	208	301
75 years old and over	2,857	567	710	2,378	1,267	259	340
Male							
18 years old and over	17,185	4,035	4,525	19,702	7,206	1,517	2,025
18 to 24 years old	3,701	282	341	965	39	19	12
25 years old and over	13,484	3,753	4,184	18,738	7,166	1,498	2,013
25 to 29 years old	1,664	360	406	2,342	388	85	87
30 to 34 years old	1,239	406	452	2,143	582	112	184
35 to 39 years old	1,228	380	416	1,974	773	115	163
40 to 44 years old	1,074	390	375	1,683	698	98	143
45 to 49 years old	1,201	382	416	1,725	787	144	161
50 to 54 years old	1,226	375	397	1,778	683	123	194
55 to 59 years old	1,327	419	453	1,748	626	147	161
60 to 64 years old	1,317	351	377	1,551	705	183	197
65 to 69 years old	1175	298	363	1431	724	148	236
70 to 74 years old	893	193	242	1,127	540	158	218
75 years old and over	1140	199	288	1,235	661	185	269
Female							
18 years old and over	18,357	4,349	6,397	21,116	9,355	1,082	1,378
18 to 24 years old	4,140	255	461	1,412	104	4	1
25 years old and over	14,217	4,094	5,936	19,704	9,251	1,078	1,377
25 to 29 years old	1,540	322	605	2,635	689	63	123
30 to 34 years old	1,188	394	553	2,290	996	130	155
35 to 39 years old	1,168	374	571	2,146	1,036	125	170
40 to 44 years old	1,034	348	485	1,880	967	103	136
45 to 49 years old	1,150	370	635	1,960	932	142	149
50 to 54 years old	1,278	408	676	1,888	804	115	103
55 to 59 years old	1,459	455	618	1,858	890	99	125
60 to 64 years old	1,428	456	603	1,649	801	93	145
65 to 69 years old	1,191	371	489	1286	901	85	116
70 to 74 years old	1065	229	280	969	629	50	83
75 years old and over	1,717	369	422	1,142	606	74	71
BLACK ALONE							
Both Sexes							
18 years old and over	6,880	1,222	1,783	4,731	1,910	188	326
18 to 24 years old	1,542	83	137	316	17	*	2
25 years old and over	5,338	1,139	1,645	4,415	1,893	188	323
25 to 29 years old	906	146	206	631	119	20	18
30 to 34 years old	633	141	207	637	198	16	53
35 to 39 years old	549	128	180	529	303	24	34
40 to 44 years old	500	126	160	524	247	26	37
45 to 49 years old	535	96	175	448	291	23	24
50 to 54 years old	514	117	185	388	182	16	28
55 to 59 years old	456	111	164	381	140	22	22
60 to 64 years old	460	112	157	348	119	11	34
65 to 69 years old	320	88	99	272	118	10	30
70 to 74 years old	220	45	82	124	77	13	17
75 years old and over	245	30	31	133	101	7	26
Male							
18 years old and over	3,048	482	688	2,034	713	73	139
18 to 24 years old	712	38	62	128	5	*	2
25 years old and over	2,336	444	625	1,906	708	73	137
25 to 29 years old	412	80	93	266	37	5	7
30 to 34 years old	303	38	76	296	58	8	19
35 to 39 years old	229	33	67	245	125	5	19
40 to 44 years old	243	40	64	224	85	10	16
45 to 49 years old	218	39	70	165	128	9	6
50 to 54 years old	215	53	67	126	62	9	10

[1]Civilian noninstitutionalized population, plus armed forces living off post or with their families on post.

Table A-24. Educational Attainment of the Population 18 Years Old and Over, by Age, Sex, Race, and Hispanic Origin, 2018—*Continued*

(Numbers in thousands; civilian noninstitutionalized population.[1])

Age, sex, race, and Hispanic origin	Total	None	1st to 4th grade	5th to 6th grade	7th to 8th grade	9th grade	10th grade	11th grade[2]	High school graduate
55 to 59 years old	1,159	5	3	6	19	16	25	74	468
60 to 64 years old	1042	2	2	3	14	20	28	55	393
65 to 69 years old	769	*	6	9	20	14	23	56	264
70 to 74 years old	543	3	2	9	21	9	15	32	188
75 years old and over	691	*	33	25	33	28	44	33	257
Female									
18 years old and over	17,100	67	75	102	227	223	432	1,013	5,099
18 to 24 years old	2,248	13	8	2	8	16	49	277	725
25 years old and over	14,852	53	67	100	219	206	383	737	4,374
25 to 29 years old	1,832	6	*	2	6	26	25	61	562
30 to 34 years old	1,585	3	10	3	12	11	25	43	390
35 to 39 years old	1,544	*	4	6	8	12	20	60	411
40 to 44 years old	1,407	2	6	5	10	15	13	34	384
45 to 49 years old	1,454	5	3	7	11	7	41	63	362
50 to 54 years old	1,454	4	3	3	10	16	34	81	415
55 to 59 years old	1,380	5	2	9	25	23	28	83	452
60 to 64 years old	1,364	10	2	11	22	18	33	110	441
65 to 69 years old	1,028	2	9	9	19	19	38	57	317
70 to 74 years old	688	4	10	23	28	18	40	55	198
75 years old and over	1,115	12	18	22	68	42	85	90	441
ASIAN ALONE									
Both Sexes									
18 years old and over	15,456	138	128	292	183	187	143	417	2,856
18 to 24 years old	1,779	4	6	6	7	17	18	134	253
25 years old and over	13,677	134	122	286	176	171	125	283	2,603
25 to 29 years old	1,656	*	*	3	16	*	7	15	218
30 to 34 years old	1,692	*	3	1	9	8	19	8	217
35 to 39 years old	1,596	2	7	6	3	11	6	33	232
40 to 44 years old	1,553	10	13	12	11	8	3	18	203
45 to 49 years old	1,426	9	3	21	12	32	15	51	288
50 to 54 years old	1,227	7	9	14	13	24	20	32	274
55 to 59 years old	1066	19	8	33	19	22	9	31	263
60 to 64 years old	1102	23	8	33	25	12	19	23	262
65 to 69 years old	829	13	20	52	14	17	9	25	229
70 to 74 years old	594	17	12	39	17	6	13	17	164
75 years old and over	936	33	38	73	37	31	6	31	253
Male									
18 years old and over	7,294	29	39	94	75	61	64	202	1,325
18 to 24 years old	913	*	2	2	7	5	12	70	144
25 years old and over	6,381	29	37	91	67	56	52	133	1,181
25 to 29 years old	826	*	*	*	6	*	6	7	116
30 to 34 years old	805	*	*	*	*	3	8	1	115
35 to 39 years old	765	*	3	3	2	2	2	20	110
40 to 44 years old	738	3	7	6	3	3	2	12	105
45 to 49 years old	681	*	1	3	10	10	4	15	140
50 to 54 years old	551	*	3	6	5	14	9	20	102
55 to 59 years old	495	6	4	16	10	*	6	16	115
60 to 64 years old	501	8	5	6	4	6	6	11	120
65 to 69 years old	377	8	4	20	8	4	*	12	99
70 to 74 years old	257	*	*	10	11	4	4	6	72
75 years old and over	385	4	11	22	8	9	4	13	87
Female									
18 years old and over	8,162	110	89	199	108	126	79	215	1,531
18 to 24 years old	866	4	4	4	*	11	6	64	109
25 years old and over	7,296	105	85	195	108	115	73	151	1,422
25 to 29 years old	830	*	*	3	10	*	*	8	102
30 to 34 years old	887	*	3	1	9	5	10	8	102
35 to 39 years old	832	2	4	3	*	9	4	14	122
40 to 44 years old	815	7	7	6	8	5	*	5	98

[1] Civilian noninstitutionalized population, plus armed forces living off post or with their families on post.
[2] Population who attained the 12th grade but received no diploma are included in this category.

Table A-24. Educational Attainment of the Population 18 Years Old and Over, by Age, Sex, Race, and Hispanic Origin, 2018—*Continued*

(Numbers in thousands; civilian noninstitutionalized population.[1])

Age, sex, race, and Hispanic origin	Educational attainment						
	Some college, no degree	Associate's degree, occupational	Associate's degree, academic	Bachelor's degree	Master's degree	Professional degree	Doctoral degree
55 to 59 years old	175	52	72	172	51	13	7
60 to 64 years old	207	46	47	159	44	5	18
65 to 69 years old	122	40	33	124	42	3	13
70 to 74 years old	102	20	27	66	34	5	11
75 years old and over	111	3	8	63	41	2	10
Female							
18 years old and over	3,832	740	1,095	2,697	1,197	115	187
18 to 24 years old	829	44	75	188	11	*	*
25 years old and over	3,002	695	1020	2,509	1,185	115	187
25 to 29 years old	495	66	112	365	81	15	10
30 to 34 years old	329	103	131	341	140	9	34
35 to 39 years old	319	95	113	284	178	19	15
40 to 44 years old	257	87	96	300	163	16	21
45 to 49 years old	318	56	105	282	162	14	18
50 to 54 years old	300	65	117	262	120	7	18
55 to 59 years old	281	58	91	209	89	9	15
60 to 64 years old	253	67	110	189	76	6	16
65 to 69 years old	198	48	66	147	76	7	17
70 to 74 years old	118	25	55	59	43	8	6
75 years old and over	135	27	23	70	60	5	17
ASIAN ALONE							
Both Sexes							
18 years old and over	1,960	382	587	4,673	2,464	358	686
18 to 24 years old	809	31	40	376	69	6	3
25 years old and over	1,151	351	547	4,297	2,395	351	683
25 to 29 years old	159	48	39	681	406	35	30
30 to 34 years old	123	45	72	637	387	46	116
35 to 39 years old	163	46	62	545	327	44	109
40 to 44 years old	106	24	100	515	375	45	111
45 to 49 years old	121	39	67	421	202	59	85
50 to 54 years old	87	24	58	326	237	28	74
55 to 59 years old	93	41	43	298	116	24	46
60 to 64 years old	104	33	45	307	141	11	55
65 to 69 years old	71	13	24	246	67	16	13
70 to 74 years old	36	13	20	148	49	23	21
75 years old and over	88	25	18	172	88	21	22
Male							
18 years old and over	1012	169	235	2,152	1,245	180	412
18 to 24 years old	432	16	18	167	32	2	3
25 years old and over	580	153	217	1,985	1,214	178	409
25 to 29 years old	85	26	16	333	204	13	13
30 to 34 years old	65	22	20	289	195	20	67
35 to 39 years old	69	16	33	257	173	21	55
40 to 44 years old	55	9	46	226	182	16	64
45 to 49 years old	68	20	31	199	89	35	55
50 to 54 years old	48	6	20	131	132	9	47
55 to 59 years old	47	20	14	127	58	18	39
60 to 64 years old	44	14	11	147	77	8	34
65 to 69 years old	42	8	9	113	31	10	10
70 to 74 years old	17	2	9	64	30	13	14
75 years old and over	40	11	9	99	43	13	12
Female							
18 years old and over	948	213	352	2,521	1,218	178	273
18 to 24 years old	377	15	22	209	37	4	*
25 years old and over	572	199	330	2,313	1,181	173	273
25 to 29 years old	74	22	23	347	202	21	17
30 to 34 years old	58	23	53	349	192	26	49
35 to 39 years old	94	30	29	287	155	23	54
40 to 44 years old	51	15	54	289	193	29	48

[1]Civilian noninstitutionalized population, plus armed forces living off post or with their families on post.

Table A-24. Educational Attainment of the Population 18 Years Old and Over, by Age, Sex, Race, and Hispanic Origin, 2018—*Continued*

(Numbers in thousands; civilian noninstitutionalized population.[1])

Age, sex, race, and Hispanic origin		Educational attainment							
	Total	None	1st to 4th grade	5th to 6th grade	7th to 8th grade	9th grade	10th grade	11th grade[2]	High school graduate
45 to 49 years old	745	9	2	18	2	22	11	37	148
50 to 54 years old	675	7	7	8	7	10	11	12	172
55 to 59 years old	571	13	4	17	9	22	2	15	148
60 to 64 years old	601	16	3	27	21	6	13	12	142
65 to 69 years old	452	5	16	33	7	12	9	13	130
70 to 74 years old	337	17	12	29	6	2	9	11	92
75 years old and over	550	29	27	51	29	22	2	17	166
HISPANIC (OF ANY RACE)									
Both Sexes									
18 years old and over	40,478	424	1,061	2,386	1,534	1,573	1,032	2,991	12,590
18 to 24 years old	6,601	19	25	46	51	63	136	1033	2,179
25 years old and over	33,877	405	1,036	2,339	1,483	1,510	896	1,958	10,412
25 to 29 years old	4,859	14	23	110	84	132	110	247	1,586
30 to 34 years old	4,422	25	65	197	137	184	110	284	1,390
35 to 39 years old	4,483	44	86	284	184	259	106	331	1,337
40 to 44 years old	3,990	41	102	276	177	203	105	217	1,367
45 to 49 years old	3,727	44	73	233	176	207	105	252	1,177
50 to 54 years old	3,234	26	102	280	146	135	87	177	982
55 to 59 years old	2,639	21	113	237	144	93	77	164	784
60 to 64 years old	2,201	31	111	255	106	94	56	101	621
65 to 69 years old	1,589	46	91	169	109	69	40	104	405
70 to 74 years old	1066	35	72	112	69	49	28	31	295
75 years old and over	1,668	78	197	187	152	84	71	49	467
Male									
18 years old and over	20,196	216	534	1,229	758	764	552	1,686	6,687
18 to 24 years old	3,350	4	17	28	27	38	89	593	1,191
25 years old and over	16,846	212	517	1,201	731	726	463	1093	5,495
25 to 29 years old	2,546	8	13	75	51	77	66	132	902
30 to 34 years old	2,272	19	35	126	70	116	60	174	763
35 to 39 years old	2,335	27	53	150	93	117	56	211	771
40 to 44 years old	1,976	29	55	141	101	89	64	117	728
45 to 49 years old	1,867	25	50	102	78	96	61	130	631
50 to 54 years old	1,618	15	45	139	79	67	39	103	513
55 to 59 years old	1,312	14	68	143	78	46	46	75	388
60 to 64 years old	1038	14	42	119	47	43	24	54	292
65 to 69 years old	747	11	37	80	53	30	11	61	198
70 to 74 years old	438	13	27	52	19	12	10	18	114
75 years old and over	696	37	93	74	62	32	26	18	196
Female									
18 years old and over	20,282	207	527	1,157	776	809	479	1,305	5,904
18 to 24 years old	3,251	15	8	19	24	25	47	440	987
25 years old and over	17,030	192	518	1,138	752	784	433	865	4,916
25 to 29 years old	2,314	5	10	34	32	55	44	115	684
30 to 34 years old	2,150	6	29	71	67	68	50	110	627
35 to 39 years old	2,148	16	32	134	91	142	50	120	566
40 to 44 years old	2,013	11	47	134	76	114	42	100	640
45 to 49 years old	1,859	20	24	131	98	111	43	122	546
50 to 54 years old	1,616	11	57	141	66	68	47	73	470
55 to 59 years old	1,327	7	45	94	66	47	31	89	397
60 to 64 years old	1163	18	70	137	59	51	32	47	330
65 to 69 years old	841	35	55	88	56	39	29	44	207
70 to 74 years old	628	22	45	60	50	37	18	13	180
75 years old and over	972	41	104	113	90	52	45	31	271

* = Quantity zero or rounds to zero.
[1] Civilian noninstitutionalized population, plus armed forces living off post or with their families on post.
[2] Population who attained the 12th grade but received no diploma are included in this category.

Table A-24. Educational Attainment of the Population 18 Years Old and Over, by Age, Sex, Race, and Hispanic Origin, 2018—*Continued*

(Numbers in thousands; civilian noninstitutionalized population.[1])

Age, sex, race, and Hispanic origin	Educational attainment						
	Some college, no degree	Associate's degree, occupational	Associate's degree, academic	Bachelor's degree	Master's degree	Professional degree	Doctoral degree
45 to 49 years old	54	20	35	222	112	24	30
50 to 54 years old	39	18	38	195	105	19	27
55 to 59 years old	46	21	29	172	59	5	7
60 to 64 years old	60	18	34	160	64	2	21
65 to 69 years old	29	6	15	133	36	6	3
70 to 74 years old	19	11	10	84	18	10	7
75 years old and over	48	14	9	74	45	8	10
HISPANIC (OF ANY RACE)							
Both Sexes							
18 years old and over	7,148	1,273	1,888	4,765	1,397	221	196
18 to 24 years old	2,251	141	291	351	12	*	3
25 years old and over	4,897	1,132	1,597	4,414	1,385	221	193
25 to 29 years old	1,070	176	302	842	138	18	8
30 to 34 years old	682	184	228	690	202	15	29
35 to 39 years old	634	144	219	605	201	35	12
40 to 44 years old	453	142	177	487	197	28	19
45 to 49 years old	506	116	165	461	163	21	27
50 to 54 years old	441	119	148	392	140	34	25
55 to 59 years old	340	87	117	313	107	18	24
60 to 64 years old	289	65	102	247	92	17	14
65 to 69 years old	199	37	67	172	56	9	14
70 to 74 years old	136	19	44	96	55	13	11
75 years old and over	146	43	30	108	34	12	9
Male							
18 years old and over	3,484	570	795	2,143	551	115	111
18 to 24 years old	1047	66	121	120	4	*	3
25 years old and over	2,437	505	673	2,022	547	115	108
25 to 29 years old	527	73	152	391	66	10	2
30 to 34 years old	337	78	101	307	69	2	15
35 to 39 years old	310	67	102	274	77	18	7
40 to 44 years old	216	65	66	205	74	14	12
45 to 49 years old	267	62	60	212	65	15	15
50 to 54 years old	230	56	43	187	61	20	20
55 to 59 years old	161	37	45	150	43	7	11
60 to 64 years old	155	31	36	137	29	10	9
65 to 69 years old	101	19	38	75	23	4	5
70 to 74 years old	66	5	17	43	27	8	6
75 years old and over	67	12	13	42	12	7	5
Female							
18 years old and over	3,663	703	1093	2,623	846	106	85
18 to 24 years old	1,204	75	169	231	7	*	*
25 years old and over	2,460	628	923	2,392	838	106	85
25 to 29 years old	543	103	150	451	72	8	7
30 to 34 years old	345	106	127	383	133	13	14
35 to 39 years old	325	77	117	331	124	17	5
40 to 44 years old	237	77	110	282	123	14	7
45 to 49 years old	239	53	106	250	98	6	12
50 to 54 years old	210	63	105	205	79	15	5
55 to 59 years old	179	51	71	163	63	11	13
60 to 64 years old	134	34	66	111	63	7	4
65 to 69 years old	98	18	29	97	33	5	9
70 to 74 years old	70	14	27	53	29	5	5
75 years old and over	79	31	16	66	22	5	4

* = Quantity zero or rounds to zero.
[1]Civilian noninstitutionalized population, plus armed forces living off post or with their families on post.

Table A-25. Educational Attainment of the Population 25 Years Old and Over, by Marital Status and Sex, 2018

(Numbers in thousands; percent; civilian noninstitutionalized population.[1])

Sex and marital status	Educational attainment									
	Total		None to 8th grade		9th to 11th grade		High school graduate		Some college, no degree	
	Number	Percent	Number	Percent	Number	Percent	Number	Percent	Number	Percent
BOTH SEXES										
Total	219,830	100.0	8,729	4.0	13,682	6.2	62,685	28.5	35,442	16.1
Married spouse present	125,323	57.0	4,587	52.5	6,345	46.4	33,015	52.7	18,522	52.3
Married spouse absent, not separated	3,569	1.6	281	3.2	277	2.0	1,044	1.7	507	1.4
Separated	4,769	2.2	341	3.9	569	4.2	1,597	2.5	889	2.5
Widowed	15,069	6.9	1,276	14.6	1,542	11.3	5,695	9.1	2,339	6.6
Divorced	25,715	11.7	741	8.5	1,701	12.4	7,929	12.6	5,064	14.3
Never married	45,386	20.6	1,504	17.2	3,249	23.7	13,406	21.4	8,120	22.9
MALE										
Total	105,862	100.0	4,256	4.0	6,939	6.6	31,325	29.6	16,981	16.0
Married spouse present	62,905	59.4	2,479	58.2	3,415	49.2	16,986	54.2	9,442	55.6
Married spouse absent, not separated	1,881	1.8	156	3.7	152	2.2	539	1.7	234	1.4
Separated	2,015	1.9	127	3.0	232	3.3	783	2.5	321	1.9
Widowed	3,399	3.2	294	6.9	329	4.7	1,220	3.9	539	3.2
Divorced	11,004	10.4	331	7.8	815	11.7	3,835	12.2	2,127	12.5
Never married	24,658	23.3	870	20.4	1,995	28.8	7,961	25.4	4,318	25.4
FEMALE										
Total	113,969	100.0	4,472	3.9	6,743	5.9	31,360	27.5	18,461	16.2
Married spouse present	62,417	54.8	2,108	47.1	2,929	43.4	16,029	51.1	9,080	49.2
Married spouse absent, not separated	1,689	1.6	125	2.9	125	1.8	505	1.6	273	1.6
Separated	2,754	2.6	213	5.0	337	4.9	814	2.6	568	3.3
Widowed	11,670	11.0	983	23.1	1,212	17.5	4,474	14.3	1,800	10.6
Divorced	14,711	13.9	410	9.6	885	12.8	4,094	13.1	2,938	17.3
Never married	20,728	19.6	634	14.9	1,255	18.1	5,445	17.4	3,802	22.4

[1]Plus armed forces living off post or with their families on post.

Table A-25. Educational Attainment of the Population 25 Years Old and Over, by Marital Status and Sex, 2018—*Continued*

(Numbers in thousands; percent; civilian noninstitutionalized population.[1])

Sex and marital status	Educational attainment									
	Associate's degree		Bachelor's degree		Master's degree		Professional degree		Doctoral degree	
	Number	Percent	Number	Percent	Number	Percent	Number	Percent	Number	Percent
BOTH SEXES										
Total	22,369	10.2	48,235	21.9	21,048	9.6	3,172	1.4	4,468	2.0
Married spouse present	13,061	58.4	30,144	62.5	14,112	67.0	2,281	71.9	3,256	72.9
Married spouse absent, not separated	294	1.3	684	1.4	350	1.7	40	1.3	94	2.1
Separated	439	2.0	656	1.4	205	1.0	32	1.0	41	0.9
Widowed	1,322	5.9	1,764	3.7	849	4.0	118	3.7	164	3.7
Divorced	3,147	14.1	4,557	9.4	2,056	9.8	245	7.7	275	6.2
Never married	4,106	18.4	10,430	21.6	3,476	16.5	456	14.4	639	14.3
MALE										
Total	9,687	9.2	23,080	21.8	9,217	8.7	1,780	1.7	2,597	2.5
Married spouse present	5,887	60.8	14,733	63.8	6,639	72.0	1,362	76.5	1,963	75.6
Married spouse absent, not separated	130	1.3	369	1.6	205	2.2	36	2.0	59	2.3
Separated	159	1.6	273	1.2	79	0.9	27	1.5	13	0.5
Widowed	259	2.7	454	2.0	195	2.1	35	2.0	74	2.8
Divorced	1,161	12.0	1,836	8.0	658	7.1	114	6.4	126	4.9
Never married	2,091	21.6	5,414	23.5	1,442	15.6	206	11.6	361	13.9
FEMALE										
Total	12,682	11.1	25,155	22.1	11,831	10.4	1,393	1.2	1,872	1.6
Married spouse present	7,174	56.6	15,411	61.3	7,473	63.2	920	66.0	1,294	69.1
Married spouse absent, not separated	164	1.7	315	1.4	145	1.6	3	0.2	35	1.3
Separated	280	2.9	383	1.7	126	1.4	5	0.3	28	1.1
Widowed	1,063	11.0	1,310	5.7	655	7.1	84	4.7	89	3.4
Divorced	1,986	20.5	2,721	11.8	1,398	15.2	131	7.4	149	5.7
Never married	2,015	20.8	5,016	21.7	2,034	22.1	251	14.1	277	10.7

[1]Plus armed forces living off post or with their families on post.

Table A-26. Educational Attainment of the Population 25 Years Old and Over, by Household Relationship and Sex, 2018

(Numbers in thousands; percent; civilian noninstitutionalized population.[1])

Sex and household relationship	Educational attainment									
	Total		None to 8th grade		9th to 11th grade		High school graduate		Some college, no degree	
	Number	Percent	Number	Percent	Number	Percent	Number	Percent	Number	Percent
BOTH SEXES										
Total	219,830	100.0	8,729	4.0	13,682	6.2	62,685	28.5	35,442	16.1
Family householder	80,086	36.4	2,679	30.7	4,739	34.6	20,577	32.8	13,735	38.8
Married spouse present	60,364	75.4	1,833	68.4	2,953	62.3	14,603	71.0	9,714	70.7
Other family householder	19,723	24.6	846	31.6	1,787	37.7	5,974	29.0	4,020	29.3
Nonfamily householder	41372	18.8	1,420	16.3	2,732	20.0	11,565	18.4	7,444	21.0
Living alone	34,274	82.8	1,282	90.3	2,369	86.7	9,880	85.4	6,240	83.8
Living with nonrelatives	7,098	17.2	138	9.7	363	13.3	1,686	14.6	1,204	16.2
Relative of householder	85455	38.9	4,066	46.6	5,357	39.2	26,243	41.9	12,342	34.8
Spouse	60,275	70.5	2,078	51.1	2,963	55.3	16,827	64.1	8,231	66.7
Other	25,180	29.5	1,989	48.9	2,394	44.7	9,417	35.9	4,111	33.3
Nonrelative	12,918	5.9	563	6.4	854	6.2	4,300	6.9	1,921	5.4
MALE										
Total	105,862	100.0	4,256	4.0	6,939	6.6	31,325	29.6	16,981	16.0
Family householder	41,742	39.4	1,377	32.4	2,221	32.0	10,844	34.6	6,816	40.1
Married spouse present	36,203	86.7	1,158	84.1	1,734	78.1	8,903	82.1	5,748	84.3
Other family householder	5,540	13.3	219	15.9	487	21.9	1,941	17.9	1,068	15.7
Nonfamily householder	19,458	18.4	648	15.2	1,300	18.7	5,503	17.6	3,546	20.9
Living alone	15,305	78.7	563	86.9	1,078	82.9	4,485	81.5	2,816	79.4
Living with nonrelatives	4,153	21.3	84	13.0	222	17.1	1018	18.5	730	20.6
Relative of householder	37,641	35.6	1,855	43.6	2,842	41.0	12,505	39.9	5,605	33.0
Spouse	24,343	64.7	994	53.6	1,439	50.6	7,280	58.2	3,399	60.6
Other	13,298	35.3	861	46.4	1,402	49.3	5,225	41.8	2,206	39.4
Nonrelative	7,021	6.6	377	8.9	576	8.3	2,473	7.9	1014	6.0
FEMALE										
Total	113,969	100.0	4,472	3.9	6,743	5.9	31,360	27.5	18,461	16.2
Family householder	38,344	33.6	1,302	29.1	2,519	37.4	9,733	31.0	6,919	37.5
Married spouse present	24,161	63.0	676	51.9	1,219	48.4	5,701	58.6	3,966	57.3
Other family householder	14,183	37.0	627	48.2	1,300	51.6	4,032	41.4	2,952	42.7
Nonfamily householder	21,914	19.2	773	17.3	1,432	21.2	6,063	19.3	3,898	21.1
Living alone	18,969	86.6	719	93.0	1,291	90.2	5,395	89.0	3,424	87.8
Living with nonrelatives	2,945	13.4	54	7.0	141	9.8	668	11.0	474	12.2
Relative of householder	47,814	42.0	2,211	49.4	2,515	37.3	13,738	43.8	6,738	36.5
Spouse	35,932	75.1	1,083	49.0	1,524	60.6	9,547	69.5	4,832	71.7
Other	11,882	24.9	1,128	51.0	991	39.4	4,192	30.5	1,905	28.3
Nonrelative	5,897	5.2	186	4.2	277	4.1	1,826	5.8	907	4.9

NOTE: Percentages may not sum to total because of rounding.
[1] Civilian noninstitutionalized population, plus armed forces living off post or with their families on post.

Table A-26. Educational Attainment of the Population 25 Years Old and Over, by Household Relationship and Sex, 2018—*Continued*

(Numbers in thousands; percent; civilian noninstitutionalized population.[1])

Sex and household relationship	Educational attainment									
	Associate degree		Bachelor's degree		Master's degree		Professional degree		Doctoral degree	
	Number	Percent	Number	Percent	Number	Percent	Number	Percent	Number	Percent
BOTH SEXES										
Total	22,369	10.2	48,235	21.9	21,048	9.6	3,172	1.4	4,468	2.0
Family householder	8,770	39.2	18,064	37.4	8,425	40.0	1,190	37.5	1,906	42.7
Married spouse present	6,379	72.7	14,849	82.2	7,241	85.9	1,078	90.6	1,714	89.9
Other family householder	2,391	27.3	3,216	17.8	1185	14.1	113	9.5	193	10.1
Nonfamily householder	4,112	18.4	8,665	18.0	4,124	19.6	554	17.5	754	16.9
Living alone	3,359	81.7	6,758	78.0	3,356	81.4	443	80.0	586	77.7
Living with nonrelatives	753	18.3	1,907	22.0	769	18.6	111	20.0	168	22.3
Relative of householder	8,404	37.6	18,613	38.6	7,505	35.7	1,285	40.5	1,640	36.7
Spouse	6,355	75.6	14,504	77.9	6,657	88.7	1,154	89.8	1,505	91.8
Other	2,048	24.4	4,109	22.1	848	11.3	130	10.1	134	8.2
Nonrelative	1,083	4.8	2,893	6.0	993	4.7	143	4.5	168	3.8
MALE										
Total	9,687	9.2	23,080	21.8	9,217	8.7	1,780	1.7	2,597	2.5
Family householder	4003	41.3	9,903	42.9	4,505	48.9	775	43.5	1,299	50.0
Married spouse present	3,476	86.8	8,956	90.4	4,243	94.2	760	98.1	1,225	94.3
Other family householder	527	13.2	947	9.6	262	5.8	15	1.9	74	5.7
Nonfamily householder	1,786	18.4	4,320	18.7	1,666	18.1	281	15.8	408	15.7
Living alone	1,356	75.9	3,236	74.9	1268	76.1	215	76.5	287	70.3
Living with nonrelatives	430	24.1	1084	25.1	398	23.9	66	23.5	121	29.7
Relative of householder	3,330	34.4	7,454	32.3	2,628	28.5	636	35.7	787	30.3
Spouse	2,275	68.3	5,395	72.4	2,286	87.0	562	88.4	713	90.6
Other	1055	31.7	2,059	27.6	342	13.0	74	11.6	74	9.4
Nonrelative	568	5.9	1,402	6.1	418	4.5	88	4.9	104	4.0
FEMALE										
Total	12,682	11.1	25,155	22.1	11,831	10.4	1,393	1.2	1,872	1.6
Family householder	4,767	37.6	8,161	32.4	3,920	33.1	416	29.9	607	32.4
Married spouse present	2,903	60.9	5,893	72.2	2,997	76.5	318	76.4	489	80.6
Other family householder	1,864	39.1	2,269	27.8	923	23.5	98	23.6	119	19.6
Nonfamily householder	2,326	18.3	4,345	17.3	2,458	20.8	273	19.6	347	18.5
Living alone	2,003	86.1	3,523	81.1	2,087	84.9	228	83.5	299	86.2
Living with nonrelatives	324	13.9	822	18.9	371	15.1	44	16.1	48	13.8
Relative of householder	5,074	40.0	11,159	44.4	4,877	41.2	649	46.6	853	45.6
Spouse	4,080	80.4	9,109	81.6	4,371	89.6	592	91.2	793	93.0
Other	994	19.6	2,050	18.4	506	10.4	56	8.6	60	7.0
Nonrelative	515	4.1	1,490	5.9	575	4.9	56	4.0	65	3.5

NOTE: Percentages may not sum to total because of rounding.
[1] Civilian noninstitutionalized population, plus armed forces living off post or with their families on post.

Table A-27. Educational Attainment of the Population 25 Years Old and Over, by Labor Force Status and Sex, 2018

(Numbers in thousands; percent; civilian noninstitutionalized population.[1])

Sex and labor force status	Total	Educational attainment								
		None to 8th grade	9th to 11th grade	High school graduate	Some college, no degree	Associate's degree	Bachelor's degree	Master's degree	Professional degree	Doctoral degree
BOTH SEXES										
Total	219,830	8,729	13,682	62,685	35,442	22,369	48,235	21,048	3,172	4,468
Employed	135,851	3,510	5,935	34,152	21,121	15,102	34,943	15,318	2,401	3,368
Unemployed	4,941	209	462	1,652	948	434	860	280	37	59
Unemployment rate	2.2	2.4	3.4	2.6	2.7	1.9	1.8	1.3	1.2	1.3
Not in civilian labor force	79,039	5,010	7,285	26,881	13,373	6,832	12,432	5,450	735	1,041
Percent	36.0	57.4	53.2	42.9	37.7	30.5	25.8	25.9	23.2	23.3
MALE										
Total	105,862	4,256	6,939	31,325	16,981	9,687	23,080	9,217	1,780	2,597
Employed	72,248	2,289	3,776	20,007	11,204	6,968	17,729	6,962	1,377	1,937
Unemployed	2,758	130	255	1,043	495	204	451	129	24	26
Unemployment rate	2.6	3.1	3.7	3.3	2.9	2.1	2.0	1.4	1.3	1.0
Not in civilian labor force	30,856	1,837	2,908	10,275	5,282	2,515	4,900	2,127	379	634
Percent	29.1	43.2	41.9	32.8	31.1	26.0	21.2	23.1	21.3	24.4
FEMALE										
Total	113,969	4,472	6,743	31,360	18,461	12,682	25,155	11,831	1,393	1,872
Employed	63,603	1,221	2,160	14,146	9,917	8,135	17,214	8,356	1,024	1,431
Unemployed	2,183	78	206	609	453	230	409	152	13	33
Unemployment rate	1.9	1.7	3.1	1.9	2.5	1.8	1.6	1.3	0.9	1.8
Not in civilian labor force	48,183	3,173	4,377	16,606	8,090	4,317	7,532	3,323	357	408
Percent	42.3	71.0	64.9	53.0	43.8	34.0	29.9	28.1	25.6	21.8

NOTE: Percentages may not sum to total because of rounding.
[1]Civilian noninstitutionalized population, plus armed forces living off post or with their families on post. May be of any race.

This page is intentionally left blank

Table A-28. Educational Attainment of Employed Civilians 25 Years Old and Over, by Occupation and Sex, 2018

(Numbers in thousands; percent; civilian noninstitutionalized population.[1])

Occupation and sex	Total Number	Total Percent	None to 8th grade Number	None to 8th grade Percent	9th to 11th grade Number	9th to 11th grade Percent	High school graduate Number	High school graduate Percent	Some college, no degree Number	Some college, no degree Percent
BOTH SEXES										
Total Employed Civilians	135,851	100.0	3,510	2.6	5,935	4.4	34,152	25.1	21,121	15.5
Occupation										
Management, business, and financial occupations	24,827	18.3	178	5.1	351	5.9	3,533	10.3	3,256	15.4
Professional and related occupations	34,439	25.4	36	1.0	145	2.4	2,098	6.1	2,981	14.1
Service occupations.................................	20,719	15.3	1,211	34.5	1,822	30.7	7,705	22.6	3,817	18.1
Sales and related occupations....................	12,341	9.1	119	3.4	460	7.8	3,379	9.9	2,426	11.5
Office and administrative occupations	14,912	11.0	76	2.2	360	6.1	4,581	13.4	3,702	17.5
Farming, forestry, and fishing occupations	892	0.7	244	7.0	120	2.0	287	0.8	87	0.4
Construction and extraction occupations....	7,165	5.3	662	18.9	927	15.6	3,185	9.3	1,090	5.2
Installation, maintenance, and repair occupations	4,331	3.2	144	4.1	305	5.1	1,805	5.3	840	4.0
Production occupations	7,664	5.6	492	14.0	671	11.3	3,463	10.1	1,395	6.6
Transportation and material moving occupations	8,562	6.3	349	9.9	775	13.1	4,117	12.1	1,527	7.2
MALE										
Total Employed Civilians	72,248	100.0	2,289	3.2	3,776	5.2	20,007	27.7	11,204	15.5
Occupation										
Management, business, and financial occupations	13,768	19.1	116	5.1	239	6.3	2,097	10.5	1,835	16.4
Professional and related occupations	15,006	20.8	15	0.7	59	1.6	854	4.3	1,347	12.0
Service occupations.................................	8,790	12.2	549	24.0	754	20.0	3,201	16.0	1,601	14.3
Sales and related occupations....................	6,567	9.1	57	2.5	202	5.3	1,678	8.4	1,268	11.3
Office and administrative occupations	3,969	5.5	34	1.5	155	4.1	1,190	5.9	964	8.6
Farming, forestry, and fishing occupations	678	0.9	181	7.9	89	2.4	235	1.2	65	0.6
Construction and extraction occupations....	6,955	9.6	650	28.4	909	24.1	3,121	15.6	1,040	9.3
Installation, maintenance, and repair occupations	4,182	5.8	144	6.3	289	7.7	1,765	8.8	814	7.3
Production occupations	5,372	7.4	280	12.2	442	11.7	2,509	12.5	1034	9.2
Transportation and material moving occupations	6,962	9.6	265	11.6	638	16.9	3,356	16.8	1,236	11.0
FEMALE										
Total Employed Civilians	63,603	100.0	1,221	1.9	2,160	3.4	14,146	22.2	9,917	15.6
Occupation										
Management, business, and financial occupations	11,059	17.4	62	5.1	111	5.1	1,436	10.2	1,421	14.3
Professional and related occupations	19,434	30.6	21	1.7	86	4.0	1,244	8.8	1,634	16.5
Service occupations.................................	11,929	18.8	662	54.2	1,068	49.4	4,505	31.8	2,217	22.4
Sales and related occupations....................	5,774	9.1	63	5.2	259	12.0	1,701	12.0	1,157	11.7
Office and administrative occupations	10,943	17.2	42	3.4	206	9.5	3,391	24.0	2,738	27.6
Farming, forestry, and fishing occupations	214	0.3	63	5.2	31	1.4	52	0.4	22	0.2
Construction and extraction occupations....	210	0.3	12	1.0	18	0.8	64	0.5	50	0.5
Installation, maintenance, and repair occupations	149	0.2	*	*	15	0.7	40	0.3	26	0.3
Production occupations	2,293	3.6	212	17.4	229	10.6	954	6.7	361	3.6
Transportation and material moving occupations	1,600	2.5	83	6.8	137	6.3	760	5.4	291	2.9

NOTE: Percentages may not sum to total because of rounding.
* = Quantity zero or rounds to zero.
[1]Civilian noninstitutionalized population plus armed forces living off post or with their families on post.

Table A-28. Educational Attainment of Employed Civilians 25 Years Old and Over, by Occupation and Sex, 2018—*Continued*

(Numbers in thousands; percent; civilian noninstitutionalized population.[1])

	Educational Attainment									
	Associate's degree		Bachelor's degree		Master's degree		Professional degree		Doctoral degree	
Occupation and sex	Number	Percent	Number	Percent	Number	Percent	Number	Percent	Number	Percent
BOTH SEXES										
Total Employed Civilians	15,102	11.1	34,943	25.7	15,318	11.3	2,401	1.8	3,368	2.5
Occupation										
Management, business, and financial										
occupations	2,260	15.0	9,884	28.3	4,576	29.9	296	12.3	492	14.6
Professional and related occupations	3,716	24.6	12,414	35.5	8,519	55.6	1,883	78.4	2,648	78.6
Service occupations.................................	2,641	17.5	2,942	8.4	449	2.9	66	2.7	66	2.0
Sales and related occupations.....................	1,407	9.3	3,711	10.6	704	4.6	55	2.3	79	2.3
Office and administrative occupations	2,096	13.9	3,384	9.7	616	4.0	50	2.1	46	1.4
Farming, forestry, and fishing										
occupations	57	0.4	77	0.2	14	0.1	3	0.1	3	0.1
Construction and extraction occupations....	656	4.3	549	1.6	78	0.5	10	0.4	8	0.2
Installation, maintenance, and repair										
occupations	750	5.0	414	1.2	62	0.4	13	0.5	*	*
Production occupations	809	5.4	665	1.9	152	1.0	7	0.3	10	0.3
Transportation and material moving										
occupations	710	4.7	904	2.6	147	1.0	18	0.7	16	0.5
MALE										
Total Employed Civilians	6,968	9.6	17,729	24.5	6,962	9.6	1,377	1.9	1,937	2.7
Occupation										
Management, business, and financial										
occupations	1,078	15.5	5,457	30.8	2,477	35.6	166	12.1	303	15.6
Professional and related occupations	1,234	17.7	5,573	31.4	3,317	47.6	1,083	78.6	1,524	78.7
Service occupations.................................	1015	14.6	1,420	8.0	203	2.9	28	2.0	21	1.1
Sales and related occupations.....................	674	9.7	2,179	12.3	422	6.1	41	3.0	47	2.4
Office and administrative occupations	415	6.0	998	5.6	184	2.6	15	1.1	13	0.7
Farming, forestry, and fishing										
occupations	41	0.6	55	0.3	9	0.1	3	0.2	*	*
Construction and extraction occupations....	636	9.1	512	2.9	70	1.0	10	0.7	6	0.3
Installation, maintenance, and repair										
occupations	729	10.5	374	2.1	57	0.8	11	0.8	*	*
Production occupations	586	8.4	414	2.3	97	1.4	4	0.3	7	0.4
Transportation and material moving										
occupations	559	8.0	748	4.2	126	1.8	18	1.3	16	0.8
FEMALE										
Total Employed Civilians	8,135	12.8	17,214	27.1	8,356	13.1	1,024	1.6	1,431	2.2
Occupation										
Management, business, and financial										
occupations	1,182	14.5	4,427	25.7	2,099	25.1	131	12.8	189	13.2
Professional and related occupations	2,482	30.5	6,842	39.7	5,202	62.3	800	78.1	1,124	78.5
Service occupations.................................	1,626	20.0	1,522	8.8	246	2.9	38	3.7	45	3.1
Sales and related occupations.....................	733	9.0	1,533	8.9	283	3.4	15	1.5	32	2.2
Office and administrative occupations	1,681	20.7	2,385	13.9	432	5.2	35	3.4	33	2.3
Farming, forestry, and fishing										
occupations	16	0.2	22	0.1	5	0.1	*	*	3	0.2
Construction and extraction occupations....	20	0.2	36	0.2	8	0.1	*	*	2	0.1
Installation, maintenance, and repair										
occupations	21	0.3	40	0.2	5	0.1	2	0.2	*	*
Production occupations	224	2.8	251	1.5	55	0.7	3	0.3	3	0.2
Transportation and material moving										
occupations	151	1.9	156	0.9	21	0.3	*	*	*	*

NOTE: Percentages may not sum to total because of rounding.
* = Quantity zero or rounds to zero.
[1]Civilian noninstitutionalized population plus armed forces living off post or with their families on post.

Table A-29. Educational Attainment of the Population 25 Years Old and Older, by Industry and Sex, 2018

(Numbers in thousands; percent; civilian noninstitutionalized population.[1])

Industry and sex	Total		None to 8th grade		9th to 11th grade		High school graduate		Some college, no degree	
	Number	Percent	Number	Percent	Number	Percent	Number	Percent	Number	Percent
BOTH SEXES										
Total Employed Civilians	135,851	100.0	3,510	2.6	5,935	4.4	34,152	25.1	21,121	15.5
Industry										
Agriculture, forestry, fishing, and hunting	2,114	1.6	321	9.1	167	2.8	766	2.2	266	1.3
Mining	690	0.5	22	0.6	34	0.6	245	0.7	123	0.6
Construction	9,649	7.1	683	19.5	1043	17.6	3,856	11.3	1,547	7.3
Manufacturing	14,442	10.6	549	15.6	802	13.5	4,752	13.9	2,255	10.7
Wholesale and retail trade	15,989	11.8	268	7.6	847	14.3	5,304	15.5	3,196	15.1
Transportation and utilities	7,649	5.6	147	4.2	360	6.1	2,829	8.3	1,635	7.7
Information	2,611	1.9	5	0.1	41	0.7	376	1.1	399	1.9
Financial activities	10,007	7.4	46	1.3	121	2.0	1,704	5.0	1,626	7.7
Professional and business services	17,166	12.6	462	13.2	601	10.1	2,837	8.3	2,138	10.1
Educational and health services	32,435	23.9	259	7.4	694	11.7	4,874	14.3	3,937	18.6
Leisure and hospitality	9,300	6.8	445	12.7	716	12.1	3,072	9.0	1,709	8.1
Other services	6,951	5.1	281	8.0	434	7.3	2,232	6.5	1,175	5.6
Public administration	6,849	5.0	22	0.6	77	1.3	1,308	3.8	1,115	5.3
MALE										
Total Employed Civilians	72,248	100.0	2,289	3.2	3,776	5.2	20,007	27.7	11,204	15.5
Industry										
Agriculture, forestry, fishing, and hunting	1,575	2.2	243	10.6	133	3.5	608	3.0	206	1.8
Mining	605	0.8	17	0.7	31	0.8	234	1.2	108	1.0
Construction	8,734	12.1	670	29.3	1015	26.9	3,603	18.0	1,340	12.0
Manufacturing	10,205	14.1	320	14.0	564	14.9	3,415	17.1	1,621	14.5
Wholesale and retail trade	8,949	12.4	162	7.1	501	13.3	2,953	14.8	1,782	15.9
Transportation and utilities	5,759	8.0	126	5.5	299	7.9	2,212	11.1	1,184	10.6
Information	1,622	2.2	2	0.1	31	0.8	265	1.3	277	2.5
Financial activities	4,693	6.5	34	1.5	70	1.9	683	3.4	619	5.5
Professional and business services	10,109	14.0	293	12.8	384	10.2	1,638	8.2	1,138	10.2
Educational and health services	8,400	11.6	47	2.1	129	3.4	1071	5.4	900	8.0
Leisure and hospitality	4,677	6.5	225	9.8	345	9.1	1,478	7.4	855	7.6
Other services	3,228	4.5	139	6.1	240	6.4	1,126	5.6	526	4.7
Public administration	3,690	5.1	8	0.3	33	0.9	723	3.6	648	5.8
FEMALE										
Total Employed Civilians	63,603	100.0	1,221	1.9	2,160	3.4	14,146	22.2	9,917	15.6
Industry										
Agriculture, forestry, fishing, and hunting	539	0.8	77	6.3	34	1.6	158	1.1	60	0.6
Mining	85	0.1	4	0	3	0.1	11	0.1	15	0.2
Construction	916	1.4	13	1.1	28	1.3	253	1.8	207	2.1
Manufacturing	4,236	6.7	229	18.8	238	11.0	1,337	9.5	634	6.4
Wholesale and retail trade	7,040	11.1	106	8.7	345	16.0	2,351	16.6	1,414	14.3
Transportation and utilities	1,889	3.0	21	1.7	61	2.8	617	4.4	451	4.5
Information	989	1.6	3	0.2	10	0.5	111	0.8	123	1.2
Financial activities	5,314	8.4	12	1.0	52	2.4	1,021	7.2	1,007	10.2
Professional and business services	7,057	11.1	169	13.8	216	10.0	1,199	8.5	1,001	10.1
Educational and health services	24,035	37.8	212	17.4	565	26.2	3,803	26.9	3,037	30.6
Leisure and hospitality	4,623	7.3	219	17.9	371	17.2	1,595	11.3	854	8.6
Other services	3,722	5.9	141	11.5	194	9.0	1,106	7.8	649	6.5
Public administration	3,159	5.0	14	1.1	44	2.0	585	4.1	467	4.7

NOTE: Percentages may not sum to total because of rounding.
[1]Civilian noninstitutionalized population plus armed forces living off post or with their families on post.

Table A-29. Educational Attainment of the Population 25 Years Old and Older, by Industry and Sex, 2018—*Continued*

(Numbers in thousands; percent; civilian noninstitutionalized population.[1])

Industry and sex	Educational Attainment									
	Associate's degree		Bachelor's degree		Master's degree		Professional degree		Doctoral degree	
	Number	Percent	Number	Percent	Number	Percent	Number	Percent	Number	Percent
BOTH SEXES										
Total Employed Civilians	15,102	11.1	34,943	25.7	15,318	11.3	2,401	1.8	3,368	2.5
Industry										
Agriculture, forestry, fishing, and hunting	178	1.2	333	1.0	67	0.4	10	0.4	7	0.2
Mining	64	0.4	120	0.3	70	0.5	7	0.3	6	0.2
Construction	936	6.2	1,273	3.6	268	1.7	21	0.9	23	0.7
Manufacturing	1,498	9.9	3,106	8.9	1,188	7.8	75	3.1	216	6.4
Wholesale and retail trade	1,809	12.0	3,655	10.5	695	4.5	65	2.7	151	4.5
Transportation and utilities	802	5.3	1,486	4.3	363	2.4	10	0.4	17	0.5
Information	230	1.5	1,111	3.2	398	2.6	35	1.5	15	0.4
Financial activities	1094	7.2	3,815	10.9	1,315	8.6	142	5.9	144	4.3
Professional and business services	1,620	10.7	5,724	16.4	2,385	15.6	744	31.0	654	19.4
Educational and health services	4,238	28.1	8,893	25.5	6,690	43.7	989	41.2	1,862	55.3
Leisure and hospitality	916	6.1	1,997	5.7	393	2.6	28	1.2	25	0.7
Other services	865	5.7	1,281	3.7	570	3.7	37	1.5	75	2.2
Public administration	851	5.6	2,149	6.2	917	6.0	237	9.9	173	5.1
MALE										
Total Employed Civilians	6,968	9.6	17,729	24.5	6,962	9.6	1,377	1.9	1,937	2.7
Industry										
Agriculture, forestry, fishing, and hunting	123	1.8	209	1.2	40	0.6	10	0.7	5	0.3
Mining	62	0.9	98	0.6	45	0.6	5	0.4	6	0.3
Construction	814	11.7	1050	5.9	206	3.0	16	1.2	19	1.0
Manufacturing	1064	15.3	2,159	12.2	848	12.2	50	3.6	163	8.4
Wholesale and retail trade	931	13.4	2,148	12.1	361	5.2	38	2.8	73	3.8
Transportation and utilities	583	8.4	1073	6.1	256	3.7	10	0.7	17	0.9
Information	135	1.9	657	3.7	220	3.2	23	1.7	11	0.6
Financial activities	364	5.2	1,955	11.0	791	11.4	91	6.6	88	4.5
Professional and business services	832	11.9	3,420	19.3	1,454	20.9	480	34.9	470	24.3
Educational and health services	772	11.1	2,165	12.2	1,869	26.8	496	36.0	951	49.1
Leisure and hospitality	462	6.6	1098	6.2	187	2.7	10	0.7	17	0.9
Other services	364	5.2	518	2.9	253	3.6	21	1.5	39	2.0
Public administration	461	6.6	1,179	6.7	432	6.2	128	9.3	79	4.1
FEMALE										
Total Employed Civilians	8,135	12.8	17,214	27.1	8,356	13.1	1,024	1.6	1,431	2.2
Industry										
Agriculture, forestry, fishing, and hunting	55	0.7	125	0.7	27	0.3	*	*	2	0.1
Mining	2	0.0	22	0.1	25	0.3	2	0.2	*	*
Construction	122	1.5	223	1.3	62	0.7	4	0.4	4	0.3
Manufacturing	434	5.3	946	5.5	340	4.1	25	2.4	53	3.7
Wholesale and retail trade	878	10.8	1,507	8.8	333	4.0	27	2.6	77	5.4
Transportation and utilities	220	2.7	413	2.4	107	1.3	*	*	*	*
Information	95	1.2	453	2.6	179	2.1	12	1.2	4	0.3
Financial activities	730	9.0	1,860	10.8	524	6.3	52	5.1	56	3.9
Professional and business services	788	9.7	2,305	13.4	931	11.1	264	25.8	183	12.8
Educational and health services	3,466	42.6	6,728	39.1	4,821	57.7	493	48.1	911	63.7
Leisure and hospitality	454	5.6	899	5.2	205	2.5	19	1.9	8	0.6
Other services	501	6.2	763	4.4	317	3.8	15	1.5	36	2.5
Public administration	390	4.8	970	5.6	486	5.8	110	10.7	95	6.6

NOTE: Percentages may not sum to total because of rounding.
[1]Civilian noninstitutionalized population plus armed forces living off post or with their families on post.

Table A-30. Educational Attainment of the Population 25 Years Old and Over, by Citizenship, Nativity, Period of Entry, and Sex, 2018

(Numbers in thousands; percent; civilian noninstitutionalized population.[1])

Citizenship, nativity, period of entry, and sex	Educational attainment									
	Total		None to 8th grade		9th to 11th grade		High school graduate		Some college, no degree	
	Number	Percent	Number	Percent	Number	Percent	Number	Percent	Number	Percent
BOTH SEXES										
Total	219,830	100.0	8,729	4.0	13,682	6.2	62,685	28.5	35,442	16.1
Native................................	180,002	81.9	3,003	1.7	9,893	5.5	52,465	29.1	31,489	17.5
Foreign-born	39,828	18.1	5,726	14.4	3,789	9.5	10,220	25.7	3,953	9.9
Native................................										
Native parentage[2]	162,848	90.5	2,526	1.6	9,041	5.6	48,255	29.6	28,529	17.5
Foreign or mixed parentage[3]	17,154	9.5	477	2.8	852	5.0	4,210	24.5	2,959	17.2
Foreign-born										
Naturalized citizen	20,319	51.0	1,924	9.5	1,322	6.5	5,180	25.5	2,372	11.7
Not a citizen	19,509	49.0	3,802	19.5	2,467	12.6	5,040	25.8	1,581	8.1
Year of entry										
2010 or later	6,971	17.5	686	9.8	480	6.9	1,502	21.5	579	8.3
2000-2009	10,492	26.3	1,548	14.8	1,183	11.3	2,743	26.1	938	8.9
1990-1999	9,784	24.6	1,408	14.4	1,013	10.4	2,704	27.6	942	9.6
1980-1989	6,555	16.5	1,085	16.6	715	10.9	1,669	25.5	726	11.1
1970-1979	3,667	9.2	629	17.2	249	6.8	924	25.2	439	12.0
Before 1970	2,360	5.9	370	15.7	149	6.3	678	28.7	330	14.0
MALE										
Total................................	105,862	100.0	4,256	4.0	6,939	6.6	31,325	29.6	16,981	16.0
Native................................	86,608	81.8	1,529	1.8	5,024	5.8	26,335	30.4	15,078	17.4
Foreign-born	19,253	18.2	2,727	14.2	1,915	9.9	4,990	25.9	1,903	9.9
Native................................										
Native parentage[2]	78,073	90.1	1,303	1.7	4,577	5.9	24,248	31.1	13,541	17.3
Foreign or mixed parentage[3]	8,536	9.9	226	2.6	447	5.2	2,087	24.4	1,537	18.0
Foreign-born										
Naturalized citizen	9,337	48.5	852	9.1	581	6.2	2,414	25.9	1,099	11.8
Not a citizen	9,916	51.5	1,875	18.9	1,335	13.5	2,576	26.0	804	8.1
Year of entry										
2010 or later	3,365	17.5	332	9.9	251	7.5	684	20.3	274	8.1
2000-2009	5,085	26.4	756	14.9	621	12.2	1,349	26.5	432	8.5
1990-1999	4,777	24.8	628	13.1	495	10.4	1,418	29.7	483	10.1
1980-1989	3,306	17.2	554	16.8	373	11.3	838	25.3	392	11.9
1970-1979	1,722	8.9	294	17.1	116	6.7	432	25.1	205	11.9
Before 1970	999	5.2	163	16.3	60	6.0	269	26.9	117	11.7
FEMALE										
Total................................	113,969	100.0	4,472	3.9	6,743	5.9	31,360	27.5	18,461	16.2
Native................................	93,394	81.9	1,474	1.6	4,869	5.2	26,131	28.0	16,410	17.6
Foreign-born	20,575	18.1	2,998	14.6	1,874	9.1	5,230	25.4	2,050	10.0
Native................................										
Native parentage[2]	84,775	90.8	1,223	1.4	4,463	5.3	24,007	28.3	14,988	17.7
Foreign or mixed parentage[3]	8,618	9.2	251	2.9	406	4.7	2,123	24.6	1,422	16.5
Foreign-born										
Naturalized citizen	10,982	53.4	1,071	9.8	742	6.8	2,766	25.2	1,273	11.6
Not a citizen	9,592	46.6	1,927	20.1	1,132	11.8	2,464	25.7	778	8.1
Year of entry										
2010 or later	3,606	17.5	354	9.8	229	6.4	818	22.7	304	8.4
2000-2009	5,407	26.3	792	14.6	562	10.4	1,393	25.8	506	9.4
1990-1999	5,007	24.3	780	15.6	518	10.3	1,285	25.7	458	9.1
1980-1989	3,249	15.8	531	16.3	343	10.6	831	25.6	334	10.3
1970-1979	1,945	9.5	335	17.2	133	6.8	493	25.3	234	12.0
Before 1970	1,361	6.6	207	15.2	89	6.5	409	30.1	214	15.7

[1]Civilian noninstitutionalized population plus armed forces living off post or with their families on post.
[2]Native parentage: Both parents born in the United States. Percent: percent of native citizens.
[3]Foreign or mixed parentage: One or both parents born outside of the United States.

Table A-30. Educational Attainment of the Population 25 Years Old and Over, by Citizenship, Nativity, Period of Entry, and Sex, 2018—*Continued*

(Numbers in thousands; percent; civilian noninstitutionalized population.[1])

Citizenship, nativity, period of entry, and sex	Educational attainment									
	Associate degree		Bachelor's degree		Master's degree		Professional degree		Doctoral degree	
	Number	Percent	Number	Percent	Number	Percent	Number	Percent	Number	Percent
BOTH SEXES										
Total	22,369	10.2	48,235	21.9	21,048	9.6	3,172	1.4	4,468	2.0
Native	19,769	11.0	40,393	22.4	17,064	9.5	2,572	1.4	3,355	1.9
Foreign-born	2,599	6.5	7,843	19.7	3,984	10.0	601	1.5	1,114	2.8
Native										
Native parentage[2]	17,901	11.0	36,169	22.2	15,286	9.4	2,207	1.4	2,934	1.8
Foreign or mixed parentage[3]	1,869	10.9	4,224	24.6	1,778	10.4	364	2.1	421	2.5
Foreign-born										
Naturalized citizen	1,718	8.5	4,631	22.8	2,143	10.5	394	1.9	636	3.1
Not a citizen	882	4.5	3,212	16.5	1,841	9.4	207	1.1	478	2.5
Year of entry										
2010 or later	351	5.0	1,944	27.9	1,117	16.0	129	1.9	183	2.6
2000-2009	683	6.5	1,971	18.8	980	9.3	113	1.1	333	3.2
1990-1999	652	6.7	1,828	18.7	835	8.5	137	1.4	265	2.7
1980-1989	466	7.1	1,109	16.9	531	8.1	90	1.4	164	2.5
1970-1979	238	6.5	660	18.0	334	9.1	85	2.3	109	3.0
Before 1970	210	8.9	330	14.0	187	7.9	46	1.9	60	2.5
MALE										
Total	9,687	9.2	23,080	21.8	9,217	8.7	1,780	1.7	2,597	2.5
Native	8,640	10.0	19,415	22.4	7,211	8.3	1,476	1.7	1,901	2.2
Foreign-born	1,047	5.4	3,665	19.0	2,006	10.4	304	1.6	696	3.6
Native										
Native parentage[2]	7,723	9.9	17,302	22.2	6,480	8.3	1,266	1.6	1,632	2.1
Foreign or mixed parentage[3]	917	10.7	2,112	24.7	731	8.6	210	2.5	269	3.2
Foreign-born										
Naturalized citizen	678	7.3	2,125	22.8	995	10.7	200	2.1	394	4.2
Not a citizen	369	3.7	1,540	15.5	1,011	10.2	104	1.0	302	3.0
Year of entry										
2010 or later	137	4.1	903	26.8	608	18.1	65	1.9	110	3.3
2000-2009	283	5.6	900	17.7	506	10.0	48	0.9	189	3.7
1990-1999	261	5.5	854	17.9	411	8.6	62	1.3	165	3.5
1980-1989	184	5.6	551	16.7	245	7.4	58	1.8	110	3.3
1970-1979	99	5.7	303	17.6	154	8.9	40	2.3	78	4.5
Before 1970	82	8.2	153	15.3	83	8.3	30	3.0	44	4.4
FEMALE										
Total	12,682	11.1	25,155	22.1	11,831	10.4	1,393	1.2	1,872	1.6
Native	11,130	11.9	20,978	22.5	9,852	10.5	1,096	1.2	1,454	1.6
Foreign-born	1,552	7.5	4,178	20.3	1,978	9.6	297	1.4	418	2.0
Native										
Native parentage[2]	10,178	12.0	18,866	22.3	8,805	10.4	942	1.1	1,302	1.5
Foreign or mixed parentage[3]	952	11.0	2,111	24.5	1,047	12.1	154	1.8	152	1.8
Foreign-born										
Naturalized citizen	1,040	9.5	2,506	22.8	1,149	10.5	194	1.8	242	2.2
Not a citizen	512	5.3	1,672	17.4	830	8.7	103	1.1	176	1.8
Year of entry										
2010 or later	214	5.9	1,041	28.9	509	14.1	64	1.8	72	2.0
2000-2009	400	7.4	1,071	19.8	474	8.8	65	1.2	144	2.7
1990-1999	391	7.8	974	19.5	425	8.5	75	1.5	100	2.0
1980-1989	281	8.6	558	17.2	286	8.8	32	1.0	54	1.7
1970-1979	138	7.1	357	18.4	180	9.3	44	2.3	32	1.6
Before 1970	128	9.4	177	13.0	104	7.6	16	1.2	16	1.2

[1] Civilian noninstitutionalized population plus armed forces living off post or with their families on post.
[2] Native parentage: Both parents born in the United States. Percent: percent of native citizens.
[3] Foreign or mixed parentage: One or both parents born outside of the United States.

Table A-31. Detailed Years of School Completed by People 25 Years and Over, by Sex, Age Groups, Race, and Hispanic Origin, 2018

(Numbers in thousands; civilian noninstitutionalized population.[1])

Detailed years of school	All races		Males		Females		25 to 34 years old		35 to 54 years old	
	Number	Percent	Number	Percent	Number	Percent	Number	Percent	Number	Percent
Total..	219,830	100.0	105,862	100.0	113,969	100.0	44,854	100.0	82,196	100.0
Elementary or High school, no diploma										
Less than 1 year, no diploma	748	0.3	328	0.3	420	0.4	79	0.2	242	0.3
1st-4th grade, no diploma	1,381	0.6	645	0.6	736	0.7	102	0.2	447	0.5
5th-6th grade, no diploma	3,082	1.4	1,534	1.5	1,548	1.4	338	0.8	1,234	1.5
7th-8th grade, no diploma	3,518	1.6	1,750	1.7	1,768	1.6	438	1.0	1,055	1.3
9th grade, no diploma	3,227	1.5	1,581	1.5	1,646	1.4	545	1.2	1,250	1.5
10th grade, no diploma	3,548	1.6	1,732	1.6	1,816	1.6	584	1.3	1,161	1.4
11th grade, no diploma	4,103	1.9	2,150	2.0	1,953	1.7	734	1.6	1,503	1.8
12th grade, no diploma	2,805	1.3	1,476	1.4	1,328	1.2	572	1.3	1,060	1.3
Elementary or High school, GED										
Less than 1 year, GED	28	*	13	*	15	*	8	*	11	*
1st-4th grade, GED	77	*	38	*	39	*	25	0.1	22	*
5th-6th grade, GED	43	*	23	*	20	*	2	*	17	*
7th-8th grade, GED	334	0.2	192	0.2	143	0.1	39	0.1	104	0.1
9th grade, GED...	648	0.3	344	0.3	304	0.3	123	0.3	194	0.2
10th grade, GED...	1,307	0.6	711	0.7	596	0.5	276	0.6	499	0.6
11th grade, GED...	2,120	1.0	1,165	1.1	956	0.8	439	1.0	843	1.0
12th grade, GED...	1,563	0.7	900	0.9	663	0.6	411	0.9	645	0.8
High school diploma...	56,564	25.7	27,939	26.4	28,624	25.1	10,136	22.6	19,345	23.5
College, no degree										
Less than 1 year college, no degree......................	5,008	2.3	2,379	2.3	2,629	2.3	1,094	2.4	1,664	2.0
One year of college, no degree.............................	11,317	5.2	5,168	4.9	6,150	5.4	2,548	5.7	3,916	4.8
Two years of college, no degree	14,135	6.4	6,816	6.4	7,319	6.4	2,918	6.5	5,056	6.2
Three years of college, no degree	3,481	1.6	1,809	1.7	1,671	1.5	901	2.0	1,264	1.5
Four or more years of college, no degree..............	1,501	0.7	809	0.8	691	0.6	394	0.9	550	0.7
Associate's degree, vocational										
Less than 1 year college, vocational/ associate's	445	0.2	174	0.2	271	0.2	104	0.2	141	0.2
One year of college, vocational/associate's	1,237	0.6	558	0.5	679	0.6	245	0.6	507	0.6
Two years of college, vocational/associate's	6,177	2.8	2,896	2.7	3,281	2.9	1,232	2.8	2,436	3.0
Three years of college, vocational/associate's........	938	0.4	413	0.4	525	0.5	200	0.5	324	0.4
Four or more years of college, vocational/ associate's	850	0.4	432	0.4	418	0.4	187	0.4	338	0.4
Associate's degree, academic										
Less than 1 year college, academic/associate's	95	*	43	*	52	0.1	15	*	33	*
One year of college, academic/associate's	755	0.3	334	0.3	421	0.4	172	0.4	286	0.4
Two years of college, academic/associate's	8,779	4.0	3,572	3.4	5,207	4.6	1,721	3.8	3,545	4.3
Three years of college, academic/associate's.........	1,611	0.7	670	0.6	941	0.8	430	1.0	667	0.8
Four or more years of college, academic/ associate's	1,482	0.7	595	0.6	887	0.8	338	0.8	612	0.7
Bachelor's degree	48,235	21.9	23,080	21.8	25,155	22.1	12,371	27.6	19,156	23.3
Master's degree[2]	21,048	9.6	9,217	8.7	11,831	10.4	3,829	8.5	9,046	11.0
Professional degree	3,172	1.4	1,780	1.7	1,393	1.2	523	1.2	1,261	1.5
Doctorate degree..	4,468	2.0	2,597	2.5	1,872	1.6	779	1.7	1,759	2.1

* = Quantity zero or rounds to zero.
[1]Excluding members of the Armed Forces living in barracks.
[2]Detail on graduate school attendance and length of master's degree program, available in previous years, discontinued due to questionnaire changes in 2015.

Table A-31. Detailed Years of School Completed by People 25 Years and Over, by Sex, Age Groups, Race, and Hispanic Origin, 2018—*Continued*

(Numbers in thousands; civilian noninstitutionalized population.[1])

Detailed years of school	55 years and older Number	Percent	White Number	Percent	Non-Hispanic White Number	Percent	Black Number	Percent	Asian Number	Percent	Hispanic (of any race) Number	Percent
Total..	92,780	100.0	172,685	100.0	142,420	100.0	27,047	100.0	13,677	100.0	33,877	100.0
Elementary or High school, no diploma												
Less than 1 year, no diploma	426	0.5	498	0.3	125	0.1	80	0.3	134	1.0	405	1.2
1st-4th grade, no diploma...............................	831	0.9	1,064	0.6	129	0.1	128	0.5	122	0.9	1,036	3.1
5th-6th grade, no diploma...............................	1,510	1.6	2,459	1.4	299	0.2	185	0.7	286	2.1	2,339	6.9
7th-8th grade, no diploma	2,025	2.2	2,814	1.6	1,450	1.0	393	1.5	176	1.3	1,483	4.4
9th grade, no diploma....................................	1,431	1.5	2,567	1.5	1,191	0.8	362	1.3	171	1.3	1,510	4.5
10th grade, no diploma..................................	1,803	1.9	2,613	1.5	1,834	1.3	669	2.5	125	0.9	896	2.6
11th grade, no diploma..................................	1,866	2.0	2,890	1.7	1,981	1.4	882	3.3	106	0.8	1,040	3.1
12th grade, no diploma..................................	1,172	1.3	1,967	1.1	1,118	0.8	564	2.1	178	1.3	918	2.7
Elementary or High school, GED												
Less than 1 year, GED	8	*	28	*	20	*	*	*	*	*	8	*
1st-4th grade, GED...	30	*	58	*	38	*	12	0.1	*	*	23	0.1
5th-6th grade, GED...	24	*	40	*	23	*	*	*	2	*	18	0.1
7th-8th grade, GED...	191	0.2	285	0.2	230	0.2	28	0.1	3	*	59	0.2
9th grade, GED...	331	0.4	513	0.3	431	0.3	86	0.3	5	*	93	0.3
10th grade, GED..	533	0.6	1,055	0.6	913	0.6	178	0.7	14	0.1	162	0.5
11th grade, GED..	839	0.9	1,656	1.0	1,452	1.0	324	1.2	27	0.2	247	0.7
12th grade, GED..	507	0.6	1,145	0.7	835	0.6	289	1.1	54	0.4	376	1.1
High school diploma..................................	27,082	29.2	44,539	25.8	36,068	25.3	7,924	29.3	2,498	18.3	9,425	27.8
College, no degree												
Less than 1 year college, no degree..................	2,249	2.4	4,051	2.4	3,513	2.5	674	2.5	104	0.8	607	1.8
One year of college, no degree........................	4,853	5.2	8,953	5.2	7,664	5.4	1,644	6.1	286	2.1	1,487	4.4
Two years of college, no degree......................	6,162	6.6	10,949	6.3	9,152	6.4	2,256	8.3	496	3.6	2,023	6.0
Three years of college, no degree	1,316	1.4	2,634	1.5	2,187	1.5	537	2.0	175	1.3	503	1.5
Four or more years of college, no degree..........	556	0.6	1,114	0.7	886	0.6	227	0.8	90	0.7	277	0.8
Associate's degree, vocational												
Less than 1 year college, vocational/ associate's	200	0.2	367	0.2	324	0.2	53	0.2	10	0.1	57	0.2
One year of college, vocational/associate's	485	0.5	1,011	0.6	853	0.6	142	0.5	34	0.3	170	0.5
Two years of college, vocational/associate's	2,509	2.7	5,032	2.9	4,427	3.1	742	2.7	221	1.6	652	1.9
Three years of college, vocational/associate's....	413	0.5	768	0.4	658	0.5	107	0.4	35	0.3	129	0.4
Four or more years of college, vocational/ associate's	325	0.4	669	0.4	567	0.4	94	0.4	51	0.4	124	0.4
Associate's degree, academic												
Less than 1 year college, academic/associate's	47	0.1	71	*	55	*	21	0.1	4	*	16	0.1
One year of college, academic/associate's	296	0.3	568	0.3	483	0.3	135	0.5	23	0.2	112	0.3
Two years of college, academic/associate's	3,512	3.8	7,040	4.1	6,168	4.3	1,077	4.0	384	2.8	1,015	3.0
Three years of college, academic/associate's....	513	0.6	1,246	0.7	1,026	0.7	222	0.8	91	0.7	232	0.7
Four or more years of college, academic/ associate's	532	0.6	1,195	0.7	997	0.7	191	0.7	46	0.3	223	0.7
Bachelor's degree	16,708	18.0	38,442	22.3	34,513	24.2	4,415	16.3	4,297	31.4	4,414	13.0
Master's degree[2]	8,173	8.8	16,417	9.5	15,217	10.7	1,893	7.0	2,395	17.5	1,385	4.1
Professional degree	1,389	1.5	2,576	1.5	2,373	1.7	188	0.7	351	2.6	221	0.7
Doctorate degree..	1,931	2.1	3,390	2.0	3,218	2.3	323	1.2	683	5.0	193	0.6

* = Quantity zero or rounds to zero.
[1]Excluding members of the Armed Forces living in barracks.
[2]Detail on graduate school attendance and length of master's degree program, available in previous years, discontinued due to questionnaire changes in 2015.

PART A

NATIONAL EDUCATION STATISTICS

- ■ **Historical Attainment Tables**

Table A-32. Percent of People 25 Years and Over Who Have Completed High School or College, by Race, Hispanic Origin, and Sex, Selected Years, 1940–2018

(Percent; civilian noninstitutionalized population.)

Age and Year	All races			White			Non-Hispanic White			Black[1]			Asian		
	Total	Male	Female	Total	Male	Female	Total	Male	Female	Total	Male	Female	Total	Male	Female
25 YEARS AND OLDER															
Completed 4 Years of High School or More															
2018..............................	89.8	89.4	90.2	90.2	89.6	90.8	94.3	93.9	94.7	87.9	87.7	88.1	90.5	92.7	88.6
2017..............................	89.6	89.1	90.0	90.1	89.5	90.6	94.1	93.7	94.5	87.3	86.5	87.9	90.9	92.6	89.4
2016..............................	89.1	88.5	89.6	89.5	88.8	90.1	93.8	93.4	94.3	87.1	86.4	87.7	90.3	91.9	89.0
2015..............................	88.4	88.0	88.8	88.8	88.3	89.3	93.3	93.0	93.5	87.0	86.4	87.6	89.1	91.0	87.4
2014..............................	88.3	87.7	88.9	88.8	88.0	89.6	93.1	92.5	93.7	85.8	85.3	86.2	89.5	91.9	87.4
2013..............................	88.2	87.6	88.6	88.6	88.0	89.2	92.9	92.7	93.2	85.1	84.1	86.0	90.1	91.5	89.0
2012[2]	87.6	87.3	88.0	88.1	87.6	88.5	92.5	92.2	92.7	85.0	84.3	85.5	88.9	90.4	87.6
2011..............................	87.6	87.1	88.0	88.1	87.4	88.6	92.4	92.0	92.8	84.5	83.8	85.0	88.6	90.4	87.1
2010..............................	87.1	86.6	87.6	87.6	86.9	88.2	92.1	91.8	92.3	84.2	83.6	84.6	88.9	91.2	87.0
2009..............................	86.7	86.2	87.1	87.1	86.5	87.7	91.6	91.4	91.9	84.1	84.0	84.1	88.2	90.4	86.2
2008..............................	86.6	85.9	87.2	87.1	86.3	87.8	91.5	91.1	91.8	83.0	81.8	84.0	88.7	90.8	86.9
2007..............................	85.7	85.0	86.4	86.2	85.3	87.1	90.6	90.2	91.0	82.3	81.9	82.6	87.8	89.8	85.9
2006..............................	85.5	85.0	85.9	86.1	85.5	86.7	90.5	90.2	90.8	80.7	80.1	81.2	87.4	89.6	85.5
2005..............................	85.2	84.9	85.5	85.8	85.2	86.2	90.1	89.9	90.3	81.1	81.0	81.2	87.6	90.4	85.2
2004..............................	85.2	84.8	85.4	85.8	85.3	86.3	90.0	89.9	90.1	80.6	80.4	80.8	86.8	88.7	85.0
2003[3]	84.6	84.1	85.0	85.1	84.5	85.7	89.4	89.0	89.7	80.0	79.6	80.3	87.6	89.5	86.0
2002..............................	84.1	83.8	84.4	84.8	84.3	85.2	88.7	88.5	88.9	78.7	78.5	78.9	NA	NA	NA
2001[4]	84.1	84.1	84.2	84.8	84.4	85.1	88.6	88.6	88.6	78.8	79.2	78.5	NA	NA	NA
2000..............................	84.1	84.2	84.0	84.9	84.8	85.0	88.4	88.5	88.4	78.5	78.7	78.3	NA	NA	NA
1999..............................	83.4	83.4	83.4	84.3	84.2	84.3	87.7	87.7	87.7	77.0	76.7	77.2	NA	NA	NA
1998..............................	82.8	82.8	82.9	83.7	83.6	83.8	87.1	87.1	87.1	76.0	75.2	76.7	NA	NA	NA
1997..............................	82.1	82.0	82.2	83.0	82.9	83.2	86.3	86.3	86.3	74.9	73.5	76.0	NA	NA	NA
1996..............................	81.7	81.9	81.6	82.8	82.7	82.8	86.0	86.1	85.9	74.3	74.3	74.2	NA	NA	NA
1995..............................	81.7	81.7	81.6	83.0	83.0	83.0	85.9	86.0	85.8	73.8	73.4	74.1	NA	NA	NA
1994..............................	80.9	81.0	80.7	82.0	82.1	81.9	84.9	85.1	84.7	72.9	71.7	73.8	NA	NA	NA
1993..............................	80.2	80.5	80.0	81.5	81.8	81.3	84.1	84.5	83.8	70.4	69.6	71.1	NA	NA	NA
1992[5]	79.4	79.7	79.2	80.9	81.1	80.7	NA	NA	NA	67.7	67.0	68.2	NA	NA	NA
1991..............................	78.4	78.5	78.3	79.9	79.8	79.9	NA	NA	NA	66.7	66.7	66.7	NA	NA	NA
1990..............................	77.6	77.7	77.5	79.1	79.1	79.0	NA	NA	NA	66.2	65.8	66.5	NA	NA	NA
1989..............................	76.9	77.2	76.6	78.4	78.6	78.2	NA	NA	NA	64.6	64.2	65.0	NA	NA	NA
1988..............................	76.2	76.4	76.0	77.7	77.7	77.6	NA	NA	NA	63.5	63.7	63.4	NA	NA	NA
1987..............................	75.6	76.0	75.3	77.0	77.3	76.7	NA	NA	NA	63.4	63.0	63.7	NA	NA	NA
1986..............................	74.7	75.1	74.4	76.2	76.5	75.9	NA	NA	NA	62.3	61.5	63.0	NA	NA	NA
1985..............................	73.9	74.4	73.5	75.5	76.0	75.1	NA	NA	NA	59.8	58.4	60.8	NA	NA	NA
1984..............................	73.3	73.7	73.0	75.0	75.4	74.6	NA	NA	NA	58.5	57.1	59.7	NA	NA	NA
1983..............................	72.1	72.7	71.5	73.8	74.4	73.3	NA	NA	NA	56.8	56.5	57.1	NA	NA	NA
1982..............................	71.0	71.7	70.3	72.8	73.4	72.3	NA	NA	NA	54.9	55.7	54.3	NA	NA	NA
1981..............................	69.7	70.3	69.1	71.6	72.1	71.2	NA	NA	NA	52.9	53.2	52.6	NA	NA	NA
1980..............................	68.6	69.2	68.1	70.5	71.0	70.1	NA	NA	NA	51.2	51.1	51.3	NA	NA	NA
1979..............................	67.7	68.4	67.1	69.7	70.3	69.2	NA	NA	NA	49.4	49.2	49.5	NA	NA	NA
1978..............................	65.9	66.8	65.2	67.9	68.6	67.2	NA	NA	NA	47.6	47.9	47.3	NA	NA	NA
1977..............................	64.9	65.6	64.4	67.0	67.5	66.5	NA	NA	NA	45.5	45.6	45.4	NA	NA	NA
1976..............................	64.1	64.7	63.5	66.1	66.7	65.5	NA	NA	NA	43.8	42.3	45.0	NA	NA	NA
1975..............................	62.5	63.1	62.1	64.5	65.0	64.1	NA	NA	NA	42.5	41.6	43.3	NA	NA	NA
1974..............................	61.2	61.6	60.9	63.3	63.6	63.0	NA	NA	NA	40.8	39.9	41.5	NA	NA	NA
1973..............................	59.8	60.0	59.6	61.9	62.1	61.7	NA	NA	NA	39.2	38.2	40.1	NA	NA	NA
1972..............................	58.2	58.2	58.2	60.4	60.3	60.5	NA	NA	NA	36.6	35.7	37.2	NA	NA	NA
1971..............................	56.4	56.3	56.6	58.6	58.4	58.8	NA	NA	NA	34.7	33.8	35.4	NA	NA	NA
1970..............................	55.2	55.0	55.4	57.4	57.2	57.6	NA	NA	NA	33.7	32.4	34.8	NA	NA	NA
1969..............................	54.0	53.6	54.4	56.3	55.7	56.7	NA	NA	NA	32.3	31.9	32.6	NA	NA	NA
1968..............................	52.6	52.0	53.2	54.9	54.3	55.5	NA	NA	NA	30.1	28.9	31.0	NA	NA	NA
1967..............................	51.1	50.5	51.7	53.4	52.8	53.8	NA	NA	NA	29.5	27.1	31.5	NA	NA	NA
1966..............................	49.9	49.0	50.8	52.2	51.3	53.0	NA	NA	NA	27.8	25.8	29.5	NA	NA	NA
1965..............................	49.0	48.0	49.9	51.3	50.2	52.2	NA	NA	NA	27.2	25.8	28.4	NA	NA	NA
1964..............................	48.0	47.0	48.9	50.3	49.3	51.2	NA	NA	NA	25.7	23.7	27.4	NA	NA	NA
1962..............................	46.3	45.0	47.5	48.7	47.4	49.9	NA	NA	NA	24.8	23.2	26.2	NA	NA	NA
1959..............................	43.7	42.2	45.2	46.1	44.5	47.7	NA	NA	NA	20.7	19.6	21.6	NA	NA	NA

Note: Starting in 2001, data are from the expanded CPS sample.
[1]Data in the column labeled "Black" include Black and other races from 1940 to 1962: from 1963 to 2003, data are for the Black population only.
[2]Starting in 2012, data were calculated using population controls based on the 2010 Census.
[3]Starting in 2003, respondents could choose more than one race. The race data in this table for White, non-Hispanic White, Black, and Asian from 2003 onward represent those respondents who indicated only one racial identity. Prior to 2003, Asians were grouped with Pacific Islanders.
[4]Starting in 2001, data were calculated using population controls based on Census 2000.
[5] Begining with data for 1992, a new question results in different categories than for earlier years: Data shown as 'Completed 4 Years of High School or more' is now collected in the category 'High School Graduate.' Data shown as 'College 1 to 3 years' is now collected in the 'Some college' and the two 'Associate degree' categories. Data shown as 'Completed 4 Years of College or more', is now collected in the categories, 'Bachelor's degree,' 'Master's degree,' 'Doctorate degree,' and 'Professional degree'. Due to the change in question format, median years of schooling cannot be derived.

Table A-32. Percent of People 25 Years and Over Who Have Completed High School or College, by Race, Hispanic Origin, and Sex, Selected Years, 1940–2018—*Continued*

(Percent; civilian noninstitutionalized population.)

Age and Year	Hispanic (of any race)			White alone or in combination			Non-Hispanic White alone or in combination			Black alone or in combination			Asian alone or in combination		
	Total	Male	Female	Total	Male	Female	Total	Male	Female	Total	Male	Female	Total	Male	Female
25 YEARS AND OLDER															
Completed 4 Years of High School or More															
2018..............................	71.6	70.7	72.5	90.2	89.5	90.7	94.3	93.9	94.6	87.9	87.6	88.2	90.7	92.9	88.8
2017..............................	70.5	69.5	71.6	90.0	89.4	90.5	94.1	93.7	94.5	87.2	86.3	88.0	91.1	92.7	89.7
2016..............................	68.5	67.2	69.7	89.4	88.8	90.1	93.8	93.4	94.3	87.2	86.5	87.7	90.6	92.0	89.4
2015..............................	66.7	65.5	67.8	88.7	88.2	89.2	93.3	93.0	93.5	87.1	86.4	87.6	89.3	91.1	87.7
2014..............................	66.5	65.1	67.9	88.7	87.9	89.5	93.1	92.6	93.7	85.8	85.2	86.3	89.9	92.2	87.9
2013..............................	66.2	64.6	67.9	88.6	88.0	89.2	92.9	92.7	93.1	85.1	84.1	85.9	90.3	91.6	89.2
2012[2]..........................	65.0	64.0	66.0	88.1	87.6	88.5	92.5	92.2	92.7	85.1	84.5	85.6	89.0	90.5	87.8
2011..............................	64.3	63.6	65.1	88.0	87.4	88.6	92.4	92.0	92.7	84.6	83.9	85.1	88.9	90.6	87.4
2010..............................	62.9	61.4	64.4	87.6	86.8	88.2	92.0	91.7	92.3	84.2	83.5	84.8	89.1	91.2	87.3
2009..............................	61.9	60.6	63.3	87.1	86.4	87.7	91.6	91.4	91.8	84.1	83.9	84.2	88.3	90.6	86.4
2008..............................	62.3	60.9	63.7	87.1	86.3	87.8	91.4	91.1	91.8	83.2	81.9	84.1	89.0	90.9	87.2
2007..............................	60.3	58.2	62.5	86.2	85.3	87.0	90.6	90.2	91.0	82.4	82.0	82.6	87.8	89.2	86.5
2006..............................	59.3	58.5	60.1	86.1	85.5	86.7	90.5	90.2	90.8	80.8	80.3	81.2	87.6	89.6	85.8
2005..............................	58.5	57.9	59.1	85.7	85.2	86.2	90.1	89.9	90.3	81.3	81.2	81.3	87.9	90.5	85.6
2004..............................	58.4	57.3	59.5	85.8	85.3	86.2	90.0	89.9	90.1	80.6	80.3	80.9	86.9	88.8	85.2
2003[3]..........................	57.0	56.3	57.8	85.1	84.5	85.7	89.4	89.0	89.6	80.0	79.5	80.3	87.8	89.7	86.1
2002..............................	57.0	56.1	57.9	NA	NA	NA	NA	NA	NA	NA	NA	NA	NA	NA	NA
2001[4]..........................	56.8	55.5	58.0	NA	NA	NA	NA	NA	NA	NA	NA	NA	NA	NA	NA
2000..............................	57.0	56.6	57.5	NA	NA	NA	NA	NA	NA	NA	NA	NA	NA	NA	NA
1999..............................	56.1	56.0	56.3	NA	NA	NA	NA	NA	NA	NA	NA	NA	NA	NA	NA
1998..............................	55.5	55.7	55.3	NA	NA	NA	NA	NA	NA	NA	NA	NA	NA	NA	NA
1997..............................	54.7	54.9	54.6	NA	NA	NA	NA	NA	NA	NA	NA	NA	NA	NA	NA
1996..............................	53.1	53.0	53.3	NA	NA	NA	NA	NA	NA	NA	NA	NA	NA	NA	NA
1995..............................	53.4	52.9	53.8	NA	NA	NA	NA	NA	NA	NA	NA	NA	NA	NA	NA
1994..............................	53.3	53.4	53.2	NA	NA	NA	NA	NA	NA	NA	NA	NA	NA	NA	NA
1993..............................	53.1	52.9	53.2	NA	NA	NA	NA	NA	NA	NA	NA	NA	NA	NA	NA
1992[5]..........................	52.6	53.7	51.5	NA	NA	NA	NA	NA	NA	NA	NA	NA	NA	NA	NA
1991..............................	51.3	51.4	51.2	NA	NA	NA	NA	NA	NA	NA	NA	NA	NA	NA	NA
1990..............................	50.8	50.3	51.3	NA	NA	NA	NA	NA	NA	NA	NA	NA	NA	NA	NA
1989..............................	50.9	51.0	50.7	NA	NA	NA	NA	NA	NA	NA	NA	NA	NA	NA	NA
1988..............................	51.0	52.0	50.0	NA	NA	NA	NA	NA	NA	NA	NA	NA	NA	NA	NA
1987..............................	50.9	51.8	50.0	NA	NA	NA	NA	NA	NA	NA	NA	NA	NA	NA	NA
1986..............................	48.5	49.2	47.8	NA	NA	NA	NA	NA	NA	NA	NA	NA	NA	NA	NA
1985..............................	47.9	48.5	47.4	NA	NA	NA	NA	NA	NA	NA	NA	NA	NA	NA	NA
1984..............................	47.1	48.6	45.7	NA	NA	NA	NA	NA	NA	NA	NA	NA	NA	NA	NA
1983..............................	46.2	48.6	44.2	NA	NA	NA	NA	NA	NA	NA	NA	NA	NA	NA	NA
1982..............................	45.9	48.1	44.1	NA	NA	NA	NA	NA	NA	NA	NA	NA	NA	NA	NA
1981..............................	44.5	45.5	43.6	NA	NA	NA	NA	NA	NA	NA	NA	NA	NA	NA	NA
1980..............................	45.3	46.4	44.1	NA	NA	NA	NA	NA	NA	NA	NA	NA	NA	NA	NA
1979..............................	42.0	42.3	41.7	NA	NA	NA	NA	NA	NA	NA	NA	NA	NA	NA	NA
1978..............................	40.8	42.2	39.6	NA	NA	NA	NA	NA	NA	NA	NA	NA	NA	NA	NA
1977..............................	39.6	42.3	37.2	NA	NA	NA	NA	NA	NA	NA	NA	NA	NA	NA	NA
1976..............................	39.3	41.4	37.3	NA	NA	NA	NA	NA	NA	NA	NA	NA	NA	NA	NA
1975..............................	37.9	39.5	36.7	NA	NA	NA	NA	NA	NA	NA	NA	NA	NA	NA	NA
1974..............................	36.5	38.3	34.9	NA	NA	NA	NA	NA	NA	NA	NA	NA	NA	NA	NA
1973..............................	NA	NA	NA	NA	NA	NA	NA	NA	NA	NA	NA	NA	NA	NA	NA
1972..............................	NA	NA	NA	NA	NA	NA	NA	NA	NA	NA	NA	NA	NA	NA	NA
1971..............................	NA	NA	NA	NA	NA	NA	NA	NA	NA	NA	NA	NA	NA	NA	NA
1970..............................	NA	NA	NA	NA	NA	NA	NA	NA	NA	NA	NA	NA	NA	NA	NA
1969..............................	NA	NA	NA	NA	NA	NA	NA	NA	NA	NA	NA	NA	NA	NA	NA
1968..............................	NA	NA	NA	NA	NA	NA	NA	NA	NA	NA	NA	NA	NA	NA	NA
1967..............................	NA	NA	NA	NA	NA	NA	NA	NA	NA	NA	NA	NA	NA	NA	NA
1966..............................	NA	NA	NA	NA	NA	NA	NA	NA	NA	NA	NA	NA	NA	NA	NA
1965..............................	NA	NA	NA	NA	NA	NA	NA	NA	NA	NA	NA	NA	NA	NA	NA
1964..............................	NA	NA	NA	NA	NA	NA	NA	NA	NA	NA	NA	NA	NA	NA	NA
1962..............................	NA	NA	NA	NA	NA	NA	NA	NA	NA	NA	NA	NA	NA	NA	NA
1959..............................	NA	NA	NA	NA	NA	NA	NA	NA	NA	NA	NA	NA	NA	NA	NA

Note: Starting in 2001, data are from the expanded CPS sample.

[2]Starting in 2012, data were calculated using population controls based on the 2010 Census.

[3]Starting in 2003, respondents could choose more than one race. The race data in this table for White, non-Hispanic White, Black, and Asian from 2003 onward represent those respondents who indicated only one racial identity. Prior to 2003, Asians were grouped with Pacific Islanders.

[4]Starting in 2001, data were calculated using population controls based on Census 2000.

[5] Begining with data for 1992, a new question results in different categories than for earlier years: Data shown as 'Completed 4 Years of High School or more' is now collected in the category 'High School Graduate.' Data shown as 'College 1 to 3 years' is now collected in the 'Some college' and the two 'Associate degree' categories. Data shown as 'Completed 4 Years of College or more', is now collected in the categories, 'Bachelor's degree,' 'Master's degree,' 'Doctorate degree,' and 'Professional degree'. Due to the change in question format, median years of schooling cannot be derived.

Table A-32. Percent of People 25 Years and Over Who Have Completed High School or College, by Race, Hispanic Origin, and Sex, Selected Years, 1940–2018—*Continued*

(Percent; civilian noninstitutionalized population.)

Age and Year	All races			White			Non-Hispanic White			Black[1]			Asian		
	Total	Male	Female	Total	Male	Female	Total	Male	Female	Total	Male	Female	Total	Male	Female
1957	41.6	39.7	43.3	43.2	41.1	45.1	NA	NA	NA	18.4	16.9	19.7	NA	NA	NA
1952	38.8	36.9	40.5	NA	NA	NA	NA	NA	NA	15.0	14.0	15.7	NA	NA	NA
1950	34.3	32.6	36.0	NA	NA	NA	NA	NA	NA	13.7	12.5	14.7	NA	NA	NA
1947	33.1	31.4	34.7	35.0	33.2	36.7	NA	NA	NA	13.6	12.7	14.5	NA	NA	NA
1940	24.5	22.7	26.3	26.1	24.2	28.1	NA	NA	NA	7.7	6.9	8.4	NA	NA	NA
Completed 4 Years of College or More															
2018	35.0	34.6	35.3	35.2	34.9	35.5	38.8	38.9	38.8	25.2	23.2	26.9	56.5	59.3	54.0
2017	34.2	33.7	34.6	34.5	34.0	35.0	38.1	37.8	38.3	23.9	22.1	25.4	54.8	56.6	53.2
2016	33.4	33.2	33.7	33.7	33.4	34.0	37.3	37.2	37.3	23.3	21.7	24.6	55.9	58.8	53.4
2015	32.5	32.3	32.7	32.8	32.6	32.9	36.2	36.3	36.1	22.5	20.6	24.0	53.9	56.8	51.5
2014	32.0	31.9	32.0	32.3	32.3	32.3	35.6	35.9	35.3	22.2	20.4	23.7	52.3	54.7	50.3
2013	31.7	32.0	31.4	32.0	32.4	31.6	35.2	36.0	34.4	21.8	19.8	23.3	53.2	56.1	50.8
2012	30.9	31.4	30.6	31.3	31.9	30.8	34.5	35.5	33.5	21.2	19.2	22.9	51.0	53.7	48.8
2011	30.4	30.8	30.1	31.0	31.5	30.5	34.0	35.0	33.1	19.9	18.0	21.4	50.3	53.4	47.7
2010	29.9	30.3	29.6	30.3	30.8	29.9	33.2	34.2	32.4	19.8	17.7	21.4	52.4	55.6	49.5
2009	29.5	30.1	29.1	29.9	30.6	29.3	32.9	33.9	31.9	19.3	17.8	20.6	52.3	55.7	49.3
2008	29.4	30.1	28.8	29.8	30.5	29.1	32.6	33.8	31.5	19.6	18.7	20.4	52.6	55.8	49.8
2007	28.7	29.5	28.0	29.1	29.9	28.3	31.8	33.2	30.6	18.5	18.0	19.0	52.1	55.2	49.3
2006	28.0	29.2	26.9	28.4	29.7	27.1	31.0	32.8	29.3	18.5	17.2	19.4	49.7	52.5	47.1
2005	27.7	28.9	26.5	28.1	29.4	26.8	30.6	32.4	28.9	17.6	16.0	18.8	50.2	54.0	46.8
2004	27.7	29.4	26.1	28.2	30.0	26.4	30.6	32.9	28.4	17.6	16.6	18.5	49.4	53.7	45.6
2003	27.2	28.9	25.7	27.6	29.4	25.9	30.0	32.3	27.9	17.3	16.7	17.8	49.8	53.9	46.1
2002	26.7	28.5	25.1	27.2	29.1	25.4	29.4	31.7	27.3	17.0	16.4	17.5	NA	NA	NA
2001	26.2	28.2	24.3	26.6	28.7	24.6	28.7	31.3	26.3	15.7	15.3	16.1	NA	NA	NA
2000	25.6	27.8	23.6	26.1	28.5	23.9	28.1	30.8	25.5	16.5	16.3	16.7	NA	NA	NA
1999	25.2	27.5	23.1	25.9	28.5	23.5	27.7	30.6	25.0	15.4	14.2	16.4	NA	NA	NA
1998	24.4	26.5	22.4	25.0	27.3	22.8	26.6	29.3	24.1	14.7	13.9	15.4	NA	NA	NA
1997	23.9	26.2	21.7	24.6	27.0	22.3	26.2	29.0	23.7	13.3	12.5	13.9	NA	NA	NA
1996	23.6	26.0	21.4	24.3	26.9	21.8	25.9	28.8	23.2	13.6	12.4	14.6	NA	NA	NA
1995	23.0	26.0	20.2	24.0	27.2	21.0	25.4	28.9	22.1	13.2	13.6	12.9	NA	NA	NA
1994	22.2	25.1	19.6	22.9	26.1	20.0	24.3	27.8	21.1	12.9	12.8	13.0	NA	NA	NA
1993	21.9	24.8	19.2	22.6	25.7	19.7	23.8	27.2	20.7	12.2	11.9	12.4	NA	NA	NA
1992	21.4	24.3	18.6	22.1	25.2	19.1	NA	NA	NA	11.9	11.9	12.0	NA	NA	NA
1991	21.4	24.3	18.8	22.2	25.4	19.3	NA	NA	NA	11.5	11.4	11.6	NA	NA	NA
1990	21.3	24.4	18.4	22.0	25.3	19.0	NA	NA	NA	11.3	11.9	10.8	NA	NA	NA
1989	21.1	24.5	18.1	21.8	25.4	18.5	NA	NA	NA	11.8	11.7	11.9	NA	NA	NA
1988	20.3	24.0	17.0	20.9	25.0	17.3	NA	NA	NA	11.2	11.1	11.4	NA	NA	NA
1987	19.9	23.6	16.5	20.5	24.5	16.9	NA	NA	NA	10.7	11.0	10.4	NA	NA	NA
1986	19.4	23.2	16.1	20.1	24.1	16.4	NA	NA	NA	10.9	11.2	10.7	NA	NA	NA
1985	19.4	23.1	16.0	20.0	24.0	16.3	NA	NA	NA	11.1	11.2	11.0	NA	NA	NA
1984	19.1	22.9	15.7	19.8	23.9	16.0	NA	NA	NA	10.4	10.4	10.4	NA	NA	NA
1983	18.8	23.0	15.1	19.5	24.0	15.4	NA	NA	NA	9.5	10.0	9.2	NA	NA	NA
1982	17.7	21.9	14.0	18.5	23.0	14.4	NA	NA	NA	8.8	9.1	8.5	NA	NA	NA
1981	17.1	21.1	13.4	17.8	22.2	13.8	NA	NA	NA	8.2	8.2	8.2	NA	NA	NA
1980	17.0	20.9	13.6	17.8	22.1	14.0	NA	NA	NA	7.9	7.7	8.1	NA	NA	NA
1979	16.4	20.4	12.9	17.2	21.4	13.3	NA	NA	NA	7.9	8.3	7.5	NA	NA	NA
1978	15.7	19.7	12.2	16.4	20.7	12.6	NA	NA	NA	7.2	7.3	7.1	NA	NA	NA
1977	15.4	19.2	12.0	16.1	20.2	12.4	NA	NA	NA	7.2	7.0	7.4	NA	NA	NA
1976	14.7	18.6	11.3	15.4	19.6	11.6	NA	NA	NA	6.6	6.3	6.8	NA	NA	NA
1975	13.9	17.6	10.6	14.5	18.4	11.0	NA	NA	NA	6.4	6.7	6.2	NA	NA	NA
1974	13.3	16.9	10.1	14.0	17.7	10.6	NA	NA	NA	5.5	5.7	5.3	NA	NA	NA
1973	12.6	16.0	9.6	13.1	16.8	9.9	NA	NA	NA	6.0	5.9	6.0	NA	NA	NA
1972	12.0	15.4	9.0	12.6	16.2	9.4	NA	NA	NA	5.1	5.5	4.8	NA	NA	NA
1971	11.4	14.6	8.5	12.0	15.5	8.9	NA	NA	NA	4.5	4.7	4.3	NA	NA	NA
1970	11.0	14.1	8.2	11.6	15.0	8.6	NA	NA	NA	4.5	4.6	4.4	NA	NA	NA
1969	10.7	13.6	8.1	11.2	14.3	8.5	NA	NA	NA	4.6	4.8	4.5	NA	NA	NA
1968	10.5	13.3	8.0	11.0	14.1	8.3	NA	NA	NA	4.3	3.7	4.8	NA	NA	NA
1967	10.1	12.8	7.6	10.6	13.6	7.9	NA	NA	NA	4.0	3.4	4.4	NA	NA	NA
1966	9.8	12.5	7.4	10.4	13.3	7.7	NA	NA	NA	3.8	3.9	3.7	NA	NA	NA
1965	9.4	12.0	7.1	9.9	12.7	7.3	NA	NA	NA	4.7	4.9	4.5	NA	NA	NA
1964	9.1	11.7	6.8	9.6	12.3	7.1	NA	NA	NA	3.9	4.5	3.4	NA	NA	NA
1962	8.9	11.4	6.7	9.5	12.2	7.0	NA	NA	NA	4.0	3.9	4.0	NA	NA	NA
1959	8.1	10.3	6.0	8.6	11.0	6.2	NA	NA	NA	3.3	3.8	2.9	NA	NA	NA
1957	7.6	9.6	5.8	8.0	10.1	6.0	NA	NA	NA	2.9	2.7	3.0	NA	NA	NA
1952	7.0	8.3	5.8	NA	NA	NA	NA	NA	NA	2.4	2.0	2.7	NA	NA	NA
1950	6.2	7.3	5.2	NA	NA	NA	NA	NA	NA	2.3	2.1	2.4	NA	NA	NA
1947	5.4	6.2	4.7	5.7	6.6	4.9	NA	NA	NA	2.5	2.4	2.6	NA	NA	NA
1940	4.6	5.5	3.8	4.9	5.9	4.0	NA	NA	NA	1.3	1.4	1.2	NA	NA	NA

Note: Starting in 2001, data are from the expanded CPS sample.
[1]Data in the column labeled "Black" include Black and other races from 1940 to 1962: from 1963 to 2003, data are for the Black population only.

Table A-32. Percent of People 25 Years and Over Who Have Completed High School or College, by Race, Hispanic Origin, and Sex, Selected Years, 1940–2018—*Continued*

(Percent; civilian noninstitutionalized population.)

Age and Year	Hispanic (of any race)			White alone or in combination			Non-Hispanic White alone or in combination			Black alone or in combination			Asian alone or in combination		
	Total	Male	Female	Total	Male	Female	Total	Male	Female	Total	Male	Female	Total	Male	Female
1957	NA	NA	NA	NA	NA	NA	NA	NA	NA	NA	NA	NA	NA	NA	NA
1952	NA	NA	NA	NA	NA	NA	NA	NA	NA	NA	NA	NA	NA	NA	NA
1950	NA	NA	NA	NA	NA	NA	NA	NA	NA	NA	NA	NA	NA	NA	NA
1947	NA	NA	NA	NA	NA	NA	NA	NA	NA	NA	NA	NA	NA	NA	NA
1940	NA	NA	NA	NA	NA	NA	NA	NA	NA	NA	NA	NA	NA	NA	NA
Completed 4 Years of College or More															
2018	18.3	16.6	20.1	35.1	34.7	35.5	38.7	38.8	38.7	25.4	23.2	27.1	56.0	58.6	53.7
2017	17.2	15.8	18.6	34.4	33.9	34.9	38.0	37.8	38.3	24.2	22.3	25.7	54.4	55.9	53.2
2016	16.4	15.4	17.4	33.6	33.3	33.9	37.2	37.1	37.3	23.5	21.8	24.9	55.4	57.9	53.3
2015	15.5	14.3	16.6	32.7	32.5	32.9	36.2	36.2	36.1	22.7	20.7	24.2	53.7	56.2	51.5
2014	15.2	14.2	16.1	32.2	32.2	32.3	35.5	35.8	35.3	22.7	20.6	24.3	52.2	54.2	50.4
2013	15.1	13.9	16.2	31.9	32.3	31.5	35.1	35.9	34.4	22.0	20.0	23.6	52.8	55.5	50.5
2012	14.5	13.3	15.8	31.2	31.8	30.7	34.4	35.4	33.4	21.4	19.4	22.9	50.4	52.6	48.6
2011	14.1	13.1	15.2	30.9	31.4	30.5	33.9	34.9	33.1	20.1	18.2	21.6	49.9	52.8	47.3
2010	13.9	12.9	14.9	30.2	30.7	29.8	33.2	34.1	32.3	19.9	17.7	21.6	51.8	54.7	49.3
2009	13.2	12.5	14.0	29.8	30.4	29.3	32.8	33.8	31.8	19.4	17.8	20.7	51.8	54.8	49.2
2008	13.3	12.6	14.1	29.7	30.3	29.0	32.5	33.6	31.4	19.8	18.8	20.5	52.0	54.6	49.8
2007	12.7	11.8	13.7	29.0	29.8	28.3	31.7	33.0	30.5	18.7	18.2	19.1	47.1	49.1	45.4
2006	12.4	11.9	12.9	28.3	29.6	27.0	30.9	32.7	29.2	18.7	17.4	19.7	49.0	51.4	46.8
2005	12.0	11.8	12.1	28.0	29.3	26.7	30.5	32.3	28.9	17.6	16.0	18.9	49.8	53.3	46.6
2004	12.1	11.8	12.3	28.0	29.9	26.3	30.5	32.8	28.3	17.7	16.5	18.6	48.9	52.8	45.4
2003	11.4	11.2	11.6	27.5	29.3	25.8	29.9	32.2	27.9	17.5	16.8	18.0	49.2	52.7	46.0
2002	11.1	11.0	11.2	NA	NA	NA	NA	NA	NA	NA	NA	NA	NA	NA	NA
2001	11.1	10.8	11.4	NA	NA	NA	NA	NA	NA	NA	NA	NA	NA	NA	NA
2000	10.6	10.7	10.6	NA	NA	NA	NA	NA	NA	NA	NA	NA	NA	NA	NA
1999	10.9	10.7	11.0	NA	NA	NA	NA	NA	NA	NA	NA	NA	NA	NA	NA
1998	11.0	11.1	10.9	NA	NA	NA	NA	NA	NA	NA	NA	NA	NA	NA	NA
1997	10.3	10.6	10.1	NA	NA	NA	NA	NA	NA	NA	NA	NA	NA	NA	NA
1996	9.3	10.3	8.3	NA	NA	NA	NA	NA	NA	NA	NA	NA	NA	NA	NA
1995	9.3	10.1	8.4	NA	NA	NA	NA	NA	NA	NA	NA	NA	NA	NA	NA
1994	9.1	9.6	8.6	NA	NA	NA	NA	NA	NA	NA	NA	NA	NA	NA	NA
1993	9.0	9.5	8.5	NA	NA	NA	NA	NA	NA	NA	NA	NA	NA	NA	NA
1992	9.3	10.2	8.5	NA	NA	NA	NA	NA	NA	NA	NA	NA	NA	NA	NA
1991	9.7	10.0	9.4	NA	NA	NA	NA	NA	NA	NA	NA	NA	NA	NA	NA
1990	9.2	9.8	8.7	NA	NA	NA	NA	NA	NA	NA	NA	NA	NA	NA	NA
1989	9.9	11.0	8.8	NA	NA	NA	NA	NA	NA	NA	NA	NA	NA	NA	NA
1988	10.1	12.3	8.1	NA	NA	NA	NA	NA	NA	NA	NA	NA	NA	NA	NA
1987	8.6	9.7	7.5	NA	NA	NA	NA	NA	NA	NA	NA	NA	NA	NA	NA
1986	8.4	9.5	7.4	NA	NA	NA	NA	NA	NA	NA	NA	NA	NA	NA	NA
1985	8.5	9.7	7.3	NA	NA	NA	NA	NA	NA	NA	NA	NA	NA	NA	NA
1984	8.2	9.5	7.0	NA	NA	NA	NA	NA	NA	NA	NA	NA	NA	NA	NA
1983	7.9	9.2	6.8	NA	NA	NA	NA	NA	NA	NA	NA	NA	NA	NA	NA
1982	7.8	9.6	6.2	NA	NA	NA	NA	NA	NA	NA	NA	NA	NA	NA	NA
1981	7.7	9.7	5.9	NA	NA	NA	NA	NA	NA	NA	NA	NA	NA	NA	NA
1980	7.9	9.7	6.2	NA	NA	NA	NA	NA	NA	NA	NA	NA	NA	NA	NA
1979	6.7	8.2	5.3	NA	NA	NA	NA	NA	NA	NA	NA	NA	NA	NA	NA
1978	7.0	8.6	5.7	NA	NA	NA	NA	NA	NA	NA	NA	NA	NA	NA	NA
1977	6.2	8.1	4.4	NA	NA	NA	NA	NA	NA	NA	NA	NA	NA	NA	NA
1976	6.1	8.6	4.0	NA	NA	NA	NA	NA	NA	NA	NA	NA	NA	NA	NA
1975	6.3	8.3	4.6	NA	NA	NA	NA	NA	NA	NA	NA	NA	NA	NA	NA
1974	5.5	7.1	4.0	NA	NA	NA	NA	NA	NA	NA	NA	NA	NA	NA	NA
1973	NA	NA	NA	NA	NA	NA	NA	NA	NA	NA	NA	NA	NA	NA	NA
1972	NA	NA	NA	NA	NA	NA	NA	NA	NA	NA	NA	NA	NA	NA	NA
1971	NA	NA	NA	NA	NA	NA	NA	NA	NA	NA	NA	NA	NA	NA	NA
1970	NA	NA	NA	NA	NA	NA	NA	NA	NA	NA	NA	NA	NA	NA	NA
1969	NA	NA	NA	NA	NA	NA	NA	NA	NA	NA	NA	NA	NA	NA	NA
1968	NA	NA	NA	NA	NA	NA	NA	NA	NA	NA	NA	NA	NA	NA	NA
1967	NA	NA	NA	NA	NA	NA	NA	NA	NA	NA	NA	NA	NA	NA	NA
1966	NA	NA	NA	NA	NA	NA	NA	NA	NA	NA	NA	NA	NA	NA	NA
1965	NA	NA	NA	NA	NA	NA	NA	NA	NA	NA	NA	NA	NA	NA	NA
1964	NA	NA	NA	NA	NA	NA	NA	NA	NA	NA	NA	NA	NA	NA	NA
1962	NA	NA	NA	NA	NA	NA	NA	NA	NA	NA	NA	NA	NA	NA	NA
1959	NA	NA	NA	NA	NA	NA	NA	NA	NA	NA	NA	NA	NA	NA	NA
1957	NA	NA	NA	NA	NA	NA	NA	NA	NA	NA	NA	NA	NA	NA	NA
1952	NA	NA	NA	NA	NA	NA	NA	NA	NA	NA	NA	NA	NA	NA	NA
1950	NA	NA	NA	NA	NA	NA	NA	NA	NA	NA	NA	NA	NA	NA	NA
1947	NA	NA	NA	NA	NA	NA	NA	NA	NA	NA	NA	NA	NA	NA	NA
1940	NA	NA	NA	NA	NA	NA	NA	NA	NA	NA	NA	NA	NA	NA	NA

Note: Starting in 2001, data are from the expanded CPS sample.

Table A-32. Percent of People 25 Years and Over Who Have Completed High School or College, by Race, Hispanic Origin, and Sex, Selected Years, 1940–2018—*Continued*

(Percent; civilian noninstitutionalized population.)

Age and Year	All races			White			Non-Hispanic White			Black[1]			Asian		
	Total	Male	Female	Total	Male	Female	Total	Male	Female	Total	Male	Female	Total	Male	Female
25 TO 29 YEARS															
Completed 4 Years of High School or More															
2018	92.9	91.9	94.0	92.9	91.7	94.1	95.6	95.0	96.3	92.0	90.7	93.1	97.5	97.6	97.4
2017	92.5	91.5	93.4	92.4	91.2	93.7	95.6	94.8	96.4	91.8	91.2	92.4	96.8	97.7	95.9
2016	91.7	90.9	92.5	91.6	90.6	92.7	95.2	94.8	95.7	90.6	90.8	90.4	96.5	95.9	97.1
2015	91.2	90.5	91.8	90.8	90.0	91.7	95.4	95.1	95.8	92.2	91.4	93.0	95.5	96.3	94.7
2014	90.8	90.1	91.5	90.9	90.2	91.7	95.6	95.4	95.9	89.8	90.2	89.4	96.7	96.3	97.2
2013	89.9	88.3	91.5	89.5	88.0	91.1	94.1	93.3	94.9	89.8	87.3	92.1	94.7	93.6	95.7
2012	89.7	88.4	91.1	89.6	88.3	90.9	94.6	93.8	95.3	88.5	87.1	89.7	95.7	96.2	95.3
2011	89.0	87.5	90.7	88.9	87.1	90.8	94.4	93.4	95.5	87.7	87.6	87.8	95.2	93.6	96.7
2010	88.8	87.4	90.2	88.5	87.3	89.9	94.5	94.6	94.4	89.0	86.7	91.0	93.2	92.3	94.1
2009	88.6	87.5	89.8	88.4	87.0	89.9	94.6	94.4	94.8	88.9	88.6	89.1	95.2	95.6	94.9
2008	87.8	85.8	89.9	87.6	85.5	89.8	93.7	92.6	94.7	87.4	85.4	89.2	95.6	95.4	95.7
2007	87.0	84.9	89.1	86.5	84.2	89.0	93.5	92.7	94.2	87.4	87.0	87.8	97.2	95.8	98.5
2006	86.4	84.4	88.5	86.1	84.1	88.3	93.4	92.3	94.6	85.6	83.1	87.8	96.6	97.2	96.0
2005	86.2	85.0	87.4	85.7	84.3	87.1	92.8	91.8	93.8	86.5	86.4	86.6	95.5	96.7	94.5
2004	86.6	85.2	88.0	85.9	83.7	88.1	93.3	92.1	94.5	87.9	90.1	86.1	96.2	96.9	95.4
2003	86.5	84.9	88.2	85.7	83.8	87.6	93.7	92.8	94.5	87.6	86.4	88.5	97.1	97.4	96.8
2002	86.4	84.7	88.1	85.9	84.1	87.7	93.0	92.1	93.8	86.6	85.0	88.0	NA	NA	NA
2001	86.8	85.3	88.3	86.4	84.6	88.3	93.4	93.1	93.7	86.3	85.4	87.0	NA	NA	NA
2000	88.1	86.7	89.4	88.3	86.6	90.0	94.0	92.9	95.2	85.9	86.6	85.3	NA	NA	NA
1999	87.8	86.1	89.5	87.6	85.8	89.3	93.0	91.9	94.1	88.2	87.7	88.6	NA	NA	NA
1998	88.1	86.6	89.6	88.1	86.3	90.0	93.6	92.5	94.6	87.6	87.6	87.6	NA	NA	NA
1997	87.4	85.8	88.9	87.6	85.8	89.4	92.9	91.7	94.0	86.2	85.2	87.1	NA	NA	NA
1996	87.3	86.5	88.1	87.5	86.3	88.8	92.6	92.0	93.1	85.6	87.2	84.2	NA	NA	NA
1995	86.8	86.3	87.4	87.4	86.6	88.2	92.5	92.0	93.0	86.5	88.1	85.1	NA	NA	NA
1994	86.1	84.5	87.6	86.5	84.7	88.3	91.1	90.0	92.3	84.1	82.9	85.0	NA	NA	NA
1993	86.7	86.0	87.4	87.3	86.1	88.5	91.2	90.6	91.8	82.8	85.0	80.9	NA	NA	NA
1992	86.3	86.1	86.5	87.0	86.5	87.6	NA	NA	NA	80.9	82.5	79.5	NA	NA	NA
1991	85.4	84.9	85.8	85.8	85.1	86.6	NA	NA	NA	81.7	83.5	80.1	NA	NA	NA
1990	85.7	84.4	87.0	86.3	84.6	88.1	NA	NA	NA	81.7	81.5	81.8	NA	NA	NA
1989	85.5	84.4	86.5	86.0	84.8	87.1	NA	NA	NA	82.2	80.6	83.6	NA	NA	NA
1988	85.7	84.4	87.0	86.5	84.8	88.2	NA	NA	NA	80.7	80.6	80.7	NA	NA	NA
1987	86.0	85.5	86.4	86.3	85.6	87.0	NA	NA	NA	83.3	84.8	82.1	NA	NA	NA
1986	86.1	85.9	86.4	86.5	85.6	87.4	NA	NA	NA	83.4	86.5	80.6	NA	NA	NA
1985	86.1	85.9	86.4	86.8	86.4	87.3	NA	NA	NA	80.6	80.8	80.4	NA	NA	NA
1984	85.9	85.6	86.3	86.9	86.8	87.0	NA	NA	NA	78.9	75.9	81.5	NA	NA	NA
1983	86.0	86.0	86.0	86.9	86.9	86.9	NA	NA	NA	79.4	78.9	79.8	NA	NA	NA
1982	86.2	86.3	86.1	86.9	87.0	86.8	NA	NA	NA	80.9	80.5	81.3	NA	NA	NA
1981	86.3	86.5	86.1	87.6	87.6	87.6	NA	NA	NA	77.3	78.4	76.4	NA	NA	NA
1980	85.4	85.4	85.5	86.9	86.8	87.0	NA	NA	NA	76.6	74.8	78.1	NA	NA	NA
1979	85.6	86.3	84.9	87.0	87.7	86.4	NA	NA	NA	74.8	73.9	75.4	NA	NA	NA
1978	85.3	86.0	84.6	86.3	86.8	85.8	NA	NA	NA	77.3	78.5	76.3	NA	NA	NA
1977	85.4	86.6	84.2	86.8	87.6	86.0	NA	NA	NA	74.4	77.5	72.0	NA	NA	NA
1976	84.7	86.0	83.5	85.9	87.3	84.6	NA	NA	NA	73.8	72.5	74.9	NA	NA	NA
1975	83.1	84.5	81.8	84.4	85.7	83.2	NA	NA	NA	71.0	72.2	70.1	NA	NA	NA
1974	81.9	83.1	80.8	83.4	84.1	82.7	NA	NA	NA	68.2	71.1	66.0	NA	NA	NA
1973	80.2	80.6	79.8	82.0	82.4	81.6	NA	NA	NA	64.2	63.1	64.9	NA	NA	NA
1972	79.8	80.5	79.2	81.5	82.3	80.8	NA	NA	NA	64.1	61.8	66.2	NA	NA	NA
1971	77.2	78.1	76.4	79.5	80.8	78.3	NA	NA	NA	57.5	54.1	60.7	NA	NA	NA
1970	75.4	76.6	74.2	77.8	79.2	76.4	NA	NA	NA	56.2	54.5	57.9	NA	NA	NA
1969	74.7	75.6	73.8	77.0	77.5	76.6	NA	NA	NA	55.8	59.8	52.3	NA	NA	NA
1968	73.2	73.7	72.7	75.3	75.5	75.0	NA	NA	NA	55.8	58.1	53.6	NA	NA	NA
1967	72.5	72.1	72.9	74.8	74.3	75.3	NA	NA	NA	53.4	51.7	55.0	NA	NA	NA
1966	71.0	70.9	71.2	73.8	73.2	74.4	NA	NA	NA	47.9	48.9	47.0	NA	NA	NA
1965	70.3	70.5	70.1	72.8	72.7	72.8	NA	NA	NA	50.3	50.3	50.4	NA	NA	NA
1964	69.2	68.8	69.5	72.1	71.8	72.4	NA	NA	NA	45.0	41.6	47.9	NA	NA	NA
1962	65.9	65.8	66.1	69.2	69.2	69.3	NA	NA	NA	41.6	38.9	43.8	NA	NA	NA
1959	63.9	63.9	64.0	67.2	66.9	67.4	NA	NA	NA	39.5	40.6	38.6	NA	NA	NA
1957	60.2	57.9	62.4	63.3	60.7	65.7	NA	NA	NA	31.6	27.4	35.2	NA	NA	NA
1952	57.1	55.3	58.7	NA	NA	NA	NA	NA	NA	28.1	27.9	28.3	NA	NA	NA
1950	52.8	50.6	55.0	NA	NA	NA	NA	NA	NA	23.6	21.3	25.5	NA	NA	NA
1947	51.4	49.4	53.3	54.9	52.9	56.8	NA	NA	NA	22.3	19.6	24.7	NA	NA	NA
1940	38.1	36.0	40.1	41.2	38.9	43.4	NA	NA	NA	12.3	10.6	13.6	NA	NA	NA

Note: Starting in 2001, data are from the expanded CPS sample.

[1]Data in the column labeled "Black" include Black and other races from 1940 to 1962: from 1963 to 2003, data are for the Black population only.

Table A-32. Percent of People 25 Years and Over Who Have Completed High School or College, by Race, Hispanic Origin, and Sex, Selected Years, 1940–2018—*Continued*

(Percent; civilian noninstitutionalized population.)

Age and Year	Hispanic (of any race)			White alone or in combination			Non-Hispanic White alone or in combination			Black alone or in combination			Asian alone or in combination		
	Total	Male	Female	Total	Male	Female	Total	Male	Female	Total	Male	Female	Total	Male	Female
25 TO 29 YEARS															
Completed 4 Years of High School or More															
2018	85.2	83.4	87.2	92.9	91.7	94.1	95.6	94.9	96.2	92.2	90.8	93.4	97.5	97.6	97.5
2017	82.7	80.7	84.8	92.3	91.2	93.5	95.6	94.8	96.3	91.8	90.9	92.6	96.9	97.9	95.9
2016	80.6	78.3	83.2	91.7	90.7	92.7	95.2	94.9	95.6	90.7	91	90.5	96.7	96.2	97.2
2015	77.1	75.7	78.6	90.8	90.0	91.6	95.4	95.2	95.6	92.2	91.5	92.8	95.5	95.8	95.1
2014	74.7	72.4	77.4	90.8	89.9	91.7	95.6	95.4	95.9	89.1	88.9	89.3	96.9	96.3	97.4
2013	75.8	73.1	78.8	89.6	88.1	91.1	94.2	93.4	95.0	89.5	87.0	91.7	94.9	94.0	95.9
2012	75.0	73.3	76.9	89.6	88.2	91.0	94.6	93.8	95.4	88.4	86.8	89.8	95.5	96.1	94.8
2011	71.5	69.2	74.3	88.9	87.1	90.8	94.4	93.3	95.5	87.9	87.6	88.3	94.7	92.8	96.5
2010	69.4	65.7	74.1	88.5	87.3	89.8	94.4	94.5	94.3	89.9	86.5	91.0	93.1	92.3	93.9
2009	68.9	66.2	72.5	88.4	87.0	89.9	94.5	94.4	94.6	88.8	88.5	89.1	95.1	95.7	94.6
2008	68.3	65.6	71.9	87.6	85.5	89.8	93.7	92.6	94.8	87.7	85.6	89.4	95.7	95.5	95.9
2007	65.0	60.5	70.7	86.5	84.2	88.8	93.4	92.7	94.1	87.4	87.0	87.8	96.3	95.8	96.8
2006	63.3	60.6	66.7	86.0	83.9	88.2	93.3	92.2	94.5	85.6	83.2	87.7	96.0	96.4	95.7
2005	63.3	63.2	63.4	85.6	84.2	87.0	92.8	91.7	93.8	86.6	86.4	86.7	95.5	96.7	94.4
2004	62.4	60.1	65.2	85.9	83.9	87.9	93.2	92.1	94.4	87.8	89.9	86.2	95.7	97.0	94.5
2003	61.7	59.6	64.2	85.7	83.9	87.6	93.6	92.8	94.4	87.4	86.4	88.5	97.2	97.5	97.0
2002	62.4	60.2	65.0	NA	NA	NA	NA	NA	NA	NA	NA	NA	NA	NA	NA
2001	62.4	58.3	67.3	NA	NA	NA	NA	NA	NA	NA	NA	NA	NA	NA	NA
2000	62.8	59.2	66.4	NA	NA	NA	NA	NA	NA	NA	NA	NA	NA	NA	NA
1999	61.6	57.4	66.0	NA	NA	NA	NA	NA	NA	NA	NA	NA	NA	NA	NA
1998	62.8	59.9	66.3	NA	NA	NA	NA	NA	NA	NA	NA	NA	NA	NA	NA
1997	61.8	59.2	64.9	NA	NA	NA	NA	NA	NA	NA	NA	NA	NA	NA	NA
1996	61.1	59.7	62.9	NA	NA	NA	NA	NA	NA	NA	NA	NA	NA	NA	NA
1995	57.1	55.7	58.7	NA	NA	NA	NA	NA	NA	NA	NA	NA	NA	NA	NA
1994	60.3	58.0	63.0	NA	NA	NA	NA	NA	NA	NA	NA	NA	NA	NA	NA
1993	60.9	58.3	64.0	NA	NA	NA	NA	NA	NA	NA	NA	NA	NA	NA	NA
1992	60.9	61.1	60.6	NA	NA	NA	NA	NA	NA	NA	NA	NA	NA	NA	NA
1991	56.7	56.4	57.1	NA	NA	NA	NA	NA	NA	NA	NA	NA	NA	NA	NA
1990	58.2	56.6	59.9	NA	NA	NA	NA	NA	NA	NA	NA	NA	NA	NA	NA
1989	61.0	61.1	61.0	NA	NA	NA	NA	NA	NA	NA	NA	NA	NA	NA	NA
1988	62.0	59.4	65.0	NA	NA	NA	NA	NA	NA	NA	NA	NA	NA	NA	NA
1987	59.8	58.6	61.0	NA	NA	NA	NA	NA	NA	NA	NA	NA	NA	NA	NA
1986	59.1	58.2	60.0	NA	NA	NA	NA	NA	NA	NA	NA	NA	NA	NA	NA
1985	60.9	58.6	63.1	NA	NA	NA	NA	NA	NA	NA	NA	NA	NA	NA	NA
1984	58.6	56.8	60.2	NA	NA	NA	NA	NA	NA	NA	NA	NA	NA	NA	NA
1983	58.3	57.8	58.9	NA	NA	NA	NA	NA	NA	NA	NA	NA	NA	NA	NA
1982	60.9	60.7	61.2	NA	NA	NA	NA	NA	NA	NA	NA	NA	NA	NA	NA
1981	59.8	59.1	60.4	NA	NA	NA	NA	NA	NA	NA	NA	NA	NA	NA	NA
1980	58.6	58.3	58.8	NA	NA	NA	NA	NA	NA	NA	NA	NA	NA	NA	NA
1979	57.0	55.5	58.5	NA	NA	NA	NA	NA	NA	NA	NA	NA	NA	NA	NA
1978	56.6	58.5	54.7	NA	NA	NA	NA	NA	NA	NA	NA	NA	NA	NA	NA
1977	58.1	62.1	54.8	NA	NA	NA	NA	NA	NA	NA	NA	NA	NA	NA	NA
1976	58.1	57.6	58.4	NA	NA	NA	NA	NA	NA	NA	NA	NA	NA	NA	NA
1975	51.7	51.1	52.1	NA	NA	NA	NA	NA	NA	NA	NA	NA	NA	NA	NA
1974	52.5	55.1	49.9	NA	NA	NA	NA	NA	NA	NA	NA	NA	NA	NA	NA
1973	NA	NA	NA	NA	NA	NA	NA	NA	NA	NA	NA	NA	NA	NA	NA
1972	NA	NA	NA	NA	NA	NA	NA	NA	NA	NA	NA	NA	NA	NA	NA
1971	NA	NA	NA	NA	NA	NA	NA	NA	NA	NA	NA	NA	NA	NA	NA
1970	NA	NA	NA	NA	NA	NA	NA	NA	NA	NA	NA	NA	NA	NA	NA
1969	NA	NA	NA	NA	NA	NA	NA	NA	NA	NA	NA	NA	NA	NA	NA
1968	NA	NA	NA	NA	NA	NA	NA	NA	NA	NA	NA	NA	NA	NA	NA
1967	NA	NA	NA	NA	NA	NA	NA	NA	NA	NA	NA	NA	NA	NA	NA
1966	NA	NA	NA	NA	NA	NA	NA	NA	NA	NA	NA	NA	NA	NA	NA
1965	NA	NA	NA	NA	NA	NA	NA	NA	NA	NA	NA	NA	NA	NA	NA
1964	NA	NA	NA	NA	NA	NA	NA	NA	NA	NA	NA	NA	NA	NA	NA
1962	NA	NA	NA	NA	NA	NA	NA	NA	NA	NA	NA	NA	NA	NA	NA
1959	NA	NA	NA	NA	NA	NA	NA	NA	NA	NA	NA	NA	NA	NA	NA
1957	NA	NA	NA	NA	NA	NA	NA	NA	NA	NA	NA	NA	NA	NA	NA
1952	NA	NA	NA	NA	NA	NA	NA	NA	NA	NA	NA	NA	NA	NA	NA
1950	NA	NA	NA	NA	NA	NA	NA	NA	NA	NA	NA	NA	NA	NA	NA
1947	NA	NA	NA	NA	NA	NA	NA	NA	NA	NA	NA	NA	NA	NA	NA
1940	NA	NA	NA	NA	NA	NA	NA	NA	NA	NA	NA	NA	NA	NA	NA

Note: Starting in 2001, data are from the expanded CPS sample.

Table A-32. Percent of People 25 Years and Over Who Have Completed High School or College, by Race, Hispanic Origin, and Sex, Selected Years, 1940–2018—Continued

(Percent; civilian noninstitutionalized population.)

Age and Year	All races			White			Non-Hispanic White			Black[1]			Asian		
	Total	Male	Female	Total	Male	Female	Total	Male	Female	Total	Male	Female	Total	Male	Female
Completed 4 Years of College or More															
2018	37.0	33.2	40.8	37.9	33.6	42.4	43.5	38.8	48.4	22.3	18.6	25.7	69.5	68.3	70.8
2017	35.7	32.0	39.3	36.4	32.2	40.7	42.1	37.7	46.5	22.2	20.4	23.9	61.9	58.1	65.9
2016	36.1	32.7	39.5	37.0	33.6	40.5	42.9	39.5	46.3	22.7	20.2	25	64.7	60.3	68.8
2015	35.6	32.4	38.9	36.7	33.2	40.3	43.0	39.5	46.6	20.5	16.5	24.2	65.0	62.8	67.2
2014	34.0	30.9	37.2	34.8	31.6	38.2	40.8	37.7	43.9	21.5	19.5	23.4	61.7	56.3	66.5
2013	33.6	30.2	37.0	34.3	30.8	37.9	40.4	37.1	43.8	20.1	16.8	23.1	59.0	54.3	63.2
2012	33.5	29.8	37.2	33.7	29.9	37.6	39.8	36.0	43.6	22.7	18.5	26.2	60.8	56.8	64.5
2011	32.2	28.4	36.1	33.1	29.2	37.4	39.2	35.5	43.0	19.6	16.1	22.8	56.2	51.5	60.6
2010	31.7	27.8	35.7	32.7	28.8	37.0	38.6	34.8	42.4	19.0	14.8	22.9	55.4	52.0	58.6
2009	30.6	26.6	34.8	31.3	27.0	36.0	37.2	32.6	42.0	19.0	15.2	22.4	59.3	58.0	60.6
2008	30.8	26.8	34.9	31.1	26.7	35.9	37.1	32.6	41.7	20.6	18.7	22.3	59.4	55.1	63.5
2007	29.6	26.3	33.0	29.8	25.8	34.0	35.5	31.9	39.2	18.9	17.9	19.9	60.9	59.8	62.0
2006	28.4	25.3	31.6	28.3	25.0	31.7	34.3	31.4	37.2	18.6	14.9	21.6	60.9	59.8	61.9
2005	28.8	25.5	32.2	28.9	25.3	32.7	34.5	30.7	38.2	17.4	14.1	20.1	61.6	60.5	62.5
2004	28.7	26.1	31.4	28.9	25.8	32.1	34.5	31.4	37.5	16.9	13.4	19.7	61.4	62.0	60.9
2003	28.4	26.0	30.9	28.3	25.3	31.5	34.2	31.4	37.1	17.2	17.5	17.0	61.6	60.9	62.3
2002	29.3	26.9	31.8	29.7	26.5	33.1	35.9	32.6	39.2	17.5	17.4	17.7	NA	NA	NA
2001	28.4	25.5	31.3	28.5	25.1	32.1	33.7	30.4	36.9	16.8	15.6	17.9	NA	NA	NA
2000	29.1	27.9	30.1	29.6	27.8	31.3	34.0	32.3	35.8	17.5	18.1	17.0	NA	NA	NA
1999	28.2	26.8	29.5	29.3	27.6	30.9	33.6	32.0	35.1	15.0	13.1	16.5	NA	NA	NA
1998	27.3	25.6	29.0	28.4	26.5	30.4	32.3	30.5	34.2	15.8	14.2	17.0	NA	NA	NA
1997	27.8	26.3	29.3	28.9	27.2	30.7	32.6	31.2	34.1	14.4	12.1	16.4	NA	NA	NA
1996	27.1	26.1	28.2	28.1	27.2	29.1	31.6	30.9	32.3	14.6	12.4	16.4	NA	NA	NA
1995	24.7	24.5	24.9	26.0	25.4	26.6	28.8	28.4	29.2	15.3	17.2	13.6	NA	NA	NA
1994	23.3	22.5	24.0	24.2	23.6	24.8	27.1	26.8	27.4	13.7	11.7	15.4	NA	NA	NA
1993	23.7	23.4	23.9	24.7	24.4	25.1	27.2	27.2	27.1	13.2	12.6	13.8	NA	NA	NA
1992	23.6	23.2	24.0	25.0	24.2	25.7	NA	NA	NA	11.3	12.0	10.6	NA	NA	NA
1991	23.2	23.0	23.4	24.6	24.1	25.0	NA	NA	NA	11.0	11.5	10.6	NA	NA	NA
1990	23.2	23.7	22.8	24.2	24.2	24.3	NA	NA	NA	13.4	15.1	11.9	NA	NA	NA
1989	23.4	23.9	22.9	24.4	24.8	24.0	NA	NA	NA	12.7	12.0	13.3	NA	NA	NA
1988	22.5	23.2	21.9	23.5	24.0	22.9	NA	NA	NA	12.2	12.6	11.9	NA	NA	NA
1987	22.0	22.3	21.7	23.0	23.3	22.8	NA	NA	NA	11.4	11.6	11.1	NA	NA	NA
1986	22.4	22.9	21.9	23.5	24.1	22.9	NA	NA	NA	11.8	10.1	13.3	NA	NA	NA
1985	22.2	23.1	21.3	23.2	24.2	22.2	NA	NA	NA	11.5	10.3	12.6	NA	NA	NA
1984	21.9	23.2	20.7	23.1	24.3	21.9	NA	NA	NA	11.6	12.9	10.5	NA	NA	NA
1983	22.5	23.9	21.1	23.4	25.0	21.8	NA	NA	NA	12.9	13.1	12.8	NA	NA	NA
1982	21.7	23.3	20.2	22.7	24.5	20.9	NA	NA	NA	12.6	11.8	13.2	NA	NA	NA
1981	21.3	23.1	19.6	22.4	24.3	20.5	NA	NA	NA	11.6	12.1	11.1	NA	NA	NA
1980	22.5	24.0	21.0	23.7	25.5	22.0	NA	NA	NA	11.6	10.5	12.5	NA	NA	NA
1979	23.1	25.6	20.5	24.3	27.1	21.5	NA	NA	NA	12.4	13.3	11.7	NA	NA	NA
1978	23.3	26.0	20.6	24.5	27.6	21.4	NA	NA	NA	11.8	10.7	12.6	NA	NA	NA
1977	24.0	27.0	21.1	25.3	28.5	22.1	NA	NA	NA	12.6	12.8	12.4	NA	NA	NA
1976	23.7	27.5	20.1	24.6	28.7	20.6	NA	NA	NA	13.0	12.0	13.6	NA	NA	NA
1975	21.9	25.1	18.7	22.8	26.3	19.4	NA	NA	NA	10.7	11.4	10.1	NA	NA	NA
1974	20.7	23.9	17.6	22.0	25.3	18.8	NA	NA	NA	7.9	8.8	7.2	NA	NA	NA
1973	19.0	21.6	16.4	19.9	22.8	17.0	NA	NA	NA	8.1	7.1	8.8	NA	NA	NA
1972	19.0	22.0	16.0	19.9	23.1	16.7	NA	NA	NA	8.3	7.1	9.4	NA	NA	NA
1971	16.9	20.1	13.8	17.9	21.3	14.6	NA	NA	NA	6.4	6.4	6.5	NA	NA	NA
1970	16.4	20.0	12.9	17.3	21.3	13.3	NA	NA	NA	7.3	6.7	8.0	NA	NA	NA
1969	16.0	19.4	12.8	17.0	20.6	13.4	NA	NA	NA	6.7	8.1	5.5	NA	NA	NA
1968	14.7	18.0	11.6	15.6	19.1	12.3	NA	NA	NA	5.3	5.3	5.3	NA	NA	NA
1967	14.6	17.2	12.1	15.5	18.3	12.7	NA	NA	NA	5.4	4.2	6.3	NA	NA	NA
1966	14.0	16.8	11.3	14.7	17.9	11.8	NA	NA	NA	5.9	5.4	6.4	NA	NA	NA
1965	12.4	15.6	9.5	13.0	16.4	9.8	NA	NA	NA	6.8	7.3	6.8	NA	NA	NA
1964	12.8	16.6	9.2	13.6	17.5	9.9	NA	NA	NA	5.5	7.5	3.9	NA	NA	NA
1962	13.1	17.2	9.2	14.3	18.7	10.0	NA	NA	NA	4.2	5.7	3.0	NA	NA	NA
1959	11.1	14.8	7.6	11.9	15.9	8.1	NA	NA	NA	4.6	5.6	3.7	NA	NA	NA
1957	10.4	13.5	7.5	11.1	14.5	7.8	NA	NA	NA	4.1	3.3	5.0	NA	NA	NA
1952	10.1	13.8	6.7	NA	NA	NA	NA	NA	NA	4.6	3.2	5.8	NA	NA	NA
1950	7.7	9.6	5.9	NA	NA	NA	NA	NA	NA	2.9	2.4	3.2	NA	NA	NA
1947	5.6	5.8	5.4	5.9	6.2	5.7	NA	NA	NA	2.8	2.6	2.9	NA	NA	NA
1940	5.9	6.9	4.9	6.4	7.5	5.3	NA	NA	NA	1.6	1.5	1.7	NA	NA	NA

Note: Starting in 2001, data are from the expanded CPS sample.
[1]Data in the column labeled "Black" include Black and other races from 1940 to 1962: from 1963 to 2003, data are for the Black population only.

Table A-32. Percent of People 25 Years and Over Who Have Completed High School or College, by Race, Hispanic Origin, and Sex, Selected Years, 1940–2018—*Continued*

(Percent; civilian noninstitutionalized population.)

Age and Year	Hispanic (of any race)			White alone or in combination			Non-Hispanic White alone or in combination			Black alone or in combination			Asian alone or in combination		
	Total	Male	Female	Total	Male	Female	Total	Male	Female	Total	Male	Female	Total	Male	Female
Completed 4 Years of College or More															
2018	20.7	18.4	23.2	37.5	33.2	42	43.1	38.4	47.9	22	18	25.5	67.5	66.3	68.7
2017	18.5	15.0	22.4	36.2	32.1	40.4	41.8	37.5	46.3	22.4	20.6	24.1	61.2	56.9	65.7
2016	18.7	16.2	21.5	36.7	33.2	40.4	42.5	38.9	46.1	22.9	20.1	25.4	63.2	58.3	67.8
2015	16.4	14.5	18.5	36.4	33.0	40.0	42.6	39.1	46.3	20.7	17.0	24.1	63.5	60.6	66.3
2014	15.1	12.4	18.3	34.5	31.2	38.0	40.6	37.4	43.8	21.4	18.7	23.9	60.0	54.4	65.3
2013	15.7	13.1	18.6	34.1	30.6	37.7	40.1	36.8	43.5	19.8	16.6	22.8	58.1	53.7	62.2
2012	14.8	12.5	17.4	33.5	29.8	37.4	39.6	35.9	43.4	22.8	18.1	27.0	59.6	55.7	63.4
2011	12.8	9.6	16.8	33.0	29.0	37.1	39.0	35.4	42.7	19.8	16.3	22.9	55.7	52.0	59.1
2010	13.5	10.8	16.8	32.6	28.6	36.8	38.4	34.6	42.3	19.3	14.8	23.5	53.7	49.6	57.6
2009	12.2	11.0	13.8	31.1	26.8	35.9	37.1	32.4	41.9	19.0	15.0	22.6	58.0	56.7	59.3
2008	12.4	10.0	15.5	31.0	26.6	35.8	36.9	32.4	41.5	20.9	19.3	22.3	57.4	52.9	61.8
2007	11.6	8.6	15.4	29.7	25.7	33.8	35.3	31.7	39.0	19.1	18.1	19.9	59.0	57.8	60.1
2006	9.5	6.9	12.8	28.1	24.8	31.6	34.1	31.2	37.0	18.9	15.0	22.3	59.4	58.4	60.5
2005	11.2	10.2	12.4	28.8	25.3	32.5	34.3	30.6	38.1	17.6	14.6	20.3	60.3	59.0	61.5
2004	10.9	9.6	12.4	28.7	25.7	31.8	34.2	31.2	37.2	16.8	13.4	19.5	59.9	61.1	58.9
2003	10.0	8.4	12.0	28.2	25.2	31.4	34.0	31.2	36.9	17.3	17.4	17.3	60.3	58.8	61.7
2002	8.9	8.3	9.7	NA	NA	NA	NA	NA	NA	NA	NA	NA	NA	NA	NA
2001	10.5	8.2	13.3	NA	NA	NA	NA	NA	NA	NA	NA	NA	NA	NA	NA
2000	9.7	8.3	11.0	NA	NA	NA	NA	NA	NA	NA	NA	NA	NA	NA	NA
1999	8.9	7.5	10.4	NA	NA	NA	NA	NA	NA	NA	NA	NA	NA	NA	NA
1998	10.4	9.5	11.3	NA	NA	NA	NA	NA	NA	NA	NA	NA	NA	NA	NA
1997	11.0	9.6	10.1	NA	NA	NA	NA	NA	NA	NA	NA	NA	NA	NA	NA
1996	10.0	10.2	9.8	NA	NA	NA	NA	NA	NA	NA	NA	NA	NA	NA	NA
1995	8.9	7.8	10.1	NA	NA	NA	NA	NA	NA	NA	NA	NA	NA	NA	NA
1994	8.0	6.6	9.8	NA	NA	NA	NA	NA	NA	NA	NA	NA	NA	NA	NA
1993	8.3	7.1	9.8	NA	NA	NA	NA	NA	NA	NA	NA	NA	NA	NA	NA
1992	9.5	8.8	10.3	NA	NA	NA	NA	NA	NA	NA	NA	NA	NA	NA	NA
1991	9.2	8.1	10.4	NA	NA	NA	NA	NA	NA	NA	NA	NA	NA	NA	NA
1990	8.1	7.3	9.1	NA	NA	NA	NA	NA	NA	NA	NA	NA	NA	NA	NA
1989	10.1	9.6	10.6	NA	NA	NA	NA	NA	NA	NA	NA	NA	NA	NA	NA
1988	11.4	12.1	10.6	NA	NA	NA	NA	NA	NA	NA	NA	NA	NA	NA	NA
1987	8.7	9.2	8.2	NA	NA	NA	NA	NA	NA	NA	NA	NA	NA	NA	NA
1986	9.0	8.9	9.1	NA	NA	NA	NA	NA	NA	NA	NA	NA	NA	NA	NA
1985	11.1	10.9	11.2	NA	NA	NA	NA	NA	NA	NA	NA	NA	NA	NA	NA
1984	10.6	9.6	11.6	NA	NA	NA	NA	NA	NA	NA	NA	NA	NA	NA	NA
1983	10.4	9.6	11.1	NA	NA	NA	NA	NA	NA	NA	NA	NA	NA	NA	NA
1982	9.7	10.7	8.7	NA	NA	NA	NA	NA	NA	NA	NA	NA	NA	NA	NA
1981	7.5	8.6	6.5	NA	NA	NA	NA	NA	NA	NA	NA	NA	NA	NA	NA
1980	7.7	8.4	6.9	NA	NA	NA	NA	NA	NA	NA	NA	NA	NA	NA	NA
1979	7.3	7.9	6.8	NA	NA	NA	NA	NA	NA	NA	NA	NA	NA	NA	NA
1978	9.6	9.6	9.7	NA	NA	NA	NA	NA	NA	NA	NA	NA	NA	NA	NA
1977	6.7	7.2	6.4	NA	NA	NA	NA	NA	NA	NA	NA	NA	NA	NA	NA
1976	7.4	10.3	4.8	NA	NA	NA	NA	NA	NA	NA	NA	NA	NA	NA	NA
1975	8.8	10.0	7.3	NA	NA	NA	NA	NA	NA	NA	NA	NA	NA	NA	NA
1974	5.7	7.2	4.6	NA	NA	NA	NA	NA	NA	NA	NA	NA	NA	NA	NA
1973	NA	NA	NA	NA	NA	NA	NA	NA	NA	NA	NA	NA	NA	NA	NA
1972	NA	NA	NA	NA	NA	NA	NA	NA	NA	NA	NA	NA	NA	NA	NA
1971	NA	NA	NA	NA	NA	NA	NA	NA	NA	NA	NA	NA	NA	NA	NA
1970	NA	NA	NA	NA	NA	NA	NA	NA	NA	NA	NA	NA	NA	NA	NA
1969	NA	NA	NA	NA	NA	NA	NA	NA	NA	NA	NA	NA	NA	NA	NA
1968	NA	NA	NA	NA	NA	NA	NA	NA	NA	NA	NA	NA	NA	NA	NA
1967	NA	NA	NA	NA	NA	NA	NA	NA	NA	NA	NA	NA	NA	NA	NA
1966	NA	NA	NA	NA	NA	NA	NA	NA	NA	NA	NA	NA	NA	NA	NA
1965	NA	NA	NA	NA	NA	NA	NA	NA	NA	NA	NA	NA	NA	NA	NA
1964	NA	NA	NA	NA	NA	NA	NA	NA	NA	NA	NA	NA	NA	NA	NA
1962	NA	NA	NA	NA	NA	NA	NA	NA	NA	NA	NA	NA	NA	NA	NA
1959	NA	NA	NA	NA	NA	NA	NA	NA	NA	NA	NA	NA	NA	NA	NA
1957	NA	NA	NA	NA	NA	NA	NA	NA	NA	NA	NA	NA	NA	NA	NA
1952	NA	NA	NA	NA	NA	NA	NA	NA	NA	NA	NA	NA	NA	NA	NA
1950	NA	NA	NA	NA	NA	NA	NA	NA	NA	NA	NA	NA	NA	NA	NA
1947	NA	NA	NA	NA	NA	NA	NA	NA	NA	NA	NA	NA	NA	NA	NA
1940	NA	NA	NA	NA	NA	NA	NA	NA	NA	NA	NA	NA	NA	NA	NA

Note: Starting in 2001, data are from the expanded CPS sample.

Table A-33. Years of School Completed by People 25 Years Old and Over, by Age and Sex, Selected Years, 1940–2018

(Numbers in thousands; civilian noninstitutionalized population, except where noted.)

Year, sex, and age	Total	Elementary		High school		College		Median years
		0 to 4 years	5 to 8 years	1 to 3 years	4 years	1 to 3 years	4 years or more	

(header spanning: "Years of school completed" over Elementary/High school/College)

Year, sex, and age	Total	0 to 4 years	5 to 8 years	1 to 3 years	4 years	1 to 3 years	4 years or more	Median years
25 YEARS OLD AND OVER								
Both Sexes								
2018	219,830	2,129	6,600	13,682	62,685	57,810	76,924	NA
2017	216,921	2,208	6,600	13,734	62,512	57,765	74,103	NA
2016	215,015	2,414	7,078	13,961	62,002	57,660	71,900	NA
2015	212,132	2,601	7,295	14,686	62,575	56,031	68,945	NA
2014	209,287	2,525	7,388	14,545	62,240	55,709	66,879	NA
2013	206,899	2,344	7,578	14,595	61,704	55,173	65,506	NA
2012	204,579	2,484	7,800	14,993	62,113	53,900	63,291	NA
2011	201,543	2,589	7,688	14,763	61,911	53,249	61,343	NA
2010	199,928	2,615	7,836	15,260	62,456	51,920	59,840	NA
2009	198,285	2,785	8,043	15,587	61,626	51,670	58,574	NA
2008	196,305	2,599	8,226	15,516	61,183	50,994	57,787	NA
2007	194,318	2,830	8,462	16,451	61,490	49,243	55,842	NA
2006	191,884	2,951	8,791	16,154	60,898	49,371	53,720	NA
2005	189,367	2,983	8,935	16,099	60,893	48,076	52,381	NA
2004	186,876	2,858	8,888	15,999	59,811	47,571	51,749	NA
2003	185,183	2,915	9,361	16,323	59,292	46,910	50,383	NA
2002	182,142	2,902	9,668	16,378	58,456	46,042	48,696	NA
2001	180,389	2,810	9,518	16,279	58,272	46,281	47,228	NA
2000	175,230	2,742	9,438	15,674	58,086	44,445	44,845	NA
1999	173,754	2,742	9,655	15,674	57,935	43,176	43,803	NA
1998	172,211	2,834	9,948	16,776	58,174	42,506	41,973	NA
1997	170,581	2,840	10,472	17,211	57,586	41,774	40,697	NA
1996	168,323	3,027	10,595	17,102	56,559	41,372	39,668	NA
1995	166,438	3,074	10,873	16,566	56,450	41,249	38,226	NA
1994	164,512	3,156	11,359	16,925	56,515	40,014	36,544	NA
1993	162,826	3,380	11,747	17,067	57,589	37,451	35,590	NA
1992	160,827	3,449	11,989	17,672	57,860	35,520	34,337	NA
1991	158,694	3,803	13,046	17,379	61,272	29,170	34,026	12.7
1990	156,538	3,833	13,758	17,461	60,119	28,075	33,291	12.7
1989	154,155	3,861	14,061	17,719	59,336	26,614	32,565	12.7
1988	151,635	3,714	14,550	17,847	58,940	25,799	30,787	12.7
1987	149,144	3,640	15,301	17,417	57,669	25,479	29,637	12.7
1986	146,606	3,894	15,672	17,484	56,338	24,729	28,489	12.6
1985	143,524	3,873	16,020	17,553	54,866	23,405	27,808	12.6
1984	140,794	3,884	16,258	17,433	54,073	22,281	26,862	12.6
1983	138,020	4,119	16,714	17,681	52,060	21,531	25,915	12.6
1982	135,526	4,119	17,232	18,006	51,426	20,692	24,050	12.6
1981	132,899	4,358	17,868	18,041	49,915	20,042	22,674	12.5
1980	130,409	4,390	18,426	18,086	47,934	19,379	22,193	12.5
1979	125,295	4,324	18,504	17,579	45,915	18,393	20,579	12.5
1978	123,019	4,445	19,309	18,175	44,381	17,379	19,332	12.4
1977	120,870	4,509	19,567	18,318	43,602	16,247	18,627	12.4
1976	118,848	4,601	19,912	18,204	43,157	15,477	17,496	12.4
1975	116,897	4,912	20,633	18,237	42,353	14,518	16,244	12.3
1974	115,005	5,106	21,200	18,274	41,460	13,665	15,300	12.3
1973	112,866	5,100	21,838	18,420	40,448	12,831	14,228	12.3
1972	111,133	5,124	22,503	18,855	39,171	12,117	13,364	12.2
1971	110,627	5,574	24,029	18,601	38,029	11,782	12,612	12.2
1970	109,310	5,747	24,519	18,682	37,134	11,164	12,062	12.2
1969	107,750	6,014	24,976	18,527	36,133	10,564	11,535	12.1
1968	106,469	6,248	25,467	18,724	34,603	10,254	11,171	12.1
1967	104,864	6,400	26,178	18,647	33,173	9,914	10,550	12.0
1966	103,876	6,705	26,478	18,859	32,391	9,235	10,212	12.0
1965	103,245	6,982	27,063	18,617	31,703	9,139	9,742	11.8
1964	102,421	7,295	27,551	18,419	30,728	9,085	9,345	11.7
1962	100,664	7,826	28,438	17,751	28,477	9,170	9,002	11.4
1960	99,465	8,303	31,218	19,140	24,440	8,747	7,617	10.6
1959	97,478	7,816	28,490	17,520	26,219	7,888	7,734	11.0
1957	95,630	8,561	29,316	16,951	24,832	6,985	7,172	10.6
1952	88,358	8,004	30,274	15,228	21,074	6,714	6,118	10.1
1950	87,484	9,491	31,617	14,817	17,625	6,246	5,272	9.3

Note: Starting in 2012, data were created using population controls based on 2010 Census data. Starting in 2001, data were created using population controls based on Census 2000 data. Also starting in 2001, data are from the expanded CPS sample. Begining with data for 1992, a new question results in different categories than for earlier years. Data shown as 'High School, 4 years' are now collected in the category 'High School Graduate.' Data shown as 'College 1 to 3 years' are now collected in the 'Some college' and the two 'Associate degree' categories. Data shown as 'College 4 years or more,' are now collected in the categories, 'Bachelor's degree,' 'Master's degree,' 'Doctorate degree,' and 'Professional degree.' Due to the change in question format, median years of schooling cannot be derived. Total includes persons who did not report on years of school completed.

Table A-33. Years of School Completed by People 25 Years Old and Over, by Age and Sex, Selected Years, 1940–2018—*Continued*

(Numbers in thousands; civilian noninstitutionalized population, except where noted.)

Year, sex, and age	Total	Elementary 0 to 4 years	Elementary 5 to 8 years	High school 1 to 3 years	High school 4 years	College 1 to 3 years	College 4 years or more	Median years
1947	82,578	8,611	32,308	13,487	16,926	5,533	4,424	9.0
1940	74,776	10,105	34,413	11,182	10,552	4,075	3,407	8.6
Male								
2018	105,862	973	3,284	6,939	31,325	26,668	36,674	NA
2017	104,324	1,090	3,312	6,934	31,296	26,581	35,112	NA
2016	103,372	1,183	3,513	7,144	30,780	26,468	34,283	NA
2015	101,887	1,243	3,669	7,278	30,997	25,778	32,923	NA
2014	100,592	1,184	3,761	7,403	30,718	25,430	32,095	NA
2013	99,305	1,127	3,836	7,314	30,014	25,283	31,731	NA
2012	98,119	1,237	3,879	7,388	30,216	24,632	30,766	NA
2011	97,220	1,234	3,883	7,443	30,370	24,319	29,971	NA
2010	96,325	1,279	3,931	7,705	30,682	23,570	29,158	NA
2009	95,518	1,372	4,027	7,754	30,025	23,634	28,706	NA
2008	94,470	1,310	4,136	7,853	29,491	23,247	28,433	NA
2007	93,421	1,458	4,249	8,294	29,604	22,219	27,596	NA
2006	92,233	1,472	4,395	7,940	29,380	22,136	26,910	NA
2005	90,899	1,505	4,402	7,787	29,151	21,794	26,259	NA
2004	89,558	1,496	4,308	7,766	27,889	21,763	26,336	NA
2003	88,597	1,482	4,566	8,026	27,356	21,568	25,598	NA
2002	86,996	1,457	4,743	7,894	26,947	21,127	24,828	NA
2001	86,096	1,419	4,673	7,615	26,956	21,120	24,313	NA
2000	83,611	1,341	4,577	7,298	26,651	20,493	23,252	NA
1999	82,917	1,339	4,651	7,736	26,368	20,043	22,782	NA
1998	82,376	1,431	4,727	8,017	26,575	19,792	21,832	NA
1997	81,620	1,454	5,023	8,212	26,226	19,332	21,374	NA
1996	80,339	1,537	5,067	7,930	25,649	19,301	20,854	NA
1995	79,463	1,598	5,231	7,691	25,378	18,933	20,631	NA
1994	78,539	1,669	5,427	7,789	25,404	18,544	19,705	NA
1993	77,644	1,709	5,594	7,821	25,766	17,521	19,234	NA
1992	76,579	1,737	5,726	8,085	25,774	16,631	18,627	NA
1991	75,487	2,018	6,299	7,887	27,189	13,720	18,373	12.8
1990	74,421	2,004	6,557	8,000	26,426	13,271	18,164	12.8
1989	73,225	1,956	6,659	8,076	25,897	12,725	17,913	12.8
1988	71,911	1,852	6,849	8,247	25,638	12,057	17,268	12.7
1987	70,677	1,794	7,259	7,909	24,998	12,062	16,654	12.7
1986	69,503	1,978	7,446	7,872	24,260	11,856	16,091	12.7
1985	67,756	1,947	7,629	7,783	23,552	11,164	15,682	12.7
1984	66,350	1,945	7,688	7,837	22,990	10,678	15,211	12.7
1983	65,004	2,103	7,750	7,867	22,048	10,310	14,926	12.7
1982	63,764	2,074	7,987	7,960	21,749	10,020	13,974	12.6
1981	62,509	2,141	8,322	8,084	21,019	9,734	13,208	12.6
1980	61,389	2,212	8,627	8,046	20,080	9,593	12,832	12.6
1979	58,986	2,190	8,785	7,636	19,250	9,100	12,025	12.6
1978	57,922	2,230	9,195	7,821	18,620	8,657	11,398	12.5
1977	56,917	2,296	9,330	7,969	18,290	8,104	10,926	12.5
1976	55,902	2,371	9,463	7,923	18,048	7,699	10,397	12.5
1975	55,036	2,568	9,760	7,985	17,769	7,274	9,679	12.4
1974	54,167	2,637	10,186	7,966	17,488	6,756	9,135	12.4
1973	53,067	2,598	10,488	8,120	17,011	6,376	8,473	12.3
1972	52,351	2,634	10,854	8,413	16,424	5,972	8,055	12.3
1971	52,357	2,933	11,703	8,264	16,008	5,798	7,653	12.2
1970	51,784	3,031	11,925	8,355	15,571	5,580	7,321	12.2
1969	51,031	3,095	12,182	8,398	15,177	5,263	6,917	12.1
1968	50,510	3,261	12,407	8,564	14,613	4,945	6,721	12.1
1967	49,756	3,417	12,736	8,463	14,015	4,755	6,372	12.0
1966	49,410	3,614	12,992	8,611	13,672	4,342	6,180	11.8
1965	49,242	3,774	13,308	8,529	13,334	4,370	5,923	11.7
1964	48,975	3,959	13,467	8,537	12,902	4,394	5,714	11.5
1962	48,283	4,213	13,927	8,399	11,932	4,315	5,497	11.1
1960	47,997	4,522	15,562	8,988	10,175	4,127	4,626	10.3
1959	47,041	4,257	14,039	8,326	10,870	3,801	4,765	10.7
1957	46,208	4,610	14,634	8,003	10,230	3,347	4,359	10.3

Note: Starting in 2012, data were created using population controls based on 2010 Census data. Starting in 2001, data were created using population controls based on Census 2000 data. Also starting in 2001, data are from the expanded CPS sample. Begining with data for 1992, a new question results in different categories than for earlier years. Data shown as 'High School, 4 years' are now collected in the category 'High School Graduate.' Data shown as 'College 1 to 3 years' are now collected in the 'Some college' and the two 'Associate degree' categories. Data shown as 'College 4 years or more,' are now collected in the categories, 'Bachelor's degree,' 'Master's degree,' 'Doctorate degree,' and 'Professional degree.' Due to the change in question format, median years of schooling cannot be derived. Total includes persons who did not report on years of school completed.

Table A-33. Years of School Completed by People 25 Years Old and Over, by Age and Sex, Selected Years, 1940–2018—*Continued*

(Numbers in thousands; civilian noninstitutionalized population, except where noted.)

Year, sex, and age	Total	Years of school completed						Median years
		Elementary		High school		College		
		0 to 4 years	5 to 8 years	1 to 3 years	4 years	1 to 3 years	4 years or more	
1952	42,368	4,396	14,876	7,048	8,760	3,164	3,480	9.7
1950	42,627	5,074	15,852	6,974	7,511	2,888	3,008	9.0
1947	40,483	4,615	16,086	6,535	7,353	2,625	2,478	8.9
1940	37,463	5,550	17,639	5,333	4,507	1,824	2,021	8.6
Female								
2018	113,969	1,156	3,316	6,743	31,360	31,142	40,251	NA
2017	112,597	1,117	3,288	6,799	31,216	31,185	38,991	NA
2016	111,643	1,231	3,565	6,817	31,221	31,192	37,617	NA
2015	110,245	1,358	3,626	7,408	31,578	30,253	36,021	NA
2014	108,695	1,341	3,627	7,142	31,522	30,279	34,784	NA
2013	107,594	1,217	3,741	7,282	31,690	29,890	33,775	NA
2012	106,460	1,246	3,920	7,604	31,898	29,267	32,524	NA
2011	104,323	1,355	3,806	7,320	31,541	28,930	31,372	NA
2010	103,603	1,336	3,904	7,555	31,774	28,350	30,683	NA
2009	102,767	1,413	4,016	7,833	31,601	28,036	29,868	NA
2008	101,835	1,289	4,090	7,663	31,692	27,747	29,354	NA
2007	100,897	1,371	4,213	8,157	31,887	27,024	28,245	NA
2006	99,651	1,479	4,395	8,215	31,518	27,234	26,810	NA
2005	98,467	1,477	4,532	8,311	31,742	26,283	26,122	NA
2004	97,319	1,363	4,580	8,233	31,921	25,808	25,413	NA
2003	96,586	1,433	4,795	8,297	31,936	25,342	24,784	NA
2002	95,146	1,445	4,926	8,484	31,509	24,915	23,868	NA
2001	94,293	1,392	4,845	8,664	31,316	25,161	22,915	NA
2000	91,620	1,400	4,861	8,378	31,435	23,953	21,594	NA
1999	90,837	1,404	5,004	8,707	31,566	23,133	21,021	NA
1998	89,835	1,403	5,220	8,758	31,599	22,714	20,142	NA
1997	88,961	1,387	5,450	8,999	31,360	22,442	19,323	NA
1996	87,984	1,491	5,528	9,171	30,911	22,071	18,813	NA
1995	86,975	1,476	5,642	8,874	31,072	22,317	17,594	NA
1994	85,973	1,487	5,932	9,135	31,111	21,470	16,838	NA
1993	85,181	1,672	6,154	9,246	31,823	19,930	16,357	NA
1992	84,248	1,712	6,263	9,587	32,086	18,889	15,709	NA
1991	83,207	1,784	6,747	9,491	34,083	15,449	15,652	12.7
1990	82,116	1,829	7,200	9,462	33,693	14,806	15,126	12.7
1989	80,930	1,904	7,402	9,643	33,440	13,888	14,652	12.6
1988	79,724	1,862	7,700	9,599	33,303	13,741	13,519	12.6
1987	78,467	1,846	8,042	9,508	32,671	13,417	12,983	12.6
1986	77,102	1,916	8,226	9,612	32,078	12,874	12,399	12.6
1985	75,768	1,926	8,390	9,770	31,314	12,242	12,126	12.6
1984	74,444	1,939	8,571	9,596	31,083	11,603	11,651	12.6
1983	73,016	2,015	8,964	9,814	30,012	11,220	10,990	12.5
1982	71,762	2,045	9,245	10,046	29,677	10,673	10,076	12.5
1981	70,390	2,217	9,545	9,957	28,896	10,309	9,466	12.5
1980	69,020	2,178	9,800	10,040	27,854	9,786	9,362	12.4
1979	66,309	2,133	9,720	9,945	26,665	9,293	8,554	12.4
1978	65,097	2,214	10,114	10,353	25,761	8,721	7,934	12.4
1977	63,953	2,213	10,236	10,349	25,312	8,142	7,701	12.4
1976	62,946	2,230	10,449	10,281	25,109	7,779	7,098	12.3
1975	61,861	2,344	10,871	10,252	24,584	7,243	6,565	12.3
1974	60,838	2,469	11,015	10,308	23,972	6,910	6,165	12.3
1973	59,799	2,502	11,350	10,300	23,437	6,454	5,755	12.2
1972	58,782	2,490	11,649	10,442	22,746	6,145	5,309	12.2
1971	58,270	2,641	12,327	10,339	22,021	5,984	4,959	12.2
1970	57,527	2,716	12,595	10,327	21,563	5,584	4,743	12.1
1969	56,719	2,919	12,796	10,131	20,955	5,301	4,619	12.1
1968	55,959	2,987	13,060	10,160	19,991	5,309	4,450	12.1
1967	55,107	2,985	13,439	10,185	19,157	5,162	4,178	12.0
1966	54,467	3,090	13,488	10,246	18,719	4,892	4,032	12.0
1965	54,004	3,207	13,753	10,085	18,369	4,767	3,820	12.0
1964	53,447	3,333	14,086	9,881	17,825	4,686	3,629	11.8
1962	52,381	3,613	14,511	9,352	16,545	4,855	3,505	11.6
1960	51,468	3,781	15,656	10,151	14,267	4,620	2,991	10.9

Note: Starting in 2012, data were created using population controls based on 2010 Census data. Starting in 2001, data were created using population controls based on Census 2000 data. Also starting in 2001, data are from the expanded CPS sample. Begining with data for 1992, a new question results in different categories than for earlier years. Data shown as 'High School, 4 years' are now collected in the category 'High School Graduate.' Data shown as 'College 1 to 3 years' are now collected in the 'Some college' and the two 'Associate degree' categories. Data shown as 'College 4 years or more,' are now collected in the categories, 'Bachelor's degree,' 'Master's degree,' 'Doctorate degree,' and 'Professional degree.' Due to the change in question format, median years of schooling cannot be derived. Total includes persons who did not report on years of school completed.

Table A-33. Years of School Completed by People 25 Years Old and Over, by Age and Sex, Selected Years, 1940–2018—*Continued*

(Numbers in thousands; civilian noninstitutionalized population, except where noted.)

| Year, sex, and age | Total | Elementary | | High school | | College | | Median years |
		0 to 4 years	5 to 8 years	1 to 3 years	4 years	1 to 3 years	4 years or more	
1959	50,437	3,559	14,451	9,194	15,349	4,087	2,969	11.2
1957	49,422	3,951	14,682	8,948	14,602	3,638	2,813	10.9
1952	45,990	3,608	15,398	8,180	12,314	3,550	2,638	10.4
1950	44,857	4,417	15,824	7,843	10,114	3,358	2,264	9.6
1947	42,095	3,996	16,222	6,952	9,573	2,908	1,946	8.9
1940	37,313	4,554	16,773	5,849	6,044	2,251	1,386	8.7
25 TO 34 YEARS								
Both Sexes								
2018	44,854	182	776	2,435	11,460	12,501	17,501	NA
2017	44,250	218	732	2,532	11,494	12,792	16,482	NA
2016	43,763	210	858	2,656	11,224	12,609	16,207	NA
2015	43,006	292	863	2,938	10,965	12,420	15,528	NA
2014	42,466	286	946	3,018	11,040	12,178	14,997	NA
2013	41,797	260	1,035	3,116	10,950	11,955	14,481	NA
2012	41,219	273	1,063	3,079	10,974	11,765	14,065	NA
2011	41,584	318	1,140	3,098	11,250	12,046	13,731	NA
2010	41,085	323	1,169	3,271	11,186	11,655	13,480	NA
2009	40,520	321	1,226	3,202	11,351	11,409	13,010	NA
2008	40,146	282	1,189	3,296	11,297	11,113	12,969	NA
2007	39,868	380	1,283	3,462	11,408	10,961	12,375	NA
2006	39,481	359	1,410	3,375	11,302	11,229	11,806	NA
2005	39,310	414	1,375	3,422	11,269	10,865	11,965	NA
2004	39,201	430	1,399	3,239	11,244	11,044	11,844	NA
2003	39,242	370	1,370	3,336	11,392	10,986	11,791	NA
2002	38,670	433	1,393	3,245	10,988	10,776	11,834	NA
2001	38,865	380	1,317	3,202	11,294	11,146	11,526	NA
2000	37,786	287	1,135	3,052	11,546	10,700	11,066	NA
1999	38,474	280	1,142	3,296	11,826	10,893	11,040	NA
1998	39,354	319	1,207	3,228	12,569	11,220	10,811	NA
1997	40,256	334	1,163	3,624	12,710	11,524	10,892	NA
1996	40,919	418	1,169	3,780	13,087	11,624	10,841	NA
1995	41,388	394	1,264	3,667	14,061	11,659	10,342	NA
1994	41,946	367	1,297	4,057	14,483	11,913	9,829	NA
1993	41,864	382	1,223	3,894	15,036	11,361	9,968	NA
1992	42,493	433	1,250	4,071	16,021	10,860	9,861	NA
1991	42,905	465	1,322	4,178	17,503	9,283	10,153	12.9
1990	43,240	505	1,413	4,041	17,635	9,320	10,326	12.9
1989	43,240	446	1,352	4,013	17,901	9,072	10,454	12.9
1988	42,953	430	1,308	4,095	17,887	9,076	10,155	12.9
1987	42,635	390	1,360	3,995	17,539	9,157	10,196	12.9
1986	42,053	387	1,359	3,797	17,311	9,104	10,094	12.9
1985	40,858	362	1,328	3,703	16,748	8,980	9,737	12.9
1984	40,173	404	1,371	3,638	16,431	8,555	9,771	12.9
1983	39,342	376	1,324	3,664	15,804	8,567	9,605	12.9
1982	38,703	337	1,371	3,598	15,893	8,304	9,200	12.9
1981	37,828	337	1,428	3,665	15,419	8,198	8,782	12.9
1980	36,615	362	1,424	3,571	14,481	7,942	8,836	12.9
1979	34,053	370	1,381	3,452	13,338	7,415	8,096	12.9
1978	33,120	325	1,459	3,515	12,993	7,008	7,821	12.9
1977	32,284	269	1,383	3,715	12,845	6,398	7,676	12.8
1976	31,148	247	1,508	3,619	12,920	5,813	7,041	12.8
1975	30,092	313	1,644	3,743	12,544	5,403	6,443	12.7
1974	28,972	352	1,654	3,763	12,362	5,056	5,785	12.7
1973	27,793	333	1,850	3,915	12,194	4,454	5,047	12.6
1972	26,517	285	1,791	3,981	11,635	4,090	4,734	12.6
1971	25,545	327	2,011	3,986	11,232	3,822	4,169	12.6
1970	24,865	329	1,937	4,251	10,929	3,491	3,926	12.5
1969	24,072	359	2,086	4,140	10,592	3,202	3,693	12.5
1968	23,285	350	2,246	4,129	10,157	2,989	3,413	12.5
1967	22,388	319	2,293	4,017	9,645	2,946	3,169	12.5
1966	22,023	430	2,208	4,158	9,546	2,647	3,037	12.4

Note: Starting in 2012, data were created using population controls based on 2010 Census data. Starting in 2001, data were created using population controls based on Census 2000 data. Also starting in 2001, data are from the expanded CPS sample. Begining with data for 1992, a new question results in different categories than for earlier years. Data shown as 'High School, 4 years' are now collected in the category 'High School Graduate.' Data shown as 'College 1 to 3 years' are now collected in the 'Some college' and the two 'Associate degree' categories. Data shown as 'College 4 years or more,' are now collected in the categories, 'Bachelor's degree,' 'Master's degree,' 'Doctorate degree,' and 'Professional degree.' Due to the change in question format, median years of schooling cannot be derived. Total includes persons who did not report on years of school completed.

Table A-33. Years of School Completed by People 25 Years Old and Over, by Age and Sex, Selected Years, 1940–2018—*Continued*

(Numbers in thousands; civilian noninstitutionalized population, except where noted.)

Year, sex, and age	Total	Years of school completed						Median years
		Elementary		High school		College		
		0 to 4 years	5 to 8 years	1 to 3 years	4 years	1 to 3 years	4 years or more	
1965	21,980	543	2,437	4,058	9,500	2,561	2,880	12.4
1964	21,997	502	2,591	4,176	9,370	2,529	2,830	12.4
1962	22,130	597	2,936	4,371	8,815	2,552	2,859	12.4
1960	22,821	709	3,738	5,135	8,166	2,572	2,499	12.4
1959	22,922	761	3,348	4,741	8,979	2,398	2,480	12.3
1957	23,437	750	3,971	4,965	8,927	2,275	2,351	12.2
1952	23,138	844	4,362	4,898	8,620	2,220	2,052	12.2
1950	23,626	1,147	5,308	5,050	7,660	2,198	1,252	11.9
1947	22,627	1,015	5,523	4,997	7,630	1,908	1,378	11.9
1940	21,339	1,377	7,676	4,553	4,702	1,554	1,288	10.0
Male								
2018	22,490	95	432	1,431	6,530	6,047	7,955	NA
2017	22,121	135	390	1,410	6,456	6,267	7,464	NA
2016	21,845	116	468	1,427	6,386	6,015	7,432	NA
2015	21,427	166	488	1,584	6,198	5,920	7,071	NA
2014	21,217	151	512	1,611	6,323	5,910	6,710	NA
2013	20,816	161	582	1,747	6,058	5,749	6,519	NA
2012	20,464	161	579	1,707	6,127	5,619	6,270	NA
2011	20,985	190	657	1,791	6,444	5,750	6,151	NA
2010	20,689	186	641	1,866	6,458	5,587	5,951	NA
2009	20,440	184	695	1,806	6,495	5,508	5,752	NA
2008	20,210	172	714	1,874	6,356	5,277	5,816	NA
2007	20,024	246	757	1,930	6,361	5,137	5,593	NA
2006	19,827	218	834	1,835	6,233	5,336	5,371	NA
2005	19,677	241	769	1,827	6,216	5,198	5,426	NA
2004	19,598	280	793	1,723	6,020	5,286	5,495	NA
2003	19,564	216	771	1,831	6,028	5,252	5,466	NA
2002	19,234	280	809	1,782	5,751	5,131	5,480	NA
2001	19,330	233	748	1,677	6,099	5,161	5,411	NA
2000	18,563	155	593	1,637	5,989	4,870	5,318	NA
1999	18,294	157	616	1,724	6,114	5,052	5,260	NA
1998	19,526	190	654	1,735	6,592	5,233	5,125	NA
1997	20,039	193	629	2,007	6,482	5,477	5,249	NA
1996	20,390	225	601	2,055	6,701	5,536	5,274	NA
1995	20,589	229	708	1,930	7,176	5,373	5,174	NA
1994	20,873	230	716	2,134	7,408	5,510	4,873	NA
1993	20,856	237	679	1,986	7,604	5,308	5,041	NA
1992	21,125	231	682	2,057	8,113	5,116	4,927	NA
1991	21,319	270	694	2,095	8,810	4,441	5,009	12.9
1990	21,462	295	759	2,153	8,649	4,392	5,215	12.9
1989	21,461	251	698	2,129	8,659	4,391	5,335	12.9
1988	21,277	237	651	2,227	8,569	4,273	5,319	12.9
1987	21,142	223	698	2,030	8,544	4,384	5,263	12.9
1986	20,956	227	715	1,887	8,359	4,488	5,279	12.9
1985	20,184	194	700	1,823	7,955	4,433	5,080	12.9
1984	19,876	231	721	1,739	7,798	4,238	5,150	12.9
1983	19,438	213	659	1,724	7,351	4,284	5,207	13.0
1982	19,090	182	659	1,654	7,380	4,162	5,053	13.0
1981	18,625	176	733	1,679	6,991	4,185	4,863	13.0
1980	18,051	198	699	1,639	6,393	4,166	4,957	13.0
1979	16,719	197	695	1,476	5,852	3,862	4,637	13.0
1978	16,263	154	717	1,526	5,701	3,698	4,471	13.1
1977	15,863	134	672	1,625	5,634	3,403	4,396	13.0
1976	15,266	134	724	1,566	5,672	3,085	4,087	12.9
1975	14,776	177	815	1,605	5,508	2,915	3,757	12.9
1974	14,222	211	859	1,617	5,491	2,672	3,372	12.8
1973	13,638	204	966	1,760	5,363	2,416	2,927	12.7
1972	13,030	157	927	1,796	5,150	2,191	2,809	12.7
1971	12,596	170	1,092	1,771	5,049	2,005	2,506	12.6
1970	12,236	189	1,063	1,896	4,833	1,842	2,412	12.6
1969	11,788	204	1,121	1,849	4,652	1,719	2,241	12.6
1968	11,381	193	1,192	1,880	4,473	1,505	2,136	12.5

Note: Starting in 2012, data were created using population controls based on 2010 Census data. Starting in 2001, data were created using population controls based on Census 2000 data. Also starting in 2001, data are from the expanded CPS sample. Begining with data for 1992, a new question results in different categories than for earlier years. Data shown as 'High School, 4 years' are now collected in the category 'High School Graduate.' Data shown as 'College 1 to 3 years' are now collected in the 'Some college' and the two 'Associate degree' categories. Data shown as 'College 4 years or more,' are now collected in the categories, 'Bachelor's degree,' 'Master's degree,' 'Doctorate degree,' and 'Professional degree.' Due to the change in question format, median years of schooling cannot be derived. Total includes persons who did not report on years of school completed.

Table A-33. Years of School Completed by People 25 Years Old and Over, by Age and Sex, Selected Years, 1940–2018—*Continued*

(Numbers in thousands; civilian noninstitutionalized population, except where noted.)

Year, sex, and age	Total	Years of school completed						Median years
		Elementary		High school		College		
		0 to 4 years	5 to 8 years	1 to 3 years	4 years	1 to 3 years	4 years or more	
1967	10,876	170	1,209	1,814	4,187	1,522	1,973	12.5
1966	10,701	241	1,162	1,839	4,191	1,374	1,894	12.5
1965	10,693	325	1,240	1,802	4,188	1,316	1,822	12.5
1964	10,729	297	1,344	1,962	4,008	1,306	1,812	12.4
1962	10,762	334	1,569	2,008	3,700	1,309	1,842	12.4
1960	11,184	420	2,026	2,441	3,356	1,316	1,624	12.2
1959	11,226	416	1,822	2,238	3,682	1,256	1,658	12.3
1957	11,368	423	2,097	2,446	3,542	1,181	1,556	12.2
1952	10,936	502	2,202	2,268	3,458	1,118	1,268	12.1
1950	11,454	631	2,705	2,426	3,250	1,117	1,037	11.5
1947	10,894	544	2,665	2,494	3,337	993	738	11.7
1940	10,521	779	3,932	2,220	2,049	692	744	9.7
Female								
2018	22,364	87	344	1,004	4,930	6,454	9,547	NA
2017	22,129	84	342	1,122	5,037	6,526	9,018	NA
2016	21,918	93	390	1,229	4,838	6,594	8,774	NA
2015	21,579	126	375	1,354	4,767	6,500	8,457	NA
2014	21,248	135	435	1,407	4,717	6,267	8,287	NA
2013	20,981	99	454	1,369	4,892	6,205	7,962	NA
2012	20,755	112	484	1,372	4,847	6,145	7,795	NA
2011	20,599	128	483	1,307	4,806	6,296	7,580	NA
2010	20,396	137	527	1,405	4,728	6,068	7,530	NA
2009	20,079	137	531	1,395	4,856	5,901	7,258	NA
2008	19,937	111	475	1,421	4,941	5,836	7,153	NA
2007	19,843	134	527	1,532	5,047	5,824	6,781	NA
2006	19,654	140	577	1,538	5,069	5,894	6,435	NA
2005	19,633	173	607	1,594	5,053	5,667	6,539	NA
2004	19,603	150	606	1,516	5,224	5,758	6,349	NA
2003	19,679	153	598	1,503	5,364	5,734	6,325	NA
2002	19,436	153	584	1,463	5,237	5,645	6,353	NA
2001	19,536	147	569	1,525	5,195	5,985	6,115	NA
2000	19,222	130	542	1,415	5,557	5,831	5,750	NA
1999	19,551	122	525	1,572	5,712	5,842	5,779	NA
1998	19,828	130	553	1,493	5,977	5,986	5,688	NA
1997	20,217	149	533	1,615	6,227	6,047	5,643	NA
1996	20,528	195	569	1,734	6,386	6,090	5,568	NA
1995	20,800	165	556	1,738	6,885	6,286	5,170	NA
1994	21,073	138	581	1,923	7,075	6,404	4,953	NA
1993	21,007	143	543	1,907	7,432	6,054	4,928	NA
1992	21,368	203	567	2,014	7,908	5,744	4,933	NA
1991	21,586	195	629	2,085	8,693	4,841	5,143	12.9
1990	21,779	209	653	1,889	8,986	4,927	5,112	12.9
1989	21,777	195	654	1,885	9,242	4,681	5,119	12.9
1988	21,675	193	657	1,869	9,319	4,801	4,836	12.9
1987	21,494	168	662	1,965	8,995	4,772	4,932	12.9
1986	21,097	160	644	1,910	8,952	4,616	4,813	12.9
1985	20,673	168	627	1,880	8,794	4,547	4,657	12.9
1984	20,297	173	649	1,904	8,634	4,319	4,621	12.9
1983	19,903	161	665	1,941	8,452	4,285	4,398	12.9
1982	19,614	155	713	1,942	8,512	4,140	4,148	12.8
1981	19,203	161	698	1,986	8,427	4,013	3,918	12.8
1980	18,565	164	725	1,932	8,087	3,777	3,879	12.8
1979	17,334	173	685	1,977	7,486	3,553	3,460	12.8
1978	16,857	172	742	1,989	7,292	3,311	3,351	12.6
1977	16,421	136	710	2,088	7,212	2,995	3,280	12.7
1976	15,882	112	784	2,054	7,248	2,731	2,954	12.7
1975	15,316	135	833	2,139	7,037	2,489	2,686	12.6
1974	14,750	142	796	2,145	6,871	2,383	2,413	12.6
1973	14,155	129	884	2,154	6,830	2,037	2,121	12.6
1972	13,487	128	862	2,184	6,485	1,899	1,926	12.5
1971	12,950	156	919	2,212	6,183	1,816	1,663	12.5
1970	12,629	140	876	2,355	6,096	1,648	1,512	12.5

Note: Starting in 2012, data were created using population controls based on 2010 Census data. Starting in 2001, data were created using population controls based on Census 2000 data. Also starting in 2001, data are from the expanded CPS sample. Begining with data for 1992, a new question results in different categories than for earlier years. Data shown as 'High School, 4 years' are now collected in the category 'High School Graduate.' Data shown as 'College 1 to 3 years' are now collected in the 'Some college' and the two 'Associate degree' categories. Data shown as 'College 4 years or more,' are now collected in the categories, 'Bachelor's degree,' 'Master's degree,' 'Doctorate degree,' and 'Professional degree.' Due to the change in question format, median years of schooling cannot be derived. Total includes persons who did not report on years of school completed.

Table A-33. Years of School Completed by People 25 Years Old and Over, by Age and Sex, Selected Years, 1940–2018—*Continued*

(Numbers in thousands; civilian noninstitutionalized population, except where noted.)

Year, sex, and age	Total	Elementary		High school		College		Median years
		0 to 4 years	5 to 8 years	1 to 3 years	4 years	1 to 3 years	4 years or more	
1969	12,285	155	965	2,291	5,941	1,481	1,451	12.4
1968	11,904	157	1,053	2,246	5,684	1,484	1,278	12.4
1967	11,512	149	1,084	2,200	5,458	1,426	1,195	12.4
1966	11,322	186	1,047	2,319	5,355	1,273	1,134	12.4
1965	11,284	218	1,197	2,256	5,310	1,244	1,060	12.4
1964	11,269	202	1,248	2,216	5,362	1,221	1,018	12.4
1962	11,368	263	1,367	2,363	5,115	1,243	1,017	12.3
1960	11,637	289	1,712	2,694	4,810	1,256	875	12.2
1959	11,696	345	1,526	2,503	5,297	1,142	822	12.3
1957	12,069	327	1,874	2,519	5,385	1,094	795	12.2
1952	12,202	342	2,160	2,630	5,162	1,102	784	12.2
1950	12,172	516	2,603	2,624	4,410	1,081	714	12.1
1947	11,733	471	2,858	2,503	4,293	915	640	12.0
1940	10,818	598	3,744	2,333	2,653	862	544	10.3
35 TO 54 YEARS								
Both Sexes								
2018	82,196	690	2,289	4,974	21,680	21,340	31,223	NA
2017	82,072	709	2,403	5,059	22,103	21,621	30,176	NA
2016	82,571	799	2,636	5,296	22,298	22,070	29,473	NA
2015	82,715	862	2,742	5,471	23,153	21,826	28,660	NA
2014	82,687	875	2,612	5,433	23,238	22,472	28,057	NA
2013	83,324	778	2,611	5,437	23,708	22,831	27,959	NA
2012	83,883	863	2,762	5,569	24,608	22,792	27,288	NA
2011	83,796	899	2,474	5,682	25,039	22,796	26,907	NA
2010	84,834	852	2,549	5,937	26,145	22,911	26,440	NA
2009	85,688	909	2,716	6,046	26,121	23,384	26,513	NA
2008	86,067	905	2,742	5,882	26,108	23,504	26,926	NA
2007	86,224	874	2,720	6,310	26,675	22,777	26,869	NA
2006	85,918	965	2,769	6,274	26,636	23,317	25,958	NA
2005	85,311	954	2,757	5,892	27,232	23,129	25,347	NA
2004	84,642	963	2,582	5,938	26,649	23,093	25,417	NA
2003	84,308	957	2,620	6,112	26,346	23,039	25,234	NA
2002	83,829	941	2,636	5,874	26,740	23,148	24,489	NA
2001	83,286	886	2,612	5,899	26,356	23,271	24,262	NA
2000	81,435	932	2,521	5,702	26,481	22,618	23,183	NA
1999	79,976	872	2,535	6,052	26,367	21,561	22,589	NA
1998	78,520	890	2,613	6,164	26,079	21,267	21,506	NA
1997	76,973	867	2,686	6,045	26,054	20,684	20,635	NA
1996	74,661	968	2,710	5,803	24,924	20,105	20,152	NA
1995	73,028	927	2,561	5,664	24,070	19,926	19,878	NA
1994	71,049	987	2,680	5,415	23,804	19,210	18,956	NA
1993	68,845	942	2,486	5,538	23,927	17,984	17,970	NA
1992	66,594	899	2,608	5,845	23,442	16,658	17,144	NA
1991	64,351	995	3,057	5,522	24,815	13,348	16,614	12.9
1990	62,499	980	3,104	5,529	24,434	12,553	15,899	12.9
1989	60,494	999	3,315	5,800	23,334	11,627	15,417	12.9
1988	58,555	958	3,272	5,889	23,049	11,017	14,369	12.8
1987	56,650	842	3,398	5,656	22,820	10,523	13,409	12.8
1986	55,170	896	3,614	5,769	22,151	10,110	12,629	12.8
1985	53,697	899	3,639	5,978	21,600	9,217	12,363	12.8
1984	52,297	893	3,754	6,158	21,290	8,702	11,500	12.7
1983	50,956	973	4,044	6,313	20,788	8,045	10,795	12.7
1982	49,722	963	4,320	6,657	20,445	7,580	9,756	12.6
1981	48,680	1,038	4,531	6,773	20,032	7,115	9,181	12.6
1980	48,124	1,034	4,676	7,063	19,584	6,943	8,822	12.6
1979	47,437	1,030	4,895	7,132	19,488	6,655	8,237	12.5
1978	46,921	1,107	5,262	7,590	19,012	6,286	7,667	12.5
1977	46,409	1,192	5,445	7,781	18,781	6,013	7,196	12.5
1976	46,271	1,245	5,729	7,671	18,893	5,957	6,776	12.5
1975	46,193	1,296	5,942	7,765	19,010	5,673	6,506	12.4
1974	46,217	1,293	6,244	7,896	19,038	5,375	6,372	12.4

Note: Starting in 2012, data were created using population controls based on 2010 Census data. Starting in 2001, data were created using population controls based on Census 2000 data. Also starting in 2001, data are from the expanded CPS sample. Begining with data for 1992, a new question results in different categories than for earlier years. Data shown as 'High School, 4 years' are now collected in the category 'High School Graduate.' Data shown as 'College 1 to 3 years' are now collected in the 'Some college' and the two 'Associate degree' categories. Data shown as 'College 4 years or more,' are now collected in the categories, 'Bachelor's degree,' 'Master's degree,' 'Doctorate degree,' and 'Professional degree.' Due to the change in question format, median years of schooling cannot be derived. Total includes persons who did not report on years of school completed.

Table A-33. Years of School Completed by People 25 Years Old and Over, by Age and Sex, Selected Years, 1940–2018—*Continued*

(Numbers in thousands; civilian noninstitutionalized population, except where noted.)

Year, sex, and age	Total	Years of school completed						Median years
		Elementary		High school		College		
		0 to 4 years	5 to 8 years	1 to 3 years	4 years	1 to 3 years	4 years or more	
1973	45,910	1,344	6,519	8,001	18,651	5,318	6,076	12.4
1972	45,956	1,367	7,004	8,521	18,400	5,074	5,589	12.3
1971	46,294	1,439	7,588	8,393	18,334	5,082	5,460	12.3
1970	46,319	1,461	7,935	8,555	18,200	4,875	5,294	12.3
1969	46,255	1,644	8,313	8,586	17,773	4,749	5,190	12.3
1968	46,396	1,654	8,698	8,838	17,362	4,642	5,200	12.2
1967	46,321	1,771	9,036	9,138	16,906	4,525	4,947	12.2
1966	46,313	1,837	9,528	9,309	16,605	4,230	4,805	12.1
1965	46,296	1,827	9,812	9,266	16,359	4,384	4,647	12.1
1964	46,089	1,905	10,259	9,289	15,760	4,397	4,482	12.1
1962	45,287	2,181	10,795	8,938	14,668	4,452	4,253	12.0
1960	44,742	2,424	12,536	9,502	12,517	4,123	3,639	11.3
1959	43,989	2,303	11,657	8,719	13,244	3,715	3,709	11.8
1957	42,645	2,658	12,349	8,384	12,041	3,248	3,360	11.3
1952	39,014	2,606	13,274	7,348	9,374	3,148	2,802	10.5
1950	38,432	3,404	14,420	6,976	7,262	2,878	2,516	9.7
1947	36,717	3,203	15,184	6,311	6,715	2,622	2,221	9.0
1940	33,845	4,549	16,270	4,972	4,217	1,836	1,540	8.6
Male								
2018	40,411	356	1,182	2,657	11,753	9,991	14,472	NA
2017	40,303	395	1,305	2,711	12,032	10,026	13,834	NA
2016	40,539	443	1,336	2,903	12,021	10,217	13,620	NA
2015	40,565	469	1,416	2,987	12,401	9,996	13,296	NA
2014	40,525	489	1,459	2,992	12,246	10,199	13,139	NA
2013	40,868	409	1,464	2,962	12,417	10,473	13,142	NA
2012	41,167	462	1,525	2,927	12,869	10,439	12,944	NA
2011	41,209	447	1,292	3,027	13,250	10,339	12,854	NA
2010	41,858	446	1,367	3,227	13,824	10,311	12,682	NA
2009	42,263	500	1,458	3,278	13,644	10,670	12,713	NA
2008	42,419	507	1,490	3,228	13,625	10,711	12,858	NA
2007	42,476	491	1,433	3,480	13,737	10,359	12,976	NA
2006	42,344	549	1,472	3,356	13,660	10,608	12,701	NA
2005	42,024	547	1,476	3,063	14,017	10,429	12,491	NA
2004	41,612	577	1,323	3,157	13,238	10,636	12,682	NA
2003	41,340	538	1,372	3,282	12,903	10,622	12,622	NA
2002	41,154	513	1,333	3,063	13,133	10,739	12,373	NA
2001	40,858	488	1,368	2,974	12,784	10,827	12,417	NA
2000	40,024	479	1,288	2,845	12,845	10,716	11,854	NA
1999	39,300	470	1,290	3,101	12,544	10,233	11,664	NA
1998	38,654	486	1,333	3,284	12,239	10,098	11,214	NA
1997	37,912	486	1,370	3,143	12,326	9,713	10,870	NA
1996	36,596	520	1,319	2,877	11,749	9,514	10,526	NA
1995	35,994	529	1,368	2,781	11,223	9,305	10,784	NA
1994	34,998	545	1,383	2,621	11,009	9,073	10,369	NA
1993	33,751	478	1,316	2,660	10,983	8,624	9,687	NA
1992	32,619	472	1,368	2,750	10,670	7,968	9,389	NA
1991	31,460	530	1,624	2,612	11,092	6,430	9,169	13.0
1990	30,623	527	1,658	2,573	10,790	6,169	8,905	13.0
1989	29,597	504	1,762	2,628	10,235	5,719	8,749	13.0
1988	28,645	498	1,725	2,654	10,100	5,327	8,340	12.9
1987	27,680	412	1,801	2,617	9,781	5,173	7,895	12.9
1986	26,925	475	1,919	2,699	9,393	5,013	7,426	12.9
1985	26,181	501	1,928	2,726	9,210	4,502	7,314	12.9
1984	25,460	506	2,014	2,831	8,926	4,257	6,929	12.8
1983	24,796	548	2,108	2,862	8,795	3,884	6,601	12.8
1982	24,164	530	2,302	2,989	8,609	3,757	5,977	12.7
1981	23,646	572	2,425	3,112	8,431	3,519	5,588	12.7
1980	23,373	590	2,492	3,202	8,278	3,442	5,370	12.7
1979	22,976	545	2,612	3,194	8,232	3,306	5,090	12.6
1978	22,719	609	2,779	3,377	8,001	3,136	4,817	12.6
1977	22,445	661	2,889	3,554	7,822	3,000	4,520	12.5
1976	22,403	730	3,004	3,473	7,904	2,969	4,323	12.5

Note: Starting in 2012, data were created using population controls based on 2010 Census data. Starting in 2001, data were created using population controls based on Census 2000 data. Also starting in 2001, data are from the expanded CPS sample. Begining with data for 1992, a new question results in different categories than for earlier years. Data shown as 'High School, 4 years' are now collected in the category 'High School Graduate.' Data shown as 'College 1 to 3 years' are now collected in the 'Some college' and the two 'Associate degree' categories. Data shown as 'College 4 years or more,' are now collected in the categories, 'Bachelor's degree,' Master's degree,' 'Doctorate degree,' and 'Professional degree.' Due to the change in question format, median years of schooling cannot be derived. Total includes persons who did not report on years of school completed.

Table A-33. Years of School Completed by People 25 Years Old and Over, by Age and Sex, Selected Years, 1940–2018—Continued

(Numbers in thousands; civilian noninstitutionalized population, except where noted.)

Year, sex, and age	Total	Elementary		High school		College		Median years
		0 to 4 years	5 to 8 years	1 to 3 years	4 years	1 to 3 years	4 years or more	
1975..	22,358	763	3,100	3,510	7,952	2,879	4,153	12.5
1974..	22,367	733	3,286	3,532	8,004	2,730	4,081	12.6
1973..	22,166	716	3,413	3,586	7,836	2,714	3,901	12.4
1972..	22,200	749	3,674	3,917	7,663	2,564	3,631	12.4
1971..	22,474	849	3,985	3,823	7,674	2,578	3,567	12.3
1970..	22,475	834	4,208	3,876	7,612	2,555	3,390	12.3
1969..	22,420	889	4,359	4,012	7,427	2,456	3,277	12.3
1968..	22,521	931	4,487	4,160	7,324	2,364	3,257	12.2
1967..	22,482	1,000	4,700	4,270	7,143	2,244	3,128	12.2
1966..	22,508	1,085	4,886	4,455	6,990	2,029	3,063	12.1
1965..	22,534	1,081	5,076	4,462	6,815	2,161	2,937	12.1
1964..	22,457	1,158	5,226	4,416	6,657	2,212	2,789	12.2
1962..	22,081	1,235	5,545	4,359	6,202	2,142	2,598	11.9
1960..	21,919	1,397	6,415	4,579	5,364	1,957	2,206	11.1
1959..	21,511	1,350	5,781	4,329	5,604	1,827	2,250	11.5
1957..	20,873	1,491	6,293	3,987	5,195	1,558	1,972	11.0
1952..	18,888	1,466	6,512	3,462	4,040	1,518	1,576	10.3
1950..	18,896	1,834	7,338	3,339	3,151	1,271	1,403	9.6
1947..	18,165	1,678	7,765	3,102	2,907	1,168	1,258	8.6
1940..	17,127	2,480	8,458	2,388	1,798	819	917	8.5
Female								
2018..	41,785	334	1,107	2,317	9,927	11,349	16,751	NA
2017..	41,769	314	1,098	2,348	10,072	11,595	16,342	NA
2016..	42,031	356	1,300	2,393	10,276	11,853	15,853	NA
2015..	42,150	394	1,326	2,484	10,752	11,830	15,364	NA
2014..	42,163	385	1,153	2,440	10,993	12,273	14,919	NA
2013..	42,456	369	1,147	2,475	11,290	12,358	14,817	NA
2012..	42,716	400	1,237	2,642	11,739	12,352	14,345	NA
2011..	42,587	452	1,183	2,654	11,789	12,457	14,053	NA
2010..	42,976	406	1,181	2,710	12,321	12,600	13,758	NA
2009..	43,424	409	1,258	2,768	12,476	12,713	13,800	NA
2008..	43,648	398	1,253	2,654	12,483	12,792	14,067	NA
2007..	43,748	382	1,288	2,830	12,938	12,419	13,892	NA
2006..	43,573	417	1,298	2,915	12,976	12,710	13,255	NA
2005..	43,287	407	1,280	2,829	13,215	12,700	12,856	NA
2004..	43,030	386	1,259	2,781	13,411	12,458	12,736	NA
2003..	42,968	419	1,248	2,830	13,443	12,417	12,611	NA
2002..	42,675	428	1,303	2,811	13,607	12,410	12,116	NA
2001..	42,428	398	1,244	2,926	13,572	12,444	11,844	NA
2000..	41,411	452	1,235	2,858	13,635	11,905	11,330	NA
1999..	40,676	402	1,248	2,950	13,825	11,326	10,925	NA
1998..	39,866	403	1,279	2,879	13,841	11,168	10,293	NA
1997..	39,061	381	1,319	2,902	13,726	10,969	9,766	NA
1996..	38,065	449	1,301	2,924	13,174	10,592	9,623	NA
1995..	37,034	396	1,192	2,881	12,846	10,623	9,096	NA
1994..	36,051	443	1,298	2,792	12,795	10,140	8,587	NA
1993..	35,093	462	1,169	2,877	12,944	9,358	8,283	NA
1992..	33,975	427	1,240	3,096	12,770	8,687	7,756	NA
1991..	32,891	464	1,431	2,910	13,723	6,919	7,443	12.8
1990..	31,876	454	1,448	2,955	13,643	6,383	6,997	12.8
1989..	30,898	498	1,552	3,171	13,099	5,908	6,669	12.8
1988..	29,908	462	1,547	3,234	12,949	5,689	6,029	12.7
1987..	28,969	430	1,598	3,039	13,038	5,349	5,513	12.7
1986..	28,244	420	1,694	3,071	12,759	5,098	5,202	12.7
1985..	27,516	398	1,710	3,252	12,391	4,715	5,049	12.7
1984..	26,838	389	1,740	3,331	12,364	4,444	4,570	12.6
1983..	26,161	427	1,935	3,450	11,993	4,161	4,193	12.6
1982..	25,555	433	2,017	3,666	11,833	3,827	3,778	12.6
1981..	25,034	467	2,105	3,661	11,599	3,605	3,595	12.5
1980..	24,751	444	2,186	3,862	11,307	3,501	3,452	12.5
1979..	24,461	486	2,282	3,935	11,258	3,353	3,147	12.5
1978..	24,202	497	2,483	4,212	11,012	3,149	2,849	12.5

Note: Starting in 2012, data were created using population controls based on 2010 Census data. Starting in 2001, data were created using population controls based on Census 2000 data. Also starting in 2001, data are from the expanded CPS sample. Begining with data for 1992, a new question results in different categories than for earlier years. Data shown as 'High School, 4 years' are now collected in the category 'High School Graduate.' Data shown as 'College 1 to 3 years' are now collected in the 'Some college' and the two 'Associate degree' categories. Data shown as 'College 4 years or more,' are now collected in the categories, 'Bachelor's degree,' 'Master's degree,' 'Doctorate degree,' and 'Professional degree.' Due to the change in question format, median years of schooling cannot be derived. Total includes persons who did not report on years of school completed.

Table A-33. Years of School Completed by People 25 Years Old and Over, by Age and Sex, Selected Years, 1940–2018—*Continued*

(Numbers in thousands; civilian noninstitutionalized population, except where noted.)

Year, sex, and age	Total	Elementary 0 to 4 years	Elementary 5 to 8 years	High school 1 to 3 years	High school 4 years	College 1 to 3 years	College 4 years or more	Median years
1977	23,964	534	2,557	4,227	10,959	3,014	2,678	12.4
1976	23,868	517	2,721	4,198	10,989	2,988	2,455	12.4
1975	23,835	533	2,842	4,256	11,058	2,793	2,352	12.4
1974	23,850	559	2,956	4,364	11,033	2,647	2,290	12.4
1973	23,744	628	3,106	4,415	10,815	2,603	2,174	12.3
1972	23,756	618	3,330	4,604	10,736	2,509	1,958	12.3
1971	23,821	590	3,604	4,570	10,660	2,505	1,894	12.3
1970	23,845	629	3,728	4,679	10,588	2,318	1,903	12.3
1969	23,834	755	3,953	4,575	10,349	2,293	1,913	12.3
1968	23,874	725	4,212	4,676	10,038	2,281	1,943	12.2
1967	23,839	773	4,334	4,868	9,762	2,282	1,819	12.2
1966	23,806	752	4,644	4,853	9,615	2,200	1,741	12.2
1965	23,765	746	4,735	4,803	9,545	2,223	1,712	12.2
1964	23,632	748	5,033	4,871	9,103	2,183	1,691	12.1
1962	23,206	946	5,250	4,579	8,466	2,310	1,655	12.1
1960	22,823	1,027	6,121	4,923	7,153	2,166	1,433	11.6
1959	22,478	953	5,876	4,390	7,640	1,888	1,459	12.0
1957	21,772	1,167	6,056	4,397	6,846	1,690	1,388	11.5
1952	20,126	1,140	6,762	3,886	5,334	1,630	1,226	10.7
1950	19,536	1,570	7,082	3,637	4,111	1,607	1,113	9.7
1947	18,552	1,525	7,419	3,209	3,808	1,454	963	9.3
1940	16,718	2,070	7,812	2,584	2,419	1,017	623	8.7

55 YEARS AND OVER

Both Sexes

Year, sex, and age	Total	0 to 4 years	5 to 8 years	1 to 3 years	4 years	1 to 3 years	4 years or more	Median years
2018	92,780	1,258	3,535	6,273	29,545	23,970	28,200	NA
2017	90,599	1,280	3,465	6,143	28,916	23,351	27,444	NA
2016	88,682	1,406	3,584	6,009	28,481	22,981	26,221	NA
2015	86,411	1,447	3,690	6,276	28,457	21,785	24,756	NA
2014	84,134	1,365	3,829	6,094	27,962	21,059	23,825	NA
2013	81,778	1,306	3,931	6,043	27,046	20,387	23,066	NA
2012	79,478	1,348	3,974	6,344	26,531	19,343	21,937	NA
2011	76,163	1,372	4,073	5,983	25,622	18,408	20,705	NA
2010	74,008	1,440	4,118	6,051	25,125	17,354	19,920	NA
2009	72,077	1,555	4,101	6,338	24,154	16,877	19,051	NA
2008	70,092	1,411	4,294	6,338	23,779	16,378	17,892	NA
2007	68,226	1,576	4,458	6,680	23,408	15,505	16,599	NA
2006	66,485	1,628	4,610	6,508	22,961	14,824	15,956	NA
2005	64,745	1,614	4,803	6,784	22,392	14,083	15,069	NA
2004	63,034	1,465	4,907	6,821	21,918	13,434	14,488	NA
2003	61,633	1,589	5,372	6,876	21,554	12,884	13,358	NA
2002	59,644	1,528	5,639	7,258	20,728	12,117	12,374	NA
2001	58,238	1,544	5,589	7,178	20,622	11,864	11,440	NA
2000	56,008	1,524	5,780	6,921	20,059	11,126	10,598	NA
1999	55,303	1,589	5,978	7,096	19,742	10,722	10,174	NA
1998	54,337	1,624	6,126	7,385	19,526	10,022	9,654	NA
1997	53,352	1,628	6,622	7,543	18,823	9,565	9,169	NA
1996	52,742	1,642	6,716	7,520	18,549	9,642	8,677	NA
1995	52,022	1,755	7,048	7,232	18,320	9,662	8,005	NA
1994	51,516	1,802	7,382	7,454	18,228	8,890	7,761	NA
1993	52,117	2,058	8,038	7,637	18,626	8,106	7,652	NA
1992	51,740	2,118	8,133	7,756	18,397	8,005	7,332	NA
1991	51,439	2,341	8,668	7,675	18,954	6,540	7,258	12.6
1990	50,798	2,349	9,239	7,893	18,050	6,202	7,064	12.3
1989	50,421	2,412	9,395	7,907	18,102	5,914	6,693	12.3
1988	50,128	2,325	9,969	7,860	18,004	5,705	6,263	12.3
1987	49,858	2,408	10,544	7,766	17,310	5,799	6,033	12.2
1986	49,383	2,611	10,699	7,917	16,876	5,515	5,767	12.2
1985	48,969	2,612	11,052	7,872	16,516	5,208	5,708	12.2
1984	48,324	2,584	11,131	7,636	16,353	5,026	5,593	12.2
1983	47,723	2,769	11,348	7,703	15,470	4,915	5,514	12.1
1982	47,102	2,818	11,541	7,751	15,091	4,807	5,095	12.1

Note: Starting in 2012, data were created using population controls based on 2010 Census data. Starting in 2001, data were created using population controls based on Census 2000 data. Also starting in 2001, data are from the expanded CPS sample. Begining with data for 1992, a new question results in different categories than for earlier years. Data shown as 'High School, 4 years' are now collected in the category 'High School Graduate.' Data shown as 'College 1 to 3 years' are now collected in the 'Some college' and the two 'Associate degree' categories. Data shown as 'College 4 years or more,' are now collected in the categories, 'Bachelor's degree,' Master's degree,' 'Doctorate degree,' and 'Professional degree.' Due to the change in question format, median years of schooling cannot be derived. Total includes persons who did not report on years of school completed.

Table A-33. Years of School Completed by People 25 Years Old and Over, by Age and Sex, Selected Years, 1940–2018—*Continued*

(Numbers in thousands; civilian noninstitutionalized population, except where noted.)

Year, sex, and age	Total	Elementary		High school		College		Median years
		0 to 4 years	5 to 8 years	1 to 3 years	4 years	1 to 3 years	4 years or more	
1981	46,391	2,983	11,909	7,600	14,464	4,721	4,711	12.0
1980	45,670	2,994	12,326	7,451	13,869	4,494	4,535	12.0
1979	43,806	2,924	12,230	6,999	13,088	4,321	4,245	12.0
1978	42,977	3,013	12,593	7,069	12,376	4,086	3,843	11.6
1977	42,176	3,047	12,740	6,823	11,977	3,835	3,754	11.3
1976	41,429	3,107	12,674	6,915	11,346	3,709	3,677	11.1
1975	40,613	3,303	13,045	6,730	10,798	3,442	3,295	10.8
1974	39,817	3,461	13,302	6,615	10,060	3,233	3,145	10.4
1973	39,163	3,424	13,467	6,504	9,604	3,060	3,105	10.2
1972	38,659	3,471	13,706	6,351	9,136	2,952	3,042	10.0
1971	38,787	3,808	14,430	6,225	8,463	2,878	2,982	9.6
1970	38,126	3,957	14,647	5,877	8,005	2,797	2,843	9.2
1969	37,424	4,012	14,576	5,801	7,768	2,615	2,653	9.1
1968	36,789	4,244	14,522	5,760	7,085	2,624	2,558	8.9
1967	36,155	4,310	14,849	5,495	6,622	2,443	2,434	8.7
1966	35,540	4,438	14,742	5,392	6,240	2,358	2,370	8.6
1965	34,969	4,612	14,814	5,293	5,844	2,194	2,215	8.5
1964	34,335	4,888	14,701	4,954	5,598	2,159	2,033	8.3
1962	33,247	5,048	14,707	4,442	4,994	2,166	1,890	8.1
1960	31,902	5,169	14,944	4,503	3,757	2,051	1,479	8.5
1959	30,567	4,752	13,485	4,060	3,996	1,775	1,545	8.1
1957	29,548	5,153	12,996	3,602	3,864	1,462	1,461	8.0
1952	26,206	4,554	12,638	2,982	3,080	1,346	1,264	7.7
1950	25,427	4,940	11,947	2,791	2,704	1,170	1,005	8.3
1947	23,234	4,393	11,601	2,179	2,581	1,003	825	7.5
1940	19,592	4,178	10,467	1,656	1,633	685	579	8.2
Male								
2018	42,961	522	1,670	2,851	13,041	10,630	14,247	NA
2017	41,901	561	1,617	2,813	12,808	10,288	13,814	NA
2016	40,988	624	1,708	2,814	12,374	10,236	13,231	NA
2015	39,895	608	1,765	2,707	12,398	9,863	12,556	NA
2014	38,850	544	1,790	2,800	12,150	9,320	12,246	NA
2013	37,621	557	1,790	2,605	11,539	9,060	12,070	NA
2012	36,489	614	1,775	2,754	11,220	8,574	11,552	NA
2011	35,027	597	1,934	2,625	10,676	8,230	10,966	NA
2010	33,778	647	1,923	2,611	10,399	7,672	10,525	NA
2009	32,814	689	1,874	2,669	9,886	7,456	10,241	NA
2008	31,841	631	1,932	2,751	9,510	7,259	9,759	NA
2007	30,920	721	2,060	2,884	9,505	6,723	9,026	NA
2006	30,060	705	2,090	2,784	9,488	6,193	8,837	NA
2005	29,198	717	2,157	2,896	8,918	6,167	8,341	NA
2004	28,347	639	2,192	2,885	8,631	5,841	8,159	NA
2003	27,694	729	2,423	2,912	8,425	5,694	7,510	NA
2002	26,608	664	2,601	3,048	8,063	5,257	6,975	NA
2001	25,908	697	2,558	2,964	8,073	5,131	6,485	NA
2000	25,023	706	2,696	2,817	7,816	4,906	6,079	NA
1999	24,694	712	2,746	2,911	7,712	4,756	5,856	NA
1998	24,197	755	2,740	3,000	7,745	4,461	5,496	NA
1997	23,668	773	3,026	3,060	7,417	4,139	5,255	NA
1996	23,352	795	3,058	2,998	7,198	4,254	5,055	NA
1995	22,881	839	3,153	2,980	6,980	4,254	4,675	NA
1994	22,669	894	3,327	3,037	6,987	3,962	4,462	NA
1993	23,038	992	3,595	3,174	7,178	3,587	4,508	NA
1992	22,836	1,033	3,676	3,277	6,991	3,549	4,312	NA
1991	22,708	1,217	3,980	3,183	7,287	2,850	4,193	12.4
1990	22,337	1,182	4,141	3,274	6,986	2,707	4,046	12.4
1989	22,167	1,202	4,198	3,317	7,003	2,616	3,829	12.3
1988	21,989	1,117	4,471	3,366	6,968	2,455	3,609	12.3
1987	21,855	1,160	4,762	3,261	6,673	2,504	3,496	12.3
1986	21,622	1,275	4,813	3,286	6,509	2,355	3,385	12.2
1985	21,391	1,252	5,001	3,234	6,387	2,229	3,289	12.2
1984	21,014	1,209	4,951	3,270	6,265	2,185	3,132	12.2

Note: Starting in 2012, data were created using population controls based on 2010 Census data. Starting in 2001, data were created using population controls based on Census 2000 data. Also starting in 2001, data are from the expanded CPS sample. Begining with data for 1992, a new question results in different categories than for earlier years. Data shown as 'High School, 4 years' are now collected in the category 'High School Graduate.' Data shown as 'College 1 to 3 years' are now collected in the 'Some college' and the two 'Associate degree' categories. Data shown as 'College 4 years or more,' are now collected in the categories, 'Bachelor's degree,' 'Master's degree,' 'Doctorate degree,' and 'Professional degree.' Due to the change in question format, median years of schooling cannot be derived. Total includes persons who did not report on years of school completed.

Table A-33. Years of School Completed by People 25 Years Old and Over, by Age and Sex, Selected Years, 1940–2018—*Continued*

(Numbers in thousands; civilian noninstitutionalized population, except where noted.)

Year, sex, and age	Total	Elementary		High school		College		Median years
		0 to 4 years	5 to 8 years	1 to 3 years	4 years	1 to 3 years	4 years or more	
1983	20,769	1,343	4,986	3,282	5,906	2,141	3,117	12.1
1982	20,508	1,362	5,026	3,313	5,759	2,102	2,946	12.1
1981	20,237	1,394	5,165	3,292	5,597	2,032	2,758	12.0
1980	19,967	1,424	5,436	3,206	5,409	1,986	2,506	11.9
1979	19,292	1,446	5,479	2,964	5,167	1,935	2,301	11.8
1978	18,939	1,467	5,701	2,919	4,919	1,824	2,110	11.4
1977	18,608	1,502	5,770	2,787	4,835	1,700	2,011	11.2
1976	18,233	1,507	5,733	2,884	4,473	1,646	1,989	11.0
1975	17,903	1,628	5,845	2,871	4,308	1,480	1,768	10.5
1974	17,579	1,693	6,042	2,817	3,993	1,356	1,682	10.1
1973	17,263	1,678	6,111	2,774	3,811	1,245	1,645	9.9
1972	17,120	1,728	6,252	2,698	3,612	1,215	1,614	9.6
1971	17,288	1,913	6,629	2,668	3,285	1,214	1,579	9.1
1970	17,074	2,011	6,655	2,583	3,127	1,182	1,516	9.0
1969	16,822	2,003	6,701	2,536	3,099	1,086	1,397	8.8
1968	16,609	2,137	6,728	2,523	2,816	1,078	1,328	8.7
1967	16,398	2,247	6,827	2,379	2,685	989	1,271	8.5
1966	16,201	2,288	6,944	2,317	2,491	939	1,223	8.3
1965	16,015	2,368	6,992	2,265	2,331	893	1,164	8.2
1964	15,789	2,504	6,897	2,159	2,237	876	1,113	8.1
1962	15,440	2,644	6,813	2,032	2,030	864	1,057	8.0
1960	14,895	2,704	7,121	1,969	1,453	853	796	8.4
1959	14,304	2,491	6,436	1,759	1,584	718	857	7.9
1957	13,967	2,696	6,244	1,570	1,493	608	831	7.7
1952	12,544	2,428	6,162	1,318	1,262	528	636	7.5
1950	12,277	2,609	5,808	1,209	1,111	500	569	8.2
1947	11,424	2,393	5,656	939	1,109	464	482	7.3
1940	9,815	2,293	5,249	724	660	313	361	8.1
Female								
2018	49,819	736	1,865	3,422	16,504	13,340	13,953	NA
2017	48,698	719	1,849	3,329	16,107	13,063	13,630	NA
2016	47,694	782	1,875	3,195	16,107	12,745	12,990	NA
2015	46,516	839	1,925	3,570	16,059	11,922	12,201	NA
2014	45,284	821	2,039	3,295	15,812	11,739	11,578	NA
2013	44,158	749	2,141	3,438	15,507	11,327	10,996	NA
2012	42,989	734	2,199	3,590	15,311	10,769	10,384	NA
2011	41,136	775	2,140	3,358	14,946	10,178	9,739	NA
2010	40,230	793	2,195	3,440	14,725	9,682	9,395	NA
2009	39,263	867	2,228	3,669	14,268	9,421	8,810	NA
2008	38,251	780	2,362	3,588	14,269	9,119	8,133	NA
2007	37,306	855	2,398	3,796	13,902	8,781	7,573	NA
2006	36,425	922	2,521	3,761	13,472	8,630	7,119	NA
2005	35,547	897	2,645	3,887	13,474	7,916	6,728	NA
2004	34,687	826	2,715	3,936	13,287	7,593	6,329	NA
2003	33,939	860	2,949	3,964	13,129	7,190	5,848	NA
2002	33,035	864	3,038	4,210	12,664	6,860	5,399	NA
2001	32,329	847	3,032	4,213	12,549	6,733	4,956	NA
2000	30,985	817	3,085	4,105	12,243	6,218	4,517	NA
1999	30,609	879	3,232	4,186	12,031	5,965	4,319	NA
1998	30,140	868	3,386	4,386	11,780	5,560	4,160	NA
1997	29,684	855	3,596	4,483	11,407	5,427	3,916	NA
1996	29,390	848	3,659	4,523	11,350	5,387	3,623	NA
1995	29,142	915	3,894	4,255	11,340	5,410	3,330	NA
1994	28,848	909	4,054	4,419	11,242	4,926	3,298	NA
1993	29,080	1,066	4,442	4,462	11,447	4,519	3,149	NA
1992	28,904	1,084	4,456	4,478	11,409	4,455	3,021	NA
1991	28,729	1,125	4,687	4,495	11,667	3,690	3,066	12.3
1990	28,461	1,167	5,098	4,619	11,063	3,495	3,019	12.3
1989	28,255	1,211	5,195	4,587	11,099	3,300	2,863	12.3
1988	28,139	1,208	5,498	4,495	11,034	3,250	2,655	12.3
1987	28,004	1,248	5,782	4,504	10,637	3,294	2,539	12.2
1986	27,762	1,336	5,886	4,630	10,367	3,160	2,382	12.2

Note: Starting in 2012, data were created using population controls based on 2010 Census data. Starting in 2001, data were created using population controls based on Census 2000 data. Also starting in 2001, data are from the expanded CPS sample. Begining with data for 1992, a new question results in different categories than for earlier years. Data shown as 'High School, 4 years' are now collected in the category 'High School Graduate.' Data shown as 'College 1 to 3 years' are now collected in the 'Some college' and the two 'Associate degree' categories. Data shown as 'College 4 years or more,' are now collected in the categories, 'Bachelor's degree,' Master's degree,' 'Doctorate degree,' and 'Professional degree.' Due to the change in question format, median years of schooling cannot be derived. Total includes persons who did not report on years of school completed.

Table A-33. Years of School Completed by People 25 Years Old and Over, by Age and Sex, Selected Years, 1940–2018—*Continued*

(Numbers in thousands; civilian noninstitutionalized population, except where noted.)

Year, sex, and age	Total	Years of school completed						Median years
		Elementary		High school		College		
		0 to 4 years	5 to 8 years	1 to 3 years	4 years	1 to 3 years	4 years or more	
1985..	27,578	1,360	6,052	4,638	10,129	2,979	2,420	12.2
1984..	27,309	1,377	6,183	4,363	10,086	2,843	2,459	12.2
1983..	26,954	1,428	6,364	4,423	9,567	2,774	2,398	12.1
1982..	26,593	1,458	6,511	4,435	9,330	2,705	2,150	12.1
1981..	26,152	1,589	6,742	4,308	8,868	2,690	1,954	12.0
1980..	25,703	1,571	6,889	4,245	8,460	2,509	2,030	12.0
1979..	24,514	1,474	6,750	4,034	7,920	2,389	1,944	12.0
1978..	24,038	1,545	6,889	4,149	7,457	2,263	1,733	11.6
1977..	23,568	1,546	6,972	4,034	7,141	2,135	1,742	11.0
1976..	23,196	1,602	6,942	4,029	6,871	2,063	1,690	11.0
1975..	22,710	1,675	7,198	3,858	6,490	1,962	1,527	10.9
1974..	22,238	1,762	7,261	3,799	6,068	1,880	1,463	10.7
1973..	21,900	1,746	7,359	3,729	5,790	1,814	1,461	10.5
1972..	21,539	1,743	7,455	3,654	5,526	1,737	1,425	10.3
1971..	21,500	1,896	7,805	3,556	5,179	1,665	1,402	9.9
1970..	21,052	1,946	7,993	3,292	4,879	1,615	1,327	9.5
1969..	20,601	2,009	7,878	3,264	4,669	1,526	1,255	9.4
1968..	20,180	2,106	7,795	3,237	4,269	1,544	1,229	9.2
1967..	19,756	2,063	8,021	3,117	3,937	1,454	1,164	8.9
1966..	19,339	2,152	7,797	3,074	3,749	1,419	1,147	8.9
1965..	18,955	2,243	7,821	3,026	3,514	1,300	1,048	8.7
1964..	18,546	2,383	7,805	2,794	3,360	1,282	920	8.5
1962..	17,807	2,404	7,894	2,410	2,964	1,302	833	8.3
1960..	17,007	2,465	7,823	2,534	2,304	1,198	683	8.6
1959..	16,263	2,261	7,049	2,301	2,412	1,057	688	8.3
1957..	15,581	2,457	6,752	2,032	2,371	854	630	8.2
1952..	13,662	2,126	6,476	1,664	1,818	818	628	7.9
1950..	13,150	2,331	6,139	1,582	1,593	670	436	8.4
1947..	11,810	2,000	5,945	1,240	1,472	539	343	7.6
1940..	9,777	1,886	5,217	932	973	372	219	8.3

Note: Starting in 2012, data were created using population controls based on 2010 Census data. Starting in 2001, data were created using population controls based on Census 2000 data. Also starting in 2001, data are from the expanded CPS sample. Begining with data for 1992, a new question results in different categories than for earlier years. Data shown as 'High School, 4 years' are now collected in the category 'High School Graduate.' Data shown as 'College 1 to 3 years' are now collected in the 'Some college' and the two 'Associate degree' categories. Data shown as 'College 4 years or more,' are now collected in the categories, 'Bachelor's degree,' 'Master's degree,' 'Doctorate degree,' and 'Professional degree.' Due to the change in question format, median years of schooling cannot be derived. Total includes persons who did not report on years of school completed.

Table A-34. Mean Earnings of Workers 18 Years Old and Over, by Educational Attainment, Race, Hispanic Origin, and Sex, 1975–2017

(Dollars except as noted)

Race, sex, year, and Hispanic origin	Total		Not a high school graduate		High school graduate		Some college or associate's degree[1]		Bachelor's degree[1]		Advanced degree[1]	
	Mean earnings	Number of workers (thousands)	Mean earnings	Number of workers (thousands)	Mean earnings	Number of workers (thousands)	Mean earnings	Number of workers (thousands)	Mean earnings	Number of workers (thousands)	Mean earnings	Number of workers (thousands)
ALL RACES												
Both Sexes												
2017..............	53,536	163,871	26,832	12,240	38,145	42,816	41,507	47,382	67,763	39,153	98,369	22,277
2016..............	51,893	162,218	27,800	12,281	36,702	42,897	40,201	48,128	67,267	37,272	95,203	21,639
2015..............	49,994	161,074	25,315	13,159	35,615	42,404	38,943	47,961	65,482	36,348	92,525	21,199
2014..............	47,653	158,000	25,236	13,197	34,099	42,529	37,945	47,023	62,466	35,305	88,056	19,944
2013..............	46,187	156,031	23,755	12,961	32,881	42,433	36,428	46,952	59,661	34,422	90,304	19,261
2012..............	45,598	155,148	21,622	13,030	32,630	41,915	35,943	47,469	60,159	33,948	89,253	18,783
2011[2]	44,729	152,711	21,107	13,594	32,493	42,129	35,585	45,999	59,415	33,188	87,981	17,800
2010..............	42,922	151,498	20,911	13,345	31,003	42,599	34,366	45,643	57,621	32,429	83,841	17,481
2009..............	42,469	152,707	20,241	14,083	30,627	44,396	34,773	45,239	56,665	32,127	85,818	16,860
2008..............	42,588	155,989	21,023	15,217	31,283	45,182	34,808	46,663	58,613	31,890	83,144	17,035
2007..............	42,064	155,738	21,484	15,330	31,286	45,393	35,138	46,577	57,181	31,832	80,977	16,604
2006..............	41,412	154,438	20,873	16,652	31,071	45,936	34,650	45,073	56,788	31,006	82,320	15,769
2005..............	39,579	152,215	19,915	16,317	29,448	45,652	33,496	45,434	54,689	29,658	79,946	15,152
2004..............	37,899	150,095	19,182	16,372	28,631	45,571	32,010	44,387	51,568	29,004	78,224	14,713
2003[3]	37,046	148,660	18,734	16,282	27,915	45,064	31,498	44,048	51,206	28,672	74,602	14,592
2002..............	36,308	148,492	18,826	16,931	27,280	45,407	31,046	43,776	51,194	28,257	72,824	14,119
2001..............	35,805	147,829	18,793	17,293	26,795	45,641	30,782	43,214	50,623	27,980	72,869	13,700
2000[4]	34,514	147,966	17,738	17,425	25,692	45,977	29,939	43,874	49,595	27,488	71,194	13,200
1999..............	32,356	144,640	16,121	16,737	24,572	46,082	28,403	42,860	45,678	26,215	67,697	12,749
1998..............	30,928	142,053	16,053	16,742	23,594	45,987	27,566	41,412	43,782	25,818	63,473	12,095
1997..............	29,514	140,367	16,124	16,962	22,895	45,976	26,235	40,802	40,478	25,035	63,229	11,591
1996..............	28,106	138,703	15,011	17,075	22,154	45,908	25,181	40,410	38,112	24,028	61,317	11,281
1995..............	26,792	136,221	14,013	16,990	21,431	44,546	23,862	40,142	36,980	23,285	56,667	11,258
1994..............	25,852	135,096	13,697	16,479	20,248	44,614	22,226	40,135	37,224	22,712	56,105	11,155
1993..............	24,674	133,119	12,820	16,575	19,422	44,779	21,539	39,429	35,121	21,815	55,789	10,521
1992..............	23,227	130,860	12,809	16,612	18,737	45,340	20,867	37,339	32,629	21,091	48,652	10,479
1991..............	22,332	130,371	12,613	17,553	18,261	46,508	20,551	35,732	31,323	20,475	46,039	10,103
1990..............	21,793	130,080	12,582	18,698	17,820	51,977	20,694	28,993	31,112	18,128	41,458	12,285
1989..............	21,414	129,094	12,242	19,137	17,594	51,846	20,255	28,078	30,736	17,767	41,019	12,265
1988..............	20,060	127,564	11,889	19,635	16,750	51,297	19,066	27,217	28,344	17,308	37,724	12,109
1987..............	19,016	124,874	11,824	19,748	15,939	50,815	18,054	26,404	26,919	16,497	35,968	11,411
1986..............	18,149	122,757	11,203	19,665	15,120	50,104	17,073	26,113	26,511	15,788	34,787	11,087
1985..............	17,181	120,651	10,726	19,692	14,457	49,674	16,349	25,402	24,877	15,373	32,909	10,510
1984..............	16,083	118,183	10,384	20,206	13,893	48,452	14,936	24,463	23,072	14,653	30,192	10,410
1983..............	15,137	115,095	9,853	20,020	13,044	47,560	14,245	23,208	21,532	13,929	28,333	10,377
1982..............	14,351	113,451	9,387	20,789	12,560	46,584	13,503	22,602	20,272	13,425	26,915	10,051
1981..............	13,624	113,301	9,357	22,296	12,109	47,332	13,176	21,759	19,006	12,579	25,281	9,336
1980..............	12,665	111,919	8,845	23,028	11,314	46,795	12,409	21,384	18,075	12,175	23,308	8,535
1979..............	11,795	110,826	8,420	23,783	10,624	45,497	11,377	21,174	16,514	11,751	21,874	8,621
1978..............	10,812	106,436	7,759	23,787	9,834	43,510	10,357	20,121	15,291	11,001	20,173	8,017
1977..............	9,887	103,119	7,066	24,854	9,013	41,696	9,607	18,905	14,207	10,357	19,077	7,309
1976..............	9,180	100,510	6,720	25,035	8,393	40,570	8,813	17,786	13,033	10,132	17,911	6,985
1975..............	8,552	97,881	6,198	24,916	7,843	39,827	8,388	16,917	12,332	9,764	16,725	6,457
Male												
2017..............	62,662	86,872	31,688	7,597	44,466	25,137	50,012	23,606	81,607	19,657	119,590	10,871
2016..............	61,232	85,718	32,463	7,695	43,534	24,908	48,123	23,891	82,089	18,627	116,617	10,595
2015..............	58,944	85,263	30,230	8,210	41,942	24,647	46,154	23,578	79,927	18,287	113,279	10,539
2014..............	56,701	83,402	29,618	8,256	39,874	24,468	46,137	23,057	76,169	17,725	110,645	9,895
2013..............	54,658	82,576	27,586	8,286	37,763	24,327	43,841	23,112	72,124	17,203	115,282	9,647
2012..............	54,118	81,979	24,955	8,183	38,454	23,783	43,593	23,267	72,546	17,175	110,501	9,570
2011[2]	52,273	80,502	25,155	8,359	38,679	23,800	43,239	22,469	71,162	16,769	109,063	9,102
2010..............	50,645	80,284	24,413	8,382	36,181	24,230	40,935	22,150	69,623	16,595	103,359	8,925
2009..............	50,186	80,799	23,036	8,851	35,468	25,143	41,773	21,895	69,479	16,226	105,636	8,683
2008..............	51,148	82,727	24,831	9,596	36,753	25,290	42,221	22,830	72,868	16,100	103,980	8,909
2007..............	50,110	82,932	24,985	9,780	36,839	25,396	41,709	22,916	70,898	16,109	100,550	8,730
2006..............	49,647	82,310	24,072	10,541	37,356	25,489	41,521	21,952	69,818	15,769	101,441	8,556
2005..............	48,034	81,258	23,222	10,273	35,248	25,348	40,995	22,173	67,980	15,217	100,379	8,245
2004..............	46,008	79,765	22,537	10,188	34,050	25,209	39,509	21,473	63,753	14,860	97,855	8,032
2003[3]	44,726	78,869	21,447	10,173	33,266	24,292	38,451	21,534	63,084	14,849	91,831	8,019

[1]For data prior to 1991, "Some college/Associate degree" equals 1 to 3 years of college completed; "Bachelor's degree" equals 4 years of college; "Advanced degree" equals 5 or more years of college completed.
[2]Starting in 2011, earnings data were created using population controls based on Census 2010 data.
[3]Starting in 2003, respondents could choose more than one race. The race data in this table from 2003 onward represent respondents who indicated only one race.
[4]Beginning in 2000, earnings data are from the expanded Current Population Survey (CPS) sample and were calculated using population controls based on Census 2000.

Table A-34. Mean Earnings of Workers 18 Years Old and Over, by Educational Attainment, Race, Hispanic Origin, and Sex, 1975–2017—*Continued*

(Dollars except as noted)

Race, sex, year, and Hispanic origin	Total		Not a high school graduate		High school graduate		Some college or associate's degree[1]		Bachelor's degree[1]		Advanced degree[1]	
	Mean earnings	Number of workers (thousands)	Mean earnings	Number of workers (thousands)	Mean earnings	Number of workers (thousands)	Mean earnings	Number of workers (thousands)	Mean earnings	Number of workers (thousands)	Mean earnings	Number of workers (thousands)
2002	44,310	78,757	22,091	10,526	32,673	24,174	38,377	21,599	63,503	14,667	90,761	7,788
2001	43,648	78,342	21,508	10,572	32,363	24,239	37,429	21,390	63,354	14,507	90,130	7,631
2000[4]	42,772	78,319	21,007	10,535	31,446	24,439	37,372	21,526	62,609	14,375	88,077	7,442
1999	40,257	76,233	18,855	9,917	30,414	24,235	35,326	21,173	57,706	13,683	84,051	7,225
1998	38,134	75,213	19,155	10,085	28,742	24,155	34,179	20,545	55,057	13,486	77,217	6,942
1997	36,556	74,596	19,575	10,348	28,307	24,152	32,641	20,359	50,056	13,008	78,032	6,728
1996	34,705	73,955	17,826	10,583	27,642	23,966	31,426	20,208	46,702	12,562	74,406	6,636
1995	33,251	72,634	16,748	10,312	26,333	23,473	29,851	19,918	46,111	12,251	69,588	6,679
1994	32,087	72,246	16,633	9,981	25,038	23,418	27,636	19,859	46,278	12,324	67,032	6,663
1993	30,568	71,183	14,946	10,151	23,973	23,388	26,614	19,532	43,499	11,810	68,221	6,302
1992	28,448	70,409	14,934	10,335	22,978	23,610	25,660	18,768	40,039	11,353	58,324	6,344
1991	27,494	70,145	15,056	10,679	22,663	24,110	25,345	18,076	38,484	11,126	54,449	6,154
1990	27,164	70,218	14,991	11,412	22,378	26,753	26,120	14,844	38,901	9,807	49,768	7,402
1989	27,025	69,798	14,727	11,774	22,508	26,469	25,555	14,384	38,692	9,737	50,144	7,434
1988	25,344	69,006	14,551	11,993	21,481	26,080	23,827	14,019	35,906	9,466	45,677	7,449
1987	24,015	67,951	14,544	12,117	20,364	25,981	22,781	13,433	33,677	9,286	43,140	7,134
1986	23,057	67,189	13,703	12,208	19,453	25,562	21,784	13,502	33,376	8,908	41,836	7,009
1985	21,823	66,439	13,124	12,137	18,575	25,496	20,698	13,385	31,433	8,794	39,768	6,627
1984	20,452	65,005	12,775	12,325	18,016	24,827	18,863	12,818	29,203	8,387	35,804	6,648
1983	19,175	63,816	12,052	12,376	16,728	24,449	18,052	12,261	27,239	8,010	33,635	6,719
1982	18,244	63,489	11,513	12,868	16,160	24,059	17,108	12,103	25,758	7,865	32,109	6,594
1981	17,542	63,547	11,668	13,701	15,900	24,435	16,870	11,784	24,353	7,393	30,072	6,235
1980	16,382	62,825	11,042	14,273	15,002	24,023	15,871	11,663	23,340	7,132	27,846	5,733
1979	15,430	62,464	10,628	14,711	14,317	23,318	14,716	11,781	21,482	6,889	26,411	5,765
1978	14,154	60,586	9,894	14,550	13,188	22,650	13,382	11,352	19,861	6,611	24,274	5,422
1977	12,888	59,441	8,939	15,369	12,092	21,846	12,393	10,848	18,187	6,341	22,786	5,038
1976	11,923	58,419	8,522	15,634	11,189	21,499	11,376	10,282	16,714	6,135	21,202	4,868
1975	11,091	57,297	7,843	15,613	10,475	21,347	10,805	9,851	15,758	5,960	19,672	4,526
Female												
2017	43,240	76,999	18,885	4,643	29,158	17,679	33,063	23,775	53,804	19,495	78,142	11,405
2016	41,429	76,500	19,974	4,586	27,242	17,988	32,391	24,236	52,461	18,645	74,656	11,043
2015	39,929	75,811	17,162	4,949	26,832	17,756	31,970	24,382	50,856	18,061	72,006	10,660
2014	37,538	74,597	17,915	4,941	26,275	18,060	30,064	23,966	48,650	17,580	65,814	10,049
2013	36,664	73,454	16,964	4,675	26,322	18,106	29,242	23,840	47,209	17,218	65,242	9,614
2012	36,404	57,409	15,250	3,682	25,487	14,107	28,861	18,881	47,596	13,383	66,934	7,355
2011[2]	35,205	72,209	14,643	5,234	24,460	18,328	28,275	23,529	47,418	16,419	65,915	8,697
2010	34,216	71,214	14,995	4,962	24,172	18,368	28,173	23,492	45,044	15,834	63,482	8,556
2009	33,797	71,907	15,514	5,232	24,304	19,253	28,207	23,344	43,589	15,900	64,771	8,176
2008	32,922	73,262	14,521	5,621	24,329	19,892	27,708	23,833	44,078	15,789	60,301	8,126
2007	32,899	72,805	15,315	5,550	24,234	19,997	28,773	23,660	43,127	15,722	59,273	7,873
2006	32,015	72,128	15,352	6,110	23,236	20,447	28,126	23,121	43,302	15,237	59,636	7,213
2005	29,897	70,956	14,294	6,044	22,208	20,304	26,348	23,260	40,684	14,440	55,553	6,906
2004	28,691	70,285	13,655	6,183	21,923	20,361	24,983	22,914	38,776	14,143	54,623	6,680
2003[3]	28,367	69,790	14,214	6,108	21,659	20,772	24,848	22,514	38,447	13,823	53,579	6,572
2002	27,271	69,735	13,459	6,404	21,141	21,233	23,905	22,176	37,909	13,589	50,756	6,330
2001	26,962	69,487	14,524	6,720	20,489	21,402	24,268	21,824	36,913	13,472	51,160	6,068
2000[4]	25,228	69,647	12,739	6,890	19,162	21,538	22,779	22,348	35,328	13,113	49,368	5,757
1999	23,551	68,409	12,145	6,819	18,092	21,847	21,644	22,687	32,546	12,533	46,307	5,523
1998	22,818	66,840	11,353	6,657	17,898	21,832	21,056	20,867	31,452	12,332	44,954	5,153
1997	21,528	65,771	10,725	6,614	16,906	21,824	19,856	20,442	30,119	12,027	42,744	4,863
1996	20,570	64,748	10,421	6,492	16,161	21,942	18,933	20,202	28,701	11,466	42,625	4,646
1995	19,414	63,587	9,790	6,678	15,970	21,073	17,962	20,224	26,841	11,034	37,813	4,578
1994	18,684	62,850	9,189	6,498	14,955	21,195	16,928	20,276	26,483	10,388	39,905	4,493
1993	17,900	61,937	9,462	6,425	14,446	21,391	16,555	19,897	25,232	10,005	37,212	4,218
1992	17,145	60,451	9,311	6,277	14,128	21,730	16,023	18,571	23,991	9,738	33,814	4,135
1991	16,320	60,226	8,818	6,875	13,523	22,398	15,643	17,657	22,802	9,348	32,929	3,948
1990	15,493	59,862	8,808	7,286	12,986	25,224	15,002	14,149	21,933	8,321	28,862	4,883
1989	14,809	59,296	8,268	7,363	12,468	25,377	14,688	13,694	21,089	8,030	26,977	4,831
1988	13,833	58,558	7,711	7,642	11,857	25,217	14,009	13,198	19,216	7,842	25,010	4,660
1987	13,049	56,923	7,504	7,631	11,309	24,834	13,158	12,971	18,217	7,211	24,004	4,277
1986	12,214	55,568	7,109	7,457	10,606	24,542	12,029	12,611	17,623	6,880	22,672	4,078
1985	11,493	54,212	6,874	7,555	10,115	24,178	11,504	12,017	16,114	6,579	21,202	3,883

[1]For data prior to 1991, "Some college/Associate degree" equals 1 to 3 years of college completed; "Bachelor's degree" equals 4 years of college; "Advanced degree" equals 5 or more years of college completed.
[2]Starting in 2011, earnings data were created using population controls based on Census 2010 data.
[3]Starting in 2003, respondents could choose more than one race. The race data in this table from 2003 onward represent respondents who indicated only one race.
[4]Beginning in 2000, earnings data are from the expanded Current Population Survey (CPS) sample and were calculated using population controls based on Census 2000.

Table A-34. Mean Earnings of Workers 18 Years Old and Over, by Educational Attainment, Race, Hispanic Origin, and Sex, 1975–2017—*Continued*

(Dollars except as noted)

Race, sex, year, and Hispanic origin	Total		Not a high school graduate		High school graduate		Some college or associate's degree[1]		Bachelor's degree[1]		Advanced degree[1]	
	Mean earnings	Number of workers (thousands)	Mean earnings	Number of workers (thousands)	Mean earnings	Number of workers (thousands)	Mean earnings	Number of workers (thousands)	Mean earnings	Number of workers (thousands)	Mean earnings	Number of workers (thousands)
1984...................	10,742	53,178	6,644	7,881	9,561	23,625	10,614	11,645	14,865	6,266	20,275	3,762
1983...................	10,111	51,279	6,292	7,644	9,147	23,111	9,981	10,947	13,808	5,919	18,593	3,658
1982...................	9,403	49,962	5,932	7,921	8,715	22,525	9,348	10,499	12,511	5,560	17,009	3,457
1981...................	8,619	49,754	5,673	8,595	8,063	22,897	8,811	9,975	11,384	5,186	15,647	3,101
1980...................	7,909	49,094	5,263	8,755	7,423	22,772	8,256	9,721	10,628	5,043	14,022	2,802
1979...................	7,099	48,362	4,840	9,072	6,741	22,179	7,190	9,393	9,474	4,862	12,717	2,856
1978...................	6,396	45,850	4,397	9,237	6,192	20,860	6,441	8,769	8,408	4,390	11,603	2,595
1977...................	5,804	43,678	4,032	9,485	5,624	19,850	5,856	8,057	7,923	4,016	10,848	2,271
1976...................	5,373	42,091	3,723	9,401	5,240	19,071	5,301	7,504	7,383	3,997	10,345	2,117
1975...................	4,968	40,584	3,438	9,303	4,802	18,480	5,019	7,066	6,963	3,804	9,818	1,931
WHITE												
Both Sexes												
2017...................	54,838	128,070	27,220	9,696	39,781	33,308	42,859	36,748	69,284	31,127	99,044	17,190
2016...................	53,178	127,241	28,489	9,615	38,326	33,491	41,583	37,481	68,538	29,950	95,647	16,701
2015...................	51,183	127,291	26,441	10,404	37,106	33,342	39,959	37,686	66,926	29,216	92,640	16,640
2014...................	48,971	125,227	26,065	10,553	35,528	33,616	39,590	36,920	63,422	28,313	88,835	15,823
2013...................	47,452	124,663	24,363	10,220	34,192	33,746	37,528	37,388	60,962	27,869	91,369	15,439
2012...................	46,844	124,316	22,048	10,491	33,928	33,498	36,493	37,706	61,527	27,651	90,948	14,967
2011[2].................	46,053	123,044	21,704	10,891	33,719	33,803	36,204	36,861	61,253	27,096	90,060	14,391
2010...................	44,142	123,870	21,471	10,820	32,067	34,611	35,180	37,071	59,188	26,950	85,070	14,415
2009...................	43,337	125,151	20,457	11,507	31,429	36,125	35,634	37,035	57,762	26,595	86,188	13,887
2008...................	43,666	127,552	21,590	12,379	32,126	36,819	35,622	37,891	59,866	26,487	84,739	13,973
2007...................	43,139	127,413	22,289	12,363	32,223	37,058	35,685	37,988	58,652	26,310	82,384	13,692
2006...................	42,395	126,570	21,464	13,582	32,083	37,362	35,338	36,878	57,932	25,763	83,185	12,983
2005...................	40,717	124,870	20,264	13,157	30,569	37,122	34,326	37,409	55,785	24,652	81,697	12,527
2004...................	38,946	123,452	19,367	13,289	29,605	37,114	32,751	36,547	52,877	24,061	79,071	12,397
2003[3].................	38,053	122,599	19,110	13,094	28,708	36,951	32,346	36,318	52,259	24,010	75,638	12,226
2002...................	37,376	122,699	19,264	13,740	28,145	37,380	31,878	36,023	52,479	23,638	73,870	11,916
2001...................	36,844	122,930	19,120	14,012	27,700	37,969	31,482	35,722	51,631	23,531	74,398	11,694
2000[4].................	35,527	123,039	18,285	14,172	26,444	38,133	30,638	36,334	50,969	23,110	71,983	11,288
1999...................	33,326	120,916	16,623	13,585	25,270	38,428	29,105	35,634	46,894	22,322	68,910	10,949
1998...................	32,057	119,201	16,474	13,531	24,409	38,397	28,318	34,540	44,852	22,266	65,379	10,467
1997...................	30,515	117,985	16,596	13,780	23,618	38,409	26,906	34,274	41,439	21,528	65,058	9,994
1996...................	28,844	117,230	15,358	13,972	22,782	38,463	25,511	34,087	38,936	20,846	61,779	9,861
1995...................	27,556	115,636	14,234	13,869	22,154	37,802	24,349	33,850	37,711	20,203	57,054	9,914
1994...................	26,696	114,586	13,941	13,119	20,911	37,562	22,648	34,006	37,996	19,917	56,475	9,981
1993...................	25,440	113,342	13,171	13,480	19,918	37,826	21,924	33,728	35,846	18,922	56,964	9,386
1992...................	23,932	112,120	13,193	13,494	19,265	38,692	21,357	32,014	33,092	18,555	49,347	9,363
1991...................	22,998	111,830	12,914	14,041	18,766	39,764	21,013	30,973	31,837	18,033	46,498	9,019
1990...................	22,401	111,972	12,773	15,191	18,257	44,635	21,095	25,105	31,626	15,993	41,908	11,049
1989...................	22,035	111,243	12,654	15,628	18,011	44,726	20,678	24,212	31,266	15,723	41,610	10,952
1988...................	20,616	110,159	12,236	16,042	17,183	44,399	19,384	23,643	28,886	15,221	38,129	10,854
1987...................	19,599	108,407	12,502	16,165	16,339	44,235	18,265	23,083	27,741	14,624	36,175	10,300
1986...................	18,698	106,384	11,605	16,094	15,514	43,593	17,371	22,653	27,061	14,055	35,265	9,987
1985...................	17,709	104,818	11,115	16,149	14,815	43,347	16,701	22,131	25,376	13,670	33,401	9,522
1984...................	16,546	103,022	10,732	16,559	14,274	42,547	15,197	21,451	23,472	13,056	30,515	9,409
1983...................	15,556	101,035	10,239	16,568	13,357	42,007	14,486	20,452	21,914	12,577	28,532	9,430
1982...................	14,767	99,488	9,719	17,132	12,854	41,157	13,799	19,967	20,760	12,103	27,040	9,127
1981...................	14,027	99,510	9,737	18,298	12,355	42,080	13,424	19,102	19,389	11,450	25,564	8,582
1980...................	13,040	98,358	9,743	18,925	11,524	41,600	12,677	18,888	18,434	11,067	23,466	7,876
1979...................	12,155	97,544	8,827	19,504	10,431	40,458	11,574	18,835	16,758	10,807	22,085	7,940
1978...................	11,135	94,002	8,135	19,516	10,020	38,915	10,504	18,022	15,463	10,171	20,531	7,376
1977...................	10,191	91,254	7,415	20,492	9,173	37,521	9,771	16,968	14,462	9,534	19,337	6,739
1976...................	9,469	89,099	7,018	20,625	8,559	36,523	8,958	16,127	13,279	9,325	18,153	6,498
1975...................	8,815	86,894	6,438	20,696	8,005	35,799	8,525	15,423	12,597	8,955	16,920	6,021
Male												
2017...................	64,266	69,222	32,096	6,277	46,284	19,933	51,974	18,724	83,478	15,913	122,160	8,373
2016...................	62,680	68,496	33,153	6,255	45,390	19,941	50,063	18,951	84,069	15,136	116,854	8,211
2015...................	60,652	68,610	31,336	6,755	43,711	19,807	47,900	18,905	82,495	14,884	115,094	8,257
2014...................	58,387	67,466	30,342	6,858	41,492	19,815	48,405	18,518	78,348	14,409	112,351	7,864

[1]For data prior to 1991, "Some college/Associate degree" equals 1 to 3 years of college completed; "Bachelor's degree" equals 4 years of college; "Advanced degree" equals 5 or more years of college completed.
[2]Starting in 2011, earnings data were created using population controls based on Census 2010 data.
[3]Starting in 2003, respondents could choose more than one race. The race data in this table from 2003 onward represent respondents who indicated only one race.
[4]Beginning in 2000, earnings data are from the expanded Current Population Survey (CPS) sample and were calculated using population controls based on Census 2000.

Table A-34. Mean Earnings of Workers 18 Years Old and Over, by Educational Attainment, Race, Hispanic Origin, and Sex, 1975–2017—*Continued*

(Dollars except as noted)

Race, sex, year, and Hispanic origin	Total		Not a high school graduate		High school graduate		Some college or associate's degree[1]		Bachelor's degree[1]		Advanced degree[1]	
	Mean earnings	Number of workers (thousands)	Mean earnings	Number of workers (thousands)	Mean earnings	Number of workers (thousands)	Mean earnings	Number of workers (thousands)	Mean earnings	Number of workers (thousands)	Mean earnings	Number of workers (thousands)
2013	56,215	67,148	28,253	6,773	39,191	19,796	45,403	18,729	74,018	14,113	117,959	7,735
2012	55,802	66,906	25,725	6,809	40,070	19,390	45,049	18,825	74,594	14,268	114,150	7,612
2011[2]	55,013	66,151	25,819	6,917	40,247	19,524	44,155	18,279	73,630	13,978	112,515	7,451
2010	52,304	66,887	25,100	7,011	37,477	20,018	42,151	18,362	71,958	14,077	105,869	7,417
2009	51,287	67,464	23,353	7,426	36,418	20,855	42,884	18,273	71,286	13,740	106,571	7,168
2008	52,672	68,816	25,386	8,113	37,852	20,899	43,463	18,849	75,053	13,596	107,099	7,356
2007	51,781	69,099	25,886	8,170	38,214	21,129	42,903	18,995	73,477	13,577	103,293	7,227
2006	51,013	68,752	24,579	8,932	38,833	21,090	42,684	18,340	71,735	13,326	103,340	7,063
2005	49,611	67,874	23,556	8,582	36,753	20,914	42,206	18,583	69,852	12,900	103,144	6,893
2004	47,404	66,677	22,598	8,591	35,360	20,781	40,639	17,990	65,652	12,555	100,084	6,758
2003[3]	46,114	66,199	21,791	8,500	34,224	20,238	39,594	18,060	65,264	12,665	94,017	6,734
2002	45,793	66,202	22,539	8,841	33,920	20,156	39,605	18,068	65,439	12,512	92,733	6,623
2001	45,071	66,216	22,006	8,833	33,545	20,465	38,501	17,957	65,046	12,396	92,304	6,562
2000[4]	44,181	66,222	21,561	8,859	32,528	20,553	38,476	18,179	64,831	12,271	89,812	6,359
1999	41,598	64,856	19,320	8,286	31,279	20,526	36,518	17,928	59,606	11,851	85,345	6,265
1998	39,638	64,181	19,632	8,430	29,782	20,388	35,277	17,407	56,620	11,874	79,734	6,083
1997	37,933	63,738	20,071	8,670	29,298	20,426	33,691	17,423	51,678	11,340	80,322	5,879
1996	35,821	63,532	18,246	8,899	28,591	20,329	32,238	17,418	48,014	11,065	75,481	5,821
1995	34,276	62,520	17,032	8,660	27,467	19,982	30,529	17,136	47,016	10,851	70,155	5,891
1994	33,292	62,029	16,835	8,133	26,125	19,833	28,240	17,091	47,575	10,992	67,629	5,979
1993	31,719	61,356	15,295	8,430	24,781	19,835	27,297	16,959	44,505	10,452	70,000	5,680
1992	29,515	60,919	15,414	8,487	23,844	20,259	26,387	16,335	40,893	10,118	59,329	5,720
1991	28,516	60,770	15,499	8,720	23,475	20,765	26,090	15,873	39,547	9,893	55,257	5,519
1990	28,105	60,676	15,319	9,476	23,135	23,088	26,841	11,003	39,780	8,770	50,385	6,731
1989	28,013	60,877	15,217	9,805	23,291	23,029	26,260	12,582	39,654	8,750	51,031	6,710
1988	26,184	60,221	14,943	10,008	22,216	22,707	24,462	12,277	36,637	8,467	46,181	6,762
1987	24,898	59,468	15,303	10,132	21,012	22,682	23,310	11,771	34,865	8,384	43,440	6,499
1986	23,892	58,932	14,168	10,239	20,128	22,392	22,303	11,846	34,273	8,041	42,480	6,413
1985	22,604	58,385	13,579	10,163	19,203	22,357	21,240	11,831	32,165	7,970	40,358	6,064
1984	21,174	57,362	13,248	10,280	18,681	21,989	19,344	11,387	29,781	7,624	36,219	6,081
1983	19,812	56,641	12,573	10,387	17,281	21,733	18,388	10,974	27,726	7,379	33,981	6,168
1982	18,859	56,364	11,952	10,816	16,662	21,436	17,571	10,822	26,404	7,242	32,266	6,047
1981	18,141	56,397	12,049	11,523	16,352	21,809	17,303	10,448	24,943	6,824	30,396	5,794
1980	16,945	55,772	11,539	11,937	15,382	21,453	16,313	10,400	23,803	6,618	27,991	5,363
1979	15,971	55,556	11,127	12,291	13,916	20,834	15,043	10,572	21,785	6,464	26,645	5,395
1978	14,627	54,113	10,358	12,141	13,534	20,328	13,589	10,350	20,085	6,205	24,635	5,088
1977	13,329	53,174	9,366	12,903	12,377	19,773	12,657	9,853	18,521	5,941	23,093	4,704
1976	12,342	52,312	8,867	13,117	11,497	19,446	11,616	9,394	16,995	5,765	21,490	4,589
1975	11,448	51,510	8,110	13,191	10,726	19,361	11,028	9,096	16,079	5,587	19,858	4,275
Female												
2017	43,749	58,847	18,270	3,419	30,089	13,374	33,390	18,023	54,436	15,213	77,089	8,816
2016	42,098	58,744	19,807	3,360	27,929	13,549	32,911	18,530	52,669	14,814	75,138	8,490
2015	40,112	58,680	17,379	3,649	27,440	13,535	31,966	18,781	50,759	14,332	70,520	8,382
2014	37,971	57,761	18,129	3,695	26,965	13,800	30,718	18,401	47,954	13,904	65,599	7,959
2013	37,222	57,515	16,718	3,446	27,097	13,949	29,622	18,658	47,565	13,755	64,670	7,704
2012	36,404	57,409	15,250	3,682	25,487	14,107	28,861	18,881	47,596	13,383	66,934	7,355
2011[2]	35,635	56,892	14,541	3,974	24,793	14,279	28,383	18,581	48,064	13,117	65,952	6,940
2010	34,561	56,982	14,791	3,808	24,645	14,593	28,339	18,709	45,223	12,873	63,021	6,997
2009	34,040	57,687	15,187	4,080	24,615	15,270	28,573	16,762	43,309	12,855	64,441	6,718
2008	33,115	58,735	14,370	4,265	24,610	15,919	27,859	19,041	43,848	12,891	59,877	6,616
2007	32,899	58,313	15,278	4,192	24,276	15,929	28,466	18,993	42,846	12,733	59,006	6,464
2006	32,148	57,818	15,483	4,650	23,334	16,272	28,069	18,537	43,142	12,437	59,141	5,920
2005	30,125	56,995	14,608	4,575	22,590	16,208	26,547	18,825	40,344	11,751	55,461	5,634
2004	28,966	56,705	13,459	4,703	22,260	16,358	25,104	18,556	38,898	11,445	53,895	5,641
2003[3]	28,591	56,400	14,149	4,593	22,028	16,712	25,177	18,258	37,739	11,344	53,102	5,492
2002	27,512	56,496	13,354	4,898	21,388	17,224	24,101	17,954	37,903	11,126	50,270	5,293
2001	27,240	56,714	14,197	5,178	20,866	17,503	24,387	17,764	36,698	11,135	51,499	5,131
2000[4]	25,441	56,816	12,823	5,313	19,330	17,579	22,790	18,155	35,273	10,838	48,982	4,929
1999	23,756	56,061	12,405	5,299	18,381	17,902	21,598	17,705	32,507	10,471	45,741	4,684
1998	23,213	55,020	11,255	5,102	18,327	18,009	21,246	17,132	31,406	10,393	45,462	4,384
1997	21,779	54,247	10,700	5,111	17,166	17,983	19,892	16,852	30,041	10,188	43,236	4,114
1996	20,590	53,697	10,290	5,073	16,270	18,134	18,482	16,669	28,667	9,781	42,049	4,041

[1]For data prior to 1991, "Some college/Associate degree" equals 1 to 3 years of college completed; "Bachelor's degree" equals 4 years of college; "Advanced degree" equals 5 or more years of college completed.
[2]Starting in 2011, earnings data were created using population controls based on Census 2010 data.
[3]Starting in 2003, respondents could choose more than one race. The race data in this table from 2003 onward represent respondents who indicated only one race.
[4]Beginning in 2000, earnings data are from the expanded Current Population Survey (CPS) sample and were calculated using population controls based on Census 2000.

Table A-34. Mean Earnings of Workers 18 Years Old and Over, by Educational Attainment, Race, Hispanic Origin, and Sex, 1975–2017—*Continued*

(Dollars except as noted)

Race, sex, year, and Hispanic origin	Total		Not a high school graduate		High school graduate		Some college or associate's degree[1]		Bachelor's degree[1]		Advanced degree[1]	
	Mean earnings	Number of workers (thousands)	Mean earnings	Number of workers (thousands)	Mean earnings	Number of workers (thousands)	Mean earnings	Number of workers (thousands)	Mean earnings	Number of workers (thousands)	Mean earnings	Number of workers (thousands)
1995.................	19,647	53,117	9,582	5,208	16,196	17,820	18,011	16,714	26,916	9,352	37,864	4,022
1994.................	18,912	52,557	9,220	4,987	15,078	17,729	16,998	16,915	26,198	8,925	39,816	4,002
1993.................	18,028	51,986	9,624	5,050	14,557	17,991	16,490	16,769	25,161	8,470	36,988	3,705
1992.................	17,289	51,200	9,428	5,007	14,233	18,434	16,116	15,679	23,738	8,437	33,675	3,643
1991.................	16,431	51,060	8,677	5,321	13,621	18,999	15,677	15,100	22,471	8,140	32,687	3,500
1990.................	15,559	50,905	8,725	5,715	13,031	21,547	14,922	12,102	21,725	7,223	28,694	4,318
1989.................	14,810	50,366	8,338	5,823	12,406	21,697	14,640	11,630	20,741	6,973	26,709	4,242
1988.................	13,902	49,938	7,747	6,034	11,915	21,692	13,898	11,366	19,169	6,754	24,824	4,092
1987.................	13,161	48,939	7,798	6,033	11,421	21,553	13,015	11,312	18,170	6,240	23,753	3,801
1986.................	12,247	47,452	7,123	5,855	10,641	21,201	11,964	10,807	17,418	6,014	22,320	3,574
1985.................	11,555	46,433	6,931	5,986	10,142	20,990	11,488	10,300	15,883	5,700	21,202	3,458
1984.................	10,732	45,660	6,614	6,279	9,561	20,558	10,504	10,064	14,617	5,432	20,092	3,328
1983.................	10,126	44,394	6,317	6,181	9,150	20,274	9,969	9,478	13,664	5,198	18,230	3,262
1982.................	9,419	43,124	5,896	6,316	8,714	19,721	9,336	9,145	12,352	4,861	16,779	3,080
1981.................	8,646	43,113	5,727	6,775	8,054	20,271	8,740	8,654	11,196	4,626	15,523	2,788
1980.................	7,926	42,586	6,675	6,988	7,415	20,147	8,221	8,488	10,447	4,449	13,809	2,513
1979.................	7,105	41,988	4,909	7,213	6,731	19,624	7,135	8,263	9,275	4,343	12,420	2,545
1978.................	6,398	39,889	4,476	7,375	6,176	18,587	6,342	7,672	8,231	3,966	11,404	2,288
1977.................	5,808	38,080	4,097	7,589	5,604	17,748	5,774	7,115	7,750	3,593	10,655	2,035
1976.................	5,383	36,787	3,788	7,508	5,214	17,077	5,250	6,733	7,262	3,560	10,131	1,909
1975.................	4,982	35,384	3,500	7,505	4,800	16,438	4,926	6,327	6,822	3,368	9,728	1,746
NON-HISPANIC WHITE												
Both Sexes												
2017.................	58,601	103,373	27,145	4,032	41,289	25,484	43,996	30,141	71,054	27,773	100,150	15,941
2016.................	56,574	103,334	27,014	3,981	39,265	25,971	42,932	30,953	70,220	26,916	96,689	15,510
2015.................	54,352	103,957	26,974	4,394	38,588	25,921	40,812	31,693	67,636	26,508	93,599	15,438
2014.................	52,171	102,756	29,080	4,344	36,826	26,583	40,487	31,236	64,462	25,783	89,735	14,808
2013.................	50,604	102,814	26,750	4,136	35,595	27,119	38,371	31,688	61,913	25,437	92,569	14,432
2012.................	49,981	102,974	23,126	4,503	35,399	26,822	37,942	32,362	62,537	25,246	91,627	14,039
2011[2]	49,147	102,365	22,642	4,849	35,365	27,313	36,992	31,780	62,389	24,891	90,659	13,529
2010.................	46,878	103,829	22,557	4,877	33,279	28,369	35,903	32,184	60,119	24,823	85,840	13,574
2009.................	45,939	105,137	21,229	5,216	32,562	29,860	36,249	32,430	58,487	24,533	86,770	13,095
2008.................	46,179	107,294	21,765	5,798	33,159	30,598	36,158	33,221	60,866	24,445	85,017	13,230
2007.................	45,542	107,434	23,015	5,908	33,094	30,855	36,290	33,431	59,727	24,366	82,900	12,871
2006.................	44,813	106,828	22,206	6,876	32,931	31,345	35,872	32,403	58,917	23,855	83,785	12,347
2005.................	42,963	106,337	21,134	6,603	31,445	31,484	34,866	33,355	56,462	23,013	82,205	11,879
2004.................	40,943	105,505	19,742	6,754	30,197	31,793	33,192	33,200	53,411	22,544	79,166	11,961
2003[3]	40,094	105,214	19,769	6,768	29,571	31,831	32,825	32,460	52,856	22,474	76,200	11,680
2002.................	39,220	105,706	19,423	7,380	28,756	32,365	32,318	32,344	53,185	22,221	74,122	11,395
2001.................	38,711	106,384	19,659	7,812	28,426	33,050	31,905	32,118	52,300	22,204	74,932	11,198
2000[4]	37,346	106,709	19,147	7,957	27,122	33,231	31,217	32,836	51,351	21,824	72,356	10,859
1999.................	34,838	106,573	16,957	8,219	25,847	34,121	29,557	32,454	47,401	21,272	68,910	10,507
1998.................	33,336	105,523	16,837	8,488	24,801	34,344	23,897	31,459	45,342	21,175	65,461	10,059
Male												
2017.................	69,548	55,091	32,263	2,530	48,476	15,170	53,779	15,353	85,885	14,239	123,866	7,797
2016.................	67,180	54,893	31,668	2,543	46,416	15,315	51,782	15,718	86,312	13,676	118,068	7,639
2015.................	64,884	56,124	33,003	2,862	45,533	15,559	48,967	16,271	83,328	13,664	116,296	7,766
2014.................	63,100	54,432	35,105	2,752	43,312	15,583	49,712	15,606	80,075	13,117	113,515	7,372
2013.................	60,804	54,529	32,329	2,717	40,991	15,819	46,713	15,873	75,345	12,910	120,004	7,208
2012.................	60,396	54,569	28,026	2,784	42,157	15,388	46,477	16,175	75,826	13,080	115,598	7,139
2011[2]	59,584	54,244	27,872	2,978	42,772	15,644	45,443	15,675	75,168	12,900	113,244	7,045
2010.................	56,417	55,094	27,375	3,030	39,284	16,186	43,272	15,846	73,149	13,010	107,125	7,019
2009.................	55,318	55,638	25,695	3,187	38,160	17,015	43,802	15,981	72,305	12,708	107,872	6,746
2008.................	56,538	56,822	26,479	3,654	39,405	17,206	44,237	16,439	76,613	12,562	107,498	6,960
2007.................	55,662	57,080	27,874	3,716	39,764	17,309	43,835	16,680	75,214	12,597	104,317	6,772
2006.................	54,843	56,843	26,100	4,289	40,180	17,470	43,589	16,024	73,376	12,321	104,031	6,738
2005.................	53,263	56,675	25,511	4,127	38,134	17,507	43,137	16,456	70,932	12,048	104,107	6,535
2004.................	50,597	55,930	23,590	4,203	36,324	17,568	41,490	16,259	66,527	11,739	100,220	6,527

[1]For data prior to 1991, "Some college/Associate degree" equals 1 to 3 years of college completed; "Bachelor's degree" equals 4 years of college; "Advanced degree" equals 5 or more years of college completed.
[2]Starting in 2011, earnings data were created using population controls based on Census 2010 data.
[3]Starting in 2003, respondents could choose more than one race. The race data in this table from 2003 onward represent respondents who indicated only one race.
[4]Beginning in 2000, earnings data are from the expanded Current Population Survey (CPS) sample and were calculated using population controls based on Census 2000.

Table A-34. Mean Earnings of Workers 18 Years Old and Over, by Educational Attainment, Race, Hispanic Origin, and Sex, 1975–2017—*Continued*

(Dollars except as noted)

Race, sex, year, and Hispanic origin	Total		Not a high school graduate		High school graduate		Some college or associate's degree[1]		Bachelor's degree[1]		Advanced degree[1]	
	Mean earnings	Number of workers (thousands)	Mean earnings	Number of workers (thousands)	Mean earnings	Number of workers (thousands)	Mean earnings	Number of workers (thousands)	Mean earnings	Number of workers (thousands)	Mean earnings	Number of workers (thousands)
2003[3]	49,386	55,774	22,957	4,224	35,589	17,225	40,316	16,048	66,390	11,849	95,029	6,427
2002	48,817	55,994	23,250	4,580	34,909	17,218	40,368	16,121	66,638	11,764	93,686	6,309
2001	47,973	56,528	23,096	4,749	34,627	17,672	39,133	16,114	66,196	11,692	92,954	6,299
2000[4]	47,084	56,675	23,296	4,763	33,669	17,733	39,379	16,435	65,459	11,594	90,150	6,149
1999	44,032	56,575	20,256	4,842	32,321	18,047	37,224	16,343	60,384	11,307	85,918	6,036
1998	41,612	56,246	20,781	5,152	30,429	18,048	29,555	15,849	57,346	11,335	79,524	5,862
Female												
2017	46,110	48,282	18,522	1,502	30,718	10,313	33,840	14,788	55,450	13,533	77,446	8,144
2016	44,556	48,441	18,777	1,437	28,989	10,656	33,801	15,235	53,598	13,240	75,942	7,871
2015	42,070	48,771	15,942	1,595	28,315	10,646	32,304	15,772	51,126	13,009	71,035	7,746
2014	39,860	48,324	18,662	1,591	27,637	10,999	31,276	15,630	48,291	12,665	66,161	7,436
2013	39,084	48,284	16,062	1,418	28,041	11,300	29,999	15,815	48,070	12,526	65,190	7,223
2012	38,240	48,405	15,189	1,718	26,303	11,433	29,413	16,187	48,247	12,165	66,824	6,900
2011[2]	37,382	48,120	14,314	1,870	25,435	11,669	28,766	16,105	48,640	11,990	66,120	6,484
2010	36,093	48,735	14,649	1,846	25,300	12,183	28,755	16,337	45,767	11,812	63,047	6,555
2009	35,396	49,498	14,216	2,029	25,147	12,845	28,911	16,448	43,636	11,825	64,351	6,349
2008	34,517	50,471	13,730	2,144	25,133	13,391	28,244	16,781	44,220	11,883	60,063	6,270
2007	34,069	50,353	14,779	2,192	24,570	13,546	28,772	16,746	43,150	11,769	59,121	6,099
2006	33,407	49,984	15,751	2,857	23,805	13,875	28,322	16,379	43,473	11,534	59,458	5,608
2005	31,208	49,661	13,837	2,476	23,004	13,977	26,812	16,899	40,562	10,964	55,422	5,344
2004	30,051	49,575	13,401	2,550	22,631	14,224	25,228	16,940	39,161	10,805	53,875	5,433
2003[3]	29,613	49,439	14,475	2,543	22,473	14,605	25,499	16,411	37,761	10,624	53,164	5,253
2002	28,410	49,712	13,163	2,800	21,762	15,146	24,318	16,222	38,049	10,457	49,845	5,085
2001	28,210	49,856	14,328	3,062	21,301	15,378	24,628	16,004	36,844	10,512	51,756	4,898
2000[4]	26,315	50,034	12,962	3,194	19,631	15,498	23,038	16,401	35,362	10,230	49,126	4,710
1999	24,436	49,998	12,227	3,378	18,579	16,074	21,779	16,112	32,667	9,964	45,943	4,470
1998	23,891	49,277	10,746	3,336	18,568	16,295	18,198	15,610	31,516	9,840	45,805	4,196
BLACK												
Both Sexes												
2017	41,570	20,112	23,690	1,329	31,889	6,293	36,777	6,816	53,938	3,740	78,350	1,932
2016	40,767	19,755	24,054	1,496	30,131	6,150	34,740	6,841	57,409	3,394	80,903	1,873
2015	39,394	19,150	19,783	1,582	29,211	6,015	34,653	6,606	55,506	3,220	80,976	1,725
2014	37,012	18,657	22,353	1,420	28,439	5,905	32,074	6,605	51,983	3,084	72,257	1,642
2013	35,817	18,023	21,403	1,590	26,670	5,689	32,137	6,228	49,904	2,997	72,496	1,517
2012	34,800	17,838	18,889	1,486	26,625	5,639	31,730	6,398	48,972	2,854	68,329	1,459
2011[2]	34,755	17,295	17,488	1,613	27,562	5,539	32,891	5,964	45,477	2,796	70,140	1,380
2010	32,808	16,840	17,644	1,559	25,757	5,518	30,351	5,927	44,311	2,596	71,000	1,237
2009	33,362	16,744	18,936	1,618	26,970	5,803	30,520	5,577	47,799	2,583	66,923	1,162
2008	32,874	17,509	18,123	1,748	27,265	6,060	30,248	5,933	46,527	2,550	66,198	1,216
2007	33,333	17,453	17,439	1,854	27,179	5,996	32,787	5,813	46,502	2,682	64,247	1,107
2006	32,443	17,234	17,823	1,943	26,368	6,159	31,234	5,581	47,903	2,503	64,834	1,045
2005	30,472	17,000	17,216	2,025	23,904	6,101	28,848	5,390	47,101	2,412	63,664	1,071
2004	29,096	16,631	17,827	2,044	23,498	6,138	27,779	5,191	42,342	2,348	65,538	909
2003[3]	28,838	16,389	16,201	2,095	23,777	5,941	27,187	5,119	42,968	2,321	64,164	911
2002	28,179	16,352	16,516	2,148	22,823	5,822	27,626	5,255	42,285	2,275	59,944	851
2001	27,031	16,683	17,248	2,382	21,743	5,729	26,907	5,481	40,165	2,212	55,771	877
2000[4]	26,204	16,756	15,201	2,434	21,789	6,020	26,324	5,431	41,513	2,060	52,373	809
1999	24,979	16,936	13,569	2,393	20,991	6,112	25,176	5,417	37,422	2,140	52,437	873
1998	22,829	16,201	13,672	2,402	19,236	6,053	23,927	4,559	36,373	1,897	44,760	764
1997	21,909	15,873	13,185	2,437	18,980	5,964	22,899	4,902	32,062	1,846	42,791	724
1996	21,978	15,255	13,110	2,383	18,722	5,844	23,628	4,783	31,955	1,655	48,731	590
1995	20,537	14,847	12,956	2,389	17,072	5,453	21,824	4,727	29,666	1,684	46,654	595
1994	19,772	14,754	12,705	2,290	16,446	5,596	19,631	4,610	30,938	1,679	48,653	579
1993	18,614	14,315	11,065	2,352	16,122	5,521	18,867	4,279	29,953	1,638	41,221	525
1992	17,416	13,836	11,077	2,451	15,260	5,379	18,719	4,054	27,457	1,429	41,439	523
1991	16,809	13,865	11,248	2,860	15,060	5,512	17,850	3,581	25,630	1,383	38,002	528
1990	16,627	13,731	11,184	2,853	14,794	6,049	18,209	3,004	26,448	1,217	32,962	607
1989	16,072	13,600	10,066	2,883	14,613	5,894	17,385	3,008	25,357	1,121	32,740	694
1988	15,318	13,356	10,202	2,970	13,835	5,760	16,760	2,802	23,689	1,204	30,802	621
1987	14,136	13,023	9,976	3,015	12,862	5,699	15,491	2,617	20,805	1,097	29,163	596
1986	13,494	12,729	9,365	3,028	12,276	5,470	14,743	2,662	21,403	1,004	27,503	564

[1]For data prior to 1991, "Some college/Associate degree" equals 1 to 3 years of college completed; "Bachelor's degree" equals 4 years of college; "Advanced degree" equals 5 or more years of college completed.
[2]Starting in 2011, earnings data were created using population controls based on Census 2010 data.
[3]Starting in 2003, respondents could choose more than one race. The race data in this table from 2003 onward represent respondents who indicated only one race.
[4]Beginning in 2000, earnings data are from the expanded Current Population Survey (CPS) sample and were calculated using population controls based on Census 2000.

Table A-34. Mean Earnings of Workers 18 Years Old and Over, by Educational Attainment, Race, Hispanic Origin, and Sex, 1975–2017—*Continued*

(Dollars except as noted)

Race, sex, year, and Hispanic origin	Total Mean earnings	Total Number of workers (thousands)	Not a high school graduate Mean earnings	Not a high school graduate Number of workers (thousands)	High school graduate Mean earnings	High school graduate Number of workers (thousands)	Some college or associate's degree[1] Mean earnings	Some college or associate's degree[1] Number of workers (thousands)	Bachelor's degree[1] Mean earnings	Bachelor's degree[1] Number of workers (thousands)	Advanced degree[1] Mean earnings	Advanced degree[1] Number of workers (thousands)
1985	12,926	12,427	9,116	3,009	11,791	5,223	13,805	2,615	20,533	1,046	26,246	535
1984	12,002	11,948	8,725	3,127	10,882	4,927	12,890	2,396	19,330	937	24,072	561
1983	11,299	11,296	7,867	3,035	10,557	4,692	12,426	2,206	17,207	828	23,506	535
1982	10,612	11,081	7,799	3,188	10,287	4,591	11,119	2,067	15,152	747	22,959	488
1981	10,117	11,088	7,520	3,514	9,994	4,388	11,456	2,078	14,587	708	19,463	398
1980	11,085	5,576	8,421	2,054	11,563	2,119	12,393	964	15,616	283	19,960	353
1979	8,720	10,856	6,424	3,776	8,723	4,267	9,895	1,826	13,473	622	18,182	366
1978	7,981	10,420	5,918	3,841	8,152	3,944	9,026	1,689	12,870	557	15,076	389
1977	7,271	10,014	5,406	3,946	7,553	3,604	8,321	1,578	11,088	532	14,749	354
1976	6,716	9,744	5,304	4,008	6,805	3,515	7,331	1,370	10,331	547	15,013	305
1975	6,190	9,368	4,989	3,922	6,281	3,495	7,212	1,193	9,473	517	12,333	241
Male												
2017	46,085	9,427	27,150	656	36,451	3,406	41,410	3,002	61,434	1,628	92,812	733
2016	46,686	9,231	26,919	769	34,968	3,235	39,407	3,004	70,026	1,531	103,465	691
2015	43,781	8,979	23,846	796	33,881	3,158	39,459	2,874	63,477	1,466	88,699	683
2014	42,454	8,645	25,516	746	32,836	3,036	37,116	2,831	60,458	1,376	91,652	653
2013	40,785	8,348	26,346	843	29,893	2,887	38,126	2,696	57,304	1,312	88,641	608
2012	38,244	8,293	19,497	800	30,276	2,891	36,043	2,804	53,983	1,210	81,253	585
2011[2]	38,633	7,951	21,035	812	31,219	2,811	38,029	2,654	49,390	1,155	85,528	518
2010	35,598	7,735	19,452	829	29,478	2,878	33,905	2,473	48,068	1,075	81,199	477
2009	37,553	7,657	21,828	861	30,723	2,996	35,889	2,301	55,655	1,030	78,574	467
2008	36,057	8,116	22,344	866	30,985	3,166	34,209	2,505	51,691	1,059	73,948	518
2007	35,668	8,088	19,705	985	29,640	2,994	34,035	2,492	53,029	1,155	74,351	459
2006	36,045	7,932	21,294	982	30,122	3,067	34,750	2,334	52,569	1,086	74,507	460
2005	34,165	7,836	19,890	1,056	27,360	3,050	33,544	2,273	52,070	1,011	77,210	444
2004	33,020	7,668	22,796	1,029	26,608	3,119	32,367	2,176	47,746	956	79,168	386
2003[3]	32,545	7,469	17,915	1,039	28,102	2,910	31,556	2,156	45,635	966	76,871	397
2002	31,790	7,483	19,294	1,072	25,582	2,832	32,764	2,283	47,018	974	75,050	321
2001	30,502	7,727	18,543	1,210	25,037	2,759	31,084	2,457	46,511	943	67,007	356
2000[4]	30,109	7,700	17,992	1,235	25,219	2,942	30,966	2,291	49,270	880	60,207	349
1999	28,821	7,806	16,391	1,199	25,849	2,934	28,442	2,338	42,530	971	59,587	365
1998	26,090	7,488	16,013	1,190	22,698	2,974	26,586	2,215	42,539	792	51,198	318
1997	25,080	7,370	15,423	1,304	22,440	2,862	27,215	2,108	35,792	818	49,940	278
1996	25,067	7,125	15,461	1,290	22,267	2,836	26,365	2,047	35,558	700	65,981	253
1995	23,876	7,090	14,877	1,280	19,514	2,812	26,846	2,047	36,026	659	57,186	293
1994	22,614	7,009	15,984	1,191	18,527	2,818	23,748	1,959	34,073	758	52,829	281
1993	21,108	6,833	13,074	1,305	18,668	2,775	21,734	1,804	35,147	721	47,372	228
1992	19,278	6,822	12,661	1,457	16,978	2,683	22,697	1,796	30,989	643	48,968	244
1991	18,607	6,830	15,714	1,624	17,352	2,731	20,548	1,570	26,075	650	43,927	255
1990	18,859	6,781	13,031	1,563	17,046	3,013	21,152	1,372	29,471	564	39,104	269
1989	18,108	6,654	11,827	1,614	16,658	2,848	20,253	1,352	27,493	515	38,166	326
1988	17,782	6,593	12,439	1,671	16,345	2,795	19,265	1,311	28,506	533	36,452	283
1987	16,171	6,505	11,899	1,711	14,800	2,769	18,081	1,250	23,345	482	34,073	294
1986	15,441	6,326	11,248	1,691	14,214	2,666	17,419	1,226	23,412	480	31,054	263
1985	14,932	6,237	10,802	1,716	13,721	2,572	16,415	1,230	23,818	477	31,947	243
1984	13,560	5,899	10,216	1,780	12,382	2,339	14,960	1,106	21,986	424	27,893	250
1983	12,789	5,707	9,094	1,768	11,956	2,312	15,113	996	20,370	363	25,466	268
1982	12,203	5,535	9,153	1,798	11,952	2,213	12,926	953	17,658	319	26,452	253
1981	11,937	5,651	9,266	1,925	11,905	2,191	13,740	1,002	16,624	327	21,082	205
1980	11,085	5,576	8,421	2,054	11,563	2,119	12,393	964	15,616	283	23,346	156
1979	10,403	5,581	7,938	2,138	10,662	2,087	11,971	931	16,161	259	21,092	166
1978	9,651	5,350	7,423	2,156	9,869	1,982	11,197	770	16,009	260	18,083	181
1977	8,710	5,220	6,648	2,230	9,332	1,770	10,023	799	12,978	234	16,385	188
1976	7,991	5,156	6,670	2,289	8,056	1,766	8,688	726	12,246	233	17,859	143
1975	7,541	4,864	6,364	2,247	7,847	1,684	8,505	599	11,318	213	13,720	121
Female												
2017	37,585	10,684	20,316	672	26,507	2,886	33,131	3,814	48,158	2,111	69,498	1,199
2016	35,576	10,524	21,023	727	24,763	2,915	31,087	3,837	47,036	1,862	67,707	1,182
2015	35,521	10,170	15,665	786	24,047	2,856	30,951	3,732	48,842	1,753	75,911	1,041
2014	32,313	10,012	18,852	674	23,785	2,868	28,290	3,773	45,149	1,707	59,429	988
2013	31,531	9,675	15,831	747	23,349	2,801	27,564	3,531	44,139	1,684	61,698	909
2012	31,808	9,544	18,178	685	22,783	2,747	28,363	3,593	25,282	1,644	59,675	874

[1]For data prior to 1991, "Some college/Associate degree" equals 1 to 3 years of college completed; "Bachelor's degree" equals 4 years of college; "Advanced degree" equals 5 or more years of college completed.
[2]Starting in 2011, earnings data were created using population controls based on Census 2010 data.
[3]Starting in 2003, respondents could choose more than one race. The race data in this table from 2003 onward represent respondents who indicated only one race.
[4]Beginning in 2000, earnings data are from the expanded Current Population Survey (CPS) sample and were calculated using population controls based on Census 2000.

Table A-34. Mean Earnings of Workers 18 Years Old and Over, by Educational Attainment, Race, Hispanic Origin, and Sex, 1975–2017—*Continued*

(Dollars except as noted)

Race, sex, year, and Hispanic origin	Total		Not a high school graduate		High school graduate		Some college or associate's degree[1]		Bachelor's degree[1]		Advanced degree[1]	
	Mean earnings	Number of workers (thousands)	Mean earnings	Number of workers (thousands)	Mean earnings	Number of workers (thousands)	Mean earnings	Number of workers (thousands)	Mean earnings	Number of workers (thousands)	Mean earnings	Number of workers (thousands)
2011[2]	31,455	9,343	13,893	801	23,795	2,728	28,771	3,310	42,721	1,640	60,889	862
2010	30,438	9,104	15,589	730	21,700	2,640	27,805	3,453	41,653	1,520	64,586	759
2009	29,831	9,087	15,644	756	22,964	2,806	26,748	3,276	42,587	1,552	59,073	694
2008	29,734	9,392	13,976	881	23,195	2,893	27,354	3,428	42,858	1,491	60,430	697
2007	31,317	9,365	14,869	868	24,724	3,001	31,850	3,320	41,560	1,526	57,076	647
2006	29,371	9,302	14,277	961	22,643	3,092	28,706	3,246	44,326	1,417	57,206	584
2005	27,314	9,163	14,300	968	20,449	3,051	25,422	3,116	43,516	1,401	54,044	626
2004	25,738	8,962	12,785	1,014	20,284	3,019	24,468	3,015	38,626	1,391	55,436	522
2003[3]	25,735	8,919	14,513	1,056	19,623	3,030	24,007	2,963	41,066	1,355	54,346	514
2002	25,131	8,868	13,748	1,075	20,209	2,989	23,679	2,972	38,741	1,301	50,766	529
2001	24,036	8,956	15,912	1,172	18,683	2,970	23,511	3,023	35,448	1,269	48,080	521
2000[4]	22,884	9,056	12,321	1,198	18,510	3,078	22,937	3,140	35,719	1,179	46,416	459
1999	21,694	9,130	10,734	1,194	16,506	3,178	22,699	3,080	33,184	1,170	47,358	509
1998	20,026	8,713	11,372	1,212	15,892	3,078	20,371	2,870	31,952	1,105	40,214	448
1997	19,161	8,503	10,607	1,132	15,789	3,102	19,643	2,794	29,091	1,027	38,392	448
1996	19,271	8,129	10,337	1,094	15,379	3,008	21,581	2,736	29,311	954	35,785	337
1995	17,485	7,757	10,739	1,108	14,473	2,641	17,985	2,679	25,577	1,025	36,585	304
1994	17,200	7,745	9,150	1,099	14,333	2,777	16,589	2,651	28,356	921	44,618	297
1993	16,336	7,481	8,562	1,048	13,550	2,746	16,778	2,475	25,865	917	36,485	296
1992	15,605	7,014	8,756	995	13,550	2,696	15,553	2,256	24,572	786	34,902	281
1991	15,065	7,034	9,151	1,237	12,810	2,781	15,743	2,010	25,235	733	32,467	273
1990	14,449	6,950	8,946	1,290	12,560	3,036	15,734	1,632	23,837	653	28,074	338
1989	14,122	6,946	7,827	1,269	12,701	3,046	15,044	1,656	23,541	606	27,933	368
1988	12,916	6,763	7,325	1,299	11,469	2,965	14,557	1,491	19,862	671	26,072	338
1987	12,106	6,518	7,452	1,304	11,030	2,930	13,123	1,367	18,815	615	24,383	302
1986	11,571	6,403	6,984	1,337	10,434	2,804	12,459	1,436	19,562	524	24,400	301
1985	10,904	6,190	6,879	1,293	9,918	2,651	11,488	1,385	17,779	569	21,502	292
1984	10,482	6,049	6,754	1,347	9,527	2,588	11,115	1,290	17,134	513	21,000	311
1983	9,778	5,589	6,154	1,267	9,197	2,380	10,215	1,210	14,738	465	21,539	267
1982	9,024	5,546	6,047	1,390	8,737	2,378	9,574	1,114	13,284	428	19,198	235
1981	8,225	5,437	5,404	1,589	8,088	2,197	9,329	1,076	12,839	381	17,743	193
1980	7,684	...	4,685	...	7,508	...	8,544	...	12,389	...	17,278	...
1979	6,940	5,275	4,448	1,638	6,866	2,180	7,735	895	11,555	363	15,766	200
ASIAN												
Both Sexes												
2017	67,599	10,215	29,306	568	35,164	1,639	38,302	1,894	71,845	3,353	109,714	2,759
2016	63,650	9,941	28,588	536	32,548	1,758	37,793	1,996	68,610	3,022	105,557	2,627
2015	61,603	9,439	23,418	571	34,215	1,533	36,914	1,847	65,558	3,056	101,667	2,429
2014	57,351	9,170	21,969	577	29,809	1,571	32,524	1,792	64,864	3,106	97,309	2,123
2013	54,752	8,732	24,616	588	30,996	1,616	34,638	1,767	57,841	2,755	96,266	2,003
2012	55,151	8,469	23,994	521	30,149	1,445	33,239	1,744	59,507	2,717	93,772	2,040
2011[2]	51,500	8,014	21,640	563	28,302	1,478	35,034	1,582	57,150	2,645	87,205	1,743
2010	49,894	7,244	20,922	534	28,579	1,374	31,273	1,432	57,183	2,338	84,657	1,565
2009	53,419	7,158	20,461	487	29,312	1,367	32,958	1,356	55,730	2,376	98,871	1,569
2008	51,063	7,118	21,200	540	29,390	1,213	32,671	1,466	58,524	2,298	83,721	1,600
2007	49,571	7,137	21,305	512	28,773	1,241	34,423	1,456	54,451	2,354	81,943	1,572
2006	50,940	7,073	20,573	599	29,426	1,301	33,238	1,350	56,197	2,268	88,408	1,553
2005	45,751	6,684	22,909	598	27,082	1,304	31,460	1,337	51,064	2,108	80,145	1,335
2004	44,361	6,369	19,684	497	28,289	1,192	29,524	1,364	47,912	2,118	81,259	1,196
2003[3]	42,163	6,190	19,558	539	25,704	1,162	27,209	1,355	48,333	1,878	74,046	1,254
2002	40,793	6,086	16,746	536	24,900	1,138	27,340	1,325	46,628	1,911	72,852	1,174
Male												
2017	79,440	5,452	35,303	283	41,576	913	45,422	964	86,369	1,694	122,087	1,597
2016	75,610	5,258	36,311	267	37,255	933	44,013	1,022	78,528	1,520	124,668	1,513
2015	71,362	5,014	26,616	303	39,038	814	39,272	894	74,452	1,587	116,397	1,414
2014	66,326	4,817	26,516	279	33,374	823	36,790	903	71,685	1,581	112,262	1,229
2013	64,019	4,690	24,897	288	35,882	881	37,731	936	66,653	1,417	112,837	1,166
2012	64,502	4,455	24,256	251	32,794	748	38,417	871	69,657	1,361	105,017	1,222
2011[2]	60,397	4,195	25,534	298	32,500	754	42,378	810	65,740	1,316	98,812	1,015
2010	57,937	3,814	24,355	280	31,783	695	35,347	741	65,448	1,181	96,699	915

[1]For data prior to 1991, "Some college/Associate degree" equals 1 to 3 years of college completed; "Bachelor's degree" equals 4 years of college; "Advanced degree" equals 5 or more years of college completed.
[2]Starting in 2011, earnings data were created using population controls based on Census 2010 data.
[3]Starting in 2003, respondents could choose more than one race. The race data in this table from 2003 onward represent respondents who indicated only one race.
[4]Beginning in 2000, earnings data are from the expanded Current Population Survey (CPS) sample and were calculated using population controls based on Census 2000.
... = Not available.

Table A-34. Mean Earnings of Workers 18 Years Old and Over, by Educational Attainment, Race, Hispanic Origin, and Sex, 1975–2017—*Continued*

(Dollars except as noted)

Race, sex, year, and Hispanic origin	Total		Not a high school graduate		High school graduate		Some college or associate's degree[1]		Bachelor's degree[1]		Advanced degree[1]	
	Mean earnings	Number of workers (thousands)	Mean earnings	Number of workers (thousands)	Mean earnings	Number of workers (thousands)	Mean earnings	Number of workers (thousands)	Mean earnings	Number of workers (thousands)	Mean earnings	Number of workers (thousands)
2009	62,328	3,811	21,167	255	33,080	695	37,691	722	62,561	1,198	113,711	940
2008	60,007	3,776	23,814	279	34,904	606	37,283	773	67,088	1,186	97,068	931
2007	57,890	3,731	24,213	244	33,607	630	41,876	773	60,356	1,156	93,604	926
2006	60,516	3,757	23,311	298	32,528	710	37,263	658	67,144	1,150	101,676	939
2005	54,257	3,564	28,150	307	30,547	721	35,401	675	60,739	1,048	92,552	811
2004	52,544	3,440	20,691	235	31,710	676	33,798	679	56,998	1,078	90,870	770
2003[3]	48,890	3,333	23,745	291	28,522	582	31,775	673	52,508	992	83,098	793
2002	48,934	3,272	17,659	298	29,547	578	32,750	664	55,198	971	82,170	758
Female												
2017	54,045	4,763	23,370	285	27,099	725	30,923	930	57,009	1,658	92,705	1,162
2016	50,220	4,683	20,875	268	27,217	824	31,258	973	58,567	1,501	79,613	1,114
2015	50,544	4,424	19,791	267	28,748	718	34,704	953	55,956	1,469	81,135	1,015
2014	47,419	4,353	17,691	297	25,886	748	28,185	888	57,793	1,525	76,741	893
2013	43,995	4,041	24,346	300	25,129	734	31,154	831	48,505	1,337	73,159	836
2012	44,770	4,013	23,751	270	27,308	697	28,077	873	49,308	1,355	76,942	817
2011[2]	41,727	3,819	17,263	265	23,926	723	27,328	772	48,647	1,329	71,001	727
2010	40,952	3,430	17,142	254	25,295	678	26,899	690	48,745	1,157	67,690	649
2009	43,270	3,346	19,684	232	25,420	672	27,574	634	48,783	1,178	76,637	628
2008	40,954	3,341	18,395	260	23,886	607	27,528	693	49,380	1,111	65,148	669
2007	40,455	3,405	18,643	267	23,785	611	25,992	683	48,748	1,197	65,206	645
2006	40,089	3,315	17,855	300	25,696	590	29,415	692	44,932	1,118	68,084	613
2005	36,033	3,119	17,383	291	22,789	582	27,439	662	41,494	1,059	60,934	524
2004	34,748	2,928	18,780	262	23,802	515	25,280	684	38,488	1,040	63,894	426
2003[3]	34,315	2,857	14,614	247	22,876	580	22,703	682	43,655	885	58,489	461
2002	31,328	2,814	15,595	237	20,094	559	21,912	661	37,766	939	55,851	415
HISPANIC[5]												
Both Sexes												
2017	38,816	27,827	27,291	6,237	34,472	8,807	37,370	7,587	54,190	3,767	83,067	1,428
2016	38,276	26,936	29,264	6,260	34,751	8,477	35,288	7,404	53,283	3,421	79,831	1,373
2015	37,083	26,263	25,697	6,630	31,647	8,240	35,780	6,887	58,152	3,096	82,499	1,409
2014	33,944	25,254	23,747	6,819	30,329	7,869	33,822	6,541	52,143	2,852	73,952	1,171
2013	32,368	24,393	22,431	6,704	28,415	7,313	32,153	6,524	50,673	2,759	74,926	1,090
2012	31,596	23,811	21,087	6,545	28,097	7,462	30,694	6,042	50,592	2,707	77,985	1,054
2011[2]	30,739	23,027	20,953	6,583	26,681	7,176	31,423	5,773	47,873	2,528	78,606	966
2010	29,917	21,566	20,534	6,301	26,381	6,750	30,708	5,327	47,980	2,290	71,647	896
2009	29,565	21,551	19,816	6,667	25,998	6,753	31,004	5,036	49,017	2,256	74,675	837
2008	30,291	21,853	21,310	6,972	27,020	6,702	31,644	5,149	48,081	2,225	77,630	802
2007	29,910	21,561	21,303	6,888	27,604	6,682	31,040	5,000	44,696	2,114	73,111	874
2006	29,155	21,209	20,581	7,134	27,508	6,495	31,380	4,863	45,371	2,038	70,432	678
2005	27,760	20,025	19,294	6,995	25,659	6,080	29,836	4,467	45,933	1,775	70,916	705
2004	27,263	19,343	19,025	6,935	25,823	5,740	29,260	4,369	45,166	1,669	69,839	629
2003[3]	25,810	18,786	18,349	6,767	23,472	5,517	28,494	4,235	43,676	1,663	62,794	603
2002	25,824	18,409	18,981	6,748	24,163	5,499	27,757	4,024	40,949	1,568	67,679	569
2001	24,786	17,575	18,334	6,533	22,866	5,265	27,523	3,842	40,586	1,416	62,194	517
2000[4]	23,855	17,161	17,156	6,428	22,009	5,145	25,276	3,737	44,661	1,395	63,908	455
1999	22,096	15,122	16,106	5,601	20,704	4,539	24,577	3,392	36,212	1,117	55,352	472
1998	22,117	14,372	15,832	5,281	20,978	4,219	23,091	3,289	35,014	1,156	62,583	425
1997	20,766	13,972	15,069	5,238	19,558	4,082	22,001	3,075	33,465	1,140	58,571	437
1996	19,439	13,365	13,287	5,062	18,528	3,783	22,209	3,096	32,955	1,027	49,873	398
1995	18,262	12,434	13,068	4,784	18,333	3,594	19,923	2,856	30,602	866	45,612	334
1994	18,568	12,035	13,733	4,686	17,323	3,444	21,041	2,723	29,165	844	51,898	337
1993	17,102	11,644	11,852	4,425	16,591	3,367	19,043	2,728	30,359	799	45,034	325
1992	16,824	10,171	11,836	3,962	16,714	2,991	19,778	2,242	28,260	702	46,736	274
1991	16,300	10,006	11,335	3,906	16,142	3,045	19,123	2,080	26,623	665	40,154	311
1990	15,943	9,729	10,368	3,929	15,417	3,282	19,206	1,534	25,703	601	38,075	382
1989	15,714	9,570	11,500	3,985	14,901	3,188	18,707	1,513	28,157	535	39,273	349
1988	15,007	9,226	11,045	3,824	14,667	2,953	18,101	1,511	23,745	596	33,843	340
1987	14,695	8,817	10,961	3,457	13,958	2,982	16,899	1,400	23,105	644	34,413	335

[1]For data prior to 1991, "Some college/Associate degree" equals 1 to 3 years of college completed; "Bachelor's degree" equals 4 years of college; "Advanced degree" equals 5 or more years of college completed.
[2]Starting in 2011, earnings data were created using population controls based on Census 2010 data.
[3]Starting in 2003, respondents could choose more than one race. The race data in this table from 2003 onward represent respondents who indicated only one race.
[4]Beginning in 2000, earnings data are from the expanded Current Population Survey (CPS) sample and were calculated using population controls based on Census 2000.
[5]May be of any race

Table A-34. Mean Earnings of Workers 18 Years Old and Over, by Educational Attainment, Race, Hispanic Origin, and Sex, 1975–2017—*Continued*

(Dollars except as noted)

Race, sex, year, and Hispanic origin	Total		Not a high school graduate		High school graduate		Some college or associate's degree[1]		Bachelor's degree[1]		Advanced degree[1]	
	Mean earnings	Number of workers (thousands)	Mean earnings	Number of workers (thousands)	Mean earnings	Number of workers (thousands)	Mean earnings	Number of workers (thousands)	Mean earnings	Number of workers (thousands)	Mean earnings	Number of workers (thousands)
1986	13,558	8,393	9,896	3,379	13,389	2,835	16,523	1,411	22,707	471	28,316	295
1985	13,120	7,840	9,956	3,223	13,044	2,661	15,318	1,226	20,878	458	28,357	273
1984	12,583	7,349	9,671	3,129	12,858	2,457	14,359	1,116	19,924	381	26,327	265
1983	11,901	6,222	9,473	2,674	12,077	2,030	13,371	976	17,972	320	24,352	222
1982	11,307	5,914	8,498	2,583	11,539	1,967	13,108	873	18,186	303	28,167	186
1981	10,872	5,930	8,645	2,648	11,046	1,966	12,971	834	16,114	320	24,082	161
1980	10,062	5,723	8,119	2,649	10,182	1,824	11,891	808	15,676	283	21,910	157
1979	9,248	5,545	7,683	2,533	9,338	1,812	10,181	768	14,940	240	18,273	190
1978	8,460	4,898	7,138	2,345	8,512	1,554	9,575	661	13,985	213	17,333	125
1977	7,761	4,752	6,547	2,306	8,079	1,461	8,172	656	12,572	210	16,660	118
1976	7,081	4,303	5,984	2,107	7,580	1,309	7,252	592	11,242	177	14,000	118
1975	6,567	4,078	5,462	2,028	6,759	1,293	7,154	474	10,573	173	15,756	111
Male												
2017	43,300	15,759	31,968	4,104	38,865	5,328	43,481	3,834	62,469	1,845	95,960	646
2016	44,237	15,189	33,701	4,124	41,541	5,136	42,172	3,652	62,670	1,643	98,834	633
2015	41,556	14,962	29,719	4,327	36,549	4,982	40,672	3,426	69,600	1,570	95,226	655
2014	38,152	14,478	27,032	4,478	34,347	4,686	40,192	3,331	59,791	1,439	92,887	542
2013	35,990	13,980	25,151	4,475	32,070	4,366	37,245	3,222	59,368	1,360	89,624	555
2012	35,423	13,622	24,012	4,379	32,313	4,460	36,238	2,949	60,552	1,308	89,780	528
2011[2]	34,135	13,134	24,189	4,277	29,872	4,272	36,660	2,928	54,936	1,200	96,359	456
2010	32,981	12,644	23,384	4,218	29,620	4,143	35,406	2,729	56,774	1,136	82,797	416
2009	32,279	12,643	21,588	4,486	28,908	4,109	36,071	2,485	58,570	1,122	84,368	439
2008	34,240	12,857	24,340	4,720	30,618	3,990	37,864	2,615	56,980	1,109	96,976	422
2007	33,040	12,885	23,923	4,726	30,932	4,111	35,861	2,510	50,805	1,057	87,195	478
2006	32,532	12,711	23,060	4,920	32,148	3,884	36,217	2,500	51,336	1,066	87,835	340
2005	31,008	12,015	21,623	4,744	29,471	3,667	34,754	2,326	54,700	896	84,033	380
2004	30,828	11,562	21,606	4,633	29,694	3,439	34,447	2,241	53,567	915	84,152	331
2003[3]	28,806	11,195	20,637	4,556	26,652	3,234	34,157	2,193	49,298	867	71,446	344
2002	29,084	10,979	21,611	4,506	27,992	3,205	32,935	2,112	46,115	815	73,836	338
2001	27,964	10,258	20,614	4,289	26,745	2,985	32,595	1,962	45,445	748	75,746	272
2000[4]	27,253	9,996	19,501	4,236	25,629	2,940	30,155	1,873	55,050	722	81,447	223
1999	24,970	8,713	18,020	3,592	23,736	2,597	29,387	1,698	42,733	577	66,745	250
1998	25,534	8,288	17,756	3,428	24,739	2,413	26,483	1,652	40,889	569	83,754	226
1997	23,520	8,261	17,447	3,444	22,253	2,391	25,471	1,598	37,963	557	68,097	272
1996	21,870	7,975	14,986	3,382	21,593	2,116	26,682	1,687	38,130	531	49,307	259
1995	20,312	7,337	14,774	3,140	20,882	2,039	22,171	1,475	35,109	466	50,802	215
1994	21,288	7,117	16,355	3,111	19,667	1,937	24,517	1,410	33,797	450	60,858	210
1993	19,460	6,957	13,572	2,928	18,765	1,954	22,417	1,444	37,554	438	52,441	194
1992	18,842	6,034	13,313	2,633	19,357	1,665	23,033	1,193	33,430	380	53,645	164
1991	18,516	5,932	13,133	2,548	18,582	1,705	21,974	1,131	31,699	356	45,873	193
1990	18,320	5,745	13,182	2,562	18,100	1,812	22,376	852	31,485	314	47,479	205
1989	18,087	5,641	13,167	2,632	17,579	1,711	22,374	810	32,767	292	49,088	196
1988	17,357	5,477	12,836	2,517	17,446	1,621	21,631	811	26,935	333	40,916	194
1987	17,048	5,248	12,823	2,281	16,774	1,616	19,414	758	26,581	383	39,014	211
1986	15,624	5,037	11,262	2,262	15,948	1,546	19,675	778	27,427	274	32,538	176
1985	15,293	4,702	11,671	2,111	15,602	1,491	18,168	678	24,723	267	32,831	155
1984	14,957	4,344	11,441	2,022	15,763	1,319	17,261	611	23,835	223	30,727	168
1983	14,265	3,577	11,353	1,678	14,584	1,074	16,626	514	21,911	170	28,680	141
1982	13,484	3,480	10,108	1,622	13,883	1,083	15,560	495	22,565	153	34,474	125
1981	13,052	3,504	10,447	1,686	13,513	1,037	15,432	489	19,201	177	27,619	114
1980	12,310	3,401	9,825	1,707	13,108	961	14,331	451	19,224	167	24,642	114
1979	11,332	2,769	9,393	1,615	11,714	952	12,489	441	18,923	142	21,299	118
1978	10,473	2,915	8,836	1,498	10,940	815	11,545	393	16,898	127	20,702	82
1977	9,655	2,833	8,192	1,460	10,386	776	9,924	391	15,189	120	19,025	85
1976	8,787	2,571	7,440	1,321	9,640	712	8,843	342	13,650	114	16,184	81
1975	8,162	2,456	6,745	1,287	8,546	691	8,807	279	12,881	113	17,991	86
Female												
2017	32,961	12,067	18,292	2,132	27,743	3,478	31,127	3,753	46,237	1,921	72,396	781
2016	30,569	11,747	20,694	2,135	24,313	3,340	28,587	3,752	44,608	1,778	63,592	740
2015	31,160	11,301	18,138	2,302	24,151	3,258	30,937	3,460	46,372	1,525	71,443	754
2014	28,291	10,775	17,461	2,340	24,412	3,183	27,210	3,209	44,347	1,412	57,642	629
2013	27,504	10,412	16,971	2,229	22,999	2,946	27,184	3,302	42,216	1,398	59,686	535
2012	26,479	10,189	15,174	2,166	21,832	3,001	25,408	3,093	41,277	1,398	66,273	528

[1]For data prior to 1991, "Some college/Associate degree" equals 1 to 3 years of college completed; "Bachelor's degree" equals 4 years of college; "Advanced degree" equals 5 or more years of college completed.
[2]Starting in 2011, earnings data were created using population controls based on Census 2010 data.
[3]Starting in 2003, respondents could choose more than one race. The race data in this table from 2003 onward represent respondents who indicated only one race.
[4]Beginning in 2000, earnings data are from the expanded Current Population Survey (CPS) sample and were calculated using population controls based on Census 2000.

Table A-34. Mean Earnings of Workers 18 Years Old and Over, by Educational Attainment, Race, Hispanic Origin, and Sex, 1975–2017—*Continued*

(Dollars except as noted)

Race, sex, year, and Hispanic origin	Total		Not a high school graduate		High school graduate		Some college or associate's degree[1]		Bachelor's degree[1]		Advanced degree[1]	
	Mean earnings	Number of workers (thousands)	Mean earnings	Number of workers (thousands)	Mean earnings	Number of workers (thousands)	Mean earnings	Number of workers (thousands)	Mean earnings	Number of workers (thousands)	Mean earnings	Number of workers (thousands)
2011[2]	26,230	9,892	14,949	2,305	21,988	2,904	26,032	2,844	41,483	1,327	62,746	510
2010	25,574	8,921	14,763	2,083	21,234	2,607	25,771	2,597	39,321	1,153	61,967	479
2009	25,713	8,907	16,170	2,180	21,473	2,644	26,065	2,550	39,566	1,134	64,405	398
2008	24,646	8,995	14,960	2,552	21,725	2,712	25,226	2,534	39,231	1,115	56,175	380
2007	25,262	8,676	15,574	2,162	22,283	2,570	26,179	2,489	38,584	1,057	56,129	396
2006	24,104	8,497	15,072	2,214	20,608	2,611	26,260	2,362	38,825	971	52,896	337
2005	22,887	8,009	14,365	2,250	19,864	2,413	24,493	2,141	37,003	879	55,554	324
2004	21,967	7,781	13,830	2,302	20,037	2,300	23,796	2,127	34,949	753	53,887	297
2003[3]	21,391	7,591	13,632	2,210	18,967	2,283	22,411	2,042	37,550	795	51,294	258
2002	21,008	7,430	13,694	2,241	18,810	2,293	22,035	1,911	35,357	753	58,623	230
2001	20,330	7,316	13,976	2,243	17,786	2,279	22,229	1,879	35,142	668	47,176	245
2000[4]	19,115	7,164	12,622	2,191	17,180	2,204	20,372	1,864	33,489	672	47,057	232
1999	18,187	6,409	12,684	2,010	16,653	1,943	19,754	1,694	29,249	540	42,503	222
1998	17,461	6,804	12,273	1,854	15,952	1,806	20,460	1,639	29,317	587	38,422	200
1997	16,781	5,711	10,503	1,794	15,747	1,691	17,759	1,477	29,173	584	43,051	165
1996	15,841	5,390	9,867	1,680	14,635	1,667	16,856	1,409	27,407	495	50,960	139
1995	15,310	5,096	9,809	1,644	14,989	1,555	17,521	1,380	25,338	399	36,255	118
1994	14,631	4,918	8,559	1,576	14,313	1,508	17,309	1,313	23,867	393	37,269	127
1993	13,602	4,687	8,489	1,498	13,584	1,413	15,250	1,284	21,627	361	34,001	131
1992	13,880	4,137	8,913	1,330	13,396	1,326	16,076	1,049	22,160	322	34,551	110
1991	13,069	4,072	4,809	1,358	13,043	1,339	15,721	948	20,791	309	30,721	117
1990	12,516	3,984	5,093	1,367	12,109	1,470	15,245	682	19,378	287	27,184	177
1989	12,307	3,929	8,256	1,353	11,799	1,477	14,482	703	22,617	243	26,700	153
1988	11,573	3,749	7,597	1,307	11,284	1,332	14,012	700	19,707	263	24,444	146
1987	11,234	3,569	7,350	1,176	10,627	1,366	13,929	642	18,003	261	26,584	124
1986	10,457	3,356	7,130	1,117	10,319	1,289	12,648	633	16,142	197	22,071	119
1985	9,865	3,138	6,699	1,112	9,784	1,170	11,791	548	15,503	191	22,480	118
1984	9,150	3,005	6,438	1,107	9,492	1,138	10,848	505	14,404	158	18,706	97
1983	8,704	2,645	6,305	996	9,261	956	9,750	462	13,507	150	16,817	81
1982	8,195	2,434	5,781	961	8,668	884	9,896	378	13,719	150	15,244	61
1981	7,723	2,426	5,486	962	8,292	929	9,483	345	12,292	143	15,503	47
1980	6,770	2,322	5,028	942	6,923	863	8,808	357	10,568	116	14,668	43
1979	6,255	2,276	4,675	918	6,708	860	7,069	327	9,168	98	13,313	72
1978	5,501	1,983	4,135	847	5,834	739	6,686	268	9,684	86	10,908	43
1977	4,964	1,919	3,707	846	5,466	685	5,588	265	9,082	90	10,569	33
1976	4,548	1,732	3,537	786	5,124	597	5,075	250	6,884	63	9,218	37
1975	4,152	1,622	3,233	741	4,708	602	4,790	195	6,226	60	8,067	25
WHITE ALONE OR IN COMBINATION												
Both Sexes												
2017	54,535	130,955	27,180	10,024	39,663	34,025	42,587	37,794	69,035	31,680	98,853	17,429
2016	52,885	129,984	28,492	9,901	38,170	34,183	41,339	38,480	68,292	30,471	95,331	16,947
2015	50,981	129,762	26,268	10,609	36,948	33,995	39,835	38,596	66,733	29,682	92,570	16,877
2014	48,772	127,557	25,894	10,790	35,354	34,216	39,403	37,756	63,404	28,754	88,614	16,039
2013	47,280	127,029	24,264	10,470	34,101	34,391	37,330	38,164	60,859	28,374	91,349	15,627
2012	46,650	126,527	22,019	10,696	33,803	34,058	36,751	38,544	61,399	28,072	90,761	15,154
2011[2]	45,898	125,256	21,648	11,080	33,584	34,425	36,139	37,718	61,173	27,455	89,895	14,575
2010	44,023	125,712	21,388	11,004	31,990	35,140	35,139	37,717	59,055	27,266	84,972	14,582
2009	43,213	127,001	20,468	11,708	31,351	36,656	35,540	37,684	57,662	26,920	86,067	14,031
2008	43,550	129,419	21,483	12,630	32,072	37,299	35,528	38,593	59,824	26,784	84,687	14,111
2007	43,000	129,203	22,245	12,568	32,126	37,570	35,565	38,664	58,565	26,583	82,309	13,816
2006	42,249	128,366	21,389	13,800	31,998	37,915	35,276	37,530	57,807	26,035	83,002	13,084
2005	40,592	126,882	20,225	13,424	30,494	37,723	34,279	38,149	55,758	24,919	81,437	12,665
2004	38,855	125,387	19,365	13,539	29,595	37,639	32,736	37,287	52,790	24,361	78,747	12,560
2003[3]	37,958	124,456	18,734	16,282	27,915	45,064	31,498	44,048	51,206	28,672	74,601	14,592
2002	37,290	124,337	19,278	13,957	28,107	37,863	31,767	36,639	52,509	23,865	73,773	12,011
Male												
2017	63,878	70,702	32,027	6,487	46,168	20,339	51,639	19,232	83,192	16,168	121,690	8,475
2016	62,320	69,912	33,197	6,429	45,231	20,309	49,685	19,464	83,750	15,397	116,488	8,312
2015	60,364	69,837	31,168	6,866	43,502	20,177	47,616	19,353	82,230	15,086	115,139	8,353

[1]For data prior to 1991, "Some college/Associate degree" equals 1 to 3 years of college completed; "Bachelor's degree" equals 4 years of college; "Advanced degree" equals 5 or more years of college completed.
[2]Starting in 2011, earnings data were created using population controls based on Census 2010 data.
[3]Starting in 2003, respondents could choose more than one race. The race data in this table from 2003 onward represent respondents who indicated only one race.
[4]Beginning in 2000, earnings data are from the expanded Current Population Survey (CPS) sample and were calculated using population controls based on Census 2000.

Table A-34. Mean Earnings of Workers 18 Years Old and Over, by Educational Attainment, Race, Hispanic Origin, and Sex, 1975–2017—*Continued*

(Dollars except as noted)

Race, sex, year, and Hispanic origin	Total		Not a high school graduate		High school graduate		Some college or associate's degree[1]		Bachelor's degree[1]		Advanced degree[1]	
	Mean earnings	Number of workers (thousands)	Mean earnings	Number of workers (thousands)	Mean earnings	Number of workers (thousands)	Mean earnings	Number of workers (thousands)	Mean earnings	Number of workers (thousands)	Mean earnings	Number of workers (thousands)
2014	58,148	68,611	30,224	6,989	41,291	20,145	48,193	18,921	78,225	14,611	112,251	7,943
2013	55,973	68,402	28,083	6,948	39,102	20,165	45,088	19,129	73,958	14,346	117,941	7,813
2012	55,544	68,068	25,701	6,940	39,910	19,715	44,814	19,246	74,396	14,465	113,877	7,700
2011[2]	54,835	67,254	25,719	7,030	40,105	19,864	44,135	18,674	73,557	14,163	112,265	7,521
2010	52,152	67,831	25,023	7,117	37,378	20,333	42,130	18,666	71,793	14,222	105,700	7,492
2009	51,133	68,426	23,327	7,561	36,321	21,162	42,760	18,567	71,166	13,886	106,451	7,248
2008	52,502	69,829	25,254	8,263	37,740	21,192	43,307	19,210	75,024	13,734	107,065	7,428
2007	51,599	70,073	25,848	8,305	38,072	21,436	42,760	19,343	73,390	13,697	103,214	7,291
2006	50,826	69,702	24,524	9,055	38,699	21,401	42,605	18,686	71,602	13,443	103,097	7,116
2005	49,437	68,987	23,526	8,740	36,608	21,289	42,139	18,954	69,821	13,045	102,904	6,957
2004	47,275	67,758	22,576	8,751	35,348	21,073	40,627	18,361	65,498	12,728	99,534	6,842
2003[3]	45,989	67,198	21,787	8,682	34,225	20,534	39,555	18,421	65,237	12,774	93,792	6,785
2002	45,682	67,082	22,601	8,977	33,846	20,430	39,439	18,377	65,548	12,621	92,575	6,675
Female												
2017	43,571	60,252	18,290	3,537	29,995	13,686	33,208	18,562	54,279	15,511	77,240	8,954
2016	41,905	60,071	19,780	3,472	27,833	13,873	32,797	19,015	52,505	15,074	74,966	8,635
2015	40,046	59,924	17,281	3,743	27,376	13,817	32,010	19,243	50,716	14,596	70,453	8,523
2014	37,859	58,945	17,930	3,801	26,854	14,070	30,572	18,835	48,092	14,143	65,422	8,095
2013	37,138	58,627	16,731	3,522	27,011	14,226	29,534	19,035	47,464	14,028	64,762	7,814
2012	36,293	58,458	15,217	3,756	25,408	14,343	28,709	19,298	47,584	13,607	66,881	7,454
2011[2]	35,534	58,001	14,581	4,050	24,687	14,561	28,299	19,044	47,976	13,292	66,041	7,053
2010	34,497	57,881	14,733	3,887	24,593	14,807	28,290	19,051	45,165	13,044	63,069	7,090
2009	33,961	58,574	15,254	4,146	24,561	15,494	28,528	19,116	43,275	13,034	64,283	6,782
2008	33,060	59,590	14,345	4,366	24,615	16,107	27,819	19,383	43,826	13,050	59,814	6,683
2007	32,810	59,130	15,226	4,263	24,226	16,134	28,362	19,321	42,807	12,886	58,951	6,525
2006	32,059	58,663	15,408	4,745	23,313	16,514	28,008	18,844	43,078	12,591	59,042	5,968
2005	30,053	57,895	14,066	4,684	22,574	16,434	25,518	19,194	40,306	11,873	55,273	5,707
2004	28,954	57,629	13,498	4,788	22,277	16,565	25,079	18,925	38,886	11,632	53,859	5,717
2003[3]	28,532	57,257	14,086	4,684	22,029	16,926	25,093	18,616	37,750	11,476	53,021	5,552
2002	27,457	57,254	13,286	4,979	21,381	17,433	24,046	18,261	37,872	11,243	50,255	5,336
NON-HISPANIC WHITE ALONE OR IN COMBINATION												
Both Sexes												
2017	58,297	105,469	26,904	4,157	41,142	26,003	43,712	30,929	70,848	28,240	100,016	16,138
2016	56,249	105,396	27,150	4,117	39,070	26,546	42,644	31,746	69,962	27,347	96,379	15,729
2015	54,138	105,849	26,738	4,515	38,446	26,400	40,705	32,404	67,469	26,896	93,459	15,633
2014	51,984	104,543	28,791	4,447	36,673	27,032	40,306	31,919	64,462	26,162	89,586	14,981
2013	50,424	104,642	26,562	4,238	35,470	27,636	38,177	32,311	61,814	25,858	92,592	14,598
2012	48,727	104,714	23,002	4,588	35,260	27,261	37,275	33,054	62,395	25,607	91,442	14,202
2011[2]	48,950	104,217	22,468	4,960	35,205	27,811	36,916	32,528	62,300	25,217	90,442	13,699
2010	46,754	105,350	22,413	4,982	33,207	28,787	35,855	32,746	59,993	25,101	85,771	13,732
2009	45,813	106,618	21,241	5,331	32,478	30,276	36,163	32,964	58,398	24,814	86,674	13,231
2008	46,050	108,823	21,579	5,959	33,105	30,982	36,042	33,806	60,818	24,717	84,996	13,358
2007	45,393	108,929	22,945	6,040	32,992	31,288	36,176	33,994	59,637	24,622	82,840	12,983
2006	44,652	108,297	22,094	6,995	32,844	31,802	35,795	32,962	58,785	24,103	83,629	12,433
2005	42,839	107,945	21,088	6,744	31,367	31,951	34,824	33,991	56,441	23,253	81,944	12,003
2004	40,847	107,086	19,667	6,892	30,195	32,216	33,192	33,200	53,335	22,814	79,166	11,961
2003[3]	39,989	106,658	19,764	6,906	29,561	32,225	32,732	33,062	52,823	22,686	76,029	11,777
2002	39,135	107,050	19,491	7,516	28,714	32,758	32,210	32,876	53,244	22,415	74,011	11,482
Male												
2017	69,152	56,133	31,964	2,602	48,321	15,471	53,400	15,721	85,654	14,456	123,474	7,881
2016	66,808	55,923	32,056	2,622	46,245	15,570	51,344	16,121	86,032	13,879	117,742	7,730
2015	64,884	56,124	33,003	2,862	45,533	15,559	48,967	16,271	83,328	13,664	116,296	7,766
2014	62,883	55,277	34,929	2,799	43,134	15,831	49,537	15,922	80,000	13,283	113,429	7,439
2013	60,564	55,448	32,072	2,770	40,829	16,130	46,426	16,176	75,330	13,088	119,984	7,282
2012	60,103	55,462	27,899	2,824	41,984	15,644	46,207	16,520	75,609	13,257	115,320	7,215
2011[2]	59,346	55,152	27,620	3,049	42,612	15,908	45,417	16,018	75,075	13,067	112,884	7,108
2010	56,252	55,855	27,218	3,086	39,192	16,430	43,238	16,108	72,990	13,140	106,988	7,088

[1]For data prior to 1991, "Some college/Associate degree" equals 1 to 3 years of college completed; "Bachelor's degree" equals 4 years of college; "Advanced degree" equals 5 or more years of college completed.
[2]Starting in 2011, earnings data were created using population controls based on Census 2010 data.
[3]Starting in 2003, respondents could choose more than one race. The race data in this table from 2003 onward represent respondents who indicated only one race.

Table A-34. Mean Earnings of Workers 18 Years Old and Over, by Educational Attainment, Race, Hispanic Origin, and Sex, 1975–2017—*Continued*

(Dollars except as noted)

Race, sex, year, and Hispanic origin	Total Mean earnings	Total Number of workers (thousands)	Not a high school graduate Mean earnings	Not a high school graduate Number of workers (thousands)	High school graduate Mean earnings	High school graduate Number of workers (thousands)	Some college or associate's degree[1] Mean earnings	Some college or associate's degree[1] Number of workers (thousands)	Bachelor's degree[1] Mean earnings	Bachelor's degree[1] Number of workers (thousands)	Advanced degree[1] Mean earnings	Advanced degree[1] Number of workers (thousands)
2009	55,161	56,390	25,612	3,262	38,049	17,253	43,680	16,218	72,222	12,834	107,782	6,821
2008	56,357	57,636	26,226	3,743	39,288	17,435	44,075	16,739	76,560	12,692	107,540	7,025
2007	55,457	57,886	27,810	3,800	39,602	17,567	43,707	16,973	75,109	12,715	104,236	6,830
2006	54,624	57,615	25,996	4,358	40,034	17,723	43,491	16,320	73,244	12,424	103,794	6,787
2005	53,084	57,553	25,469	4,213	38,034	17,787	43,083	16,769	70,891	12,187	103,850	6,593
2004	50,488	56,761	23,520	4,287	36,323	17,817	41,490	16,259	66,467	11,869	100,220	6,527
2003[3]	49,227	56,549	22,947	4,313	35,550	17,549	40,196	16,358	66,368	11,946	94,830	6,471
2002	48,700	56,714	23,426	4,663	34,830	17,446	40,195	16,390	66,776	11,859	100,412	6,510
Female												
2017	45,948	49,335	18,429	1,554	30,597	10,532	33,698	15,208	55,319	13,783	77,626	8,257
2016	44,314	49,473	18,546	1,495	28,808	10,886	33,667	15,625	53,401	13,468	75,732	7,998
2015	42,009	49,725	15,893	1,653	28,275	10,840	32,372	16,132	51,092	13,232	70,913	7,866
2014	39,755	49,266	18,362	1,647	27,542	11,201	31,118	15,997	48,436	12,879	66,065	7,541
2013	38,994	49,193	16,163	1,468	27,957	11,505	29,907	16,135	47,960	12,769	65,324	7,315
2012	38,106	49,251	15,161	1,763	26,205	11,617	29,250	16,534	48,210	12,349	66,783	6,986
2011[2]	37,264	49,065	14,246	1,910	25,304	11,902	28,668	16,510	48,561	12,150	66,241	6,591
2010	36,034	49,495	14,590	1,895	25,249	12,356	28,707	16,637	45,715	11,960	63,134	6,644
2009	35,318	50,227	14,347	2,068	25,096	13,022	28,882	16,745	43,589	11,980	64,211	6,409
2008	34,445	51,187	13,726	2,215	25,148	13,547	28,163	17,067	44,203	12,025	59,983	6,332
2007	33,979	51,043	14,690	2,239	24,530	13,721	28,665	17,020	43,115	11,907	59,092	6,153
2006	33,316	50,682	15,642	2,636	23,794	14,079	28,248	16,641	43,402	11,678	59,389	5,646
2005	31,139	50,391	13,793	2,530	22,994	14,163	26,782	17,222	40,527	11,065	55,242	5,409
2004	29,972	50,324	13,325	2,605	22,613	14,399	25,228	16,940	39,092	10,945	53,875	5,433
2003[3]	29,564	50,108	14,469	2,592	22,479	14,765	25,422	16,704	37,757	10,739	53,102	5,306
2002	28,359	50,335	13,060	2,853	21,745	15,312	24,271	16,485	38,042	10,556	49,827	5,127
BLACK ALONE OR IN COMBINATION												
Both Sexes												
2017	41,274	21,401	23,937	1,484	31,926	6,656	36,242	7,272	53,964	3,948	77,781	2,039
2016	40,580	20,976	24,895	1,638	30,186	6,459	34,166	7,299	57,751	3,598	79,881	1,981
2015	39,326	20,228	19,655	1,677	29,060	6,260	34,345	7,059	55,584	3,393	81,381	1,837
2014	36,922	19,750	22,204	1,514	28,241	6,204	31,932	7,047	52,652	3,257	71,738	1,725
2013	35,571	19,045	20,951	1,726	26,594	5,960	31,867	6,541	49,351	3,229	72,413	1,587
2012	34,798	18,798	18,964	1,599	26,408	5,885	31,438	6,743	49,385	3,021	69,209	1,548
2011[2]	34,640	18,098	17,330	1,701	27,323	5,766	32,580	6,274	45,809	2,922	70,880	1,433
2010	32,934	17,524	17,406	1,641	25,842	5,709	30,521	6,172	44,519	2,712	71,305	1,288
2009	33,294	17,389	18,841	1,691	26,805	5,972	30,451	5,823	47,773	2,696	67,075	1,205
2008	32,878	18,157	18,049	1,826	27,123	6,220	30,266	6,207	46,983	2,654	66,247	1,248
2007	33,318	18,023	17,555	1,903	27,096	6,149	32,580	6,056	46,555	2,761	64,714	1,152
2006	32,384	17,721	17,842	1,995	26,290	6,305	31,175	5,759	47,740	2,580	64,563	1,080
2005	30,521	17,540	17,264	2,097	23,810	6,246	28,817	5,576	47,641	2,501	63,065	1,118
2004	29,031	17,109	17,821	2,085	23,458	6,298	27,801	5,369	42,131	2,414	64,545	941
2003[3]	28,854	16,871	16,238	2,177	23,956	6,082	27,095	5,296	42,991	2,374	63,966	940
2002	28,255	16,833	17,114	2,217	22,762	5,940	27,582	5,441	42,099	2,348	60,458	884
Male												
2017	45,864	10,030	27,639	747	36,658	3,602	40,854	3,197	61,668	1,708	92,018	775
2016	46,496	9,842	28,803	868	35,148	3,389	38,631	3,230	70,663	1,626	101,400	727
2015	43,773	9,472	23,797	848	33,581	3,287	39,238	3,084	63,992	1,537	90,477	714
2014	42,302	9,139	25,531	802	32,701	3,179	37,034	3,034	60,583	1,446	91,907	675
2013	40,318	8,860	25,377	934	29,742	3,044	37,568	2,852	56,800	1,387	88,936	640
2012	38,147	8,772	19,877	869	29,982	3,033	35,733	2,973	54,486	1,270	81,457	625
2011[2]	38,722	8,350	20,704	861	31,081	2,927	37,776	2,799	50,163	1,218	87,635	543
2010	35,899	8,067	19,116	875	29,746	2,974	34,307	2,592	48,406	1,117	81,533	507
2009	37,500	7,963	21,585	912	30,541	3,087	35,842	2,409	55,824	1,068	79,551	485
2008	36,386	8,442	21,894	913	30,690	3,263	34,159	2,631	52,773	1,103	73,362	530
2007	35,669	8,405	19,932	1,019	29,508	3,083	33,845	2,621	52,951	1,200	75,355	480
2006	36,026	8,170	21,361	1,006	29,973	3,146	34,784	2,417	52,382	1,124	74,769	475
2005	34,258	8,127	19,996	1,093	27,189	3,142	33,449	2,380	53,556	1,049	76,407	462
2004	32,919	7,884	22,755	1,049	26,575	3,202	32,466	2,258	47,448	976	77,648	398

[1]For data prior to 1991, "Some college/Associate degree" equals 1 to 3 years of college completed; "Bachelor's degree" equals 4 years of college; "Advanced degree" equals 5 or more years of college completed.
[2]Starting in 2011, earnings data were created using population controls based on Census 2010 data.
[3]Starting in 2003, respondents could choose more than one race. The race data in this table from 2003 onward represent respondents who indicated only one race.

Table A-34. Mean Earnings of Workers 18 Years Old and Over, by Educational Attainment, Race, Hispanic Origin, and Sex, 1975–2017—*Continued*

(Dollars except as noted)

Race, sex, year, and Hispanic origin	Total		Not a high school graduate		High school graduate		Some college or associate's degree[1]		Bachelor's degree[1]		Advanced degree[1]	
	Mean earnings	Number of workers (thousands)	Mean earnings	Number of workers (thousands)	Mean earnings	Number of workers (thousands)	Mean earnings	Number of workers (thousands)	Mean earnings	Number of workers (thousands)	Mean earnings	Number of workers (thousands)
2003[3]	32,574	7,689	17,982	1,088	28,323	2,981	31,591	2,233	45,705	982	76,954	402
2002	31,967	7,734	20,537	1,114	25,510	2,902	32,696	2,375	46,942	1,009	76,003	332
Female												
2017	37,224	11,370	20,184	737	26,345	3,054	32,623	4,074	48,089	2,240	69,040	1,263
2016	35,351	11,134	20,483	769	24,709	3,069	30,622	4,069	47,094	1,971	67,406	1,254
2015	35,411	10,756	15,420	829	24,060	2,972	30,548	3,974	48,620	1,855	75,598	1,123
2014	32,288	10,611	18,457	712	23,553	3,025	28,073	4,013	46,315	1,810	58,757	1,050
2013	31,442	10,185	15,723	791	23,309	2,916	27,457	3,688	43,738	1,841	61,233	946
2012	31,867	10,026	17,876	730	22,606	2,851	28,051	3,769	45,688	1,751	60,912	923
2011[2]	31,144	9,748	13,869	840	23,449	2,839	28,395	3,475	42,696	1,704	60,632	889
2010	30,405	9,456	15,449	765	21,597	2,735	27,779	3,579	41,796	1,595	64,662	781
2009	29,740	9,426	15,631	779	22,805	2,884	26,646	3,414	42,487	1,627	58,664	719
2008	29,829	9,715	14,204	913	23,187	2,957	27,399	3,575	42,861	1,550	60,996	718
2007	31,263	9,618	14,816	884	24,669	3,065	31,614	3,435	41,636	1,561	57,105	672
2006	29,268	9,551	14,257	988	22,622	3,159	28,565	3,342	44,157	1,456	56,541	605
2005	27,295	9,413	14,289	1,003	20,389	3,104	25,366	3,195	43,369	1,452	53,669	656
2004	25,707	9,224	12,818	1,035	20,236	3,096	24,415	3,111	38,522	1,438	54,931	543
2003[3]	25,739	9,182	14,495	1,089	19,765	3,100	23,816	3,063	41,073	1,391	54,265	538
2002	25,099	9,098	13,656	1,103	20,137	3,038	23,621	3,066	38,447	1,339	51,101	552
ASIAN ALONE OR IN COMBINATION												
Both Sexes												
2017	66,240	10,932	29,126	602	35,168	1,758	37,559	2,149	70,857	3,573	109,132	2,848
2016	62,413	10,599	27,996	567	32,276	1,866	37,279	2,246	67,706	3,189	104,680	2,729
2015	60,892	10,057	23,340	591	33,847	1,652	38,217	2,051	64,314	3,259	101,782	2,501
2014	56,577	9,805	21,960	610	29,376	1,703	32,506	1,974	64,665	3,294	96,335	2,222
2013	54,320	9,367	24,499	613	31,088	1,726	33,613	1,984	58,218	2,948	96,346	2,094
2012	54,277	9,067	23,974	543	30,241	1,555	32,728	1,989	58,891	2,865	93,791	2,113
2011[2]	50,943	8,587	21,649	592	28,304	1,609	34,825	1,796	57,118	2,784	87,273	1,804
2010	49,145	7,711	20,791	555	28,544	1,468	30,951	1,608	56,521	2,459	84,367	1,621
2009	61,575	4,022	20,995	267	32,985	747	37,106	793	62,504	1,237	113,267	976
2008	50,622	7,553	21,195	569	29,163	1,300	32,577	1,630	58,179	2,403	84,523	1,649
2007	48,865	7,563	21,399	530	28,524	1,331	33,846	1,630	54,204	2,454	81,694	1,615
2006	50,094	7,501	20,142	631	29,502	1,413	33,050	1,495	55,827	2,375	87,887	1,585
2005	45,269	7,131	22,330	629	27,059	1,413	31,332	1,504	51,750	2,204	79,229	1,379
2004	43,856	6,771	19,536	524	27,946	1,292	29,377	1,490	47,711	2,226	81,310	1,237
2003[3]	41,563	6,560	19,548	564	25,554	1,256	27,083	1,495	47,945	1,948	73,812	1,295
2002	40,323	6,424	16,969	559	25,038	1,221	27,146	1,456	46,218	1,984	72,943	1,202
Male												
2017	77,742	5,821	34,659	300	41,564	981	43,886	1,100	85,215	1,806	121,921	1,633
2016	74,131	5,602	34,904	289	37,283	984	43,483	1,171	77,744	1,604	124,132	1,554
2015	70,202	5,322	26,205	315	38,246	886	39,357	1,004	73,370	1,671	117,211	1,444
2014	65,545	5,124	26,738	294	32,798	887	37,109	998	71,395	1,677	112,206	1,266
2013	63,189	5,032	24,585	302	36,133	951	36,128	1,060	67,355	1,521	113,152	1,196
2012	63,269	4,759	24,720	262	32,762	819	37,917	981	68,713	1,439	104,757	1,256
2011[2]	59,326	4,489	25,638	318	32,392	828	41,887	918	65,569	1,392	98,425	1,032
2010	56,907	4,048	24,137	292	31,788	741	34,995	827	64,573	1,253	96,286	933
2009	61,575	4,022	20,995	267	32,985	747	37,106	793	62,504	1,237	113,267	976
2008	59,565	4,007	23,204	297	34,568	655	37,228	865	66,880	1,228	98,718	959
2007	56,990	3,945	24,261	254	33,105	685	40,965	875	60,606	1,187	93,566	942
2006	59,328	3,980	22,631	318	32,716	783	37,104	736	66,740	1,191	101,474	950
2005	53,761	3,797	27,107	328	30,490	790	35,583	758	62,247	1,097	92,170	823
2004	52,032	3,633	20,799	251	31,194	730	34,237	736	56,581	1,126	91,406	788
2003[3]	48,062	3,522	23,122	308	28,514	635	31,430	746	52,179	1,024	83,131	807
2002	48,128	3,469	18,101	312	29,493	633	32,427	744	54,683	1,006	82,134	772

[1]For data prior to 1991, "Some college/Associate degree" equals 1 to 3 years of college completed; "Bachelor's degree" equals 4 years of college; "Advanced degree" equals 5 or more years of college completed.
[2]Starting in 2011, earnings data were created using population controls based on Census 2010 data.
[3]Starting in 2003, respondents could choose more than one race. The race data in this table from 2003 onward represent respondents who indicated only one race.

Table A-34. Mean Earnings of Workers 18 Years Old and Over, by Educational Attainment, Race, Hispanic Origin, and Sex, 1975–2017—*Continued*

(Dollars except as noted)

Race, sex, year, and Hispanic origin	Total		Not a high school graduate		High school graduate		Some college or associate's degree[1]		Bachelor's degree[1]		Advanced degree[1]	
	Mean earnings	Number of workers (thousands)	Mean earnings	Number of workers (thousands)	Mean earnings	Number of workers (thousands)	Mean earnings	Number of workers (thousands)	Mean earnings	Number of workers (thousands)	Mean earnings	Number of workers (thousands)
Female												
2017..................	53,139	5,111	23,640	302	27,100	777	30,923	1,049	56,176	1,766	91,932	1,214
2016..................	49,273	4,996	20,803	277	26,695	882	30,524	1,075	57,544	1,584	78,963	1,175
2015..................	50,426	4,734	20,074	276	28,752	765	37,124	1,046	54,785	1,588	80,694	1,056
2014..................	46,761	4,681	17,496	315	25,652	815	27,803	976	57,684	1,617	75,320	956
2013..................	44,026	4,335	24,416	311	24,895	775	30,727	924	48,470	1,426	73,960	898
2012..................	44,342	4,307	23,277	280	27,432	735	27,683	1,008	48,971	1,425	77,697	856
2011[2]	41,759	4,097	17,012	274	23,973	781	27,441	878	48,660	1,391	72,373	772
2010..................	40,566	3,663	17,055	262	25,230	726	26,667	780	48,151	1,205	68,200	687
2009..................	42,848	3,561	20,121	239	25,448	713	27,565	717	48,655	1,241	76,052	650
2008..................	40,518	3,546	18,999	272	23,665	644	27,315	764	49,076	1,174	64,802	690
2007..................	40,002	3,617	18,753	275	23,660	645	25,597	755	48,200	1,266	65,098	673
2006..................	39,652	3,520	17,610	313	25,508	630	29,116	759	44,846	1,183	67,514	634
2005..................	35,593	3,333	17,122	301	22,703	622	27,007	745	41,350	1,107	60,077	556
2004..................	34,387	3,137	18,375	273	23,721	561	24,634	754	38,618	1,099	63,553	448
2003[3]	34,031	3,038	15,233	255	22,530	621	22,750	748	43,252	924	58,391	487
2002..................	31,157	2,954	15,536	247	20,242	588	21,615	711	37,507	978	56,417	429

[1]For data prior to 1991, "Some college/Associate degree" equals 1 to 3 years of college completed; "Bachelor's degree" equals 4 years of college; "Advanced degree" equals 5 or more years of college completed.

[2]Starting in 2011, earnings data were created using population controls based on Census 2010 data.

[3]Starting in 2003, respondents could choose more than one race. The race data in this table from 2003 onward represent respondents who indicated only one race.

Table A-35. Median Annual Earnings and Number of Full-Time Year-Round Workers 25 Years Old and Over, by Highest Level of Educational Attainment and Sex: 1991–2017

(Dollars except as noted; people 25 years old and over as of March of the following year; income in current and 2017 CPI-U-RS adjusted dollars.)

	Total			Elementary/secondary					
				Less than 9th Grade			Some high school, no diploma		
Sex and year	Number of persons with earnings who worked full time, year round (thousands)	Median annual earnings		Number of persons with earnings who worked full time, year round (thousands)	Median annual earnings		Number of persons with earnings who worked full time, year round (thousands)	Median annual earnings	
		Current dollars	2017 dollars		Current dollars	2017 dollars		Current dollars	2017 dollars
Male									
2017	101,040	45,256	45,256	3,903	21,899	21,899	6,249	24,085	24,085
2016	99,369	42,747	43,666	4,021	21,263	21,720	6,172	23,165	23,663
2015	98,367	41,886	43,339	4,328	20,877	21,601	6,420	22,214	22,984
2014	96,753	40,846	42,335	4,467	19,553	20,266	6,445	21,701	22,492
2013	95,921	40,328	42,506	4,682	18,503	19,502	6,120	20,021	21,102
2013	95,253	39,602	41,741	4,464	19,701	20,765	6,557	21,417	22,574
2012	94,263	38,428	41,104	4,510	18,002	19,255	6,418	19,780	21,157
2011	93,141	37,653	41,128	4,633	17,505	19,120	6,650	20,437	22,323
2010	92,242	36,852	41,522	4,757	16,384	18,460	6,625	19,356	21,809
2009	91,745	36,801	42,148	4,736	16,473	18,867	6,948	19,720	22,585
2008	91,653	37,463	42,757	4,973	17,043	19,452	7,158	20,845	23,791
2007	90,647	37,828	44,832	5,036	16,625	19,703	7,200	20,643	24,465
2006	89,816	36,847	44,908	5,283	17,169	20,925	7,684	21,184	25,818
2005	88,804	35,758	44,994	5,475	16,321	20,536	7,276	20,934	26,341
2004	87,570	34,823	45,301	5,520	16,171	21,037	7,254	19,593	25,489
2003	86,532	33,517	44,780	5,405	15,461	20,657	7,245	18,990	25,372
2002	85,668	32,471	44,368	5,705	15,130	20,673	7,488	19,802	27,057
2001	84,389	32,494	45,099	5,809	14,594	20,255	7,421	19,434	26,973
2000	83,860	32,155	45,899	5,724	14,131	20,171	7,226	18,915	27,000
1999	82,795	31,545	46,557	5,728	13,529	19,967	7,085	17,653	26,054
1998	80,869	30,654	46,205	5,641	12,571	18,948	7,366	17,462	26,321
1997	80,263	28,919	44,180	5,839	12,157	18,572	7,601	16,818	25,693
1996	79,423	27,248	42,527	6,139	12,174	19,000	7,671	16,058	25,062
1995	78,264	26,346	42,214	6,277	11,723	18,784	7,490	15,791	25,302
1994	77,546	25,465	41,786	6,507	11,324	18,582	7,286	14,584	23,931
1993	76,419	24,605	41,218	6,734	10,895	18,251	7,377	14,550	24,374
1992	75,872	23,894	41,036	7,000	10,374	17,816	7,524	14,218	24,418
1991	75,137	23,686	41,690	7,143	10,319	18,163	7,759	14,736	25,937
Female									
2017	103,352	27,709	27,709	3,294	12,365	12,365	5,471	13,801	13,801
2016	101,906	27,259	27,845	3,212	12,045	12,304	5,471	13,666	13,960
2015	101,006	26,282	27,193	3,569	11,863	12,274	5,508	12,768	13,211
2014	99,193	25,071	25,985	3,644	11,558	11,979	5,934	12,364	12,815
2013	98,670	24,773	26,111	3,664	11,249	11,857	5,692	11,840	12,480
2013	96,915	24,756	26,093	3,633	11,395	12,010	5,677	11,869	12,510
2012	96,256	23,946	25,613	3,674	10,841	11,596	5,898	11,981	12,815
2011	95,404	23,395	25,554	3,839	11,113	12,139	6,235	12,193	13,318
2010	94,679	22,934	25,840	3,897	10,680	12,033	6,003	12,075	13,605
2009	93,426	23,159	26,524	4,036	10,516	12,044	6,175	12,278	14,062
2008	93,143	22,944	26,186	4,201	10,625	12,127	6,413	11,904	13,586
2007	92,075	23,052	27,320	4,070	10,539	12,490	6,286	11,982	14,201
2006	91,315	21,900	26,691	4,257	10,451	12,737	6,750	11,914	14,520
2005	90,762	20,806	26,180	4,579	9,496	11,949	6,812	11,136	14,012
2004	89,794	20,147	26,209	4,742	9,576	12,457	6,982	10,751	13,986
2003	89,118	19,679	26,292	4,734	9,296	12,420	6,965	10,786	14,411
2002	88,903	18,965	25,914	5,015	8,965	12,250	7,103	10,613	14,501
2001	88,075	18,549	25,745	5,196	8,846	12,278	7,376	10,330	14,337
2000	87,619	18,032	25,740	5,195	8,546	12,199	7,565	10,063	14,364
1999	87,229	17,022	25,122	5,397	8,261	12,192	7,525	9,632	14,216
1998	84,819	16,258	24,506	5,419	7,914	11,929	7,559	9,582	14,443
1997	83,821	15,573	23,791	5,647	7,505	11,466	7,661	8,861	13,537
1996	83,056	14,682	22,915	5,775	7,276	11,356	7,929	8,544	13,335
1995	82,457	13,821	22,145	6,020	7,096	11,370	8,122	8,057	12,910
1994	81,829	12,766	20,948	6,183	6,865	11,265	7,943	7,618	12,500
1993	80,898	12,234	20,494	6,423	6,480	10,855	8,152	7,187	12,039
1992	79,854	11,922	20,475	6,921	6,337	10,883	8,248	7,293	12,525
1991	79,383	11,580	20,382	7,065	6,268	11,032	8,561	7,055	12,418

100,000+ = The medians were topcoded. Beginning with 2009 income data, the Census Bureau expanded the upper income interval used to calculate medians and Gini indexes from $100,000 to $250,000.

Table A-35. Median Annual Earnings and Number of Full-Time Year-Round Workers 25 Years Old and Over, by Highest Level of Educational Attainment and Sex: 1991–2017—Continued

(Dollars except as noted; people 25 years old and over as of March of the following year; income in current and 2017 CPI-U-RS adjusted dollars.)

	Elementary/secondary			College								
	High school completion (includes equivalency)			Some college, no degree			Associate degree			Bachelor's or higher degree Total		
	Number of persons	Median annual earnings		Number of persons	Median annual earnings		Number of persons	Median annual earnings		Number of persons	Median annual earnings	
Sex and year	with earnings who worked full time, year round (thousands)	Current dollars	2017 dollars	with earnings who worked full time, year round (thousands)	Current dollars	2017 dollars	with earnings who worked full time, year round (thousands)	Current dollars	2017 dollars	with earnings who worked full time, year round (thousands)	Current dollars	2017 dollars
Male												
2017	29,381	35,276	35,276	16,300	40,912	40,912	9,401	46,518	46,518	35,807	72,315	72,315
2016	29,326	33,516	34,237	16,171	40,232	41,097	9,355	45,987	46,976	34,324	70,853	72,377
2015	28,760	32,307	33,427	16,218	39,823	41,204	9,171	43,785	45,303	33,470	70,437	72,880
2014	28,988	32,080	33,250	15,963	37,865	39,246	8,728	43,871	45,471	32,162	67,367	69,823
2013	29,036	31,188	32,873	16,248	37,741	39,780	8,509	42,717	45,024	31,326	69,639	73,401
2013	28,677	31,288	32,978	15,615	37,424	39,445	8,654	42,176	44,454	31,285	65,526	69,065
2012	28,115	31,064	33,227	15,752	37,062	39,643	8,499	41,731	44,637	30,969	63,272	67,678
2011	28,295	30,616	33,441	15,301	36,552	39,925	8,286	41,916	45,784	29,976	62,282	68,030
2010	28,307	30,250	34,083	15,395	36,226	40,816	7,924	40,974	46,166	29,234	61,522	69,318
2009	28,946	30,303	34,706	15,184	36,693	42,025	7,399	42,163	48,289	28,532	61,280	70,184
2008	28,450	30,879	35,243	15,523	37,297	42,568	7,375	42,608	48,629	28,174	63,277	72,219
2007	27,988	31,337	37,139	15,321	37,447	44,381	7,244	43,006	50,969	27,857	62,421	73,979
2006	28,253	31,009	37,793	14,526	37,271	45,425	6,973	41,807	50,953	27,097	61,168	74,550
2005	28,077	30,134	37,917	14,505	36,930	46,468	7,000	41,903	52,726	26,470	58,114	73,124
2004	27,799	29,332	38,158	14,405	36,162	47,043	6,782	39,765	51,730	25,810	56,434	73,415
2003	26,800	28,763	38,429	14,586	35,073	46,859	6,618	39,015	52,126	25,879	55,751	74,486
2002	26,298	27,526	37,611	14,747	35,023	47,855	6,274	37,970	51,882	25,155	55,188	75,408
2001	25,954	28,343	39,338	14,340	33,777	46,880	6,352	38,870	53,949	24,512	54,069	75,044
2000	26,175	27,480	39,226	14,433	33,319	47,561	6,272	38,026	54,280	24,028	53,488	76,351
1999	26,278	27,188	40,126	14,440	32,575	48,077	5,939	36,558	53,955	23,325	52,246	77,109
1998	25,636	26,542	40,007	13,935	31,627	47,672	5,766	35,962	54,206	22,525	50,272	75,775
1997	25,777	25,453	38,885	13,892	30,536	46,650	5,591	32,930	50,308	21,563	47,126	71,995
1996	25,510	24,814	38,728	13,756	29,160	45,511	5,210	33,065	51,606	21,136	44,161	68,924
1995	24,909	23,365	37,438	13,715	28,004	44,871	5,230	31,027	49,715	20,644	43,322	69,415
1994	24,704	22,387	36,735	13,573	26,768	43,924	5,046	30,643	50,282	20,429	42,027	68,962
1993	24,682	21,782	36,489	13,247	26,323	44,096	4,901	29,736	49,813	19,479	41,649	69,769
1992	25,143	21,645	37,173	12,728	26,318	45,199	4,540	28,791	49,446	18,937	40,557	69,653
1991	25,297	21,546	37,923	12,366	26,591	46,803	4,083	29,358	51,674	18,490	39,803	70,058
Female												
2017	27,672	20,199	20,199	16,919	25,161	25,161	11,905	30,406	30,406	38,092	48,223	48,223
2016	27,483	19,904	20,332	17,033	25,433	25,980	11,870	29,538	30,173	36,837	46,788	47,794
2015	27,607	19,810	20,497	17,437	24,512	25,362	11,409	28,664	29,658	35,477	45,170	46,737
2014	27,688	19,208	19,908	16,851	23,504	24,361	11,069	27,122	28,111	34,007	43,330	44,910
2013	27,640	20,060	21,144	16,776	22,301	23,506	11,265	27,340	28,817	33,633	42,063	44,335
2013	27,482	18,325	19,315	16,800	22,814	24,046	10,887	27,340	28,817	32,432	43,115	45,444
2012	27,717	18,213	19,481	16,625	22,469	24,034	10,757	27,159	29,050	31,585	42,027	44,953
2011	28,051	17,887	19,538	16,427	22,499	24,575	10,353	27,180	29,688	30,498	41,338	45,153
2010	28,314	17,826	20,085	16,661	22,808	25,698	10,197	28,147	31,714	29,606	41,112	46,322
2009	28,154	18,340	21,005	16,208	23,107	26,465	9,936	27,027	30,954	28,917	40,766	46,689
2008	28,217	18,293	20,878	16,329	23,252	26,538	9,662	27,715	31,632	28,321	40,801	46,567
2007	28,134	18,162	21,525	16,600	23,532	27,889	9,166	27,668	32,791	27,820	40,712	48,250
2006	28,538	17,546	21,385	16,099	22,709	27,677	9,043	26,295	32,048	26,626	39,450	48,081
2005	28,409	16,695	21,007	16,402	21,545	27,110	9,070	26,074	32,808	25,490	37,055	46,625
2004	28,561	16,165	21,029	15,791	21,159	27,526	8,861	25,199	32,781	24,857	35,726	46,476
2003	28,976	15,962	21,326	15,691	21,007	28,066	8,523	24,808	33,145	24,229	35,125	46,929
2002	29,161	15,972	21,824	15,616	20,602	28,150	8,323	23,766	32,474	23,686	34,292	46,856
2001	28,945	15,665	21,742	15,420	20,101	27,899	8,177	22,638	31,420	22,961	33,842	46,970
2000	28,968	15,153	21,630	15,825	20,166	28,786	8,108	23,124	33,008	21,958	33,148	47,317
1999	29,798	14,652	21,625	15,693	19,599	28,926	7,482	21,916	32,345	21,334	31,604	46,644
1998	29,330	13,786	20,780	15,173	18,445	27,802	6,931	21,290	32,091	20,409	30,692	46,262
1997	29,332	13,407	20,482	14,677	17,153	26,205	6,914	21,073	32,194	19,590	29,781	45,497
1996	29,212	12,702	19,825	14,528	16,255	25,370	6,839	20,460	31,933	18,775	27,556	43,008
1995	28,785	12,046	19,301	14,619	15,552	24,919	6,642	19,450	31,165	18,269	26,843	43,011
1994	29,110	11,390	18,690	14,911	14,585	23,933	6,573	17,954	29,461	17,109	26,237	43,053
1993	29,171	11,089	18,576	14,390	14,489	24,272	6,282	18,346	30,733	16,480	25,246	42,291
1992	29,596	10,901	18,722	13,615	14,401	24,732	5,539	17,331	29,764	15,933	25,093	43,095
1991	30,149	10,818	19,041	13,013	13,963	24,577	5,236	17,364	30,563	15,359	23,627	41,586

100,000+ = The medians were topcoded. Beginning with 2009 income data, the Census Bureau expanded the upper income interval used to calculate medians and Gini indexes from $100,000 to $250,000.

Table A-35. Median Annual Earnings and Number of Full-Time Year-Round Workers 25 Years Old and Over, by Highest Level of Educational Attainment and Sex: 1991–2017—*Continued*

(Dollars except as noted; people 25 years old and over as of March of the following year; income in current and 2017 CPI-U-RS adjusted dollars.)

	College											
	Bachelor's or higher degree											
	Bachelor's degree			Master's degree			Professional degree			Doctorate degree		
	Number of persons with earnings who worked full time, year round (thousands)	Median annual earnings		Number of persons with earnings who worked full time, year round (thousands)	Median annual earnings		Number of persons with earnings who worked full time, year round (thousands)	Median annual earnings		Number of persons with earnings who worked full time, year round (thousands)	Median annual earnings	
Sex and year		Current dollars	2017 dollars		Current dollars	2017 dollars		Current dollars	2017 dollars		Current dollars	2017 dollars
Male												
2017	22,462	65,325	65,325	9,059	82,722	82,722	1,724	110,651	110,651	2,561	102,423	102,423
2016	21,342	63,269	64,630	8,880	80,083	81,805	1,735	107,506	109,818	2,367	101,591	103,776
2015	20,772	62,304	64,465	8,594	78,222	80,935	1,824	111,881	115,761	2,281	91,604	94,781
2014	20,147	60,933	63,155	7,992	76,386	79,171	1,940	107,050	110,953	2,082	91,770	95,116
2013	19,388	60,808	64,093	7,867	75,525	79,604	1,762	102,353	107,882	2,309	101,336	106,810
2013	19,513	58,170	61,312	7,705	75,407	79,480	1,802	101,504	106,987	2,265	93,712	98,774
2012	19,320	56,656	60,601	7,652	71,364	76,333	1,847	100,064	107,031	2,150	91,742	98,130
2011	18,859	56,404	61,609	7,238	71,537	78,139	1,903	98,883	108,008	1,976	82,376	89,978
2010	18,378	55,225	62,223	7,100	69,576	78,392	1,856	96,212	108,404	1,900	86,200	97,123
2009	18,205	54,091	61,951	6,728	69,825	79,971	1,844	102,398	117,277	1,755	89,845	102,900
2008	17,726	57,278	65,373	6,896	70,973	81,003	1,930	100,000+	X	1,622	90,575	103,375
2007	17,654	56,826	67,348	6,759	71,097	84,261	1,843	100,000+	X	1,601	86,171	102,126
2006	17,129	54,403	66,305	6,350	67,425	82,176	1,969	96,926	118,131	1,649	90,511	110,312
2005	16,764	51,700	65,053	6,137	64,468	81,119	1,912	90,878	114,350	1,656	76,937	96,808
2004	16,302	51,081	66,451	6,059	63,260	82,295	1,876	90,210	117,354	1,573	80,033	104,115
2003	16,295	50,916	68,026	6,076	61,698	82,431	1,901	88,530	118,280	1,606	73,853	98,671
2002	16,057	50,600	69,139	5,768	60,830	83,117	1,816	88,216	120,537	1,514	76,147	104,046
2001	15,723	49,985	69,376	5,522	61,960	85,996	1,779	81,602	113,258	1,488	72,642	100,822
2000	15,452	49,080	70,059	5,346	59,732	85,264	1,711	83,701	119,478	1,520	71,271	101,735
1999	14,922	47,289	69,793	5,178	59,189	87,356	1,774	81,545	120,351	1,451	70,461	103,992
1998	14,614	45,749	68,958	4,772	55,784	84,084	1,695	76,362	115,101	1,443	65,319	98,456
1997	13,900	41,949	64,086	4,583	52,530	80,251	1,741	72,274	110,414	1,338	68,643	104,867
1996	13,510	39,624	61,843	4,709	50,003	78,042	1,702	71,869	112,169	1,215	62,255	97,164
1995	13,065	39,040	62,554	4,774	49,076	78,635	1,657	66,257	106,164	1,149	57,356	91,902
1994	12,997	38,701	63,505	4,558	46,635	76,524	1,691	61,739	101,308	1,183	57,478	94,316
1993	12,360	37,474	62,775	4,320	45,597	76,383	1,650	69,678	116,723	1,149	55,751	93,393
1992	11,938	36,745	63,106	4,308	44,293	76,069	1,639	68,429	117,521	1,053	51,681	88,758
1991	11,657	36,067	63,482	4,356	43,125	75,905	1,547	63,741	112,192	929	51,845	91,253
Female												
2017	23,562	41,827	41,827	11,379	56,806	56,806	1,335	77,090	77,090	1,817	77,766	77,766
2016	22,865	41,045	41,928	11,009	54,571	55,745	1,333	76,523	78,169	1,629	72,018	73,567
2015	22,045	40,115	41,506	10,558	51,494	53,280	1,278	65,012	67,267	1,595	68,887	71,276
2014	21,336	40,033	41,493	9,876	50,255	52,087	1,319	63,353	65,663	1,475	62,388	64,663
2013	21,508	37,424	39,445	9,661	49,731	52,417	1,224	61,224	64,531	1,241	65,673	69,220
2013	20,430	39,201	41,318	9,397	50,507	53,235	1,294	68,826	72,544	1,310	64,001	67,458
2012	20,125	37,285	39,881	9,124	49,703	53,164	1,126	67,428	72,123	1,210	67,057	71,726
2011	19,629	36,812	40,209	8,650	48,738	53,236	1,098	61,206	66,854	1,121	63,913	69,811
2010	18,909	36,359	40,966	8,507	48,488	54,632	1,053	60,477	68,140	1,136	70,417	79,340
2009	18,844	35,972	41,199	7,945	50,576	57,925	1,142	60,259	69,015	987	65,587	75,117
2008	18,381	36,294	41,423	7,801	48,000	54,783	1,197	58,364	66,612	942	60,619	69,186
2007	18,347	36,167	42,864	7,590	48,077	56,979	1,060	61,875	73,332	823	61,554	72,951
2006	17,931	35,094	42,772	6,876	46,250	56,368	1,037	60,463	73,691	782	61,091	74,456
2005	17,090	32,668	41,105	6,560	44,385	55,849	1,090	59,934	75,414	749	56,820	71,495
2004	16,668	31,585	41,089	6,464	42,243	54,954	991	50,311	65,450	734	55,996	72,845
2003	16,198	31,309	41,830	6,268	41,334	55,224	990	48,536	64,846	773	53,003	70,815
2002	16,003	30,788	42,068	6,073	40,939	55,939	946	44,748	61,143	663	52,336	71,511
2001	15,660	30,973	42,988	5,749	40,744	56,550	899	46,635	64,726	653	52,181	72,423
2000	15,102	30,418	43,420	5,421	40,619	57,981	852	46,084	65,782	584	51,460	73,456
1999	14,690	28,520	42,092	5,220	39,712	58,610	824	45,432	67,052	600	46,511	68,645
1998	14,218	27,415	41,323	4,837	36,888	55,602	788	43,490	65,553	567	46,275	69,751
1997	13,787	26,401	40,333	4,488	35,882	54,818	807	45,199	69,051	508	46,545	71,108
1996	13,247	25,192	39,318	4,285	33,302	51,976	715	42,059	65,643	527	42,431	66,224
1995	12,875	24,065	38,560	4,205	33,509	53,692	732	38,588	61,830	457	39,821	63,806
1994	11,773	23,405	38,405	4,166	32,069	52,622	709	35,806	58,754	462	40,793	66,938
1993	11,447	22,452	37,611	4,003	31,389	52,582	583	32,742	54,849	447	42,737	71,592
1992	11,133	22,383	38,441	3,873	30,169	51,813	569	36,640	62,926	358	39,322	67,532
1991	10,721	20,967	36,904	3,745	29,747	52,358	556	34,064	59,957	337	37,242	65,550

100,000+ = The medians were topcoded. Beginning with 2009 income data, the Census Bureau expanded the upper income interval used to calculate medians and Gini indexes from $100,000 to $250,000.
X = Not available.

Table A-36. Unemployment Rates of Persons 16 to 64 Years Old, by Age Group and Highest Level of Educational Attainment: Selected Years, 1975–2018

(Number; percent.)

Year	16 to 19 years old				20 to 24 years old				
	Unemployment rate for all education levels	Less than high school completion	High school completion	At least some college	Unemployment rate for all education levels	Less than high school completion	High school completion	At least some college	Bachelor's or higher degree
2018......................	15.4	16.3	16.7	9.5	8.7	19.5	11.1	5.3	5.3
2017......................	14.8	21.7	12.6	9.2	8.1	16.0	9.7	6.4	4.7
2016......................	20.2	21.6	22.0	11.8	10.5	17.3	12.2	9.9	4.9
2015......................	22.5	25.6	23.3	13.2	12.3	19.9	15.8	9.6	5.1
2014......................	22.9	22.9	25.0	15.1	14.9	25.3	18.9	12.2	6.7
2013......................	29.4	36.3	29.2	16.2	15.2	29.2	17.5	12.2	7.0
2012......................	30.6	41.1	28.7	19.6	15.5	27.6	18.3	12.7	6.0
2011......................	28.8	35.1	28.9	16.2	18.1	30.1	21.6	14.0	8.7
2010......................	31.9	41.7	29.6	18.1	18.8	32.3	22.3	14.2	7.9
2009......................	30.3	38.9	29.1	18.1	17.0	29.0	20.3	12.1	7.9
2008......................	20.9	30.8	17.2	11.3	10.7	19.2	13.0	6.8	4.5
2007......................	19.5	28.6	15.1	8.9	9.3	18.6	9.4	7.2	3.4
2006......................	20.6	25.8	17.6	17.7	9.3	15.7	10.4	7.1	3.9
2005......................	22.8	30.3	19.1	15.8	10.9	18.9	12.0	7.3	5.4
2000......................	17.2	21.4	15.3	‡	9.2	16.6	10.0	5.2	5.0
1995......................	21.0	30.3	15.1	12.4	10.7	19.5	12.0	7.3	4.1
1990......................	17.0	26.2	11.7	‡	8.2	17.4	7.8	4.8	3.1
1985......................	NA	NA	NA	NA	NA	NA	NA	NA	NA
1980......................	NA	NA	NA	NA	NA	NA	NA	NA	NA
1975......................	NA	NA	NA	NA	NA	NA	NA	NA	NA

NA = Not available.
‡ = Reporting standards not met.

Table A-36. Unemployment Rates of Persons 16 to 64 Years Old, by Age Group and Highest Level of Educational Attainment: Selected Years, 1975–2018—*Continued*

(Number; percent.)

Year	25 to 34 years old					35 to 44 years old				
	Unemployment rate for all education levels	Less than high school completion	High school completion	At least some college	Bachelor's or higher degree	Unemployment rate for all education levels	Less than high school completion	High school completion	At least some college	Bachelor's or higher degree
2018...............	4.3	9.1	6.4	4.7	2.0	3.3	5.5	4.9	3.2	2.1
2017...............	4.9	13.2	7.2	4.4	2.5	4.0	6.9	5.7	4.4	2.3
2016...............	5.6	13.1	8.6	5.6	2.4	4.1	6.2	6.6	4.5	2.0
2015...............	5.9	12.5	8.9	6.5	2.4	4.4	8.4	6.3	4.5	2.1
2014...............	7.4	13.7	10.5	7.8	3.7	5.7	11.5	7.4	6.1	2.8
2013...............	8.0	15.1	12.1	8.0	3.6	6.4	11.5	8.5	6.7	3.6
2012...............	9.2	16.8	12.8	10.1	4.1	7.1	14.1	9.1	7.4	3.6
2011...............	10.0	19.7	14.3	10.1	4.3	8.2	15.9	11.3	7.5	4.6
2010...............	10.8	20.3	15.9	10.6	4.5	9.2	17.8	11.9	9.2	4.6
2009...............	10.1	19.9	14.1	9.8	4.5	7.9	15.3	10.6	7.2	4.2
2008...............	5.9	14.2	8.5	5.0	2.2	4.3	9.1	6.0	3.8	1.9
2007...............	4.9	10.3	6.2	4.6	2.2	3.7	9.3	4.8	3.0	1.5
2006...............	5.5	11.0	6.5	5.3	2.8	4.1	8.6	5.1	3.7	2.0
2005...............	5.8	11.6	7.7	5.4	2.6	4.2	8.7	5.2	3.9	2.0
2000...............	4.0	10.3	4.8	3.6	1.6	3.5	8.4	3.9	3.1	1.8
1995...............	5.8	12.9	6.8	5.0	2.7	4.6	10.5	5.1	4.7	2.2
1990...............	4.8	12.0	5.1	3.8	1.9	3.3	8.3	3.7	2.8	1.6
1985...............	7.3	15.5	9.1	5.4	2.8	5.6	12.4	6.1	4.8	2.2
1980...............	6.8	13.7	7.9	6.0	2.5	4.3	9.0	4.2	3.1	1.6
1975...............	8.6	17.2	9.4	6.7	2.9	6.4	11.2	5.7	4.6	2.3

Table A-36. Unemployment Rates of Persons 16 to 64 Years Old, by Age Group and Highest Level of Educational Attainment: Selected Years, 1975–2018—*Continued*

(Number; percent.)

Year	45 to 54 years old					55 to 64 years old				
	Unemployment rate for all education levels	Less than high school completion	High school completion	At least some college	Bachelor's or higher degree	Unemployment rate for all education levels	Less than high school completion	High school completion	At least some college	Bachelor's or higher degree
2018...............	3.2	6.5	3.5	3.3	2.2	3.3	5.6	4.0	3.2	2.2
2017...............	3.3	6.9	4.3	2.9	2.1	3.2	6.0	3.6	3.2	2.4
2016...............	3.7	6.6	5.0	3.4	2.3	3.9	6.5	4.1	4.1	3.2
2015...............	4.1	8.6	5.2	4.1	2.2	4.2	6.9	4.4	4.3	3.3
2014...............	4.9	8.0	6.1	4.8	3.2	5.2	8.2	5.6	5.5	4.0
2013...............	6.0	12.3	7.8	5.2	3.8	5.7	11.2	6.4	5.8	4.2
2012...............	6.8	13.5	7.8	6.9	3.9	6.6	11.5	7.1	7.1	4.8
2011...............	7.5	16.3	9.3	7.1	4.0	6.9	10.0	8.4	7.3	4.9
2010...............	8.4	15.6	11.0	7.6	4.8	7.3	10.1	9.3	7.7	5.0
2009...............	7.4	13.6	8.8	7.5	4.3	6.7	12.7	7.8	7.0	4.3
2008...............	3.9	8.9	4.7	4.0	1.9	3.3	5.6	3.4	3.7	2.4
2007...............	3.5	7.3	4.0	3.7	1.8	3.1	5.3	3.7	3.5	1.8
2006...............	3.4	5.9	3.9	3.4	2.3	2.9	6.0	2.9	3.1	2.0
2005...............	3.9	7.0	4.6	3.7	2.5	3.7	7.5	4.3	3.5	2.3
2000...............	2.4	6.1	2.7	2.4	1.3	2.8	5.2	3.1	2.8	1.4
1995...............	3.9	7.9	4.0	3.9	2.4	3.9	6.7	3.4	3.2	3.3
1990...............	2.5	4.7	2.3	2.6	1.4	2.8	3.9	3.0	2.2	1.8
1985...............	5.4	10.2	5.4	3.2	2.1	4.6	7.1	4.5	3.0	2.2
1980...............	3.9	6.6	3.4	3.0	1.3	3.2	5.2	2.7	2.0	‡
1975...............	5.9	8.5	5.6	4.7	2.0	5.5	7.1	5.1	4.1	1.5

‡ = Reporting standards not met.

Table A-37. Degrees Conferred by Post-Secondary Institutions, by Level of Degree and Sex of Student, 1970-1971 through 2016–2017

(Number.)

Degree conferred, level of degree, and sex of student (when available)	1970-71	1971-72	1972-73	1973-74	1974-75	1975-76	1976-77	1977-78	1978-79	1979-80
Agriculture and Natural Resources										
Bachelor's degrees, total	12,672	13,516	14,756	16,253	17,528	19,402	21,467	22,650	23,134	22,802
Male	12,136	12,779	13,661	14,684	15,061	15,845	16,690	17,069	16,854	16,045
Female	536	737	1,095	1,569	2,467	3,557	4,777	5,581	6,280	6,757
Master's degrees, total	2,457	2,680	2,807	2,928	3,067	3,340	3,724	4,023	3,994	3,976
Male	2,313	2,490	2,588	2,640	2,703	2,862	3,177	3,268	3,187	3,082
Female	144	190	219	288	364	478	547	755	807	894
Doctor's degrees, total	1,086	971	1,059	930	991	928	893	971	950	991
Male	1,055	945	1,031	897	958	867	831	909	877	879
Female	31	26	28	33	33	61	62	62	73	112
Architecture and Related Services										
Bachelor's degrees, total	5,570	6,440	6,962	7,822	8,226	9,146	9,222	9,250	9,273	9,132
Male	4,906	5,667	6,042	6,665	6,791	7,396	7,249	7,054	6,876	6,596
Female	664	773	920	1,157	1,435	1,750	1,973	2,196	2,397	2,536
Master's degrees, total	1,705	1,899	2,307	2,702	2,938	3,215	3,213	3,115	3,113	3,139
Male	1,469	1,626	1,943	2,208	2,343	2,545	2,489	2,304	2,226	2,245
Female	236	273	364	494	595	670	724	811	887	894
Doctor's degrees, total	36	50	58	69	69	82	73	73	96	79
Male	33	43	54	65	58	69	62	57	74	66
Female	3	7	4	4	11	13	11	16	22	13
Biological and Biomedical Sciences										
Bachelor's degrees, total	35,705	37,269	42,207	48,244	51,609	54,154	53,464	51,360	48,713	46,254
Male	25,319	26,314	29,625	33,217	34,580	35,498	34,178	31,673	29,173	26,797
Female	10,386	10,955	12,582	15,027	17,029	18,656	19,286	19,687	19,540	19,457
Master's degrees, total	5,625	5,989	6,156	6,408	6,429	6,457	6,953	6,651	6,638	6,339
Male	3,782	4,056	4,317	4,512	4,554	4,466	4,670	4,353	4,198	4,042
Female	1,843	1,933	1,839	1,896	1,875	1,991	2,283	2,298	2,440	2,297
Doctor's degrees, total	3,603	3,587	3,583	3,358	3,334	3,347	3,335	3,255	3,459	3,568
Male	3,018	2,981	2,892	2,684	2,612	2,631	2,627	2,481	2,593	2,651
Female	585	606	691	674	722	716	708	774	866	917
Biology, Microbiology, and Zoology										
Biology, general										
Bachelor's degree	26,294	27,473	31,185	36,188	38,748	40,163	39,530	37,598	35,962	33,523
Master's degree	2,665	2,943	2,959	3,186	3,109	3,177	3,322	3,094	3,093	2,911
Doctor's degree	536	580	627	657	637	624	608	664	663	718
Microbiology										
Bachelor's degree	1,475	1,548	1,940	2,311	2,767	2,927	2,884	2,695	2,670	2,631
Master's degree	456	470	517	505	552	585	659	615	597	596
Doctor's degree	365	351	344	384	345	364	325	353	395	376
Zoology										
Bachelor's degree	5,721	5,518	5,763	6,128	6,110	6,077	5,574	5,096	4,738	4,301
Master's degree	1,027	1,040	1,042	1,091	1,039	976	985	958	946	922
Doctor's degree	878	836	803	677	697	645	696	624	669	639
Business										
Bachelor's degrees, total	115,396	121,917	126,717	132,304	133,639	143,171	152,010	160,775	172,392	186,264
Male	104,936	110,331	113,337	115,363	111,983	114,986	116,394	117,103	119,765	123,639
Female	10,460	11,586	13,380	16,941	21,656	28,185	35,616	43,672	52,627	62,625
Master's degrees, total	26,490	30,509	31,208	32,691	36,315	42,592	46,505	48,347	50,397	55,008
Male	25,458	29,317	29,689	30,557	33,274	37,654	39,852	40,224	40,766	42,744
Female	1,032	1,192	1,519	2,134	3,041	4,938	6,653	8,123	9,631	12,264
Doctor's degrees, total	774	876	917	922	939	906	839	834	852	767
Male	753	857	864	873	900	856	785	760	752	650
Female	21	19	53	49	39	50	54	74	100	117
Communication, Journalism, and Related Programs in Communication Technologies										
Bachelor's degrees, total	10,802	12,340	14,317	17,096	19,248	21,282	23,214	25,400	26,457	28,616
Male	6,989	7,964	9,074	10,536	11,455	12,458	12,932	13,480	13,266	13,656
Female	3,813	4,376	5,243	6,560	7,793	8,824	10,282	11,920	13,191	14,960
Master's degrees, total	1,856	2,200	2,406	2,640	2,794	3,126	3,091	3,296	2,882	3,082
Male	1,214	1,443	1,546	1,668	1,618	1,818	1,719	1,673	1,483	1,527
Female	642	757	860	972	1,176	1,308	1,372	1,623	1,399	1,555
Doctor's degrees, total	145	111	139	175	165	204	171	191	192	193
Male	126	96	114	146	119	154	130	138	138	121
Female	19	15	25	29	46	50	41	53	54	72

NOTE: Data are for postsecondary institutions participating in Title IV federal financial aid programs.

Table A-37. Degrees Conferred by Post-Secondary Institutions, by Level of Degree and Sex of Student, 1970-1971 through 2016–2017—*Continued*

(Number.)

Degree conferred, level of degree, and sex of student (when available)	1980-81	1981-82	1982-83	1983-84	1984-85	1985-86	1986-87	1987-88	1988-89	1989-90	1990-91
Agriculture and Natural Resources											
Bachelor's degrees, total	21,886	21,029	20,909	19,317	18,107	16,823	14,991	14,222	13,492	12,900	13,124
Male	15,154	14,443	14,085	13,206	12,477	11,544	10,314	9,744	9,298	8,822	8,832
Female	6,732	6,586	6,824	6,111	5,630	5,279	4,677	4,478	4,194	4,078	4,292
Master's degrees, total	4,003	4,163	4,254	4,178	3,928	3,801	3,522	3,479	3,245	3,382	3,295
Male	3,061	3,114	3,129	2,989	2,846	2,701	2,460	2,427	2,231	2,239	2,160
Female	942	1,049	1,125	1,189	1,082	1,100	1,062	1,052	1,014	1,143	1,135
Doctor's degrees, total	1,067	1,079	1,149	1,172	1,213	1,158	1,049	1,142	1,183	1,295	1,185
Male	940	925	1,004	1,001	1,036	966	871	926	950	1,038	953
Female	127	154	145	171	177	192	178	216	233	257	232
Architecture and Related Services											
Bachelor's degrees, total	9,455	9,728	9,823	9,186	9,325	9,119	8,950	8,603	9,150	9,364	9,781
Male	6,800	6,825	6,403	5,895	6,019	5,824	5,617	5,271	5,545	5,703	5,788
Female	2,655	2,903	3,420	3,291	3,306	3,295	3,333	3,332	3,605	3,661	3,993
Master's degrees, total	3,153	3,327	3,357	3,223	3,275	3,260	3,163	3,159	3,383	3,499	3,490
Male	2,234	2,242	2,224	2,197	2,148	2,129	2,086	2,042	2,192	2,228	2,244
Female	919	1,085	1,133	1,026	1,127	1,131	1,077	1,117	1,191	1,271	1,246
Doctor's degrees, total	93	80	97	84	89	73	92	98	86	103	135
Male	73	58	74	62	66	56	66	66	63	73	101
Female	20	22	23	22	23	17	26	32	23	30	34
Biological and Biomedical Sciences											
Bachelor's degrees, total	43,078	41,501	39,924	38,593	38,354	38,395	38,074	36,688	36,068	37,304	39,482
Male	24,124	22,722	21,572	20,565	20,071	20,000	19,684	18,267	17,998	18,363	19,418
Female	18,954	18,779	18,352	18,028	18,283	18,395	18,390	18,421	18,070	18,941	20,064
Master's degrees, total	5,766	5,679	5,711	5,489	5,109	5,064	4,995	4,871	5,034	4,941	4,834
Male	3,602	3,384	3,298	3,123	2,775	2,733	2,646	2,530	2,598	2,509	2,417
Female	2,164	2,295	2,413	2,366	2,334	2,331	2,349	2,341	2,436	2,432	2,417
Doctor's degrees, total	3,640	3,662	3,386	3,496	3,465	3,405	3,469	3,688	3,617	3,922	4,152
Male	2,620	2,611	2,306	2,416	2,335	2,273	2,268	2,389	2,299	2,478	2,618
Female	1,020	1,051	1,080	1,080	1,130	1,132	1,201	1,299	1,318	1,444	1,534
Biology, Microbiology, and Zoology											
Biology, general											
Bachelor's degree	31,323	29,651	28,022	27,379	27,593	27,618	27,465	26,838	26,229	27,213	29,285
Master's degree	2,598	2,579	2,354	2,313	2,130	2,173	2,022	1,981	2,097	1,998	1,956
Doctor's degree	734	678	521	617	658	574	537	576	527	551	632
Microbiology											
Bachelor's degree	2,414	2,377	2,324	2,349	2,207	2,257	2,159	2,061	1,833	1,973	1,788
Master's degree	482	470	499	505	471	392	451	404	449	403	343
Doctor's degree	370	350	358	388	319	362	380	442	423	441	443
Zoology											
Bachelor's degree	3,873	3,615	3,407	3,231	3,069	2,894	2,791	2,537	2,549	2,473	2,641
Master's degree	881	868	738	700	664	618	623	629	634	548	551
Doctor's degree	613	625	533	521	508	548	464	492	466	545	516
Business											
Bachelor's degrees, total	200,521	215,190	226,442	229,013	232,282	236,700	240,346	242,859	246,262	248,568	249,165
Male	126,798	130,693	131,451	129,296	127,467	128,415	128,506	129,467	131,098	132,284	131,557
Female	73,723	84,497	94,991	99,717	104,815	108,285	111,840	113,392	115,164	116,284	117,608
Master's degrees, total	57,888	61,251	64,741	66,129	66,981	66,676	67,093	69,230	73,065	76,676	78,255
Male	43,411	44,230	45,987	46,167	46,199	45,927	44,913	45,980	48,540	50,585	50,883
Female	14,477	17,021	18,754	19,962	20,782	20,749	22,180	23,250	24,525	26,091	27,372
Doctor's degrees, total	808	826	770	926	827	923	1,062	1,063	1,100	1,093	1,185
Male	686	676	638	727	685	720	808	810	800	818	876
Female	122	150	132	199	142	203	254	253	300	275	309
Communication, Journalism, and Related Programs in Communication Technologies											
Bachelor's degrees, total	31,282	34,222	38,647	40,203	42,102	43,145	45,521	46,916	48,889	51,572	53,047
Male	14,179	14,917	16,213	16,662	17,233	17,681	18,201	18,672	19,357	20,374	20,806
Female	17,103	19,305	22,434	23,541	24,869	25,464	27,320	28,244	29,532	31,198	32,241
Master's degrees, total	3,105	3,327	3,600	3,620	3,657	3,808	3,881	3,916	4,249	4,353	4,327
Male	1,448	1,578	1,660	1,578	1,574	1,603	1,584	1,568	1,734	1,705	1,711
Female	1,657	1,749	1,940	2,042	2,083	2,205	2,297	2,348	2,515	2,648	2,616
Doctor's degrees, total	182	200	208	216	232	218	275	233	248	272	272
Male	107	136	123	129	141	116	158	133	137	145	150
Female	75	64	85	87	91	102	117	100	111	127	122

NOTE: Data are for postsecondary institutions participating in Title IV federal financial aid programs.

Table A-37. Degrees Conferred by Post-Secondary Institutions, by Level of Degree and Sex of Student, 1970-1971 through 2016–2017—*Continued*

(Number.)

Degree conferred, level of degree, and sex of student (when available)	1970-71	1971-72	1972-73	1973-74	1974-75	1975-76	1976-77	1977-78	1978-79	1979-80
Computer and Information Sciences										
Bachelor's degrees, total	2,388	3,402	4,304	4,756	5,033	5,652	6,407	7,201	8,719	11,154
Male	2,064	2,941	3,664	3,976	4,080	4,534	4,876	5,349	6,272	7,782
Female	324	461	640	780	953	1,118	1,531	1,852	2,447	3,372
Master's degrees, total	1,588	1,977	2,113	2,276	2,299	2,603	2,798	3,038	3,055	3,647
Male	1,424	1,752	1,888	1,983	1,961	2,226	2,332	2,471	2,480	2,883
Female	164	225	225	293	338	377	466	567	575	764
Doctor's degrees, total	128	167	196	198	213	244	216	196	236	240
Male	125	155	181	189	199	221	197	181	206	213
Female	3	12	15	9	14	23	19	15	30	27
Education										
Bachelor's degrees, total	176,307	190,880	193,984	184,907	166,758	154,437	143,234	135,821	125,873	118,038
Male	44,896	49,344	51,300	48,997	44,463	42,004	39,867	37,410	33,743	30,901
Female	131,411	141,536	142,684	135,910	122,295	112,433	103,367	98,411	92,130	87,137
Master's degrees, total	87,666	96,668	103,777	110,402	117,841	126,061	124,267	116,916	109,866	101,819
Male	38,365	41,141	43,298	44,112	44,430	44,831	42,308	37,662	34,410	30,300
Female	49,301	55,527	60,479	66,290	73,411	81,230	81,959	79,254	75,456	71,519
Doctor's degrees, total	6,041	6,648	6,857	6,757	6,975	7,202	7,338	7,018	7,170	7,314
Male	4,771	5,104	5,191	4,974	4,856	4,826	4,832	4,281	4,174	4,100
Female	1,270	1,544	1,666	1,783	2,119	2,376	2,506	2,737	2,996	3,214
Engineering and Engineering Technologies										
Bachelor's degrees, total	50,182	51,258	51,384	50,412	47,131	46,676	49,482	56,150	62,898	69,387
Male	49,775	50,726	50,766	49,611	46,105	45,184	47,238	52,353	57,603	62,877
Female	407	532	618	801	1,026	1,492	2,244	3,797	5,295	6,510
Master's degrees, total	16,947	17,299	16,988	15,851	15,837	16,800	16,659	16,887	16,012	16,765
Male	16,734	17,009	16,694	15,470	15,426	16,174	15,891	15,940	14,971	15,535
Female	213	290	294	381	411	626	768	947	1,041	1,230
Doctor's degrees, total	3,688	3,708	3,513	3,374	3,181	2,874	2,622	2,483	2,545	2,546
Male	3,663	3,685	3,459	3,318	3,113	2,805	2,547	2,424	2,459	2,447
Female	25	23	54	56	68	69	75	59	86	99
Chemical, Civil, Electrical, and Mechanical Engineering										
Chemical engineering										
Bachelor's degree	3,579	3,625	3,578	3,399	3,070	3,140	3,524	4,569	5,568	6,320
Master's degree	1,100	1,154	1,051	1,044	990	1,031	1,086	1,235	1,149	1,270
Doctor's degree	406	394	397	400	346	308	291	259	304	284
Civil engineering										
Bachelor's degree	6,526	6,803	7,390	8,017	7,651	7,923	8,228	9,135	9,809	10,326
Master's degree	2,425	2,487	2,627	2,652	2,769	2,999	2,964	2,685	2,646	2,683
Doctor's degree	446	415	397	368	356	370	309	277	253	270
Electrical, electronics, and communications engineering										
Bachelor's degree	12,198	12,101	12,313	11,316	10,161	9,791	9,936	11,133	12,338	13,821
Master's degree	4,282	4,206	3,895	3,499	3,469	3,774	3,788	3,740	3,591	3,836
Doctor's degree	879	824	791	705	701	649	566	503	586	525
Mechanical engineering										
Bachelor's degree	8,858	8,530	8,523	7,677	6,890	6,800	7,703	8,875	10,107	11,808
Master's degree	2,237	2,282	2,141	1,843	1,858	1,907	1,952	1,942	1,877	2,060
Doctor's degree	438	411	370	385	340	305	283	279	271	281
English Language and Literature/Letters										
Bachelor's degrees, total	63,914	63,707	60,607	54,190	47,062	41,452	37,343	34,799	33,218	32,187
Male	22,005	22,580	22,022	20,082	17,689	15,898	14,135	12,972	12,085	11,237
Female	41,909	41,127	38,585	34,108	29,373	25,554	23,208	21,827	21,133	20,950
Master's degrees, total	10,441	10,412	10,035	9,573	9,178	8,599	7,824	7,444	6,503	6,026
Male	4,126	4,066	3,988	3,824	3,463	3,290	2,907	2,623	2,307	2,181
Female	6,315	6,346	6,047	5,749	5,715	5,309	4,917	4,821	4,196	3,845
Doctor's degrees, total	1,554	1,734	1,817	1,755	1,595	1,514	1,373	1,272	1,186	1,196
Male	1,107	1,173	1,189	1,142	974	895	768	698	639	635
Female	447	561	628	613	621	619	605	574	547	561
Foreign Languages and Literatures										
Bachelor's degrees, total	20,988	19,890	20,170	20,197	19,103	17,068	15,496	14,334	13,211	12,480
Male	5,508	5,196	5,119	5,063	4,723	4,270	3,965	3,684	3,391	3,226
Female	15,480	14,694	15,051	15,134	14,380	12,798	11,531	10,650	9,820	9,254
Master's degrees, total	5,480	5,283	5,068	4,851	4,721	4,432	4,056	3,624	3,248	3,067
Male	1,961	1,919	1,909	1,788	1,672	1,581	1,365	1,194	1,092	1,026

NOTE: Data are for postsecondary institutions participating in Title IV federal financial aid programs.

Table A-37. Degrees Conferred by Post-Secondary Institutions, by Level of Degree and Sex of Student, 1970-1971 through 2016–2017—*Continued*

(Number.)

Degree conferred, level of degree, and sex of student (when available)	1980-81	1981-82	1982-83	1983-84	1984-85	1985-86	1986-87	1987-88	1988-89	1989-90	1990-91
Computer and Information Sciences											
Bachelor's degrees, total	15,121	20,267	24,565	32,439	39,121	42,337	39,767	34,651	30,560	27,347	25,159
Male	10,202	13,218	15,641	20,416	24,737	27,208	25,962	23,414	21,143	19,159	17,771
Female	4,919	7,049	8,924	12,023	14,384	15,129	13,805	11,237	9,417	8,188	7,388
Master's degrees, total	4,218	4,935	5,321	6,190	7,101	8,070	8,481	9,197	9,414	9,677	9,324
Male	3,247	3,625	3,813	4,379	5,064	5,658	5,985	6,726	6,775	6,960	6,563
Female	971	1,310	1,508	1,811	2,037	2,412	2,496	2,471	2,639	2,717	2,761
Doctor's degrees, total	252	251	262	251	248	344	374	428	551	627	676
Male	227	230	228	225	223	299	322	380	466	534	584
Female	25	21	34	26	25	45	52	48	85	93	92
Education											
Bachelor's degrees, total	108,074	100,932	97,908	92,310	88,078	87,147	86,788	90,928	96,740	105,112	110,807
Male	27,039	24,380	23,651	22,200	21,254	20,982	20,705	20,947	21,643	23,007	23,417
Female	81,035	76,552	74,257	70,110	66,824	66,165	66,083	69,981	75,097	82,105	87,390
Master's degrees, total	96,713	91,601	83,254	75,700	74,667	74,816	72,619	75,270	79,793	84,890	87,352
Male	27,548	25,339	22,824	21,164	20,539	20,302	18,955	18,777	19,616	20,469	20,448
Female	69,165	66,262	60,430	54,536	54,128	54,514	53,664	56,493	60,177	64,421	66,904
Doctor's degrees, total	7,279	6,999	7,063	6,914	6,614	6,610	5,905	5,568	5,884	6,503	6,189
Male	3,843	3,612	3,550	3,448	3,174	3,088	2,745	2,530	2,522	2,776	2,614
Female	3,436	3,387	3,513	3,466	3,440	3,522	3,160	3,038	3,362	3,727	3,575
Engineering and Engineering Technologies											
Bachelor's degrees, total	75,355	80,632	89,811	95,295	97,099	97,122	93,560	89,406	85,982	82,480	79,751
Male	67,573	71,305	78,673	82,841	83,991	84,050	80,543	76,886	74,020	70,859	68,482
Female	7,782	9,327	11,138	12,454	13,108	13,072	13,017	12,520	11,962	11,621	11,269
Master's degrees, total	17,216	18,475	19,949	21,197	22,124	22,146	23,101	23,839	25,066	25,294	25,450
Male	15,761	16,747	18,038	18,916	19,688	19,545	20,137	20,815	21,731	21,753	21,780
Female	1,455	1,728	1,911	2,281	2,436	2,601	2,964	3,024	3,335	3,541	3,670
Doctor's degrees, total	2,608	2,676	2,871	3,032	3,269	3,456	3,854	4,237	4,572	5,030	5,330
Male	2,499	2,532	2,742	2,864	3,055	3,220	3,585	3,941	4,160	4,576	4,834
Female	109	144	129	168	214	236	269	296	412	454	496
Chemical, Civil, Electrical, and Mechanical Engineering											
Chemical engineering											
Bachelor's degree	6,527	6,740	7,185	7,475	7,146	5,877	4,991	3,917	3,663	3,430	3,444
Master's degree	1,267	1,285	1,368	1,514	1,544	1,361	1,184	1,088	1,093	1,035	903
Doctor's degree	300	311	319	330	418	446	497	579	602	562	611
Civil engineering											
Bachelor's degree	10,678	10,524	9,989	9,693	9,162	8,679	8,147	7,488	7,312	7,252	7,314
Master's degree	2,891	2,995	3,074	3,146	3,172	2,926	2,901	2,836	2,903	2,812	2,927
Doctor's degree	325	329	340	369	377	395	451	481	505	516	536
Electrical, electronics, and communications engineering											
Bachelor's degree	14,938	16,455	18,049	19,943	21,691	23,742	24,547	23,597	21,908	20,711	19,320
Master's degree	3,901	4,462	4,531	5,078	5,153	5,534	6,183	6,688	7,028	7,225	7,095
Doctor's degree	535	526	550	585	660	722	724	860	998	1,162	1,220
Mechanical engineering											
Bachelor's degree	13,329	13,922	15,675	16,629	16,794	16,194	15,450	14,900	14,843	14,336	13,977
Master's degree	2,291	2,399	2,511	2,797	3,053	3,075	3,198	3,329	3,498	3,424	3,516
Doctor's degree	276	333	299	319	409	426	528	596	633	742	757
English Language and Literature/Letters											
Bachelor's degrees, total	31,922	33,078	31,327	32,296	32,686	34,083	35,667	38,106	41,786	46,803	51,064
Male	11,082	11,300	10,699	11,007	11,195	11,657	12,133	12,687	13,729	15,437	16,891
Female	20,840	21,778	20,628	21,289	21,491	22,426	23,534	25,419	28,057	31,366	34,173
Master's degrees, total	5,742	5,593	4,866	4,814	4,987	5,335	5,298	5,366	5,716	6,317	6,784
Male	2,026	1,916	1,653	1,681	1,723	1,811	1,819	1,796	1,930	2,125	2,203
Female	3,716	3,677	3,213	3,133	3,264	3,524	3,479	3,570	3,786	4,192	4,581
Doctor's degrees, total	1,040	986	877	899	915	895	853	858	929	986	1,056
Male	497	467	419	413	414	390	367	380	405	444	469
Female	543	519	458	486	501	505	486	478	524	542	587
Foreign Languages and Literatures											
Bachelor's degrees, total	11,638	11,175	11,170	10,985	11,436	11,550	11,706	11,515	12,403	13,133	13,937
Male	3,013	2,919	3,048	3,098	3,186	3,374	3,374	3,223	3,432	3,625	4,008
Female	8,625	8,256	8,122	7,887	8,250	8,176	8,332	8,292	8,971	9,508	9,929
Master's degrees, total	2,934	2,892	2,706	2,814	2,708	2,690	2,574	2,680	2,837	3,018	3,049
Male	1,039	997	1,001	984	932	878	847	931	955	987	1,018

NOTE: Data are for postsecondary institutions participating in Title IV federal financial aid programs.

Table A-37. Degrees Conferred by Post-Secondary Institutions, by Level of Degree and Sex of Student, 1970-1971 through 2016–2017—*Continued*

(Number.)

Degree conferred, level of degree, and sex of student (when available)	1970-71	1971-72	1972-73	1973-74	1974-75	1975-76	1976-77	1977-78	1978-79	1979-80
Female	3,519	3,364	3,159	3,063	3,049	2,851	2,691	2,430	2,156	2,041
Doctor's degrees, total	1,084	1,134	1,347	1,248	1,220	1,245	1,103	1,002	960	857
Male	714	742	829	703	665	643	574	490	471	412
Female	370	392	518	545	555	602	529	512	489	445
French, German, Italian, and Spanish Language and Literature										
French										
Bachelor's degree	7,306	6,822	6,705	6,263	5,745	4,783	4,228	3,708	3,558	3,285
Master's degree	1,437	1,421	1,277	1,195	1,077	914	875	692	576	513
Doctor's degree	192	193	203	213	200	190	177	155	143	128
German										
Bachelor's degree	2,601	2,477	2,520	2,425	2,289	1,983	1,820	1,647	1,524	1,466
Master's degree	690	608	598	550	480	471	394	357	344	309
Doctor's degree	144	167	176	149	147	164	126	101	106	94
Italian										
Bachelor's degree	201	287	313	292	329	342	325	301	236	272
Master's degree	87	104	78	81	100	85	89	58	60	49
Doctor's degree	10	19	27	19	13	19	16	19	14	9
Spanish										
Bachelor's degree	7,068	6,847	7,209	7,250	6,719	5,984	5,359	4,832	4,563	4,331
Master's degree	1,456	1,421	1,298	1,217	1,228	1,080	930	822	720	685
Doctor's degree	168	152	206	203	202	176	153	113	118	103
Arabic, Chinese, Korean, and Russian Language and Literature										
Arabic										
Bachelor's degree	15	10	12	20	13	10	7	8	4	13
Master's degree	6	4	3	5	11	7	15	3	4	2
Doctor's degree	4	0	1	1	2	2	1	1	5	5
Chinese										
Bachelor's degree	89	103	98	121	141	150	112	116	91	79
Master's degree	22	20	29	37	26	23	32	23	22	33
Doctor's degree	8	11	13	5	12	6	6	4	12	7
Korean										
Bachelor's degree	NA	NA	NA	NA	NA	NA	NA	NA	NA	NA
Master's degree	NA	NA	NA	NA	NA	NA	NA	NA	NA	NA
Doctor's degree	NA	NA	NA	NA	NA	NA	NA	NA	NA	NA
Russian										
Bachelor's degree	715	658	622	624	598	531	528	442	465	402
Master's degree	110	150	120	100	106	81	66	50	51	60
Doctor's degree	14	15	27	27	20	13	19	12	9	6
Health Professions and Related Programs										
Bachelor's degrees, total	25,223	28,611	33,562	41,421	49,002	53,885	57,222	59,445	62,095	63,848
Male	5,785	7,005	7,752	9,347	10,844	11,386	11,896	11,600	11,214	11,330
Female	19,438	21,606	25,810	32,074	38,158	42,499	45,326	47,845	50,881	52,518
Master's degrees, total	5,330	6,811	7,978	9,232	10,277	12,164	12,627	14,027	15,110	15,374
Male	2,165	2,749	3,189	3,444	3,686	3,837	3,865	3,972	4,155	4,060
Female	3,165	4,062	4,789	5,788	6,591	8,327	8,762	10,055	10,955	11,314
Doctor's degrees, total	15,988	16,538	18,215	20,094	22,191	25,267	24,972	26,516	27,766	28,190
Male	14,863	15,373	16,870	18,287	19,808	21,980	21,022	21,622	22,194	22,157
Female	1,125	1,165	1,345	1,807	2,383	3,287	3,950	4,894	5,572	6,033
Mathematics and Statistics										
Bachelor's degrees, total	24,801	23,713	23,067	21,635	18,181	15,984	14,196	12,569	11,806	11,378
Male	15,369	14,454	13,796	12,791	10,586	9,475	8,303	7,398	6,899	6,562
Female	9,432	9,259	9,271	8,844	7,595	6,509	5,893	5,171	4,907	4,816
Master's degrees, total	5,191	5,198	5,028	4,834	4,327	3,857	3,695	3,373	3,036	2,860
Male	3,673	3,655	3,525	3,337	2,905	2,547	2,396	2,228	1,985	1,828
Female	1,518	1,543	1,503	1,497	1,422	1,310	1,299	1,145	1,051	1,032
Doctor's degrees, total	1,199	1,128	1,068	1,031	975	856	823	805	730	724
Male	1,106	1,039	966	931	865	762	714	681	608	624
Female	93	89	102	100	110	94	109	124	122	100
Physical Sciences and Science Technologies										
Bachelor's degrees, total	21,410	20,743	20,692	21,170	20,770	21,458	22,482	22,975	23,197	23,407
Male	18,457	17,661	17,622	17,669	16,986	17,349	17,985	18,083	17,976	17,861
Female	2,953	3,082	3,070	3,501	3,784	4,109	4,497	4,892	5,221	5,546

NOTE: Data are for postsecondary institutions participating in Title IV federal financial aid programs.
NA = Not available.

Table A-37. Degrees Conferred by Post-Secondary Institutions, by Level of Degree and Sex of Student, 1970-1971 through 2016–2017—*Continued*

(Number.)

Degree conferred, level of degree, and sex of student (when available)	1980-81	1981-82	1982-83	1983-84	1984-85	1985-86	1986-87	1987-88	1988-89	1989-90	1990-91
Female	1,895	1,895	1,705	1,830	1,776	1,812	1,727	1,749	1,882	2,031	2,031
Doctor's degrees, total	931	869	790	779	761	768	769	725	727	816	889
Male	460	407	362	353	342	338	332	330	317	348	396
Female	471	462	428	426	419	430	437	395	410	468	493
French, German, Italian, and Spanish Language and Literature											
French											
Bachelor's degree	3,178	3,054	2,871	2,876	2,991	3,015	3,062	3,082	3,297	3,259	3,355
Master's degree	460	485	360	418	385	409	421	437	444	478	480
Doctor's degree	115	92	106	86	74	86	85	89	83	115	98
German											
Bachelor's degree	1,286	1,327	1,367	1,292	1,411	1,396	1,366	1,350	1,428	1,437	1,543
Master's degree	294	324	281	241	240	249	234	244	263	253	242
Doctor's degree	79	76	68	63	58	73	70	71	59	67	58
Italian											
Bachelor's degree	205	208	224	206	190	240	219	224	239	247	253
Master's degree	65	55	45	41	44	42	53	45	45	38	36
Doctor's degree	13	14	18	13	9	10	17	7	17	19	21
Spanish											
Bachelor's degree	3,870	3,633	3,349	3,254	3,415	3,385	3,450	3,416	3,748	4,176	4,480
Master's degree	592	568	506	537	505	521	504	553	552	573	609
Doctor's degree	131	140	129	102	115	95	104	93	101	108	125
Arabic, Chinese, Korean, and Russian Language and Literature											
Arabic											
Bachelor's degree	6	15	12	6	9	5	8	9	6	4	9
Master's degree	7	4	4	2	4	4	1	4	2	0	0
Doctor's degree	0	4	1	0	0	0	1	0	1	1	1
Chinese											
Bachelor's degree	73	68	92	115	97	87	110	103	138	144	150
Master's degree	20	14	15	14	21	23	16	31	27	33	24
Doctor's degree	6	10	7	10	3	11	10	9	8	8	9
Korean											
Bachelor's degree	NA	NA	NA	NA	NA	NA	NA	NA	NA	NA	NA
Master's degree	NA	NA	NA	NA	NA	NA	NA	NA	NA	NA	NA
Doctor's degree	NA	NA	NA	NA	NA	NA	NA	NA	NA	NA	NA
Russian											
Bachelor's degree	409	324	342	340	432	493	502	472	469	549	593
Master's degree	68	49	33	39	47	33	54	54	55	52	70
Doctor's degree	8	7	5	3	6	3	8	8	6	5	6
Health Professions and Related Programs											
Bachelor's degrees, total	63,665	63,660	65,642	65,305	65,331	65,309	63,963	61,614	59,850	58,983	59,875
Male	10,531	10,110	10,247	10,068	9,741	9,629	9,137	8,955	8,878	9,075	9,619
Female	53,134	53,550	55,395	55,237	55,590	55,680	54,826	52,659	50,972	49,908	50,256
Master's degrees, total	16,176	16,212	16,941	17,351	17,442	18,603	18,442	18,774	19,493	20,406	21,354
Male	4,024	3,743	4,138	4,124	4,046	4,355	3,818	4,004	4,197	4,486	4,423
Female	12,152	12,469	12,803	13,227	13,396	14,248	14,624	14,770	15,296	15,920	16,931
Doctor's degrees, total	29,595	30,096	30,800	31,655	31,493	31,922	29,500	30,060	30,546	30,101	29,842
Male	22,792	22,968	22,920	22,851	22,045	22,069	19,686	19,853	19,893	19,118	18,492
Female	6,803	7,128	7,880	8,804	9,448	9,853	9,814	10,207	10,653	10,983	11,350
Mathematics and Statistics											
Bachelor's degrees, total	11,078	11,599	12,294	13,087	15,009	16,122	16,257	15,712	15,017	14,276	14,393
Male	6,342	6,593	6,888	7,290	8,080	8,623	8,673	8,408	8,081	7,674	7,580
Female	4,736	5,006	5,406	5,797	6,929	7,499	7,584	7,304	6,936	6,602	6,813
Master's degrees, total	2,567	2,727	2,810	2,723	2,859	3,131	3,283	3,413	3,405	3,624	3,549
Male	1,692	1,821	1,838	1,773	1,858	2,028	1,995	2,052	2,061	2,172	2,096
Female	875	906	972	950	1,001	1,103	1,288	1,361	1,344	1,452	1,453
Doctor's degrees, total	728	681	697	695	699	742	723	750	866	917	978
Male	614	587	581	569	590	618	598	625	700	754	790
Female	114	94	116	126	109	124	125	125	166	163	188
Physical Sciences and Science Technologies											
Bachelor's degrees, total	23,936	24,045	23,374	23,645	23,694	21,711	20,060	17,797	17,179	16,056	16,334
Male	18,052	17,861	16,988	17,112	17,065	15,750	14,365	12,385	12,071	11,026	11,170
Female	5,884	6,184	6,386	6,533	6,629	5,961	5,695	5,412	5,108	5,030	5,164

NOTE: Data are for postsecondary institutions participating in Title IV federal financial aid programs.
NA = Not available.

Table A-37. Degrees Conferred by Post-Secondary Institutions, by Level of Degree and Sex of Student, 1970-1971 through 2016–2017—*Continued*

(Number.)

Degree conferred, level of degree, and sex of student (when available)	1970-71	1971-72	1972-73	1973-74	1974-75	1975-76	1976-77	1977-78	1978-79	1979-80
Master's degrees, total	6,336	6,268	6,230	6,019	5,782	5,428	5,281	5,507	5,418	5,167
Male	5,495	5,390	5,388	5,157	4,949	4,622	4,411	4,583	4,438	4,210
Female	841	878	842	862	833	806	870	924	980	957
Doctor's degrees, total	4,324	4,075	3,961	3,558	3,577	3,388	3,295	3,073	3,061	3,044
Male	4,082	3,805	3,698	3,312	3,284	3,097	2,981	2,763	2,717	2,669
Female	242	270	263	246	293	291	314	310	344	375
Chemistry, Geology and Earth Science, and Physics										
Chemistry										
Bachelor's degree	11,061	10,588	10,124	10,430	10,541	11,015	11,200	11,304	11,499	11,229
Master's degree	2,244	2,229	2,198	2,082	1,961	1,745	1,717	1,832	1,724	1,671
Doctor's degree	2,093	1,943	1,827	1,755	1,773	1,578	1,522	1,461	1,475	1,500
Geology and earth science[1]										
Bachelor's degree	3,312	3,766	4,117	4,526	4,566	4,677	5,280	5,648	5,753	5,785
Master's degree	1,074	1,233	1,296	1,479	1,320	1,384	1,446	1,633	1,596	1,623
Doctor's degree	408	433	430	416	433	445	480	419	414	440
Physics[2]										
Bachelor's degree	5,071	4,634	4,259	3,952	3,706	3,544	3,420	3,330	3,337	3,396
Master's degree	2,188	2,033	1,747	1,655	1,574	1,451	1,319	1,294	1,319	1,192
Doctor's degree	1,482	1,344	1,338	1,115	1,080	997	945	873	918	830
Psychology										
Bachelor's degrees, total	38,187	43,433	47,940	52,139	51,245	50,278	47,861	44,879	42,697	42,093
Male	21,227	23,352	25,117	25,868	24,284	22,898	20,627	18,422	16,540	15,440
Female	16,960	20,081	22,823	26,271	26,961	27,380	27,234	26,457	26,157	26,653
Master's degrees, total	5,717	6,764	7,619	8,796	9,394	10,167	10,859	10,282	10,132	9,938
Male	3,395	3,934	4,325	4,983	5,035	5,136	5,293	4,670	4,405	4,096
Female	2,322	2,830	3,294	3,813	4,359	5,031	5,566	5,612	5,727	5,842
Doctor's degrees, total	2,144	2,277	2,550	2,872	2,913	3,157	3,386	3,164	3,228	3,395
Male	1,629	1,694	1,797	1,987	1,979	2,115	2,127	1,974	1,895	1,921
Female	515	583	753	885	934	1,042	1,259	1,190	1,333	1,474
Public Administration and Social Services										
Bachelor's degrees, total	5,466	7,508	10,690	11,966	13,661	15,440	16,136	16,607	17,328	16,644
Male	1,726	2,588	3,998	4,266	4,630	5,706	5,544	5,096	4,938	4,451
Female	3,740	4,920	6,692	7,700	9,031	9,734	10,592	11,511	12,390	12,193
Master's degrees, total	7,785	8,756	10,068	11,415	13,617	15,209	17,026	17,337	17,306	17,560
Male	3,893	4,537	5,271	6,028	7,200	7,969	8,810	8,513	8,051	7,866
Female	3,892	4,219	4,797	5,387	6,417	7,240	8,216	8,824	9,255	9,694
Doctor's degrees, total	174	193	198	201	257	292	292	357	315	342
Male	132	150	160	154	192	192	197	237	215	216
Female	42	43	38	47	65	100	95	120	100	126
Social Sciences and History										
Bachelor's degrees, total	155,324	158,060	155,970	150,320	135,190	126,396	117,040	112,952	108,059	103,662
Male	98,173	100,895	99,735	95,650	84,826	78,691	71,128	67,217	62,852	58,511
Female	57,151	57,165	56,235	54,670	50,364	47,705	45,912	45,735	45,207	45,151
Master's degrees, total	16,539	17,445	17,477	17,293	16,977	15,953	15,533	14,718	12,963	12,176
Male	11,833	12,540	12,605	12,321	11,875	10,918	10,413	9,845	8,395	7,794
Female	4,706	4,905	4,872	4,972	5,102	5,035	5,120	4,873	4,568	4,382
Doctor's degrees, total	3,660	4,081	4,234	4,124	4,212	4,157	3,802	3,594	3,371	3,230
Male	3,153	3,483	3,573	3,383	3,334	3,262	2,957	2,722	2,501	2,357
Female	507	598	661	741	878	895	845	872	870	873
Economics, History, Political Science and Government, and Sociology										
Economics										
Bachelor's degree	15,758	15,231	14,770	14,285	14,046	14,741	15,296	15,661	16,409	17,863
Master's degree	1,995	2,224	2,225	2,141	2,127	2,087	2,158	1,995	1,955	1,821
Doctor's degree	721	794	845	788	815	763	758	706	712	677
History										
Bachelor's degree	44,663	43,695	40,943	37,049	31,470	28,400	25,433	23,004	21,019	19,301
Master's degree	5,157	5,217	5,030	4,533	4,226	3,658	3,393	3,033	2,536	2,367
Doctor's degree	991	1,133	1,140	1,114	1,117	1,014	921	813	756	712
Political science and government										
Bachelor's degree	27,482	28,135	30,100	30,744	29,126	28,302	26,411	26,069	25,628	25,457
Master's degree	2,318	2,451	2,398	2,448	2,333	2,191	2,222	2,069	2,037	1,938
Doctor's degree	700	758	747	766	680	723	641	636	563	535

NOTE: Data are for postsecondary institutions participating in Title IV federal financial aid programs.
[1] Includes geology/earth science, general; geochemistry; geophysics; paleontology; hydrology; oceanography; and geological and earth sciences, other.
[2] Includes physics, general; atomic/molecular physics; elementary particle physics; nuclear physics; optics; acoustics; theoretical physics; and physics, other.

Table A-37. Degrees Conferred by Post-Secondary Institutions, by Level of Degree and Sex of Student, 1970-1971 through 2016–2017—*Continued*

(Number.)

Degree conferred, level of degree, and sex of student (when available)	1980-81	1981-82	1982-83	1983-84	1984-85	1985-86	1986-87	1987-88	1988-89	1989-90	1990-91
Master's degrees, total	5,246	5,446	5,250	5,541	5,752	5,860	5,586	5,696	5,691	5,410	5,281
Male	4,172	4,274	4,131	4,249	4,425	4,443	4,193	4,300	4,180	3,996	3,823
Female	1,074	1,172	1,119	1,292	1,327	1,417	1,393	1,396	1,511	1,414	1,458
Doctor's degrees, total	3,105	3,246	3,214	3,269	3,349	3,521	3,629	3,758	3,795	4,116	4,248
Male	2,733	2,804	2,767	2,789	2,808	2,946	3,004	3,085	3,046	3,328	3,417
Female	372	442	447	480	541	575	625	673	749	788	831
Chemistry, Geology and Earth Science, and Physics											
Chemistry											
Bachelor's degree	11,331	11,058	10,789	10,698	10,472	10,110	9,660	9,043	8,618	8,122	8,311
Master's degree	1,616	1,683	1,582	1,632	1,675	1,712	1,695	1,671	1,742	1,643	1,637
Doctor's degree	1,586	1,682	1,691	1,707	1,735	1,878	1,932	1,944	1,974	2,135	2,196
Geology and earth science[1]											
Bachelor's degree	6,332	6,650	6,981	7,524	7,194	5,760	3,943	3,204	2,847	2,372	2,367
Master's degree	1,702	1,848	1,784	1,747	1,927	2,036	1,835	1,722	1,609	1,399	1,336
Doctor's degree	404	452	406	408	401	395	399	462	492	562	600
Physics[2]											
Bachelor's degree	3,441	3,472	3,793	3,907	4,097	4,180	4,318	4,100	4,352	4,155	4,236
Master's degree	1,294	1,284	1,369	1,532	1,523	1,501	1,543	1,675	1,736	1,831	1,725
Doctor's degree	866	873	873	953	951	1,010	1,074	1,093	1,112	1,192	1,209
Psychology											
Bachelor's degrees, total	41,068	41,212	40,460	39,955	39,900	40,628	43,152	45,371	49,083	53,952	58,655
Male	14,332	13,645	13,131	12,812	12,706	12,605	13,395	13,579	14,265	15,336	16,067
Female	26,736	27,567	27,329	27,143	27,194	28,023	29,757	31,792	34,818	38,616	42,588
Master's degrees, total	10,223	9,947	9,981	9,525	9,891	9,845	11,000	10,488	11,329	10,730	11,349
Male	4,066	3,823	3,647	3,400	3,452	3,347	3,516	3,256	3,465	3,377	3,329
Female	6,157	6,124	6,334	6,125	6,439	6,498	7,484	7,232	7,864	7,353	8,020
Doctor's degrees, total	3,576	3,461	3,602	3,535	3,447	3,593	4,062	3,973	4,143	3,811	3,932
Male	2,002	1,856	1,838	1,774	1,739	1,724	1,801	1,783	1,773	1,566	1,520
Female	1,574	1,605	1,764	1,761	1,708	1,869	2,261	2,190	2,370	2,245	2,412
Public Administration and Social Services											
Bachelor's degrees, total	16,707	16,495	14,414	12,570	11,754	11,887	12,328	12,385	13,162	13,908	14,350
Male	4,248	4,176	3,343	2,998	2,829	2,966	2,993	2,923	3,214	3,334	3,215
Female	12,459	12,319	11,071	9,572	8,925	8,921	9,335	9,462	9,948	10,574	11,135
Master's degrees, total	17,803	17,416	16,046	15,060	15,575	15,692	16,432	16,424	17,020	17,399	17,905
Male	7,460	6,975	5,961	5,634	5,573	5,594	5,673	5,631	5,615	5,634	5,679
Female	10,343	10,441	10,085	9,426	10,002	10,098	10,759	10,793	11,405	11,765	12,226
Doctor's degrees, total	362	372	347	420	431	382	398	470	428	508	430
Male	212	205	184	230	213	171	216	238	210	235	190
Female	150	167	163	190	218	211	182	232	218	273	240
Social Sciences and History											
Bachelor's degrees, total	100,513	99,705	95,228	93,323	91,570	93,840	96,342	100,460	108,151	118,083	125,107
Male	56,131	55,196	52,771	52,154	51,226	52,724	53,949	56,377	60,121	65,887	68,701
Female	44,382	44,509	42,457	41,169	40,344	41,116	42,393	44,083	48,030	52,196	56,406
Master's degrees, total	11,945	12,002	11,205	10,577	10,503	10,564	10,506	10,412	11,023	11,634	12,233
Male	7,457	7,468	6,974	6,551	6,475	6,419	6,373	6,310	6,599	6,898	7,016
Female	4,488	4,534	4,231	4,026	4,028	4,145	4,133	4,102	4,424	4,736	5,217
Doctor's degrees, total	3,122	3,061	2,931	2,911	2,851	2,955	2,916	2,781	2,885	3,010	3,012
Male	2,274	2,237	2,042	2,030	1,933	1,970	2,026	1,849	1,949	2,019	1,956
Female	848	824	889	881	918	985	890	932	936	991	1,056
Economics, History, Political Science and Government, and Sociology											
Economics											
Bachelor's degree	18,753	19,876	20,517	20,719	20,711	21,602	22,378	22,911	23,454	23,923	23,488
Master's degree	1,911	1,964	1,972	1,891	1,992	1,937	1,855	1,847	1,886	1,950	1,951
Doctor's degree	727	677	734	729	749	789	750	770	827	806	802
History											
Bachelor's degree	18,301	17,146	16,467	16,643	16,049	16,415	16,997	18,207	20,159	22,476	24,541
Master's degree	2,237	2,210	2,041	1,940	1,921	1,961	2,021	2,093	2,121	2,369	2,591
Doctor's degree	643	636	575	561	468	497	534	517	487	570	606
Political science and government											
Bachelor's degree	24,977	25,658	25,791	25,719	25,834	26,439	26,817	27,207	30,450	33,560	35,737
Master's degree	1,875	1,954	1,829	1,769	1,500	1,704	1,618	1,579	1,598	1,580	1,772
Doctor's degree	484	513	435	457	441	439	435	391	452	480	468

NOTE: Data are for postsecondary institutions participating in Title IV federal financial aid programs.

[1] Includes geology/earth science, general; geochemistry; geophysics; paleontology; hydrology; oceanography; and geological and earth sciences, other.

[2] Includes physics, general; atomic/molecular physics; elementary particle physics; nuclear physics; optics; acoustics; theoretical physics; and physics, other.

Table A-37. Degrees Conferred by Post-Secondary Institutions, by Level of Degree and Sex of Student, 1970-1971 through 2016–2017—*Continued*

(Number.)

Degree conferred, level of degree, and sex of student (when available)	1970-71	1971-72	1972-73	1973-74	1974-75	1975-76	1976-77	1977-78	1978-79	1979-80
Sociology										
Bachelor's degree	33,263	35,216	35,436	35,491	31,488	27,634	24,713	22,750	20,285	18,881
Master's degree	1,808	1,944	1,923	2,196	2,112	2,009	1,830	1,611	1,415	1,341
Doctor's degree	574	636	583	632	693	729	714	599	612	583
Visual and Performing Arts										
Bachelor's degrees, total	30,394	33,831	36,017	39,730	40,782	42,138	41,793	40,951	40,969	40,892
Male	12,256	13,580	14,267	15,821	15,532	16,491	16,166	15,572	15,380	15,065
Female	18,138	20,251	21,750	23,909	25,250	25,647	25,627	25,379	25,589	25,827
Master's degrees, total	6,675	7,537	7,254	8,001	8,362	8,817	8,636	9,036	8,524	8,708
Male	3,510	4,049	4,005	4,325	4,448	4,507	4,211	4,327	3,933	4,067
Female	3,165	3,488	3,249	3,676	3,914	4,310	4,425	4,709	4,591	4,641
Doctor's degrees, total	621	572	616	585	649	620	662	708	700	655
Male	483	428	449	440	446	447	447	448	454	413
Female	138	144	167	145	203	173	215	260	246	242

NOTE: Data are for postsecondary institutions participating in Title IV federal financial aid programs.

Table A-37. Degrees Conferred by Post-Secondary Institutions, by Level of Degree and Sex of Student, 1970-1971 through 2016–2017—*Continued*

(Number.)

Degree conferred, level of degree, and sex of student (when available)	1980-81	1981-82	1982-83	1983-84	1984-85	1985-86	1986-87	1987-88	1988-89	1989-90	1990-91
Sociology											
Bachelor's degree	17,272	16,042	14,105	13,145	11,968	12,271	12,239	13,024	14,435	16,035	17,550
Master's degree	1,240	1,145	1,112	1,008	1,022	965	950	984	1,135	1,198	1,260
Doctor's degree	610	558	522	520	480	504	451	452	451	432	465
Visual and Performing Arts											
Bachelor's degrees, total	40,479	40,422	39,804	40,131	38,285	37,241	36,873	37,150	38,420	39,934	42,186
Male	14,798	14,819	14,695	15,089	14,518	14,236	13,980	14,225	14,698	15,189	15,761
Female	25,681	25,603	25,109	25,042	23,767	23,005	22,893	22,925	23,722	24,745	26,425
Master's degrees, total	8,629	8,746	8,763	8,526	8,720	8,420	8,508	7,939	8,267	8,481	8,657
Male	4,056	3,866	4,013	3,897	3,896	3,775	3,756	3,442	3,611	3,706	3,830
Female	4,573	4,880	4,750	4,629	4,824	4,645	4,752	4,497	4,656	4,775	4,827
Doctor's degrees, total	654	670	692	730	696	722	793	727	753	849	838
Male	396	380	404	406	407	396	447	424	446	472	466
Female	258	290	288	324	289	326	346	303	307	377	372

NOTE: Data are for postsecondary institutions participating in Title IV federal financial aid programs.

Table A-37. Degrees Conferred by Post-Secondary Institutions, by Level of Degree and Sex of Student, 1970-1971 through 2016–2017—*Continued*

(Number.)

Degree conferred, level of degree, and sex of student (when available)	1991-92	1992-93	1993-94	1994-95	1995-96	1996-97	1997-98	1998-99	1999-2000	2000-01	2001-02	2002-03	2003-04
Agriculture and Natural Resources													
Bachelor's degrees, total	15,113	16,769	18,056	19,832	21,425	22,597	23,276	24,179	24,238	23,370	23,331	23,348	22,835
Male	9,867	11,079	11,746	12,686	13,531	13,791	13,806	14,045	13,843	12,840	12,630	12,343	11,889
Female	5,246	5,690	6,310	7,146	7,894	8,806	9,470	10,134	10,395	10,530	10,701	11,005	10,946
Master's degrees, total	3,730	3,959	4,110	4,234	4,551	4,505	4,464	4,376	4,360	4,272	4,503	4,492	4,783
Male	2,409	2,474	2,512	2,541	2,642	2,601	2,545	2,360	2,356	2,251	2,340	2,232	2,306
Female	1,321	1,485	1,598	1,693	1,909	1,904	1,919	2,016	2,004	2,021	2,163	2,260	2,477
Doctor's degrees, total	1,205	1,159	1,262	1,256	1,259	1,202	1,290	1,249	1,168	1,127	1,148	1,229	1,185
Male	955	869	969	955	926	875	924	869	803	741	760	790	758
Female	250	290	293	301	333	327	366	380	365	386	388	439	427
Architecture and Related Services													
Bachelor's degrees, total	8,753	9,167	8,975	8,756	8,352	7,944	7,652	8,245	8,462	8,480	8,808	9,056	8,838
Male	5,805	5,940	5,764	5,741	5,340	5,090	4,966	5,145	5,193	5,086	5,224	5,331	5,059
Female	2,948	3,227	3,211	3,015	3,012	2,854	2,686	3,100	3,269	3,394	3,584	3,725	3,779
Master's degrees, total	3,640	3,808	3,943	3,923	3,993	4,034	4,347	4,235	4,268	4,302	4,566	4,925	5,424
Male	2,271	2,376	2,428	2,310	2,361	2,336	2,537	2,435	2,508	2,515	2,606	2,832	3,049
Female	1,369	1,432	1,515	1,613	1,632	1,698	1,810	1,800	1,760	1,787	1,960	2,093	2,375
Doctor's degrees, total	132	148	161	141	141	135	131	119	129	153	183	152	173
Male	93	105	111	95	96	93	80	76	85	83	117	83	94
Female	39	43	50	46	45	42	51	43	44	70	66	69	79
Biological and Biomedical Sciences													
Bachelor's degrees, total	42,892	47,009	51,296	55,983	61,014	63,973	65,917	65,310	63,630	60,576	60,309	61,294	62,624
Male	20,816	22,870	25,071	26,734	28,921	29,562	29,663	28,507	26,579	24,600	23,694	23,356	23,691
Female	22,076	24,139	26,225	29,249	32,093	34,411	36,254	36,803	37,051	35,976	36,615	37,938	38,933
Master's degrees, total	4,862	5,026	5,462	5,873	6,593	6,986	6,848	6,966	6,850	7,017	7,011	7,050	7,732
Male	2,437	2,540	2,681	2,920	3,212	3,419	3,336	3,279	3,171	3,075	3,033	3,015	3,271
Female	2,425	2,486	2,781	2,953	3,381	3,567	3,512	3,687	3,679	3,942	3,978	4,035	4,461
Doctor's degrees, total	4,442	4,749	4,891	5,069	5,250	5,313	5,474	5,250	5,463	5,225	5,104	5,268	5,538
Male	2,749	2,866	2,910	3,012	3,062	3,014	3,123	3,010	3,068	2,923	2,836	2,866	2,975
Female	1,693	1,883	1,981	2,057	2,188	2,299	2,351	2,240	2,395	2,302	2,268	2,402	2,563
Biology, Microbiology, and Zoology													
Biology, general													
Bachelor's degree	31,909	34,932	38,103	41,658	44,818	46,632	47,054	46,172	44,982	42,310	42,281	42,699	43,465
Master's degree	1,995	2,000	2,178	2,350	2,606	2,742	2,617	2,616	2,599	2,582	2,424	2,340	2,529
Doctor's degree	657	671	665	729	768	693	809	718	727	780	689	680	681
Microbiology													
Bachelor's degree	1,750	1,798	1,872	1,992	2,220	2,530	2,926	2,885	3,049	2,779	2,622	2,455	2,365
Master's degree	372	367	359	326	364	363	401	406	383	334	325	297	350
Doctor's degree	532	621	591	572	606	612	585	544	551	553	538	507	599
Zoology													
Bachelor's degree	2,811	3,036	3,162	3,149	3,463	3,438	3,653	3,508	3,226	3,045	2,979	2,488	2,454
Master's degree	530	559	658	586	677	720	685	606	616	560	578	379	367
Doctor's degree	494	465	503	487	501	474	465	462	481	380	413	355	245
Business													
Bachelor's degrees, total	256,298	256,473	246,265	233,895	226,623	225,934	232,079	239,924	256,070	263,515	278,217	293,391	307,149
Male	135,263	135,368	128,946	121,663	116,545	116,023	119,379	121,741	128,521	132,275	138,343	145,075	152,513
Female	121,035	121,105	117,319	112,232	110,078	109,911	112,700	118,183	127,549	131,240	139,874	148,316	154,636
Master's degrees, total	84,517	89,425	93,285	93,540	93,554	97,204	101,652	106,830	111,532	115,602	119,725	127,685	139,347
Male	54,609	57,504	59,223	58,931	58,400	59,333	62,357	64,271	67,078	68,471	70,463	75,239	80,858
Female	29,908	31,921	34,062	34,609	35,154	37,871	39,295	42,559	44,454	47,131	49,262	52,446	58,489
Doctor's degrees, total	1,242	1,346	1,364	1,391	1,366	1,336	1,290	1,216	1,194	1,180	1,156	1,252	1,481
Male	953	969	980	1,011	972	947	885	848	812	783	746	820	960
Female	289	377	384	380	394	389	405	368	382	397	410	432	521
Communication, Journalism, and Related Programs in Communication Technologies													
Bachelor's degrees, total	55,144	54,907	52,033	48,969	48,173	47,894	50,263	52,397	57,058	59,191	64,036	69,828	73,002
Male	21,601	22,154	21,484	20,501	19,868	19,771	20,103	20,943	22,152	22,542	23,692	25,338	25,813
Female	33,543	32,753	30,549	28,468	28,305	28,123	30,160	31,454	34,906	36,649	40,344	44,490	47,189
Master's degrees, total	4,463	5,179	5,388	5,559	5,561	5,552	6,097	5,582	5,525	5,645	5,980	6,495	6,900
Male	1,692	1,969	2,088	2,086	2,153	1,989	2,369	2,001	2,030	1,964	2,169	2,301	2,329
Female	2,771	3,210	3,300	3,473	3,408	3,563	3,728	3,581	3,495	3,681	3,811	4,194	4,571
Doctor's degrees, total	255	301	345	321	345	300	359	348	357	370	383	398	426
Male	132	146	174	162	190	155	171	182	168	190	168	179	186
Female	123	155	171	159	155	145	188	166	189	180	215	219	240

NOTE: Data are for postsecondary institutions participating in Title IV federal financial aid programs.

Table A-37. Degrees Conferred by Post-Secondary Institutions, by Level of Degree and Sex of Student, 1970-1971 through 2016–2017—*Continued*

(Number.)

Degree conferred, level of degree, and sex of student (when available)	2004-05	2005-06	2006-07	2007-08	2008-09	2009-10	2010-11	2011-12	2012-13	2013-14	2014-15	2015-16	2016-17
Agriculture and Natural Resources													
Bachelor's degrees, total	23,002	23,053	23,133	24,113	24,982	26,343	28,630	30,972	33,592	35,125	36,278	37,005	37,719
Male	11,987	12,063	12,309	12,634	13,096	13,524	14,678	15,485	16,618	17,254	17,585	17,622	17,816
Female	11,015	10,990	10,824	11,479	11,886	12,819	13,952	15,487	16,974	17,871	18,693	19,383	19,903
Master's degrees, total	4,746	4,640	4,623	4,684	4,878	5,215	5,766	6,390	6,336	6,544	6,426	6,681	6,844
Male	2,288	2,280	2,174	2,180	2,328	2,512	2,746	3,026	2,912	2,966	2,904	2,955	3,038
Female	2,458	2,360	2,449	2,504	2,550	2,703	3,020	3,364	3,424	3,578	3,522	3,726	3,806
Doctor's degrees, total	1,173	1,194	1,272	1,257	1,328	1,149	1,246	1,333	1,411	1,407	1,561	1,508	1,561
Male	763	710	768	742	741	626	675	721	767	739	811	816	805
Female	410	484	504	515	587	523	571	612	644	668	750	692	756
Architecture and Related Services													
Bachelor's degrees, total	9,237	9,515	9,717	9,805	10,119	10,051	9,831	9,727	9,757	9,149	9,090	8,823	8,573
Male	5,222	5,414	5,393	5,579	5,797	5,694	5,698	5,566	5,581	5,174	5,116	4,854	4,585
Female	4,015	4,101	4,324	4,226	4,322	4,357	4,133	4,161	4,176	3,975	3,974	3,969	3,988
Master's degrees, total	5,674	5,743	5,951	6,065	6,587	7,280	7,788	8,448	8,095	8,048	8,006	7,986	7,911
Male	3,180	3,165	3,304	3,252	3,657	4,012	4,265	4,504	4,261	4,122	4,147	4,163	4,014
Female	2,494	2,578	2,647	2,813	2,930	3,268	3,523	3,944	3,834	3,926	3,859	3,823	3,897
Doctor's degrees, total	179	201	178	199	212	210	205	255	247	247	272	236	291
Male	110	108	104	103	113	116	110	147	134	134	145	122	146
Female	69	93	74	96	99	94	95	108	113	113	127	114	145
Biological and Biomedical Sciences													
Bachelor's degrees, total	65,915	70,607	76,832	79,829	82,828	86,391	89,984	95,850	100,397	104,657	109,904	113,794	116,759
Male	25,104	27,183	30,600	32,401	33,707	35,866	36,888	39,542	41,556	43,440	45,104	45,613	45,515
Female	40,811	43,424	46,232	47,428	49,121	50,525	53,096	56,308	58,841	61,217	64,800	68,181	71,244
Master's degrees, total	8,284	8,781	8,898	9,689	10,018	10,730	11,324	12,419	13,300	13,964	14,655	15,717	16,284
Male	3,361	3,709	3,639	4,094	4,250	4,612	4,869	5,378	5,783	6,073	6,252	6,707	6,840
Female	4,923	5,072	5,259	5,595	5,768	6,118	6,455	7,041	7,517	7,891	8,403	9,010	9,444
Doctor's degrees, total	5,935	6,162	6,764	7,400	7,499	7,672	7,693	7,935	7,939	8,302	8,053	7,939	8,087
Male	3,025	3,138	3,440	3,645	3,549	3,603	3,648	3,708	3,689	3,884	3,763	3,733	3,852
Female	2,910	3,024	3,324	3,755	3,950	4,069	4,045	4,227	4,250	4,418	4,290	4,206	4,235
Biology, Microbiology, and Zoology													
Biology, general													
Bachelor's degree	45,540	48,855	52,527	54,384	55,859	58,700	61,236	64,616	66,692	69,425	71,622	73,044	74,048
Master's degree	2,564	2,719	2,679	2,935	2,987	3,087	3,283	3,494	3,479	3,465	3,432	3,448	3,439
Doctor's degree	712	776	788	866	896	919	935	964	1,003	1,053	976	948	1,020
Microbiology													
Bachelor's degree	2,318	2,243	2,347	2,458	2,480	2,449	2,466	2,532	2,582	2,572	2,567	2,637	2,744
Master's degree	390	372	369	353	291	303	337	395	402	465	510	524	491
Doctor's degree	610	612	667	734	716	767	739	687	704	674	688	643	649
Zoology													
Bachelor's degree	2,159	2,140	2,223	2,235	2,140	2,147	2,062	2,174	2,246	2,269	2,250	2,311	2,315
Master's degree	384	384	416	381	347	360	338	346	416	464	421	501	398
Doctor's degree	268	254	263	281	297	243	230	258	231	217	230	271	233
Business													
Bachelor's degrees, total	311,574	318,042	327,531	335,254	348,056	358,119	365,133	367,235	360,887	358,132	363,741	371,690	381,353
Male	155,940	159,683	166,350	170,978	177,924	183,272	187,116	190,180	187,843	188,468	191,288	196,309	201,886
Female	155,634	158,359	161,181	164,276	170,132	174,847	178,017	177,055	173,044	169,664	172,453	175,381	179,467
Master's degrees, total	142,617	146,406	150,211	155,637	168,404	177,748	187,178	191,606	188,617	189,364	185,236	186,835	187,404
Male	82,151	83,550	84,115	86,258	91,991	96,742	101,440	103,250	101,599	101,061	98,593	99,488	98,768
Female	60,466	62,856	66,096	69,379	76,413	81,006	85,738	88,356	87,018	88,303	86,643	87,347	88,636
Doctor's degrees, total	1,498	1,711	2,029	2,084	2,123	2,249	2,286	2,538	2,828	3,039	3,116	3,325	3,329
Male	901	1,049	1,188	1,250	1,302	1,338	1,357	1,461	1,605	1,722	1,716	1,933	1,854
Female	597	662	841	834	821	911	929	1,077	1,223	1,317	1,400	1,392	1,475
Communication, Journalism, and Related Programs in Communication Technologies													
Bachelor's degrees, total	75,238	76,936	78,420	81,048	83,084	86,062	88,089	88,754	89,805	92,603	95,793	97,375	98,393
Male	26,926	28,142	29,009	30,384	31,207	32,048	33,018	33,525	33,670	34,393	35,220	35,540	35,357
Female	48,312	48,794	49,411	50,664	51,877	54,014	55,071	55,229	56,135	58,210	60,573	61,835	63,036
Master's degrees, total	7,195	7,745	7,272	7,546	7,517	8,093	8,804	9,502	9,337	9,930	10,135	10,167	10,667
Male	2,535	2,611	2,485	2,580	2,446	2,656	2,819	3,068	3,021	3,131	3,111	3,104	3,220
Female	4,660	5,134	4,787	4,966	5,071	5,437	5,985	6,434	6,316	6,799	7,024	7,063	7,447
Doctor's degrees, total	468	464	480	496	535	573	578	567	612	614	644	633	615
Male	195	207	188	209	225	225	207	242	246	267	259	258	208
Female	273	257	292	287	310	348	371	325	366	347	385	375	407

NOTE: Data are for postsecondary institutions participating in Title IV federal financial aid programs.

Table A-37. Degrees Conferred by Post-Secondary Institutions, by Level of Degree and Sex of Student, 1970-1971 through 2016–2017—*Continued*

(Number.)

Degree conferred, level of degree, and sex of student (when available)	1991-92	1992-93	1993-94	1994-95	1995-96	1996-97	1997-98	1998-99	1999-2000	2000-01	2001-02	2002-03	2003-04
Computer and Information Sciences													
Bachelor's degrees, total	24,821	24,519	24,527	24,737	24,506	25,422	27,829	30,552	37,788	44,142	50,365	57,433	59,488
Male	17,685	17,606	17,528	17,684	17,757	18,527	20,372	22,289	27,185	31,923	36,462	41,950	44,585
Female	7,136	6,913	6,999	7,053	6,749	6,895	7,457	8,263	10,603	12,219	13,903	15,483	14,903
Master's degrees, total	9,655	10,353	10,568	10,595	10,579	10,513	11,765	12,843	14,990	16,911	17,173	19,509	20,143
Male	6,980	7,557	7,836	7,805	7,729	7,526	8,343	8,866	9,978	11,195	11,447	13,267	13,868
Female	2,675	2,796	2,732	2,790	2,850	2,987	3,422	3,977	5,012	5,716	5,726	6,242	6,275
Doctor's degrees, total	772	805	810	887	869	857	858	806	779	768	752	816	909
Male	669	689	685	726	743	721	718	656	648	632	581	648	709
Female	103	116	125	161	126	136	140	150	131	136	171	168	200
Education													
Bachelor's degrees, total	107,836	107,578	107,440	105,929	105,384	105,116	105,833	107,372	108,034	105,458	106,295	105,845	106,278
Male	22,655	23,199	24,424	25,619	26,214	26,242	26,285	26,321	26,103	24,580	24,049	22,604	22,802
Female	85,181	84,379	83,016	80,310	79,170	78,874	79,548	81,051	81,931	80,878	82,246	83,241	83,476
Master's degrees, total	91,225	94,497	97,427	99,835	104,936	108,720	113,374	118,226	123,045	127,829	135,189	147,883	162,345
Male	20,897	21,857	22,656	23,511	24,955	25,518	26,814	28,077	29,081	29,997	31,907	34,033	37,843
Female	70,328	72,640	74,771	76,324	79,981	83,202	86,560	90,149	93,964	97,832	103,282	113,850	124,502
Doctor's degrees, total	6,423	6,581	6,450	6,475	6,246	6,297	6,261	6,471	6,409	6,284	6,549	6,832	7,088
Male	2,652	2,712	2,555	2,490	2,404	2,367	2,334	2,297	2,295	2,237	2,211	2,314	2,403
Female	3,771	3,869	3,895	3,985	3,842	3,930	3,927	4,174	4,114	4,047	4,338	4,518	4,685
Engineering and Engineering Technologies													
Bachelor's degrees, total	78,036	78,619	78,580	78,483	77,997	75,659	74,557	72,796	73,323	72,869	74,588	77,231	78,079
Male	67,086	67,214	66,867	66,157	65,362	62,994	61,880	59,859	59,668	59,489	60,417	62,821	63,401
Female	10,950	11,405	11,713	12,326	12,635	12,665	12,677	12,937	13,655	13,380	14,171	14,410	14,678
Master's degrees, total	26,373	29,103	30,102	29,949	28,843	27,016	27,244	26,689	26,648	27,187	26,987	30,583	35,053
Male	22,397	24,721	25,394	25,028	23,840	22,047	21,800	21,348	21,047	21,341	21,212	24,097	27,561
Female	3,976	4,382	4,708	4,921	5,003	4,969	5,444	5,341	5,601	5,846	5,775	6,486	7,492
Doctor's degrees, total	5,499	5,870	5,954	6,108	6,354	6,166	5,966	5,413	5,367	5,547	5,181	5,252	5,859
Male	4,967	5,300	5,288	5,378	5,559	5,408	5,230	4,643	4,539	4,630	4,285	4,353	4,821
Female	532	570	666	730	795	758	736	770	828	917	896	899	1,038
Chemical, Civil, Electrical, and Mechanical Engineering													
Chemical engineering													
Bachelor's degree	3,754	4,459	5,163	5,901	6,319	6,564	6,319	6,038	5,807	5,611	5,462	5,109	4,742
Master's degree	956	990	1,032	1,085	1,176	1,131	1,128	1,130	1,078	1,083	973	1,065	1,165
Doctor's degree	590	595	604	571	670	650	652	575	590	610	605	542	623
Civil engineering													
Bachelor's degree	8,034	8,868	9,479	9,927	10,607	10,437	9,926	9,178	8,136	7,588	7,665	7,836	7,827
Master's degree	3,113	3,610	3,873	4,077	3,905	3,833	3,795	3,656	3,433	3,310	3,295	3,596	3,790
Doctor's degree	540	577	651	625	616	640	610	534	543	571	574	599	636
Electrical, electronics, and communications engineering													
Bachelor's degree	17,958	17,281	15,823	14,929	13,900	13,336	12,995	12,606	12,930	13,091	13,056	13,627	14,123
Master's degree	7,360	7,870	7,791	7,693	7,103	6,393	6,737	6,708	6,926	6,815	6,587	7,621	9,511
Doctor's degree	1,282	1,413	1,470	1,543	1,591	1,512	1,458	1,309	1,392	1,417	1,235	1,256	1,440
Mechanical engineering													
Bachelor's degree	14,067	14,464	15,030	14,794	14,177	13,493	13,071	12,753	12,807	12,817	13,058	13,693	14,050
Master's degree	3,653	3,982	4,099	4,213	3,881	3,608	3,441	3,268	3,273	3,371	3,391	3,695	4,420
Doctor's degree	851	871	887	890	940	913	933	788	776	849	772	747	787
English Language and Literature/Letters													
Bachelor's degrees, total	54,250	55,289	53,150	51,170	49,928	48,641	49,016	49,877	50,106	50,569	52,375	53,699	53,984
Male	18,314	19,007	18,214	17,581	17,007	16,325	16,280	16,332	16,124	15,997	16,457	16,738	16,792
Female	35,936	36,282	34,936	33,589	32,921	32,316	32,736	33,545	33,982	34,572	35,918	36,961	37,192
Master's degrees, total	7,215	7,537	7,611	7,612	7,657	7,487	7,587	7,326	7,022	6,763	7,097	7,428	7,956
Male	2,441	2,570	2,620	2,672	2,727	2,650	2,568	2,452	2,315	2,160	2,270	2,433	2,459
Female	4,774	4,967	4,991	4,940	4,930	4,837	5,019	4,874	4,707	4,603	4,827	4,995	5,497
Doctor's degrees, total	1,142	1,201	1,205	1,393	1,395	1,431	1,489	1,412	1,470	1,330	1,291	1,246	1,207
Male	484	495	512	589	535	610	611	554	611	533	532	492	479
Female	658	706	693	804	860	821	878	858	859	797	759	754	728
Foreign Languages and Literatures													
Bachelor's degrees, total	14,634	15,305	15,242	14,558	14,832	14,487	15,279	15,835	15,886	16,128	16,258	16,912	17,754
Male	4,225	4,435	4,573	4,496	4,514	4,388	4,585	4,738	4,616	4,695	4,685	4,996	5,215
Female	10,409	10,870	10,669	10,062	10,318	10,099	10,694	11,097	11,270	11,433	11,573	11,916	12,539
Master's degrees, total	3,229	3,513	3,612	3,439	3,443	3,361	3,181	3,109	3,037	3,035	3,075	3,049	3,124
Male	1,074	1,182	1,199	1,124	1,141	1,104	1,033	976	944	969	958	874	957
Female	2,155	2,331	2,413	2,315	2,302	2,257	2,148	2,133	2,093	2,066	2,117	2,175	2,167

NOTE: Data are for postsecondary institutions participating in Title IV federal financial aid programs.

Table A-37. Degrees Conferred by Post-Secondary Institutions, by Level of Degree and Sex of Student, 1970-1971 through 2016–2017—*Continued*

(Number.)

Degree conferred, level of degree, and sex of student (when available)	2004-05	2005-06	2006-07	2007-08	2008-09	2009-10	2010-11	2011-12	2012-13	2013-14	2014-15	2015-16	2016-17
Computer and Information Sciences													
Bachelor's degrees, total	54,111	47,480	42,170	38,476	37,992	39,593	43,066	47,406	50,961	55,271	59,586	64,402	71,420
Male	42,125	37,705	34,342	31,694	31,213	32,414	35,477	38,796	41,874	45,320	48,844	52,330	57,766
Female	11,986	9,775	7,828	6,782	6,779	7,179	7,589	8,610	9,087	9,951	10,742	12,072	13,654
Master's degrees, total	18,416	17,055	16,232	17,087	17,907	17,955	19,516	20,925	22,782	24,514	31,475	40,130	46,555
Male	13,136	12,470	11,985	12,513	13,063	13,019	14,010	15,132	16,539	17,472	21,893	27,788	32,173
Female	5,280	4,585	4,247	4,574	4,844	4,936	5,506	5,793	6,243	7,042	9,582	12,342	14,382
Doctor's degrees, total	1,119	1,416	1,595	1,698	1,580	1,599	1,588	1,698	1,834	1,982	1,998	1,989	1,982
Male	905	1,109	1,267	1,323	1,226	1,250	1,267	1,332	1,480	1,566	1,548	1,591	1,538
Female	214	307	328	375	354	349	321	366	354	416	450	398	444
Education													
Bachelor's degrees, total	105,451	107,238	105,641	102,582	101,716	101,287	104,008	105,656	104,698	98,838	91,596	87,221	85,118
Male	22,513	22,448	22,516	21,828	21,163	20,739	21,206	21,714	21,824	20,357	18,467	17,429	16,067
Female	82,938	84,790	83,125	80,754	80,553	80,548	82,802	83,942	82,874	78,481	73,129	69,792	69,051
Master's degrees, total	167,490	174,620	176,572	175,880	178,538	182,165	185,127	179,047	164,652	154,655	146,581	145,792	145,680
Male	38,863	40,700	40,164	40,055	40,312	41,284	42,043	41,364	37,816	35,974	33,963	33,791	33,177
Female	128,627	133,920	136,408	135,825	138,226	140,881	143,084	137,683	126,836	118,681	112,618	112,001	112,503
Doctor's degrees, total	7,681	7,584	8,261	8,491	9,028	9,237	9,642	10,118	10,572	10,929	11,772	11,838	12,687
Male	2,557	2,664	2,681	2,773	2,956	3,023	3,070	3,262	3,418	3,464	3,838	3,693	4,013
Female	5,124	4,920	5,580	5,718	6,072	6,214	6,572	6,856	7,154	7,465	7,934	8,145	8,674
Engineering and Engineering Technologies													
Bachelor's degrees, total	79,544	81,406	81,854	83,608	84,404	88,735	93,097	98,654	102,997	108,976	115,105	123,948	133,761
Male	65,033	66,866	68,081	69,540	70,504	73,838	77,080	81,364	84,645	88,941	93,541	99,568	106,539
Female	14,511	14,540	13,773	14,068	13,900	14,897	16,017	17,290	18,352	20,035	21,564	24,380	27,222
Master's degrees, total	34,988	33,389	31,989	34,430	38,008	39,391	43,179	45,116	45,328	47,343	51,441	57,713	60,244
Male	27,049	25,568	24,746	26,461	29,458	30,554	33,372	34,712	34,496	35,791	38,453	43,198	45,220
Female	7,939	7,821	7,243	7,969	8,550	8,837	9,807	10,404	10,832	11,552	12,988	14,515	15,024
Doctor's degrees, total	6,467	7,318	7,928	7,977	7,803	7,773	8,425	8,856	9,467	10,117	10,362	10,398	10,523
Male	5,263	5,848	6,285	6,263	6,123	5,986	6,548	6,838	7,305	7,820	7,958	7,960	8,027
Female	1,204	1,470	1,643	1,714	1,680	1,787	1,877	2,018	2,162	2,297	2,404	2,438	2,496
Chemical, Civil, Electrical, and Mechanical Engineering													
Chemical engineering													
Bachelor's degree	4,397	4,326	4,492	4,795	5,036	5,740	6,311	7,027	7,529	8,104	8,980	9,917	10,915
Master's degree	1,183	1,116	957	933	994	1,043	1,283	1,389	1,450	1,518	1,626	1,699	1,797
Doctor's degree	773	819	835	853	789	830	831	823	835	992	1,015	1,009	989
Civil engineering													
Bachelor's degree	8,186	9,090	9,671	10,455	10,785	11,335	12,557	12,808	13,262	12,995	12,673	13,244	13,593
Master's degree	3,834	3,768	3,482	3,595	3,794	4,079	4,860	5,359	5,353	5,501	5,365	5,626	5,682
Doctor's degree	713	750	805	752	763	717	751	787	868	972	1,031	1,015	1,077
Electrical, electronics, and communications engineering													
Bachelor's degree	14,171	13,966	13,089	12,375	11,620	11,450	11,575	12,110	12,835	13,856	14,599	15,680	16,916
Master's degree	9,054	8,123	7,777	8,631	9,178	9,052	9,691	9,696	9,485	9,829	11,917	13,782	12,799
Doctor's degree	1,566	1,860	2,042	1,996	1,812	1,869	2,037	2,119	2,118	2,301	2,320	2,258	2,290
Mechanical engineering													
Bachelor's degree	14,609	15,850	16,601	17,367	17,352	18,498	19,171	20,541	21,990	24,301	26,394	29,216	32,306
Master's degree	4,637	4,443	4,294	4,497	4,620	4,818	5,802	5,840	5,872	6,182	6,841	7,558	8,281
Doctor's degree	915	1,096	1,106	1,109	1,142	996	1,106	1,213	1,321	1,387	1,526	1,470	1,450
English Language and Literature/Letters													
Bachelor's degrees, total	54,379	55,096	55,122	55,038	55,465	53,229	52,754	53,765	52,401	50,464	45,851	42,797	41,317
Male	17,154	17,316	17,475	17,681	17,973	17,050	16,917	16,976	16,508	15,831	14,055	12,777	12,247
Female	37,225	37,780	37,647	37,357	37,492	36,179	35,837	36,789	35,893	34,633	31,796	30,020	29,070
Master's degrees, total	8,468	8,845	8,742	9,161	9,262	9,202	9,475	9,938	9,755	9,294	8,928	8,581	8,247
Male	2,615	2,860	2,867	3,027	3,000	3,006	3,137	3,403	3,213	3,115	3,052	2,884	2,739
Female	5,853	5,985	5,875	6,134	6,262	6,196	6,338	6,535	6,542	6,179	5,876	5,697	5,508
Doctor's degrees, total	1,212	1,254	1,178	1,262	1,271	1,334	1,344	1,427	1,377	1,393	1,418	1,402	1,347
Male	494	510	478	453	464	523	529	548	554	557	554	522	519
Female	718	744	700	809	807	811	815	879	823	836	864	880	828
Foreign Languages and Literatures													
Bachelor's degrees, total	18,386	19,410	20,275	20,977	21,169	21,507	21,705	21,756	21,647	20,332	19,493	18,436	17,642
Male	5,370	5,842	6,173	6,254	6,305	6,607	6,719	6,629	6,842	6,266	6,066	5,755	5,561
Female	13,016	13,568	14,102	14,723	14,864	14,900	14,986	15,127	14,805	14,066	13,427	12,681	12,081
Master's degrees, total	3,407	3,539	3,443	3,565	3,592	3,756	3,727	3,827	3,708	3,482	3,566	3,407	3,274
Male	1,056	1,049	1,058	1,128	1,211	1,254	1,256	1,280	1,235	1,222	1,241	1,174	1,170
Female	2,351	2,490	2,385	2,437	2,381	2,502	2,471	2,547	2,473	2,260	2,325	2,233	2,104

NOTE: Data are for postsecondary institutions participating in Title IV federal financial aid programs.

Table A-37. Degrees Conferred by Post-Secondary Institutions, by Level of Degree and Sex of Student, 1970-1971 through 2016–2017—*Continued*

(Number.)

Degree conferred, level of degree, and sex of student (when available)	1991-92	1992-93	1993-94	1994-95	1995-96	1996-97	1997-98	1998-99	1999-2000	2000-01	2001-02	2002-03	2003-04
Doctor's degrees, total	984	977	1,033	1,081	1,020	1,064	1,118	1,049	1,086	1,078	1,003	1,042	1,031
Male	434	417	418	479	446	450	473	443	446	420	418	424	410
Female	550	560	615	602	574	614	645	606	640	658	585	618	621
French, German, Italian, and Spanish Language and Literature													
French													
Bachelor's degree	3,371	3,280	3,094	2,764	2,655	2,468	2,530	2,565	2,514	2,371	2,396	2,294	2,362
Master's degree	465	513	479	470	446	414	389	365	343	376	356	348	361
Doctor's degree	112	98	104	118	113	119	104	115	129	115	89	75	85
German													
Bachelor's degree	1,616	1,572	1,580	1,352	1,290	1,214	1,181	1,237	1,125	1,143	1,092	1,097	1,031
Master's degree	273	317	298	278	305	281	209	242	184	242	208	188	153
Doctor's degree	85	86	61	83	75	80	94	78	76	73	64	77	30
Italian													
Bachelor's degree	238	274	264	271	232	234	252	257	237	286	263	307	279
Master's degree	55	50	47	69	44	49	60	41	48	42	46	54	49
Doctor's degree	18	13	24	31	22	18	25	12	13	11	15	20	31
Spanish													
Bachelor's degree	4,768	5,233	5,505	5,602	5,995	6,161	6,595	6,992	7,031	7,164	7,243	7,619	7,991
Master's degree	647	667	691	709	769	677	781	697	718	716	792	791	833
Doctor's degree	143	145	160	161	151	175	160	153	175	185	193	190	199
Arabic, Chinese, Korean, and Russian Language and Literature													
Arabic													
Bachelor's degree	13	8	8	10	8	9	16	13	6	7	13	13	13
Master's degree	0	3	2	1	3	3	2	3	4	2	2	3	3
Doctor's degree	0	2	0	1	2	0	1	1	5	3	2	0	1
Chinese													
Bachelor's degree	183	129	112	107	136	152	161	178	183	183	189	190	186
Master's degree	36	54	48	63	42	31	21	20	18	13	16	12	15
Doctor's degree	14	8	18	16	19	15	13	14	15	7	12	9	5
Korean													
Bachelor's degree	NA	NA	NA	NA	NA	NA	NA	NA	NA	NA	NA	5	9
Master's degree	NA	NA	NA	NA	NA	NA	NA	NA	NA	NA	NA	0	2
Doctor's degree	NA	NA	NA	NA	NA	NA	NA	NA	NA	NA	NA	0	1
Russian													
Bachelor's degree	629	612	611	572	494	455	383	398	340	335	277	271	301
Master's degree	68	68	71	66	58	46	49	29	33	24	34	16	21
Doctor's degree	7	4	3	3	7	9	9	4	10	7	5	6	3
Health Professions and Related Programs													
Bachelor's degrees, total	62,779	68,434	75,890	81,596	86,087	87,997	86,843	84,989	80,863	75,933	72,887	71,261	73,934
Male	10,330	11,605	13,377	14,812	15,942	16,440	15,700	15,191	13,342	12,514	10,869	10,096	10,017
Female	52,449	56,829	62,513	66,784	70,145	71,557	71,143	69,798	67,521	63,419	62,018	61,165	63,917
Master's degrees, total	23,671	26,190	28,442	31,770	33,920	36,162	39,567	40,628	42,593	43,623	43,560	42,748	44,939
Male	4,794	5,249	5,813	6,718	7,017	7,536	8,644	9,152	9,500	9,711	9,588	9,280	9,670
Female	18,877	20,941	22,629	25,052	26,903	28,626	30,923	31,476	33,093	33,912	33,972	33,468	35,269
Doctor's degrees, total	31,479	31,089	30,959	32,124	32,678	34,971	35,369	35,939	37,829	39,019	39,435	39,799	41,861
Male	19,362	18,446	17,988	18,463	18,495	19,619	19,370	19,673	19,984	20,260	19,760	19,493	19,587
Female	12,117	12,643	12,971	13,661	14,183	15,352	15,999	16,266	17,845	18,759	19,675	20,306	22,274
Mathematics and Statistics													
Bachelor's degrees, total	14,468	14,384	14,171	13,494	12,713	12,401	11,795	12,011	11,418	11,171	11,950	12,505	13,327
Male	7,668	7,566	7,594	7,154	6,847	6,649	6,247	6,206	5,955	5,791	6,333	6,784	7,203
Female	6,800	6,818	6,577	6,340	5,866	5,752	5,548	5,805	5,463	5,380	5,617	5,721	6,124
Master's degrees, total	3,558	3,644	3,682	3,820	3,651	3,504	3,409	3,304	3,208	3,209	3,350	3,620	4,191
Male	2,151	2,151	2,237	2,289	2,178	2,055	1,985	1,912	1,749	1,857	1,913	1,996	2,302
Female	1,407	1,493	1,445	1,531	1,473	1,449	1,424	1,392	1,459	1,352	1,437	1,624	1,889
Doctor's degrees, total	1,048	1,138	1,125	1,181	1,158	1,134	1,215	1,107	1,075	997	923	1,007	1,060
Male	825	867	880	919	919	861	903	812	803	715	658	734	762
Female	223	271	245	262	239	273	312	295	272	282	265	273	298
Physical Sciences and Science Technologies													
Bachelor's degrees, total	16,970	17,577	18,474	19,247	19,716	19,594	19,454	18,448	18,427	18,025	17,890	18,038	18,131
Male	11,443	11,853	12,271	12,556	12,634	12,285	11,999	11,119	11,019	10,628	10,349	10,625	10,577
Female	5,527	5,724	6,203	6,691	7,082	7,309	7,455	7,329	7,408	7,397	7,541	7,413	7,554
Master's degrees, total	5,397	5,392	5,718	5,798	5,910	5,616	5,411	5,241	4,888	5,134	5,082	5,196	5,714

NOTE: Data are for postsecondary institutions participating in Title IV federal financial aid programs.
NA = Not available.

Table A-37. Degrees Conferred by Post-Secondary Institutions, by Level of Degree and Sex of Student, 1970-1971 through 2016–2017—*Continued*

(Number.)

Degree conferred, level of degree, and sex of student (when available)	2004-05	2005-06	2006-07	2007-08	2008-09	2009-10	2010-11	2011-12	2012-13	2013-14	2014-15	2015-16	2016-17
Doctor's degrees, total	1,027	1,074	1,059	1,078	1,111	1,091	1,158	1,231	1,304	1,230	1,243	1,278	1,168
Male	410	436	437	431	426	446	477	497	531	498	532	514	479
Female	617	638	622	647	685	645	681	734	773	732	711	764	689
French, German, Italian, and Spanish Language and Literature													
French													
Bachelor's degree	2,394	2,410	2,462	2,432	2,450	2,488	2,490	2,358	2,278	2,043	1,916	1,750	1,625
Master's degree	356	395	364	359	386	391	366	341	332	308	270	306	265
Doctor's degree	80	84	95	102	86	87	81	96	115	107	110	95	85
German													
Bachelor's degree	1,103	1,106	1,055	1,085	1,058	1,028	1,019	1,001	931	878	828	809	753
Master's degree	180	172	158	173	163	143	156	130	102	123	115	88	96
Doctor's degree	56	48	56	51	47	46	43	67	52	44	52	64	49
Italian													
Bachelor's degree	277	321	280	359	341	336	313	332	284	271	231	191	183
Master's degree	70	94	97	88	76	73	83	72	73	58	55	34	56
Doctor's degree	12	17	20	25	34	23	28	35	27	29	23	27	35
Spanish													
Bachelor's degree	8,304	8,690	9,013	9,278	9,333	9,138	8,920	8,714	8,419	8,034	7,508	6,875	6,420
Master's degree	919	981	982	990	878	962	955	991	928	832	830	747	740
Doctor's degree	190	192	195	193	218	199	179	189	205	192	198	197	171
Arabic, Chinese, Korean, and Russian Language and Literature													
Arabic													
Bachelor's degree	21	26	68	57	85	121	141	143	167	165	169	155	160
Master's degree	5	4	2	8	14	10	5	8	12	6	4	18	8
Doctor's degree	0	2	0	1	1	6	1	7	1	0	2	1	2
Chinese													
Bachelor's degree	208	241	261	289	384	456	449	496	510	497	509	482	450
Master's degree	21	20	30	35	45	51	51	46	61	46	48	44	51
Doctor's degree	8	10	2	5	11	12	8	9	12	3	6	7	14
Korean													
Bachelor's degree	8	17	13	15	24	27	28	38	43	32	43	54	67
Master's degree	0	4	0	4	2	19	10	8	14	10	8	6	5
Doctor's degree	0	3	0	1	1	1	3	3	0	8	2	2	2
Russian													
Bachelor's degree	298	279	311	294	325	356	340	392	392	371	339	304	296
Master's degree	18	28	18	20	21	19	11	17	11	14	15	13	13
Doctor's degree	0	7	4	1	1	1	3	2	5	1	4	0	4
Health Professions and Related Programs													
Bachelor's degrees, total	80,685	91,973	101,810	111,478	120,420	129,623	143,463	163,675	181,149	198,777	216,228	228,907	238,014
Male	10,858	12,914	14,325	16,286	17,776	19,309	21,540	24,905	28,208	30,932	33,658	36,262	37,758
Female	69,827	79,059	87,485	95,192	102,644	110,314	121,923	138,770	152,941	167,845	182,570	192,645	200,256
Master's degrees, total	46,703	51,380	54,531	58,120	62,642	69,112	75,571	84,355	90,933	97,416	103,052	110,350	119,273
Male	9,816	10,630	10,636	11,010	11,848	12,874	14,034	15,675	16,747	17,751	18,793	20,424	21,982
Female	36,887	40,750	43,895	47,110	50,794	56,238	61,537	68,680	74,186	79,665	84,259	89,926	97,291
Doctor's degrees, total	44,201	45,677	48,943	51,675	54,846	57,750	60,221	62,097	64,192	67,447	71,004	73,687	77,693
Male	19,697	19,640	20,522	21,616	22,678	23,946	25,386	26,074	26,852	28,082	29,427	30,387	31,845
Female	24,504	26,037	28,421	30,059	32,168	33,804	34,835	36,023	37,340	39,365	41,577	43,300	45,848
Mathematics and Statistics													
Bachelor's degrees, total	14,351	14,770	14,954	15,192	15,507	16,029	17,182	18,841	20,449	20,987	21,854	22,778	24,073
Male	7,937	8,115	8,360	8,490	8,801	9,087	9,782	10,722	11,599	11,970	12,462	13,090	14,002
Female	6,414	6,655	6,594	6,702	6,706	6,942	7,400	8,119	8,850	9,017	9,392	9,688	10,071
Master's degrees, total	4,477	4,730	4,884	4,980	5,211	5,639	5,866	6,246	6,957	7,273	7,589	8,451	9,086
Male	2,525	2,712	2,859	2,860	3,064	3,378	3,459	3,695	4,178	4,256	4,508	4,924	5,116
Female	1,952	2,018	2,025	2,120	2,147	2,261	2,407	2,551	2,779	3,017	3,081	3,527	3,970
Doctor's degrees, total	1,176	1,293	1,351	1,360	1,535	1,596	1,586	1,669	1,823	1,863	1,801	1,855	1,925
Male	841	911	949	938	1,059	1,118	1,132	1,198	1,292	1,325	1,298	1,324	1,403
Female	335	382	402	422	476	478	454	471	531	538	503	531	522
Physical Sciences and Science Technologies													
Bachelor's degrees, total	19,104	20,522	21,291	22,179	22,691	23,381	24,705	26,664	28,053	29,307	30,042	30,483	31,268
Male	11,065	11,978	12,604	13,143	13,465	13,866	14,778	15,972	17,142	17,804	18,480	18,671	18,860
Female	8,039	8,544	8,687	9,036	9,226	9,515	9,927	10,692	10,911	11,503	11,562	11,812	12,408
Master's degrees, total	5,823	6,063	6,012	6,061	5,862	6,066	6,386	6,911	7,014	6,984	7,100	7,131	7,143

NOTE: Data are for postsecondary institutions participating in Title IV federal financial aid programs.

Table A-37. Degrees Conferred by Post-Secondary Institutions, by Level of Degree and Sex of Student, 1970-1971 through 2016–2017—*Continued*

(Number.)

Degree conferred, level of degree, and sex of student (when available)	1991-92	1992-93	1993-94	1994-95	1995-96	1996-97	1997-98	1998-99	1999-2000	2000-01	2001-02	2002-03	2003-04
Male	3,935	3,840	4,069	4,058	4,031	3,799	3,484	3,454	3,167	3,276	3,186	3,284	3,470
Female	1,462	1,552	1,649	1,740	1,879	1,817	1,927	1,787	1,721	1,858	1,896	1,912	2,244
Doctor's degrees, total	4,378	4,372	4,652	4,486	4,589	4,501	4,592	4,229	4,017	3,968	3,824	3,939	3,937
Male	3,433	3,426	3,657	3,443	3,543	3,479	3,451	3,206	3,002	2,914	2,766	2,854	2,855
Female	945	946	995	1,043	1,046	1,022	1,141	1,023	1,015	1,054	1,058	1,085	1,082
Chemistry, Geology and Earth Science, and Physics													
Chemistry													
Bachelor's degree	8,629	8,903	9,417	9,706	10,395	10,609	10,528	10,109	9,989	9,466	9,084	9,013	9,016
Master's degree	1,746	1,822	1,968	2,062	2,214	2,203	2,108	2,019	1,857	1,952	1,823	1,777	2,009
Doctor's degree	2,233	2,216	2,298	2,211	2,228	2,202	2,291	2,175	2,028	2,056	1,984	2,092	2,033
Geology and earth science[1]													
Bachelor's degree	2,784	3,123	3,456	4,032	4,019	4,023	3,866	3,570	3,516	3,495	3,449	3,381	3,312
Master's degree	1,245	1,195	1,221	1,280	1,288	1,258	1,227	1,196	1,186	1,220	1,263	1,323	1,389
Doctor's degree	549	626	577	539	555	564	588	533	492	472	494	466	463
Physics[2]													
Bachelor's degree	4,098	4,063	4,001	3,823	3,679	3,376	3,441	3,200	3,342	3,418	3,627	3,900	4,118
Master's degree	1,834	1,777	1,945	1,817	1,678	1,496	1,371	1,326	1,232	1,365	1,344	1,438	1,625
Doctor's degree	1,337	1,277	1,465	1,424	1,462	1,410	1,393	1,257	1,208	1,169	1,096	1,089	1,119
Psychology													
Bachelor's degrees, total	63,683	66,931	69,419	72,233	73,416	74,308	74,107	73,747	74,194	73,645	76,775	78,650	82,098
Male	17,062	17,942	18,668	19,570	19,836	19,408	18,976	18,376	17,451	16,585	17,284	17,514	18,193
Female	46,621	48,989	50,751	52,663	53,580	54,900	55,131	55,371	56,743	57,060	59,491	61,136	63,905
Master's degrees, total	11,659	12,518	13,723	15,378	15,152	15,769	15,142	15,560	15,740	16,539	16,357	17,161	17,898
Male	3,335	3,380	3,763	4,210	4,090	4,155	3,978	3,959	3,821	3,892	3,814	3,839	3,789
Female	8,324	9,138	9,960	11,168	11,062	11,614	11,164	11,601	11,919	12,647	12,543	13,322	14,109
Doctor's degrees, total	3,814	4,100	4,021	4,252	4,141	4,507	4,541	4,678	4,731	5,091	4,759	4,835	4,827
Male	1,490	1,570	1,497	1,562	1,380	1,495	1,470	1,528	1,529	1,598	1,503	1,483	1,496
Female	2,324	2,530	2,524	2,690	2,761	3,012	3,071	3,150	3,202	3,493	3,256	3,352	3,331
Public Administration and Social Services													
Bachelor's degrees, total	15,987	16,775	17,815	18,586	19,849	20,649	20,408	20,323	20,185	19,447	19,392	19,900	20,552
Male	3,479	3,801	3,919	3,935	4,205	4,177	3,881	3,799	3,816	3,670	3,706	3,726	3,793
Female	12,508	12,974	13,896	14,651	15,644	16,472	16,527	16,524	16,369	15,777	15,686	16,174	16,759
Master's degrees, total	19,243	20,634	21,833	23,501	24,229	24,781	25,144	25,038	25,594	25,268	25,448	25,903	28,250
Male	5,769	6,105	6,406	6,870	6,927	6,957	7,025	6,621	6,808	6,544	6,505	6,391	7,001
Female	13,474	14,529	15,427	16,631	17,302	17,824	18,119	18,417	18,786	18,724	18,943	19,512	21,249
Doctor's degrees, total	432	459	519	556	499	518	499	534	537	574	571	599	649
Male	204	215	238	274	220	243	223	240	227	263	250	265	275
Female	228	244	281	282	279	275	276	294	310	311	321	334	374
Social Sciences and History													
Bachelor's degrees, total	133,974	135,703	133,680	128,154	126,479	124,891	125,040	124,815	127,101	128,036	132,874	143,256	150,357
Male	73,001	73,589	72,006	68,139	65,872	64,115	63,537	61,843	62,062	61,749	64,170	69,517	73,834
Female	60,973	62,114	61,674	60,015	60,607	60,776	61,503	62,972	65,039	66,287	68,704	73,739	76,523
Master's degrees, total	12,702	13,471	14,561	14,845	15,012	14,787	14,938	14,396	14,066	13,791	14,112	14,630	16,110
Male	7,237	7,671	8,152	8,207	8,093	7,830	7,960	7,440	7,024	6,816	6,941	7,202	7,810
Female	5,465	5,800	6,409	6,638	6,919	6,957	6,978	6,956	7,042	6,975	7,171	7,428	8,300
Doctor's degrees, total	3,218	3,460	3,627	3,725	3,760	3,989	4,127	3,873	4,095	3,930	3,902	3,850	3,811
Male	2,126	2,203	2,317	2,319	2,339	2,479	2,445	2,290	2,407	2,302	2,219	2,196	2,188
Female	1,092	1,257	1,310	1,406	1,421	1,510	1,682	1,583	1,688	1,628	1,683	1,654	1,623
Economics, History, Political Science and Government, and Sociology													
Economics													
Bachelor's degree	23,423	21,321	19,496	17,673	16,674	16,539	17,074	17,577	18,441	19,437	20,927	23,007	24,069
Master's degree	2,106	2,292	2,521	2,400	2,533	2,433	2,435	2,332	2,168	2,139	2,330	2,582	2,824
Doctor's degree	866	879	869	910	916	968	928	819	851	851	826	836	849
History													
Bachelor's degree	26,966	27,774	27,503	26,598	26,005	25,214	25,726	24,742	25,247	25,090	26,001	27,757	29,808
Master's degree	2,754	2,952	3,009	3,091	2,898	2,901	2,895	2,618	2,573	2,365	2,420	2,521	2,522
Doctor's degree	644	690	752	816	805	873	937	931	984	931	924	861	855
Political science and government													
Bachelor's degree	37,805	37,931	36,097	33,013	30,775	28,969	28,044	27,476	27,635	27,792	29,354	33,205	35,581
Master's degree	1,908	1,943	2,147	2,019	2,024	1,909	1,957	1,667	1,627	1,596	1,641	1,664	1,869
Doctor's degree	535	529	616	637	634	686	705	694	693	688	625	671	618
Sociology													

NOTE: Data are for postsecondary institutions participating in Title IV federal financial aid programs.
[1] Includes geology/earth science, general; geochemistry; geophysics; paleontology; hydrology; oceanography; and geological and earth sciences, other.
[2] Includes physics, general; atomic/molecular physics; elementary particle physics; nuclear physics; optics; acoustics; theoretical physics; and physics, other.

Table A-37. Degrees Conferred by Post-Secondary Institutions, by Level of Degree and Sex of Student, 1970-1971 through 2016–2017—*Continued*

(Number.)

Degree conferred, level of degree, and sex of student (when available)	2004-05	2005-06	2006-07	2007-08	2008-09	2009-10	2010-11	2011-12	2012-13	2013-14	2014-15	2015-16	2016-17
Male	3,569	3,666	3,675	3,762	3,576	3,654	3,907	4,299	4,377	4,312	4,438	4,435	4,418
Female	2,254	2,397	2,337	2,299	2,286	2,412	2,479	2,612	2,637	2,672	2,662	2,696	2,725
Doctor's degrees, total	4,248	4,642	5,041	4,994	5,237	5,065	5,295	5,370	5,514	5,806	5,823	6,057	6,027
Male	3,071	3,258	3,454	3,513	3,554	3,406	3,608	3,609	3,646	3,873	3,826	4,102	4,072
Female	1,177	1,384	1,587	1,481	1,683	1,659	1,687	1,761	1,868	1,933	1,997	1,955	1,955
Chemistry, Geology and Earth Science, and Physics													
Chemistry													
Bachelor's degree	9,664	10,606	10,994	11,568	11,852	12,107	12,656	13,473	13,814	14,443	14,447	14,483	14,954
Master's degree	1,879	2,044	2,097	2,194	2,085	2,123	2,272	2,435	2,396	2,357	2,425	2,455	2,494
Doctor's degree	2,148	2,403	2,514	2,410	2,556	2,470	2,599	2,537	2,617	2,796	2,792	2,894	2,887
Geology and earth science[1]													
Bachelor's degree	3,276	3,322	3,319	3,561	3,809	4,093	4,611	5,111	5,539	5,959	6,405	6,552	6,615
Master's degree	1,420	1,476	1,437	1,350	1,352	1,447	1,568	1,807	1,845	1,933	1,955	1,912	1,941
Doctor's degree	476	505	640	577	614	613	567	612	657	735	681	771	737
Physics[2]													
Bachelor's degree	4,182	4,541	4,843	4,862	4,824	4,984	5,199	5,531	6,082	6,263	6,658	6,948	7,109
Master's degree	1,785	1,846	1,777	1,791	1,653	1,793	1,769	1,873	1,975	1,866	1,926	1,956	1,850
Doctor's degree	1,254	1,341	1,442	1,507	1,580	1,571	1,670	1,752	1,740	1,768	1,840	1,845	1,826
Psychology													
Bachelor's degrees, total	85,614	88,134	90,039	92,587	94,273	97,215	100,906	109,099	114,446	117,312	117,573	117,447	116,861
Male	19,000	19,865	20,343	21,202	21,490	22,262	23,230	25,420	26,814	27,306	26,803	26,277	25,526
Female	66,614	68,269	69,696	71,385	72,783	74,953	77,676	83,679	87,632	90,006	90,770	91,170	91,335
Master's degrees, total	18,830	19,770	21,037	21,431	23,415	23,763	25,062	27,052	27,787	27,926	26,772	27,645	27,542
Male	3,900	4,079	4,265	4,356	4,789	4,799	5,127	5,482	5,715	5,729	5,538	5,571	5,588
Female	14,930	15,691	16,772	17,075	18,626	18,964	19,935	21,570	22,072	22,197	21,234	22,074	21,954
Doctor's degrees, total	5,106	4,921	5,153	5,296	5,477	5,540	5,851	5,936	6,326	6,634	6,583	6,540	6,702
Male	1,466	1,347	1,382	1,440	1,478	1,478	1,481	1,525	1,628	1,680	1,624	1,658	1,691
Female	3,640	3,574	3,771	3,856	3,999	4,062	4,370	4,411	4,698	4,954	4,959	4,882	5,011
Public Administration and Social Services													
Bachelor's degrees, total	21,769	21,986	23,147	23,493	23,852	25,421	26,799	29,695	31,950	33,483	34,364	34,433	35,464
Male	4,209	4,126	4,354	4,202	4,373	4,578	4,913	5,386	5,664	5,916	6,146	6,023	6,238
Female	17,560	17,860	18,793	19,291	19,479	20,843	21,886	24,309	26,286	27,567	28,218	28,410	29,226
Master's degrees, total	29,552	30,510	31,131	33,029	33,934	35,740	38,614	41,737	43,591	44,508	45,948	46,754	45,393
Male	7,370	7,572	7,758	8,140	8,346	8,868	9,791	10,494	10,864	10,834	11,181	11,184	10,799
Female	22,182	22,938	23,373	24,889	25,588	26,872	28,823	31,243	32,727	33,674	34,767	35,570	34,594
Doctor's degrees, total	673	704	726	760	812	838	851	890	979	1,047	1,123	1,066	1,116
Male	272	285	253	269	306	323	327	343	351	346	374	354	381
Female	401	419	473	491	506	515	524	547	628	701	749	712	735
Social Sciences and History													
Bachelor's degrees, total	156,892	161,485	164,183	167,363	168,517	172,782	177,169	178,534	177,767	173,132	166,971	161,211	159,099
Male	77,702	80,799	82,417	84,868	85,202	87,404	89,809	90,628	90,143	88,254	85,484	81,292	79,568
Female	79,190	80,686	81,766	82,495	83,315	85,378	87,360	87,906	87,624	84,878	81,487	79,919	79,531
Master's degrees, total	16,952	17,369	17,665	18,495	19,241	20,234	21,085	21,891	21,591	21,497	20,533	19,861	20,015
Male	8,256	8,415	8,577	9,349	9,605	9,967	10,578	10,987	10,811	10,764	10,318	10,010	9,914
Female	8,696	8,954	9,088	9,146	9,636	10,267	10,507	10,904	10,780	10,733	10,215	9,851	10,101
Doctor's degrees, total	3,819	3,914	3,844	4,059	4,234	4,238	4,390	4,597	4,610	4,724	4,828	4,706	4,706
Male	2,184	2,218	2,110	2,194	2,353	2,292	2,331	2,464	2,461	2,494	2,589	2,594	2,572
Female	1,635	1,696	1,734	1,865	1,881	1,946	2,059	2,133	2,149	2,230	2,239	2,112	2,134
Economics, History, Political Science and Government, and Sociology													
Economics													
Bachelor's degree	24,217	23,807	23,916	25,278	26,301	27,623	28,517	27,994	28,449	29,999	32,683	33,474	34,051
Master's degree	3,092	2,941	2,962	3,187	3,233	3,358	3,731	3,890	3,872	4,115	3,993	3,953	4,045
Doctor's degree	973	930	941	1,025	1,015	983	1,018	1,130	1,076	1,059	1,128	1,162	1,150
History													
Bachelor's degree	31,398	33,153	34,446	34,441	34,713	35,191	35,008	35,122	34,188	31,122	28,038	25,589	24,058
Master's degree	2,893	2,992	3,144	3,403	3,543	3,858	4,003	4,155	4,083	3,955	3,703	3,465	3,436
Doctor's degree	819	852	807	860	918	888	908	969	1,003	1,040	986	980	925
Political science and government													
Bachelor's degree	38,107	39,409	39,899	40,259	39,202	39,462	40,133	39,792	38,466	37,360	35,442	33,955	34,191
Master's degree	1,983	2,054	2,102	2,156	2,171	2,252	2,488	2,510	2,332	2,294	2,082	1,983	1,842
Doctor's degree	636	649	614	639	709	745	722	746	821	792	844	793	796
Sociology													

NOTE: Data are for postsecondary institutions participating in Title IV federal financial aid programs.
[1] Includes geology/earth science, general; geochemistry; geophysics; paleontology; hydrology; oceanography; and geological and earth sciences, other.
[2] Includes physics, general; atomic/molecular physics; elementary particle physics; nuclear physics; optics; acoustics; theoretical physics; and physics, other.

Table A-37. Degrees Conferred by Post-Secondary Institutions, by Level of Degree and Sex of Student, 1970-1971 through 2016–2017—*Continued*

(Number.)

Degree conferred, level of degree, and sex of student (when available)	1991-92	1992-93	1993-94	1994-95	1995-96	1996-97	1997-98	1998-99	1999-2000	2000-01	2001-02	2002-03	2003-04
Bachelor's degree............................	19,568	20,896	22,368	22,886	24,071	24,672	24,806	24,979	25,598	25,268	25,202	26,095	26,939
Master's degree..............................	1,347	1,521	1,639	1,748	1,772	1,731	1,737	1,940	1,996	1,845	1,928	1,897	2,009
Doctor's degree...............................	501	536	530	546	527	591	596	521	595	546	534	591	558
Visual and Performing Arts													
Bachelor's degrees, total.....................	46,522	47,761	49,053	48,690	49,296	50,083	52,077	54,446	58,791	61,148	66,773	71,482	77,181
Male...	17,616	18,610	19,538	19,781	20,126	20,729	21,483	22,270	24,003	24,967	27,130	27,922	30,037
Female	28,906	29,151	29,515	28,909	29,170	29,354	30,594	32,176	34,788	36,181	39,643	43,560	47,144
Master's degrees, total........................	9,353	9,440	9,925	10,277	10,280	10,627	11,145	10,762	10,918	11,404	11,595	11,982	12,906
Male...	4,078	4,099	4,229	4,374	4,361	4,470	4,596	4,544	4,672	4,788	4,912	4,975	5,531
Female	5,275	5,341	5,696	5,903	5,919	6,157	6,549	6,218	6,246	6,616	6,683	7,007	7,375
Doctor's degrees, total........................	906	882	1,054	1,080	1,067	1,060	1,163	1,117	1,127	1,167	1,114	1,293	1,282
Male...	504	478	585	545	524	525	566	567	537	568	490	613	572
Female	402	404	469	535	543	535	597	550	590	599	624	680	710

NOTE: Data are for postsecondary institutions participating in Title IV federal financial aid programs.

Table A-37. Degrees Conferred by Post-Secondary Institutions, by Level of Degree and Sex of Student, 1970-1971 through 2016–2017—*Continued*

(Number.)

Degree conferred, level of degree, and sex of student (when available)	2004-05	2005-06	2006-07	2007-08	2008-09	2009-10	2010-11	2011-12	2012-13	2013-14	2014-15	2015-16	2016-17
Bachelor's degree	28,473	28,467	28,960	28,815	28,735	28,650	29,281	30,136	30,531	30,070	29,000	28,001	27,443
Master's degree	1,499	1,547	1,545	1,560	1,580	1,428	1,559	1,696	1,603	1,611	1,447	1,363	1,397
Doctor's degree	527	562	569	585	628	603	656	626	615	674	722	646	682
Visual and Performing Arts													
Bachelor's degrees, total	80,955	83,297	85,186	87,703	89,143	91,798	93,939	95,806	97,799	97,414	95,840	92,979	91,262
Male	31,355	32,117	32,729	33,862	35,055	35,768	36,342	37,164	38,063	38,177	38,024	36,712	35,296
Female	49,600	51,180	52,457	53,841	54,088	56,030	57,597	58,642	59,736	59,237	57,816	56,267	55,966
Master's degrees, total	13,183	13,530	13,767	14,164	14,918	15,562	16,277	17,307	17,869	17,869	17,756	18,052	17,523
Male	5,646	5,801	5,910	5,998	6,325	6,531	6,881	7,320	7,610	7,712	7,643	7,679	7,565
Female	7,537	7,729	7,857	8,166	8,593	9,031	9,396	9,987	10,259	10,157	10,113	10,373	9,958
Doctor's degrees, total	1,278	1,383	1,364	1,453	1,569	1,599	1,646	1,728	1,814	1,778	1,793	1,809	1,774
Male	594	639	625	675	726	700	770	790	850	869	837	853	812
Female	684	744	739	778	843	899	876	938	964	909	956	956	962

NOTE: Data are for postsecondary institutions participating in Title IV federal financial aid programs.

NOTES AND DEFINITIONS: NATIONAL SCHOOL ENROLLMENT, EDUCATIONAL ATTAINMENT, AND POSTSECONDARY EDUCATION

ENROLLMENT TABLES A-1 THROUGH A-8 AND A-10 THROUGH A-17

Source: U.S. Census Bureau. School Enrollment in the United States. *Current Population Survey (CPS) Report.*
https://www.census.gov/data/tables/2017/demo/school-enrollment/2017-cps.html and https://www.census.gov/data/tables/time-series/demo/school-enrollment/cps-historical-time-series.html

ATTAINMENT TABLES A-24 THROUGH A-35

Source: U.S. Census Bureau. Educational Attainment in the United States. *Current Population Survey (CPS) Report.*
https://www.census.gov/data/tables/2018/demo/education-attainment/cps-detailed-tables.html and https://www.census.gov/data/tables/time-series/demo/educational-attainment/cps-historical-time-series.html.

POSTSECONDARY EDUCATION ENROLLMENT AND ATTAINMENT TABLES A-9, A-18 THROUGH A-24, A-36, AND A-37

Source: U.S. Department of Education, National Center for Education Statistics, Institute of Education Sciences, *Digest of Education Statistics, 2017 and 2018.*
https://nces.ed.gov/programs/digest/current_tables.asp

SCHOOL ENROLLMENT AND EDUCATIONAL ATTAINMENT TABLES

The School Enrollment and Educational Attainment tables in Part A are derived from the Current Population Survey (CPS). The Census Bureau disseminated comparable tables in the P-20 series of *Current Population Reports* (CPR) for most years between 1947 and 1994. Since then, these tables have not been available in printed form. However, they can be found on the Census Bureau website at www.census.gov. In the historical series, data before 1992 are not strictly comparable to data after 1992. Before 1992, the CPS did not ask questions about degrees received; educational attainment was gauged only by years of school completed.

Age. Age classification is based on the age of the person at his or her last birthday.

Citizenship status. There are five categories of citizenship status: (1) born in the United States; (2) born in Puerto Rico or another outlying area of the United States; (3) born abroad to U.S. citizen parents; (4) naturalized citizens; and (5) non-citizens. Place of birth was asked for every household member and for the parents of every household member in the CPS sample. People born in the United States or its outlying areas, or whose parents were born in the United States or its outlying areas, were not asked citizenship questions. Citizenship statuses (1), (2), and (3) were assigned during the editing phase of data preparation, based on the place of birth of the household member or the place of birth of his or her parents. People born outside the United States and its outlying areas, whose parents were born outside the United States and its outlying areas, were asked, "Are you a citizen of the United States?" 'Yes' answers were assigned to the "naturalized citizen" category (4), and 'No' answers were assigned to the "not a citizen" category (5) during the editing process. People for whom no birthplace was provided were also assigned a citizenship status during the editing process; for example, the citizenship status of a child might have been assigned based on the citizenship status of his or her mother.

Dropouts. See School, Dropout rate, annual high school.

Earnings. See Income.

Educational attainment. Data on educational attainment are derived from a single question that asks, "What is the highest grade of school . . . completed, or the highest degree . . . received?"

The single educational attainment question now in use was introduced into the CPS in January 1992. It is similar to the question used in the 1990 Decennial Census of Population and Housing. Consequently, data on educational attainment from the 1992 CPS are not directly comparable to CPS data from earlier years. The new question replaces the previous two-part question used in the CPS, which asked respondents to report the highest grade they attended and whether or not they completed that grade.

The question concerning educational attainment applies only to progress in "regular" schools. Such schools include graded public, private, and parochial elementary and high schools (both junior and senior high schools), colleges, universities, and professional schools, and both day schools and night schools. Thus, regular schooling is that which may advance a person toward an elementary school certificate, a high school diploma, or a college, university, or professional school degree. Non-regular schooling was counted only if the credits obtained were regarded as transferable to a school within the regular school system.

Family. A family is a group of two people or more residing together (including the householder) related by birth, marriage, or adoption; all such people (including related subfamily members) are considered members of one family. Beginning with the 1980 Current Population Survey, unrelated subfamilies (formerly referred to as secondary families) are no longer included in the count of families, nor are members of unrelated subfamilies included in the count of family members. The number of families is equal to the number of family households; however, the count of family members differs from the count of family household members, as family household members include any non-relatives living in the household.

Family household. A family household is a household maintained by a householder within a family (as defined above). It includes any unrelated people (unrelated subfamily members and/or secondary individuals) residing in the household. The number of family households is equal to the number of families; however, the count of family household members differs from the count of family members. Family household members include all people living in the household, whereas family members include only the householder and his or her relatives. (See Family for more information.)

Hispanic origin. People of Hispanic origin were identified by a question that asked respondents to self-identify their origin or descent. Respondents were asked to select their origin (and the origin of other household members) from a "flash card" listing different ethnicities. People of Hispanic origin were those who indicated that their descent was of Mexican, Puerto Rican, Cuban, Central or South American, or some other Hispanic origin. It should be noted that people of Hispanic origin may be of any race.

People who were of non-Hispanic White origin were identified by crossing the responses to two self-identification questions: (1) origin or descent; and (2) race. Respondents were asked to select their race (and the race of other household members) from a "flash card" listing racial groups. Since March 1989, the population has been divided into five groups on the basis of race: White; Black; American Indian, Eskimo, or Aleut; Asian or Pacific Islander; and Other races. The last category includes any race other than the four indicated races. Respondents who identified their race as White and did not select one of the Hispanic origin subgroups

(Mexican, Puerto Rican, Cuban, Central or South American) were classified as non-Hispanic White.

Household. A household consists of all the people who occupy a housing unit. A house, apartment, group of rooms, or single room is regarded as a housing unit when it is occupied or intended for occupancy as separate living quarters (meaning that occupants do not live and eat with any other persons in the structure and have direct access to their dwelling from outside or through a common hall). A household includes related family members and all unrelated people—such as lodgers, foster children, wards, or employees—who share the housing unit. A person living alone in a housing unit, or a group of unrelated people sharing a dwelling (such as partners or roomers), are also counted as a household. The count of households excludes group quarters. There are two major categories of households: "family" and "nonfamily." (See Family household and Nonfamily household for more information.)

Householder. The householder is the person (or one of the people) in whose name the housing unit is owned or rented (maintained). If there is no such person, any adult member of the household—excluding roomers, boarders, and paid employees—can be counted as the householder. If a married couple jointly owns or rents the housing unit, the householder may be either the husband or the wife. The person designated as the householder is the "reference person" to whom the relationship of all other household members, if any, is recorded.

The number of householders is equal to the number of households. The number of family householders is also equal to the number of families.

Head versus householder. The Census Bureau discontinued the use of the terms "head of household" and "head of family" beginning with the 1980 CPS. Instead, the terms "householder" and "family householder" are used. Recent social changes have resulted in a greater sharing of household responsibilities among the adult members. This has made the term "head" increasingly inappropriate in the analysis of household and family data. Specifically, beginning in 1980, the Census Bureau discontinued its longtime practice of always classifying the husband as the reference person (head of household) when he was living with his wife.

INCOME. Definitions of income and the types of income are found below.

Income, Official definition of. For each person age 15 years and over in the sample, the CPS asks questions about the amount of money income received during the preceding calendar year from each of the following sources: earnings; unemployment compensation; workers' compensation; Social Security; Supplemental Security Income; public assistance or welfare payments; veterans' payments; survivor benefits; disability benefits; pension or retirement income; interest, dividends, rents, royalties, and estates and trusts; educational assistance; child support; alimony; financial assistance from outside the household; and other income.

Although the income statistics refer to receipts during the preceding calendar year, demographic characteristics such as age, labor force status, and family or household composition are as of the survey date. The income of the family/household does not include amounts received by members who were members of the family/household during all or part of the income year if these people no longer resided in the family/household at the time of interview. However, the CPS collects income data for people who are current residents, but who did not reside in the household during the income year.

Data on consumer income collected in the CPS by the Census Bureau cover money income (exclusive of certain money receipts, such as capital gains) received before payments for personal income taxes, Social Security, union dues, Medicare deductions, and so on. Therefore, money income does not reflect the fact that some families receive part of their income in the form of noncash benefits, such as food stamps, health benefits, rent-free housing, and goods produced and consumed on the farm. Money income also does not reflect the fact that noncash benefits are also received by some nonfarm residents. These benefits often take the form of the use of business transportation and facilities, full or partial payments by business for retirement programs, medical and educational expenses, and so on. Data users should consider these elements when comparing income levels. Moreover, readers should be aware that respondents in household surveys tend to underreport their income for many different reasons. Based on an analysis of independently derived income estimates, the Census Bureau determined that respondents report income earned from wages or salaries much more accurately than income earned from other sources of income, and that the reported wage and salary income is nearly equal to independent estimates of aggregate income.

The Census Bureau collects data for the following income sources:

Alimony. Alimony includes all periodic payments received from ex-spouses. It excludes one-time property settlements.

Child support. Child support includes all periodic payments received from an absent parent for the support of his or her children, even if these payments are made through a state or local government office.

Disability benefits. Disability benefits include payments people received due to a health problem or disability (other than those received from Social Security). Respondents can report payments from 10

sources, including workers' compensation, companies or unions, federal government (civil service), military, state or local governments, railroad retirement, accident or disability insurance, Black Lung payments, state temporary sickness, or other disability payments.

Dividends. Dividends include income received from stock holdings and mutual fund shares. The CPS does not include capital gains from the sale of stock holdings as income.

Earnings. The Census Bureau classifies earnings from respondents' longest job (or self-employment) and other employment earnings into three types:

- Money wage or salary income, is the total income people receive for work performed as an employee during the income year. This category includes wages, salary, armed forces pay, commissions, tips, piece-rate payments, and cash bonuses earned, before deductions are made for items such as taxes, bonds, pensions, and union dues.

- Net income from nonfarm self-employment is the net money income (gross receipts minus expenses) from a respondent's own business, professional enterprise, or partnership. Gross receipts include the value of all goods sold and all services rendered. Expenses include items such as the costs of goods purchased; rent, heat, power, and depreciation charges; wages and salaries paid; and business taxes (but not personal income taxes). In general, the Census Bureau considers inventory changes in determining net income from nonfarm self-employment; replies based on income tax returns or other official records reflect inventory changes. However, when respondents do not report values of inventory changes, interviewers will accept net income figures exclusive of inventory changes. The Census Bureau does not include the value of saleable merchandise consumed by the proprietors of retail stores as part of net income.

- Net income from farm self-employment is the net money income (gross receipts minus operating expenses) from the operation of a farm by a person acting on their own account as owner, renter, or sharecropper. Gross receipts include the value of all products sold, payments from government farm programs, money received from renting farm equipment to others, rent received from farm property if payment is based on the percentage of crops produced, and incidental receipts from the sale of items such as wood, sand, and gravel.

- Operating expenses include items such as the cost of feed, fertilizer, seed, and other farming supplies; cash wages paid to farmhands; depreciation charges; cash rent; interest on farm mortgages; farm building repairs; and farm taxes (not state and federal personal income taxes). The Census Bureau does not include the value of fuel, food, or other farm products used for family living as part of net income, and only considers inventory changes in determining net income when they are accounted for in income tax returns or other official records. Otherwise, the Census Bureau does not take inventory changes into account.

Educational assistance. Educational assistance includes Pell Grants, other government educational assistance, scholarships or grants, and any financial assistance received from employers, friends, or relatives not residing in the student's household.

Financial assistance from outside the household. Financial assistance from outside the household includes periodic payments received from nonhousehold members. This type of assistance excludes gifts and sporadic assistance.

Government transfers. Government transfers include payments received from the following sources: unemployment compensation, state workers' compensation, Social Security, Supplemental Security Income (SSI), public assistance, veterans' payments, government survivor benefits, government disability benefits, government pensions, and government educational assistance.

Interest income. Interest income includes payments received or credited to accounts from bonds, treasury notes, individual retirement accounts (IRAs), certificates of deposit, interest-bearing savings and checking accounts, and all other interest-paying investments.

Other income. Other income includes any other unclassified payments received regularly. Some examples are state programs such as foster child payments, military family allotments, and income received from foreign government pensions.

Pension or retirement income. Pension or retirement income includes payments received from eight sources, including companies or unions; federal government (civil service); military; state or local governments; railroad retirement; annuities or paid-up insurance policies; IRAs, Keogh, or 401(k) payments; or other retirement income.

Public assistance or welfare payments. Public assistance or welfare payments include cash payments to low-income persons, including payments given under programs such as Aid to Families with Dependent Children (AFDC, ADC) and Temporary Assistance to Needy Families (TANF), emergency assistance, and other general assistance.

Rents, royalties, and estates and trusts. Rents, royalties, and estates and trusts include net income received from the rental of a house, a store, or other property; receipts from boarders or lodgers; net royalty income; and periodic payments from estate or trust funds.

Social Security. Social Security includes pensions, survivors' benefits, and permanent disability insurance payments made by the Social Security Administration prior to medical insurance deductions. The Census Bureau does not include Medicare reimbursements for health services as Social Security benefits.

Supplemental Security Income. Supplemental Security Income includes federal, state, and local welfare agency payments to low-income people age 65 years and over and to blind or disabled people of any age.

Survivor benefits. Survivor benefits include payments received from survivors' or widows' pensions, estates, trusts, annuities, or any other types of survivors' benefits. Respondents can report payments from 10 different sources, including private companies or unions, federal government (civil service), military, state or local governments, railroad retirement, workers' compensation, Black Lung payments, estates and trusts, annuities or paid-up insurance policies, and other survivor payments.

Unemployment compensation. Unemployment compensation includes payments made to the respondent from government unemployment agencies or private companies during periods of unemployment. It also accounts for any strike benefits the respondent received from union funds.

Veterans' payments. Veterans' payments include periodic payments from the Department of Veterans Affairs to disabled members of the armed forces or survivors of deceased veterans for education and on-the-job training. These payments also include means-tested assistance to veterans.

Workers' compensation. Workers' compensation includes periodic payments from public or private insurance companies for work-related injuries.

The Census Bureau does not count the following receipts as income: (1) capital gains (or losses) from the sale of property, including stocks, bonds, houses, or cars (unless the person was engaged in the business of selling such property, in which case the CPS counts the net proceeds as income from self-employment); (2) withdrawals of bank deposits; (3) money borrowed; (4) tax refunds; (5) gifts; and (6) lump-sum inheritances or insurance payments.

The Census Bureau combines all sources of income into two major types:

Total money earnings. Total money earnings is the algebraic sum of money wages, salary, and net income from farm and nonfarm self-employment.

Income other than earnings. Income other than earnings is the algebraic sum of all sources of money income, except wages and salaries and income from self-employment.

Mean (average) income. Mean (average) income is the amount obtained by dividing the total aggregate income of a group by the number of units in that group. The means for households, families, and unrelated individuals are based respectively on all households, all families, and all unrelated individuals. The means (averages) for people are based on people age 15 years and over with income.

Median income. Median income is the amount that divides the income distribution into two equal groups. Half of all people have incomes above the median, and half of all people have incomes below the median. The medians for households, families, and unrelated individuals are respectively based on all households, all families, and all unrelated individuals. The medians for people are based on people age 15 years and over with income.

LABOR FORCE STATUS. Definitions of labor force characteristics are found below:

Civilian labor force. Consists of people classified as employed or unemployed. Excluded are institutionalized people and people on active duty in the United States Armed Forces. The entire labor force consists of people classified as employed or unemployed and people in the armed forces.

Current job (basic data). A worker's current job is the job held during the reference week (the week before the survey). A person holding two or more jobs is classified as being in the job at which he or she spent the most hours during the reference week. The unemployed are classified according to their most recent full-time job of two weeks or more, or by the job (either the full-time or part-time job) from which they were laid off. The occupation/industry classification system for the 1990 Decennial Census of Population was first used to code CPS data for the January 1992 file. The occupation/industry classification system for the 2000 Decennial Census of Population was first used to code CPS data for the January 2003 file.

Employed. Employed persons include all civilians who, during the survey week, did any work at all (for at least one hour) as paid employees or in their own business or profession, or on their own farm, or who worked 15 hours or more as unpaid workers on a farm or a business operated by a member of the family; and all people who had jobs but were not working due to illness, bad weather, vacation, labor-management dispute, or personal reasons, whether or not they were seeking other jobs. Each employed person is counted only once. People who held two or more jobs are counted as working in the job at which they worked the greatest number of hours during the survey week. If a person worked an equal number of hours at two or more jobs, he or she is counted as working at the job that they have held the longest.

Labor force. Workers are classified as being in the labor force if they are employed, unemployed, or in the armed forces during the survey week. The "civilian labor force" includes all civilians classified as employed or unemployed. The file includes labor force data for civilians age 15 years and over. However, the official definition of the civilian labor force consists of workers age 16 years and over.

Not in labor force. All civilians age 15 years and over who are not classified as employed or unemployed are considered not to be in the labor force. These people are further classified as being engaged in a major activity such as keeping house, going to school, unable to work because of long-term physical or mental illness, and "other," which is mostly composed of retired persons. Those who report doing unpaid work on a family-owned farm or in a family-owned business for less than 15 hours are also classified as not in the labor force.

For persons not in the labor force, questions about previous work experience, intentions to seek work again, current desire for a job, and reasons for not seeking work are only asked of households in the fourth and eighth months of the sample. These are the "outgoing" groups—those that were in the sample for three previous months and would not be in it for the subsequent month.

Finally, it should be noted that the unemployment rate represents the number of unemployed persons as a percentage of the civilian labor force age 16 years and over. This measure can be computed for groups within the labor force by sex, age, marital status, race, and so on. The job loser, job leaver, reentrant, and new entrant rates are each calculated as a percentage of the civilian labor force age 16 years and over; the sum of the rates for the four groups thus equals the total unemployment rate.

Unemployed. Unemployed persons are civilians who, during the survey week, had no employment but were available for work and had engaged in any specific job-seeking activity within the past four previous weeks, such as registering at a public or private employment office, meeting with prospective employers, checking with friends or relatives, placing and answering advertisements, writing letters of application, or being on a union or professional register. Others in this category were waiting to be called back to a job from which they had been laid off or were within 30 days of starting a new wage or salary job. This category consists of job leavers, job losers, new job entrants, and job reentrants.

Work experience. A person with work experience is one who did any work for pay or profit or worked without pay on a family-operated farm or business at any time during the preceding calendar year, on a part-time or full-time basis. A full-time worker is a worker who worked 35 hours or more per week during a majority of the weeks in the preceding calendar year. A year-round worker is a worker who worked for 50 weeks or more during the preceding calendar year. A full-time, year-round worker is a person who worked full-time (35 or more hours per week) for 50 or more weeks during the previous calendar year.

Level of school completed. The statistics on level of school completed indicate the number of persons enrolled at each of five levels: nursery school, kindergarten, elementary school (first to eighth grades), high school (ninth to twelfth grades), and college or professional school. The last group includes graduate students at colleges and universities. Those enrolled in elementary school, middle school, intermediate school, or junior high through eighth grade are classified as being in elementary school. All persons enrolled in ninth through twelfth grade are classified as being in high school.

Modal grade. See School, Modal grade.

Nativity. There are two major categories of nativity, native born and foreign born. A person who is native is a citizen at birth. All people with the following citizenship status are native born: (1) born in the United States; (2) born in Puerto Rico or an outlying area of the United States; and (3) born abroad of American parents. (See Citizenship status for more information.) All other people are classified as foreign born.

Nonfamily household. A nonfamily household consists of a householder living alone (a one-person household) or a household shared exclusively by unrelated people.

Population coverage. The sample for the CPS includes the civilian noninstitutional population of the United States, along with members of the armed forces in the United States living off post or with their families on post. It excludes all other members of the armed forces. The information on the Hispanic population from the CPS was collected in the 50 states and the District of Columbia and does not include residents of outlying areas or of U.S. territories such as Guam, Puerto Rico, and the U.S. Virgin Islands.

Race. The race of individuals was identified through a question requiring self-identification of the person's race. Respondents were asked to select their race from a "flash card" listing racial groups. Since March 1989, the population has been divided into five groups on the basis of race: White; Black; American Indian, Eskimo or Aleut; Asian or Pacific Islander; and Other races. The last category includes any other race except the five mentioned. In most of the published tables, "Other races" are included in the total population data line but are not shown individually.

Reference person. The reference person serves as the central point for determining relationships within the household. The household reference person is the person listed as the householder. (See Householder for more information.) The subfamily reference person is either the single parent or the husband or wife in a married-couple situation.

Rounding. Percentages are rounded to the nearest 10th of a percent; therefore, the percentages in a distribution do not always sum to exactly 100 percent.

School, Dropout rate, annual high school. The annual high school dropout rate is an estimate of the proportion of students who drop out of school in a single year. This section briefly explains how the annual dropout rate is calculated; for further explanation and details of its derivation, see *Current Population Report (Series P-20, No. 413): "School Enrollment—Social and Economic Characteristics of Students: October 1983."*

Annual dropout rates for a single grade (X) are estimated as the ratio between the number of people enrolled in grade (X) in the year preceding the survey who did not complete grade (X) and are not currently enrolled in grade (X) at the start of the year preceding this survey. People reported as enrolled last year but not currently enrolled are presented by the highest grade completed in Table 8 of the *Current Population Report* on school enrollment. They are presumed to have dropped out of the succeeding grade (except for those who graduated this year). Thus, individuals counted as 10th grade dropouts are those whose highest grade completed is the 9th grade, but who are not currently enrolled in school. (The dropout classification also includes those people who finished the 9th grade in the spring preceding the survey and were not enrolled on the survey date.) These estimates form the numerator of the annual grade-specific dropout rate.

People currently enrolled in high school are presumed to have been enrolled in and have successfully completed the preceding grade during the preceding year. For example, those who have successfully completed the

10th grade would be enrolled in the 11th grade. Along with the people who dropped out of that grade, they comprise the denominator of the estimate of the annual grade-specific dropout rate:

$$\text{Dropout from Grade n} = \frac{\text{Not enrolled and highest grade completed} = n-1}{\left(\begin{array}{c}\text{Enrolled in } n+1 \ + \ \text{Not enrolled and} \\ \text{highest grade completed} = n-1\end{array}\right)}$$

It cannot be presumed that all 12th grade graduates will enroll in college. The estimate of the number of people enrolled in the 12th grade one year before the survey is constructed as the sum of the number of people reported to have graduated from high school "this year" (whether or not they are currently enrolled in college) and those not currently enrolled who were enrolled last year and whose highest grade completed is the 11th grade (dropouts). The annual dropout rate for all grades during one year can be obtained by summing the components of the rates for the individual grades—the sum of all people previously enrolled in the 10th, 11th, or 12th grade last year, but who are not currently enrolled and do not have a high school diploma.

In addition to the annual rate, two other estimates of dropouts are frequently used. The annual dropout rate is different from a "pool" (or status) measure, such as the proportion of high school dropouts within an age group. A third measure of dropouts is the "cohort measure," most commonly from a longitudinal study, in which the proportion of a specific group of people enrolled in a specific year is calculated. These people did not receive diplomas (and are no longer in school) some years later. For example, the proportion of a cohort enrolled in 9th grade in year X, who were not enrolled and had not received a diploma by year X equals 4.

School enrollment. The school enrollment statistics from the CPS are based on replies to inquiries concerning current regular school enrollment. Those counted as enrolled had attended a public, parochial, or other private school in the regular school system at any time during the current or previous school year. Such schools include nursery schools, kindergartens, elementary schools, high schools, colleges, universities, and professional schools. Attendance could have been on either a full-time or part-time basis during the day or night. Regular schooling is that which advances a person toward an elementary or high school diploma or toward a college, university, or professional school degree. Children enrolled in nursery schools and kindergarten are included in the enrollment figures for regular schools and are shown separately.

Enrollment in schools not in the regular school system, such as trade schools, business colleges, and schools for the mentally handicapped is not included, as these schools do not advance students toward regular school degrees.

People enrolled in classes not requiring their physical presence in school, such as correspondence courses or other courses of independent study, and those enrolled in training courses given directly on the job, are also excluded from the count of those enrolled in school, unless such courses are being counted for credit at a regular school.

School enrollment in the year preceding current survey. All respondents were asked to state their school enrollment status as of October of the preceding year. Before 1988, this question was only asked of people not currently attending regular school and people who were enrolled in college. In the tabulations of previous year's secondary school enrollment, those currently enrolled in high school were assumed to have been enrolled the previous year.

Comparability of enrollment data in previous years. Changes in the edit and tabulation packages used to process the October CPS school enrollment supplement caused some minor revisions to the estimates. The current

edit and tabulation package began with 1987 data. The 1986 data published in the *Current Population Report (Series P-20 No. 429)* were reprocessed with the rewritten programs in order to clarify comparability. Time series tables usually show only the revised estimates for 1986. The previous edit and tabulation package was used from 1967 to 1986.

Major changes in the data caused by the 1987 edit revisions were: (1) Among 14- and 15-year-olds, an edit improvement allowed people with unreported enrollment data, who were previously imputed as "not enrolled," to be enrolled; (2) Revisions in the tabulation of enrollment in the previous year simplified the calculation of an annual high school dropout rate; (3) Edit improvements caused increases in college enrollment estimates, most notably above the age of 24. This age group was largely ignored in earlier edits; (4) Type of college is fully allocated (discussed earlier in the section); (5) Tabulations of type of college (2-year and 4-year colleges) were made available by race; (6) Dependent family members became consistently defined; (7) New tabulations of employment status, vocational course enrollment, college retention and re-entry, and families with children enrolled in public and private school became available beginning in 1987.

In the series of reports on school enrollment for 1987 to 1992, race and Hispanic origin were erroneously tabulated for a small percentage of children age 3 to 14 years. Race and Hispanic origin of an adult in the household were attributed to the child, rather than using the child's reported characteristics. In the vast majority of cases, these characteristics were the same for family members, but for a small percentage of children, they were different. The correction made the following proportional changes in the numbers of children in each group: White (-0.5 percent), Black (+3.1 percent), and Hispanic (-4.6 percent).

Published data on enrollment from the October CPS for 1981 to 1993 used population controls based on the 1980 census. Beginning in 1994, estimates used 1990 census–based population controls, including adjustment for undercount. Time series tables show two sets of data for 1993; the data labeled "1993r" were processed using population controls based on the 1990 census with adjustments for undercount. The change in 1994 from a paper-and-pencil survey to a computer-assisted survey had some affect on the data. Most notably, the enrollment question for children age 3 to 5 years was different from the question for older children—it included a reference to nursery school. In 1994, reported nursery school enrollment was significantly higher than in earlier years.

Attendance, full-time and part-time. College students are classified according to their attendance status. A student is categorized as attending college full-time if he or she was taking 12 or more hours of classes during the average school week, and part-time if he or she was taking less than 12 hours of classes per average school week.

College enrollment. The college enrollment statistics are based on reports of school enrollment, including the grade in which the respondent was enrolled. Students enrolled in college at any time during the current term or school year were counted as enrolled, except those who had left for the remainder of the term. Thus, regular college enrollment includes those attending two-year or four-year colleges, universities, or professional schools (such as medical or law schools) in courses that advance students toward a recognized college or university degree (such as a B.A. or an M.A.). Attendance may be full-time or part-time during the day or night. The college student need not be working toward a degree, but he or she must be enrolled in a class for which credit would be applied toward a degree. (See school enrollment for more information.) Students are classified by year of college, based on the academic year (not calendar year). The undergraduate years are the first through

fourth year, or freshman through senior years. Graduate or professional school years include the fifth year and higher.

Two-year and four-year colleges. College students were asked if their school was a two-year college (junior or community college) or a four-year college or university. Students enrolled in the first four years of college (undergraduates) were classified by the type of school that they attended. Graduate students are shown as a separate group.

Vocational school enrollment. Vocational school enrollment includes enrollment in business, vocational, technical, secretarial, trade, or correspondence courses that are not counted as regular school enrollment. This category excludes recreation or adult education classes. Courses that counted as college enrollment are also excluded.

School, Modal grade. Enrolled people are classified according to their relative progress in school and whether the grade or year in which they were enrolled was below, at, or above the modal (or typical) grade for students of their age at the time of the survey. The modal grade is the year of school in which the largest proportion of students of a given age were enrolled.

School, Nursery. A nursery school is defined as a group or class that has been organized to provide educational experiences for children during the year or years preceding kindergarten. It includes instruction as an important and integral phase of its childcare program. Private homes, in which essentially custodial care is provided, are not considered nursery schools. Children attending nursery school are classified as attending for part of the day or for the full day. Part-day attendance refers to those who attend either in the morning or in the afternoon. Full-day attendance refers to those who attend in the morning and in the afternoon. Children enrolled in Head Start programs or similar local agency-sponsored programs that provide preschool education to young children are counted as being enrolled in nursery school.

School, Public or private. A public school is defined as any educational institution operated by publicly elected or appointed school officials and supported by public funds. Private schools include educational institutions established and operated by religious bodies, as well as those that are under other private controls. In cases in which a school or college was both publicly and privately controlled or supported, enrollment was counted according to whether the school was primarily public or private.

Undocumented immigrants or illegal aliens. Since all residents of the United States living in households are represented in the sample of households interviewed by the CPS, undocumented immigrants or illegal aliens are probably included in CPS data. Because the CPS makes no attempt to ascertain the legal status of any person interviewed, these individuals cannot be identified from CPS data.

POSTSECONDARY EDUCATION TABLES

Tables A-29 through A-37 were adapted from the most current published tables from the National Center for Education Statistics, Institute of Education Sciences: *Digest of Education Statistics.*

Consumer Price Index. This price index measures the average change in the cost of a fixed market basket of goods and services purchased by consumers.

Control of institution describes whether an institution is operated by publicly elected or appointed officials (public control) or by privately elected or appointed officials and derives its major source of funds from private sources (private not-for-profit or private for-profit control). There are nine institutional categories resulting from dividing

the universe according to control and level. Control categories are public, private not-for-profit, and private for-profit. Level categories are 4-year and higher (4 year), 2-but-less-than 4-year (2 year), and less than 2-year. For example: Public, 4-year is one of the institution sectors.

Fall enrollment. IPEDS collects data on the number of students enrolled in the fall at postsecondary institutions. Students reported are those enrolled in courses creditable toward a degree or other formal award; students enrolled in courses that are part of a vocational or occupational program, including those enrolled in off-campus or extension centers; and high school students taking regular college courses for credit. Institutions report annually the number of full- and part-time students, by gender, race/ethnicity, and level (undergraduate, graduate, first-professional); the total number of undergraduate entering students (first-time, full- and part-time students, transfer-ins, and nondegree students); and retention rates. In even-numbered years, data are collected for state of residence of first-time students and for the number of those students who graduated from high school or received high school equivalent certificates in the past 12 months. Also in even-numbered years, 4-year institutions are required to provide enrollment data by gender, race/ethnicity, and level for selected fields of study. In odd-numbered years, data are collected for enrollment by age category by student level and gender.

Data through 1995 are for institutions of higher education, while later data are for degree-granting institutions. Degree-granting institutions grant associate's or higher degrees and participate in Title IV federal financial aid programs. The degree-granting classification is very similar to the earlier higher education classification, but it includes more 2-year colleges and excludes a few higher education institutions that did not grant degrees.

Nonresident alien is a person who is not a citizen or national of the United States and who is in this country on a visa or temporary basis and does not have the right to remain indefinitely.

A **Postbaccalaureate student** is a student with a bachelor's degree who is enrolled in graduate-level or first-professional courses.

Price of attendance includes tuition and required fees, books and supplies, room and board charges, and other expenses. Amounts are institutional averages as reported by the institution, not average amounts paid by students (for example, charges are not weighted by enrollment). Out-of-state average tuition and required fees were used for private institutions that reported varying tuitions by residency. The 2,578 institutions with academic calendars that differ by program or allow continuous enrollment are not included. U.S. service academies are not included. All amounts from 2011–2012 were converted to 2013–2014 dollars using the average Consumer Price Index values for the 12-month periods ending in October 2011 and October 2013. On-campus average price is based on those institutions that offer on-campus housing and/or meal service. Off-campus average price is based on those institutions that do not require full-time, first-time students to live on campus. For public institutions, "in district" refers to the charges paid by a student who lives in the locality surrounding the institution, such as a county.

Race/ethnicity categories were developed in 1997 by the Office of Management and Budget (OMB) and are used to describe groups to which individuals belong, identify with, or belong in the eyes of the community. The categories do not denote scientific definitions of anthropological origins. The designations are used to categorize U.S. citizens, resident aliens, and other eligible non-citizens. Individuals are asked to first designate ethnicity as Hispanic/Latino or not Hispanic/Latino. Hispanic/Latino refers to a person of Cuban, Mexican, Puerto Rican, South or Central American, or other Spanish culture or origin, regardless of race. Second, individuals are asked to indicate all races that apply among the following:

American Indian or Alaska Native (A person having origins in any of the original peoples of North and South America (including Central America) who maintains cultural identification through tribal affiliation or community attachment.

Asian (A person having origins in any of the original peoples of the Far East, Southeast Asia, or the Indian Subcontinent, including, for example, Cambodia, China, India, Japan, Korea, Malaysia, Pakistan, the Philippine Islands, Thailand, and Vietnam).

Black or African American (A person having origins in any of the black racial groups of Africa).

Native Hawaiian or Other Pacific Islander (A person having origins in any of the original peoples of Hawaii, Guam, Samoa, or other Pacific Islands.)

White (A person having origins in any of the original peoples of Europe, the Middle East, or North Africa.)

Before 1997, slightly different race/ethnicity categories were used and persons could identify with only one racial category.

Tuition and required fees is the amount of tuition and required fees covering a full academic year most frequently charged to students. These values represent what a typical student would be charged and may not be the same for all students at an institution. If tuition is charged on a per-credit-hour basis, the average full-time credit hour load for an entire academic year is used to estimate average tuition. Required fees include all fixed sum charges that are required of such a large proportion of all students that the student who does not pay the charges is an exception.

PART B
REGION AND STATE EDUCATION STATISTICS

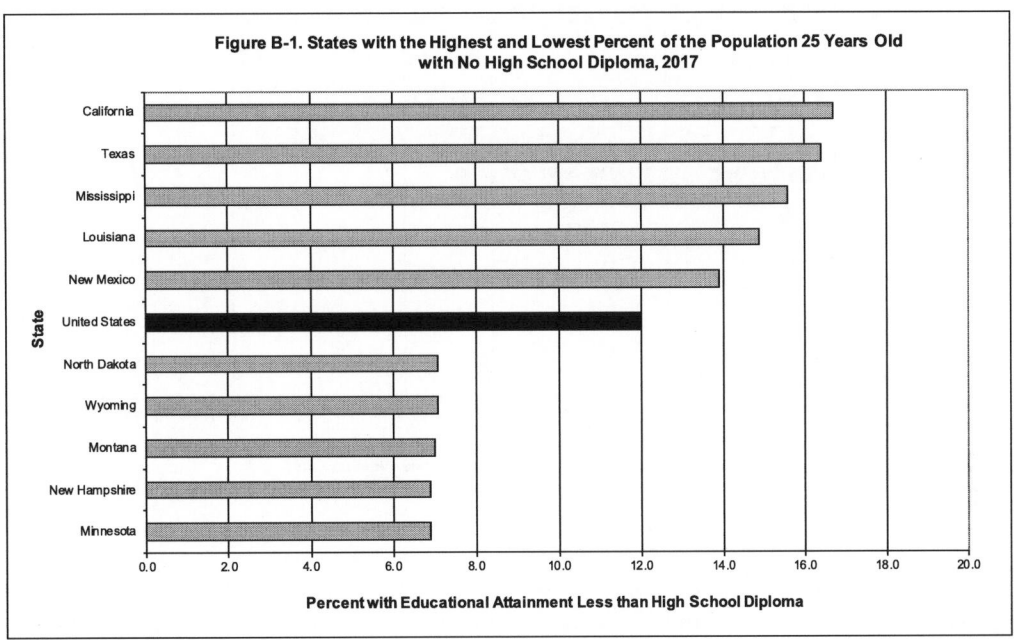

Figure B-1. States with the Highest and Lowest Percent of the Population 25 Years Old with No High School Diploma, 2017

In 2017, 88.0 percent of the U.S. population 25 years old and over had graduated from high school and/or a higher education establishment. The West region had the lowest average high-school attainment rate of 86.6 percent, followed by the South (86.9 percent), the Northeast (89.2 percent) and the Midwest (90.5 percent). All states had high-school attainment levels of more than 80 percent. California had the lowest level at 83.3 percent. Minnesota and New Hampshire had the highest high-school graduation rate of 93.1 percent. (Table B-2)

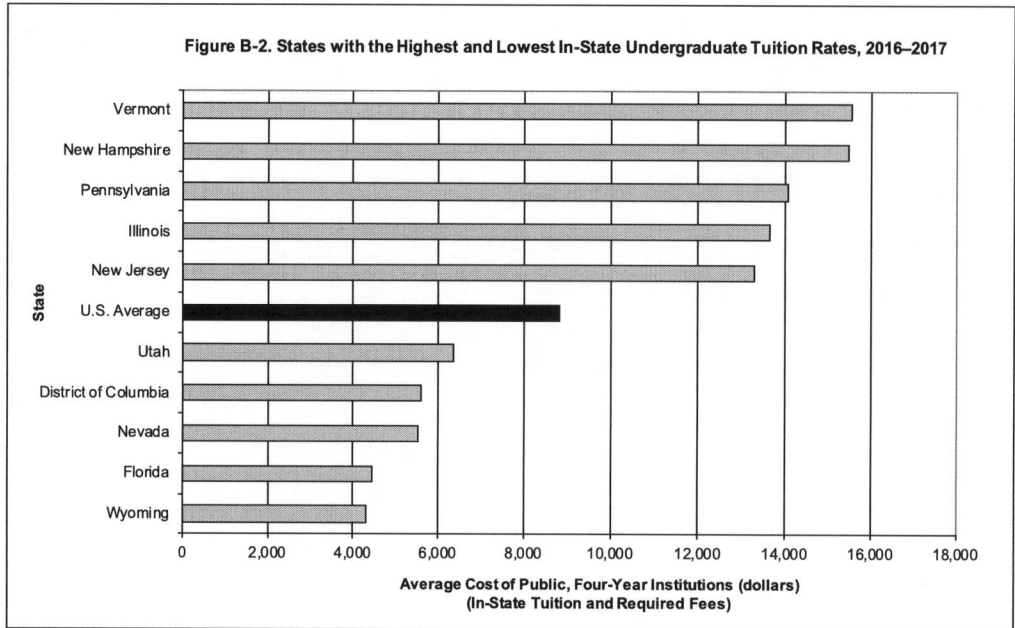

Figure B-2. States with the Highest and Lowest In-State Undergraduate Tuition Rates, 2016–2017

The average cost of in-state tuition and fees at public, 4-year colleges during the 2016-2017 school year was $8,804. Out-of-state tuition at public, 4-year colleges averaged $24,854, and the average tuition and fees at private, 4-year colleges was $29,478. Vermont was the state with the highest in-state tuition and fees ($15,537), and Wyoming was the state with the lowest average in-state tuition and fees ($4,311). Vermont had the most expensive out-of-state tuition and fees at a cost of $37,991 per year, which was $22,454 more than the average in-state tuition rate. The District of Columbia had the lowest out-of-state cost with a tuition rate of $11,756 for non-residents. Michigan had the greatest difference between in-state and out-of-state tuition, with its out-of-state tuition rate ($36,714) being $24,824 more than the in-state rate ($11,890). (Table B-15)

There are several ways to measure high school dropouts. "Event dropout rates" provide the state's estimate of students who have left their schools with no documented reason (for example, transfer, move, or illness). In 2016, 5.8 percent of the population 16 to 24 years old were estimated to have dropped out of school before graduation because they are no longer enrolled in school and not high school graduates. Of the states, North Dakota had the lowest percentage of these dropouts (2.7 percent) and Louisiana had the highest percentage (8.7 percent). (Table B-11)

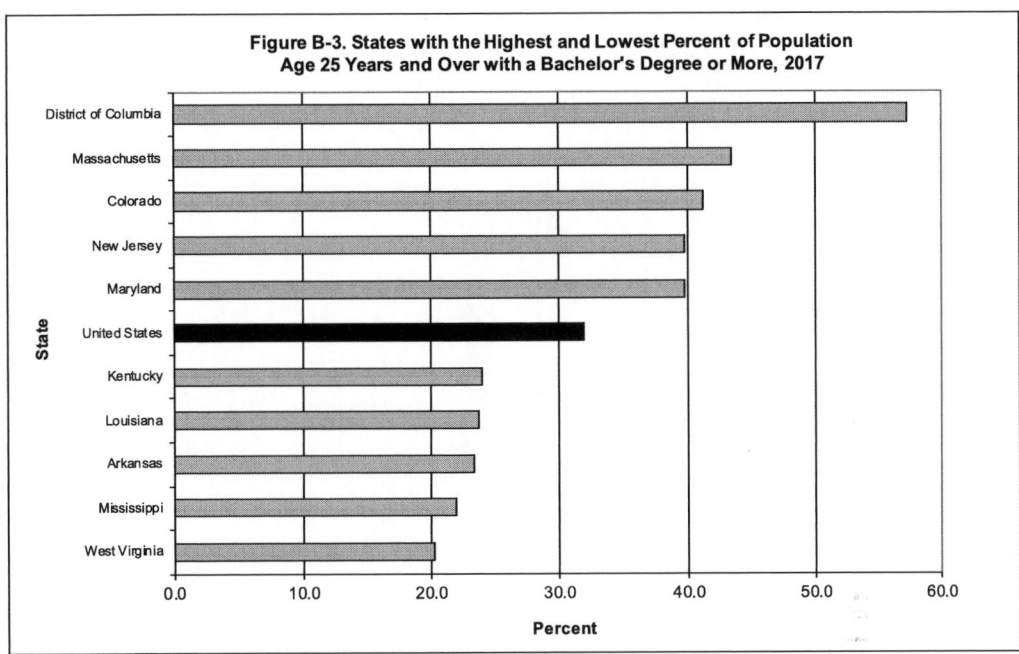

Figure B-3. States with the Highest and Lowest Percent of Population Age 25 Years and Over with a Bachelor's Degree or More, 2017

The proportion of the U.S. population with a bachelor's degree or more was 32.0 percent for the population age 25 and over in 2017. In the District of Columbia, 57.3 percent of residents held a bachelor's degree or more, the highest rate in the nation. Among the states, 12 had proportions of college graduates exceeding 35 percent. West Virginia had the lowest college attainment level of 20.2 percent. (Table B-2)

The Northeast region had the highest college attainment rate (36.5 percent), followed by the West (33.2 percent), the Midwest (30.6 percent), and the South (29.8 percent).

Among people age 25 years old and older, people who self-identified as Asian had the highest college attainment (53.8 percent), followed by White (33.4 percent), Black (21.4 percent), and Hispanic (16.0 percent) individuals. The District of Columbia had the highest percent of White and Asian individuals with bachelor's degrees or more. Vermont was the state with the highest percent of Black and Hispanic individuals with bachelor's degrees or more (37.1 percent and 46.2 percent, respectively). (Table B-2)

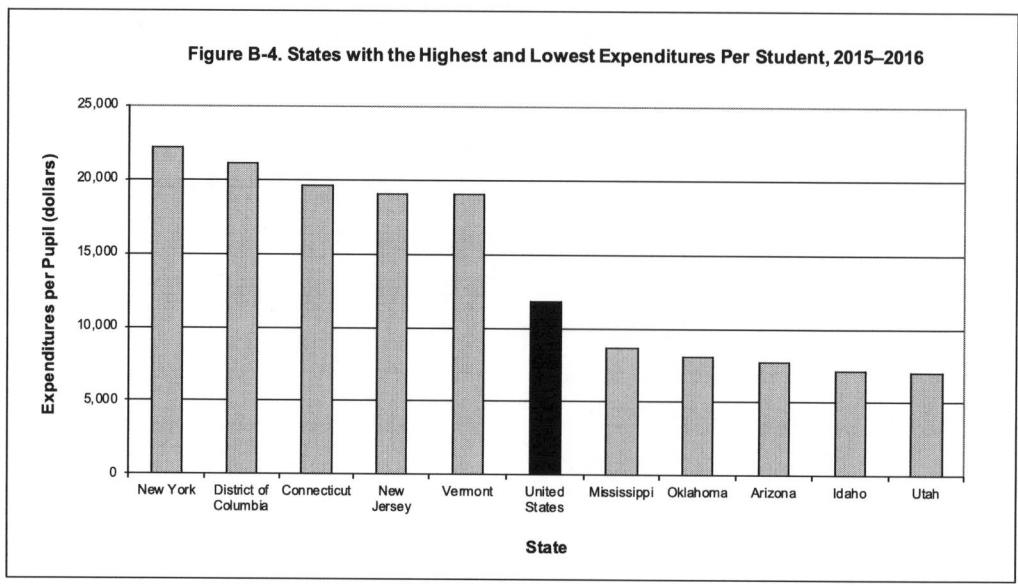

Figure B-4. States with the Highest and Lowest Expenditures Per Student, 2015–2016

Nationally, expenditures for 2015–2016 were 60.9 percent for instruction, 34.9 percent for support services, and 4.2 percent for non-instruction related expenses. New York had the highest proportion of instruction-related expenditures, with 70.9 percent of the state's total expenditures for elementary and secondary programs used for this purpose. Arizona had the lowest at 53.7 percent. The national average expenditure per student was $12,330 in 2015-2016. The state with the largest expenditure per student was New York, where the expenditure per pupil was $23,150 per student. Utah, the state with the smallest expenditure per student spent $7,296 per student. (Table B-10)

Schools can be divided into four locales: city, suburban, town, or rural. Nevada was the state with the most students in a city school in 2015–2016 (50.4 percent). New Jersey had the highest percent of students in suburban schools (79.7 percent), Wyoming had the largest percent of students attending schools located in towns (44.1 percent), and Vermont had the highest percent of students in rural schools (55.7 percent). (Table B-4)

Nationally, the student-teacher ratio was 16.0 in Fall 2015. California and Arizona exceeded an average of 23 students per teacher. North Dakota and Vermont had the lowest student-teacher ratios (11.8 and 10.5 students per teacher, respectively). (Table B-9)

During the 2015–2016 school year, 52.1 percent of students nationwide were eligible for free or reduced-price lunch. The District of Columbia had the highest percent of students eligible for free or reduced-price lunch (76.4 percent), followed by Mississippi (74.9 percent), and New Mexico (71.7 percent). The states with the most English language learner students were California (20.2 percent), Texas (17.2 percent), and Nevada (15.9 percent). (Table B-7)

Table B-1. Educational Attainment of the Population 18 Years and Over, by Region, Age, and Sex, 2017

(Number; percent.)

Characteristic	United States Number	United States Percent	Northeast Number	Northeast Percent	Midwest Number	Midwest Percent	South Number	South Percent	West Number	West Percent
Total...	252,070,495	100.0	44,723,331	100.0	52,663,682	100.0	95,147,033	100.0	59,536,449	100.0
18 to 24 years...	30,820,412	12.2	5,318,411	11.9	6,505,037	12.4	11,660,530	12.3	7,336,434	12.3
Less than 9th grade	427,514	1.4	71,625	1.3	83,739	1.3	184,374	1.6	87,776	1.2
9th to 12th grade, no diploma......................	3,491,623	11.3	523,267	9.8	727,192	11.2	1,442,499	12.4	798,665	10.9
High school graduate (includes equivalency)	9,772,204	31.7	1,540,794	29.0	2,035,077	31.3	3,830,475	32.8	2,365,858	32.2
Some college, no degree..............................	12,125,401	39.3	2,091,144	39.3	2,575,919	39.6	4,477,384	38.4	2,980,954	40.6
Associate's degree	1,630,242	5.3	256,250	4.8	349,273	5.4	634,363	5.4	390,356	5.3
Bachelor's degree..	3,132,559	10.2	763,147	14.3	683,785	10.5	1,015,744	8.7	669,883	9.1
Graduate or professional degree	240,869	0.8	72,184	1.4	50,052	0.8	75,691	0.6	42,942	0.6
25 to 34 years...	44,965,735	17.8	7,725,981	17.3	8,991,999	17.1	16,803,365	17.7	11,444,390	19.2
Less than 9th grade	1,260,205	2.8	196,469	2.5	207,217	2.3	516,346	3.1	340,173	3.0
9th to 12th grade, no diploma......................	2,821,519	6.3	395,398	5.1	484,204	5.4	1,191,675	7.1	750,242	6.6
High school graduate (includes equivalency)	10,819,034	24.1	1,738,046	22.5	2,100,861	23.4	4,374,383	26.0	2,605,744	22.8
Some college, no degree..............................	9,983,342	22.2	1,340,228	17.3	2,031,242	22.6	3,848,795	22.9	2,763,077	24.1
Associate's degree	4,071,987	9.1	642,953	8.3	926,686	10.3	1,513,088	9.0	989,260	8.6
Bachelor's degree..	11,121,057	24.7	2,231,530	28.9	2,288,678	25.5	3,739,339	22.3	2,861,510	25.0
Graduate or professional degree	4,888,591	10.9	1,181,357	15.3	953,111	10.6	1,619,739	9.6	1,134,384	9.9
35 to 44 years...	41,117,905	16.3	6,873,096	15.4	8,289,709	15.7	15,809,172	16.6	10,145,928	17.0
Less than 9th grade	1,923,095	4.7	269,588	3.9	259,791	3.1	745,561	4.7	648,155	6.4
9th to 12th grade, no diploma......................	2,839,471	6.9	383,403	5.6	474,450	5.7	1,231,156	7.8	750,462	7.4
High school graduate (includes equivalency)	9,700,245	23.6	1,640,413	23.9	1,962,891	23.7	3,965,806	25.1	2,131,135	21.0
Some college, no degree..............................	8,075,770	19.6	1,078,827	15.7	1,737,073	21.0	3,177,825	20.1	2,082,045	20.5
Associate's degree	3,830,614	9.3	598,541	8.7	910,402	11.0	1,453,056	9.2	868,615	8.6
Bachelor's degree..	8,898,332	21.6	1,630,933	23.7	1,813,434	21.9	3,191,103	20.2	2,262,862	22.3
Graduate or professional degree	5,850,378	14.2	1,271,391	18.5	1,131,668	13.7	2,044,665	12.9	1,402,654	13.8
45 to 64 years...	84,350,731	33.5	15,446,077	34.5	17,953,835	34.1	31,670,956	33.3	19,279,863	32.4
Less than 9th grade	4,153,706	4.9	616,637	4.0	519,159	2.9	1,551,195	4.9	1,466,715	7.6
9th to 12th grade, no diploma......................	5,674,190	6.7	911,104	5.9	1,034,948	5.8	2,418,405	7.6	1,309,733	6.8
High school graduate (includes equivalency)	23,693,642	28.1	4,629,312	30.0	5,484,594	30.5	9,253,047	29.2	4,326,689	22.4
Some college, no degree..............................	17,150,418	20.3	2,483,793	16.1	3,839,177	21.4	6,482,956	20.5	4,344,492	22.5
Associate's degree	7,707,075	9.1	1,439,839	9.3	1,821,998	10.1	2,751,549	8.7	1,693,689	8.8
Bachelor's degree..	15,865,356	18.8	3,106,581	20.1	3,270,595	18.2	5,706,048	18.0	3,782,132	19.6
Graduate or professional degree	10,106,344	12.0	2,258,811	14.6	1,983,364	11.0	3,507,756	11.1	2,356,413	12.2
65 years and over	50,815,712	20.2	9,359,766	20.9	10,923,102	20.7	19,203,010	20.2	11,329,834	19.0
Less than 9th grade	3,930,052	7.7	740,976	7.9	567,201	5.2	1,593,525	8.3	1,028,350	9.1
9th to 12th grade, no diploma......................	3,979,973	7.8	755,657	8.1	825,510	7.6	1,705,351	8.9	693,455	6.1
High school graduate (includes equivalency)	15,818,624	31.1	3,215,405	34.4	4,005,659	36.7	5,949,706	31.0	2,647,854	23.4
Some college, no degree..............................	9,900,123	19.5	1,371,494	14.7	2,199,190	20.1	3,751,651	19.5	2,577,788	22.8
Associate's degree	3,151,083	6.2	559,265	6.0	630,201	5.8	1,131,005	5.9	830,612	7.3
Bachelor's degree..	7,700,283	15.2	1,369,632	14.6	1,500,476	13.7	2,822,938	14.7	2,007,237	17.7
Graduate or professional degree	6,335,574	12.5	1,347,337	14.4	1,194,865	10.9	2,248,834	11.7	1,544,538	13.6
Male	122,729,360	48.7	21,520,099	48.1	25,715,281	48.8	46,036,758	48.4	29,457,222	49.5
18 to 24 years...	15,827,557	12.9	2,695,135	12.5	3,333,287	13.0	5,997,526	13.0	3,801,609	12.9
Less than 9th grade	256,186	1.6	44,306	1.6	45,361	1.4	111,404	1.9	55,115	1.4
9th to 12th grade, no diploma......................	2,037,693	12.9	306,116	11.4	424,132	12.7	838,473	14.0	468,972	12.3
High school graduate (includes equivalency)	5,514,948	34.8	855,908	31.8	1,145,593	34.4	2,178,309	36.3	1,335,138	35.1
Some college, no degree..............................	5,875,382	37.1	1,008,542	37.4	1,250,720	37.5	2,136,876	35.6	1,479,244	38.9
Associate's degree	727,060	4.6	124,460	4.6	157,956	4.7	278,145	4.6	166,499	4.4
Bachelor's degree..	1,319,109	8.3	327,433	12.1	287,548	8.6	425,016	7.1	279,112	7.3
Graduate or professional degree	97,179	0.6	28,370	1.1	21,977	0.7	29,303	0.5	17,529	0.5
25 to 34 years...	22,744,325	18.5	3,886,729	18.1	4,557,487	17.7	8,405,541	18.3	5,894,568	20.0
Less than 9th grade	723,506	3.2	112,791	2.9	115,313	2.5	304,314	3.6	191,088	3.2
9th to 12th grade, no diploma......................	1,643,052	7.2	227,696	5.9	286,823	6.3	689,231	8.2	439,302	7.5
High school graduate (includes equivalency)	6,267,885	27.6	1,018,947	26.2	1,226,144	26.9	2,524,527	30.0	1,498,267	25.4
Some college, no degree..............................	5,071,147	22.3	687,800	17.7	1,037,611	22.8	1,895,951	22.6	1,449,785	24.6
Associate's degree	1,844,839	8.1	305,833	7.9	420,539	9.2	651,245	7.7	467,222	7.9
Bachelor's degree..	5,165,125	22.7	1,059,875	27.3	1,073,624	23.6	1,680,894	20.0	1,350,732	22.9
Graduate or professional degree	2,028,771	8.9	473,787	12.2	397,433	8.7	659,379	7.8	498,172	8.5
35 to 44 years...	20,471,735	16.7	3,396,397	15.8	4,149,527	16.1	7,801,724	16.9	5,124,087	17.4
Less than 9th grade	1,040,662	5.1	145,199	4.3	138,487	3.3	417,020	5.3	339,956	6.6
9th to 12th grade, no diploma......................	1,600,666	7.8	210,792	6.2	269,958	6.5	700,664	9.0	419,252	8.2
High school graduate (includes equivalency)	5,484,998	26.8	927,956	27.3	1,138,211	27.4	2,231,797	28.6	1,187,034	23.2
Some college, no degree..............................	4,048,105	19.8	548,369	16.1	898,227	21.6	1,542,437	19.8	1,059,072	20.7
Associate's degree	1,674,333	8.2	263,651	7.8	398,803	9.6	608,862	7.8	403,017	7.9
Bachelor's degree..	4,098,085	20.0	759,520	22.4	833,691	20.1	1,433,792	18.4	1,071,082	20.9
Graduate or professional degree	2,524,886	12.3	540,910	15.9	472,150	11.4	867,152	11.1	644,674	12.6

Table B-1. Educational Attainment of the Population 18 Years and Over, by Region, Age, and Sex, 2017—*Continued*

(Number; percent.)

Characteristic	United States Number	Percent	Northeast Number	Percent	Midwest Number	Percent	South Number	Percent	West Number	Percent
45 to 64 years	41,165,294	33.5	7,488,448	34.8	8,836,569	34.4	15,333,964	33.3	9,506,313	32.3
Less than 9th grade	2,132,675	5.2	310,953	4.2	276,135	3.1	825,554	5.4	720,033	7.6
9th to 12th grade, no diploma	3,110,624	7.6	500,113	6.7	573,127	6.5	1,332,700	8.7	704,684	7.4
High school graduate (includes equivalency)	12,276,005	29.8	2,403,758	32.1	2,889,850	32.7	4,741,241	30.9	2,241,156	23.6
Some college, no degree	8,153,061	19.8	1,190,392	15.9	1,837,786	20.8	3,014,273	19.7	2,110,610	22.2
Associate's degree	3,204,920	7.8	580,631	7.8	767,648	8.7	1,119,219	7.3	737,422	7.8
Bachelor's degree	7,446,535	18.1	1,450,523	19.4	1,543,678	17.5	2,635,150	17.2	1,817,184	19.1
Graduate or professional degree	4,841,474	11.8	1,052,078	14.0	948,345	10.7	1,665,827	10.9	1,175,224	12.4
65 years and over	22,520,449	18.3	4,053,390	18.8	4,838,411	18.8	8,498,003	18.5	5,130,645	17.4
Less than 9th grade	1,680,126	7.5	298,849	7.4	255,531	5.3	712,617	8.4	413,129	8.1
9th to 12th grade, no diploma	1,639,486	7.3	320,281	7.9	349,569	7.2	686,934	8.1	282,702	5.5
High school graduate (includes equivalency)	6,119,537	27.2	1,212,444	29.9	1,581,758	32.7	2,289,284	26.9	1,036,051	20.2
Some college, no degree	4,322,076	19.2	606,257	15.0	972,134	20.1	1,624,520	19.1	1,119,165	21.8
Associate's degree	1,354,837	6.0	229,049	5.7	271,246	5.6	483,579	5.7	370,963	7.2
Bachelor's degree	3,908,741	17.4	679,774	16.8	750,352	15.5	1,457,441	17.2	1,021,174	19.9
Graduate or professional degree	3,495,646	15.5	706,736	17.4	657,821	13.6	1,243,628	14.6	887,461	17.3
Female	129,341,135	51.3	23,203,232	51.9	26,948,401	51.2	49,110,275	51.6	30,079,227	50.5
18 to 24 years	14,992,855	11.6	2,623,276	11.3	3,171,750	11.8	5,663,004	11.5	3,534,825	11.8
Less than 9th grade	171,328	1.1	27,319	1.0	38,378	1.2	72,970	1.3	32,661	0.9
9th to 12th grade, no diploma	1,453,930	9.7	217,151	8.3	303,060	9.6	604,026	10.7	329,693	9.3
High school graduate (includes equivalency)	4,257,256	28.4	684,886	26.1	889,484	28.0	1,652,166	29.2	1,030,720	29.2
Some college, no degree	6,250,019	41.7	1,082,602	41.3	1,325,199	41.8	2,340,508	41.3	1,501,710	42.5
Associate's degree	903,182	6.0	131,790	5.0	191,317	6.0	356,218	6.3	223,857	6.3
Bachelor's degree	1,813,450	12.1	435,714	16.6	396,237	12.5	590,728	10.4	390,771	11.1
Graduate or professional degree	143,690	1.0	43,814	1.7	28,075	0.9	46,388	0.8	25,413	0.7
25 to 34 years	22,221,410	17.2	3,839,252	16.5	4,434,512	16.5	8,397,824	17.1	5,549,822	18.5
Less than 9th grade	536,699	2.4	83,678	2.2	91,904	2.1	212,032	2.5	149,085	2.7
9th to 12th grade, no diploma	1,178,467	5.3	167,702	4.4	197,381	4.5	502,444	6.0	310,940	5.6
High school graduate (includes equivalency)	4,551,149	20.5	719,099	18.7	874,717	19.7	1,849,856	22.0	1,107,477	20.0
Some college, no degree	4,912,195	22.1	652,428	17.0	993,631	22.4	1,952,844	23.3	1,313,292	23.7
Associate's degree	2,227,148	10.0	337,120	8.8	506,147	11.4	861,843	10.3	522,038	9.4
Bachelor's degree	5,955,932	26.8	1,171,655	30.5	1,215,054	27.4	2,058,445	24.5	1,510,778	27.2
Graduate or professional degree	2,859,820	12.9	707,570	18.4	555,678	12.5	960,360	11.4	636,212	11.5
35 to 44 years	20,646,170	16.0	3,476,699	15.0	4,140,182	15.4	8,007,448	16.3	5,021,841	16.7
Less than 9th grade	882,433	4.3	124,389	3.6	121,304	2.9	328,541	4.1	308,199	6.1
9th to 12th grade, no diploma	1,238,805	6.0	172,611	5.0	204,492	4.9	530,492	6.6	331,210	6.6
High school graduate (includes equivalency)	4,215,247	20.4	712,457	20.5	824,680	19.9	1,734,009	21.7	944,101	18.8
Some college, no degree	4,027,665	19.5	530,458	15.3	838,846	20.3	1,635,388	20.4	1,022,973	20.4
Associate's degree	2,156,281	10.4	334,890	9.6	511,599	12.4	844,194	10.5	465,598	9.3
Bachelor's degree	4,800,247	23.3	871,413	25.1	979,743	23.7	1,757,311	21.9	1,191,780	23.7
Graduate or professional degree	3,325,492	16.1	730,481	21.0	659,518	15.9	1,177,513	14.7	757,980	15.1
45 to 64 years	43,185,437	33.4	7,957,629	34.3	9,117,266	33.8	16,336,992	33.3	9,773,550	32.5
Less than 9th grade	2,021,031	4.7	305,684	3.8	243,024	2.7	725,641	4.4	746,682	7.6
9th to 12th grade, no diploma	2,563,566	5.9	410,991	5.2	461,821	5.1	1,085,705	6.6	605,049	6.2
High school graduate (includes equivalency)	11,417,637	26.4	2,225,554	28.0	2,594,744	28.5	4,511,806	27.6	2,085,533	21.3
Some college, no degree	8,997,357	20.8	1,293,401	16.3	2,001,391	22.0	3,468,683	21.2	2,233,882	22.9
Associate's degree	4,502,155	10.4	859,208	10.8	1,054,350	11.6	1,632,330	10.0	956,267	9.8
Bachelor's degree	8,418,821	19.5	1,656,058	20.8	1,726,917	18.9	3,070,898	18.8	1,964,948	20.1
Graduate or professional degree	5,264,870	12.2	1,206,733	15.2	1,035,019	11.4	1,841,929	11.3	1,181,189	12.1
65 years and over	28,295,263	21.9	5,306,376	22.9	6,084,691	22.6	10,705,007	21.8	6,199,189	20.6
Less than 9th grade	2,249,926	8.0	442,127	8.3	311,670	5.1	880,908	8.2	615,221	9.9
9th to 12th grade, no diploma	2,340,487	8.3	435,376	8.2	475,941	7.8	1,018,417	9.5	410,753	6.6
High school graduate (includes equivalency)	9,699,087	34.3	2,002,961	37.7	2,423,901	39.8	3,660,422	34.2	1,611,803	26.0
Some college, no degree	5,578,047	19.7	765,237	14.4	1,227,056	20.2	2,127,131	19.9	1,458,623	23.5
Associate's degree	1,796,246	6.3	330,216	6.2	358,955	5.9	647,426	6.0	459,649	7.4
Bachelor's degree	3,791,542	13.4	689,858	13.0	750,124	12.3	1,365,497	12.8	986,063	15.9
Graduate or professional degree	2,839,928	10.0	640,601	12.1	537,044	8.8	1,005,206	9.4	657,077	10.6

Table B-2. Educational Attainment of the Population 25 Years Old and Over, by Sex, Race, Hispanic Origin, and Region or State, 2017

(Number; percent.)

Region or State	Population	Less than 9th grade	9th to 12th grade, no diploma	High school graduate (includes equivalency)	Some college, no degree	Associate degree	Bachelor's degree	Graduate or professional degree	High school graduate or higher (percent)	Bachelor's degree or higher (percent)
United States..........	221,250,083	11,267,058	15,315,153	60,031,545	45,109,653	18,760,759	43,585,028	27,180,887	88.0	32.0
Northeast Region.........	39,404,920	1,823,670	2,445,562	11,223,176	6,274,342	3,240,598	8,338,676	6,058,896	89.2	36.5
Midwest Region............	46,158,645	1,553,368	2,819,112	13,554,005	9,806,682	4,289,287	8,873,183	5,263,008	90.5	30.6
South Region...............	83,486,503	4,406,627	6,546,587	23,542,942	17,261,227	6,848,698	15,459,428	9,420,994	86.9	29.8
West Region.................	52,200,015	3,483,393	3,503,892	11,711,422	11,767,402	4,382,176	10,913,741	6,437,989	86.6	33.2
Alabama......................	3,309,607	137,386	309,557	1,029,982	709,100	278,878	528,019	316,685	86.5	25.5
Alaska........................	481,561	14,246	25,790	133,132	126,985	42,724	86,444	52,240	91.7	28.8
Arizona.......................	4,711,362	254,700	350,198	1,136,493	1,178,809	408,070	863,062	520,030	87.2	29.4
Arkansas.....................	2,008,398	92,735	174,807	683,285	443,935	143,522	301,294	168,820	86.7	23.4
California....................	26,679,273	2,459,993	1,989,309	5,541,182	5,641,881	2,070,661	5,616,449	3,359,798	83.3	33.6
Colorado.....................	3,822,068	129,351	190,285	815,595	798,831	313,309	994,894	579,803	91.6	41.2
Connecticut.................	2,493,854	102,064	137,225	676,911	411,854	201,193	533,791	430,816	90.4	38.7
Delaware.....................	673,686	23,460	40,091	218,309	127,966	51,777	121,442	90,641	90.6	31.5
District of Columbia	494,614	21,119	27,212	85,033	62,009	15,722	118,172	165,347	90.2	57.3
Florida........................	15,020,177	710,891	1,035,042	4,330,040	2,982,278	1,507,434	2,839,500	1,614,992	88.4	29.7
Georgia.......................	6,896,026	313,025	580,411	1,936,501	1,394,047	540,564	1,311,611	819,867	87.0	30.9
Hawaii.........................	997,744	34,495	42,636	280,494	204,452	106,987	216,993	111,687	92.3	32.9
Idaho..........................	1,111,788	36,681	65,058	313,029	291,857	107,505	202,800	94,858	90.8	26.8
Illinois........................	8,707,057	424,494	525,386	2,272,174	1,794,526	692,672	1,829,903	1,167,902	89.1	34.4
Indiana........................	4,435,317	161,138	343,724	1,450,767	896,138	394,092	753,268	436,190	88.6	26.8
Iowa...........................	2,093,909	65,578	100,027	639,230	440,516	242,738	406,630	199,190	92.1	28.9
Kansas........................	1,904,528	66,505	104,758	490,769	432,206	167,548	403,542	239,200	91.0	33.7
Kentucky.....................	3,018,953	164,235	248,251	997,060	644,270	241,585	423,916	299,636	86.3	24.0
Louisiana	3,120,277	152,771	311,048	1,061,526	666,998	185,409	482,439	260,086	85.1	23.8
Maine.........................	971,740	25,574	49,213	300,716	184,416	100,214	193,860	117,747	92.3	32.1
Maryland.....................	4,167,604	165,505	254,504	1,020,828	788,808	285,379	889,090	763,490	89.9	39.7
Massachusetts..............	4,788,573	207,140	235,318	1,163,526	743,218	360,700	1,146,586	932,085	90.8	43.4
Michigan	6,819,310	192,884	427,082	1,969,839	1,594,025	649,916	1,201,375	784,189	90.9	29.1
Minnesota...................	3,778,416	114,437	147,197	938,908	788,988	426,760	888,880	473,246	93.1	36.1
Mississippi..................	1,959,341	94,490	211,478	595,611	431,185	198,080	265,220	163,277	84.4	21.9
Missouri......................	4,150,275	129,072	298,467	1,277,505	912,962	326,430	743,797	462,042	89.7	29.1
Montana......................	723,666	16,155	34,574	203,141	170,207	65,772	157,326	76,491	93.0	32.3
Nebraska.....................	1,259,254	48,755	60,668	331,081	291,423	128,547	263,330	135,450	91.3	31.7
Nevada........................	2,063,180	107,354	165,663	592,846	518,529	165,508	340,110	173,170	86.8	24.9
New Hampshire.............	958,005	18,164	48,396	268,564	171,011	97,978	216,750	137,142	93.1	36.9
New Jersey	6,234,538	298,109	330,076	1,696,858	1,014,640	418,148	1,506,899	969,808	89.9	39.7
New Mexico	1,391,475	80,805	112,760	370,599	333,280	117,531	211,995	164,505	86.1	27.1
New York.....................	13,821,132	842,286	1,012,659	3,634,065	2,133,828	1,218,132	2,794,920	2,185,242	86.6	36.0
North Carolina..............	6,991,185	314,734	539,055	1,800,555	1,487,938	658,224	1,406,739	783,940	87.8	31.3
North Dakota................	495,904	13,936	21,087	130,900	111,306	66,236	108,045	44,394	92.9	30.7
Ohio...........................	7,981,885	218,232	559,456	2,661,209	1,612,818	698,820	1,381,934	849,416	90.3	28.0
Oklahoma....................	2,586,414	104,975	204,039	804,245	603,902	208,717	437,243	223,293	88.1	25.5
Oregon........................	2,901,195	102,453	159,928	673,810	730,804	255,783	609,160	369,257	91.0	33.7
Pennsylvania................	8,960,842	283,386	560,910	3,134,497	1,416,816	747,997	1,697,397	1,119,839	90.6	31.4
Rhode Island................	736,969	37,301	48,991	220,613	124,664	58,876	149,699	96,825	88.3	33.5
South Carolina	3,443,851	139,309	295,539	1,016,072	698,438	330,153	607,024	357,316	87.4	28.0
South Dakota	574,559	16,831	30,795	176,709	126,282	62,204	109,803	51,935	91.7	28.1
Tennessee	4,588,453	200,536	359,348	1,488,080	953,734	332,593	790,840	463,322	87.8	27.3
Texas..........................	18,149,346	1,473,004	1,496,019	4,552,676	3,932,201	1,323,957	3,510,311	1,861,178	83.6	29.6
Utah...........................	1,827,035	50,122	93,413	408,078	469,981	172,999	416,804	215,638	92.1	34.6
Vermont......................	439,267	9,646	22,774	127,426	73,895	37,360	98,774	69,392	92.6	38.3
Virginia.......................	5,779,221	240,260	353,117	1,396,487	1,095,931	456,210	1,270,190	967,026	89.7	38.7
Washington..................	5,101,968	189,334	254,629	1,128,284	1,203,615	514,987	1,130,392	680,727	91.3	35.5
West Virginia................	1,279,350	58,192	107,069	526,652	238,487	90,494	156,378	102,078	87.1	20.2
Wisconsin....................	3,958,231	101,506	200,465	1,214,914	805,492	433,324	782,676	419,854	92.4	30.4
Wyoming	387,700	7,704	19,649	114,739	98,171	40,340	67,312	39,785	92.9	27.6

Table B-2. Educational Attainment of the Population 25 Years Old and Over, by Sex, Race, Hispanic Origin, and Region or State, 2017—*Continued*

(Number; percent.)

Region or State	Population	Less than 9th grade	9th to 12th grade, no diploma	High school graduate (includes equivalency)	Some college, no degree	Associate degree	Bachelor's degree	Graduate or professional degree	High school graduate or higher (percent)	Bachelor's degree or higher (percent)
				Male, age 25 years and over						
United States	106,901,803	5,576,969	7,993,828	30,148,425	21,594,389	8,078,929	20,618,486	12,890,777	87.3	31.3
Northeast Region	18,824,964	867,792	1,258,882	5,563,105	3,032,818	1,379,164	3,949,692	2,773,511	88.7	35.7
Midwest Region	22,381,994	785,466	1,479,477	6,835,963	4,745,758	1,858,236	4,201,345	2,475,749	89.9	29.8
South Region	40,039,232	2,259,505	3,409,529	11,786,849	8,077,181	2,862,905	7,207,277	4,435,986	85.8	29.1
West Region	25,655,613	1,664,206	1,845,940	5,962,508	5,738,632	1,978,624	5,260,172	3,205,531	86.3	33.0
Alabama	1,565,244	71,748	155,237	509,811	327,801	111,785	242,582	146,280	85.5	24.8
Alaska	250,605	6,031	14,647	80,671	65,565	20,307	39,090	24,294	91.7	25.3
Arizona	2,306,351	132,383	182,307	564,349	560,568	185,702	421,514	259,528	86.4	29.5
Arkansas	968,413	49,256	90,762	354,410	202,599	54,286	141,893	75,207	85.5	22.4
California	13,058,109	1,150,285	1,044,728	2,804,668	2,766,398	929,539	2,693,031	1,669,460	83.2	33.4
Colorado	1,898,797	66,752	99,503	425,029	396,421	140,223	484,314	286,555	91.2	40.6
Connecticut	1,190,675	52,642	71,929	340,717	192,063	82,023	253,151	198,150	89.5	37.9
Delaware	319,385	12,354	22,988	107,629	59,235	18,515	58,029	40,635	88.9	30.9
District of Columbia	232,163	11,119	12,718	39,518	27,278	6,772	55,931	78,827	89.7	58.0
Florida	7,204,003	356,399	529,274	2,117,800	1,424,389	640,108	1,335,158	800,875	87.7	29.7
Georgia	3,272,064	162,047	304,175	968,901	640,019	219,179	614,256	363,487	85.8	29.9
Hawaii	490,056	12,871	21,514	141,943	107,102	51,643	100,525	54,458	93.0	31.6
Idaho	548,879	18,879	36,376	159,834	136,704	48,436	97,903	50,747	89.9	27.1
Illinois	4,203,875	208,726	280,398	1,120,023	871,338	305,166	876,478	541,746	88.4	33.7
Indiana	2,138,329	83,021	177,700	723,346	431,223	166,188	352,009	204,842	87.8	26.0
Iowa	1,021,693	32,926	54,399	330,875	213,202	177,609	189,790	92,892	91.5	27.7
Kansas	932,690	35,258	55,807	250,641	211,004	72,097	193,207	114,676	90.2	33.0
Kentucky	1,452,947	85,926	132,170	510,675	298,263	94,440	203,082	128,391	85.0	22.8
Louisiana	1,486,544	81,791	165,577	528,014	311,150	75,731	211,189	113,092	83.4	21.8
Maine	467,767	14,996	29,250	152,120	91,567	43,543	85,562	50,729	90.5	29.1
Maryland	1,972,491	86,115	129,756	517,988	365,018	115,182	410,803	347,629	89.1	38.5
Massachusetts	2,281,288	93,928	121,768	593,543	351,818	144,696	541,895	433,640	90.5	42.8
Michigan	3,296,886	98,288	224,504	991,579	768,725	268,868	569,277	375,645	90.2	28.7
Minnesota	1,859,930	55,574	81,705	486,120	387,672	195,318	427,993	225,548	92.6	35.1
Mississippi	920,497	51,647	109,220	300,708	200,360	73,542	118,283	66,737	82.5	20.1
Missouri	1,993,985	65,630	153,634	649,276	427,276	138,593	347,259	212,317	89.0	28.1
Montana	359,169	9,473	18,356	108,584	82,918	29,236	73,383	37,219	92.3	30.8
Nebraska	619,219	24,447	32,147	171,892	137,440	65,322	122,835	65,136	90.9	30.4
Nevada	1,025,274	53,286	83,989	301,305	255,619	78,058	167,190	85,827	86.6	24.7
New Hampshire	467,449	10,292	25,237	143,036	82,895	40,664	101,959	63,366	92.4	35.4
New Jersey	2,980,708	140,261	166,181	817,276	500,580	173,839	707,327	475,244	89.7	39.7
New Mexico	677,505	39,828	59,400	191,417	159,290	51,753	99,627	76,190	85.4	26.0
New York	6,566,617	391,317	516,788	1,799,580	1,043,342	526,111	1,327,412	962,067	86.2	34.9
North Carolina	3,308,297	166,453	290,885	904,571	684,993	263,668	641,514	356,213	86.2	30.2
North Dakota	252,434	7,959	10,292	72,604	57,461	33,438	51,215	19,465	92.8	28.0
Ohio	3,831,440	111,943	280,185	1,319,887	783,006	280,577	658,148	397,694	89.8	27.6
Oklahoma	1,254,892	57,841	105,858	407,886	286,036	90,701	199,322	107,248	87.0	24.4
Oregon	1,417,459	52,951	86,806	347,265	345,144	118,563	291,360	175,370	90.1	32.9
Pennsylvania	4,308,022	141,466	288,956	1,534,639	681,593	327,177	817,555	516,636	90.0	31.0
Rhode Island	350,267	17,714	23,632	112,724	55,054	26,029	71,311	43,803	88.2	32.9
South Carolina	1,626,956	73,061	156,588	496,855	319,932	137,196	286,633	156,111	85.8	27.2
South Dakota	286,447	8,697	16,613	94,462	61,391	27,138	51,419	26,727	91.2	27.3
Tennessee	2,191,574	107,074	183,941	742,070	436,493	136,629	373,333	212,034	86.7	26.7
Texas	8,857,031	728,038	786,091	2,296,264	1,877,903	601,565	1,645,023	922,147	82.9	29.0
Utah	906,645	26,170	49,562	193,125	228,696	74,215	206,048	128,829	91.6	36.9
Vermont	212,171	5,176	15,141	69,470	33,906	15,082	43,520	29,876	90.4	34.6
Virginia	2,785,654	125,602	179,054	710,802	505,956	191,791	595,764	476,685	89.1	38.5
Washington	2,519,954	90,703	138,301	580,676	584,902	233,499	554,337	337,536	90.9	35.4
West Virginia	621,077	32,454	55,235	272,947	109,756	31,815	74,482	44,388	85.9	19.1
Wisconsin	1,945,066	52,997	112,093	625,258	396,020	197,922	361,715	199,061	91.5	28.8
Wyoming	196,810	4,594	10,451	63,642	49,305	17,450	31,850	19,518	92.4	26.1

Table B-2. Educational Attainment of the Population 25 Years Old and Over, by Sex, Race, Hispanic Origin, and Region or State, 2017—*Continued*

(Number; percent.)

Region or State	Population	Less than 9th grade	9th to 12th grade, no diploma	High school graduate (includes equivalency)	Some college, no degree	Associate degree	Bachelor's degree	Graduate or professional degree	High school graduate or higher (percent)	Bachelor's degree or higher (percent)
				Female, age 25 years and over						
United States............	114,348,280	5,690,089	7,321,325	29,883,120	23,515,264	10,681,830	22,966,542	14,290,110	88.6	32.6
Northeast Region...........	20,579,956	955,878	1,186,680	5,660,071	3,241,524	1,861,434	4,388,984	3,285,385	89.6	37.3
Midwest Region.............	23,776,651	767,902	1,339,635	6,718,042	5,060,924	2,431,051	4,671,838	2,787,259	91.1	31.4
South Region................	43,447,271	2,147,122	3,137,058	11,756,093	9,184,046	3,985,793	8,252,151	4,985,008	87.8	30.5
West Region..................	26,544,402	1,819,187	1,657,952	5,748,914	6,028,770	2,403,552	5,653,569	3,232,458	86.9	33.5
Alabama......................	1,744,363	65,638	154,320	520,171	381,299	167,093	285,437	170,405	87.4	26.1
Alaska	230,956	8,215	11,143	52,461	61,420	22,417	47,354	27,946	91.6	32.6
Arizona........................	2,405,011	122,317	167,891	572,144	618,241	222,368	441,548	260,502	87.9	29.2
Arkansas	1,039,985	43,479	84,045	328,875	241,336	89,236	159,401	93,613	87.7	24.3
California.....................	13,621,164	1,309,708	944,581	2,736,514	2,875,483	1,141,122	2,923,418	1,690,338	83.5	33.9
Colorado	1,923,271	62,599	90,782	390,566	402,410	173,086	510,580	293,248	92.0	41.8
Connecticut..................	1,303,179	49,422	65,296	336,194	219,791	119,170	280,640	232,666	91.2	39.4
Delaware	354,301	11,106	17,103	110,680	68,731	33,262	63,413	50,006	92.0	32.0
District of Columbia	262,451	10,000	14,494	45,515	34,731	8,950	62,241	86,520	90.7	56.7
Florida.........................	7,816,174	354,492	505,768	2,212,240	1,557,889	867,326	1,504,342	814,117	89.0	29.7
Georgia	3,623,962	150,978	276,236	967,600	754,028	321,385	697,355	456,380	88.2	31.8
Hawaii	507,688	21,624	21,122	138,551	97,350	55,344	116,468	57,229	91.6	34.2
Idaho..........................	562,909	17,802	28,682	153,195	155,153	59,069	104,897	44,111	91.7	26.5
Illinois.........................	4,503,182	215,768	244,988	1,152,151	923,188	387,506	953,425	626,156	89.8	35.1
Indiana........................	2,296,988	78,117	166,024	727,421	464,915	227,904	401,259	231,348	89.4	27.5
Iowa...........................	1,072,216	32,652	45,628	308,355	227,314	135,129	216,840	106,298	92.7	30.1
Kansas	971,838	31,247	48,951	240,128	221,202	95,451	210,335	124,524	91.7	34.5
Kentucky	1,566,006	78,309	116,081	486,385	346,007	147,145	220,834	171,245	87.6	25.0
Louisiana	1,633,733	70,980	145,471	533,512	355,848	109,678	271,250	146,994	86.8	25.6
Maine..........................	503,973	10,578	19,963	148,596	92,849	56,671	108,298	67,018	93.9	34.8
Maryland......................	2,195,113	79,390	124,748	502,840	423,790	170,197	478,287	415,861	90.7	40.7
Massachusetts..............	2,507,285	113,212	113,550	569,983	391,400	216,004	604,691	498,445	91.0	44.0
Michigan	3,522,424	94,596	202,578	978,260	825,300	381,048	632,098	408,544	91.6	29.5
Minnesota	1,918,486	58,863	65,492	452,788	401,316	231,442	460,887	247,698	93.5	36.9
Mississippi...................	1,038,844	42,843	102,258	294,903	230,825	124,538	146,937	96,540	86.0	23.4
Missouri......................	2,156,290	63,442	144,833	628,229	485,686	187,837	396,538	249,725	90.3	30.0
Montana......................	364,497	6,682	16,218	94,557	87,289	36,536	83,943	39,272	93.7	33.8
Nebraska.....................	640,035	24,308	28,521	159,189	153,983	63,225	140,495	70,314	91.7	32.9
Nevada........................	1,037,906	54,068	81,674	291,541	262,910	87,450	172,920	87,343	86.9	25.1
New Hampshire..............	490,556	7,872	23,159	125,528	88,116	57,314	114,791	73,776	93.7	38.4
New Jersey	3,253,830	157,848	163,895	879,582	514,060	244,309	799,572	494,564	90.1	39.8
New Mexico	713,970	40,977	53,360	179,182	173,990	65,778	112,368	88,315	86.8	28.1
New York......................	7,254,515	450,969	495,871	1,834,485	1,090,486	692,021	1,467,508	1,223,175	86.9	37.1
North Carolina..............	3,682,888	148,281	248,170	895,984	802,945	394,556	765,225	427,727	89.2	32.4
North Dakota.................	243,470	5,977	10,795	58,296	53,845	32,798	56,830	24,929	93.1	33.6
Ohio	4,150,445	106,289	279,271	1,341,322	829,812	418,243	723,786	451,722	90.7	28.3
Oklahoma....................	1,331,522	47,134	98,181	396,359	317,866	118,016	237,921	116,045	89.1	26.6
Oregon........................	1,483,736	49,502	73,122	326,545	385,660	137,220	317,800	193,887	91.7	34.5
Pennsylvania.................	4,652,820	141,920	271,954	1,599,858	735,223	420,820	879,842	603,203	91.1	31.9
Rhode Island.................	386,702	19,587	25,359	107,889	69,610	32,847	78,388	53,022	88.4	34.0
South Carolina	1,816,895	65,668	138,951	519,217	378,506	192,957	320,391	201,205	88.7	28.7
South Dakota	288,112	8,134	14,182	82,247	64,891	35,066	58,384	25,208	92.3	29.0
Tennessee	2,396,879	93,462	175,407	746,010	517,241	195,964	417,507	251,288	88.8	27.9
Texas..........................	9,292,315	744,966	709,928	2,256,412	2,054,298	722,392	1,865,288	939,031	84.3	30.2
Utah	920,390	23,952	43,851	214,953	241,285	98,784	210,756	86,809	92.6	32.3
Vermont	227,096	4,470	7,633	57,956	39,989	22,278	55,254	39,516	94.7	41.7
Virginia........................	2,993,567	114,658	174,063	685,685	589,975	264,419	674,426	490,341	90.4	38.9
Washington...................	2,582,014	98,631	116,328	547,608	618,713	281,488	576,055	343,191	91.7	35.6
West Virginia.................	658,273	25,738	51,834	253,705	128,731	58,679	81,896	57,690	88.2	21.2
Wisconsin	2,013,165	48,509	88,372	589,656	409,472	235,402	420,961	220,793	93.2	31.9
Wyoming	190,890	3,110	9,198	51,097	48,866	22,890	35,462	20,267	93.6	29.2

Table B-2. Educational Attainment of the Population 25 Years Old and Over, by Sex, Race, Hispanic Origin, and Region or State, 2017—*Continued*

(Number; percent.)

Region or State	Population	White alone, age 25 years and over					
		Less than a high school diploma	High school graduate (includes equivalency)	Some college or associate's degree	Bachelor's degree or higher	High school graduate or higher (percent)	Bachelor's degree or higher (percent)
United States.............	165,626,125	16,661,262	45,195,831	48,475,584	55,293,448	89.9	33.4
Northeast Region	29,609,840	2,442,263	8,534,743	7,238,290	11,394,544	91.8	38.5
Midwest Region	38,426,997	3,077,319	11,462,665	11,761,647	12,125,366	92.0	31.6
South Region	61,022,481	7,238,379	17,037,306	17,595,736	19,151,060	88.1	31.4
West Region....................	36,566,807	3,903,301	8,161,117	11,879,911	12,622,478	89.3	34.5
Alabama..........................	2,342,850	277,121	705,815	692,909	667,005	88.2	28.5
Alaska	334,466	15,809	85,266	117,933	115,458	95.3	34.5
Arizona...........................	3,800,035	424,760	899,917	1,307,602	1,167,756	88.8	30.7
Arkansas	1,600,041	180,782	549,855	470,295	399,109	88.7	24.9
California........................	16,205,852	2,235,946	3,323,946	4,994,698	5,651,262	86.2	34.9
Colorado	3,293,204	233,168	687,030	961,208	1,411,798	92.9	42.9
Connecticut....................	1,965,707	147,994	514,121	486,740	816,852	92.5	41.6
Delaware	486,639	43,790	152,325	130,916	159,608	91.0	32.8
District of Columbia	218,184	4,804	6,690	13,554	193,136	97.8	88.5
Florida............................	11,774,810	1,209,342	3,366,245	3,525,905	3,673,318	89.7	31.2
Georgia	4,251,758	482,843	1,157,813	1,181,111	1,429,991	88.6	33.6
Hawaii	270,276	8,537	53,722	88,537	119,219	96.7	44.1
Idaho..............................	1,021,668	82,508	289,351	370,190	279,619	91.9	27.4
Illinois	6,438,389	543,699	1,709,695	1,849,991	2,335,004	91.6	36.3
Indiana	3,822,117	400,098	1,272,929	1,110,479	1,038,611	89.5	27.2
Iowa...............................	1,935,933	132,438	600,999	637,296	565,200	93.2	29.2
Kansas	1,653,177	127,419	424,353	524,513	576,892	92.3	34.9
Kentucky	2,690,118	367,438	895,945	779,852	646,883	86.3	24.0
Louisiana	2,038,970	233,743	685,250	553,379	566,598	88.5	27.8
Maine..............................	932,606	68,781	290,725	272,650	300,450	92.6	32.2
Maryland.........................	2,403,782	181,492	571,136	591,773	1,059,381	92.4	44.1
Massachusetts	3,884,683	285,435	946,671	907,708	1,744,869	92.7	44.9
Michigan	5,525,976	436,177	1,616,597	1,816,368	1,656,834	92.1	30.0
Minnesota	3,263,895	153,189	824,851	1,070,061	1,215,794	95.3	37.2
Mississippi.....................	1,211,539	154,386	351,272	399,017	306,864	87.3	25.3
Missouri..........................	3,511,414	331,646	1,090,074	1,036,629	1,053,065	90.6	30.0
Montana..........................	658,190	41,472	184,928	211,680	220,110	93.7	33.4
Nebraska.........................	1,131,814	82,797	297,812	383,305	367,900	92.7	32.5
Nevada............................	1,395,786	147,773	400,627	478,180	369,206	89.4	26.5
New Hampshire...............	902,395	60,080	255,421	256,636	330,258	93.3	36.6
New Jersey	4,360,008	371,158	1,228,972	1,013,378	1,746,500	91.5	40.1
New Mexico	1,087,117	135,132	283,835	349,647	318,503	87.6	29.3
New York.........................	9,034,087	795,168	2,333,603	2,248,501	3,656,815	91.2	40.5
North Carolina................	5,024,276	521,598	1,242,257	1,550,099	1,710,322	89.6	34.0
North Dakota	441,932	28,065	117,387	159,140	137,340	93.6	31.1
Ohio	6,695,975	589,563	2,274,830	1,902,838	1,928,744	91.2	28.8
Oklahoma.......................	1,976,555	214,298	612,107	613,535	536,615	89.2	27.1
Oregon............................	2,526,224	199,389	596,681	874,242	855,912	92.1	33.9
Pennsylvania...................	7,482,827	619,475	2,656,740	1,785,550	2,421,062	91.7	32.4
Rhode Island..................	627,563	65,285	184,924	160,372	216,982	89.6	34.6
South Carolina	2,423,368	243,990	662,099	726,305	790,974	89.9	32.6
South Dakota	507,840	33,025	156,126	166,963	151,726	93.5	29.9
Tennessee	3,682,954	428,068	1,201,936	1,012,966	1,039,984	88.4	28.2
Texas..............................	13,642,801	2,189,376	3,416,382	3,967,837	4,069,206	84.0	29.8
Utah................................	1,600,310	91,685	348,293	584,039	576,293	94.3	36.0
Vermont..........................	419,964	28,887	123,566	106,755	160,756	93.1	38.3
Virginia...........................	4,045,095	348,637	959,515	1,077,360	1,659,583	91.4	41.0
Washington.....................	4,012,319	263,304	899,675	1,413,548	1,435,792	93.4	35.8
West Virginia..................	1,208,741	156,671	500,664	308,923	242,483	87.0	20.1
Wisconsin	3,498,535	219,203	1,077,012	1,104,064	1,098,256	93.7	31.4
Wyoming	361,360	23,557	107,846	128,407	101,550	93.5	28.1

Table B-2. Educational Attainment of the Population 25 Years Old and Over, by Sex, Race, Hispanic Origin, and Region or State, 2017—*Continued*

(Number; percent.)

Region or State	Population	Black or African American alone, age 25 years and over					
		Less than a high school diploma	High school graduate (includes equivalency)	Some college or associate's degree	Bachelor's degree or higher	High school graduate or higher (percent)	Bachelor's degree or higher (percent)
United States...............	26,472,921	3,742,027	8,386,809	8,687,482	5,656,603	85.9	21.4
Northeast Region.............	4,453,882	659,500	1,484,904	1,283,365	1,026,113	85.2	23.0
Midwest Region...............	4,415,512	634,999	1,371,840	1,589,222	819,451	85.6	18.6
South Region...................	15,218,867	2,203,974	4,928,477	4,876,093	3,210,323	85.5	21.1
West Region....................	2,384,660	243,554	601,588	938,802	600,716	89.8	25.2
Alabama.........................	833,006	140,459	289,457	262,726	140,364	83.1	16.9
Alaska............................	13,931	1,196	4,596	5,638	2,501	91.4	18.0
Arizona..........................	192,907	18,015	50,929	76,989	46,974	90.7	24.4
Arkansas........................	278,042	46,437	101,104	86,613	43,888	83.3	15.8
California........................	1,553,323	161,526	375,863	618,995	396,939	89.6	25.6
Colorado	146,066	13,195	42,665	49,019	41,187	91.0	28.2
Connecticut....................	245,862	32,747	91,548	72,696	48,871	86.7	19.9
Delaware........................	137,339	12,669	53,729	40,111	30,830	90.8	22.4
District of Columbia	217,915	29,348	72,512	57,888	58,167	86.5	26.7
Florida...........................	2,137,020	349,311	714,011	671,461	402,237	83.7	18.8
Georgia	2,079,786	287,095	657,556	649,970	485,165	86.2	23.3
Hawaii	15,653	802	2,923	6,470	5,458	94.9	34.9
Idaho.............................	6,498	637	2,068	2,204	1,589	90.2	24.5
Illinois...........................	1,168,603	154,916	338,129	429,491	246,067	86.7	21.1
Indiana..........................	383,579	56,883	126,779	126,211	73,706	85.2	19.2
Iowa..............................	57,195	8,299	17,167	20,471	11,258	85.5	19.7
Kansas...........................	101,011	13,593	30,321	36,852	20,245	86.5	20.0
Kentucky	224,307	25,808	78,347	77,530	42,622	88.5	19.0
Louisiana	935,496	193,996	339,351	265,697	136,452	79.3	14.6
Maine............................	8,870	1,671	2,192	2,896	2,111	81.2	23.8
Maryland........................	1,216,114	122,477	354,449	380,929	358,259	89.9	29.5
Massachusetts.................	337,720	49,530	99,013	101,740	87,437	85.3	25.9
Michigan	875,432	121,306	270,593	331,007	152,526	86.1	17.4
Minnesota......................	196,415	36,804	48,793	67,667	43,151	81.3	22.0
Mississippi......................	689,164	137,891	230,451	215,085	105,737	80.0	15.3
Missouri.........................	432,245	65,080	140,088	152,463	74,614	84.9	17.3
Montana.........................	3,105	321	669	1,573	542	89.7	17.5
Nebraska........................	53,583	7,603	16,524	19,827	9,629	85.8	18.0
Nevada..........................	175,821	19,284	54,818	69,250	32,469	89.0	18.5
New Hampshire................	13,572	1,823	4,888	3,338	3,523	86.6	26.0
New Jersey	802,713	102,805	265,545	236,185	198,178	87.2	24.7
New Mexico	27,850	3,240	5,925	12,430	6,255	88.4	22.5
New York........................	2,098,464	348,045	658,826	589,788	501,805	83.4	23.9
North Carolina.................	1,439,450	209,828	443,646	481,318	304,658	85.4	21.2
North Dakota...................	13,448	1,431	3,769	4,834	3,414	89.4	25.4
Ohio..............................	911,989	133,965	301,733	323,268	153,023	85.3	16.8
Oklahoma.......................	176,022	18,370	59,048	63,829	34,775	89.6	19.8
Oregon	49,421	5,722	11,662	17,765	14,272	88.4	28.9
Pennsylvania...................	904,357	115,452	347,274	267,102	174,529	87.2	19.3
Rhode Island...................	38,569	7,041	14,436	8,826	8,266	81.7	21.4
South Carolina	867,504	158,101	315,915	264,805	128,683	81.8	14.8
South Dakota	9,548	674	3,751	3,811	1,312	92.9	13.7
Tennessee	710,141	91,717	244,580	231,211	142,633	87.1	20.1
Texas............................	2,156,713	227,297	629,162	777,810	522,444	89.5	24.2
Utah	19,072	2,605	3,752	6,629	6,086	86.3	31.9
Vermont	3,755	386	1,182	794	1,393	89.7	37.1
Virginia..........................	1,074,928	148,588	325,607	334,416	266,317	86.2	24.8
Washington.....................	177,786	16,840	45,129	69,984	45,833	90.5	25.8
West Virginia...................	45,920	4,582	19,552	14,694	7,092	90.0	15.4
Wisconsin	212,464	34,445	74,193	73,320	30,506	83.8	14.4
Wyoming	...	...	...	...	...	...	...

... = Not available

Table B-2. Educational Attainment of the Population 25 Years Old and Over, by Sex, Race, Hispanic Origin, and Region or State, 2017—*Continued*

(Number; percent.)

Region or State	Population	Asian alone, age 25 years and over					
		Less than a high school diploma	High school graduate (includes equivalency)	Some college or associate's degree	Bachelor's degree or higher	High school graduate or higher (percent)	Bachelor's degree or higher (percent)
United States.............	12,886,236	1,681,683	1,932,148	2,333,566	6,938,839	86.9	53.8
Northeast Region...........	2,653,189	433,353	407,153	349,825	1,462,858	83.7	55.1
Midwest Region.............	1,447,629	179,711	196,066	224,417	847,435	87.6	58.5
South Region.................	2,928,919	355,021	417,678	492,080	1,664,140	87.9	56.8
West Region..................	5,856,499	713,598	911,251	1,267,244	2,964,406	87.8	50.6
Alabama........................	43,607	5,673	9,042	8,120	20,772	87.0	47.6
Alaska..........................	32,240	6,583	7,586	9,775	8,296	79.6	25.7
Arizona.........................	161,708	18,045	19,866	32,024	91,773	88.8	56.8
Arkansas.......................	30,297	6,261	4,165	5,175	14,696	79.3	48.5
California.......................	4,234,099	528,362	602,917	881,521	2,221,299	87.5	52.5
Colorado.......................	118,758	19,147	16,920	20,443	62,248	83.9	52.4
Connecticut...................	113,851	12,668	14,663	13,560	72,960	88.9	64.1
Delaware.......................	26,990	1,819	4,886	2,295	17,990	93.3	66.7
District of Columbia........	21,767	1,053	812	2,080	17,822	95.2	81.9
Florida..........................	421,720	56,641	67,332	83,401	214,346	86.6	50.8
Georgia.........................	281,696	37,345	49,732	42,724	151,895	86.7	53.9
Hawaii..........................	434,390	44,687	116,577	125,661	147,465	89.7	33.9
Idaho...........................	15,127	1,727	2,944	3,490	6,966	88.6	46.1
Illinois..........................	488,920	44,394	55,079	70,405	319,042	90.9	65.3
Indiana.........................	89,487	14,637	10,653	13,053	51,144	83.6	57.2
Iowa............................	49,562	10,645	7,832	10,091	20,994	78.5	42.4
Kansas.........................	57,486	7,690	10,196	10,704	28,896	86.6	50.3
Kentucky.......................	40,370	6,253	7,283	7,236	19,598	84.5	48.5
Louisiana......................	55,217	12,011	11,439	8,238	23,529	78.2	42.6
Maine...........................	9,790	1,583	2,594	1,194	4,419	83.8	45.1
Maryland.......................	280,663	26,648	35,046	45,221	173,748	90.5	61.9
Massachusetts...............	309,727	43,893	41,336	34,113	190,385	85.8	61.5
Michigan.......................	204,155	21,735	24,554	31,132	126,734	89.4	62.1
Minnesota.....................	167,233	32,090	28,170	32,800	74,173	80.8	44.4
Mississippi....................	18,444	3,566	3,915	4,485	6,478	80.7	35.1
Missouri........................	82,661	7,908	11,885	13,931	48,937	90.4	59.2
Montana........................	6,262	877	1,093	1,609	2,683	86.0	42.8
Nebraska.......................	28,432	6,387	4,432	3,332	14,281	77.5	50.2
Nevada.........................	193,401	17,133	42,675	56,162	77,431	91.1	40.0
New Hampshire..............	24,677	3,457	3,408	2,888	14,924	86.0	60.5
New Jersey....................	628,099	49,304	63,826	74,437	440,532	92.2	70.1
New Mexico...................	21,405	1,724	3,022	3,646	13,013	91.9	60.8
New York.......................	1,238,032	268,325	232,504	180,545	556,658	78.3	45.0
North Carolina...............	194,787	27,251	25,290	26,180	116,066	86.0	59.6
North Dakota.................	8,091	841	870	851	5,529	89.6	68.3
Ohio.............................	172,454	19,591	25,694	20,198	106,971	88.6	62.0
Oklahoma.....................	56,009	10,919	9,039	12,889	23,162	80.5	41.4
Oregon.........................	128,319	15,665	17,664	25,922	69,068	87.8	53.8
Pennsylvania.................	297,517	48,588	43,727	39,073	166,129	83.7	55.8
Rhode Island.................	24,590	3,261	3,922	3,287	14,120	86.7	57.4
South Carolina	53,449	7,258	9,997	9,365	26,829	86.4	50.2
South Dakota	6,312	569	1,637	1,251	2,855	91.0	45.2
Tennessee	82,433	10,402	12,874	11,636	47,521	87.4	57.6
Texas...........................	929,639	107,411	112,854	158,849	550,525	88.4	59.2
Utah	49,406	5,278	9,922	8,755	25,451	89.3	51.5
Vermont........................	6,906	2,274	1,173	728	2,731	67.1	39.5
Virginia.........................	382,715	33,188	52,327	63,119	234,081	91.3	61.2
Washington....................	458,135	54,213	69,504	97,432	236,986	88.2	51.7
West Virginia.................	9,116	1,322	1,645	1,067	5,082	85.5	55.7
Wisconsin	92,836	13,224	15,064	16,669	47,879	85.8	51.6
Wyoming	3,249	157	561	804	1,727	95	53

Table B-2. Educational Attainment of the Population 25 Years Old and Over, by Sex, Race, Hispanic Origin, and Region or State, 2017—*Continued*

(Number; percent.)

	Hispanic or Latino[1], age 25 years and over						
	Population	Less than a high school diploma	High school graduate (includes equivalency)	Some college or associate's degree	Bachelor's degree or higher	High school graduate or higher (percent)	Bachelor's degree or higher (percent)
United States............	33,474,043	10,478,009	9,411,822	8,223,621	5,360,591	68.7	16.0
Northeast Region	4,897,946	1,370,404	1,508,791	1,121,716	897,035	72.0	18.3
Midwest Region	2,813,704	908,584	817,827	661,532	425,761	67.7	15.1
South Region	12,653,773	3,833,714	3,518,633	3,026,044	2,275,382	69.7	18.0
West Region..................	13,108,620	4,365,307	3,566,571	3,414,329	1,762,413	66.7	13.4
Alabama	95,591	33,950	26,051	19,069	16,521	64.5	17.3
Alaska	26,452	2,942	5,482	12,209	5,819	88.9	22.0
Arizona........................	1,203,000	369,946	340,667	336,361	156,026	69.2	13.0
Arkansas	107,132	45,534	30,907	18,864	11,827	57.5	11.0
California......................	8,921,445	3,142,727	2,345,304	2,274,496	1,158,918	64.8	13.0
Colorado......................	670,114	178,880	206,337	177,275	107,622	73.3	16.1
Connecticut..................	330,633	93,981	108,620	75,050	52,982	71.6	16.0
Delaware	47,762	17,422	16,488	8,696	5,156	63.5	10.8
District of Columbia	48,455	15,761	6,050	5,520	21,124	67.5	43.6
Florida.........................	3,545,630	705,958	1,029,627	955,778	854,267	80.1	24.1
Georgia	520,525	203,559	137,589	92,137	87,240	60.9	16.8
Hawaii	76,514	7,388	24,916	28,677	15,533	90.3	20.3
Idaho...........................	104,078	35,679	30,376	27,745	10,278	65.7	9.9
Illinois.........................	1,234,633	419,537	364,088	274,837	176,171	66.0	14.3
Indiana........................	230,550	82,244	65,493	49,312	33,501	64.3	14.5
Iowa............................	88,561	33,013	26,259	17,642	11,647	62.7	13.2
Kansas	169,377	57,174	47,109	42,294	22,800	66.2	13.5
Kentucky	76,434	20,363	21,592	18,250	16,229	73.4	21.2
Louisiana	140,423	43,269	40,430	34,754	21,970	69.2	15.6
Maine	10,628	1,315	3,072	2,898	3,343	87.6	31.5
Maryland......................	345,734	122,404	81,361	67,220	74,749	64.6	21.6
Massachusetts	454,608	124,828	138,162	108,450	83,168	72.5	18.3
Michigan	259,188	70,637	74,045	70,196	44,310	72.7	17.1
Minnesota	146,906	49,911	37,454	34,866	24,675	66.0	16.8
Mississippi...................	42,000	13,533	12,350	8,602	7,515	67.8	17.9
Missouri.......................	128,571	34,377	35,365	33,158	25,671	73.3	20.0
Montana.......................	18,729	5,227	4,864	5,191	3,447	72.1	18.4
Nebraska......................	102,067	42,817	26,528	21,563	11,159	58.1	10.9
Nevada	483,686	163,851	155,636	114,166	50,033	66.1	10.3
New Hampshire.............	26,931	4,613	8,016	7,631	6,671	82.9	24.8
New Jersey	1,117,438	275,755	363,117	259,252	219,314	75.3	19.6
New Mexico	606,602	136,296	187,089	185,739	97,478	77.5	16.1
New York......................	2,365,690	714,499	678,001	535,912	437,278	69.8	18.5
North Carolina..............	476,705	190,812	115,596	98,539	71,758	60.0	15.1
North Dakota................	13,249	2,699	4,684	4,217	1,649	79.6	12.4
Ohio	227,001	52,742	72,235	60,128	41,896	76.8	18.5
Oklahoma.....................	197,987	71,654	58,876	44,203	23,254	63.8	11.7
Oregon.........................	277,055	88,051	70,223	72,982	45,799	68.2	16.5
Pennsylvania.................	497,044	134,238	169,533	113,443	79,830	73.0	16.1
Rhode Island.................	89,333	20,353	39,704	17,435	11,841	77.2	13.3
South Carolina	151,542	48,737	43,558	35,625	23,622	67.8	15.6
South Dakota	15,743	3,953	5,960	3,030	2,800	74.9	17.8
Tennessee	176,098	66,039	53,399	29,816	26,844	62.5	15.2
Texas...........................	6,230,377	2,105,928	1,735,689	1,487,596	901,164	66.2	14.5
Utah	215,503	64,395	66,320	53,822	30,966	70.1	14.4
Vermont.......................	5,641	822	566	1,645	2,608	85.4	46.2
Virginia........................	439,050	126,574	105,785	97,558	109,133	71.2	24.9
Washington...................	474,071	162,211	118,854	116,963	76,043	65.8	16.0
West Virginia.................	12,328	2,217	3,285	3,817	3,009	82.0	24.4
Wisconsin	197,858	59,480	58,607	50,289	29,482	69.9	14.9
Wyoming	31,371	7,714	10,503	8,703	4,451	75.4	14.2

[1]May be of any race.

Table B-3. Selected Characteristics of Children and the School-Age Population, by Region and State, 2017

(Number; dollars; percent.)

Region or State	Population			Median income for a family of four, (2016 inflation-adjusted dollars)	Poverty status	
	Total	5 to 17 years old	5 to 17 years old (percent)		Total children under 18 years old for whom poverty status is determined	Children under 18 years old in poverty (percent)
UNITED STATES.............................	325,719,178	53,853,524	16.5	$90,748	72,404,453	18.4
Northeast Region	56,470,581	8,608,716	15.2	$106,744	11,543,236	16.4
Midwest Region	68,179,351	11,362,810	16.7	$91,742	15,204,473	17.0
South Region	123,658,624	20,844,756	16.9	$81,836	28,083,648	20.8
West Region......................................	77,410,622	13,037,242	16.8	$92,272	17,573,096	17.1
Alabama..	4,874,747	805,164	16.5	$76,585	1,078,449	24.6
Alaska...	739,795	132,262	17.9	$97,465	179,806	14.8
Arizona..	7,016,270	1,197,687	17.1	$79,026	1,600,270	20.7
Arkansas...	3,004,279	521,793	17.4	$66,712	696,150	22.5
California...	39,536,653	6,596,961	16.7	$94,505	8,917,200	18.1
Colorado..	5,607,154	929,766	16.6	$102,233	1,240,167	12.0
Connecticut.......................................	3,588,184	560,084	15.6	$114,110	733,472	12.6
Delaware	961,939	149,406	15.5	$97,540	199,186	18.5
District of Columbia	693,972	79,533	11.5	$129,135	123,345	25.6
Florida...	20,984,400	3,071,458	14.6	$76,953	4,134,720	20.3
Georgia	10,429,379	1,859,542	17.8	$80,510	2,473,799	20.9
Hawaii...	1,427,538	216,424	15.2	$102,125	298,916	11.5
Idaho...	1,716,943	327,059	19.0	$72,381	437,797	15.3
Illinois...	12,802,023	2,127,742	16.6	$96,252	2,855,100	17.0
Indiana..	6,666,818	1,154,479	17.3	$85,368	1,537,250	18.3
Iowa..	3,145,711	531,727	16.9	$92,135	715,835	12.2
Kansas..	2,913,123	519,526	17.8	$83,114	698,794	14.8
Kentucky...	4,454,189	738,248	16.6	$77,069	991,662	22.4
Louisiana	4,684,333	803,029	17.1	$76,618	1,093,807	28.0
Maine..	1,335,907	189,812	14.2	$94,215	247,870	12.9
Maryland..	6,052,177	983,637	16.3	$115,771	1,332,136	12.0
Massachusetts...................................	6,859,819	1,010,248	14.7	$127,579	1,347,369	13.5
Michigan	9,962,311	1,603,491	16.1	$90,531	2,125,728	19.7
Minnesota..	5,576,606	943,922	16.9	$109,211	1,271,150	11.7
Mississippi..	2,984,100	532,086	17.8	$65,138	703,315	26.9
Missouri..	6,113,532	1,013,660	16.6	$83,609	1,352,564	18.6
Montana..	1,050,493	168,490	16.0	$92,646	223,522	14.7
Nebraska...	1,920,076	342,918	17.9	$91,136	465,209	14.1
Nevada..	2,998,039	499,902	16.7	$82,970	670,816	18.5
New Hampshire..................................	1,342,795	194,672	14.5	$113,991	252,034	10.2
New Jersey	9,005,644	1,458,435	16.2	$122,474	1,952,390	13.9
New Mexico	2,088,070	363,295	17.4	$67,924	479,624	27.2
New York	19,849,399	2,995,900	15.1	$99,943	4,072,194	19.6
North Carolina...................................	10,273,419	1,700,009	16.5	$82,994	2,270,261	21.1
North Dakota.....................................	755,393	120,334	15.9	$102,402	169,236	10.9
Ohio..	11,658,609	1,906,867	16.4	$87,321	2,552,429	20.1
Oklahoma..	3,930,864	698,922	17.8	$72,569	942,400	21.5
Oregon..	4,142,776	641,521	15.5	$88,440	855,053	16.4
Pennsylvania.....................................	12,805,537	1,959,953	15.3	$97,692	2,618,598	17.0
Rhode Island.....................................	1,059,639	151,953	14.3	$101,338	203,444	16.5
South Carolina	5,024,369	812,181	16.2	$75,646	1,082,717	22.6
South Dakota	869,666	152,768	17.6	$86,627	206,638	16.6
Tennessee	6,715,984	1,103,124	16.4	$77,260	1,483,612	21.2
Texas..	28,304,596	5,344,999	18.9	$81,958	7,276,522	20.9
Utah..	3,101,833	672,005	21.7	$86,717	913,357	10.7
Vermont..	623,657	87,659	14.1	$86,315	115,865	13.8
Virginia...	8,470,020	1,366,109	16.1	$102,751	1,839,624	14.0
Washington..	7,405,743	1,191,718	16.1	$105,074	1,621,235	14.3
West Virginia.....................................	1,815,857	275,516	15.2	$73,337	361,943	25.8
Wisconsin	5,795,483	945,376	16.3	$96,972	1,254,540	14.5
Wyoming	579,315	100,152	17.3	$89,527	135,333	13.3

Table B-3. Selected Characteristics of Children and the School-Age Population, by Region and State, 2017—*Continued*

(Number; dollars; percent.)

Region or State	Health insurance		Language spoken at home					
	Total children under 18 years old	Children under 18 years with no health insurance (percent)	Population 5 to 17 years old	English only (percent)	Language other than English (percent)			
					Spanish	Other Indo-European Languages	Asian and Pacific Island Languages	Other languages
UNITED STATES...............	78,075,324	5.0	53,853,524	77.5	2.8	0.5	0.4	0.2
Northeast Region.................	12,502,407	3.1	8,608,716	76.5	2.1	1.0	0.5	0.2
Midwest Region....................	16,450,425	4.1	11,362,810	87.0	1.3	0.4	0.3	0.3
South Region.......................	30,235,401	6.8	20,844,756	79.3	2.9	0.4	0.3	0.1
West Region.........................	18,887,091	4.2	13,037,242	66.8	4.6	0.4	0.7	0.2
Alabama...............................	1,169,489	3.1	805,164	93.1	0.9	0.1	0.1	0.0
Alaska..................................	194,383	9.6	132,262	86.3	0.4	0.4	0.9	0.9
Arizona................................	1,729,440	7.7	1,197,687	70.7	4.6	0.2	0.2	0.4
Arkansas..............................	751,794	4.4	521,793	90.2	1.5	0.1	0.2	0.0
California..............................	9,567,473	3.1	6,596,961	55.9	6.1	0.5	1.0	0.2
Colorado..............................	1,334,235	4.3	929,766	79.6	2.7	0.3	0.3	0.2
Connecticut..........................	792,881	3.1	560,084	78.1	2.3	0.8	0.3	0.2
Delaware..............................	218,473	3.5	149,406	83.0	2.0	0.4	0.3	0.1
District of Columbia.............	133,635	1.2	79,533	80.1	1.8	0.3	0.1	0.2
Florida.................................	4,450,443	7.3	3,071,458	70.4	3.5	0.8	0.2	0.1
Georgia................................	2,670,877	7.5	1,859,542	84.1	2.2	0.3	0.3	0.2
Hawaii..................................	320,949	2.2	216,424	83.3	0.3	0.2	2.2	0.1
Idaho...................................	471,739	4.6	327,059	88.8	1.9	0.1	0.2	0.1
Illinois.................................	3,069,418	2.9	2,127,742	75.4	3.1	0.7	0.3	0.2
Indiana................................	1,670,417	6.3	1,154,479	89.1	1.2	0.4	0.3	0.1
Iowa....................................	775,929	3.1	531,727	90.3	1.0	0.3	0.2	0.1
Kansas................................	755,441	5.2	519,526	86.2	2.1	0.2	0.3	0.1
Kentucky.............................	1,078,842	3.8	738,248	93.8	0.5	0.3	0.1	0.1
Louisiana.............................	1,175,200	3.1	803,029	93.9	0.8	0.2	0.1	0.0
Maine...................................	271,746	4.9	189,812	95.6	0.2	0.3	0.1	0.1
Maryland..............................	1,419,540	3.8	983,637	80.5	2.0	0.6	0.5	0.2
Massachusetts.....................	1,478,961	1.5	1,010,248	76.7	1.7	1.1	0.5	0.2
Michigan..............................	2,312,692	3.0	1,603,491	88.7	0.7	0.4	0.2	0.5
Minnesota............................	1,372,988	3.4	943,922	84.9	1.1	0.3	0.7	0.7
Mississippi..........................	763,456	4.8	532,086	96.5	0.5	0.1	0.1	0.0
Missouri..............................	1,464,725	5.1	1,013,660	93.3	0.6	0.3	0.2	0.1
Montana..............................	240,764	5.8	168,490	95.3	0.4	0.3	0.0	0.1
Nebraska.............................	500,004	5.1	342,918	85.2	2.1	0.3	0.3	0.2
Nevada................................	718,836	8.0	499,902	67.5	4.9	0.2	0.5	0.2
New Hampshire....................	275,977	2.3	194,672	93.2	0.4	0.3	0.2	0.1
New Jersey...........................	2,093,669	3.7	1,458,435	69.2	3.3	1.0	0.7	0.3
New Mexico..........................	522,820	5.1	363,295	72.3	4.2	0.1	0.1	0.8
New York..............................	4,403,144	2.7	2,995,900	69.7	2.6	1.3	0.6	0.3
North Carolina......................	2,450,911	4.8	1,700,009	84.5	2.1	0.2	0.3	0.1
North Dakota........................	183,593	7.5	120,334	95.9	0.4	0.1	0.1	0.0
Ohio....................................	2,759,296	4.5	1,906,867	92.1	0.5	0.5	0.1	0.2
Oklahoma............................	1,018,753	8.1	698,922	88.4	1.8	0.1	0.2	0.1
Oregon................................	928,115	3.6	641,521	79.0	2.4	0.4	0.4	0.2
Pennsylvania.......................	2,834,916	4.4	1,959,953	87.4	1.0	0.6	0.3	0.1
Rhode Island........................	224,008	2.1	151,953	77.0	2.5	0.6	0.3	0.2
South Carolina.....................	1,169,363	5.1	812,181	91.1	1.1	0.2	0.1	0.0
South Dakota.......................	224,414	6.2	152,768	93.9	0.4	0.3	0.1	0.3
Tennessee............................	1,600,422	4.4	1,103,124	90.8	1.1	0.2	0.1	0.2
Texas...................................	7,781,845	10.7	5,344,999	64.5	6.3	0.3	0.4	0.2
Utah....................................	972,601	7.3	672,005	85.0	2.8	0.2	0.4	0.2
Vermont...............................	127,105	1.6	87,659	94.7	0.2	0.4	0.2	0.0
Virginia................................	1,983,006	5.1	1,366,109	83.5	1.6	0.5	0.4	0.3
Washington..........................	1,739,832	2.6	1,191,718	77.5	2.3	0.7	0.7	0.2
West Virginia........................	399,352	2.6	275,516	98.2	0.2	0.0	0.0	0.0
Wisconsin............................	1,361,508	3.9	945,376	89.2	1.2	0.3	0.3	0.1
Wyoming..............................	145,904	9.5	100,152	90.3	1.4	0.1	0.1	0.2

Table B-3. Selected Characteristics of Children and the School-Age Population, by Region and State, 2017—*Continued*

(Number; dollars; percent.)

Region or State	Total, children under 18 years old in households	White (percent)	Black (percent)	Hispanic or Latino (may be of any race) (percent)	Asian (percent)	Asian and Pacific Islander (percent)	American Indian, Alaska Native (percent)	Some other race (percent)	Two or more races (percent)
UNITED STATES	73,403,167	66.7	14.0	25.2	4.9	0.2	1.0	6.6	6.6
Northeast Region	11,690,288	66.6	13.6	20.4	6.4	0.0	0.3	7.1	5.9
Midwest Region	15,461,994	74.6	12.0	12.2	3.2	0.1	0.8	3.4	6.0
South Region	28,431,519	64.8	21.1	24.4	3.2	0.1	0.7	4.5	5.6
West Region	17,819,366	62.9	4.5	40.8	8.0	0.6	2.0	12.6	9.3
Alabama	1,091,883	62.1	29.6	7.5	1.5	0.0	0.3	2.5	3.9
Alaska	184,438	53.6	2.1	9.3	6.5	1.6	19.1	1.1	16.0
Arizona	1,627,338	71.3	4.9	44.2	2.7	0.3	5.7	7.6	7.6
Arkansas	705,930	69.1	17.6	12.5	1.8	0.4	0.6	5.0	5.5
California	9,032,652	54.3	5.3	52.1	11.5	0.4	0.8	18.6	9.1
Colorado	1,258,171	79.8	4.5	31.2	3.2	0.2	0.9	5.0	6.5
Connecticut	740,420	68.0	12.4	24.1	4.4	0.0	0.4	7.4	7.4
Delaware	203,417	60.8	24.5	15.8	4.0	0.0	0.1	3.3	7.2
District of Columbia	123,954	27.5	54.4	16.7	2.2	0.0	0.2	10.3	5.4
Florida	4,187,312	66.8	20.7	31.2	2.6	0.1	0.3	3.7	5.7
Georgia	2,509,016	52.8	33.8	14.6	3.5	0.2	0.4	3.8	5.6
Hawaii	303,497	18.0	1.2	18.1	25.0	13.1	0.1	1.8	40.8
Idaho	442,350	87.1	0.7	18.4	1.2	0.1	1.2	4.0	5.6
Illinois	2,888,885	65.5	15.4	24.7	4.7	0.1	0.2	8.7	5.5
Indiana	1,566,737	78.4	10.9	11.1	2.2	0.0	0.1	2.7	5.7
Iowa	726,303	85.3	4.4	9.7	2.7	0.3	0.5	1.7	5.2
Kansas	709,879	80.2	6.1	18.3	2.6	0.1	0.6	3.2	7.0
Kentucky	1,010,289	82.2	9.1	5.9	1.8	0.1	0.1	1.5	5.2
Louisiana	1,107,039	54.7	37.2	6.6	1.7	0.0	0.5	2.1	3.9
Maine	252,402	89.8	2.1	3.1	1.3	0.1	1.0	0.2	5.5
Maryland	1,344,571	47.8	30.8	15.2	5.9	0.0	0.3	7.8	7.4
Massachusetts	1,363,970	71.7	9.5	18.4	6.3	0.0	0.3	5.4	6.7
Michigan	2,168,603	72.6	15.7	8.3	3.0	0.0	0.6	1.6	6.5
Minnesota	1,292,083	73.8	9.6	8.7	5.7	0.0	1.5	3.0	6.4
Mississippi	711,030	51.2	42.8	4.3	0.9	0.0	0.6	1.5	2.9
Missouri	1,379,986	76.6	13.1	6.8	1.8	0.2	0.4	2.2	5.7
Montana	228,139	81.9	0.3	6.1	0.2	0.1	9.9	0.9	6.6
Nebraska	472,329	82.4	5.1	17.4	2.7	0.0	1.1	2.9	5.9
Nevada	682,316	57.8	10.2	41.2	6.1	0.7	1.4	14.7	9.3
New Hampshire	257,131	90.0	2.1	6.4	2.5	0.0	0.2	0.3	4.9
New Jersey	1,972,533	63.2	14.0	27.0	9.5	0.0	0.2	7.8	5.2
New Mexico	487,638	70.9	2.0	60.0	0.9	0.1	11.8	8.2	6.1
New York	4,126,648	57.5	17.1	24.8	7.9	0.0	0.4	11.2	5.8
North Carolina	2,295,201	61.8	22.7	16.1	3.1	0.1	1.3	5.1	5.9
North Dakota	172,607	80.5	4.3	5.1	1.1	0.0	8.5	1.3	4.3
Ohio	2,595,692	75.3	14.3	6.1	2.2	0.0	0.2	1.3	6.6
Oklahoma	958,572	63.9	8.0	17.1	2.0	0.1	9.4	3.4	13.1
Oregon	870,422	78.4	2.4	22.1	3.7	0.5	1.5	4.5	9.1
Pennsylvania	2,653,661	73.9	13.7	12.1	3.6	0.0	0.2	2.7	5.9
Rhode Island	206,099	73.7	8.7	25.2	3.5	0.2	0.7	6.4	6.8
South Carolina	1,097,351	60.3	30.4	9.1	1.5	0.2	0.3	2.6	4.7
South Dakota	210,920	76.4	2.7	5.6	1.0	0.1	13.8	0.5	5.4
Tennessee	1,503,833	72.2	18.9	9.5	1.8	0.1	0.1	2.2	4.7
Texas	7,347,905	71.7	12.1	49.5	4.3	0.1	0.5	6.8	4.7
Utah	922,324	82.9	1.4	17.6	1.8	0.9	1.0	6.8	5.1
Vermont	117,424	90.6	2.1	2.9	2.2	0.1	0.2	0.1	4.8
Virginia	1,862,534	61.5	20.1	13.8	5.9	0.1	0.2	3.8	8.4
Washington	1,642,581	67.7	3.9	21.2	7.0	0.7	1.6	7.0	12.2
West Virginia	371,682	88.7	4.3	1.9	0.8	0.0	0.1	1.4	4.6
Wisconsin	1,277,970	77.7	8.8	11.8	3.4	0.1	0.9	3.4	5.7
Wyoming	137,500	87.0	1.5	14.4	0.4	0.0	3.3	2.0	5.8

Table B-4. Number and Percent of Students in City, Suburban, Town, and Rural Regular Public Elementary and Secondary Schools, by State, 2015–2016

(Number; percent.)

Region or State	Total number of operating schools[1]	Total number of students[2]	City Number of schools	City Percent of students	Suburban Number of schools	Suburban Percent of students	Town Number of schools	Town Percent of students	Rural Number of schools	Rural Percent of students
UNITED STATES	88,835	49,312,454	23,756	30.2	28,291	39.7	11,582	11.3	25,188	18.7
Alabama......................................	1,315	740,713	289	23.7	232	21.9	195	14.6	599	39.7
Alaska	474	129,054	88	35.4	14	8.6	82	25.8	290	30.2
Arizona......................................	1,910	1,090,144	895	48.6	476	31.3	243	10.3	296	9.8
Arkansas....................................	1,052	491,390	227	28.6	120	14.2	233	23.6	472	33.6
California....................................	8,788	6,044,665	3,592	42.7	3,592	45.8	632	5.7	972	5.8
Colorado	1,756	878,804	585	38.5	545	39.0	198	9.0	428	13.5
Connecticut................................	1,062	519,528	296	29.7	557	55.5	38	2.8	157	12.0
Delaware	196	124,161	36	13.3	99	52.8	31	16.7	30	17.3
District of Columbia	212	80,914	211	100.0	0	0.0	0	0.0	0	0.0
Florida.......................................	3,472	2,727,105	961	25.6	1,856	58.5	217	4.4	438	11.5
Georgia......................................	2,237	1,753,296	406	15.8	847	46.4	270	10.5	714	27.3
Hawaii..	288	181,870	68	23.9	107	45.2	72	21.8	41	9.1
Idaho...	635	286,447	114	23.3	119	27.8	143	23.9	258	24.8
Illinois.......................................	3,908	2,012,523	965	30.0	1,635	49.0	499	10.2	809	10.8
Indiana......................................	1,862	1,045,085	514	30.8	394	26.9	288	14.4	664	27.9
Iowa..	1,323	497,345	233	27.4	109	12.8	321	25.5	660	34.2
Kansas	1,311	488,382	249	28.3	148	17.4	321	26.3	593	28.1
Kentucky	1,221	676,793	159	16.0	224	22.1	307	25.5	531	36.5
Louisiana...................................	1,337	714,923	367	29.5	324	29.0	231	14.2	415	27.3
Maine..	581	176,396	48	12.7	66	16.6	77	17.1	390	53.6
Maryland....................................	1,329	861,595	299	20.6	762	62.0	55	3.6	213	13.8
Massachusetts............................	1,793	914,148	328	17.7	1,226	72.0	39	1.4	200	8.8
Michigan....................................	2,939	1,412,050	665	23.6	1,079	43.7	368	11.5	827	21.1
Minnesota..................................	1,666	832,485	329	21.4	426	36.2	325	20.6	586	21.7
Mississippi.................................	908	486,910	103	10.7	86	14.0	267	28.4	452	46.9
Missouri.....................................	2,220	913,246	378	18.5	529	34.7	388	20.3	925	26.6
Montana.....................................	817	145,240	64	25.2	11	2.0	138	36.7	604	36.1
Nebraska....................................	1,001	316,014	211	38.8	85	14.8	190	21.0	515	25.4
Nevada......................................	609	464,272	260	50.4	173	36.0	71	7.5	105	6.1
New Hampshire...........................	488	181,307	49	14.8	133	36.9	71	14.1	235	34.2
New Jersey	2,374	1,337,561	232	10.4	1,884	79.7	63	2.1	195	7.8
New Mexico................................	834	330,429	219	34.4	83	13.6	227	27.3	305	24.7
New York....................................	4,617	2,634,356	2,037	45.4	1,484	36.8	352	6.3	744	11.4
North Carolina............................	2,495	1,536,724	653	28.6	485	23.8	307	10.5	1,050	37.0
North Dakota..............................	471	106,372	61	27.7	24	11.6	64	21.5	322	39.2
Ohio..	3,479	1,708,484	751	19.1	1,288	45.3	506	13.3	934	22.3
Oklahoma...................................	1,791	692,546	279	23.7	219	22.2	388	23.6	905	30.5
Oregon.......................................	1,207	562,870	326	34.7	254	27.0	291	23.8	336	14.5
Pennsylvania..............................	2,921	1,692,726	569	20.8	1,344	51.3	286	9.0	722	18.8
Rhode Island..............................	297	136,719	72	24.5	188	65.4	0	0.0	37	10.1
South Carolina	1,182	761,721	216	19.6	345	35.4	151	11.3	470	33.6
South Dakota	650	132,433	56	26.8	6	1.7	99	30.2	489	41.3
Tennessee	1,744	991,648	572	32.5	277	20.5	281	16.6	614	30.3
Texas..	7,851	5,224,531	2,923	41.5	1,988	32.3	1,004	9.8	1,935	16.4
Utah..	928	636,734	149	16.0	495	62.9	118	10.8	166	10.3
Vermont.....................................	298	84,355	14	7.8	17	9.4	52	27.1	215	55.7
Virginia......................................	1,846	1,281,866	429	23.0	676	45.4	161	7.0	580	24.5
Washington................................	1,961	1,040,890	572	32.8	683	42.7	266	12.5	440	12.1
West Virginia..............................	677	276,449	81	15.4	126	20.6	123	21.6	347	42.4
Wisconsin	2,145	861,518	504	29.2	445	28.1	419	19.7	777	23.0
Wyoming....................................	358	94,717	52	25.0	6	2.0	114	44.1	186	28.9

[1]The total number of schools is limited to regular, operational schools with membership and excludes schools also reported by the Bureau of Indian Education (BIE). The number of operating schools shared with the BIE include one in Arizona, one in Michigan, and eight in North Dakota.
[2]Total number of students is the count of students enrolled on October 1 of the reported school year.

Table B-5. Population 3 Years and Over Enrolled in Public or Private School, by Selected Grade Levels and Region or State, 2017

(Number; percent.)

Region or State	Total enrolled population	Percent in public school	Percent in private school	Nursery school Total enrolled	Nursery school Percent in public school	Nursery school Percent in private school
UNITED STATES............................	81,273,337	83.9	16.1	4,889,724	59.5	40.5
Northeast Region	13,571,641	77.4	22.6	858,131	55.0	45.0
Midwest Region	16,923,790	83.6	16.4	1,062,439	63.6	36.4
South Region	30,899,072	85.3	14.7	1,830,549	60.6	39.4
West Region.......................................	19,878,834	86.4	13.6	1,138,605	57.3	42.7
Alabama...	1,188,014	86.7	13.3	63,400	58.3	41.7
Alaska..	186,461	88.3	11.7	9,307	72.3	27.7
Arizona...	1,757,544	88.8	11.2	88,736	65.4	34.6
Arkansas..	743,696	88.6	11.4	47,292	72.5	27.5
California..	10,455,915	86.0	14.0	599,565	57.6	42.4
Colorado	1,394,563	88.4	11.6	83,333	62.7	37.3
Connecticut..	898,609	80.0	20.0	53,459	59.1	40.9
Delaware..	233,046	84.4	15.6	13,536	52.5	47.5
District of Columbia	167,649	58.1	41.9	13,119	69.3	30.7
Florida..	4,770,596	82.1	17.9	288,668	55.3	44.7
Georgia	2,748,599	85.9	14.1	175,165	64.5	35.5
Hawaii..	324,608	77.9	22.1	23,360	44.2	55.8
Idaho..	454,019	86.3	13.7	25,462	49.8	50.2
Illinois..	3,216,701	81.7	18.3	214,728	62.6	37.4
Indiana...	1,661,841	83.6	16.4	101,850	59.3	40.7
Iowa...	802,489	84.4	15.6	52,310	69.7	30.3
Kansas...	777,271	85.8	14.2	56,855	67.1	32.9
Kentucky..	1,051,294	83.9	16.1	62,924	61.5	38.5
Louisiana..	1,176,248	79.9	20.1	80,379	60.0	40.0
Maine...	289,898	82.4	17.6	14,496	54.4	45.6
Maryland..	1,536,509	81.5	18.5	97,926	51.3	48.7
Massachusetts...................................	1,714,245	72.8	27.2	105,212	52.2	47.8
Michigan..	2,452,202	87.2	12.8	142,421	67.4	32.6
Minnesota..	1,404,105	84.7	15.3	95,941	66.8	33.2
Mississippi...	779,151	87.1	12.9	48,060	70.5	29.5
Missouri...	1,484,234	81.2	18.8	96,353	56.7	43.3
Montana...	236,016	84.6	15.4	14,864	53.4	46.6
Nebraska..	507,288	82.0	18.0	36,089	62.2	37.8
Nevada...	697,092	88.5	11.5	33,886	58.8	41.2
New Hampshire...................................	300,223	79.2	20.8	16,793	52.0	48.0
New Jersey	2,226,989	81.7	18.3	163,607	55.6	44.4
New Mexico	536,849	90.5	9.5	26,850	76.1	23.9
New York..	4,794,761	76.8	23.2	298,614	58.9	41.1
North Carolina....................................	2,521,781	85.1	14.9	131,763	54.3	45.7
North Dakota......................................	179,366	90.6	9.4	8,882	74.0	26.0
Ohio...	2,812,859	82.1	17.9	167,505	59.5	40.5
Oklahoma...	1,011,241	88.8	11.2	67,039	76.7	23.3
Oregon...	953,051	84.9	15.1	57,027	45.0	55.0
Pennsylvania......................................	2,941,997	76.4	23.6	183,290	48.5	51.5
Rhode Island......................................	260,894	73.9	26.1	12,667	50.4	49.6
South Carolina	1,183,515	86.2	13.8	58,869	58.7	41.3
South Dakota	214,085	87.8	12.2	16,008	68.2	31.8
Tennessee	1,573,379	82.8	17.2	83,123	58.2	41.8
Texas..	7,679,163	89.2	10.8	453,117	65.6	34.4
Utah...	984,783	85.9	14.1	57,982	56.7	43.3
Vermont..	144,025	80.5	19.5	9,993	67.1	32.9
Virginia...	2,138,155	83.3	16.7	124,910	46.6	53.4
Washington...	1,750,825	85.0	15.0	109,547	49.9	50.1
West Virginia......................................	397,036	88.8	11.2	21,259	82.5	17.5
Wisconsin...	1,411,349	84.1	15.9	73,497	70.2	29.8
Wyoming	147,108	91.1	8.9	8,686	64.9	35.1

Table B-5. Population 3 Years and Over Enrolled in Public or Private School, by Selected Grade Levels and Region or State, 2017—*Continued*

(Number; percent.)

Region or State	Kindergarten			Elementary: grades 1-4		
	Total enrolled	Percent in public school	Percent in private school	Total enrolled	Percent in public school	Percent in private school
UNITED STATES	4,001,570	87.9	12.1	16,214,534	89.8	10.2
Northeast Region	618,212	85.9	14.1	2,547,747	88.4	11.6
Midwest Region	835,126	86.9	13.1	3,402,156	88.0	12.0
South Region	1,551,675	88.3	11.7	6,379,413	90.4	9.6
West Region	996,557	89.3	10.7	3,885,218	91.4	8.6
Alabama	59,093	87.5	12.5	243,468	89.8	10.2
Alaska	11,597	85.2	14.8	41,482	89.0	11.0
Arizona	81,544	90.0	10.0	358,912	92.3	7.7
Arkansas	41,214	92.4	7.6	161,784	93.0	7.0
California	526,390	90.6	9.4	1,913,684	91.6	8.4
Colorado	69,643	89.3	10.7	280,158	93.2	6.8
Connecticut	35,155	91.5	8.5	159,854	91.6	8.4
Delaware	12,247	91.5	8.5	44,179	88.7	11.3
District of Columbia	9,551	92.7	7.3	28,102	86.0	14.0
Florida	227,092	85.0	15.0	937,216	87.1	12.9
Georgia	135,124	89.0	11.0	564,728	91.6	8.4
Hawaii	17,003	82.5	17.5	62,754	87.1	12.9
Idaho	20,784	84.7	15.3	98,136	91.8	8.2
Illinois	146,425	85.4	14.6	639,018	88.9	11.1
Indiana	86,800	88.2	11.8	342,785	87.6	12.4
Iowa	42,019	86.9	13.1	161,163	89.2	10.8
Kansas	40,024	89.2	10.8	161,763	87.0	13.0
Kentucky	51,244	87.8	12.2	225,646	88.6	11.4
Louisiana	57,360	83.4	16.6	255,479	81.7	18.3
Maine	13,560	94.4	5.6	57,763	89.7	10.3
Maryland	68,537	85.3	14.7	297,598	88.3	11.7
Massachusetts	74,584	87.4	12.6	292,593	92.3	7.7
Michigan	119,322	89.9	10.1	469,242	89.8	10.2
Minnesota	71,612	88.7	11.3	284,573	88.8	11.2
Mississippi	40,442	86.5	13.5	166,341	90.2	9.8
Missouri	68,973	83.8	16.2	307,220	87.0	13.0
Montana	13,248	82.1	17.9	51,731	89.2	10.8
Nebraska	26,168	85.5	14.5	101,353	85.0	15.0
Nevada	35,952	85.9	14.1	157,056	93.2	6.8
New Hampshire	12,460	87.0	13.0	54,042	90.7	9.3
New Jersey	106,420	85.7	14.3	431,700	90.2	9.8
New Mexico	26,975	91.4	8.6	112,494	92.1	7.9
New York	227,537	84.9	15.1	899,624	86.9	13.1
North Carolina	122,843	88.7	11.3	512,899	90.7	9.3
North Dakota	9,831	94.3	5.7	38,210	93.2	6.8
Ohio	132,663	85.0	15.0	572,527	87.1	12.9
Oklahoma	54,586	91.6	8.4	217,580	92.2	7.8
Oregon	44,108	84.7	15.3	196,128	89.9	10.1
Pennsylvania	133,054	84.7	15.3	581,812	86.2	13.8
Rhode Island	9,484	83.6	16.4	46,113	89.2	10.8
South Carolina	69,252	88.6	11.4	252,902	91.2	8.8
South Dakota	11,779	94.9	5.1	46,710	89.9	10.1
Tennessee	81,990	87.6	12.4	325,173	88.6	11.4
Texas	395,408	91.1	8.9	1,648,578	93.6	6.4
Utah	49,078	92.2	7.8	209,268	92.3	7.7
Vermont	5,958	89.6	10.4	24,246	91.5	8.5
Virginia	105,228	85.2	14.8	412,626	90.3	9.7
Washington	93,487	86.8	13.2	369,758	88.2	11.8
West Virginia	20,464	92.9	7.1	85,114	92.8	7.2
Wisconsin	79,510	85.6	14.4	277,592	85.2	14.8
Wyoming	6,748	93.9	6.1	33,657	92.7	7.3

Table B-5. Population 3 Years and Over Enrolled in Public or Private School, by Selected Grade Levels and Region or State, 2017—*Continued*

(Number; percent.)

Region or State	Elementary: grades 5-8			High school: grades 9-12		
	Total enrolled	Percent in public school	Percent in private school	Total enrolled	Percent in public school	Percent in private school
UNITED STATES..........................	16,723,145	89.6	10.4	17,150,113	90.1	9.9
Northeast Region	2,681,647	88.0	12.0	2,827,126	87.3	12.7
Midwest Region	3,525,724	88.4	11.6	3,613,630	89.9	10.1
South Region	6,468,071	89.7	10.3	6,578,424	90.0	10.0
West Region.......................................	4,047,703	91.4	8.6	4,130,933	92.2	7.8
Alabama...	254,196	89.0	11.0	257,748	89.0	11.0
Alaska..	39,218	92.4	7.6	40,414	90.2	9.8
Arizona...	379,836	91.8	8.2	383,592	93.9	6.1
Arkansas..	155,521	92.1	7.9	161,292	91.7	8.3
California..	2,057,417	91.3	8.7	2,128,815	91.9	8.1
Colorado	290,539	92.9	7.1	293,248	93.6	6.4
Connecticut..	179,062	89.7	10.3	195,883	88.0	12.0
Delaware..	48,957	88.2	11.8	45,142	86.2	13.8
District of Columbia	20,475	79.0	21.0	22,217	81.9	18.1
Florida..	953,102	86.5	13.5	991,018	88.4	11.6
Georgia	585,268	90.9	9.1	596,264	90.2	9.8
Hawaii..	67,349	80.9	19.1	61,609	79.9	20.1
Idaho..	103,929	92.2	7.8	102,332	92.8	7.2
Illinois..	669,320	89.0	11.0	693,053	90.7	9.3
Indiana...	355,064	87.6	12.4	357,731	89.0	11.0
Iowa...	165,472	91.3	8.7	162,157	92.3	7.7
Kansas...	153,863	89.2	10.8	158,337	89.6	10.4
Kentucky	223,295	87.4	12.6	227,670	86.3	13.7
Louisiana	250,090	81.7	18.3	254,665	81.1	18.9
Maine	57,962	90.9	9.1	63,486	88.3	11.7
Maryland..	302,196	86.9	13.1	314,534	87.1	12.9
Massachusetts...................................	312,939	90.2	9.8	345,019	88.1	11.9
Michigan	494,444	90.0	10.0	537,262	91.5	8.5
Minnesota	293,480	89.8	10.2	297,221	92.1	7.9
Mississippi...	163,972	89.9	10.1	166,614	88.3	11.7
Missouri...	316,308	87.0	13.0	314,456	87.4	12.6
Montana...	49,810	85.5	14.5	49,577	89.7	10.3
Nebraska..	107,746	87.0	13.0	101,575	87.6	12.4
Nevada...	150,139	93.1	6.9	156,129	92.9	7.1
New Hampshire...................................	60,888	90.5	9.5	65,444	88.0	12.0
New Jersey	448,758	90.2	9.8	478,940	88.9	11.1
New Mexico	116,494	93.7	6.3	111,753	92.8	7.2
New York..	933,829	86.4	13.6	981,434	86.3	13.7
North Carolina....................................	519,451	89.1	10.9	555,649	89.7	10.3
North Dakota......................................	34,472	93.9	6.1	33,543	92.9	7.1
Ohio...	590,878	86.9	13.1	614,190	86.9	13.1
Oklahoma...	217,345	91.7	8.3	213,310	91.7	8.3
Oregon...	195,706	90.1	9.9	204,773	92.0	8.0
Pennsylvania......................................	610,633	86.2	13.8	621,429	87.0	13.0
Rhode Island......................................	48,434	90.6	9.4	46,956	87.0	13.0
South Carolina	250,106	90.4	9.6	249,181	91.2	8.8
South Dakota	45,810	92.3	7.7	44,865	93.0	7.0
Tennessee..	345,471	87.7	12.3	349,861	86.7	13.3
Texas..	1,673,664	93.5	6.5	1,657,752	93.7	6.3
Utah...	207,178	94.4	5.6	203,783	94.0	6.0
Vermont..	29,142	90.9	9.1	28,535	87.6	12.4
Virginia...	418,786	89.5	10.5	431,758	91.0	9.0
Washington...	359,071	90.1	9.9	364,765	92.0	8.0
West Virginia......................................	86,176	90.8	9.2	83,749	91.0	9.0
Wisconsin...	298,867	85.5	14.5	299,240	91.6	8.4
Wyoming	31,017	95.0	5.0	30,143	93.4	6.6

Table B-5. Population 3 Years and Over Enrolled in Public or Private School, by Selected Grade Levels and Region or State, 2017—*Continued*

(Number; percent.)

Region or State	College, undergraduate			Graduate, professional school		
	Total enrolled	Percent in public school	Percent in private school	Total enrolled	Percent in public school	Percent in private school
UNITED STATES............................	18,105,312	78.9	21.1	4,188,939	59.7	40.3
Northeast Region................................	3,178,852	64.7	35.3	859,926	42.2	57.8
Midwest Region..................................	3,631,711	78.6	21.4	853,004	63.7	36.3
South Region......................................	6,584,347	81.9	18.1	1,506,593	66.1	33.9
West Region..	4,710,402	84.4	15.6	969,416	61.6	38.4
Alabama..	261,639	88.0	12.0	48,470	76.4	23.6
Alaska...	35,247	87.1	12.9	9,196	83.5	16.5
Arizona..	384,659	87.0	13.0	80,265	67.1	32.9
Arkansas...	148,402	83.3	16.7	28,191	76.4	23.6
California..	2,699,808	84.9	15.1	530,236	55.2	44.8
Colorado	300,066	86.8	13.2	77,576	66.7	33.3
Connecticut...	216,701	67.5	32.5	58,495	50.4	49.6
Delaware...	55,239	86.9	13.1	13,746	65.5	34.5
District of Columbia...........................	50,096	26.9	73.1	24,089	30.7	69.3
Florida...	1,120,457	80.0	20.0	253,043	59.9	40.1
Georgia	553,921	81.2	18.8	138,129	65.2	34.8
Hawaii...	75,435	78.3	21.7	17,098	65.2	34.8
Idaho...	87,793	77.7	22.3	15,583	79.3	20.7
Illinois...	675,272	73.0	27.0	178,885	46.4	53.6
Indiana..	342,704	78.1	21.9	74,907	73.0	27.0
Iowa..	183,287	75.3	24.7	36,081	61.3	38.7
Kansas	164,915	85.6	14.4	41,514	76.6	23.4
Kentucky...	210,426	80.8	19.2	50,089	73.6	26.4
Louisiana..	232,404	82.5	17.5	45,871	69.4	30.6
Maine..	66,555	73.6	26.4	16,076	54.7	45.3
Maryland...	341,883	81.1	18.9	113,835	58.5	41.5
Massachusetts.....................................	444,343	52.3	47.7	139,555	28.3	71.7
Michigan	568,355	84.7	15.3	121,156	78.8	21.2
Minnesota..	292,129	77.9	22.1	69,149	63.2	36.8
Mississippi..	163,564	87.5	12.5	30,158	73.2	26.8
Missouri..	301,024	76.6	23.4	79,900	56.1	43.9
Montana..	47,632	84.9	15.1	9,154	80.3	19.7
Nebraska...	106,963	78.6	21.4	27,394	65.7	34.3
Nevada..	134,682	84.7	15.3	29,248	71.1	28.9
New Hampshire....................................	73,373	65.6	34.4	17,223	48.8	51.2
New Jersey	472,948	74.8	25.2	124,616	51.4	48.6
New Mexico...	117,022	89.7	10.3	25,261	76.6	23.4
New York...	1,142,643	66.1	33.9	311,080	39.6	60.4
North Carolina.....................................	560,380	82.1	17.9	118,796	65.6	34.4
North Dakota.......................................	44,572	89.4	10.6	9,856	77.8	22.2
Ohio..	593,862	76.8	23.2	141,234	67.8	32.2
Oklahoma..	200,554	84.3	15.7	40,827	77.1	22.9
Oregon..	209,352	83.4	16.6	45,957	67.2	32.8
Pennsylvania.......................................	644,150	62.2	37.8	167,629	46.2	53.8
Rhode Island..	81,612	57.0	43.0	15,628	38.3	61.7
South Carolina	258,896	80.1	19.9	44,309	73.2	26.8
South Dakota	40,599	84.1	15.9	8,314	69.4	30.6
Tennessee...	316,592	77.6	22.4	71,169	59.3	40.7
Texas...	1,530,060	85.0	15.0	320,584	71.7	28.3
Utah..	217,147	73.8	26.2	40,347	67.1	32.9
Vermont...	36,527	66.9	33.1	9,624	59.7	40.3
Virginia..	499,749	80.2	19.8	145,098	63.5	36.5
Washington..	373,438	83.9	16.1	80,759	67.4	32.6
West Virginia.......................................	80,085	83.1	16.9	20,189	79.2	20.8
Wisconsin..	318,029	81.7	18.3	64,614	62.9	37.1
Wyoming	28,121	90.2	9.8	8,736	90.3	9.7

Table B-6. School Districts and Public Schools, by School Type, Title I Eligibility, and State, 2015–2016

(Number; percent.)

Region or state	Number of school districts	Type of school					Charter schools	Magnet schools	Title I status	
		Total schools	Regular schools	Special education schools	Vocational schools	Alternative schools			Title I eligible schools	Title I schoolwide schools
UNITED STATES............	18,328	98,456	89,644	2,011	1,419	5,382	6,857	3,237	68,614	53,669
Alabama................................	180	1,509	1,326	34	68	81	0	40	‡	‡
Alaska..................................	54	508	478	3	3	24	28	32	358	337
Arizona................................	692	2,284	1,963	20	242	59	552	0	1,724	1,306
Arkansas..............................	289	1,088	1,052	4	26	6	65	30	988	924
California..............................	1,163	10,303	8,936	151	74	1,142	1224	504	7,339	5,640
Colorado..............................	265	1,862	1,756	6	6	94	226	28	690	539
Connecticut..........................	205	1,369	1,062	168	17	122	24	85	608	270
Delaware..............................	50	223	198	13	6	6	28	3	151	151
District of Columbia................	64	228	216	3	0	9	115	6	186	181
Florida.................................	76	4,322	3,716	174	53	379	653	536	3,109	2,950
Georgia...............................	223	2,297	2,237	19	0	41	82	80	1,630	1,548
Hawaii.................................	1	290	288	1	0	1	34	*	192	192
Idaho..................................	159	744	635	18	14	77	54	19	576	504
Illinois.................................	1052	4175	3929	108	0	138	64	105	3312	2095
Indiana................................	418	1,921	1,863	22	28	8	88	30	1,510	1,219
Iowa....................................	345	1,349	1,324	3	0	22	3	0	923	512
Kansas................................	317	1,320	1,315	4	0	1	10	32	1137	873
Kentucky..............................	186	1,541	1,230	8	121	182	*	66	1,119	1084
Louisiana.............................	179	1,390	1,341	32	12	5	138	36	1,239	1,212
Maine..................................	267	611	582	2	27	0	7	1	527	392
Maryland..............................	25	1437	1329	37	27	44	50	97	800	704
Massachusetts......................	408	1862	1796	7	38	21	81	‡	1061	596
Michigan..............................	902	3,468	2,962	187	4	315	370	386	2302	1523
Minnesota............................	564	2,478	1,686	292	9	491	216	80	965	454
Mississippi...........................	157	1,076	915	2	91	68	2	17	738	736
Missouri...............................	567	2,424	2,247	53	63	61	70	29	1887	1569
Montana...............................	490	823	817	2	0	4	*	0	720	436
Nebraska..............................	284	1,085	1,009	25	0	51	*	*	454	345
Nevada................................	19	662	610	14	0	38	47	44	349	347
New Hampshire......................	299	490	490	0	0	0	31	1	434	164
New Jersey............................	694	2588	2384	64	56	84	89	0	1764	553
New Mexico...........................	158	884	846	6	0	32	99	*	788	767
New York..............................	989	4824	4618	131	21	54	256	‡	3578	2937
North Carolina.......................	297	2,603	2,498	24	7	74	158	123	2,112	1987
North Dakota.........................	222	518	474	31	13	0	*	*	259	109
Ohio....................................	1103	3,619	3,495	51	73	0	373	NA	2,887	2,267
Oklahoma.............................	605	1,800	1,791	4	0	5	45	*	1,602	1,112
Oregon................................	221	1242	1209	1	0	32	126	*	572	486
Pennsylvania.........................	784	3,019	2,925	4	84	6	175	50	2,417	1,707
Rhode Island.........................	64	313	297	1	10	5	29	*	241	154
South Carolina.......................	102	1,248	1,185	9	42	12	68	111	587	587
South Dakota........................	168	698	651	12	3	32	0	*	588	329
Tennessee............................	146	1859	1806	16	15	22	100	126	1575	1516
Texas..................................	1232	8826	7872	14	0	940	702	258	7080	6770
Utah....................................	152	1,033	935	64	6	28	117	22	321	250
Vermont...............................	357	314	298	0	15	1	*	2	226	200
Virginia................................	222	2,133	1,864	53	89	127	7	140	737	584
Washington...........................	330	2,427	1,998	96	20	313	9	NA	1,535	1,283
West Virginia.........................	57	744	682	3	30	29	*	0	350	348
Wisconsin.............................	465	2255	2147	12	6	90	242	8	2205	833
Wyoming..............................	60	370	361	3	0	6	0	0	162	87

* Not applicable. Some states/jurisdictions do not have charter school authorization and some states/jurisdictions do not designate magnet schools.
‡ Reporting standards not met. Data missing for more than 80 percent of schools in the state or jurisdiction.
NA = Not available.

Table B-7. Participation in Public School Services, by State, School Year 2015–2016

(Number; percent.)

State	Enrollment in public elementary and secondary schools (2015-2016)	Percent of students eligible for free or reduced-price lunch (2015-2016)	Percent of students with IEP (2015-2016)	Percent English language learner students (Fall 2016)	Percent homeless students (2015-2016)
UNITED STATES................................	49,753,676	52.1	13.2	9.6	2.6
Alabama...	742,919	51.1	11.3	2.8	1.9
Alaska..	132,466	42.7	13.9	11.0	2.9
Arizona..	973,369	50.2	12.0	6.3	2.2
Arkansas..	491,485	63.6	13.9	8.4	2.4
California...	6,208,436	58.9	11.5	20.2	3.9
Colorado..	899,008	41.8	10.6	11.7	2.6
Connecticut..	537,536	37.9	13.9	6.8	0.7
Delaware..	133,792	37.7	15.4	7.9	2.4
District of Columbia	83,009	76.4	14.6	7.7	7.5
Florida...	2,791,193	58.8	13.3	10.3	2.6
Georgia..	1,756,579	62.4	11.5	6.5	2.2
Hawaii...	181,991	49.6	10.6	7.0	2.1
Idaho...	292,233	46.9	10.2	5.4	2.4
Illinois...	2,018,688	49.9	14.5	9.8	2.5
Indiana..	1,045,235	48.3	16.4	4.5	1.7
Iowa..	500,102	41.4	12.6	5.6	1.3
Kansas...	488,568	49.2	14.3	11.1	1.9
Kentucky..	686,113	59.4	14.5	3.2	4.0
Louisiana...	683,839	61.3	11.7	3.2	2.8
Maine..	176,400	46.0	17.9	2.9	1.3
Maryland..	879,580	45.0	12.0	7.8	1.8
Massachusetts..	953,423	39.9	17.4	9.0	2.2
Michigan..	1,484,270	46.1	12.8	6.2	2.5
Minnesota..	863,719	38.1	14.8	8.2	1.9
Mississippi...	487,195	74.9	13.7	2.7	1.9
Missouri...	917,862	50.1	13.7	3.4	3.5
Montana..	140,868	46.2	12.0	2.0	2.1
Nebraska..	316,009	44.2	15.1	7.1	1.1
Nevada...	455,144	58.8	11.9	15.9	4.4
New Hampshire.......................................	181,307	28.3	15.8	2.4	1.8
New Jersey	1,368,639	37.6	16.5	5.0	0.7
New Mexico	334,061	71.7	14.8	13.4	3.0
New York..	2,660,164	49.5	18.4	8.7	5.2
North Carolina..	1,544,677	57.4	12.9	6.0	1.7
North Dakota..	106,358	29.9	12.8	2.9	2.1
Ohio..	1,707,833	44.9	14.8	3.3	1.7
Oklahoma..	682,309	62.2	15.7	6.7	3.8
Oregon..	549,322	51.4	13.9	9.8	3.8
Pennsylvania..	1,665,328	48.2	17.7	3.3	1.3
Rhode Island..	140,427	47.0	16.6	7.8	0.7
South Carolina	763,483	60.0	13.3	5.7	1.9
South Dakota	133,746	41.7	14.5	3.4	1.5
Tennessee..	974,752	58.8	12.9	4.3	1.5
Texas...	5,300,136	58.9	8.7	17.2	2.2
Utah..	647,843	36.4	12.3	6.3	2.3
Vermont...	84,355	38.4	15.8	1.7	1.2
Virginia..	1,271,067	41.2	12.8	7.8	1.4
Washington..	1,086,805	45.4	12.5	11.1	3.6
West Virginia..	277,445	49.4	16.3	0.9	3.4
Wisconsin..	857,907	39.9	13.9	5.4	2.1
Wyoming	94,681	37.5	16.5	3.0	1.7

Table B-8. Number of Private Schools, Students, Teachers, High School Graduates, and Percent Change in Enrollment, by State, Fall 2015

State	Private schools				
	Number of private schools, Fall 2015	Total teachers, Fall 2015	High school graduates, 2014–2015	Enrollment in Pre-K to 12th grade, Fall 2015	Enrollment percent change, Fall 2005 to Fall 2015
UNITED STATES......................	34,580	481,560	343,250	5,750,520	-5.3
Alabama...............................	350	5,870	4,710	75,070	-18.6
Alaska.................................	50	480	220	5,540	-26.1
Arizona................................	320	4,110	3,030	56,610	-15.3
Arkansas..............................	330	3,670	1,800	37,930	7.2
California..............................	3,420	49,520	36,930	627,170	-15.0
Colorado	600	5,680	2,790	68,140	-3.7
Connecticut..........................	420	7,770	7,140	66,710	-12.5
Delaware..............................	100	1,650	1,180	19,660	-34.1
District of Columbia	90	2,050	1,500	17,110	-13.9
Florida.................................	2,200	30,520	22,770	389,310	-1.9
Georgia	1,220	19,930	11,630	189,630	24.3
Hawaii.................................	140	3,730	3,510	45,600	39.0
Idaho...................................	260	1,420	640	20,230	32.0
Illinois.................................	1,500	19,600	16800	280,440	-11.8
Indiana................................	1,660	11,940	7,130	171,570	23.1
Iowa....................................	510	5,120	2,580	70,870	16.3
Kansas................................	210	3,210	2,550	42,270	-10.3
Kentucky..............................	330	5,670	4,520	70,090	-11.1
Louisiana	580	12,640	11,420	166,560	20.5
Maine..................................	140	2,020	2,700	18,600	-10.1
Maryland..............................	760	13,810	9,130	142,630	-16.3
Massachusetts......................	760	14,440	9,270	123,230	-21.9
Michigan..............................	890	13,550	10,960	172,130	3.1
Minnesota............................	470	5,860	4,430	75,630	-27.8
Mississippi...........................	180	3,530	2,700	43,580	-24.8
Missouri...............................	870	10,340	8,540	125,290	-9.1
Montana...............................	120	980	400	11,690	NA
Nebraska.............................	350	3,120	2,460	48,960	15.4
Nevada................................	150	1,540	1240	23,910	-17.9
New Hampshire.....................	260	2,670	2,430	25,330	-23.8
New Jersey	1,270	19,170	14320	213,170	-16.8
New Mexico	170	2,010	1,440	22,230	-11.2
New York..............................	1,940	46,140	35,600	520,660	1.9
North Carolina.......................	650	11,830	7,490	124,030	5.8
North Dakota.........................	50	630	370	7,830	7.4
Ohio	1,360	18,380	12,920	255,690	0.5
Oklahoma.............................	180	2,740	1,570	32,160	-9.0
Oregon.................................	410	4,210	3470	57,310	-17.7
Pennsylvania........................	2,740	26,350	19,640	315,830	-5.1
Rhode Island.........................	130	1,900	1,460	20,620	-32.6
South Carolina	370	5,310	3,130	62,830	-10.5
South Dakota	70	830	380	10,740	-15.4
Tennessee	500	8,730	6,040	91,950	-12.6
Texas..................................	2,400	30,430	16,540	351,270	15.5
Utah....................................	160	1,800	1,490	21,140	-0.4
Vermont...............................	110	1,280	1080	10,040	-12.9
Virginia................................	950	12,850	7,150	140,350	-9.6
Washington...........................	640	7,680	5,650	100,140	-16.3
West Virginia.........................	130	1,330	850	14,780	-8.3
Wisconsin	1,050	11,310	5,540	144,020	1.2
Wyoming..............................	40	220	30	2,240	-3.0

NOTE: Includes special education, vocational/technical education, and alternative schools. Tabulation includes schools that offer kindergarten or higher grade. Includes enrollment of students in prekindergarten through grade 12 in schools that offer kindergarten or higher grade. Detail may not sum to totals because of rounding.
NA = Not available.

Table B-9. Staff Employed by Public Elementary and Secondary School Systems, Fall 2015

State	Total staff	Student/ Teacher Ratio	Student/ Staff Ratio	School staff										
				Principals and assistant principals		School and library support staff		Teachers		Instructional aides		Guidance counselors	
				Number	Percent	Number	Percent	Number	Percent	Number	Percent	Number	Percent
UNITED STATES..........	6,382,816	16.0	7.9	182,006	2.9	279,128	4.4	3,151,497	49.4	764,537	12.0	108,376	1.7
Alabama....................	71,628	18.2	10.4	3,311	4.6	2,211	3.1	40,766	56.9	5,380	7.5	1,516	2.1
Alaska.....................	16,982	16.9	7.8	647	3.8	1,129	6.6	7,832	46.1	2,490	14.7	308	1.8
Arizona....................	103,175	23.1	10.7	2,461	2.4	3,877	3.8	47,944	46.5	15,107	14.6	1,228	1.2
Arkansas..................	73,658	13.7	6.7	1,797	2.4	3,109	4.2	35,804	48.6	8,963	12.2	1,303	1.8
California.................	577,836	23.9	10.9	17,158	3.0	33,874	5.9	263,475	45.6	78,999	13.7	8,800	1.5
Colorado	111,939	17.4	8.0	3,434	3.1	5,903	5.3	51,798	46.3	17,396	15.5	2,392	2.1
Connecticut..............	98,166	12.3	5.5	2,402	2.4	3,509	3.6	43,772	44.6	16,516	16.8	1,170	1.2
Delaware..................	17,097	15.0	7.9	465	2.7	395	2.3	8,962	52.4	2,127	12.4	320	1.9
District of Columbia.............	14,106	12.4	6.0	656	4.7	823	5.8	6,789	48.1	1,733	12.3	172	1.2
Florida....................	345,645	15.3	8.1	8,687	2.5	16,879	4.9	182,586	52.8	32,096	9.3	5,770	1.7
Georgia	224,488	15.5	7.8	6,396	2.8	10,154	4.5	113,031	50.4	24,508	10.9	3,690	1.6
Hawaii.....................	22,596	15.5	8.1	668	3.0	1,016	4.5	11,747	52.0	2,547	11.3	634	2.8
Idaho......................	27,186	18.7	10.8	673	2.5	1,178	4.3	15,656	57.6	2,928	10.8	500	1.8
Illinois....................	260,463	15.7	7.8	8,125	3.1	11,397	4.4	129,948	49.9	26,577	10.2	3,011	1.2
Indiana....................	152,826	18.1	6.8	3,336	2.2	7,998	5.2	57,675	37.7	17,033	11.1	1,964	1.3
Iowa.......................	72,887	14.2	7.0	1,719	2.4	2,751	3.8	35,687	49.0	11,900	16.3	1,218	1.7
Kansas....................	73,272	12.4	6.8	1,895	2.6	2,704	3.7	40,035	54.6	9,065	12.4	1,111	1.5
Kentucky..................	97,712	16.4	7.0	3,475	3.6	5,697	5.8	41,902	42.9	12,857	13.2	1,553	1.6
Louisiana	107,600	12.3	6.7	3,711	3.4	4,238	3.9	58,469	54.3	13,640	12.7	1,828	1.7
Maine......................	35,241	12.2	5.2	940	2.7	1,700	4.8	14,857	42.2	5,743	16.3	564	1.6
Maryland..................	115,517	14.8	7.6	3,566	3.1	6,258	5.4	59,414	51.4	11,042	9.6	2,361	2.0
Massachusetts..................	128,291	13.4	7.5	4,816	3.8	6,797	5.3	71,969	56.1	25,530	19.9	2,349	1.8
Michigan	181,468	18.2	8.5	6,633	3.7	11,534	6.4	84,181	46.4	19,856	10.9	2,064	1.1
Minnesota	117,236	15.4	7.4	2,392	2.0	4,633	4.0	55,985	47.8	18,897	16.1	1,246	1.1
Mississippi...............	67,757	15.1	7.2	2,003	3.0	2,511	3.7	32,175	47.5	8,187	12.1	1,120	1.7
Missouri..................	128,938	13.6	7.1	3,288	2.6	336	0.3	67,635	52.5	13,802	10.7	2,637	2.0
Montana...................	21,330	14.0	6.8	523	2.5	728	3.4	10,412	48.8	2,633	12.3	449	2.1
Nebraska..................	47,292	13.6	6.7	1,081	2.3	1,920	4.1	23,308	49.3	6,838	14.5	831	1.8
Nevada....................	26,430	20.6	17.7	1,151	4.4	NA	NA	22,702	85.9	NA	NA	965	3.6
New Hampshire..................	31,980	12.4	5.7	496	1.6	736	2.3	14,770	46.2	7,044	22.0	828	2.6
New Jersey	236,558	12.3	6.0	5,069	2.1	9,922	4.2	114,968	48.6	37,615	15.9	3,816	1.6
New Mexico	37,573	15.5	8.9	1,184	3.2	2,113	5.6	21,722	57.8	5,884	15.7	713	1.9
New York..................	372,692	13.2	7.3	10,258	2.8	8,508	2.3	206,086	55.3	43,977	11.8	6,933	1.9
North Carolina....................	190,855	15.5	8.1	5,808	3.0	7,278	3.8	99,355	52.1	21,900	11.5	4,124	2.2
North Dakota.............	17,983	11.8	6.0	478	2.7	776	4.3	9,195	51.1	2,540	14.1	359	2.0
Ohio.......................	322,611	16.9	5.3	5,464	1.7	14,088	4.4	101,742	31.5	21,601	6.7	3,881	1.2
Oklahoma.................	85,915	16.3	8.1	2,328	2.7	4,524	5.3	42,452	49.4	10,051	11.7	1,611	1.9
Oregon....................	65,928	20.9	9.2	1,656	2.5	4,735	7.2	29,086	44.1	10,468	15.9	1,127	1.7
Pennsylvania..................	241,548	14.2	7.1	4,991	2.1	11,168	4.6	120,893	50.0	31,340	13.0	4,317	1.8
Rhode Island..................	19,483	13.4	7.3	539	2.8	660	3.4	10,631	54.6	2,371	12.2	335	1.7
South Carolina	78,108	15.2	9.8	3,151	4.0	2,252	2.9	50,237	64.3	11,143	14.3	2,079	2.7
South Dakota	19,543	13.9	6.9	440	2.2	674	3.4	9,638	49.3	2,645	13.5	346	1.8
Tennessee	128,469	15.1	7.8	3,643	2.8	5,272	4.1	66,488	51.8	16,417	12.8	2,980	2.3
Texas......................	690,077	15.3	7.7	25,580	3.7	27,829	4.0	347,329	50.3	66,089	9.6	11,943	1.7
Utah.......................	56,146	22.9	11.5	1,431	2.5	2,796	5.0	28,348	50.5	8,891	15.8	952	1.7
Vermont...................	18,183	10.5	4.8	495	2.7	880	4.8	8,338	45.9	3,938	21.7	451	2.5
Virginia....................	178,551	14.2	7.2	4,235	2.4	8,335	4.7	90,255	50.5	19,132	10.7	3,334	1.9
Washington................	94,883	18.8	11.5	3,215	3.4	5,385	5.7	57,942	61.1	11,731	12.4	2,131	2.2
West Virginia..............	38,452	14.1	7.2	1,145	3.0	475	1.2	19,664	51.1	3,663	9.5	731	1.9
Wisconsin	101,250	14.9	8.6	2,601	2.6	4,456	4.4	58,185	57.5	9,228	9.1	1,891	1.9
Wyoming	17,269	12.4	5.5	392	2.3	1,006	5.8	7,653	44.3	2,480	14.4	421	2.4

NA = Not available.

Table B-9. Staff Employed by Public Elementary and Secondary School Systems, Fall 2015—*Continued*

State	School staff — Librarians		School district staff — Officials and administrators		School district staff — Administrative support staff		School district staff — Instruction coordinators		Student support staff		Other support services staff	
	Number	Percent	Number	Percent	Number	Percent	Number	Percent	Number	Percent	Number	Percent
UNITED STATES	43,368	0.7	67,778	1.1	190,681	3.0	87,495	1.4	338,888	5.3	1,169,063	18.3
Alabama	957	1.3	13	0.0	612	0.9	17	0.0	1,929	2.7	14,916	20.8
Alaska	118	0.7	600	3.5	793	4.7	0	0.0	622	3.7	2,444	14.4
Arizona	445	0.4	1,385	1.3	4,159	4.0	624	0.6	11,685	11.3	14,260	13.8
Arkansas	948	1.3	614	0.8	2,596	3.5	996	1.4	7,685	10.4	9,842	13.4
California	105	0.0	3,312	0.6	20,672	3.6	22,630	3.9	19,214	3.3	109,597	19.0
Colorado	583	0.5	1,348	1.2	4,630	4.1	3,335	3.0	6,774	6.1	14,347	12.8
Connecticut	760	0.8	2,324	2.4	1,584	1.6	5,217	5.3	3,620	3.7	17,291	17.6
Delaware	122	0.7	430	2.5	329	1.9	307	1.8	771	4.5	2,870	16.8
District of Columbia	99	0.7	434	3.1	927	6.6	403	2.9	1,308	9.3	761	5.4
Florida	2,061	0.6	2,146	0.6	15,502	4.5	682	0.2	11,323	3.3	67,914	19.6
Georgia	2,086	0.9	2,411	1.1	2,573	1.1	3,372	1.5	8,237	3.7	48,031	21.4
Hawaii	160	0.7	275	1.2	697	3.1	616	2.7	1,726	7.6	2,511	11.1
Idaho	48	0.2	128	0.5	648	2.4	241	0.9	540	2.0	4,644	17.1
Illinois	1,645	0.6	3,902	1.5	6,993	2.7	1,600	0.6	37,001	14.2	30,264	11.6
Indiana	692	0.5	1,170	0.8	739	0.5	3,995	2.6	18,819	12.3	39,404	25.8
Iowa	421	0.6	1,710	2.3	2,009	2.8	808	1.1	4,363	6.0	10,300	14.1
Kansas	630	0.9	488	0.7	1,362	1.9	992	1.4	4,400	6.0	10,589	14.5
Kentucky	1,053	1.1	945	1.0	2,254	2.3	1,598	1.6	3,130	3.2	23,248	23.8
Louisiana	1,194	1.1	106	0.1	453	0.4	1,569	1.5	4,300	4.0	18,092	16.8
Maine	195	0.6	629	1.8	704	2.0	427	1.2	4,098	11.6	5,384	15.3
Maryland	1,181	1.0	3,570	3.1	2,077	1.8	1,641	1.4	4,991	4.3	19,415	16.8
Massachusetts	659	0.5	2,207	1.7	2,828	2.2	429	0.3	9,068	7.1	1,638	1.3
Michigan	451	0.2	4,201	2.3	1,119	0.6	1,281	0.7	13,922	7.7	36,226	20.0
Minnesota	588	0.5	2,331	2.0	2,214	1.9	2,731	2.3	13,288	11.3	12,930	11.0
Mississippi	808	1.2	976	1.4	2,076	3.1	708	1.0	3,206	4.7	13,986	20.6
Missouri	1,391	1.1	872	0.7	7,013	5.4	1,453	1.1	5,314	4.1	25,196	19.5
Montana	368	1.7	429	2.0	716	3.4	163	0.8	989	4.6	3,920	18.4
Nebraska	550	1.2	629	1.3	1,353	2.9	808	1.7	1,561	3.3	8,413	17.8
Nevada	328	1.2	41	0.2	NA	NA	NA	NA	338	1.3	905	3.4
New Hampshire	321	1.0	758	2.4	726	2.3	273	0.9	730	2.3	5,300	16.6
New Jersey	1,415	0.6	1,406	0.6	5,512	2.3	3,964	1.7	13,349	5.6	39,522	16.7
New Mexico	232	0.6	216	0.6	34	0.1	385	1.0	1,417	3.8	3,670	9.8
New York	2,407	0.6	3,004	0.8	18,735	5.0	1,688	0.5	11,012	3.0	60,085	16.1
North Carolina	2,158	1.1	1,664	0.9	5,524	2.9	1,226	0.6	10,827	5.7	30,990	16.2
North Dakota	192	1.1	498	2.8	274	1.5	225	1.3	893	5.0	2,554	14.2
Ohio	869	0.3	2,502	0.8	14,414	4.5	2,592	0.8	26,170	8.1	129,289	40.1
Oklahoma	1,000	1.2	605	0.7	3,058	3.6	339	0.4	4,948	5.8	14,998	17.5
Oregon	164	0.2	464	0.7	2,586	3.9	494	0.7	2,684	4.1	12,465	18.9
Pennsylvania	1,719	0.7	2,435	1.0	7,182	3.0	1,634	0.7	8,178	3.4	47,691	19.7
Rhode Island	193	1.0	266	1.4	547	2.8	187	1.0	2,012	10.3	1,742	8.9
South Carolina	1,087	1.4	767	1.0	2,352	3.0	1,482	1.9	3,556	4.6	2	0.0
South Dakota	101	0.5	718	3.7	372	1.9	208	1.1	981	5.0	3,422	17.5
Tennessee	1,725	1.3	213	0.2	1,367	1.1	817	0.6	1,550	1.2	27,997	21.8
Texas	4,577	0.7	6,532	0.9	25,087	3.6	3,840	0.6	26,747	3.9	144,525	20.9
Utah	252	0.4	409	0.7	752	1.3	1,986	3.5	1,208	2.2	9,122	16.2
Vermont	209	1.2	134	0.7	463	2.5	265	1.5	963	5.3	2,047	11.3
Virginia	1,693	0.9	1,831	1.0	4,248	2.4	1,840	1.0	4,680	2.6	38,967	21.8
Washington	1,108	1.2	1,322	1.4	3,046	3.2	3,324	3.5	3,384	3.6	2,295	2.4
West Virginia	280	0.7	903	2.3	1,415	3.7	401	1.0	1,154	3.0	8,622	22.4
Wisconsin	914	0.9	1,093	1.1	2,860	2.8	1,312	1.3	7,485	7.4	11,226	11.1
Wyoming	108	0.6	412	2.4	496	2.9	369	2.1	738	4.3	3,193	18.5

NA = Not available.

Table B-10. Revenues and Expenditures for Public Elementary and Secondary Schools, by State, 2015–2016

(Dollars in thousands except as noted; percent.)

State	Revenues for public elementary and secondary schools, by source				Current expenditures for public elementary and secondary schools, by function				
	Total revenue (thousands of dollars)	Percent from:			Total current expenditures (thousands of dollars)	Current expenditure per pupil (dollars)	Percent for:		
		Federal government	State government	Local government			Instruction	Support services	Non-instruction
UNITED STATES..........	678,378,476	8.3	47.0	44.8	596,135,643	12,330	60.9	34.9	4.2
Alabama..............................	7,586,636	11.2	54.7	34.2	6,885,677	9,640	56.9	36.0	7.1
Alaska	2,497,340	12.4	64.6	23.0	2,319,662	18,234	54.0	42.4	3.6
Arizona..............................	10,225,235	12.6	45.9	41.4	8,551,673	8,094	53.7	40.9	5.4
Arkansas............................	5,383,382	11.6	51.1	37.3	4,872,214	10,310	56.1	38.4	5.5
California...........................	85,779,627	8.5	59.4	32.1	72,003,129	11,893	59.2	36.7	4.2
Colorado............................	10,237,008	7.1	43.7	49.2	8,648,369	10,017	56.3	39.7	4.0
Connecticut........................	11,697,383	4.3	40.3	55.3	10,551,327	20,426	63.1	33.8	3.1
Delaware............................	2,190,905	8.3	57.4	34.3	1,941,408	14,992	62.7	33.8	3.4
District of Columbia	2,274,302	9.9	NA	90.1	1,775,833	22,009	55.4	40.8	3.7
Florida...............................	27,929,250	11.6	39.3	49.2	25,621,239	9,555	61.5	33.5	5.0
Georgia	19,617,068	9.5	45.8	44.6	17,283,295	10,242	61.9	32.4	5.7
Hawaii................................	3,031,312	8.6	89.4	1.9	2,502,117	14,317	58.7	36.0	5.3
Idaho.................................	2,413,672	10.6	65.3	24.1	2,097,992	7,475	59.3	35.5	5.2
Illinois...............................	27,704,831	8.4	24.1	67.4	29,253,457	14,920	62.1	35.3	2.7
Indiana..............................	12,437,534	8.0	55.6	36.4	10,144,064	10,092	57.5	37.6	4.9
Iowa..................................	6,657,857	7.3	53.8	38.9	5,663,444	11,609	60.6	34.9	4.5
Kansas...............................	6,297,498	8.4	63.1	28.4	5,065,968	10,638	59.8	35.4	4.9
Kentucky............................	7,634,758	11.6	54.7	33.6	6,750,052	10,238	57.9	35.5	6.5
Louisiana	8,930,136	12.7	43.5	43.8	8,027,058	11,631	56.3	38.3	5.4
Maine................................	2,809,790	7.0	39.4	53.6	2,579,299	14,789	58.8	37.1	4.1
Maryland............................	14,420,623	5.8	43.9	50.2	12,774,063	15,123	62.9	34.2	2.9
Massachusetts....................	17,962,854	5.0	37.8	57.2	16,374,676	17,688	64.1	33.2	2.7
Michigan............................	19,835,653	8.9	60.2	30.9	16,977,163	11,508	57.5	38.8	3.7
Minnesota..........................	12,725,423	5.6	66.8	27.5	10,687,048	12,875	65.0	30.3	4.7
Mississippi.........................	4,712,456	14.7	51.2	34.1	4,234,977	9,052	57.0	36.9	6.1
Missouri.............................	11,147,752	8.6	33.0	58.4	9,545,816	10,814	59.2	36.1	4.7
Montana.............................	1,781,468	12.6	47.7	39.6	1,652,848	11,844	58.7	36.5	4.8
Nebraska............................	4,351,337	8.3	33.0	58.6	3,911,805	12,890	63.6	29.6	6.8
Nevada...............................	4,683,088	8.9	35.6	55.5	4,092,457	9,115	58.6	37.4	4.0
New Hampshire...................	3,055,956	5.7	32.9	61.4	2,833,893	16,177	63.7	33.9	2.5
New Jersey	29,671,607	4.2	42.7	53.1	26,825,114	19,828	60.1	36.7	3.2
New Mexico........................	3,987,279	13.7	70.0	16.2	3,343,152	10,371	56.9	38.2	4.9
New York............................	65,776,757	5.0	41.7	53.2	59,161,439	23,150	70.9	27.1	2.0
North Carolina....................	14,072,129	11.6	62.1	26.3	13,466,942	9,077	62.3	32.2	5.5
North Dakota......................	1,705,036	9.1	57.8	33.1	1,451,309	13,911	59.9	32.7	7.4
Ohio..................................	24,956,848	7.7	44.9	47.4	20,484,182	12,427	58.4	38.3	3.4
Oklahoma...........................	6,270,084	11.5	48.3	40.2	5,606,044	8,426	55.8	36.9	7.4
Oregon...............................	7,377,456	7.6	52.3	40.0	6,238,574	11,271	58.5	37.9	3.6
Pennsylvania......................	29,892,129	6.8	37.6	55.6	26,045,127	15,792	61.8	34.5	3.8
Rhode Island......................	2,485,803	7.7	41.4	50.9	2,283,927	16,747	61.0	36.3	2.7
South Carolina	9,442,258	9.5	47.7	42.8	7,669,725	10,460	55.2	39.1	5.6
South Dakota	1,461,886	13.8	30.4	55.8	1,253,268	9,721	58.3	35.7	6.0
Tennessee..........................	9,596,867	11.5	46.2	42.3	8,886,994	9,243	61.5	33.0	5.5
Texas.................................	58,954,734	10.6	40.9	48.6	49,577,688	9,738	58.4	35.9	5.7
Utah..................................	5,447,070	8.3	54.6	37.0	4,539,291	7,296	63.2	31.3	5.6
Vermont.............................	1,724,527	6.6	89.3	4.0	1,671,433	19,809	63.5	33.7	2.8
Virginia..............................	15,927,348	6.6	39.5	53.8	14,677,698	11,908	60.9	35.2	3.9
Washington.........................	14,830,244	7.4	62.2	30.4	12,483,668	11,959	57.8	38.3	3.9
West Virginia......................	3,433,438	10.4	55.5	34.1	3,169,684	11,897	57.6	36.1	6.4
Wisconsin	11,309,921	7.1	45.5	47.3	10,122,041	12,146	59.5	36.8	3.7
Wyoming	2,042,925	6.0	57.6	36.4	1,556,321	17,111	59.4	37.6	3.0

NA = Not applicable.

Table B-11. Percentage of High School Dropouts Among Persons 16 to 24 Years Old, by Race/Ethnicity and State, 2016

(Percent.)

State	Total	White	Black	Hispanic	Asian	Pacific Islander	American Indian/Alaska Native	Two or more races
UNITED STATES	5.8	4.5	7.0	9.1	2.0	6.9	11.0	4.8
Alabama	6.9	6.7	6.5	12.4	NA	NA	NA	3.2
Alaska	5.6	1.9	NA	NA	NA	NA	19.0	10.1
Arizona	7.6	5.0	8.9	10.6	NA	NA	11.1	3.3
Arkansas	7.2	5.8	10.7	9.1	NA	NA	NA	8.2
California	5.3	3.0	5.7	7.7	1.6	NA	3.6	3.6
Colorado	6.4	3.5	9.0	12.5	2.5	NA	12.1	6.1
Connecticut	3.1	1.9	2.5	8.1	NA	NA	NA	NA
Delaware	7.1	3.4	10.3	18.0	NA	NA	NA	NA
District of Columbia	3.5	NA	6.0	6.4	NA	NA	NA	NA
Florida	6.6	5.4	7.1	8.7	2.2	NA	NA	5.2
Georgia	6.9	5.9	7.3	12.0	2.8	NA	NA	5.6
Hawaii	3.6	3.9	NA	5.0	1.2	9.0	NA	3.4
Idaho	4.1	3.6	NA	7.2	NA	NA	NA	NA
Illinois	4.8	3.2	7.4	7.5	2.1	NA	NA	5.4
Indiana	7.0	6.2	8.2	13.6	NA	NA	NA	5.0
Iowa	4.5	4.0	12.2	6.6	NA	NA	NA	NA
Kansas	5.3	4.6	5.2	10.4	NA	NA	NA	4.0
Kentucky	6.6	6.4	7.2	12.4	NA	NA	NA	NA
Louisiana	8.7	6.6	11.9	7.5	NA	NA	NA	7.0
Maine	4.1	4.2	NA	NA	NA	NA	NA	NA
Maryland	5.2	3.4	5.2	14.4	NA	NA	NA	4.8
Massachusetts	3.8	2.3	6.9	10.0	1.4	NA	NA	2.1
Michigan	6.1	5.6	9.0	7.3	1.1	NA	9.7	6.6
Minnesota	4.3	3.5	5.9	10.5	NA	NA	17.6	6.8
Mississippi	6.2	5.6	6.5	9.0	NA	NA	NA	NA
Missouri	5.8	4.8	7.9	11.9	NA	NA	NA	7.3
Montana	5.2	5.0	NA	NA	NA	NA	11.3	NA
Nebraska	5.1	3.6	12.4	13.1	NA	NA	NA	NA
Nevada	8.2	6.1	9.5	11.9	1.8	NA	NA	3.1
New Hampshire	3.9	3.5	NA	NA	NA	NA	NA	NA
New Jersey	3.7	2.1	4.9	7.3	1.4	NA	NA	2.5
New Mexico	8.2	5.4	NA	9.3	NA	NA	10.7	NA
New York	5.5	3.7	7.7	9.5	2.1	NA	NA	4.5
North Carolina	6.0	5.3	5.7	10.7	2.3	NA	11.1	5.3
North Dakota	2.7	2.2	NA	NA	NA	NA	NA	NA
Ohio	6.2	5.3	9.7	9.3	NA	NA	NA	9.1
Oklahoma	7.9	5.8	14.8	10.3	NA	NA	12.5	7.4
Oregon	5.5	5.2	NA	7.6	NA	NA	16.5	4.4
Pennsylvania	5.3	5.0	4.8	10.7	2.4	NA	NA	3.2
Rhode Island	4.1	2.6	NA	8.5	NA	NA	NA	NA
South Carolina	5.9	5.7	5.9	8.9	NA	NA	NA	6.1
South Dakota	5.1	3.1	NA	NA	NA	NA	22.0	NA
Tennessee	4.8	4.2	6.2	9.5	NA	NA	NA	NA
Texas	6.7	4.4	6.0	9.2	2.6	NA	5.3	2.1
Utah	4.7	3.7	NA	9.9	NA	NA	13.8	3.9
Vermont	4.5	4.8	NA	NA	NA	NA	NA	NA
Virginia	3.9	2.8	4.3	9.9	3.1	NA	NA	1.7
Washington	7.5	5.8	10.5	13.2	4.1	12.2	11.7	9.4
West Virginia	6.6	6.6	9.5	NA	NA	NA	NA	NA
Wisconsin	4.7	3.8	9.3	9.3	2.7	NA	NA	NA
Wyoming	5.2	5.2	NA	NA	NA	NA	NA	NA

NA = Not available. Reporting standards not met.
NOTE: Dropouts are 16- to 24-year-olds who are not enrolled in school and who have not completed a high school program, regardless of when they left school. People who have received GED credentials are counted as high school completers. Data are based on sample surveys of the entire population in the given age range residing within the United States, including both noninstitutionalized persons (e.g., those living in households, college housing, or military housing located within the United States) and institutionalized persons (e.g., those living in prisons, nursing facilities, or other healthcare facilities). Totals include other racial/ethnic groups not separately shown. Race categories exclude persons of Hispanic ethnicity.

Table B-12. Total Fall Enrollment in Degree-Granting Postsecondary Institutions, by Level and Control of School, and State, Fall 2016

(Number.)

State	Public Undergraduate Total	Public Undergraduate 4-year	Public Undergraduate 2-year	Public Post-baccalaureate	Private Undergraduate Total	Private Undergraduate Nonprofit 4-year	Private Undergraduate For-profit 4-year	Private Undergraduate Nonprofit 2-year	Private Undergraduate For-profit 2-year	Private Postbaccalaureate Total	Private Postbaccalaureate Nonprofit 4-year	Private Postbaccalaureate For-profit 4-year
UNITED STATES...	13,141,086	7,300,010	5,841,076	1,441,886	3,728,126	2,762,212	716,745	50,557	198,612	1,529,916	1,265,028	264,888
Alabama	216,115	135,080	81,035	34,923	41,893	19,891	19,627	386	1,989	11,121	4,679	6,442
Alaska	25,146	24,958	188	2,206	851	348	0	79	424	243	243	0
Arizona	329,282	141,410	187,872	32,118	181,083	4,928	166,124	0	10,031	65,601	4,872	60,729
Arkansas	130,299	81,842	48,457	19,084	15,661	14,085	279	1,178	119	2,276	2,183	93
California	2,120,578	838,948	1,281,630	108,354	295,702	164,797	98,805	1,602	30,498	175,472	137,762	37,710
Colorado	235,434	162,875	72,559	37,233	57,830	21,271	29,349	265	6,945	21,799	12,733	9,066
Connecticut	103,564	53,016	50,548	13,781	57,088	49,388	7,700	0	0	23,578	22,956	622
Delaware	37,687	37,687	0	4,129	11,360	10,944	246	170	0	7,963	7,908	55
District of Columbia	3,950	3,950	0	637	44,998	38,681	5,838	0	479	43,455	40,257	3,198
Florida	728,374	698,976	29,398	68,674	219,432	134,631	48,248	18,185	18,368	59,016	52,507	6,509
Georgia	376,377	264,674	111,703	45,782	80,750	52,698	19,073	1,981	6,998	29,998	21,418	8,580
Hawaii	47,903	22,488	25,415	5,515	10,440	8,497	1,426	0	517	2,000	1,317	683
Idaho	66,855	44,662	22,193	7,812	48,404	47,767	197	0	440	725	725	0
Illinois	443,681	139,508	304,173	48,897	182,387	131,672	45,300	368	5,047	102,755	86,243	16,512
Indiana	279,127	200,217	78,910	40,454	81,368	72,770	5,458	582	2,558	18,254	18,152	102
Iowa	156,060	65,251	90,809	15,015	73,392	40,477	32,655	0	260	22,046	12,998	9,048
Kansas	158,127	78,570	79,557	22,043	28,504	18,830	8,391	0	1,283	5,627	4,228	1,399
Kentucky	182,322	102,912	79,410	23,109	34,556	27,290	6,635	0	631	15,085	14,042	1,043
Louisiana	186,093	120,077	66,016	22,161	23,437	17,771	802	368	4,496	7,596	7,546	50
Maine	43,952	26,699	17,253	3,811	18,504	16,801	1,182	220	301	5,849	5,716	133
Maryland	262,794	138,358	124,436	42,956	31,264	26,063	3,162	0	2,039	28,653	27,818	835
Massachusetts	191,295	98,813	92,482	27,170	176,441	172,807	1,948	1,122	564	110,817	110,585	232
Michigan	426,809	269,111	157,698	65,963	73,242	70,528	1,593	0	1,121	17,021	16,769	252
Minnesota	228,839	109,041	119,798	24,399	75,101	48,933	25,704	77	387	94,453	21,346	73,107
Mississippi	138,113	66,918	71,195	15,092	13,478	11,908	242	0	1,328	6,029	5,949	80
Missouri	216,882	126,166	90,716	28,042	107,276	97,018	4,636	854	4,768	48,894	48,582	312
Montana	41,222	32,846	8,376	5,038	4,490	4,030	0	425	35	166	166	0
Nebraska	86,641	46,688	39,953	14,391	23,695	22,328	1,059	150	158	11,375	11,273	102
Nevada	98,046	87,173	10,873	8,150	6,763	954	2,334	287	3,188	3,071	2,816	255
New Hampshire	37,200	23,756	13,444	3,970	67,121	66,940	0	181	0	24,845	24,845	0
New Jersey	298,857	148,389	150,468	38,233	58,595	48,576	6,980	0	3,039	25,692	25,246	446
New Mexico	116,054	46,967	69,087	12,984	4,638	856	2,355	0	1,427	931	802	129
New York	633,226	329,353	303,873	67,666	400,116	358,908	25,621	2,594	12,993	172,643	169,436	3,207
North Carolina	404,100	182,462	221,638	46,062	84,840	71,823	8,870	687	3,460	26,494	24,811	1,683
North Dakota	41,686	34,708	6,978	6,278	4,983	4,434	549	0	0	1,256	1,256	0
Ohio	439,769	269,254	170,515	61,705	127,945	108,668	6,803	1,269	11,205	28,810	28,409	401
Oklahoma	157,278	99,101	58,177	20,363	25,477	19,832	2,379	1,194	2,072	5,227	5,201	26
Oregon	179,220	86,594	92,626	17,978	24,764	21,411	2,370	0	983	14,273	14,023	250
Pennsylvania	357,105	230,479	126,626	49,240	227,384	192,694	10,729	7,822	16,139	92,041	91,475	566
Rhode Island	37,311	22,210	15,101	4,058	35,185	35,185	0	0	0	6,794	6,794	0
South Carolina	179,618	92,223	87,395	20,677	40,600	30,213	6,215	991	3,181	5,668	3,902	1,766
South Dakota	38,410	31,874	6,536	5,895	8,318	6,163	2,155	0	0	1,062	1,062	0
Tennessee	197,712	112,781	84,931	23,576	76,953	61,818	6,052	682	8,401	23,510	21,925	1,585
Texas	1,269,436	574,688	694,748	151,538	140,457	100,699	16,623	1,941	21,194	41,828	39,618	2,210
Utah	162,096	132,195	29,901	13,212	110,508	104,750	3,247	2,119	392	25,718	24,658	1,060
Vermont	23,158	17,295	5,863	2,578	14,626	14,326	300	0	0	4,357	4,357	0
Virginia	343,785	170,510	173,275	45,661	118,567	87,164	26,372	747	4,284	49,448	44,949	4,499
Washington	290,938	229,566	61,372	24,418	38,506	29,988	5,087	1,513	1,918	12,300	12,106	194
West Virginia	72,861	55,212	17,649	12,243	50,668	7,419	40,464	0	2,785	10,586	1,390	9,196
Wisconsin	254,431	166,647	87,784	24,011	47,922	42,194	5,561	0	167	15,495	14,974	521
Wyoming	30,224	9,788	20,436	2,578	563	45	0	518	0	0	0	0

NOTE: Degree-granting institutions grant associate's or higher degrees and participate in Title IV federal financial aid programs.

Table B-13. Degrees Conferred by Institutions of Higher Education, by State, 2015–2016

(Number.)

State	Total degrees	Associate's degrees				Bachelor's degrees			
		Total	Public	Private not-for-profit	Private for-profit	Total	Public	Private not-for-profit	Private for-profit
UNITED STATES......................	3,892,494	1,008,314	848,168	56,593	103,553	1,920,718	1,240,405	560,752	119,561
Alabama...............................	58,509	12,880	9,871	122	2,887	31,123	23,878	3,669	3,576
Alaska..................................	4,052	1,372	1,312	17	43	1,957	1,915	42	0
Arizona................................	121,149	33,564	19,050	243	14,271	56,625	27,439	803	28,383
Arkansas..............................	31,104	8,767	8,524	173	70	16,019	13,311	2,613	95
California.............................	443,463	143,570	129,583	1,801	12,186	203,864	142,743	40,121	21,000
Colorado..............................	65,510	14,027	9,920	554	3,553	33,580	25,332	4,094	4,154
Connecticut.........................	42,922	7,320	6,053	918	349	22,721	11,381	10,248	1,092
Delaware..............................	13,368	2,059	1,900	151	8	6,988	4,717	2,253	18
District of Columbia.............	24,948	603	244	223	136	9,337	387	8,577	373
Florida.................................	238,100	93,341	74,502	11,743	7,096	101,876	70,860	23,554	7,462
Georgia................................	93,951	19,815	16,142	1,020	2,653	50,827	37,778	10,029	3,020
Hawaii..................................	13,937	4,571	4,113	446	12	6,922	4,841	1,749	332
Idaho...................................	19,285	5,588	3,637	1,729	222	11,424	6,560	4,813	51
Illinois.................................	167,081	40,410	35,544	1,048	3,818	75,687	33,121	31,347	11,219
Indiana................................	80,767	14,703	11,688	1,439	1,576	47,614	32,180	15,094	340
Iowa....................................	54,462	15,639	11,374	412	3,853	27,761	13,021	9,851	4,889
Kansas.................................	40,315	11,008	9,421	370	1,217	20,249	15,512	3,731	1,006
Kentucky..............................	47,143	12,276	10,348	288	1,640	23,221	18,082	4,668	471
Louisiana.............................	40,060	7,396	6,183	244	969	22,602	18,517	3,873	212
Maine...................................	13,563	3,103	2,677	129	297	7,652	4,275	3,211	166
Maryland..............................	72,531	16,999	16,594	21	384	33,882	27,095	6,404	383
Massachusetts......................	121,724	13,777	12,097	1,245	435	61,082	20,917	39,798	367
Michigan..............................	117,343	29,787	26,215	3,303	269	60,305	46,838	13,103	364
Minnesota............................	85,421	19,526	16,400	652	2,474	36,580	21,329	11,075	4,176
Mississippi...........................	34,834	13,759	13,419	51	289	14,702	12,517	2,175	10
Missouri...............................	86,614	18,305	12,456	3,744	2,105	41,447	22,367	18,334	746
Montana...............................	9,976	2,339	2,177	162	0	6,011	5,186	825	0
Nebraska..............................	26,650	5,144	4,666	258	220	14,301	8,658	5,506	137
Nevada.................................	17,980	6,097	5,180	115	802	8,638	7,778	358	502
New Hampshire.....................	23,031	3,076	2,048	1,028	0	12,527	5,129	7,398	0
New Jersey............................	86,283	23,847	22,356	131	1,360	42,479	31,807	9,882	790
New Mexico..........................	22,486	9,435	8,967	0	468	9,183	8,450	149	584
New York..............................	292,341	66,966	52,406	6,960	7,600	139,136	64,545	70,404	4,187
North Carolina......................	108,400	32,108	29,631	1,046	1,431	53,526	38,211	14,656	659
North Dakota........................	10,714	2,222	2,024	130	68	6,298	5,663	611	24
Ohio.....................................	131,806	31,495	24,595	2,870	4,030	70,052	47,601	21,539	912
Oklahoma.............................	41,289	12,027	10,896	379	752	21,024	16,928	3,921	175
Oregon.................................	47,513	12,955	12,374	35	546	22,563	17,419	4,872	272
Pennsylvania........................	165,256	25,877	16,546	3,380	5,951	92,362	47,775	43,127	1,460
Rhode Island........................	18,663	3,291	1,649	1,642	0	11,982	4,563	7,419	0
South Carolina......................	44,584	11,517	10,050	381	1,086	25,107	18,632	5,440	1,035
South Dakota........................	10,251	2,236	1,919	137	180	6,040	4,750	1,098	192
Tennessee............................	63,991	13,225	10,703	787	1,735	35,255	21,737	12,700	818
Texas...................................	276,328	86,838	80,767	1,399	4,672	126,083	102,981	20,498	2,604
Utah.....................................	59,829	13,367	11,483	1,245	639	34,118	15,934	17,642	542
Vermont...............................	9,996	1,176	970	143	63	6,222	3,298	2,884	40
Virginia................................	113,688	25,123	19,137	1,703	4,283	58,642	37,954	16,726	3,962
Washington..........................	76,530	30,591	29,700	161	730	33,598	25,836	7,152	610
West Virginia........................	30,421	6,498	3,488	103	2,907	16,519	9,661	1,274	5,584
Wisconsin.............................	63,406	13,929	12,501	210	1,218	37,493	27,489	9,437	567
Wyoming..............................	5,575	2,770	2,668	102	0	2,164	2,159	5	0

NOTE: Data are for postsecondary institutions participating in Title IV federal financial aid programs.

Table B-13. Degrees Conferred by Institutions of Higher Education, by State, 2015–2016—*Continued*

(Number.)

State	Master's degrees				Doctoral degrees[1]			
	Total	Public	Private not-for-profit	Private for-profit	Total	Public	Private not-for-profit	Private for-profit
UNITED STATES	785,595	364,526	350,721	70,348	177,867	89,786	80,044	8,037
Alabama	12,074	9,173	858	2,043	2,432	1,913	503	16
Alaska	670	612	58	0	53	48	5	0
Arizona	27,353	9,066	559	17,728	3,607	1,912	737	958
Arkansas	5,277	4,759	498	20	1,041	938	103	0
California	77,453	32,077	36,402	8,974	18,576	6,753	9,784	2,039
Colorado	14,934	8,104	3,766	3,064	2,969	1,883	622	464
Connecticut	10,829	3,140	7,396	293	2,052	780	1,272	0
Delaware	3,903	968	2,910	25	418	338	80	0
District of Columbia	11,512	106	10,846	560	3,496	97	3,399	0
Florida	33,785	17,585	13,776	2,424	9,098	4,882	3,796	420
Georgia	18,558	11,064	5,219	2,275	4,751	2,592	1,803	356
Hawaii	1,917	1,126	582	209	527	472	0	55
Idaho	1,860	1,614	244	2	413	398	15	0
Illinois	42,124	13,288	24,331	4,505	8,860	3,063	5,486	311
Indiana	14,841	9,424	5,372	45	3,609	2,671	938	0
Iowa	8,341	2,803	2,569	2,969	2,721	1,379	1,213	129
Kansas	7,480	5,308	1,615	557	1,578	1,372	206	0
Kentucky	9,503	5,722	3,317	464	2,143	1,657	387	99
Louisiana	7,508	5,261	2,176	71	2,554	1,625	929	0
Maine	2,237	863	1,350	24	571	169	402	0
Maryland	18,829	10,822	7,735	272	2,821	2,033	788	0
Massachusetts	38,390	6,129	32,152	109	8,475	812	7,663	0
Michigan	21,675	17,218	4,299	158	5,576	4,371	1,205	0
Minnesota	23,882	5,203	5,580	13,099	5,433	1,877	1,015	2,541
Mississippi	5,029	3,361	1,645	23	1,344	1,023	321	0
Missouri	22,162	8,576	13,471	115	4,700	1,632	3,068	0
Montana	1,196	1,114	82	0	430	430	0	0
Nebraska	5,506	2,835	2,635	36	1,699	839	860	0
Nevada	2,229	1,700	372	157	1,016	550	466	0
New Hampshire	6,960	1,089	5,871	0	468	147	321	0
New Jersey	16,970	9,688	7,167	115	2,987	2,096	891	0
New Mexico	3,212	2,844	267	101	656	656	0	0
New York	71,571	18,427	51,876	1,268	14,668	3,132	11,534	2
North Carolina	18,159	11,822	5,903	434	4,607	2,694	1,913	0
North Dakota	1,625	1,311	314	0	569	491	78	0
Ohio	24,213	16,045	7,938	230	6,046	4,496	1,549	1
Oklahoma	6,576	5,011	1,536	29	1,662	1,363	299	0
Oregon	10,021	4,214	5,734	73	1,974	1,012	962	0
Pennsylvania	36,940	12,240	24,495	205	10,077	3,359	6,718	0
Rhode Island	2,674	807	1,867	0	716	255	461	0
South Carolina	6,068	4,589	1,128	351	1,892	1,490	196	206
South Dakota	1,538	1,241	297	0	437	431	6	0
Tennessee	11,841	5,570	5,824	447	3,670	1,889	1,695	86
Texas	52,453	40,980	10,486	987	10,954	8,467	2,465	22
Utah	11,081	3,360	7,490	231	1,263	817	253	193
Vermont	2,251	481	1,770	0	347	221	126	0
Virginia	24,665	11,133	11,432	2,100	5,258	3,342	1,783	133
Washington	9,750	6,044	3,583	123	2,591	1,915	670	6
West Virginia	6,244	2,630	344	3,270	1,160	1,044	116	0
Wisconsin	9,298	5,551	3,584	163	2,686	1,744	942	0
Wyoming	425	425	0	0	216	216	0	0

[1]Includes Ph.D., Ed.D., and comparable degrees at the doctoral level. Includes most degrees formerly classified as first-professional, such as M.D., D.D.S., and law degrees.
NOTE: Data are for postsecondary institutions participating in Title IV federal financial aid programs.

Table B-14. Race/Ethnicity of Students Enrolled in Institutions of Higher Education, Fall 2017

(Number; percent.)

State	Total enrolled	Percent of U.S. resident students							Nonresident alien (percent)
		White (percent)	Black (percent)	Hispanic or Latino (may be of any race) (percent)	Asian (percent)	Pacific Islander (percent)	American Indian/ Alaska Native (percent)	Two or more races (percent)	
UNITED STATES..............	19,765,598	56.0	13.6	18.9	6.8	0.3	0.7	3.7	5.1
Alabama..................................	306,822	63.9	27.1	3.8	2.0	0.1	0.7	2.5	2.9
Alaska....................................	26,905	61.0	3.0	8.3	6.4	0.8	10.5	10.1	2.1
Arizona..................................	591,626	50.5	13.1	25.6	3.9	0.5	2.4	3.9	3.4
Arkansas................................	164,082	71.0	16.4	6.3	1.8	0.1	0.8	3.6	3.5
California...............................	2,714,051	29.7	6.7	42.3	15.6	0.5	0.4	4.8	5.5
Colorado	360,236	64.6	7.6	18.1	3.8	0.3	0.9	4.6	3.5
Connecticut............................	197,534	60.7	13.6	16.3	5.8	0.1	0.3	3.2	5.8
Delaware................................	60,338	59.8	22.9	9.6	3.9	0.1	0.6	3.0	8.2
District of Columbia	95,999	49.5	28.6	10.3	7.8	0.2	0.3	3.5	11.4
Florida...................................	1,071,484	45.7	18.6	28.2	3.7	0.2	0.3	3.3	4.3
Georgia	538,124	50.2	32.7	8.0	5.6	0.1	0.3	3.0	4.3
Hawaii	64,125	17.9	2.4	12.4	32.6	7.1	0.3	27.4	6.2
Idaho.....................................	131,803	81.4	1.2	9.8	1.7	0.5	0.8	4.7	8.3
Illinois...................................	757,002	56.3	13.5	19.6	7.3	0.1	0.2	2.8	5.6
Indiana	398,804	76.0	10.2	6.7	3.4	0.1	0.2	3.4	6.3
Iowa......................................	260,954	76.3	9.4	7.9	3.0	0.2	0.5	2.7	4.9
Kansas	213,962	71.6	9.4	10.7	3.0	0.2	1.4	3.8	6.0
Kentucky	258,498	81.9	8.8	3.9	1.9	0.1	0.2	3.2	4.1
Louisiana	242,065	56.4	31.9	5.5	2.6	0.1	0.7	2.7	3.0
Maine....................................	71,811	85.3	4.2	3.2	2.8	0.1	0.9	3.6	2.2
Maryland................................	364,207	47.8	29.6	9.7	8.0	0.3	0.3	4.2	6.0
Massachusetts........................	503,508	64.3	10.0	12.7	9.2	0.1	0.2	3.5	11.9
Michigan................................	558,053	73.5	12.4	5.4	4.4	0.1	0.6	3.5	5.5
Minnesota	412,966	68.7	15.4	5.7	5.7	0.2	0.8	3.6	3.9
Mississippi.............................	171,751	56.6	37.5	2.4	1.3	0.1	0.5	1.7	1.9
Missouri.................................	383,489	74.5	12.5	5.5	3.4	0.2	0.5	3.4	4.6
Montana.................................	50,642	82.2	0.9	4.2	1.6	0.2	7.3	3.6	2.9
Nebraska................................	135,864	76.5	5.5	10.6	3.2	0.2	0.7	3.2	4.2
Nevada..................................	117,574	44.5	7.8	28.3	11.0	1.1	0.7	6.6	2.0
New Hampshire.......................	149,184	73.6	12.5	8.0	2.9	0.3	0.6	2.2	2.2
New Jersey	419,037	50.0	14.8	22.4	10.0	0.3	0.3	2.2	5.2
New Mexico	129,494	33.3	3.0	49.2	2.1	0.2	9.8	2.3	2.7
New York................................	1,260,240	51.9	14.8	19.5	10.6	0.2	0.4	2.7	8.6
North Carolina........................	563,831	60.0	23.3	8.3	3.7	0.2	1.1	3.4	3.5
North Dakota..........................	53,749	83.5	3.5	3.8	1.5	0.2	4.3	3.2	4.7
Ohio	649,687	76.7	12.1	4.4	3.0	0.1	0.3	3.5	4.9
Oklahoma...............................	202,051	60.6	8.8	9.4	3.2	0.2	7.7	10.2	5.0
Oregon	229,936	68.2	3.2	14.0	6.4	0.7	1.1	6.4	5.3
Pennsylvania..........................	717,289	70.6	12.0	7.8	6.1	0.1	0.2	3.2	6.6
Rhode Island..........................	82,766	69.0	7.7	14.0	5.0	0.1	0.4	3.8	5.8
South Carolina	246,388	64.3	25.2	4.9	1.9	0.1	0.4	3.2	2.1
South Dakota	53,620	83.7	3.5	3.3	1.3	0.1	5.5	2.5	3.6
Tennessee	323,157	69.9	19.2	4.7	2.7	0.1	0.3	3.1	2.8
Texas.....................................	1,630,516	38.0	13.1	39.2	6.4	0.2	0.4	2.8	4.3
Utah......................................	332,334	76.9	4.6	10.4	2.9	0.7	0.8	3.6	2.2
Vermont.................................	43,855	83.1	3.9	5.8	2.9	0.1	0.5	3.8	4.3
Virginia..................................	554,212	59.0	20.4	8.9	6.9	0.2	0.4	4.3	3.6
Washington............................	367,944	61.4	4.8	13.8	10.2	0.7	1.2	7.9	6.4
West Virginia..........................	142,963	77.5	10.2	6.2	1.8	0.4	0.4	3.4	3.0
Wisconsin	340,770	79.5	5.5	7.0	4.1	0.1	0.7	3.0	3.6
Wyoming	33,015	83.4	1.2	9.4	1.0	0.2	1.4	3.3	3.2

NA = Not available.
NOTE: Includes special education, vocational/technical education, and alternative schools. Tabulation includes schools that offer kindergarten or higher grade. Includes enrollment of students in prekindergarten through grade 12 in schools that offer kindergarten or higher grade. Detail may not sum to totals because of rounding.

Table B-15. Average Undergraduate Tuition, Fees, and Room and Board Rates for Full-Time College Students, by State, 2016–2017

(Dollars.)

State	Public 4-year					Private 4-year				Public 2-year, tuition and required fees	
	In-state				Out-of-state tuition and required fees						
	Total	Tuition and required fees	Room	Board		Total	Tuition and required fees	Room	Board	In-state	Out-of-state
UNITED STATES.......	19,488	8,804	6,017	4,666	24,854	41,468	29,478	6,717	5,273	3,156	7,668
Alabama..........................	19,052	9,466	5,386	4,200	24,000	24,710	15,422	4,677	4,611	4,362	9,075
Alaska.............................	17,370	7,210	5,830	4,330	21,431	26,132	18,876	3,623	3,632	3,820	3,820
Arizona...........................	21,491	10,057	6,697	4,737	25,061	22,559	13,140	5,100	4,319	2,129	7,931
Arkansas.........................	16,871	7,924	4,959	3,989	19,323	29,804	21,710	4,100	3,994	3,195	4,582
California.........................	21,356	7,896	7,532	5,928	28,253	44,722	31,495	7,467	5,759	1,262	7,120
Colorado	20,943	9,352	5,672	5,919	28,986	34,337	22,627	6,827	4,883	3,565	10,152
Connecticut.....................	24,174	11,726	6,715	5,733	32,836	53,198	38,975	8,110	6,113	4,189	12,528
Delaware	21,698	9,578	7,259	4,862	28,497	25,996	14,383	5,798	5,815	NA	NA
District of Columbia	NA	5,612	NA	NA	11,756	55,669	40,618	9,649	5,402	NA	NA
Florida............................	14,806	4,435	5,860	4,512	18,304	35,876	24,360	6,473	5,042	2,552	9,122
Georgia	17,353	7,010	6,043	4,300	21,377	39,118	27,220	6,618	5,279	2,895	7,958
Hawaii............................	21,016	9,712	5,756	5,547	30,929	28,393	15,949	5,444	6,999	3,080	8,216
Idaho..............................	14,457	7,005	3,582	3,870	21,370	13,010	5,925	2,733	4,352	3,227	7,589
Illinois	24,541	13,636	5,975	4,930	28,167	43,382	31,298	6,986	5,097	3,749	10,748
Indiana	19,001	8,876	5,419	4,705	28,315	41,847	30,926	5,684	5,237	4,175	8,052
Iowa...............................	17,604	8,361	5,236	4,007	24,912	35,780	26,742	4,391	4,648	4,791	6,406
Kansas	17,560	8,489	4,669	4,402	22,000	28,746	20,291	4,046	4,408	3,222	4,548
Kentucky	19,673	10,014	5,547	4,112	23,539	34,893	25,845	4,623	4,426	3,962	13,321
Louisiana	18,319	8,813	5,700	3,806	22,771	47,559	35,190	6,798	5,571	4,031	6,496
Maine	19,073	9,219	4,937	4,917	26,004	48,107	35,547	6,290	6,270	3,673	6,494
Maryland.........................	20,647	9,083	6,600	4,964	22,437	53,775	40,209	7,767	5,798	3,983	9,170
Massachusetts	24,473	12,331	7,528	4,614	28,740	57,363	42,655	8,448	6,260	4,785	9,785
Michigan	21,832	11,890	4,936	5,006	36,714	33,498	24,058	4,543	4,897	3,423	6,474
Minnesota	19,727	10,883	4,772	4,072	19,088	40,939	30,925	5,237	4,777	5,310	6,053
Mississippi......................	16,843	7,472	5,539	3,833	19,138	24,698	16,949	4,036	3,713	2,830	5,176
Missouri..........................	17,639	8,176	5,844	3,619	18,940	33,433	23,702	5,511	4,221	3,028	5,737
Montana..........................	15,241	6,503	4,019	4,719	22,956	32,375	23,657	4,139	4,579	3,381	8,210
Nebraska.........................	17,379	7,732	5,297	4,350	19,483	32,200	23,109	4,751	4,340	2,991	3,941
Nevada	17,145	5,520	5,661	5,964	20,672	35,053	21,423	7,295	6,335	2,910	9,555
New Hampshire................	26,968	15,491	6,838	4,639	27,201	46,533	33,235	8,302	4,996	7,002	15,157
New Jersey	26,070	13,297	7,856	4,917	28,051	48,439	35,224	7,634	5,580	4,366	7,692
New Mexico	15,528	6,825	4,429	4,275	17,272	32,373	22,535	5,539	4,299	1,590	4,749
New York.........................	21,750	7,709	9,099	4,942	21,454	51,790	37,580	8,664	5,546	5,122	8,857
North Carolina.................	16,635	7,218	5,409	4,008	23,778	42,312	30,701	5,993	5,618	2,470	8,481
North Dakota...................	15,388	7,376	3,205	4,806	18,288	20,964	14,290	2,997	3,677	4,562	9,484
Ohio	20,961	9,827	6,306	4,827	23,434	40,980	30,296	5,567	5,118	3,655	5,721
Oklahoma........................	15,754	7,219	4,579	3,957	19,174	33,883	24,776	4,545	4,562	3,627	8,582
Oregon	21,324	9,739	6,828	4,757	29,330	48,703	37,088	6,048	5,566	4,263	8,410
Pennsylvania...................	25,331	14,068	6,545	4,719	26,328	52,132	39,185	7,076	5,870	5,048	12,833
Rhode Island...................	23,135	11,386	7,352	4,397	27,815	52,874	38,855	8,389	5,629	4,266	11,496
South Carolina	21,508	12,153	5,745	3,610	29,888	33,748	24,523	4,660	4,564	4,418	9,730
South Dakota	16,054	8,301	3,724	4,029	11,845	30,926	23,147	3,844	3,935	5,803	5,660
Tennessee	18,340	9,287	4,856	4,197	24,802	35,929	25,985	5,625	4,319	4,048	15,540
Texas..............................	17,799	8,375	4,931	4,493	23,511	41,979	31,009	6,125	4,845	2,099	6,100
Utah	13,709	6,334	3,210	4,165	19,407	15,212	7,445	3,901	3,865	3,690	11,728
Vermont..........................	26,786	15,537	7,110	4,139	37,991	54,003	41,063	7,108	5,831	6,222	12,294
Virginia...........................	22,567	12,126	5,907	4,534	32,250	32,616	22,286	5,511	4,819	4,962	11,080
Washington......................	18,053	6,903	5,886	5,264	28,128	46,746	35,288	6,111	5,347	3,848	6,647
West Virginia...................	17,096	7,241	5,245	4,609	20,030	20,898	12,206	4,250	4,442	4,009	9,241
Wisconsin	16,246	8,419	4,699	3,128	22,574	41,503	31,662	5,655	4,186	4,292	6,223
Wyoming	14,354	4,311	4,493	5,550	13,239	NA	18,021	NA	NA	2,987	7,292

NA = Not applicable.

NOTES AND DEFINITIONS: REGION AND STATE EDUCATION STATISTICS

This section provides details about each item's source and relevant definitions. Internet references are provided when available. In some cases, the Internet reference will lead to a general website instead of to the precise data included in this volume. Additional data sources, such as the U.S. Census Bureau's online FactFinder and online databases from the National Center for Education Statistics (NCES), were often used.

TABLE B-1

EDUCATIONAL ATTAINMENT

Source: U.S. Census Bureau. *American Community Survey, 2017*. Table B15001. Educational Attainment of the Population 18 Years and Over, by Region, Sex, and Age, 2017. (ACS 1-Year Estimates) https://factfinder.census.gov.

Statistics for educational attainment only include persons 25 years old and over. Respondents are classified according to the highest degree or the highest level of school completed. The question includes instructions for people currently enrolled in school to report the level of the previous grade attended or the highest degree received.

High school graduate or more. This category includes persons who have received a high school diploma or its equivalent, and those who reported any level higher than a high school diploma.

Bachelor's degree or more. This category includes persons who have received bachelor's degrees, master's degrees, professional school degrees (such as law school or medical school degrees), and doctoral degrees.

TABLE B-2

Source: U.S. Census Bureau. *American Community Survey, 2017*. 1-year estimates. Tables K201501, C15002, C15002A, C15002B, C15002D, and C15002I. Attainment of the Population 25 Over, by Region, State, Sex, Race, and Hispanic Origin, 2017. https://factfinder.census.gov.

Tables B-1 and B-2 are from the American Community Survey (ACS), the sample survey that has replaced the long form of the decennial census. The sample data are estimates of the actual figures that would have been obtained from a complete count. Estimates derived from a sample are expected to be different from the 100-percent figures because they are subject to sampling and nonsampling errors. Sampling error in data arises from the selection of people and housing units included in the sample. Nonsampling error affects both sample and 100-percent data. It is introduced as a result of errors that may occur during the data collection and processing phases of the census. Conclusions should not be based on small numbers or small differences and users should consult the ACS website to determine the appropriate margins of error. The ACS is ongoing and data are released on an annual basis for all regions and states.

For additional information about the American Community Survey, see www.census.gov/acs/www/.

Educational Attainment. In the ACS, respondents are classified according to the highest degree or the highest level of school completed. The question includes instructions for people currently enrolled in school to report the level of the previous grade attended or the highest degree received.

High school graduate or higher. This category includes persons who have received a high school diploma or its equivalent (for example, GED), and those who reported any level higher than a high school diploma.

Bachelor's degree or higher. This category includes persons who have received bachelor's degrees, master's degrees, professional school degrees (such as law school or medical school degrees), and doctoral degrees.

Geographic Definitions

Data are presented for the four major regions of the United States. These groups of states are as follows:

Northeast: Connecticut, Maine, Massachusetts, New Hampshire, New Jersey, New York, Pennsylvania, Rhode Island, and Vermont

Midwest: Illinois, Indiana, Iowa, Kansas, Michigan, Minnesota, Missouri, Nebraska, North Dakota, Ohio, South Dakota, and Wisconsin

South: Alabama, Arkansas, Delaware, District of Columbia, Florida, Georgia, Kentucky, Louisiana, Maryland, Mississippi, North Carolina, Oklahoma, South Carolina, Tennessee, Texas, Virginia, and West Virginia

West: Alaska, Arizona, California, Colorado, Hawaii, Idaho, Montana, Nevada, New Mexico, Oregon, Utah, Washington, and Wyoming

TABLE B-3

POPULATION
Source: U.S. Census Bureau. *Population Estimates Program.* 2017 American Community Survey. https://factfinder.census.gov

The population data for 2017 are U.S. Census Bureau estimates of the resident population as of July 1, 2017.

INCOME, POVERTY, AND HEALTH INSURANCE
Source: U.S. Census Bureau. American Community Survey, 2017 1-Year Estimates.

The Census Bureau reports income from several major household surveys and programs. Each of these surveys differs from the others in some way, such as the length and detail of its questionnaire, the number of households included (sample size), and the methodology used to collect and process the data. The American Community Survey (ACS) is preferred for subnational data on income and poverty by detailed demographic characteristics, because of its large sample size. The Census Bureau recommends using the ACS for single-year estimates of income and poverty at the state level.

The median income for a family of four is from ACS table B19119 on American FactFinder. "Total income" is the sum of the amounts reported separately for wages, salary, commissions, bonuses, or tips; self-employment income from own nonfarm or farm businesses, including proprietorships and partnerships; interest, dividends, net rental income, royalty income, or income from estates and trusts; Social Security or Railroad Retirement income; Supplemental Security Income (SSI); any public assistance or welfare payments from the state or local welfare office; retirement, survivor, or disability pensions; and any other sources of income received regularly such as Veterans' (VA) payments, unemployment compensation, child support, or alimony. Receipts not counted as income include various "lump sum" payments, such as capital gains or inheritances. The total represents the amount of income received before deductions for personal income taxes, Social Security, bond purchases, union dues, Medicare deductions, and the like.

Poverty status is based on the definition prescribed by the U.S. Office of Management and Budget as the standard to be used by federal agencies for statistical purposes.

Persons lacking health insurance coverage include those not covered by a private health plan or by Medicaid, Medicare, or a military health plan.

LANGUAGE SPOKEN AT HOME
Source: U.S. Census Bureau, *American Community Survey, 2017.* 1-year estimates. Tables S1601 and S1603. https://factfinder. census.gov.

RACE AND ETHNICITY ORIGIN
Source: U.S. Census Bureau, *American Community Survey, 2017.* 1-year estimates. Table S0901. https://factfinder.census.gov.

TABLE B-4

CITY, SUBURBAN, TOWN, OR RURAL SCHOOLS
Source: U.S. Department of Education, National Center for Education Statistics (NCES), Common Core of Data (CCD), "Public Elementary/Secondary School Universe Survey", Provisional Version 1a, and the NCES Education Demographic and Geographic Estimates (EDGE), "Public Elementary/Secondary School Universe - Geographic Data," 2015-16. Table 4. https:// nces.ed.gov/pubs2018/2018052/tables/ table_04.asp

The locales of "city", "suburban", "town", and "rural" are a collapse of the 12 category, urban-centric locale code.

TABLE B-5

SCHOOL ENROLLMENT OF RESI-DENT POPULATION
Source: U.S. Census Bureau. American Community Survey, 2017 1-Year Estimates

Table S1401 from American FactFinder.

School enrollment is enrollment in a regular school, either public or private, including nursery schools, kindergarten, and elementary schools, as well as schooling that leads to a high school diploma or college degree. Schools supported and controlled primarily by the federal, state, or local government are defined as public schools (including tribal schools). Schools primarily supported and controlled by religious organizations or other private groups are considered private schools.

TABLE B-6

NUMBER AND TYPE OF SCHOOLS
Sources: U.S. Department of Education. National Center for Education Statistics. *Common Core of Data, 2016–2017; Public Elementary/Secondary School Universe Survey, SY 2016–17 Provisional Version 1a;* nces.ed.gov/ccd

The state data are from the CCD school universe. Almost 99,000 schools are represented, including all those that were operating in 2016–2017.

Regular schools do not focus primarily on special, vocational, or alternative education, though they may offer these programs in addition to the regular curriculum. Special education schools focus primarily on special education, with materials and instructional approaches adapted to meet students' needs. Vocational education schools focus on vocational, technical, or career education. They provide education or training in at least one semi-skilled or technical occupation. Alternative education schools address students' needs that typically cannot be met in a regular school setting. These schools provide nontraditional educational experiences.

A charter school is a school that provides free public elementary and/or secondary education to eligible students under a specific charter granted by the state legislature or other appropriate authority; the school must have also been designated as a charter school by these authorities. Charter schools can be administered by regular school districts, State Education Agencies (SEAs), or chartering organizations.

A magnet school or program is a special school or program designed to attract students of different racial and ethnic backgrounds for the purpose of reducing, preventing, or eliminating racial isolation and/or to provide an academic or social focus on a particular theme.

A Title I eligible school is a school designated under appropriate state and federal regulations as being high poverty and eligible for participation in programs (such as remedial reading or remedial math) authorized by Title I of P.L. 107–110. A Title I school is one in which the percentage of children from low-income families is at least as high as the percentage of children from low-income families served by the LEA as a whole, or a school designated by the LEA as Title I eligible because 35 percent or more of the children are from low-income families. A Title I schoolwide school is a school in which all the students are designated under appropriate state and federal regulations as eligible for participation in Title I programs authorized by Title I of P.L. 107–110. The number of students who received Title I services is from the Public School Data File of the Schools and Staffing Survey.

TABLE B-7
Sources: U.S. Department of Education. National Center for Education Statistics. *Digest of Education Statistics*, tables 204.10, 204.20, 204.70, and 204.75c. nces.ed.gov/programs/digest/current_tables.asp

STUDENTS WHO ARE ELIGIBLE FOR FREE OR REDUCED-PRICE LUNCH

The Free and Reduced-Price Lunch Program is a program under the National School Lunch Act that provides cash subsidies for free or reduced-price meals to students based on family size and income criteria. Participation in the Free and Reduced-Price Lunch Program depends on income, and eligibility is often used to estimate student needs.

STUDENTS WITH INDIVIDUAL EDUCATION PROGRAM

An Individualized Education Program (IEP) is a written instructional plan for students with disabilities who are designated as special education students under IDEA (Individuals with Disabilities Education Act). An IEP includes a statement of present levels of educational performance of a child; a statement of annual goals, including short-term instructional objectives; a statement of specific educational services to be provided and the extent to which the child will be able to participate in regular educational programs; a projected date for initiation and the anticipated duration of services; appropriate objectives, criteria, and evaluation procedures; and schedules for determining, on at least an annual basis, whether instructional objectives are being achieved.

STUDENTS WHO ARE ENGLISH-LANGUAGE LEARNERS

This category includes the number of students who are served in appropriate programs of language assistance (e.g., English as a Second Language, High Intensity Language Training, and bilingual education). This designation changed from Limited-English Proficient (LEP) to English-Language Learners (ELL) in the 2001–2002 school year.

TABLE B-8

PRIVATE SCHOOLS
Sources: U.S. Department of Education, National Center for Education Statistics, Private School Universe Survey (PSS), 2005-06 through 2015-16. Table 205.80. https://nces.ed.gov/programs/digest/d16/tables/dt16_205.80.asp

Since 1989, the Census Bureau has conducted the biennial Private School Universe Survey (PSS) for NCES. The PSS is designed to generate biennial data on the total number of private schools, students, and teachers and to build a universe of private schools in all of the states and the District of Columbia to serve as a sampling frame of private schools for NCES sample surveys. The target population for the PSS is every school in all of the states and the District of Columbia that are not primarily supported by public funds, provide instruction for one or more grades between kindergarten and grade 12 (or comparable ungraded levels), and have one or more teachers. Organizations or institutions that provide support for home schooling, but do not provide classroom instruction, are not included. Although the PSS has begun to collect limited data on the many private schools for which kindergarten is the highest grade, the data in this volume are for (traditional) schools that include at least one grade between grades 1 and 12.

A private school is controlled by an individual or agency other than a state, a subdivision of a state, or the federal government; is usually supported primarily by nonpublic funds; and the operation of its program does not rest with publicly elected or appointed officials. Private schools include both nonprofit and proprietary institutions.

Data for private schools in Arkansas, Colorado, Washington, D.C., Idaho, Indiana, and Nebraska, should be interpreted with caution. The coefficient of variation for these estimates is larger than 25 percent.

TABLE B-9

Sources: U.S. Department of Education. National Center for Education Statistics. *Digest of Education Statistics*, tables 213.50 and 213.20. nces.ed.gov/programs/digest/current_tables.asp

PUBLIC SCHOOL STAFF

The number of teachers represents full-time equivalent teachers employed within the state. Instructional aides directly assist teachers in providing instruction. Instructional

coordinators help teachers through curriculum development and in-service training. Support staff includes those involved with food, health, library, maintenance, transportation, security, and other services in public schools. School administrators are principals and assistant principals. School district administrators include the Local Education Agency (LEA) superintendents, deputies, assistant superintendents, and other persons with district-wide responsibilities.

TABLE B-10

REVENUES

Source: U.S. Department of Education. National Center for Education Statistics. "Digest of Education Statistics." Tables 235. 20.nces.ed.gov/programs/digest/current_tables. asp

The state data include adjustments made by NCES. Values that were missing and not reported elsewhere in the survey were imputed based on corresponding proportions in reporting states. Other adjustments were made when a single value was reported that included two or more categories. NCES distributed portions of the single reported value to the missing items. In Nebraska and Wyoming, the fiscal data do not include prekindergarten. In Illinois and Wisconsin, revenues for charter schools are not included. In addition to these adjustments, the NPEFS may also include state-run education programs. Consequently, these numbers may differ from the state totals in Table C, which are derived from a different survey.

Revenues from federal sources include direct grants-in-aid from the federal government, federal grants-in-aid through the state or an intermediate agency, and other revenue in lieu of taxes to compensate a school district for nontaxable federal institutions within a district's boundaries.

State revenues include revenues that can be used without restriction, revenues for categorical purposes, and revenues in lieu of taxation. Also included are revenues from payments made by a state for the benefit of the Local Education Agency (LEA) or contributions of equipment or supplies. Such revenues include the payment of a pension fund by the state on behalf of an LEA employee for services rendered and contributions of fixed assets (property, plant, or equipment), such as school buses and textbooks.

Revenues from local sources include local property and non-property tax revenues, taxes levied or assessed by an LEA, revenues from a local government to the LEA, tuition received, transportation fees, earnings on investments from LEA holdings, net revenues from food services (gross receipts less gross expenditures), net revenues from student activities (gross receipts less gross expenditures), and other revenues (textbook sales, donations, and property rentals). Intermediate revenues were included in local revenue totals. Intermediate revenues are derived from sources other than Local or State Education Agencies; these sources operate at an intermediate level between Local and State Education Agencies and possess independent fundraising capabilities (such as county or municipal agencies).

EXPENDITURES
Source: U.S. Department of Education. National Center for Education Statistics. "Digest of Education Statistics." Tables 236.30 and 236.65. nces.ed.gov/programs/digest/current_tables.asp

The state data include adjustments made by NCES. Values that were missing and not reported elsewhere in the survey were imputed based on proportions in reporting states. Other adjustments were made when a single value was reported that included two or more categories. NCES distributed portions of the single reported value to the missing items. In Nebraska and Wyoming, the fiscal data do not include prekindergarten. In Illinois and Wisconsin, expenditures for charter

schools are not included. In addition to these adjustments, the NPEFS may include state-run education programs. Consequently, these numbers may differ from the state totals in Table C, which come from a different survey.

Current expenditures consist of expenditures for the categories of instruction, support services, and non-instructional services for salaries; employee benefits; purchased services and supplies; and payments by the state made for or on behalf of school systems. These expenditures do not include expenditures for debt service, capital outlay, and property (e.g., equipment), or direct costs (e.g., Head Start, adult education, community colleges, etc.) and community services expenditures.

Instruction and instruction-related expenses comprise current expenditures for activities that deal directly with the interaction between students and teachers. These expenditures include teacher salaries and benefits, supplies (such as textbooks), instructional staff support (for example, salaries for librarians and instructional specialists), and purchased instructional services.

Support services expenditures consist of current expenditures for activities supporting instruction. These services include operation and maintenance of buildings, school administration, student support services (e.g., nurses, therapists, and guidance counselors), student transportation, school district administration, business services, research, and data processing.

Non-instruction expenditures are mostly for food service, but also consist of expenditures for enterprise operations, such as bookstores and interscholastic athletics.

TABLE B-11

DROPOUTS
Source: U.S. Department of Commerce, Census Bureau, American Community Survey

(ACS), 1-year sample, 2016. NCES, *Digest of Education Statistics*, Table 219.85a. https://nces.ed.gov/programs/digest/d17/tables/dt17_219.85a.asp

"Status" dropouts are 16- to 24-year-olds who are not enrolled in school and who have not completed a high school program, regardless of when they left school. People who have received GED credentials are counted as high school completers. Data are based on sample surveys of the entire population in the given age range residing within the United States, including both noninstitutionalized persons (e.g., those living in households, college housing, or military housing located within the United States) and institutionalized persons (e.g., those living in prisons, nursing facilities, or other healthcare facilities). Totals include other racial/ethnic groups not separately shown. Race categories exclude persons of Hispanic ethnicity.

TABLES B-12 to B-15

HIGHER EDUCATION
Sources: U.S. Department of Education. National Center for Education Statistics. Integrated Postsecondary Education Data System (IPEDS). *Digest of Education Statistics, 2017.* Tables 304.80, 319.10, 306.60, and 330.20.

The Integrated Postsecondary Education Data System (IPEDS) surveys approximately 10,000 postsecondary institutions, including universities, colleges, and institutions offering technical and vocational education beyond the high school level. This survey, which began in 1986, replaced the Higher Education General Information Survey (HEGIS). IPEDS is made up of eight integrated components that obtain information on who provides postsecondary education (institutions), who participates in it and completes it (students), what programs are offered and which ones are completed, and the specific human and financial resources involved in the provision of institutionally

based postsecondary education. These components are organized into the following categories: Institutional Characteristics, including instructional activity; Fall Enrollment, including age and residence; Enrollment in Occupationally Specific Programs; Completions; Finance; Staff; Salaries of Full-Time Instructional Faculty; and Academic Libraries.

Institutions of higher education include those with courses leading to an associate's degree or higher, or those with courses accepted for credit toward such degrees. A public institution is controlled and operated by publicly elected or appointed officials and derives its primary support from public funds. A private institution is controlled by an individual or agency other than a state, a subdivision of a state, or the federal government; it is usually primarily supported by nonpublic funds, and the operation of its program does not rest with publicly elected or appointed officials. Private institutions comprise both not-for-profit and proprietary institutions.

Full-time students include undergraduate students enrolled for 12 or more semester credits, 12 or more quarter credits, or 24 or more contact hours a week each term; graduate students enrolled for 9 or more semester credits or 9 or more quarter credits, or students involved in thesis or dissertation preparation who are considered full time students by the institution; and first-professional students (as defined by the institution).

Types of institutions include the following:

- Degree-granting institutions, which offer associate's, bachelor's, master's, doctoral and/or first-professional degrees.

- Level categories include four-year and higher (four-year) institutions, at least two but less than four-year (two-year) institutions, and less than two-year institutions.

A four-year institution is a postsecondary institution that offers programs of at least four years' duration or programs at or above the baccalaureate level. This category includes schools that only offer post-baccalaureate certificates and those that only offer graduate programs. Also included are freestanding medical, law, and other first-professional schools.

A two-year institution is a postsecondary institution that offers programs of at least two years' duration but less than four years' duration. This category includes occupational and vocational schools with programs of at least 1,800 hours and academic institutions with programs of less than four years' duration. It does not include bachelor's degree–granting institutions where the baccalaureate program can be completed in three years.

Control categories are public, private not-for-profit, and private for-profit.

Undergraduate students are registered at an institution of higher education and are working in a program leading to a baccalaureate degree or other formal award below the baccalaureate, such as an associate degree.

Postbaccalaureate students are working towards master's or doctor's degree or are enrolled in graduate-level classes, but not enrolled in degree programs.

Race/ethnicity categories are categories used to describe groups to which individuals belong, identify with, or belong to in the eyes of the community. A person may be counted in only one group. Classification is based on self-identification. Race categories exclude persons of Hispanic ethnicity.

A nonresident alien is a person who is not a citizen or national of the United States, and who is in this country on a visa or temporary basis; a nonresident alien does not have the right to remain in the United States indefinitely.

Migration refers to the movement of students from their home state of residence to another state to attend a postsecondary institution. The percentages in columns 123 and 124 refer to all first-time postsecondary students enrolled in degree granting institutions in fall 2012.

An associate's degree is a degree granted for the successful completion of a sub-baccalaureate program of studies, and usually requires at least two years (or the equivalent) of full-time college-level study. This category also includes degrees granted in a cooperative or work-study program.

A bachelor's degree is a degree granted for the successful completion of a baccalaureate program of studies, and usually requires at least four years (or the equivalent) of full-time college-level study. This category includes degrees granted in a cooperative or work-study program.

A master's degree is awarded for successful completion of a program generally requiring 1 or 2 years of full-time, college-level study beyond the bachelor's degree. One type of master's degree, including the master of arts degree (M.A.), and the master of science degree (M.S.), is awarded in the liberal arts and sciences for advanced scholarship in a subject field or discipline and demonstrated ability to perform scholarly research. A second type of master's degree is awarded for the completion of a professionally oriented program. These include master's degrees in education (M.Ed.), business administration (M.B.A.), fine arts (M.F.A.), music (M.M.), social work (M.S.W.), and public administration (M.P.A.) A third type of master's degree is awarded in professional fields for study beyond the first-professional degree, such as the master of laws (LL.M.) and the masters of science in various medical specializations. Some master's degrees—such as divinity degrees (M.Div. or M.H.L./Rav), which were formerly classified as "first-professional"—may require more than 2 years of full-time study beyond the bachelor's degree.

A doctor's degree is an earned degree that generally carries the title of Doctor. The Doctor of Philosophy degree (Ph.D.) is the highest academic degree and requires mastery within a field of knowledge and demonstrated ability to perform scholarly research. Other doctor's degrees are awarded for fulfilling specialized requirements in professional fields, such as education (Ed.D.), musical arts (D.M.A.), business administration (D.B.A.), and engineering (D.Eng. or D.E.S.). Many doctor's degrees in academic and professional fields require an earned master's degree as a prerequisite. The doctor's degree classification includes most degrees that NCES formerly classified as first-professional degrees. Such degrees are awarded in the fields of dentistry (D.D.S. or D.M.D.), medicine (M.D.), optometry (O.D.), osteopathic medicine (D.O.), pharmacy (Pharm.D.), podiatry (D.P.M., Pod.D., or D.P.), veterinary medicine (D.V.M.), chiropractic (D.C. or D.C.M.), and law (L.L.B. or J.D.).

Tuition and required fees are payments or charges for instruction or compensation for services, privileges, or the use of equipment, books, or other goods. Data are for the entire academic year and are average charges. In-state tuition and fees were weighted by the number of full-time-equivalent undergraduates, but were not adjusted to reflect student residency. Out-of-state tuition and fees were weighted by the number of first-time freshmen attending the institution in fall 2016 from out of state.

PART C

COUNTY EDUCATION STATISTICS

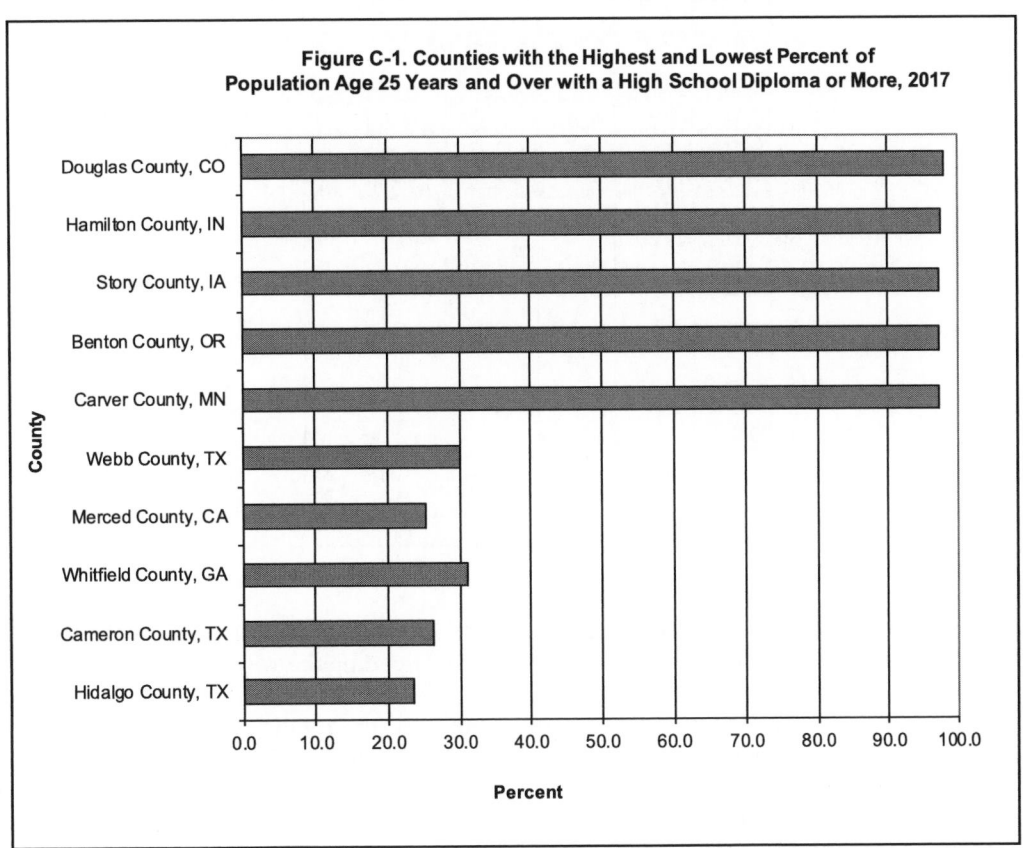

Figure C-1. Counties with the Highest and Lowest Percent of
Population Age 25 Years and Over with a High School Diploma or More, 2017

In 2017, there were 44 counties where more than 95 percent of the population age 25 years old and over had graduated from high school. The highest proportion was 98.0 percent of the population in Douglas County, Colorado. Five counties had high school attainment levels of less than 70 percent, including three counties in Texas along with Whitfield County, Georgia, and Merced County, California. (Table C-2)

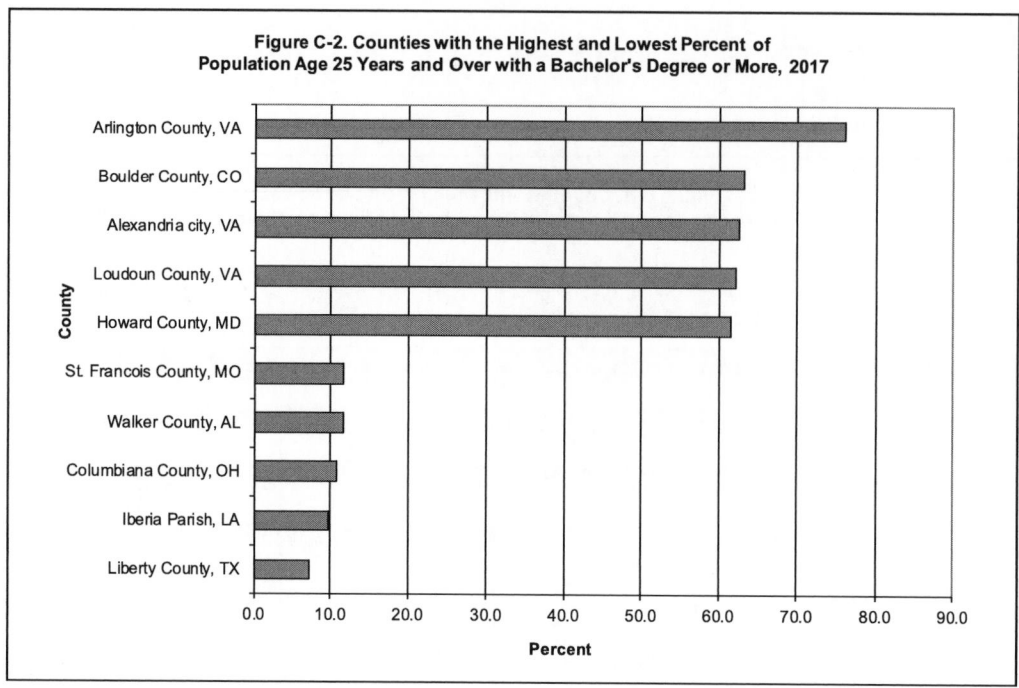

Figure C-2. Counties with the Highest and Lowest Percent of Population Age 25 Years and Over with a Bachelor's Degree or More, 2017

In 2017, eight counties had college attainment levels of 60 percent or more, with Arlington County, Virginia (which is near Washington, DC), leading the way with 76.0 percent of population age 25 years and over having bachelor's degrees or more. Five of the top ten counties were in the Washington, DC, metropolitan area. The others were Boulder County, Colorado (63.2 percent with college degrees), New York County, New York (60.5 percent), Williamson County, Tennessee (60.0 percent), Hamilton County, Indiana (59.9 percent), and Douglas County, Colorado (58.6 percent). Liberty County, Texas, had the lowest college attainment rate, with just 7.3 percent of the population having a bachelor's degree or more. (Table C-2)

Figure C-3. Counties with the Highest and Lowest Median Earnings for Population Age 25 Years and Over with Bachelor's Degrees, 2017

Arlington County also had the highest median earnings for 2017 at $75,904. Four counties had median earnings over $65,000. Otero County, New Mexico, had the lowest median earnings, $24,623. Twenty-eight counties had median earnings less than $30,000. (Table C-2)

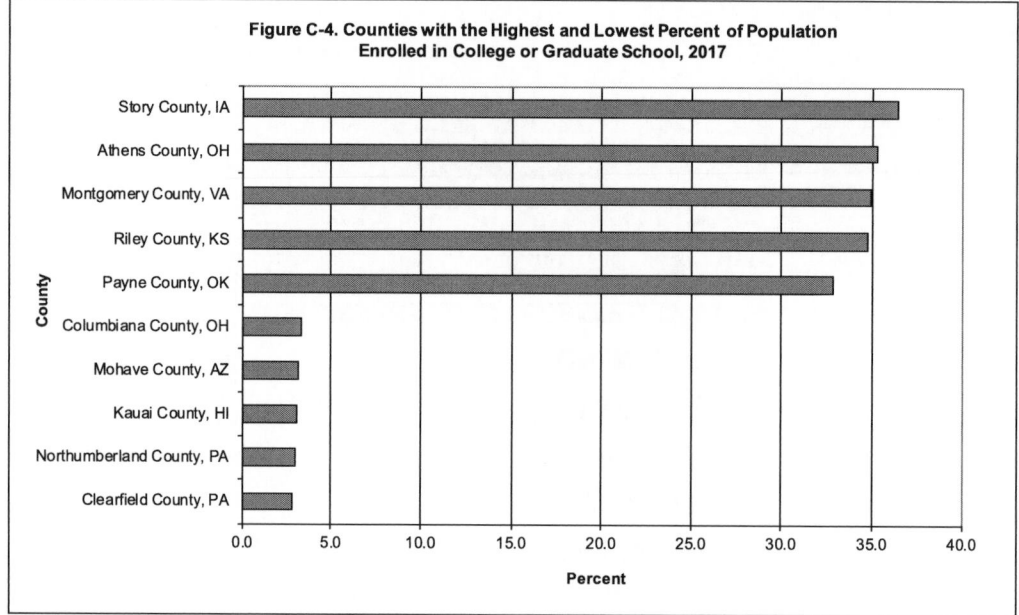

Figure C-4. Counties with the Highest and Lowest Percent of Population Enrolled in College or Graduate School, 2017

The counties with the highest percent of population enrolled in college or graduate school in 2017 were: Story County, Iowa, where Iowa State is located (36.4 percent), Athens County, Ohio, home to Ohio University (35.2 percent), and Montgomery County, Virginia, which is the home of Virginia Tech (34.9 percent). (Table C-3)

Table C-1. Population and Poverty Characteristics, by State and Selected Counties, 2017

(Number; percent.)

State/County	Population		Children under 18 years old in poverty (percent)	Children under 19 years with no health insurance (percent)
	Total under 18 years old	Percent under 18 years old		
UNITED STATES...	73,648,683	22.6	18.4	5.0
ALABAMA	1,094,061	22.4	24.6	3.1
Baldwin County, Alabama...............................	46,021	21.6	10.9	4.4
Calhoun County, Alabama...............................	25,000	21.8	22.4	1.0
Cullman County, Alabama...............................	18,092	21.9	14.8	4.2
DeKalb County, Alabama................................	17,240	24.1	29.8	1.8
Elmore County, Alabama................................	18,095	22.2	12.9	2.1
Etowah County, Alabama...............................	22,340	21.7	32.0	3.1
Houston County, Alabama..............................	24,189	23.2	27.1	1.4
Jefferson County, Alabama............................	150,754	22.9	23.5	4.6
Lauderdale County, Alabama..........................	18,377	19.9	15.3	3.0
Lee County, Alabama.....................................	34,395	21.3	23.6	3.4
Limestone County, Alabama...........................	21,228	22.5	18.8	0.7
Madison County, Alabama..............................	79,506	22.0	20.3	5.1
Marshall County, Alabama..............................	23,678	24.8	35.7	2.8
Mobile County, Alabama.................................	97,669	23.6	32.1	3.3
Montgomery County, Alabama.........................	53,448	23.6	36.8	2.0
Morgan County, Alabama...............................	26,887	22.6	20.4	1.0
St. Clair County, Alabama..............................	20,545	23.3	18.7	0.3
Shelby County, Alabama	50,675	23.7	8.9	2.7
Talladega County, Alabama............................	17,398	21.7	28.9	0.5
Tuscaloosa County, Alabama..........................	43,561	21.0	18.1	0.8
Walker County, Alabama	14,054	21.9	17.1	2.4
ALASKA...	185,181	25.0	14.9	9.6
Anchorage Municipality, Alaska......................	72,042	24.5	14.3	8.0
Fairbanks North Star Borough, Alaska	23,932	24.0	4.9	10.2
Matanuska-Susitna Borough, Alaska....................	29,150	27.4	14.0	11.2
ARIZONA	1,632,728	23.3	20.8	7.7
Apache County, Arizona	19,779	27.6	44.1	26.1
Cochise County, Arizona	27,074	21.7	19.4	4.5
Coconino County, Arizona	29,569	21.0	20.7	7.9
Maricopa County, Arizona	1,045,263	24.3	19.2	8.0
Mohave County, Arizona	36,199	17.5	27.0	11.1
Navajo County, Arizona	29,445	27.0	37.6	9.8
Pima County, Arizona	217,019	21.2	22.4	5.8
Pinal County, Arizona	99,004	23.0	14.7	4.6
Yavapai County, Arizona................................	37,443	16.4	19.3	7.8
Yuma County, Arizona	52,497	25.3	24.9	7.2
ARKANSAS..	708,433	23.6	22.5	4.4
Benton County, Arkansas	70,752	26.6	11.9	5.1
Craighead County, Arkansas	26,201	24.5	15.1	4.7
Faulkner County, Arkansas.............................	28,730	23.2	13.3	4.4
Garland County, Arkansas..............................	19,842	20.1	23.2	12.0
Jefferson County, Arkansas............................	15,486	22.4	38.3	4.4
Lonoke County, Arkansas...............................	19,027	26.1	16.1	4.1
Pulaski County, Arkansas...............................	92,337	23.4	19.1	2.8
Saline County, Arkansas................................	27,964	23.4	6.8	5.6
Sebastian County, Arkansas...........................	30,953	24.2	31.7	7.9
Washington County, Arkansas	56,973	24.6	16.4	9.1
White County, Arkansas	18,518	23.4	20.3	2.8
CALIFORNIA	9,057,386	22.9	18.1	3.1
Alameda County, California	344,662	20.7	10.1	2.4
Butte County, California..................................	45,869	20.0	22.3	1.2
Contra Costa County, California	262,014	22.8	11.9	3.5
El Dorado County, California	37,749	20.0	9.1	2.8
Fresno County, California	281,683	28.5	28.5	2.7
Humboldt County, California	26,095	19.1	27.2	8.7
Imperial County, California..............................	52,551	28.7	28.1	3.9
Kern County, California	259,222	29.0	29.8	3.0
Kings County, California.................................	40,967	27.3	26.8	3.3
Lake County, California	13,168	20.5	33.4	1.8
Los Angeles County, California........................	2,224,905	21.9	20.8	3.6
Madera County, California	42,580	27.1	32.0	3.1
Marin County, California.................................	52,268	20.0	10.2	1.8
Mendocino County, California	18,921	21.5	17.3	6.3
Merced County, California	80,514	29.5	37.1	2.4
Monterey County, California............................	115,143	26.3	15.9	2.2
Napa County, California..................................	29,484	20.9	3.2	4.5

Table C-1. Population and Poverty Characteristics, by State and Selected Counties, 2017—*Continued*

(Number; percent.)

State/County	Population		Children under 18 years old in poverty (percent)	Children under 19 years with no health insurance (percent)
	Total under 18 years old	Percent under 18 years old		
CALIFORNIA—*(Continued)*				
Nevada County, California	17,283	17.3	14.8	5.7
Orange County, California	705,999	22.1	15.8	3.3
Placer County, California	86,249	22.3	7.4	2.3
Riverside County, California	616,210	25.4	15.9	3.9
Sacramento County, California	364,311	23.8	18.1	3.0
San Bernardino County, California	571,670	26.5	23.0	2.7
San Diego County, California	728,528	21.8	15.7	3.9
San Francisco County, California	118,584	13.4	11.4	1.4
San Joaquin County, California	203,135	27.3	22.5	3.0
San Luis Obispo County, California	50,790	17.9	12.3	4.0
San Mateo County, California	160,264	20.8	6.9	2.0
Santa Barbara County, California	99,712	22.2	18.8	3.6
Santa Clara County, California	430,081	22.2	8.0	2.0
Santa Cruz County, California	53,426	19.4	12.7	3.7
Shasta County, California	38,695	21.5	23.3	4.6
Solano County, California	99,059	22.2	15.1	1.7
Sonoma County, California	99,696	19.8	10.8	2.3
Stanislaus County, California	148,237	27.1	17.8	1.2
Sutter County, California	25,064	25.9	15.3	4.5
Tulare County, California	143,725	30.9	33.2	1.8
Ventura County, California	198,663	23.3	13.2	4.0
Yolo County, California	46,228	21.1	14.1	0.7
Yuba County, California	21,041	27.3	16.6	0.5
COLORADO	1,262,359	22.5	12.0	4.3
Adams County, Colorado	135,396	26.9	14.0	4.1
Arapahoe County, Colorado	153,056	23.8	8.2	3.5
Boulder County, Colorado	62,936	19.5	12.0	2.2
Broomfield County, Colorado	16,070	23.5	3.2	1.6
Denver County, Colorado	140,204	19.9	17.2	5.3
Douglas County, Colorado	89,024	26.6	3.4	1.6
El Paso County, Colorado	170,006	24.3	14.2	3.1
Jefferson County, Colorado	114,968	20.0	8.7	3.2
Larimer County, Colorado	68,426	19.9	9.0	5.9
Mesa County, Colorado	33,045	21.8	20.3	3.2
Pueblo County, Colorado	37,899	22.8	24.5	4.9
Weld County, Colorado	80,530	26.4	8.8	4.8
CONNECTICUT	742,278	20.7	12.6	3.1
Fairfield County, Connecticut	214,749	22.6	11.3	5.3
Hartford County, Connecticut	188,504	21.1	15.2	2.5
Litchfield County, Connecticut	33,087	18.2	6.3	1.3
Middlesex County, Connecticut	29,541	18.1	8.0	0.9
New Haven County, Connecticut	174,842	20.3	14.4	2.1
New London County, Connecticut	52,659	19.6	11.5	1.8
Tolland County, Connecticut	26,464	17.5	4.8	3.3
Windham County, Connecticut	22,432	19.3	16.3	2.6
DELAWARE	204,313	21.2	18.5	3.5
Kent County, Delaware	40,793	23.1	21.3	6.8
New Castle County, Delaware	121,285	21.7	16.2	2.3
Sussex County, Delaware	42,235	18.7	22.1	3.9
DISTRICT OF COLUMBIA	124,598	18.0	25.6	1.2
District of Columbia, District of Columbia	124,598	18.0	25.6	1.2
FLORIDA	4,200,780	20.0	20.3	7.3
Alachua County, Florida	48,047	18.0	18.8	4.4
Bay County, Florida	39,870	21.7	20.6	5.3
Brevard County, Florida	108,791	18.5	18.6	5.7
Broward County, Florida	411,799	21.3	17.9	8.9
Charlotte County, Florida	22,648	12.4	11.1	15.0
Citrus County, Florida	21,242	14.6	26.1	5.8
Clay County, Florida	50,558	23.8	13.1	7.6
Collier County, Florida	64,723	17.4	25.6	10.7
Columbia County, Florida	15,218	21.9	11.8	5.5
Duval County, Florida	211,042	22.5	23.4	6.9
Escambia County, Florida	65,715	21.0	26.1	6.3
Flagler County, Florida	19,041	17.2	29.7	11.2
Hernando County, Florida	35,317	18.9	16.9	10.3
Highlands County, Florida	18,291	17.8	37.6	4.9

Table C-1. Population and Poverty Characteristics, by State and Selected Counties, 2017—*Continued*

(Number; percent.)

State/County	Population		Children under 18 years old in poverty (percent)	Children under 19 years with no health insurance (percent)
	Total under 18 years old	Percent under 18 years old		
FLORIDA—(*Continued*)				
Hillsborough County, Florida	321,546	22.8	21.8	7.9
Indian River County, Florida	25,527	16.5	8.5	4.9
Lake County, Florida	67,026	19.4	22.0	9.3
Lee County, Florida	131,867	17.8	20.8	9.1
Leon County, Florida	54,381	18.7	15.0	3.6
Manatee County, Florida	71,655	18.6	14.1	6.2
Marion County, Florida	66,845	18.9	25.4	4.6
Martin County, Florida	26,456	16.5	14.6	12.3
Miami-Dade County, Florida	557,238	20.2	21.8	6.7
Monroe County, Florida	11,780	15.3	17.8	17.5
Nassau County, Florida	16,179	19.6	9.5	11.1
Okaloosa County, Florida	45,039	22.2	15.8	9.2
Orange County, Florida	301,904	22.4	22.4	8.6
Osceola County, Florida	87,372	24.8	20.9	7.0
Palm Beach County, Florida	283,151	19.2	16.5	8.4
Pasco County, Florida	106,936	20.3	18.3	4.2
Pinellas County, Florida	159,887	16.5	15.8	6.2
Polk County, Florida	153,232	22.3	26.2	6.5
Putnam County, Florida	15,793	21.5	51.2	5.3
St. Johns County, Florida	53,762	22.1	11.1	4.5
St. Lucie County, Florida	63,050	20.1	16.1	6.2
Santa Rosa County, Florida	38,218	21.9	15.4	4.3
Sarasota County, Florida	60,085	14.3	11.4	9.3
Seminole County, Florida	97,833	21.1	14.1	2.2
Sumter County, Florida	8,483	6.8	12.9	8.2
Volusia County, Florida	95,971	17.8	25.7	5.2
Walton County, Florida	13,839	20.2	39.4	6.9
GEORGIA	2,514,765	24.1	21.0	7.5
Barrow County, Georgia	20,907	26.4	15.6	7.1
Bartow County, Georgia	25,556	24.3	21.0	9.6
Bibb County, Georgia	37,690	24.7	37.2	7.1
Bulloch County, Georgia	15,335	20.1	26.5	2.4
Carroll County, Georgia	28,185	23.9	28.8	7.3
Catoosa County, Georgia	15,262	22.9	9.6	7.0
Chatham County, Georgia	62,765	21.6	22.4	7.0
Cherokee County, Georgia	61,639	24.9	9.6	5.2
Clarke County, Georgia	21,956	17.3	24.8	11.4
Clayton County, Georgia	79,861	28.0	21.8	7.1
Cobb County, Georgia	181,098	24.0	10.3	9.0
Columbia County, Georgia	38,835	25.6	4.9	1.2
Coweta County, Georgia	35,457	24.8	15.3	3.7
DeKalb County, Georgia	175,205	23.3	24.3	6.3
Dougherty County, Georgia	21,790	24.3	41.1	4.2
Douglas County, Georgia	37,559	26.1	11.7	9.3
Fayette County, Georgia	26,307	23.4	7.8	5.9
Floyd County, Georgia	22,585	23.1	30.3	1.8
Forsyth County, Georgia	63,627	27.9	6.3	10.5
Fulton County, Georgia	232,078	22.3	20.1	5.9
Glynn County, Georgia	18,996	22.3	31.7	8.4
Gwinnett County, Georgia	250,115	27.2	15.9	11.4
Hall County, Georgia	51,008	25.6	22.6	8.5
Henry County, Georgia	59,010	26.1	16.4	6.5
Houston County, Georgia	39,516	25.7	22.4	7.6
Jackson County, Georgia	16,661	24.7	15.0	9.1
Lowndes County, Georgia	27,913	24.2	31.0	5.1
Muscogee County, Georgia	48,369	24.9	37.3	3.5
Newton County, Georgia	28,409	26.3	13.5	2.9
Paulding County, Georgia	43,146	27.1	11.9	9.3
Richmond County, Georgia	46,867	23.2	35.9	8.6
Rockdale County, Georgia	22,593	25.0	19.3	13.4
Spalding County, Georgia	16,096	24.6	31.6	4.0
Troup County, Georgia	17,450	25.0	29.4	6.4
Walker County, Georgia	15,217	22.1	25.2	11.6
Walton County, Georgia	22,786	24.9	15.0	2.4
Whitfield County, Georgia	27,682	26.4	30.4	10.2
HAWAII	305,997	21.4	11.5	2.2
Hawaii County, Hawaii	43,717	21.8	19.6	2.9
Honolulu County, Hawaii	209,809	21.2	10.2	1.8
Kauai County, Hawaii	16,263	22.5	11.9	0.7
Maui County, Hawaii	36,201	21.8	9.3	4.3

Table C-1. Population and Poverty Characteristics, by State and Selected Counties, 2017—*Continued*

(Number; percent.)

State/County	Population		Children under 18 years old in poverty (percent)	Children under 19 years with no health insurance (percent)
	Total under 18 years old	Percent under 18 years old		
IDAHO...	443,285	25.8	15.3	4.6
Ada County, Idaho...........................	110,529	24.2	12.0	4.2
Bannock County, Idaho	21,974	25.8	12.8	3.8
Bonneville County, Idaho.................	35,365	30.9	12.5	1.9
Canyon County, Idaho.....................	61,969	28.6	18.5	3.0
Kootenai County, Idaho...................	36,433	23.1	17.6	3.0
Twin Falls County, Idaho	23,860	28.0	16.3	9.5
ILLINOIS	2,895,090	22.6	17.0	2.9
Adams County, Illinois	14,890	22.5	18.8	6.2
Champaign County, Illinois	39,831	19.0	16.1	0.9
Cook County, Illinois.......................	1,146,736	22.0	20.1	3.0
DeKalb County, Illinois....................	22,678	21.7	12.9	0.0
DuPage County, Illinois...................	212,281	22.8	7.5	3.7
Kane County, Illinois	138,472	25.9	14.4	2.1
Kankakee County, Illinois................	25,450	23.2	20.9	3.1
Kendall County, Illinois...................	36,304	28.8	7.7	5.3
Lake County, Illinois.......................	171,813	24.4	9.5	2.8
LaSalle County, Illinois...................	23,718	21.5	26.9	0.6
McHenry County, Illinois.................	74,136	24.0	7.2	3.0
McLean County, Illinois...................	37,500	21.8	18.7	3.5
Macon County, Illinois....................	23,421	22.1	18.2	1.7
Madison County, Illinois.................	58,097	21.9	19.7	2.8
Peoria County, Illinois	43,640	23.8	17.2	5.2
Rock Island County, Illinois.............	32,276	22.3	17.7	2.6
St. Clair County, Illinois..................	62,007	23.6	24.2	2.4
Sangamon County, Illinois	44,106	22.5	26.6	1.3
Tazewell County, Illinois.................	30,181	22.6	9.8	2.9
Vermilion County, Illinois................	18,601	23.9	33.0	4.3
Will County, Illinois........................	174,511	25.2	8.8	2.3
Williamson County, Illinois..............	14,623	21.7	20.1	1.6
Winnebago County, Illinois	66,784	23.5	20.9	3.2
INDIANA......................................	1,574,031	23.6	18.4	6.3
Allen County, Indiana	96,420	25.9	18.9	7.0
Bartholomew County, Indiana	19,505	23.8	22.6	8.0
Boone County, Indiana	17,237	26.2	4.6	2.9
Clark County, Indiana	26,531	22.7	18.6	5.5
Delaware County, Indiana................	20,580	17.9	18.1	4.6
Elkhart County, Indiana...................	56,596	27.6	14.3	9.6
Floyd County, Indiana.....................	18,298	23.7	11.5	1.8
Grant County, Indiana	14,096	21.2	29.6	3.4
Hamilton County, Indiana................	89,002	27.5	3.8	2.9
Hancock County, Indiana.................	18,479	24.6	6.3	2.5
Hendricks County, Indiana	41,080	25.1	5.0	3.7
Howard County, Indiana..................	18,678	22.7	22.2	3.8
Johnson County, Indiana.................	38,103	24.8	17.8	5.8
Kosciusko County, Indiana..............	18,888	23.8	18.5	12.0
Lake County, Indiana......................	115,237	23.7	23.4	6.8
LaPorte County, Indiana..................	23,682	21.5	20.5	5.7
Madison County, Indiana.................	28,116	21.7	25.9	4.1
Marion County, Indiana...................	234,704	24.7	24.7	7.2
Monroe County, Indiana..................	23,415	15.9	20.1	2.9
Morgan County, Indiana..................	15,857	22.7	13.0	0.7
Porter County, Indiana	37,848	22.5	15.9	1.3
St. Joseph County, Indiana	64,055	23.7	21.3	4.9
Tippecanoe County, Indiana	39,738	20.9	16.8	3.3
Vanderburgh County, Indiana..........	38,975	21.5	26.9	5.2
Vigo County, Indiana......................	22,322	20.8	25.3	2.9
Wayne County, Indiana...................	14,566	22.0	23.8	8.6
IOWA...	730,350	23.2	12.3	3.1
Black Hawk County, Iowa................	28,836	21.7	18.6	3.9
Dallas County, Iowa.......................	24,511	28.1	3.9	2.0
Dubuque County, Iowa....................	22,334	23.0	10.2	0.8
Johnson County, Iowa.....................	30,192	20.2	9.1	2.0
Linn County, Iowa	52,888	23.6	12.8	2.4
Polk County, Iowa	120,594	25.0	13.2	2.3
Pottawattamie County, Iowa............	21,891	23.4	11.1	3.5
Scott County, Iowa.........................	41,227	23.9	13.3	2.0
Story County, Iowa.........................	16,128	16.5	6.9	5.2
Woodbury County, Iowa..................	26,841	26.2	15.7	1.9

Table C-1. Population and Poverty Characteristics, by State and Selected Counties, 2017—*Continued*

(Number; percent.)

State/County	Population		Children under 18 years old in poverty (percent)	Children under 19 years with no health insurance (percent)
	Total under 18 years old	Percent under 18 years old		
KANSAS	712,575	24.5	14.8	5.2
Butler County, Kansas	17,077	25.5	15.9	5.3
Douglas County, Kansas	22,473	18.6	12.6	4.2
Johnson County, Kansas	145,914	24.7	6.5	5.1
Leavenworth County, Kansas	20,008	24.7	3.6	4.8
Riley County, Kansas..................................	12,428	16.8	12.8	1.3
Sedgwick County, Kansas	132,969	25.9	18.5	4.5
Shawnee County, Kansas	42,028	23.6	13.2	5.9
Wyandotte County, Kansas	46,263	28.0	23.3	6.6
KENTUCKY...	1,014,604	22.8	22.4	3.8
Boone County, Kentucky	34,012	26.0	10.1	1.2
Bullitt County, Kentucky	17,848	22.2	7.7	1.6
Campbell County, Kentucky	19,257	20.8	7.4	0.3
Christian County, Kentucky	19,120	27.2	29.9	6.5
Daviess County, Kentucky	24,488	24.4	29.3	1.5
Fayette County, Kentucky	67,885	21.1	18.1	4.2
Hardin County, Kentucky	26,804	24.8	16.5	4.3
Jefferson County, Kentucky..........................	171,898	22.3	20.7	3.0
Kenton County, Kentucky	39,406	23.8	13.6	4.7
McCracken County, Kentucky.......................	14,586	22.3	16.6	1.5
Madison County, Kentucky	19,065	20.9	17.4	4.0
Oldham County, Kentucky	18,061	27.2	3.2	0.2
Warren County, Kentucky.............................	29,324	22.8	21.9	1.4
LOUISIANA..	1,109,242	23.7	28.0	3.1
Ascension Parish, Louisiana	33,079	26.9	16.9	1.4
Bossier Parish, Louisiana	32,484	25.5	29.5	2.2
Caddo Parish, Louisiana	59,159	24.0	42.6	1.4
Calcasieu Parish, Louisiana.........................	50,403	24.9	18.5	2.7
East Baton Rouge Parish, Louisiana	101,496	22.7	26.1	3.4
Iberia Parish, Louisiana...............................	19,254	26.7	34.4	3.0
Jefferson Parish, Louisiana..........................	96,152	21.9	28.0	3.5
Lafayette Parish, Louisiana	58,258	24.0	24.4	6.7
Lafourche Parish, Louisiana	23,019	23.4	21.6	4.2
Livingston Parish, Louisiana	35,799	25.9	12.0	4.4
Orleans Parish, Louisiana	79,093	20.1	39.3	3.9
Ouachita Parish, Louisiana..........................	38,912	25.0	41.2	2.6
Rapides Parish, Louisiana............................	32,941	25.0	24.2	3.5
St. Landry Parish, Louisiana	22,749	27.2	39.5	2.2
St. Tammany Parish, Louisiana	61,864	24.1	15.5	2.6
Tangipahoa Parish, Louisiana......................	32,649	24.6	32.8	1.4
Terrebonne Parish, Louisiana.......................	28,724	25.6	22.6	2.9
MAINE...	254,202	19.0	13.1	4.9
Androscoggin County, Maine	23,417	21.8	10.7	4.7
Aroostook County, Maine	12,624	18.7	14.8	4.4
Cumberland County, Maine..........................	55,443	19.0	9.3	4.2
Kennebec County, Maine	23,718	19.5	13.9	2.8
Penobscot County, Maine	27,489	18.1	18.4	3.4
York County, Maine.....................................	38,380	18.8	6.1	4.4
MARYLAND..	1,346,950	22.3	12.0	3.8
Allegany County, Maryland...........................	12,713	17.8	22.8	5.3
Anne Arundel County, Maryland....................	127,463	22.2	7.1	2.5
Baltimore County, Maryland.........................	180,025	21.6	8.7	2.7
Calvert County, Maryland	21,405	23.4	5.0	2.4
Carroll County, Maryland.............................	36,567	21.8	3.5	1.9
Cecil County, Maryland	23,435	22.8	10.0	3.2
Charles County, Maryland	38,576	24.2	10.2	3.8
Frederick County, Maryland.........................	58,738	23.3	7.8	1.4
Harford County, Maryland............................	56,595	22.4	8.2	2.8
Howard County, Maryland............................	78,314	24.4	7.9	2.7
Montgomery County, Maryland.....................	246,273	23.3	9.4	3.4
Prince George's County, Maryland	203,325	22.3	11.0	6.3
St. Mary's County, Maryland	27,605	24.5	13.1	4.8
Washington County, Maryland	33,140	22.0	22.0	6.5
Wicomico County, Maryland.........................	22,739	22.1	16.7	5.9
Baltimore city, Maryland	126,007	20.6	32.6	5.1

Table C-1. Population and Poverty Characteristics, by State and Selected Counties, 2017—*Continued*

(Number; percent.)

State/County	Population		Children under 18 years old in poverty (percent)	Children under 19 years with no health insurance (percent)
	Total under 18 years old	Percent under 18 years old		
MASSACHUSETTS	1,370,584	20.0	13.5	1.5
Barnstable County, Massachusetts	33,157	15.5	9.0	1.8
Berkshire County, Massachusetts	21,511	17.0	11.8	0.7
Bristol County, Massachusetts.............................	116,081	20.7	17.8	1.6
Essex County, Massachusetts	168,312	21.4	14.1	2.2
Franklin County, Massachusetts...........................	12,724	18.0	10.1	0.3
Hampden County, Massachusetts	101,795	21.7	26.1	1.2
Hampshire County, Massachusetts	23,901	14.8	7.9	0.5
Middlesex County, Massachusetts	319,235	19.9	9.4	1.8
Norfolk County, Massachusetts	147,871	21.1	8.2	1.0
Plymouth County, Massachusetts.........................	111,412	21.6	7.4	0.8
Suffolk County, Massachusetts............................	133,694	16.8	24.7	0.8
Worcester County, Massachusetts	175,489	21.2	12.5	1.9
MICHIGAN	2,175,861	21.8	19.7	3.0
Allegan County, Michigan...................................	28,355	24.4	12.5	2.1
Bay County, Michigan	21,276	20.4	19.6	2.6
Berrien County, Michigan	33,921	22.0	29.6	4.4
Calhoun County, Michigan	30,647	22.8	34.0	2.3
Clinton County, Michigan	17,431	22.2	4.9	2.0
Eaton County, Michigan	23,057	21.1	12.1	2.0
Genesee County, Michigan	92,644	22.7	26.2	3.3
Grand Traverse County, Michigan	18,198	19.8	12.5	6.4
Ingham County, Michigan	57,752	19.9	25.9	2.1
Isabella County, Michigan	12,055	17.0	16.3	8.2
Jackson County, Michigan	34,287	21.6	22.8	4.6
Kalamazoo County, Michigan	57,117	21.7	15.8	2.9
Kent County, Michigan	158,210	24.4	14.3	3.5
Lapeer County, Michigan....................................	18,376	20.8	8.4	4.1
Lenawee County, Michigan	20,854	21.1	12.6	1.5
Livingston County, Michigan...............................	41,152	21.7	6.9	1.3
Macomb County, Michigan	185,217	21.3	16.7	2.9
Marquette County, Michigan	12,034	18.1	23.7	3.0
Midland County, Michigan..................................	17,899	21.5	12.8	2.0
Monroe County, Michigan	32,413	21.7	17.8	2.1
Muskegon County, Michigan...............................	39,977	23.0	20.8	0.2
Oakland County, Michigan..................................	265,816	21.3	9.1	2.3
Ottawa County, Michigan	69,190	24.2	9.7	2.8
Saginaw County, Michigan.................................	40,863	21.3	23.2	1.4
St. Clair County, Michigan..................................	33,598	21.1	20.8	1.4
Shiawassee County, Michigan.............................	14,894	21.8	13.2	2.7
Van Buren County, Michigan	17,825	23.7	14.5	2.6
Washtenaw County, Michigan	68,710	18.7	11.3	1.1
Wayne County, Michigan...................................	416,178	23.7	34.0	2.5
MINNESOTA...	1,297,782	23.3	11.8	3.4
Anoka County, Minnesota	84,277	24.0	6.1	3.5
Blue Earth County, Minnesota.............................	12,874	19.2	10.4	5.3
Carver County, Minnesota..................................	27,643	27.1	3.6	5.4
Dakota County, Minnesota	103,530	24.5	6.5	2.1
Hennepin County, Minnesota	275,389	22.0	14.5	3.2
Olmsted County, Minnesota...............................	37,911	24.5	12.0	1.2
Ramsey County, Minnesota................................	127,780	23.3	20.2	2.8
Rice County, Minnesota	14,314	21.7	21.4	1.5
St. Louis County, Minnesota	38,060	19.0	15.2	3.4
Scott County, Minnesota....................................	40,627	27.9	1.9	1.8
Sherburne County, Minnesota.............................	24,812	26.2	0.2	1.8
Stearns County, Minnesota	36,335	23.0	14.9	3.2
Washington County, Minnesota	63,147	24.6	4.5	3.7
Wright County, Minnesota..................................	37,714	28.1	4.5	1.8
MISSISSIPPI	714,553	23.9	26.9	4.8
DeSoto County, Mississippi	46,358	25.9	12.0	1.3
Forrest County, Mississippi	17,368	23.0	21.2	3.2
Harrison County, Mississippi	49,302	24.0	32.6	5.9
Hinds County, Mississippi..................................	58,574	24.5	27.2	3.4
Jackson County, Mississippi...............................	33,819	23.8	20.9	8.0
Jones County, Mississippi..................................	17,219	25.3	26.0	7.5
Lauderdale County, Mississippi...........................	18,009	23.6	28.0	2.2
Lee County, Mississippi	21,862	25.7	14.3	4.6
Madison County, Mississippi	26,301	25.1	13.5	4.9
Rankin County, Mississippi................................	36,209	23.8	8.9	4.5

Table C-1. Population and Poverty Characteristics, by State and Selected Counties, 2017—*Continued*

(Number; percent.)

State/County	Population		Children under 18 years old in poverty (percent)	Children under 19 years with no health insurance (percent)
	Total under 18 years old	Percent under 18 years old		
MISSOURI...	1,387,661	22.7	18.6	5.1
Boone County, Missouri..	36,044	20.2	12.3	4.5
Buchanan County, Missouri	20,458	23.0	21.7	5.4
Cape Girardeau County, Missouri........................	16,511	21.1	23.3	3.2
Cass County, Missouri	25,181	24.3	17.2	3.0
Christian County, Missouri.................................	21,687	25.4	10.7	3.4
Clay County, Missouri	58,721	24.2	10.3	2.1
Cole County, Missouri..	16,751	21.8	21.8	5.7
Franklin County, Missouri	24,028	23.3	17.4	3.8
Greene County, Missouri....................................	60,461	20.9	22.6	5.7
Jackson County, Missouri	166,200	23.8	21.1	6.6
Jasper County, Missouri	30,461	25.3	27.8	9.1
Jefferson County, Missouri	52,062	23.3	17.1	4.8
Platte County, Missouri	24,008	23.7	6.8	0.7
St. Charles County, Missouri..............................	93,438	23.6	7.4	2.5
St. Francois County, Missouri	13,972	20.9	24.7	0.3
St. Louis County, Missouri.................................	219,579	22.0	13.5	3.1
St. Louis city, Missouri	59,831	19.4	28.4	5.2
MONTANA	229,895	21.9	14.7	5.8
Cascade County, Montana..................................	18,201	22.3	11.1	3.4
Flathead County, Montana..................................	22,076	22.1	10.1	6.4
Gallatin County, Montana	21,657	20.1	6.9	2.2
Lewis and Clark County, Montana......................	14,599	21.5	4.7	1.9
Missoula County, Montana.................................	22,644	19.3	17.7	2.5
Yellowstone County, Montana............................	37,417	23.5	13.7	5.2
NEBRASKA	474,597	24.7	14.1	5.1
Douglas County, Nebraska	144,408	25.7	16.5	5.3
Lancaster County, Nebraska..............................	72,247	23.0	10.7	3.7
Sarpy County, Nebraska....................................	50,140	27.6	4.5	4.8
NEVADA	683,957	22.8	18.5	8.0
Clark County, Nevada	514,191	23.3	20.3	7.9
Washoe County, Nevada....................................	100,677	21.9	12.7	8.8
NEW HAMPSHIRE...................................	258,195	19.2	10.3	2.3
Cheshire County, New Hampshire......................	13,465	17.7	9.9	2.4
Grafton County, New Hampshire........................	14,892	16.7	15.2	3.4
Hillsborough County, New Hampshire	84,642	20.7	11.7	1.7
Merrimack County, New Hampshire....................	28,714	19.2	9.7	3.6
Rockingham County, New Hampshire..................	60,112	19.6	5.9	2.0
Strafford County, New Hampshire......................	23,799	18.5	8.2	2.3
NEW JERSEY...	1,978,796	22.0	13.9	3.7
Atlantic County, New Jersey..............................	58,004	21.5	22.3	5.3
Bergen County, New Jersey...............................	201,470	21.2	6.2	5.0
Burlington County, New Jersey	93,897	20.9	8.5	2.4
Camden County, New Jersey..............................	116,574	22.8	16.3	2.4
Cape May County, New Jersey	16,226	17.3	12.9	2.3
Cumberland County, New Jersey	35,909	23.5	32.5	6.3
Essex County, New Jersey	190,780	23.6	21.1	5.5
Gloucester County, New Jersey.........................	64,660	22.1	9.2	2.8
Hudson County, New Jersey	140,021	20.2	20.6	4.1
Hunterdon County, New Jersey.........................	25,185	20.1	1.2	4.3
Mercer County, New Jersey...............................	79,885	21.3	16.5	2.5
Middlesex County, New Jersey..........................	182,068	21.6	11.5	3.7
Monmouth County, New Jersey	133,950	21.4	9.7	2.3
Morris County, New Jersey	107,093	21.4	5.2	1.5
Ocean County, New Jersey................................	141,981	23.7	15.3	3.1
Passaic County, New Jersey..............................	122,793	24.0	25.1	5.0
Salem County, New Jersey................................	13,537	21.6	31.1	7.7
Somerset County, New Jersey	74,088	22.1	4.8	2.4
Sussex County, New Jersey	27,726	19.6	5.9	2.4
Union County, New Jersey	131,375	23.3	13.4	4.2
Warren County, New Jersey	21,574	20.2	9.8	4.0
NEW MEXICO..	489,722	23.5	27.2	5.1
Bernalillo County, New Mexico...........................	149,684	22.1	19.0	2.6
Chaves County, New Mexico	17,469	26.9	18.0	12.2
Doña Ana County, New Mexico	53,451	24.8	42.3	4.1
Lea County, New Mexico...................................	20,747	30.2	14.9	3.9

Table C-1. Population and Poverty Characteristics, by State and Selected Counties, 2017—*Continued*

(Number; percent.)

State/County	Population		Children under 18 years old in poverty (percent)	Children under 19 years with no health insurance (percent)
	Total under 18 years old	Percent under 18 years old		
NEW MEXICO—(*Continued*)				
McKinley County, New Mexico	21,412	29.5	50.4	14.2
Otero County, New Mexico	15,429	23.4	24.0	3.9
Sandoval County, New Mexico	33,537	23.5	24.2	6.8
San Juan County, New Mexico	34,183	26.9	32.7	10.2
Santa Fe County, New Mexico	27,222	18.3	18.2	7.1
Valencia County, New Mexico	17,964	23.7	20.9	2.3
NEW YORK	4,153,497	20.9	19.7	2.7
Albany County, New York	57,503	18.6	10.7	1.5
Bronx County, New York	365,215	24.8	39.6	2.5
Broome County, New York	37,667	19.5	20.2	1.5
Cattaraugus County, New York	17,251	22.3	22.3	4.6
Cayuga County, New York	15,402	19.8	18.1	7.0
Chautauqua County, New York	26,409	20.5	28.2	4.6
Chemung County, New York	18,201	21.3	24.3	1.0
Clinton County, New York	14,626	18.1	15.0	0.9
Dutchess County, New York	56,452	19.1	15.4	3.1
Erie County, New York	188,721	20.4	22.1	1.9
Jefferson County, New York	27,173	23.8	23.1	1.9
Kings County, New York	605,465	22.9	26.4	2.4
Livingston County, New York	11,391	17.9	13.6	1.0
Madison County, New York	14,168	20.0	10.6	5.0
Monroe County, New York	156,670	21.0	23.2	1.7
Nassau County, New York	295,264	21.6	7.3	3.1
New York County, New York	239,573	14.4	23.0	2.5
Niagara County, New York	42,437	20.1	15.6	2.9
Oneida County, New York	49,155	21.2	25.9	4.6
Onondaga County, New York	99,680	21.4	20.6	2.7
Ontario County, New York	22,479	20.5	13.8	0.2
Orange County, New York	97,503	25.5	15.2	1.5
Oswego County, New York	24,666	20.8	26.8	1.2
Putnam County, New York	19,740	19.9	2.2	3.1
Queens County, New York	473,974	20.1	15.6	3.4
Rensselaer County, New York	31,247	19.6	14.5	1.2
Richmond County, New York	104,842	21.9	16.5	1.4
Rockland County, New York	91,816	27.9	22.9	1.4
St. Lawrence County, New York	21,842	19.9	37.2	16.2
Saratoga County, New York	46,654	20.3	7.8	1.2
Schenectady County, New York	33,529	21.6	18.0	1.1
Steuben County, New York	20,787	21.6	16.7	7.1
Suffolk County, New York	319,379	21.4	8.3	1.8
Sullivan County, New York	15,352	20.3	21.2	2.5
Tompkins County, New York	15,185	14.5	15.9	2.0
Ulster County, New York	32,054	17.9	19.0	4.1
Warren County, New York	11,560	17.9	8.3	0.6
Wayne County, New York	19,549	21.6	16.7	4.8
Westchester County, New York	217,265	22.2	10.1	2.9
NORTH CAROLINA	2,301,190	22.4	21.2	4.8
Alamance County, North Carolina	36,545	22.5	21.6	6.2
Brunswick County, North Carolina	20,954	16.0	17.4	4.3
Buncombe County, North Carolina	48,315	18.8	15.2	2.5
Burke County, North Carolina	17,202	19.3	20.1	3.2
Cabarrus County, North Carolina	53,988	26.1	16.1	1.4
Caldwell County, North Carolina	16,637	20.3	22.2	2.4
Carteret County, North Carolina	12,693	18.4	23.2	5.6
Catawba County, North Carolina	35,520	22.5	18.2	2.1
Chatham County, North Carolina	14,733	20.6	20.5	7.6
Cleveland County, North Carolina	21,617	22.2	25.1	3.6
Craven County, North Carolina	23,097	22.5	34.0	11.5
Cumberland County, North Carolina	81,939	24.6	24.9	4.0
Davidson County, North Carolina	36,951	22.3	23.3	4.9
Durham County, North Carolina	65,684	21.1	26.9	6.8
Forsyth County, North Carolina	87,189	23.2	26.0	4.2
Franklin County, North Carolina	14,768	22.3	29.8	9.9
Gaston County, North Carolina	49,878	22.7	21.5	3.6
Guilford County, North Carolina	118,236	22.4	18.7	3.7
Harnett County, North Carolina	35,178	26.5	25.6	5.0
Henderson County, North Carolina	22,296	19.3	12.1	7.7
Iredell County, North Carolina	41,139	23.4	19.6	2.9
Johnston County, North Carolina	50,493	25.7	27.4	7.8

Table C-1. Population and Poverty Characteristics, by State and Selected Counties, 2017—*Continued*

(Number; percent.)

State/County	Population		Children under 18 years old in poverty (percent)	Children under 19 years with no health insurance (percent)
	Total under 18 years old	Percent under 18 years old		
NORTH CAROLINA—(*Continued*)				
Lincoln County, North Carolina	17,667	21.4	14.3	8.8
Mecklenburg County, North Carolina	257,325	23.9	16.5	5.5
Moore County, North Carolina	21,222	21.8	5.8	5.6
Nash County, North Carolina	20,934	22.3	21.3	4.7
New Hanover County, North Carolina	42,677	18.8	23.8	6.6
Onslow County, North Carolina	47,324	24.4	15.6	2.6
Orange County, North Carolina	28,721	19.8	9.5	4.0
Pitt County, North Carolina	38,105	21.3	33.1	2.2
Randolph County, North Carolina	32,036	22.4	28.1	9.5
Robeson County, North Carolina	33,165	25.0	45.4	4.2
Rockingham County, North Carolina	18,578	20.4	21.9	8.4
Rowan County, North Carolina	31,209	22.2	21.0	4.0
Rutherford County, North Carolina	14,031	21.1	12.5	6.9
Surry County, North Carolina	15,406	21.3	19.1	3.4
Union County, North Carolina	63,058	27.3	13.1	4.0
Wake County, North Carolina	259,374	24.2	12.0	4.9
Wayne County, North Carolina	29,220	23.5	34.3	5.0
Wilkes County, North Carolina	14,066	20.5	25.4	3.7
Wilson County, North Carolina	18,944	23.2	27.4	2.6
NORTH DAKOTA	173,136	22.9	10.9	7.5
Burleigh County, North Dakota	22,691	23.9	7.6	5.0
Cass County, North Dakota	39,131	22.0	5.8	4.6
Grand Forks County, North Dakota	14,237	20.1	17.1	1.6
Ward County, North Dakota	15,983	23.2	15.7	3.7
OHIO	2,601,997	22.3	20.1	4.5
Allen County, Ohio	23,877	23.1	24.6	6.2
Ashtabula County, Ohio	21,702	22.2	31.0	9.4
Athens County, Ohio	9,742	14.6	33.9	5.1
Belmont County, Ohio	12,941	19.0	3.7	1.1
Butler County, Ohio	89,870	23.6	12.5	3.4
Clark County, Ohio	30,186	22.4	20.8	2.2
Clermont County, Ohio	47,155	23.1	12.6	2.3
Columbiana County, Ohio	21,082	20.5	24.2	5.8
Cuyahoga County, Ohio	260,986	20.9	26.8	3.0
Delaware County, Ohio	53,778	26.8	8.5	3.2
Erie County, Ohio	15,314	20.5	15.0	4.7
Fairfield County, Ohio	37,105	24.0	13.0	6.7
Franklin County, Ohio	302,183	23.4	22.5	4.4
Geauga County, Ohio	21,674	23.1	6.0	14.4
Greene County, Ohio	34,672	20.8	11.1	2.0
Hamilton County, Ohio	187,795	23.1	26.0	3.5
Hancock County, Ohio	16,901	22.3	10.5	4.4
Jefferson County, Ohio	12,974	19.6	23.6	4.0
Lake County, Ohio	46,537	20.2	13.2	3.6
Licking County, Ohio	40,164	23.2	9.4	4.3
Lorain County, Ohio	68,577	22.3	21.0	2.7
Lucas County, Ohio	99,382	23.1	25.8	2.7
Mahoning County, Ohio	45,985	20.0	30.8	1.1
Marion County, Ohio	13,452	20.7	21.6	4.0
Medina County, Ohio	40,393	22.6	8.1	1.8
Miami County, Ohio	24,161	23.0	10.0	2.1
Montgomery County, Ohio	117,368	22.1	23.2	4.2
Muskingum County, Ohio	19,641	22.8	18.2	4.4
Portage County, Ohio	30,714	18.9	13.3	2.1
Richland County, Ohio	26,248	21.8	16.6	16.1
Ross County, Ohio	16,512	21.4	22.8	1.3
Scioto County, Ohio	16,291	21.5	28.7	2.8
Stark County, Ohio	80,191	21.5	24.3	5.1
Summit County, Ohio	114,107	21.1	18.3	2.9
Trumbull County, Ohio	40,908	20.4	24.9	6.6
Tuscarawas County, Ohio	21,171	22.9	20.3	3.9
Warren County, Ohio	57,385	25.1	4.5	2.7
Wayne County, Ohio	28,184	24.3	25.3	26.2
Wood County, Ohio	26,418	20.2	8.9	2.3
OKLAHOMA	961,483	24.5	21.5	8.1
Canadian County, Oklahoma	36,476	26.1	7.6	5.5
Cleveland County, Oklahoma	61,144	21.9	12.3	5.1
Comanche County, Oklahoma	28,851	23.7	24.5	7.5

Table C-1. Population and Poverty Characteristics, by State and Selected Counties, 2017—*Continued*

(Number; percent.)

State/County	Population		Children under 18 years old in poverty (percent)	Children under 19 years with no health insurance (percent)
	Total under 18 years old	Percent under 18 years old		
OKLAHOMA—*(Continued)*				
Creek County, Oklahoma	17,290	24.1	28.9	4.4
Muskogee County, Oklahoma	16,917	24.5	40.4	13.8
Oklahoma County, Oklahoma	202,849	25.7	23.7	6.5
Payne County, Oklahoma	16,348	20.0	21.4	8.2
Pottawatomie County, Oklahoma	17,202	23.8	15.8	5.4
Rogers County, Oklahoma	21,722	23.8	13.3	7.2
Tulsa County, Oklahoma	164,069	25.4	20.8	7.2
Wagoner County, Oklahoma	19,323	24.6	11.6	5.2
OREGON	873,774	21.1	16.5	3.6
Benton County, Oregon	15,126	16.6	9.7	2.6
Clackamas County, Oregon	89,401	21.7	10.5	2.7
Deschutes County, Oregon	38,589	20.6	10.7	3.1
Douglas County, Oregon	21,002	19.2	21.0	3.0
Jackson County, Oregon	45,104	20.7	22.3	6.3
Josephine County, Oregon	16,851	19.5	24.3	4.6
Klamath County, Oregon	14,425	21.6	22.9	9.3
Lane County, Oregon	70,098	18.7	17.9	4.5
Linn County, Oregon	28,631	22.9	15.4	3.6
Marion County, Oregon	84,788	24.8	21.6	4.0
Multnomah County, Oregon	154,317	19.1	17.8	2.4
Polk County, Oregon	19,678	23.5	25.0	4.3
Umatilla County, Oregon	19,505	25.3	21.9	4.3
Washington County, Oregon	137,043	23.3	9.3	2.4
Yamhill County, Oregon	23,686	22.4	9.6	0.4
PENNSYLVANIA	2,664,971	20.8	17.0	4.4
Adams County, Pennsylvania	20,481	20.0	10.2	3.8
Allegheny County, Pennsylvania	230,313	18.8	15.1	2.1
Armstrong County, Pennsylvania	12,599	19.2	16.7	0.6
Beaver County, Pennsylvania	32,434	19.5	13.9	1.0
Berks County, Pennsylvania	94,114	22.5	17.4	5.0
Blair County, Pennsylvania	25,347	20.5	17.3	3.6
Bucks County, Pennsylvania	129,967	20.7	8.1	2.4
Butler County, Pennsylvania	37,746	20.2	9.9	1.0
Cambria County, Pennsylvania	25,430	19.1	27.2	1.4
Carbon County, Pennsylvania	12,367	19.4	20.8	2.6
Centre County, Pennsylvania	24,389	15.0	12.3	4.6
Chester County, Pennsylvania	118,914	22.9	6.4	4.0
Clearfield County, Pennsylvania	14,596	18.3	23.1	2.2
Columbia County, Pennsylvania	11,945	18.1	11.9	1.0
Crawford County, Pennsylvania	17,722	20.6	19.2	10.7
Cumberland County, Pennsylvania	51,108	20.4	8.7	4.8
Dauphin County, Pennsylvania	61,769	22.4	17.9	3.6
Delaware County, Pennsylvania	124,148	22.0	12.9	1.8
Erie County, Pennsylvania	59,103	21.5	24.9	2.4
Fayette County, Pennsylvania	25,403	19.3	30.5	2.9
Franklin County, Pennsylvania	34,409	22.3	12.6	7.6
Indiana County, Pennsylvania	15,320	18.0	15.8	12.9
Lackawanna County, Pennsylvania	42,896	20.4	22.5	0.3
Lancaster County, Pennsylvania	128,891	23.7	13.6	19.6
Lawrence County, Pennsylvania	17,481	20.1	16.5	5.7
Lebanon County, Pennsylvania	32,020	22.9	15.8	11.3
Lehigh County, Pennsylvania	83,247	22.7	19.2	4.5
Luzerne County, Pennsylvania	62,151	19.6	26.6	3.2
Lycoming County, Pennsylvania	23,346	20.5	16.9	6.3
Mercer County, Pennsylvania	21,619	19.3	16.5	7.8
Monroe County, Pennsylvania	33,410	19.9	10.5	5.0
Montgomery County, Pennsylvania	178,522	21.6	6.7	1.8
Northampton County, Pennsylvania	60,641	20.0	16.6	2.9
Northumberland County, Pennsylvania	17,870	19.4	17.3	4.3
Philadelphia County, Pennsylvania	344,138	21.8	31.9	3.6
Schuylkill County, Pennsylvania	27,834	19.5	19.3	2.4
Somerset County, Pennsylvania	13,975	18.8	17.2	4.3
Washington County, Pennsylvania	40,409	19.5	11.5	1.9
Westmoreland County, Pennsylvania	65,053	18.4	11.8	0.7
York County, Pennsylvania	98,853	22.2	13.5	4.7
RHODE ISLAND	206,972	19.5	16.6	2.1
Kent County, Rhode Island	30,866	18.8	6.9	2.1
Newport County, Rhode Island	14,465	17.3	10.8	1.4

Table C-1. Population and Poverty Characteristics, by State and Selected Counties, 2017—*Continued*

(Number; percent.)

State/County	Population		Children under 18 years old in poverty (percent)	Children under 19 years with no health insurance (percent)
	Total under 18 years old	Percent under 18 years old		
RHODE ISLAND—(*Continued*)				
Providence County, Rhode Island	131,450	20.6	21.0	2.4
Washington County, Rhode Island	20,953	16.6	12.1	0.4
SOUTH CAROLINA	1,101,720	21.9	22.6	5.1
Aiken County, South Carolina	36,341	21.6	22.9	3.3
Anderson County, South Carolina	45,593	22.9	21.2	8.4
Beaufort County, South Carolina	35,515	19.0	17.3	11.7
Berkeley County, South Carolina	52,403	24.0	17.6	6.0
Charleston County, South Carolina	79,588	19.8	20.2	8.5
Darlington County, South Carolina	15,229	22.6	32.0	4.3
Dorchester County, South Carolina	38,675	24.7	11.2	8.8
Florence County, South Carolina	33,276	24.0	27.8	1.7
Greenville County, South Carolina	117,643	23.2	18.6	5.3
Greenwood County, South Carolina	15,034	21.4	33.8	5.2
Horry County, South Carolina	61,223	18.4	31.0	7.8
Kershaw County, South Carolina	15,243	23.4	14.8	3.2
Lancaster County, South Carolina	19,876	21.5	21.3	0.8
Laurens County, South Carolina	14,742	22.1	31.8	4.7
Lexington County, South Carolina	67,793	23.3	18.3	4.8
Oconee County, South Carolina	15,339	19.9	25.7	2.5
Orangeburg County, South Carolina	19,059	21.8	34.3	2.5
Pickens County, South Carolina	24,090	19.5	11.0	5.5
Richland County, South Carolina	88,447	21.5	19.7	3.5
Spartanburg County, South Carolina	70,883	23.1	19.8	4.9
Sumter County, South Carolina	24,999	23.4	29.7	5.3
York County, South Carolina	65,027	24.4	17.5	2.3
SOUTH DAKOTA	213,228	24.5	16.6	6.2
Minnehaha County, South Dakota	47,880	25.4	8.6	3.6
Pennington County, South Dakota	25,321	23.0	13.5	7.6
TENNESSEE	1,508,252	22.5	21.2	4.4
Anderson County, Tennessee	16,329	21.4	21.8	2.0
Blount County, Tennessee	26,585	20.5	20.6	4.2
Bradley County, Tennessee	23,360	22.1	23.9	3.7
Davidson County, Tennessee	145,690	21.1	23.7	8.4
Greene County, Tennessee	13,549	19.7	27.4	1.3
Hamilton County, Tennessee	75,521	20.9	16.4	5.6
Knox County, Tennessee	97,573	21.1	17.8	2.4
Madison County, Tennessee	21,498	22.0	24.2	5.5
Maury County, Tennessee	21,622	23.5	8.2	4.6
Montgomery County, Tennessee	53,571	26.8	16.6	3.2
Putnam County, Tennessee	16,533	21.3	34.4	1.4
Robertson County, Tennessee	16,972	24.2	22.6	2.8
Rutherford County, Tennessee	78,325	24.7	14.5	5.7
Sevier County, Tennessee	20,279	20.8	15.1	4.7
Shelby County, Tennessee	233,989	25.0	30.2	4.9
Sullivan County, Tennessee	30,575	19.5	26.2	2.1
Sumner County, Tennessee	43,495	23.7	8.6	2.2
Washington County, Tennessee	24,576	19.2	17.5	6.3
Williamson County, Tennessee	62,244	27.5	2.8	3.8
Wilson County, Tennessee	32,502	23.8	13.5	6.8
TEXAS	7,365,163	26.0	20.9	10.7
Angelina County, Texas	22,406	25.5	26.1	13.7
Bastrop County, Texas	22,134	26.1	7.4	7.7
Bell County, Texas	97,043	27.9	20.9	4.2
Bexar County, Texas	505,220	25.8	22.8	7.9
Bowie County, Texas	22,302	23.7	16.4	3.8
Brazoria County, Texas	96,293	26.6	10.5	8.6
Brazos County, Texas	46,396	20.8	21.2	9.7
Cameron County, Texas	130,192	30.7	39.2	16.7
Collin County, Texas	254,918	26.3	6.0	8.0
Comal County, Texas	32,511	23.1	17.8	5.7
Coryell County, Texas	17,488	23.3	18.4	9.1
Dallas County, Texas	691,940	26.4	22.5	14.3
Denton County, Texas	210,066	25.1	8.0	7.7
Ector County, Texas	47,146	30.0	11.3	14.7
Ellis County, Texas	46,662	26.9	10.4	10.6
El Paso County, Texas	231,104	27.5	30.2	9.4
Fort Bend County, Texas	211,880	27.7	10.5	7.7

Table C-1. Population and Poverty Characteristics, by State and Selected Counties, 2017—Continued

(Number; percent.)

State/County	Population		Children under 18 years old in poverty (percent)	Children under 19 years with no health insurance (percent)
	Total under 18 years old	Percent under 18 years old		
TEXAS—(Continued)				
Galveston County, Texas	81,904	24.4	16.7	3.9
Grayson County, Texas	31,218	23.8	20.0	10.7
Gregg County, Texas	31,900	25.9	21.6	11.9
Guadalupe County, Texas	40,628	25.4	12.1	5.9
Harris County, Texas	1,249,482	26.9	23.9	11.4
Harrison County, Texas	17,282	25.9	18.3	8.9
Hays County, Texas	50,081	23.3	13.1	10.3
Henderson County, Texas	17,301	21.3	24.2	13.2
Hidalgo County, Texas	284,500	33.1	42.4	14.1
Hunt County, Texas	22,604	24.1	26.4	12.1
Jefferson County, Texas	61,474	24.0	28.5	11.3
Johnson County, Texas	43,535	26.0	12.5	8.6
Kaufman County, Texas	34,350	28.0	10.2	9.8
Liberty County, Texas	21,814	26.1	19.1	19.1
Lubbock County, Texas	73,451	24.1	23.1	7.5
McLennan County, Texas	61,915	24.6	23.0	7.8
Midland County, Texas	46,567	28.2	16.8	17.1
Montgomery County, Texas	151,043	26.5	12.1	11.0
Nacogdoches County, Texas	15,360	23.4	42.9	14.6
Nueces County, Texas	89,611	24.8	20.7	9.8
Orange County, Texas	21,226	25.0	17.2	8.9
Parker County, Texas	32,634	24.5	9.7	10.7
Potter County, Texas	33,064	27.4	20.8	15.8
Randall County, Texas	32,099	23.9	7.2	4.3
Rockwall County, Texas	26,390	27.3	9.5	6.1
San Patricio County, Texas	17,538	26.1	31.0	13.2
Smith County, Texas	56,044	24.6	19.7	10.7
Tarrant County, Texas	545,278	26.5	17.6	11.7
Taylor County, Texas	33,706	24.7	19.5	5.8
Tom Green County, Texas	28,029	23.7	15.0	14.6
Travis County, Texas	271,403	22.1	15.0	7.7
Victoria County, Texas	23,573	25.6	22.0	18.4
Walker County, Texas	11,053	15.3	21.5	10.0
Webb County, Texas	91,760	33.4	37.0	13.7
Wichita County, Texas	29,685	22.5	19.6	9.1
Williamson County, Texas	142,588	26.0	7.2	5.4
Wise County, Texas	16,167	24.4	15.3	23.2
UTAH	925,094	29.8	10.7	7.3
Cache County, Utah	37,744	30.3	13.9	5.6
Davis County, Utah	113,069	32.5	5.3	3.9
Salt Lake County, Utah	312,340	27.5	10.8	8.6
Tooele County, Utah	22,288	33.0	8.1	4.0
Utah County, Utah	205,469	33.9	9.5	5.0
Washington County, Utah	44,020	26.6	15.1	15.1
Weber County, Utah	71,895	28.6	13.5	6.7
VERMONT	117,755	18.9	13.8	1.6
Chittenden County, Vermont	29,068	17.9	15.8	1.9
VIRGINIA	1,868,081	22.1	14.0	5.1
Albemarle County, Virginia	21,636	20.1	11.6	4.9
Arlington County, Virginia	41,977	17.9	3.0	3.3
Augusta County, Virginia	14,476	19.3	10.0	3.9
Bedford County, Virginia	15,015	19.3	13.5	3.3
Chesterfield County, Virginia	82,056	23.9	7.9	3.9
Fairfax County, Virginia	268,833	23.4	9.8	4.5
Fauquier County, Virginia	16,709	24.1	4.8	5.8
Frederick County, Virginia	20,109	23.3	3.4	2.2
Hanover County, Virginia	23,526	22.2	5.7	5.6
Henrico County, Virginia	75,007	22.9	16.8	6.5
James City County, Virginia	15,964	21.1	9.1	2.7
Loudoun County, Virginia	113,338	28.5	2.1	3.7
Montgomery County, Virginia	14,889	15.1	19.8	3.2
Prince William County, Virginia	126,162	27.2	8.1	8.0
Roanoke County, Virginia	18,361	19.6	10.0	3.9
Rockingham County, Virginia	17,824	22.2	10.4	19.0
Spotsylvania County, Virginia	33,279	25.0	9.7	3.7
Stafford County, Virginia	38,373	26.2	2.4	6.2
York County, Virginia	16,158	23.9	4.4	1.8
Alexandria city, Virginia	28,865	18.0	24.6	4.2

Table C-1. Population and Poverty Characteristics, by State and Selected Counties, 2017—*Continued*

(Number; percent.)

State/County	Population		Children under 18 years old in poverty (percent)	Children under 19 years with no health insurance (percent)
	Total under 18 years old	Percent under 18 years old		
VIRGINIA—(*Continued*)				
Chesapeake city, Virginia	58,425	24.3	18.1	4.7
Hampton city, Virginia	28,133	20.9	26.3	2.2
Lynchburg city, Virginia	15,723	19.4	21.8	2.4
Newport News city, Virginia	41,691	23.2	26.1	8.5
Norfolk city, Virginia	48,416	19.8	28.1	5.1
Portsmouth city, Virginia	21,795	23.0	35.3	4.0
Richmond city, Virginia	40,329	17.8	38.4	6.1
Roanoke city, Virginia	21,643	21.7	25.6	3.9
Suffolk city, Virginia	22,014	24.4	19.4	2.4
Virginia Beach city, Virginia	100,408	22.3	10.6	3.0
WASHINGTON	1,646,733	22.2	14.3	2.6
Benton County, Washington	52,968	26.7	18.0	2.1
Chelan County, Washington	18,481	24.1	21.8	3.4
Clallam County, Washington	12,778	16.9	34.7	2.5
Clark County, Washington	115,419	24.3	14.4	3.2
Cowlitz County, Washington	24,515	22.9	20.5	0.6
Franklin County, Washington	29,411	31.9	17.9	0.9
Grant County, Washington	28,308	29.7	24.0	1.8
Grays Harbor County, Washington	15,020	20.7	25.8	5.3
Island County, Washington	15,300	18.4	15.4	2.7
King County, Washington	447,348	20.4	12.0	1.9
Kitsap County, Washington	55,081	20.7	9.8	2.8
Lewis County, Washington	16,943	21.7	20.9	7.9
Pierce County, Washington	206,928	23.6	11.4	3.2
Skagit County, Washington	27,869	22.2	15.8	3.3
Snohomish County, Washington	182,236	22.7	8.2	3.0
Spokane County, Washington	112,390	22.2	16.7	3.0
Thurston County, Washington	61,271	21.8	12.6	1.3
Whatcom County, Washington	43,196	19.5	11.1	2.0
Yakima County, Washington	74,372	29.7	27.6	3.1
WEST VIRGINIA	373,403	20.6	25.9	2.6
Berkeley County, West Virginia	27,102	23.6	17.7	1.9
Cabell County, West Virginia	18,826	19.8	40.8	3.6
Harrison County, West Virginia	14,646	21.6	22.2	9.2
Kanawha County, West Virginia	37,795	20.6	26.9	1.3
Monongalia County, West Virginia	17,218	16.4	10.7	0.4
Raleigh County, West Virginia	15,723	21.0	26.6	1.9
Wood County, West Virginia	18,209	21.4	29.9	0.6
WISCONSIN	1,279,361	22.1	14.5	3.9
Brown County, Wisconsin	62,929	24.0	13.5	4.4
Dane County, Wisconsin	110,838	20.7	9.7	2.1
Dodge County, Wisconsin	17,767	20.2	8.9	2.6
Eau Claire County, Wisconsin	20,983	20.2	15.1	7.0
Fond du Lac County, Wisconsin	21,772	21.2	12.3	3.5
Jefferson County, Wisconsin	18,045	21.3	11.6	1.3
Kenosha County, Wisconsin	39,134	23.2	17.0	3.5
La Crosse County, Wisconsin	23,563	19.9	7.0	3.2
Manitowoc County, Wisconsin	16,520	20.9	13.9	3.0
Marathon County, Wisconsin	31,229	23.0	13.4	6.8
Milwaukee County, Wisconsin	228,624	24.0	25.8	3.0
Outagamie County, Wisconsin	44,167	23.7	7.9	1.8
Ozaukee County, Wisconsin	18,824	21.3	5.8	1.8
Portage County, Wisconsin	13,506	19.2	10.0	2.7
Racine County, Wisconsin	45,524	23.2	18.2	3.2
Rock County, Wisconsin	38,098	23.5	18.7	3.5
St. Croix County, Wisconsin	22,746	25.6	3.3	4.8
Sheboygan County, Wisconsin	25,653	22.2	6.6	2.8
Walworth County, Wisconsin	21,527	20.9	9.1	6.6
Washington County, Wisconsin	29,981	22.2	3.9	2.0
Waukesha County, Wisconsin	86,872	21.7	5.4	1.8
Winnebago County, Wisconsin	35,105.0	20.6	16.1	3.3
Wood County, Wisconsin	15,762.0	21.6	11.4	1.3
WYOMING	138,062.0	23.8	13.3	9.5
Laramie County, Wyoming	22,679.0	23.1	9.5	4.2
Natrona County, Wyoming	20,496.0	25.8	10.6	11.3

Table C-2. Educational Attainment of the Population, by Selected Counties, 2017

(Number; percent; dollars.)

State/County	Population 18 to 24 years				
	Total	Less than high school graduate (percent)	High school graduate (includes equivalency) (percent)	Some college or associate's degree (percent)	Bachelor's degree or higher (percent)
ALABAMA					
Baldwin County, Alabama	14,570	15.2	33.6	42.7	8.5
Calhoun County, Alabama	10,146	16.2	35.1	42.7	6.0
Cullman County, Alabama	6,747	14.6	34.9	45.8	4.7
DeKalb County, Alabama	6,773	15.7	34.8	48.1	1.4
Elmore County, Alabama	7,800	20.5	51.7	20.6	7.2
Etowah County, Alabama	8,569	16.5	35.0	42.8	5.7
Houston County, Alabama	8,008	16.9	38.4	36.7	8.0
Jefferson County, Alabama	60,333	12.0	31.3	42.4	14.3
Lauderdale County, Alabama	10,236	9.8	20.1	63.7	6.3
Lee County, Alabama	30,374	4.6	22.8	65.7	6.9
Limestone County, Alabama	8,155	17.1	29.0	43.4	10.5
Madison County, Alabama	33,947	8.5	26.4	55.3	9.9
Marshall County, Alabama	9,198	23.1	37.8	36.7	2.4
Mobile County, Alabama	38,031	16.9	34.4	42.7	6.0
Montgomery County, Alabama	22,656	15.2	34.5	47.0	3.3
Morgan County, Alabama	9,770	19.3	32.4	46.7	1.5
St. Clair County, Alabama	5,753	7.2	67.4	22.5	2.9
Shelby County, Alabama	18,170	9.6	33.2	45.0	12.1
Talladega County, Alabama	6,474	8.8	48.2	41.2	1.7
Tuscaloosa County, Alabama	35,254	6.5	22.2	66.4	4.9
Walker County, Alabama	5,167	7.8	53.3	38.6	0.2
ALASKA					
Anchorage Municipality, Alaska	29,848	13.2	37.5	41.8	7.5
Fairbanks North Star Borough, Alaska	13,857	8.8	28.1	54.2	8.8
Matanuska-Susitna Borough, Alaska	9,409	20.7	44.6	28.9	5.9
ARIZONA					
Apache County, Arizona	7,255	25.8	32.3	41.9	0.0
Cochise County, Arizona	10,871	17.3	43.0	37.3	2.4
Coconino County, Arizona	27,775	5.9	35.1	52.6	6.3
Maricopa County, Arizona	397,294	14.6	34.3	41.7	9.4
Mohave County, Arizona	12,221	38.2	37.8	21.7	2.3
Navajo County, Arizona	9,466	23.7	44.0	31.5	0.8
Pima County, Arizona	121,317	17.0	29.4	45.9	7.8
Pinal County, Arizona	33,662	27.6	40.3	28.9	3.3
Yavapai County, Arizona	14,796	17.4	26.0	53.7	2.9
Yuma County, Arizona	23,765	13.4	30.9	54.5	1.2
ARKANSAS					
Benton County, Arkansas	21,352	10.4	42.1	37.5	10.0
Craighead County, Arkansas	11,583	7.5	21.2	54.4	16.8
Faulkner County, Arkansas	18,951	6.1	29.6	53.0	11.4
Garland County, Arkansas	7,381	20.8	32.0	45.6	1.6
Jefferson County, Arkansas	7,205	14.6	25.7	50.5	9.1
Lonoke County, Arkansas	5,809	10.6	45.4	29.9	14.1
Pulaski County, Arkansas	33,955	17.4	39.6	30.4	12.6
Saline County, Arkansas	8,873	21.4	26.0	43.1	9.5
Sebastian County, Arkansas	12,116	15.4	39.3	42.7	2.6
Washington County, Arkansas	35,018	6.0	30.4	51.4	12.3
White County, Arkansas	9,156	3.8	31.7	58.8	5.8
CALIFORNIA					
Alameda County, California	140,475	9.1	29.1	45.4	16.4
Butte County, California	32,324	7.6	33.2	51.1	8.2
Contra Costa County, California	94,314	9.9	29.9	49.3	11.0
El Dorado County, California	13,956	9.0	43.9	38.1	9.0
Fresno County, California	99,039	16.0	30.0	48.8	5.2
Humboldt County, California	18,382	10.5	27.5	58.4	3.7
Imperial County, California	19,025	14.7	28.7	53.0	3.6
Kern County, California	91,460	18.0	43.7	35.0	3.3
Kings County, California	16,011	20.3	43.6	32.5	3.6
Lake County, California	3,049	1.8	39.3	56.7	2.2
Los Angeles County, California	983,483	10.9	27.2	50.8	11.1
Madera County, California	14,893	19.2	34.3	43.6	3.0
Marin County, California	17,052	17.3	28.5	36.7	17.5
Mendocino County, California	6,264	8.7	53.0	36.6	1.8
Merced County, California	30,106	11.0	24.8	57.2	6.9
Monterey County, California	44,246	17.0	27.3	49.0	6.6
Napa County, California	12,875	10.5	29.1	50.9	9.5

Table C-2. Educational Attainment of the Population, by Selected Counties, 2017—*Continued*

(Number; percent; dollars.)

State/County	Population 25 years and over							
	Total	Less than 9th grade (percent)	9th to 12th grade, no diploma (percent)	High school graduate (includes equivalency) (percent)	Some college, no degree (percent)	Associate's degree (percent)	Bachelor's degree (percent)	Graduate or professional degree (percent)
ALABAMA								
Baldwin County, Alabama	152,037	2.8	8.0	25.2	22.6	7.9	23.0	10.6
Calhoun County, Alabama	79,582	4.3	10.4	34.0	24.7	7.3	10.6	8.7
Cullman County, Alabama	57,916	4.3	13.5	35.9	22.5	11.4	7.7	4.7
DeKalb County, Alabama	47,604	9.0	13.7	37.4	17.3	7.5	9.8	5.3
Elmore County, Alabama	55,782	3.6	9.7	31.4	20.1	10.3	16.0	8.9
Etowah County, Alabama	71,846	4.0	12.1	33.2	22.8	8.6	11.7	7.7
Houston County, Alabama	72,149	3.5	9.5	32.5	22.2	10.3	13.7	8.4
Jefferson County, Alabama	448,110	2.8	7.3	26.3	21.4	8.9	20.6	12.7
Lauderdale County, Alabama	63,925	2.4	9.2	37.4	21.0	6.0	15.0	9.0
Lee County, Alabama	96,835	2.7	5.6	25.3	23.4	9.5	18.0	15.5
Limestone County, Alabama	65,019	4.6	7.7	27.2	22.1	9.1	20.2	9.1
Madison County, Alabama	247,593	2.7	6.1	20.6	21.2	8.0	25.0	16.3
Marshall County, Alabama	62,672	7.9	11.3	29.6	22.9	8.5	12.8	7.0
Mobile County, Alabama	278,255	3.4	9.2	35.3	21.0	8.1	14.8	8.3
Montgomery County, Alabama	150,542	4.4	9.6	26.5	19.8	7.0	19.5	13.2
Morgan County, Alabama	82,161	4.7	8.8	32.7	23.5	10.3	14.1	5.8
St. Clair County, Alabama	61,901	4.5	9.3	34.7	26.5	8.6	11.0	5.3
Shelby County, Alabama	144,760	1.9	5.2	19.9	21.7	8.0	27.7	15.6
Talladega County, Alabama	56,193	5.2	11.1	34.4	23.8	11.3	8.9	5.4
Tuscaloosa County, Alabama	128,996	4.4	9.4	28.4	19.0	6.2	19.3	13.4
Walker County, Alabama	44,837	6.1	11.7	36.2	25.6	8.8	7.3	4.3
ALASKA								
Anchorage Municipality, Alaska	192,466	3.0	4.6	22.8	24.9	9.6	21.4	13.7
Fairbanks North Star Borough, Alaska	61,914	1.9	5.0	23.1	31.0	9.4	16.6	13.0
Matanuska-Susitna Borough, Alaska	67,973	2.9	5.6	33.7	27.7	8.3	14.7	7.2
ARIZONA								
Apache County, Arizona	44,572	9.4	11.3	28.9	29.7	8.6	8.3	3.8
Cochise County, Arizona	86,811	4.6	7.1	21.2	31.8	10.5	14.0	10.7
Coconino County, Arizona	83,432	3.3	5.5	23.1	23.7	7.1	21.7	15.6
Maricopa County, Arizona	2,864,476	5.7	6.7	22.8	23.8	8.7	20.6	11.7
Mohave County, Arizona	158,780	4.2	9.5	35.7	28.5	8.6	8.0	5.5
Navajo County, Arizona	70,045	6.1	10.5	28.7	30.2	6.4	10.7	7.4
Pima County, Arizona	684,433	3.7	6.8	21.6	25.0	9.3	19.5	14.0
Pinal County, Arizona	297,571	5.2	10.2	31.5	26.0	7.5	12.7	6.8
Yavapai County, Arizona	175,929	3.1	6.1	25.9	30.9	10.3	13.4	10.3
Yuma County, Arizona	131,272	12.9	14.8	26.6	24.0	8.2	8.2	5.4
ARKANSAS								
Benton County, Arkansas	174,196	4.9	5.9	29.2	20.1	5.9	23.2	10.8
Craighead County, Arkansas	69,331	4.1	6.7	34.5	17.7	9.5	16.9	10.6
Faulkner County, Arkansas	75,973	1.7	6.0	31.2	21.0	7.3	20.0	12.9
Garland County, Arkansas	71,435	3.7	7.9	30.7	30.8	7.4	12.7	6.8
Jefferson County, Arkansas	46,424	2.9	9.6	40.6	23.8	4.7	12.4	6.0
Lonoke County, Arkansas	48,062	3.5	6.1	35.3	19.5	12.1	17.6	5.8
Pulaski County, Arkansas	267,664	2.7	6.2	27.2	22.7	6.5	20.4	14.4
Saline County, Arkansas	82,486	2.2	6.0	30.2	25.2	10.8	16.6	9.1
Sebastian County, Arkansas	85,038	5.8	10.5	30.3	23.5	8.1	14.3	7.4
Washington County, Arkansas	140,005	6.6	9.8	24.3	21.9	4.6	20.3	12.5
White County, Arkansas	51,342	5.2	10.9	38.7	15.2	6.7	15.0	8.3
CALIFORNIA								
Alameda County, California	1,178,053	5.8	6.2	18.0	17.5	6.1	26.9	19.5
Butte County, California	151,101	3.7	6.5	22.1	30.0	11.1	16.7	9.9
Contra Costa County, California	791,111	6.1	5.3	16.6	21.3	8.6	26.7	15.5
El Dorado County, California	137,282	2.2	4.7	20.0	26.5	12.4	22.7	11.5
Fresno County, California	608,533	13.1	10.6	23.1	24.0	8.9	13.8	6.6
Humboldt County, California	92,277	2.3	6.1	21.9	25.6	10.4	21.5	12.1
Imperial County, California	111,254	15.1	13.5	28.2	23.0	5.2	10.4	4.7
Kern County, California	542,437	14.4	12.4	27.9	21.9	7.4	10.4	5.6
Kings County, California	93,123	14.8	11.7	24.7	27.1	8.4	9.4	3.8
Lake County, California	48,029	6.0	7.4	34.0	27.0	12.0	9.5	4.2
Los Angeles County, California	6,955,119	12.2	8.5	20.8	19.3	7.0	21.1	11.1
Madera County, California	99,417	16.7	12.3	23.0	24.3	8.3	10.6	4.7
Marin County, California	191,635	3.3	2.6	10.5	17.9	7.2	32.8	25.8
Mendocino County, California	62,833	4.9	6.0	26.8	29.0	7.2	16.2	9.9
Merced County, California	162,053	19.1	11.9	25.2	22.9	7.6	8.7	4.7
Monterey County, California	278,518	21.6	7.6	20.9	17.9	7.3	14.9	9.9
Napa County, California	98,614	9.2	5.0	17.8	22.5	9.4	23.4	12.8

Table C-2. Educational Attainment of the Population, by Selected Counties, 2017—*Continued*

(Number; percent; dollars.)

State/County	Population 18 to 24 years				
	Total	Less than high school graduate (percent)	High school graduate (includes equivalency) (percent)	Some college or associate's degree (percent)	Bachelor's degree or higher (percent)
CALIFORNIA—*(Continued)*					
Nevada County, California	5,580	13.6	37.5	43.1	5.8
Orange County, California	297,063	8.5	27.4	51.2	12.9
Placer County, California	28,641	8.8	33.0	48.5	9.7
Riverside County, California	239,444	10.0	41.1	42.8	6.1
Sacramento County, California	131,898	11.0	36.3	45.1	7.7
San Bernardino County, California	227,781	11.3	36.9	45.7	6.2
San Diego County, California	346,417	8.1	34.4	46.6	11.0
San Francisco County, California	63,254	4.8	21.2	40.0	34.0
San Joaquin County, California	71,715	14.3	37.2	43.7	4.8
San Luis Obispo County, California	43,604	7.8	22.3	58.9	11.0
San Mateo County, California	55,586	8.4	27.3	40.7	23.7
Santa Barbara County, California	71,301	9.2	19.4	61.0	10.4
Santa Clara County, California	163,769	8.6	23.8	44.4	23.1
Santa Cruz County, California	41,064	7.4	28.7	53.7	10.2
Shasta County, California	14,769	12.1	40.9	39.9	7.1
Solano County, California	39,762	9.7	37.6	44.8	8.0
Sonoma County, California	41,789	10.2	32.3	48.3	9.3
Stanislaus County, California	52,511	13.9	36.3	43.2	6.7
Sutter County, California	7,721	27.0	20.2	48.2	4.6
Tulare County, California	46,760	13.4	35.8	48.3	2.5
Ventura County, California	81,185	10.0	30.3	52.2	7.5
Yolo County, California	44,732	4.5	24.4	59.9	11.3
Yuba County, California	6,328	5.2	42.8	48.3	3.7
COLORADO					
Adams County, Colorado	43,586	19.2	41.5	32.3	7.0
Arapahoe County, Colorado	53,381	12.4	33.8	38.2	15.7
Boulder County, Colorado	47,345	5.6	18.1	63.4	13.0
Broomfield County, Colorado	5,111	8.2	27.2	40.6	23.9
Denver County, Colorado	56,753	7.5	30.4	43.7	18.4
Douglas County, Colorado	24,371	12.3	31.5	38.5	17.6
El Paso County, Colorado	77,014	8.8	35.3	46.1	9.9
Jefferson County, Colorado	44,514	12.8	28.6	43.9	14.7
Larimer County, Colorado	49,096	5.8	29.9	44.7	19.7
Mesa County, Colorado	15,363	12.9	28.0	52.5	6.6
Pueblo County, Colorado	15,084	22.5	34.2	34.1	9.1
Weld County, Colorado	28,350	7.1	40.4	47.7	4.8
CONNECTICUT					
Fairfield County, Connecticut	87,447	13.3	25.8	39.4	21.4
Hartford County, Connecticut	81,609	9.8	28.1	43.7	18.3
Litchfield County, Connecticut	12,676	6.6	32.3	47.4	13.7
Middlesex County, Connecticut	14,527	11.9	25.8	47.1	15.2
New Haven County, Connecticut	86,733	10.3	33.1	41.0	15.6
New London County, Connecticut	27,764	14.4	32.0	36.8	16.9
Tolland County, Connecticut	28,511	3.6	18.1	66.8	11.5
Windham County, Connecticut	12,785	8.1	23.9	60.7	7.3
DELAWARE					
Kent County, Delaware	17,685	8.7	24.7	55.8	10.8
New Castle County, Delaware	52,815	10.4	37.7	42.5	9.5
Sussex County, Delaware	13,440	22.3	29.8	42.7	5.1
DISTRICT OF COLUMBIA					
District of Columbia, District of Columbia	74,760	9.8	22.8	44.4	23.0
FLORIDA					
Alachua County, Florida	57,001	4.3	18.3	59.7	17.7
Bay County, Florida	15,071	21.5	30.0	41.6	6.9
Brevard County, Florida	44,086	16.7	30.6	41.8	10.9
Broward County, Florida	154,038	15.6	28.8	45.7	10.0
Charlotte County, Florida	8,511	15.8	48.9	30.0	5.3
Citrus County, Florida	7,922	10.5	54.4	31.4	3.7
Clay County, Florida	17,034	16.0	45.1	35.9	3.1
Collier County, Florida	24,562	11.5	35.2	39.8	13.4
Columbia County, Florida	6,330	33.5	44.4	20.7	1.4
Duval County, Florida	85,232	16.1	32.5	41.9	9.4
Escambia County, Florida	36,825	11.7	30.7	50.4	7.2
Flagler County, Florida	7,939	10.8	40.9	41.4	6.8
Hernando County, Florida	12,373	19.2	33.8	42.9	4.1

Table C-2. Educational Attainment of the Population, by Selected Counties, 2017—*Continued*

(Number; percent; dollars.)

State/County	Population 25 years and over							
	Total	Less than 9th grade (percent)	9th to 12th grade, no diploma (percent)	High school graduate (includes equivalency) (percent)	Some college, no degree (percent)	Associate's degree (percent)	Bachelor's degree (percent)	Graduate or professional degree (percent)
CALIFORNIA—*(Continued)*								
Nevada County, California	76,951	1.4	3.8	17.2	29.5	11.2	22.6	14.3
Orange County, California	2,187,338	8.0	7.0	17.3	19.7	7.7	26.1	14.2
Placer County, California	271,276	2.3	3.2	19.8	27.0	10.6	24.4	12.8
Riverside County, California	1,567,612	9.1	8.5	27.4	24.5	8.3	14.3	7.9
Sacramento County, California	1,034,406	6.6	5.9	23.1	24.3	9.5	20.0	10.6
San Bernardino County, California	1,357,953	8.6	11.5	26.4	24.5	8.5	13.6	6.9
San Diego County, California	2,262,740	6.7	5.8	18.6	22.1	8.2	23.7	15.0
San Francisco County, California	702,525	7.3	4.4	11.5	14.1	4.8	35.1	22.7
San Joaquin County, California	470,574	10.3	8.6	30.0	23.2	9.0	13.1	5.7
San Luis Obispo County, California	189,011	3.8	4.2	20.7	26.5	10.3	19.8	14.8
San Mateo County, California	555,560	6.1	3.6	14.8	17.0	6.8	28.6	23.0
Santa Barbara County, California	277,137	12.6	6.6	17.0	21.0	7.6	21.2	14.1
Santa Clara County, California	1,344,303	6.4	5.1	14.7	15.6	6.4	26.9	24.7
Santa Cruz County, California	181,407	8.4	4.9	17.0	21.1	8.4	23.8	16.4
Shasta County, California	126,457	3.3	6.1	27.4	29.9	10.3	15.2	7.8
Solano County, California	306,637	6.7	6.3	22.9	27.5	9.9	18.4	8.3
Sonoma County, California	362,732	5.5	5.2	19.3	24.9	9.3	22.6	13.3
Stanislaus County, California	347,151	11.6	9.2	30.1	24.6	7.0	12.0	5.5
Sutter County, California	63,863	11.5	9.5	25.5	24.8	11.9	11.7	5.2
Tulare County, California	274,008	17.8	11.7	27.5	21.1	7.6	10.1	4.2
Ventura County, California	574,375	9.2	5.6	19.1	23.4	9.1	21.9	11.6
Yolo County, California	128,156	7.0	6.7	18.2	22.7	6.7	20.1	18.7
Yuba County, California	49,662	6.8	13.1	24.3	28.4	9.4	13.9	3.9
COLORADO								
Adams County, Colorado	324,185	6.3	9.7	29.6	22.3	9.3	16.2	6.7
Arapahoe County, Colorado	436,615	3.3	4.6	21.0	19.4	7.9	28.4	15.2
Boulder County, Colorado	212,233	1.8	2.8	11.1	14.8	6.4	35.2	28.0
Broomfield County, Colorado	47,160	1.3	1.8	16.2	15.6	10.0	36.2	18.9
Denver County, Colorado	507,664	5.8	5.8	17.4	16.4	5.3	30.1	19.2
Douglas County, Colorado	221,904	0.6	1.4	11.9	20.1	7.4	38.3	20.3
El Paso County, Colorado	452,212	2.2	4.1	19.5	24.6	10.3	23.6	15.6
Jefferson County, Colorado	415,131	1.4	4.0	20.7	20.7	7.7	28.8	16.8
Larimer County, Colorado	226,454	1.8	2.9	19.5	19.2	8.8	27.9	20.0
Mesa County, Colorado	103,208	2.5	6.0	27.7	28.4	9.7	17.3	8.6
Pueblo County, Colorado	113,492	3.2	5.6	30.0	29.0	10.2	14.9	7.3
Weld County, Colorado	195,753	5.9	6.6	27.1	23.4	9.4	19.0	8.5
CONNECTICUT								
Fairfield County, Connecticut	647,725	5.8	5.2	21.4	14.0	6.5	26.0	21.2
Hartford County, Connecticut	625,275	4.6	6.1	27.1	16.0	8.5	20.9	16.8
Litchfield County, Connecticut	136,414	2.5	4.9	28.3	17.4	10.4	21.4	15.1
Middlesex County, Connecticut	119,342	1.4	4.0	28.4	16.8	9.5	23.1	16.6
New Haven County, Connecticut	598,860	3.5	5.8	31.3	17.2	8.1	18.4	15.8
New London County, Connecticut	188,610	2.4	5.5	28.7	21.3	8.7	17.8	15.6
Tolland County, Connecticut	96,486	1.7	2.9	28.8	18.4	8.3	22.4	17.6
Windham County, Connecticut	81,142	4.1	7.7	33.7	20.7	9.5	15.1	9.2
DELAWARE								
Kent County, Delaware	118,346	4.2	7.4	32.2	23.7	9.1	14.5	8.8
New Castle County, Delaware	385,693	2.8	4.8	33.6	17.1	6.5	20.1	15.1
Sussex County, Delaware	169,647	4.5	7.5	29.8	20.0	9.4	15.8	13.0
DISTRICT OF COLUMBIA								
District of Columbia, District of Columbia	494,614	4.3	5.5	17.2	12.5	3.2	23.9	33.4
FLORIDA								
Alachua County, Florida	161,896	2.3	6.0	22.8	17.6	10.6	20.3	20.4
Bay County, Florida	128,622	3.0	6.0	30.3	26.1	11.0	15.2	8.5
Brevard County, Florida	436,285	2.4	5.7	27.7	21.4	12.8	18.4	11.6
Broward County, Florida	1,370,041	4.9	5.7	27.4	19.6	9.7	20.5	12.2
Charlotte County, Florida	150,874	2.9	5.5	34.3	24.5	9.2	15.5	8.1
Citrus County, Florida	116,483	2.2	9.2	39.3	23.4	9.1	11.2	5.7
Clay County, Florida	144,638	1.6	8.1	32.6	24.1	11.6	14.4	7.6
Collier County, Florida	283,595	7.2	4.5	27.0	16.2	8.1	22.4	14.6
Columbia County, Florida	48,064	3.7	7.4	35.4	27.1	8.9	13.2	4.3
Duval County, Florida	641,660	2.9	7.2	28.1	22.0	10.4	19.9	9.6
Escambia County, Florida	210,972	2.3	7.6	26.1	24.8	12.8	17.3	9.2
Flagler County, Florida	83,530	2.6	5.0	34.8	22.8	9.8	15.7	9.3
Hernando County, Florida	138,863	3.4	7.9	37.8	24.2	7.9	12.2	6.7

Table C-2. Educational Attainment of the Population, by Selected Counties, 2017—*Continued*

(Number; percent; dollars.)

State/County		Population 18 to 24 years			
	Total	Less than high school graduate (percent)	High school graduate (includes equivalency) (percent)	Some college or associate's degree (percent)	Bachelor's degree or higher (percent)
FLORIDA—(*Continued*)					
Highlands County, Florida	5,184	25.9	33.9	38.5	1.6
Hillsborough County, Florida	126,110	15.5	28.0	44.2	12.4
Indian River County, Florida	11,750	27.6	26.3	36.2	9.9
Lake County, Florida	25,295	13.9	44.0	36.6	5.5
Lee County, Florida	52,203	22.3	32.3	39.5	5.9
Leon County, Florida	62,086	5.9	14.0	65.5	14.6
Manatee County, Florida	26,388	26.6	34.9	32.0	6.5
Marion County, Florida	22,991	27.5	36.2	33.4	2.9
Martin County, Florida	11,494	26.6	34.6	33.9	4.9
Miami-Dade County, Florida	233,195	14.9	30.3	45.2	9.5
Monroe County, Florida	4,464	0.2	33.2	58.7	7.8
Nassau County, Florida	5,896	14.6	43.2	30.4	11.8
Okaloosa County, Florida	18,451	9.8	34.3	44.3	11.6
Orange County, Florida	142,667	11.8	26.1	51.5	10.6
Osceola County, Florida	34,428	13.9	35.1	49.1	1.9
Palm Beach County, Florida	110,899	15.9	26.1	46.0	12.0
Pasco County, Florida	37,414	15.6	36.8	40.8	6.7
Pinellas County, Florida	64,582	15.2	37.0	36.7	11.0
Polk County, Florida	56,853	15.7	40.0	38.0	6.3
Putnam County, Florida	5,327	18.0	53.2	22.0	6.8
St. Johns County, Florida	17,114	11.6	32.2	45.4	10.8
St. Lucie County, Florida	25,626	16.5	37.8	38.1	7.6
Santa Rosa County, Florida	15,272	22.3	50.0	22.6	5.1
Sarasota County, Florida	23,958	16.0	34.0	40.0	10.0
Seminole County, Florida	38,891	13.1	20.8	58.2	7.9
Sumter County, Florida	4,497	12.6	51.3	35.2	0.9
Volusia County, Florida	44,321	15.8	32.6	46.2	5.5
Walton County, Florida	3,793	11.8	43.8	41.9	2.5
GEORGIA					
Barrow County, Georgia	6,311	18.7	44.5	28.8	8.0
Bartow County, Georgia	8,424	20.5	35.7	38.4	5.5
Bibb County, Georgia	15,815	16.6	23.8	52.0	7.6
Bulloch County, Georgia	18,606	3.5	21.9	68.4	6.3
Carroll County, Georgia	14,620	14.2	35.1	44.6	6.2
Catoosa County, Georgia	6,786	19.4	50.2	24.6	5.7
Chatham County, Georgia	32,655	10.1	31.4	47.2	11.3
Cherokee County, Georgia	20,523	12.5	27.6	53.8	6.2
Clarke County, Georgia	35,021	2.5	14.8	71.5	11.2
Clayton County, Georgia	28,602	22.6	40.6	31.6	5.2
Cobb County, Georgia	68,095	12.7	27.4	47.6	12.3
Columbia County, Georgia	14,232	10.3	41.4	43.0	5.3
Coweta County, Georgia	13,490	15.6	36.8	41.3	6.2
DeKalb County, Georgia	64,140	15.6	30.2	38.7	15.6
Dougherty County, Georgia	10,082	17.4	37.0	44.7	1.0
Douglas County, Georgia	12,278	22.7	29.1	37.7	10.5
Fayette County, Georgia	7,850	16.5	37.5	39.7	6.3
Floyd County, Georgia	10,789	20.7	41.2	32.9	5.3
Forsyth County, Georgia	15,896	13.7	41.5	33.1	11.7
Fulton County, Georgia	106,108	9.7	28.5	42.1	19.6
Glynn County, Georgia	7,257	16.1	36.5	30.5	16.9
Gwinnett County, Georgia	83,076	17.8	34.0	36.1	12.1
Hall County, Georgia	18,621	17.2	37.3	38.9	6.7
Henry County, Georgia	22,474	13.6	43.0	37.5	5.9
Houston County, Georgia	13,072	18.0	27.5	42.2	12.3
Jackson County, Georgia	4,305	12.1	38.6	38.8	10.5
Lowndes County, Georgia	19,514	8.7	35.7	45.9	9.7
Muscogee County, Georgia	19,935	8.0	36.7	50.9	4.4
Newton County, Georgia	11,072	21.3	47.9	27.3	3.6
Paulding County, Georgia	13,463	15.8	38.3	42.4	3.5
Richmond County, Georgia	23,500	13.3	43.2	40.0	3.4
Rockdale County, Georgia	10,451	21.0	26.4	40.4	12.2
Spalding County, Georgia	5,075	20.1	50.9	20.5	8.5
Troup County, Georgia	7,330	25.9	44.3	25.8	4.0
Walker County, Georgia	5,116	9.1	45.5	44.4	0.9
Walton County, Georgia	7,271	18.8	45.9	34.6	0.6
Whitfield County, Georgia	10,139	15.7	28.4	47.8	8.2

Table C-2. Educational Attainment of the Population, by Selected Counties, 2017—*Continued*

(Number; percent; dollars.)

State/County	Total	Less than 9th grade (percent)	9th to 12th grade, no diploma (percent)	High school graduate (includes equivalency) (percent)	Some college, no degree (percent)	Associate's degree (percent)	Bachelor's degree (percent)	Graduate or professional degree (percent)
FLORIDA—*(Continued)*								
Highlands County, Florida	79,408	5.0	10.6	38.1	20.8	7.6	11.1	6.8
Hillsborough County, Florida	960,910	4.3	6.5	27.8	18.7	9.4	21.4	11.9
Indian River County, Florida	117,106	3.4	6.2	32.5	17.8	9.7	19.3	11.1
Lake County, Florida	253,696	3.0	8.1	32.3	20.9	11.2	15.3	9.2
Lee County, Florida	555,154	5.1	5.9	32.0	20.1	9.6	16.9	10.4
Leon County, Florida	173,825	1.7	3.4	18.4	19.7	9.9	25.9	21.0
Manatee County, Florida	287,528	3.4	5.8	28.7	21.0	9.1	20.0	12.0
Marion County, Florida	264,517	3.4	10.8	35.5	20.7	7.7	14.5	7.4
Martin County, Florida	121,973	3.1	7.1	27.4	21.4	9.5	21.7	10.0
Miami-Dade County, Florida	1,961,363	9.9	8.3	27.9	15.0	9.6	18.9	10.5
Monroe County, Florida	60,769	5.1	5.0	26.1	23.1	7.2	21.7	11.7
Nassau County, Florida	60,646	2.6	4.6	31.3	18.1	10.0	21.3	12.2
Okaloosa County, Florida	139,480	2.0	4.5	24.0	25.7	12.5	19.8	11.5
Orange County, Florida	904,404	4.1	6.2	24.2	18.8	12.6	22.8	11.2
Osceola County, Florida	230,380	5.0	8.7	28.9	25.6	12.7	13.5	5.7
Palm Beach County, Florida	1,077,100	5.6	5.6	24.5	19.4	8.7	22.4	13.8
Pasco County, Florida	381,293	3.0	7.6	34.7	21.8	9.7	15.5	7.8
Pinellas County, Florida	746,168	3.0	5.9	28.4	21.2	10.2	20.2	11.2
Polk County, Florida	476,398	5.9	8.7	34.2	23.0	9.1	12.3	6.7
Putnam County, Florida	52,344	5.9	13.0	43.7	17.9	6.7	8.2	4.6
St. Johns County, Florida	172,936	2.2	6.1	22.6	17.5	7.7	27.6	16.2
St. Lucie County, Florida	224,830	5.6	8.0	34.1	21.6	8.7	14.7	7.3
Santa Rosa County, Florida	120,782	1.9	5.9	27.3	20.9	16.7	17.6	9.8
Sarasota County, Florida	335,076	3.0	5.3	29.8	19.0	8.7	20.1	14.1
Seminole County, Florida	325,935	1.3	3.3	18.3	18.0	17.5	28.8	12.9
Sumter County, Florida	112,185	1.8	6.8	28.1	22.2	8.2	20.5	12.5
Volusia County, Florida	398,400	3.2	7.2	32.9	23.7	10.3	14.3	8.4
Walton County, Florida	50,744	3.2	10.5	27.1	20.9	9.9	16.9	11.5
GEORGIA								
Barrow County, Georgia	51,843	5.4	8.8	36.3	22.1	8.9	12.2	6.3
Bartow County, Georgia	71,074	5.3	11.3	31.8	23.7	6.9	13.9	7.1
Bibb County, Georgia	99,357	3.2	10.2	31.6	24.1	6.0	14.2	10.7
Bulloch County, Georgia	42,208	3.5	9.2	30.1	22.2	8.6	14.5	12.0
Carroll County, Georgia	75,007	4.2	9.5	32.8	23.0	7.5	15.1	7.9
Catoosa County, Georgia	44,502	2.7	8.2	35.4	26.6	9.2	12.6	5.4
Chatham County, Georgia	195,081	2.5	9.0	24.1	23.3	8.3	19.3	13.4
Cherokee County, Georgia	165,411	2.5	4.8	22.3	25.8	8.0	24.1	12.4
Clarke County, Georgia	70,087	4.4	7.4	21.5	15.7	7.0	22.0	22.1
Clayton County, Georgia	176,690	5.9	10.8	36.4	21.6	9.0	10.7	5.7
Cobb County, Georgia	506,561	3.5	4.1	19.3	19.0	7.4	29.6	17.1
Columbia County, Georgia	98,512	4.6	4.6	23.2	20.4	11.8	22.2	13.3
Coweta County, Georgia	94,167	4.2	5.9	26.4	25.1	7.0	22.5	8.8
DeKalb County, Georgia	513,908	4.8	6.2	21.8	18.3	6.1	24.5	18.2
Dougherty County, Georgia	57,630	4.1	9.6	31.4	23.0	7.3	12.3	12.3
Douglas County, Georgia	94,045	4.3	10.4	30.8	20.2	7.4	15.7	11.2
Fayette County, Georgia	78,392	0.8	4.8	20.8	19.9	7.6	28.1	18.0
Floyd County, Georgia	64,239	7.8	11.6	34.8	18.8	8.0	10.3	8.5
Forsyth County, Georgia	148,444	3.0	4.3	14.8	15.6	7.1	36.0	19.2
Fulton County, Georgia	703,237	2.6	4.9	18.5	16.4	6.4	30.9	20.3
Glynn County, Georgia	59,029	2.3	8.6	25.9	23.1	8.7	19.8	11.6
Gwinnett County, Georgia	587,069	6.4	5.8	23.1	18.5	9.7	23.8	12.6
Hall County, Georgia	129,706	10.9	10.4	28.2	19.6	4.7	16.1	10.2
Henry County, Georgia	144,329	1.9	5.7	32.0	22.8	8.0	19.5	10.2
Houston County, Georgia	100,891	2.1	4.3	27.4	25.9	9.2	20.4	10.8
Jackson County, Georgia	46,553	5.6	9.6	32.4	20.4	9.4	14.2	8.4
Lowndes County, Georgia	68,062	4.9	10.7	31.3	15.4	8.5	17.3	11.9
Muscogee County, Georgia	125,754	4.3	8.2	29.2	24.3	8.3	17.1	8.5
Newton County, Georgia	68,597	2.3	8.3	37.0	23.0	8.6	11.0	9.8
Paulding County, Georgia	102,836	2.1	8.0	33.5	26.1	8.7	13.5	8.2
Richmond County, Georgia	131,433	4.5	13.1	29.9	22.3	9.0	13.3	7.8
Rockdale County, Georgia	57,268	5.8	5.5	30.1	23.8	9.2	15.5	10.1
Spalding County, Georgia	44,209	2.0	15.2	41.7	15.3	6.6	12.7	6.5
Troup County, Georgia	45,006	4.9	13.2	34.1	21.2	6.2	13.6	6.8
Walker County, Georgia	48,606	3.0	11.3	38.4	20.3	8.8	11.2	7.0
Walton County, Georgia	61,543	1.4	9.4	44.2	18.0	7.9	14.1	5.0
Whitfield County, Georgia	66,837	14.5	17.8	31.1	15.6	4.7	10.3	6.1

Table C-2. Educational Attainment of the Population, by Selected Counties, 2017—*Continued*

(Number; percent; dollars.)

State/County	Population 18 to 24 years				
	Total	Less than high school graduate (percent)	High school graduate (includes equivalency) (percent)	Some college or associate's degree (percent)	Bachelor's degree or higher (percent)
HAWAII					
Hawaii County, Hawaii	14,518	7.4	45.9	40.5	6.2
Honolulu County, Hawaii	92,917	5.3	39.0	46.5	9.2
Kauai County, Hawaii	5,190	9.7	42.4	44.8	3.1
Maui County, Hawaii	11,172	13.7	45.6	33.7	7.0
IDAHO					
Ada County, Idaho	38,689	11.1	29.1	49.2	10.6
Bannock County, Idaho	10,291	5.5	32.7	55.7	6.0
Bonneville County, Idaho	10,107	11.4	34.7	41.2	12.7
Canyon County, Idaho	21,417	16.0	43.6	33.5	6.9
Kootenai County, Idaho	12,351	16.5	42.3	40.0	1.2
Twin Falls County, Idaho	6,607	13.2	46.1	40.8	0.0
ILLINOIS					
Adams County, Illinois	5,247	12.8	40.6	38.0	8.7
Champaign County, Illinois	49,095	3.5	15.3	67.0	14.1
Cook County, Illinois	467,035	12.7	27.3	43.5	16.6
DeKalb County, Illinois	19,132	7.2	18.8	62.0	11.9
DuPage County, Illinois	81,091	11.2	23.7	44.3	20.8
Kane County, Illinois	49,299	13.2	31.5	43.2	12.1
Kankakee County, Illinois	11,467	10.6	40.9	45.1	3.4
Kendall County, Illinois	9,124	27.7	36.2	30.4	5.7
Lake County, Illinois	72,376	13.8	36.5	37.0	12.7
LaSalle County, Illinois	9,311	16.3	33.3	44.2	6.2
McHenry County, Illinois	26,291	12.7	32.4	43.2	11.6
McLean County, Illinois	30,163	7.5	13.2	69.8	9.4
Macon County, Illinois	9,932	17.5	32.6	43.0	6.9
Madison County, Illinois	21,858	14.4	35.8	41.7	8.1
Peoria County, Illinois	16,410	17.3	21.3	52.9	8.5
Rock Island County, Illinois	13,144	13.5	32.5	45.1	9.0
St. Clair County, Illinois	22,686	20.8	33.1	41.7	4.4
Sangamon County, Illinois	15,797	15.5	37.0	34.4	13.2
Tazewell County, Illinois	10,394	17.9	39.1	36.4	6.6
Vermilion County, Illinois	6,328	22.0	40.0	35.2	2.8
Will County, Illinois	63,735	12.1	32.7	43.7	11.5
Williamson County, Illinois	4,516	10.4	39.9	46.3	3.4
Winnebago County, Illinois	23,122	17.0	36.0	39.7	7.4
INDIANA					
Allen County, Indiana	33,641	18.3	34.1	38.8	8.8
Bartholomew County, Indiana	6,498	4.6	43.9	27.7	23.7
Boone County, Indiana	5,091	13.8	33.9	23.6	28.7
Clark County, Indiana	9,293	4.6	51.0	40.2	4.2
Delaware County, Indiana	23,221	5.7	19.6	68.3	6.4
Elkhart County, Indiana	18,498	24.4	41.2	28.4	6.0
Floyd County, Indiana	6,144	16.5	29.6	41.4	12.5
Grant County, Indiana	8,357	13.5	22.9	57.6	5.9
Hamilton County, Indiana	22,680	16.5	31.1	33.7	18.7
Hancock County, Indiana	5,334	19.9	31.5	43.6	5.0
Hendricks County, Indiana	14,530	22.9	25.1	38.3	13.6
Howard County, Indiana	6,691	11.6	46.6	38.6	3.2
Johnson County, Indiana	12,441	12.1	32.9	39.2	15.8
Kosciusko County, Indiana	7,278	25.4	39.0	29.0	6.6
Lake County, Indiana	42,237	13.7	37.9	40.5	7.8
LaPorte County, Indiana	8,520	23.7	37.4	26.4	12.5
Madison County, Indiana	10,782	25.2	39.9	30.3	4.5
Marion County, Indiana	88,702	15.4	37.5	33.4	13.7
Monroe County, Indiana	38,380	3.6	15.9	67.3	13.2
Morgan County, Indiana	5,385	31.4	22.1	44.6	1.9
Porter County, Indiana	15,594	10.2	39.5	39.0	11.3
St. Joseph County, Indiana	30,017	12.5	29.3	48.4	9.8
Tippecanoe County, Indiana	45,353	3.3	26.1	54.2	16.5
Vanderburgh County, Indiana	18,319	19.2	27.7	43.1	9.9
Vigo County, Indiana	16,405	11.3	26.6	50.4	11.7
Wayne County, Indiana	6,133	14.0	39.3	44.9	1.8
IOWA					
Black Hawk County, Iowa	19,962	9.2	18.0	63.7	9.1
Dallas County, Iowa	6,075	10.0	16.6	27.0	46.4
Dubuque County, Iowa	10,430	9.2	22.8	56.8	11.2

Table C-2. Educational Attainment of the Population, by Selected Counties, 2017—*Continued*

(Number; percent; dollars.)

State/County	Population 25 years and over							
	Total	Less than 9th grade (percent)	9th to 12th grade, no diploma (percent)	High school graduate (includes equivalency) (percent)	Some college, no degree (percent)	Associate's degree (percent)	Bachelor's degree (percent)	Graduate or professional degree (percent)
HAWAII								
Hawaii County, Hawaii	142,146	2.1	4.7	29.8	23.3	9.3	20.9	9.8
Honolulu County, Hawaii	685,924	3.5	4.2	27.0	19.6	10.9	22.8	12.0
Kauai County, Hawaii	50,706	5.5	4.2	30.9	17.7	12.9	19.0	9.8
Maui County, Hawaii	118,898	3.7	4.5	31.2	23.5	10.1	18.1	8.9
IDAHO								
Ada County, Idaho	307,631	1.6	4.1	24.8	23.7	9.6	23.5	12.6
Bannock County, Idaho	53,004	1.3	5.2	28.0	25.8	10.1	21.0	8.6
Bonneville County, Idaho	69,123	2.8	4.8	24.2	28.5	8.4	23.1	8.3
Canyon County, Idaho	133,313	6.0	8.3	33.0	27.2	7.4	13.3	4.8
Kootenai County, Idaho	108,853	0.7	4.5	26.7	31.6	10.4	18.9	7.1
Twin Falls County, Idaho	54,657	5.5	6.3	26.8	28.2	12.9	14.2	6.1
ILLINOIS								
Adams County, Illinois	46,097	2.4	5.6	33.7	24.1	7.9	14.4	11.9
Champaign County, Illinois	120,473	1.7	2.5	20.8	20.9	9.3	21.7	23.1
Cook County, Illinois	3,597,492	6.6	6.4	23.2	18.7	6.5	23.1	15.6
DeKalb County, Illinois	62,923	4.0	4.8	27.8	23.9	10.4	18.2	10.9
DuPage County, Illinois	636,756	3.6	3.5	18.2	17.5	7.1	30.3	19.9
Kane County, Illinois	346,896	8.3	7.2	23.6	21.6	6.8	21.4	11.0
Kankakee County, Illinois	72,688	4.1	8.0	31.9	25.0	10.2	13.2	7.6
Kendall County, Illinois	80,790	5.3	4.9	23.8	24.9	9.4	21.0	10.7
Lake County, Illinois	459,331	4.4	5.0	22.0	17.4	6.4	25.9	19.0
LaSalle County, Illinois	77,038	2.7	7.5	37.1	25.1	8.9	12.0	6.7
McHenry County, Illinois	208,695	3.0	4.4	26.1	23.7	8.5	23.1	11.1
McLean County, Illinois	104,627	1.8	1.8	24.4	19.8	6.9	31.9	13.4
Macon County, Illinois	72,448	2.2	5.9	32.8	25.7	10.3	15.2	8.0
Madison County, Illinois	185,473	2.5	5.8	30.6	23.8	10.0	16.5	10.9
Peoria County, Illinois	122,961	3.3	7.4	25.6	23.3	9.3	17.8	13.4
Rock Island County, Illinois	99,388	4.1	7.2	30.5	24.7	10.7	14.2	8.7
St. Clair County, Illinois	177,786	1.9	6.1	29.5	23.3	10.6	16.1	12.4
Sangamon County, Illinois	136,549	1.7	5.2	27.8	24.1	8.2	20.2	12.8
Tazewell County, Illinois	92,951	1.5	6.9	31.2	21.3	10.3	20.0	8.8
Vermilion County, Illinois	52,980	2.4	11.6	38.9	20.4	9.8	11.4	5.4
Will County, Illinois	454,415	4.3	5.4	26.9	22.3	8.4	21.7	11.0
Williamson County, Illinois	48,189	3.1	5.4	28.8	29.0	10.9	13.2	9.5
Winnebago County, Illinois	194,872	4.7	7.3	32.8	23.9	10.0	13.1	8.3
INDIANA								
Allen County, Indiana	242,816	4.3	6.3	29.5	22.1	11.5	17.6	8.7
Bartholomew County, Indiana	56,037	2.9	6.0	31.0	16.8	8.2	20.3	14.9
Boone County, Indiana	43,547	1.3	4.6	18.1	17.4	6.4	31.7	20.6
Clark County, Indiana	81,149	2.4	7.7	37.1	23.2	10.9	13.0	5.8
Delaware County, Indiana	71,383	2.9	8.0	33.8	19.9	10.7	13.8	10.8
Elkhart County, Indiana	129,938	8.3	11.1	32.1	20.8	7.4	12.7	7.5
Floyd County, Indiana	52,629	1.2	9.6	30.0	19.1	10.2	18.8	11.1
Grant County, Indiana	44,038	2.1	7.0	36.7	23.0	9.0	12.7	9.5
Hamilton County, Indiana	212,065	0.6	1.9	14.1	17.1	6.4	37.2	22.7
Hancock County, Indiana	51,172	1.4	5.1	31.3	20.9	8.5	22.2	10.5
Hendricks County, Indiana	108,075	2.0	3.2	27.4	21.6	10.2	23.1	12.5
Howard County, Indiana	56,994	3.9	6.1	39.2	19.7	10.7	15.1	5.4
Johnson County, Indiana	103,353	1.5	5.6	28.7	21.7	8.4	22.3	11.9
Kosciusko County, Indiana	53,040	4.6	7.8	33.8	19.4	9.3	17.4	7.5
Lake County, Indiana	328,166	4.1	7.7	34.0	23.0	8.7	15.1	7.5
LaPorte County, Indiana	77,827	2.6	9.0	40.2	21.9	9.4	11.7	5.2
Madison County, Indiana	90,600	2.2	9.0	38.7	21.6	9.7	12.7	6.1
Marion County, Indiana	626,646	5.1	9.9	27.7	18.0	7.3	20.1	11.9
Monroe County, Indiana	85,191	2.9	6.5	20.3	18.7	6.5	24.2	20.8
Morgan County, Indiana	48,471	2.3	11.2	36.9	20.9	10.1	12.8	5.8
Porter County, Indiana	114,962	1.3	4.9	35.4	20.3	8.2	19.0	11.0
St. Joseph County, Indiana	176,362	3.4	8.0	29.2	20.9	8.6	17.4	12.4
Tippecanoe County, Indiana	105,496	2.6	4.5	25.2	17.7	8.6	22.8	18.5
Vanderburgh County, Indiana	124,322	2.0	8.1	26.9	22.8	10.9	19.2	10.1
Vigo County, Indiana	68,789	2.3	11.9	30.8	23.2	8.6	13.3	9.9
Wayne County, Indiana	45,486	3.3	9.5	34.2	23.1	9.2	12.4	8.3
IOWA								
Black Hawk County, Iowa	83,850	3.4	6.5	28.5	20.2	13.0	18.4	9.8
Dallas County, Iowa	56,649	1.6	2.7	17.0	17.4	11.2	34.8	15.3
Dubuque County, Iowa	64,277	2.6	4.8	29.3	21.1	9.3	20.2	12.7

Table C-2. Educational Attainment of the Population, by Selected Counties, 2017—*Continued*

(Number; percent; dollars.)

| State/County | Population 18 to 24 years | | | | |
	Total	Less than high school graduate (percent)	High school graduate (includes equivalency) (percent)	Some college or associate's degree (percent)	Bachelor's degree or higher (percent)
IOWA—*(Continued)*					
Johnson County, Iowa	32,642	1.8	23.2	56.8	18.2
Linn County, Iowa	21,366	11.1	36.7	39.8	12.4
Polk County, Iowa	42,665	15.3	24.9	44.2	15.6
Pottawattamie County, Iowa	8,275	9.7	43.4	41.5	5.3
Scott County, Iowa	14,728	12.1	27.8	46.2	13.9
Story County, Iowa	29,418	2.1	17.5	72.2	8.2
Woodbury County, Iowa	9,862	13.6	24.3	56.3	5.8
KANSAS					
Butler County, Kansas	5,531	12.1	18.7	64.4	4.8
Douglas County, Kansas	27,367	3.7	21.1	58.0	17.3
Johnson County, Kansas	46,281	11.9	26.0	40.5	21.6
Leavenworth County, Kansas	6,506	15.3	32.1	43.2	9.4
Riley County, Kansas	25,032	1.4	19.8	69.8	9.0
Sedgwick County, Kansas	46,507	13.6	32.4	42.9	11.1
Shawnee County, Kansas	15,055	13.6	37.8	38.2	10.4
Wyandotte County, Kansas	14,469	22.4	29.7	39.7	8.2
KENTUCKY					
Boone County, Kentucky	10,654	14.5	37.9	37.0	10.6
Bullitt County, Kentucky	6,454	16.3	50.9	27.0	5.8
Campbell County, Kentucky	9,075	6.3	33.0	42.0	18.7
Christian County, Kentucky	11,515	4.0	46.3	42.8	6.9
Daviess County, Kentucky	8,384	13.0	37.5	36.2	13.2
Fayette County, Kentucky	44,871	8.6	26.8	50.5	14.1
Hardin County, Kentucky	8,805	9.8	58.0	25.9	6.3
Jefferson County, Kentucky	66,217	10.6	35.2	38.9	15.3
Kenton County, Kentucky	12,709	13.6	28.0	44.7	13.7
McCracken County, Kentucky	4,610	20.1	27.9	41.7	10.4
Madison County, Kentucky	16,268	4.7	29.2	54.2	11.9
Oldham County, Kentucky	5,682	15.0	31.3	48.8	4.9
Warren County, Kentucky	20,888	6.6	33.4	49.5	10.4
LOUISIANA					
Ascension Parish, Louisiana	10,710	18.2	25.1	47.2	9.5
Bossier Parish, Louisiana	12,546	13.4	38.2	38.6	9.8
Caddo Parish, Louisiana	20,555	21.5	37.8	36.7	4.0
Calcasieu Parish, Louisiana	18,419	8.8	41.0	38.7	11.6
East Baton Rouge Parish, Louisiana	62,646	13.3	20.3	57.1	9.2
Iberia Parish, Louisiana	6,565	25.1	42.3	30.7	1.9
Jefferson Parish, Louisiana	35,180	14.5	31.0	43.3	11.2
Lafayette Parish, Louisiana	23,170	15.7	26.2	50.6	7.5
Lafourche Parish, Louisiana	9,067	18.5	30.1	45.9	5.5
Livingston Parish, Louisiana	11,076	12.6	45.1	38.9	3.3
Orleans Parish, Louisiana	35,570	11.0	23.9	53.3	11.8
Ouachita Parish, Louisiana	15,838	16.1	23.5	49.1	11.2
Rapides Parish, Louisiana	11,838	31.3	27.4	34.0	7.3
St. Landry Parish, Louisiana	6,897	29.9	38.2	30.1	1.8
St. Tammany Parish, Louisiana	20,421	15.7	41.9	30.7	11.8
Tangipahoa Parish, Louisiana	13,710	12.2	38.9	40.8	8.1
Terrebonne Parish, Louisiana	10,334	45.1	22.1	26.6	6.3
MAINE					
Androscoggin County, Maine	9,530	11.1	35.9	47.1	5.9
Aroostook County, Maine	5,021	14.2	33.7	42.2	9.9
Cumberland County, Maine	25,196	7.0	28.4	48.5	16.0
Kennebec County, Maine	10,738	11.5	33.0	44.9	10.6
Penobscot County, Maine	15,928	8.5	30.1	51.7	9.7
York County, Maine	15,805	11.6	31.7	45.8	10.9
MARYLAND					
Allegany County, Maryland	8,853	7.2	28.5	58.8	5.6
Anne Arundel County, Maryland	50,389	10.5	32.3	43.5	13.7
Baltimore County, Maryland	73,907	9.2	32.5	45.7	12.6
Calvert County, Maryland	7,460	3.8	36.3	50.2	9.7
Carroll County, Maryland	13,828	9.1	35.0	44.2	11.6
Cecil County, Maryland	8,724	16.0	47.8	22.7	13.5
Charles County, Maryland	13,400	10.6	39.2	44.1	6.1
Frederick County, Maryland	20,701	9.9	35.4	38.4	16.3
Harford County, Maryland	20,943	5.0	41.4	42.0	11.6

Table C-2. Educational Attainment of the Population, by Selected Counties, 2017—*Continued*

(Number; percent; dollars.)

State/County	Population 25 years and over							
	Total	Less than 9th grade (percent)	9th to 12th grade, no diploma (percent)	High school graduate (includes equivalency) (percent)	Some college, no degree (percent)	Associate's degree (percent)	Bachelor's degree (percent)	Graduate or professional degree (percent)
IOWA—(*Continued*)								
Johnson County, Iowa	86,376	1.6	1.9	14.8	17.0	7.7	30.3	26.6
Linn County, Iowa	149,861	1.4	3.6	26.7	22.4	12.5	24.5	8.9
Polk County, Iowa	318,571	4.0	5.0	25.1	20.8	9.8	24.3	10.9
Pottawattamie County, Iowa	63,220	4.9	6.5	32.1	23.3	10.9	13.9	8.4
Scott County, Iowa	116,554	3.0	4.6	29.5	20.4	10.9	19.8	11.9
Story County, Iowa	51,956	0.5	2.2	18.0	18.6	7.7	31.3	21.7
Woodbury County, Iowa	65,726	7.9	6.2	31.5	19.7	11.2	17.1	6.4
KANSAS								
Butler County, Kansas	44,270	2.0	5.9	27.8	24.5	9.6	20.1	10.2
Douglas County, Kansas	70,953	0.5	3.3	18.7	22.2	8.0	23.9	23.4
Johnson County, Kansas	398,983	1.4	3.0	13.8	18.3	7.6	34.0	21.8
Leavenworth County, Kansas	54,581	2.5	7.9	26.8	20.5	9.7	19.7	12.9
Riley County, Kansas	36,712	1.3	3.6	18.3	20.0	8.3	24.0	24.4
Sedgwick County, Kansas	334,211	3.8	6.3	26.5	23.6	8.8	19.8	11.2
Shawnee County, Kansas	121,104	1.7	3.9	31.5	22.1	6.8	21.5	12.5
Wyandotte County, Kansas	104,556	8.0	11.3	32.7	23.5	7.8	11.4	5.3
KENTUCKY								
Boone County, Kentucky	86,062	2.0	5.8	28.1	26.3	7.3	18.6	11.9
Bullitt County, Kentucky	55,944	3.6	8.6	41.7	22.9	9.7	8.8	4.7
Campbell County, Kentucky	64,156	2.1	5.3	28.5	20.3	7.1	23.3	13.4
Christian County, Kentucky	39,781	6.9	7.7	31.6	28.6	8.9	8.7	7.7
Daviess County, Kentucky	67,502	3.1	5.6	35.4	22.6	11.0	13.8	8.5
Fayette County, Kentucky	209,203	3.0	4.8	19.4	21.8	7.5	25.9	17.6
Hardin County, Kentucky	72,462	1.8	6.2	31.1	26.1	12.9	12.7	9.1
Jefferson County, Kentucky	533,043	2.9	6.1	27.6	22.7	7.3	19.6	13.9
Kenton County, Kentucky	113,284	3.1	6.8	29.6	21.1	7.4	19.0	13.1
McCracken County, Kentucky	46,189	2.9	5.2	32.2	21.8	12.9	16.0	8.9
Madison County, Kentucky	55,893	5.9	6.3	26.8	20.8	9.1	18.6	12.5
Oldham County, Kentucky	42,672	3.4	3.3	20.5	23.9	7.4	24.0	17.5
Warren County, Kentucky	78,633	6.2	7.3	28.9	21.2	8.0	16.4	12.1
LOUISIANA								
Ascension Parish, Louisiana	79,159	4.4	6.7	30.3	24.3	8.5	17.7	8.1
Bossier Parish, Louisiana	82,604	2.6	7.3	29.7	27.5	9.8	14.9	8.2
Caddo Parish, Louisiana	166,867	3.5	10.4	33.3	23.6	5.9	14.0	9.2
Calcasieu Parish, Louisiana	133,623	2.6	8.1	34.3	22.7	7.4	17.9	7.0
East Baton Rouge Parish, Louisiana	282,126	2.6	8.1	26.7	23.1	4.4	21.6	13.5
Iberia Parish, Louisiana	46,357	7.7	10.5	48.9	18.0	5.0	6.7	3.1
Jefferson Parish, Louisiana	307,704	5.6	9.4	31.3	22.9	5.7	15.8	9.4
Lafayette Parish, Louisiana	161,057	3.7	8.5	32.5	17.4	5.1	22.3	10.6
Lafourche Parish, Louisiana	66,340	9.2	12.2	41.4	13.9	5.8	11.9	5.5
Livingston Parish, Louisiana	91,353	5.2	8.1	42.0	21.3	7.0	11.7	4.7
Orleans Parish, Louisiana	278,629	4.3	9.5	23.9	21.9	5.1	20.0	15.3
Ouachita Parish, Louisiana	101,124	3.7	8.9	35.0	22.7	6.1	17.3	6.3
Rapides Parish, Louisiana	86,869	5.3	10.1	36.0	22.4	5.2	13.2	7.9
St. Landry Parish, Louisiana	53,851	9.2	11.8	41.4	16.0	6.2	10.4	5.0
St. Tammany Parish, Louisiana	174,042	2.5	6.7	25.4	22.9	6.7	23.4	12.5
Tangipahoa Parish, Louisiana	86,138	5.0	11.7	40.2	20.3	3.7	13.7	5.4
Terrebonne Parish, Louisiana	73,028	12.2	11.9	37.7	19.1	4.4	10.4	4.3
MAINE								
Androscoggin County, Maine	74,704	3.4	5.7	35.1	20.9	10.3	16.8	7.9
Aroostook County, Maine	50,008	4.9	6.8	37.1	20.2	11.9	12.3	6.7
Cumberland County, Maine	211,861	2.0	3.5	21.7	17.0	8.7	29.0	18.2
Kennebec County, Maine	87,365	3.9	4.1	31.2	20.6	11.6	18.0	10.6
Penobscot County, Maine	108,540	2.4	5.5	33.7	18.9	10.3	17.6	11.6
York County, Maine	150,006	2.7	5.0	28.6	20.5	10.7	21.0	11.5
MARYLAND								
Allegany County, Maryland	50,049	2.8	8.0	40.8	22.6	8.8	9.8	7.2
Anne Arundel County, Maryland	395,383	2.6	5.6	23.6	19.7	7.8	23.6	17.1
Baltimore County, Maryland	578,536	3.0	5.8	26.0	19.6	6.6	22.5	16.6
Calvert County, Maryland	62,637	1.6	3.8	30.7	21.9	8.2	20.6	13.2
Carroll County, Maryland	117,386	1.8	5.6	29.7	18.7	7.9	23.1	13.1
Cecil County, Maryland	70,587	3.7	6.5	32.9	24.4	7.8	14.2	10.5
Charles County, Maryland	107,724	2.4	6.0	28.0	24.0	8.2	19.0	12.5
Frederick County, Maryland	172,583	3.1	5.0	21.5	19.7	8.4	24.1	18.1
Harford County, Maryland	174,622	2.4	5.5	26.3	20.9	9.6	20.5	14.8

Table C-2. Educational Attainment of the Population, by Selected Counties, 2017—*Continued*

(Number; percent; dollars.)

State/County		Population 18 to 24 years			
	Total	Less than high school graduate (percent)	High school graduate (includes equivalency) (percent)	Some college or associate's degree (percent)	Bachelor's degree or higher (percent)
MARYLAND—(*Continued*)					
Howard County, Maryland	25,567	9.2	23.1	47.8	20.0
Montgomery County, Maryland	84,206	10.7	29.8	40.4	19.0
Prince George's County, Maryland	90,094	11.8	28.1	50.1	9.9
St. Mary's County, Maryland	11,061	8.6	39.3	40.4	11.7
Washington County, Maryland	12,198	12.5	40.3	41.0	6.1
Wicomico County, Maryland	15,488	10.5	21.2	51.7	16.6
Baltimore city, Maryland	58,959	13.0	26.5	44.8	15.8
MASSACHUSETTS					
Barnstable County, Massachusetts	14,853	15.3	39.8	24.3	20.5
Berkshire County, Massachusetts	12,237	10.7	38.0	42.3	8.9
Bristol County, Massachusetts	51,110	13.7	34.9	39.7	11.8
Essex County, Massachusetts	72,911	16.1	28.0	39.7	16.2
Franklin County, Massachusetts	5,044	10.5	42.4	34.2	12.9
Hampden County, Massachusetts	49,131	15.3	25.0	51.8	7.9
Hampshire County, Massachusetts	38,327	2.7	15.3	76.4	5.6
Middlesex County, Massachusetts	158,704	9.6	26.7	37.9	25.8
Norfolk County, Massachusetts	61,175	11.0	25.8	40.9	22.4
Plymouth County, Massachusetts	44,331	13.1	23.4	48.4	15.1
Suffolk County, Massachusetts	109,533	6.9	18.8	51.7	22.6
Worcester County, Massachusetts	81,189	11.8	31.7	41.7	14.9
MICHIGAN					
Allegan County, Michigan	9,702	24.5	41.2	29.7	4.6
Bay County, Michigan	7,760	14.6	36.5	41.6	7.2
Berrien County, Michigan	11,971	20.4	30.4	42.9	6.3
Calhoun County, Michigan	11,251	15.5	31.0	51.1	2.5
Clinton County, Michigan	6,939	8.8	26.7	54.5	10.0
Eaton County, Michigan	9,790	9.8	30.7	45.3	14.2
Genesee County, Michigan	35,359	15.3	38.3	39.7	6.8
Grand Traverse County, Michigan	6,850	15.2	32.5	45.8	6.6
Ingham County, Michigan	56,590	5.0	25.8	57.0	12.2
Isabella County, Michigan	20,199	5.4	18.9	66.5	9.2
Jackson County, Michigan	13,805	13.1	37.8	43.2	5.9
Kalamazoo County, Michigan	41,383	7.0	23.0	60.3	9.8
Kent County, Michigan	61,767	15.5	25.9	41.4	17.3
Lapeer County, Michigan	6,885	13.4	48.5	32.5	5.6
Lenawee County, Michigan	8,749	14.2	34.3	43.7	7.8
Livingston County, Michigan	15,661	11.3	37.6	38.5	12.5
Macomb County, Michigan	72,237	9.6	36.3	42.8	11.3
Marquette County, Michigan	9,937	6.5	27.3	61.9	4.2
Midland County, Michigan	7,227	5.5	36.8	37.8	19.9
Monroe County, Michigan	11,318	17.7	39.5	33.4	9.5
Muskegon County, Michigan	15,657	19.0	28.3	47.9	4.8
Oakland County, Michigan	102,671	11.1	29.9	41.7	17.4
Ottawa County, Michigan	38,794	5.6	33.9	50.0	10.5
Saginaw County, Michigan	17,197	14.9	34.7	47.2	3.3
St. Clair County, Michigan	12,519	16.6	37.5	42.6	3.3
Shiawassee County, Michigan	5,606	12.1	31.1	55.0	1.8
Van Buren County, Michigan	6,052	19.9	35.7	39.2	5.2
Washtenaw County, Michigan	69,317	5.2	17.0	58.7	19.1
Wayne County, Michigan	154,715	14.5	35.2	41.6	8.8
MINNESOTA					
Anoka County, Minnesota	27,972	17.8	31.2	43.0	8.0
Blue Earth County, Minnesota	15,576	1.8	9.4	79.9	8.9
Carver County, Minnesota	8,393	13.4	24.4	49.1	13.1
Dakota County, Minnesota	32,353	16.0	34.0	32.6	17.4
Hennepin County, Minnesota	107,374	10.8	26.0	40.9	22.4
Olmsted County, Minnesota	11,734	11.4	20.6	41.4	26.6
Ramsey County, Minnesota	54,915	11.2	25.3	46.3	17.2
Rice County, Minnesota	9,314	9.6	13.6	71.9	4.9
St. Louis County, Minnesota	25,680	11.2	20.3	57.6	10.8
Scott County, Minnesota	11,003	12.5	29.7	40.7	17.2
Sherburne County, Minnesota	7,974	10.9	33.1	44.6	11.3
Stearns County, Minnesota	24,222	7.3	18.1	63.6	11.0
Washington County, Minnesota	19,492	12.4	37.8	34.1	15.8
Wright County, Minnesota	9,974	13.6	32.5	44.9	9.0

Table C-2. Educational Attainment of the Population, by Selected Counties, 2017—*Continued*

(Number; percent; dollars.)

State/County	Total	Population 25 years and over						
		Less than 9th grade (percent)	9th to 12th grade, no diploma (percent)	High school graduate (includes equivalency) (percent)	Some college, no degree (percent)	Associate's degree (percent)	Bachelor's degree (percent)	Graduate or professional degree (percent)
MARYLAND—(*Continued*)								
Howard County, Maryland	217,232	2.0	2.5	13.6	14.2	6.2	30.6	31.0
Montgomery County, Maryland	728,331	5.0	4.0	13.9	13.5	5.7	27.0	30.8
Prince George's County, Maryland	619,337	6.5	6.4	26.9	21.8	6.4	18.1	14.0
St. Mary's County, Maryland	74,001	3.7	6.1	31.2	19.3	8.0	18.4	13.4
Washington County, Maryland	105,240	3.6	9.3	33.7	20.9	8.6	14.1	9.9
Wicomico County, Maryland	64,696	3.8	10.3	31.5	17.4	7.3	18.3	11.4
Baltimore city, Maryland	426,682	5.1	10.6	29.3	19.3	5.1	15.0	15.6
MASSACHUSETTS								
Barnstable County, Massachusetts	165,434	1.8	3.4	23.6	17.5	9.1	24.9	19.6
Berkshire County, Massachusetts	92,565	2.4	6.4	29.4	20.6	8.9	17.0	15.3
Bristol County, Massachusetts	394,292	8.0	6.5	29.8	18.0	8.9	18.3	10.6
Essex County, Massachusetts	543,982	5.5	5.1	25.8	16.2	7.6	24.3	15.5
Franklin County, Massachusetts	52,934	1.4	4.1	30.2	16.0	9.2	21.0	18.2
Hampden County, Massachusetts	318,892	5.7	9.3	29.6	19.1	9.0	16.6	10.7
Hampshire County, Massachusetts	99,606	1.1	3.4	25.4	13.6	9.1	24.9	22.4
Middlesex County, Massachusetts	1,125,008	3.6	3.2	19.3	12.0	5.9	27.2	28.8
Norfolk County, Massachusetts	491,276	3.0	3.6	18.7	13.8	7.4	29.0	24.5
Plymouth County, Massachusetts	359,399	2.8	4.3	27.5	19.2	10.3	22.1	13.9
Suffolk County, Massachusetts	554,712	7.0	5.8	23.8	14.1	4.7	24.2	20.5
Worcester County, Massachusetts	569,438	3.0	5.9	28.0	17.6	8.9	22.3	14.2
MICHIGAN								
Allegan County, Michigan	78,390	2.8	5.5	36.7	23.6	7.9	15.9	7.7
Bay County, Michigan	75,203	3.4	6.3	34.2	24.3	10.0	14.2	7.7
Berrien County, Michigan	108,367	3.0	7.7	30.6	23.7	9.4	15.3	10.3
Calhoun County, Michigan	92,230	2.3	5.9	36.0	25.7	8.2	13.6	8.3
Clinton County, Michigan	54,073	1.0	4.1	27.7	24.0	10.7	18.7	13.8
Eaton County, Michigan	76,180	1.8	3.5	27.3	28.1	10.3	16.0	13.0
Genesee County, Michigan	279,382	2.3	6.6	31.3	28.3	10.6	13.2	7.7
Grand Traverse County, Michigan	66,759	0.9	3.1	21.6	25.0	8.4	25.4	15.5
Ingham County, Michigan	175,844	2.6	5.3	22.2	22.1	9.2	20.6	17.9
Isabella County, Michigan	38,809	2.1	5.8	29.0	22.1	8.8	18.8	13.4
Jackson County, Michigan	110,548	2.1	6.1	33.0	26.1	10.6	15.0	7.2
Kalamazoo County, Michigan	164,485	1.2	4.6	20.8	23.4	10.1	23.9	16.0
Kent County, Michigan	428,617	4.0	5.2	24.6	20.5	9.2	24.2	12.4
Lapeer County, Michigan	62,913	1.9	6.1	36.6	26.9	11.5	12.2	4.8
Lenawee County, Michigan	69,020	1.7	6.1	35.5	25.0	10.2	13.8	7.7
Livingston County, Michigan	132,838	0.9	3.6	25.3	22.3	9.8	25.7	12.5
Macomb County, Michigan	613,921	3.7	6.8	28.6	25.2	11.0	16.1	8.7
Marquette County, Michigan	44,531	2.2	3.3	29.3	22.0	10.9	23.1	9.3
Midland County, Michigan	58,285	2.4	3.4	27.9	20.0	9.2	22.8	14.4
Monroe County, Michigan	105,918	1.5	7.1	37.7	24.0	12.2	10.6	6.9
Muskegon County, Michigan	118,059	3.5	5.8	34.5	24.9	11.9	13.9	5.5
Oakland County, Michigan	882,349	2.0	3.9	19.2	19.6	7.9	26.5	20.9
Ottawa County, Michigan	178,399	2.9	4.3	26.7	22.1	9.8	23.3	10.8
Saginaw County, Michigan	133,874	3.1	7.4	31.8	25.8	11.5	12.6	7.8
St. Clair County, Michigan	113,233	1.1	7.3	34.6	25.9	12.7	10.8	7.6
Shiawassee County, Michigan	47,946	1.6	6.6	38.7	26.8	10.1	9.8	6.2
Van Buren County, Michigan	51,476	3.9	7.3	30.6	26.7	10.6	14.4	6.4
Washtenaw County, Michigan	229,600	1.4	3.3	16.0	17.6	7.2	25.2	29.3
Wayne County, Michigan	1,182,723	4.1	9.1	30.3	24.4	8.7	13.9	9.4
MINNESOTA								
Anoka County, Minnesota	239,124	2.0	3.8	30.4	22.2	12.1	20.3	9.4
Blue Earth County, Minnesota	38,523	1.3	3.1	23.3	21.6	12.6	24.0	14.1
Carver County, Minnesota	66,083	1.3	1.6	18.3	16.7	12.2	34.7	15.3
Dakota County, Minnesota	285,868	2.2	4.0	21.2	20.7	11.0	27.8	13.2
Hennepin County, Minnesota	869,261	3.5	2.9	16.4	18.3	8.7	31.3	18.8
Olmsted County, Minnesota	105,285	2.3	2.2	21.5	17.5	10.7	26.3	19.5
Ramsey County, Minnesota	365,279	6.2	4.3	20.0	18.6	8.5	24.9	17.5
Rice County, Minnesota	42,340	4.5	5.5	30.7	20.9	10.9	18.2	9.4
St. Louis County, Minnesota	136,260	1.3	4.5	26.5	24.8	12.9	20.6	9.4
Scott County, Minnesota	94,197	2.3	2.6	21.0	21.0	11.4	28.8	12.9
Sherburne County, Minnesota	61,784	2.1	3.8	28.0	25.1	12.9	21.4	6.6
Stearns County, Minnesota	97,265	4.9	3.5	26.0	21.4	13.6	20.5	10.1
Washington County, Minnesota	173,709	1.2	2.0	21.4	20.3	11.5	28.1	15.4
Wright County, Minnesota	86,598	1.6	3.7	30.7	22.7	13.0	21.3	7.0

Table C-2. Educational Attainment of the Population, by Selected Counties, 2017—*Continued*

(Number; percent; dollars.)

State/County	Population 18 to 24 years				
	Total	Less than high school graduate (percent)	High school graduate (includes equivalency) (percent)	Some college or associate's degree (percent)	Bachelor's degree or higher (percent)
MISSISSIPPI					
DeSoto County, Mississippi	15,974	14.6	41.2	37.3	6.9
Forrest County, Mississippi	11,580	12.5	19.5	64.2	3.8
Harrison County, Mississippi	20,446	11.1	39.5	38.3	11.1
Hinds County, Mississippi	26,314	9.0	33.1	49.1	8.9
Jackson County, Mississippi	13,438	14.1	41.8	39.5	4.6
Jones County, Mississippi	6,792	19.7	40.6	38.5	1.2
Lauderdale County, Mississippi	6,826	24.6	34.9	36.7	3.9
Lee County, Mississippi	6,998	19.9	44.4	34.5	1.2
Madison County, Mississippi	9,843	10.8	27.5	37.5	24.3
Rankin County, Mississippi	10,995	14.4	35.9	28.5	21.3
MISSOURI					
Boone County, Missouri	34,768	3.5	10.6	70.9	15.0
Buchanan County, Missouri	8,779	15.4	46.2	33.6	4.7
Cape Girardeau County, Missouri	11,877	7.7	24.0	58.9	9.4
Cass County, Missouri	7,550	22.1	39.9	29.6	8.5
Christian County, Missouri	6,974	13.0	39.3	45.8	1.9
Clay County, Missouri	21,304	10.7	31.9	39.7	17.7
Cole County, Missouri	7,548	18.5	39.9	34.0	7.6
Franklin County, Missouri	7,716	7.6	40.7	45.9	5.8
Greene County, Missouri	40,528	8.5	25.5	54.5	11.5
Jackson County, Missouri	57,913	10.9	35.2	38.4	15.4
Jasper County, Missouri	10,947	17.3	43.0	36.1	3.6
Jefferson County, Missouri	16,467	12.5	39.5	42.5	5.5
Platte County, Missouri	8,417	13.5	30.3	40.2	16.0
St. Charles County, Missouri	33,457	8.3	28.1	54.1	9.5
St. Francois County, Missouri	4,185	33.7	32.8	31.9	1.6
St. Louis County, Missouri	86,004	12.5	29.8	40.3	17.5
St. Louis city, Missouri	28,885	11.7	26.4	46.9	15.0
MONTANA					
Cascade County, Montana	7,726	8.8	45.4	38.6	7.2
Flathead County, Montana	6,819	6.5	61.0	27.9	4.6
Gallatin County, Montana	17,385	3.4	24.9	52.9	18.7
Lewis and Clark County, Montana	5,229	13.8	27.2	59.0	0.0
Missoula County, Montana	16,010	6.6	24.7	55.0	13.7
Yellowstone County, Montana	11,741	11.7	42.1	34.1	12.1
NEBRASKA					
Douglas County, Nebraska	51,065	11.0	29.0	45.9	14.1
Lancaster County, Nebraska	47,246	6.9	24.8	53.7	14.5
Sarpy County, Nebraska	15,428	6.9	34.3	49.3	9.5
NEVADA					
Clark County, Nevada	184,051	15.7	41.0	38.1	5.2
Washoe County, Nevada	41,267	11.1	32.7	47.5	8.7
NEW HAMPSHIRE					
Cheshire County, New Hampshire	9,488	6.0	21.1	68.8	4.1
Grafton County, New Hampshire	11,595	8.1	29.5	53.7	8.6
Hillsborough County, New Hampshire	35,746	10.8	36.7	39.2	13.4
Merrimack County, New Hampshire	13,458	9.2	34.3	43.4	13.0
Rockingham County, New Hampshire	23,607	10.7	37.4	33.7	18.3
Strafford County, New Hampshire	20,519	4.0	25.9	57.5	12.6
NEW JERSEY					
Atlantic County, New Jersey	26,367	8.2	34.2	48.8	8.8
Bergen County, New Jersey	77,731	10.5	21.9	42.5	25.0
Burlington County, New Jersey	38,342	13.5	35.6	41.1	9.9
Camden County, New Jersey	43,432	14.2	30.2	38.6	17.0
Cape May County, New Jersey	6,880	6.6	41.7	41.2	10.6
Cumberland County, New Jersey	13,482	13.5	45.6	30.6	10.3
Essex County, New Jersey	73,009	10.7	31.4	46.4	11.5
Gloucester County, New Jersey	26,537	8.6	26.6	49.6	15.2
Hudson County, New Jersey	56,739	10.6	24.5	42.0	22.9
Hunterdon County, New Jersey	11,452	18.8	34.0	31.9	15.4
Mercer County, New Jersey	42,939	7.0	27.4	51.2	14.4
Middlesex County, New Jersey	79,500	7.8	21.2	56.0	15.0
Monmouth County, New Jersey	53,850	13.1	25.3	42.4	19.2

Table C-2. Educational Attainment of the Population, by Selected Counties, 2017—*Continued*

(Number; percent; dollars.)

State/County	Total	Less than 9th grade (percent)	9th to 12th grade, no diploma (percent)	High school graduate (includes equivalency) (percent)	Some college, no degree (percent)	Associate's degree (percent)	Bachelor's degree (percent)	Graduate or professional degree (percent)
MISSISSIPPI								
DeSoto County, Mississippi	116,419	2.2	5.9	31.7	25.3	12.0	14.5	8.2
Forrest County, Mississippi	46,523	4.1	7.1	24.9	23.5	7.5	22.3	10.6
Harrison County, Mississippi	135,279	3.0	7.8	28.3	25.6	10.4	15.8	9.0
Hinds County, Mississippi	154,609	3.7	10.2	25.3	22.1	10.0	16.5	12.2
Jackson County, Mississippi	94,895	3.6	7.1	31.2	23.5	12.6	14.7	7.3
Jones County, Mississippi	43,919	5.2	9.8	34.4	25.4	8.4	8.5	8.4
Lauderdale County, Mississippi	51,320	3.9	10.9	26.2	23.1	11.6	14.2	10.1
Lee County, Mississippi	56,073	5.2	13.6	23.9	22.1	11.4	13.7	10.0
Madison County, Mississippi	68,474	2.4	6.9	16.2	16.5	9.0	29.0	20.1
Rankin County, Mississippi	104,876	2.3	7.9	26.4	24.3	10.5	18.8	9.7
MISSOURI								
Boone County, Missouri	107,459	1.8	3.7	22.5	19.2	7.1	27.1	18.7
Buchanan County, Missouri	59,828	3.4	7.4	40.8	22.9	7.0	11.6	6.8
Cape Girardeau County, Missouri	49,773	2.9	5.1	34.2	20.3	5.8	20.7	11.1
Cass County, Missouri	70,993	3.6	5.7	33.8	21.1	9.4	17.4	9.0
Christian County, Missouri	56,771	2.1	5.4	32.1	19.9	9.3	21.6	9.7
Clay County, Missouri	162,849	1.8	5.2	28.1	24.2	8.1	21.3	11.3
Cole County, Missouri	52,409	1.7	6.3	31.5	23.8	5.5	20.9	10.2
Franklin County, Missouri	71,586	3.0	10.1	32.5	23.1	10.5	12.0	8.7
Greene County, Missouri	188,816	1.8	6.5	26.8	25.5	8.1	19.7	11.6
Jackson County, Missouri	474,782	3.0	7.4	28.5	23.7	7.0	19.4	11.0
Jasper County, Missouri	78,809	3.6	9.5	32.0	24.6	7.4	17.1	5.8
Jefferson County, Missouri	155,281	2.3	8.0	29.9	25.2	11.8	15.1	7.6
Platte County, Missouri	68,762	1.1	3.5	22.1	23.2	7.7	23.8	18.5
St. Charles County, Missouri	268,609	1.3	3.4	25.2	21.2	9.4	25.6	13.8
St. Francois County, Missouri	48,548	6.6	10.7	36.7	22.9	11.4	7.0	4.7
St. Louis County, Missouri	691,143	1.9	4.6	21.3	21.7	7.7	24.4	18.4
St. Louis city, Missouri	219,910	3.0	8.8	23.7	20.9	6.5	20.1	17.0
MONTANA								
Cascade County, Montana	55,727	3.8	6.2	33.6	20.5	9.7	17.0	9.3
Flathead County, Montana	71,105	1.5	5.8	27.5	24.8	11.0	19.4	10.0
Gallatin County, Montana	68,768	0.9	2.5	18.2	23.1	4.7	34.7	15.9
Lewis and Clark County, Montana	47,945	1.8	2.6	23.1	23.9	9.0	25.3	14.3
Missoula County, Montana	78,787	1.3	2.8	20.5	21.2	8.3	28.5	17.5
Yellowstone County, Montana	109,822	2.4	5.2	27.6	22.3	10.8	21.6	10.2
NEBRASKA								
Douglas County, Nebraska	366,147	4.4	5.4	21.0	22.9	7.6	25.1	13.6
Lancaster County, Nebraska	194,865	2.8	3.9	21.3	22.6	10.9	24.2	14.3
Sarpy County, Nebraska	115,871	2.4	2.5	21.1	21.7	10.1	27.8	14.4
NEVADA								
Clark County, Nevada	1,505,837	5.8	8.1	29.1	24.8	7.7	16.3	8.1
Washoe County, Nevada	318,643	3.7	6.9	24.4	25.3	8.6	20.3	10.8
NEW HAMPSHIRE								
Cheshire County, New Hampshire	53,007	1.8	4.7	29.4	18.7	11.4	21.4	12.5
Grafton County, New Hampshire	62,899	2.0	4.0	26.7	16.8	8.5	23.0	18.9
Hillsborough County, New Hampshire	289,309	2.2	5.4	26.9	16.8	11.2	23.6	14.0
Merrimack County, New Hampshire	107,044	1.9	4.7	30.4	18.1	10.1	21.0	13.8
Rockingham County, New Hampshire	222,644	1.3	3.9	24.9	18.4	9.4	26.1	16.0
Strafford County, New Hampshire	84,295	1.9	6.7	29.3	18.7	10.5	19.9	13.0
NEW JERSEY								
Atlantic County, New Jersey	185,547	4.8	8.1	32.1	19.2	7.4	17.8	10.5
Bergen County, New Jersey	669,205	3.8	3.8	23.8	13.9	5.8	30.1	18.8
Burlington County, New Jersey	316,357	2.5	4.2	28.3	18.3	9.4	23.6	13.7
Camden County, New Jersey	350,713	4.0	7.1	29.3	19.6	7.3	20.0	12.7
Cape May County, New Jersey	70,447	2.5	3.8	31.4	20.4	8.4	21.4	12.1
Cumberland County, New Jersey	103,147	8.7	11.1	36.4	19.6	6.0	12.0	6.0
Essex County, New Jersey	544,496	7.4	7.4	27.5	16.0	6.1	21.1	14.4
Gloucester County, New Jersey	201,009	1.8	4.0	31.3	19.4	9.1	22.2	12.3
Hudson County, New Jersey	494,883	8.2	6.5	25.5	13.0	4.4	27.1	15.4
Hunterdon County, New Jersey	88,422	2.4	2.3	20.8	14.3	7.1	30.6	22.4
Mercer County, New Jersey	251,909	5.2	6.0	23.9	15.6	5.4	23.2	20.7
Middlesex County, New Jersey	581,230	4.8	5.1	24.9	14.1	6.6	26.4	18.1
Monmouth County, New Jersey	438,551	2.9	4.0	23.2	16.6	7.6	27.8	17.8

Table C-2. Educational Attainment of the Population, by Selected Counties, 2017—*Continued*

(Number; percent; dollars.)

State/County		Population 18 to 24 years			
	Total	Less than high school graduate (percent)	High school graduate (includes equivalency) (percent)	Some college or associate's degree (percent)	Bachelor's degree or higher (percent)
NEW JERSEY—(*Continued*)					
Morris County, New Jersey	43,360	8.3	26.0	42.6	23.0
Ocean County, New Jersey	44,361	12.1	29.9	44.2	13.7
Passaic County, New Jersey	50,066	11.2	37.6	41.2	10.0
Salem County, New Jersey	5,295	18.3	33.1	37.0	11.5
Somerset County, New Jersey	28,271	12.2	28.5	36.9	22.4
Sussex County, New Jersey	12,195	11.8	34.6	32.7	20.9
Union County, New Jersey	48,773	12.1	29.3	43.1	15.5
Warren County, New Jersey	9,729	6.2	36.3	44.8	12.8
NEW MEXICO					
Bernalillo County, New Mexico	61,982	15.4	28.2	47.4	9.0
Chaves County, New Mexico	6,342	20.9	35.9	39.4	3.9
Doña Ana County, New Mexico	32,599	16.1	31.4	44.2	8.4
Lea County, New Mexico	6,528	16.7	36.3	45.9	1.1
McKinley County, New Mexico	6,841	19.2	43.8	36.3	0.7
Otero County, New Mexico	7,314	14.9	31.0	49.2	4.9
Sandoval County, New Mexico	10,987	11.6	34.5	47.1	6.8
San Juan County, New Mexico	11,622	28.1	34.1	37.1	0.8
Santa Fe County, New Mexico	11,127	23.4	29.7	41.7	5.2
Valencia County, New Mexico	7,326	26.7	39.0	33.1	1.3
NEW YORK					
Albany County, New York	46,843	9.0	23.7	47.0	20.3
Bronx County, New York	152,674	20.8	27.2	43.1	8.9
Broome County, New York	28,093	11.2	24.1	50.9	13.8
Cattaraugus County, New York	7,291	16.0	43.2	33.9	6.9
Cayuga County, New York	6,212	14.2	28.6	49.5	7.6
Chautauqua County, New York	13,747	18.9	28.6	45.9	6.6
Chemung County, New York	7,074	19.7	47.1	30.8	2.5
Clinton County, New York	11,221	9.4	23.4	57.0	10.2
Dutchess County, New York	32,876	9.5	28.8	50.5	11.2
Erie County, New York	86,847	7.8	27.3	51.8	13.2
Jefferson County, New York	14,751	7.5	52.5	34.4	5.6
Kings County, New York	222,446	13.7	24.9	42.9	18.5
Livingston County, New York	9,477	8.0	18.3	67.2	6.5
Madison County, New York	8,689	3.7	31.7	55.8	8.8
Monroe County, New York	75,827	7.6	27.7	49.4	15.2
Nassau County, New York	122,645	7.2	24.1	45.5	23.3
New York County, New York	151,885	8.4	18.8	38.6	34.2
Niagara County, New York	17,887	14.6	29.8	43.1	12.5
Oneida County, New York	21,676	17.9	26.1	44.0	12.0
Onondaga County, New York	48,554	9.1	20.9	57.4	12.6
Ontario County, New York	9,421	5.4	37.3	41.4	15.9
Orange County, New York	40,000	10.9	32.1	44.7	12.2
Oswego County, New York	13,617	6.3	29.4	59.6	4.6
Putnam County, New York	8,136	13.9	30.1	33.2	22.8
Queens County, New York	189,306	11.4	22.5	50.4	15.7
Rensselaer County, New York	17,428	9.8	30.2	41.3	18.7
Richmond County, New York	40,537	9.7	27.2	44.8	18.4
Rockland County, New York	31,067	15.8	29.6	38.2	16.3
St. Lawrence County, New York	15,226	8.3	32.9	51.0	7.9
Saratoga County, New York	18,801	9.9	23.5	47.3	19.3
Schenectady County, New York	14,583	13.7	29.5	46.5	10.3
Steuben County, New York	7,483	25.0	37.7	25.8	11.5
Suffolk County, New York	136,628	9.4	29.7	43.7	17.1
Sullivan County, New York	6,823	26.4	24.5	36.0	13.1
Tompkins County, New York	27,696	0.9	21.9	50.8	26.3
Ulster County, New York	16,451	8.0	33.3	47.5	11.3
Warren County, New York	4,587	16.7	24.2	46.8	12.3
Wayne County, New York	7,516	11.2	30.8	48.3	9.7
Westchester County, New York	87,411	10.8	25.8	39.2	24.2
NORTH CAROLINA					
Alamance County, North Carolina	15,887	14.7	24.4	55.0	6.0
Brunswick County, North Carolina	7,097	12.8	43.6	36.9	6.7
Buncombe County, North Carolina	20,040	7.4	36.5	44.2	11.9
Burke County, North Carolina	7,924	35.9	25.3	33.6	5.2
Cabarrus County, North Carolina	15,858	21.1	28.9	41.5	8.4
Caldwell County, North Carolina	6,682	27.4	36.3	32.1	4.2

Table C-2. Educational Attainment of the Population, by Selected Counties, 2017—*Continued*

(Number; percent; dollars.)

State/County	Total	Less than 9th grade (percent)	9th to 12th grade, no diploma (percent)	High school graduate (includes equivalency) (percent)	Some college, no degree (percent)	Associate's degree (percent)	Bachelor's degree (percent)	Graduate or professional degree (percent)
NEW JERSEY—*(Continued)*								
Morris County, New Jersey	349,240	3.6	2.8	20.0	14.3	6.9	30.2	22.3
Ocean County, New Jersey	411,601	2.5	5.1	33.2	20.5	8.2	20.3	10.2
Passaic County, New Jersey	339,748	8.8	7.2	35.1	15.7	5.4	19.0	8.9
Salem County, New Jersey	43,960	3.5	7.4	35.9	20.6	10.3	14.8	7.6
Somerset County, New Jersey	233,073	2.2	2.5	22.6	14.2	5.8	27.9	24.6
Sussex County, New Jersey	101,761	1.9	3.2	31.7	17.9	8.5	24.0	12.7
Union County, New Jersey	383,744	7.0	5.7	29.4	17.1	6.0	20.8	14.0
Warren County, New Jersey	75,495	3.3	5.3	29.8	18.2	10.1	20.8	12.6
NEW MEXICO								
Bernalillo County, New Mexico	465,107	3.9	5.8	23.0	23.8	8.3	19.1	16.1
Chaves County, New Mexico	41,055	13.2	8.8	29.2	22.9	9.0	10.7	6.2
Doña Ana County, New Mexico	129,529	12.0	9.1	21.7	24.0	8.3	15.1	9.8
Lea County, New Mexico	41,484	9.8	14.2	33.7	23.0	6.7	7.3	5.2
McKinley County, New Mexico	44,311	10.4	12.3	35.2	20.7	8.0	6.2	7.2
Otero County, New Mexico	43,074	5.8	7.3	27.5	31.0	9.7	11.5	7.1
Sandoval County, New Mexico	97,983	2.6	7.7	26.6	25.0	9.3	16.8	11.9
San Juan County, New Mexico	81,121	6.8	9.4	31.8	27.3	10.7	9.0	5.0
Santa Fe County, New Mexico	110,401	4.4	5.0	23.6	20.8	5.9	20.3	20.1
Valencia County, New Mexico	50,650	5.5	10.1	32.7	27.5	9.4	9.1	5.6
NEW YORK								
Albany County, New York	205,266	2.1	5.3	22.6	15.5	11.7	22.1	20.7
Bronx County, New York	953,271	13.8	14.3	27.6	17.4	7.3	12.6	7.1
Broome County, New York	127,879	3.4	6.2	30.8	19.1	13.1	15.3	12.1
Cattaraugus County, New York	52,806	2.4	8.1	37.4	17.9	14.0	11.1	9.0
Cayuga County, New York	55,989	4.1	8.9	32.6	18.9	13.0	14.3	8.1
Chautauqua County, New York	88,890	3.0	7.5	34.4	18.2	14.0	12.4	10.4
Chemung County, New York	60,282	3.1	7.5	37.1	18.7	9.7	12.4	11.4
Clinton County, New York	55,133	4.0	8.8	39.7	15.4	9.9	12.9	9.2
Dutchess County, New York	206,240	3.1	5.1	26.9	18.7	11.8	18.1	16.5
Erie County, New York	649,960	2.5	5.6	27.3	18.6	11.6	19.9	14.5
Jefferson County, New York	72,243	2.4	8.0	34.8	22.7	10.9	12.8	8.4
Kings County, New York	1,820,860	8.6	8.5	26.5	13.0	6.3	22.1	15.0
Livingston County, New York	42,931	2.4	5.4	31.4	19.4	15.7	15.1	10.6
Madison County, New York	48,108	2.2	4.7	37.2	15.5	13.0	16.1	11.4
Monroe County, New York	515,145	2.9	6.5	24.5	17.2	11.7	20.2	17.1
Nassau County, New York	951,605	4.7	4.4	23.0	14.5	8.3	24.9	20.2
New York County, New York	1,273,269	6.9	7.1	12.1	9.3	4.1	30.6	29.9
Niagara County, New York	151,004	2.6	6.1	33.4	20.4	13.0	13.3	11.1
Oneida County, New York	160,501	4.6	7.6	31.5	19.4	13.2	14.0	9.6
Onondaga County, New York	317,164	2.5	6.3	25.9	16.6	12.8	20.1	15.9
Ontario County, New York	77,999	1.9	4.7	25.2	16.5	14.9	21.9	14.8
Orange County, New York	244,723	3.0	7.1	29.1	20.0	9.8	18.1	12.9
Oswego County, New York	80,195	2.7	9.8	37.7	17.2	14.4	9.9	8.3
Putnam County, New York	71,447	3.1	4.0	28.8	16.3	9.1	20.9	17.8
Queens County, New York	1,695,302	9.8	8.2	29.1	14.4	7.6	19.8	11.1
Rensselaer County, New York	111,047	2.5	5.7	28.6	18.4	13.0	18.1	13.6
Richmond County, New York	334,079	5.1	6.6	30.2	17.3	7.7	19.8	13.3
Rockland County, New York	205,985	4.6	6.6	22.8	17.3	7.7	22.7	18.3
St. Lawrence County, New York	72,555	4.4	8.3	35.6	17.6	10.1	11.4	12.6
Saratoga County, New York	164,414	1.8	4.7	23.7	15.4	12.3	23.0	19.0
Schenectady County, New York	107,453	2.7	6.7	29.9	17.9	14.9	16.0	11.9
Steuben County, New York	68,011	3.4	6.1	38.1	16.3	14.1	11.0	10.9
Suffolk County, New York	1,036,946	4.6	5.3	26.7	17.4	9.6	20.1	16.4
Sullivan County, New York	53,310	4.1	7.7	32.4	14.3	12.6	17.4	11.5
Tompkins County, New York	61,921	1.6	5.4	17.9	13.0	9.8	22.1	30.1
Ulster County, New York	130,912	2.4	5.6	29.6	19.8	9.9	17.9	14.8
Warren County, New York	48,385	2.3	6.4	30.3	19.7	10.1	15.0	16.2
Wayne County, New York	63,605	3.3	8.7	34.3	17.7	14.2	13.8	8.0
Westchester County, New York	675,568	6.4	6.1	20.0	12.9	6.7	23.6	24.3
NORTH CAROLINA								
Alamance County, North Carolina	109,959	6.4	9.3	29.4	22.0	9.6	15.5	7.8
Brunswick County, North Carolina	102,846	2.2	6.3	29.5	22.2	9.5	18.9	11.4
Buncombe County, North Carolina	189,252	2.8	5.8	23.2	16.6	9.5	26.8	15.4
Burke County, North Carolina	64,167	7.0	10.4	33.0	20.3	12.8	9.5	7.2
Cabarrus County, North Carolina	137,026	4.4	7.1	25.0	23.1	8.6	20.4	11.4
Caldwell County, North Carolina	58,662	8.0	13.3	34.2	18.5	10.4	8.6	7.0

Table C-2. Educational Attainment of the Population, by Selected Counties, 2017—*Continued*

(Number; percent; dollars.)

State/County	Population 18 to 24 years				
	Total	Less than high school graduate (percent)	High school graduate (includes equivalency) (percent)	Some college or associate's degree (percent)	Bachelor's degree or higher (percent)
NORTH CAROLINA—(*Continued*)					
Carteret County, North Carolina	4,287	20.6	38.9	36.4	4.1
Catawba County, North Carolina	13,745	12.2	40.2	39.7	8.0
Chatham County, North Carolina	3,442	15.4	44.3	22.0	18.2
Cleveland County, North Carolina	9,339	15.2	38.2	43.1	3.4
Craven County, North Carolina	12,687	7.8	34.5	54.5	3.2
Cumberland County, North Carolina	44,642	11.4	39.3	42.5	6.7
Davidson County, North Carolina	11,244	20.1	36.1	37.7	6.0
Durham County, North Carolina	30,867	10.6	21.9	47.0	20.5
Forsyth County, North Carolina	36,638	14.3	35.6	40.6	9.5
Franklin County, North Carolina	5,942	11.4	31.6	45.8	11.3
Gaston County, North Carolina	18,254	17.4	33.0	44.6	5.0
Guilford County, North Carolina	55,504	10.9	21.1	58.7	9.3
Harnett County, North Carolina	12,483	14.3	23.3	52.0	10.4
Henderson County, North Carolina	7,638	21.5	31.3	41.7	5.5
Iredell County, North Carolina	14,501	11.6	33.5	45.2	9.7
Johnston County, North Carolina	14,925	21.6	31.8	43.0	3.6
Lincoln County, North Carolina	6,235	12.3	36.9	46.0	4.8
Mecklenburg County, North Carolina	96,675	12.6	22.9	46.3	18.2
Moore County, North Carolina	6,542	10.3	30.0	52.6	7.2
Nash County, North Carolina	9,298	10.8	28.5	52.0	8.7
New Hanover County, North Carolina	27,278	9.1	14.5	66.0	10.5
Onslow County, North Carolina	42,611	4.5	55.4	39.1	1.1
Orange County, North Carolina	25,183	4.7	23.9	55.5	15.9
Pitt County, North Carolina	33,274	1.7	19.5	69.4	9.4
Randolph County, North Carolina	10,592	23.7	32.0	40.4	3.9
Robeson County, North Carolina	13,825	20.0	30.2	44.3	5.5
Rockingham County, North Carolina	7,926	29.0	39.5	28.8	2.7
Rowan County, North Carolina	12,497	17.9	35.6	42.0	4.5
Rutherford County, North Carolina	5,079	15.4	44.8	28.0	11.9
Surry County, North Carolina	5,571	19.1	32.6	43.6	4.7
Union County, North Carolina	19,389	14.7	38.3	40.1	6.9
Wake County, North Carolina	96,931	12.5	25.7	41.8	20.0
Wayne County, North Carolina	12,610	11.1	38.3	47.3	3.3
Wilkes County, North Carolina	5,055	27.3	19.9	47.0	5.8
Wilson County, North Carolina	6,774	32.2	29.5	29.7	8.6
NORTH DAKOTA					
Burleigh County, North Dakota	7,976	16.1	28.9	40.0	15.0
Cass County, North Dakota	25,015	6.2	28.3	48.9	16.6
Grand Forks County, North Dakota	14,278	5.0	27.0	57.1	10.9
Ward County, North Dakota	9,806	3.1	41.2	45.9	9.7
OHIO					
Allen County, Ohio	9,623	19.5	43.1	33.8	3.5
Ashtabula County, Ohio	7,485	27.7	42.4	26.9	3.0
Athens County, Ohio	20,255	0.9	25.8	72.2	1.1
Belmont County, Ohio	4,532	15.4	48.7	24.4	11.5
Butler County, Ohio	47,101	7.0	35.2	49.7	8.1
Clark County, Ohio	12,696	12.9	46.4	36.1	4.6
Clermont County, Ohio	15,774	14.0	41.1	36.0	8.9
Columbiana County, Ohio	8,013	20.9	44.8	31.6	2.8
Cuyahoga County, Ohio	110,866	14.0	31.0	41.3	13.7
Delaware County, Ohio	15,399	15.1	32.0	45.6	7.3
Erie County, Ohio	5,683	11.4	34.7	39.6	14.3
Fairfield County, Ohio	13,602	19.0	41.1	29.7	10.2
Franklin County, Ohio	128,174	12.9	26.3	45.3	15.4
Geauga County, Ohio	7,763	33.0	32.3	25.0	9.6
Greene County, Ohio	21,522	4.2	23.9	60.0	11.9
Hamilton County, Ohio	75,823	11.0	34.1	42.0	12.9
Hancock County, Ohio	6,736	5.9	42.5	41.6	10.0
Jefferson County, Ohio	5,680	10.1	35.4	43.2	11.2
Lake County, Ohio	17,678	13.4	33.0	39.3	14.3
Licking County, Ohio	14,700	11.9	42.7	40.1	5.4
Lorain County, Ohio	26,655	17.8	29.4	44.5	8.2
Lucas County, Ohio	38,884	15.8	29.5	44.1	10.7
Mahoning County, Ohio	19,769	15.3	35.7	38.6	10.5
Marion County, Ohio	4,872	15.4	41.3	37.5	5.8
Medina County, Ohio	13,740	7.7	36.7	43.4	12.2
Miami County, Ohio	7,343	12.3	46.3	30.7	10.6

Table C-2. Educational Attainment of the Population, by Selected Counties, 2017—*Continued*

(Number; percent; dollars.)

State/County	Population 25 years and over							
	Total	Less than 9th grade (percent)	9th to 12th grade, no diploma (percent)	High school graduate (includes equivalency) (percent)	Some college, no degree (percent)	Associate's degree (percent)	Bachelor's degree (percent)	Graduate or professional degree (percent)
NORTH CAROLINA—(*Continued*)								
Carteret County, North Carolina	51,901	1.7	6.3	25.1	29.2	12.0	15.6	10.2
Catawba County, North Carolina	108,709	6.0	9.6	30.1	22.2	12.3	13.3	6.6
Chatham County, North Carolina	53,297	4.0	6.5	24.5	18.3	7.8	22.0	17.0
Cleveland County, North Carolina	66,378	4.1	10.2	34.9	23.6	9.6	11.2	6.4
Craven County, North Carolina	66,794	5.2	7.8	21.8	25.9	11.2	18.7	9.4
Cumberland County, North Carolina	205,965	2.9	6.4	27.1	29.2	10.4	16.3	7.7
Davidson County, North Carolina	117,271	4.6	11.6	31.1	23.3	12.1	12.2	5.1
Durham County, North Carolina	215,089	5.7	6.9	17.2	16.4	5.4	25.9	22.5
Forsyth County, North Carolina	252,493	4.1	6.4	25.5	21.9	8.0	21.9	12.2
Franklin County, North Carolina	45,458	4.6	9.5	32.0	22.7	10.3	14.8	6.2
Gaston County, North Carolina	152,050	4.7	10.1	31.4	22.7	10.4	14.3	6.3
Guilford County, North Carolina	353,213	3.4	6.8	23.5	21.1	9.5	23.3	12.3
Harnett County, North Carolina	85,093	4.2	8.6	28.9	25.2	11.2	15.0	6.9
Henderson County, North Carolina	85,774	3.3	5.7	21.6	24.7	10.5	22.9	11.3
Iredell County, North Carolina	120,071	4.4	5.2	29.6	22.6	10.7	19.8	7.6
Johnston County, North Carolina	131,290	5.1	8.5	28.4	23.7	12.2	16.0	6.0
Lincoln County, North Carolina	58,501	3.4	9.5	30.7	23.5	11.0	14.7	7.1
Mecklenburg County, North Carolina	722,837	4.6	4.5	17.3	19.9	7.6	30.5	15.6
Moore County, North Carolina	69,500	1.7	5.0	20.5	21.1	10.0	25.2	16.5
Nash County, North Carolina	63,759	4.9	8.0	35.9	21.5	7.6	15.9	6.1
New Hanover County, North Carolina	157,243	1.8	6.0	21.5	21.0	9.5	26.3	13.9
Onslow County, North Carolina	103,958	2.0	5.4	29.3	29.1	11.8	15.0	7.2
Orange County, North Carolina	91,042	4.3	3.3	15.7	14.3	5.8	24.6	31.9
Pitt County, North Carolina	107,663	2.1	7.7	20.5	21.7	13.4	22.1	12.5
Randolph County, North Carolina	100,654	5.5	12.6	33.7	21.5	10.6	12.3	3.8
Robeson County, North Carolina	85,616	8.1	14.0	34.6	20.8	8.7	8.3	5.4
Rockingham County, North Carolina	64,445	4.2	12.2	29.8	26.2	11.3	11.1	5.2
Rowan County, North Carolina	96,938	4.6	10.6	33.3	23.5	8.7	13.4	5.8
Rutherford County, North Carolina	47,441	4.0	10.2	35.5	18.5	12.2	11.7	8.1
Surry County, North Carolina	51,247	8.1	12.9	26.1	21.3	11.0	14.5	6.1
Union County, North Carolina	148,919	3.6	6.5	25.7	20.8	10.1	22.6	10.6
Wake County, North Carolina	715,898	3.6	4.2	15.0	17.5	7.6	32.4	19.8
Wayne County, North Carolina	82,342	6.3	8.5	32.0	20.4	12.4	14.9	5.4
Wilkes County, North Carolina	49,455	7.8	13.3	30.9	21.1	10.5	11.7	4.6
Wilson County, North Carolina	55,953	5.5	13.3	32.4	21.5	8.7	14.4	4.2
NORTH DAKOTA								
Burleigh County, North Dakota	64,363	2.6	2.7	24.0	22.0	13.4	24.0	11.3
Cass County, North Dakota	113,641	1.7	3.4	17.6	20.8	14.7	29.0	12.8
Grand Forks County, North Dakota	42,280	2.1	3.6	19.8	25.9	13.2	21.6	13.9
Ward County, North Dakota	43,157	2.3	2.8	33.5	20.1	9.6	22.9	8.8
OHIO								
Allen County, Ohio	69,698	2.2	8.1	37.9	21.2	10.9	11.9	7.7
Ashtabula County, Ohio	68,620	4.1	9.3	46.9	17.6	7.5	10.5	4.1
Athens County, Ohio	36,600	2.7	7.6	35.2	14.7	7.4	14.8	17.5
Belmont County, Ohio	50,556	2.4	6.1	43.1	20.3	13.7	8.3	6.1
Butler County, Ohio	243,633	2.2	6.0	33.6	20.5	8.4	18.5	10.8
Clark County, Ohio	91,675	2.9	9.5	38.2	21.6	7.8	10.7	9.3
Clermont County, Ohio	141,285	3.6	6.8	32.6	20.0	9.7	17.4	9.8
Columbiana County, Ohio	73,982	3.6	9.9	46.0	19.9	9.8	7.3	3.5
Cuyahoga County, Ohio	876,662	2.7	7.1	27.9	22.2	7.5	19.2	13.5
Delaware County, Ohio	131,287	1.0	3.0	16.8	18.1	6.8	34.8	19.4
Erie County, Ohio	53,820	1.9	5.9	35.9	19.9	11.1	15.7	9.5
Fairfield County, Ohio	104,026	1.7	6.7	32.5	23.4	8.7	17.9	9.2
Franklin County, Ohio	861,624	2.9	6.1	25.5	19.6	7.2	24.2	14.5
Geauga County, Ohio	64,481	5.6	5.3	23.8	19.4	7.3	23.5	15.2
Greene County, Ohio	110,558	2.6	4.6	23.8	19.0	9.6	20.7	19.7
Hamilton County, Ohio	550,204	2.5	6.8	26.4	18.2	8.8	22.5	14.8
Hancock County, Ohio	52,117	1.1	7.3	34.5	18.0	11.4	17.9	9.9
Jefferson County, Ohio	47,705	1.4	5.6	45.0	21.4	12.2	10.1	4.3
Lake County, Ohio	165,902	3.0	6.0	30.0	23.0	11.4	16.6	10.0
Licking County, Ohio	118,584	2.4	7.1	34.6	21.4	8.5	17.8	8.1
Lorain County, Ohio	212,692	1.9	8.8	31.4	23.9	10.5	15.5	8.0
Lucas County, Ohio	292,621	2.3	10.0	29.6	22.2	9.4	16.4	10.1
Mahoning County, Ohio	164,042	2.2	6.3	40.7	19.2	8.9	15.2	7.4
Marion County, Ohio	46,643	3.4	7.1	41.1	24.0	8.3	9.3	6.9
Medina County, Ohio	124,238	1.3	3.9	30.6	21.3	10.6	21.1	11.1
Miami County, Ohio	73,618	1.0	5.9	39.9	20.3	9.1	14.9	8.9

Table C-2. Educational Attainment of the Population, by Selected Counties, 2017—*Continued*

(Number; percent; dollars.)

State/County	Total	\[Population 18 to 24 years\] Less than high school graduate (percent)	High school graduate (includes equivalency) (percent)	Some college or associate's degree (percent)	Bachelor's degree or higher (percent)
NORTH CAROLINA					
Montgomery County, Ohio	48,154	8.5	30.1	51.9	9.5
Muskingum County, Ohio	7,660	4.4	45.3	47.1	3.1
Portage County, Ohio	26,948	6.1	20.3	62.9	10.7
Richland County, Ohio	9,791	21.1	40.1	33.8	4.9
Ross County, Ohio	6,367	16.4	47.9	34.0	1.7
Scioto County, Ohio	6,497	17.7	40.9	37.2	4.1
Stark County, Ohio	32,427	13.4	35.5	43.3	7.8
Summit County, Ohio	46,446	11.5	31.8	46.3	10.4
Trumbull County, Ohio	15,364	23.0	40.7	29.9	6.4
Tuscarawas County, Ohio	7,154	28.3	47.8	21.0	2.9
Warren County, Ohio	17,059	15.0	43.8	30.9	10.3
Wayne County, Ohio	11,259	14.4	32.0	43.4	10.2
Wood County, Ohio	23,023	2.8	16.3	65.2	15.8
OKLAHOMA					
Canadian County, Oklahoma	11,566	15.8	42.2	29.4	12.6
Cleveland County, Oklahoma	40,270	8.6	23.0	58.0	10.4
Comanche County, Oklahoma	16,472	6.6	48.0	37.7	7.8
Creek County, Oklahoma	6,097	21.6	37.7	36.0	4.7
Muskogee County, Oklahoma	6,901	16.1	44.2	35.5	4.1
Oklahoma County, Oklahoma	70,809	15.0	29.2	46.5	9.3
Payne County, Oklahoma	22,204	3.5	12.5	71.5	12.5
Pottawatomie County, Oklahoma	7,070	17.5	29.4	47.1	5.9
Rogers County, Oklahoma	8,226	12.0	47.2	37.4	3.4
Tulsa County, Oklahoma	57,277	17.6	33.3	38.7	10.3
Wagoner County, Oklahoma	5,466	19.4	46.0	29.6	5.0
OREGON					
Benton County, Oregon	20,498	3.0	14.8	70.4	11.8
Clackamas County, Oregon	31,826	17.8	29.1	46.6	6.4
Deschutes County, Oregon	12,944	9.6	45.6	37.7	7.0
Douglas County, Oregon	7,628	14.4	55.3	24.6	5.7
Jackson County, Oregon	18,094	16.8	43.1	36.9	3.2
Josephine County, Oregon	5,405	11.3	34.0	54.7	0.0
Klamath County, Oregon	5,612	4.6	40.3	55.1	0.0
Lane County, Oregon	47,513	12.4	27.6	48.7	11.4
Linn County, Oregon	9,194	24.5	41.0	32.5	1.9
Marion County, Oregon	31,116	18.4	33.4	43.0	5.3
Multnomah County, Oregon	65,427	10.6	32.9	41.4	15.1
Polk County, Oregon	11,609	24.5	22.6	42.9	10.0
Umatilla County, Oregon	7,488	23.2	40.0	36.3	0.6
Washington County, Oregon	47,837	13.8	25.5	50.3	10.4
Yamhill County, Oregon	11,085	20.7	21.3	51.7	6.3
PENNSYLVANIA					
Adams County, Pennsylvania	9,737	6.1	35.5	50.8	7.6
Allegheny County, Pennsylvania	108,641	8.3	29.6	41.0	21.1
Armstrong County, Pennsylvania	4,846	17.8	50.6	22.8	8.9
Beaver County, Pennsylvania	12,464	15.6	35.4	36.9	12.1
Berks County, Pennsylvania	40,777	12.7	36.3	41.0	10.0
Blair County, Pennsylvania	9,301	11.3	44.0	39.5	5.2
Bucks County, Pennsylvania	49,600	11.7	34.2	34.7	19.3
Butler County, Pennsylvania	16,469	10.6	34.5	43.1	11.7
Cambria County, Pennsylvania	12,460	6.3	41.7	47.4	4.6
Carbon County, Pennsylvania	4,219	17.4	39.3	38.9	4.4
Centre County, Pennsylvania	39,968	2.4	26.7	58.9	12.0
Chester County, Pennsylvania	46,480	12.1	27.5	39.2	21.2
Clearfield County, Pennsylvania	6,013	13.4	50.0	30.2	6.4
Columbia County, Pennsylvania	10,129	7.6	24.9	56.8	10.7
Crawford County, Pennsylvania	7,884	10.9	42.0	41.8	5.2
Cumberland County, Pennsylvania	23,818	11.5	25.4	52.1	10.9
Dauphin County, Pennsylvania	22,596	16.3	34.6	33.9	15.2
Delaware County, Pennsylvania	56,748	10.8	30.8	46.8	11.6
Erie County, Pennsylvania	27,789	11.0	33.9	41.6	13.6
Fayette County, Pennsylvania	9,627	8.5	43.0	36.8	11.7
Franklin County, Pennsylvania	11,296	20.7	36.9	32.1	10.3
Indiana County, Pennsylvania	14,411	9.2	33.1	52.1	5.7
Lackawanna County, Pennsylvania	19,521	16.1	22.1	51.2	10.6
Lancaster County, Pennsylvania	49,103	23.6	33.1	31.8	11.5

Table C-2. Educational Attainment of the Population, by Selected Counties, 2017—*Continued*

(Number; percent; dollars.)

State/County	Total	Less than 9th grade (percent)	9th to 12th grade, no diploma (percent)	High school graduate (includes equivalency) (percent)	Some college, no degree (percent)	Associate's degree (percent)	Bachelor's degree (percent)	Graduate or professional degree (percent)
NORTH CAROLINA								
Montgomery County, Ohio	366,020	2.7	7.8	28.1	23.3	10.3	16.5	11.4
Muskingum County, Ohio	58,848	3.2	8.3	42.7	17.7	12.1	10.2	5.8
Portage County, Ohio	104,615	1.6	7.3	35.6	17.7	7.7	18.4	11.7
Richland County, Ohio	84,550	3.8	9.8	39.1	20.1	8.4	13.7	5.1
Ross County, Ohio	54,434	2.2	9.7	42.1	19.2	10.2	10.2	6.4
Scioto County, Ohio	53,141	5.1	13.6	39.5	17.9	7.3	8.3	8.4
Stark County, Ohio	259,924	1.8	7.2	38.1	22.8	8.0	14.2	7.9
Summit County, Ohio	380,675	1.8	5.8	30.2	20.8	8.6	21.0	11.8
Trumbull County, Ohio	144,108	3.1	6.6	46.3	18.5	6.7	12.4	6.2
Tuscarawas County, Ohio	63,972	3.7	7.8	48.0	18.9	7.8	8.7	5.1
Warren County, Ohio	154,438	2.0	4.1	27.4	15.6	8.6	26.2	16.3
Wayne County, Ohio	76,595	8.0	5.3	38.8	18.5	7.0	14.0	8.3
Wood County, Ohio	81,051	1.3	3.6	31.2	20.8	10.6	19.3	13.2
OKLAHOMA								
Canadian County, Oklahoma	91,884	2.9	3.9	27.7	28.1	10.2	20.0	7.3
Cleveland County, Oklahoma	178,227	2.3	6.3	25.3	24.3	8.1	21.6	12.0
Comanche County, Oklahoma	76,203	2.5	5.9	29.4	30.2	7.9	13.9	10.3
Creek County, Oklahoma	48,317	3.4	8.6	40.9	23.0	7.8	11.0	5.4
Muskogee County, Oklahoma	45,268	4.0	13.7	36.8	19.5	8.5	11.6	6.0
Oklahoma County, Oklahoma	514,300	4.7	7.2	25.9	22.2	7.4	20.9	11.8
Payne County, Oklahoma	43,023	1.5	8.6	29.8	16.8	6.7	22.4	14.3
Pottawatomie County, Oklahoma	47,954	3.1	9.6	36.7	22.9	10.0	10.3	7.5
Rogers County, Oklahoma	61,496	2.1	5.8	32.3	26.1	8.0	17.0	8.7
Tulsa County, Oklahoma	424,920	4.3	6.0	24.9	24.0	9.1	21.3	10.4
Wagoner County, Oklahoma	53,868	2.2	8.4	30.8	23.3	10.8	16.6	7.9
OREGON								
Benton County, Oregon	55,327	1.2	1.5	13.2	20.1	10.2	28.8	25.0
Clackamas County, Oregon	291,445	2.1	3.7	21.3	25.4	9.1	24.1	14.3
Deschutes County, Oregon	135,342	1.6	4.4	24.4	25.8	10.1	22.1	11.6
Douglas County, Oregon	80,775	3.0	8.2	33.2	28.5	9.8	10.9	6.4
Jackson County, Oregon	154,281	2.9	6.0	25.9	28.3	8.6	18.1	10.3
Josephine County, Oregon	64,096	2.0	6.7	31.0	31.9	9.5	11.6	7.3
Klamath County, Oregon	46,898	4.6	6.9	33.6	23.2	12.3	13.0	6.4
Lane County, Oregon	257,137	2.4	5.1	22.5	29.4	9.5	18.2	12.8
Linn County, Oregon	87,222	3.4	7.2	31.4	29.3	11.4	12.9	4.5
Marion County, Oregon	225,382	8.3	8.0	28.6	23.5	8.6	15.8	7.2
Multnomah County, Oregon	587,811	3.5	4.4	18.1	21.2	7.5	27.3	18.1
Polk County, Oregon	52,409	4.0	7.0	21.3	27.3	9.6	17.9	13.0
Umatilla County, Oregon	49,992	7.1	11.0	28.6	27.0	9.1	9.8	7.4
Washington County, Oregon	404,077	3.2	3.7	17.1	22.0	8.2	29.3	16.5
Yamhill County, Oregon	70,951	4.4	5.8	23.6	27.9	10.8	17.0	10.5
PENNSYLVANIA								
Adams County, Pennsylvania	72,118	3.8	7.3	40.2	17.7	8.1	13.8	9.1
Allegheny County, Pennsylvania	884,094	1.7	3.8	27.0	16.2	9.9	23.8	17.6
Armstrong County, Pennsylvania	48,197	2.1	8.3	48.5	15.2	10.6	10.6	4.7
Beaver County, Pennsylvania	121,242	1.3	4.2	39.9	20.1	10.7	15.7	8.0
Berks County, Pennsylvania	282,963	5.2	8.4	36.9	17.7	7.9	15.6	8.3
Blair County, Pennsylvania	88,809	2.4	6.5	42.5	17.7	9.8	14.8	6.1
Bucks County, Pennsylvania	448,774	1.9	4.1	27.8	17.4	7.5	24.2	17.2
Butler County, Pennsylvania	132,893	1.2	4.1	31.9	15.9	10.6	23.8	12.4
Cambria County, Pennsylvania	95,164	2.3	6.6	44.9	13.7	11.2	13.7	7.5
Carbon County, Pennsylvania	47,267	3.1	6.3	46.1	18.1	11.8	9.9	4.6
Centre County, Pennsylvania	98,303	2.1	4.3	28.0	12.1	8.1	24.4	21.1
Chester County, Pennsylvania	353,899	2.7	4.0	22.2	12.7	6.1	30.9	21.3
Clearfield County, Pennsylvania	59,076	5.0	7.9	48.0	13.1	8.7	12.0	5.3
Columbia County, Pennsylvania	43,858	1.2	7.5	43.0	15.7	9.2	13.0	10.4
Crawford County, Pennsylvania	60,553	4.3	7.2	47.5	13.9	5.7	14.6	6.8
Cumberland County, Pennsylvania	175,140	2.5	4.9	30.7	15.8	8.8	21.3	16.1
Dauphin County, Pennsylvania	191,345	2.7	6.1	36.8	17.5	7.7	17.4	11.8
Delaware County, Pennsylvania	383,800	2.3	3.9	29.9	16.3	7.2	22.6	17.7
Erie County, Pennsylvania	187,649	3.3	6.1	38.3	15.6	9.6	17.4	9.7
Fayette County, Pennsylvania	96,474	2.9	8.7	46.9	15.4	8.0	13.1	5.0
Franklin County, Pennsylvania	108,529	3.5	8.1	41.1	15.5	8.1	13.2	10.5
Indiana County, Pennsylvania	55,222	3.2	6.4	42.4	13.4	10.3	14.5	9.8
Lackawanna County, Pennsylvania	148,344	2.7	5.4	37.4	17.2	8.2	18.5	10.7
Lancaster County, Pennsylvania	364,909	7.2	8.2	35.2	13.8	7.6	17.4	10.7

Table C-2. Educational Attainment of the Population, by Selected Counties, 2017—*Continued*

(Number; percent; dollars.)

State/County	Total	Less than high school graduate (percent)	High school graduate (includes equivalency) (percent)	Some college or associate's degree (percent)	Bachelor's degree or higher (percent)
			Population 18 to 24 years		
PENNSYLVANIA—*(Continued)*					
Lawrence County, Pennsylvania	7,043	14.8	28.9	50.0	6.2
Lebanon County, Pennsylvania	11,970	22.0	38.7	35.4	3.9
Lehigh County, Pennsylvania	34,255	13.0	29.9	46.1	11.0
Luzerne County, Pennsylvania	27,953	12.8	35.4	42.3	9.4
Lycoming County, Pennsylvania	10,180	9.6	34.3	51.1	4.9
Mercer County, Pennsylvania	11,067	13.4	36.3	41.0	9.3
Monroe County, Pennsylvania	17,725	9.1	49.0	33.8	8.1
Montgomery County, Pennsylvania	67,097	9.7	31.0	38.2	21.1
Northampton County, Pennsylvania	29,938	5.4	28.7	55.6	10.3
Northumberland County, Pennsylvania	7,084	18.3	38.2	35.3	8.2
Philadelphia County, Pennsylvania	160,872	10.7	33.6	41.5	14.2
Schuylkill County, Pennsylvania	10,175	17.2	44.0	31.7	7.0
Somerset County, Pennsylvania	5,303	21.6	39.0	31.1	8.3
Washington County, Pennsylvania	18,016	13.8	35.1	42.1	9.0
Westmoreland County, Pennsylvania	26,567	10.6	36.3	40.6	12.5
York County, Pennsylvania	36,444	16.9	38.8	31.3	13.0
RHODE ISLAND					
Kent County, Rhode Island	12,041	10.9	32.9	41.2	15.0
Newport County, Rhode Island	8,525	6.0	26.5	44.7	22.8
Providence County, Rhode Island	70,295	9.1	33.9	47.8	9.1
Washington County, Rhode Island	19,422	5.3	27.4	57.5	9.8
SOUTH CAROLINA					
Aiken County, South Carolina	13,220	11.3	33.2	50.1	5.4
Anderson County, South Carolina	16,662	11.0	28.9	54.2	5.9
Beaufort County, South Carolina	18,641	14.9	38.1	38.6	8.4
Berkeley County, South Carolina	19,890	16.5	30.9	45.6	7.0
Charleston County, South Carolina	35,992	8.1	21.2	53.1	17.6
Darlington County, South Carolina	5,250	20.3	38.6	35.4	5.7
Dorchester County, South Carolina	11,959	22.9	33.5	37.9	5.6
Florence County, South Carolina	11,982	16.1	31.7	46.8	5.3
Greenville County, South Carolina	44,246	13.1	33.4	41.1	12.4
Greenwood County, South Carolina	6,696	10.2	27.9	52.2	9.8
Horry County, South Carolina	25,656	11.7	34.0	45.0	9.3
Kershaw County, South Carolina	5,133	14.9	33.4	44.3	7.4
Lancaster County, South Carolina	6,104	22.2	43.7	29.8	4.2
Laurens County, South Carolina	5,908	14.4	40.4	35.1	10.2
Lexington County, South Carolina	22,704	16.3	43.3	30.3	10.2
Oconee County, South Carolina	5,832	10.8	36.0	47.4	5.8
Orangeburg County, South Carolina	9,567	15.1	29.0	52.5	3.4
Pickens County, South Carolina	21,680	10.4	20.3	60.7	8.6
Richland County, South Carolina	64,502	8.5	31.6	50.0	9.9
Spartanburg County, South Carolina	28,920	12.2	33.2	45.7	8.9
Sumter County, South Carolina	10,743	12.8	42.0	42.7	2.5
York County, South Carolina	23,880	8.4	29.7	47.5	14.3
SOUTH DAKOTA					
Minnehaha County, South Dakota	16,598	13.1	24.3	47.8	14.8
Pennington County, South Dakota	9,304	12.6	30.5	45.3	11.6
TENNESSEE					
Anderson County, Tennessee	5,843	26.0	27.9	31.2	14.9
Blount County, Tennessee	9,801	7.5	30.1	53.9	8.4
Bradley County, Tennessee	10,240	4.5	34.8	54.0	6.7
Davidson County, Tennessee	68,293	12.5	26.9	41.8	18.9
Greene County, Tennessee	5,631	14.7	44.4	39.7	1.2
Hamilton County, Tennessee	30,795	12.0	19.4	56.4	12.2
Knox County, Tennessee	54,928	9.3	30.7	47.8	12.1
Madison County, Tennessee	11,986	9.4	48.1	36.5	6.0
Maury County, Tennessee	8,186	14.4	51.7	29.1	4.8
Montgomery County, Tennessee	22,742	6.8	36.4	49.3	7.6
Putnam County, Tennessee	11,310	3.1	29.4	66.3	1.3
Robertson County, Tennessee	5,909	14.6	46.3	34.0	5.1
Rutherford County, Tennessee	38,887	9.6	31.7	48.1	10.7
Sevier County, Tennessee	8,170	20.0	35.8	39.7	4.5
Shelby County, Tennessee	88,698	12.9	33.1	42.7	11.3
Sullivan County, Tennessee	11,640	11.4	43.8	37.3	7.5
Sumner County, Tennessee	13,933	16.8	30.0	42.3	10.9

Table C-2. Educational Attainment of the Population, by Selected Counties, 2017—*Continued*

(Number; percent; dollars.)

State/County	Population 25 years and over							
	Total	Less than 9th grade (percent)	9th to 12th grade, no diploma (percent)	High school graduate (includes equivalency) (percent)	Some college, no degree (percent)	Associate's degree (percent)	Bachelor's degree (percent)	Graduate or professional degree (percent)
PENNSYLVANIA—*(Continued)*								
Lawrence County, Pennsylvania	62,545	3.2	5.8	42.0	16.5	9.8	15.4	7.3
Lebanon County, Pennsylvania	95,764	3.4	7.9	43.2	14.8	8.4	14.5	7.8
Lehigh County, Pennsylvania	248,992	4.2	7.6	32.7	16.3	9.8	17.8	11.6
Luzerne County, Pennsylvania	227,239	3.4	7.5	38.5	17.0	9.7	15.3	8.5
Lycoming County, Pennsylvania	80,315	1.8	6.5	38.9	17.3	11.4	16.2	7.9
Mercer County, Pennsylvania	79,064	2.3	6.7	43.4	15.3	7.9	16.4	7.9
Monroe County, Pennsylvania	116,911	3.4	8.4	32.7	22.2	9.2	14.8	9.3
Montgomery County, Pennsylvania	580,456	1.8	3.4	23.4	14.4	6.9	28.0	22.1
Northampton County, Pennsylvania	212,826	3.3	6.0	35.0	16.8	9.0	18.9	11.0
Northumberland County, Pennsylvania	67,075	2.7	9.8	51.7	13.2	6.5	11.7	4.2
Philadelphia County, Pennsylvania	1,075,853	5.3	9.4	35.7	15.5	5.7	16.4	11.9
Schuylkill County, Pennsylvania	104,560	2.9	7.7	46.2	16.0	10.5	11.9	4.7
Somerset County, Pennsylvania	55,223	3.9	7.4	52.5	14.6	7.2	9.9	4.5
Washington County, Pennsylvania	148,873	1.5	5.0	36.9	15.3	9.9	20.4	10.9
Westmoreland County, Pennsylvania	261,007	1.9	3.8	35.9	16.8	11.1	19.7	10.9
York County, Pennsylvania	310,781	3.1	7.2	38.5	15.3	10.6	16.4	8.9
RHODE ISLAND								
Kent County, Rhode Island	120,853	3.3	5.9	27.1	18.9	11.3	21.3	12.2
Newport County, Rhode Island	60,470	1.7	4.3	22.2	17.9	6.1	28.4	19.4
Providence County, Rhode Island	435,612	6.7	7.8	33.6	16.1	7.1	17.8	10.9
Washington County, Rhode Island	85,775	2.4	3.2	23.3	18.1	9.6	25.4	17.9
SOUTH CAROLINA								
Aiken County, South Carolina	118,618	4.6	7.9	34.0	19.5	7.5	17.0	9.5
Anderson County, South Carolina	136,504	4.4	11.6	32.9	18.9	11.4	13.9	6.9
Beaufort County, South Carolina	132,688	2.2	5.9	22.7	17.3	10.7	23.6	17.6
Berkeley County, South Carolina	145,644	3.6	7.7	29.0	25.1	9.8	16.2	8.6
Charleston County, South Carolina	285,858	2.6	5.2	25.2	17.0	7.7	27.0	15.5
Darlington County, South Carolina	46,786	4.3	9.6	34.0	22.6	6.2	15.2	8.0
Dorchester County, South Carolina	105,822	3.2	5.8	26.8	21.4	12.8	19.5	10.4
Florence County, South Carolina	93,308	4.8	13.4	30.8	17.0	9.5	15.5	9.0
Greenville County, South Carolina	344,948	3.9	7.9	23.8	20.0	9.9	20.9	13.5
Greenwood County, South Carolina	48,625	6.0	10.9	31.6	16.0	12.2	13.4	9.9
Horry County, South Carolina	246,389	3.0	6.4	34.8	23.0	10.2	15.1	7.6
Kershaw County, South Carolina	44,660	3.3	5.8	34.0	22.2	12.0	13.6	9.0
Lancaster County, South Carolina	66,570	4.2	11.3	30.0	17.3	9.9	18.1	9.1
Laurens County, South Carolina	46,198	5.9	13.6	35.7	21.6	7.6	9.9	5.8
Lexington County, South Carolina	200,145	3.2	7.6	30.0	20.2	8.6	19.7	10.7
Oconee County, South Carolina	56,099	6.2	9.0	28.6	17.2	12.2	15.8	11.0
Orangeburg County, South Carolina	58,850	5.8	10.8	25.9	19.3	17.6	11.7	8.9
Pickens County, South Carolina	77,709	5.4	10.2	25.7	22.9	11.4	13.8	10.6
Richland County, South Carolina	258,643	2.7	6.2	23.8	22.9	7.0	22.2	15.2
Spartanburg County, South Carolina	207,051	4.5	8.6	28.5	22.0	11.3	15.6	9.5
Sumter County, South Carolina	71,105	4.5	10.6	33.1	23.4	8.8	12.7	6.9
York County, South Carolina	177,532	3.3	6.5	24.5	21.0	10.1	23.2	11.4
SOUTH DAKOTA								
Minnehaha County, South Dakota	124,138	2.3	3.6	28.2	22.3	12.2	21.3	10.1
Pennington County, South Dakota	75,516	1.1	5.8	27.4	25.5	10.5	18.0	11.7
TENNESSEE								
Anderson County, Tennessee	54,085	3.5	10.0	34.5	19.5	9.1	12.5	11.0
Blount County, Tennessee	93,543	3.8	7.2	35.7	22.5	7.6	14.4	8.7
Bradley County, Tennessee	71,960	4.5	9.1	33.9	23.0	7.9	12.2	9.6
Davidson County, Tennessee	477,260	4.1	5.5	22.2	19.9	6.5	27.1	14.7
Greene County, Tennessee	49,628	5.0	10.0	39.7	23.8	7.2	9.1	5.1
Hamilton County, Tennessee	255,297	2.9	5.3	29.2	21.0	8.9	21.6	10.9
Knox County, Tennessee	309,359	2.7	5.6	25.2	21.1	8.1	22.5	14.8
Madison County, Tennessee	64,159	5.2	7.0	36.9	19.2	5.9	14.9	10.9
Maury County, Tennessee	62,355	2.7	7.4	39.2	19.5	7.3	16.7	7.3
Montgomery County, Tennessee	123,869	2.9	5.2	25.9	28.2	9.7	17.5	10.6
Putnam County, Tennessee	49,831	5.7	7.9	37.5	19.5	5.7	13.8	9.8
Robertson County, Tennessee	47,296	4.2	7.8	39.3	21.0	8.6	11.9	7.3
Rutherford County, Tennessee	199,945	2.7	6.7	26.0	21.6	8.4	24.7	9.9
Sevier County, Tennessee	69,189	4.1	10.5	37.3	24.0	7.7	11.4	5.1
Shelby County, Tennessee	614,274	4.0	7.1	27.7	23.0	6.5	18.4	13.3
Sullivan County, Tennessee	114,943	4.4	9.9	35.0	19.1	7.8	14.7	9.0
Sumner County, Tennessee	126,117	3.2	6.5	29.5	23.4	9.3	18.9	9.2

Table C-2. Educational Attainment of the Population, by Selected Counties, 2017—*Continued*

(Number; percent; dollars.)

State/County	Population 18 to 24 years				
	Total	Less than high school graduate (percent)	High school graduate (includes equivalency) (percent)	Some college or associate's degree (percent)	Bachelor's degree or higher (percent)
TENNESSEE—*(Continued)*					
Washington County, Tennessee...............	14,745	8.6	27.7	53.3	10.4
Williamson County, Tennessee...............	16,766	9.4	31.8	43.3	15.5
Wilson County, Tennessee	10,332	13.6	33.7	38.4	14.4
TEXAS					
Angelina County, Texas	8,291	11.5	42.3	45.4	0.9
Bastrop County, Texas........................	7,929	15.7	61.5	21.5	1.3
Bell County, Texas	40,464	13.7	33.9	42.2	10.1
Bexar County, Texas	203,646	14.1	33.1	43.8	9.0
Bowie County, Texas	9,072	13.8	53.3	31.9	1.1
Brazoria County, Texas.......................	29,548	13.5	33.6	45.1	7.8
Brazos County, Texas.........................	58,671	5.4	18.7	65.0	10.9
Cameron County, Texas......................	45,142	13.4	42.6	40.0	4.0
Collin County, Texas..........................	79,151	11.0	32.9	39.7	16.4
Comal County, Texas.........................	10,579	15.1	31.2	45.3	8.4
Coryell County, Texas........................	9,286	12.4	47.4	33.9	6.3
Dallas County, Texas	250,197	15.8	33.9	39.7	10.6
Denton County, Texas........................	78,246	9.2	28.2	50.8	11.9
Ector County, Texas..........................	17,068	24.3	39.6	33.4	2.8
Ellis County, Texas	15,298	18.4	31.7	45.2	4.6
El Paso County, Texas........................	94,577	13.4	29.9	50.5	6.2
Fort Bend County, Texas.....................	63,058	14.3	31.5	42.7	11.5
Galveston County, Texas	28,206	15.9	32.9	35.2	16.1
Grayson County, Texas.......................	11,316	8.1	27.3	59.9	4.7
Gregg County, Texas	11,353	7.9	46.2	42.7	3.2
Guadalupe County, Texas	14,047	9.0	57.1	29.5	4.4
Harris County, Texas	432,641	17.0	31.1	42.0	9.9
Harrison County, Texas.......................	5,549	17.5	41.7	35.2	5.6
Hays County, Texas...........................	36,824	5.4	25.6	64.3	4.7
Henderson County, Texas....................	5,717	17.0	36.2	38.9	7.9
Hidalgo County, Texas........................	93,819	16.9	32.8	44.0	6.3
Hunt County, Texas	9,711	11.1	24.2	55.3	9.4
Jefferson County, Texas	25,901	11.8	37.7	43.8	6.7
Johnson County, Texas.......................	14,167	10.9	50.9	29.1	9.2
Kaufman County, Texas......................	10,000	14.6	35.7	42.3	7.4
Liberty County, Texas........................	7,446	23.1	44.6	31.3	0.9
Lubbock County, Texas.......................	51,258	7.8	30.1	51.8	10.3
McLennan County, Texas	36,055	9.8	28.1	55.2	6.9
Midland County, Texas.......................	15,500	25.7	33.7	36.0	4.5
Montgomery County, Texas..................	46,383	25.7	27.4	39.4	7.5
Nacogdoches County, Texas.................	12,483	10.4	23.6	60.6	5.3
Nueces County, Texas	35,692	16.2	31.3	47.8	4.7
Orange County, Texas........................	7,401	26.6	39.4	32.5	1.5
Parker County, Texas.........................	10,462	20.8	36.2	38.0	4.9
Potter County, Texas.........................	10,493	23.1	37.3	33.4	6.1
Randall County, Texas	13,660	13.4	28.5	50.7	7.5
Rockwall County, Texas......................	7,299	24.5	26.1	40.6	8.7
San Patricio County, Texas	6,845	22.1	50.2	25.3	2.4
Smith County, Texas..........................	23,146	14.6	27.2	52.1	6.1
Tarrant County, Texas........................	191,638	13.9	33.6	42.3	10.2
Taylor County, Texas.........................	19,360	6.0	35.6	49.2	9.2
Tom Green County, Texas	13,196	8.1	32.3	53.0	6.5
Travis County, Texas..........................	112,997	9.5	24.3	49.8	16.4
Victoria County, Texas.......................	8,813	18.9	27.9	46.1	7.1
Walker County, Texas........................	14,349	2.3	14.3	81.7	1.6
Webb County, Texas..........................	30,893	14.9	41.6	38.4	5.0
Wichita County, Texas........................	19,222	4.4	49.8	40.5	5.3
Williamson County, Texas	44,700	18.5	30.8	40.2	10.6
Wise County, Texas...........................	5,446	15.2	65.4	15.9	3.5
UTAH					
Cache County, Utah...........................	24,527	7.4	18.8	67.3	6.5
Davis County, Utah...........................	30,478	12.5	36.0	45.5	5.9
Salt Lake County, Utah.......................	106,526	11.5	33.2	46.7	8.6
Tooele County, Utah..........................	6,176	12.9	42.0	42.7	2.4
Utah County, Utah............................	101,195	7.3	25.9	59.6	7.2
Washington County, Utah....................	14,407	11.5	30.3	55.0	3.2
Weber County, Utah..........................	25,302	9.7	42.4	43.1	4.8

Table C-2. Educational Attainment of the Population, by Selected Counties, 2017—*Continued*

(Number; percent; dollars.)

State/County		Population 25 years and over						
	Total	Less than 9th grade (percent)	9th to 12th grade, no diploma (percent)	High school graduate (includes equivalency) (percent)	Some college, no degree (percent)	Associate's degree (percent)	Bachelor's degree (percent)	Graduate or professional degree (percent)
TENNESSEE—*(Continued)*								
Washington County, Tennessee	88,485	2.6	7.5	28.9	20.6	7.5	19.0	13.9
Williamson County, Tennessee	147,247	1.6	3.0	13.6	16.1	5.6	36.1	23.9
Wilson County, Tennessee	93,608	2.4	4.8	29.5	23.4	8.2	23.1	8.7
TEXAS								
Angelina County, Texas	57,108	6.4	10.5	30.7	26.5	9.5	10.8	5.5
Bastrop County, Texas	54,698	7.8	9.9	27.4	20.6	9.0	18.6	6.7
Bell County, Texas	210,326	3.1	5.0	24.8	27.8	12.3	17.6	9.3
Bexar County, Texas	1,249,712	6.9	8.4	25.8	22.8	8.3	17.5	10.3
Bowie County, Texas	62,638	2.5	6.5	36.2	25.9	6.7	15.0	7.2
Brazoria County, Texas	236,616	4.6	7.0	23.0	24.4	8.6	20.4	11.9
Brazos County, Texas	117,763	7.2	6.5	19.4	19.2	6.8	22.8	18.1
Cameron County, Texas	248,391	19.4	13.7	26.2	14.9	7.7	12.8	5.3
Collin County, Texas	635,534	2.9	3.3	14.6	19.8	7.4	33.3	18.6
Comal County, Texas	97,919	2.3	3.3	24.3	26.1	5.7	25.2	13.2
Coryell County, Texas	48,139	4.0	6.3	28.2	33.3	11.3	11.8	5.1
Dallas County, Texas	1,676,011	11.0	9.6	23.4	19.8	5.7	19.6	11.0
Denton County, Texas	547,898	3.5	3.8	17.0	21.4	8.3	30.4	15.7
Ector County, Texas	92,873	10.3	14.9	29.1	24.8	7.0	10.4	3.4
Ellis County, Texas	111,660	6.6	7.4	30.5	25.2	8.2	15.5	6.6
El Paso County, Texas	514,729	13.3	8.3	24.1	23.6	7.9	15.0	7.9
Fort Bend County, Texas	489,890	5.1	4.9	16.9	18.4	7.9	28.5	18.2
Galveston County, Texas	224,926	3.9	6.5	27.0	22.7	8.7	20.0	11.2
Grayson County, Texas	88,606	3.9	7.4	29.7	29.2	9.8	13.7	6.3
Gregg County, Texas	80,114	5.9	9.3	28.0	29.7	8.6	13.3	5.3
Guadalupe County, Texas	104,984	4.7	7.3	30.1	23.0	8.0	17.2	9.7
Harris County, Texas	2,970,857	10.4	8.5	23.3	20.0	7.0	19.7	11.1
Harrison County, Texas	43,830	3.3	9.2	33.9	27.4	6.9	13.6	5.7
Hays County, Texas	127,580	2.7	5.9	20.3	25.1	6.7	25.6	13.7
Henderson County, Texas	58,046	3.8	12.6	33.8	24.7	7.8	9.5	7.7
Hidalgo County, Texas	482,342	21.8	13.0	23.5	18.3	4.8	13.3	5.4
Hunt County, Texas	61,557	3.9	6.9	35.3	21.9	8.2	14.5	9.3
Jefferson County, Texas	168,924	6.3	8.0	32.2	27.5	7.0	12.8	6.1
Johnson County, Texas	109,599	4.2	10.0	34.2	25.0	8.1	13.1	5.4
Kaufman County, Texas	78,533	5.9	9.0	32.5	21.0	9.2	14.2	8.3
Liberty County, Texas	54,398	9.4	14.5	37.9	26.8	4.2	5.8	1.5
Lubbock County, Texas	180,516	5.7	8.1	26.2	23.6	6.5	18.9	11.0
McLennan County, Texas	153,289	7.2	9.2	25.7	23.5	9.8	16.4	8.2
Midland County, Texas	102,982	5.8	9.2	28.7	20.4	8.2	20.4	7.3
Montgomery County, Texas	373,508	4.9	6.4	24.1	24.2	7.4	22.1	11.0
Nacogdoches County, Texas	37,737	6.4	7.6	31.8	23.4	6.6	14.4	9.8
Nueces County, Texas	235,918	7.8	9.9	29.6	24.1	7.5	13.6	7.4
Orange County, Texas	56,420	2.6	10.2	34.6	30.3	7.3	12.5	2.6
Parker County, Texas	90,367	3.9	6.6	27.5	25.3	10.4	18.8	7.6
Potter County, Texas	76,901	11.3	12.7	32.4	19.7	7.9	10.7	5.3
Randall County, Texas	88,683	1.4	5.6	24.9	27.6	9.5	22.4	8.7
Rockwall County, Texas	63,099	3.6	6.1	15.9	20.1	11.7	25.6	17.0
San Patricio County, Texas	42,832	8.6	12.2	32.6	23.8	9.1	7.9	5.8
Smith County, Texas	148,537	5.6	7.2	21.5	28.8	10.0	18.4	8.3
Tarrant County, Texas	1,317,559	7.0	7.8	23.6	22.7	7.4	21.2	10.3
Taylor County, Texas	83,224	4.8	7.7	30.5	24.4	8.4	15.2	9.1
Tom Green County, Texas	76,794	5.2	5.8	31.8	26.3	7.6	15.5	7.8
Travis County, Texas	842,298	4.8	4.9	18.1	16.9	5.9	31.6	17.8
Victoria County, Texas	59,698	6.5	11.2	30.1	23.8	8.8	12.9	6.8
Walker County, Texas	46,843	4.9	7.3	40.9	17.5	6.8	15.8	6.9
Webb County, Texas	152,141	18.9	11.9	30.0	15.5	6.6	11.9	5.2
Wichita County, Texas	83,093	4.1	7.8	34.4	22.9	8.5	16.6	5.8
Williamson County, Texas	360,257	3.6	3.4	21.5	22.2	8.4	27.4	13.5
Wise County, Texas	44,568	6.6	11.5	35.8	21.1	10.3	9.3	5.5
UTAH								
Cache County, Utah	62,167	3.5	3.2	18.6	25.8	8.2	27.1	13.6
Davis County, Utah	204,090	1.1	3.0	21.2	26.0	9.9	26.5	12.4
Salt Lake County, Utah	716,783	3.2	5.8	22.1	24.3	8.6	22.8	13.2
Tooele County, Utah	38,992	0.9	8.0	25.6	27.7	10.4	18.0	9.5
Utah County, Utah	299,761	2.0	3.6	15.2	26.8	10.6	28.9	12.9
Washington County, Utah	107,235	4.3	5.8	22.7	28.4	11.9	17.4	9.5
Weber County, Utah	154,572	3.7	6.9	28.6	26.3	9.2	17.2	8.2

Table C-2. Educational Attainment of the Population, by Selected Counties, 2017—*Continued*

(Number; percent; dollars.)

State/County		Population 18 to 24 years			
	Total	Less than high school graduate (percent)	High school graduate (includes equivalency) (percent)	Some college or associate's degree (percent)	Bachelor's degree or higher (percent)
VERMONT					
Chittenden County, Vermont	25,988	6.7	23.4	52.4	17.4
VIRGINIA					
Albemarle County, Virginia	14,250	4.9	40.1	41.3	13.7
Arlington County, Virginia	19,316	6.6	12.8	22.3	58.3
Augusta County, Virginia	5,467	22.2	44.1	21.0	12.7
Bedford County, Virginia	5,516	3.6	49.8	40.3	6.3
Chesterfield County, Virginia	29,864	14.0	31.6	46.0	8.4
Fairfax County, Virginia	95,698	12.6	23.8	40.2	23.4
Fauquier County, Virginia	4,990	7.2	34.9	40.7	17.2
Frederick County, Virginia	6,884	17.0	32.9	39.7	10.4
Hanover County, Virginia	9,101	9.8	32.8	45.8	11.6
Henrico County, Virginia	25,896	9.3	32.4	37.2	21.0
James City County, Virginia	6,724	2.4	29.0	56.1	12.6
Loudoun County, Virginia	28,481	12.2	29.9	40.4	17.5
Montgomery County, Virginia	29,100	1.5	11.6	73.6	13.3
Prince William County, Virginia	40,379	14.1	30.6	45.0	10.3
Roanoke County, Virginia	7,853	13.5	25.7	40.9	19.9
Rockingham County, Virginia	7,924	21.9	31.8	37.8	8.5
Spotsylvania County, Virginia	11,654	16.8	32.2	41.2	9.7
Stafford County, Virginia	15,349	16.2	35.1	39.2	9.4
York County, Virginia	5,979	3.4	30.3	42.6	23.7
Alexandria city, Virginia	9,465	11.0	31.4	33.3	24.3
Chesapeake city, Virginia	21,185	11.0	32.2	43.3	13.4
Hampton city, Virginia	15,755	9.6	34.5	54.6	1.2
Lynchburg city, Virginia	20,804	5.0	25.9	57.1	12.0
Newport News city, Virginia	21,457	2.4	31.5	56.8	9.4
Norfolk city, Virginia	44,380	4.2	28.2	59.0	8.6
Portsmouth city, Virginia	9,336	15.1	44.6	33.7	6.5
Richmond city, Virginia	29,416	7.6	24.8	53.6	14.0
Roanoke city, Virginia	6,831	14.8	30.6	46.0	8.6
Suffolk city, Virginia	6,373	10.4	52.2	28.2	9.3
Virginia Beach city, Virginia	42,623	6.6	32.8	47.9	12.6
WASHINGTON					
Benton County, Washington	16,574	17.4	33.4	44.6	4.6
Chelan County, Washington	6,889	48.9	20.1	27.4	3.7
Clallam County, Washington	4,686	11.0	51.5	33.7	3.8
Clark County, Washington	37,340	13.1	38.2	41.3	7.4
Cowlitz County, Washington	7,671	15.3	38.3	42.8	3.5
Franklin County, Washington	9,084	9.8	42.0	41.5	6.8
Grant County, Washington	9,464	25.1	33.6	29.9	11.4
Grays Harbor County, Washington	4,772	13.9	36.5	42.1	7.5
Island County, Washington	7,047	11.1	36.7	50.2	2.0
King County, Washington	178,561	12.1	25.8	42.0	20.2
Kitsap County, Washington	26,459	12.1	40.8	41.8	5.3
Lewis County, Washington	5,520	23.3	28.9	45.0	2.9
Pierce County, Washington	79,909	15.7	38.8	37.3	8.2
Skagit County, Washington	9,794	15.1	35.0	45.4	4.5
Snohomish County, Washington	64,158	16.0	32.9	39.8	11.3
Spokane County, Washington	49,541	10.2	29.3	53.5	6.9
Thurston County, Washington	23,186	15.3	31.8	45.3	7.6
Whatcom County, Washington	30,964	4.2	23.0	64.7	8.1
Yakima County, Washington	24,004	26.2	35.3	33.8	4.8
WEST VIRGINIA					
Berkeley County, West Virginia	9,882	23.0	33.7	39.7	3.7
Cabell County, West Virginia	12,397	9.7	36.1	41.7	12.5
Harrison County, West Virginia	4,947	22.2	36.6	31.2	10.0
Kanawha County, West Virginia	13,004	12.6	47.4	36.2	3.9
Monongalia County, West Virginia	22,705	4.9	19.1	61.7	14.3
Raleigh County, West Virginia	5,927	6.9	46.0	41.8	5.4
Wood County, West Virginia	6,439	12.7	33.1	45.0	9.2
WISCONSIN					
Brown County, Wisconsin	24,093	14.2	35.9	37.9	12.0
Dane County, Wisconsin	75,117	6.4	23.5	44.8	25.3
Dodge County, Wisconsin	6,540	13.1	34.5	46.8	5.6
Eau Claire County, Wisconsin	17,239	5.5	28.4	56.7	9.4

Table C-2. Educational Attainment of the Population, by Selected Counties, 2017—*Continued*

(Number; percent; dollars.)

State/County	Total	Population 25 years and over						
		Less than 9th grade (percent)	9th to 12th grade, no diploma (percent)	High school graduate (includes equivalency) (percent)	Some college, no degree (percent)	Associate's degree (percent)	Bachelor's degree (percent)	Graduate or professional degree (percent)
VERMONT								
Chittenden County, Vermont	107,316	2.3	3.7	20.9	15.5	9.4	28.1	20.1
VIRGINIA								
Albemarle County, Virginia	71,816	2.4	5.5	16.7	15.8	4.4	32.2	23.0
Arlington County, Virginia	173,672	4.3	2.3	7.5	6.6	3.5	35.5	40.5
Augusta County, Virginia	55,201	3.9	8.2	44.0	16.3	6.3	11.3	9.9
Bedford County, Virginia	57,443	3.3	4.9	34.8	21.0	9.0	16.4	10.7
Chesterfield County, Virginia	231,679	2.7	4.8	24.2	19.7	8.8	25.4	14.5
Fairfax County, Virginia	783,902	4.3	3.1	13.7	12.2	5.4	30.8	30.6
Fauquier County, Virginia	47,766	2.5	4.4	28.6	19.9	10.0	22.7	11.9
Frederick County, Virginia	59,491	4.6	7.4	31.0	20.3	9.6	16.5	10.6
Hanover County, Virginia	73,296	1.6	5.8	27.2	18.9	7.8	25.7	12.9
Henrico County, Virginia	226,995	3.1	4.9	20.5	18.4	7.7	26.5	18.9
James City County, Virginia	52,836	1.9	5.1	16.8	17.1	8.2	27.5	23.5
Loudoun County, Virginia	256,261	3.1	3.0	12.8	13.8	5.3	34.8	27.3
Montgomery County, Virginia	54,570	1.1	6.7	27.9	18.1	4.6	19.5	22.1
Prince William County, Virginia	296,482	6.1	5.4	22.0	18.5	7.9	23.7	16.3
Roanoke County, Virginia	67,516	3.5	3.9	26.1	20.4	11.4	23.9	10.9
Rockingham County, Virginia	54,479	7.9	9.1	38.0	14.2	6.0	14.2	10.5
Spotsylvania County, Virginia	88,100	2.5	5.9	28.1	21.9	8.2	21.3	12.1
Stafford County, Virginia	92,927	2.6	3.8	21.0	22.1	9.2	24.9	16.4
York County, Virginia	45,602	1.7	3.6	18.7	21.2	9.6	25.8	19.4
Alexandria city, Virginia	121,705	5.5	2.8	11.5	12.2	5.6	31.3	31.2
Chesapeake city, Virginia	160,787	1.3	4.4	24.4	24.7	10.1	21.0	14.1
Hampton city, Virginia	90,781	2.0	6.2	26.8	28.2	8.7	16.4	11.7
Lynchburg city, Virginia	44,468	4.5	7.1	23.6	21.8	9.7	20.9	12.4
Newport News city, Virginia	116,240	3.3	6.7	28.9	25.7	10.1	16.6	8.7
Norfolk city, Virginia	151,907	3.6	8.9	24.8	24.4	9.2	18.0	11.1
Portsmouth city, Virginia	63,441	3.6	6.8	30.1	28.4	8.7	14.7	7.7
Richmond city, Virginia	157,287	5.1	9.8	22.4	20.0	4.0	23.0	15.6
Roanoke city, Virginia	71,363	6.4	9.5	29.8	20.2	10.9	13.2	10.0
Suffolk city, Virginia	61,850	4.0	7.9	28.5	24.0	9.5	14.5	11.6
Virginia Beach city, Virginia	307,404	2.0	4.4	21.6	25.4	11.1	22.2	13.1
WASHINGTON								
Benton County, Washington	128,629	5.5	5.8	24.9	25.0	9.0	17.8	11.9
Chelan County, Washington	51,163	7.6	9.2	24.3	23.6	8.3	17.1	9.9
Clallam County, Washington	58,010	1.7	6.1	26.7	28.9	10.0	14.4	12.2
Clark County, Washington	321,884	2.0	5.1	23.6	26.6	11.1	20.7	10.9
Cowlitz County, Washington	74,724	2.0	9.2	29.5	31.4	10.7	10.0	7.3
Franklin County, Washington	53,630	14.9	8.1	26.8	25.7	8.5	11.4	4.7
Grant County, Washington	57,386	14.6	9.0	28.2	23.0	8.5	10.4	6.3
Grays Harbor County, Washington	52,905	3.7	7.0	34.8	29.2	11.4	9.4	4.6
Island County, Washington	60,812	1.3	3.3	23.7	29.8	8.7	20.4	12.8
King County, Washington	1,562,740	3.7	3.5	15.3	17.9	8.2	30.8	20.7
Kitsap County, Washington	184,874	1.9	4.3	22.1	28.2	9.9	21.5	12.0
Lewis County, Washington	55,737	4.3	8.1	28.1	29.0	12.8	9.9	7.8
Pierce County, Washington	589,927	2.6	5.8	28.5	25.7	11.5	16.7	9.3
Skagit County, Washington	87,956	4.9	5.2	25.8	24.7	11.3	17.9	10.1
Snohomish County, Washington	555,239	2.5	4.7	23.5	26.4	11.0	22.1	9.8
Spokane County, Washington	344,221	1.9	4.3	23.1	25.7	14.3	19.6	11.3
Thurston County, Washington	196,131	2.0	3.3	21.0	27.2	10.8	22.1	13.6
Whatcom County, Washington	147,244	2.3	4.1	21.6	24.1	12.1	24.9	10.9
Yakima County, Washington	151,817	15.1	11.8	25.9	21.3	8.2	10.6	7.0
WEST VIRGINIA								
Berkeley County, West Virginia	77,936	3.9	5.3	37.7	22.4	9.0	15.3	6.4
Cabell County, West Virginia	63,735	3.4	7.7	35.7	19.6	6.5	16.9	10.1
Harrison County, West Virginia	48,218	4.0	6.9	39.0	21.2	7.6	12.8	8.5
Kanawha County, West Virginia	132,494	3.1	8.4	36.8	18.8	7.2	15.7	9.9
Monongalia County, West Virginia	65,107	1.5	7.1	25.4	19.6	5.2	21.9	19.3
Raleigh County, West Virginia	53,372	3.4	7.4	41.5	21.4	6.1	13.8	6.5
Wood County, West Virginia	60,456	3.7	6.5	34.2	21.0	12.3	13.9	8.3
WISCONSIN								
Brown County, Wisconsin	175,030	3.0	5.8	28.0	17.6	12.3	21.7	11.6
Dane County, Wisconsin	350,461	1.1	2.7	17.4	17.1	10.3	30.0	21.5
Dodge County, Wisconsin	63,479	2.5	6.6	41.2	21.7	11.8	11.6	4.7
Eau Claire County, Wisconsin	65,449	3.4	3.0	24.7	20.9	15.2	19.9	12.9

Table C-2. Educational Attainment of the Population, by Selected Counties, 2017—*Continued*

(Number; percent; dollars.)

State/County	Population 18 to 24 years				
	Total	Less than high school graduate (percent)	High school graduate (includes equivalency) (percent)	Some college or associate's degree (percent)	Bachelor's degree or higher (percent)
WISCONSIN—(*Continued*)					
Fond du Lac County, Wisconsin...........................	8,730	10.2	39.2	46.4	4.1
Jefferson County, Wisconsin................................	7,875	11.8	30.9	52.2	5.2
Kenosha County, Wisconsin.................................	16,581	11.4	42.9	35.3	10.4
La Crosse County, Wisconsin..............................	18,867	4.9	28.1	56.1	10.8
Manitowoc County, Wisconsin.............................	5,896	10.1	41.3	39.4	9.2
Marathon County, Wisconsin..............................	10,684	10.0	47.6	35.1	7.4
Milwaukee County, Wisconsin.............................	92,658	12.5	31.6	45.8	10.1
Outagamie County, Wisconsin	15,498	9.7	35.2	48.2	6.9
Ozaukee County, Wisconsin	7,778	9.9	26.1	48.3	15.7
Portage County, Wisconsin	12,057	3.8	27.2	64.1	4.9
Racine County, Wisconsin...................................	17,666	15.5	37.0	41.7	5.9
Rock County, Wisconsin	13,883	10.0	41.2	45.3	3.5
St. Croix County, Wisconsin................................	6,556	10.0	33.8	48.4	7.9
Sheboygan County, Wisconsin............................	9,707	13.8	38.2	41.4	6.6
Walworth County, Wisconsin	13,189	7.5	28.3	57.1	7.2
Washington County, Wisconsin	9,796	15.1	32.5	36.2	16.1
Waukesha County, Wisconsin	30,968	9.2	34.0	42.1	14.7
Winnebago County, Wisconsin	20,814	6.8	29.9	54.9	8.3
Wood County, Wisconsin....................................	5,019	14.8	25.7	53.8	5.6
WYOMING					
Laramie County, Wyoming.................................	8,202	10.7	36.5	47.2	5.6
Natrona County, Wyoming	5,570	11.5	57.3	26.5	4.7

Table C-2. Educational Attainment of the Population, by Selected Counties, 2017—*Continued*

(Number; percent; dollars.)

State/County	Population 25 years and over							
	Total	Less than 9th grade (percent)	9th to 12th grade, no diploma (percent)	High school graduate (includes equivalency) (percent)	Some college, no degree (percent)	Associate's degree (percent)	Bachelor's degree (percent)	Graduate or professional degree (percent)
WISCONSIN—(*Continued*)								
Fond du Lac County, Wisconsin............................	72,046	2.7	5.2	34.9	20.3	12.1	16.9	7.8
Jefferson County, Wisconsin...............................	58,912	2.9	5.6	29.9	22.6	13.8	16.5	8.6
Kenosha County, Wisconsin................................	112,806	3.8	5.6	31.7	22.9	10.2	16.9	8.8
La Crosse County, Wisconsin..............................	75,844	2.7	4.1	27.3	20.4	13.6	22.0	9.8
Manitowoc County, Wisconsin.............................	56,759	2.2	4.9	35.3	23.8	14.9	13.3	5.6
Marathon County, Wisconsin..............................	93,819	3.5	4.4	34.3	18.1	14.0	16.6	9.2
Milwaukee County, Wisconsin.............................	630,803	4.2	7.2	29.9	20.4	7.7	19.3	11.4
Outagamie County, Wisconsin	126,394	1.6	4.3	29.8	19.8	14.5	20.1	9.9
Ozaukee County, Wisconsin	61,827	2.1	3.1	19.3	17.6	7.3	30.8	19.9
Portage County, Wisconsin.................................	44,911	2.4	3.3	31.7	19.6	9.7	24.2	9.1
Racine County, Wisconsin..................................	132,881	2.8	5.2	31.4	23.3	9.4	18.3	9.5
Rock County, Wisconsin.....................................	110,328	3.0	6.3	36.7	20.2	12.5	14.7	6.6
St. Croix County, Wisconsin...............................	59,401	1.1	2.7	27.1	20.8	13.0	23.8	11.5
Sheboygan County, Wisconsin............................	79,984	2.3	4.5	34.9	21.4	11.7	17.6	7.6
Walworth County, Wisconsin	68,366	2.8	6.2	30.5	22.3	7.9	19.1	11.1
Washington County, Wisconsin	95,324	1.6	3.1	29.7	23.7	10.8	22.3	8.7
Waukesha County, Wisconsin.............................	282,781	1.2	2.5	22.6	18.8	9.4	30.4	15.1
Winnebago County, Wisconsin	114,495	1.3	4.9	35.4	19.1	9.8	20.4	9.0
Wood County, Wisconsin....................................	52,345	1.7	4.9	36.7	23.2	12.7	13.1	7.7
WYOMING								
Laramie County, Wyoming.................................	67,446	1.9	6.1	25.7	25.1	13.1	16.0	11.9
Natrona County, Wyoming	53,481	1.8	5.1	28.8	27.4	12.7	15.8	8.5

Table C-2. Educational Attainment of the Population, by Selected Counties, 2017—*Continued*

(Number; percent; dollars.)

State/County	Population 25 to 34 years			Population 35 to 44 years		
	Total	High school graduate or more (percent)	Bachelor's degree or more (percent)	Total	High school graduate or more (percent)	Bachelor's degree or more (percent)
ALABAMA						
Baldwin County, Alabama	25,425	83.9	30.9	26,549	93.9	40.1
Calhoun County, Alabama	15,103	85.8	15.6	14,286	88.9	22.6
Cullman County, Alabama	10,397	88.2	10.0	10,128	78.4	14.4
DeKalb County, Alabama	7,890	78.8	15.7	9,452	79.2	14.1
Elmore County, Alabama	10,357	78.6	17.8	11,367	85.3	26.0
Etowah County, Alabama	12,259	88.9	16.7	12,597	79.8	28.9
Houston County, Alabama	13,907	92.8	26.7	12,592	90.4	20.5
Jefferson County, Alabama	93,773	92.1	40.5	82,879	91.2	35.4
Lauderdale County, Alabama	11,256	90.7	26.4	10,280	90.0	31.7
Lee County, Alabama	24,102	97.6	31.3	18,031	91.9	34.4
Limestone County, Alabama	12,776	92.5	34.8	12,020	89.1	29.7
Madison County, Alabama	50,080	90.6	34.9	44,610	92.1	44.4
Marshall County, Alabama	11,924	76.3	15.4	11,176	78.3	16.5
Mobile County, Alabama	56,688	87.3	24.3	49,489	91.5	26.8
Montgomery County, Alabama	32,474	84.4	29.4	28,793	89.7	32.9
Morgan County, Alabama	14,949	85.2	15.8	14,964	92.5	19.7
St. Clair County, Alabama	11,413	87.3	12.2	11,543	84.9	23.3
Shelby County, Alabama	25,294	94.8	46.9	29,940	93.0	49.2
Talladega County, Alabama	9,992	84.9	3.2	10,263	92.2	20.2
Tuscaloosa County, Alabama	30,197	88.4	42.7	24,274	87.8	31.0
Walker County, Alabama	7,676	90.9	19.1	6,914	76.4	15.2
ALASKA						
Anchorage Municipality, Alaska	50,018	91.8	31.0	41,496	94.3	37.4
Fairbanks North Star Borough, Alaska	19,456	89.4	21.7	12,194	98.8	35.3
Matanuska-Susitna Borough, Alaska	14,308	92.6	16.3	14,151	93.0	20.7
ARIZONA						
Apache County, Arizona	8,975	93.8	9.4	7,860	85.4	14.3
Cochise County, Arizona	15,800	89.8	22.0	13,156	92.5	26.7
Coconino County, Arizona	19,077	91.6	35.4	15,580	89.9	33.8
Maricopa County, Arizona	623,248	89.3	31.9	560,348	85.7	34.8
Mohave County, Arizona	20,950	80.6	11.7	18,501	81.3	17.1
Navajo County, Arizona	11,803	81.6	8.5	11,791	91.9	16.0
Pima County, Arizona	128,248	92.0	33.3	116,606	88.8	32.0
Pinal County, Arizona	56,470	80.6	16.4	56,805	84.2	19.7
Yavapai County, Arizona	21,016	91.7	18.9	20,243	84.7	18.3
Yuma County, Arizona	28,471	82.2	14.8	22,505	75.3	17.4
ARKANSAS						
Benton County, Arkansas	39,291	91.6	37.2	38,065	87.4	37.2
Craighead County, Arkansas	16,245	95.2	33.7	14,267	90.8	30.1
Faulkner County, Arkansas	17,082	94.5	40.5	14,358	94.4	33.3
Garland County, Arkansas	11,426	92.1	15.8	10,393	88.4	19.2
Jefferson County, Arkansas	8,657	83.4	17.0	7,849	90.0	16.7
Lonoke County, Arkansas	10,447	92.9	23.4	9,723	95.4	25.7
Pulaski County, Arkansas	58,707	93.3	35.9	50,140	92.4	44.9
Saline County, Arkansas	15,708	90.6	24.4	16,134	93.7	30.9
Sebastian County, Arkansas	15,518	86.8	25.4	14,980	80.0	19.2
Washington County, Arkansas	33,837	88.6	41.4	32,084	79.1	33.2
White County, Arkansas	9,288	89.8	23.2	9,401	88.3	29.3
CALIFORNIA						
Alameda County, California	277,096	92.5	54.6	248,521	88.8	52.7
Butte County, California	29,298	94.6	22.8	25,783	86.7	23.5
Contra Costa County, California	146,524	90.8	36.6	153,578	85.6	44.5
El Dorado County, California	18,976	89.5	34.9	21,815	88.2	41.2
Fresno County, California	151,781	83.4	20.9	123,214	74.6	20.2
Humboldt County, California	16,864	89.7	26.3	18,262	91.5	43.3
Imperial County, California	26,875	83.0	22.8	22,081	79.5	15.3
Kern County, California	139,012	81.6	13.0	113,052	70.4	16.9
Kings County, California	26,108	78.3	11.1	20,181	74.9	13.9
Lake County, California	6,788	94.4	11.1	7,792	77.7	7.5
Los Angeles County, California	1,639,556	89.2	37.7	1,388,427	80.3	35.4
Madera County, California	22,530	74.8	9.0	20,099	62.1	15.4
Marin County, California	22,840	88.6	49.5	31,176	91.4	63.0
Mendocino County, California	10,706	88.1	16.7	10,288	83.7	27.2
Merced County, California	39,802	79.8	15.2	33,294	70.1	10.2
Monterey County, California	63,128	76.0	22.8	57,309	62.8	22.0
Napa County, California	17,295	90.5	34.3	17,973	83.9	36.0

Table C-2. Educational Attainment of the Population, by Selected Counties, 2017—*Continued*

(Number; percent; dollars.)

State/County	Population 45 to 64 years			Population 65 years and over		
	Total	High school graduate or more (percent)	Bachelor's degree or more (percent)	Total	High school graduate or more (percent)	Bachelor's degree or more (percent)
ALABAMA						
Baldwin County, Alabama	57,561	91.4	35.4	42,502	86.7	28.6
Calhoun County, Alabama	30,218	84.5	18.9	19,975	83.5	20.4
Cullman County, Alabama	22,515	84.0	13.6	14,876	77.8	10.8
DeKalb County, Alabama	18,298	78.7	16.3	11,964	72.7	13.8
Elmore County, Alabama	21,935	91.2	27.1	12,123	86.4	25.7
Etowah County, Alabama	27,783	87.8	17.6	19,207	77.9	17.2
Houston County, Alabama	27,668	85.7	21.6	17,982	82.3	20.1
Jefferson County, Alabama	170,376	91.2	31.2	101,082	84.6	28.5
Lauderdale County, Alabama	24,075	87.0	20.7	18,314	87.8	22.6
Lee County, Alabama	35,886	91.4	31.5	18,816	84.5	38.8
Limestone County, Alabama	25,710	91.6	30.8	14,513	75.1	21.1
Madison County, Alabama	99,653	94.1	46.7	53,250	85.5	34.8
Marshall County, Alabama	23,710	84.1	20.1	15,862	81.2	25.1
Mobile County, Alabama	106,630	89.4	22.4	65,448	81.2	20.3
Montgomery County, Alabama	56,210	87.5	34.2	33,065	81.8	33.3
Morgan County, Alabama	31,409	84.0	23.8	20,839	86.9	17.0
St. Clair County, Alabama	24,350	89.0	19.9	14,595	81.5	8.2
Shelby County, Alabama	57,371	94.3	44.4	32,155	89.0	33.1
Talladega County, Alabama	22,003	84.0	14.9	13,935	75.9	16.9
Tuscaloosa County, Alabama	47,798	87.1	33.1	26,727	80.5	22.0
Walker County, Alabama	18,189	83.9	7.2	12,058	77.6	11.3
ALASKA						
Anchorage Municipality, Alaska	69,991	93.3	35.8	30,961	88.4	36.9
Fairbanks North Star Borough, Alaska	20,735	93.9	30.4	9,529	91.8	36.8
Matanuska-Susitna Borough, Alaska	27,353	90.4	23.2	12,161	91.0	26.8
ARIZONA						
Apache County, Arizona	16,984	79.6	12.5	10,753	62.1	12.2
Cochise County, Arizona	31,039	87.3	22.5	26,816	86.3	27.9
Coconino County, Arizona	32,103	93.1	35.6	16,672	88.4	45.9
Maricopa County, Arizona	1,042,244	86.7	31.8	638,636	89.1	31.1
Mohave County, Arizona	57,779	86.4	12.0	61,550	89.6	14.4
Navajo County, Arizona	28,043	82.2	17.7	18,408	81.1	26.2
Pima County, Arizona	243,056	88.8	31.5	196,523	89.0	37.2
Pinal County, Arizona	98,230	86.6	19.0	86,066	85.2	22.0
Yavapai County, Arizona	64,392	89.2	20.9	70,278	93.7	29.2
Yuma County, Arizona	42,546	67.0	13.6	37,750	69.0	10.2
ARKANSAS						
Benton County, Arkansas	61,955	88.5	32.4	34,885	89.6	29.5
Craighead County, Arkansas	23,799	94.4	25.8	15,020	72.9	21.1
Faulkner County, Arkansas	29,261	91.1	32.4	15,272	90.2	24.5
Garland County, Arkansas	26,017	87.1	18.2	23,599	88.0	22.9
Jefferson County, Arkansas	18,242	91.5	21.0	11,676	82.4	16.3
Lonoke County, Arkansas	18,276	88.3	24.8	9,616	86.4	18.6
Pulaski County, Arkansas	99,762	90.5	33.0	59,055	89.0	27.8
Saline County, Arkansas	30,187	92.8	26.6	20,457	89.9	21.3
Sebastian County, Arkansas	35,194	83.9	23.0	19,346	83.3	18.2
Washington County, Arkansas	47,737	81.0	25.2	26,347	87.3	34.8
White County, Arkansas	20,110	82.0	21.3	12,543	79.2	22.4
CALIFORNIA						
Alameda County, California	428,265	87.7	42.9	224,171	82.1	36.2
Butte County, California	54,597	88.6	25.9	41,423	89.8	32.2
Contra Costa County, California	315,345	89.2	44.1	175,664	88.4	41.2
El Dorado County, California	58,034	94.4	32.3	38,457	95.5	32.9
Fresno County, California	215,018	74.0	19.3	118,520	73.1	21.9
Humboldt County, California	34,056	90.1	30.0	23,095	95.3	36.6
Imperial County, California	38,694	72.1	13.1	23,604	49.4	9.3
Kern County, California	195,398	70.5	16.0	94,975	69.8	19.4
Kings County, California	31,924	70.9	14.3	14,910	68.6	13.6
Lake County, California	19,210	85.8	14.2	14,239	89.0	17.6
Los Angeles County, California	2,583,175	75.9	29.3	1,343,961	72.6	28.2
Madera County, California	35,575	72.7	18.7	21,213	72.2	15.9
Marin County, California	80,819	96.6	64.1	56,800	94.5	51.9
Mendocino County, California	22,832	89.9	20.3	19,007	91.7	37.9
Merced County, California	59,063	64.9	13.7	29,894	61.3	13.8
Monterey County, California	100,259	68.6	22.2	57,822	77.1	34.2
Napa County, California	37,286	84.6	35.6	26,060	85.9	38.3

Table C-2. Educational Attainment of the Population, by Selected Counties, 2017—*Continued*

(Number; percent; dollars.)

State/County	Population 25 to 34 years			Population 35 to 44 years		
	Total	High school graduate or more (percent)	Bachelor's degree or more (percent)	Total	High school graduate or more (percent)	Bachelor's degree or more (percent)
CALIFORNIA—(*Continued*)						
Nevada County, California	9,666	92.0	25.7	11,253	96.8	42.2
Orange County, California	461,007	89.7	42.6	414,137	84.4	44.2
Placer County, California	42,555	94.3	32.5	49,674	95.4	44.3
Riverside County, California	336,737	89.3	20.0	308,515	82.4	22.1
Sacramento County, California	240,672	90.8	31.7	201,246	87.9	32.1
San Bernardino County, California	327,565	88.0	21.4	276,420	79.5	21.9
San Diego County, California	549,650	92.6	40.3	444,445	88.2	42.0
San Francisco County, California	207,492	97.0	75.2	138,769	94.2	68.6
San Joaquin County, California	104,130	85.2	17.9	96,899	83.0	21.1
San Luis Obispo County, California	32,239	93.2	31.4	30,008	88.8	33.1
San Mateo County, California	114,948	94.5	57.7	110,336	92.4	59.2
Santa Barbara County, California	59,383	82.8	33.1	50,396	76.1	33.5
Santa Clara County, California	311,887	93.6	60.5	280,115	89.5	57.2
Santa Cruz County, California	33,348	88.2	34.0	32,770	80.2	45.5
Shasta County, California	22,294	90.2	24.5	19,255	92.9	31.6
Solano County, California	65,557	88.7	24.3	55,779	88.0	27.3
Sonoma County, California	66,635	89.2	30.8	62,955	86.1	34.9
Stanislaus County, California	80,217	90.0	16.8	68,288	79.2	20.4
Sutter County, California	14,657	91.0	16.2	11,319	77.1	11.0
Tulare County, California	66,334	82.2	12.0	57,893	68.7	14.6
Ventura County, California	113,653	89.2	30.2	105,819	83.2	32.0
Yolo County, California	29,511	91.6	36.9	25,976	87.9	39.6
Yuba County, California	12,374	89.0	23.2	10,362	77.1	18.0
COLORADO						
Adams County, Colorado	81,747	86.3	26.8	74,053	82.1	24.6
Arapahoe County, Colorado	99,666	92.9	44.0	91,408	89.3	45.4
Boulder County, Colorado	43,996	96.2	63.9	40,514	92.0	60.7
Broomfield County, Colorado	9,990	99.1	57.8	10,010	98.8	69.1
Denver County, Colorado	161,633	93.8	59.2	111,783	87.1	51.8
Douglas County, Colorado	36,930	97.5	58.7	50,763	98.7	65.5
El Paso County, Colorado	109,108	94.2	31.5	89,883	92.7	45.9
Jefferson County, Colorado	83,051	94.6	46.8	77,210	94.8	51.3
Larimer County, Colorado	50,343	96.3	44.1	41,501	91.2	53.4
Mesa County, Colorado	18,495	92.7	20.6	18,690	85.4	23.2
Pueblo County, Colorado	21,897	91.2	20.1	18,881	91.6	27.7
Weld County, Colorado	46,408	88.4	31.2	40,703	88.2	27.6
CONNECTICUT						
Fairfield County, Connecticut	108,583	89.5	46.6	117,937	89.9	49.3
Hartford County, Connecticut	118,202	90.8	42.4	109,091	91.4	44.7
Litchfield County, Connecticut	19,845	95.8	36.6	18,937	96.5	44.2
Middlesex County, Connecticut	18,019	98.1	43.4	18,059	97.2	48.2
New Haven County, Connecticut	114,823	93.1	42.8	100,513	92.3	39.3
New London County, Connecticut	34,032	92.5	33.9	27,889	94.9	36.1
Tolland County, Connecticut	16,907	95.7	47.2	14,803	98.8	51.2
Windham County, Connecticut	13,730	92.0	29.6	14,151	88.8	29.2
DELAWARE						
Kent County, Delaware	24,147	93.4	26.9	20,485	82.5	19.1
New Castle County, Delaware	82,145	91.6	34.3	68,271	92.5	40.3
Sussex County, Delaware	24,657	90.9	23.1	22,312	80.9	22.9
DISTRICT OF COLUMBIA						
District of Columbia, District of Columbia	162,354	95.7	72.3	102,128	90.1	62.4
FLORIDA						
Alachua County, Florida	40,752	96.0	44.6	29,672	89.4	51.0
Bay County, Florida	25,237	92.2	25.9	22,296	92.5	26.1
Brevard County, Florida	64,880	96.2	29.3	60,326	91.0	33.2
Broward County, Florida	262,479	92.8	33.6	257,255	92.6	37.8
Charlotte County, Florida	13,565	88.7	20.6	14,285	91.3	22.3
Citrus County, Florida	11,016	80.5	11.3	12,395	88.6	15.9
Clay County, Florida	24,044	85.7	14.8	28,037	90.5	26.4
Collier County, Florida	36,119	85.5	25.0	36,191	82.3	27.7
Columbia County, Florida	8,275	84.9	18.1	9,011	87.4	13.5
Duval County, Florida	155,646	90.8	32.2	117,723	91.3	33.5
Escambia County, Florida	45,826	92.7	27.7	34,832	87.5	26.1
Flagler County, Florida	9,362	98.7	19.1	11,323	97.8	21.5

Table C-2. Educational Attainment of the Population, by Selected Counties, 2017—*Continued*

(Number; percent; dollars.)

State/County	Population 45 to 64 years			Population 65 years and over		
	Total	High school graduate or more (percent)	Bachelor's degree or more (percent)	Total	High school graduate or more (percent)	Bachelor's degree or more (percent)
CALIFORNIA—(*Continued*)						
Nevada County, California	29,577	96.9	37.5	26,455	92.4	38.1
Orange County, California	855,163	83.3	38.4	457,031	84.1	37.9
Placer County, California	105,130	95.5	38.6	73,917	92.7	33.1
Riverside County, California	581,988	78.6	21.4	340,372	81.7	25.8
Sacramento County, California	383,202	86.4	29.8	209,286	85.1	29.2
San Bernardino County, California	511,256	77.8	19.8	242,712	74.1	19.2
San Diego County, California	814,117	86.0	37.1	454,528	83.8	36.8
San Francisco County, California	220,039	85.2	47.1	136,225	73.8	37.8
San Joaquin County, California	176,103	80.9	18.6	93,442	74.8	18.2
San Luis Obispo County, California	71,658	90.5	33.1	55,106	95.1	39.1
San Mateo County, California	208,069	89.6	49.7	122,207	85.8	42.4
Santa Barbara County, California	100,948	79.5	34.5	66,410	84.5	39.7
Santa Clara County, California	497,154	87.5	48.1	255,147	83.0	42.0
Santa Cruz County, California	72,291	87.1	39.4	42,998	89.6	42.2
Shasta County, California	48,312	91.8	21.5	36,596	88.1	19.6
Solano County, California	118,018	85.6	25.9	67,283	86.8	29.5
Sonoma County, California	138,199	88.4	35.5	94,943	93.0	40.4
Stanislaus County, California	127,823	75.6	16.8	70,823	73.3	16.8
Sutter County, California	23,341	77.0	21.2	14,546	71.3	15.0
Tulare County, California	98,849	66.2	15.3	50,932	65.3	14.8
Ventura County, California	227,191	83.9	35.1	127,712	85.3	34.6
Yolo County, California	46,202	85.4	40.0	26,467	80.5	38.0
Yuba County, California	18,342	77.5	16.6	8,584	76.2	12.7
COLORADO						
Adams County, Colorado	116,682	83.3	21.0	51,703	85.0	18.4
Arapahoe County, Colorado	164,344	92.8	42.7	81,197	92.4	43.5
Boulder County, Colorado	83,585	96.3	66.1	44,138	96.0	59.2
Broomfield County, Colorado	18,333	96.3	52.7	8,827	93.7	41.3
Denver County, Colorado	152,373	85.4	40.9	81,875	85.2	42.1
Douglas County, Colorado	95,865	98.2	58.5	38,346	96.7	49.1
El Paso County, Colorado	166,257	95.6	41.1	86,964	90.4	38.3
Jefferson County, Colorado	162,901	94.9	43.9	91,969	94.0	42.7
Larimer County, Colorado	82,587	96.5	50.3	52,023	95.8	43.5
Mesa County, Colorado	37,251	94.5	29.7	28,772	90.9	25.9
Pueblo County, Colorado	42,786	93.0	20.0	29,928	88.6	23.2
Weld County, Colorado	72,679	87.3	27.3	35,963	85.5	23.2
CONNECTICUT						
Fairfield County, Connecticut	273,692	90.3	50.6	147,513	85.5	39.4
Hartford County, Connecticut	247,702	90.6	36.8	150,280	84.5	30.6
Litchfield County, Connecticut	60,961	92.3	33.8	36,671	89.6	37.0
Middlesex County, Connecticut	51,130	94.6	39.0	32,134	90.9	34.1
New Haven County, Connecticut	237,947	91.9	31.7	145,577	85.8	27.8
New London County, Connecticut	79,499	93.8	34.2	47,190	87.0	30.1
Tolland County, Connecticut	42,236	96.4	35.6	22,540	91.2	35.5
Windham County, Connecticut	34,072	88.0	19.6	19,189	85.3	25.2
DELAWARE						
Kent County, Delaware	44,683	88.6	22.1	29,031	87.9	25.0
New Castle County, Delaware	150,917	94.1	37.0	84,360	90.1	28.7
Sussex County, Delaware	62,852	90.3	30.8	59,826	87.0	31.2
DISTRICT OF COLUMBIA						
District of Columbia, District of Columbia	146,140	88.8	45.1	83,992	82.3	43.6
FLORIDA						
Alachua County, Florida	55,142	91.5	36.6	36,330	89.1	34.1
Bay County, Florida	50,228	92.3	20.4	30,861	86.9	25.4
Brevard County, Florida	174,600	93.6	31.7	136,479	88.1	26.8
Broward County, Florida	535,988	90.1	32.6	314,319	82.9	27.9
Charlotte County, Florida	51,320	91.1	21.8	71,704	92.5	25.7
Citrus County, Florida	40,079	91.0	16.1	52,993	88.4	18.7
Clay County, Florida	59,441	92.5	21.6	33,116	89.3	24.1
Collier County, Florida	93,993	87.5	36.2	117,292	91.6	44.2
Columbia County, Florida	17,544	92.4	18.3	13,234	87.8	18.9
Duval County, Florida	239,862	90.6	26.6	128,429	86.4	27.5
Escambia County, Florida	79,248	90.9	26.1	51,066	88.5	26.2
Flagler County, Florida	30,319	90.2	24.2	32,526	90.8	28.7

Table C-2. Educational Attainment of the Population, by Selected Counties, 2017—*Continued*

(Number; percent; dollars.)

	Population 25 to 34 years			Population 35 to 44 years		
State/County	Total	High school graduate or more (percent)	Bachelor's degree or more (percent)	Total	High school graduate or more (percent)	Bachelor's degree or more (percent)
FLORIDA—(*Continued*)						
Hernando County, Florida	18,554	86.7	11.8	18,267	88.7	21.2
Highlands County, Florida	10,349	78.8	9.5	9,289	81.5	17.3
Hillsborough County, Florida	213,630	90.8	35.5	190,942	88.8	37.5
Indian River County, Florida	12,300	88.7	31.1	13,536	85.7	26.0
Lake County, Florida	33,826	91.1	25.0	38,873	83.9	28.5
Lee County, Florida	79,182	88.4	20.5	75,574	84.3	22.4
Leon County, Florida	42,227	95.7	50.1	32,300	98.4	44.9
Manatee County, Florida	39,197	88.9	27.4	41,082	90.2	31.5
Marion County, Florida	37,238	83.0	24.9	35,668	83.2	22.3
Martin County, Florida	13,469	82.5	31.7	14,649	84.1	36.1
Miami-Dade County, Florida	395,237	91.0	33.7	379,990	87.5	34.3
Monroe County, Florida	9,203	87.1	23.9	10,478	85.7	33.0
Nassau County, Florida	8,783	93.1	23.4	9,255	93.5	39.0
Okaloosa County, Florida	31,189	94.5	29.7	23,955	93.7	28.4
Orange County, Florida	227,501	92.7	35.7	189,625	90.8	36.4
Osceola County, Florida	47,858	89.2	19.5	51,986	86.3	21.6
Palm Beach County, Florida	176,115	87.7	33.8	168,222	86.7	35.6
Pasco County, Florida	58,175	91.4	27.0	62,736	91.0	28.0
Pinellas County, Florida	117,195	90.3	32.8	105,627	92.0	35.9
Polk County, Florida	88,113	86.5	17.2	81,100	87.2	20.7
Putnam County, Florida	8,383	80.8	12.2	6,615	88.8	11.6
St. Johns County, Florida	24,345	91.6	46.5	30,129	92.0	54.2
St. Lucie County, Florida	33,150	87.1	18.6	34,441	89.8	21.6
Santa Rosa County, Florida	22,651	92.8	24.6	21,686	95.0	26.8
Sarasota County, Florida	35,463	91.6	25.6	35,875	91.5	36.8
Seminole County, Florida	67,303	96.6	37.9	62,952	97.8	51.1
Sumter County, Florida	6,717	78.2	1.9	7,633	89.0	11.3
Volusia County, Florida	61,974	88.5	17.2	56,526	89.2	27.0
Walton County, Florida	8,640	75.8	12.1	8,250	93.6	27.7
GEORGIA						
Barrow County, Georgia	12,012	92.8	26.0	10,887	87.2	15.2
Bartow County, Georgia	14,608	77.5	18.3	13,102	88.7	23.6
Bibb County, Georgia	19,952	82.6	24.3	17,293	88.6	30.6
Bulloch County, Georgia	9,528	86.2	28.0	7,784	93.0	34.5
Carroll County, Georgia	14,768	94.7	32.8	15,660	88.4	24.8
Catoosa County, Georgia	6,710	88.3	16.8	8,932	93.8	18.6
Chatham County, Georgia	48,272	90.6	29.5	35,299	90.2	35.3
Cherokee County, Georgia	27,944	95.2	38.5	34,893	93.7	42.1
Clarke County, Georgia	18,976	97.1	53.2	14,714	85.7	49.6
Clayton County, Georgia	43,111	85.6	14.7	37,723	81.4	20.5
Cobb County, Georgia	109,820	92.4	45.9	108,159	91.4	50.8
Columbia County, Georgia	20,798	84.1	30.4	19,199	96.5	50.9
Coweta County, Georgia	14,962	94.3	32.5	18,752	90.7	40.6
DeKalb County, Georgia	126,908	89.3	47.0	107,699	88.8	45.2
Dougherty County, Georgia	12,241	91.0	21.2	11,871	88.5	35.9
Douglas County, Georgia	18,558	86.3	29.0	20,684	89.4	29.4
Fayette County, Georgia	11,703	89.4	51.6	13,122	95.4	48.7
Floyd County, Georgia	12,012	73.4	12.7	12,290	71.4	23.3
Forsyth County, Georgia	22,494	86.9	55.2	37,378	92.5	63.9
Fulton County, Georgia	175,013	94.0	53.6	148,569	93.9	55.6
Glynn County, Georgia	9,559	84.7	21.5	10,205	87.5	34.2
Gwinnett County, Georgia	122,495	88.3	35.5	135,008	86.7	38.4
Hall County, Georgia	25,151	79.3	20.1	25,432	74.0	27.5
Henry County, Georgia	24,852	94.3	32.3	32,676	94.9	34.4
Houston County, Georgia	22,117	97.0	32.7	21,533	95.1	37.0
Jackson County, Georgia	9,081	87.6	22.0	9,927	83.1	25.5
Lowndes County, Georgia	17,520	87.5	29.8	13,241	86.9	35.8
Muscogee County, Georgia	30,407	92.9	26.9	24,648	91.7	29.3
Newton County, Georgia	11,790	95.7	20.6	14,675	87.8	25.2
Paulding County, Georgia	20,021	98.1	26.0	24,031	90.7	23.9
Richmond County, Georgia	32,135	85.1	22.3	23,189	83.3	24.1
Rockdale County, Georgia	7,567	86.8	26.6	12,926	89.7	25.7
Spalding County, Georgia	8,369	84.9	19.2	7,727	83.1	28.2
Troup County, Georgia	8,134	88.8	15.8	8,624	81.3	21.8
Walker County, Georgia	8,475	83.7	26.4	8,258	86.9	16.7
Walton County, Georgia	11,661	89.1	18.5	10,744	92.9	17.0
Whitfield County, Georgia	13,374	80.5	19.0	14,435	49.8	10.2

Table C-2. Educational Attainment of the Population, by Selected Counties, 2017—*Continued*

(Number; percent; dollars.)

	Population 45 to 64 years			Population 65 years and over		
State/County	Total	High school graduate or more (percent)	Bachelor's degree or more (percent)	Total	High school graduate or more (percent)	Bachelor's degree or more (percent)
FLORIDA—(*Continued*)						
Hernando County, Florida	50,462	90.1	21.1	51,580	88.1	18.4
Highlands County, Florida	24,020	85.4	18.9	35,750	86.2	19.7
Hillsborough County, Florida	359,182	90.1	32.8	197,156	86.3	27.8
Indian River County, Florida	42,253	90.6	28.7	49,017	91.9	32.8
Lake County, Florida	89,260	89.9	24.8	91,737	89.2	22.6
Lee County, Florida	193,207	89.7	26.6	207,191	90.3	32.2
Leon County, Florida	62,129	93.7	46.1	37,169	93.1	46.5
Manatee County, Florida	102,845	89.9	31.4	104,404	92.7	34.5
Marion County, Florida	90,381	86.7	18.9	101,230	86.9	23.4
Martin County, Florida	45,487	90.6	30.4	48,368	93.0	31.5
Miami-Dade County, Florida	747,173	82.9	28.1	438,963	66.7	23.2
Monroe County, Florida	24,338	93.4	35.5	16,750	89.1	36.0
Nassau County, Florida	24,776	94.8	33.7	17,832	89.8	35.4
Okaloosa County, Florida	52,258	93.2	30.4	32,078	92.7	36.6
Orange County, Florida	329,316	90.8	34.3	157,962	81.5	28.5
Osceola County, Florida	84,844	92.8	18.5	45,692	71.2	17.1
Palm Beach County, Florida	386,230	89.2	35.7	346,533	89.7	38.2
Pasco County, Florida	141,885	89.4	22.6	118,497	87.6	19.7
Pinellas County, Florida	288,164	91.4	30.2	235,182	90.8	29.9
Polk County, Florida	168,893	85.6	20.4	138,292	83.3	17.6
Putnam County, Florida	20,886	78.0	9.9	16,460	82.0	17.0
St. Johns County, Florida	71,032	92.5	39.6	47,430	90.1	42.1
St. Lucie County, Florida	82,916	86.5	20.0	74,323	84.4	26.0
Santa Rosa County, Florida	49,366	91.3	29.9	27,079	90.9	25.3
Sarasota County, Florida	111,793	91.0	32.4	151,945	92.3	37.0
Seminole County, Florida	125,284	95.5	41.9	70,396	91.7	36.4
Sumter County, Florida	26,932	88.9	31.3	70,903	93.9	38.9
Volusia County, Florida	150,050	91.4	23.8	129,850	88.3	22.2
Walton County, Florida	20,143	84.8	30.4	13,711	90.8	36.0
GEORGIA						
Barrow County, Georgia	19,829	85.8	16.9	9,115	74.8	15.9
Bartow County, Georgia	28,539	88.0	23.6	14,825	75.6	16.3
Bibb County, Georgia	39,165	91.2	24.2	22,947	80.8	22.3
Bulloch County, Georgia	16,564	88.1	22.2	8,332	81.7	25.6
Carroll County, Georgia	29,725	84.7	19.1	14,854	78.6	19.1
Catoosa County, Georgia	17,709	88.1	14.5	11,151	87.3	23.5
Chatham County, Georgia	69,576	88.2	31.7	41,934	85.0	35.9
Cherokee County, Georgia	70,518	92.8	37.4	32,056	89.4	26.9
Clarke County, Georgia	22,953	84.0	35.9	13,444	85.9	38.8
Clayton County, Georgia	70,159	84.3	17.3	25,697	79.9	10.7
Cobb County, Georgia	199,179	94.5	48.8	89,403	88.5	37.9
Columbia County, Georgia	39,028	92.6	34.5	19,487	89.0	27.6
Coweta County, Georgia	41,054	89.3	30.3	19,399	86.9	23.4
DeKalb County, Georgia	188,825	90.8	40.9	90,476	85.0	37.6
Dougherty County, Georgia	19,865	82.8	22.1	13,653	85.1	21.7
Douglas County, Georgia	38,123	87.7	28.8	16,680	73.7	17.4
Fayette County, Georgia	33,410	95.6	48.3	20,157	94.7	37.8
Floyd County, Georgia	23,981	83.7	17.6	15,956	88.4	22.0
Forsyth County, Georgia	62,088	95.3	56.0	26,484	92.0	40.9
Fulton County, Georgia	261,572	93.4	51.9	118,083	86.3	40.9
Glynn County, Georgia	22,675	93.7	30.8	16,590	86.2	36.2
Gwinnett County, Georgia	241,124	89.2	37.6	88,442	84.8	31.8
Hall County, Georgia	50,292	78.8	27.5	28,831	82.4	28.3
Henry County, Georgia	61,802	93.5	30.3	24,999	84.4	19.0
Houston County, Georgia	38,456	93.5	32.9	18,785	88.5	19.3
Jackson County, Georgia	17,359	88.0	25.7	10,186	78.7	14.8
Lowndes County, Georgia	23,997	85.7	28.6	13,304	75.3	22.8
Muscogee County, Georgia	45,624	85.2	25.1	25,075	81.0	21.6
Newton County, Georgia	27,864	89.9	16.7	14,268	85.0	24.5
Paulding County, Georgia	42,436	90.9	20.3	16,348	76.4	16.5
Richmond County, Georgia	48,857	84.0	20.9	27,252	75.5	17.4
Rockdale County, Georgia	24,369	91.8	27.4	12,406	82.8	21.5
Spalding County, Georgia	16,612	86.6	20.2	11,501	75.7	11.6
Troup County, Georgia	17,837	81.9	18.1	10,411	76.7	26.8
Walker County, Georgia	19,044	87.9	15.8	12,829	83.1	17.6
Walton County, Georgia	24,963	88.3	21.1	14,175	88.1	17.6
Whitfield County, Georgia	25,240	68.0	17.8	13,788	73.8	17.9

Table C-2. Educational Attainment of the Population, by Selected Counties, 2017—*Continued*

(Number; percent; dollars.)

State/County	Population 25 to 34 years			Population 35 to 44 years		
	Total	High school graduate or more (percent)	Bachelor's degree or more (percent)	Total	High school graduate or more (percent)	Bachelor's degree or more (percent)
HAWAII						
Hawaii County, Hawaii	23,894	92.7	21.4	23,500	92.4	30.2
Honolulu County, Hawaii	152,516	96.5	34.0	125,019	96.4	41.2
Kauai County, Hawaii	8,468	92.4	25.6	10,159	93.5	30.7
Maui County, Hawaii	21,186	94.6	20.0	23,141	94.2	25.2
IDAHO						
Ada County, Idaho	65,110	93.2	35.2	63,061	95.7	39.6
Bannock County, Idaho	12,719	93.8	29.7	10,048	98.3	32.3
Bonneville County, Idaho	15,930	93.3	31.8	14,328	96.3	37.2
Canyon County, Idaho	28,821	87.3	13.1	27,282	84.7	23.1
Kootenai County, Idaho	20,151	95.9	21.1	19,336	97.7	28.1
Twin Falls County, Idaho	11,361	94.1	18.7	12,149	83.1	21.1
ILLINOIS						
Adams County, Illinois	7,997	90.9	28.4	7,437	95.5	31.6
Champaign County, Illinois	29,088	97.4	55.3	23,834	96.2	48.0
Cook County, Illinois	848,731	92.8	49.9	700,528	89.1	42.2
DeKalb County, Illinois	15,574	92.2	22.5	11,962	90.6	32.7
DuPage County, Illinois	117,557	94.9	54.4	119,705	92.3	57.9
Kane County, Illinois	61,504	86.4	33.7	73,615	80.4	31.3
Kankakee County, Illinois	12,591	89.9	29.0	13,341	89.5	14.2
Kendall County, Illinois	16,550	92.3	25.9	19,728	86.9	44.7
Lake County, Illinois	78,275	92.4	39.3	87,564	89.4	46.6
LaSalle County, Illinois	12,918	91.2	21.0	13,331	88.3	20.0
McHenry County, Illinois	34,262	93.5	35.3	39,186	91.9	40.3
McLean County, Illinois	22,026	99.9	48.9	20,510	97.3	53.2
Macon County, Illinois	12,121	95.0	21.2	12,525	87.5	25.7
Madison County, Illinois	36,094	91.4	30.0	32,568	95.2	34.2
Peoria County, Illinois	24,353	88.6	32.9	22,305	93.3	42.0
Rock Island County, Illinois	17,358	89.3	24.2	18,044	87.0	26.1
St. Clair County, Illinois	34,140	94.9	29.8	32,829	91.7	28.2
Sangamon County, Illinois	24,664	93.6	38.1	23,901	90.5	35.6
Tazewell County, Illinois	15,805	89.4	29.6	17,127	96.9	41.5
Vermilion County, Illinois	9,053	88.5	16.5	8,925	84.4	20.0
Will County, Illinois	81,769	92.7	34.6	94,418	89.9	39.2
Williamson County, Illinois	9,150	92.6	19.2	8,862	91.5	29.9
Winnebago County, Illinois	36,007	90.5	20.0	33,458	85.1	20.3
INDIANA						
Allen County, Indiana	51,676	90.0	29.4	45,729	88.5	28.5
Bartholomew County, Indiana	12,947	85.2	37.2	9,448	97.8	38.0
Boone County, Indiana	7,716	93.5	57.7	8,998	92.6	53.6
Clark County, Indiana	16,250	95.6	20.2	16,077	89.8	19.3
Delaware County, Indiana	13,421	92.3	32.0	11,315	89.2	24.5
Elkhart County, Indiana	25,615	76.7	16.0	25,774	81.6	19.0
Floyd County, Indiana	9,383	92.1	37.5	9,728	89.3	34.3
Grant County, Indiana	6,688	94.2	24.3	7,195	92.3	15.7
Hamilton County, Indiana	39,920	98.2	62.6	48,677	98.6	67.5
Hancock County, Indiana	8,597	99.3	32.0	9,749	91.6	38.2
Hendricks County, Indiana	20,833	97.8	37.7	22,266	94.6	45.8
Howard County, Indiana	9,464	88.2	34.9	9,426	95.9	22.0
Johnson County, Indiana	21,338	94.8	40.7	21,183	91.9	36.8
Kosciusko County, Indiana	11,012	88.0	30.1	8,293	89.8	30.0
Lake County, Indiana	59,376	89.2	27.7	60,862	89.2	23.5
LaPorte County, Indiana	15,463	86.6	14.3	13,041	87.3	16.1
Madison County, Indiana	15,787	89.0	18.3	16,683	89.8	23.5
Marion County, Indiana	159,449	87.2	40.5	121,940	80.7	31.3
Monroe County, Indiana	21,036	93.0	56.3	15,343	90.6	50.0
Morgan County, Indiana	7,966	91.3	16.5	8,190	93.8	24.7
Porter County, Indiana	19,816	93.7	39.4	22,482	96.9	37.5
St. Joseph County, Indiana	35,769	91.6	36.2	32,053	87.1	34.6
Tippecanoe County, Indiana	26,362	95.4	50.0	20,260	90.3	49.4
Vanderburgh County, Indiana	26,767	92.1	32.7	20,831	91.2	36.8
Vigo County, Indiana	13,495	86.4	23.8	12,050	82.1	23.9
Wayne County, Indiana	7,500	83.7	14.9	7,794	90.6	27.0
IOWA						
Black Hawk County, Iowa	17,103	83.7	30.8	14,372	97.3	28.2
Dallas County, Iowa	12,087	96.7	61.0	14,334	95.5	62.0
Dubuque County, Iowa	12,261	93.8	36.4	10,451	94.9	44.3

Table C-2. Educational Attainment of the Population, by Selected Counties, 2017—*Continued*

(Number; percent; dollars.)

State/County	Population 45 to 64 years			Population 65 years and over		
	Total	High school graduate or more (percent)	Bachelor's degree or more (percent)	Total	High school graduate or more (percent)	Bachelor's degree or more (percent)
HAWAII						
Hawaii County, Hawaii	54,662	95.1	31.5	40,090	91.4	35.6
Honolulu County, Hawaii	237,701	91.4	35.0	170,688	86.8	30.3
Kauai County, Hawaii	18,111	91.9	25.0	13,968	84.5	34.3
Maui County, Hawaii	45,569	93.0	26.6	29,002	86.0	34.1
IDAHO						
Ada County, Idaho	116,357	93.8	34.5	63,103	95.0	36.6
Bannock County, Idaho	18,665	92.6	27.4	11,572	90.2	30.5
Bonneville County, Idaho	24,156	87.9	29.0	14,709	95.1	28.9
Canyon County, Idaho	48,171	86.9	19.0	29,039	83.0	17.0
Kootenai County, Idaho	40,471	95.4	26.8	28,895	91.4	26.9
Twin Falls County, Idaho	18,663	88.7	20.5	12,484	87.0	20.7
ILLINOIS						
Adams County, Illinois	17,156	94.0	26.6	13,507	88.2	21.9
Champaign County, Illinois	41,484	95.4	39.5	26,067	94.3	38.7
Cook County, Illinois	1,304,462	85.6	34.5	743,771	80.7	29.7
DeKalb County, Illinois	22,735	90.9	30.3	12,652	91.0	31.6
DuPage County, Illinois	260,189	94.2	50.5	139,305	89.1	39.0
Kane County, Illinois	141,750	85.0	35.3	70,027	85.8	26.6
Kankakee County, Illinois	28,744	90.0	21.4	18,012	82.1	18.9
Kendall County, Illinois	31,250	91.9	31.2	13,262	85.9	20.9
Lake County, Illinois	197,249	91.0	47.5	96,243	89.5	42.7
LaSalle County, Illinois	30,826	91.9	17.7	19,963	86.8	17.9
McHenry County, Illinois	92,634	93.2	36.4	42,613	91.1	23.2
McLean County, Illinois	39,909	97.7	44.5	22,182	89.7	36.1
Macon County, Illinois	27,251	94.7	24.7	20,551	89.3	20.8
Madison County, Illinois	71,932	91.8	26.5	44,879	89.2	21.6
Peoria County, Illinois	45,686	90.7	28.5	30,617	84.8	25.9
Rock Island County, Illinois	36,938	89.9	22.3	27,048	87.7	20.8
St. Clair County, Illinois	70,607	93.1	30.4	40,210	87.9	24.4
Sangamon County, Illinois	54,453	94.4	32.4	33,531	92.4	28.5
Tazewell County, Illinois	36,011	92.1	26.8	24,008	88.4	21.9
Vermilion County, Illinois	19,871	88.8	15.1	15,131	81.7	17.3
Will County, Illinois	190,791	91.2	32.9	87,437	86.8	23.5
Williamson County, Illinois	17,672	91.9	24.8	12,505	89.8	17.1
Winnebago County, Illinois	76,700	88.0	23.2	48,707	88.3	20.1
INDIANA						
Allen County, Indiana	92,223	90.2	25.6	53,188	88.0	22.7
Bartholomew County, Indiana	20,506	90.6	33.9	13,136	93.1	32.9
Boone County, Indiana	18,255	95.0	51.8	8,578	94.7	46.8
Clark County, Indiana	30,847	89.2	20.4	17,975	86.2	14.2
Delaware County, Indiana	27,321	91.9	25.7	19,326	82.7	18.2
Elkhart County, Indiana	49,319	82.0	21.1	29,230	80.8	23.5
Floyd County, Indiana	21,577	90.5	28.3	11,941	84.5	23.3
Grant County, Indiana	17,378	93.6	25.8	12,777	85.0	20.0
Hamilton County, Indiana	85,274	97.3	61.7	38,194	96.1	43.4
Hancock County, Indiana	21,252	93.9	34.6	11,574	90.0	25.2
Hendricks County, Indiana	42,938	95.6	35.7	22,038	90.7	23.3
Howard County, Indiana	22,488	90.7	19.1	15,616	86.6	12.6
Johnson County, Indiana	38,551	94.5	35.0	22,281	89.3	24.1
Kosciusko County, Indiana	21,021	85.6	22.2	12,714	88.9	21.8
Lake County, Indiana	129,807	90.4	23.1	78,121	83.1	17.3
LaPorte County, Indiana	30,135	88.6	14.8	19,188	90.3	22.9
Madison County, Indiana	35,275	90.4	15.4	22,855	85.4	21.2
Marion County, Indiana	228,089	87.2	29.6	117,168	82.4	26.1
Monroe County, Indiana	30,239	91.3	38.2	18,573	86.7	39.1
Morgan County, Indiana	20,909	84.2	16.9	11,406	82.1	18.7
Porter County, Indiana	45,818	94.3	25.7	26,846	90.7	24.2
St. Joseph County, Indiana	66,427	89.0	26.0	42,113	86.2	26.9
Tippecanoe County, Indiana	37,726	93.8	35.1	21,148	90.8	33.9
Vanderburgh County, Indiana	47,089	90.5	27.3	29,635	86.1	24.1
Vigo County, Indiana	25,957	87.2	21.9	17,287	85.8	23.9
Wayne County, Indiana	18,203	91.7	22.9	11,989	80.6	17.1
IOWA						
Black Hawk County, Iowa	31,389	89.9	29.7	20,986	90.6	23.9
Dallas County, Iowa	20,172	95.9	42.2	10,056	94.6	35.7
Dubuque County, Iowa	24,946	92.6	29.9	16,619	90.5	27.8

Table C-2. Educational Attainment of the Population, by Selected Counties, 2017—*Continued*

(Number; percent; dollars.)

State/County	Population 25 to 34 years			Population 35 to 44 years		
	Total	High school graduate or more (percent)	Bachelor's degree or more (percent)	Total	High school graduate or more (percent)	Bachelor's degree or more (percent)
IOWA—*(Continued)*						
Johnson County, Iowa	21,846	98.2	68.2	17,413	99.8	56.0
Linn County, Iowa	30,335	91.5	36.9	27,718	96.6	40.0
Polk County, Iowa	74,029	93.1	39.8	65,328	89.6	41.2
Pottawattamie County, Iowa	10,788	92.6	29.1	11,636	84.5	26.0
Scott County, Iowa	22,352	94.9	33.2	21,591	94.2	38.7
Story County, Iowa	13,718	99.3	60.4	9,354	95.5	54.9
Woodbury County, Iowa	13,322	88.2	21.7	12,461	79.2	26.3
KANSAS						
Butler County, Kansas	8,022	83.7	36.2	7,900	95.9	35.6
Douglas County, Kansas	19,333	96.2	45.0	14,399	95.4	42.2
Johnson County, Kansas	80,648	94.9	57.5	82,940	94.7	59.6
Leavenworth County, Kansas	10,439	89.6	37.8	11,394	86.2	26.1
Riley County, Kansas	13,306	96.5	51.0	6,176	95.6	51.6
Sedgwick County, Kansas	74,256	90.3	34.1	63,213	89.9	33.8
Shawnee County, Kansas	23,338	95.1	33.0	20,107	95.2	44.7
Wyandotte County, Kansas	24,513	85.0	20.4	21,303	77.4	20.4
KENTUCKY						
Boone County, Kentucky	16,213	92.1	30.0	18,509	93.4	41.1
Bullitt County, Kentucky	10,565	96.6	16.2	10,156	94.1	21.4
Campbell County, Kentucky	14,015	95.6	49.1	11,430	94.0	45.7
Christian County, Kentucky	10,657	93.3	11.7	7,597	85.8	23.0
Daviess County, Kentucky	12,574	96.9	24.5	11,868	87.7	20.9
Fayette County, Kentucky	50,494	96.3	50.6	42,447	94.0	44.0
Hardin County, Kentucky	14,967	95.3	18.8	14,233	93.5	29.2
Jefferson County, Kentucky	114,136	94.9	38.1	96,315	90.8	36.6
Kenton County, Kentucky	25,665	92.4	40.1	21,302	93.5	38.5
McCracken County, Kentucky	7,762	99.2	33.8	7,473	96.4	17.6
Madison County, Kentucky	11,303	96.6	28.6	11,656	95.2	38.9
Oldham County, Kentucky	6,577	96.1	34.1	9,235	97.2	51.3
Warren County, Kentucky	18,010	92.5	34.6	14,694	85.9	34.2
LOUISIANA						
Ascension Parish, Louisiana	16,984	93.4	25.6	18,660	94.9	35.3
Bossier Parish, Louisiana	18,426	93.6	23.2	17,971	83.9	23.9
Caddo Parish, Louisiana	35,329	86.9	21.4	29,267	90.8	24.2
Calcasieu Parish, Louisiana	29,986	92.1	26.9	24,386	93.2	29.1
East Baton Rouge Parish, Louisiana	65,744	91.0	34.5	52,156	85.8	38.5
Iberia Parish, Louisiana	10,100	83.0	4.5	7,734	87.1	14.7
Jefferson Parish, Louisiana	64,038	87.9	29.3	54,493	84.6	28.1
Lafayette Parish, Louisiana	39,265	92.1	37.9	32,116	91.7	45.6
Lafourche Parish, Louisiana	13,812	87.8	24.1	11,450	79.5	21.8
Livingston Parish, Louisiana	19,971	85.5	12.5	18,657	89.6	29.1
Orleans Parish, Louisiana	71,100	91.1	40.9	52,551	90.6	39.7
Ouachita Parish, Louisiana	22,165	86.1	19.1	18,973	89.7	25.7
Rapides Parish, Louisiana	16,707	89.5	23.3	15,813	86.8	24.4
St. Landry Parish, Louisiana	10,198	80.2	19.9	9,395	84.8	18.4
St. Tammany Parish, Louisiana	28,633	91.4	37.2	33,019	91.4	45.8
Tangipahoa Parish, Louisiana	19,224	86.1	25.8	17,114	82.7	21.5
Terrebonne Parish, Louisiana	15,180	78.4	20.5	14,023	76.9	18.1
MAINE						
Androscoggin County, Maine	12,827	95.9	35.2	12,877	94.9	29.7
Aroostook County, Maine	6,847	95.1	32.4	6,912	94.1	33.0
Cumberland County, Maine	40,799	97.5	50.6	35,191	95.4	47.0
Kennebec County, Maine	14,042	96.6	26.9	13,496	95.6	36.2
Penobscot County, Maine	20,662	94.1	33.7	16,874	96.6	35.6
York County, Maine	23,587	93.7	30.6	24,057	94.7	36.5
MARYLAND						
Allegany County, Maryland	8,543	86.4	17.6	8,346	86.4	20.4
Anne Arundel County, Maryland	81,451	92.5	39.7	75,159	92.2	49.1
Baltimore County, Maryland	115,018	92.1	40.2	100,804	92.4	48.4
Calvert County, Maryland	10,288	99.7	40.4	10,705	98.2	32.9
Carroll County, Maryland	19,799	90.8	37.9	18,639	98.1	52.1
Cecil County, Maryland	13,800	93.4	28.4	11,649	92.8	26.4
Charles County, Maryland	21,199	91.7	27.2	20,622	94.3	42.7
Frederick County, Maryland	31,570	93.3	45.6	33,686	91.6	46.0

Table C-2. Educational Attainment of the Population, by Selected Counties, 2017—*Continued*

(Number; percent; dollars.)

State/County	Population 45 to 64 years			Population 65 years and over		
	Total	High school graduate or more (percent)	Bachelor's degree or more (percent)	Total	High school graduate or more (percent)	Bachelor's degree or more (percent)
IOWA—(*Continued*)						
Johnson County, Iowa	29,991	96.8	55.5	17,126	90.6	46.1
Linn County, Iowa	57,303	95.9	34.0	34,505	95.4	24.0
Polk County, Iowa	118,183	91.2	32.7	61,031	89.8	28.3
Pottawattamie County, Iowa	24,748	89.7	19.4	16,048	87.5	19.6
Scott County, Iowa	45,388	92.9	31.5	27,223	88.3	25.3
Story County, Iowa	17,670	98.0	52.3	11,214	95.4	43.3
Woodbury County, Iowa	24,707	86.2	21.7	15,236	88.9	25.5
KANSAS						
Butler County, Kansas	18,356	97.7	29.3	9,992	85.6	22.9
Douglas County, Kansas	22,970	97.4	49.0	14,251	95.0	52.8
Johnson County, Kansas	153,344	96.6	56.9	82,051	95.2	48.4
Leavenworth County, Kansas	21,669	90.9	34.9	11,079	91.0	29.9
Riley County, Kansas	10,332	91.3	46.7	6,898	97.7	43.5
Sedgwick County, Kansas	124,729	90.1	28.3	72,013	89.2	30.2
Shawnee County, Kansas	46,348	94.3	31.8	31,311	93.4	31.3
Wyandotte County, Kansas	39,125	82.1	12.0	19,615	76.0	17.1
KENTUCKY						
Boone County, Kentucky	34,567	94.0	28.5	16,773	87.4	23.6
Bullitt County, Kentucky	22,871	85.4	12.2	12,352	79.4	7.0
Campbell County, Kentucky	24,781	92.9	32.1	13,930	87.9	25.1
Christian County, Kentucky	13,081	81.9	18.1	8,446	80.7	13.6
Daviess County, Kentucky	26,456	93.0	23.6	16,604	86.9	19.4
Fayette County, Kentucky	74,879	91.5	42.3	41,383	87.1	36.8
Hardin County, Kentucky	28,788	93.3	24.9	14,474	84.2	11.7
Jefferson County, Kentucky	201,329	91.2	32.1	121,263	87.3	28.9
Kenton County, Kentucky	42,924	88.2	27.7	23,393	88.1	25.5
McCracken County, Kentucky	18,677	92.8	26.7	12,277	82.9	21.0
Madison County, Kentucky	20,639	85.0	32.5	12,295	77.2	23.6
Oldham County, Kentucky	18,688	91.6	45.2	8,172	91.0	28.3
Warren County, Kentucky	29,813	87.0	23.2	16,116	79.7	26.0
LOUISIANA						
Ascension Parish, Louisiana	29,860	88.3	23.7	13,655	76.5	17.8
Bossier Parish, Louisiana	29,111	92.4	24.0	17,096	88.9	20.7
Caddo Parish, Louisiana	61,166	87.5	23.3	41,105	79.9	24.0
Calcasieu Parish, Louisiana	50,001	88.4	23.9	29,250	84.8	20.9
East Baton Rouge Parish, Louisiana	103,657	90.4	33.7	60,569	88.5	35.2
Iberia Parish, Louisiana	18,354	78.8	10.5	10,169	82.0	10.1
Jefferson Parish, Louisiana	116,574	83.9	22.8	72,599	84.4	23.0
Lafayette Parish, Louisiana	59,387	86.6	26.4	30,289	80.6	25.7
Lafourche Parish, Louisiana	26,603	77.8	14.1	14,475	70.7	13.7
Livingston Parish, Louisiana	34,425	89.7	13.0	18,300	79.4	14.2
Orleans Parish, Louisiana	99,686	83.2	31.7	55,292	81.1	30.3
Ouachita Parish, Louisiana	37,947	90.4	25.9	22,039	81.6	22.2
Rapides Parish, Louisiana	33,553	82.7	18.4	20,796	82.2	21.1
St. Landry Parish, Louisiana	21,071	80.1	11.6	13,187	72.4	15.8
St. Tammany Parish, Louisiana	70,886	92.6	33.7	41,504	87.0	31.1
Tangipahoa Parish, Louisiana	31,522	82.8	16.7	18,278	81.8	13.9
Terrebonne Parish, Louisiana	28,051	78.2	13.0	15,774	68.3	9.1
MAINE						
Androscoggin County, Maine	30,380	94.0	19.3	18,620	79.9	22.6
Aroostook County, Maine	20,507	90.6	14.9	15,742	79.7	12.6
Cumberland County, Maine	83,218	95.1	49.9	52,653	90.6	40.3
Kennebec County, Maine	36,597	91.9	27.0	23,230	87.3	27.7
Penobscot County, Maine	43,676	93.4	27.2	27,328	85.5	24.9
York County, Maine	62,024	93.9	33.1	40,338	87.4	30.6
MARYLAND						
Allegany County, Maryland	19,084	92.7	15.6	14,076	87.8	16.5
Anne Arundel County, Maryland	157,321	92.8	40.4	81,452	88.8	34.6
Baltimore County, Maryland	223,835	92.4	36.8	138,879	87.7	35.0
Calvert County, Maryland	28,342	95.2	32.0	13,302	86.3	33.2
Carroll County, Maryland	51,949	94.1	35.3	26,999	86.9	25.9
Cecil County, Maryland	29,528	88.9	25.2	15,610	86.2	19.1
Charles County, Maryland	46,208	92.2	32.6	19,695	87.5	21.7
Frederick County, Maryland	72,002	93.6	43.5	35,325	87.4	33.0

Table C-2. Educational Attainment of the Population, by Selected Counties, 2017—*Continued*

(Number; percent; dollars.)

State/County	Population 25 to 34 years			Population 35 to 44 years		
	Total	High school graduate or more (percent)	Bachelor's degree or more (percent)	Total	High school graduate or more (percent)	Bachelor's degree or more (percent)
MARYLAND—(*Continued*)						
Harford County, Maryland	29,960	95.3	42.0	30,733	94.8	45.0
Howard County, Maryland	39,426	97.3	59.7	45,128	96.3	67.7
Montgomery County, Maryland	135,842	93.4	57.9	145,465	89.2	57.7
Prince George's County, Maryland	134,234	88.4	33.6	122,730	84.1	35.3
St. Mary's County, Maryland	14,970	94.3	38.9	14,290	93.6	31.2
Washington County, Maryland	19,196	88.5	21.3	18,486	88.6	32.3
Wicomico County, Maryland	12,738	77.8	30.8	10,559	87.9	32.6
Baltimore city, Maryland	117,493	88.9	43.4	75,659	86.5	33.9
MASSACHUSETTS						
Barnstable County, Massachusetts	18,794	94.8	29.1	17,864	94.5	45.0
Berkshire County, Massachusetts	13,816	91.3	27.6	12,795	90.9	33.8
Bristol County, Massachusetts	71,324	92.0	34.5	69,168	92.2	32.2
Essex County, Massachusetts	96,522	92.7	41.7	93,398	88.3	44.7
Franklin County, Massachusetts	7,920	93.8	26.6	8,201	97.8	36.5
Hampden County, Massachusetts	61,765	85.9	30.0	54,714	87.6	27.7
Hampshire County, Massachusetts	17,328	98.0	48.5	16,324	96.8	44.4
Middlesex County, Massachusetts	245,929	95.5	66.7	209,151	94.4	61.2
Norfolk County, Massachusetts	87,848	96.4	63.6	89,297	93.8	66.8
Plymouth County, Massachusetts	54,670	93.4	31.3	59,544	93.6	42.8
Suffolk County, Massachusetts	185,451	94.1	63.8	103,363	87.3	42.3
Worcester County, Massachusetts	106,153	92.2	41.7	99,240	92.5	44.4
MICHIGAN						
Allegan County, Michigan	13,440	90.4	25.3	13,287	93.8	26.9
Bay County, Michigan	13,111	94.0	27.8	11,738	93.0	28.1
Berrien County, Michigan	18,613	85.9	27.7	17,377	86.9	29.0
Calhoun County, Michigan	15,797	90.3	18.1	16,167	95.2	28.1
Clinton County, Michigan	9,579	96.0	37.8	9,103	97.5	44.7
Eaton County, Michigan	13,431	95.2	33.1	12,250	93.8	31.4
Genesee County, Michigan	48,459	89.8	22.4	47,048	93.0	24.2
Grand Traverse County, Michigan	11,945	93.7	39.6	10,383	98.8	46.7
Ingham County, Michigan	40,753	93.2	45.3	32,679	90.5	45.3
Isabella County, Michigan	8,595	94.0	39.3	6,788	89.7	35.8
Jackson County, Michigan	19,858	92.5	22.1	18,035	91.1	23.7
Kalamazoo County, Michigan	35,043	94.8	40.5	30,215	94.6	47.2
Kent County, Michigan	101,322	91.4	44.4	80,988	89.6	39.5
Lapeer County, Michigan	9,561	92.2	21.0	9,992	92.8	21.3
Lenawee County, Michigan	12,308	94.8	19.7	11,219	91.1	27.2
Livingston County, Michigan	20,546	95.2	38.3	21,431	96.9	44.4
Macomb County, Michigan	114,243	91.9	31.1	105,107	91.3	29.0
Marquette County, Michigan	7,804	92.3	41.9	7,226	94.6	37.1
Midland County, Michigan	10,149	96.5	42.4	9,618	91.0	46.6
Monroe County, Michigan	18,012	91.8	17.7	16,992	93.5	22.5
Muskegon County, Michigan	21,823	92.8	16.9	20,922	90.4	21.2
Oakland County, Michigan	162,114	95.8	55.7	155,375	95.8	55.4
Ottawa County, Michigan	34,534	95.8	41.5	33,346	93.1	34.8
Saginaw County, Michigan	25,033	89.7	20.7	21,113	91.0	26.9
St. Clair County, Michigan	17,717	92.6	16.7	17,705	93.3	21.0
Shiawassee County, Michigan	7,606	95.1	22.7	7,887	90.3	13.6
Van Buren County, Michigan	7,740	85.3	11.8	8,503	90.3	24.1
Washtenaw County, Michigan	52,374	98.0	63.0	42,053	95.3	57.6
Wayne County, Michigan	243,308	89.9	25.7	206,301	87.8	25.8
MINNESOTA						
Anoka County, Minnesota	45,253	95.5	33.5	48,022	93.4	33.0
Blue Earth County, Minnesota	8,568	99.0	44.5	7,203	96.5	40.5
Carver County, Minnesota	11,413	97.2	48.2	14,561	97.7	57.5
Dakota County, Minnesota	56,429	94.5	43.0	55,845	92.5	45.0
Hennepin County, Minnesota	214,281	94.6	55.9	168,328	93.2	55.8
Olmsted County, Minnesota	22,645	97.2	54.0	20,082	97.4	56.6
Ramsey County, Minnesota	91,083	90.9	48.2	67,540	86.7	40.3
Rice County, Minnesota	7,315	87.5	25.8	8,255	82.8	21.2
St. Louis County, Minnesota	22,928	93.1	41.6	22,538	96.8	32.7
Scott County, Minnesota	18,166	96.9	47.4	21,827	95.9	51.5
Sherburne County, Minnesota	12,764	95.8	33.6	13,147	90.4	31.9
Stearns County, Minnesota	19,514	91.8	31.8	17,511	91.9	37.9
Washington County, Minnesota	30,538	95.7	43.2	33,484	97.7	56.0
Wright County, Minnesota	15,483	98.6	26.5	19,213	94.1	41.4

Table C-2. Educational Attainment of the Population, by Selected Counties, 2017—*Continued*

(Number; percent; dollars.)

State/County	Population 45 to 64 years			Population 65 years and over		
	Total	High school graduate or more (percent)	Bachelor's degree or more (percent)	Total	High school graduate or more (percent)	Bachelor's degree or more (percent)
MARYLAND—(*Continued*)						
Harford County, Maryland	74,256	93.3	34.1	39,673	85.6	24.9
Howard County, Maryland	89,507	96.2	64.5	43,171	91.8	50.8
Montgomery County, Maryland	288,546	91.8	59.4	158,478	89.1	55.1
Prince George's County, Maryland	245,420	88.3	31.5	116,953	86.2	28.3
St. Mary's County, Maryland	30,553	89.3	33.4	14,188	84.7	21.5
Washington County, Maryland	42,270	88.4	23.4	25,288	82.8	20.7
Wicomico County, Maryland	26,117	89.1	29.8	15,282	85.6	26.6
Baltimore city, Maryland	150,978	84.3	22.6	82,552	76.0	23.9
MASSACHUSETTS						
Barnstable County, Massachusetts	65,240	94.6	43.0	63,536	95.1	50.6
Berkshire County, Massachusetts	37,349	92.6	30.0	28,605	89.3	36.9
Bristol County, Massachusetts	159,984	87.6	29.5	93,816	72.2	21.3
Essex County, Massachusetts	223,227	91.1	40.8	130,835	85.1	33.4
Franklin County, Massachusetts	21,786	94.1	41.3	15,027	93.8	44.1
Hampden County, Massachusetts	124,616	87.0	28.1	77,797	79.3	23.4
Hampshire County, Massachusetts	39,268	96.8	51.8	26,686	91.0	41.6
Middlesex County, Massachusetts	429,816	93.9	54.9	240,112	88.7	42.4
Norfolk County, Massachusetts	198,063	94.7	51.0	116,068	88.7	39.9
Plymouth County, Massachusetts	155,140	93.8	36.8	90,045	90.7	32.9
Suffolk County, Massachusetts	172,344	85.6	34.9	93,554	76.6	27.3
Worcester County, Massachusetts	237,995	92.7	34.4	126,050	86.0	29.9
MICHIGAN						
Allegan County, Michigan	33,166	93.9	21.2	18,497	87.5	24.0
Bay County, Michigan	29,625	92.3	17.9	20,729	83.6	20.1
Berrien County, Michigan	42,676	91.4	24.0	29,701	89.6	24.7
Calhoun County, Michigan	37,359	92.0	21.1	22,907	90.4	21.6
Clinton County, Michigan	22,513	95.3	31.0	12,878	91.8	22.8
Eaton County, Michigan	31,171	97.0	31.0	19,328	91.1	21.2
Genesee County, Michigan	114,930	93.3	21.4	68,945	86.9	16.7
Grand Traverse County, Michigan	26,804	97.1	39.3	17,627	94.1	40.7
Ingham County, Michigan	63,717	93.3	31.5	38,695	90.2	37.0
Isabella County, Michigan	14,596	94.9	30.4	8,830	87.2	25.2
Jackson County, Michigan	45,385	93.0	20.6	27,270	89.9	23.9
Kalamazoo County, Michigan	61,052	94.8	38.7	38,175	92.2	35.5
Kent County, Michigan	160,380	92.3	34.5	85,927	88.4	28.3
Lapeer County, Michigan	27,774	92.8	16.9	15,586	90.4	12.2
Lenawee County, Michigan	27,706	95.3	22.6	17,787	86.2	17.5
Livingston County, Michigan	59,875	95.5	40.5	30,986	94.8	29.3
Macomb County, Michigan	249,425	90.7	23.7	145,146	84.3	18.7
Marquette County, Michigan	17,382	96.6	27.8	12,119	92.9	29.9
Midland County, Michigan	23,496	96.0	37.1	15,022	91.9	27.4
Monroe County, Michigan	44,598	93.4	17.0	26,316	86.3	14.8
Muskegon County, Michigan	47,055	91.9	19.5	28,259	87.4	19.8
Oakland County, Michigan	359,735	94.5	46.5	205,125	90.9	36.4
Ottawa County, Michigan	68,770	93.9	33.7	41,749	88.2	27.9
Saginaw County, Michigan	51,681	91.8	18.5	36,047	85.2	18.9
St. Clair County, Michigan	48,366	92.6	17.8	29,445	88.4	18.8
Shiawassee County, Michigan	20,263	94.1	15.6	12,190	86.9	14.3
Van Buren County, Michigan	22,496	89.9	22.0	12,737	87.7	22.1
Washtenaw County, Michigan	85,982	95.3	51.0	49,191	92.4	48.9
Wayne County, Michigan	468,638	87.4	23.4	264,476	81.9	19.2
MINNESOTA						
Anoka County, Minnesota	98,680	95.1	30.7	47,169	92.3	20.1
Blue Earth County, Minnesota	13,880	95.0	34.1	8,872	92.6	36.3
Carver County, Minnesota	28,699	97.3	52.5	11,410	95.7	35.8
Dakota County, Minnesota	116,420	94.7	42.0	57,174	92.6	33.0
Hennepin County, Minnesota	315,507	93.8	48.6	171,145	92.5	40.5
Olmsted County, Minnesota	39,427	95.9	40.5	23,131	91.6	37.6
Ramsey County, Minnesota	129,572	89.2	41.9	77,084	90.6	38.1
Rice County, Minnesota	16,413	96.7	31.4	10,357	87.2	27.9
St. Louis County, Minnesota	53,487	95.4	25.5	37,307	91.7	27.6
Scott County, Minnesota	39,445	95.6	38.4	14,759	90.2	29.1
Sherburne County, Minnesota	25,372	96.9	26.0	10,501	89.4	20.9
Stearns County, Minnesota	37,191	95.5	31.3	23,049	84.9	22.7
Washington County, Minnesota	72,421	97.5	42.7	37,266	95.6	34.3
Wright County, Minnesota	35,258	95.7	28.0	16,644	89.7	15.5

Table C-2. Educational Attainment of the Population, by Selected Counties, 2017—*Continued*

(Number; percent; dollars.)

State/County	Population 25 to 34 years			Population 35 to 44 years		
	Total	High school graduate or more (percent)	Bachelor's degree or more (percent)	Total	High school graduate or more (percent)	Bachelor's degree or more (percent)
MISSISSIPPI						
DeSoto County, Mississippi	22,588	93.2	22.1	26,520	92.9	29.5
Forrest County, Mississippi	11,193	89.0	40.9	8,999	90.6	33.3
Harrison County, Mississippi	29,248	93.1	25.3	24,443	89.8	23.1
Hinds County, Mississippi	34,622	87.7	27.1	28,334	90.2	31.8
Jackson County, Mississippi	16,664	86.5	26.6	17,063	95.2	27.8
Jones County, Mississippi	7,968	81.1	12.8	7,192	90.5	13.1
Lauderdale County, Mississippi	10,161	85.4	26.7	9,074	91.1	28.4
Lee County, Mississippi	11,149	74.3	14.0	10,859	80.8	25.2
Madison County, Mississippi	12,713	92.4	44.6	14,893	89.6	55.5
Rankin County, Mississippi	20,946	93.5	25.7	23,115	88.3	27.6
MISSOURI						
Boone County, Missouri	26,950	96.2	54.1	21,474	93.4	48.2
Buchanan County, Missouri	13,087	87.7	20.4	10,111	91.9	20.1
Cape Girardeau County, Missouri	9,409	98.0	29.1	8,711	94.2	39.3
Cass County, Missouri	13,566	86.4	23.3	12,517	93.0	32.7
Christian County, Missouri	10,942	90.7	32.3	10,777	89.6	32.3
Clay County, Missouri	32,565	94.4	37.2	34,296	94.6	35.4
Cole County, Missouri	10,647	90.2	35.8	9,686	93.4	35.6
Franklin County, Missouri	12,550	84.6	18.0	11,487	95.4	26.8
Greene County, Missouri	39,331	91.5	33.3	32,510	92.3	33.9
Jackson County, Missouri	107,842	90.8	34.8	86,756	90.5	35.9
Jasper County, Missouri	17,394	84.9	23.9	14,991	84.6	23.4
Jefferson County, Missouri	28,921	92.4	27.9	29,007	89.7	22.9
Platte County, Missouri	13,481	95.6	44.0	13,298	97.0	55.2
St. Charles County, Missouri	51,822	96.8	48.6	51,706	96.5	49.7
St. Francois County, Missouri	11,446	87.6	11.5	8,803	86.6	13.5
St. Louis County, Missouri	127,461	94.5	45.0	117,355	95.1	51.0
St. Louis city, Missouri	61,937	93.2	50.1	40,360	89.5	41.9
MONTANA						
Cascade County, Montana	11,294	89.7	27.4	9,076	87.6	28.6
Flathead County, Montana	12,019	93.2	27.7	12,165	93.8	28.3
Gallatin County, Montana	17,356	93.9	47.0	14,516	99.8	55.9
Lewis and Clark County, Montana	8,662	96.6	36.5	8,254	94.4	44.3
Missoula County, Montana	18,221	97.9	42.8	15,238	92.1	50.7
Yellowstone County, Montana	21,889	95.5	34.1	19,457	94.5	33.9
NEBRASKA						
Douglas County, Nebraska	87,926	90.9	43.4	74,333	87.4	42.4
Lancaster County, Nebraska	43,547	94.7	46.3	38,854	92.6	41.4
Sarpy County, Nebraska	26,360	95.3	46.3	25,092	96.6	50.9
NEVADA						
Clark County, Nevada	329,846	87.9	23.4	304,861	85.2	25.1
Washoe County, Nevada	68,809	90.7	30.5	55,708	89.0	33.1
NEW HAMPSHIRE						
Cheshire County, New Hampshire	9,150	97.1	31.6	7,590	90.1	30.1
Grafton County, New Hampshire	10,846	97.9	51.5	8,752	93.5	42.6
Hillsborough County, New Hampshire	54,297	92.6	42.5	49,660	95.1	40.2
Merrimack County, New Hampshire	17,764	93.5	39.3	17,285	95.5	32.2
Rockingham County, New Hampshire	35,303	95.8	49.4	35,494	96.5	48.7
Strafford County, New Hampshire	17,460	91.1	33.9	13,719	96.9	47.2
NEW JERSEY						
Atlantic County, New Jersey	30,474	91.3	28.2	31,057	86.3	33.4
Bergen County, New Jersey	110,581	96.6	58.8	125,343	95.8	60.3
Burlington County, New Jersey	55,867	95.7	44.3	54,874	95.3	42.4
Camden County, New Jersey	70,365	91.5	36.7	64,549	91.3	36.9
Cape May County, New Jersey	9,734	97.6	26.8	8,499	93.8	32.7
Cumberland County, New Jersey	20,219	82.2	21.3	21,110	81.5	16.5
Essex County, New Jersey	111,125	90.7	37.9	113,547	87.2	39.2
Gloucester County, New Jersey	34,794	98.6	40.2	37,127	94.6	46.5
Hudson County, New Jersey	146,900	93.4	59.2	109,368	90.0	50.0
Hunterdon County, New Jersey	10,968	97.4	55.1	12,990	97.2	63.9
Mercer County, New Jersey	47,046	90.7	45.4	47,788	87.0	42.3
Middlesex County, New Jersey	116,343	94.9	55.7	115,981	92.5	55.6
Monmouth County, New Jersey	67,201	94.9	52.0	71,720	92.4	53.3

Table C-2. Educational Attainment of the Population, by Selected Counties, 2017—*Continued*

(Number; percent; dollars.)

State/County	Population 45 to 64 years			Population 65 years and over		
	Total	High school graduate or more (percent)	Bachelor's degree or more (percent)	Total	High school graduate or more (percent)	Bachelor's degree or more (percent)
MISSISSIPPI						
DeSoto County, Mississippi	44,195	93.6	23.0	23,116	85.9	15.3
Forrest County, Mississippi	16,097	90.7	29.1	10,234	84.0	30.0
Harrison County, Mississippi	51,697	89.3	25.0	29,891	84.7	25.6
Hinds County, Mississippi	57,948	88.4	27.9	33,705	77.3	29.2
Jackson County, Mississippi	39,028	90.4	20.7	22,140	84.8	16.2
Jones County, Mississippi	17,338	87.3	20.0	11,421	81.0	17.4
Lauderdale County, Mississippi	19,339	86.0	19.0	12,746	79.8	27.8
Lee County, Mississippi	21,687	86.2	28.8	12,378	79.1	22.2
Madison County, Mississippi	27,072	94.8	51.3	13,796	82.4	41.9
Rankin County, Mississippi	38,356	90.2	32.3	22,459	86.9	25.5
MISSOURI						
Boone County, Missouri	37,510	94.7	42.4	21,525	93.1	38.7
Buchanan County, Missouri	21,936	92.0	20.6	14,694	84.6	12.4
Cape Girardeau County, Missouri	18,867	89.8	31.7	12,786	89.3	28.9
Cass County, Missouri	27,872	91.7	25.3	17,038	90.7	26.3
Christian County, Missouri	21,904	95.2	35.9	13,148	92.0	22.0
Clay County, Missouri	61,976	95.3	33.3	34,012	85.5	23.8
Cole County, Missouri	19,697	93.1	29.6	12,379	90.6	26.1
Franklin County, Missouri	29,885	87.7	23.2	17,664	81.6	14.4
Greene County, Missouri	69,890	92.1	32.2	47,085	90.6	26.3
Jackson County, Missouri	178,590	89.4	28.3	101,594	88.0	25.1
Jasper County, Missouri	28,321	88.0	23.5	18,103	88.9	20.6
Jefferson County, Missouri	64,300	90.7	23.4	33,053	85.3	16.7
Platte County, Missouri	27,787	96.3	39.3	14,196	91.6	34.5
St. Charles County, Missouri	106,792	96.1	37.2	58,289	91.1	26.3
St. Francois County, Missouri	17,472	80.1	12.7	10,827	78.7	8.8
St. Louis County, Missouri	269,983	94.1	43.5	176,344	90.6	34.6
St. Louis city, Missouri	77,790	86.9	30.0	39,823	81.4	25.9
MONTANA						
Cascade County, Montana	20,257	90.6	24.5	15,100	91.1	26.2
Flathead County, Montana	28,416	93.9	32.0	18,505	89.9	27.3
Gallatin County, Montana	23,918	97.0	52.9	12,978	95.8	45.3
Lewis and Clark County, Montana	18,872	95.9	41.3	12,157	95.2	36.2
Missoula County, Montana	27,505	97.3	42.3	17,823	95.2	50.9
Yellowstone County, Montana	41,975	91.2	29.0	26,501	90.3	32.8
NEBRASKA						
Douglas County, Nebraska	132,995	91.0	36.2	70,893	90.8	33.8
Lancaster County, Nebraska	70,170	93.1	35.5	42,294	92.8	32.7
Sarpy County, Nebraska	43,546	96.5	39.9	20,873	89.9	31.3
NEVADA						
Clark County, Nevada	554,014	85.2	24.2	317,116	86.5	25.1
Washoe County, Nevada	120,772	88.9	29.6	73,354	89.2	32.8
NEW HAMPSHIRE						
Cheshire County, New Hampshire	21,628	93.6	36.5	14,639	92.6	33.5
Grafton County, New Hampshire	25,433	94.5	43.6	17,868	91.1	33.6
Hillsborough County, New Hampshire	122,742	93.7	37.3	62,610	87.9	32.0
Merrimack County, New Hampshire	45,255	93.3	33.5	26,740	92.0	35.8
Rockingham County, New Hampshire	99,190	95.4	42.1	52,657	91.9	33.0
Strafford County, New Hampshire	34,035	93.3	29.4	19,081	84.4	28.2
NEW JERSEY						
Atlantic County, New Jersey	77,408	89.2	28.6	46,608	81.3	24.7
Bergen County, New Jersey	273,703	92.8	46.8	159,578	86.2	36.7
Burlington County, New Jersey	130,878	94.4	36.9	74,738	88.2	29.3
Camden County, New Jersey	137,889	90.4	31.7	77,910	81.8	27.2
Cape May County, New Jersey	28,187	93.3	34.7	24,027	92.6	35.2
Cumberland County, New Jersey	38,954	80.3	17.0	22,864	77.0	18.4
Essex County, New Jersey	212,182	85.6	35.5	107,642	76.8	29.5
Gloucester County, New Jersey	84,370	95.4	32.5	44,718	88.2	23.6
Hudson County, New Jersey	158,732	84.1	32.3	79,883	66.6	21.7
Hunterdon County, New Jersey	42,765	97.4	57.9	21,699	88.8	35.8
Mercer County, New Jersey	101,729	91.2	47.0	55,346	84.7	38.3
Middlesex County, New Jersey	226,634	90.0	40.4	122,272	83.3	31.1
Monmouth County, New Jersey	193,238	94.2	46.5	106,392	90.3	35.1

Table C-2. Educational Attainment of the Population, by Selected Counties, 2017—*Continued*

(Number; percent; dollars.)

State/County	Population 25 to 34 years			Population 35 to 44 years		
	Total	High school graduate or more (percent)	Bachelor's degree or more (percent)	Total	High school graduate or more (percent)	Bachelor's degree or more (percent)
NEW JERSEY—(*Continued*)						
Morris County, New Jersey	53,468	97.6	60.2	61,406	93.9	59.1
Ocean County, New Jersey	66,094	94.1	38.9	59,794	91.1	36.1
Passaic County, New Jersey	68,854	90.0	31.5	65,328	82.8	30.5
Salem County, New Jersey	7,469	92.4	26.7	7,345	91.4	32.3
Somerset County, New Jersey	36,786	96.6	53.8	44,509	96.2	60.1
Sussex County, New Jersey	14,560	97.7	44.2	16,638	95.5	40.9
Union County, New Jersey	72,308	92.7	36.2	78,486	85.9	37.9
Warren County, New Jersey	11,238	97.6	38.2	12,332	93.9	39.1
NEW MEXICO						
Bernalillo County, New Mexico	99,872	92.8	34.7	87,351	88.9	34.5
Chaves County, New Mexico	9,052	87.6	21.1	7,470	70.4	11.9
Doña Ana County, New Mexico	27,153	89.9	24.5	22,640	81.5	21.7
Lea County, New Mexico	9,999	85.9	11.5	8,506	77.6	12.5
McKinley County, New Mexico	10,976	88.3	8.9	8,231	78.1	8.9
Otero County, New Mexico	9,925	89.3	26.4	7,922	90.2	15.1
Sandoval County, New Mexico	17,329	87.7	23.3	18,517	86.6	24.5
San Juan County, New Mexico	16,827	88.5	14.5	16,421	80.2	11.7
Santa Fe County, New Mexico	16,491	91.2	26.0	16,564	81.7	29.0
Valencia County, New Mexico	8,974	87.5	6.3	9,232	85.7	12.6
NEW YORK						
Albany County, New York	39,216	95.3	54.3	36,238	93.5	50.7
Bronx County, New York	237,759	81.3	23.4	186,598	72.7	19.2
Broome County, New York	21,114	92.4	37.5	19,349	91.6	32.0
Cattaraugus County, New York	8,171	93.2	18.7	8,528	92.0	17.7
Cayuga County, New York	9,945	81.1	16.9	9,068	90.7	29.8
Chautauqua County, New York	14,483	91.1	22.9	13,652	92.5	21.7
Chemung County, New York	11,018	89.2	25.7	9,550	91.0	29.9
Clinton County, New York	10,197	84.0	15.6	9,640	90.3	18.5
Dutchess County, New York	34,578	90.8	35.9	33,795	91.8	37.9
Erie County, New York	131,635	93.1	42.5	102,186	93.9	43.0
Jefferson County, New York	19,092	89.2	25.5	12,681	93.3	23.6
Kings County, New York	488,903	91.2	52.5	367,676	87.2	43.4
Livingston County, New York	7,124	89.5	23.3	6,430	91.2	28.1
Madison County, New York	7,111	97.9	27.5	7,377	93.1	28.7
Monroe County, New York	105,574	91.3	39.7	84,153	92.1	43.0
Nassau County, New York	159,487	94.2	51.0	163,083	90.0	53.3
New York County, New York	374,994	93.5	74.3	238,266	90.3	64.9
Niagara County, New York	26,199	95.6	31.3	23,374	92.5	32.6
Oneida County, New York	29,466	87.4	25.6	24,303	88.8	23.8
Onondaga County, New York	61,763	92.6	43.0	51,497	91.5	38.4
Ontario County, New York	12,036	94.0	38.9	11,896	92.8	44.2
Orange County, New York	44,679	89.1	27.7	45,702	87.0	36.2
Oswego County, New York	14,104	85.9	24.5	13,134	94.2	24.4
Putnam County, New York	11,129	95.5	34.7	12,033	95.8	51.4
Queens County, New York	386,253	90.8	43.8	325,972	86.0	35.3
Rensselaer County, New York	21,772	94.6	37.9	18,506	89.5	43.7
Richmond County, New York	64,076	91.8	42.8	61,066	90.0	44.0
Rockland County, New York	37,067	87.5	34.1	37,215	82.3	40.0
St. Lawrence County, New York	13,405	83.7	30.0	11,976	87.3	23.0
Saratoga County, New York	27,176	92.2	44.6	29,229	95.3	54.1
Schenectady County, New York	18,643	96.1	34.5	19,473	89.6	28.5
Steuben County, New York	10,937	90.5	28.8	10,758	94.3	32.0
Suffolk County, New York	175,719	91.1	40.3	176,332	88.5	42.4
Sullivan County, New York	8,361	94.5	36.6	8,521	84.5	22.2
Tompkins County, New York	13,663	93.9	61.3	11,811	89.7	59.2
Ulster County, New York	21,710	89.3	24.7	20,932	94.8	38.0
Warren County, New York	7,819	89.5	28.1	7,008	96.7	38.5
Wayne County, New York	9,645	91.8	25.6	9,864	87.0	21.3
Westchester County, New York	112,661	88.8	47.4	124,979	86.5	51.9
NORTH CAROLINA						
Alamance County, North Carolina	19,661	86.1	25.5	19,006	85.6	24.7
Brunswick County, North Carolina	12,323	89.5	19.5	11,320	87.6	26.3
Buncombe County, North Carolina	33,556	93.5	39.9	35,592	89.9	39.4
Burke County, North Carolina	9,470	84.6	10.7	10,975	84.0	11.0
Cabarrus County, North Carolina	25,921	88.6	29.4	29,278	90.3	41.4
Caldwell County, North Carolina	8,850	80.2	16.5	9,080	83.2	16.3

Table C-2. Educational Attainment of the Population, by Selected Counties, 2017—*Continued*

(Number; percent; dollars.)

State/County	Population 45 to 64 years			Population 65 years and over		
	Total	High school graduate or more (percent)	Bachelor's degree or more (percent)	Total	High school graduate or more (percent)	Bachelor's degree or more (percent)
NEW JERSEY—(*Continued*)						
Morris County, New Jersey	151,464	94.8	54.6	82,902	88.9	38.9
Ocean County, New Jersey	151,998	94.6	28.4	133,715	89.7	26.2
Passaic County, New Jersey	132,777	84.1	26.7	72,789	79.5	24.2
Salem County, New Jersey	17,827	91.8	22.6	11,319	81.3	12.6
Somerset County, New Jersey	100,862	97.2	55.5	50,916	89.4	39.0
Sussex County, New Jersey	47,231	94.4	35.3	23,332	93.5	31.9
Union County, New Jersey	153,341	89.6	35.0	79,609	79.6	30.0
Warren County, New Jersey	33,712	91.7	32.2	18,213	85.2	28.5
NEW MEXICO						
Bernalillo County, New Mexico	171,305	89.9	34.4	106,579	89.7	37.8
Chaves County, New Mexico	14,334	79.3	16.2	10,199	73.5	17.9
Doña Ana County, New Mexico	46,602	76.0	23.9	33,134	72.1	28.9
Lea County, New Mexico	14,996	73.6	13.4	7,983	65.8	12.1
McKinley County, New Mexico	16,667	76.5	17.2	8,437	63.9	16.0
Otero County, New Mexico	15,033	84.3	15.0	10,194	85.9	19.2
Sandoval County, New Mexico	37,777	90.5	31.8	24,360	91.9	31.0
San Juan County, New Mexico	29,709	86.7	14.0	18,164	78.4	15.7
Santa Fe County, New Mexico	43,176	90.8	40.1	34,170	94.5	53.1
Valencia County, New Mexico	19,404	82.4	17.8	13,040	84.4	17.5
NEW YORK						
Albany County, New York	79,294	93.4	40.5	50,518	88.7	31.8
Bronx County, New York	347,206	71.6	19.3	181,708	59.3	15.9
Broome County, New York	51,241	89.7	25.6	36,175	89.6	21.5
Cattaraugus County, New York	21,731	91.2	21.0	14,376	83.2	21.0
Cayuga County, New York	22,617	90.8	22.9	14,359	82.7	20.8
Chautauqua County, New York	35,205	89.9	23.8	25,550	86.3	21.8
Chemung County, New York	24,237	92.3	21.4	15,477	83.9	22.7
Clinton County, New York	22,268	90.9	25.9	13,028	81.0	23.5
Dutchess County, New York	87,595	94.6	35.3	50,272	87.9	29.9
Erie County, New York	254,524	92.9	31.9	161,615	88.2	26.1
Jefferson County, New York	25,529	88.7	18.3	14,941	88.5	18.6
Kings County, New York	607,298	80.8	28.8	356,983	70.6	23.8
Livingston County, New York	18,562	95.5	23.0	10,815	88.7	30.4
Madison County, New York	21,197	91.9	26.7	12,423	92.3	28.0
Monroe County, New York	200,290	91.4	35.1	125,128	87.7	35.0
Nassau County, New York	390,815	92.5	45.8	238,220	86.9	34.5
New York County, New York	393,786	83.1	54.4	266,223	76.1	46.5
Niagara County, New York	62,434	92.5	23.0	38,997	85.8	17.2
Oneida County, New York	64,289	88.8	24.7	42,443	85.8	20.4
Onondaga County, New York	127,326	92.6	35.5	76,578	87.9	29.3
Ontario County, New York	33,096	93.0	36.5	20,971	93.8	31.7
Orange County, New York	102,262	92.4	32.6	52,080	87.9	26.0
Oswego County, New York	34,239	88.5	14.8	18,718	82.5	15.7
Putnam County, New York	32,340	94.4	38.5	15,945	85.7	32.3
Queens County, New York	628,123	80.9	25.8	354,954	70.7	21.8
Rensselaer County, New York	43,899	93.5	27.8	26,870	88.4	25.0
Richmond County, New York	133,176	88.8	30.9	75,761	83.2	20.1
Rockland County, New York	80,853	92.7	44.7	50,850	88.4	41.0
St. Lawrence County, New York	29,005	91.3	24.4	18,169	83.8	19.8
Saratoga County, New York	68,083	95.5	41.7	39,926	89.8	32.3
Schenectady County, New York	43,101	90.5	22.9	26,236	87.6	30.8
Steuben County, New York	27,838	90.8	18.2	18,478	87.6	17.5
Suffolk County, New York	440,142	91.3	35.7	244,753	88.5	30.7
Sullivan County, New York	22,543	90.8	26.1	13,885	82.4	32.8
Tompkins County, New York	22,177	93.6	43.5	14,270	93.7	51.1
Ulster County, New York	54,175	93.9	34.1	34,095	88.9	32.2
Warren County, New York	19,401	92.0	28.8	14,157	88.5	32.5
Wayne County, New York	27,468	90.5	19.3	16,628	82.2	23.9
Westchester County, New York	274,962	89.9	51.0	162,966	83.4	39.9
NORTH CAROLINA						
Alamance County, North Carolina	44,238	83.9	24.1	27,054	82.8	19.6
Brunswick County, North Carolina	38,816	91.2	29.3	40,387	93.5	35.7
Buncombe County, North Carolina	69,880	91.3	42.8	50,224	91.4	44.8
Burke County, North Carolina	26,542	80.8	16.9	17,180	83.5	23.0
Cabarrus County, North Carolina	55,185	89.3	35.1	26,642	84.6	16.8
Caldwell County, North Carolina	24,921	76.2	17.2	15,811	79.0	12.2

Table C-2. Educational Attainment of the Population, by Selected Counties, 2017—*Continued*

(Number; percent; dollars.)

State/County	Population 25 to 34 years			Population 35 to 44 years		
	Total	High school graduate or more (percent)	Bachelor's degree or more (percent)	Total	High school graduate or more (percent)	Bachelor's degree or more (percent)
NORTH CAROLINA—(*Continued*)						
Carteret County, North Carolina	6,741	92.4	23.1	7,663	88.5	19.3
Catawba County, North Carolina	18,620	89.3	20.6	18,819	85.8	21.0
Chatham County, North Carolina	7,340	87.2	23.9	8,934	83.7	48.9
Cleveland County, North Carolina	10,723	90.0	20.1	10,006	88.4	15.0
Craven County, North Carolina	12,983	94.5	18.8	11,422	77.8	26.2
Cumberland County, North Carolina	56,963	92.8	22.6	38,599	92.4	33.0
Davidson County, North Carolina	19,803	89.2	12.7	19,037	79.0	23.0
Durham County, North Carolina	56,307	90.7	57.5	43,843	82.9	48.6
Forsyth County, North Carolina	48,949	91.0	37.0	45,855	86.6	37.6
Franklin County, North Carolina	7,301	79.3	25.1	7,283	84.5	15.4
Gaston County, North Carolina	28,211	89.9	24.1	28,177	87.6	24.4
Guilford County, North Carolina	72,265	90.8	34.5	65,562	89.3	38.5
Harnett County, North Carolina	20,163	95.2	30.1	18,201	87.0	26.2
Henderson County, North Carolina	10,901	97.5	30.6	13,599	87.9	34.7
Iredell County, North Carolina	20,475	90.5	29.8	21,975	93.6	31.8
Johnston County, North Carolina	24,078	90.4	22.2	28,004	82.7	21.1
Lincoln County, North Carolina	8,959	82.3	22.2	10,403	92.1	28.8
Mecklenburg County, North Carolina	181,936	92.4	52.3	159,182	90.4	51.4
Moore County, North Carolina	12,050	96.7	54.5	10,701	92.6	31.3
Nash County, North Carolina	10,064	85.9	20.5	11,397	94.7	31.6
New Hanover County, North Carolina	31,167	89.5	40.1	28,247	94.7	49.2
Onslow County, North Carolina	35,215	96.6	25.6	18,630	91.7	34.8
Orange County, North Carolina	18,901	94.1	59.7	17,058	92.1	59.6
Pitt County, North Carolina	24,689	91.9	39.2	20,162	96.4	43.8
Randolph County, North Carolina	17,257	87.1	14.6	17,893	78.9	15.9
Robeson County, North Carolina	16,436	84.1	12.4	16,300	74.0	12.2
Rockingham County, North Carolina	8,547	85.8	15.6	11,357	81.0	13.7
Rowan County, North Carolina	16,358	86.6	20.1	15,903	82.0	18.3
Rutherford County, North Carolina	6,307	89.1	15.8	7,573	80.3	26.9
Surry County, North Carolina	7,913	90.5	28.8	8,559	79.7	24.8
Union County, North Carolina	22,715	92.9	29.4	32,492	88.1	44.4
Wake County, North Carolina	159,113	91.8	56.4	160,353	92.3	58.3
Wayne County, North Carolina	16,007	82.9	25.7	15,742	81.3	21.2
Wilkes County, North Carolina	7,915	90.9	16.7	7,527	91.7	23.0
Wilson County, North Carolina	10,636	84.7	14.5	9,143	79.5	15.7
NORTH DAKOTA						
Burleigh County, North Dakota	14,067	97.2	48.2	11,998	96.6	40.2
Cass County, North Dakota	31,574	96.1	49.1	22,739	98.4	53.0
Grand Forks County, North Dakota	11,680	94.8	40.8	7,116	96.7	36.8
Ward County, North Dakota	11,986	99.3	38.8	8,135	94.4	36.0
OHIO						
Allen County, Ohio	12,872	95.5	22.5	12,075	91.1	27.3
Ashtabula County, Ohio	11,795	82.2	12.2	10,727	91.8	18.4
Athens County, Ohio	7,997	87.5	40.0	6,622	94.1	38.1
Belmont County, Ohio	8,168	93.7	12.1	8,495	90.5	17.8
Butler County, Ohio	45,253	95.8	30.8	45,288	94.1	35.4
Clark County, Ohio	15,885	92.7	18.6	14,396	88.1	22.6
Clermont County, Ohio	25,294	95.6	30.7	25,455	93.7	32.7
Columbiana County, Ohio	11,534	91.4	12.1	12,023	86.3	16.9
Cuyahoga County, Ohio	172,776	93.3	38.3	142,143	90.9	38.4
Delaware County, Ohio	20,560	98.0	53.7	30,123	98.0	67.2
Erie County, Ohio	9,370	86.5	23.4	7,412	98.2	30.8
Fairfield County, Ohio	18,541	85.8	28.9	20,277	94.8	33.0
Franklin County, Ohio	234,432	93.9	46.2	171,371	91.9	43.5
Geauga County, Ohio	7,841	82.6	44.4	9,652	91.5	42.0
Greene County, Ohio	21,587	95.2	44.5	17,893	96.3	50.3
Hamilton County, Ohio	123,291	92.3	43.1	94,995	91.7	43.6
Hancock County, Ohio	10,399	93.5	31.6	9,137	90.2	39.2
Jefferson County, Ohio	7,410	94.2	18.5	7,456	96.1	14.2
Lake County, Ohio	26,380	95.6	34.8	26,816	89.7	26.9
Licking County, Ohio	20,905	92.4	22.8	21,009	92.6	38.9
Lorain County, Ohio	34,162	90.8	26.4	37,695	91.1	28.9
Lucas County, Ohio	61,195	91.0	31.8	49,229	90.7	29.1
Mahoning County, Ohio	27,344	92.2	25.4	25,686	90.9	24.9
Marion County, Ohio	8,649	92.9	17.6	8,036	81.0	13.1
Medina County, Ohio	19,864	97.6	43.3	22,241	97.3	42.5
Miami County, Ohio	12,597	95.8	27.3	12,815	99.1	33.5

Table C-2. Educational Attainment of the Population, by Selected Counties, 2017—*Continued*

(Number; percent; dollars.)

State/County	Population 45 to 64 years			Population 65 years and over		
	Total	High school graduate or more (percent)	Bachelor's degree or more (percent)	Total	High school graduate or more (percent)	Bachelor's degree or more (percent)
NORTH CAROLINA—(*Continued*)						
Carteret County, North Carolina	20,854	93.9	28.3	16,643	91.2	26.7
Catawba County, North Carolina	43,142	87.8	21.3	28,128	75.2	16.4
Chatham County, North Carolina	19,580	91.8	42.3	17,443	90.9	36.4
Cleveland County, North Carolina	27,957	87.1	18.6	17,692	79.1	15.7
Craven County, North Carolina	23,294	89.7	33.4	19,095	84.0	29.1
Cumberland County, North Carolina	71,350	92.2	21.6	39,053	82.9	21.1
Davidson County, North Carolina	49,098	86.2	16.7	29,333	79.1	17.5
Durham County, North Carolina	75,700	88.5	46.9	39,239	86.2	38.3
Forsyth County, North Carolina	99,712	90.8	34.4	57,977	88.1	28.2
Franklin County, North Carolina	20,356	91.8	26.3	10,518	80.0	11.6
Gaston County, North Carolina	60,751	85.6	20.2	34,911	78.8	15.6
Guilford County, North Carolina	137,190	90.5	36.9	78,196	88.0	32.1
Harnett County, North Carolina	30,519	88.6	18.5	16,210	74.6	12.9
Henderson County, North Carolina	32,554	89.3	29.8	28,720	91.9	40.4
Iredell County, North Carolina	49,924	91.1	28.9	27,697	86.4	19.5
Johnston County, North Carolina	53,661	89.5	23.1	25,547	80.4	20.9
Lincoln County, North Carolina	24,587	90.4	21.1	14,552	80.6	17.8
Mecklenburg County, North Carolina	263,896	92.2	44.3	117,823	85.9	33.1
Moore County, North Carolina	24,108	95.3	42.2	22,641	89.6	39.5
Nash County, North Carolina	25,528	86.4	19.5	16,770	83.8	20.1
New Hanover County, North Carolina	58,896	93.9	39.0	38,933	90.0	35.6
Onslow County, North Carolina	32,126	95.2	16.4	17,987	80.7	13.2
Orange County, North Carolina	35,247	91.2	54.8	19,836	93.1	53.8
Pitt County, North Carolina	39,957	93.8	31.8	22,855	76.6	26.3
Randolph County, North Carolina	40,780	83.9	16.1	24,724	77.3	17.5
Robeson County, North Carolina	33,111	80.2	14.4	19,769	71.9	14.7
Rockingham County, North Carolina	26,486	87.4	17.2	18,055	78.6	16.8
Rowan County, North Carolina	39,930	87.7	19.3	24,747	81.0	19.3
Rutherford County, North Carolina	19,389	86.5	20.5	14,172	86.5	16.5
Surry County, North Carolina	20,332	75.7	18.6	14,443	76.8	16.3
Union County, North Carolina	65,705	91.2	35.3	28,007	86.6	18.9
Wake County, North Carolina	275,987	93.5	52.0	120,445	89.8	39.2
Wayne County, North Carolina	30,806	90.7	17.6	19,787	81.6	19.5
Wilkes County, North Carolina	19,961	75.1	19.3	14,052	70.5	8.5
Wilson County, North Carolina	21,987	84.3	22.0	14,187	75.0	18.2
NORTH DAKOTA						
Burleigh County, North Dakota	23,617	95.2	32.3	14,681	90.0	23.7
Cass County, North Dakota	38,851	95.3	36.5	20,477	88.3	28.2
Grand Forks County, North Dakota	15,004	92.5	33.2	8,480	95.0	31.0
Ward County, North Dakota	14,374	94.7	28.3	8,662	89.5	23.4
OHIO						
Allen County, Ohio	26,787	89.3	17.3	17,964	85.4	16.1
Ashtabula County, Ohio	27,825	89.2	16.3	18,273	82.3	11.3
Athens County, Ohio	13,721	89.6	28.9	8,260	88.4	26.2
Belmont County, Ohio	20,254	92.6	17.4	13,639	89.1	9.2
Butler County, Ohio	98,946	93.0	28.1	54,146	84.6	25.1
Clark County, Ohio	35,600	86.2	17.5	25,794	86.1	23.1
Clermont County, Ohio	58,420	90.7	24.4	32,116	79.8	25.4
Columbiana County, Ohio	30,151	85.6	8.7	20,274	85.3	9.5
Cuyahoga County, Ohio	339,896	91.1	31.4	221,847	86.0	26.4
Delaware County, Ohio	54,373	95.7	53.9	26,231	92.5	40.6
Erie County, Ohio	20,995	93.9	27.8	16,043	90.3	20.2
Fairfield County, Ohio	41,284	93.8	27.5	23,924	89.9	20.0
Franklin County, Ohio	304,676	89.9	34.3	151,145	87.4	30.4
Geauga County, Ohio	28,097	92.5	37.6	18,891	85.7	36.2
Greene County, Ohio	43,719	94.5	40.7	27,359	85.5	30.1
Hamilton County, Ohio	209,650	91.6	34.8	122,268	86.6	31.1
Hancock County, Ohio	20,312	94.1	23.0	12,269	87.1	24.0
Jefferson County, Ohio	19,143	92.2	13.7	13,696	92.0	13.5
Lake County, Ohio	67,288	92.9	27.6	45,418	86.1	20.0
Licking County, Ohio	48,664	91.6	25.5	28,006	85.6	19.4
Lorain County, Ohio	85,956	90.1	21.7	54,879	85.8	21.1
Lucas County, Ohio	114,501	87.0	24.5	67,696	84.0	23.3
Mahoning County, Ohio	64,271	93.4	21.5	46,741	88.7	21.5
Marion County, Ohio	18,766	93.1	16.6	11,192	87.2	16.6
Medina County, Ohio	51,258	94.6	28.8	30,875	91.2	23.1
Miami County, Ohio	29,077	93.9	21.0	19,129	86.0	19.2

Table C-2. Educational Attainment of the Population, by Selected Counties, 2017—*Continued*

(Number; percent; dollars.)

State/County	Population 25 to 34 years			Population 35 to 44 years		
	Total	High school graduate or more (percent)	Bachelor's degree or more (percent)	Total	High school graduate or more (percent)	Bachelor's degree or more (percent)
OHIO—(*Continued*)						
Montgomery County, Ohio	72,153	90.0	28.6	60,313	90.7	33.5
Muskingum County, Ohio	10,523	93.7	21.7	9,908	91.2	16.6
Portage County, Ohio	18,308	91.9	34.9	16,251	97.9	31.1
Richland County, Ohio	14,244	82.6	20.5	15,212	87.6	17.3
Ross County, Ohio	10,197	92.7	17.2	9,793	87.3	19.4
Scioto County, Ohio	10,212	82.6	21.8	9,006	94.4	25.7
Stark County, Ohio	42,895	92.3	22.4	41,939	90.1	27.5
Summit County, Ohio	71,659	93.4	34.8	62,850	94.7	41.3
Trumbull County, Ohio	22,696	89.0	21.5	21,778	91.9	19.4
Tuscarawas County, Ohio	10,476	83.6	15.8	10,527	91.8	22.6
Warren County, Ohio	26,390	93.4	42.7	31,025	94.7	57.6
Wayne County, Ohio	13,758	90.2	24.8	12,659	79.1	20.3
Wood County, Ohio	15,667	96.2	41.9	14,804	95.3	40.6
OKLAHOMA						
Canadian County, Oklahoma	19,638	95.1	28.0	19,853	93.3	31.9
Cleveland County, Oklahoma	41,043	93.4	41.4	36,612	95.6	35.7
Comanche County, Oklahoma	18,774	94.6	29.0	15,035	90.2	18.2
Creek County, Oklahoma	8,499	85.8	15.9	8,484	90.3	16.6
Muskogee County, Oklahoma	8,255	86.1	17.1	8,966	78.3	16.6
Oklahoma County, Oklahoma	124,576	91.0	36.1	100,664	83.9	33.2
Payne County, Oklahoma	11,304	91.9	35.2	7,853	89.9	41.3
Pottawatomie County, Oklahoma	9,023	87.7	15.9	9,340	91.0	24.0
Rogers County, Oklahoma	11,107	91.9	25.5	11,217	94.2	24.3
Tulsa County, Oklahoma	95,669	88.9	29.7	82,534	88.8	34.0
Wagoner County, Oklahoma	10,359	96.7	24.2	10,227	85.5	29.7
OREGON						
Benton County, Oregon	12,866	98.8	56.8	8,732	98.1	57.7
Clackamas County, Oregon	50,101	92.2	37.6	54,525	96.2	40.4
Deschutes County, Oregon	23,160	95.1	33.6	23,916	88.6	32.8
Douglas County, Oregon	11,804	83.7	16.0	10,908	86.5	14.1
Jackson County, Oregon	25,974	88.2	24.0	24,525	90.5	30.7
Josephine County, Oregon	8,773	97.0	16.4	9,405	88.7	19.5
Klamath County, Oregon	7,547	88.6	15.2	6,989	83.2	22.0
Lane County, Oregon	48,225	95.3	33.1	45,496	88.3	34.9
Linn County, Oregon	16,140	85.1	17.0	15,646	89.5	21.6
Marion County, Oregon	47,266	86.5	25.1	43,947	78.2	22.6
Multnomah County, Oregon	150,572	94.0	50.4	132,021	92.0	51.7
Polk County, Oregon	8,809	90.5	26.5	9,692	84.5	34.8
Umatilla County, Oregon	10,701	82.7	15.0	9,160	71.9	20.7
Washington County, Oregon	91,117	94.5	49.1	88,566	92.2	51.4
Yamhill County, Oregon	13,285	84.5	31.9	13,696	86.7	31.9
PENNSYLVANIA						
Adams County, Pennsylvania	11,325	91.0	30.5	11,163	93.7	27.3
Allegheny County, Pennsylvania	187,301	96.8	55.9	140,739	96.0	53.3
Armstrong County, Pennsylvania	7,118	82.1	22.9	7,369	94.4	19.3
Beaver County, Pennsylvania	18,561	97.2	32.9	19,115	94.0	29.1
Berks County, Pennsylvania	50,943	89.3	25.1	48,175	88.1	32.4
Blair County, Pennsylvania	15,616	96.3	25.5	13,934	97.0	25.2
Bucks County, Pennsylvania	69,886	96.3	45.6	73,745	94.9	48.7
Butler County, Pennsylvania	21,165	98.1	47.1	21,751	95.3	49.6
Cambria County, Pennsylvania	13,648	93.7	33.6	14,396	92.7	32.3
Carbon County, Pennsylvania	7,429	87.4	13.8	6,838	95.4	24.6
Centre County, Pennsylvania	22,213	94.4	52.5	16,766	95.5	55.9
Chester County, Pennsylvania	60,907	91.7	50.7	63,183	93.6	62.5
Clearfield County, Pennsylvania	9,619	86.2	16.3	9,669	90.1	23.3
Columbia County, Pennsylvania	6,824	92.9	34.8	6,811	97.5	36.6
Crawford County, Pennsylvania	9,533	83.4	19.7	8,945	92.6	30.0
Cumberland County, Pennsylvania	33,355	95.0	42.7	30,222	95.0	42.4
Dauphin County, Pennsylvania	37,842	91.0	39.6	33,383	90.8	33.5
Delaware County, Pennsylvania	73,383	94.6	45.1	66,514	96.1	47.5
Erie County, Pennsylvania	35,171	92.2	35.7	31,506	92.2	30.0
Fayette County, Pennsylvania	14,912	93.3	24.0	14,986	95.2	24.0
Franklin County, Pennsylvania	18,683	90.4	27.4	18,265	87.1	27.6
Indiana County, Pennsylvania	8,780	92.0	37.7	8,343	88.8	30.0
Lackawanna County, Pennsylvania	25,036	93.2	42.7	24,639	91.9	33.6
Lancaster County, Pennsylvania	70,915	85.9	33.0	61,015	82.6	28.6

Table C-2. Educational Attainment of the Population, by Selected Counties, 2017—*Continued*

(Number; percent; dollars.)

State/County	Population 45 to 64 years			Population 65 years and over		
	Total	High school graduate or more (percent)	Bachelor's degree or more (percent)	Total	High school graduate or more (percent)	Bachelor's degree or more (percent)
OHIO—(*Continued*)						
Montgomery County, Ohio	140,088	91.1	26.8	93,466	86.2	25.4
Muskingum County, Ohio	23,503	88.1	16.3	14,914	83.7	11.1
Portage County, Ohio	44,009	89.4	27.4	26,047	89.2	30.8
Richland County, Ohio	31,718	91.3	20.6	23,376	81.3	16.2
Ross County, Ohio	22,269	87.2	16.6	12,175	86.6	14.0
Scioto County, Ohio	20,172	78.4	15.9	13,751	76.1	8.0
Stark County, Ohio	103,924	91.6	21.1	71,166	90.1	20.1
Summit County, Ohio	152,038	93.0	30.9	94,128	89.1	28.8
Trumbull County, Ohio	57,330	90.8	19.9	42,304	89.1	15.1
Tuscarawas County, Ohio	24,932	90.3	11.7	18,037	87.0	10.4
Warren County, Ohio	65,029	95.7	42.7	31,994	90.1	27.1
Wayne County, Ohio	29,803	90.0	23.1	20,375	84.3	20.8
Wood County, Ohio	31,168	95.8	31.0	19,412	93.0	21.1
OKLAHOMA						
Canadian County, Oklahoma	34,704	92.8	26.3	17,689	91.5	23.0
Cleveland County, Oklahoma	64,636	91.5	30.5	35,936	84.6	28.2
Comanche County, Oklahoma	26,964	92.3	24.4	15,430	88.1	23.9
Creek County, Oklahoma	19,338	91.0	17.3	11,996	83.3	15.1
Muskogee County, Oklahoma	16,794	86.2	19.5	11,253	77.0	15.6
Oklahoma County, Oklahoma	184,370	88.4	32.0	104,690	88.3	29.2
Payne County, Oklahoma	13,865	90.0	36.6	10,001	87.5	34.7
Pottawatomie County, Oklahoma	17,790	87.7	15.5	11,801	83.9	17.6
Rogers County, Oklahoma	24,601	92.6	28.0	14,571	89.9	23.2
Tulsa County, Oklahoma	156,283	90.3	32.1	90,434	90.1	31.1
Wagoner County, Oklahoma	20,909	90.9	25.5	12,373	84.0	18.7
OREGON						
Benton County, Oregon	19,634	97.3	57.0	14,095	95.3	44.2
Clackamas County, Oregon	114,400	94.9	39.6	72,419	92.8	35.6
Deschutes County, Oregon	52,398	95.9	32.0	35,868	94.3	36.9
Douglas County, Oregon	31,153	88.8	16.5	26,910	91.9	20.0
Jackson County, Oregon	56,965	92.0	27.4	46,817	91.8	30.8
Josephine County, Oregon	24,251	92.4	18.2	21,667	89.0	20.4
Klamath County, Oregon	17,939	88.5	15.6	14,423	90.9	25.1
Lane County, Oregon	92,809	92.3	27.1	70,607	93.4	32.6
Linn County, Oregon	32,502	90.4	15.6	22,934	91.0	17.1
Marion County, Oregon	82,288	84.2	22.3	51,881	85.2	22.4
Multnomah County, Oregon	200,275	91.2	40.4	104,943	91.2	39.7
Polk County, Oregon	19,073	88.3	26.6	14,835	91.8	36.4
Umatilla County, Oregon	18,776	83.1	15.7	11,355	87.3	19.2
Washington County, Oregon	148,417	92.7	42.6	75,977	93.3	41.6
Yamhill County, Oregon	26,054	92.8	25.1	17,916	91.6	24.4
PENNSYLVANIA						
Adams County, Pennsylvania	29,411	88.8	20.3	20,219	85.1	20.0
Allegheny County, Pennsylvania	330,439	95.3	37.6	225,615	90.4	27.4
Armstrong County, Pennsylvania	19,771	93.8	14.8	13,939	84.7	10.0
Beaver County, Pennsylvania	48,296	95.7	22.6	35,270	91.4	17.7
Berks County, Pennsylvania	113,009	87.9	22.0	70,836	80.7	20.0
Blair County, Pennsylvania	34,557	89.9	21.5	24,702	86.0	15.0
Bucks County, Pennsylvania	190,845	94.6	42.0	114,298	91.1	33.0
Butler County, Pennsylvania	55,641	95.2	32.8	34,336	91.4	26.8
Cambria County, Pennsylvania	37,712	93.1	16.7	29,408	86.6	16.1
Carbon County, Pennsylvania	20,082	94.9	12.9	12,918	83.1	12.2
Centre County, Pennsylvania	36,903	94.6	42.8	22,421	89.8	35.1
Chester County, Pennsylvania	148,052	95.1	53.3	81,757	91.2	43.7
Clearfield County, Pennsylvania	23,784	87.3	18.0	16,004	85.6	13.1
Columbia County, Pennsylvania	17,947	92.3	21.0	12,276	85.3	13.2
Crawford County, Pennsylvania	24,759	89.6	18.5	17,316	87.7	22.0
Cumberland County, Pennsylvania	66,235	93.7	36.8	45,328	87.7	30.8
Dauphin County, Pennsylvania	74,505	93.2	27.0	45,615	88.2	20.9
Delaware County, Pennsylvania	153,175	95.1	39.8	90,728	88.9	32.1
Erie County, Pennsylvania	73,654	91.0	23.1	47,318	87.8	24.9
Fayette County, Pennsylvania	39,964	88.1	15.6	26,612	82.2	15.3
Franklin County, Pennsylvania	42,133	88.3	19.0	29,448	88.0	25.8
Indiana County, Pennsylvania	22,135	92.0	21.7	15,964	88.0	17.6
Lackawanna County, Pennsylvania	57,566	93.2	28.6	41,103	89.5	19.1
Lancaster County, Pennsylvania	138,249	85.8	26.1	94,730	83.0	26.8

Table C-2. Educational Attainment of the Population, by Selected Counties, 2017—*Continued*

(Number; percent; dollars.)

State/County	Population 25 to 34 years			Population 35 to 44 years		
	Total	High school graduate or more (percent)	Bachelor's degree or more (percent)	Total	High school graduate or more (percent)	Bachelor's degree or more (percent)
PENNSYLVANIA—(*Continued*)						
Lawrence County, Pennsylvania	9,312	91.5	23.7	9,013	93.9	28.0
Lebanon County, Pennsylvania	16,514	91.5	24.7	15,673	92.5	21.9
Lehigh County, Pennsylvania	46,932	91.0	30.2	45,562	89.3	31.8
Luzerne County, Pennsylvania	40,528	89.7	28.1	35,726	89.6	29.4
Lycoming County, Pennsylvania	15,419	96.7	31.0	12,766	95.4	35.5
Mercer County, Pennsylvania	11,412	93.3	22.2	11,741	92.5	26.1
Monroe County, Pennsylvania	18,621	93.5	23.4	19,443	85.5	27.0
Montgomery County, Pennsylvania	103,102	96.0	58.1	102,141	95.6	60.4
Northampton County, Pennsylvania	36,186	94.1	36.6	35,332	94.1	35.1
Northumberland County, Pennsylvania	11,047	86.3	15.8	10,373	88.7	24.4
Philadelphia County, Pennsylvania	299,973	93.1	42.8	195,085	87.1	30.8
Schuylkill County, Pennsylvania	16,493	95.5	23.9	17,596	93.1	18.0
Somerset County, Pennsylvania	8,421	91.3	17.8	8,730	95.0	19.6
Washington County, Pennsylvania	22,692	94.0	44.7	23,731	97.0	37.3
Westmoreland County, Pennsylvania	37,409	96.5	36.7	37,881	95.2	41.4
York County, Pennsylvania	53,998	93.0	29.3	54,229	92.1	31.0
RHODE ISLAND						
Kent County, Rhode Island	21,609	94.4	43.9	19,888	94.6	35.4
Newport County, Rhode Island	10,124	98.7	58.6	8,670	97.2	52.8
Providence County, Rhode Island	96,708	91.5	29.7	77,849	89.9	38.1
Washington County, Rhode Island	12,113	95.3	52.2	11,581	100.0	49.4
SOUTH CAROLINA						
Aiken County, South Carolina	21,665	85.4	23.7	19,483	91.9	20.0
Anderson County, South Carolina	24,345	83.7	24.8	23,217	85.6	22.8
Beaufort County, South Carolina	20,028	90.2	29.3	19,082	79.0	28.4
Berkeley County, South Carolina	31,766	90.0	24.0	29,370	91.0	28.9
Charleston County, South Carolina	69,005	93.0	44.4	52,313	92.3	45.7
Darlington County, South Carolina	7,836	90.0	13.2	8,610	91.7	23.6
Dorchester County, South Carolina	22,498	92.9	30.2	21,553	94.4	33.9
Florence County, South Carolina	17,542	82.8	29.4	16,685	87.6	30.9
Greenville County, South Carolina	70,470	90.3	37.2	65,888	90.3	38.9
Greenwood County, South Carolina	9,143	90.4	14.1	7,987	88.0	29.5
Horry County, South Carolina	38,112	89.1	23.4	38,689	90.4	23.6
Kershaw County, South Carolina	7,396	92.5	14.0	8,153	96.5	31.3
Lancaster County, South Carolina	11,257	84.3	29.4	11,706	83.1	37.4
Laurens County, South Carolina	8,267	78.6	18.9	7,588	78.2	12.3
Lexington County, South Carolina	38,622	89.2	32.1	38,042	87.4	34.2
Oconee County, South Carolina	8,476	81.9	17.2	7,939	88.0	26.6
Orangeburg County, South Carolina	8,856	95.1	22.2	11,088	77.9	27.4
Pickens County, South Carolina	14,211	86.3	31.7	13,724	83.4	28.4
Richland County, South Carolina	61,269	93.7	36.6	51,233	91.3	40.0
Spartanburg County, South Carolina	39,608	91.3	26.8	37,973	89.5	28.2
Sumter County, South Carolina	15,108	90.1	16.0	12,435	92.2	24.0
York County, South Carolina	31,006	90.2	39.8	37,779	91.5	41.0
SOUTH DAKOTA						
Minnehaha County, South Dakota	29,582	95.8	32.3	23,133	94.6	38.1
Pennington County, South Dakota	16,279	89.7	28.2	12,510	88.6	27.4
TENNESSEE						
Anderson County, Tennessee	9,251	91.9	22.2	8,376	88.6	18.0
Blount County, Tennessee	14,706	85.9	22.4	15,719	90.5	25.5
Bradley County, Tennessee	13,785	93.2	16.1	12,625	87.0	30.6
Davidson County, Tennessee	138,183	94.1	53.7	94,116	88.4	43.1
Greene County, Tennessee	7,211	94.3	13.5	7,991	88.6	15.0
Hamilton County, Tennessee	53,041	93.2	31.1	45,127	93.5	39.3
Knox County, Tennessee	62,840	95.3	42.9	57,195	94.9	44.2
Madison County, Tennessee	11,351	97.3	32.7	10,891	88.8	30.8
Maury County, Tennessee	11,506	95.3	37.9	11,229	91.7	28.8
Montgomery County, Tennessee	38,038	96.1	32.0	26,827	93.9	26.2
Putnam County, Tennessee	9,935	95.6	31.3	8,738	90.8	18.8
Robertson County, Tennessee	8,348	90.0	31.8	8,927	88.0	15.4
Rutherford County, Tennessee	46,900	93.7	36.3	46,517	87.5	40.6
Sevier County, Tennessee	11,907	90.4	16.1	10,562	86.0	22.7
Shelby County, Tennessee	137,908	90.0	33.2	117,012	86.9	33.2
Sullivan County, Tennessee	18,022	92.5	24.7	18,091	88.4	27.2
Sumner County, Tennessee	22,976	93.7	29.4	24,064	95.4	34.6

Table C-2. Educational Attainment of the Population, by Selected Counties, 2017—*Continued*

(Number; percent; dollars.)

State/County	Population 45 to 64 years			Population 65 years and over		
	Total	High school graduate or more (percent)	Bachelor's degree or more (percent)	Total	High school graduate or more (percent)	Bachelor's degree or more (percent)
PENNSYLVANIA—(*Continued*)						
Lawrence County, Pennsylvania	25,412	92.8	20.9	18,808	87.2	22.1
Lebanon County, Pennsylvania	36,499	91.6	22.9	27,078	80.7	19.9
Lehigh County, Pennsylvania	97,362	89.7	31.3	59,136	82.7	23.9
Luzerne County, Pennsylvania	88,630	92.1	25.1	62,355	84.1	16.2
Lycoming County, Pennsylvania	30,961	92.1	19.7	21,169	85.4	18.6
Mercer County, Pennsylvania	32,223	92.7	26.4	23,688	86.7	21.8
Monroe County, Pennsylvania	50,668	90.3	22.9	28,179	82.7	24.8
Montgomery County, Pennsylvania	231,980	95.8	49.1	143,233	91.6	39.0
Northampton County, Pennsylvania	84,829	93.1	29.5	56,479	82.8	23.1
Northumberland County, Pennsylvania	26,489	92.2	14.8	19,166	80.9	13.1
Philadelphia County, Pennsylvania	369,079	84.5	20.7	211,716	74.0	18.9
Schuylkill County, Pennsylvania	41,730	89.8	15.6	28,741	82.9	13.2
Somerset County, Pennsylvania	21,779	90.8	14.4	16,293	81.2	9.9
Washington County, Pennsylvania	61,034	95.2	30.7	41,416	88.8	21.4
Westmoreland County, Pennsylvania	107,994	95.4	30.2	77,723	91.5	22.7
York County, Pennsylvania	127,222	91.8	24.9	75,332	81.8	18.9
RHODE ISLAND						
Kent County, Rhode Island	49,388	93.0	34.1	29,968	82.1	23.7
Newport County, Rhode Island	24,351	93.2	42.6	17,325	90.9	46.2
Providence County, Rhode Island	165,679	84.3	27.1	95,376	77.9	22.8
Washington County, Rhode Island	37,555	95.6	40.7	24,526	89.2	39.9
SOUTH CAROLINA						
Aiken County, South Carolina	45,491	87.0	27.3	31,979	86.9	31.0
Anderson County, South Carolina	53,194	87.7	19.4	35,748	77.7	18.8
Beaufort County, South Carolina	44,356	94.5	39.6	49,222	95.3	52.3
Berkeley County, South Carolina	54,209	89.0	25.2	30,299	84.4	21.0
Charleston County, South Carolina	101,520	92.8	42.1	63,020	90.6	38.3
Darlington County, South Carolina	17,904	88.9	26.6	12,436	75.6	24.2
Dorchester County, South Carolina	41,529	91.7	31.3	20,242	83.5	22.5
Florence County, South Carolina	36,095	84.6	23.0	22,986	72.5	18.5
Greenville County, South Carolina	130,851	88.3	32.7	77,739	84.1	31.2
Greenwood County, South Carolina	18,674	83.1	24.3	12,821	75.1	24.6
Horry County, South Carolina	92,177	91.3	21.5	77,411	90.8	23.3
Kershaw County, South Carolina	17,584	93.2	22.8	11,527	82.3	21.8
Lancaster County, South Carolina	24,352	83.8	17.6	19,255	86.3	32.0
Laurens County, South Carolina	18,165	81.2	16.1	12,178	82.3	14.8
Lexington County, South Carolina	78,721	90.2	27.8	44,760	89.0	30.0
Oconee County, South Carolina	21,990	84.5	24.9	17,694	85.2	33.9
Orangeburg County, South Carolina	22,198	88.1	18.5	16,708	74.6	18.2
Pickens County, South Carolina	29,938	86.4	22.2	19,836	80.3	19.7
Richland County, South Carolina	95,312	91.4	38.4	50,829	87.1	34.1
Spartanburg County, South Carolina	80,843	87.0	23.1	48,627	81.2	24.9
Sumter County, South Carolina	26,217	86.9	21.0	17,345	72.1	17.4
York County, South Carolina	71,352	90.3	32.3	37,395	89.0	28.3
SOUTH DAKOTA						
Minnehaha County, South Dakota	47,040	94.4	29.6	24,383	91.1	27.7
Pennington County, South Dakota	28,083	96.0	30.2	18,644	94.6	31.9
TENNESSEE						
Anderson County, Tennessee	21,460	83.9	21.3	14,998	85.8	30.6
Blount County, Tennessee	37,127	92.4	23.7	25,991	85.0	21.1
Bradley County, Tennessee	28,411	86.1	22.0	17,139	81.4	19.5
Davidson County, Tennessee	163,094	89.8	34.2	81,867	87.6	35.2
Greene County, Tennessee	19,983	86.2	14.2	14,443	76.7	14.2
Hamilton County, Tennessee	94,872	91.0	32.8	62,257	90.3	28.4
Knox County, Tennessee	118,749	90.0	35.2	70,575	89.0	30.4
Madison County, Tennessee	25,861	86.0	21.2	16,056	83.3	25.2
Maury County, Tennessee	25,765	92.2	18.4	13,855	79.7	18.6
Montgomery County, Tennessee	40,979	88.8	28.6	18,025	86.9	21.2
Putnam County, Tennessee	18,434	85.1	22.1	12,724	78.1	23.1
Robertson County, Tennessee	20,128	88.6	16.9	9,893	85.2	16.6
Rutherford County, Tennessee	75,152	92.5	31.5	31,376	86.2	30.6
Sevier County, Tennessee	28,049	85.9	14.1	18,671	81.4	16.7
Shelby County, Tennessee	236,877	91.2	32.1	122,477	85.2	28.1
Sullivan County, Tennessee	44,951	87.1	24.2	33,879	78.8	20.7
Sumner County, Tennessee	51,431	89.9	27.5	27,646	83.8	22.6

Table C-2. Educational Attainment of the Population, by Selected Counties, 2017—*Continued*

(Number; percent; dollars.)

State/County	Population 25 to 34 years			Population 35 to 44 years		
	Total	High school graduate or more (percent)	Bachelor's degree or more (percent)	Total	High school graduate or more (percent)	Bachelor's degree or more (percent)
TENNESSEE—(*Continued*)						
Washington County, Tennessee	16,443	96.0	41.5	15,094	92.1	39.2
Williamson County, Tennessee	22,082	96.9	62.9	32,569	95.1	73.8
Wilson County, Tennessee	15,427	93.1	35.6	18,800	97.5	42.6
TEXAS						
Angelina County, Texas	10,628	88.7	14.3	10,068	88.1	13.9
Bastrop County, Texas	8,517	79.9	19.9	10,782	81.4	32.7
Bell County, Texas	57,520	95.8	26.8	45,230	90.5	26.5
Bexar County, Texas	310,755	89.6	29.1	262,874	85.4	29.4
Bowie County, Texas	11,942	88.1	26.6	12,618	93.4	15.9
Brazoria County, Texas	51,226	89.6	34.8	53,505	88.4	39.9
Brazos County, Texas	34,900	90.7	43.8	24,920	83.3	42.9
Cameron County, Texas	51,668	84.2	16.8	51,770	68.2	18.6
Collin County, Texas	121,656	93.2	49.8	154,256	94.3	57.8
Comal County, Texas	16,244	95.8	37.7	16,489	93.3	37.8
Coryell County, Texas	15,030	92.9	17.2	10,681	90.9	16.4
Dallas County, Texas	427,020	85.4	34.6	361,049	75.4	30.1
Denton County, Texas	123,683	94.6	48.0	128,100	92.9	49.7
Ector County, Texas	26,229	80.3	16.2	19,911	81.4	13.5
Ellis County, Texas	22,824	87.1	20.9	22,395	86.6	24.4
El Paso County, Texas	124,297	91.7	24.4	104,366	86.3	29.9
Fort Bend County, Texas	93,181	93.7	44.6	116,681	89.7	53.8
Galveston County, Texas	44,089	91.6	30.3	44,446	91.6	33.7
Grayson County, Texas	15,408	96.0	23.5	15,264	89.9	16.0
Gregg County, Texas	16,858	81.7	17.3	14,534	78.7	13.1
Guadalupe County, Texas	20,670	91.5	22.5	21,857	92.3	31.2
Harris County, Texas	750,294	86.6	32.8	663,606	78.8	30.4
Harrison County, Texas	8,181	93.1	24.5	7,907	89.1	12.9
Hays County, Texas	29,790	92.1	39.6	28,719	91.8	43.3
Henderson County, Texas	9,462	81.8	12.1	9,511	83.3	17.7
Hidalgo County, Texas	113,388	81.3	19.5	111,705	70.3	17.7
Hunt County, Texas	11,377	91.4	23.1	11,149	93.2	21.3
Jefferson County, Texas	36,265	91.4	17.9	31,656	83.7	20.7
Johnson County, Texas	21,164	87.0	19.7	21,886	85.4	21.8
Kaufman County, Texas	16,226	84.3	24.7	17,168	89.8	24.1
Liberty County, Texas	11,681	86.0	11.5	10,581	69.3	10.2
Lubbock County, Texas	45,184	94.0	33.0	35,553	88.4	33.8
McLennan County, Texas	33,005	83.8	21.1	28,889	80.9	25.2
Midland County, Texas	28,587	87.8	32.4	21,885	83.4	23.9
Montgomery County, Texas	71,947	88.0	36.2	78,037	84.7	33.0
Nacogdoches County, Texas	7,907	87.0	25.9	5,971	91.6	24.1
Nueces County, Texas	52,742	88.1	21.2	44,805	84.9	19.1
Orange County, Texas	10,548	88.7	14.9	10,420	88.3	22.0
Parker County, Texas	15,756	93.0	23.7	17,111	86.6	30.6
Potter County, Texas	17,307	83.0	18.3	16,567	72.7	14.4
Randall County, Texas	20,257	92.4	30.9	17,053	93.2	35.0
Rockwall County, Texas	10,947	94.4	41.6	13,927	86.5	47.2
San Patricio County, Texas	7,867	73.1	8.9	9,271	90.0	16.2
Smith County, Texas	28,702	86.2	23.7	28,016	88.4	27.0
Tarrant County, Texas	306,177	88.3	32.1	280,505	83.9	33.1
Taylor County, Texas	20,142	91.6	23.3	15,085	89.3	21.8
Tom Green County, Texas	18,965	91.9	24.0	14,073	92.5	25.1
Travis County, Texas	246,262	93.3	51.6	193,600	88.3	49.7
Victoria County, Texas	12,399	84.7	19.6	11,367	82.8	19.6
Walker County, Texas	9,973	94.6	28.1	10,382	85.9	17.4
Webb County, Texas	36,695	82.9	17.9	35,498	76.8	21.0
Wichita County, Texas	19,313	87.9	22.0	14,642	87.8	20.6
Williamson County, Texas	75,123	93.9	41.1	88,217	94.0	43.8
Wise County, Texas	7,723	86.1	13.7	8,811	85.1	15.0
UTAH						
Cache County, Utah	16,705	97.4	44.9	15,302	86.6	42.1
Davis County, Utah	49,933	96.1	36.8	50,070	96.9	43.4
Salt Lake County, Utah	187,157	92.3	37.3	166,562	91.2	39.1
Tooele County, Utah	8,553	93.6	27.1	10,347	90.1	35.2
Utah County, Utah	86,389	95.1	41.4	77,036	94.4	44.7
Washington County, Utah	19,008	87.8	15.9	18,901	87.4	26.4
Weber County, Utah	37,943	91.0	21.4	34,215	88.5	29.3

Table C-2. Educational Attainment of the Population, by Selected Counties, 2017—*Continued*

(Number; percent; dollars.)

State/County	Population 45 to 64 years			Population 65 years and over		
	Total	High school graduate or more (percent)	Bachelor's degree or more (percent)	Total	High school graduate or more (percent)	Bachelor's degree or more (percent)
TENNESSEE—(*Continued*)						
Washington County, Tennessee...............	34,323	89.7	31.0	22,625	84.3	25.3
Williamson County, Tennessee...............	63,121	96.3	58.2	29,475	92.4	46.6
Wilson County, Tennessee	38,048	92.7	31.6	21,333	88.9	19.9
TEXAS						
Angelina County, Texas	21,914	80.2	15.5	14,498	79.8	20.6
Bastrop County, Texas............................	24,833	79.0	25.4	10,566	92.9	21.9
Bell County, Texas..................................	70,496	92.4	27.2	37,080	86.8	27.2
Bexar County, Texas...............................	444,386	84.2	26.7	231,697	78.1	26.3
Bowie County, Texas..............................	23,316	94.3	22.5	14,762	86.1	23.6
Brazoria County, Texas...........................	90,208	88.7	28.6	41,677	86.0	27.9
Brazos County, Texas.............................	38,764	83.2	36.9	19,179	88.5	41.1
Cameron County, Texas...........................	88,891	66.4	19.5	56,062	50.6	16.6
Collin County, Texas...............................	255,676	94.3	52.9	103,946	92.6	43.6
Comal County, Texas..............................	39,719	95.7	39.8	25,467	91.7	36.8
Coryell County, Texas.............................	15,382	85.2	15.1	7,046	90.5	20.8
Dallas County, Texas..............................	613,353	77.6	27.8	274,589	79.4	31.1
Denton County, Texas.............................	213,856	92.9	45.9	82,259	89.5	38.3
Ector County, Texas...............................	31,643	71.3	13.5	15,090	63.8	11.0
Ellis County, Texas.................................	44,682	84.2	21.3	21,759	88.1	22.8
El Paso County, Texas............................	186,184	77.8	22.0	99,882	55.0	15.4
Fort Bend County, Texas.........................	198,725	90.2	46.0	81,303	85.4	40.7
Galveston County, Texas.........................	89,973	89.0	31.6	46,418	87.0	28.9
Grayson County, Texas...........................	35,185	86.8	19.3	22,749	85.9	21.2
Gregg County, Texas..............................	29,333	87.8	21.7	19,389	87.7	19.1
Guadalupe County, Texas........................	41,043	89.5	29.9	21,414	77.8	21.1
Harris County, Texas..............................	1,082,768	79.6	29.6	474,189	78.7	30.6
Harrison County, Texas	16,821	90.6	21.1	10,921	77.3	17.2
Hays County, Texas................................	46,968	91.4	35.9	22,103	89.8	40.8
Henderson County, Texas........................	20,926	85.7	19.7	18,147	82.1	16.9
Hidalgo County, Texas............................	164,407	61.9	21.0	92,842	45.8	14.6
Hunt County, Texas................................	24,175	87.6	21.0	14,856	87.3	31.0
Jefferson County, Texas..........................	65,349	85.4	18.0	35,654	81.9	19.7
Johnson County, Texas	43,130	87.2	16.3	23,419	82.5	18.3
Kaufman County, Texas...........................	30,832	82.8	20.3	14,307	85.5	22.5
Liberty County, Texas.............................	21,913	75.4	4.0	10,223	73.5	6.5
Lubbock County, Texas	63,079	83.6	25.9	36,700	79.0	29.1
McLennan County, Texas	55,756	85.6	26.0	35,639	82.4	25.2
Midland County, Texas............................	35,297	86.9	25.5	17,213	78.6	29.4
Montgomery County, Texas......................	150,778	90.6	34.5	72,746	90.2	27.4
Nacogdoches County, Texas....................	14,147	83.5	21.4	9,712	85.5	26.8
Nueces County, Texas............................	87,385	82.0	21.6	50,986	74.1	21.4
Orange County, Texas............................	22,463	89.5	14.0	12,989	81.0	11.5
Parker County, Texas..............................	36,239	90.1	26.7	21,261	88.2	24.4
Potter County, Texas..............................	29,051	73.3	14.6	13,976	77.0	18.3
Randall County, Texas............................	31,650	95.3	27.9	19,723	89.7	32.7
Rockwall County, Texas..........................	26,967	89.7	45.8	11,258	92.2	30.0
San Patricio County, Texas.....................	15,852	81.1	14.0	9,842	70.9	14.6
Smith County, Texas...............................	54,900	86.8	26.1	36,919	87.5	30.0
Tarrant County, Texas.............................	504,302	84.6	30.7	226,575	83.8	30.0
Taylor County, Texas..............................	28,341	85.1	23.0	19,656	85.7	28.9
Tom Green County, Texas.......................	25,849	89.6	26.7	17,907	82.3	16.2
Travis County, Texas..............................	285,348	90.4	49.3	117,088	87.2	44.8
Victoria County, Texas............................	21,437	84.2	19.6	14,495	77.3	19.9
Walker County, Texas.............................	17,646	84.8	19.0	8,842	87.5	30.2
Webb County, Texas...............................	54,466	64.9	16.5	25,482	47.8	11.9
Wichita County, Texas............................	29,987	88.4	25.6	19,151	88.3	18.9
Williamson County, Texas	130,940	92.5	40.0	65,977	91.6	38.5
Wise County, Texas................................	18,071	82.0	16.7	9,963	76.0	11.9
UTAH						
Cache County, Utah................................	19,077	94.7	37.7	11,083	94.2	37.8
Davis County, Utah.................................	68,827	95.6	39.3	35,260	94.7	34.6
Salt Lake County, Utah...........................	243,299	89.6	33.5	119,765	91.5	34.8
Tooele County, Utah...............................	14,136	89.4	25.1	5,956	93.6	20.1
Utah County, Utah..................................	90,670	94.3	41.9	45,666	93.4	37.4
Washington County, Utah........................	34,503	90.1	28.8	34,823	92.1	31.2
Weber County, Utah................................	54,054	89.4	26.9	28,360	88.7	23.1

Table C-2. Educational Attainment of the Population, by Selected Counties, 2017—*Continued*

(Number; percent; dollars.)

State/County	Population 25 to 34 years			Population 35 to 44 years		
	Total	High school graduate or more (percent)	Bachelor's degree or more (percent)	Total	High school graduate or more (percent)	Bachelor's degree or more (percent)
VERMONT						
Chittenden County, Vermont	23,743	93.3	51.6	18,303	92.8	56.2
VIRGINIA						
Albemarle County, Virginia	13,575	95.2	63.4	12,721	94.3	52.5
Arlington County, Virginia	56,929	95.4	85.7	39,709	91.5	75.6
Augusta County, Virginia	8,689	90.8	20.0	8,829	90.0	25.1
Bedford County, Virginia	7,618	95.4	26.5	8,087	95.7	30.0
Chesterfield County, Virginia	40,623	92.9	35.9	46,671	92.1	43.2
Fairfax County, Virginia	154,004	92.4	60.7	165,774	91.3	64.1
Fauquier County, Virginia	7,842	90.4	26.6	8,710	94.3	36.5
Frederick County, Virginia	9,630	86.7	26.7	9,780	94.4	32.4
Hanover County, Virginia	10,432	95.3	45.4	12,417	92.5	46.2
Henrico County, Virginia	46,651	92.1	49.9	43,682	93.3	49.7
James City County, Virginia	6,479	89.3	42.6	8,231	86.5	53.7
Loudoun County, Virginia	48,640	96.1	66.2	68,075	94.0	68.6
Montgomery County, Virginia	13,449	95.1	50.4	9,885	97.2	56.7
Prince William County, Virginia	63,035	89.7	36.6	70,578	86.6	42.5
Roanoke County, Virginia	10,300	95.8	38.4	11,476	94.7	49.6
Rockingham County, Virginia	8,928	93.6	26.6	9,266	82.9	26.0
Spotsylvania County, Virginia	16,253	94.7	33.7	17,268	92.3	38.1
Stafford County, Virginia	16,567	90.3	35.7	22,438	92.1	45.2
York County, Virginia	8,240	96.1	40.8	8,609	91.9	51.0
Alexandria city, Virginia	34,997	97.1	68.7	31,416	88.8	61.2
Chesapeake city, Virginia	32,451	95.5	35.5	32,348	95.4	37.5
Hampton city, Virginia	20,937	97.7	24.8	15,978	93.9	28.9
Lynchburg city, Virginia	10,957	95.6	46.9	7,743	93.1	32.9
Newport News city, Virginia	30,571	92.7	27.3	20,871	88.2	26.9
Norfolk city, Virginia	46,961	92.9	31.3	27,211	88.3	35.8
Portsmouth city, Virginia	14,693	93.7	25.9	11,869	95.5	24.7
Richmond city, Virginia	48,706	89.4	51.0	26,831	84.6	36.2
Roanoke city, Virginia	15,328	87.0	27.2	12,948	86.3	25.4
Suffolk city, Virginia	13,074	91.9	26.4	11,159	94.4	27.6
Virginia Beach city, Virginia	75,016	96.5	33.5	58,380	94.7	38.2
WASHINGTON						
Benton County, Washington	26,889	88.5	21.8	25,039	89.6	39.3
Chelan County, Washington	8,151	90.4	33.5	8,347	76.9	23.0
Clallam County, Washington	7,589	89.8	19.6	7,555	90.9	21.1
Clark County, Washington	62,046	91.7	28.9	63,508	90.3	36.0
Cowlitz County, Washington	13,426	91.3	14.7	11,784	87.2	20.2
Franklin County, Washington	14,293	82.0	15.6	12,674	76.1	21.3
Grant County, Washington	12,451	75.1	13.2	11,137	77.9	22.0
Grays Harbor County, Washington	8,621	91.6	7.0	8,619	87.6	17.2
Island County, Washington	11,977	97.2	30.1	8,217	93.8	30.1
King County, Washington	390,742	94.8	58.8	326,747	93.0	56.4
Kitsap County, Washington	37,401	95.8	32.8	30,627	93.6	30.6
Lewis County, Washington	8,435	90.9	17.5	10,184	82.8	19.0
Pierce County, Washington	136,674	90.6	23.5	113,043	90.5	26.3
Skagit County, Washington	15,217	92.4	24.2	14,474	83.4	28.7
Snohomish County, Washington	117,156	95.3	34.4	112,758	92.5	33.5
Spokane County, Washington	73,010	93.6	28.8	61,881	94.6	32.2
Thurston County, Washington	39,241	95.1	29.1	37,549	93.6	42.5
Whatcom County, Washington	29,207	94.7	34.3	26,431	92.8	39.4
Yakima County, Washington	33,648	78.2	17.1	29,034	67.7	17.8
WEST VIRGINIA						
Berkeley County, West Virginia	14,365	96.0	26.9	15,909	94.9	22.9
Cabell County, West Virginia	12,397	88.7	26.6	10,963	95.4	39.0
Harrison County, West Virginia	8,045	93.5	31.0	8,196	92.4	24.5
Kanawha County, West Virginia	22,305	89.4	29.2	21,900	94.2	26.5
Monongalia County, West Virginia	17,419	95.3	56.2	12,234	92.3	39.6
Raleigh County, West Virginia	8,812	94.7	21.4	9,406	93.7	26.4
Wood County, West Virginia	9,340	89.7	26.8	10,274	94.9	22.6
WISCONSIN						
Brown County, Wisconsin	35,129	94.3	37.0	33,949	85.6	37.3
Dane County, Wisconsin	80,907	97.7	60.3	71,945	95.5	59.0
Dodge County, Wisconsin	10,879	93.1	14.6	10,976	96.5	22.5
Eau Claire County, Wisconsin	13,765	95.9	32.7	11,569	93.1	42.1

Table C-2. Educational Attainment of the Population, by Selected Counties, 2017—*Continued*

(Number; percent; dollars.)

State/County	Population 45 to 64 years			Population 65 years and over		
	Total	High school graduate or more (percent)	Bachelor's degree or more (percent)	Total	High school graduate or more (percent)	Bachelor's degree or more (percent)
VERMONT						
Chittenden County, Vermont	41,784	95.9	46.6	23,486	91.9	41.3
VIRGINIA						
Albemarle County, Virginia	27,105	93.7	58.7	18,415	85.9	45.9
Arlington County, Virginia	53,148	93.0	73.6	23,886	93.1	58.5
Augusta County, Virginia	22,110	88.4	21.2	15,573	84.3	19.8
Bedford County, Virginia	24,663	94.3	27.8	17,075	84.9	25.0
Chesterfield County, Virginia	95,080	94.6	42.7	49,305	88.8	34.4
Fairfax County, Virginia	313,847	93.8	62.1	150,277	91.9	57.7
Fauquier County, Virginia	20,201	94.5	35.6	11,013	91.3	37.1
Frederick County, Virginia	25,578	89.7	26.7	14,503	81.1	24.3
Hanover County, Virginia	32,185	94.2	41.2	18,262	88.2	25.2
Henrico County, Virginia	87,581	92.7	46.0	49,081	89.4	36.3
James City County, Virginia	19,958	95.5	48.2	18,168	94.5	55.7
Loudoun County, Virginia	103,891	93.8	60.6	35,655	91.4	48.6
Montgomery County, Virginia	19,277	88.3	31.9	11,959	90.9	34.5
Prince William County, Virginia	119,061	89.0	41.1	43,808	88.4	38.2
Roanoke County, Virginia	25,645	93.0	32.6	20,095	89.3	27.5
Rockingham County, Virginia	21,154	84.4	25.5	15,131	74.7	21.8
Spotsylvania County, Virginia	36,345	93.3	31.0	18,234	85.1	33.7
Stafford County, Virginia	38,959	96.3	42.8	14,963	92.3	37.4
York County, Virginia	18,654	96.7	48.0	10,099	92.4	38.7
Alexandria city, Virginia	37,402	90.7	60.1	17,890	88.8	57.5
Chesapeake city, Virginia	65,120	94.7	38.1	30,868	91.2	26.0
Hampton city, Virginia	33,614	90.4	29.0	20,252	86.4	29.7
Lynchburg city, Virginia	14,221	86.8	30.0	11,547	80.5	24.7
Newport News city, Virginia	42,089	91.0	23.6	22,709	86.4	24.5
Norfolk city, Virginia	50,958	87.4	27.5	26,777	77.4	22.1
Portsmouth city, Virginia	23,026	87.2	20.7	13,853	84.3	19.8
Richmond city, Virginia	52,938	85.2	32.1	28,812	78.2	31.7
Roanoke city, Virginia	26,220	81.6	18.1	16,867	83.9	25.9
Suffolk city, Virginia	24,831	88.8	27.1	12,786	77.4	22.6
Virginia Beach city, Virginia	112,473	94.2	36.4	61,535	87.6	33.0
WASHINGTON						
Benton County, Washington	48,092	89.6	29.8	28,609	86.7	28.8
Chelan County, Washington	20,636	77.2	25.7	14,029	91.3	27.5
Clallam County, Washington	20,798	92.1	23.7	22,068	93.5	33.6
Clark County, Washington	125,433	94.5	31.4	70,897	93.4	30.5
Cowlitz County, Washington	29,792	90.9	15.3	19,722	85.2	20.2
Franklin County, Washington	18,168	73.9	11.2	8,495	76.9	19.9
Grant County, Washington	20,654	75.6	16.0	13,144	77.9	16.7
Grays Harbor County, Washington	20,518	87.9	14.5	15,147	91.0	15.5
Island County, Washington	20,683	94.4	29.4	19,935	96.0	40.4
King County, Washington	561,293	92.7	47.6	283,958	90.4	43.4
Kitsap County, Washington	70,431	93.2	35.0	46,415	92.9	33.7
Lewis County, Washington	20,893	89.2	19.3	16,225	86.8	14.8
Pierce County, Washington	222,353	93.2	26.1	117,857	91.0	28.4
Skagit County, Washington	32,571	90.6	25.6	25,694	91.1	32.9
Snohomish County, Washington	221,107	92.4	31.6	104,218	91.0	27.9
Spokane County, Washington	129,944	94.4	32.8	79,386	92.6	28.4
Thurston County, Washington	71,529	96.7	35.4	47,812	92.2	36.3
Whatcom County, Washington	53,863	94.2	34.2	37,743	92.3	36.7
Yakima County, Washington	55,453	71.9	16.8	33,682	74.3	19.1
WEST VIRGINIA						
Berkeley County, West Virginia	31,255	89.5	20.0	16,407	84.6	19.2
Cabell County, West Virginia	22,842	88.7	22.4	17,533	85.1	25.9
Harrison County, West Virginia	18,739	87.4	17.3	13,238	86.7	19.1
Kanawha County, West Virginia	51,488	90.2	24.2	36,801	82.4	25.2
Monongalia County, West Virginia	22,887	92.4	37.7	12,567	83.6	28.3
Raleigh County, West Virginia	20,080	86.5	19.8	15,074	86.9	16.3
Wood County, West Virginia	24,108	93.3	25.6	16,734	81.3	14.6
WISCONSIN						
Brown County, Wisconsin	68,607	92.5	32.9	37,345	91.1	27.1
Dane County, Wisconsin	125,750	96.5	46.1	71,859	94.8	43.3
Dodge County, Wisconsin	26,606	90.4	16.4	15,018	86.1	12.8
Eau Claire County, Wisconsin	23,894	94.4	30.2	16,221	90.9	30.1

Table C-2. Educational Attainment of the Population, by Selected Counties, 2017—*Continued*

(Number; percent; dollars.)

State/County	Population 25 to 34 years			Population 35 to 44 years		
	Total	High school graduate or more (percent)	Bachelor's degree or more (percent)	Total	High school graduate or more (percent)	Bachelor's degree or more (percent)
WISCONSIN—(*Continued*)						
Fond du Lac County, Wisconsin	12,163	92.9	32.4	11,747	90.8	34.7
Jefferson County, Wisconsin	10,167	95.4	29.1	10,692	91.7	29.9
Kenosha County, Wisconsin	21,808	92.4	28.2	20,593	91.6	29.2
La Crosse County, Wisconsin	14,693	97.0	35.3	13,711	91.9	38.8
Manitowoc County, Wisconsin	8,413	94.4	22.1	9,110	96.2	26.4
Marathon County, Wisconsin	16,146	95.3	34.5	16,710	90.7	28.0
Milwaukee County, Wisconsin	155,229	93.0	38.4	121,145	89.5	31.9
Outagamie County, Wisconsin	24,131	94.4	35.7	24,814	95.7	39.1
Ozaukee County, Wisconsin	8,231	99.0	53.7	9,752	98.1	64.8
Portage County, Wisconsin	8,380	97.1	37.2	7,558	95.6	42.6
Racine County, Wisconsin	22,555	89.4	29.0	23,070	94.7	31.1
Rock County, Wisconsin	20,425	95.3	21.9	19,705	87.9	27.7
St. Croix County, Wisconsin	9,537	97.2	43.5	12,239	96.0	34.8
Sheboygan County, Wisconsin	12,808	98.0	27.8	14,292	95.2	28.0
Walworth County, Wisconsin	11,417	91.5	26.3	10,521	87.3	22.0
Washington County, Wisconsin	14,248	97.4	39.9	16,275	95.6	35.3
Waukesha County, Wisconsin	42,024	96.9	53.1	48,737	97.3	58.2
Winnebago County, Wisconsin	22,148	94.8	39.8	19,829	94.5	31.6
Wood County, Wisconsin	8,238	94.1	20.6	8,475	89.7	28.1
WYOMING						
Laramie County, Wyoming	14,892	94.4	27.0	12,823	87.8	28.3
Natrona County, Wyoming	11,658	98.4	19.2	10,124	90.1	24.7

Table C-2. Educational Attainment of the Population, by Selected Counties, 2017—*Continued*

(Number; percent; dollars.)

State/County	Population 45 to 64 years			Population 65 years and over		
	Total	High school graduate or more (percent)	Bachelor's degree or more (percent)	Total	High school graduate or more (percent)	Bachelor's degree or more (percent)
WISCONSIN—(*Continued*)						
Fond du Lac County, Wisconsin............................	29,735	94.7	22.4	18,401	88.2	17.1
Jefferson County, Wisconsin................................	24,188	93.8	24.9	13,865	84.2	19.1
Kenosha County, Wisconsin................................	47,714	91.9	24.5	22,691	85.3	23.0
La Crosse County, Wisconsin..............................	28,808	95.8	30.9	18,632	86.9	25.2
Manitowoc County, Wisconsin.............................	23,521	94.0	17.0	15,715	88.7	15.7
Marathon County, Wisconsin	37,960	93.2	25.2	23,003	89.2	19.0
Milwaukee County, Wisconsin.............................	228,348	87.6	27.1	126,081	84.4	26.4
Outagamie County, Wisconsin	50,890	95.6	28.7	26,559	89.5	18.5
Ozaukee County, Wisconsin	26,490	95.0	48.2	17,354	90.7	45.1
Portage County, Wisconsin	17,590	95.5	34.5	11,383	89.5	22.1
Racine County, Wisconsin..................................	55,792	93.0	28.3	31,464	90.0	23.8
Rock County, Wisconsin	44,249	90.1	19.6	25,949	90.2	19.1
St. Croix County, Wisconsin...............................	25,562	97.3	34.1	12,063	93.4	32.1
Sheboygan County, Wisconsin............................	32,601	93.9	27.1	20,283	87.5	18.2
Walworth County, Wisconsin	28,700	90.6	34.3	17,728	93.4	30.9
Washington County, Wisconsin	41,487	97.4	31.7	23,314	90.2	21.5
Waukesha County, Wisconsin.............................	118,797	97.2	45.2	73,223	93.8	33.0
Winnebago County, Wisconsin	45,755	94.2	28.2	26,763	91.7	21.3
Wood County, Wisconsin....................................	20,933	96.6	19.2	14,699	90.5	18.8
WYOMING						
Laramie County, Wyoming..................................	24,563	92.3	28.3	15,168	92.4	27.9
Natrona County, Wyoming	20,373	92.8	26.4	11,326	91.2	25.3

Table C-2. Educational Attainment of the Population, by Selected Counties, 2017—*Continued*

(Number; percent; dollars.)

State/County	Educational attainment by race/ethnicity, 25 years and over					
	White alone			White alone, not Hispanic		
	Total	High school graduate or more (percent)	Bachelor's degree or more (percent)	Total	High school graduate or more (percent)	Bachelor's degree or more (percent)
ALABAMA						
Baldwin County, Alabama	134,486	91.2	35.4	129,590	92.1	35.9
Calhoun County, Alabama	61,374	85.9	20.7	60,256	86.1	20.7
Cullman County, Alabama	55,434	82.2	12.3	54,316	82.5	12.1
DeKalb County, Alabama	42,535	79.2	15.2	41,348	79.7	15.6
Elmore County, Alabama	43,015	90.7	29.2	42,392	91.1	29.2
Etowah County, Alabama	59,443	85.0	19.0	58,311	85.1	19.4
Houston County, Alabama	52,643	89.6	24.6	50,937	90.3	24.8
Jefferson County, Alabama	246,166	92.6	44.6	239,611	93.0	44.9
Lauderdale County, Alabama	56,173	88.9	24.9	55,202	89.0	25.1
Lee County, Alabama	69,027	94.5	39.9	66,091	94.7	39.9
Limestone County, Alabama	53,615	89.4	28.5	51,955	89.8	27.7
Madison County, Alabama	175,651	92.7	44.3	168,933	93.8	45.2
Marshall County, Alabama	58,722	81.9	20.4	55,236	84.5	21.7
Mobile County, Alabama	174,007	88.5	26.0	168,854	88.7	26.2
Montgomery County, Alabama	60,496	91.8	46.2	58,174	93.1	47.2
Morgan County, Alabama	68,171	88.1	20.6	65,845	89.5	21.1
St. Clair County, Alabama	54,702	86.9	16.1	53,877	86.8	15.5
Shelby County, Alabama	120,108	93.8	45.0	117,078	94.1	45.4
Talladega County, Alabama	37,053	85.6	16.7	36,872	85.5	16.4
Tuscaloosa County, Alabama	85,011	87.8	36.5	83,493	88.2	36.5
Walker County, Alabama	41,076	82.6	12.1	40,899	82.6	12.1
ALASKA						
Anchorage Municipality, Alaska	130,282	96.4	42.0	123,384	96.5	42.6
Fairbanks North Star Borough, Alaska	48,844	94.8	31.1	46,477	94.6	31.4
Matanuska-Susitna Borough, Alaska	59,091	92.4	23.3	57,240	92.5	23.1
ARIZONA						
Apache County, Arizona	11,644	90.2	19.5	10,085	93.9	20.8
Cochise County, Arizona	76,480	88.2	23.6	53,468	93.0	28.5
Coconino County, Arizona	56,613	96.3	46.7	48,746	97.0	50.2
Maricopa County, Arizona	2,305,777	89.1	33.3	1,790,220	95.2	39.0
Mohave County, Arizona	145,621	87.4	13.8	128,730	90.1	14.3
Navajo County, Arizona	37,006	91.4	26.5	32,917	92.4	28.4
Pima County, Arizona	545,434	91.5	36.5	405,537	95.6	41.9
Pinal County, Arizona	250,923	86.2	20.7	188,163	92.0	24.4
Yavapai County, Arizona	165,309	92.0	24.2	149,535	93.8	25.7
Yuma County, Arizona	108,800	72.0	12.6	50,855	88.8	17.5
ARKANSAS						
Benton County, Arkansas	154,748	90.1	32.8	135,394	94.4	34.9
Craighead County, Arkansas	58,286	90.8	29.8	56,848	91.2	30.0
Faulkner County, Arkansas	64,055	93.6	33.2	62,705	93.9	33.4
Garland County, Arkansas	63,544	89.7	21.1	61,590	90.0	21.4
Jefferson County, Arkansas	20,684	91.8	17.5	20,293	92.7	17.3
Lonoke County, Arkansas	43,461	90.9	23.7	42,227	90.9	24.0
Pulaski County, Arkansas	162,223	93.6	41.7	155,395	94.4	42.8
Saline County, Arkansas	74,167	92.5	26.3	72,007	93.5	26.6
Sebastian County, Arkansas	66,867	88.5	24.4	64,190	90.2	25.4
Washington County, Arkansas	114,030	90.3	36.1	108,311	91.4	37.4
White County, Arkansas	47,284	84.6	23.0	46,619	85.1	23.0
CALIFORNIA						
Alameda County, California	500,815	92.8	52.4	411,120	97.1	58.8
Butte County, California	127,645	91.7	27.3	116,683	92.2	28.2
Contra Costa County, California	475,836	91.4	45.4	383,303	96.7	51.4
El Dorado County, California	123,044	93.3	33.5	111,969	94.7	34.7
Fresno County, California	409,466	79.4	21.9	218,219	93.6	32.4
Humboldt County, California	78,499	93.1	35.2	74,434	93.7	36.1
Imperial County, California	66,611	75.0	17.5	14,523	93.5	24.8
Kern County, California	417,317	73.0	15.5	220,856	89.3	23.6
Kings County, California	61,353	76.7	14.4	34,306	93.3	21.4
Lake County, California	38,350	93.2	14.8	36,319	94.1	15.3
Los Angeles County, California	3,570,835	81.9	35.3	2,091,520	94.8	49.8
Madera County, California	68,987	74.0	16.5	41,349	91.0	20.7
Marin County, California	153,793	97.0	62.7	144,271	98.0	64.6
Mendocino County, California	54,317	91.0	27.9	45,453	94.3	31.1
Merced County, California	95,323	77.7	16.3	55,319	89.7	22.9
Monterey County, California	150,199	85.2	34.7	102,897	94.0	44.2

Table C-2. Educational Attainment of the Population, by Selected Counties, 2017—*Continued*

(Number; percent; dollars.)

| State/County | Educational attainment by race/ethnicity, 25 years and over | | | | | |
| | Black alone | | | American Indian or Alaska Native alone | | |
	Total	High school graduate or more (percent)	Bachelor's degree or more (percent)	Total	High school graduate or more (percent)	Bachelor's degree or more (percent)
ALABAMA						
Baldwin County, Alabama	12,509	74.3	20.2	N	N	N
Calhoun County, Alabama	14,862	88.8	15.3	N	N	N
Cullman County, Alabama	N	N	N	N	N	N
DeKalb County, Alabama	N	N	N	N	N	N
Elmore County, Alabama	10,953	73.8	11.1	N	N	N
Etowah County, Alabama	10,358	78.3	21.9	N	N	N
Houston County, Alabama	17,517	79.5	13.5	N	N	N
Jefferson County, Alabama	184,514	86.9	18.1	N	N	N
Lauderdale County, Alabama	6,698	85.7	18.9	N	N	N
Lee County, Alabama	21,973	85.0	12.8	N	N	N
Limestone County, Alabama	8,926	77.2	29.7	N	N	N
Madison County, Alabama	55,185	87.8	31.5	1,778	97.5	24.0
Marshall County, Alabama	1,401	66.3	10.3	N	N	N
Mobile County, Alabama	91,877	86.3	16.8	N	N	N
Montgomery County, Alabama	83,125	81.3	21.8	N	N	N
Morgan County, Alabama	9,388	80.9	10.9	N	N	N
St. Clair County, Alabama	5,907	79.4	22.4	N	N	N
Shelby County, Alabama	16,686	91.7	33.3	N	N	N
Talladega County, Alabama	17,845	82.5	9.6	N	N	N
Tuscaloosa County, Alabama	39,214	85.3	22.1	N	N	N
Walker County, Alabama	2,447	90.1	5.3	N	N	N
ALASKA						
Anchorage Municipality, Alaska	9,829	89.2	17.8	12,421	81.0	13.1
Fairbanks North Star Borough, Alaska	N	N	N	4,535	81.0	16.0
Matanuska-Susitna Borough, Alaska	N	N	N	3,196	86.8	7.9
ARIZONA						
Apache County, Arizona	N	N	N	31,981	76.0	8.9
Cochise County, Arizona	3,135	93.0	37.7	N	N	N
Coconino County, Arizona	N	N	N	20,890	77.5	9.5
Maricopa County, Arizona	144,741	91.8	24.5	51,871	83.5	14.4
Mohave County, Arizona	N	N	N	3,140	88.9	1.6
Navajo County, Arizona	N	N	N	27,293	75.6	7.4
Pima County, Arizona	22,597	90.8	30.5	24,676	70.9	11.6
Pinal County, Arizona	13,372	82.2	13.7	13,106	65.1	2.4
Yavapai County, Arizona	N	N	N	1,968	68.2	5.9
Yuma County, Arizona	3,451	93.1	21.0	N	N	N
ARKANSAS						
Benton County, Arkansas	3,079	95.8	32.9	2,860	85.1	19.9
Craighead County, Arkansas	7,484	81.0	8.9	N	N	N
Faulkner County, Arkansas	8,295	94.5	32.0	N	N	N
Garland County, Arkansas	5,222	80.1	4.0	N	N	N
Jefferson County, Arkansas	24,216	84.1	18.8	N	N	N
Lonoke County, Arkansas	3,130	81.2	26.9	N	N	N
Pulaski County, Arkansas	87,756	88.3	22.7	N	N	N
Saline County, Arkansas	5,052	91.5	23.8	N	N	N
Sebastian County, Arkansas	5,100	79.0	8.6	N	N	N
Washington County, Arkansas	N	N	N	N	N	N
White County, Arkansas	1,930	83.3	30.4	N	N	N
CALIFORNIA						
Alameda County, California	125,465	89.7	28.6	8,132	81.1	21.3
Butte County, California	3,399	89.4	27.4	2,346	76.9	3.2
Contra Costa County, California	64,109	88.4	26.5	3,380	82.2	25.6
El Dorado County, California	N	N	N	N	N	N
Fresno County, California	28,607	85.3	16.7	6,307	70.9	12.6
Humboldt County, California	N	N	N	3,455	84.5	12.3
Imperial County, California	3,219	66.5	0.7	1,113	86.4	1.5
Kern County, California	28,589	81.1	13.6	5,267	67.5	3.2
Kings County, California	6,402	82.0	4.1	1,714	64.6	16.4
Lake County, California	N	N	N	N	N	N
Los Angeles County, California	584,575	89.6	26.8	49,616	72.3	15.4
Madera County, California	4,505	86.0	12.0	N	N	N
Marin County, California	3,721	78.0	17.1	N	N	N
Mendocino County, California	N	N	N	2,190	62.5	1.1
Merced County, California	6,186	88.3	21.7	N	N	N
Monterey County, California	8,330	89.3	21.1	N	N	N

N = Data for this geographic area cannot be displayed because the number of sample cases is too small.

Table C-2. Educational Attainment of the Population, by Selected Counties, 2017—*Continued*

(Number; percent; dollars.)

State/County	Educational attainment by race/ethnicity, 25 years and over					
	White alone			White alone, not Hispanic		
	Total	High school graduate or more (percent)	Bachelor's degree or more (percent)	Total	High school graduate or more (percent)	Bachelor's degree or more (percent)
CALIFORNIA—*(Continued)*						
Napa County, California	77,499	88.9	38.8	59,010	97.1	45.5
Nevada County, California	72,499	94.7	36.6	67,064	95.8	38.6
Orange County, California	1,352,816	88.9	40.9	988,571	96.4	49.3
Placer County, California	227,970	95.2	35.8	207,403	96.7	37.0
Riverside County, California	944,744	87.2	24.8	656,533	94.6	29.8
Sacramento County, California	618,796	91.4	32.5	518,395	94.1	34.4
San Bernardino County, California	860,221	81.0	19.4	457,985	91.4	26.3
San Diego County, California	1,619,153	88.3	39.4	1,142,237	96.2	48.9
San Francisco County, California	336,920	96.8	74.1	301,377	98.4	77.1
San Joaquin County, California	268,623	83.4	19.2	178,141	90.9	24.6
San Luis Obispo County, California	167,183	92.6	35.5	140,624	96.9	38.9
San Mateo County, California	281,394	93.8	57.0	233,451	97.3	63.7
Santa Barbara County, California	220,526	81.4	36.4	142,987	97.2	51.0
Santa Clara County, California	612,432	91.9	51.7	469,940	97.0	60.6
Santa Cruz County, California	140,004	91.2	45.1	116,864	96.4	50.6
Shasta County, California	113,189	91.2	22.9	106,317	91.9	23.2
Solano County, California	168,458	88.9	27.3	130,760	94.8	31.9
Sonoma County, California	281,885	93.4	39.2	251,211	95.8	41.4
Stanislaus County, California	270,762	80.4	17.1	169,949	91.1	23.3
Sutter County, California	43,431	81.1	15.4	32,483	89.0	18.7
Tulare County, California	212,220	70.6	14.6	97,803	90.0	23.8
Ventura County, California	469,312	85.3	32.0	294,239	96.2	43.6
Yolo County, California	95,928	87.7	39.3	68,770	95.1	49.5
Yuba County, California	39,336	79.3	14.4	29,607	83.9	15.4
COLORADO						
Adams County, Colorado	276,448	85.3	23.1	185,447	94.1	29.6
Arapahoe County, Colorado	330,994	94.0	47.0	288,634	96.7	51.4
Boulder County, Colorado	192,347	96.5	63.7	173,744	98.4	66.6
Broomfield County, Colorado	41,249	97.6	55.3	37,743	97.9	55.9
Denver County, Colorado	395,903	91.1	55.4	311,030	97.5	66.2
Douglas County, Colorado	197,968	98.4	58.9	185,753	98.6	60.2
El Paso County, Colorado	373,671	94.6	41.3	335,072	96.2	43.1
Jefferson County, Colorado	381,577	95.5	46.2	338,872	97.1	49.3
Larimer County, Colorado	211,626	95.2	47.6	195,453	96.9	49.4
Mesa County, Colorado	97,935	91.8	26.2	88,831	94.5	27.6
Pueblo County, Colorado	93,782	92.8	24.1	65,688	94.8	27.4
Weld County, Colorado	180,637	88.5	27.9	140,404	95.4	33.4
CONNECTICUT						
Fairfield County, Connecticut	488,628	92.1	52.7	419,714	95.4	57.7
Hartford County, Connecticut	463,180	91.9	41.3	413,100	94.4	44.1
Litchfield County, Connecticut	127,664	92.6	37.2	122,015	92.9	37.1
Middlesex County, Connecticut	107,660	94.7	39.8	103,292	95.1	40.5
New Haven County, Connecticut	461,388	92.2	36.8	409,247	94.2	39.5
New London County, Connecticut	157,452	93.4	35.4	150,424	93.9	35.3
Tolland County, Connecticut	86,230	96.4	39.4	83,913	96.3	39.4
Windham County, Connecticut	73,505	89.9	25.4	70,889	90.4	25.8
DELAWARE						
Kent County, Delaware	84,035	87.8	22.5	78,507	89.8	23.4
New Castle County, Delaware	260,243	92.6	36.8	237,884	95.2	39.0
Sussex County, Delaware	142,361	90.0	31.6	135,940	91.5	32.8
DISTRICT OF COLUMBIA						
District of Columbia, District of Columbia	218,184	97.8	88.5	197,526	99.3	90.8
FLORIDA						
Alachua County, Florida	115,737	93.0	42.7	105,668	93.8	43.1
Bay County, Florida	108,842	92.2	24.4	103,461	92.1	24.5
Brevard County, Florida	372,065	93.4	30.3	342,491	93.5	29.9
Broward County, Florida	885,982	91.1	36.4	555,443	93.7	39.1
Charlotte County, Florida	138,781	92.4	23.8	130,735	93.4	24.1
Citrus County, Florida	108,635	88.4	15.7	104,499	88.2	15.0
Clay County, Florida	117,076	90.7	21.3	110,082	91.1	20.9
Collier County, Florida	258,360	89.3	38.0	198,962	95.6	44.1
Columbia County, Florida	38,977	88.7	18.3	37,313	89.0	17.7
Duval County, Florida	407,843	91.6	32.8	370,166	91.8	33.3
Escambia County, Florida	151,233	92.9	30.0	145,404	92.9	29.7

Table C-2. Educational Attainment of the Population, by Selected Counties, 2017—*Continued*

(Number; percent; dollars.)

| | Educational attainment by race/ethnicity, 25 years and over | | | | | |
| | Black alone | | | American Indian or Alaska Native alone | | |
State/County	Total	High school graduate or more (percent)	Bachelor's degree or more (percent)	Total	High school graduate or more (percent)	Bachelor's degree or more (percent)
CALIFORNIA—(*Continued*)						
Napa County, California	1,717	87.9	24.6	N	N	N
Nevada County, California	N	N	N	N	N	N
Orange County, California	39,235	92.7	35.4	11,595	77.6	14.5
Placer County, California	4,266	94.7	49.3	N	N	N
Riverside County, California	102,539	92.5	25.4	12,612	79.5	12.8
Sacramento County, California	97,476	90.2	21.5	7,960	81.0	16.4
San Bernardino County, California	111,123	89.5	21.3	12,447	76.4	9.4
San Diego County, California	109,119	91.5	25.6	17,075	80.7	16.9
San Francisco County, California	34,695	88.6	30.1	N	N	N
San Joaquin County, California	33,768	90.3	19.0	2,878	79.9	10.1
San Luis Obispo County, California	4,058	76.7	7.7	N	N	N
San Mateo County, California	14,156	90.3	31.3	N	N	N
Santa Barbara County, California	4,941	90.7	26.6	2,489	91.1	7.4
Santa Clara County, California	33,613	91.8	36.0	7,038	80.7	12.3
Santa Cruz County, California	N	N	N	N	N	N
Shasta County, California	N	N	N	3,901	85.6	7.9
Solano County, California	43,117	90.4	22.6	N	N	N
Sonoma County, California	5,714	89.8	36.8	N	N	N
Stanislaus County, California	11,034	93.0	12.8	2,919	70.3	12.5
Sutter County, California	N	N	N	N	N	N
Tulare County, California	4,375	85.6	29.4	3,932	66.0	8.5
Ventura County, California	11,054	95.0	40.7	4,405	81.7	19.7
Yolo County, California	3,054	87.3	21.0	N	N	N
Yuba County, California	N	N	N	N	N	N
COLORADO						
Adams County, Colorado	10,207	85.1	21.4	2,748	90.1	11.0
Arapahoe County, Colorado	43,127	90.6	31.8	3,128	84.9	30.3
Boulder County, Colorado	2,149	80.0	40.1	N	N	N
Broomfield County, Colorado	N	N	N	N	N	N
Denver County, Colorado	43,415	90.8	24.3	5,426	81.7	17.7
Douglas County, Colorado	3,309	96.6	52.2	N	N	N
El Paso County, Colorado	27,013	93.6	28.7	4,375	90.3	29.1
Jefferson County, Colorado	3,833	93.9	36.1	3,558	73.2	7.9
Larimer County, Colorado	1,939	100.0	43.1	N	N	N
Mesa County, Colorado	N	N	N	N	N	N
Pueblo County, Colorado	1,963	90.9	28.0	4,163	78.2	2.4
Weld County, Colorado	1,714	86.3	36.6	N	N	N
CONNECTICUT						
Fairfield County, Connecticut	67,831	85.2	21.2	N	N	N
Hartford County, Connecticut	80,811	85.8	19.5	N	N	N
Litchfield County, Connecticut	3,023	88.1	20.9	N	N	N
Middlesex County, Connecticut	5,887	89.3	25.1	N	N	N
New Haven County, Connecticut	74,634	88.6	19.7	N	N	N
New London County, Connecticut	9,268	89.3	13.3	N	N	N
Tolland County, Connecticut	2,809	90.1	14.9	N	N	N
Windham County, Connecticut	N	N	N	N	N	N
DELAWARE						
Kent County, Delaware	27,463	89.0	23.8	N	N	N
New Castle County, Delaware	91,597	92.9	24.2	N	N	N
Sussex County, Delaware	18,279	82.9	11.8	N	N	N
DISTRICT OF COLUMBIA						
District of Columbia, District of Columbia	217,915	86.5	26.7	N	N	N
FLORIDA						
Alachua County, Florida	31,188	85.6	22.9	N	N	N
Bay County, Florida	12,300	86.8	18.6	N	N	N
Brevard County, Florida	37,324	82.3	22.3	N	N	N
Broward County, Florida	355,241	85.7	21.3	3,804	82.6	25.6
Charlotte County, Florida	6,846	85.1	16.9	N	N	N
Citrus County, Florida	3,024	84.2	14.4	N	N	N
Clay County, Florida	13,980	93.5	19.2	N	N	N
Collier County, Florida	15,794	75.0	21.0	N	N	N
Columbia County, Florida	7,498	89.6	14.8	N	N	N
Duval County, Florida	173,119	87.9	18.1	N	N	N
Escambia County, Florida	42,895	84.6	13.9	N	N	N

N = Data for this geographic area cannot be displayed because the number of sample cases is too small.

Table C-2. Educational Attainment of the Population, by Selected Counties, 2017—*Continued*

(Number; percent; dollars.)

State/County	Educational attainment by race/ethnicity, 25 years and over					
	White alone			White alone, not Hispanic		
	Total	High school graduate or more (percent)	Bachelor's degree or more (percent)	Total	High school graduate or more (percent)	Bachelor's degree or more (percent)
FLORIDA—(*Continued*)						
Flagler County, Florida	71,515	92.8	24.1	66,063	93.4	25.1
Hernando County, Florida	127,999	88.6	18.2	113,886	90.2	18.8
Highlands County, Florida	67,959	85.7	17.5	58,026	89.6	18.8
Hillsborough County, Florida	724,828	90.3	34.6	513,246	93.9	39.9
Indian River County, Florida	106,276	90.8	30.7	96,228	93.6	31.7
Lake County, Florida	215,088	90.6	25.3	191,304	92.1	25.9
Lee County, Florida	486,954	90.2	28.7	409,722	93.5	31.5
Leon County, Florida	113,796	96.5	50.8	106,729	97.1	51.7
Manatee County, Florida	252,451	91.8	32.9	224,631	93.7	33.8
Marion County, Florida	225,227	87.5	22.9	198,589	88.5	23.7
Martin County, Florida	111,926	92.1	33.0	103,020	94.3	34.5
Miami-Dade County, Florida	1,507,270	82.4	31.6	253,434	94.7	54.1
Monroe County, Florida	54,404	90.8	35.6	42,544	95.3	38.8
Nassau County, Florida	55,550	93.2	34.2	53,855	93.3	34.3
Okaloosa County, Florida	115,000	95.1	32.2	108,172	95.0	32.7
Orange County, Florida	584,751	92.0	37.9	395,138	95.1	44.2
Osceola County, Florida	168,704	86.9	18.7	83,343	91.0	23.1
Palm Beach County, Florida	830,336	91.8	40.1	651,992	95.6	44.2
Pasco County, Florida	342,134	89.9	22.5	299,907	91.1	22.4
Pinellas County, Florida	629,051	92.2	32.8	583,645	93.1	33.5
Polk County, Florida	382,364	85.9	19.2	310,843	89.3	20.6
Putnam County, Florida	43,438	83.7	13.7	40,259	85.2	13.8
St. Johns County, Florida	155,957	92.3	45.1	147,422	92.6	45.0
St. Lucie County, Florida	177,108	88.4	23.6	144,844	92.8	25.0
Santa Rosa County, Florida	105,948	93.9	28.7	102,878	94.3	28.9
Sarasota County, Florida	312,134	92.4	34.9	291,155	93.4	36.2
Seminole County, Florida	258,445	96.0	42.8	208,191	96.8	45.6
Sumter County, Florida	101,267	92.6	35.4	97,482	94.0	36.7
Volusia County, Florida	337,384	91.0	23.0	305,683	91.5	23.5
Walton County, Florida	44,184	88.7	30.0	43,640	88.7	30.0
GEORGIA						
Barrow County, Georgia	42,202	87.6	20.6	39,068	88.7	21.4
Bartow County, Georgia	60,089	84.7	20.2	56,738	86.1	20.8
Bibb County, Georgia	45,085	91.5	36.3	43,396	91.4	36.0
Bulloch County, Georgia	29,289	90.2	33.0	28,889	90.1	33.3
Carroll County, Georgia	58,878	89.5	25.8	55,877	90.4	26.6
Catoosa County, Georgia	41,495	89.7	18.5	41,115	89.6	18.7
Chatham County, Georgia	112,578	92.0	43.9	104,711	93.0	45.1
Cherokee County, Georgia	147,985	93.0	36.7	136,363	94.2	38.0
Clarke County, Georgia	43,963	92.8	55.2	39,528	96.0	58.2
Clayton County, Georgia	30,825	74.6	9.7	23,041	81.6	10.9
Cobb County, Georgia	318,583	92.5	49.0	284,776	96.0	52.3
Columbia County, Georgia	76,641	91.1	33.2	71,551	95.9	34.7
Coweta County, Georgia	74,929	92.2	32.9	70,765	94.0	34.6
DeKalb County, Georgia	186,208	93.3	63.1	167,662	97.7	68.1
Dougherty County, Georgia	17,920	89.0	31.6	17,624	89.9	32.1
Douglas County, Georgia	47,471	82.0	24.1	42,768	84.6	26.3
Fayette County, Georgia	53,415	94.9	44.7	50,619	96.3	45.3
Floyd County, Georgia	54,038	80.2	20.0	49,325	85.4	21.6
Forsyth County, Georgia	121,173	92.0	51.2	109,563	94.6	53.3
Fulton County, Georgia	334,891	96.2	67.6	303,406	98.1	71.1
Glynn County, Georgia	43,691	93.2	38.0	41,154	94.4	38.8
Gwinnett County, Georgia	298,036	90.8	40.0	245,616	95.6	44.1
Hall County, Georgia	114,500	79.4	27.3	88,801	89.9	33.5
Henry County, Georgia	75,858	91.7	24.2	69,125	91.8	23.2
Houston County, Georgia	65,772	94.9	30.7	60,842	96.1	31.6
Jackson County, Georgia	40,716	85.4	23.6	38,156	87.2	25.2
Lowndes County, Georgia	40,120	89.0	32.2	39,384	88.8	31.8
Muscogee County, Georgia	58,681	89.3	34.8	54,913	89.7	35.1
Newton County, Georgia	37,197	90.6	19.0	35,466	91.4	18.4
Paulding County, Georgia	81,618	89.6	19.4	76,580	90.3	19.7
Richmond County, Georgia	53,799	85.9	25.6	50,732	86.0	25.9
Rockdale County, Georgia	24,351	83.6	20.6	21,909	88.0	21.7
Spalding County, Georgia	28,957	84.9	21.1	28,081	85.5	20.2
Troup County, Georgia	27,240	87.2	26.5	27,048	87.4	26.7
Walker County, Georgia	45,045	85.9	17.1	44,816	86.1	17.2
Walton County, Georgia	49,610	93.5	20.0	47,744	94.4	20.6
Whitfield County, Georgia	61,389	67.2	16.7	44,284	81.5	22.1

Table C-2. Educational Attainment of the Population, by Selected Counties, 2017—*Continued*

(Number; percent; dollars.)

	Educational attainment by race/ethnicity, 25 years and over					
	Black alone			American Indian or Alaska Native alone		
State/County	Total	High school graduate or more (percent)	Bachelor's degree or more (percent)	Total	High school graduate or more (percent)	Bachelor's degree or more (percent)
FLORIDA—(*Continued*)						
Flagler County, Florida............................	7,865	91.0	23.9	N	N	N
Hernando County, Florida........................	6,521	90.1	23.3	N	N	N
Highlands County, Florida........................	6,968	74.8	19.3	N	N	N
Hillsborough County, Florida....................	146,706	88.5	22.6	3,289	85.2	28.9
Indian River County, Florida....................	8,154	87.9	18.8	N	N	N
Lake County, Florida..............................	22,849	80.2	15.8	N	N	N
Lee County, Florida	37,143	84.3	12.4	N	N	N
Leon County, Florida..............................	47,994	92.0	33.1	N	N	N
Manatee County, Florida.........................	20,693	85.0	16.1	N	N	N
Marion County, Florida...........................	29,127	74.5	12.6	N	N	N
Martin County, Florida............................	5,333	75.7	15.3	N	N	N
Miami-Dade County, Florida.....................	312,050	79.2	16.8	N	N	N
Monroe County, Florida...........................	N	N	N	N	N	N
Nassau County, Florida	3,557	84.4	22.7	N	N	N
Okaloosa County, Florida........................	12,387	89.2	26.6	N	N	N
Orange County, Florida...........................	177,513	85.6	21.7	2,457	85.3	15.3
Osceola County, Florida..........................	26,038	88.5	22.1	N	N	N
Palm Beach County, Florida	175,906	78.4	17.3	2,303	64.5	18.5
Pasco County, Florida	19,635	84.3	23.0	N	N	N
Pinellas County, Florida..........................	65,677	86.6	15.4	2,300	91.0	15.3
Polk County, Florida...............................	65,402	84.8	16.2	2,386	77.6	19.2
Putnam County, Florida...........................	7,563	67.5	5.5	N	N	N
St. Johns County, Florida........................	8,252	85.1	13.4	N	N	N
St. Lucie County, Florida	37,977	78.8	15.1	N	N	N
Santa Rosa County, Florida.....................	6,294	76.8	18.9	N	N	N
Sarasota County, Florida.........................	12,272	77.3	15.5	N	N	N
Seminole County, Florida........................	37,566	94.2	29.0	N	N	N
Sumter County, Florida...........................	7,688	78.0	4.5	N	N	N
Volusia County, Florida...........................	35,884	85.8	17.8	N	N	N
Walton County, Florida...........................	2,654	77.8	6.7	N	N	N
GEORGIA						
Barrow County, Georgia	5,911	72.9	5.3	N	N	N
Bartow County, Georgia	5,709	81.5	27.5	N	N	N
Bibb County, Georgia	50,480	82.5	14.6	N	N	N
Bulloch County, Georgia..........................	10,883	83.5	10.6	N	N	N
Carroll County, Georgia...........................	13,764	79.3	10.9	N	N	N
Catoosa County, Georgia.........................	N	N	N	N	N	N
Chatham County, Georgia	70,737	83.2	14.0	N	N	N
Cherokee County, Georgia.......................	9,367	96.2	38.1	N	N	N
Clarke County, Georgia...........................	20,032	82.4	18.5	N	N	N
Clayton County, Georgia..........................	124,621	89.9	19.4	N	N	N
Cobb County, Georgia	133,177	95.9	39.6	N	N	N
Columbia County, Georgia.......................	15,030	94.1	39.8	N	N	N
Coweta County, Georgia..........................	15,295	79.2	22.4	N	N	N
DeKalb County, Georgia	268,019	89.2	29.3	5,424	49.0	10.9
Dougherty County, Georgia......................	37,655	85.1	19.7	N	N	N
Douglas County, Georgia.........................	41,984	91.7	29.7	N	N	N
Fayette County, Georgia	17,851	91.7	51.3	N	N	N
Floyd County, Georgia.............................	8,209	81.5	11.8	N	N	N
Forsyth County, Georgia..........................	5,049	95.7	38.9	N	N	N
Fulton County, Georgia...........................	296,281	88.4	28.7	N	N	N
Glynn County, Georgia	13,461	76.0	10.8	N	N	N
Gwinnett County, Georgia	155,450	94.1	34.3	3,490	74.2	15.6
Hall County, Georgia	9,136	81.4	15.6	N	N	N
Henry County, Georgia	61,039	94.5	35.0	N	N	N
Houston County, Georgia	29,489	92.1	31.3	N	N	N
Jackson County, Georgia.........................	N	N	N	N	N	N
Lowndes County, Georgia	23,072	79.3	23.3	N	N	N
Muscogee County, Georgia	57,285	85.6	15.8	N	N	N
Newton County, Georgia	27,311	87.1	21.3	N	N	N
Paulding County, Georgia........................	18,473	92.2	28.6	N	N	N
Richmond County, Georgia	71,105	79.4	16.4	N	N	N
Rockdale County, Georgia........................	29,252	95.1	31.6	N	N	N
Spalding County, Georgia........................	13,671	77.6	12.1	N	N	N
Troup County, Georgia	15,295	72.1	8.9	N	N	N
Walker County, Georgia..........................	N	N	N	N	N	N
Walton County, Georgia	9,577	75.4	10.6	N	N	N
Whitfield County, Georgia	2,857	86.1	15.5	N	N	N

N = Data for this geographic area cannot be displayed because the number of sample cases is too small.

Table C-2. Educational Attainment of the Population, by Selected Counties, 2017—*Continued*

(Number; percent; dollars.)

	Educational attainment by race/ethnicity, 25 years and over					
	White alone			White alone, not Hispanic		
State/County	Total	High school graduate or more (percent)	Bachelor's degree or more (percent)	Total	High school graduate or more (percent)	Bachelor's degree or more (percent)
HAWAII						
Hawaii County, Hawaii	57,313	96.9	42.3	51,453	97.9	45.1
Honolulu County, Hawaii	145,703	97.0	47.1	130,573	97.0	49.2
Kauai County, Hawaii	19,373	96.5	42.3	17,408	96.8	44.6
Maui County, Hawaii	47,887	95.8	37.9	42,364	97.2	41.6
IDAHO						
Ada County, Idaho	282,444	95.0	36.2	268,076	95.1	36.7
Bannock County, Idaho	49,019	94.4	30.1	46,801	94.2	30.4
Bonneville County, Idaho	62,351	94.6	32.8	59,974	94.8	33.7
Canyon County, Idaho	116,166	88.3	19.8	102,129	92.5	21.6
Kootenai County, Idaho	103,528	95.1	26.2	100,753	94.9	26.4
Twin Falls County, Idaho	50,787	88.1	20.8	45,135	92.5	22.7
ILLINOIS						
Adams County, Illinois	43,659	94.4	27.1	43,213	94.5	26.9
Champaign County, Illinois	93,993	96.8	43.7	89,426	97.3	44.1
Cook County, Illinois	2,131,810	90.0	45.4	1,691,185	95.1	52.7
DeKalb County, Illinois	55,001	92.1	29.9	51,243	93.8	31.3
DuPage County, Illinois	502,680	94.1	49.2	450,663	96.5	52.4
Kane County, Illinois	263,482	90.6	37.5	221,534	96.3	42.3
Kankakee County, Illinois	60,510	90.1	21.2	55,997	92.3	22.1
Kendall County, Illinois	65,515	94.3	35.6	58,370	97.4	37.8
Lake County, Illinois	352,805	93.1	48.0	307,434	96.7	53.1
LaSalle County, Illinois	71,463	92.1	19.4	68,799	92.4	19.4
McHenry County, Illinois	195,873	92.7	33.8	177,487	95.6	35.7
McLean County, Illinois	90,140	96.3	43.6	86,924	96.8	44.5
Macon County, Illinois	59,875	93.0	25.1	59,163	93.1	25.2
Madison County, Illinois	166,840	91.9	28.3	163,672	92.2	28.6
Peoria County, Illinois	97,078	91.9	33.2	93,489	92.9	34.0
Rock Island County, Illinois	85,147	91.0	23.2	77,510	92.7	24.3
St. Clair County, Illinois	120,337	95.2	32.3	117,586	95.6	32.4
Sangamon County, Illinois	117,498	94.5	34.8	115,625	94.6	34.6
Tazewell County, Illinois	89,814	91.5	28.4	88,940	91.6	28.2
Vermilion County, Illinois	46,094	87.6	17.7	44,186	88.2	18.2
Will County, Illinois	341,395	92.9	33.0	308,895	95.5	34.9
Williamson County, Illinois	43,963	92.2	23.6	43,784	92.3	23.6
Winnebago County, Illinois	161,509	89.7	22.8	147,512	92.3	24.1
INDIANA						
Allen County, Indiana	201,180	91.8	27.9	191,357	93.1	28.8
Bartholomew County, Indiana	48,586	93.0	32.1	47,536	93.0	31.8
Boone County, Indiana	40,677	94.5	52.1	39,824	94.4	53.1
Clark County, Indiana	73,035	89.5	18.9	70,225	90.8	19.3
Delaware County, Indiana	64,495	89.1	25.6	64,100	89.0	25.5
Elkhart County, Indiana	117,932	81.1	21.3	104,685	85.6	23.6
Floyd County, Indiana	48,533	88.9	30.3	48,253	89.3	30.4
Grant County, Indiana	39,302	90.4	23.7	38,726	90.5	23.7
Hamilton County, Indiana	186,284	97.6	59.4	180,192	98.1	60.3
Hancock County, Indiana	48,813	93.5	31.9	48,236	93.7	31.6
Hendricks County, Indiana	97,105	95.2	36.7	94,597	95.4	37.0
Howard County, Indiana	51,215	90.7	20.7	50,267	91.4	20.9
Johnson County, Indiana	95,874	93.4	32.9	93,266	93.6	32.5
Kosciusko County, Indiana	50,666	87.5	24.0	48,006	89.2	25.3
Lake County, Indiana	215,707	90.8	25.5	194,641	92.7	26.2
LaPorte County, Indiana	66,608	90.3	18.0	64,231	90.5	18.6
Madison County, Indiana	80,431	89.4	18.7	79,144	90.0	18.8
Marion County, Indiana	421,546	86.9	36.1	385,639	90.1	38.2
Monroe County, Indiana	75,767	90.8	44.4	73,894	91.5	44.2
Morgan County, Indiana	47,725	86.9	18.6	47,180	86.8	18.5
Porter County, Indiana	107,626	93.7	29.3	99,494	94.7	30.4
St. Joseph County, Indiana	145,755	89.9	32.1	138,410	91.0	32.6
Tippecanoe County, Indiana	91,497	93.1	38.5	86,214	94.8	39.1
Vanderburgh County, Indiana	109,572	90.9	30.4	108,515	90.9	30.3
Vigo County, Indiana	61,635	86.5	23.5	60,906	86.5	23.8
Wayne County, Indiana	42,284	87.4	20.8	41,654	87.5	21.1
IOWA						
Black Hawk County, Iowa	73,351	91.8	28.7	71,579	92.1	29.1
Dallas County, Iowa	51,683	96.7	49.6	49,591	97.8	51.3
Dubuque County, Iowa	61,218	93.2	33.4	60,837	93.4	33.6

Table C-2. Educational Attainment of the Population, by Selected Counties, 2017—*Continued*

(Number; percent; dollars.)

| | Educational attainment by race/ethnicity, 25 years and over | | | | | |
| | Black alone | | | American Indian or Alaska Native alone | | |
State/County	Total	High school graduate or more (percent)	Bachelor's degree or more (percent)	Total	High school graduate or more (percent)	Bachelor's degree or more (percent)
HAWAII						
Hawaii County, Hawaii	N	N	N	N	N	N
Honolulu County, Hawaii	13,860	97.4	36.5	N	N	N
Kauai County, Hawaii	N	N	N	N	N	N
Maui County, Hawaii	N	N	N	N	N	N
IDAHO						
Ada County, Idaho	3,596	86.9	22.6	N	N	N
Bannock County, Idaho	N	N	N	N	N	N
Bonneville County, Idaho	N	N	N	N	N	N
Canyon County, Idaho	N	N	N	N	N	N
Kootenai County, Idaho	N	N	N	N	N	N
Twin Falls County, Idaho	N	N	N	N	N	N
ILLINOIS						
Adams County, Illinois	N	N	N	N	N	N
Champaign County, Illinois	13,668	91.5	24.0	N	N	N
Cook County, Illinois	810,969	87.4	22.1	8,927	73.3	24.4
DeKalb County, Illinois	4,691	98.5	18.5	N	N	N
DuPage County, Illinois	28,011	94.2	39.7	N	N	N
Kane County, Illinois	16,058	86.3	13.7	N	N	N
Kankakee County, Illinois	9,898	79.0	18.7	N	N	N
Kendall County, Illinois	N	N	N	N	N	N
Lake County, Illinois	29,751	88.2	18.8	N	N	N
LaSalle County, Illinois	N	N	N	N	N	N
McHenry County, Illinois	2,745	89.4	25.4	N	N	N
McLean County, Illinois	7,554	95.7	35.8	N	N	N
Macon County, Illinois	8,104	88.1	9.5	N	N	N
Madison County, Illinois	13,555	90.5	14.0	N	N	N
Peoria County, Illinois	18,369	75.1	10.8	N	N	N
Rock Island County, Illinois	8,282	73.7	17.5	N	N	N
St. Clair County, Illinois	48,709	86.0	18.7	N	N	N
Sangamon County, Illinois	14,610	82.7	13.7	N	N	N
Tazewell County, Illinois	N	N	N	N	N	N
Vermilion County, Illinois	5,623	73.3	3.2	N	N	N
Will County, Illinois	50,994	89.0	27.4	N	N	N
Williamson County, Illinois	N	N	N	N	N	N
Winnebago County, Illinois	21,397	83.8	9.9	N	N	N
INDIANA						
Allen County, Indiana	24,610	82.8	15.7	N	N	N
Bartholomew County, Indiana	N	N	N	N	N	N
Boone County, Indiana	N	N	N	N	N	N
Clark County, Indiana	5,592	93.3	13.8	N	N	N
Delaware County, Indiana	5,592	89.8	14.9	N	N	N
Elkhart County, Indiana	6,371	77.3	5.9	N	N	N
Floyd County, Indiana	2,677	96.6	16.4	N	N	N
Grant County, Indiana	3,642	96.0	7.2	N	N	N
Hamilton County, Indiana	8,778	97.7	54.5	N	N	N
Hancock County, Indiana	N	N	N	N	N	N
Hendricks County, Indiana	7,112	96.0	26.4	N	N	N
Howard County, Indiana	4,537	82.2	15.0	N	N	N
Johnson County, Indiana	N	N	N	N	N	N
Kosciusko County, Indiana	N	N	N	N	N	N
Lake County, Indiana	72,194	88.1	16.8	N	N	N
LaPorte County, Indiana	8,264	80.7	11.0	N	N	N
Madison County, Indiana	7,453	84.4	15.0	N	N	N
Marion County, Indiana	162,144	83.0	20.8	N	N	N
Monroe County, Indiana	N	N	N	N	N	N
Morgan County, Indiana	N	N	N	N	N	N
Porter County, Indiana	3,534	97.2	45.7	N	N	N
St. Joseph County, Indiana	20,164	83.3	13.8	N	N	N
Tippecanoe County, Indiana	4,580	94.9	40.3	N	N	N
Vanderburgh County, Indiana	10,424	81.0	13.7	N	N	N
Vigo County, Indiana	2,984	82.9	14.6	N	N	N
Wayne County, Indiana	N	N	N	N	N	N
IOWA						
Black Hawk County, Iowa	7,129	80.7	20.5	N	N	N
Dallas County, Iowa	N	N	N	N	N	N
Dubuque County, Iowa	N	N	N	N	N	N

N = Data for this geographic area cannot be displayed because the number of sample cases is too small.

Table C-2. Educational Attainment of the Population, by Selected Counties, 2017—*Continued*

(Number; percent; dollars.)

State/County	Educational attainment by race/ethnicity, 25 years and over					
	White alone			White alone, not Hispanic		
	Total	High school graduate or more (percent)	Bachelor's degree or more (percent)	Total	High school graduate or more (percent)	Bachelor's degree or more (percent)
IOWA—*(Continued)*						
Johnson County, Iowa	74,280	97.4	57.5	71,786	97.7	58.2
Linn County, Iowa	136,930	96.0	33.9	134,370	96.4	33.9
Polk County, Iowa	278,220	93.4	37.5	263,872	95.1	38.9
Pottawattamie County, Iowa	59,429	89.7	23.0	57,718	90.6	23.0
Scott County, Iowa	104,166	93.3	32.4	99,002	94.1	33.6
Story County, Iowa	45,116	97.0	50.6	44,076	97.1	50.5
Woodbury County, Iowa	58,221	87.9	24.4	52,323	93.3	26.3
KANSAS						
Butler County, Kansas	41,429	92.8	30.2	39,951	93.4	30.3
Douglas County, Kansas	60,179	95.9	47.6	57,180	96.1	48.2
Johnson County, Kansas	349,651	96.6	57.0	331,176	97.8	58.7
Leavenworth County, Kansas	46,739	91.2	35.6	44,608	91.6	36.9
Riley County, Kansas	31,843	95.4	47.9	29,684	96.8	49.2
Sedgwick County, Kansas	265,375	92.6	33.7	245,977	94.4	35.1
Shawnee County, Kansas	103,844	95.8	35.6	95,836	96.7	37.3
Wyandotte County, Kansas	65,866	82.3	18.8	50,301	88.0	21.8
KENTUCKY						
Boone County, Kentucky	78,673	93.0	31.1	77,170	93.2	31.1
Bullitt County, Kentucky	54,657	87.6	13.6	53,665	87.5	13.8
Campbell County, Kentucky	60,769	92.5	36.4	60,240	92.4	36.0
Christian County, Kentucky	29,727	85.5	14.8	28,248	87.4	15.3
Daviess County, Kentucky	63,201	92.5	23.0	61,980	92.6	23.0
Fayette County, Kentucky	163,994	93.5	46.7	156,064	94.1	47.6
Hardin County, Kentucky	59,891	91.0	21.3	56,380	90.5	20.7
Jefferson County, Kentucky	402,135	92.1	36.6	384,537	92.6	37.3
Kenton County, Kentucky	104,021	90.5	32.6	102,660	90.7	32.8
McCracken County, Kentucky	40,588	92.2	26.0	39,941	92.0	26.0
Madison County, Kentucky	51,923	88.1	32.0	50,960	88.9	32.5
Oldham County, Kentucky	40,148	93.4	41.8	39,303	94.7	42.4
Warren County, Kentucky	66,331	87.6	30.7	64,671	88.4	30.7
LOUISIANA						
Ascension Parish, Louisiana	59,458	91.5	29.0	57,076	92.0	29.8
Bossier Parish, Louisiana	62,172	91.5	24.7	59,135	93.0	25.5
Caddo Parish, Louisiana	84,954	91.2	30.2	82,617	91.4	30.5
Calcasieu Parish, Louisiana	98,337	91.2	27.6	95,293	91.8	27.8
East Baton Rouge Parish, Louisiana	144,137	95.1	47.6	138,234	96.1	48.4
Iberia Parish, Louisiana	30,390	85.7	13.1	29,979	86.1	13.1
Jefferson Parish, Louisiana	201,064	88.3	28.4	175,390	90.4	30.6
Lafayette Parish, Louisiana	117,199	92.0	37.7	112,990	92.2	38.7
Lafourche Parish, Louisiana	54,787	81.0	19.6	53,894	81.2	19.4
Livingston Parish, Louisiana	84,296	87.5	16.9	81,942	87.5	17.2
Orleans Parish, Louisiana	106,409	95.2	61.8	96,947	95.8	63.3
Ouachita Parish, Louisiana	65,332	91.0	28.0	63,996	91.2	28.0
Rapides Parish, Louisiana	58,214	88.8	24.7	56,722	89.4	24.4
St. Landry Parish, Louisiana	32,249	81.8	17.5	31,480	82.7	17.5
St. Tammany Parish, Louisiana	147,366	92.3	37.9	141,375	93.2	38.5
Tangipahoa Parish, Louisiana	62,053	83.8	21.5	58,978	84.5	21.9
Terrebonne Parish, Louisiana	54,023	80.4	16.3	52,918	80.1	16.4
MAINE						
Androscoggin County, Maine	70,858	91.2	25.0	70,329	91.1	24.6
Aroostook County, Maine	48,201	88.7	19.0	47,968	88.8	19.0
Cumberland County, Maine	198,704	95.4	48.1	196,101	95.5	48.4
Kennebec County, Maine	84,893	92.6	28.3	84,395	92.6	28.2
Penobscot County, Maine	103,084	92.0	28.7	102,563	91.9	28.8
York County, Maine	144,614	92.3	33.1	143,159	92.3	33.2
MARYLAND						
Allegany County, Maryland	44,943	90.9	18.4	44,613	91.2	18.4
Anne Arundel County, Maryland	295,916	93.6	43.4	283,243	94.3	43.7
Baltimore County, Maryland	369,525	92.1	40.5	355,179	93.1	41.1
Calvert County, Maryland	51,367	95.2	33.2	49,941	95.2	33.5
Carroll County, Maryland	108,063	93.3	37.1	106,060	93.7	37.5
Cecil County, Maryland	63,719	90.0	24.4	62,407	90.3	24.5
Charles County, Maryland	51,945	92.0	30.1	47,376	92.8	29.1
Frederick County, Maryland	141,271	92.9	42.6	132,806	93.7	43.1

Table C-2. Educational Attainment of the Population, by Selected Counties, 2017—*Continued*

(Number; percent; dollars.)

| | Educational attainment by race/ethnicity, 25 years and over | | | | | |
| | Black alone | | | American Indian or Alaska Native alone | | |
State/County	Total	High school graduate or more (percent)	Bachelor's degree or more (percent)	Total	High school graduate or more (percent)	Bachelor's degree or more (percent)
IOWA—(*Continued*)						
Johnson County, Iowa	4,802	93.4	31.8	N	N	N
Linn County, Iowa	6,746	83.0	20.2	N	N	N
Polk County, Iowa	16,438	86.9	17.1	N	N	N
Pottawattamie County, Iowa	N	N	N	N	N	N
Scott County, Iowa	6,910	84.1	19.0	N	N	N
Story County, Iowa	N	N	N	N	N	N
Woodbury County, Iowa	N	N	N	N	N	N
KANSAS						
Butler County, Kansas	N	N	N	N	N	N
Douglas County, Kansas	N	N	N	N	N	N
Johnson County, Kansas	17,567	91.7	36.0	1,759	93.9	31.8
Leavenworth County, Kansas	5,927	76.0	12.5	N	N	N
Riley County, Kansas	N	N	N	N	N	N
Sedgwick County, Kansas	26,646	86.9	16.1	2,107	78.7	12.8
Shawnee County, Kansas	9,279	87.8	15.5	N	N	N
Wyandotte County, Kansas	23,781	85.4	14.4	N	N	N
KENTUCKY						
Boone County, Kentucky	3,392	90.2	14.5	N	N	N
Bullitt County, Kentucky	N	N	N	N	N	N
Campbell County, Kentucky	N	N	N	N	N	N
Christian County, Kentucky	8,874	84.2	17.6	N	N	N
Daviess County, Kentucky	N	N	N	N	N	N
Fayette County, Kentucky	28,162	88.2	20.0	N	N	N
Hardin County, Kentucky	7,962	97.3	18.6	N	N	N
Jefferson County, Kentucky	103,864	88.2	20.0	N	N	N
Kenton County, Kentucky	5,002	93.3	17.9	N	N	N
McCracken County, Kentucky	4,649	90.6	15.8	N	N	N
Madison County, Kentucky	N	N	N	N	N	N
Oldham County, Kentucky	N	N	N	N	N	N
Warren County, Kentucky	6,263	93.7	12.1	N	N	N
LOUISIANA						
Ascension Parish, Louisiana	16,782	81.0	15.4	N	N	N
Bossier Parish, Louisiana	17,236	85.6	15.8	N	N	N
Caddo Parish, Louisiana	74,445	79.5	14.4	N	N	N
Calcasieu Parish, Louisiana	31,102	84.0	15.1	N	N	N
East Baton Rouge Parish, Louisiana	120,614	84.5	19.9	N	N	N
Iberia Parish, Louisiana	13,915	77.7	3.2	N	N	N
Jefferson Parish, Louisiana	75,082	82.5	16.8	N	N	N
Lafayette Parish, Louisiana	37,899	75.5	18.0	N	N	N
Lafourche Parish, Louisiana	7,710	71.8	4.9	N	N	N
Livingston Parish, Louisiana	6,472	79.0	9.2	N	N	N
Orleans Parish, Louisiana	156,245	80.7	17.0	N	N	N
Ouachita Parish, Louisiana	34,229	80.4	14.0	N	N	N
Rapides Parish, Louisiana	25,385	76.1	11.9	N	N	N
St. Landry Parish, Louisiana	20,742	74.8	11.8	N	N	N
St. Tammany Parish, Louisiana	18,023	84.2	16.4	N	N	N
Tangipahoa Parish, Louisiana	22,347	81.6	12.1	N	N	N
Terrebonne Parish, Louisiana	13,020	63.3	7.0	3,661	60.2	9.2
MAINE						
Androscoggin County, Maine	N	N	N	N	N	N
Aroostook County, Maine	N	N	N	N	N	N
Cumberland County, Maine	4,710	76.1	20.0	N	N	N
Kennebec County, Maine	N	N	N	N	N	N
Penobscot County, Maine	N	N	N	1,454	94.1	12.0
York County, Maine	N	N	N	N	N	N
MARYLAND						
Allegany County, Maryland	N	N	N	N	N	N
Anne Arundel County, Maryland	63,701	91.3	30.5	N	N	N
Baltimore County, Maryland	155,379	91.6	32.7	N	N	N
Calvert County, Maryland	8,329	90.6	30.1	N	N	N
Carroll County, Maryland	4,518	83.5	21.8	N	N	N
Cecil County, Maryland	4,553	84.2	22.6	N	N	N
Charles County, Maryland	46,702	91.6	31.6	N	N	N
Frederick County, Maryland	14,642	94.2	38.8	N	N	N

N = Data for this geographic area cannot be displayed because the number of sample cases is too small.

Table C-2. Educational Attainment of the Population, by Selected Counties, 2017—*Continued*

(Number; percent; dollars.)

| | Educational attainment by race/ethnicity, 25 years and over | | | | | |
| | White alone | | | White alone, not Hispanic | | |
State/County	Total	High school graduate or more (percent)	Bachelor's degree or more (percent)	Total	High school graduate or more (percent)	Bachelor's degree or more (percent)
MARYLAND—(*Continued*)						
Harford County, Maryland	141,906	93.0	34.9	138,614	92.9	35.2
Howard County, Maryland	128,936	96.7	61.4	119,944	97.4	63.5
Montgomery County, Maryland	397,082	94.4	66.5	342,451	97.3	71.5
Prince George's County, Maryland	107,855	89.5	43.0	86,936	95.6	48.2
St. Mary's County, Maryland	60,043	93.2	35.4	57,262	93.7	35.3
Washington County, Maryland	88,801	88.0	25.5	87,344	88.1	25.5
Wicomico County, Maryland	43,853	91.1	33.5	43,158	91.6	33.8
Baltimore city, Maryland	141,610	89.2	54.6	132,750	90.0	56.0
MASSACHUSETTS						
Barnstable County, Massachusetts	155,669	95.8	45.8	152,611	95.8	46.1
Berkshire County, Massachusetts	85,239	91.8	33.3	83,847	91.9	33.7
Bristol County, Massachusetts	343,564	86.3	30.1	336,316	86.6	30.2
Essex County, Massachusetts	467,009	91.7	41.7	411,485	94.6	45.6
Franklin County, Massachusetts	50,408	94.5	39.0	49,453	94.4	39.3
Hampden County, Massachusetts	266,852	86.5	28.2	220,458	90.8	32.3
Hampshire County, Massachusetts	91,951	96.0	47.7	88,627	96.2	48.5
Middlesex County, Massachusetts	891,718	94.6	56.4	844,466	95.4	57.4
Norfolk County, Massachusetts	390,209	95.6	55.1	378,045	96.0	55.1
Plymouth County, Massachusetts	306,437	95.6	38.3	299,514	95.8	38.6
Suffolk County, Massachusetts	325,716	91.3	56.5	272,659	94.8	63.3
Worcester County, Massachusetts	490,163	92.5	36.4	459,046	93.9	38.0
MICHIGAN						
Allegan County, Michigan	74,792	92.0	24.0	72,101	92.8	24.6
Bay County, Michigan	71,975	90.7	22.1	69,451	90.9	22.3
Berrien County, Michigan	88,968	91.3	26.6	85,746	91.7	26.7
Calhoun County, Michigan	77,738	91.6	22.1	74,522	92.6	22.4
Clinton County, Michigan	51,390	95.8	32.6	49,927	95.8	32.8
Eaton County, Michigan	67,630	94.7	28.2	65,583	94.8	28.5
Genesee County, Michigan	218,598	92.4	22.7	213,121	92.7	22.7
Grand Traverse County, Michigan	63,602	95.8	40.7	62,590	96.1	40.3
Ingham County, Michigan	138,837	93.5	38.8	131,143	94.0	40.0
Isabella County, Michigan	35,171	92.5	31.6	34,530	92.7	31.7
Jackson County, Michigan	99,203	92.5	23.2	96,837	92.8	23.3
Kalamazoo County, Michigan	140,288	94.6	39.8	135,601	95.2	39.8
Kent County, Michigan	358,890	93.4	39.3	339,692	94.9	40.7
Lapeer County, Michigan	60,441	92.4	17.2	58,393	93.2	17.4
Lenawee County, Michigan	64,983	92.4	21.6	61,252	92.8	22.2
Livingston County, Michigan	129,198	95.5	37.8	126,816	95.8	37.8
Macomb County, Michigan	513,940	90.1	24.9	506,448	90.1	24.9
Marquette County, Michigan	41,963	95.6	33.3	41,488	96.1	33.4
Midland County, Michigan	55,362	94.2	36.0	54,538	94.1	35.7
Monroe County, Michigan	101,324	91.9	17.8	98,316	91.7	17.8
Muskegon County, Michigan	99,137	92.0	21.2	95,685	92.7	21.7
Oakland County, Michigan	678,098	94.6	47.0	657,711	95.2	47.5
Ottawa County, Michigan	165,532	93.9	34.4	155,695	95.1	35.7
Saginaw County, Michigan	104,341	91.5	22.0	97,961	92.5	22.6
St. Clair County, Michigan	107,836	91.9	18.0	105,544	92.0	18.2
Shiawassee County, Michigan	46,690	92.0	16.1	45,792	92.4	16.3
Van Buren County, Michigan	45,978	91.4	21.4	44,167	92.0	22.3
Washtenaw County, Michigan	176,531	96.3	55.8	169,428	96.6	56.6
Wayne County, Michigan	661,672	89.0	28.3	628,217	90.1	29.1
MINNESOTA						
Anoka County, Minnesota	207,435	96.0	30.2	204,745	96.3	30.3
Blue Earth County, Minnesota	36,575	95.5	38.1	35,744	96.1	38.5
Carver County, Minnesota	62,451	97.5	50.1	60,473	97.7	51.0
Dakota County, Minnesota	243,122	96.0	43.3	235,893	96.8	44.0
Hennepin County, Minnesota	670,406	97.4	55.4	651,791	98.0	56.1
Olmsted County, Minnesota	91,454	97.0	46.5	88,489	97.0	46.6
Ramsey County, Minnesota	267,443	95.4	48.2	255,083	97.0	49.7
Rice County, Minnesota	38,157	94.7	29.6	36,636	95.7	30.4
St. Louis County, Minnesota	128,391	95.0	30.3	127,808	95.0	30.3
Scott County, Minnesota	81,100	97.3	42.8	79,050	97.8	43.7
Sherburne County, Minnesota	58,318	94.5	28.6	57,638	94.7	28.9
Stearns County, Minnesota	90,185	93.6	31.7	88,747	94.1	31.9
Washington County, Minnesota	153,407	97.7	43.5	148,718	98.0	44.2
Wright County, Minnesota	82,578	95.3	28.4	81,566	95.5	28.6

Table C-2. Educational Attainment of the Population, by Selected Counties, 2017—*Continued*

(Number; percent; dollars.)

State/County	Educational attainment by race/ethnicity, 25 years and over					
	Black alone			American Indian or Alaska Native alone		
	Total	High school graduate or more (percent)	Bachelor's degree or more (percent)	Total	High school graduate or more (percent)	Bachelor's degree or more (percent)
MARYLAND—(*Continued*)						
Harford County, Maryland	21,334	90.5	36.1	N	N	N
Howard County, Maryland	39,290	94.7	52.3	N	N	N
Montgomery County, Maryland	128,807	94.6	43.2	2,645	47.1	11.2
Prince George's County, Maryland	401,798	93.7	32.1	N	N	N
St. Mary's County, Maryland	9,920	75.6	7.4	N	N	N
Washington County, Maryland	10,443	81.4	12.9	N	N	N
Wicomico County, Maryland	15,963	74.9	19.5	N	N	N
Baltimore city, Maryland	257,208	82.1	15.8	N	N	N
MASSACHUSETTS						
Barnstable County, Massachusetts	4,122	76.6	17.9	N	N	N
Berkshire County, Massachusetts	N	N	N	N	N	N
Bristol County, Massachusetts	14,208	86.7	19.3	N	N	N
Essex County, Massachusetts	22,262	83.6	22.9	N	N	N
Franklin County, Massachusetts	N	N	N	N	N	N
Hampden County, Massachusetts	27,442	84.7	23.6	N	N	N
Hampshire County, Massachusetts	N	N	N	N	N	N
Middlesex County, Massachusetts	55,748	89.5	35.8	N	N	N
Norfolk County, Massachusetts	32,223	88.5	41.1	N	N	N
Plymouth County, Massachusetts	30,117	78.4	20.9	N	N	N
Suffolk County, Massachusetts	121,668	84.6	20.3	1,607	82.4	19.7
Worcester County, Massachusetts	24,799	86.8	30.4	N	N	N
MICHIGAN						
Allegan County, Michigan	N	N	N	N	N	N
Bay County, Michigan	N	N	N	N	N	N
Berrien County, Michigan	13,378	80.0	12.6	N	N	N
Calhoun County, Michigan	9,434	93.0	14.3	N	N	N
Clinton County, Michigan	N	N	N	N	N	N
Eaton County, Michigan	5,170	94.7	38.7	N	N	N
Genesee County, Michigan	50,103	87.5	13.2	N	N	N
Grand Traverse County, Michigan	N	N	N	N	N	N
Ingham County, Michigan	18,111	85.8	21.9	N	N	N
Isabella County, Michigan	N	N	N	N	N	N
Jackson County, Michigan	8,422	85.0	7.9	N	N	N
Kalamazoo County, Michigan	14,823	91.8	28.2	N	N	N
Kent County, Michigan	36,895	85.7	22.5	N	N	N
Lapeer County, Michigan	N	N	N	N	N	N
Lenawee County, Michigan	N	N	N	N	N	N
Livingston County, Michigan	N	N	N	N	N	N
Macomb County, Michigan	62,324	87.5	15.6	1,900	89.6	14.5
Marquette County, Michigan	N	N	N	N	N	N
Midland County, Michigan	N	N	N	N	N	N
Monroe County, Michigan	2,507	78.9	9.6	N	N	N
Muskegon County, Michigan	14,819	82.3	8.0	N	N	N
Oakland County, Michigan	117,257	92.4	33.8	2,681	85.6	43.5
Ottawa County, Michigan	1,848	88.8	17.3	N	N	N
Saginaw County, Michigan	22,714	82.9	10.1	N	N	N
St. Clair County, Michigan	2,526	87.8	32.8	N	N	N
Shiawassee County, Michigan	N	N	N	N	N	N
Van Buren County, Michigan	1,856	76.9	20.7	N	N	N
Washtenaw County, Michigan	25,132	88.5	27.1	N	N	N
Wayne County, Michigan	440,639	84.6	13.4	4,505	79.9	20.5
MINNESOTA						
Anoka County, Minnesota	12,169	83.9	19.5	N	N	N
Blue Earth County, Minnesota	N	N	N	N	N	N
Carver County, Minnesota	N	N	N	N	N	N
Dakota County, Minnesota	16,168	87.7	21.4	N	N	N
Hennepin County, Minnesota	92,795	82.1	22.0	6,246	78.2	27.0
Olmsted County, Minnesota	4,669	84.3	26.3	N	N	N
Ramsey County, Minnesota	36,712	80.2	23.4	2,209	88.0	29.6
Rice County, Minnesota	N	N	N	N	N	N
St. Louis County, Minnesota	1,896	76.4	25.2	2,243	80.0	11.6
Scott County, Minnesota	3,409	86.0	41.4	N	N	N
Sherburne County, Minnesota	1,689	80.9	21.6	N	N	N
Stearns County, Minnesota	3,862	62.3	15.1	N	N	N
Washington County, Minnesota	6,876	89.9	27.8	N	N	N
Wright County, Minnesota	1,169	79.3	39.7	N	N	N

N = Data for this geographic area cannot be displayed because the number of sample cases is too small.

Table C-2. Educational Attainment of the Population, by Selected Counties, 2017—*Continued*

(Number; percent; dollars.)

| | Educational attainment by race/ethnicity, 25 years and over | | | | | |
| | White alone | | | White alone, not Hispanic | | |
State/County	Total	High school graduate or more (percent)	Bachelor's degree or more (percent)	Total	High school graduate or more (percent)	Bachelor's degree or more (percent)
MISSISSIPPI						
DeSoto County, Mississippi	81,155	92.6	24.0	79,859	92.6	24.0
Forrest County, Mississippi	29,174	89.7	36.4	28,432	90.2	36.6
Harrison County, Mississippi	96,921	89.9	27.6	92,611	89.9	27.4
Hinds County, Mississippi	44,539	93.6	44.5	43,623	93.7	43.5
Jackson County, Mississippi	71,762	90.3	23.6	68,963	90.5	23.9
Jones County, Mississippi	32,231	85.7	17.8	30,984	87.8	17.8
Lauderdale County, Mississippi	29,646	90.0	29.5	28,924	90.3	30.0
Lee County, Mississippi	40,051	82.8	26.9	39,244	84.4	27.3
Madison County, Mississippi	40,733	95.6	58.8	40,027	95.8	59.0
Rankin County, Mississippi	81,018	92.0	32.3	79,979	92.5	32.4
MISSOURI						
Boone County, Missouri	90,392	94.6	46.4	88,230	94.6	47.0
Buchanan County, Missouri	53,461	90.6	19.2	52,129	91.6	19.7
Cape Girardeau County, Missouri	45,637	93.1	33.3	45,167	93.1	33.2
Cass County, Missouri	65,184	91.4	26.9	63,669	91.7	27.5
Christian County, Missouri	55,276	92.7	31.0	54,497	92.9	31.2
Clay County, Missouri	143,569	93.5	33.1	138,813	93.7	33.5
Cole County, Missouri	45,849	93.3	32.9	44,933	93.9	33.1
Franklin County, Missouri	69,409	87.3	20.8	68,816	87.8	20.9
Greene County, Missouri	175,039	91.9	31.3	171,148	92.0	31.5
Jackson County, Missouri	335,986	92.6	36.0	320,073	93.4	36.6
Jasper County, Missouri	72,019	88.1	23.2	69,376	90.1	23.7
Jefferson County, Missouri	150,136	89.9	22.6	147,885	89.8	22.8
Platte County, Missouri	59,498	95.8	42.7	57,918	96.2	42.5
St. Charles County, Missouri	244,726	95.3	39.0	239,874	95.4	39.0
St. Francois County, Missouri	45,273	83.8	11.7	44,574	83.5	11.9
St. Louis County, Missouri	494,252	95.5	48.2	484,288	95.6	48.2
St. Louis city, Missouri	113,938	93.7	54.1	108,837	94.1	54.7
MONTANA						
Cascade County, Montana	49,977	91.8	27.5	49,048	92.1	27.5
Flathead County, Montana	67,771	93.5	30.2	66,973	93.4	30.3
Gallatin County, Montana	65,690	96.5	51.2	64,521	96.7	51.1
Lewis and Clark County, Montana	45,351	95.8	40.3	44,526	95.9	40.4
Missoula County, Montana	73,077	96.7	46.6	71,805	96.9	47.0
Yellowstone County, Montana	101,151	92.6	32.5	97,722	94.4	33.5
NEBRASKA						
Douglas County, Nebraska	303,770	92.2	41.8	276,440	96.1	44.9
Lancaster County, Nebraska	173,368	94.9	39.2	165,906	96.0	40.2
Sarpy County, Nebraska	103,503	96.0	43.3	97,790	97.4	44.5
NEVADA						
Clark County, Nevada	933,226	88.8	26.1	730,353	94.1	30.1
Washoe County, Nevada	257,465	91.2	32.4	219,820	94.8	35.8
NEW HAMPSHIRE						
Cheshire County, New Hampshire	51,189	93.6	34.1	51,041	93.6	34.0
Grafton County, New Hampshire	59,250	94.7	41.4	58,562	94.8	41.6
Hillsborough County, New Hampshire	264,425	92.7	36.7	253,838	93.5	37.4
Merrimack County, New Hampshire	101,607	94.1	34.8	100,487	94.2	34.7
Rockingham County, New Hampshire	213,246	94.8	41.8	209,014	94.9	41.9
Strafford County, New Hampshire	79,024	92.6	33.1	77,615	92.6	33.4
NEW JERSEY						
Atlantic County, New Jersey	128,411	91.4	31.9	114,225	94.0	34.0
Bergen County, New Jersey	486,574	92.7	45.9	388,571	94.6	49.8
Burlington County, New Jersey	236,556	93.9	38.8	222,675	94.4	39.3
Camden County, New Jersey	241,148	91.0	35.2	215,443	93.3	37.6
Cape May County, New Jersey	65,414	94.0	35.1	62,005	94.4	35.7
Cumberland County, New Jersey	73,335	82.0	20.5	54,579	89.4	24.9
Essex County, New Jersey	242,160	88.3	46.7	180,558	91.7	54.5
Gloucester County, New Jersey	168,876	95.2	34.2	163,839	95.3	34.0
Hudson County, New Jersey	278,955	84.6	41.0	154,923	92.7	57.3
Hunterdon County, New Jersey	82,039	95.4	52.5	78,281	95.8	53.1
Mercer County, New Jersey	165,556	90.2	46.1	134,227	96.5	52.3
Middlesex County, New Jersey	346,728	89.9	35.4	272,087	94.8	40.2
Monmouth County, New Jersey	366,795	94.6	47.0	341,485	96.1	48.5

Table C-2. Educational Attainment of the Population, by Selected Counties, 2017—*Continued*

(Number; percent; dollars.)

	Educational attainment by race/ethnicity, 25 years and over					
	Black alone			American Indian or Alaska Native alone		
State/County	Total	High school graduate or more (percent)	Bachelor's degree or more (percent)	Total	High school graduate or more (percent)	Bachelor's degree or more (percent)
MISSISSIPPI						
DeSoto County, Mississippi	29,185	92.2	20.3	N	N	N
Forrest County, Mississippi	15,800	88.1	25.4	N	N	N
Harrison County, Mississippi	30,517	88.7	16.0	N	N	N
Hinds County, Mississippi	107,673	83.0	21.6	N	N	N
Jackson County, Mississippi	18,732	86.7	13.8	N	N	N
Jones County, Mississippi	11,112	82.7	12.4	N	N	N
Lauderdale County, Mississippi	21,003	78.3	15.7	N	N	N
Lee County, Mississippi	14,720	76.7	14.6	N	N	N
Madison County, Mississippi	24,721	85.1	31.8	N	N	N
Rankin County, Mississippi	20,726	83.9	12.0	N	N	N
MISSOURI						
Boone County, Missouri	7,956	95.1	15.7	N	N	N
Buchanan County, Missouri	N	N	N	N	N	N
Cape Girardeau County, Missouri	2,434	75.7	8.6	N	N	N
Cass County, Missouri	2,407	93.4	20.6	N	N	N
Christian County, Missouri	N	N	N	N	N	N
Clay County, Missouri	7,850	95.8	27.8	N	N	N
Cole County, Missouri	4,695	79.2	17.1	N	N	N
Franklin County, Missouri	N	N	N	N	N	N
Greene County, Missouri	4,527	91.3	16.9	N	N	N
Jackson County, Missouri	102,610	85.4	14.6	2,196	98.7	34.6
Jasper County, Missouri	N	N	N	N	N	N
Jefferson County, Missouri	N	N	N	N	N	N
Platte County, Missouri	3,899	88.1	24.6	N	N	N
St. Charles County, Missouri	9,757	94.4	28.6	N	N	N
St. Francois County, Missouri	N	N	N	N	N	N
St. Louis County, Missouri	151,022	87.7	20.7	N	N	N
St. Louis city, Missouri	93,611	81.2	15.5	N	N	N
MONTANA						
Cascade County, Montana	N	N	N	2,349	66.1	5.9
Flathead County, Montana	N	N	N	N	N	N
Gallatin County, Montana	N	N	N	N	N	N
Lewis and Clark County, Montana	N	N	N	N	N	N
Missoula County, Montana	N	N	N	N	N	N
Yellowstone County, Montana	N	N	N	3,654	90.6	17.3
NEBRASKA						
Douglas County, Nebraska	36,451	84.2	14.6	1,392	92.8	16.3
Lancaster County, Nebraska	6,579	88.2	23.7	N	N	N
Sarpy County, Nebraska	4,457	96.1	35.2	N	N	N
NEVADA						
Clark County, Nevada	164,287	88.9	18.6	10,981	83.0	10.9
Washoe County, Nevada	7,039	95.9	24.0	5,128	84.2	10.2
NEW HAMPSHIRE						
Cheshire County, New Hampshire	N	N	N	N	N	N
Grafton County, New Hampshire	N	N	N	N	N	N
Hillsborough County, New Hampshire	7,824	87.9	25.3	N	N	N
Merrimack County, New Hampshire	N	N	N	N	N	N
Rockingham County, New Hampshire	N	N	N	N	N	N
Strafford County, New Hampshire	N	N	N	N	N	N
NEW JERSEY						
Atlantic County, New Jersey	24,198	82.5	14.4	N	N	N
Bergen County, New Jersey	39,796	90.1	39.2	1,136	93.1	39.7
Burlington County, New Jersey	51,248	92.4	28.8	N	N	N
Camden County, New Jersey	61,502	87.8	21.8	N	N	N
Cape May County, New Jersey	2,945	91.3	11.5	N	N	N
Cumberland County, New Jersey	19,428	77.7	10.4	1,269	75.3	15.9
Essex County, New Jersey	214,214	85.7	22.2	N	N	N
Gloucester County, New Jersey	19,302	88.0	28.0	N	N	N
Hudson County, New Jersey	53,809	83.9	27.3	N	N	N
Hunterdon County, New Jersey	N	N	N	N	N	N
Mercer County, New Jersey	49,692	81.4	18.8	N	N	N
Middlesex County, New Jersey	57,351	93.8	36.0	N	N	N
Monmouth County, New Jersey	30,094	86.1	22.6	N	N	N

N = Data for this geographic area cannot be displayed because the number of sample cases is too small.

Table C-2. Educational Attainment of the Population, by Selected Counties, 2017—*Continued*

(Number; percent; dollars.)

| | Educational attainment by race/ethnicity, 25 years and over | | | | | |
| | White alone | | | White alone, not Hispanic | | |
State/County	Total	High school graduate or more (percent)	Bachelor's degree or more (percent)	Total	High school graduate or more (percent)	Bachelor's degree or more (percent)
NEW JERSEY—(*Continued*)						
Morris County, New Jersey	288,198	94.7	50.5	255,392	96.3	54.1
Ocean County, New Jersey	377,348	93.0	30.4	356,842	94.1	31.1
Passaic County, New Jersey	229,902	85.8	30.7	153,087	93.6	38.9
Salem County, New Jersey	36,732	89.6	24.2	34,692	90.6	25.4
Somerset County, New Jersey	162,546	95.6	48.6	138,353	96.9	53.5
Sussex County, New Jersey	94,139	95.3	36.7	89,355	95.6	37.4
Union County, New Jersey	219,590	90.0	41.8	164,599	93.0	48.4
Warren County, New Jersey	69,006	91.3	33.2	64,391	93.1	34.4
NEW MEXICO						
Bernalillo County, New Mexico	369,730	91.3	36.6	208,608	96.0	48.6
Chaves County, New Mexico	36,331	78.6	16.5	19,011	94.2	26.3
Doña Ana County, New Mexico	111,679	80.1	25.0	42,889	95.1	44.2
Lea County, New Mexico	36,035	75.7	12.6	17,778	95.8	22.1
McKinley County, New Mexico	7,876	80.4	34.9	4,414	91.2	50.1
Otero County, New Mexico	35,966	86.7	20.2	24,156	96.6	21.2
Sandoval County, New Mexico	76,600	91.8	31.7	48,356	98.1	38.7
San Juan County, New Mexico	44,901	87.0	20.3	36,250	90.3	21.6
Santa Fe County, New Mexico	94,549	92.8	43.0	55,202	98.9	60.3
Valencia County, New Mexico	42,366	85.3	15.3	19,623	90.6	22.1
NEW YORK						
Albany County, New York	163,649	94.5	44.2	158,060	95.3	44.5
Bronx County, New York	232,858	74.9	26.0	101,864	87.2	38.7
Broome County, New York	115,737	91.5	27.6	113,539	91.8	27.5
Cattaraugus County, New York	49,997	89.5	20.5	49,472	89.6	20.7
Cayuga County, New York	51,741	89.1	23.4	51,186	89.4	23.5
Chautauqua County, New York	83,982	90.3	22.7	81,696	90.5	23.1
Chemung County, New York	53,728	90.5	23.7	52,999	90.6	23.9
Clinton County, New York	50,467	88.3	22.8	50,254	88.5	22.8
Dutchess County, New York	167,459	93.9	36.2	153,969	94.4	37.5
Erie County, New York	530,042	94.3	36.8	519,026	94.7	37.1
Jefferson County, New York	64,187	90.2	20.8	61,748	90.9	21.2
Kings County, New York	802,233	89.0	50.9	675,204	91.6	56.0
Livingston County, New York	39,921	93.0	27.0	39,312	93.3	27.2
Madison County, New York	46,479	92.9	26.8	46,027	92.9	26.3
Monroe County, New York	409,521	94.0	41.5	388,852	94.9	42.6
Nassau County, New York	658,097	93.9	48.3	595,769	95.8	50.6
New York County, New York	743,972	94.5	76.6	630,114	98.3	83.7
Niagara County, New York	136,370	92.7	25.4	134,306	93.0	25.5
Oneida County, New York	143,045	90.5	24.7	138,221	91.6	25.2
Onondaga County, New York	266,677	94.0	38.5	259,747	94.4	39.0
Ontario County, New York	72,608	95.0	37.9	71,457	95.1	38.0
Orange County, New York	186,535	91.5	31.6	164,346	93.3	33.2
Oswego County, New York	77,925	87.5	17.6	77,274	87.7	17.8
Putnam County, New York	63,280	93.6	39.1	57,424	94.6	40.0
Queens County, New York	664,072	86.2	36.2	458,814	91.1	44.0
Rensselaer County, New York	99,310	93.4	32.9	97,633	93.5	33.0
Richmond County, New York	252,900	90.8	34.1	215,582	93.0	37.3
Rockland County, New York	150,495	90.3	43.0	129,293	93.1	46.0
St. Lawrence County, New York	67,773	89.5	24.2	67,469	89.6	24.3
Saratoga County, New York	154,075	93.8	40.8	150,856	94.2	41.2
Schenectady County, New York	87,373	93.3	30.0	83,910	94.0	30.5
Steuben County, New York	65,001	90.5	21.0	64,358	90.5	20.9
Suffolk County, New York	860,037	91.7	37.4	741,751	95.0	40.5
Sullivan County, New York	43,783	88.9	31.5	40,651	89.1	32.1
Tompkins County, New York	53,403	92.9	51.0	51,023	93.1	50.6
Ulster County, New York	113,206	93.2	34.9	107,916	93.1	34.5
Warren County, New York	46,560	91.4	31.8	45,597	91.8	32.1
Wayne County, New York	60,423	89.1	22.4	59,151	89.1	22.8
Westchester County, New York	439,458	91.5	56.2	380,539	94.2	60.2
NORTH CAROLINA						
Alamance County, North Carolina	80,952	86.9	25.4	75,459	90.5	26.9
Brunswick County, North Carolina	89,377	92.8	33.1	87,892	92.7	33.3
Buncombe County, North Carolina	172,235	92.6	43.6	164,251	93.6	44.8
Burke County, North Carolina	58,262	82.9	17.6	55,780	83.8	18.0
Cabarrus County, North Carolina	103,224	88.6	30.8	96,905	91.5	31.9
Caldwell County, North Carolina	53,634	79.7	15.9	53,277	80.0	16.0

Table C-2. Educational Attainment of the Population, by Selected Counties, 2017—*Continued*

(Number; percent; dollars.)

| | Educational attainment by race/ethnicity, 25 years and over | | | | | |
| | Black alone | | | American Indian or Alaska Native alone | | |
State/County	Total	High school graduate or more (percent)	Bachelor's degree or more (percent)	Total	High school graduate or more (percent)	Bachelor's degree or more (percent)
NEW JERSEY—(*Continued*)						
Morris County, New Jersey	11,224	88.9	42.6	N	N	N
Ocean County, New Jersey	12,131	93.4	31.7	N	N	N
Passaic County, New Jersey	36,668	83.0	16.2	N	N	N
Salem County, New Jersey	5,608	84.6	11.7	N	N	N
Somerset County, New Jersey	21,153	94.8	39.5	N	N	N
Sussex County, New Jersey	N	N	N	N	N	N
Union County, New Jersey	85,722	89.1	21.4	N	N	N
Warren County, New Jersey	2,756	98.4	21.7	N	N	N
NEW MEXICO						
Bernalillo County, New Mexico	12,041	92.8	24.7	21,461	89.9	19.4
Chaves County, New Mexico	N	N	N	N	N	N
Doña Ana County, New Mexico	N	N	N	1,377	78.0	33.6
Lea County, New Mexico	2,033	71.1	0.0	N	N	N
McKinley County, New Mexico	N	N	N	33,031	76.3	6.6
Otero County, New Mexico	N	N	N	2,590	88.7	8.9
Sandoval County, New Mexico	N	N	N	10,693	75.4	9.8
San Juan County, New Mexico	N	N	N	30,166	80.7	5.3
Santa Fe County, New Mexico	N	N	N	3,108	93.5	14.6
Valencia County, New Mexico	N	N	N	N	N	N
NEW YORK						
Albany County, New York	21,912	83.2	23.3	N	N	N
Bronx County, New York	336,037	79.1	21.3	8,180	69.1	20.3
Broome County, New York	5,283	83.9	15.7	N	N	N
Cattaraugus County, New York	N	N	N	1,449	87.7	6.6
Cayuga County, New York	N	N	N	N	N	N
Chautauqua County, New York	1,049	66.4	6.3	N	N	N
Chemung County, New York	3,708	73.5	18.0	N	N	N
Clinton County, New York	N	N	N	N	N	N
Dutchess County, New York	20,184	83.6	15.7	N	N	N
Erie County, New York	76,753	82.7	16.2	3,604	93.2	15.6
Jefferson County, New York	3,834	92.6	20.2	N	N	N
Kings County, New York	587,275	85.8	24.3	5,348	75.2	25.8
Livingston County, New York	N	N	N	N	N	N
Madison County, New York	N	N	N	N	N	N
Monroe County, New York	68,988	76.5	13.1	N	N	N
Nassau County, New York	109,414	89.2	31.3	N	N	N
New York County, New York	182,348	78.9	30.4	N	N	N
Niagara County, New York	9,129	86.2	9.9	1,759	50.3	5.7
Oneida County, New York	8,029	68.8	13.4	N	N	N
Onondaga County, New York	29,528	77.0	12.2	N	N	N
Ontario County, New York	N	N	N	N	N	N
Orange County, New York	26,864	90.9	33.1	N	N	N
Oswego County, New York	N	N	N	N	N	N
Putnam County, New York	N	N	N	N	N	N
Queens County, New York	301,515	86.3	24.9	6,348	70.3	14.1
Rensselaer County, New York	5,717	80.9	8.8	N	N	N
Richmond County, New York	31,414	85.4	27.5	N	N	N
Rockland County, New York	26,236	85.8	28.9	N	N	N
St. Lawrence County, New York	N	N	N	N	N	N
Saratoga County, New York	N	N	N	N	N	N
Schenectady County, New York	10,781	80.6	12.3	N	N	N
Steuben County, New York	1,275	85.9	30.7	N	N	N
Suffolk County, New York	79,277	84.3	24.9	2,467	79.1	39.6
Sullivan County, New York	4,944	82.0	16.8	N	N	N
Tompkins County, New York	N	N	N	N	N	N
Ulster County, New York	7,389	88.7	18.4	N	N	N
Warren County, New York	N	N	N	N	N	N
Wayne County, New York	N	N	N	N	N	N
Westchester County, New York	99,638	85.3	29.7	3,475	57.5	9.8
NORTH CAROLINA						
Alamance County, North Carolina	21,300	80.9	17.1	N	N	N
Brunswick County, North Carolina	9,283	87.8	12.2	N	N	N
Buncombe County, North Carolina	10,395	82.5	21.0	N	N	N
Burke County, North Carolina	N	N	N	N	N	N
Cabarrus County, North Carolina	23,313	90.0	29.8	N	N	N
Caldwell County, North Carolina	2,822	79.8	11.3	N	N	N

N = Data for this geographic area cannot be displayed because the number of sample cases is too small.

Table C-2. Educational Attainment of the Population, by Selected Counties, 2017—*Continued*

(Number; percent; dollars.)

	Educational attainment by race/ethnicity, 25 years and over					
	White alone			White alone, not Hispanic		
State/County	Total	High school graduate or more (percent)	Bachelor's degree or more (percent)	Total	High school graduate or more (percent)	Bachelor's degree or more (percent)
NORTH CAROLINA—(*Continued*)						
Carteret County, North Carolina	47,596	92.1	26.6	46,427	92.4	27.1
Catawba County, North Carolina	90,038	87.0	22.0	88,170	87.8	22.4
Chatham County, North Carolina	43,750	91.0	43.4	40,080	94.8	46.3
Cleveland County, North Carolina	52,172	88.6	19.7	51,113	89.4	20.0
Craven County, North Carolina	48,491	94.4	34.3	47,370	94.8	34.4
Cumberland County, North Carolina	106,477	91.5	25.3	95,267	92.3	25.1
Davidson County, North Carolina	102,468	84.5	18.6	97,190	86.3	19.4
Durham County, North Carolina	119,215	89.6	57.8	103,284	96.9	63.5
Forsyth County, North Carolina	176,809	90.8	37.8	158,505	94.0	40.9
Franklin County, North Carolina	31,784	92.1	22.8	30,246	93.8	23.7
Gaston County, North Carolina	122,768	85.7	20.0	116,561	87.3	20.5
Guilford County, North Carolina	212,510	92.3	41.7	197,642	94.8	43.8
Harnett County, North Carolina	60,108	89.8	22.8	56,522	90.8	23.5
Henderson County, North Carolina	80,031	92.0	34.4	75,194	94.1	35.8
Iredell County, North Carolina	100,977	91.4	29.6	95,698	93.3	30.3
Johnston County, North Carolina	105,241	87.2	22.8	94,871	90.9	24.6
Lincoln County, North Carolina	53,055	87.7	23.2	51,490	87.7	23.0
Mecklenburg County, North Carolina	412,489	94.3	55.3	372,496	96.9	58.2
Moore County, North Carolina	59,855	95.0	45.3	56,979	95.0	45.8
Nash County, North Carolina	35,412	89.7	26.2	34,353	90.9	26.6
New Hanover County, North Carolina	130,118	93.0	44.2	125,681	94.0	44.6
Onslow County, North Carolina	80,059	94.3	22.6	72,674	94.2	22.7
Orange County, North Carolina	69,829	93.8	60.5	65,506	96.7	63.1
Pitt County, North Carolina	64,542	93.5	44.0	61,859	93.8	44.5
Randolph County, North Carolina	86,305	83.6	16.6	83,160	85.1	16.7
Robeson County, North Carolina	27,185	83.0	17.3	25,067	87.4	18.3
Rockingham County, North Carolina	51,225	85.1	16.7	49,480	85.9	16.8
Rowan County, North Carolina	77,103	84.4	19.6	74,414	85.8	20.1
Rutherford County, North Carolina	42,349	86.4	20.9	41,122	87.3	21.4
Surry County, North Carolina	47,038	79.4	21.4	44,896	81.5	21.9
Union County, North Carolina	121,763	91.3	33.7	111,804	93.9	35.2
Wake County, North Carolina	487,515	94.7	57.3	456,344	96.7	59.2
Wayne County, North Carolina	53,713	84.2	24.3	47,922	91.3	26.3
Wilkes County, North Carolina	45,859	78.6	16.4	44,441	79.5	16.8
Wilson County, North Carolina	31,100	87.0	25.6	28,839	88.5	26.6
NORTH DAKOTA						
Burleigh County, North Dakota	59,930	94.8	35.5	58,965	95.3	35.7
Cass County, North Dakota	100,548	96.1	42.3	98,982	96.2	42.8
Grand Forks County, North Dakota	37,022	97.0	37.6	35,825	97.3	38.5
Ward County, North Dakota	38,775	94.7	30.0	37,706	94.6	30.8
OHIO						
Allen County, Ohio	59,343	91.5	20.9	58,236	91.4	20.7
Ashtabula County, Ohio	64,588	86.9	15.1	62,989	86.8	15.4
Athens County, Ohio	34,398	89.5	30.0	34,386	89.5	30.0
Belmont County, Ohio	47,227	92.6	14.7	47,085	92.6	14.7
Butler County, Ohio	211,462	92.5	28.7	205,223	92.9	29.0
Clark County, Ohio	81,586	87.3	20.2	80,465	87.2	20.3
Clermont County, Ohio	135,674	89.6	26.6	133,505	89.6	26.7
Columbiana County, Ohio	70,986	86.9	10.8	70,561	86.8	10.9
Cuyahoga County, Ohio	580,766	92.9	38.7	556,319	93.4	39.5
Delaware County, Ohio	116,401	96.4	52.6	114,231	96.8	52.6
Erie County, Ohio	48,218	92.9	26.9	46,604	94.2	27.5
Fairfield County, Ohio	93,273	93.0	27.7	92,610	93.0	27.6
Franklin County, Ohio	607,547	92.7	43.3	587,694	93.3	44.0
Geauga County, Ohio	62,603	89.1	39.1	61,894	89.4	39.2
Greene County, Ohio	98,961	93.1	40.4	97,381	93.1	40.4
Hamilton County, Ohio	391,457	92.8	43.2	381,878	93.4	43.4
Hancock County, Ohio	49,363	92.7	28.8	47,543	93.4	29.6
Jefferson County, Ohio	43,972	92.9	13.8	43,715	93.1	13.7
Lake County, Ohio	152,956	91.9	27.2	150,461	92.7	27.5
Licking County, Ohio	109,937	90.1	25.5	108,727	90.1	25.6
Lorain County, Ohio	188,169	89.7	24.1	175,709	90.8	25.4
Lucas County, Ohio	224,058	90.0	29.6	215,675	90.5	30.2
Mahoning County, Ohio	135,816	93.5	24.9	131,098	93.8	25.6
Marion County, Ohio	41,951	91.1	17.2	41,394	91.3	17.3
Medina County, Ohio	119,952	94.9	31.6	118,350	94.9	31.7
Miami County, Ohio	69,771	93.3	23.5	68,903	93.4	23.6

Table C-2. Educational Attainment of the Population, by Selected Counties, 2017—*Continued*

(Number; percent; dollars.)

State/County	Educational attainment by race/ethnicity, 25 years and over					
	Black alone			American Indian or Alaska Native alone		
	Total	High school graduate or more (percent)	Bachelor's degree or more (percent)	Total	High school graduate or more (percent)	Bachelor's degree or more (percent)
NORTH CAROLINA—(*Continued*)						
Carteret County, North Carolina	2,442	91.4	13.3	N	N	N
Catawba County, North Carolina	8,067	78.0	12.0	N	N	N
Chatham County, North Carolina	7,338	85.2	15.3	N	N	N
Cleveland County, North Carolina	12,406	73.6	9.1	N	N	N
Craven County, North Carolina	14,174	75.7	12.8	N	N	N
Cumberland County, North Carolina	77,262	91.7	22.3	2,428	70.7	10.8
Davidson County, North Carolina	9,189	85.1	5.4	N	N	N
Durham County, North Carolina	74,922	84.4	31.2	N	N	N
Forsyth County, North Carolina	62,605	88.4	21.9	N	N	N
Franklin County, North Carolina	11,479	71.1	18.0	N	N	N
Gaston County, North Carolina	22,925	84.5	20.5	N	N	N
Guilford County, North Carolina	112,675	88.3	23.9	1,880	80.4	22.9
Harnett County, North Carolina	17,897	85.1	19.5	N	N	N
Henderson County, North Carolina	2,907	78.8	23.5	N	N	N
Iredell County, North Carolina	13,398	86.2	11.0	N	N	N
Johnston County, North Carolina	21,385	87.7	20.5	N	N	N
Lincoln County, North Carolina	3,443	79.8	7.4	N	N	N
Mecklenburg County, North Carolina	217,897	91.2	31.8	3,060	49.3	12.9
Moore County, North Carolina	7,303	78.0	17.6	N	N	N
Nash County, North Carolina	25,333	86.1	16.9	N	N	N
New Hanover County, North Carolina	20,747	91.8	15.7	N	N	N
Onslow County, North Carolina	16,213	86.1	20.7	N	N	N
Orange County, North Carolina	11,390	89.6	25.9	N	N	N
Pitt County, North Carolina	37,670	85.6	19.7	N	N	N
Randolph County, North Carolina	5,880	77.0	22.9	N	N	N
Robeson County, North Carolina	19,752	77.8	8.2	33,836	76.9	14.5
Rockingham County, North Carolina	12,201	79.6	14.2	N	N	N
Rowan County, North Carolina	14,182	90.8	18.6	N	N	N
Rutherford County, North Carolina	4,187	88.8	11.5	N	N	N
Surry County, North Carolina	2,176	77.3	10.0	N	N	N
Union County, North Carolina	16,987	84.9	23.2	N	N	N
Wake County, North Carolina	138,202	90.5	32.3	2,806	84.2	27.5
Wayne County, North Carolina	25,715	87.4	10.9	N	N	N
Wilkes County, North Carolina	2,013	79.8	5.8	N	N	N
Wilson County, North Carolina	22,214	75.9	7.3	N	N	N
NORTH DAKOTA						
Burleigh County, North Dakota	N	N	N	N	N	N
Cass County, North Dakota	5,611	81.5	13.0	N	N	N
Grand Forks County, North Dakota	N	N	N	N	N	N
Ward County, North Dakota	N	N	N	N	N	N
OHIO						
Allen County, Ohio	8,012	82.8	10.0	N	N	N
Ashtabula County, Ohio	2,925	75.5	0.0	N	N	N
Athens County, Ohio	N	N	N	N	N	N
Belmont County, Ohio	N	N	N	N	N	N
Butler County, Ohio	17,965	89.4	26.5	N	N	N
Clark County, Ohio	7,754	92.3	16.5	N	N	N
Clermont County, Ohio	N	N	N	N	N	N
Columbiana County, Ohio	N	N	N	N	N	N
Cuyahoga County, Ohio	239,411	84.9	15.8	2,332	70.2	10.1
Delaware County, Ohio	4,696	95.3	51.9	N	N	N
Erie County, Ohio	4,098	82.1	7.3	N	N	N
Fairfield County, Ohio	7,078	92.8	23.6	N	N	N
Franklin County, Ohio	174,732	87.5	20.2	1,898	93.0	40.4
Geauga County, Ohio	N	N	N	N	N	N
Greene County, Ohio	5,628	81.5	15.7	N	N	N
Hamilton County, Ohio	130,057	85.1	16.5	N	N	N
Hancock County, Ohio	N	N	N	N	N	N
Jefferson County, Ohio	3,033	94.3	20.9	N	N	N
Lake County, Ohio	6,184	92.6	8.4	N	N	N
Licking County, Ohio	4,595	99.8	34.5	N	N	N
Lorain County, Ohio	16,410	88.0	11.9	N	N	N
Lucas County, Ohio	50,619	79.4	10.0	N	N	N
Mahoning County, Ohio	21,283	82.6	8.8	N	N	N
Marion County, Ohio	2,764	65.0	4.6	N	N	N
Medina County, Ohio	N	N	N	N	N	N
Miami County, Ohio	N	N	N	N	N	N

N = Data for this geographic area cannot be displayed because the number of sample cases is too small.

Table C-2. Educational Attainment of the Population, by Selected Counties, 2017—*Continued*

(Number; percent; dollars.)

State/County	Educational attainment by race/ethnicity, 25 years and over					
	White alone			White alone, not Hispanic		
	Total	High school graduate or more (percent)	Bachelor's degree or more (percent)	Total	High school graduate or more (percent)	Bachelor's degree or more (percent)
OHIO—(*Continued*)						
Montgomery County, Ohio	276,704	91.1	29.4	270,815	91.7	29.5
Muskingum County, Ohio	54,982	88.3	16.4	54,982	88.3	16.4
Portage County, Ohio	97,520	91.5	29.0	96,994	91.5	29.1
Richland County, Ohio	74,787	87.4	19.2	73,960	87.6	19.2
Ross County, Ohio	49,789	88.8	17.1	49,481	88.8	17.1
Scioto County, Ohio	50,178	82.1	17.2	49,784	81.9	17.3
Stark County, Ohio	235,216	91.7	22.8	232,057	91.8	22.7
Summit County, Ohio	312,434	93.7	35.6	307,464	93.8	35.5
Trumbull County, Ohio	129,506	89.9	18.9	128,330	90.0	18.7
Tuscarawas County, Ohio	62,550	88.6	13.9	61,649	89.2	14.1
Warren County, Ohio	137,816	94.3	39.8	135,123	94.5	40.2
Wayne County, Ohio	73,409	86.5	22.0	72,805	86.5	21.8
Wood County, Ohio	76,269	95.1	31.5	73,594	95.6	31.6
OKLAHOMA						
Canadian County, Oklahoma	77,709	95.0	28.8	74,484	95.4	29.1
Cleveland County, Oklahoma	143,082	91.9	34.0	135,298	92.3	34.3
Comanche County, Oklahoma	50,994	92.6	25.6	47,221	92.6	26.9
Creek County, Oklahoma	40,495	88.3	16.6	39,354	88.6	16.6
Muskogee County, Oklahoma	29,532	81.7	15.1	29,099	82.1	15.4
Oklahoma County, Oklahoma	368,927	89.3	35.8	322,260	93.5	39.5
Payne County, Oklahoma	36,526	89.8	35.8	35,548	89.8	36.4
Pottawatomie County, Oklahoma	38,555	87.2	18.2	37,288	88.6	18.6
Rogers County, Oklahoma	48,573	92.5	26.3	47,366	93.0	26.2
Tulsa County, Oklahoma	317,310	91.8	34.9	291,617	93.9	36.8
Wagoner County, Oklahoma	42,256	90.3	25.0	40,853	90.6	25.2
OREGON						
Benton County, Oregon	49,265	97.6	53.4	47,183	98.1	53.8
Clackamas County, Oregon	263,193	94.3	37.6	248,756	95.3	38.7
Deschutes County, Oregon	129,025	94.6	33.7	122,319	95.2	34.3
Douglas County, Oregon	75,323	88.5	17.6	72,825	88.7	18.1
Jackson County, Oregon	144,502	91.4	28.5	133,151	93.9	29.8
Josephine County, Oregon	60,789	91.6	18.8	57,066	92.2	19.5
Klamath County, Oregon	42,076	89.8	19.7	38,942	92.3	20.8
Lane County, Oregon	231,234	93.5	31.3	221,618	94.1	31.5
Linn County, Oregon	81,006	90.2	17.7	77,031	91.0	17.9
Marion County, Oregon	192,841	86.7	24.8	164,534	91.7	27.6
Multnomah County, Oregon	476,196	94.1	48.4	439,486	96.1	50.4
Polk County, Oregon	48,948	89.7	31.5	44,810	92.6	31.9
Umatilla County, Oregon	43,274	84.2	18.2	36,868	89.7	20.3
Washington County, Oregon	316,461	94.6	44.7	286,322	96.7	47.3
Yamhill County, Oregon	64,021	90.2	28.3	58,072	94.6	30.6
PENNSYLVANIA						
Adams County, Pennsylvania	67,831	89.4	23.0	66,455	89.8	23.0
Allegheny County, Pennsylvania	734,736	95.3	42.9	725,092	95.3	42.8
Armstrong County, Pennsylvania	47,479	89.5	15.1	47,313	89.5	15.1
Beaver County, Pennsylvania	112,200	94.4	24.7	111,449	94.4	24.6
Berks County, Pennsylvania	242,853	88.2	25.2	221,765	90.1	27.0
Blair County, Pennsylvania	85,460	91.0	21.0	84,744	91.0	21.1
Bucks County, Pennsylvania	401,233	94.6	41.0	387,519	95.3	41.7
Butler County, Pennsylvania	129,099	94.8	35.7	127,589	94.9	35.8
Cambria County, Pennsylvania	91,165	91.4	21.2	90,443	91.4	21.2
Carbon County, Pennsylvania	45,667	90.4	15.0	44,174	90.3	15.1
Centre County, Pennsylvania	89,050	94.1	44.4	87,463	94.1	44.7
Chester County, Pennsylvania	308,092	94.0	52.9	291,927	95.7	54.9
Clearfield County, Pennsylvania	55,601	88.6	18.0	54,695	88.9	18.0
Columbia County, Pennsylvania	42,581	91.3	23.1	41,857	91.2	22.9
Crawford County, Pennsylvania	58,004	88.4	20.9	57,763	88.4	20.8
Cumberland County, Pennsylvania	157,654	93.2	37.0	154,535	93.4	37.2
Dauphin County, Pennsylvania	144,361	92.2	31.8	136,657	93.1	32.8
Delaware County, Pennsylvania	277,014	95.5	43.4	272,243	95.7	43.5
Erie County, Pennsylvania	170,062	91.9	28.2	166,221	92.3	28.2
Fayette County, Pennsylvania	90,625	89.1	18.7	90,109	89.0	18.7
Franklin County, Pennsylvania	102,048	89.7	24.2	98,557	90.9	24.4
Indiana County, Pennsylvania	53,939	90.4	24.2	53,698	90.4	24.4
Lackawanna County, Pennsylvania	139,529	92.7	29.3	133,300	93.9	30.2
Lancaster County, Pennsylvania	331,594	85.1	28.4	311,785	85.6	29.1

Table C-2. Educational Attainment of the Population, by Selected Counties, 2017—*Continued*

(Number; percent; dollars.)

| | Educational attainment by race/ethnicity, 25 years and over | | | | | |
| | Black alone | | | American Indian or Alaska Native alone | | |
State/County	Total	High school graduate or more (percent)	Bachelor's degree or more (percent)	Total	High school graduate or more (percent)	Bachelor's degree or more (percent)
OHIO—(*Continued*)						
Montgomery County, Ohio	70,517	84.2	18.9	N	N	N
Muskingum County, Ohio	N	N	N	N	N	N
Portage County, Ohio	3,720	92.5	57.8	N	N	N
Richland County, Ohio	7,262	76.8	11.3	N	N	N
Ross County, Ohio	N	N	N	N	N	N
Scioto County, Ohio	N	N	N	N	N	N
Stark County, Ohio	15,872	83.0	11.6	N	N	N
Summit County, Ohio	49,243	86.8	14.5	N	N	N
Trumbull County, Ohio	10,541	94.1	14.9	N	N	N
Tuscarawas County, Ohio	N	N	N	N	N	N
Warren County, Ohio	6,226	79.9	44.6	N	N	N
Wayne County, Ohio	N	N	N	N	N	N
Wood County, Ohio	N	N	N	N	N	N
OKLAHOMA						
Canadian County, Oklahoma	N	N	N	2,843	91.6	12.6
Cleveland County, Oklahoma	8,555	95.0	23.0	6,354	88.9	26.7
Comanche County, Oklahoma	11,713	93.9	25.1	4,130	85.5	8.3
Creek County, Oklahoma	N	N	N	5,137	87.0	14.7
Muskogee County, Oklahoma	4,444	85.8	21.1	7,283	82.9	23.5
Oklahoma County, Oklahoma	73,631	88.5	20.5	12,909	90.7	22.3
Payne County, Oklahoma	N	N	N	N	N	N
Pottawatomie County, Oklahoma	N	N	N	6,134	86.3	13.0
Rogers County, Oklahoma	N	N	N	6,781	91.0	19.4
Tulsa County, Oklahoma	38,707	90.2	18.8	19,526	90.2	26.3
Wagoner County, Oklahoma	2,007	88.1	36.2	5,048	86.3	17.2
OREGON						
Benton County, Oregon	N	N	N	N	N	N
Clackamas County, Oregon	N	N	N	N	N	N
Deschutes County, Oregon	N	N	N	N	N	N
Douglas County, Oregon	N	N	N	N	N	N
Jackson County, Oregon	N	N	N	N	N	N
Josephine County, Oregon	N	N	N	N	N	N
Klamath County, Oregon	N	N	N	N	N	N
Lane County, Oregon	N	N	N	N	N	N
Linn County, Oregon	N	N	N	N	N	N
Marion County, Oregon	N	N	N	N	N	N
Multnomah County, Oregon	29,053	85.3	25.1	6,070	89.5	10.3
Polk County, Oregon	N	N	N	N	N	N
Umatilla County, Oregon	N	N	N	2,037	80.5	13.1
Washington County, Oregon	7,733	93.7	46.2	2,654	79.7	26.4
Yamhill County, Oregon	N	N	N	N	N	N
PENNSYLVANIA						
Adams County, Pennsylvania	N	N	N	N	N	N
Allegheny County, Pennsylvania	100,041	91.5	22.4	N	N	N
Armstrong County, Pennsylvania	N	N	N	N	N	N
Beaver County, Pennsylvania	6,181	95.3	11.3	N	N	N
Berks County, Pennsylvania	13,960	81.5	14.4	N	N	N
Blair County, Pennsylvania	N	N	N	N	N	N
Bucks County, Pennsylvania	16,350	88.3	28.7	N	N	N
Butler County, Pennsylvania	N	N	N	N	N	N
Cambria County, Pennsylvania	2,423	81.1	9.2	N	N	N
Carbon County, Pennsylvania	N	N	N	N	N	N
Centre County, Pennsylvania	N	N	N	N	N	N
Chester County, Pennsylvania	19,261	91.0	21.3	N	N	N
Clearfield County, Pennsylvania	N	N	N	N	N	N
Columbia County, Pennsylvania	N	N	N	N	N	N
Crawford County, Pennsylvania	N	N	N	N	N	N
Cumberland County, Pennsylvania	4,524	85.3	23.7	N	N	N
Dauphin County, Pennsylvania	32,372	89.4	14.5	N	N	N
Delaware County, Pennsylvania	73,323	92.6	23.9	N	N	N
Erie County, Pennsylvania	10,718	82.0	13.7	N	N	N
Fayette County, Pennsylvania	4,251	80.6	12.8	N	N	N
Franklin County, Pennsylvania	3,797	63.9	6.0	N	N	N
Indiana County, Pennsylvania	N	N	N	N	N	N
Lackawanna County, Pennsylvania	2,972	71.9	17.3	N	N	N
Lancaster County, Pennsylvania	12,956	81.6	16.9	N	N	N

N = Data for this geographic area cannot be displayed because the number of sample cases is too small.

Table C-2. Educational Attainment of the Population, by Selected Counties, 2017—*Continued*

(Number; percent; dollars.)

	Educational attainment by race/ethnicity, 25 years and over					
	White alone			White alone, not Hispanic		
State/County	Total	High school graduate or more (percent)	Bachelor's degree or more (percent)	Total	High school graduate or more (percent)	Bachelor's degree or more (percent)
PENNSYLVANIA—(*Continued*)						
Lawrence County, Pennsylvania	59,452	91.4	23.2	59,019	91.5	23.3
Lebanon County, Pennsylvania	85,979	88.9	22.9	83,111	89.0	22.8
Lehigh County, Pennsylvania	207,114	90.1	30.8	177,432	92.6	34.6
Luzerne County, Pennsylvania	209,246	90.2	24.3	197,367	91.4	25.1
Lycoming County, Pennsylvania	75,939	91.6	24.4	74,876	91.6	23.8
Mercer County, Pennsylvania	73,375	91.9	25.5	72,632	91.8	25.6
Monroe County, Pennsylvania	91,899	88.8	24.1	82,383	89.9	24.7
Montgomery County, Pennsylvania	471,904	95.8	50.2	455,397	96.6	50.9
Northampton County, Pennsylvania	188,614	91.2	30.3	172,878	92.7	31.8
Northumberland County, Pennsylvania	64,285	87.8	16.3	63,476	87.8	16.2
Philadelphia County, Pennsylvania	489,978	88.7	37.9	424,594	91.7	40.8
Schuylkill County, Pennsylvania	98,815	89.7	17.0	96,771	90.1	17.2
Somerset County, Pennsylvania	53,112	88.9	14.6	52,655	88.8	14.7
Washington County, Pennsylvania	141,359	93.9	31.8	140,015	94.0	31.9
Westmoreland County, Pennsylvania	250,664	94.6	30.7	248,732	94.7	30.8
York County, Pennsylvania	284,417	90.0	26.0	271,193	90.6	26.5
RHODE ISLAND						
Kent County, Rhode Island	113,188	91.2	32.8	110,055	91.5	33.4
Newport County, Rhode Island	55,770	94.6	49.3	54,354	94.4	49.2
Providence County, Rhode Island	344,222	87.2	29.8	293,664	88.3	32.5
Washington County, Rhode Island	81,790	94.3	44.0	80,589	94.4	44.3
SOUTH CAROLINA						
Aiken County, South Carolina	86,929	89.6	31.3	82,858	91.0	32.3
Anderson County, South Carolina	112,616	85.1	22.3	109,697	85.3	22.7
Beaufort County, South Carolina	105,314	93.7	47.1	99,039	95.9	49.1
Berkeley County, South Carolina	102,402	92.0	28.4	97,272	92.1	28.7
Charleston County, South Carolina	204,747	95.1	52.4	194,389	96.5	54.3
Darlington County, South Carolina	27,541	88.9	26.0	27,045	89.3	26.2
Dorchester County, South Carolina	74,272	94.2	33.5	70,937	94.3	34.2
Florence County, South Carolina	53,308	87.1	30.8	52,177	88.0	31.4
Greenville County, South Carolina	262,790	90.1	39.0	248,131	91.4	39.9
Greenwood County, South Carolina	32,859	85.9	30.6	30,703	89.2	30.7
Horry County, South Carolina	208,717	92.2	24.2	202,156	93.0	24.6
Kershaw County, South Carolina	32,695	89.4	26.2	32,027	89.5	26.3
Lancaster County, South Carolina	51,031	86.5	30.8	48,698	87.0	31.0
Laurens County, South Carolina	33,216	82.9	19.0	32,670	83.6	19.2
Lexington County, South Carolina	164,489	90.3	32.2	157,596	91.6	33.1
Oconee County, South Carolina	50,459	87.0	28.0	49,158	87.7	28.6
Orangeburg County, South Carolina	22,607	90.8	19.9	21,681	90.4	19.9
Pickens County, South Carolina	69,760	84.3	24.3	68,593	84.5	24.6
Richland County, South Carolina	120,727	95.5	51.3	116,076	95.8	51.4
Spartanburg County, South Carolina	156,091	89.4	28.5	149,390	89.9	29.3
Sumter County, South Carolina	35,370	90.0	23.4	33,818	89.5	24.0
York County, South Carolina	137,519	91.7	36.5	132,621	92.1	36.9
SOUTH DAKOTA						
Minnehaha County, South Dakota	111,675	94.3	33.5	108,455	95.0	33.9
Pennington County, South Dakota	66,101	95.7	31.9	64,656	96.4	32.3
TENNESSEE						
Anderson County, Tennessee	49,997	86.7	22.4	49,641	86.6	22.2
Blount County, Tennessee	88,753	88.5	22.4	86,558	89.3	22.8
Bradley County, Tennessee	65,522	87.1	22.4	64,076	87.4	22.6
Davidson County, Tennessee	324,870	91.3	46.1	294,848	93.9	49.2
Greene County, Tennessee	47,646	85.1	14.7	47,267	85.4	14.8
Hamilton County, Tennessee	199,694	92.9	35.6	190,924	94.0	36.3
Knox County, Tennessee	269,415	92.3	38.1	263,016	92.7	38.2
Madison County, Tennessee	41,038	88.0	32.6	39,991	88.4	33.4
Maury County, Tennessee	54,345	90.4	25.7	52,473	90.0	25.4
Montgomery County, Tennessee	90,664	92.9	29.7	83,326	93.8	30.6
Putnam County, Tennessee	47,345	87.4	23.7	45,517	87.9	24.4
Robertson County, Tennessee	42,331	89.9	20.2	41,425	90.5	20.4
Rutherford County, Tennessee	160,469	91.2	34.0	149,057	93.6	35.5
Sevier County, Tennessee	67,320	85.2	16.3	64,558	86.1	16.9
Shelby County, Tennessee	262,570	94.4	46.5	248,353	96.2	47.7
Sullivan County, Tennessee	109,365	85.7	23.9	108,724	85.8	23.9
Sumner County, Tennessee	112,454	90.6	27.6	109,340	91.0	28.1

Table C-2. Educational Attainment of the Population, by Selected Counties, 2017—*Continued*

(Number; percent; dollars.)

	Educational attainment by race/ethnicity, 25 years and over					
	Black alone			American Indian or Alaska Native alone		
State/County	Total	High school graduate or more (percent)	Bachelor's degree or more (percent)	Total	High school graduate or more (percent)	Bachelor's degree or more (percent)
PENNSYLVANIA—(*Continued*)						
Lawrence County, Pennsylvania...........................	2,047	82.0	12.6	N	N	N
Lebanon County, Pennsylvania	N	N	N	N	N	N
Lehigh County, Pennsylvania	15,757	86.0	23.2	N	N	N
Luzerne County, Pennsylvania.............................	8,412	82.1	9.1	N	N	N
Lycoming County, Pennsylvania...........................	3,059	94.5	14.0	N	N	N
Mercer County, Pennsylvania..............................	4,049	87.0	6.9	N	N	N
Monroe County, Pennsylvania..............................	16,106	86.5	21.2	N	N	N
Montgomery County, Pennsylvania......................	51,720	91.9	34.8	N	N	N
Northampton County, Pennsylvania	11,564	82.8	13.5	N	N	N
Northumberland County, Pennsylvania	N	N	N	N	N	N
Philadelphia County, Pennsylvania......................	428,784	86.0	17.8	3,740	90.8	25.8
Schuylkill County, Pennsylvania..........................	N	N	N	N	N	N
Somerset County, Pennsylvania..........................	N	N	N	N	N	N
Washington County, Pennsylvania......................	4,246	84.5	13.6	N	N	N
Westmoreland County, Pennsylvania	5,622	86.5	13.2	N	N	N
York County, Pennsylvania..................................	15,467	87.0	13.5	N	N	N
RHODE ISLAND						
Kent County, Rhode Island...................................	N	N	N	N	N	N
Newport County, Rhode Island.............................	N	N	N	N	N	N
Providence County, Rhode Island	34,151	81.6	19.8	N	N	N
Washington County, Rhode Island.......................	N	N	N	N	N	N
SOUTH CAROLINA						
Aiken County, South Carolina..............................	26,720	82.9	10.9	N	N	N
Anderson County, South Carolina	20,283	77.3	8.4	N	N	N
Beaufort County, South Carolina.........................	21,422	87.0	13.7	N	N	N
Berkeley County, South Carolina	33,920	81.1	14.3	N	N	N
Charleston County, South Carolina.....................	72,192	84.8	13.1	N	N	N
Darlington County, South Carolina......................	18,375	81.2	19.7	N	N	N
Dorchester County, South Carolina	26,420	84.5	19.8	N	N	N
Florence County, South Carolina.........................	37,081	73.1	14.7	N	N	N
Greenville County, South Carolina......................	56,378	82.7	16.4	N	N	N
Greenwood County, South Carolina	14,966	77.9	8.6	N	N	N
Horry County, South Carolina	27,006	82.5	14.6	N	N	N
Kershaw County, South Carolina.........................	10,605	94.5	13.8	N	N	N
Lancaster County, South Carolina	13,156	76.2	10.0	N	N	N
Laurens County, South Carolina.........................	11,279	74.4	6.3	N	N	N
Lexington County, South Carolina.......................	27,119	83.8	16.5	N	N	N
Oconee County, South Carolina..........................	3,544	73.1	15.3	N	N	N
Orangeburg County, South Carolina....................	35,002	79.1	20.7	N	N	N
Pickens County, South Carolina..........................	5,445	84.9	14.6	N	N	N
Richland County, South Carolina.........................	120,366	88.5	23.3	N	N	N
Spartanburg County, South Carolina...................	39,844	79.5	12.9	N	N	N
Sumter County, South Carolina...........................	32,130	79.4	14.3	N	N	N
York County, South Carolina	31,270	87.6	25.4	1,006	95.3	12.8
SOUTH DAKOTA						
Minnehaha County, South Dakota........................	5,569	94.2	14.9	N	N	N
Pennington County, South Dakota	N	N	N	5,124	57.2	7.9
TENNESSEE						
Anderson County, Tennessee	N	N	N	N	N	N
Blount County, Tennessee	2,433	98.2	23.0	N	N	N
Bradley County, Tennessee..................................	3,286	96.5	19.8	N	N	N
Davidson County, Tennessee...............................	119,743	90.5	29.3	N	N	N
Greene County, Tennessee..................................	N	N	N	N	N	N
Hamilton County, Tennessee	44,929	89.1	17.1	N	N	N
Knox County, Tennessee	24,821	92.4	21.4	N	N	N
Madison County, Tennessee................................	21,911	88.5	13.5	N	N	N
Maury County, Tennessee	6,630	88.4	6.0	N	N	N
Montgomery County, Tennessee.........................	23,759	92.3	23.4	N	N	N
Putnam County, Tennessee..................................	N	N	N	N	N	N
Robertson County, Tennessee.............................	3,000	75.9	13.3	N	N	N
Rutherford County, Tennessee	27,253	86.8	36.9	N	N	N
Sevier County, Tennessee...................................	N	N	N	N	N	N
Shelby County, Tennessee..................................	313,065	86.5	18.5	N	N	N
Sullivan County, Tennessee................................	2,364	76.9	7.6	N	N	N
Sumner County, Tennessee.................................	8,762	89.1	32.2	N	N	N

N = Data for this geographic area cannot be displayed because the number of sample cases is too small.

Table C-2. Educational Attainment of the Population, by Selected Counties, 2017—*Continued*

(Number; percent; dollars.)

| State/County | | Educational attainment by race/ethnicity, 25 years and over | | | | |
| | | White alone | | | White alone, not Hispanic | | |
	Total	High school graduate or more (percent)	Bachelor's degree or more (percent)	Total	High school graduate or more (percent)	Bachelor's degree or more (percent)
TENNESSEE—(*Continued*)						
Washington County, Tennessee............	81,198	90.2	32.2	79,850	90.5	32.3
Williamson County, Tennessee............	132,063	96.2	60.4	126,822	97.2	61.8
Wilson County, Tennessee	83,929	93.2	31.6	81,999	93.8	31.9
TEXAS						
Angelina County, Texas	46,519	84.3	17.3	38,106	88.4	18.2
Bastrop County, Texas......................	41,834	86.6	28.6	32,408	92.4	30.1
Bell County, Texas...........................	139,829	91.4	29.5	106,975	94.6	34.0
Bexar County, Texas.........................	996,393	84.8	27.8	394,126	95.9	44.1
Bowie County, Texas.........................	45,411	92.2	25.6	43,014	93.1	27.0
Brazoria County, Texas......................	172,397	89.2	28.2	121,956	94.5	30.3
Brazos County, Texas........................	91,370	86.7	42.5	68,543	96.0	51.0
Cameron County, Texas.....................	230,233	68.3	18.3	29,749	90.9	34.7
Collin County, Texas.........................	450,900	93.7	49.1	386,725	97.3	53.2
Comal County, Texas........................	91,308	94.5	38.0	70,721	97.5	42.3
Coryell County, Texas.......................	35,696	88.7	16.1	29,641	90.7	17.6
Dallas County, Texas........................	1,051,497	77.0	32.4	591,656	95.0	49.7
Denton County, Texas.......................	418,844	93.3	44.6	348,148	97.3	49.0
Ector County, Texas.........................	71,476	76.9	13.7	36,114	89.9	18.1
Ellis County, Texas...........................	93,184	86.4	22.5	73,955	93.3	27.2
El Paso County, Texas.......................	391,206	80.8	24.4	69,906	95.9	44.5
Fort Bend County, Texas....................	261,198	89.5	44.8	175,113	97.4	53.2
Galveston County, Texas....................	181,048	90.4	32.2	138,544	94.4	37.8
Grayson County, Texas......................	79,657	89.1	20.3	71,906	92.2	22.1
Gregg County, Texas.........................	61,751	83.5	18.3	50,987	91.8	21.5
Guadalupe County, Texas...................	76,600	90.4	27.8	56,882	95.0	32.4
Harris County, Texas.........................	1,905,616	80.2	32.1	1,022,483	95.8	48.2
Harrison County, Texas......................	32,762	89.0	21.3	30,023	91.9	23.1
Hays County, Texas..........................	114,275	91.0	38.4	75,400	97.7	48.2
Henderson County, Texas...................	52,228	84.3	18.4	47,549	86.6	19.3
Hidalgo County, Texas.......................	415,087	67.0	18.6	42,153	92.1	34.9
Hunt County, Texas..........................	52,352	90.5	24.4	48,140	91.8	25.2
Jefferson County, Texas.....................	102,394	87.1	22.1	77,938	93.6	26.8
Johnson County, Texas......................	101,548	85.8	18.3	84,433	91.4	20.0
Kaufman County, Texas.....................	66,110	85.5	21.9	54,784	90.3	23.5
Liberty County, Texas.......................	43,348	76.9	8.5	37,189	82.5	8.8
Lubbock County, Texas......................	152,707	87.1	31.7	104,308	94.1	38.6
McLennan County, Texas....................	121,591	84.1	26.6	94,031	91.7	32.0
Midland County, Texas......................	87,909	86.0	29.6	53,347	96.2	40.8
Montgomery County, Texas.................	326,445	88.7	32.7	265,661	95.6	35.5
Nacogdoches County, Texas................	28,530	86.0	27.5	24,797	90.8	30.6
Nueces County, Texas.......................	214,076	82.0	20.4	79,362	92.9	32.2
Orange County, Texas.......................	49,791	87.2	15.9	47,582	86.6	15.9
Parker County, Texas........................	85,399	89.5	26.5	78,067	91.9	27.7
Potter County, Texas........................	61,136	78.7	16.9	39,172	90.9	23.5
Randall County, Texas.......................	79,175	93.6	32.3	67,828	95.4	34.0
Rockwall County, Texas.....................	52,858	92.0	42.1	47,007	95.2	44.9
San Patricio County, Texas.................	39,097	79.9	14.7	18,529	93.5	21.3
Smith County, Texas.........................	117,955	86.9	27.7	98,224	93.5	32.3
Tarrant County, Texas.......................	906,717	87.4	34.6	694,401	94.8	40.6
Taylor County, Texas........................	63,881	91.7	27.7	57,109	94.9	29.5
Tom Green County, Texas...................	63,871	90.5	25.6	45,133	95.2	31.4
Travis County, Texas.........................	618,099	92.3	54.4	459,372	97.3	62.5
Victoria County, Texas......................	52,719	83.9	20.3	30,000	93.3	29.2
Walker County, Texas.......................	34,741	88.6	25.1	27,485	92.6	28.9
Webb County, Texas.........................	144,701	68.7	16.6	7,015	85.1	29.8
Wichita County, Texas.......................	65,834	91.2	24.2	59,217	93.0	26.2
Williamson County, Texas	294,309	92.6	39.0	231,519	96.4	43.2
Wise County, Texas..........................	41,946	82.2	14.4	35,965	87.1	16.7
UTAH						
Cache County, Utah..........................	57,597	94.3	40.8	53,797	97.7	43.2
Davis County, Utah..........................	186,016	96.2	39.9	173,904	96.9	41.1
Salt Lake County, Utah	580,635	94.7	38.8	540,452	95.8	40.2
Tooele County, Utah.........................	36,061	94.8	29.1	33,501	94.9	29.6
Utah County, Utah...........................	276,972	95.1	42.0	251,913	97.0	43.7
Washington County, Utah...................	99,073	92.0	27.7	94,132	93.1	28.7
Weber County, Utah.........................	139,343	91.1	26.2	125,080	93.9	28.1

Table C-2. Educational Attainment of the Population, by Selected Counties, 2017—*Continued*

(Number; percent; dollars.)

| State/County | Educational attainment by race/ethnicity, 25 years and over | | | | | |
| | Black alone | | | American Indian or Alaska Native alone | | |
	Total	High school graduate or more (percent)	Bachelor's degree or more (percent)	Total	High school graduate or more (percent)	Bachelor's degree or more (percent)
TENNESSEE—(*Continued*)						
Washington County, Tennessee............................	4,124	88.8	40.1	N	N	N
Williamson County, Tennessee............................	6,351	76.0	28.7	N	N	N
Wilson County, Tennessee	5,531	95.8	19.6	N	N	N
TEXAS						
Angelina County, Texas	8,024	79.1	9.0	N	N	N
Bastrop County, Texas......................................	4,830	83.9	24.9	N	N	N
Bell County, Texas	46,174	94.2	23.2	N	N	N
Bexar County, Texas...	95,264	93.2	28.6	5,885	87.1	28.2
Bowie County, Texas	14,635	88.4	9.2	N	N	N
Brazoria County, Texas.....................................	33,449	89.2	43.3	N	N	N
Brazos County, Texas	12,737	87.7	15.8	N	N	N
Cameron County, Texas.....................................	N	N	N	N	N	N
Collin County, Texas	59,215	96.7	45.7	2,605	95.9	35.9
Comal County, Texas	N	N	N	N	N	N
Coryell County, Texas.......................................	6,335	92.5	17.5	N	N	N
Dallas County, Texas..	379,811	89.3	21.9	6,290	82.0	11.5
Denton County, Texas.......................................	52,474	96.1	45.5	N	N	N
Ector County, Texas	3,986	98.1	22.8	N	N	N
Ellis County, Texas	10,716	94.0	25.7	N	N	N
El Paso County, Texas	16,055	97.6	29.6	3,141	85.1	24.9
Fort Bend County, Texas....................................	99,145	93.6	38.4	N	N	N
Galveston County, Texas	27,126	86.0	21.6	N	N	N
Grayson County, Texas......................................	5,181	89.1	12.1	N	N	N
Gregg County, Texas	14,424	90.6	17.5	N	N	N
Guadalupe County, Texas..................................	9,354	87.8	42.8	N	N	N
Harris County, Texas	560,751	89.5	24.0	11,929	75.3	28.3
Harrison County, Texas	9,065	83.4	13.6	N	N	N
Hays County, Texas..	N	N	N	N	N	N
Henderson County, Texas..................................	3,487	82.2	2.2	N	N	N
Hidalgo County, Texas......................................	N	N	N	N	N	N
Hunt County, Texas..	3,927	88.0	24.1	N	N	N
Jefferson County, Texas....................................	53,714	85.5	12.7	N	N	N
Johnson County, Texas	4,020	87.4	18.8	N	N	N
Kaufman County, Texas.....................................	8,689	92.8	27.6	N	N	N
Liberty County, Texas.......................................	6,182	85.4	1.7	N	N	N
Lubbock County, Texas	12,587	86.5	8.5	N	N	N
McLennan County, Texas...................................	20,674	86.9	9.1	N	N	N
Midland County, Texas	6,625	84.5	11.5	N	N	N
Montgomery County, Texas................................	18,665	94.9	26.3	N	N	N
Nacogdoches County, Texas...............................	6,651	93.8	11.7	N	N	N
Nueces County, Texas.......................................	8,822	91.2	25.0	N	N	N
Orange County, Texas.......................................	4,491	91.9	3.5	N	N	N
Parker County, Texas..	N	N	N	N	N	N
Potter County, Texas..	8,133	73.3	3.8	N	N	N
Randall County, Texas......................................	N	N	N	N	N	N
Rockwall County, Texas....................................	4,204	87.9	62.3	N	N	N
San Patricio County, Texas................................	N	N	N	N	N	N
Smith County, Texas...	24,087	88.1	16.7	N	N	N
Tarrant County, Texas.......................................	207,560	90.5	24.6	5,758	84.5	21.4
Taylor County, Texas	5,659	83.8	12.5	N	N	N
Tom Green County, Texas..................................	N	N	N	N	N	N
Travis County, Texas...	67,670	90.2	27.7	5,468	92.2	41.5
Victoria County, Texas......................................	3,932	81.2	11.1	N	N	N
Walker County, Texas	10,663	84.4	15.0	N	N	N
Webb County, Texas...	N	N	N	N	N	N
Wichita County, Texas......................................	8,006	84.0	16.2	N	N	N
Williamson County, Texas	20,318	95.5	53.2	N	N	N
Wise County, Texas..	N	N	N	N	N	N
UTAH						
Cache County, Utah..	N	N	N	N	N	N
Davis County, Utah...	3,092	95.4	32.3	N	N	N
Salt Lake County, Utah	10,948	80.0	33.0	5,566	79.9	23.6
Tooele County, Utah	N	N	N	N	N	N
Utah County, Utah	N	N	N	N	N	N
Washington County, Utah..................................	N	N	N	N	N	N
Weber County, Utah...	N	N	N	N	N	N

N = Data for this geographic area cannot be displayed because the number of sample cases is too small.

Table C-2. Educational Attainment of the Population, by Selected Counties, 2017—*Continued*

(Number; percent; dollars.)

State/County	Educational attainment by race/ethnicity, 25 years and over					
	White alone			White alone, not Hispanic		
	Total	High school graduate or more (percent)	Bachelor's degree or more (percent)	Total	High school graduate or more (percent)	Bachelor's degree or more (percent)
VERMONT						
Chittenden County, Vermont	98,573	95.5	48.6	97,135	95.4	48.1
VIRGINIA						
Albemarle County, Virginia	61,455	92.7	57.2	58,736	93.2	58.7
Arlington County, Virginia	125,489	96.8	82.0	111,499	99.0	85.5
Augusta County, Virginia	51,375	88.9	21.4	50,691	89.1	21.5
Bedford County, Virginia	51,496	91.5	27.6	50,571	91.9	28.1
Chesterfield County, Virginia	165,733	92.3	42.4	152,538	94.2	44.0
Fairfax County, Virginia	493,307	95.1	66.6	418,959	98.2	72.7
Fauquier County, Virginia	42,399	93.6	35.3	39,515	95.2	36.3
Frederick County, Virginia	55,221	87.8	27.2	51,896	89.9	28.4
Hanover County, Virginia	63,658	92.8	39.0	62,212	93.0	39.2
Henrico County, Virginia	133,322	94.6	50.2	128,637	95.8	51.0
James City County, Virginia	45,413	94.9	53.2	43,226	96.1	54.1
Loudoun County, Virginia	169,129	95.5	61.7	148,621	98.0	65.3
Montgomery County, Virginia	49,410	92.6	39.3	48,957	92.9	39.4
Prince William County, Virginia	171,268	90.0	43.1	137,477	95.8	49.1
Roanoke County, Virginia	60,889	92.6	34.7	59,405	93.1	35.1
Rockingham County, Virginia	51,813	83.6	25.0	50,521	84.3	25.5
Spotsylvania County, Virginia	65,910	93.2	35.1	63,392	93.3	34.8
Stafford County, Virginia	66,746	95.3	41.5	60,990	95.7	42.6
York County, Virginia	34,443	95.1	47.9	33,230	95.4	48.1
Alexandria city, Virginia	77,987	94.5	73.3	66,949	98.6	81.2
Chesapeake city, Virginia	100,799	94.7	35.5	96,555	95.5	36.1
Hampton city, Virginia	40,037	93.2	29.3	38,129	93.7	29.8
Lynchburg city, Virginia	29,629	90.8	43.1	28,889	91.5	43.4
Newport News city, Virginia	60,131	92.4	29.8	54,357	94.7	31.3
Norfolk city, Virginia	76,060	93.4	39.3	72,582	93.3	39.2
Portsmouth city, Virginia	27,664	92.0	27.7	26,490	91.6	27.4
Richmond city, Virginia	77,164	92.1	59.7	71,963	96.0	63.3
Roanoke city, Virginia	46,959	84.3	28.2	44,961	86.2	29.4
Suffolk city, Virginia	33,641	92.8	27.6	31,990	93.3	27.3
Virginia Beach city, Virginia	211,151	94.8	38.3	200,473	95.1	38.5
WASHINGTON						
Benton County, Washington	110,602	91.7	31.2	98,969	93.5	33.0
Chelan County, Washington	45,340	85.6	28.7	39,507	93.3	32.2
Clallam County, Washington	52,058	93.7	27.9	50,035	93.5	28.5
Clark County, Washington	281,241	93.1	30.9	265,519	94.4	31.6
Cowlitz County, Washington	68,645	89.0	17.2	65,220	89.4	17.2
Franklin County, Washington	37,722	87.2	19.8	26,272	97.0	25.4
Grant County, Washington	41,436	89.1	19.9	36,632	92.6	21.8
Grays Harbor County, Washington	47,677	89.9	13.3	44,532	92.2	14.1
Island County, Washington	52,389	96.0	34.9	50,340	96.0	34.9
King County, Washington	1,055,279	96.3	54.5	1,004,360	97.2	55.6
Kitsap County, Washington	157,135	94.6	34.8	149,409	95.1	35.6
Lewis County, Washington	50,838	88.7	16.7	48,841	90.5	17.2
Pierce County, Washington	453,594	93.0	27.2	424,789	93.9	28.0
Skagit County, Washington	75,852	92.6	29.6	71,669	94.4	30.8
Snohomish County, Washington	435,064	94.2	31.1	410,472	95.1	31.5
Spokane County, Washington	312,458	94.6	31.4	303,782	94.9	31.3
Thurston County, Washington	164,981	95.9	36.2	155,602	96.0	36.1
Whatcom County, Washington	127,397	95.3	36.8	122,275	96.0	37.2
Yakima County, Washington	121,531	76.4	18.9	81,343	89.6	26.2
WEST VIRGINIA						
Berkeley County, West Virginia	69,767	91.5	21.2	68,314	92.1	20.9
Cabell County, West Virginia	58,667	88.4	26.6	58,050	88.6	26.6
Harrison County, West Virginia	46,252	89.3	21.5	45,986	89.4	21.6
Kanawha County, West Virginia	120,065	87.9	25.6	119,222	87.8	25.5
Monongalia County, West Virginia	59,200	91.7	40.8	58,464	91.6	40.6
Raleigh County, West Virginia	47,451	88.9	21.1	47,394	88.8	21.1
Wood County, West Virginia	58,996	89.5	22.2	58,623	89.8	22.2
WISCONSIN						
Brown County, Wisconsin	154,990	93.4	34.3	150,803	94.8	34.7
Dane County, Wisconsin	305,902	97.1	51.6	294,858	97.7	52.5
Dodge County, Wisconsin	59,318	91.3	16.5	58,029	91.9	16.7
Eau Claire County, Wisconsin	61,568	94.1	33.0	60,645	94.9	33.5

Table C-2. Educational Attainment of the Population, by Selected Counties, 2017—*Continued*

(Number; percent; dollars.)

| | Educational attainment by race/ethnicity, 25 years and over | | | | | |
| | Black alone | | | American Indian or Alaska Native alone | | |
State/County	Total	High school graduate or more (percent)	Bachelor's degree or more (percent)	Total	High school graduate or more (percent)	Bachelor's degree or more (percent)
VERMONT						
Chittenden County, Vermont	N	N	N	N	N	N
VIRGINIA						
Albemarle County, Virginia	6,167	88.8	34.9	N	N	N
Arlington County, Virginia	15,284	89.4	49.0	N	N	N
Augusta County, Virginia	N	N	N	N	N	N
Bedford County, Virginia	N	N	N	N	N	N
Chesterfield County, Virginia	49,993	94.6	31.4	N	N	N
Fairfax County, Virginia	74,713	91.8	45.2	2,963	91.9	33.1
Fauquier County, Virginia	3,587	84.5	19.4	N	N	N
Frederick County, Virginia	N	N	N	N	N	N
Hanover County, Virginia	7,153	91.2	29.7	N	N	N
Henrico County, Virginia	64,929	89.6	27.8	N	N	N
James City County, Virginia	6,466	80.1	32.3	N	N	N
Loudoun County, Virginia	21,110	93.8	56.0	1,031	77.4	45.4
Montgomery County, Virginia	N	N	N	N	N	N
Prince William County, Virginia	63,371	93.8	38.8	N	N	N
Roanoke County, Virginia	3,736	88.8	26.3	N	N	N
Rockingham County, Virginia	1,187	82.5	22.8	N	N	N
Spotsylvania County, Virginia	13,182	89.4	28.1	N	N	N
Stafford County, Virginia	15,454	96.0	47.6	N	N	N
York County, Virginia	6,086	95.0	33.1	N	N	N
Alexandria city, Virginia	27,312	91.3	39.1	N	N	N
Chesapeake city, Virginia	47,639	93.8	33.4	N	N	N
Hampton city, Virginia	43,270	91.9	24.0	N	N	N
Lynchburg city, Virginia	12,316	85.1	12.8	N	N	N
Newport News city, Virginia	45,911	88.1	18.1	N	N	N
Norfolk city, Virginia	60,817	81.2	15.3	N	N	N
Portsmouth city, Virginia	32,381	87.3	17.7	N	N	N
Richmond city, Virginia	71,078	77.6	15.2	N	N	N
Roanoke city, Virginia	19,378	88.1	11.1	N	N	N
Suffolk city, Virginia	24,931	81.5	22.6	N	N	N
Virginia Beach city, Virginia	55,416	91.3	26.5	N	N	N
WASHINGTON						
Benton County, Washington	N	N	N	N	N	N
Chelan County, Washington	N	N	N	N	N	N
Clallam County, Washington	N	N	N	2,471	70.0	2.6
Clark County, Washington	5,931	98.8	27.3	N	N	N
Cowlitz County, Washington	N	N	N	N	N	N
Franklin County, Washington	N	N	N	N	N	N
Grant County, Washington	N	N	N	N	N	N
Grays Harbor County, Washington	N	N	N	2,008	83.7	8.6
Island County, Washington	N	N	N	N	N	N
King County, Washington	89,246	88.5	27.9	6,211	84.6	32.2
Kitsap County, Washington	4,441	97.8	25.1	1,856	75.5	13.5
Lewis County, Washington	N	N	N	N	N	N
Pierce County, Washington	40,061	92.9	23.2	6,277	87.4	8.6
Skagit County, Washington	N	N	N	1,524	84.1	9.1
Snohomish County, Washington	15,584	92.5	24.4	3,813	79.2	7.2
Spokane County, Washington	4,623	93.9	14.0	3,937	85.4	20.2
Thurston County, Washington	5,469	85.7	40.6	N	N	N
Whatcom County, Washington	N	N	N	4,707	78.6	8.8
Yakima County, Washington	N	N	N	5,535	76.1	8.4
WEST VIRGINIA						
Berkeley County, West Virginia	5,335	83.3	22.5	N	N	N
Cabell County, West Virginia	2,846	96.2	22.3	N	N	N
Harrison County, West Virginia	N	N	N	N	N	N
Kanawha County, West Virginia	9,665	97.9	21.9	N	N	N
Monongalia County, West Virginia	N	N	N	N	N	N
Raleigh County, West Virginia	4,883	91.4	6.7	N	N	N
Wood County, West Virginia	N	N	N	N	N	N
WISCONSIN						
Brown County, Wisconsin	3,512	75.5	13.6	3,650	88.1	15.4
Dane County, Wisconsin	14,485	89.8	31.7	N	N	N
Dodge County, Wisconsin	N	N	N	N	N	N
Eau Claire County, Wisconsin	N	N	N	N	N	N

N = Data for this geographic area cannot be displayed because the number of sample cases is too small.

Table C-2. Educational Attainment of the Population, by Selected Counties, 2017—*Continued*

(Number; percent; dollars.)

State/County	Educational attainment by race/ethnicity, 25 years and over					
	White alone			White alone, not Hispanic		
	Total	High school graduate or more (percent)	Bachelor's degree or more (percent)	Total	High school graduate or more (percent)	Bachelor's degree or more (percent)
WISCONSIN— (*Continued*)						
Fond du Lac County, Wisconsin	68,112	93.0	23.9	66,582	93.6	24.3
Jefferson County, Wisconsin	56,507	92.5	25.4	54,342	93.5	25.9
Kenosha County, Wisconsin	99,274	91.6	26.8	91,634	93.0	28.1
La Crosse County, Wisconsin	70,388	94.1	33.0	69,789	94.2	32.9
Manitowoc County, Wisconsin	54,611	93.5	19.3	53,311	93.6	19.7
Marathon County, Wisconsin	87,678	93.7	26.0	86,511	93.9	26.3
Milwaukee County, Wisconsin	410,712	92.6	38.2	372,170	94.8	40.5
Outagamie County, Wisconsin	116,103	95.1	30.6	113,870	95.2	31.0
Ozaukee County, Wisconsin	58,447	96.4	51.5	57,417	96.4	51.5
Portage County, Wisconsin	42,903	94.7	33.0	42,495	94.9	33.2
Racine County, Wisconsin	114,171	94.0	29.8	104,773	95.6	30.4
Rock County, Wisconsin	100,510	92.2	22.6	96,715	93.0	23.0
St. Croix County, Wisconsin	57,687	96.2	35.7	56,953	96.4	35.8
Sheboygan County, Wisconsin	72,995	94.6	25.6	71,077	95.3	26.2
Walworth County, Wisconsin	64,391	92.5	31.6	60,868	94.8	32.8
Washington County, Wisconsin	92,061	95.6	31.0	90,354	95.5	31.0
Waukesha County, Wisconsin	264,507	96.4	44.7	256,389	96.9	45.2
Winnebago County, Wisconsin	107,782	94.6	29.5	105,406	94.7	29.8
Wood County, Wisconsin	49,405	94.3	20.3	48,918	94.4	20.3
WYOMING						
Laramie County, Wyoming	60,589	93.3	29.8	54,782	95.1	32.0
Natrona County, Wyoming	51,675	93.1	24.7	48,352	94.3	25.3

Table C-2. Educational Attainment of the Population, by Selected Counties, 2017—*Continued*

(Number; percent; dollars.)

| | Educational attainment by race/ethnicity, 25 years and over | | | | | |
| | Black alone | | | American Indian or Alaska Native alone | | |
State/County	Total	High school graduate or more (percent)	Bachelor's degree or more (percent)	Total	High school graduate or more (percent)	Bachelor's degree or more (percent)
WISCONSIN—(*Continued*)						
Fond du Lac County, Wisconsin	N	N	N	N	N	N
Jefferson County, Wisconsin	N	N	N	N	N	N
Kenosha County, Wisconsin	6,309	85.7	8.2	N	N	N
La Crosse County, Wisconsin	N	N	N	N	N	N
Manitowoc County, Wisconsin	N	N	N	N	N	N
Marathon County, Wisconsin	N	N	N	N	N	N
Milwaukee County, Wisconsin	146,107	84.4	13.1	2,977	83.5	14.7
Outagamie County, Wisconsin	N	N	N	N	N	N
Ozaukee County, Wisconsin	N	N	N	N	N	N
Portage County, Wisconsin	N	N	N	N	N	N
Racine County, Wisconsin	11,707	77.9	8.7	N	N	N
Rock County, Wisconsin	4,320	81.1	2.9	N	N	N
St. Croix County, Wisconsin	N	N	N	N	N	N
Sheboygan County, Wisconsin	N	N	N	N	N	N
Walworth County, Wisconsin	N	N	N	N	N	N
Washington County, Wisconsin	N	N	N	N	N	N
Waukesha County, Wisconsin	3,912	94.8	30.9	N	N	N
Winnebago County, Wisconsin	2,186	69.6	11.5	N	N	N
Wood County, Wisconsin	N	N	N	N	N	N
WYOMING						
Laramie County, Wyoming	N	N	N	N	N	N
Natrona County, Wyoming	N	N	N	N	N	N

N = Data for this geographic area cannot be displayed because the number of sample cases is too small.

Table C-2. Educational Attainment of the Population, by Selected Counties, 2017—*Continued*

(Number; percent; dollars.)

	Educational attainment by race/ethnicity, 25 years and over								
	Asian alone			Native Hawaiian or Other Pacific Islander alone			Some other race alone		
State/County	Total	High school graduate or more (percent)	Bachelor's degree or more (percent)	Total	High school graduate or more (percent)	Bachelor's degree or more (percent)	Total	High school graduate or more (percent)	Bachelor's degree or more (percent)
ALABAMA									
Baldwin County, Alabama	N	N	N	N	N	N	N	N	N
Calhoun County, Alabama	N	N	N	N	N	N	N	N	N
Cullman County, Alabama	N	N	N	N	N	N	N	N	N
DeKalb County, Alabama	N	N	N	N	N	N	N	N	N
Elmore County, Alabama	N	N	N	N	N	N	N	N	N
Etowah County, Alabama	N	N	N	N	N	N	N	N	N
Houston County, Alabama	583	87.3	53.9	N	N	N	N	N	N
Jefferson County, Alabama	7,923	97.1	54.6	N	N	N	4,526	54.9	6.5
Lauderdale County, Alabama	N	N	N	N	N	N	N	N	N
Lee County, Alabama	3,888	84.0	41.7	N	N	N	N	N	N
Limestone County, Alabama	N	N	N	N	N	N	N	N	N
Madison County, Alabama	7,244	89.9	54.8	N	N	N	3,150	61.4	16.1
Marshall County, Alabama	N	N	N	N	N	N	N	N	N
Mobile County, Alabama	4,716	70.5	33.6	N	N	N	2,455	87.9	22.9
Montgomery County, Alabama	4,240	98.1	58.4	N	N	N	N	N	N
Morgan County, Alabama	N	N	N	N	N	N	N	N	N
St. Clair County, Alabama	N	N	N	N	N	N	N	N	N
Shelby County, Alabama	N	N	N	N	N	N	N	N	N
Talladega County, Alabama	N	N	N	N	N	N	N	N	N
Tuscaloosa County, Alabama	N	N	N	N	N	N	N	N	N
Walker County, Alabama	N	N	N	N	N	N	N	N	N
ALASKA									
Anchorage Municipality, Alaska	18,643	76.0	26.0	4,389	84.7	12.2	4,714	84.7	12.0
Fairbanks North Star Borough, Alaska	N	N	N	N	N	N	N	N	N
Matanuska-Susitna Borough, Alaska	N	N	N	N	N	N	N	N	N
ARIZONA									
Apache County, Arizona	N	N	N	N	N	N	N	N	N
Cochise County, Arizona	N	N	N	N	N	N	2,349	80.7	19.3
Coconino County, Arizona	N	N	N	N	N	N	N	N	N
Maricopa County, Arizona	125,077	89.4	58.6	5,792	89.2	18.5	166,142	62.5	10.6
Mohave County, Arizona	N	N	N	N	N	N	3,247	39.6	7.1
Navajo County, Arizona	N	N	N	N	N	N	2,531	46.0	3.0
Pima County, Arizona	19,838	88.8	50.0	N	N	N	47,927	79.0	10.6
Pinal County, Arizona	5,204	90.2	50.2	N	N	N	7,008	64.3	1.9
Yavapai County, Arizona	N	N	N	N	N	N	2,608	67.9	11.4
Yuma County, Arizona	N	N	N	N	N	N	13,225	66.7	12.8
ARKANSAS									
Benton County, Arkansas	7,002	87.0	73.6	N	N	N	2,954	57.3	25.8
Craighead County, Arkansas	N	N	N	N	N	N	N	N	N
Faulkner County, Arkansas	N	N	N	N	N	N	N	N	N
Garland County, Arkansas	N	N	N	N	N	N	N	N	N
Jefferson County, Arkansas	N	N	N	N	N	N	N	N	N
Lonoke County, Arkansas	N	N	N	N	N	N	N	N	N
Pulaski County, Arkansas	6,525	82.2	58.9	N	N	N	4,859	71.3	0.9
Saline County, Arkansas	N	N	N	N	N	N	N	N	N
Sebastian County, Arkansas	3,426	66.6	14.0	N	N	N	5,656	39.9	5.1
Washington County, Arkansas	2,999	70.3	54.5	N	N	N	12,378	32.6	3.3
White County, Arkansas	N	N	N	N	N	N	N	N	N
CALIFORNIA									
Alameda County, California	367,605	87.9	55.9	9,621	83.3	16.9	112,287	64.0	13.5
Butte County, California	6,019	86.7	43.3	N	N	N	5,843	58.8	12.9
Contra Costa County, California	142,212	90.2	54.3	N	N	N	63,484	65.0	13.1
El Dorado County, California	6,000	92.9	60.3	N	N	N	N	N	N
Fresno County, California	63,794	74.6	29.3	N	N	N	81,386	58.0	7.7
Humboldt County, California	1,685	82.3	32.2	N	N	N	2,366	69.4	4.6
Imperial County, California	N	N	N	N	N	N	35,682	63.0	9.7
Kern County, California	31,242	82.3	36.2	N	N	N	47,640	61.7	8.3
Kings County, California	4,175	82.3	37.5	N	N	N	15,499	51.0	6.2
Lake County, California	N	N	N	N	N	N	5,194	61.4	7.6
Los Angeles County, California	1,143,195	88.0	52.7	18,167	88.1	19.9	1,396,848	60.3	10.0
Madera County, California	2,386	84.9	43.5	N	N	N	20,029	53.0	8.0
Marin County, California	12,909	95.1	73.6	N	N	N	13,494	66.0	16.7

N = Data for this geographic area cannot be displayed because the number of sample cases is too small.

Table C-2. Educational Attainment of the Population, by Selected Counties, 2017—*Continued*

(Number; percent; dollars.)

State/County	Median earnings in the past 12 months (2017 inflation-adjusted dollars)					
	Two or more races			Hispanic or Latino (of any race)		
	Total	High school graduate or more (percent)	Bachelor's degree or more (percent)	Total	High school graduate or more (percent)	Bachelor's degree or more (percent)
ALABAMA						
Baldwin County, Alabama	N	N	N	6,074	69.2	22.5
Calhoun County, Alabama	N	N	N	2,475	55.6	9.1
Cullman County, Alabama	N	N	N	N	N	N
DeKalb County, Alabama	N	N	N	4,044	53.4	4.6
Elmore County, Alabama	N	N	N	N	N	N
Etowah County, Alabama	N	N	N	N	N	N
Houston County, Alabama	1,225	89.1	22.6	1,906	67.2	18.0
Jefferson County, Alabama	3,691	93.0	36.9	11,384	70.0	22.8
Lauderdale County, Alabama	N	N	N	N	N	N
Lee County, Alabama	N	N	N	3,679	84.6	35.8
Limestone County, Alabama	N	N	N	N	N	N
Madison County, Alabama	4,585	94.8	48.9	9,842	67.4	19.7
Marshall County, Alabama	N	N	N	4,226	41.3	0.9
Mobile County, Alabama	3,105	87.6	33.0	7,058	85.7	17.4
Montgomery County, Alabama	1,487	88.1	34.2	3,343	62.5	18.4
Morgan County, Alabama	N	N	N	4,539	49.5	2.5
St. Clair County, Alabama	N	N	N	N	N	N
Shelby County, Alabama	N	N	N	6,305	75.1	25.7
Talladega County, Alabama	N	N	N	N	N	N
Tuscaloosa County, Alabama	N	N	N	N	N	N
Walker County, Alabama	N	N	N	N	N	N
ALASKA						
Anchorage Municipality, Alaska	12,188	94.1	28.0	13,938	87.2	22.8
Fairbanks North Star Borough, Alaska	N	N	N	N	N	N
Matanuska-Susitna Borough, Alaska	3,739	88.2	14.4	2,446	93.1	23.7
ARIZONA						
Apache County, Arizona	N	N	N	2,144	64.9	15.5
Cochise County, Arizona	N	N	N	25,892	77.2	12.6
Coconino County, Arizona	N	N	N	9,893	86.1	24.1
Maricopa County, Arizona	65,076	88.8	32.2	715,587	67.0	12.7
Mohave County, Arizona	2,693	84.4	2.3	21,151	63.3	8.4
Navajo County, Arizona	N	N	N	7,147	69.0	6.8
Pima County, Arizona	22,943	81.9	25.7	212,649	78.6	17.7
Pinal County, Arizona	6,885	86.9	14.7	74,106	68.7	8.7
Yavapai County, Arizona	2,907	89.5	15.6	18,924	74.3	10.3
Yuma County, Arizona	N	N	N	73,620	59.2	9.1
ARKANSAS						
Benton County, Arkansas	2,650	90.1	30.4	22,853	59.7	18.0
Craighead County, Arkansas	N	N	N	2,888	71.2	15.4
Faulkner County, Arkansas	N	N	N	2,254	53.4	12.6
Garland County, Arkansas	N	N	N	2,748	81.4	8.3
Jefferson County, Arkansas	N	N	N	N	N	N
Lonoke County, Arkansas	N	N	N	N	N	N
Pulaski County, Arkansas	5,705	92.1	24.4	12,246	72.9	11.0
Saline County, Arkansas	N	N	N	N	N	N
Sebastian County, Arkansas	3,050	87.6	23.2	8,689	42.8	3.9
Washington County, Arkansas	3,972	84.3	29.9	18,294	45.9	7.3
White County, Arkansas	N	N	N	N	N	N
CALIFORNIA						
Alameda County, California	54,128	92.3	45.2	222,651	69.9	18.4
Butte County, California	5,758	86.1	16.8	19,452	77.1	16.2
Contra Costa County, California	38,155	88.1	35.5	170,187	68.3	17.7
El Dorado County, California	4,668	91.3	26.8	13,866	81.0	19.0
Fresno County, California	17,959	82.7	21.2	283,830	62.4	9.5
Humboldt County, California	3,314	94.4	24.2	7,215	79.5	13.5
Imperial County, California	2,752	81.0	35.1	89,880	67.8	13.4
Kern County, California	11,542	86.4	23.2	251,021	56.4	6.7
Kings County, California	3,971	92.5	10.8	44,735	55.2	6.1
Lake County, California	N	N	N	7,708	65.9	6.4
Los Angeles County, California	191,883	87.7	39.1	2,995,069	62.4	12.7
Madera County, California	1,787	78.8	17.2	48,481	50.4	9.0
Marin County, California	6,929	95.7	48.4	24,730	72.4	24.0

N = Data for this geographic area cannot be displayed because the number of sample cases is too small.

Table C-2. Educational Attainment of the Population, by Selected Counties, 2017—*Continued*

(Number; percent; dollars.)

	Educational attainment by race/ethnicity, 25 years and over								
	Asian alone			Native Hawaiian or Other Pacific Islander alone			Some other race alone		
State/County	Total	High school graduate or more (percent)	Bachelor's degree or more (percent)	Total	High school graduate or more (percent)	Bachelor's degree or more (percent)	Total	High school graduate or more (percent)	Bachelor's degree or more (percent)
CALIFORNIA—(*Continued*)									
Mendocino County, California	N	N	N	N	N	N	2,224	68.0	14.4
Merced County, California	12,653	60.2	20.3	N	N	N	40,253	46.1	3.5
Monterey County, California	18,462	90.6	40.6	N	N	N	90,286	39.6	5.2
Napa County, California	7,713	88.5	50.1	N	N	N	7,996	51.9	5.6
Nevada County, California	N	N	N	N	N	N	N	N	N
Orange County, California	478,737	87.7	54.3	5,868	91.6	24.1	238,235	54.8	10.5
Placer County, California	20,968	94.3	61.4	N	N	N	7,598	81.8	20.0
Riverside County, California	113,224	88.9	44.6	3,897	81.4	22.9	350,386	63.7	7.0
Sacramento County, California	168,251	81.7	41.1	12,348	84.2	12.4	80,027	65.2	10.3
San Bernardino County, California	113,015	90.6	51.0	3,972	86.5	30.6	213,748	63.4	8.4
San Diego County, California	292,593	89.9	53.3	9,942	91.8	21.8	138,574	69.3	14.9
San Francisco County, California	248,212	79.8	47.0	N	N	N	48,568	69.6	26.2
San Joaquin County, California	75,034	77.9	31.0	2,702	87.8	9.0	44,231	65.5	3.9
San Luis Obispo County, California	5,999	95.7	53.1	N	N	N	4,623	75.9	18.5
San Mateo County, California	170,059	92.1	58.9	7,214	88.1	28.3	61,064	68.2	17.4
Santa Barbara County, California	13,856	90.5	55.8	N	N	N	26,343	63.9	17.5
Santa Clara County, California	515,892	90.1	64.1	4,608	85.6	15.7	129,682	64.0	11.1
Santa Cruz County, California	8,310	90.7	49.8	N	N	N	22,970	54.6	8.2
Shasta County, California	3,278	85.3	44.2	N	N	N	N	N	N
Solano County, California	52,426	88.8	35.4	2,777	86.6	29.6	25,478	62.1	9.2
Sonoma County, California	15,420	91.5	46.1	N	N	N	40,263	58.1	10.6
Stanislaus County, California	20,483	86.9	38.0	N	N	N	29,548	54.2	6.0
Sutter County, California	11,770	76.1	23.7	N	N	N	3,151	69.7	10.4
Tulare County, California	10,297	85.5	36.9	N	N	N	35,130	60.8	5.2
Ventura County, California	47,726	94.0	57.7	N	N	N	24,209	54.5	10.9
Yolo County, California	14,767	87.8	53.9	N	N	N	7,435	65.0	16.0
Yuba County, California	3,348	85.5	33.5	N	N	N	N	N	N
COLORADO									
Adams County, Colorado	14,501	69.3	32.4	N	N	N	12,351	72.4	5.3
Arapahoe County, Colorado	25,366	84.0	48.1	N	N	N	19,762	74.5	13.5
Boulder County, Colorado	9,981	89.4	72.0	N	N	N	3,301	68.8	29.9
Broomfield County, Colorado	3,472	93.8	62.0	N	N	N	N	N	N
Denver County, Colorado	19,044	79.9	52.0	N	N	N	29,953	54.5	11.2
Douglas County, Colorado	11,056	93.3	68.6	N	N	N	4,439	92.0	39.7
El Paso County, Colorado	11,656	77.7	45.2	N	N	N	17,306	82.9	18.7
Jefferson County, Colorado	11,293	88.1	52.6	N	N	N	6,937	74.4	21.8
Larimer County, Colorado	N	N	N	N	N	N	2,482	90.6	32.6
Mesa County, Colorado	N	N	N	N	N	N	N	N	N
Pueblo County, Colorado	N	N	N	N	N	N	9,429	82.8	9.0
Weld County, Colorado	2,874	87.9	46.8	N	N	N	6,130	51.0	10.2
CONNECTICUT									
Fairfield County, Connecticut	37,237	90.6	70.2	N	N	N	41,287	58.0	9.4
Hartford County, Connecticut	33,739	85.9	64.4	N	N	N	32,885	66.0	10.0
Litchfield County, Connecticut	N	N	N	N	N	N	N	N	N
Middlesex County, Connecticut	N	N	N	N	N	N	N	N	N
New Haven County, Connecticut	24,085	88.4	61.4	N	N	N	28,842	75.8	11.3
New London County, Connecticut	8,084	84.5	38.1	N	N	N	5,954	78.3	5.4
Tolland County, Connecticut	N	N	N	N	N	N	N	N	N
Windham County, Connecticut	N	N	N	N	N	N	N	N	N
DELAWARE									
Kent County, Delaware	N	N	N	N	N	N	N	N	N
New Castle County, Delaware	22,252	94.2	68.4	N	N	N	5,155	68.5	14.1
Sussex County, Delaware	2,318	84.7	53.7	N	N	N	3,734	43.7	2.2
DISTRICT OF COLUMBIA									
District of Columbia, District of Columbia	21,767	95.2	81.9	N	N	N	23,645	49.4	24.3
FLORIDA									
Alachua County, Florida	9,085	94.5	75.3	N	N	N	N	N	N
Bay County, Florida	2,982	63.7	21.3	N	N	N	N	N	N
Brevard County, Florida	10,275	88.5	47.6	N	N	N	7,257	76.8	26.6
Broward County, Florida	50,402	91.5	54.3	N	N	N	41,662	82.3	23.9
Charlotte County, Florida	N	N	N	N	N	N	N	N	N
Citrus County, Florida	N	N	N	N	N	N	N	N	N

N = Data for this geographic area cannot be displayed because the number of sample cases is too small.

Table C-2. Educational Attainment of the Population, by Selected Counties, 2017—*Continued*

(Number; percent; dollars.)

| State/County | Median earnings in the past 12 months (2017 inflation-adjusted dollars) | | | | | |
| | Two or more races | | | Hispanic or Latino (of any race) | | |
	Total	High school graduate or more (percent)	Bachelor's degree or more (percent)	Total	High school graduate or more (percent)	Bachelor's degree or more (percent)
CALIFORNIA—(*Continued*)						
Mendocino County, California	N	N	N	12,058	70.8	11.5
Merced County, California	5,603	86.1	13.0	85,085	54.5	5.8
Monterey County, California	8,469	90.4	30.2	140,854	49.1	8.6
Napa County, California	2,627	93.8	33.6	27,306	60.2	14.3
Nevada County, California	2,649	98.1	35.6	5,905	82.3	14.4
Orange County, California	60,852	89.9	41.4	629,551	63.8	15.6
Placer County, California	7,976	89.6	28.8	31,067	81.6	23.1
Riverside County, California	40,210	86.5	25.8	663,529	67.0	10.1
Sacramento County, California	49,548	89.9	28.3	198,188	73.4	17.1
San Bernardino County, California	43,427	87.9	23.1	644,867	67.7	10.6
San Diego County, California	76,284	92.7	39.6	654,276	70.1	16.6
San Francisco County, California	29,305	93.1	53.6	94,519	76.6	34.8
San Joaquin County, California	43,338	80.1	12.0	166,337	69.1	7.2
San Luis Obispo County, California	4,914	97.5	26.4	34,872	73.2	16.9
San Mateo County, California	18,685	94.8	47.2	116,168	72.8	20.0
Santa Barbara County, California	8,645	91.4	41.4	108,204	56.0	11.2
Santa Clara County, California	41,038	93.3	47.0	289,294	70.2	16.9
Santa Cruz County, California	7,054	94.7	38.2	49,878	61.6	15.0
Shasta County, California	2,474	98.0	31.1	9,800	78.3	13.9
Solano County, California	13,538	92.2	29.6	66,461	66.9	11.5
Sonoma County, California	14,949	95.7	34.1	76,574	66.9	16.3
Stanislaus County, California	9,817	87.8	25.3	135,830	61.4	6.8
Sutter County, California	2,164	62.6	13.5	15,882	59.1	7.1
Tulare County, California	7,659	81.7	10.8	155,736	56.1	6.5
Ventura County, California	16,699	94.9	36.8	210,445	66.6	13.1
Yolo County, California	5,276	84.0	33.2	37,001	69.5	14.5
Yuba County, California	N	N	N	11,429	63.5	11.3
COLORADO						
Adams County, Colorado	7,930	80.6	31.1	108,799	68.1	9.9
Arapahoe County, Colorado	13,413	91.9	39.8	66,598	75.5	16.9
Boulder County, Colorado	N	N	N	22,948	76.9	34.4
Broomfield County, Colorado	N	N	N	4,485	90.7	44.3
Denver County, Colorado	13,580	92.3	47.1	122,622	65.1	14.9
Douglas County, Colorado	4,131	96.9	44.2	16,790	94.1	36.0
El Paso County, Colorado	16,246	94.3	31.8	62,382	81.9	21.4
Jefferson County, Colorado	7,639	89.3	45.5	52,781	80.9	20.6
Larimer County, Colorado	3,480	100.0	51.4	20,171	79.2	25.4
Mesa County, Colorado	N	N	N	10,765	67.0	13.6
Pueblo County, Colorado	2,943	84.2	13.1	43,047	85.8	13.6
Weld County, Colorado	3,401	95.6	23.1	47,354	63.6	8.6
CONNECTICUT						
Fairfield County, Connecticut	10,699	86.3	28.8	112,811	66.7	17.0
Hartford County, Connecticut	12,798	89.4	29.2	91,724	69.7	14.9
Litchfield County, Connecticut	N	N	N	7,442	87.8	32.5
Middlesex County, Connecticut	N	N	N	5,845	80.8	20.5
New Haven County, Connecticut	8,846	86.5	26.2	86,616	76.4	13.2
New London County, Connecticut	6,345	82.7	28.3	14,702	79.2	20.7
Tolland County, Connecticut	1,653	87.2	38.9	4,673	84.3	28.8
Windham County, Connecticut	N	N	N	6,820	66.0	9.5
DELAWARE						
Kent County, Delaware	2,903	96.8	9.6	7,183	66.0	11.5
New Castle County, Delaware	5,381	92.8	32.2	30,178	66.1	12.2
Sussex County, Delaware	2,378	82.5	7.8	10,401	54.2	6.2
DISTRICT OF COLUMBIA						
District of Columbia, District of Columbia	11,613	91.2	70.0	48,455	67.5	43.6
FLORIDA						
Alachua County, Florida	3,404	95.3	36.6	13,457	87.3	38.9
Bay County, Florida	2,827	100.0	29.1	6,697	91.8	20.2
Brevard County, Florida	6,491	84.0	31.1	38,312	88.6	31.6
Broward County, Florida	32,552	90.9	33.3	391,593	86.4	30.4
Charlotte County, Florida	N	N	N	9,261	75.9	18.9
Citrus County, Florida	N	N	N	5,550	94.7	43.5

N = Data for this geographic area cannot be displayed because the number of sample cases is too small.

Table C-2. Educational Attainment of the Population, by Selected Counties, 2017—*Continued*

(Number; percent; dollars.)

	Educational attainment by race/ethnicity, 25 years and over								
	Asian alone			Native Hawaiian or Other Pacific Islander alone			Some other race alone		
State/County	Total	High school graduate or more (percent)	Bachelor's degree or more (percent)	Total	High school graduate or more (percent)	Bachelor's degree or more (percent)	Total	High school graduate or more (percent)	Bachelor's degree or more (percent)
FLORIDA—(*Continued*)									
Clay County, Florida	4,960	76.1	49.0	N	N	N	N	N	N
Collier County, Florida	4,224	88.7	44.3	N	N	N	2,562	69.9	24.8
Columbia County, Florida	N	N	N	N	N	N	N	N	N
Duval County, Florida	33,687	83.7	47.9	N	N	N	12,108	78.2	20.3
Escambia County, Florida	6,571	80.9	25.8	N	N	N	N	N	N
Flagler County, Florida	N	N	N	N	N	N	N	N	N
Hernando County, Florida	1,813	86.0	50.1	N	N	N	N	N	N
Highlands County, Florida	N	N	N	N	N	N	N	N	N
Hillsborough County, Florida	41,915	85.5	55.0	N	N	N	24,174	71.0	19.0
Indian River County, Florida	N	N	N	N	N	N	N	N	N
Lake County, Florida	5,670	89.6	52.6	N	N	N	N	N	N
Lee County, Florida	9,116	89.2	41.8	N	N	N	15,717	66.5	8.2
Leon County, Florida	6,653	93.1	83.1	N	N	N	N	N	N
Manatee County, Florida	5,686	88.7	68.3	N	N	N	5,150	72.4	6.7
Marion County, Florida	4,267	82.4	40.1	N	N	N	N	N	N
Martin County, Florida	N	N	N	N	N	N	N	N	N
Miami-Dade County, Florida	35,494	83.1	50.4	N	N	N	76,390	80.6	24.6
Monroe County, Florida	N	N	N	N	N	N	N	N	N
Nassau County, Florida	N	N	N	N	N	N	N	N	N
Okaloosa County, Florida	4,920	85.5	25.8	N	N	N	N	N	N
Orange County, Florida	49,296	84.9	51.0	N	N	N	65,852	82.4	19.2
Osceola County, Florida	6,203	95.9	47.7	N	N	N	20,774	79.7	11.6
Palm Beach County, Florida	29,101	93.5	57.0	N	N	N	24,420	62.2	12.7
Pasco County, Florida	9,594	81.4	47.9	N	N	N	3,432	80.8	21.2
Pinellas County, Florida	25,260	80.8	45.3	N	N	N	11,065	86.5	14.2
Polk County, Florida	9,482	87.6	44.2	N	N	N	8,814	67.7	8.9
Putnam County, Florida	N	N	N	N	N	N	N	N	N
St. Johns County, Florida	N	N	N	N	N	N	N	N	N
St. Lucie County, Florida	3,714	72.3	23.7	N	N	N	N	N	N
Santa Rosa County, Florida	2,378	100.0	15.7	N	N	N	N	N	N
Sarasota County, Florida	5,680	85.6	40.2	N	N	N	N	N	N
Seminole County, Florida	15,217	89.1	55.5	N	N	N	6,779	93.4	33.9
Sumter County, Florida	N	N	N	N	N	N	N	N	N
Volusia County, Florida	6,966	77.7	46.1	N	N	N	12,344	68.9	13.6
Walton County, Florida	N	N	N	N	N	N	N	N	N
GEORGIA									
Barrow County, Georgia	1,821	77.8	13.2	N	N	N	N	N	N
Bartow County, Georgia	N	N	N	N	N	N	N	N	N
Bibb County, Georgia	N	N	N	N	N	N	N	N	N
Bulloch County, Georgia	N	N	N	N	N	N	N	N	N
Carroll County, Georgia	N	N	N	N	N	N	N	N	N
Catoosa County, Georgia	N	N	N	N	N	N	N	N	N
Chatham County, Georgia	4,291	92.3	57.6	N	N	N	N	N	N
Cherokee County, Georgia	3,369	95.4	31.8	N	N	N	N	N	N
Clarke County, Georgia	N	N	N	N	N	N	N	N	N
Clayton County, Georgia	10,531	66.5	9.1	N	N	N	7,329	31.8	0.9
Cobb County, Georgia	28,299	92.0	72.2	N	N	N	16,208	62.2	16.7
Columbia County, Georgia	N	N	N	N	N	N	N	N	N
Coweta County, Georgia	N	N	N	N	N	N	N	N	N
DeKalb County, Georgia	31,463	73.4	49.0	N	N	N	7,358	64.0	22.3
Dougherty County, Georgia	N	N	N	N	N	N	N	N	N
Douglas County, Georgia	N	N	N	N	N	N	N	N	N
Fayette County, Georgia	3,570	99.6	40.7	N	N	N	N	N	N
Floyd County, Georgia	N	N	N	N	N	N	N	N	N
Forsyth County, Georgia	18,342	97.2	86.2	N	N	N	N	N	N
Fulton County, Georgia	49,661	95.0	77.9	N	N	N	9,308	75.7	41.6
Glynn County, Georgia	N	N	N	N	N	N	N	N	N
Gwinnett County, Georgia	74,244	86.9	43.6	N	N	N	40,470	46.2	7.8
Hall County, Georgia	N	N	N	N	N	N	N	N	N
Henry County, Georgia	4,879	77.7	48.0	N	N	N	N	N	N
Houston County, Georgia	3,130	81.4	40.4	N	N	N	N	N	N
Jackson County, Georgia	N	N	N	N	N	N	N	N	N
Lowndes County, Georgia	N	N	N	N	N	N	N	N	N
Muscogee County, Georgia	3,934	93.1	43.4	N	N	N	3,025	72.9	11.1
Newton County, Georgia	N	N	N	N	N	N	N	N	N
Paulding County, Georgia	N	N	N	N	N	N	N	N	N

N = Data for this geographic area cannot be displayed because the number of sample cases is too small.

Table C-2. Educational Attainment of the Population, by Selected Counties, 2017—*Continued*

(Number; percent; dollars.)

| | Median earnings in the past 12 months (2017 inflation-adjusted dollars) | | | | | |
| | Two or more races | | | Hispanic or Latino (of any race) | | |
State/County	Total	High school graduate or more (percent)	Bachelor's degree or more (percent)	Total	High school graduate or more (percent)	Bachelor's degree or more (percent)
FLORIDA—(*Continued*)						
Clay County, Florida	4,404	88.0	30.6	12,461	82.9	23.0
Collier County, Florida	N	N	N	62,589	68.1	17.4
Columbia County, Florida	N	N	N	2,207	80.9	26.4
Duval County, Florida	13,709	92.7	34.0	53,961	87.5	26.7
Escambia County, Florida	6,584	78.7	27.9	9,724	81.7	33.1
Flagler County, Florida	N	N	N	7,147	83.4	16.9
Hernando County, Florida	N	N	N	15,736	77.7	12.7
Highlands County, Florida	N	N	N	12,658	64.0	8.2
Hillsborough County, Florida	19,763	85.9	37.8	249,283	80.7	21.1
Indian River County, Florida	N	N	N	10,567	63.1	23.1
Lake County, Florida	N	N	N	31,091	75.7	18.1
Lee County, Florida	5,114	81.3	27.4	94,139	71.3	12.9
Leon County, Florida	N	N	N	9,307	86.7	36.3
Manatee County, Florida	N	N	N	34,282	76.5	22.7
Marion County, Florida	2,627	87.0	18.8	28,839	79.1	16.7
Martin County, Florida	N	N	N	11,647	59.6	13.7
Miami-Dade County, Florida	27,246	84.8	33.7	1,376,484	79.9	26.8
Monroe County, Florida	N	N	N	13,130	75.4	22.0
Nassau County, Florida	N	N	N	1,918	91.9	37.2
Okaloosa County, Florida	3,553	96.3	31.2	10,518	86.0	25.9
Orange County, Florida	23,547	91.0	40.7	266,955	84.5	23.4
Osceola County, Florida	7,281	76.9	19.2	117,115	82.9	14.6
Palm Beach County, Florida	14,952	78.2	40.2	209,185	75.7	23.6
Pasco County, Florida	5,009	95.2	26.5	48,610	81.7	23.7
Pinellas County, Florida	12,198	84.5	26.3	59,239	80.2	23.2
Polk County, Florida	7,500	86.5	18.5	86,813	71.0	12.7
Putnam County, Florida	N	N	N	3,653	59.1	12.6
St. Johns County, Florida	N	N	N	10,059	80.6	44.2
St. Lucie County, Florida	N	N	N	35,271	70.0	16.8
Santa Rosa County, Florida	2,949	74.0	18.2	5,541	83.2	16.0
Sarasota County, Florida	N	N	N	23,027	79.3	18.1
Seminole County, Florida	6,690	97.9	48.6	63,537	92.9	31.4
Sumter County, Florida	N	N	N	4,941	60.4	2.0
Volusia County, Florida	4,008	85.3	33.5	45,794	81.5	16.6
Walton County, Florida	N	N	N	2,360	55.2	7.4
GEORGIA						
Barrow County, Georgia	N	N	N	4,648	79.5	12.5
Bartow County, Georgia	N	N	N	4,663	57.2	7.2
Bibb County, Georgia	N	N	N	N	N	N
Bulloch County, Georgia	N	N	N	N	N	N
Carroll County, Georgia	N	N	N	N	N	N
Catoosa County, Georgia	N	N	N	N	N	N
Chatham County, Georgia	N	N	N	10,585	76.7	24.7
Cherokee County, Georgia	N	N	N	14,032	77.5	19.1
Clarke County, Georgia	N	N	N	6,366	59.0	23.9
Clayton County, Georgia	2,724	84.8	25.0	18,293	47.5	8.5
Cobb County, Georgia	9,613	90.4	41.7	51,942	63.7	20.1
Columbia County, Georgia	N	N	N	5,849	32.8	17.0
Coweta County, Georgia	N	N	N	5,309	65.7	17.9
DeKalb County, Georgia	15,212	91.4	39.1	33,584	56.1	17.3
Dougherty County, Georgia	N	N	N	N	N	N
Douglas County, Georgia	N	N	N	7,742	62.1	8.8
Fayette County, Georgia	N	N	N	4,461	77.5	38.1
Floyd County, Georgia	N	N	N	4,875	28.7	4.6
Forsyth County, Georgia	N	N	N	12,333	68.3	31.3
Fulton County, Georgia	12,083	93.2	51.7	42,123	77.5	34.1
Glynn County, Georgia	N	N	N	N	N	N
Gwinnett County, Georgia	15,115	81.7	36.7	103,572	59.5	15.5
Hall County, Georgia	N	N	N	28,572	42.2	5.6
Henry County, Georgia	N	N	N	7,664	90.4	35.5
Houston County, Georgia	N	N	N	6,046	82.0	16.1
Jackson County, Georgia	N	N	N	N	N	N
Lowndes County, Georgia	N	N	N	3,050	56.5	15.0
Muscogee County, Georgia	N	N	N	7,513	81.8	22.1
Newton County, Georgia	N	N	N	N	N	N
Paulding County, Georgia	N	N	N	6,279	82.4	19.4

N = Data for this geographic area cannot be displayed because the number of sample cases is too small.

Table C-2. Educational Attainment of the Population, by Selected Counties, 2017—*Continued*

(Number; percent; dollars.)

| | Educational attainment by race/ethnicity, 25 years and over | | | | | | | | |
| | Asian alone | | | Native Hawaiian or Other Pacific Islander alone | | | Some other race alone | | |
State/County	Total	High school graduate or more (percent)	Bachelor's degree or more (percent)	Total	High school graduate or more (percent)	Bachelor's degree or more (percent)	Total	High school graduate or more (percent)	Bachelor's degree or more (percent)
GEORGIA—(*Continued*)									
Richmond County, Georgia	N	N	N	N	N	N	N	N	N
Rockdale County, Georgia	N	N	N	N	N	N	N	N	N
Spalding County, Georgia	N	N	N	N	N	N	N	N	N
Troup County, Georgia	N	N	N	N	N	N	N	N	N
Walker County, Georgia	N	N	N	N	N	N	N	N	N
Walton County, Georgia	N	N	N	N	N	N	N	N	N
Whitfield County, Georgia	N	N	N	N	N	N	N	N	N
HAWAII									
Hawaii County, Hawaii	35,600	93.1	34.6	15,310	88.6	14.0	2,837	71.1	9.7
Honolulu County, Hawaii	341,618	89.6	35.7	58,771	87.1	14.7	7,890	94.0	33.5
Kauai County, Hawaii	19,222	85.4	22.8	4,437	91.4	18.0	N	N	N
Maui County, Hawaii	37,910	89.6	23.5	12,239	88.0	10.8	N	N	N
IDAHO									
Ada County, Idaho	7,288	88.6	57.0	N	N	N	4,383	58.2	15.9
Bannock County, Idaho	N	N	N	N	N	N	N	N	N
Bonneville County, Idaho	N	N	N	N	N	N	4,168	57.1	6.4
Canyon County, Idaho	N	N	N	N	N	N	10,984	59.9	0.3
Kootenai County, Idaho	N	N	N	N	N	N	N	N	N
Twin Falls County, Idaho	N	N	N	N	N	N	N	N	N
ILLINOIS									
Adams County, Illinois	N	N	N	N	N	N	N	N	N
Champaign County, Illinois	N	N	N	N	N	N	N	N	N
Cook County, Illinois	278,344	89.9	64.0	N	N	N	300,123	61.4	10.6
DeKalb County, Illinois	N	N	N	N	N	N	N	N	N
DuPage County, Illinois	76,291	91.9	70.2	N	N	N	19,946	62.9	14.1
Kane County, Illinois	14,923	87.2	49.2	N	N	N	42,032	47.9	5.1
Kankakee County, Illinois	N	N	N	N	N	N	N	N	N
Kendall County, Illinois	N	N	N	N	N	N	N	N	N
Lake County, Illinois	37,017	95.9	70.9	N	N	N	31,481	58.3	9.5
LaSalle County, Illinois	N	N	N	N	N	N	N	N	N
McHenry County, Illinois	5,654	97.1	66.1	N	N	N	1,986	69.8	10.5
McLean County, Illinois	5,741	99.4	86.0	N	N	N	N	N	N
Macon County, Illinois	N	N	N	N	N	N	N	N	N
Madison County, Illinois	N	N	N	N	N	N	N	N	N
Peoria County, Illinois	4,713	93.1	73.9	N	N	N	N	N	N
Rock Island County, Illinois	N	N	N	N	N	N	N	N	N
St. Clair County, Illinois	2,161	88.5	33.0	N	N	N	N	N	N
Sangamon County, Illinois	2,387	90.5	64.2	N	N	N	N	N	N
Tazewell County, Illinois	N	N	N	N	N	N	N	N	N
Vermilion County, Illinois	N	N	N	N	N	N	N	N	N
Will County, Illinois	26,416	93.0	68.1	N	N	N	28,322	60.1	6.7
Williamson County, Illinois	N	N	N	N	N	N	N	N	N
Winnebago County, Illinois	5,337	88.3	40.4	N	N	N	3,021	46.7	5.3
INDIANA									
Allen County, Indiana	8,444	61.6	28.7	N	N	N	3,205	63.8	4.6
Bartholomew County, Indiana	N	N	N	N	N	N	N	N	N
Boone County, Indiana	N	N	N	N	N	N	N	N	N
Clark County, Indiana	N	N	N	N	N	N	N	N	N
Delaware County, Indiana	N	N	N	N	N	N	N	N	N
Elkhart County, Indiana	1,383	78.2	27.9	N	N	N	2,097	60.2	5.8
Floyd County, Indiana	N	N	N	N	N	N	N	N	N
Grant County, Indiana	N	N	N	N	N	N	N	N	N
Hamilton County, Indiana	12,752	96.4	75.1	N	N	N	N	N	N
Hancock County, Indiana	N	N	N	N	N	N	N	N	N
Hendricks County, Indiana	N	N	N	N	N	N	N	N	N
Howard County, Indiana	N	N	N	N	N	N	N	N	N
Johnson County, Indiana	N	N	N	N	N	N	N	N	N
Kosciusko County, Indiana	N	N	N	N	N	N	N	N	N
Lake County, Indiana	4,875	90.4	53.0	N	N	N	27,382	68.3	10.2
LaPorte County, Indiana	N	N	N	N	N	N	N	N	N
Madison County, Indiana	N	N	N	N	N	N	N	N	N
Marion County, Indiana	18,907	72.2	41.9	N	N	N	11,070	61.3	18.1
Monroe County, Indiana	N	N	N	N	N	N	N	N	N

N = Data for this geographic area cannot be displayed because the number of sample cases is too small.

Table C-2. Educational Attainment of the Population, by Selected Counties, 2017—*Continued*

(Number; percent; dollars.)

| State/County | Median earnings in the past 12 months (2017 inflation-adjusted dollars) | | | | | |
| | Two or more races | | | Hispanic or Latino (of any race) | | |
	Total	High school graduate or more (percent)	Bachelor's degree or more (percent)	Total	High school graduate or more (percent)	Bachelor's degree or more (percent)
GEORGIA—(*Continued*)						
Richmond County, Georgia	N	N	N	5,005	77.8	20.9
Rockdale County, Georgia	N	N	N	N	N	N
Spalding County, Georgia	N	N	N	N	N	N
Troup County, Georgia	N	N	N	N	N	N
Walker County, Georgia	N	N	N	N	N	N
Walton County, Georgia	N	N	N	2,310	61.0	4.7
Whitfield County, Georgia	N	N	N	18,439	30.3	2.9
HAWAII						
Hawaii County, Hawaii	29,706	90.7	14.4	12,715	80.9	13.5
Honolulu County, Hawaii	117,075	96.2	26.5	48,927	94.5	24.3
Kauai County, Hawaii	6,747	87.8	16.3	4,460	87.6	20.0
Maui County, Hawaii	18,483	90.4	17.9	10,412	83.5	9.9
IDAHO						
Ada County, Idaho	7,539	98.2	38.5	19,823	85.2	22.2
Bannock County, Idaho	N	N	N	3,008	94.2	22.2
Bonneville County, Idaho	N	N	N	6,678	69.4	7.2
Canyon County, Idaho	2,964	90.0	7.9	26,211	60.0	5.3
Kootenai County, Idaho	N	N	N	3,872	99.6	16.9
Twin Falls County, Idaho	N	N	N	7,133	57.0	5.0
ILLINOIS						
Adams County, Illinois	N	N	N	N	N	N
Champaign County, Illinois	N	N	N	5,521	83.5	33.3
Cook County, Illinois	66,572	88.5	44.3	771,410	67.2	15.0
DeKalb County, Illinois	N	N	N	5,535	60.8	7.5
DuPage County, Illinois	8,504	94.3	44.9	73,219	70.2	19.0
Kane County, Illinois	6,627	81.8	28.0	91,175	54.6	9.2
Kankakee County, Illinois	N	N	N	5,725	59.6	9.5
Kendall County, Illinois	N	N	N	13,965	53.6	10.0
Lake County, Illinois	6,530	93.4	30.5	79,917	64.5	11.6
LaSalle County, Illinois	N	N	N	5,089	62.2	10.5
McHenry County, Illinois	2,299	93.0	28.0	21,055	66.7	14.3
McLean County, Illinois	N	N	N	3,541	84.4	19.8
Macon County, Illinois	3,265	84.0	12.4	N	N	N
Madison County, Illinois	N	N	N	4,273	71.9	10.3
Peoria County, Illinois	N	N	N	4,506	69.8	15.8
Rock Island County, Illinois	N	N	N	9,921	70.4	11.8
St. Clair County, Illinois	3,253	92.3	31.7	5,917	69.7	29.7
Sangamon County, Illinois	N	N	N	2,693	88.7	43.7
Tazewell County, Illinois	N	N	N	N	N	N
Vermilion County, Illinois	N	N	N	N	N	N
Will County, Illinois	6,381	86.2	28.5	64,265	65.6	11.7
Williamson County, Illinois	N	N	N	N	N	N
Winnebago County, Illinois	2,851	66.0	12.9	18,184	60.0	7.8
INDIANA						
Allen County, Indiana	4,736	86.6	21.3	13,735	64.3	9.1
Bartholomew County, Indiana	N	N	N	N	N	N
Boone County, Indiana	N	N	N	N	N	N
Clark County, Indiana	N	N	N	2,972	58.7	9.6
Delaware County, Indiana	N	N	N	N	N	N
Elkhart County, Indiana	2,079	83.9	9.9	15,434	47.7	3.5
Floyd County, Indiana	N	N	N	N	N	N
Grant County, Indiana	N	N	N	N	N	N
Hamilton County, Indiana	N	N	N	7,183	82.7	36.0
Hancock County, Indiana	N	N	N	N	N	N
Hendricks County, Indiana	N	N	N	3,613	83.7	22.8
Howard County, Indiana	N	N	N	N	N	N
Johnson County, Indiana	N	N	N	N	N	N
Kosciusko County, Indiana	N	N	N	3,195	57.7	3.6
Lake County, Indiana	6,738	85.6	22.1	52,794	71.1	14.6
LaPorte County, Indiana	N	N	N	4,163	70.5	2.6
Madison County, Indiana	N	N	N	1,870	57.0	8.4
Marion County, Indiana	11,575	89.4	42.0	47,853	54.3	13.4
Monroe County, Indiana	N	N	N	N	N	N

N = Data for this geographic area cannot be displayed because the number of sample cases is too small.

Table C-2. Educational Attainment of the Population, by Selected Counties, 2017—*Continued*

(Number; percent; dollars.)

	Educational attainment by race/ethnicity, 25 years and over								
	Asian alone			Native Hawaiian or Other Pacific Islander alone			Some other race alone		
State/County	Total	High school graduate or more (percent)	Bachelor's degree or more (percent)	Total	High school graduate or more (percent)	Bachelor's degree or more (percent)	Total	High school graduate or more (percent)	Bachelor's degree or more (percent)
INDIANA—(*Continued*)									
Morgan County, Indiana	N	N	N	N	N	N	N	N	N
Porter County, Indiana	N	N	N	N	N	N	N	N	N
St. Joseph County, Indiana	N	N	N	N	N	N	N	N	N
Tippecanoe County, Indiana	N	N	N	N	N	N	N	N	N
Vanderburgh County, Indiana	N	N	N	N	N	N	N	N	N
Vigo County, Indiana	1,472	88.9	64.8	N	N	N	N	N	N
Wayne County, Indiana	N	N	N	N	N	N	N	N	N
IOWA									
Black Hawk County, Iowa	2,072	71.4	46.5	N	N	N	N	N	N
Dallas County, Iowa	N	N	N	N	N	N	N	N	N
Dubuque County, Iowa	N	N	N	N	N	N	N	N	N
Johnson County, Iowa	4,530	100.0	73.5	N	N	N	N	N	N
Linn County, Iowa	N	N	N	N	N	N	N	N	N
Polk County, Iowa	15,008	64.4	22.2	N	N	N	3,376	46.5	3.6
Pottawattamie County, Iowa	N	N	N	N	N	N	N	N	N
Scott County, Iowa	3,510	81.0	45.6	N	N	N	N	N	N
Story County, Iowa	N	N	N	N	N	N	N	N	N
Woodbury County, Iowa	2,157	74.7	25.8	N	N	N	N	N	N
KANSAS									
Butler County, Kansas	N	N	N	N	N	N	N	N	N
Douglas County, Kansas	N	N	N	N	N	N	N	N	N
Johnson County, Kansas	20,118	89.5	66.0	N	N	N	4,606	63.9	18.0
Leavenworth County, Kansas	N	N	N	N	N	N	N	N	N
Riley County, Kansas	N	N	N	N	N	N	N	N	N
Sedgwick County, Kansas	16,079	82.0	39.2	N	N	N	14,149	55.6	9.7
Shawnee County, Kansas	N	N	N	N	N	N	2,225	68.8	19.5
Wyandotte County, Kansas	4,053	68.3	14.8	N	N	N	7,192	54.3	3.5
KENTUCKY									
Boone County, Kentucky	N	N	N	N	N	N	N	N	N
Bullitt County, Kentucky	N	N	N	N	N	N	N	N	N
Campbell County, Kentucky	N	N	N	N	N	N	N	N	N
Christian County, Kentucky	N	N	N	N	N	N	N	N	N
Daviess County, Kentucky	N	N	N	N	N	N	N	N	N
Fayette County, Kentucky	8,121	88.4	61.7	N	N	N	3,808	79.7	42.0
Hardin County, Kentucky	2,035	96.0	35.9	N	N	N	N	N	N
Jefferson County, Kentucky	14,970	81.2	45.1	N	N	N	4,147	88.4	20.6
Kenton County, Kentucky	N	N	N	N	N	N	N	N	N
McCracken County, Kentucky	N	N	N	N	N	N	N	N	N
Madison County, Kentucky	N	N	N	N	N	N	N	N	N
Oldham County, Kentucky	N	N	N	N	N	N	N	N	N
Warren County, Kentucky	2,285	48.2	28.4	N	N	N	N	N	N
LOUISIANA									
Ascension Parish, Louisiana	N	N	N	N	N	N	N	N	N
Bossier Parish, Louisiana	N	N	N	N	N	N	N	N	N
Caddo Parish, Louisiana	2,503	89.6	56.9	N	N	N	N	N	N
Calcasieu Parish, Louisiana	2,073	88.4	44.4	N	N	N	N	N	N
East Baton Rouge Parish, Louisiana	9,949	76.5	46.0	N	N	N	4,029	62.9	19.8
Iberia Parish, Louisiana	N	N	N	N	N	N	N	N	N
Jefferson Parish, Louisiana	12,516	74.5	39.8	N	N	N	14,266	59.6	10.9
Lafayette Parish, Louisiana	N	N	N	N	N	N	N	N	N
Lafourche Parish, Louisiana	N	N	N	N	N	N	N	N	N
Livingston Parish, Louisiana	N	N	N	N	N	N	N	N	N
Orleans Parish, Louisiana	7,770	70.6	40.1	N	N	N	3,599	80.4	19.8
Ouachita Parish, Louisiana	N	N	N	N	N	N	N	N	N
Rapides Parish, Louisiana	N	N	N	N	N	N	N	N	N
St. Landry Parish, Louisiana	N	N	N	N	N	N	N	N	N
St. Tammany Parish, Louisiana	N	N	N	N	N	N	N	N	N
Tangipahoa Parish, Louisiana	N	N	N	N	N	N	N	N	N
Terrebonne Parish, Louisiana	N	N	N	N	N	N	N	N	N
MAINE									
Androscoggin County, Maine	N	N	N	N	N	N	N	N	N
Aroostook County, Maine	N	N	N	N	N	N	N	N	N

N = Data for this geographic area cannot be displayed because the number of sample cases is too small.

Table C-2. Educational Attainment of the Population, by Selected Counties, 2017—*Continued*

(Number; percent; dollars.)

	Median earnings in the past 12 months (2017 inflation-adjusted dollars)					
	Two or more races			Hispanic or Latino (of any race)		
State/County	Total	High school graduate or more (percent)	Bachelor's degree or more (percent)	Total	High school graduate or more (percent)	Bachelor's degree or more (percent)
INDIANA—(*Continued*)						
Morgan County, Indiana	N	N	N	N	N	N
Porter County, Indiana	N	N	N	9,072	83.2	16.2
St. Joseph County, Indiana	3,458	92.7	21.0	11,040	68.0	19.1
Tippecanoe County, Indiana	N	N	N	7,261	67.6	29.4
Vanderburgh County, Indiana	N	N	N	2,093	82.9	23.1
Vigo County, Indiana	N	N	N	N	N	N
Wayne County, Indiana	N	N	N	N	N	N
IOWA						
Black Hawk County, Iowa	N	N	N	N	N	N
Dallas County, Iowa	N	N	N	2,481	64.5	12.1
Dubuque County, Iowa	N	N	N	N	N	N
Johnson County, Iowa	N	N	N	3,842	75.8	36.9
Linn County, Iowa	N	N	N	3,583	67.7	26.2
Polk County, Iowa	3,910	85.0	26.7	19,182	59.1	11.2
Pottawattamie County, Iowa	N	N	N	3,450	53.2	15.7
Scott County, Iowa	N	N	N	5,771	80.3	9.3
Story County, Iowa	N	N	N	N	N	N
Woodbury County, Iowa	N	N	N	7,658	44.7	5.8
KANSAS						
Butler County, Kansas	N	N	N	N	N	N
Douglas County, Kansas	N	N	N	3,798	93.3	36.3
Johnson County, Kansas	5,096	91.3	47.9	23,760	72.7	24.0
Leavenworth County, Kansas	N	N	N	N	N	N
Riley County, Kansas	N	N	N	2,804	69.6	24.9
Sedgwick County, Kansas	9,505	90.8	20.0	35,750	65.9	13.0
Shawnee County, Kansas	2,398	84.3	25.9	11,024	80.4	16.4
Wyandotte County, Kansas	3,151	88.8	20.9	23,917	61.6	7.9
KENTUCKY						
Boone County, Kentucky	N	N	N	2,879	68.6	19.3
Bullitt County, Kentucky	N	N	N	N	N	N
Campbell County, Kentucky	N	N	N	N	N	N
Christian County, Kentucky	N	N	N	N	N	N
Daviess County, Kentucky	N	N	N	N	N	N
Fayette County, Kentucky	4,494	92.6	40.9	11,439	79.1	29.0
Hardin County, Kentucky	N	N	N	3,979	98.8	33.9
Jefferson County, Kentucky	6,949	93.2	36.2	22,544	82.6	21.1
Kenton County, Kentucky	N	N	N	2,396	53.4	14.6
McCracken County, Kentucky	N	N	N	N	N	N
Madison County, Kentucky	N	N	N	N	N	N
Oldham County, Kentucky	N	N	N	N	N	N
Warren County, Kentucky	N	N	N	3,026	59.6	24.6
LOUISIANA						
Ascension Parish, Louisiana	N	N	N	3,566	78.2	8.7
Bossier Parish, Louisiana	N	N	N	4,143	68.1	19.0
Caddo Parish, Louisiana	N	N	N	4,026	89.0	22.2
Calcasieu Parish, Louisiana	N	N	N	4,234	68.2	16.0
East Baton Rouge Parish, Louisiana	N	N	N	10,315	64.0	23.3
Iberia Parish, Louisiana	N	N	N	N	N	N
Jefferson Parish, Louisiana	3,943	94.9	24.6	40,809	67.5	10.1
Lafayette Parish, Louisiana	N	N	N	5,848	74.4	8.9
Lafourche Parish, Louisiana	N	N	N	2,235	57.8	16.8
Livingston Parish, Louisiana	N	N	N	N	N	N
Orleans Parish, Louisiana	4,129	93.9	48.3	14,804	83.6	34.8
Ouachita Parish, Louisiana	N	N	N	N	N	N
Rapides Parish, Louisiana	N	N	N	2,039	59.5	27.5
St. Landry Parish, Louisiana	N	N	N	N	N	N
St. Tammany Parish, Louisiana	N	N	N	8,817	62.2	20.3
Tangipahoa Parish, Louisiana	N	N	N	N	N	N
Terrebonne Parish, Louisiana	N	N	N	N	N	N
MAINE						
Androscoggin County, Maine	2,539	96.8	22.4	N	N	N
Aroostook County, Maine	N	N	N	N	N	N

N = Data for this geographic area cannot be displayed because the number of sample cases is too small.

Table C-2. Educational Attainment of the Population, by Selected Counties, 2017—*Continued*

(Number; percent; dollars.)

	Educational attainment by race/ethnicity, 25 years and over								
	Asian alone			Native Hawaiian or Other Pacific Islander alone			Some other race alone		
State/County	Total	High school graduate or more (percent)	Bachelor's degree or more (percent)	Total	High school graduate or more (percent)	Bachelor's degree or more (percent)	Total	High school graduate or more (percent)	Bachelor's degree or more (percent)
MAINE—(*Continued*)									
Cumberland County, Maine	4,608	81.9	42.0	N	N	N	N	N	N
Kennebec County, Maine	N	N	N	N	N	N	N	N	N
Penobscot County, Maine	N	N	N	N	N	N	N	N	N
York County, Maine	1,730	83.4	18.3	N	N	N	N	N	N
MARYLAND									
Allegany County, Maryland	N	N	N	N	N	N	N	N	N
Anne Arundel County, Maryland	16,348	87.4	47.9	N	N	N	9,699	47.4	12.5
Baltimore County, Maryland	34,955	84.1	54.6	N	N	N	6,325	68.3	29.5
Calvert County, Maryland	N	N	N	N	N	N	N	N	N
Carroll County, Maryland	2,383	93.2	46.8	N	N	N	N	N	N
Cecil County, Maryland	N	N	N	N	N	N	N	N	N
Charles County, Maryland	4,503	86.5	41.3	N	N	N	N	N	N
Frederick County, Maryland	8,363	86.7	51.8	N	N	N	3,362	64.0	24.4
Harford County, Maryland	5,860	96.5	58.2	N	N	N	N	N	N
Howard County, Maryland	40,474	93.5	72.1	N	N	N	N	N	N
Montgomery County, Maryland	118,092	91.9	66.8	N	N	N	62,121	61.8	16.4
Prince George's County, Maryland	28,635	90.5	53.6	N	N	N	67,269	42.7	5.5
St. Mary's County, Maryland	N	N	N	N	N	N	N	N	N
Washington County, Maryland	N	N	N	N	N	N	N	N	N
Wicomico County, Maryland	N	N	N	N	N	N	N	N	N
Baltimore city, Maryland	12,140	89.5	71.4	N	N	N	6,667	55.1	15.2
MASSACHUSETTS									
Barnstable County, Massachusetts	1,951	72.8	47.9	N	N	N	N	N	N
Berkshire County, Massachusetts	N	N	N	N	N	N	N	N	N
Bristol County, Massachusetts	8,450	88.9	58.5	N	N	N	20,359	69.0	7.1
Essex County, Massachusetts	18,660	84.4	59.4	N	N	N	25,284	62.7	12.1
Franklin County, Massachusetts	N	N	N	N	N	N	N	N	N
Hampden County, Massachusetts	7,975	68.8	40.7	N	N	N	10,751	65.9	11.5
Hampshire County, Massachusetts	3,352	82.0	62.9	N	N	N	N	N	N
Middlesex County, Massachusetts	133,059	90.1	69.2	N	N	N	24,688	70.0	17.7
Norfolk County, Massachusetts	53,481	82.8	53.7	N	N	N	7,683	83.4	30.7
Plymouth County, Massachusetts	4,953	85.2	55.7	N	N	N	13,725	69.7	11.8
Suffolk County, Massachusetts	48,673	80.9	55.5	N	N	N	36,435	76.3	15.3
Worcester County, Massachusetts	27,311	85.9	61.2	N	N	N	13,658	67.7	9.7
MICHIGAN									
Allegan County, Michigan	N	N	N	N	N	N	N	N	N
Bay County, Michigan	N	N	N	N	N	N	N	N	N
Berrien County, Michigan	2,388	92.0	63.0	N	N	N	N	N	N
Calhoun County, Michigan	2,266	91.7	53.3	N	N	N	N	N	N
Clinton County, Michigan	N	N	N	N	N	N	N	N	N
Eaton County, Michigan	N	N	N	N	N	N	N	N	N
Genesee County, Michigan	3,133	74.4	38.8	N	N	N	N	N	N
Grand Traverse County, Michigan	N	N	N	N	N	N	N	N	N
Ingham County, Michigan	10,155	88.2	67.1	N	N	N	2,048	98.0	45.5
Isabella County, Michigan	N	N	N	N	N	N	N	N	N
Jackson County, Michigan	N	N	N	N	N	N	N	N	N
Kalamazoo County, Michigan	N	N	N	N	N	N	N	N	N
Kent County, Michigan	12,565	70.3	33.4	N	N	N	11,587	49.9	3.7
Lapeer County, Michigan	N	N	N	N	N	N	N	N	N
Lenawee County, Michigan	N	N	N	N	N	N	N	N	N
Livingston County, Michigan	1,253	100.0	56.8	N	N	N	N	N	N
Macomb County, Michigan	23,214	87.0	48.1	N	N	N	4,537	66.6	19.5
Marquette County, Michigan	N	N	N	N	N	N	N	N	N
Midland County, Michigan	N	N	N	N	N	N	N	N	N
Monroe County, Michigan	N	N	N	N	N	N	N	N	N
Muskegon County, Michigan	N	N	N	N	N	N	N	N	N
Oakland County, Michigan	64,451	94.3	76.7	N	N	N	6,082	81.0	33.9
Ottawa County, Michigan	5,036	83.5	39.9	N	N	N	3,512	50.1	11.4
Saginaw County, Michigan	N	N	N	N	N	N	2,175	72.6	11.6
St. Clair County, Michigan	N	N	N	N	N	N	N	N	N
Shiawassee County, Michigan	N	N	N	N	N	N	N	N	N
Van Buren County, Michigan	N	N	N	N	N	N	1,913	52.9	5.1
Washtenaw County, Michigan	19,264	95.7	79.7	N	N	N	1,462	89.4	35.6
Wayne County, Michigan	39,008	87.2	54.9	N	N	N	16,782	55.9	10.2

N = Data for this geographic area cannot be displayed because the number of sample cases is too small.

Table C-2. Educational Attainment of the Population, by Selected Counties, 2017—*Continued*

(Number; percent; dollars.)

| | Median earnings in the past 12 months (2017 inflation-adjusted dollars) | | | | | |
| | Two or more races | | | Hispanic or Latino (of any race) | | |
State/County	Total	High school graduate or more (percent)	Bachelor's degree or more (percent)	Total	High school graduate or more (percent)	Bachelor's degree or more (percent)
MAINE—(*Continued*)						
Cumberland County, Maine	2,950	88.9	33.5	3,523	85.7	37.2
Kennebec County, Maine	N	N	N	N	N	N
Penobscot County, Maine	N	N	N	N	N	N
York County, Maine	N	N	N	N	N	N
MARYLAND						
Allegany County, Maryland	N	N	N	N	N	N
Anne Arundel County, Maryland	8,607	93.0	48.4	24,261	67.4	26.0
Baltimore County, Maryland	10,412	95.5	39.3	24,486	65.9	26.5
Calvert County, Maryland	N	N	N	1,829	96.5	31.5
Carroll County, Maryland	N	N	N	3,626	71.1	9.8
Cecil County, Maryland	N	N	N	N	N	N
Charles County, Maryland	3,194	97.6	36.7	5,408	83.7	39.6
Frederick County, Maryland	4,436	83.8	39.4	13,233	75.5	32.3
Harford County, Maryland	2,628	95.2	28.7	6,186	75.1	20.0
Howard County, Maryland	N	N	N	12,992	88.2	36.5
Montgomery County, Maryland	19,206	91.0	64.6	122,342	68.4	25.1
Prince George's County, Maryland	11,259	84.9	30.9	94,598	50.6	9.8
St. Mary's County, Maryland	N	N	N	3,778	78.5	37.8
Washington County, Maryland	N	N	N	3,537	73.7	13.5
Wicomico County, Maryland	N	N	N	N	N	N
Baltimore city, Maryland	7,208	89.1	39.9	17,946	67.0	24.6
MASSACHUSETTS						
Barnstable County, Massachusetts	N	N	N	3,694	95.7	30.2
Berkshire County, Massachusetts	N	N	N	3,007	90.5	14.4
Bristol County, Massachusetts	7,711	90.7	19.5	22,380	72.5	12.5
Essex County, Massachusetts	9,683	78.2	27.3	91,403	67.8	12.4
Franklin County, Massachusetts	N	N	N	N	N	N
Hampden County, Massachusetts	5,112	76.8	13.5	63,214	65.6	9.6
Hampshire County, Massachusetts	1,601	95.1	55.8	4,300	89.1	24.8
Middlesex County, Massachusetts	18,516	91.2	56.3	73,578	76.8	32.4
Norfolk County, Massachusetts	6,756	86.0	52.4	18,962	85.3	41.7
Plymouth County, Massachusetts	3,641	84.3	29.1	10,906	83.6	23.8
Suffolk County, Massachusetts	20,573	72.2	29.1	110,252	73.0	18.2
Worcester County, Massachusetts	11,698	81.7	28.1	51,557	70.8	10.9
MICHIGAN						
Allegan County, Michigan	N	N	N	3,824	68.5	5.2
Bay County, Michigan	N	N	N	3,086	79.1	15.1
Berrien County, Michigan	1,510	95.6	31.9	4,500	69.9	20.0
Calhoun County, Michigan	N	N	N	3,922	72.7	13.9
Clinton County, Michigan	N	N	N	2,189	81.3	17.4
Eaton County, Michigan	N	N	N	3,213	86.1	12.3
Genesee County, Michigan	5,338	85.7	11.6	7,827	82.3	20.9
Grand Traverse County, Michigan	N	N	N	N	N	N
Ingham County, Michigan	5,788	82.1	32.0	11,639	86.3	23.4
Isabella County, Michigan	N	N	N	890	77.5	26.7
Jackson County, Michigan	N	N	N	3,037	79.4	13.6
Kalamazoo County, Michigan	4,367	86.6	43.8	5,743	78.1	37.9
Kent County, Michigan	6,912	90.4	34.9	32,677	61.2	10.9
Lapeer County, Michigan	N	N	N	2,451	71.0	13.5
Lenawee County, Michigan	N	N	N	4,644	84.7	9.9
Livingston County, Michigan	N	N	N	2,591	77.7	36.9
Macomb County, Michigan	7,766	88.7	25.5	12,139	82.4	20.5
Marquette County, Michigan	N	N	N	N	N	N
Midland County, Michigan	N	N	N	N	N	N
Monroe County, Michigan	N	N	N	3,291	93.0	15.3
Muskegon County, Michigan	2,224	98.3	19.5	4,356	75.3	8.3
Oakland County, Michigan	13,658	93.2	52.1	27,767	75.7	32.4
Ottawa County, Michigan	N	N	N	13,979	70.0	13.7
Saginaw County, Michigan	N	N	N	8,730	74.8	12.7
St. Clair County, Michigan	1,365	88.4	9.8	3,092	83.5	7.6
Shiawassee County, Michigan	N	N	N	N	N	N
Van Buren County, Michigan	N	N	N	3,859	61.9	0.7
Washtenaw County, Michigan	6,300	94.2	57.8	8,929	90.0	37.5
Wayne County, Michigan	20,034	87.5	29.8	54,037	63.9	11.4

N = Data for this geographic area cannot be displayed because the number of sample cases is too small.

Table C-2. Educational Attainment of the Population, by Selected Counties, 2017—*Continued*

(Number; percent; dollars.)

	Educational attainment by race/ethnicity, 25 years and over								
	Asian alone			Native Hawaiian or Other Pacific Islander alone			Some other race alone		
State/County	Total	High school graduate or more (percent)	Bachelor's degree or more (percent)	Total	High school graduate or more (percent)	Bachelor's degree or more (percent)	Total	High school graduate or more (percent)	Bachelor's degree or more (percent)
MINNESOTA									
Anoka County, Minnesota	10,230	89.4	42.6	N	N	N	4,462	59.7	8.9
Blue Earth County, Minnesota	N	N	N	N	N	N	N	N	N
Carver County, Minnesota	N	N	N	N	N	N	N	N	N
Dakota County, Minnesota	14,211	84.3	46.2	N	N	N	6,968	50.7	12.8
Hennepin County, Minnesota	58,991	88.2	56.0	N	N	N	23,569	50.1	11.5
Olmsted County, Minnesota	6,058	84.1	56.3	N	N	N	N	N	N
Ramsey County, Minnesota	45,435	66.3	30.1	N	N	N	7,009	59.6	16.9
Rice County, Minnesota	N	N	N	N	N	N	N	N	N
St. Louis County, Minnesota	N	N	N	N	N	N	N	N	N
Scott County, Minnesota	5,663	85.3	43.5	N	N	N	N	N	N
Sherburne County, Minnesota	N	N	N	N	N	N	N	N	N
Stearns County, Minnesota	N	N	N	N	N	N	N	N	N
Washington County, Minnesota	9,154	93.7	61.6	N	N	N	N	N	N
Wright County, Minnesota	N	N	N	N	N	N	N	N	N
MISSISSIPPI									
DeSoto County, Mississippi	N	N	N	N	N	N	2,607	71.0	16.3
Forrest County, Mississippi	N	N	N	N	N	N	N	N	N
Harrison County, Mississippi	4,282	76.4	17.1	N	N	N	N	N	N
Hinds County, Mississippi	N	N	N	N	N	N	N	N	N
Jackson County, Mississippi	N	N	N	N	N	N	N	N	N
Jones County, Mississippi	N	N	N	N	N	N	N	N	N
Lauderdale County, Mississippi	N	N	N	N	N	N	N	N	N
Lee County, Mississippi	662	81.7	32.6	N	N	N	N	N	N
Madison County, Mississippi	N	N	N	N	N	N	N	N	N
Rankin County, Mississippi	N	N	N	N	N	N	N	N	N
MISSOURI									
Boone County, Missouri	N	N	N	N	N	N	N	N	N
Buchanan County, Missouri	N	N	N	N	N	N	N	N	N
Cape Girardeau County, Missouri	N	N	N	N	N	N	N	N	N
Cass County, Missouri	N	N	N	N	N	N	N	N	N
Christian County, Missouri	N	N	N	N	N	N	N	N	N
Clay County, Missouri	3,813	87.9	43.2	N	N	N	N	N	N
Cole County, Missouri	N	N	N	N	N	N	N	N	N
Franklin County, Missouri	414	83.1	16.9	N	N	N	N	N	N
Greene County, Missouri	3,710	89.2	52.5	N	N	N	N	N	N
Jackson County, Missouri	9,162	79.3	42.9	N	N	N	15,775	56.7	7.7
Jasper County, Missouri	N	N	N	N	N	N	N	N	N
Jefferson County, Missouri	1,146	82.7	42.2	N	N	N	N	N	N
Platte County, Missouri	N	N	N	N	N	N	N	N	N
St. Charles County, Missouri	6,983	93.2	70.9	N	N	N	N	N	N
St. Francois County, Missouri	N	N	N	N	N	N	N	N	N
St. Louis County, Missouri	29,218	94.5	73.9	N	N	N	6,107	72.2	23.1
St. Louis city, Missouri	7,291	88.5	54.2	N	N	N	N	N	N
MONTANA									
Cascade County, Montana	N	N	N	N	N	N	N	N	N
Flathead County, Montana	N	N	N	N	N	N	N	N	N
Gallatin County, Montana	N	N	N	N	N	N	N	N	N
Lewis and Clark County, Montana	N	N	N	N	N	N	N	N	N
Missoula County, Montana	N	N	N	N	N	N	N	N	N
Yellowstone County, Montana	N	N	N	N	N	N	N	N	N
NEBRASKA									
Douglas County, Nebraska	13,140	72.2	54.2	N	N	N	5,916	65.7	11.6
Lancaster County, Nebraska	8,417	78.4	47.7	N	N	N	N	N	N
Sarpy County, Nebraska	3,098	94.4	56.4	N	N	N	N	N	N
NEVADA									
Clark County, Nevada	170,885	91.3	39.2	10,894	91.2	9.7	167,995	60.9	7.9
Washoe County, Nevada	18,450	92.5	48.6	N	N	N	18,915	61.6	7.3
NEW HAMPSHIRE									
Cheshire County, New Hampshire	N	N	N	N	N	N	N	N	N
Grafton County, New Hampshire	2,026	73.5	34.4	N	N	N	N	N	N
Hillsborough County, New Hampshire	11,394	89.2	70.9	N	N	N	N	N	N

N = Data for this geographic area cannot be displayed because the number of sample cases is too small.

Table C-2. Educational Attainment of the Population, by Selected Counties, 2017—*Continued*

(Number; percent; dollars.)

State/County	Median earnings in the past 12 months (2017 inflation-adjusted dollars)					
	Two or more races			Hispanic or Latino (of any race)		
	Total	High school graduate or more (percent)	Bachelor's degree or more (percent)	Total	High school graduate or more (percent)	Bachelor's degree or more (percent)
MINNESOTA						
Anoka County, Minnesota	3,534	90.5	26.3	7,999	66.2	14.0
Blue Earth County, Minnesota	N	N	N	N	N	N
Carver County, Minnesota	N	N	N	N	N	N
Dakota County, Minnesota	4,018	92.8	23.0	14,920	63.7	15.5
Hennepin County, Minnesota	17,086	93.4	41.1	44,815	61.5	19.5
Olmsted County, Minnesota	2,063	91.7	42.8	3,930	94.1	37.1
Ramsey County, Minnesota	6,348	92.1	29.2	20,970	63.2	15.9
Rice County, Minnesota	N	N	N	2,835	55.7	6.2
St. Louis County, Minnesota	2,272	89.2	33.5	1,075	71.2	23.4
Scott County, Minnesota	N	N	N	3,908	61.8	10.5
Sherburne County, Minnesota	N	N	N	N	N	N
Stearns County, Minnesota	N	N	N	2,287	49.9	8.9
Washington County, Minnesota	2,935	90.6	31.4	5,783	86.8	25.0
Wright County, Minnesota	N	N	N	1,921	63.7	21.3
MISSISSIPPI						
DeSoto County, Mississippi	N	N	N	4,046	78.8	16.7
Forrest County, Mississippi	N	N	N	N	N	N
Harrison County, Mississippi	N	N	N	5,118	83.8	28.0
Hinds County, Mississippi	N	N	N	N	N	N
Jackson County, Mississippi	N	N	N	4,070	86.4	26.9
Jones County, Mississippi	N	N	N	N	N	N
Lauderdale County, Mississippi	N	N	N	N	N	N
Lee County, Mississippi	N	N	N	N	N	N
Madison County, Mississippi	N	N	N	N	N	N
Rankin County, Mississippi	N	N	N	N	N	N
MISSOURI						
Boone County, Missouri	N	N	N	N	N	N
Buchanan County, Missouri	N	N	N	2,435	61.6	1.7
Cape Girardeau County, Missouri	N	N	N	N	N	N
Cass County, Missouri	N	N	N	2,719	59.5	5.6
Christian County, Missouri	N	N	N	N	N	N
Clay County, Missouri	4,003	89.6	30.7	8,568	80.6	15.2
Cole County, Missouri	N	N	N	N	N	N
Franklin County, Missouri	N	N	N	N	N	N
Greene County, Missouri	3,720	87.8	28.2	4,821	82.3	22.6
Jackson County, Missouri	7,777	96.0	36.9	33,051	66.1	15.1
Jasper County, Missouri	N	N	N	4,471	37.6	12.0
Jefferson County, Missouri	2,342	76.9	23.1	N	N	N
Platte County, Missouri	N	N	N	3,197	85.8	53.0
St. Charles County, Missouri	5,831	99.8	41.3	7,049	88.3	35.5
St. Francois County, Missouri	N	N	N	N	N	N
St. Louis County, Missouri	9,486	90.3	33.0	15,811	78.7	33.2
St. Louis city, Missouri	2,699	92.4	40.9	7,110	85.2	38.2
MONTANA						
Cascade County, Montana	N	N	N	N	N	N
Flathead County, Montana	N	N	N	N	N	N
Gallatin County, Montana	N	N	N	N	N	N
Lewis and Clark County, Montana	N	N	N	N	N	N
Missoula County, Montana	N	N	N	2,069	81.2	28.8
Yellowstone County, Montana	N	N	N	4,467	48.4	7.7
NEBRASKA						
Douglas County, Nebraska	5,266	89.0	24.2	33,652	54.8	11.0
Lancaster County, Nebraska	3,948	87.4	31.1	9,789	68.2	15.5
Sarpy County, Nebraska	1,898	97.1	17.9	8,228	69.5	20.4
NEVADA						
Clark County, Nevada	47,569	91.7	22.3	388,465	66.2	10.2
Washoe County, Nevada	9,957	89.2	29.9	61,001	67.9	10.2
NEW HAMPSHIRE						
Cheshire County, New Hampshire	N	N	N	N	N	N
Grafton County, New Hampshire	N	N	N	N	N	N
Hillsborough County, New Hampshire	3,518	96.6	24.9	14,800	75.5	19.0

N = Data for this geographic area cannot be displayed because the number of sample cases is too small.

Table C-2. Educational Attainment of the Population, by Selected Counties, 2017—*Continued*

(Number; percent; dollars.)

| | Educational attainment by race/ethnicity, 25 years and over | | | | | | | | |
| | Asian alone | | | Native Hawaiian or Other Pacific Islander alone | | | Some other race alone | | |
State/County	Total	High school graduate or more (percent)	Bachelor's degree or more (percent)	Total	High school graduate or more (percent)	Bachelor's degree or more (percent)	Total	High school graduate or more (percent)	Bachelor's degree or more (percent)
NEW HAMPSHIRE—(*Continued*)									
Merrimack County, New Hampshire	N	N	N	N	N	N	N	N	N
Rockingham County, New Hampshire	4,273	90.3	64.5	N	N	N	N	N	N
Strafford County, New Hampshire	3,068	72.4	42.7	N	N	N	N	N	N
NEW JERSEY									
Atlantic County, New Jersey	15,446	75.7	34.0	N	N	N	12,438	62.6	6.9
Bergen County, New Jersey	117,221	93.2	68.3	N	N	N	14,341	86.5	23.0
Burlington County, New Jersey	16,027	86.1	52.5	N	N	N	4,349	92.9	18.3
Camden County, New Jersey	21,088	88.2	55.7	N	N	N	18,301	65.0	9.7
Cape May County, New Jersey	N	N	N	N	N	N	N	N	N
Cumberland County, New Jersey	N	N	N	N	N	N	4,732	61.6	1.4
Essex County, New Jersey	31,570	93.7	71.1	N	N	N	45,409	60.3	10.6
Gloucester County, New Jersey	5,846	93.9	61.4	N	N	N	4,048	81.1	27.9
Hudson County, New Jersey	83,651	93.1	73.5	N	N	N	63,030	80.2	21.0
Hunterdon County, New Jersey	N	N	N	N	N	N	N	N	N
Mercer County, New Jersey	28,311	96.5	79.5	N	N	N	4,243	67.4	20.5
Middlesex County, New Jersey	143,601	91.4	74.2	N	N	N	22,382	77.1	20.6
Monmouth County, New Jersey	25,553	93.7	71.0	N	N	N	10,672	59.9	10.9
Morris County, New Jersey	37,612	93.5	78.9	N	N	N	7,406	68.2	19.4
Ocean County, New Jersey	8,535	89.7	52.7	N	N	N	8,487	73.6	13.3
Passaic County, New Jersey	19,310	93.3	62.4	N	N	N	47,783	71.5	9.9
Salem County, New Jersey	N	N	N	N	N	N	N	N	N
Somerset County, New Jersey	42,423	95.1	78.0	N	N	N	4,023	82.9	18.0
Sussex County, New Jersey	2,660	86.7	52.3	N	N	N	N	N	N
Union County, New Jersey	20,986	89.1	70.0	N	N	N	50,696	72.4	13.1
Warren County, New Jersey	N	N	N	N	N	N	N	N	N
NEW MEXICO									
Bernalillo County, New Mexico	12,296	90.1	64.8	N	N	N	36,033	78.6	23.2
Chaves County, New Mexico	N	N	N	N	N	N	2,818	73.9	20.0
Doña Ana County, New Mexico	N	N	N	N	N	N	11,140	63.1	13.9
Lea County, New Mexico	N	N	N	N	N	N	2,162	88.1	27.7
McKinley County, New Mexico	N	N	N	N	N	N	N	N	N
Otero County, New Mexico	N	N	N	N	N	N	N	N	N
Sandoval County, New Mexico	1,574	100.0	50.3	N	N	N	4,264	81.1	14.4
San Juan County, New Mexico	N	N	N	N	N	N	3,154	65.0	7.2
Santa Fe County, New Mexico	N	N	N	N	N	N	8,155	63.5	13.2
Valencia County, New Mexico	N	N	N	N	N	N	3,587	66.2	3.2
NEW YORK									
Albany County, New York	12,510	92.1	66.3	N	N	N	N	N	N
Bronx County, New York	40,540	70.4	30.1	N	N	N	308,174	61.9	11.4
Broome County, New York	4,051	79.2	46.2	N	N	N	N	N	N
Cattaraugus County, New York	N	N	N	N	N	N	N	N	N
Cayuga County, New York	N	N	N	N	N	N	N	N	N
Chautauqua County, New York	N	N	N	N	N	N	2,297	63.5	17.8
Chemung County, New York	N	N	N	N	N	N	N	N	N
Clinton County, New York	N	N	N	N	N	N	N	N	N
Dutchess County, New York	7,974	90.2	67.4	N	N	N	5,869	67.0	16.8
Erie County, New York	19,614	77.4	53.4	N	N	N	11,790	71.2	16.3
Jefferson County, New York	N	N	N	N	N	N	N	N	N
Kings County, New York	231,400	67.9	34.7	N	N	N	151,243	60.9	14.1
Livingston County, New York	N	N	N	N	N	N	N	N	N
Madison County, New York	N	N	N	N	N	N	N	N	N
Monroe County, New York	18,240	81.4	56.2	N	N	N	8,025	69.5	11.3
Nassau County, New York	93,107	91.3	62.5	N	N	N	67,778	69.9	19.4
New York County, New York	164,649	75.5	60.1	N	N	N	131,966	64.8	19.9
Niagara County, New York	N	N	N	N	N	N	N	N	N
Oneida County, New York	5,231	48.4	14.7	N	N	N	1,910	56.2	21.5
Onondaga County, New York	10,635	69.8	48.8	N	N	N	2,050	76.5	15.6
Ontario County, New York	N	N	N	N	N	N	1,474	59.5	11.0
Orange County, New York	6,955	84.9	54.9	N	N	N	17,999	75.2	16.7
Oswego County, New York	N	N	N	N	N	N	N	N	N
Putnam County, New York	N	N	N	N	N	N	N	N	N
Queens County, New York	455,519	78.9	35.9	N	N	N	223,134	70.4	13.3
Rensselaer County, New York	N	N	N	N	N	N	N	N	N
Richmond County, New York	32,951	76.3	38.0	N	N	N	11,981	73.3	11.0

N = Data for this geographic area cannot be displayed because the number of sample cases is too small.

Table C-2. Educational Attainment of the Population, by Selected Counties, 2017—*Continued*

(Number; percent; dollars.)

| State/County | Median earnings in the past 12 months (2017 inflation-adjusted dollars) | | | | | |
| | Two or more races | | | Hispanic or Latino (of any race) | | |
	Total	High school graduate or more (percent)	Bachelor's degree or more (percent)	Total	High school graduate or more (percent)	Bachelor's degree or more (percent)
NEW HAMPSHIRE—(*Continued*)						
Merrimack County, New Hampshire.....................	N	N	N	1,621	84.5	35.9
Rockingham County, New Hampshire..................	2,336	99.7	38.4	5,294	92.2	35.4
Strafford County, New Hampshire........................	N	N	N	N	N	N
NEW JERSEY						
Atlantic County, New Jersey...............................	4,121	93.6	43.9	29,022	68.2	12.5
Bergen County, New Jersey	9,559	87.9	46.3	120,942	85.5	30.1
Burlington County, New Jersey	7,734	95.1	29.1	21,149	89.4	27.2
Camden County, New Jersey	7,480	92.6	34.1	47,880	70.0	13.1
Cape May County, New Jersey	N	N	N	3,803	85.4	20.4
Cumberland County, New Jersey	2,647	85.2	19.2	25,951	59.8	6.8
Essex County, New Jersey..................................	10,264	88.3	54.3	114,456	71.5	19.5
Gloucester County, New Jersey..........................	2,696	96.6	41.9	9,891	87.7	36.5
Hudson County, New Jersey...............................	13,434	83.4	44.7	198,903	75.9	20.8
Hunterdon County, New Jersey...........................	N	N	N	4,617	84.7	33.8
Mercer County, New Jersey................................	3,990	95.9	37.8	38,133	63.3	19.1
Middlesex County, New Jersey...........................	9,870	84.8	34.8	105,246	74.5	20.3
Monmouth County, New Jersey	4,722	91.3	27.9	38,680	71.3	21.7
Morris County, New Jersey	4,021	80.8	44.3	42,724	78.4	21.6
Ocean County, New Jersey.................................	4,706	81.2	26.2	30,864	73.3	16.4
Passaic County, New Jersey...............................	5,745	93.3	24.9	128,308	71.0	13.0
Salem County, New Jersey.................................	N	N	N	2,994	79.8	6.4
Somerset County, New Jersey............................	2,671	97.4	42.1	29,795	88.0	21.0
Sussex County, New Jersey	N	N	N	6,799	89.3	19.1
Union County, New Jersey	5,566	88.6	34.9	111,542	77.1	17.1
Warren County, New Jersey	N	N	N	5,739	70.8	16.0
NEW MEXICO						
Bernalillo County, New Mexico............................	13,047	92.4	38.2	207,172	84.1	21.4
Chaves County, New Mexico...............................	N	N	N	20,504	63.1	7.6
Doña Ana County, New Mexico	N	N	N	81,788	69.8	13.8
Lea County, New Mexico....................................	N	N	N	21,074	59.8	5.9
McKinley County, New Mexico	N	N	N	5,877	66.6	11.3
Otero County, New Mexico.................................	N	N	N	13,732	68.3	16.2
Sandoval County, New Mexico............................	2,565	93.6	29.5	34,054	80.8	18.9
San Juan County, New Mexico...........................	N	N	N	12,938	72.6	12.2
Santa Fe County, New Mexico	1,959	93.0	51.9	49,001	80.7	17.7
Valencia County, New Mexico	N	N	N	27,978	79.6	9.3
NEW YORK						
Albany County, New York.....................................	4,258	85.1	28.7	9,246	70.0	28.5
Bronx County, New York	26,538	74.5	22.1	508,908	64.1	13.9
Broome County, New York	1,768	86.9	16.9	3,623	67.5	24.3
Cattaraugus County, New York............................	N	N	N	N	N	N
Cayuga County, New York...................................	N	N	N	1,508	62.7	14.9
Chautauqua County, New York............................	N	N	N	4,684	72.6	12.3
Chemung County, New York................................	N	N	N	N	N	N
Clinton County, New York....................................	N	N	N	N	N	N
Dutchess County, New York................................	4,130	96.4	24.3	21,377	80.2	20.8
Erie County, New York..	7,956	85.8	31.6	26,157	74.3	22.3
Jefferson County, New York................................	N	N	N	3,523	69.1	8.7
Kings County, New York......................................	42,902	89.1	49.4	322,726	68.7	18.1
Livingston County, New York	N	N	N	N	N	N
Madison County, New York.................................	N	N	N	N	N	N
Monroe County, New York	8,177	88.2	24.5	34,981	74.1	15.0
Nassau County, New York...................................	21,164	76.5	27.8	142,922	71.4	21.9
New York County, New York................................	46,260	78.6	42.9	304,306	68.3	26.4
Niagara County, New York..................................	N	N	N	3,130	74.9	15.6
Oneida County, New York...................................	N	N	N	7,143	60.9	14.2
Onondaga County, New York...............................	6,878	86.7	26.8	10,924	79.6	18.3
Ontario County, New York	N	N	N	3,105	72.1	16.1
Orange County, New York...................................	5,188	81.0	22.8	44,075	78.0	19.0
Oswego County, New York..................................	1,000	98.8	37.1	N	N	N
Putnam County, New York	N	N	N	9,451	80.7	28.2
Queens County, New York...................................	43,630	82.9	31.2	434,181	73.4	16.7
Rensselaer County, New York.............................	2,194	79.3	25.3	4,057	79.0	21.7
Richmond County, New York	4,126	99.0	40.8	52,371	77.4	15.9

N = Data for this geographic area cannot be displayed because the number of sample cases is too small.

Table C-2. Educational Attainment of the Population, by Selected Counties, 2017—*Continued*

(Number; percent; dollars.)

State/County	Educational attainment by race/ethnicity, 25 years and over								
	Asian alone			Native Hawaiian or Other Pacific Islander alone			Some other race alone		
	Total	High school graduate or more (percent)	Bachelor's degree or more (percent)	Total	High school graduate or more (percent)	Bachelor's degree or more (percent)	Total	High school graduate or more (percent)	Bachelor's degree or more (percent)
NEW YORK—(*Continued*)									
Rockland County, New York	15,265	90.3	60.4	N	N	N	9,744	69.2	16.5
St. Lawrence County, New York	N	N	N	N	N	N	N	N	N
Saratoga County, New York	4,667	94.0	75.7	N	N	N	N	N	N
Schenectady County, New York	4,049	85.8	46.6	N	N	N	N	N	N
Steuben County, New York	N	N	N	N	N	N	N	N	N
Suffolk County, New York	39,491	92.5	61.1	N	N	N	40,398	66.1	13.8
Sullivan County, New York	N	N	N	N	N	N	N	N	N
Tompkins County, New York	N	N	N	N	N	N	N	N	N
Ulster County, New York	2,524	87.1	41.2	N	N	N	3,770	75.3	9.4
Warren County, New York	N	N	N	N	N	N	N	N	N
Wayne County, New York	N	N	N	N	N	N	N	N	N
Westchester County, New York	43,756	93.1	71.4	N	N	N	77,528	65.5	14.0
NORTH CAROLINA									
Alamance County, North Carolina	N	N	N	N	N	N	4,240	55.9	2.6
Brunswick County, North Carolina	N	N	N	N	N	N	N	N	N
Buncombe County, North Carolina	N	N	N	N	N	N	N	N	N
Burke County, North Carolina	N	N	N	N	N	N	N	N	N
Cabarrus County, North Carolina	N	N	N	N	N	N	N	N	N
Caldwell County, North Carolina	N	N	N	N	N	N	N	N	N
Carteret County, North Carolina	N	N	N	N	N	N	N	N	N
Catawba County, North Carolina	3,772	69.9	17.6	N	N	N	5,429	63.7	1.9
Chatham County, North Carolina	N	N	N	N	N	N	N	N	N
Cleveland County, North Carolina	N	N	N	N	N	N	N	N	N
Craven County, North Carolina	N	N	N	N	N	N	N	N	N
Cumberland County, North Carolina	6,121	82.2	41.9	N	N	N	6,066	79.2	6.8
Davidson County, North Carolina	N	N	N	N	N	N	N	N	N
Durham County, North Carolina	10,224	95.4	79.7	N	N	N	5,318	61.8	23.7
Forsyth County, North Carolina	5,990	80.0	54.8	N	N	N	2,614	53.9	21.2
Franklin County, North Carolina	N	N	N	N	N	N	N	N	N
Gaston County, North Carolina	2,300	85.7	56.6	N	N	N	N	N	N
Guilford County, North Carolina	17,004	75.3	43.3	N	N	N	4,665	69.9	22.3
Harnett County, North Carolina	N	N	N	N	N	N	3,889	52.2	8.7
Henderson County, North Carolina	N	N	N	N	N	N	N	N	N
Iredell County, North Carolina	2,445	87.6	31.9	N	N	N	N	N	N
Johnston County, North Carolina	N	N	N	N	N	N	N	N	N
Lincoln County, North Carolina	N	N	N	N	N	N	N	N	N
Mecklenburg County, North Carolina	42,595	82.4	58.4	N	N	N	33,329	60.3	10.9
Moore County, North Carolina	N	N	N	N	N	N	N	N	N
Nash County, North Carolina	N	N	N	N	N	N	N	N	N
New Hanover County, North Carolina	N	N	N	N	N	N	N	N	N
Onslow County, North Carolina	3,153	82.6	33.6	N	N	N	N	N	N
Orange County, North Carolina	6,881	92.7	71.9	N	N	N	N	N	N
Pitt County, North Carolina	N	N	N	N	N	N	N	N	N
Randolph County, North Carolina	N	N	N	N	N	N	4,864	56.2	2.2
Robeson County, North Carolina	N	N	N	N	N	N	N	N	N
Rockingham County, North Carolina	N	N	N	N	N	N	N	N	N
Rowan County, North Carolina	N	N	N	N	N	N	N	N	N
Rutherford County, North Carolina	N	N	N	N	N	N	N	N	N
Surry County, North Carolina	N	N	N	N	N	N	N	N	N
Union County, North Carolina	4,763	89.8	64.6	N	N	N	2,931	53.8	8.4
Wake County, North Carolina	51,347	94.2	78.3	N	N	N	24,709	49.4	11.9
Wayne County, North Carolina	N	N	N	N	N	N	N	N	N
Wilkes County, North Carolina	N	N	N	N	N	N	N	N	N
Wilson County, North Carolina	N	N	N	N	N	N	N	N	N
NORTH DAKOTA									
Burleigh County, North Dakota	N	N	N	N	N	N	N	N	N
Cass County, North Dakota	N	N	N	N	N	N	N	N	N
Grand Forks County, North Dakota	N	N	N	N	N	N	N	N	N
Ward County, North Dakota	N	N	N	N	N	N	N	N	N
OHIO									
Allen County, Ohio	N	N	N	N	N	N	N	N	N
Ashtabula County, Ohio	N	N	N	N	N	N	N	N	N
Athens County, Ohio	N	N	N	N	N	N	N	N	N
Belmont County, Ohio	N	N	N	N	N	N	N	N	N

N = Data for this geographic area cannot be displayed because the number of sample cases is too small.

Table C-2. Educational Attainment of the Population, by Selected Counties, 2017—*Continued*

(Number; percent; dollars.)

	Median earnings in the past 12 months (2017 inflation-adjusted dollars)					
	Two or more races			Hispanic or Latino (of any race)		
State/County	Total	High school graduate or more (percent)	Bachelor's degree or more (percent)	Total	High school graduate or more (percent)	Bachelor's degree or more (percent)
NEW YORK—(*Continued*)						
Rockland County, New York	3,872	97.3	31.7	33,907	73.6	23.4
St. Lawrence County, New York	N	N	N	N	N	N
Saratoga County, New York	N	N	N	4,246	72.9	22.3
Schenectady County, New York	N	N	N	4,812	74.4	19.2
Steuben County, New York	N	N	N	N	N	N
Suffolk County, New York	15,276	86.7	37.9	169,516	70.2	17.6
Sullivan County, New York	N	N	N	5,934	85.2	13.4
Tompkins County, New York	N	N	N	N	N	N
Ulster County, New York	3,493	83.9	13.0	11,021	87.4	25.9
Warren County, New York	N	N	N	1,235	76.4	16.8
Wayne County, New York	N	N	N	N	N	N
Westchester County, New York	11,158	91.6	39.4	148,420	68.7	20.4
NORTH CAROLINA						
Alamance County, North Carolina	N	N	N	9,924	45.7	4.2
Brunswick County, North Carolina	N	N	N	3,071	74.7	10.0
Buncombe County, North Carolina	N	N	N	9,666	69.1	16.8
Burke County, North Carolina	N	N	N	N	N	N
Cabarrus County, North Carolina	N	N	N	10,829	52.9	12.8
Caldwell County, North Carolina	N	N	N	N	N	N
Carteret County, North Carolina	N	N	N	N	N	N
Catawba County, North Carolina	N	N	N	7,585	60.4	2.2
Chatham County, North Carolina	N	N	N	5,062	50.4	11.3
Cleveland County, North Carolina	N	N	N	1,875	61.8	5.8
Craven County, North Carolina	N	N	N	3,310	44.0	15.9
Cumberland County, North Carolina	6,974	91.9	26.3	19,605	84.1	18.9
Davidson County, North Carolina	N	N	N	5,686	49.5	3.6
Durham County, North Carolina	4,703	92.6	47.7	21,607	46.7	21.5
Forsyth County, North Carolina	3,587	83.0	37.6	22,690	63.3	13.2
Franklin County, North Carolina	N	N	N	N	N	N
Gaston County, North Carolina	N	N	N	7,819	56.1	9.5
Guilford County, North Carolina	4,390	88.5	34.8	20,662	61.2	16.1
Harnett County, North Carolina	N	N	N	7,830	63.3	13.2
Henderson County, North Carolina	N	N	N	5,881	59.1	18.2
Iredell County, North Carolina	1,595	100.0	40.8	7,276	59.3	15.2
Johnston County, North Carolina	N	N	N	13,137	51.1	5.4
Lincoln County, North Carolina	N	N	N	N	N	N
Mecklenburg County, North Carolina	13,315	90.9	48.1	76,319	65.5	21.0
Moore County, North Carolina	N	N	N	3,513	93.4	31.2
Nash County, North Carolina	N	N	N	N	N	N
New Hanover County, North Carolina	N	N	N	6,323	61.2	26.3
Onslow County, North Carolina	N	N	N	10,161	93.0	19.7
Orange County, North Carolina	N	N	N	6,017	51.6	23.8
Pitt County, North Carolina	N	N	N	5,160	78.8	17.8
Randolph County, North Carolina	N	N	N	8,290	53.8	7.7
Robeson County, North Carolina	N	N	N	4,826	31.6	3.9
Rockingham County, North Carolina	N	N	N	N	N	N
Rowan County, North Carolina	N	N	N	5,705	60.0	10.2
Rutherford County, North Carolina	N	N	N	N	N	N
Surry County, North Carolina	N	N	N	3,472	49.6	11.0
Union County, North Carolina	N	N	N	13,227	62.0	15.2
Wake County, North Carolina	11,005	90.5	54.5	57,401	58.4	20.9
Wayne County, North Carolina	N	N	N	6,716	33.9	10.2
Wilkes County, North Carolina	N	N	N	N	N	N
Wilson County, North Carolina	N	N	N	3,855	53.6	7.4
NORTH DAKOTA						
Burleigh County, North Dakota	N	N	N	N	N	N
Cass County, North Dakota	N	N	N	N	N	N
Grand Forks County, North Dakota	N	N	N	N	N	N
Ward County, North Dakota	N	N	N	N	N	N
OHIO						
Allen County, Ohio	N	N	N	1,819	82.4	35.1
Ashtabula County, Ohio	N	N	N	N	N	N
Athens County, Ohio	N	N	N	N	N	N
Belmont County, Ohio	N	N	N	N	N	N

N = Data for this geographic area cannot be displayed because the number of sample cases is too small.

Table C-2. Educational Attainment of the Population, by Selected Counties, 2017—*Continued*

(Number; percent; dollars.)

State/County	Educational attainment by race/ethnicity, 25 years and over								
	Asian alone			Native Hawaiian or Other Pacific Islander alone			Some other race alone		
	Total	High school graduate or more (percent)	Bachelor's degree or more (percent)	Total	High school graduate or more (percent)	Bachelor's degree or more (percent)	Total	High school graduate or more (percent)	Bachelor's degree or more (percent)
OHIO—(*Continued*)									
Butler County, Ohio	7,863	82.1	54.6	N	N	N	2,412	92.0	33.1
Clark County, Ohio	N	N	N	N	N	N	N	N	N
Clermont County, Ohio	N	N	N	N	N	N	N	N	N
Columbiana County, Ohio	N	N	N	N	N	N	N	N	N
Cuyahoga County, Ohio	26,105	89.9	66.1	N	N	N	12,681	80.5	10.2
Delaware County, Ohio	8,471	89.2	79.0	N	N	N	N	N	N
Erie County, Ohio	N	N	N	N	N	N	N	N	N
Fairfield County, Ohio	N	N	N	N	N	N	N	N	N
Franklin County, Ohio	45,943	86.4	57.9	N	N	N	12,197	67.6	15.3
Geauga County, Ohio	N	N	N	N	N	N	N	N	N
Greene County, Ohio	N	N	N	N	N	N	N	N	N
Hamilton County, Ohio	15,043	90.7	70.4	N	N	N	N	N	N
Hancock County, Ohio	N	N	N	N	N	N	N	N	N
Jefferson County, Ohio	N	N	N	N	N	N	N	N	N
Lake County, Ohio	2,180	77.3	44.8	N	N	N	N	N	N
Licking County, Ohio	N	N	N	N	N	N	N	N	N
Lorain County, Ohio	N	N	N	N	N	N	1,691	77.6	17.6
Lucas County, Ohio	5,079	90.9	71.1	N	N	N	6,050	76.6	12.2
Mahoning County, Ohio	N	N	N	N	N	N	N	N	N
Marion County, Ohio	N	N	N	N	N	N	N	N	N
Medina County, Ohio	N	N	N	N	N	N	N	N	N
Miami County, Ohio	N	N	N	N	N	N	N	N	N
Montgomery County, Ohio	8,268	91.7	62.4	N	N	N	2,743	53.9	2.4
Muskingum County, Ohio	N	N	N	N	N	N	N	N	N
Portage County, Ohio	N	N	N	N	N	N	N	N	N
Richland County, Ohio	N	N	N	N	N	N	N	N	N
Ross County, Ohio	N	N	N	N	N	N	N	N	N
Scioto County, Ohio	N	N	N	N	N	N	N	N	N
Stark County, Ohio	N	N	N	N	N	N	N	N	N
Summit County, Ohio	11,886	83.9	37.5	N	N	N	N	N	N
Trumbull County, Ohio	N	N	N	N	N	N	N	N	N
Tuscarawas County, Ohio	N	N	N	N	N	N	N	N	N
Warren County, Ohio	N	N	N	N	N	N	N	N	N
Wayne County, Ohio	N	N	N	N	N	N	N	N	N
Wood County, Ohio	N	N	N	N	N	N	N	N	N
OKLAHOMA									
Canadian County, Oklahoma	N	N	N	N	N	N	N	N	N
Cleveland County, Oklahoma	7,204	87.8	55.2	N	N	N	N	N	N
Comanche County, Oklahoma	2,664	88.2	41.7	N	N	N	2,260	83.8	14.7
Creek County, Oklahoma	N	N	N	N	N	N	N	N	N
Muskogee County, Oklahoma	N	N	N	N	N	N	N	N	N
Oklahoma County, Oklahoma	18,900	85.1	47.0	N	N	N	15,577	55.8	12.4
Payne County, Oklahoma	N	N	N	N	N	N	N	N	N
Pottawatomie County, Oklahoma	N	N	N	N	N	N	N	N	N
Rogers County, Oklahoma	N	N	N	N	N	N	N	N	N
Tulsa County, Oklahoma	14,095	69.5	34.3	N	N	N	11,632	49.6	5.0
Wagoner County, Oklahoma	N	N	N	N	N	N	N	N	N
OREGON									
Benton County, Oregon	N	N	N	N	N	N	N	N	N
Clackamas County, Oregon	12,395	93.3	57.8	N	N	N	2,593	92.9	44.5
Deschutes County, Oregon	N	N	N	N	N	N	N	N	N
Douglas County, Oregon	N	N	N	N	N	N	N	N	N
Jackson County, Oregon	N	N	N	N	N	N	N	N	N
Josephine County, Oregon	N	N	N	N	N	N	N	N	N
Klamath County, Oregon	N	N	N	N	N	N	N	N	N
Lane County, Oregon	6,870	86.1	56.8	N	N	N	5,609	70.9	14.6
Linn County, Oregon	N	N	N	N	N	N	N	N	N
Marion County, Oregon	5,334	74.9	39.1	N	N	N	10,539	45.2	2.8
Multnomah County, Oregon	43,894	81.4	41.3	N	N	N	10,959	70.5	15.4
Polk County, Oregon	N	N	N	N	N	N	N	N	N
Umatilla County, Oregon	N	N	N	N	N	N	N	N	N
Washington County, Oregon	45,018	93.7	68.7	N	N	N	16,432	66.9	17.8
Yamhill County, Oregon	N	N	N	N	N	N	N	N	N

N = Data for this geographic area cannot be displayed because the number of sample cases is too small.

Table C-2. Educational Attainment of the Population, by Selected Counties, 2017—*Continued*

(Number; percent; dollars.)

State/County	Median earnings in the past 12 months (2017 inflation-adjusted dollars)					
	Two or more races			Hispanic or Latino (of any race)		
	Total	High school graduate or more (percent)	Bachelor's degree or more (percent)	Total	High school graduate or more (percent)	Bachelor's degree or more (percent)
OHIO—(*Continued*)						
Butler County, Ohio	3,162	93.5	24.3	8,543	83.6	20.9
Clark County, Ohio	N	N	N	N	N	N
Clermont County, Ohio	N	N	N	N	N	N
Columbiana County, Ohio	N	N	N	N	N	N
Cuyahoga County, Ohio	15,367	84.8	29.8	41,539	80.2	17.1
Delaware County, Ohio	N	N	N	N	N	N
Erie County, Ohio	N	N	N	2,109	65.1	12.7
Fairfield County, Ohio	N	N	N	N	N	N
Franklin County, Ohio	19,128	90.5	31.2	35,268	74.6	20.0
Geauga County, Ohio	N	N	N	N	N	N
Greene County, Ohio	N	N	N	N	N	N
Hamilton County, Ohio	9,025	89.7	29.9	13,145	67.3	34.3
Hancock County, Ohio	N	N	N	2,444	73.6	6.3
Jefferson County, Ohio	N	N	N	N	N	N
Lake County, Ohio	2,716	71.5	26.1	4,904	43.8	9.4
Licking County, Ohio	2,721	100.0	25.7	1,639	92.7	21.4
Lorain County, Ohio	3,280	86.2	23.4	16,432	74.1	7.5
Lucas County, Ohio	5,710	84.9	30.3	15,386	77.1	12.7
Mahoning County, Ohio	3,353	76.7	5.2	8,023	73.1	4.5
Marion County, Ohio	N	N	N	N	N	N
Medina County, Ohio	N	N	N	1,769	97.1	26.1
Miami County, Ohio	N	N	N	N	N	N
Montgomery County, Ohio	6,906	96.0	29.1	8,195	60.1	16.6
Muskingum County, Ohio	N	N	N	N	N	N
Portage County, Ohio	N	N	N	N	N	N
Richland County, Ohio	N	N	N	1,358	73.6	24.2
Ross County, Ohio	N	N	N	N	N	N
Scioto County, Ohio	N	N	N	N	N	N
Stark County, Ohio	5,854	90.5	18.7	3,780	88.3	20.7
Summit County, Ohio	5,046	90.4	34.4	6,397	84.6	41.0
Trumbull County, Ohio	N	N	N	1,968	76.5	27.2
Tuscarawas County, Ohio	N	N	N	N	N	N
Warren County, Ohio	N	N	N	3,205	84.4	19.5
Wayne County, Ohio	N	N	N	N	N	N
Wood County, Ohio	N	N	N	3,727	81.5	29.1
OKLAHOMA						
Canadian County, Oklahoma	4,355	88.8	22.4	5,756	68.6	14.7
Cleveland County, Oklahoma	9,654	93.4	32.6	11,828	79.8	25.9
Comanche County, Oklahoma	4,151	84.1	15.4	7,663	90.9	11.0
Creek County, Oklahoma	N	N	N	1,300	68.8	14.1
Muskogee County, Oklahoma	2,416	95.4	18.9	1,672	62.0	11.7
Oklahoma County, Oklahoma	24,160	90.5	29.9	65,590	60.1	11.1
Payne County, Oklahoma	N	N	N	N	N	N
Pottawatomie County, Oklahoma	1,398	91.6	34.0	1,615	56.2	5.8
Rogers County, Oklahoma	3,915	95.1	29.7	1,947	65.3	20.6
Tulsa County, Oklahoma	23,225	91.6	26.7	39,453	63.3	11.8
Wagoner County, Oklahoma	2,883	91.5	29.9	2,436	74.1	11.2
OREGON						
Benton County, Oregon	N	N	N	3,252	86.4	39.0
Clackamas County, Oregon	8,197	96.5	40.3	18,853	78.9	22.7
Deschutes County, Oregon	N	N	N	7,854	84.7	24.2
Douglas County, Oregon	3,195	94.2	4.5	3,680	88.3	7.9
Jackson County, Oregon	4,133	93.3	20.7	13,563	66.9	16.7
Josephine County, Oregon	N	N	N	4,095	84.6	8.0
Klamath County, Oregon	N	N	N	4,257	60.3	8.0
Lane County, Oregon	8,861	85.0	18.1	16,297	78.4	22.2
Linn County, Oregon	2,580	83.7	4.7	5,860	70.5	15.0
Marion County, Oregon	11,307	75.7	11.1	44,490	54.7	7.2
Multnomah County, Oregon	19,054	91.9	42.1	51,926	71.7	23.6
Polk County, Oregon	N	N	N	4,743	63.0	29.2
Umatilla County, Oregon	1,474	72.7	13.8	9,648	51.5	6.0
Washington County, Oregon	14,432	90.2	34.1	51,907	72.5	21.4
Yamhill County, Oregon	N	N	N	8,804	56.1	6.2

N = Data for this geographic area cannot be displayed because the number of sample cases is too small.

Table C-2. Educational Attainment of the Population, by Selected Counties, 2017—*Continued*

(Number; percent; dollars.)

	Educational attainment by race/ethnicity, 25 years and over								
	Asian alone			Native Hawaiian or Other Pacific Islander alone			Some other race alone		
State/County	Total	High school graduate or more (percent)	Bachelor's degree or more (percent)	Total	High school graduate or more (percent)	Bachelor's degree or more (percent)	Total	High school graduate or more (percent)	Bachelor's degree or more (percent)
PENNSYLVANIA									
Adams County, Pennsylvania	N	N	N	N	N	N	1,702	63.7	22.9
Allegheny County, Pennsylvania	29,988	86.9	70.1	N	N	N	3,365	91.2	45.5
Armstrong County, Pennsylvania	N	N	N	N	N	N	N	N	N
Beaver County, Pennsylvania	N	N	N	N	N	N	N	N	N
Berks County, Pennsylvania	4,457	89.0	51.0	N	N	N	10,149	68.9	9.2
Blair County, Pennsylvania	N	N	N	N	N	N	N	N	N
Bucks County, Pennsylvania	21,404	91.6	60.8	N	N	N	4,158	75.4	25.4
Butler County, Pennsylvania	1,826	97.7	78.5	N	N	N	N	N	N
Cambria County, Pennsylvania	N	N	N	N	N	N	N	N	N
Carbon County, Pennsylvania	N	N	N	N	N	N	N	N	N
Centre County, Pennsylvania	N	N	N	N	N	N	N	N	N
Chester County, Pennsylvania	19,471	93.8	80.9	N	N	N	3,432	44.9	16.4
Clearfield County, Pennsylvania	N	N	N	N	N	N	N	N	N
Columbia County, Pennsylvania	N	N	N	N	N	N	N	N	N
Crawford County, Pennsylvania	N	N	N	N	N	N	N	N	N
Cumberland County, Pennsylvania	7,741	89.4	58.0	N	N	N	N	N	N
Dauphin County, Pennsylvania	7,638	83.3	46.4	N	N	N	N	N	N
Delaware County, Pennsylvania	22,132	83.6	61.1	N	N	N	5,120	76.2	23.4
Erie County, Pennsylvania	2,519	70.6	36.2	N	N	N	N	N	N
Fayette County, Pennsylvania	N	N	N	N	N	N	N	N	N
Franklin County, Pennsylvania	N	N	N	N	N	N	N	N	N
Indiana County, Pennsylvania	N	N	N	N	N	N	N	N	N
Lackawanna County, Pennsylvania	3,606	82.6	40.4	N	N	N	N	N	N
Lancaster County, Pennsylvania	8,031	80.0	39.9	N	N	N	6,644	67.9	11.5
Lawrence County, Pennsylvania	N	N	N	N	N	N	N	N	N
Lebanon County, Pennsylvania	N	N	N	N	N	N	5,457	88.1	1.9
Lehigh County, Pennsylvania	9,123	87.2	45.9	N	N	N	12,459	67.3	6.1
Luzerne County, Pennsylvania	3,137	84.8	47.3	N	N	N	4,599	53.9	22.2
Lycoming County, Pennsylvania	N	N	N	N	N	N	N	N	N
Mercer County, Pennsylvania	N	N	N	N	N	N	N	N	N
Monroe County, Pennsylvania	N	N	N	N	N	N	3,365	70.5	19.3
Montgomery County, Pennsylvania	43,634	92.4	73.5	N	N	N	5,769	57.9	16.8
Northampton County, Pennsylvania	5,457	96.7	71.0	N	N	N	N	N	N
Northumberland County, Pennsylvania	N	N	N	N	N	N	N	N	N
Philadelphia County, Pennsylvania	79,453	70.1	38.4	N	N	N	54,300	70.4	7.6
Schuylkill County, Pennsylvania	N	N	N	N	N	N	N	N	N
Somerset County, Pennsylvania	N	N	N	N	N	N	N	N	N
Washington County, Pennsylvania	N	N	N	N	N	N	N	N	N
Westmoreland County, Pennsylvania	N	N	N	N	N	N	N	N	N
York County, Pennsylvania	4,563	80.9	32.8	N	N	N	2,121	77.8	18.1
RHODE ISLAND									
Kent County, Rhode Island	3,750	86.3	55.7	N	N	N	N	N	N
Newport County, Rhode Island	N	N	N	N	N	N	N	N	N
Providence County, Rhode Island	17,374	85.1	57.9	N	N	N	26,491	69.5	7.8
Washington County, Rhode Island	N	N	N	N	N	N	N	N	N
SOUTH CAROLINA									
Aiken County, South Carolina	N	N	N	N	N	N	N	N	N
Anderson County, South Carolina	N	N	N	N	N	N	N	N	N
Beaufort County, South Carolina	N	N	N	N	N	N	N	N	N
Berkeley County, South Carolina	3,397	87.5	31.6	N	N	N	N	N	N
Charleston County, South Carolina	N	N	N	N	N	N	N	N	N
Darlington County, South Carolina	N	N	N	N	N	N	N	N	N
Dorchester County, South Carolina	N	N	N	N	N	N	N	N	N
Florence County, South Carolina	N	N	N	N	N	N	N	N	N
Greenville County, South Carolina	8,384	90.1	53.8	N	N	N	8,459	67.1	8.3
Greenwood County, South Carolina	N	N	N	N	N	N	N	N	N
Horry County, South Carolina	N	N	N	N	N	N	4,074	77.4	2.4
Kershaw County, South Carolina	N	N	N	N	N	N	N	N	N
Lancaster County, South Carolina	N	N	N	N	N	N	N	N	N
Laurens County, South Carolina	N	N	N	N	N	N	N	N	N
Lexington County, South Carolina	3,978	95.9	62.0	N	N	N	N	N	N
Oconee County, South Carolina	N	N	N	N	N	N	N	N	N
Orangeburg County, South Carolina	N	N	N	N	N	N	N	N	N
Pickens County, South Carolina	N	N	N	N	N	N	N	N	N
Richland County, South Carolina	7,658	97.4	61.2	N	N	N	6,072	45.8	14.0

N = Data for this geographic area cannot be displayed because the number of sample cases is too small.

Table C-2. Educational Attainment of the Population, by Selected Counties, 2017—*Continued*

(Number; percent; dollars.)

State/County	Median earnings in the past 12 months (2017 inflation-adjusted dollars)					
	Two or more races			Hispanic or Latino (of any race)		
	Total	High school graduate or more (percent)	Bachelor's degree or more (percent)	Total	High school graduate or more (percent)	Bachelor's degree or more (percent)
PENNSYLVANIA						
Adams County, Pennsylvania	N	N	N	3,315	69.0	24.0
Allegheny County, Pennsylvania	14,375	91.4	36.0	15,204	93.1	41.5
Armstrong County, Pennsylvania	N	N	N	N	N	N
Beaver County, Pennsylvania	N	N	N	N	N	N
Berks County, Pennsylvania	10,191	70.8	10.0	44,253	67.4	7.2
Blair County, Pennsylvania	N	N	N	N	N	N
Bucks County, Pennsylvania	4,703	92.2	41.5	19,170	76.4	21.1
Butler County, Pennsylvania	N	N	N	N	N	N
Cambria County, Pennsylvania	N	N	N	1,067	90.1	17.6
Carbon County, Pennsylvania	N	N	N	N	N	N
Centre County, Pennsylvania	N	N	N	2,117	91.4	24.4
Chester County, Pennsylvania	3,325	95.1	44.7	20,309	60.3	17.3
Clearfield County, Pennsylvania	N	N	N	N	N	N
Columbia County, Pennsylvania	N	N	N	N	N	N
Crawford County, Pennsylvania	N	N	N	N	N	N
Cumberland County, Pennsylvania	3,221	95.3	32.3	5,546	78.5	23.9
Dauphin County, Pennsylvania	4,146	88.4	20.2	12,749	75.4	12.8
Delaware County, Pennsylvania	5,547	80.9	38.1	11,156	77.9	28.9
Erie County, Pennsylvania	2,086	85.4	23.3	5,688	70.9	18.5
Fayette County, Pennsylvania	N	N	N	N	N	N
Franklin County, Pennsylvania	N	N	N	4,407	55.1	15.3
Indiana County, Pennsylvania	N	N	N	N	N	N
Lackawanna County, Pennsylvania	N	N	N	7,119	67.8	10.6
Lancaster County, Pennsylvania	5,385	87.3	35.4	30,231	74.3	17.7
Lawrence County, Pennsylvania	N	N	N	N	N	N
Lebanon County, Pennsylvania	N	N	N	8,917	88.1	13.5
Lehigh County, Pennsylvania	3,649	71.1	22.2	48,051	71.9	7.3
Luzerne County, Pennsylvania	1,419	91.8	9.2	18,587	67.5	13.0
Lycoming County, Pennsylvania	N	N	N	N	N	N
Mercer County, Pennsylvania	N	N	N	N	N	N
Monroe County, Pennsylvania	N	N	N	14,889	77.0	17.7
Montgomery County, Pennsylvania	6,710	92.3	49.3	23,246	69.8	27.7
Northampton County, Pennsylvania	3,420	77.7	23.4	21,992	75.5	12.4
Northumberland County, Pennsylvania	N	N	N	N	N	N
Philadelphia County, Pennsylvania	19,334	85.7	38.9	129,277	70.6	15.1
Schuylkill County, Pennsylvania	N	N	N	3,214	72.4	4.0
Somerset County, Pennsylvania	N	N	N	N	N	N
Washington County, Pennsylvania	N	N	N	1,921	83.3	25.5
Westmoreland County, Pennsylvania	2,247	92.4	19.0	2,516	75.1	18.1
York County, Pennsylvania	3,556	94.5	10.9	16,787	78.3	15.6
RHODE ISLAND						
Kent County, Rhode Island	N	N	N	4,265	76.6	9.8
Newport County, Rhode Island	N	N	N	N	N	N
Providence County, Rhode Island	10,412	87.9	25.6	80,295	76.2	12.1
Washington County, Rhode Island	N	N	N	N	N	N
SOUTH CAROLINA						
Aiken County, South Carolina	N	N	N	5,074	62.3	9.4
Anderson County, South Carolina	N	N	N	3,929	81.1	18.1
Beaufort County, South Carolina	N	N	N	10,122	61.8	13.7
Berkeley County, South Carolina	2,696	92.7	12.6	7,808	78.9	24.3
Charleston County, South Carolina	3,778	97.4	50.7	11,206	69.0	16.2
Darlington County, South Carolina	N	N	N	N	N	N
Dorchester County, South Carolina	N	N	N	4,643	86.8	15.1
Florence County, South Carolina	N	N	N	1,840	58.9	14.2
Greenville County, South Carolina	6,307	79.1	30.3	25,344	67.9	17.5
Greenwood County, South Carolina	N	N	N	N	N	N
Horry County, South Carolina	N	N	N	11,075	72.9	7.8
Kershaw County, South Carolina	N	N	N	N	N	N
Lancaster County, South Carolina	N	N	N	N	N	N
Laurens County, South Carolina	N	N	N	N	N	N
Lexington County, South Carolina	2,177	100.0	28.3	8,615	57.3	10.3
Oconee County, South Carolina	N	N	N	N	N	N
Orangeburg County, South Carolina	N	N	N	N	N	N
Pickens County, South Carolina	N	N	N	N	N	N
Richland County, South Carolina	N	N	N	11,296	66.8	27.9

N = Data for this geographic area cannot be displayed because the number of sample cases is too small.

Table C-2. Educational Attainment of the Population, by Selected Counties, 2017—*Continued*

(Number; percent; dollars.)

	Educational attainment by race/ethnicity, 25 years and over								
	Asian alone			Native Hawaiian or Other Pacific Islander alone			Some other race alone		
State/County	Total	High school graduate or more (percent)	Bachelor's degree or more (percent)	Total	High school graduate or more (percent)	Bachelor's degree or more (percent)	Total	High school graduate or more (percent)	Bachelor's degree or more (percent)
SOUTH CAROLINA—(*Continued*)									
Spartanburg County, South Carolina	4,485	87.0	32.2	N	N	N	2,953	62.3	13.3
Sumter County, South Carolina	N	N	N	N	N	N	N	N	N
York County, South Carolina	3,997	75.7	42.9	N	N	N	N	N	N
SOUTH DAKOTA									
Minnehaha County, South Dakota	N	N	N	N	N	N	N	N	N
Pennington County, South Dakota	N	N	N	N	N	N	N	N	N
TENNESSEE									
Anderson County, Tennessee	N	N	N	N	N	N	N	N	N
Blount County, Tennessee	N	N	N	N	N	N	N	N	N
Bradley County, Tennessee	N	N	N	N	N	N	N	N	N
Davidson County, Tennessee	16,670	81.1	56.3	N	N	N	6,234	57.7	16.5
Greene County, Tennessee	N	N	N	N	N	N	N	N	N
Hamilton County, Tennessee	5,478	82.0	49.2	N	N	N	N	N	N
Knox County, Tennessee	8,156	87.3	69.3	N	N	N	N	N	N
Madison County, Tennessee	N	N	N	N	N	N	N	N	N
Maury County, Tennessee	N	N	N	N	N	N	N	N	N
Montgomery County, Tennessee	2,696	61.8	34.8	N	N	N	N	N	N
Putnam County, Tennessee	N	N	N	N	N	N	N	N	N
Robertson County, Tennessee	N	N	N	N	N	N	N	N	N
Rutherford County, Tennessee	7,665	91.2	40.2	N	N	N	N	N	N
Sevier County, Tennessee	N	N	N	N	N	N	N	N	N
Shelby County, Tennessee	16,924	89.7	65.0	N	N	N	13,292	37.5	6.1
Sullivan County, Tennessee	N	N	N	N	N	N	N	N	N
Sumner County, Tennessee	N	N	N	N	N	N	N	N	N
Washington County, Tennessee	N	N	N	N	N	N	N	N	N
Williamson County, Tennessee	N	N	N	N	N	N	N	N	N
Wilson County, Tennessee	N	N	N	N	N	N	N	N	N
TEXAS									
Angelina County, Texas	N	N	N	N	N	N	N	N	N
Bastrop County, Texas	N	N	N	N	N	N	6,987	54.9	6.3
Bell County, Texas	7,982	84.7	28.5	N	N	N	6,833	90.7	11.2
Bexar County, Texas	36,426	85.1	53.8	N	N	N	83,122	71.4	14.5
Bowie County, Texas	N	N	N	N	N	N	N	N	N
Brazoria County, Texas	15,467	90.6	69.7	N	N	N	9,004	66.0	7.3
Brazos County, Texas	7,036	95.0	85.1	N	N	N	3,710	53.8	3.5
Cameron County, Texas	N	N	N	N	N	N	12,944	37.4	5.6
Collin County, Texas	93,836	95.0	75.0	N	N	N	15,622	76.8	24.7
Comal County, Texas	N	N	N	N	N	N	N	N	N
Coryell County, Texas	N	N	N	N	N	N	N	N	N
Dallas County, Texas	116,074	85.9	57.6	N	N	N	91,668	55.0	10.0
Denton County, Texas	49,419	92.2	69.0	N	N	N	13,288	69.4	18.4
Ector County, Texas	N	N	N	N	N	N	14,760	57.2	9.6
Ellis County, Texas	N	N	N	N	N	N	2,951	54.7	7.2
El Paso County, Texas	7,273	89.4	53.8	N	N	N	87,187	61.9	11.2
Fort Bend County, Texas	106,206	91.2	63.5	N	N	N	17,946	70.9	19.7
Galveston County, Texas	8,347	92.0	52.4	N	N	N	N	N	N
Grayson County, Texas	N	N	N	N	N	N	N	N	N
Gregg County, Texas	N	N	N	N	N	N	N	N	N
Guadalupe County, Texas	1,839	84.9	41.7	N	N	N	13,801	75.1	11.0
Harris County, Texas	238,085	86.8	53.9	N	N	N	204,526	58.1	9.6
Harrison County, Texas	N	N	N	N	N	N	N	N	N
Hays County, Texas	N	N	N	N	N	N	4,390	87.3	42.8
Henderson County, Texas	N	N	N	N	N	N	N	N	N
Hidalgo County, Texas	5,713	94.6	56.8	N	N	N	53,043	47.7	16.0
Hunt County, Texas	N	N	N	N	N	N	N	N	N
Jefferson County, Texas	6,841	73.3	28.2	N	N	N	2,893	52.8	9.3
Johnson County, Texas	N	N	N	N	N	N	N	N	N
Kaufman County, Texas	N	N	N	N	N	N	N	N	N
Liberty County, Texas	N	N	N	N	N	N	N	N	N
Lubbock County, Texas	N	N	N	N	N	N	7,031	67.2	13.4
McLennan County, Texas	2,619	82.2	65.1	N	N	N	5,758	61.9	14.2
Midland County, Texas	1,900	61.7	42.7	N	N	N	5,123	75.4	14.2
Montgomery County, Texas	12,231	90.8	60.7	N	N	N	9,433	78.0	28.2
Nacogdoches County, Texas	N	N	N	N	N	N	N	N	N

N = Data for this geographic area cannot be displayed because the number of sample cases is too small.

Table C-2. Educational Attainment of the Population, by Selected Counties, 2017—*Continued*

(Number; percent; dollars.)

State/County	Median earnings in the past 12 months (2017 inflation-adjusted dollars)					
	Two or more races			Hispanic or Latino (of any race)		
	Total	High school graduate or more (percent)	Bachelor's degree or more (percent)	Total	High school graduate or more (percent)	Bachelor's degree or more (percent)
SOUTH CAROLINA—(*Continued*)						
Spartanburg County, South Carolina	3,193	81.7	13.4	10,006	73.2	11.3
Sumter County, South Carolina	N	N	N	N	N	N
York County, South Carolina	N	N	N	7,333	76.0	28.0
SOUTH DAKOTA						
Minnehaha County, South Dakota	N	N	N	4,233	74.7	17.8
Pennington County, South Dakota	N	N	N	2,217	69.1	17.6
TENNESSEE						
Anderson County, Tennessee	N	N	N	N	N	N
Blount County, Tennessee	N	N	N	N	N	N
Bradley County, Tennessee	N	N	N	3,201	61.6	9.9
Davidson County, Tennessee	7,879	95.6	43.8	36,507	65.0	16.7
Greene County, Tennessee	N	N	N	N	N	N
Hamilton County, Tennessee	2,224	94.5	41.4	11,089	66.4	17.0
Knox County, Tennessee	3,098	93.1	39.3	9,152	64.8	25.8
Madison County, Tennessee	N	N	N	N	N	N
Maury County, Tennessee	N	N	N	N	N	N
Montgomery County, Tennessee	3,902	88.7	24.9	9,888	81.7	17.2
Putnam County, Tennessee	N	N	N	2,292	67.8	4.9
Robertson County, Tennessee	N	N	N	N	N	N
Rutherford County, Tennessee	2,875	100.0	27.3	13,355	62.0	16.1
Sevier County, Tennessee	N	N	N	N	N	N
Shelby County, Tennessee	6,293	86.5	31.7	28,425	51.2	15.2
Sullivan County, Tennessee	N	N	N	1,533	69.7	19.3
Sumner County, Tennessee	N	N	N	4,710	78.2	17.4
Washington County, Tennessee	N	N	N	2,335	81.4	24.0
Williamson County, Tennessee	N	N	N	5,483	71.9	24.9
Wilson County, Tennessee	N	N	N	2,699	67.0	15.9
TEXAS						
Angelina County, Texas	N	N	N	9,651	64.5	11.5
Bastrop County, Texas	N	N	N	16,597	62.0	16.1
Bell County, Texas	6,176	97.8	20.0	45,197	84.2	15.0
Bexar County, Texas	30,763	88.5	29.2	705,290	77.1	17.0
Bowie County, Texas	N	N	N	N	N	N
Brazoria County, Texas	N	N	N	62,061	74.1	20.0
Brazos County, Texas	N	N	N	27,533	58.5	16.8
Cameron County, Texas	N	N	N	214,231	63.1	15.2
Collin County, Texas	13,083	95.3	49.7	81,770	73.4	24.5
Comal County, Texas	N	N	N	22,936	84.8	22.6
Coryell County, Texas	2,765	86.2	5.0	7,980	81.4	9.9
Dallas County, Texas	30,016	89.2	37.8	561,848	54.3	10.3
Denton County, Texas	10,912	89.8	47.7	88,903	72.8	22.9
Ector County, Texas	N	N	N	51,257	61.9	9.2
Ellis County, Texas	3,190	81.6	9.4	23,978	59.0	4.6
El Paso County, Texas	9,297	93.0	32.0	416,704	74.5	18.3
Fort Bend County, Texas	4,968	86.6	53.2	107,165	72.6	26.2
Galveston County, Texas	4,691	87.0	24.5	47,057	77.1	14.3
Grayson County, Texas	N	N	N	8,496	61.7	6.1
Gregg County, Texas	N	N	N	11,875	45.7	4.2
Guadalupe County, Texas	3,006	88.5	17.0	35,546	77.0	13.1
Harris County, Texas	48,562	86.2	33.0	1,117,608	61.5	12.8
Harrison County, Texas	N	N	N	N	N	N
Hays County, Texas	N	N	N	44,876	79.7	22.7
Henderson County, Texas	N	N	N	5,690	61.5	9.5
Hidalgo County, Texas	4,710	61.0	11.8	431,520	62.1	16.6
Hunt County, Texas	N	N	N	7,255	72.9	11.1
Jefferson County, Texas	N	N	N	29,030	66.6	6.3
Johnson County, Texas	N	N	N	18,606	59.0	9.7
Kaufman County, Texas	N	N	N	13,421	60.4	14.1
Liberty County, Texas	N	N	N	10,098	45.9	4.4
Lubbock County, Texas	2,162	89.8	22.1	57,389	71.7	16.1
McLennan County, Texas	N	N	N	33,305	59.1	8.5
Midland County, Texas	N	N	N	40,602	70.5	12.5
Montgomery County, Texas	5,256	92.1	35.1	72,473	61.8	21.3
Nacogdoches County, Texas	N	N	N	5,327	53.4	4.7

N = Data for this geographic area cannot be displayed because the number of sample cases is too small.

Table C-2. Educational Attainment of the Population, by Selected Counties, 2017—*Continued*

(Number; percent; dollars.)

State/County	Educational attainment by race/ethnicity, 25 years and over								
	Asian alone			Native Hawaiian or Other Pacific Islander alone			Some other race alone		
	Total	High school graduate or more (percent)	Bachelor's degree or more (percent)	Total	High school graduate or more (percent)	Bachelor's degree or more (percent)	Total	High school graduate or more (percent)	Bachelor's degree or more (percent)
TEXAS—(*Continued*)									
Nueces County, Texas	5,062	87.5	45.0	N	N	N	3,518	69.1	10.5
Orange County, Texas	N	N	N	N	N	N	N	N	N
Parker County, Texas	N	N	N	N	N	N	N	N	N
Potter County, Texas	N	N	N	N	N	N	N	N	N
Randall County, Texas	N	N	N	N	N	N	2,373	63.9	11.5
Rockwall County, Texas	N	N	N	N	N	N	N	N	N
San Patricio County, Texas	N	N	N	N	N	N	N	N	N
Smith County, Texas	N	N	N	N	N	N	N	N	N
Tarrant County, Texas	74,274	80.7	44.3	N	N	N	95,671	54.0	7.4
Taylor County, Texas	2,214	82.2	55.6	N	N	N	10,016	62.9	4.0
Tom Green County, Texas	N	N	N	N	N	N	7,827	75.2	5.6
Travis County, Texas	57,235	93.7	72.7	N	N	N	72,320	70.9	11.1
Victoria County, Texas	N	N	N	N	N	N	N	N	N
Walker County, Texas	N	N	N	N	N	N	N	N	N
Webb County, Texas	N	N	N	N	N	N	4,996	71.0	13.0
Wichita County, Texas	N	N	N	N	N	N	5,917	62.7	7.7
Williamson County, Texas	23,695	98.2	68.6	N	N	N	10,247	82.6	15.7
Wise County, Texas	N	N	N	N	N	N	N	N	N
UTAH									
Cache County, Utah	N	N	N	N	N	N	N	N	N
Davis County, Utah	5,415	90.5	43.7	N	N	N	3,011	87.3	17.2
Salt Lake County, Utah	31,448	87.4	51.4	8,652	92.5	12.1	64,531	62.7	8.6
Tooele County, Utah	N	N	N	N	N	N	N	N	N
Utah County, Utah	5,455	94.9	54.1	3,131	97.7	27.5	6,979	67.1	22.7
Washington County, Utah	N	N	N	N	N	N	3,749	37.5	0.0
Weber County, Utah	N	N	N	N	N	N	7,312	59.6	3.5
VERMONT									
Chittenden County, Vermont	4,765	62.5	39.1	N	N	N	N	N	N
VIRGINIA									
Albemarle County, Virginia	N	N	N	N	N	N	N	N	N
Arlington County, Virginia	19,636	95.9	82.7	N	N	N	8,943	49.5	25.2
Augusta County, Virginia	N	N	N	N	N	N	N	N	N
Bedford County, Virginia	N	N	N	N	N	N	N	N	N
Chesterfield County, Virginia	9,302	92.5	45.6	N	N	N	2,205	72.2	13.2
Fairfax County, Virginia	158,692	91.8	63.2	N	N	N	28,853	59.8	18.1
Fauquier County, Virginia	N	N	N	N	N	N	N	N	N
Frederick County, Virginia	N	N	N	N	N	N	N	N	N
Hanover County, Virginia	N	N	N	N	N	N	N	N	N
Henrico County, Virginia	19,577	90.8	75.2	N	N	N	5,065	60.2	24.4
James City County, Virginia	N	N	N	N	N	N	N	N	N
Loudoun County, Virginia	50,301	93.7	74.7	N	N	N	7,699	63.8	24.6
Montgomery County, Virginia	N	N	N	N	N	N	N	N	N
Prince William County, Virginia	26,431	90.9	46.4	N	N	N	23,143	58.7	9.6
Roanoke County, Virginia	N	N	N	N	N	N	N	N	N
Rockingham County, Virginia	N	N	N	N	N	N	N	N	N
Spotsylvania County, Virginia	2,458	89.1	44.8	N	N	N	4,068	73.3	21.1
Stafford County, Virginia	N	N	N	N	N	N	N	N	N
York County, Virginia	2,713	85.1	45.3	N	N	N	N	N	N
Alexandria city, Virginia	7,629	88.2	66.1	N	N	N	4,102	58.2	19.6
Chesapeake city, Virginia	5,650	88.3	34.8	N	N	N	N	N	N
Hampton city, Virginia	N	N	N	N	N	N	N	N	N
Lynchburg city, Virginia	1,061	90.1	31.3	N	N	N	N	N	N
Newport News city, Virginia	4,256	76.7	39.6	N	N	N	N	N	N
Norfolk city, Virginia	6,328	91.9	51.3	N	N	N	4,330	64.5	17.4
Portsmouth city, Virginia	N	N	N	N	N	N	N	N	N
Richmond city, Virginia	N	N	N	N	N	N	N	N	N
Roanoke city, Virginia	2,517	53.4	37.9	N	N	N	N	N	N
Suffolk city, Virginia	N	N	N	N	N	N	N	N	N
Virginia Beach city, Virginia	23,826	90.4	35.4	N	N	N	6,856	80.8	31.4
WASHINGTON									
Benton County, Washington	4,581	93.3	46.5	N	N	N	8,111	44.0	7.0
Chelan County, Washington	N	N	N	N	N	N	N	N	N
Clallam County, Washington	N	N	N	N	N	N	N	N	N

N = Data for this geographic area cannot be displayed because the number of sample cases is too small.

Table C-2. Educational Attainment of the Population, by Selected Counties, 2017—*Continued*

(Number; percent; dollars.)

State/County	Median earnings in the past 12 months (2017 inflation-adjusted dollars)					
	Two or more races			Hispanic or Latino (of any race)		
	Total	High school graduate or more (percent)	Bachelor's degree or more (percent)	Total	High school graduate or more (percent)	Bachelor's degree or more (percent)
TEXAS—(*Continued*)						
Nueces County, Texas	3,305	74.8	29.3	140,237	75.5	13.3
Orange County, Texas	N	N	N	3,077	96.1	17.2
Parker County, Texas	N	N	N	8,273	64.6	13.9
Potter County, Texas	N	N	N	24,549	56.4	6.3
Randall County, Texas	N	N	N	15,641	81.7	21.0
Rockwall County, Texas	N	N	N	9,057	64.1	15.9
San Patricio County, Texas	N	N	N	22,160	67.2	8.2
Smith County, Texas	N	N	N	21,950	55.5	8.6
Tarrant County, Texas	25,146	92.6	31.6	314,482	60.9	12.6
Taylor County, Texas	N	N	N	17,359	64.7	7.2
Tom Green County, Texas	N	N	N	26,982	78.3	9.7
Travis County, Texas	21,298	89.5	46.3	243,060	76.1	25.2
Victoria County, Texas	N	N	N	24,972	70.4	9.0
Walker County, Texas	N	N	N	7,568	73.5	10.3
Webb County, Texas	N	N	N	143,378	68.1	15.9
Wichita County, Texas	N	N	N	12,765	68.8	6.6
Williamson County, Texas	10,691	96.8	35.4	75,815	79.9	22.3
Wise County, Texas	N	N	N	6,811	54.0	0.3
UTAH						
Cache County, Utah	N	N	N	5,452	50.0	7.3
Davis County, Utah	4,085	96.1	25.4	16,902	86.8	21.0
Salt Lake County, Utah	15,003	88.6	31.4	107,075	69.5	12.8
Tooele County, Utah	N	N	N	4,415	62.4	13.1
Utah County, Utah	4,678	96.9	55.7	32,787	74.1	24.9
Washington County, Utah	N	N	N	8,532	56.0	5.9
Weber County, Utah	2,843	81.4	28.7	23,166	64.0	7.6
VERMONT						
Chittenden County, Vermont	N	N	N	N	N	N
VIRGINIA						
Albemarle County, Virginia	N	N	N	3,111	81.5	25.2
Arlington County, Virginia	N	N	N	24,403	67.9	43.3
Augusta County, Virginia	N	N	N	N	N	N
Bedford County, Virginia	N	N	N	N	N	N
Chesterfield County, Virginia	N	N	N	16,308	71.0	21.4
Fairfax County, Virginia	24,681	89.6	49.7	111,100	72.5	28.4
Fauquier County, Virginia	N	N	N	3,501	77.1	23.7
Frederick County, Virginia	N	N	N	N	N	N
Hanover County, Virginia	N	N	N	1,729	88.4	32.6
Henrico County, Virginia	3,691	92.5	54.7	10,028	62.1	27.4
James City County, Virginia	N	N	N	N	N	N
Loudoun County, Virginia	6,842	95.6	44.4	31,690	74.6	34.8
Montgomery County, Virginia	N	N	N	N	N	N
Prince William County, Virginia	11,022	94.5	51.7	61,401	64.8	15.9
Roanoke County, Virginia	N	N	N	N	N	N
Rockingham County, Virginia	N	N	N	2,354	59.0	2.3
Spotsylvania County, Virginia	1,966	94.4	28.8	7,137	82.2	30.8
Stafford County, Virginia	N	N	N	9,945	78.6	17.3
York County, Virginia	N	N	N	1,815	84.4	38.5
Alexandria city, Virginia	4,361	82.1	53.5	16,947	68.0	24.6
Chesapeake city, Virginia	4,307	98.3	45.4	7,711	85.6	36.5
Hampton city, Virginia	N	N	N	4,229	83.6	25.9
Lynchburg city, Virginia	N	N	N	N	N	N
Newport News city, Virginia	3,356	99.0	29.8	8,438	73.8	15.1
Norfolk city, Virginia	3,934	90.6	24.3	9,176	80.0	25.0
Portsmouth city, Virginia	N	N	N	N	N	N
Richmond city, Virginia	4,274	77.7	34.4	7,337	51.6	12.0
Roanoke city, Virginia	N	N	N	3,733	62.9	2.5
Suffolk city, Virginia	N	N	N	2,281	84.5	34.5
Virginia Beach city, Virginia	8,916	95.6	27.0	20,863	84.7	29.8
WASHINGTON						
Benton County, Washington	2,496	85.9	14.6	20,509	64.3	12.2
Chelan County, Washington	N	N	N	9,452	39.4	6.8
Clallam County, Washington	N	N	N	2,688	96.1	10.7

N = Data for this geographic area cannot be displayed because the number of sample cases is too small.

Table C-2. Educational Attainment of the Population, by Selected Counties, 2017—*Continued*

(Number; percent; dollars.)

| | Educational attainment by race/ethnicity, 25 years and over | | | | | | | | |
| | Asian alone | | | Native Hawaiian or Other Pacific Islander alone | | | Some other race alone | | |
State/County	Total	High school graduate or more (percent)	Bachelor's degree or more (percent)	Total	High school graduate or more (percent)	Bachelor's degree or more (percent)	Total	High school graduate or more (percent)	Bachelor's degree or more (percent)
WASHINGTON—(*Continued*)									
Clark County, Washington	16,334	93.6	46.8	2,654	100.0	37.3	4,611	67.4	10.1
Cowlitz County, Washington	N	N	N	N	N	N	N	N	N
Franklin County, Washington	N	N	N	N	N	N	9,408	43.1	0.0
Grant County, Washington	N	N	N	N	N	N	13,240	34.7	5.0
Grays Harbor County, Washington	N	N	N	N	N	N	N	N	N
Island County, Washington	3,142	82.0	19.7	N	N	N	N	N	N
King County, Washington	279,761	88.2	58.5	9,733	90.6	19.6	59,984	58.9	14.2
Kitsap County, Washington	10,520	87.1	34.8	N	N	N	2,303	73.7	21.2
Lewis County, Washington	N	N	N	N	N	N	N	N	N
Pierce County, Washington	39,880	86.1	30.7	8,461	93.8	5.3	13,372	58.8	14.0
Skagit County, Washington	1,816	95.1	34.4	N	N	N	6,175	53.4	7.3
Snohomish County, Washington	61,999	91.2	48.6	N	N	N	13,945	64.3	13.1
Spokane County, Washington	8,217	73.0	39.3	N	N	N	3,463	93.1	21.3
Thurston County, Washington	10,441	91.2	36.2	N	N	N	2,805	69.1	23.7
Whatcom County, Washington	6,040	79.9	33.2	N	N	N	2,523	68.3	10.3
Yakima County, Washington	N	N	N	N	N	N	18,352	46.5	10.0
WEST VIRGINIA									
Berkeley County, West Virginia	N	N	N	N	N	N	N	N	N
Cabell County, West Virginia	N	N	N	N	N	N	N	N	N
Harrison County, West Virginia	N	N	N	N	N	N	N	N	N
Kanawha County, West Virginia	N	N	N	N	N	N	N	N	N
Monongalia County, West Virginia	2,201	94.8	69.8	N	N	N	N	N	N
Raleigh County, West Virginia	N	N	N	N	N	N	N	N	N
Wood County, West Virginia	N	N	N	N	N	N	N	N	N
WISCONSIN									
Brown County, Wisconsin	5,277	90.5	65.1	N	N	N	5,510	44.1	4.0
Dane County, Wisconsin	18,257	95.0	70.2	N	N	N	5,226	69.0	32.8
Dodge County, Wisconsin	N	N	N	N	N	N	N	N	N
Eau Claire County, Wisconsin	N	N	N	N	N	N	N	N	N
Fond du Lac County, Wisconsin	N	N	N	N	N	N	N	N	N
Jefferson County, Wisconsin	N	N	N	N	N	N	N	N	N
Kenosha County, Wisconsin	N	N	N	N	N	N	2,933	69.6	11.7
La Crosse County, Wisconsin	3,263	68.4	6.8	N	N	N	N	N	N
Manitowoc County, Wisconsin	N	N	N	N	N	N	N	N	N
Marathon County, Wisconsin	3,941	72.9	31.6	N	N	N	N	N	N
Milwaukee County, Wisconsin	25,219	77.4	41.4	N	N	N	31,881	65.0	7.2
Outagamie County, Wisconsin	3,927	80.4	38.3	N	N	N	N	N	N
Ozaukee County, Wisconsin	N	N	N	N	N	N	N	N	N
Portage County, Wisconsin	N	N	N	N	N	N	N	N	N
Racine County, Wisconsin	N	N	N	N	N	N	N	N	N
Rock County, Wisconsin	N	N	N	N	N	N	2,866	49.4	0.2
St. Croix County, Wisconsin	N	N	N	N	N	N	N	N	N
Sheboygan County, Wisconsin	3,210	77.4	18.9	N	N	N	1,317	79.7	10.5
Walworth County, Wisconsin	N	N	N	N	N	N	N	N	N
Washington County, Wisconsin	N	N	N	N	N	N	N	N	N
Waukesha County, Wisconsin	8,981	96.0	77.2	N	N	N	N	N	N
Winnebago County, Wisconsin	2,388	93.7	51.3	N	N	N	N	N	N
Wood County, Wisconsin	N	N	N	N	N	N	N	N	N
WYOMING									
Laramie County, Wyoming	N	N	N	N	N	N	N	N	N
Natrona County, Wyoming	N	N	N	N	N	N	N	N	N

N = Data for this geographic area cannot be displayed because the number of sample cases is too small.

Table C-2. Educational Attainment of the Population, by Selected Counties, 2017—*Continued*

(Number; percent; dollars.)

State/County	Median earnings in the past 12 months (2017 inflation-adjusted dollars)					
	Two or more races			Hispanic or Latino (of any race)		
	Total	High school graduate or more (percent)	Bachelor's degree or more (percent)	Total	High school graduate or more (percent)	Bachelor's degree or more (percent)
WASHINGTON—(*Continued*)						
Clark County, Washington	9,566	96.0	37.0	21,830	71.3	19.6
Cowlitz County, Washington	N	N	N	4,850	87.1	16.9
Franklin County, Washington	N	N	N	23,431	55.6	6.2
Grant County, Washington	N	N	N	18,529	43.0	5.1
Grays Harbor County, Washington	N	N	N	3,765	56.5	5.5
Island County, Washington	2,238	95.6	26.1	3,409	97.4	29.5
King County, Washington	62,526	95.2	45.6	118,659	69.9	23.9
Kitsap County, Washington	6,723	93.3	26.1	10,837	82.3	19.0
Lewis County, Washington	2,645	87.1	20.8	N	N	N
Pierce County, Washington	28,282	91.9	20.4	47,443	75.2	13.8
Skagit County, Washington	1,668	97.1	37.8	10,786	58.4	9.2
Snohomish County, Washington	22,080	90.5	24.9	42,070	73.8	18.9
Spokane County, Washington	9,870	90.6	27.3	14,390	88.9	28.1
Thurston County, Washington	9,750	91.9	33.8	12,971	85.2	34.0
Whatcom County, Washington	4,346	94.6	50.5	9,717	75.4	21.9
Yakima County, Washington	3,739	79.5	21.0	59,577	48.9	6.2
WEST VIRGINIA						
Berkeley County, West Virginia	N	N	N	2,630	61.8	30.4
Cabell County, West Virginia	N	N	N	N	N	N
Harrison County, West Virginia	N	N	N	N	N	N
Kanawha County, West Virginia	N	N	N	N	N	N
Monongalia County, West Virginia	N	N	N	N	N	N
Raleigh County, West Virginia	N	N	N	N	N	N
Wood County, West Virginia	N	N	N	N	N	N
WISCONSIN						
Brown County, Wisconsin	2,091	84.3	22.4	10,457	46.7	11.0
Dane County, Wisconsin	5,248	98.0	58.0	16,140	76.1	27.7
Dodge County, Wisconsin	N	N	N	2,002	66.6	7.6
Eau Claire County, Wisconsin	N	N	N	N	N	N
Fond du Lac County, Wisconsin	N	N	N	2,741	57.8	11.5
Jefferson County, Wisconsin	N	N	N	3,184	60.4	8.1
Kenosha County, Wisconsin	2,338	88.5	27.1	11,116	73.6	11.0
La Crosse County, Wisconsin	N	N	N	N	N	N
Manitowoc County, Wisconsin	N	N	N	N	N	N
Marathon County, Wisconsin	N	N	N	2,111	58.0	6.1
Milwaukee County, Wisconsin	13,750	93.2	31.0	74,946	69.3	11.7
Outagamie County, Wisconsin	N	N	N	3,784	80.4	7.8
Ozaukee County, Wisconsin	N	N	N	1,609	90.3	40.9
Portage County, Wisconsin	N	N	N	N	N	N
Racine County, Wisconsin	N	N	N	12,693	75.2	18.4
Rock County, Wisconsin	N	N	N	6,939	64.3	7.2
St. Croix County, Wisconsin	N	N	N	N	N	N
Sheboygan County, Wisconsin	N	N	N	3,455	74.6	9.3
Walworth County, Wisconsin	N	N	N	5,609	52.1	8.5
Washington County, Wisconsin	N	N	N	N	N	N
Waukesha County, Wisconsin	2,642	99.6	58.8	10,143	79.6	27.0
Winnebago County, Wisconsin	N	N	N	3,103	82.5	12.1
Wood County, Wisconsin	N	N	N	N	N	N
WYOMING						
Laramie County, Wyoming	N	N	N	8,276	69.5	8.3
Natrona County, Wyoming	N	N	N	3,853	79.6	16.1

N = Data for this geographic area cannot be displayed because the number of sample cases is too small.

Table C-2. Educational Attainment of the Population, by Selected Counties, 2017—*Continued*

(Number; percent; dollars.)

State/County	Median earnings in the past 12 months (2017 inflation-adjusted dollars)					
	Population 25 years and over with earnings					
	Total	Less than high school graduate	High school graduate (includes equivalency)	Some college or associate's degree	Bachelor's degree	Graduate or professional degree
ALABAMA						
Baldwin County, Alabama	36,780	22,182	30,709	32,171	47,534	54,748
Calhoun County, Alabama	32,123	25,792	31,841	30,691	40,228	57,352
Cullman County, Alabama	33,388	31,565	27,346	34,444	42,255	55,767
DeKalb County, Alabama	33,075	26,287	27,399	38,222	45,502	50,712
Elmore County, Alabama	42,300	21,831	31,236	45,086	59,016	57,233
Etowah County, Alabama	31,866	18,706	24,756	35,622	40,499	49,086
Houston County, Alabama	32,061	20,858	28,015	32,071	43,620	60,808
Jefferson County, Alabama	36,903	19,754	29,148	31,701	48,801	62,051
Lauderdale County, Alabama	32,391	24,292	31,991	28,323	42,021	55,351
Lee County, Alabama	35,529	27,263	29,917	29,931	40,650	54,081
Limestone County, Alabama	34,780	20,091	27,493	30,129	53,813	65,052
Madison County, Alabama	41,339	22,152	28,521	31,183	61,748	81,095
Marshall County, Alabama	32,482	21,168	29,938	34,082	40,617	61,951
Mobile County, Alabama	35,815	19,152	30,843	31,927	48,316	52,612
Montgomery County, Alabama	31,860	15,932	23,739	30,473	42,477	61,379
Morgan County, Alabama	31,711	17,152	22,137	35,144	41,730	75,379
St. Clair County, Alabama	37,401	29,466	30,782	37,769	46,030	59,173
Shelby County, Alabama	47,478	27,770	36,889	40,429	55,842	57,529
Talladega County, Alabama	31,712	20,919	30,442	30,315	52,302	54,938
Tuscaloosa County, Alabama	40,004	30,033	30,614	32,238	51,095	55,975
Walker County, Alabama	32,469	20,855	31,223	36,436	48,289	67,604
ALASKA						
Anchorage Municipality, Alaska	47,168	27,221	36,498	42,868	60,905	77,136
Fairbanks North Star Borough, Alaska	48,055	35,455	42,208	46,471	47,755	77,235
Matanuska-Susitna Borough, Alaska	42,430	21,484	42,359	39,175	60,833	59,439
ARIZONA						
Apache County, Arizona	30,616	15,601	25,539	33,670	49,770	41,870
Cochise County, Arizona	31,985	16,669	23,568	31,074	53,949	56,194
Coconino County, Arizona	35,516	20,073	29,112	31,765	40,582	52,990
Maricopa County, Arizona	39,934	23,159	30,409	37,485	54,818	69,689
Mohave County, Arizona	29,879	15,652	23,895	32,174	41,675	69,428
Navajo County, Arizona	29,024	15,261	24,162	28,318	46,702	52,116
Pima County, Arizona	34,196	20,620	24,566	32,070	44,156	61,828
Pinal County, Arizona	35,539	22,682	31,129	36,965	42,349	51,789
Yavapai County, Arizona	32,030	26,056	28,442	31,577	36,042	51,784
Yuma County, Arizona	30,673	19,029	25,222	35,768	36,991	60,203
ARKANSAS						
Benton County, Arkansas	41,007	24,432	33,229	35,954	61,314	71,868
Craighead County, Arkansas	34,827	23,131	26,882	31,701	43,566	65,348
Faulkner County, Arkansas	37,581	18,481	29,007	33,950	46,483	55,972
Garland County, Arkansas	32,187	26,538	28,715	31,051	37,856	57,392
Jefferson County, Arkansas	31,494	22,518	25,957	33,024	47,250	43,642
Lonoke County, Arkansas	36,682	33,131	28,672	35,695	52,515	70,405
Pulaski County, Arkansas	37,078	24,608	31,179	33,493	46,360	66,224
Saline County, Arkansas	41,935	25,492	32,489	41,267	50,456	65,978
Sebastian County, Arkansas	32,144	23,405	26,332	32,613	48,586	61,603
Washington County, Arkansas	34,533	26,245	27,402	34,310	45,114	61,207
White County, Arkansas	36,979	18,889	30,871	34,917	45,084	50,419
CALIFORNIA						
Alameda County, California	52,487	26,824	37,144	46,310	71,203	97,388
Butte County, California	33,761	26,273	24,886	26,795	51,656	66,575
Contra Costa County, California	51,711	26,270	35,235	41,982	74,637	95,745
El Dorado County, California	48,503	30,481	27,615	41,867	72,380	80,630
Fresno County, California	31,786	18,447	26,963	32,676	49,552	81,176
Humboldt County, California	33,519	28,482	28,729	34,135	31,597	60,042
Imperial County, California	31,490	17,475	27,484	35,837	41,576	61,193
Kern County, California	31,683	20,738	29,789	34,094	62,037	80,026
Kings County, California	31,495	21,110	28,111	36,702	52,142	64,654
Lake County, California	27,068	19,574	26,971	23,852	53,517	50,807
Los Angeles County, California	36,954	21,901	28,882	36,535	54,442	77,200
Madera County, California	26,771	16,882	28,605	29,565	50,868	61,166
Marin County, California	61,537	23,385	29,532	41,855	80,024	95,639
Mendocino County, California	30,131	22,650	27,062	30,267	36,884	46,179
Merced County, California	30,346	23,992	29,224	31,843	57,794	62,376
Monterey County, California	31,711	21,492	30,906	35,221	60,923	75,708

Table C-2. Educational Attainment of the Population, by Selected Counties, 2017—*Continued*

(Number; percent; dollars.)

State/County	Median earnings in the past 12 months (2017 inflation-adjusted dollars)					
	Population 25 years and over with earnings					
	Total	Less than high school graduate	High school graduate (includes equivalency)	Some college or associate's degree	Bachelor's degree	Graduate or professional degree
CALIFORNIA—(*Continued*)						
Napa County, California	43,928	27,047	27,934	44,360	63,811	67,339
Nevada County, California	40,427	26,739	25,249	35,081	57,550	67,892
Orange County, California	42,884	23,328	31,311	40,499	61,202	87,277
Placer County, California	51,524	28,482	40,709	42,343	68,509	79,545
Riverside County, California	36,321	25,340	30,829	36,943	55,461	80,064
Sacramento County, California	40,907	24,631	30,517	38,874	55,132	75,650
San Bernardino County, California	36,684	23,642	30,663	36,977	53,264	75,241
San Diego County, California	42,178	22,499	31,122	38,484	57,697	81,872
San Francisco County, California	65,451	21,977	30,473	40,902	81,683	102,424
San Joaquin County, California	37,315	25,365	32,260	40,595	57,781	80,086
San Luis Obispo County, California	44,314	34,663	31,625	40,209	52,174	71,371
San Mateo County, California	59,997	26,619	34,052	42,788	75,675	108,560
Santa Barbara County, California	38,759	22,153	32,955	36,779	60,221	81,466
Santa Clara County, California	60,812	27,268	34,527	45,771	81,702	117,292
Santa Cruz County, California	45,583	23,068	30,240	38,361	64,480	72,094
Shasta County, California	34,181	15,222	30,616	31,967	49,958	61,372
Solano County, California	43,044	25,814	36,915	42,480	60,737	80,312
Sonoma County, California	42,386	28,098	34,257	40,972	54,012	70,102
Stanislaus County, California	35,731	25,789	31,543	35,320	60,400	80,035
Sutter County, California	34,629	21,612	30,132	37,150	66,120	76,577
Tulare County, California	30,318	20,067	29,053	33,946	53,516	80,925
Ventura County, California	41,828	24,257	32,248	41,224	59,798	85,173
Yolo County, California	41,643	24,119	33,029	38,340	57,034	80,959
Yuba County, California	41,123	23,849	41,475	39,370	50,442	64,397
COLORADO						
Adams County, Colorado	38,566	26,881	35,722	40,703	46,651	65,682
Arapahoe County, Colorado	44,767	24,354	35,597	40,564	53,222	67,499
Boulder County, Colorado	50,100	26,850	31,584	36,461	53,118	72,575
Broomfield County, Colorado	54,585	14,939	40,470	46,369	61,713	71,691
Denver County, Colorado	46,962	25,847	31,240	37,367	55,687	70,657
Douglas County, Colorado	62,410	25,804	44,561	48,786	72,207	85,478
El Paso County, Colorado	40,758	20,187	28,919	36,351	51,524	65,477
Jefferson County, Colorado	47,109	30,273	36,020	40,968	55,277	71,787
Larimer County, Colorado	42,261	35,484	32,023	35,704	47,427	66,122
Mesa County, Colorado	35,939	23,649	31,216	33,417	45,359	51,254
Pueblo County, Colorado	31,702	16,256	27,302	30,297	43,619	53,060
Weld County, Colorado	41,089	26,975	35,738	40,524	51,329	65,809
CONNECTICUT						
Fairfield County, Connecticut	50,395	25,363	31,350	41,280	71,078	93,162
Hartford County, Connecticut	48,082	22,298	35,030	42,031	61,562	78,751
Litchfield County, Connecticut	46,412	31,399	36,287	45,379	51,952	65,875
Middlesex County, Connecticut	52,002	26,785	34,389	45,508	66,753	85,036
New Haven County, Connecticut	47,660	25,324	35,617	42,518	56,785	74,058
New London County, Connecticut	45,849	25,389	33,278	41,707	59,821	78,707
Tolland County, Connecticut	51,242	24,964	37,518	47,491	62,040	75,461
Windham County, Connecticut	42,044	30,515	38,050	40,975	54,223	52,154
DELAWARE						
Kent County, Delaware	36,660	26,733	31,766	32,312	46,236	60,792
New Castle County, Delaware	47,680	26,770	35,516	38,603	62,448	78,601
Sussex County, Delaware	36,658	25,177	30,021	35,851	44,207	61,763
DISTRICT OF COLUMBIA						
District of Columbia, District of Columbia	61,641	26,686	30,469	41,297	65,056	91,724
FLORIDA						
Alachua County, Florida	36,177	27,060	25,795	34,124	41,860	50,528
Bay County, Florida	33,336	21,365	28,122	31,519	44,687	50,922
Brevard County, Florida	35,137	26,061	26,904	31,201	50,976	62,865
Broward County, Florida	36,042	21,851	27,298	34,614	46,577	62,681
Charlotte County, Florida	30,899	21,234	29,717	30,448	36,413	45,688
Citrus County, Florida	28,652	21,447	26,779	30,698	35,199	51,042
Clay County, Florida	36,385	20,276	31,402	37,363	47,234	59,851
Collier County, Florida	31,855	18,228	30,435	31,192	44,456	60,226
Columbia County, Florida	30,614	25,709	26,749	28,426	41,609	59,955
Duval County, Florida	36,201	24,533	28,452	34,508	47,079	60,479
Escambia County, Florida	32,482	20,640	26,355	31,827	40,954	64,260

Table C-2. Educational Attainment of the Population, by Selected Counties, 2017—*Continued*

(Number; percent; dollars.)

| State/County | Median earnings in the past 12 months (2017 inflation-adjusted dollars) | | | | | |
| | Population 25 years and over with earnings | | | | | |
	Total	Less than high school graduate	High school graduate (includes equivalency)	Some college or associate's degree	Bachelor's degree	Graduate or professional degree
FLORIDA—(*Continued*)						
Flagler County, Florida........................	30,476	22,624	29,739	29,607	35,822	31,648
Hernando County, Florida....................	30,845	24,630	26,265	30,373	41,316	53,978
Highlands County, Florida...................	25,518	20,384	21,265	26,808	40,695	66,046
Hillsborough County, Florida...............	37,008	20,099	26,293	36,230	51,116	66,496
Indian River County, Florida...............	30,265	23,528	27,934	27,104	36,335	60,474
Lake County, Florida..........................	32,871	27,890	29,000	30,612	42,828	51,642
Lee County, Florida	31,793	21,593	27,568	32,388	44,284	51,222
Leon County, Florida..........................	38,103	16,902	26,363	32,105	44,155	61,472
Manatee County, Florida.....................	34,036	28,976	25,947	35,507	45,335	56,147
Marion County, Florida.......................	31,016	22,085	25,674	30,379	41,417	51,034
Martin County, Florida........................	36,333	25,534	25,648	35,100	48,263	52,178
Miami-Dade County, Florida................	30,960	21,569	24,630	31,269	41,302	58,283
Monroe County, Florida......................	36,647	23,569	35,093	37,318	45,558	42,149
Nassau County, Florida......................	37,479	36,571	30,557	36,492	52,895	71,756
Okaloosa County, Florida....................	35,686	17,144	26,962	36,334	42,584	80,192
Orange County, Florida.......................	32,406	20,200	24,889	30,120	45,273	62,360
Osceola County, Florida......................	27,245	22,073	25,624	26,400	36,660	55,900
Palm Beach County, Florida	36,515	21,171	27,196	35,870	50,543	65,769
Pasco County, Florida........................	36,384	21,387	30,143	35,837	51,103	63,376
Pinellas County, Florida......................	35,646	22,059	28,019	32,977	48,411	62,330
Polk County, Florida...........................	31,490	23,066	26,870	31,536	45,286	50,573
Putnam County, Florida......................	27,484	21,590	28,287	26,710	35,491	46,728
St. Johns County, Florida...................	44,344	24,405	29,895	37,127	53,232	76,503
St. Lucie County, Florida	31,332	21,794	28,141	34,605	41,452	51,181
Santa Rosa County, Florida................	36,721	15,950	30,221	34,078	47,099	63,292
Sarasota County, Florida....................	35,203	24,311	29,564	32,945	48,507	55,150
Seminole County, Florida....................	40,864	21,691	26,514	34,481	51,546	71,961
Sumter County, Florida......................	25,296	14,879	22,546	24,248	38,497	58,859
Volusia County, Florida.......................	32,679	22,462	29,602	32,170	41,423	60,731
Walton County, Florida.......................	32,323	22,200	24,523	30,460	55,702	60,203
GEORGIA						
Barrow County, Georgia	33,602	32,551	27,803	34,524	41,058	55,074
Bartow County, Georgia	34,993	31,345	29,387	33,189	50,123	56,689
Bibb County, Georgia	31,911	21,463	27,790	29,434	44,089	67,035
Bulloch County, Georgia.....................	31,001	13,639	27,461	30,010	44,783	52,195
Carroll County, Georgia......................	36,561	21,705	32,570	38,693	41,194	50,850
Catoosa County, Georgia....................	37,306	20,021	31,805	39,836	38,507	65,558
Chatham County, Georgia...................	35,995	20,857	27,307	33,079	46,863	60,600
Cherokee County, Georgia..................	46,746	23,986	32,831	41,428	61,343	61,873
Clarke County, Georgia......................	32,205	23,412	23,584	31,238	39,245	52,184
Clayton County, Georgia.....................	30,627	21,861	28,113	31,179	40,164	47,160
Cobb County, Georgia........................	46,214	22,482	31,189	37,497	60,721	76,935
Columbia County, Georgia..................	41,290	23,671	29,664	35,288	61,024	71,380
Coweta County, Georgia.....................	42,132	17,989	36,134	39,119	59,685	65,326
DeKalb County, Georgia.....................	40,308	20,189	25,968	33,140	52,264	71,201
Dougherty County, Georgia.................	30,035	16,128	27,559	22,262	42,279	50,108
Douglas County, Georgia....................	37,477	28,065	30,556	35,971	49,531	70,156
Fayette County, Georgia	50,593	22,087	33,584	38,491	57,349	70,889
Floyd County, Georgia........................	31,736	21,240	29,264	36,503	45,409	60,288
Forsyth County, Georgia.....................	60,628	26,104	35,046	48,265	77,307	86,552
Fulton County, Georgia.......................	45,944	19,482	26,411	36,250	61,542	81,192
Glynn County, Georgia.......................	35,765	25,743	25,546	31,952	45,068	64,586
Gwinnett County, Georgia	38,298	25,985	29,401	37,351	52,357	61,515
Hall County, Georgia	34,319	21,164	29,140	35,131	51,256	65,364
Henry County, Georgia.......................	40,335	22,453	35,046	39,366	45,920	61,138
Houston County, Georgia...................	35,697	22,712	26,992	35,530	45,986	65,876
Jackson County, Georgia....................	40,136	25,485	32,332	42,269	45,998	53,615
Lowndes County, Georgia...................	37,368	18,551	26,851	36,352	41,951	54,856
Muscogee County, Georgia	32,437	21,284	22,186	33,843	43,650	58,596
Newton County, Georgia.....................	36,622	22,361	36,102	31,872	34,944	50,152
Paulding County, Georgia...................	41,383	30,005	33,935	37,677	57,826	64,328
Richmond County, Georgia.................	26,401	17,607	21,515	26,888	35,517	60,959
Rockdale County, Georgia..................	41,621	34,516	30,457	38,252	57,033	59,125
Spalding County, Georgia...................	33,347	22,474	25,723	36,211	45,436	52,311
Troup County, Georgia.......................	30,972	16,142	26,904	30,928	43,466	61,112
Walker County, Georgia......................	34,486	23,772	32,892	35,329	32,937	56,121
Walton County, Georgia	37,368	25,833	30,911	41,617	47,155	48,279
Whitfield County, Georgia	32,227	29,829	30,613	32,580	47,301	62,139

Table C-2. Educational Attainment of the Population, by Selected Counties, 2017—*Continued*

(Number; percent; dollars.)

State/County	Median earnings in the past 12 months (2017 inflation-adjusted dollars)					
	Population 25 years and over with earnings					
	Total	Less than high school graduate	High school graduate (includes equivalency)	Some college or associate's degree	Bachelor's degree	Graduate or professional degree
HAWAII						
Hawaii County, Hawaii	35,881	25,590	31,284	35,209	40,861	57,240
Honolulu County, Hawaii	42,298	26,985	32,337	40,355	51,799	71,638
Kauai County, Hawaii	40,927	27,214	40,093	41,207	46,861	47,602
Maui County, Hawaii	41,128	31,534	36,565	41,144	47,392	61,456
IDAHO						
Ada County, Idaho	38,289	21,837	31,479	32,155	50,346	65,066
Bannock County, Idaho	31,391	14,491	27,725	26,282	41,831	50,167
Bonneville County, Idaho	32,377	22,441	30,394	27,734	41,033	88,663
Canyon County, Idaho	28,210	22,291	22,195	28,652	42,823	45,326
Kootenai County, Idaho	35,371	27,463	31,044	32,237	43,808	61,062
Twin Falls County, Idaho	31,377	25,765	26,529	33,405	34,959	75,201
ILLINOIS						
Adams County, Illinois	36,289	23,799	32,562	31,828	42,094	60,090
Champaign County, Illinois	39,608	18,406	31,183	31,365	42,159	57,615
Cook County, Illinois	41,710	25,215	30,110	36,124	56,953	75,179
DeKalb County, Illinois	37,719	25,925	34,335	34,979	49,296	54,126
DuPage County, Illinois	51,970	25,736	35,772	42,240	61,436	85,523
Kane County, Illinois	42,361	25,726	35,478	40,835	65,922	77,273
Kankakee County, Illinois	40,382	20,996	40,664	37,358	44,899	58,466
Kendall County, Illinois	45,367	25,440	36,685	42,659	64,075	75,474
Lake County, Illinois	47,241	25,435	31,120	40,857	67,892	90,161
LaSalle County, Illinois	36,861	19,308	33,636	34,629	51,155	60,341
McHenry County, Illinois	47,609	26,902	36,964	42,186	64,355	80,004
McLean County, Illinois	50,274	25,849	31,764	40,075	66,628	64,980
Macon County, Illinois	36,569	15,662	26,200	36,048	58,645	54,174
Madison County, Illinois	40,937	20,863	31,127	36,141	50,375	65,589
Peoria County, Illinois	39,143	27,479	26,434	31,900	50,034	69,877
Rock Island County, Illinois	34,253	24,669	30,247	30,828	50,442	62,052
St. Clair County, Illinois	36,441	21,182	28,472	35,081	50,317	63,188
Sangamon County, Illinois	42,466	24,919	33,686	37,498	59,199	70,108
Tazewell County, Illinois	39,919	14,724	32,536	34,091	57,080	63,355
Vermilion County, Illinois	32,360	17,269	30,755	30,089	51,681	44,583
Will County, Illinois	48,794	27,175	35,219	42,886	61,299	80,447
Williamson County, Illinois	34,600	11,031	24,950	34,702	44,654	60,556
Winnebago County, Illinois	37,013	25,760	31,730	36,681	51,414	56,591
INDIANA						
Allen County, Indiana	36,318	24,587	31,838	34,914	47,537	56,810
Bartholomew County, Indiana	38,460	30,187	30,595	35,831	51,536	77,311
Boone County, Indiana	50,344	22,290	37,865	42,059	65,095	76,394
Clark County, Indiana	34,754	24,696	30,666	35,434	41,955	52,500
Delaware County, Indiana	35,660	16,218	29,555	35,393	41,845	58,696
Elkhart County, Indiana	38,430	30,586	36,401	36,653	46,906	62,492
Floyd County, Indiana	39,660	17,135	33,118	39,246	49,553	65,246
Grant County, Indiana	35,045	12,274	31,937	30,378	43,325	52,039
Hamilton County, Indiana	56,909	19,953	35,176	40,255	66,966	81,394
Hancock County, Indiana	41,686	30,545	37,440	40,492	52,377	51,557
Hendricks County, Indiana	45,763	21,002	36,705	38,600	60,435	73,894
Howard County, Indiana	32,299	17,965	25,387	34,662	45,219	61,478
Johnson County, Indiana	48,121	22,045	40,557	44,255	57,061	72,538
Kosciusko County, Indiana	37,167	30,505	35,550	37,342	41,086	61,444
Lake County, Indiana	40,343	27,001	32,751	39,312	49,530	60,482
LaPorte County, Indiana	32,825	22,595	31,023	30,858	46,884	62,053
Madison County, Indiana	32,421	14,329	28,262	31,464	43,366	54,618
Marion County, Indiana	35,853	22,257	27,109	33,202	47,314	61,847
Monroe County, Indiana	36,070	14,394	31,232	32,333	38,870	60,515
Morgan County, Indiana	39,130	22,037	36,335	40,039	63,054	53,592
Porter County, Indiana	45,884	26,321	37,219	37,300	57,000	62,011
St. Joseph County, Indiana	35,889	22,456	29,308	34,141	45,727	61,317
Tippecanoe County, Indiana	37,587	21,824	30,004	31,874	50,170	66,456
Vanderburgh County, Indiana	36,950	16,652	27,821	35,917	51,056	61,881
Vigo County, Indiana	32,096	21,556	26,314	33,392	39,713	70,590
Wayne County, Indiana	31,434	18,100	26,989	35,218	37,486	51,958
IOWA						
Black Hawk County, Iowa	35,550	26,404	34,584	28,281	45,273	61,244
Dallas County, Iowa	59,420	27,778	37,332	47,915	80,210	90,671

Table C-2. Educational Attainment of the Population, by Selected Counties, 2017—*Continued*

(Number; percent; dollars.)

State/County	Median earnings in the past 12 months (2017 inflation-adjusted dollars)					
	Population 25 years and over with earnings					
	Total	Less than high school graduate	High school graduate (includes equivalency)	Some college or associate's degree	Bachelor's degree	Graduate or professional degree
IOWA—*(Continued)*						
Dubuque County, Iowa	40,898	33,073	32,016	35,544	50,221	60,624
Johnson County, Iowa	45,619	18,022	29,650	37,659	48,107	62,846
Linn County, Iowa	40,262	25,211	31,169	37,720	50,895	70,678
Polk County, Iowa	41,938	26,876	32,087	39,072	56,915	70,372
Pottawattamie County, Iowa	40,384	32,143	34,065	39,667	52,389	67,290
Scott County, Iowa	40,757	22,332	31,069	35,447	51,951	65,067
Story County, Iowa	42,121	31,622	25,008	40,208	45,863	72,026
Woodbury County, Iowa	37,405	29,950	29,943	36,018	49,873	66,066
KANSAS						
Butler County, Kansas	46,054	27,263	40,286	41,562	50,804	59,889
Douglas County, Kansas	37,355	15,096	30,528	31,966	44,838	60,092
Johnson County, Kansas	50,487	27,048	33,621	37,343	60,872	69,068
Leavenworth County, Kansas	41,018	27,750	35,899	36,185	46,672	81,268
Riley County, Kansas	36,874	21,203	22,744	32,477	45,701	54,475
Sedgwick County, Kansas	36,472	26,586	29,120	31,765	46,228	63,029
Shawnee County, Kansas	40,860	32,173	27,315	39,996	45,657	60,808
Wyandotte County, Kansas	33,225	21,889	30,926	36,334	40,407	50,000
KENTUCKY						
Boone County, Kentucky	42,518	21,335	31,543	41,565	66,344	75,617
Bullitt County, Kentucky	41,424	19,631	40,178	41,527	45,646	61,256
Campbell County, Kentucky	42,245	24,234	30,888	41,526	52,168	61,292
Christian County, Kentucky	34,238	35,622	30,831	32,778	33,004	50,945
Daviess County, Kentucky	35,891	25,713	29,644	31,561	42,407	61,750
Fayette County, Kentucky	37,062	20,535	26,860	30,669	48,665	58,169
Hardin County, Kentucky	36,946	19,098	25,966	35,747	52,205	59,471
Jefferson County, Kentucky	38,121	23,300	30,680	34,564	47,598	63,284
Kenton County, Kentucky	40,271	28,467	30,374	37,636	52,051	61,183
McCracken County, Kentucky	36,180	15,873	27,408	35,631	45,104	69,649
Madison County, Kentucky	36,194	17,494	25,619	30,741	40,982	56,816
Oldham County, Kentucky	52,355	25,785	41,609	43,991	55,222	96,301
Warren County, Kentucky	34,658	23,569	29,608	31,198	47,471	53,773
LOUISIANA						
Ascension Parish, Louisiana	49,438	31,155	46,095	41,990	62,112	58,929
Bossier Parish, Louisiana	38,760	30,168	29,719	36,339	51,191	57,152
Caddo Parish, Louisiana	29,796	20,648	21,854	29,372	43,484	54,555
Calcasieu Parish, Louisiana	38,277	19,178	30,523	37,283	50,861	60,698
East Baton Rouge Parish, Louisiana	40,520	25,634	26,524	32,777	51,865	63,886
Iberia Parish, Louisiana	31,220	27,961	29,471	29,178	61,660	61,337
Jefferson Parish, Louisiana	36,166	22,458	30,411	35,817	47,480	61,009
Lafayette Parish, Louisiana	36,942	25,952	26,365	30,993	51,663	58,942
Lafourche Parish, Louisiana	40,556	27,309	36,793	35,643	50,147	63,281
Livingston Parish, Louisiana	41,494	15,088	33,388	48,546	55,904	45,088
Orleans Parish, Louisiana	32,258	19,397	21,354	26,550	45,071	60,945
Ouachita Parish, Louisiana	31,967	12,233	26,976	31,147	51,242	41,961
Rapides Parish, Louisiana	31,634	19,833	26,045	30,710	43,507	69,789
St. Landry Parish, Louisiana	28,237	12,597	23,925	28,086	38,329	51,839
St. Tammany Parish, Louisiana	41,526	23,378	31,224	36,646	55,451	70,692
Tangipahoa Parish, Louisiana	33,290	21,238	30,299	27,342	48,311	48,804
Terrebonne Parish, Louisiana	40,379	26,376	39,981	32,160	43,792	53,079
MAINE						
Androscoggin County, Maine	34,184	17,957	27,240	37,291	44,063	51,802
Aroostook County, Maine	33,383	16,218	28,284	35,665	37,645	52,158
Cumberland County, Maine	42,342	26,328	28,014	37,020	51,149	62,025
Kennebec County, Maine	36,060	21,518	30,449	34,360	39,951	56,765
Penobscot County, Maine	34,872	25,782	28,100	31,322	41,811	55,740
York County, Maine	40,771	28,611	34,213	39,134	47,204	63,356
MARYLAND						
Allegany County, Maryland	32,289	22,492	30,718	30,486	42,263	52,700
Anne Arundel County, Maryland	53,872	29,002	38,406	50,001	65,298	91,835
Baltimore County, Maryland	49,759	22,089	38,322	44,261	60,763	73,052
Calvert County, Maryland	57,422	21,700	41,028	51,673	82,377	85,512
Carroll County, Maryland	52,338	28,093	41,117	50,904	66,082	76,895
Cecil County, Maryland	49,989	19,896	42,118	45,676	62,294	70,137
Charles County, Maryland	60,774	26,902	41,052	57,968	75,938	88,637

Table C-2. Educational Attainment of the Population, by Selected Counties, 2017—*Continued*

(Number; percent; dollars.)

State/County	Median earnings in the past 12 months (2017 inflation-adjusted dollars)					
	Population 25 years and over with earnings					
	Total	Less than high school graduate	High school graduate (includes equivalency)	Some college or associate's degree	Bachelor's degree	Graduate or professional degree
MARYLAND—(*Continued*)						
Frederick County, Maryland	52,264	27,666	39,998	47,609	64,238	77,046
Harford County, Maryland	51,786	26,258	36,782	50,248	64,772	79,971
Howard County, Maryland	64,451	34,951	37,431	46,786	71,484	95,707
Montgomery County, Maryland	55,550	26,175	32,043	40,500	62,460	96,584
Prince George's County, Maryland	46,670	30,020	37,321	45,278	61,112	82,041
St. Mary's County, Maryland	52,358	28,561	40,640	48,816	72,288	95,342
Washington County, Maryland	40,998	25,677	31,548	40,172	63,179	71,745
Wicomico County, Maryland	36,153	21,262	26,570	31,927	46,457	65,220
Baltimore city, Maryland	39,144	23,832	28,398	33,961	52,717	67,759
MASSACHUSETTS						
Barnstable County, Massachusetts	41,172	37,194	31,337	37,196	48,636	63,377
Berkshire County, Massachusetts	36,943	21,322	32,312	32,004	46,955	56,688
Bristol County, Massachusetts	47,503	31,047	40,477	40,867	61,550	80,982
Essex County, Massachusetts	47,597	24,493	34,317	39,203	61,551	79,729
Franklin County, Massachusetts	40,090	40,490	31,849	36,089	42,033	55,194
Hampden County, Massachusetts	41,526	24,920	33,082	38,793	52,221	64,492
Hampshire County, Massachusetts	45,972	18,835	44,460	41,207	48,198	64,327
Middlesex County, Massachusetts	60,084	25,028	37,401	44,331	69,580	85,521
Norfolk County, Massachusetts	60,683	22,147	34,268	48,591	70,624	90,987
Plymouth County, Massachusetts	51,283	29,690	41,638	42,628	66,006	80,100
Suffolk County, Massachusetts	47,016	24,487	30,463	36,508	61,684	71,912
Worcester County, Massachusetts	47,364	26,119	37,337	41,776	59,217	76,347
MICHIGAN						
Allegan County, Michigan	40,773	31,051	32,840	40,466	53,135	55,905
Bay County, Michigan	32,062	25,784	28,961	31,705	41,024	52,023
Berrien County, Michigan	32,176	20,997	27,241	32,216	45,641	57,821
Calhoun County, Michigan	35,041	18,662	25,949	35,753	47,232	63,545
Clinton County, Michigan	41,771	16,875	33,586	37,214	54,452	71,717
Eaton County, Michigan	40,307	27,394	29,772	36,799	58,733	55,645
Genesee County, Michigan	32,388	19,185	25,670	31,424	48,468	67,173
Grand Traverse County, Michigan	35,829	37,652	27,381	33,216	45,922	52,351
Ingham County, Michigan	37,295	16,951	27,831	34,048	44,193	65,988
Isabella County, Michigan	33,071	20,801	23,211	30,728	40,467	59,230
Jackson County, Michigan	32,544	15,764	27,477	35,921	40,287	59,035
Kalamazoo County, Michigan	40,549	24,925	30,190	33,529	46,476	64,629
Kent County, Michigan	37,764	20,663	30,249	35,260	49,203	61,524
Lapeer County, Michigan	36,662	31,157	32,070	37,237	50,075	68,125
Lenawee County, Michigan	35,990	20,931	31,481	34,347	50,491	59,471
Livingston County, Michigan	50,663	35,247	37,012	42,339	61,305	78,529
Macomb County, Michigan	40,950	21,771	31,344	40,577	56,973	72,071
Marquette County, Michigan	31,733	21,941	26,842	31,283	33,968	52,830
Midland County, Michigan	41,286	13,620	28,955	31,183	59,332	101,125
Monroe County, Michigan	40,726	20,914	33,461	40,876	58,196	75,835
Muskegon County, Michigan	34,816	21,112	27,711	34,363	47,020	59,438
Oakland County, Michigan	51,478	23,597	31,268	37,940	63,262	84,535
Ottawa County, Michigan	39,839	30,763	33,623	35,097	50,493	70,197
Saginaw County, Michigan	31,653	18,540	25,792	30,574	49,852	62,305
St. Clair County, Michigan	37,286	26,973	32,409	36,686	48,105	70,237
Shiawassee County, Michigan	36,257	26,075	32,041	38,591	38,975	47,695
Van Buren County, Michigan	31,459	22,023	25,010	31,583	42,009	65,174
Washtenaw County, Michigan	46,662	22,028	30,476	34,383	51,296	68,957
Wayne County, Michigan	35,668	21,528	28,203	32,406	51,311	71,010
MINNESOTA						
Anoka County, Minnesota	45,982	25,012	36,759	42,179	61,544	78,797
Blue Earth County, Minnesota	39,950	23,442	33,596	33,450	45,947	63,125
Carver County, Minnesota	53,130	32,389	36,470	47,645	66,938	73,777
Dakota County, Minnesota	50,312	22,302	36,345	43,989	63,358	80,050
Hennepin County, Minnesota	49,587	23,044	30,007	40,477	60,734	76,528
Olmsted County, Minnesota	49,775	21,285	30,943	40,850	58,394	71,616
Ramsey County, Minnesota	40,639	24,488	29,331	35,025	49,231	70,084
Rice County, Minnesota	39,261	21,454	31,275	37,869	51,892	68,878
St. Louis County, Minnesota	39,791	16,393	27,127	40,179	46,557	65,580
Scott County, Minnesota	53,705	28,438	39,665	48,658	73,518	71,853
Sherburne County, Minnesota	49,091	34,394	38,822	45,123	65,030	65,481
Stearns County, Minnesota	40,575	25,811	32,159	35,080	51,085	69,735
Washington County, Minnesota	52,913	31,614	35,377	44,573	70,274	82,473
Wright County, Minnesota	47,086	45,028	39,654	45,180	60,602	72,480

Table C-2. Educational Attainment of the Population, by Selected Counties, 2017—*Continued*

(Number; percent; dollars.)

State/County	Median earnings in the past 12 months (2017 inflation-adjusted dollars)					
	Population 25 years and over with earnings					
	Total	Less than high school graduate	High school graduate (includes equivalency)	Some college or associate's degree	Bachelor's degree	Graduate or professional degree
MISSISSIPPI						
DeSoto County, Mississippi	40,869	25,615	32,113	39,246	60,440	65,345
Forrest County, Mississippi	30,560	22,178	19,717	29,745	31,479	54,577
Harrison County, Mississippi	31,886	18,516	25,244	31,337	36,362	67,052
Hinds County, Mississippi	31,835	19,830	25,775	30,251	41,934	50,163
Jackson County, Mississippi	36,303	32,508	26,482	36,347	39,858	60,579
Jones County, Mississippi	31,688	33,726	26,892	30,965	46,713	47,206
Lauderdale County, Mississippi	35,195	21,408	30,311	29,528	46,971	75,245
Lee County, Mississippi	36,356	25,507	30,809	35,174	48,957	52,689
Madison County, Mississippi	44,192	30,761	27,582	37,864	51,622	61,100
Rankin County, Mississippi	39,335	24,637	30,494	37,358	55,088	57,403
MISSOURI						
Boone County, Missouri	36,350	22,335	26,209	31,051	42,047	56,688
Buchanan County, Missouri	33,555	26,259	31,426	30,394	41,592	52,328
Cape Girardeau County, Missouri	32,361	22,089	26,552	30,722	50,076	46,649
Cass County, Missouri	42,714	25,664	39,564	40,530	55,370	58,484
Christian County, Missouri	36,320	17,010	31,511	30,998	45,628	50,562
Clay County, Missouri	41,350	28,506	32,100	37,203	56,823	59,993
Cole County, Missouri	36,802	20,122	28,391	32,243	50,382	53,450
Franklin County, Missouri	36,216	17,119	32,334	36,086	47,420	49,563
Greene County, Missouri	32,669	18,974	29,287	30,909	39,042	51,495
Jackson County, Missouri	38,355	25,786	30,679	36,656	49,984	57,068
Jasper County, Missouri	35,231	23,324	30,433	35,293	42,033	56,477
Jefferson County, Missouri	40,192	27,691	31,999	38,052	52,127	57,283
Platte County, Missouri	48,074	15,977	35,305	41,100	51,927	69,042
St. Charles County, Missouri	48,303	22,337	37,366	42,099	57,894	69,259
St. Francois County, Missouri	27,996	9,531	27,709	27,397	45,794	47,376
St. Louis County, Missouri	42,933	22,101	30,466	35,413	56,269	73,128
St. Louis city, Missouri	35,245	17,350	25,079	30,089	48,564	57,682
MONTANA						
Cascade County, Montana	32,284	21,611	27,842	32,415	37,494	58,080
Flathead County, Montana	33,069	27,809	32,184	26,198	41,321	52,182
Gallatin County, Montana	39,565	30,207	30,815	30,934	42,100	53,082
Lewis and Clark County, Montana	37,480	19,648	30,073	31,084	51,208	69,008
Missoula County, Montana	32,585	22,289	30,116	29,557	31,937	54,917
Yellowstone County, Montana	35,757	24,273	29,622	32,321	41,771	60,561
NEBRASKA						
Douglas County, Nebraska	41,221	22,433	30,962	37,415	52,806	61,972
Lancaster County, Nebraska	40,550	28,362	29,268	35,905	47,099	59,199
Sarpy County, Nebraska	48,785	26,537	36,753	41,165	52,496	72,034
NEVADA						
Clark County, Nevada	35,918	26,740	30,941	36,220	48,881	66,101
Washoe County, Nevada	39,298	25,290	31,167	38,761	50,894	62,262
NEW HAMPSHIRE						
Cheshire County, New Hampshire	37,492	30,699	32,149	37,813	41,952	49,415
Grafton County, New Hampshire	36,939	19,485	26,451	35,309	48,763	62,141
Hillsborough County, New Hampshire	49,013	30,402	35,488	43,345	62,907	76,777
Merrimack County, New Hampshire	41,732	30,113	38,263	37,504	50,261	61,242
Rockingham County, New Hampshire	51,438	32,292	40,555	45,264	65,260	79,423
Strafford County, New Hampshire	42,325	20,140	33,625	45,036	55,091	61,058
NEW JERSEY						
Atlantic County, New Jersey	37,139	21,577	27,981	36,163	51,413	77,169
Bergen County, New Jersey	55,496	29,265	36,516	46,166	70,362	89,093
Burlington County, New Jersey	51,264	29,663	35,528	44,954	64,090	82,711
Camden County, New Jersey	43,086	18,118	32,459	38,293	59,019	82,134
Cape May County, New Jersey	40,576	20,282	31,572	35,988	48,413	62,068
Cumberland County, New Jersey	31,146	19,881	27,264	31,282	49,334	65,807
Essex County, New Jersey	43,133	22,706	30,517	40,509	58,276	86,054
Gloucester County, New Jersey	50,848	31,748	38,305	42,905	63,054	83,842
Hudson County, New Jersey	43,186	21,614	27,473	34,263	64,846	86,290
Hunterdon County, New Jersey	66,767	24,313	47,605	50,060	76,852	90,510
Mercer County, New Jersey	49,042	22,190	33,421	42,288	61,126	90,620
Middlesex County, New Jersey	50,892	24,516	35,779	41,318	61,363	85,226
Monmouth County, New Jersey	56,592	18,784	40,788	42,884	72,118	89,717

Table C-2. Educational Attainment of the Population, by Selected Counties, 2017—*Continued*

(Number; percent; dollars.)

| State/County | Median earnings in the past 12 months (2017 inflation-adjusted dollars) | | | | | |
| | Population 25 years and over with earnings | | | | | |
	Total	Less than high school graduate	High school graduate (includes equivalency)	Some college or associate's degree	Bachelor's degree	Graduate or professional degree
NEW JERSEY—(*Continued*)						
Morris County, New Jersey	62,408	26,812	40,085	46,754	76,148	100,855
Ocean County, New Jersey	46,628	30,866	37,337	40,966	57,994	72,773
Passaic County, New Jersey	40,039	21,030	31,209	40,748	57,086	73,288
Salem County, New Jersey	42,239	21,152	31,505	45,555	69,139	66,143
Somerset County, New Jersey	61,576	31,005	33,475	43,265	74,580	108,734
Sussex County, New Jersey	51,541	31,319	41,615	43,333	59,971	88,161
Union County, New Jersey	43,808	24,037	35,548	37,259	63,007	81,927
Warren County, New Jersey	50,134	16,153	41,884	46,561	60,111	66,259
NEW MEXICO						
Bernalillo County, New Mexico	35,915	22,687	27,857	31,447	43,153	62,145
Chaves County, New Mexico	31,601	21,446	29,974	31,138	44,221	52,865
Doña Ana County, New Mexico	29,891	14,254	23,628	30,651	42,800	52,792
Lea County, New Mexico	39,245	31,025	37,129	37,061	50,104	65,234
McKinley County, New Mexico	25,093	15,013	22,322	23,895	31,179	58,443
Otero County, New Mexico	24,623	10,233	24,124	26,387	35,880	35,402
Sandoval County, New Mexico	36,235	21,386	28,416	35,703	47,904	63,660
San Juan County, New Mexico	30,663	20,361	24,452	30,297	47,276	63,577
Santa Fe County, New Mexico	35,135	24,297	30,468	33,750	37,055	60,297
Valencia County, New Mexico	30,807	27,817	27,854	28,991	46,978	61,875
NEW YORK						
Albany County, New York	47,496	25,823	31,388	40,954	55,251	70,325
Bronx County, New York	29,737	19,933	25,674	31,280	43,262	59,744
Broome County, New York	37,140	21,429	29,231	35,015	50,148	60,333
Cattaraugus County, New York	35,622	20,919	31,751	31,854	43,011	56,267
Cayuga County, New York	37,197	24,077	31,675	35,577	58,750	65,505
Chautauqua County, New York	32,243	20,176	25,020	35,158	38,797	56,858
Chemung County, New York	34,363	22,455	24,031	31,713	42,030	65,837
Clinton County, New York	40,249	28,705	34,212	37,307	53,531	53,447
Dutchess County, New York	47,461	23,906	36,392	41,364	63,301	79,099
Erie County, New York	40,608	22,481	30,591	35,903	51,215	60,208
Jefferson County, New York	32,049	29,750	25,324	32,679	43,627	60,878
Kings County, New York	41,264	21,190	30,114	36,707	57,330	70,564
Livingston County, New York	40,651	20,260	35,272	36,477	47,127	60,671
Madison County, New York	36,706	30,865	30,643	35,520	45,250	60,736
Monroe County, New York	39,823	20,006	30,423	34,697	50,687	61,537
Nassau County, New York	56,845	26,804	36,094	49,530	71,059	90,104
New York County, New York	63,890	20,752	30,171	38,068	78,344	100,594
Niagara County, New York	38,949	21,676	30,451	36,956	52,354	58,793
Oneida County, New York	36,794	21,379	29,910	35,563	50,741	65,719
Onondaga County, New York	42,443	28,879	33,193	37,072	56,498	65,006
Ontario County, New York	42,130	28,922	28,446	35,453	52,314	66,131
Orange County, New York	48,315	30,245	37,208	44,176	56,244	77,975
Oswego County, New York	36,089	21,701	31,593	34,436	45,940	65,481
Putnam County, New York	51,413	28,816	36,514	49,150	65,859	88,674
Queens County, New York	40,276	23,490	30,969	40,260	53,564	70,899
Rensselaer County, New York	47,495	21,765	35,148	42,000	61,789	66,351
Richmond County, New York	51,735	30,680	37,575	48,710	69,057	72,101
Rockland County, New York	49,388	23,999	35,318	41,691	66,246	84,250
St. Lawrence County, New York	35,092	19,943	26,101	38,908	43,310	55,723
Saratoga County, New York	51,124	22,299	36,678	46,629	67,911	75,070
Schenectady County, New York	41,000	20,655	26,723	41,738	55,675	69,703
Steuben County, New York	34,308	18,492	27,459	35,397	44,628	60,951
Suffolk County, New York	50,534	29,098	38,397	46,431	62,649	84,547
Sullivan County, New York	40,740	31,502	32,556	42,346	36,185	50,751
Tompkins County, New York	38,285	13,331	30,194	34,586	39,674	51,128
Ulster County, New York	38,874	25,612	31,575	34,052	51,083	66,282
Warren County, New York	40,495	25,882	34,263	38,666	47,188	66,140
Wayne County, New York	33,162	28,006	31,102	32,142	50,269	52,175
Westchester County, New York	52,663	23,852	32,234	41,248	72,227	100,284
NORTH CAROLINA						
Alamance County, North Carolina	33,925	24,648	28,300	35,774	43,549	59,711
Brunswick County, North Carolina	31,051	24,550	25,164	30,764	51,325	41,961
Buncombe County, North Carolina	32,400	22,775	25,634	30,167	40,387	51,647
Burke County, North Carolina	26,248	24,234	23,886	25,658	37,167	50,496
Cabarrus County, North Carolina	40,425	30,063	35,016	33,593	50,289	84,178
Caldwell County, North Carolina	30,848	22,130	26,246	30,703	41,672	46,667

Table C-2. Educational Attainment of the Population, by Selected Counties, 2017—*Continued*

(Number; percent; dollars.)

State/County	Median earnings in the past 12 months (2017 inflation-adjusted dollars)					
	Population 25 years and over with earnings					
	Total	Less than high school graduate	High school graduate (includes equivalency)	Some college or associate's degree	Bachelor's degree	Graduate or professional degree
NORTH CAROLINA—(*Continued*)						
Carteret County, North Carolina	31,528	12,271	25,072	30,619	46,992	61,457
Catawba County, North Carolina	32,557	23,064	28,677	33,881	49,843	52,158
Chatham County, North Carolina	39,031	21,503	21,848	36,981	57,584	75,500
Cleveland County, North Carolina	30,241	21,588	22,674	31,029	42,635	49,794
Craven County, North Carolina	32,702	21,181	27,602	31,135	50,219	59,857
Cumberland County, North Carolina	31,547	20,188	24,633	30,340	42,292	62,972
Davidson County, North Carolina	32,640	23,917	29,586	32,492	49,319	45,099
Durham County, North Carolina	42,001	21,546	26,689	35,389	50,267	63,170
Forsyth County, North Carolina	36,482	22,662	27,175	33,464	45,418	61,160
Franklin County, North Carolina	34,078	19,274	31,716	31,185	36,885	66,077
Gaston County, North Carolina	35,370	22,295	30,034	35,256	49,118	55,008
Guilford County, North Carolina	35,987	25,950	26,508	30,928	47,887	58,578
Harnett County, North Carolina	35,446	26,367	30,198	32,198	42,951	61,210
Henderson County, North Carolina	31,530	16,693	21,966	32,364	39,271	44,823
Iredell County, North Carolina	36,769	20,515	31,995	32,044	53,492	65,941
Johnston County, North Carolina	37,911	24,320	35,824	36,800	57,929	47,410
Lincoln County, North Carolina	39,414	15,810	34,129	36,613	53,792	51,619
Mecklenburg County, North Carolina	42,225	22,408	28,683	32,716	57,364	70,110
Moore County, North Carolina	40,880	19,076	29,532	33,879	52,621	70,327
Nash County, North Carolina	35,040	20,110	27,203	35,553	46,735	60,083
New Hanover County, North Carolina	37,718	24,881	26,549	34,556	47,041	60,850
Onslow County, North Carolina	36,229	17,467	30,504	32,112	41,622	55,527
Orange County, North Carolina	43,426	18,279	30,629	36,575	50,002	74,156
Pitt County, North Carolina	35,883	12,150	24,807	32,976	41,625	61,025
Randolph County, North Carolina	31,867	17,274	27,686	32,923	49,850	55,947
Robeson County, North Carolina	29,954	21,127	26,576	29,416	39,388	44,504
Rockingham County, North Carolina	31,853	28,022	26,184	33,135	36,875	45,732
Rowan County, North Carolina	32,388	22,364	30,068	34,324	45,967	43,664
Rutherford County, North Carolina	30,862	20,435	30,397	28,473	36,491	66,474
Surry County, North Carolina	32,441	25,356	22,461	31,325	42,103	51,235
Union County, North Carolina	45,034	23,433	32,237	43,747	60,742	80,606
Wake County, North Carolina	47,061	21,679	30,307	37,863	59,504	71,324
Wayne County, North Carolina	30,171	20,271	24,727	28,074	43,684	47,400
Wilkes County, North Carolina	31,772	18,166	30,426	32,207	57,960	50,060
Wilson County, North Carolina	30,491	20,759	24,551	35,643	45,500	59,617
NORTH DAKOTA						
Burleigh County, North Dakota	45,180	30,380	35,277	41,862	51,109	61,656
Cass County, North Dakota	41,593	22,701	35,824	38,018	50,778	60,569
Grand Forks County, North Dakota	40,508	33,175	38,051	35,066	47,835	69,343
Ward County, North Dakota	42,044	50,617	29,583	41,567	51,005	81,024
OHIO						
Allen County, Ohio	36,362	21,994	31,530	35,108	45,961	70,232
Ashtabula County, Ohio	30,558	22,119	27,967	33,788	33,779	47,062
Athens County, Ohio	36,197	19,405	30,276	34,264	41,041	54,618
Belmont County, Ohio	31,446	18,613	26,314	36,725	39,418	61,190
Butler County, Ohio	40,989	30,016	31,923	39,579	51,716	70,215
Clark County, Ohio	33,727	17,324	30,920	31,900	48,125	59,281
Clermont County, Ohio	41,039	28,851	32,325	40,112	51,322	71,116
Columbiana County, Ohio	30,896	21,944	31,434	29,293	36,395	60,143
Cuyahoga County, Ohio	37,260	21,079	27,153	32,376	50,953	66,936
Delaware County, Ohio	61,156	21,425	35,725	45,042	75,079	92,863
Erie County, Ohio	38,484	21,954	29,337	38,176	49,481	63,837
Fairfield County, Ohio	41,197	23,013	32,103	39,327	56,723	66,452
Franklin County, Ohio	39,919	22,096	30,541	33,270	52,127	67,343
Geauga County, Ohio	47,975	30,873	38,399	42,200	60,285	90,271
Greene County, Ohio	46,389	23,037	30,662	40,049	55,651	77,419
Hamilton County, Ohio	40,828	17,914	30,277	36,692	52,007	67,729
Hancock County, Ohio	38,066	26,712	35,445	34,757	50,017	60,071
Jefferson County, Ohio	31,757	20,865	30,812	30,210	41,216	42,083
Lake County, Ohio	40,593	33,810	32,453	37,452	51,130	70,825
Licking County, Ohio	41,608	22,494	30,163	38,421	60,408	70,127
Lorain County, Ohio	37,711	17,454	30,523	35,623	57,612	68,333
Lucas County, Ohio	36,778	16,838	29,119	35,921	48,372	60,163
Mahoning County, Ohio	31,676	20,302	24,218	31,780	50,324	62,705
Marion County, Ohio	34,698	14,527	30,748	36,906	40,435	56,250
Medina County, Ohio	45,615	21,558	35,810	40,803	61,041	77,514
Miami County, Ohio	37,624	21,280	28,856	35,350	54,792	62,148

Table C-2. Educational Attainment of the Population, by Selected Counties, 2017—*Continued*

(Number; percent; dollars.)

| State/County | Median earnings in the past 12 months (2017 inflation-adjusted dollars) | | | | | |
| | Population 25 years and over with earnings | | | | | |
	Total	Less than high school graduate	High school graduate (includes equivalency)	Some college or associate's degree	Bachelor's degree	Graduate or professional degree
OHIO—(*Continued*)						
Montgomery County, Ohio	36,149	21,192	27,193	34,319	48,763	70,316
Muskingum County, Ohio	31,827	17,188	26,703	32,783	50,029	55,152
Portage County, Ohio	40,856	19,536	37,330	36,914	51,255	57,762
Richland County, Ohio	33,679	24,997	27,684	34,844	40,647	68,059
Ross County, Ohio	32,219	30,844	26,745	29,599	49,182	58,497
Scioto County, Ohio	35,411	25,227	31,285	29,742	47,236	64,099
Stark County, Ohio	34,819	20,702	29,379	33,014	55,189	65,441
Summit County, Ohio	37,369	17,106	30,149	32,941	50,513	68,742
Trumbull County, Ohio	32,312	32,197	27,511	29,710	42,345	52,345
Tuscarawas County, Ohio	34,398	31,888	28,081	36,142	50,132	61,549
Warren County, Ohio	53,870	28,750	34,943	46,376	67,402	81,805
Wayne County, Ohio	32,386	31,380	29,733	32,513	45,343	51,931
Wood County, Ohio	40,710	24,758	30,157	40,342	49,454	62,298
OKLAHOMA						
Canadian County, Oklahoma	41,038	24,490	34,136	37,125	52,459	54,063
Cleveland County, Oklahoma	38,336	29,623	30,529	36,235	41,973	57,352
Comanche County, Oklahoma	32,443	23,533	22,408	31,581	42,990	55,410
Creek County, Oklahoma	37,048	29,933	35,523	36,867	40,561	56,897
Muskogee County, Oklahoma	30,956	23,861	25,657	31,037	37,706	56,717
Oklahoma County, Oklahoma	35,782	24,987	26,512	32,328	47,823	65,432
Payne County, Oklahoma	31,756	19,571	26,281	31,282	38,833	45,821
Pottawatomie County, Oklahoma	32,072	21,271	28,695	34,132	40,368	47,558
Rogers County, Oklahoma	39,624	24,550	34,761	37,398	49,117	53,851
Tulsa County, Oklahoma	36,518	23,539	29,627	34,403	49,546	59,928
Wagoner County, Oklahoma	38,511	26,066	31,167	39,624	47,267	56,600
OREGON						
Benton County, Oregon	38,955	36,081	31,545	28,151	39,839	56,398
Clackamas County, Oregon	47,175	23,446	36,394	43,994	58,004	72,470
Deschutes County, Oregon	35,658	37,787	26,660	34,319	39,588	56,641
Douglas County, Oregon	29,912	19,120	29,087	29,390	35,625	61,585
Jackson County, Oregon	32,530	22,255	31,995	31,617	40,613	57,011
Josephine County, Oregon	30,173	12,203	23,370	28,827	38,203	80,634
Klamath County, Oregon	30,207	16,575	29,688	26,513	34,912	51,663
Lane County, Oregon	31,363	25,650	27,069	30,348	37,386	49,142
Linn County, Oregon	34,577	23,138	30,432	36,357	50,320	57,975
Marion County, Oregon	35,291	25,450	30,934	35,123	51,033	64,491
Multnomah County, Oregon	40,412	23,426	27,383	32,941	49,348	64,179
Polk County, Oregon	32,462	20,417	26,580	31,640	54,554	51,496
Umatilla County, Oregon	34,239	24,285	34,414	33,377	45,650	66,901
Washington County, Oregon	45,700	23,427	30,218	40,948	52,627	81,837
Yamhill County, Oregon	39,105	24,688	30,604	39,077	53,326	56,678
PENNSYLVANIA						
Adams County, Pennsylvania	40,861	32,343	32,465	41,694	53,513	65,521
Allegheny County, Pennsylvania	42,096	21,645	29,423	36,504	51,663	67,747
Armstrong County, Pennsylvania	33,708	22,460	31,227	31,096	45,729	45,237
Beaver County, Pennsylvania	39,345	23,007	33,419	36,125	50,075	62,780
Berks County, Pennsylvania	40,365	24,661	33,416	38,827	52,506	67,596
Blair County, Pennsylvania	33,136	20,385	26,213	36,225	46,522	52,440
Bucks County, Pennsylvania	50,745	22,716	39,300	42,075	65,242	85,841
Butler County, Pennsylvania	45,865	18,372	34,634	41,616	56,791	74,036
Cambria County, Pennsylvania	35,001	22,386	30,472	32,784	41,665	61,687
Carbon County, Pennsylvania	36,818	22,119	30,236	40,393	50,675	44,706
Centre County, Pennsylvania	41,445	30,737	28,343	38,779	46,207	62,155
Chester County, Pennsylvania	54,045	25,868	36,991	41,243	66,263	90,994
Clearfield County, Pennsylvania	30,463	16,047	27,462	31,875	37,297	50,547
Columbia County, Pennsylvania	36,368	29,768	30,495	34,808	41,123	64,267
Crawford County, Pennsylvania	33,499	34,228	30,030	31,150	40,839	60,083
Cumberland County, Pennsylvania	44,249	30,192	31,865	41,723	55,458	69,398
Dauphin County, Pennsylvania	40,736	25,917	32,609	39,133	51,919	60,936
Delaware County, Pennsylvania	48,443	22,140	34,482	41,802	58,432	80,136
Erie County, Pennsylvania	35,149	20,781	27,370	35,143	45,451	61,845
Fayette County, Pennsylvania	32,634	20,753	28,210	35,625	41,392	60,750
Franklin County, Pennsylvania	38,343	26,244	32,802	42,000	45,779	59,611
Indiana County, Pennsylvania	32,729	29,703	30,319	32,380	38,005	53,945
Lackawanna County, Pennsylvania	37,019	24,252	31,642	34,961	41,708	62,552
Lancaster County, Pennsylvania	40,352	31,576	35,051	34,463	48,946	62,380

Table C-2. Educational Attainment of the Population, by Selected Counties, 2017—*Continued*

(Number; percent; dollars.)

State/County	Median earnings in the past 12 months (2017 inflation-adjusted dollars)					
	Population 25 years and over with earnings					
	Total	Less than high school graduate	High school graduate (includes equivalency)	Some college or associate's degree	Bachelor's degree	Graduate or professional degree
PENNSYLVANIA—(*Continued*)						
Lawrence County, Pennsylvania	33,229	21,565	29,010	32,179	47,488	61,449
Lebanon County, Pennsylvania	39,120	31,936	31,758	40,505	50,642	61,042
Lehigh County, Pennsylvania	39,263	22,405	30,968	35,939	55,898	76,855
Luzerne County, Pennsylvania	35,833	25,044	30,006	34,987	46,952	62,314
Lycoming County, Pennsylvania	34,956	27,123	26,990	35,296	42,201	61,703
Mercer County, Pennsylvania	33,550	29,356	30,329	27,570	46,720	59,746
Monroe County, Pennsylvania	37,690	33,040	32,946	36,828	49,176	51,483
Montgomery County, Pennsylvania	52,220	28,963	35,761	43,010	61,722	81,575
Northampton County, Pennsylvania	41,444	23,969	33,788	40,512	52,230	68,213
Northumberland County, Pennsylvania	33,115	22,214	30,051	35,129	43,601	65,137
Philadelphia County, Pennsylvania	36,789	20,794	30,124	32,485	48,454	61,986
Schuylkill County, Pennsylvania	36,287	34,215	32,234	35,400	44,885	62,274
Somerset County, Pennsylvania	31,113	20,158	26,877	31,284	45,260	53,513
Washington County, Pennsylvania	40,328	21,736	31,102	35,260	56,968	66,967
Westmoreland County, Pennsylvania	40,265	19,575	31,393	36,185	52,438	67,121
York County, Pennsylvania	40,817	22,877	34,682	40,353	53,588	67,539
RHODE ISLAND						
Kent County, Rhode Island	50,120	30,745	40,111	45,785	60,236	70,717
Newport County, Rhode Island	45,595	25,483	33,336	38,013	50,951	79,764
Providence County, Rhode Island	40,278	21,650	31,787	36,999	53,087	71,953
Washington County, Rhode Island	52,045	36,326	42,781	37,983	63,651	85,040
SOUTH CAROLINA						
Aiken County, South Carolina	32,787	24,798	27,416	32,394	45,956	50,237
Anderson County, South Carolina	33,173	21,701	28,432	35,077	41,932	66,646
Beaufort County, South Carolina	31,312	22,634	22,340	30,635	41,492	51,026
Berkeley County, South Carolina	36,819	22,391	30,232	36,250	50,119	61,419
Charleston County, South Carolina	38,601	19,439	26,007	30,274	51,064	72,702
Darlington County, South Carolina	30,180	15,221	27,112	22,482	40,429	49,596
Dorchester County, South Carolina	41,237	21,717	32,317	39,985	50,598	58,659
Florence County, South Carolina	31,036	20,378	27,386	30,247	39,017	45,356
Greenville County, South Carolina	37,135	22,548	27,178	34,587	51,000	57,979
Greenwood County, South Carolina	30,487	20,310	30,298	26,877	37,172	54,183
Horry County, South Carolina	30,063	17,948	23,823	30,814	38,259	51,574
Kershaw County, South Carolina	39,027	42,378	30,753	35,741	47,376	56,897
Lancaster County, South Carolina	35,069	25,777	32,247	31,654	46,159	60,888
Laurens County, South Carolina	26,747	13,539	24,375	30,678	42,035	38,136
Lexington County, South Carolina	37,221	18,968	30,505	34,680	51,582	57,064
Oconee County, South Carolina	30,985	17,017	26,812	32,112	39,283	62,117
Orangeburg County, South Carolina	30,550	18,423	27,111	30,036	32,210	43,910
Pickens County, South Carolina	32,084	24,075	30,195	30,680	40,313	59,597
Richland County, South Carolina	35,754	19,515	25,672	30,793	49,792	59,580
Spartanburg County, South Carolina	34,612	25,213	27,113	31,920	45,348	51,598
Sumter County, South Carolina	31,738	21,466	30,179	30,169	37,088	61,416
York County, South Carolina	40,521	22,386	27,281	40,679	52,455	61,375
SOUTH DAKOTA						
Minnehaha County, South Dakota	37,337	28,095	30,817	36,603	46,640	62,087
Pennington County, South Dakota	31,700	20,615	28,601	29,127	42,111	59,543
TENNESSEE						
Anderson County, Tennessee	33,529	20,873	27,313	31,130	51,429	67,092
Blount County, Tennessee	33,809	16,892	26,894	34,857	45,735	61,995
Bradley County, Tennessee	36,357	27,911	31,624	32,344	44,819	51,171
Davidson County, Tennessee	37,956	22,192	28,003	35,318	45,895	60,553
Greene County, Tennessee	28,095	14,216	23,781	27,635	39,136	52,257
Hamilton County, Tennessee	36,719	18,854	29,511	31,661	49,090	63,085
Knox County, Tennessee	38,588	25,251	27,784	35,470	47,462	58,369
Madison County, Tennessee	32,469	25,169	27,990	31,304	37,336	66,512
Maury County, Tennessee	35,908	25,881	31,220	40,204	37,471	50,808
Montgomery County, Tennessee	36,734	17,029	31,547	36,275	46,472	50,316
Putnam County, Tennessee	30,110	21,496	25,615	27,375	37,291	48,108
Robertson County, Tennessee	34,308	30,011	30,703	32,575	47,644	60,546
Rutherford County, Tennessee	40,327	21,958	36,125	37,940	45,470	60,832
Sevier County, Tennessee	27,029	18,414	23,750	27,101	41,035	45,281
Shelby County, Tennessee	35,795	21,328	26,548	32,131	49,239	65,672
Sullivan County, Tennessee	31,037	20,475	23,339	31,846	45,201	61,246
Sumner County, Tennessee	39,468	26,445	30,319	38,164	51,785	62,708

Table C-2. Educational Attainment of the Population, by Selected Counties, 2017—*Continued*

(Number; percent; dollars.)

State/County	Median earnings in the past 12 months (2017 inflation-adjusted dollars)					
	Population 25 years and over with earnings					
	Total	Less than high school graduate	High school graduate (includes equivalency)	Some college or associate's degree	Bachelor's degree	Graduate or professional degree
TENNESSEE—(*Continued*)						
Washington County, Tennessee..........................	35,171	17,055	29,150	27,365	43,861	60,929
Williamson County, Tennessee............................	59,471	24,605	35,420	40,998	65,957	80,931
Wilson County, Tennessee	42,052	22,314	36,508	41,690	61,268	52,445
TEXAS						
Angelina County, Texas	30,533	20,669	25,331	31,669	46,719	51,735
Bastrop County, Texas.......................................	40,252	35,879	36,094	27,105	52,326	61,319
Bell County, Texas...	35,829	22,788	26,390	34,189	47,671	60,581
Bexar County, Texas..	35,044	21,506	27,814	32,179	52,325	61,722
Bowie County, Texas..	40,487	21,120	40,767	31,669	55,565	51,202
Brazoria County, Texas......................................	50,229	29,157	37,213	48,182	60,659	81,376
Brazos County, Texas..	36,407	24,005	32,606	31,743	45,394	51,066
Cameron County, Texas.....................................	24,920	17,008	21,494	28,515	44,032	50,347
Collin County, Texas..	55,700	24,326	32,042	46,283	68,053	84,658
Comal County, Texas...	45,560	24,993	31,993	40,274	56,419	86,787
Coryell County, Texas..	31,506	24,718	23,218	36,548	33,562	42,078
Dallas County, Texas...	36,774	25,240	29,708	36,217	56,135	74,205
Denton County, Texas..	50,995	26,232	37,357	44,036	60,781	76,084
Ector County, Texas...	39,076	31,559	36,821	41,473	51,046	55,369
Ellis County, Texas..	43,453	31,827	38,665	42,463	59,157	67,935
El Paso County, Texas	29,530	16,354	25,076	30,186	42,205	61,235
Fort Bend County, Texas....................................	50,883	27,438	30,721	41,388	61,519	85,714
Galveston County, Texas...................................	47,238	23,551	31,898	45,303	65,198	77,074
Grayson County, Texas......................................	35,966	23,381	36,609	32,117	50,838	56,011
Gregg County, Texas...	31,803	30,670	23,730	32,197	44,707	33,084
Guadalupe County, Texas..................................	40,227	21,899	32,292	41,343	51,240	67,432
Harris County, Texas	38,623	22,348	30,613	36,613	57,077	73,555
Harrison County, Texas	40,236	28,138	32,571	35,753	42,325	70,307
Hays County, Texas...	42,755	27,053	33,453	38,663	51,111	56,381
Henderson County, Texas..................................	31,127	21,124	22,391	31,827	46,378	50,475
Hidalgo County, Texas.......................................	24,760	15,233	22,031	27,824	46,366	61,688
Hunt County, Texas...	40,506	31,168	36,583	40,091	45,314	52,390
Jefferson County, Texas	35,583	23,444	26,887	36,371	50,331	61,304
Johnson County, Texas......................................	42,152	27,168	36,770	45,344	51,070	57,968
Kaufman County, Texas.....................................	42,223	31,857	31,528	47,111	52,075	75,030
Liberty County, Texas..	38,209	30,818	34,373	41,495	46,425	21,543
Lubbock County, Texas......................................	32,594	20,745	27,871	31,232	49,161	59,966
McLennan County, Texas...................................	32,066	21,641	26,266	32,147	50,915	57,837
Midland County, Texas	50,060	31,232	40,734	49,891	64,414	67,320
Montgomery County, Texas................................	45,273	24,521	35,280	42,161	62,413	80,124
Nacogdoches County, Texas..............................	30,052	23,312	28,025	24,962	41,031	62,143
Nueces County, Texas.......................................	35,018	21,206	30,236	34,569	49,275	63,113
Orange County, Texas.......................................	40,972	19,516	37,098	40,121	54,824	59,874
Parker County, Texas...	41,614	30,181	31,306	40,331	57,184	86,110
Potter County, Texas...	31,226	27,037	28,392	31,824	51,151	51,834
Randall County, Texas.......................................	40,760	24,462	30,059	36,430	50,860	69,112
Rockwall County, Texas.....................................	52,667	21,275	41,376	47,462	61,962	80,748
San Patricio County, Texas................................	31,040	16,817	28,980	27,467	52,406	64,286
Smith County, Texas..	36,568	22,776	26,925	33,717	47,788	88,766
Tarrant County, Texas..	41,439	27,327	32,285	38,994	56,358	72,398
Taylor County, Texas...	35,210	21,349	27,036	32,923	48,097	64,230
Tom Green County, Texas..................................	32,345	19,881	26,457	32,854	42,654	46,793
Travis County, Texas...	46,337	25,092	31,116	37,397	55,261	75,512
Victoria County, Texas.......................................	35,120	16,994	31,595	34,941	51,692	64,511
Walker County, Texas..	37,160	18,206	35,050	39,289	43,720	40,789
Webb County, Texas..	28,488	16,988	25,689	32,129	47,291	66,107
Wichita County, Texas.......................................	32,641	31,492	30,208	29,743	43,734	58,275
Williamson County, Texas..................................	46,818	31,176	32,434	44,013	55,433	80,269
Wise County, Texas...	36,454	26,488	·31,217	37,046	58,180	66,773
UTAH						
Cache County, Utah...	32,231	30,713	30,811	28,847	33,659	57,942
Davis County, Utah..	45,072	29,880	31,735	40,090	52,063	80,167
Salt Lake County, Utah......................................	39,872	26,563	31,941	36,230	48,025	70,972
Tooele County, Utah..	39,373	21,650	36,681	34,070	53,295	67,002
Utah County, Utah...	40,414	32,020	31,474	32,223	45,451	76,245
Washington County, Utah...................................	30,852	28,848	25,199	28,494	38,080	56,897
Weber County, Utah...	37,428	28,492	30,622	34,774	48,319	61,666

Table C-2. Educational Attainment of the Population, by Selected Counties, 2017—*Continued*

(Number; percent; dollars.)

State/County	Median earnings in the past 12 months (2017 inflation-adjusted dollars)					
	Population 25 years and over with earnings					
	Total	Less than high school graduate	High school graduate (includes equivalency)	Some college or associate's degree	Bachelor's degree	Graduate or professional degree
VERMONT						
Chittenden County, Vermont	43,785	25,083	31,600	42,417	47,547	66,659
VIRGINIA						
Albemarle County, Virginia	44,985	27,313	30,285	36,106	51,443	67,088
Arlington County, Virginia	75,904	24,396	35,663	45,241	77,442	98,043
Augusta County, Virginia	34,760	21,682	29,404	39,328	46,771	48,102
Bedford County, Virginia	39,485	17,606	33,823	36,191	44,427	65,596
Chesterfield County, Virginia	45,792	35,099	33,140	41,565	56,141	67,340
Fairfax County, Virginia	62,241	25,101	30,710	43,204	73,752	102,413
Fauquier County, Virginia	51,895	27,194	46,609	50,808	61,911	76,638
Frederick County, Virginia	46,582	30,450	42,893	42,098	57,087	60,350
Hanover County, Virginia	50,742	36,068	40,566	47,843	59,191	63,098
Henrico County, Virginia	44,547	22,264	29,636	34,789	56,385	66,703
James City County, Virginia	41,993	22,200	24,808	37,180	44,429	72,598
Loudoun County, Virginia	70,257	30,714	38,367	51,192	81,107	105,279
Montgomery County, Virginia	40,647	36,612	30,313	37,531	43,892	55,332
Prince William County, Virginia	52,647	36,966	40,054	44,676	65,271	92,210
Roanoke County, Virginia	41,671	35,792	31,631	40,048	52,512	55,832
Rockingham County, Virginia	38,319	20,954	33,927	41,032	42,160	52,961
Spotsylvania County, Virginia	47,548	22,868	36,424	46,898	62,318	82,226
Stafford County, Virginia	58,989	28,331	41,045	48,469	77,081	101,241
York County, Virginia	48,143	24,236	36,599	35,701	52,484	75,167
Alexandria city, Virginia	60,498	28,774	29,051	37,126	68,979	99,290
Chesapeake city, Virginia	46,079	19,870	32,203	40,578	51,003	77,518
Hampton city, Virginia	35,622	24,973	27,354	35,441	41,033	56,593
Lynchburg city, Virginia	33,574	26,293	26,146	29,919	40,632	47,340
Newport News city, Virginia	36,533	20,589	32,252	36,242	47,996	52,063
Norfolk city, Virginia	33,070	21,447	24,626	31,771	46,000	65,556
Portsmouth city, Virginia	34,061	23,893	27,020	35,329	37,787	51,970
Richmond city, Virginia	35,153	18,363	21,930	28,274	45,541	54,843
Roanoke city, Virginia	31,428	21,275	26,363	30,788	45,531	57,546
Suffolk city, Virginia	41,865	22,042	36,278	36,979	52,216	61,453
Virginia Beach city, Virginia	42,356	24,973	32,273	37,445	51,879	70,232
WASHINGTON						
Benton County, Washington	42,278	26,755	31,982	37,154	61,805	80,948
Chelan County, Washington	35,396	27,592	26,929	35,566	41,763	80,913
Clallam County, Washington	37,449	17,761	28,276	36,853	42,301	65,697
Clark County, Washington	45,358	30,614	34,135	41,328	61,236	72,225
Cowlitz County, Washington	32,480	26,238	30,740	29,407	43,981	63,843
Franklin County, Washington	35,297	20,796	35,224	39,692	52,211	66,417
Grant County, Washington	35,008	25,696	32,472	36,498	42,823	64,280
Grays Harbor County, Washington	33,360	21,380	33,440	32,216	43,394	70,902
Island County, Washington	35,942	31,064	36,205	30,497	45,829	60,945
King County, Washington	55,396	24,013	35,289	41,954	68,948	88,873
Kitsap County, Washington	45,620	34,030	31,268	41,767	54,325	75,855
Lewis County, Washington	31,906	25,707	30,048	31,157	36,823	66,357
Pierce County, Washington	42,758	26,912	35,868	41,284	55,301	69,195
Skagit County, Washington	41,350	31,828	35,472	36,747	50,709	75,378
Snohomish County, Washington	49,251	35,003	40,030	43,543	62,263	75,455
Spokane County, Washington	37,497	19,576	30,996	32,170	47,682	65,815
Thurston County, Washington	42,697	17,246	36,223	39,911	51,068	65,972
Whatcom County, Washington	40,822	30,591	31,988	39,332	41,786	68,983
Yakima County, Washington	31,260	24,590	28,065	33,900	46,082	60,359
WEST VIRGINIA						
Berkeley County, West Virginia	39,353	29,676	33,631	43,915	41,894	48,990
Cabell County, West Virginia	36,838	11,484	31,415	29,538	50,768	63,253
Harrison County, West Virginia	39,595	24,302	28,844	39,939	47,460	51,819
Kanawha County, West Virginia	34,853	14,618	26,747	34,770	46,101	55,350
Monongalia County, West Virginia	36,956	12,228	26,373	27,334	41,860	73,137
Raleigh County, West Virginia	32,359	21,196	27,266	32,392	40,871	49,719
Wood County, West Virginia	34,295	29,904	25,439	30,342	44,160	68,570
WISCONSIN						
Brown County, Wisconsin	41,155	26,379	32,964	39,047	48,529	65,028
Dane County, Wisconsin	47,217	28,096	34,118	40,644	52,551	65,363
Dodge County, Wisconsin	38,083	30,307	35,686	38,753	48,086	55,188
Eau Claire County, Wisconsin	40,886	31,942	28,931	34,375	49,713	62,064

Table C-2. Educational Attainment of the Population, by Selected Counties, 2017—*Continued*

(Number; percent; dollars.)

State/County	Median earnings in the past 12 months (2017 inflation-adjusted dollars)					
	Population 25 years and over with earnings					
	Total	Less than high school graduate	High school graduate (includes equivalency)	Some college or associate's degree	Bachelor's degree	Graduate or professional degree
WISCONSIN—(*Continued*)						
Fond du Lac County, Wisconsin	40,180	25,550	37,105	36,619	50,047	58,703
Jefferson County, Wisconsin	36,441	21,569	34,803	33,202	44,654	54,397
Kenosha County, Wisconsin	40,833	26,512	31,496	38,327	54,546	65,666
La Crosse County, Wisconsin	39,142	30,723	30,014	35,701	48,355	57,021
Manitowoc County, Wisconsin	40,106	38,003	35,387	40,658	43,415	60,833
Marathon County, Wisconsin	38,447	30,489	31,691	37,234	51,924	62,044
Milwaukee County, Wisconsin	37,271	24,020	30,057	34,426	50,040	64,280
Outagamie County, Wisconsin	42,111	24,675	33,640	41,804	51,925	61,422
Ozaukee County, Wisconsin	50,286	23,759	33,428	40,121	56,476	70,934
Portage County, Wisconsin	38,017	20,875	31,123	36,986	42,852	56,250
Racine County, Wisconsin	45,352	26,729	36,883	40,052	60,501	72,184
Rock County, Wisconsin	36,890	26,389	30,641	35,749	48,691	58,200
St. Croix County, Wisconsin	48,620	32,206	33,832	46,674	65,298	72,469
Sheboygan County, Wisconsin	40,135	25,414	35,717	37,279	52,336	67,127
Walworth County, Wisconsin	40,206	33,848	29,448	36,243	50,577	65,469
Washington County, Wisconsin	46,999	50,299	36,597	41,279	60,923	77,048
Waukesha County, Wisconsin	51,872	27,473	37,101	45,502	61,749	76,578
Winnebago County, Wisconsin	40,532	26,217	32,162	38,813	46,292	67,667
Wood County, Wisconsin	37,214	31,016	32,444	35,955	46,351	62,206
WYOMING						
Laramie County, Wyoming	39,366	34,049	26,750	35,890	47,421	65,184
Natrona County, Wyoming	44,730	39,850	30,732	43,470	50,915	56,282

Table C-3. College Enrollment of the Population, by Selected Counties, 2017

(Number.)

State/County	Total population	Population enrolled in college or graduate school	Male			Female		
			Total population	Enrolled in public college or graduate school	Enrolled in private college or graduate school	Total population	Enrolled in public college or graduate school	Enrolled in private college or graduate school
ALABAMA								
Baldwin County, Alabama	174,771	7,816	84,805	1,576	700	89,966	4,162	1,378
Calhoun County, Alabama	94,269	6,917	44,660	2,738	329	49,609	3,669	181
DeKalb County, Alabama	57,171	4,270	27,774	1,344	270	29,397	2,146	510
Elmore County, Alabama	67,089	3,670	31,868	1,047	547	35,221	1,703	373
Houston County, Alabama	84,547	5,106	39,851	1,358	248	44,696	2,834	666
Jefferson County, Alabama	532,961	45,756	247,348	15,073	2,869	285,613	23,731	4,083
Lauderdale County, Alabama	77,709	8,408	36,162	3,444	340	41,547	4,517	107
Lee County, Alabama	132,624	29,472	64,437	13,717	1,047	68,187	13,607	1,101
Limestone County, Alabama	77,546	5,794	38,819	3,523	202	38,727	1,601	468
Madison County, Alabama	295,575	33,483	143,115	13,897	1,702	152,460	14,301	3,583
Marshall County, Alabama	75,721	4,979	36,380	1,683	199	39,341	2,903	194
Mobile County, Alabama	333,554	23,778	156,002	8,473	1,148	177,552	10,817	3,340
Montgomery County, Alabama	182,224	15,580	84,423	5,083	1,318	97,801	7,484	1,695
Morgan County, Alabama	96,713	6,076	47,608	2,572	501	49,105	2,496	507
Shelby County, Alabama	172,317	12,321	82,158	3,737	1,357	90,159	6,564	663
Talladega County, Alabama	65,947	3,950	31,620	1,235	403	34,327	2,097	215
Tuscaloosa County, Alabama	171,914	25,916	82,427	11,159	67	89,487	14,312	378
ALASKA								
Anchorage Municipality, Alaska	233,032	19,498	118,903	7,670	1,575	114,129	8,863	1,390
Fairbanks North Star Borough, Alaska	78,943	9,467	42,835	4,820	442	36,108	4,045	160
Matanuska-Susitna Borough, Alaska	82,207	5,341	42,984	1,844	420	39,223	2,180	897
ARIZONA								
Apache County, Arizona	55,391	3,598	27,216	1,792	274	28,175	1,222	310
Cochise County, Arizona	102,038	6,369	52,297	2,658	557	49,741	2,669	485
Coconino County, Arizona	116,743	24,270	57,922	8,961	137	58,821	14,262	910
Maricopa County, Arizona	3,440,203	279,213	1,688,069	105,174	25,665	1,752,134	118,154	30,220
Mohave County, Arizona	177,646	5,648	88,861	1,470	199	88,785	3,108	871
Navajo County, Arizona	84,410	3,848	42,539	1,523	210	41,871	1,713	402
Pima County, Arizona	843,632	87,491	411,393	37,371	2,788	432,239	43,779	3,553
Pinal County, Arizona	347,931	18,956	182,511	6,667	1,342	165,420	8,400	2,547
Yavapai County, Arizona	197,536	14,838	95,886	4,907	3,024	101,650	5,827	1,080
Yuma County, Arizona	163,610	13,528	83,876	5,832	230	79,734	6,845	621
ARKANSAS								
Benton County, Arkansas	206,753	11,056	101,179	3,009	1,648	105,574	5,082	1,317
Craighead County, Arkansas	85,356	9,343	41,241	3,170	362	44,115	5,703	108
Faulkner County, Arkansas	99,592	14,485	48,090	5,223	1,742	51,502	5,383	2,137
Garland County, Arkansas	82,347	6,304	39,335	3,368	235	43,012	2,282	419
Jefferson County, Arkansas	56,440	4,949	27,451	1,679	342	28,989	2,290	638
Lonoke County, Arkansas	57,554	3,271	27,556	1,128	110	29,998	1,925	108
Pulaski County, Arkansas	315,726	23,679	148,129	8,600	1,932	167,597	10,573	2,574
Saline County, Arkansas	96,125	7,575	47,417	2,189	335	48,708	4,508	543
Sebastian County, Arkansas	103,234	6,793	50,068	2,828	251	53,166	3,109	605
Washington County, Arkansas	184,189	24,967	91,817	11,519	1,122	92,372	10,336	1,990
White County, Arkansas	63,728	6,270	30,779	684	1,945	32,949	1,139	2,502
CALIFORNIA								
Alameda County, California	1,373,625	136,306	669,677	55,728	8,291	703,948	61,771	10,516
Butte County, California	191,239	30,224	93,950	12,706	708	97,289	15,908	902
Contra Costa County, California	932,835	85,326	451,704	30,679	6,408	481,131	36,395	11,844
El Dorado County, California	158,378	9,451	78,665	3,422	828	79,713	3,989	1,212
Fresno County, California	751,868	69,699	371,887	26,673	3,548	379,981	33,513	5,965
Humboldt County, California	115,181	13,185	57,095	4,845	227	58,086	7,981	132
Imperial County, California	138,544	12,816	70,647	5,113	1,399	67,897	5,921	383
Kern County, California	675,556	57,596	347,892	20,628	4,789	327,664	25,042	7,137
Kings County, California	115,675	9,277	65,269	2,438	2,220	50,406	3,448	1,171
Los Angeles County, California	8,319,325	879,088	4,065,825	315,669	87,166	4,253,500	366,286	109,967
Madera County, California	121,521	8,747	58,027	2,623	884	63,494	3,493	1,747
Marin County, California	218,600	12,928	106,306	4,995	1,130	112,294	4,747	2,056
Mendocino County, California	72,277	4,532	35,557	1,616	242	36,720	2,049	625
Merced County, California	206,066	25,163	104,242	10,386	305	101,824	13,226	1,246
Monterey County, California	341,304	33,844	173,046	11,659	3,381	168,258	16,267	2,537
Napa County, California	116,974	9,846	57,475	2,975	1,641	59,499	3,929	1,301
Nevada County, California	86,093	3,903	42,105	1,250	263	43,988	1,843	547
Orange County, California	2,609,605	285,707	1,277,805	107,900	27,003	1,331,800	118,749	32,055
Placer County, California	315,598	22,219	152,023	8,316	1,684	163,575	9,641	2,578
Riverside County, California	1,915,485	182,877	947,278	67,793	15,529	968,207	76,894	22,661

Table C-3. College Enrollment of the Population, by Selected Counties, 2017—*Continued*

(Number.)

State/County	Total population	Population enrolled in college or graduate school	Male Total population	Male Enrolled in public college or graduate school	Male Enrolled in private college or graduate school	Female Total population	Female Enrolled in public college or graduate school	Female Enrolled in private college or graduate school
CALIFORNIA— (*Continued*)								
Sacramento County, California	1,226,647	111,387	593,153	44,603	6,973	633,494	51,312	8,499
San Bernardino County, California	1,683,712	177,774	831,965	64,817	16,910	851,747	73,497	22,550
San Diego County, California	2,727,051	303,740	1,366,626	120,244	26,476	1,360,425	123,539	33,481
San Francisco County, California	782,395	68,459	398,505	21,216	9,432	383,890	26,353	11,458
San Joaquin County, California	576,908	44,296	284,360	13,843	5,918	292,548	18,039	6,496
San Luis Obispo County, California	241,433	36,415	122,192	17,648	1,346	119,241	15,672	1,749
San Mateo County, California	637,252	51,488	311,926	18,174	5,601	325,326	22,031	5,682
Santa Barbara County, California	364,300	57,456	181,464	25,389	1,406	182,836	28,003	2,658
Santa Clara County, California	1,578,462	158,887	795,160	57,346	19,588	783,302	56,850	25,103
Santa Cruz County, California	231,159	39,441	114,009	14,880	2,485	117,150	16,942	5,134
Shasta County, California	148,209	10,144	72,026	4,456	540	76,183	4,019	1,129
Solano County, California	363,162	31,662	179,182	11,407	2,882	183,980	13,028	4,345
Sonoma County, California	421,680	35,765	204,293	13,818	1,492	217,387	18,696	1,759
Stanislaus County, California	425,063	35,384	209,182	14,390	1,406	215,881	16,977	2,611
Sutter County, California	75,798	6,007	37,577	2,810	251	38,221	2,754	192
Tulare County, California	343,722	27,770	170,840	9,824	1,891	172,882	13,360	2,695
Ventura County, California	690,521	62,354	340,219	22,184	7,349	350,302	26,309	6,512
Yolo County, California	180,734	44,554	86,903	18,386	521	93,831	23,755	1,892
Yuba County, California	58,915	5,271	30,680	2,702	35	28,235	2,188	346
COLORADO								
Adams County, Colorado	389,870	21,932	195,716	8,231	1,775	194,154	10,764	1,162
Arapahoe County, Colorado	516,032	37,073	253,617	12,587	4,511	262,415	15,104	4,871
Boulder County, Colorado	270,921	46,803	136,207	21,766	3,383	134,714	19,144	2,510
Broomfield County, Colorado	55,559	3,610	27,125	1,472	200	28,434	1,659	279
Denver County, Colorado	584,559	51,682	291,796	18,477	6,239	292,763	19,086	7,880
Douglas County, Colorado	263,494	17,246	130,087	6,084	1,593	133,407	7,640	1,929
El Paso County, Colorado	557,371	53,036	280,683	23,103	4,269	276,688	20,218	5,446
Jefferson County, Colorado	480,459	33,812	238,464	14,233	3,241	241,995	12,978	3,360
Larimer County, Colorado	286,828	39,104	143,099	17,396	1,138	143,729	18,838	1,732
Mesa County, Colorado	124,004	10,804	60,962	4,781	1,129	63,042	4,250	644
Pueblo County, Colorado	135,226	9,907	66,023	3,906	818	69,203	4,621	562
Weld County, Colorado	236,641	20,503	118,351	8,401	1,068	118,290	9,980	1,054
CONNECTICUT								
Fairfield County, Connecticut	775,421	69,317	373,826	17,213	12,054	401,595	23,236	16,814
Hartford County, Connecticut	742,016	62,905	356,964	19,372	7,881	385,052	25,112	10,540
Litchfield County, Connecticut	156,083	8,148	76,811	2,677	697	79,272	3,695	1,079
Middlesex County, Connecticut	139,588	11,471	67,266	3,389	2,489	72,322	2,766	2,827
New Haven County, Connecticut	718,207	69,436	342,599	14,630	15,253	375,608	20,292	19,261
New London County, Connecticut	226,024	17,235	112,907	5,127	3,319	113,117	4,615	4,174
Tolland County, Connecticut	131,216	26,645	65,042	12,299	708	66,174	12,439	1,199
Windham County, Connecticut	98,282	10,039	47,089	3,455	443	51,193	5,399	742
DELAWARE								
Kent County, Delaware	142,777	17,042	67,521	4,612	1,135	75,256	9,481	1,814
New Castle County, Delaware	459,687	44,233	220,321	15,989	3,474	239,366	20,780	3,990
Sussex County, Delaware	190,047	7,710	91,311	2,755	949	98,736	3,371	635
DISTRICT OF COLUMBIA								
District of Columbia, District of Columbia	585,161	74,185	274,333	9,304	20,504	310,828	11,599	32,778
FLORIDA								
Alachua County, Florida	226,417	55,425	108,736	25,082	601	117,681	28,692	1,050
Bay County, Florida	150,310	9,318	74,334	3,193	1,282	75,976	3,702	1,141
Brevard County, Florida	500,390	36,466	241,283	11,132	5,898	259,107	14,314	5,122
Broward County, Florida	1,596,640	143,803	771,479	51,755	14,242	825,161	53,473	24,333
Charlotte County, Florida	163,572	5,536	79,534	1,528	1,022	84,038	2,413	573
Citrus County, Florida	128,917	4,484	62,243	824	160	66,674	2,417	1,083
Clay County, Florida	171,120	12,242	83,503	5,734	953	87,617	4,624	931
Collier County, Florida	319,073	15,045	155,431	5,072	2,100	163,642	5,306	2,567
Duval County, Florida	759,457	60,451	363,048	19,909	6,003	396,409	28,320	6,219
Escambia County, Florida	258,352	24,874	127,729	7,351	3,550	130,623	10,255	3,718
Flagler County, Florida	95,382	5,384	45,577	1,215	842	49,805	2,756	571
Hernando County, Florida	157,556	7,518	74,332	2,082	581	83,224	3,357	1,498
Hillsborough County, Florida	1,141,158	110,865	550,221	37,773	10,897	590,937	44,802	17,393
Indian River County, Florida	134,501	7,026	63,135	2,274	653	71,366	3,697	402
Lake County, Florida	291,650	16,480	139,172	5,493	1,613	152,478	7,284	2,090
Lee County, Florida	630,562	37,755	306,058	12,011	5,504	324,504	15,611	4,629

Table C-3. College Enrollment of the Population, by Selected Counties, 2017—*Continued*

(Number.)

State/County	Total population	Population enrolled in college or graduate school	Male Total population	Male Enrolled in public college or graduate school	Male Enrolled in private college or graduate school	Female Total population	Female Enrolled in public college or graduate school	Female Enrolled in private college or graduate school
FLORIDA—(*Continued*)								
Leon County, Florida	244,849	56,913	114,742	24,801	1,589	130,107	29,249	1,274
Manatee County, Florida	326,868	14,375	156,360	5,807	772	170,508	5,485	2,311
Marion County, Florida	299,171	14,094	141,694	4,471	1,170	157,477	6,325	2,128
Martin County, Florida	137,787	7,133	67,698	3,177	374	70,089	2,929	653
Miami-Dade County, Florida	2,288,674	208,641	1,099,277	65,917	25,791	1,189,397	79,237	37,696
Nassau County, Florida	69,437	3,847	33,594	1,713	103	35,843	1,673	358
Okaloosa County, Florida	164,718	11,515	84,297	5,246	1,088	80,421	4,466	715
Orange County, Florida	1,098,711	117,462	534,282	41,990	12,035	564,429	48,740	14,697
Osceola County, Florida	280,938	20,041	136,429	7,155	1,148	144,509	8,633	3,105
Palm Beach County, Florida	1,238,348	92,657	594,673	29,806	8,972	643,675	40,601	13,278
Pasco County, Florida	437,847	26,108	210,727	8,465	3,188	227,120	10,015	4,440
Pinellas County, Florida	839,330	55,087	398,780	19,768	4,833	440,550	25,327	5,159
Polk County, Florida	560,058	34,019	271,552	8,519	4,973	288,506	13,204	7,323
St. Johns County, Florida	200,219	11,344	97,551	2,602	2,085	102,668	4,073	2,584
St. Lucie County, Florida	261,894	16,606	126,268	5,286	2,069	135,626	6,322	2,929
Santa Rosa County, Florida	143,461	8,836	73,432	3,139	499	70,029	3,859	1,339
Sarasota County, Florida	370,323	13,121	174,376	4,521	704	195,947	6,386	1,510
Seminole County, Florida	382,480	37,547	183,096	15,727	2,333	199,384	15,439	4,048
Volusia County, Florida	459,573	31,523	222,667	8,424	5,425	236,906	12,351	5,323
GEORGIA								
Barrow County, Georgia	61,367	3,920	28,959	1,090	318	32,408	1,911	601
Bibb County, Georgia	121,708	11,339	55,533	3,406	1,482	66,175	3,790	2,661
Bulloch County, Georgia	63,128	16,971	30,137	8,169	406	32,991	7,918	478
Carroll County, Georgia	94,481	9,987	45,042	2,703	564	49,439	6,167	553
Chatham County, Georgia	237,411	29,781	112,576	8,352	4,115	124,835	12,004	5,310
Cherokee County, Georgia	197,604	18,562	95,414	5,259	1,400	102,190	8,776	3,127
Clarke County, Georgia	108,839	33,261	51,100	15,299	105	57,739	16,876	981
Clayton County, Georgia	218,503	16,201	99,766	4,803	1,667	118,737	7,545	2,186
Cobb County, Georgia	606,636	56,489	289,927	21,862	3,266	316,709	25,548	5,813
Columbia County, Georgia	120,444	13,887	58,673	4,908	326	61,771	7,870	783
Coweta County, Georgia	114,284	5,995	55,494	2,538	544	58,790	2,351	562
DeKalb County, Georgia	604,760	55,228	280,111	13,725	9,933	324,649	14,884	16,686
Dougherty County, Georgia	71,321	9,372	32,418	2,176	236	38,903	6,400	560
Douglas County, Georgia	112,976	7,364	52,597	2,048	235	60,379	3,800	1,281
Fayette County, Georgia	91,954	5,283	44,299	2,375	330	47,655	1,995	583
Floyd County, Georgia	78,865	5,322	37,017	933	801	41,848	1,716	1,872
Forsyth County, Georgia	175,755	11,609	86,739	4,309	968	89,016	4,645	1,687
Fulton County, Georgia	849,356	82,262	406,377	29,015	8,830	442,979	31,346	13,071
Glynn County, Georgia	69,845	5,031	32,612	1,506	477	37,233	1,904	1,144
Gwinnett County, Georgia	715,809	55,486	346,836	20,263	5,094	368,973	21,944	8,185
Hall County, Georgia	157,308	9,333	78,033	3,357	506	79,275	4,094	1,376
Henry County, Georgia	177,764	12,932	83,593	3,774	1,467	94,171	5,068	2,623
Houston County, Georgia	121,141	9,411	57,638	3,035	422	63,503	4,664	1,290
Jackson County, Georgia	53,394	3,258	27,481	838	209	25,913	1,949	262
Lowndes County, Georgia	92,076	11,159	44,213	3,015	628	47,863	7,291	225
Muscogee County, Georgia	152,763	15,191	73,368	5,564	125	79,395	8,227	1,275
Newton County, Georgia	85,133	5,724	39,698	1,115	448	45,435	3,458	703
Paulding County, Georgia	123,461	6,421	58,707	2,201	483	64,754	3,189	548
Richmond County, Georgia	162,127	14,686	77,519	4,473	1,926	84,608	5,915	2,372
Troup County, Georgia	54,909	2,519	25,747	946	0	29,162	1,291	282
Walton County, Georgia	72,992	4,306	34,835	1,580	262	38,157	1,919	545
HAWAII								
Hawaii County, Hawaii	163,192	8,893	80,573	3,115	523	82,619	4,131	1,124
Honolulu County, Hawaii	810,403	76,780	406,553	29,166	8,908	403,850	28,810	9,896
Kauai County, Hawaii	58,137	1,758	28,298	413	161	29,839	1,083	101
Maui County, Hawaii	136,018	5,102	67,558	1,818	1,215	68,460	1,658	411
IDAHO								
Ada County, Idaho	366,150	31,704	183,062	13,678	1,564	183,088	15,254	1,208
Bannock County, Idaho	67,430	8,118	33,220	3,979	208	34,210	3,641	290
Bonneville County, Idaho	84,863	5,856	41,977	2,703	726	42,886	1,824	603
Canyon County, Idaho	165,207	11,885	81,632	3,411	1,807	83,575	4,654	2,013
Kootenai County, Idaho	127,325	6,100	62,283	2,891	80	65,042	2,332	797
Twin Falls County, Idaho	65,030	4,176	31,546	1,645	621	33,484	1,530	380
ILLINOIS								
Adams County, Illinois	53,741	3,108	26,070	853	206	27,671	1,105	944
Champaign County, Illinois	176,438	49,292	87,702	24,969	378	88,736	22,939	1,006

Table C-3. College Enrollment of the Population, by Selected Counties, 2017—*Continued*

(Number.)

State/County	Total population	Population enrolled in college or graduate school	Male Total population	Male Enrolled in public college or graduate school	Male Enrolled in private college or graduate school	Female Total population	Female Enrolled in public college or graduate school	Female Enrolled in private college or graduate school
ILLINOIS—(*Continued*)								
Cook County, Illinois	4,255,478	352,960	2,044,280	88,225	66,416	2,211,198	106,757	91,562
DeKalb County, Illinois	85,981	15,935	41,937	7,032	906	44,044	7,541	456
DuPage County, Illinois	756,133	65,024	368,162	17,269	12,106	387,971	20,055	15,594
Kane County, Illinois	421,743	34,996	209,031	11,177	5,016	212,712	14,089	4,714
Kankakee County, Illinois	88,876	7,798	43,308	1,848	1,530	45,568	2,565	1,855
Lake County, Illinois	564,682	43,299	280,722	14,942	6,517	283,960	15,560	6,280
LaSalle County, Illinois	90,836	4,410	45,478	2,173	302	45,358	1,559	376
McHenry County, Illinois	250,242	18,054	123,678	6,046	686	126,564	9,045	2,277
McLean County, Illinois	141,202	24,761	67,916	9,347	736	73,286	13,321	1,357
Macon County, Illinois	86,209	4,742	40,505	801	1,036	45,704	2,405	500
Madison County, Illinois	217,451	17,372	104,779	6,864	1,510	112,672	7,872	1,126
Peoria County, Illinois	146,324	11,682	69,927	2,206	3,041	76,397	4,108	2,327
Rock Island County, Illinois	117,765	8,708	57,077	1,895	1,559	60,688	3,505	1,749
St. Clair County, Illinois	210,927	13,971	100,815	4,152	1,797	110,112	6,408	1,614
Sangamon County, Illinois	159,988	10,358	75,340	3,444	980	84,648	4,754	1,180
Tazewell County, Illinois	108,413	6,787	52,739	1,945	1,120	55,674	2,546	1,176
Vermilion County, Illinois	61,976	2,858	30,911	1,248	177	31,065	1,164	269
Will County, Illinois	552,023	41,873	272,359	13,254	5,210	279,664	15,733	7,676
Winnebago County, Illinois	230,082	12,670	110,837	3,818	1,391	119,245	5,542	1,919
INDIANA								
Allen County, Indiana	292,672	20,749	141,076	6,042	2,874	151,596	9,080	2,753
Bartholomew County, Indiana	65,622	2,804	32,585	611	140	33,037	1,846	207
Clark County, Indiana	95,084	6,050	45,637	2,571	202	49,447	2,407	870
Delaware County, Indiana	98,016	18,258	46,671	8,609	249	51,345	8,779	621
Elkhart County, Indiana	157,774	8,594	77,542	3,196	1,006	80,232	2,620	1,772
Floyd County, Indiana	62,793	4,660	30,747	2,097	216	32,046	1,741	606
Grant County, Indiana	54,923	6,563	25,579	359	1,675	29,344	744	3,785
Hamilton County, Indiana	249,221	13,429	119,379	5,013	1,572	129,842	5,786	1,058
Hancock County, Indiana	60,484	3,443	29,260	1,679	0	31,224	1,242	522
Hendricks County, Indiana	129,414	10,186	63,899	4,161	553	65,515	4,744	728
Johnson County, Indiana	122,087	8,278	59,152	2,513	1,272	62,935	2,437	2,056
Kosciusko County, Indiana	63,933	3,381	32,063	295	742	31,870	1,650	694
Lake County, Indiana	391,178	25,266	186,438	8,629	2,099	204,740	11,798	2,740
LaPorte County, Indiana	90,392	3,487	46,573	821	267	43,819	1,428	971
Madison County, Indiana	106,271	4,726	52,707	1,622	426	53,564	1,757	921
Marion County, Indiana	752,148	57,771	356,226	19,991	5,566	395,922	22,070	10,144
Monroe County, Indiana	127,549	38,879	63,462	18,823	687	64,087	18,960	409
Porter County, Indiana	138,106	8,886	68,563	1,774	1,661	69,543	3,356	2,095
St. Joseph County, Indiana	217,316	24,138	104,348	2,655	7,219	112,968	6,029	8,235
Tippecanoe County, Indiana	157,198	40,645	80,199	22,378	378	76,999	17,096	793
Vanderburgh County, Indiana	148,540	12,720	70,909	4,083	1,907	77,631	5,949	781
Vigo County, Indiana	89,163	12,752	45,009	4,806	1,715	44,154	5,693	538
Wayne County, Indiana	54,294	3,636	26,162	997	713	28,132	1,225	701
IOWA								
Black Hawk County, Iowa	108,544	15,583	52,069	5,343	357	56,475	9,095	788
Dallas County, Iowa	66,438	4,027	32,188	1,275	209	34,250	2,076	467
Dubuque County, Iowa	78,504	8,502	38,234	1,172	3,152	40,270	2,184	1,994
Johnson County, Iowa	123,221	32,525	60,905	15,499	982	62,316	14,777	1,267
Linn County, Iowa	180,002	12,718	87,964	3,713	2,214	92,038	4,722	2,069
Polk County, Iowa	380,247	28,772	185,665	7,091	5,607	194,582	9,600	6,474
Pottawattamie County, Iowa	75,158	4,723	36,448	1,571	430	38,710	2,312	410
Scott County, Iowa	138,386	9,600	67,463	2,256	1,619	70,923	2,997	2,728
Story County, Iowa	84,014	30,577	44,625	18,345	818	39,389	11,058	356
Woodbury County, Iowa	80,070	5,070	39,519	601	1,663	40,551	1,494	1,312
KANSAS								
Butler County, Kansas	52,845	3,730	27,109	1,581	212	25,736	1,722	215
Douglas County, Kansas	102,366	22,463	49,850	10,522	504	52,516	10,728	709
Johnson County, Kansas	470,549	34,964	228,536	12,870	2,958	242,013	14,583	4,553
Leavenworth County, Kansas	64,363	5,731	34,817	2,140	1,231	29,546	2,098	262
Riley County, Kansas	63,251	21,983	33,411	11,065	263	29,840	10,276	379
Sedgwick County, Kansas	402,934	33,829	197,577	11,818	3,034	205,357	15,096	3,881
Shawnee County, Kansas	143,234	8,433	68,956	3,210	575	74,278	4,124	524
Wyandotte County, Kansas	125,851	7,779	61,498	1,655	1,030	64,353	3,586	1,508
KENTUCKY								
Boone County, Kentucky	102,560	6,050	50,285	2,172	334	52,275	3,125	419
Campbell County, Kentucky	76,781	7,335	37,110	3,005	454	39,671	3,459	417

Table C-3. College Enrollment of the Population, by Selected Counties, 2017—*Continued*

(Number.)

			Male			Female		
State/County	Total population	Population enrolled in college or graduate school	Total population	Enrolled in public college or graduate school	Enrolled in private college or graduate school	Total population	Enrolled in public college or graduate school	Enrolled in private college or graduate school
KENTUCKY—(*Continued*)								
Christian County, Kentucky	53,651	4,074	28,614	1,428	106	25,037	1,979	561
Daviess County, Kentucky	79,904	4,612	38,361	1,820	330	41,543	1,983	479
Fayette County, Kentucky	264,428	37,023	128,363	15,708	1,457	136,065	18,022	1,836
Hardin County, Kentucky	85,407	6,782	42,087	2,854	767	43,320	2,098	1,063
Jefferson County, Kentucky	627,663	44,352	300,223	14,995	5,555	327,440	17,234	6,568
Kenton County, Kentucky	132,065	8,358	64,663	2,837	1,012	67,402	3,597	912
Madison County, Kentucky	75,463	11,818	36,540	3,919	921	38,923	5,687	1,291
Oldham County, Kentucky	51,975	4,315	26,828	1,197	260	25,147	1,970	888
Warren County, Kentucky	104,142	17,469	50,232	7,755	504	53,910	8,263	947
LOUISIANA								
Ascension Parish, Louisiana	95,403	6,733	45,868	1,300	155	49,535	4,170	1,108
Bossier Parish, Louisiana	100,126	6,057	48,549	1,689	301	51,577	3,772	295
Caddo Parish, Louisiana	196,936	11,292	92,073	3,725	207	104,863	6,350	1,010
Calcasieu Parish, Louisiana	159,980	10,022	76,763	3,875	624	83,217	5,044	479
East Baton Rouge Parish, Louisiana	361,281	47,405	171,048	19,130	2,670	190,233	21,288	4,317
Jefferson Parish, Louisiana	358,166	25,576	171,621	7,533	2,629	186,545	11,111	4,303
Lafayette Parish, Louisiana	193,526	18,126	93,298	7,052	756	100,228	9,065	1,253
Lafourche Parish, Louisiana	79,547	4,829	38,560	1,662	107	40,987	2,438	622
Livingston Parish, Louisiana	108,730	5,219	51,787	1,313	746	56,943	1,447	1,713
Orleans Parish, Louisiana	326,015	34,500	152,759	6,750	6,147	173,256	11,222	10,381
Ouachita Parish, Louisiana	123,576	9,333	58,310	3,768	216	65,266	4,797	552
Rapides Parish, Louisiana	104,273	7,219	49,493	1,634	593	54,780	4,102	890
St. Tammany Parish, Louisiana	205,043	11,134	98,853	4,663	344	106,190	5,327	800
Tangipahoa Parish, Louisiana	104,988	7,418	50,289	2,396	353	54,699	4,669	0
Terrebonne Parish, Louisiana	89,441	3,076	43,826	850	494	45,615	1,688	44
MAINE								
Androscoggin County, Maine	88,069	7,573	43,011	2,235	1,033	45,058	2,788	1,517
Aroostook County, Maine	57,437	2,836	28,312	1,021	362	29,125	1,165	288
Cumberland County, Maine	247,038	23,914	118,390	5,745	3,489	128,648	9,356	5,324
Kennebec County, Maine	102,798	6,645	49,544	1,582	1,575	53,254	1,949	1,539
Penobscot County, Maine	129,684	15,765	63,812	6,620	1,053	65,872	6,582	1,510
York County, Maine	172,790	9,579	83,984	2,303	1,616	88,806	3,700	1,960
MARYLAND								
Allegany County, Maryland	61,280	6,020	32,270	2,180	226	29,010	3,559	55
Anne Arundel County, Maryland	466,794	38,433	229,796	13,526	3,718	236,998	16,528	4,661
Baltimore County, Maryland	683,122	65,303	319,112	20,983	6,582	364,010	29,123	8,615
Calvert County, Maryland	74,637	4,606	36,453	2,192	432	38,184	1,579	403
Carroll County, Maryland	138,408	10,035	68,005	2,214	1,778	70,403	3,908	2,135
Cecil County, Maryland	83,733	6,316	41,455	951	285	42,278	4,070	1,010
Charles County, Maryland	127,979	10,524	60,855	3,997	823	67,124	4,679	1,025
Frederick County, Maryland	204,293	18,430	99,414	5,320	2,393	104,879	6,858	3,859
Harford County, Maryland	206,070	16,290	100,189	5,796	1,262	105,881	7,403	1,829
Howard County, Maryland	257,222	26,850	123,769	9,463	3,054	133,453	10,836	3,497
Montgomery County, Maryland	854,720	75,622	407,979	27,759	8,529	446,741	29,353	9,981
Prince George's County, Maryland	741,842	79,191	352,751	28,154	6,311	389,091	34,469	10,257
St. Mary's County, Maryland	89,991	8,881	44,140	2,992	771	45,851	3,997	1,121
Washington County, Maryland	123,807	6,947	62,822	2,706	565	60,985	2,849	827
Wicomico County, Maryland	83,559	11,357	39,363	4,175	240	44,196	6,707	235
Baltimore city, Maryland	504,714	56,270	232,785	13,514	9,112	271,929	20,854	12,790
MASSACHUSETTS								
Barnstable County, Massachusetts	187,271	7,511	88,944	2,010	1,431	98,327	2,696	1,374
Berkshire County, Massachusetts	109,337	8,703	52,357	2,030	1,811	56,980	2,565	2,297
Bristol County, Massachusetts	466,486	35,858	222,612	10,405	4,650	243,874	13,674	7,129
Essex County, Massachusetts	647,461	49,642	308,705	11,426	8,641	338,756	17,129	12,446
Franklin County, Massachusetts	60,491	4,217	29,189	1,101	342	31,302	2,092	682
Hampden County, Massachusetts	386,883	35,768	184,809	9,309	5,641	202,074	13,330	7,488
Hampshire County, Massachusetts	142,726	36,679	64,983	13,156	1,516	77,743	13,822	8,185
Middlesex County, Massachusetts	1,340,180	144,686	650,288	25,654	44,236	689,892	26,893	47,903
Norfolk County, Massachusetts	579,885	50,983	275,154	8,952	13,111	304,731	10,802	18,118
Plymouth County, Massachusetts	424,991	33,857	204,566	11,071	4,531	220,425	11,748	6,507
Suffolk County, Massachusetts	685,736	112,046	329,859	11,786	37,964	355,877	15,610	46,686
Worcester County, Massachusetts	683,332	62,964	334,707	15,398	12,963	348,625	18,604	15,999
MICHIGAN								
Allegan County, Michigan	93,113	4,827	46,498	1,273	322	46,615	2,753	479
Bay County, Michigan	86,619	5,976	42,341	2,724	295	44,278	2,821	136
Berrien County, Michigan	126,103	7,058	61,351	1,476	1,412	64,752	2,791	1,379

Table C-3. College Enrollment of the Population, by Selected Counties, 2017—*Continued*

(Number.)

State/County	Total population	Population enrolled in college or graduate school	Male			Female		
			Total population	Enrolled in public college or graduate school	Enrolled in private college or graduate school	Total population	Enrolled in public college or graduate school	Enrolled in private college or graduate school
MICHIGAN—(*Continued*)								
Calhoun County, Michigan	109,298	7,101	52,933	2,010	862	56,365	3,128	1,101
Clinton County, Michigan	64,206	5,486	31,401	1,727	404	32,805	3,116	239
Eaton County, Michigan	90,517	6,253	44,192	1,508	1,073	46,325	2,794	878
Genesee County, Michigan	331,522	21,473	157,316	8,221	2,668	174,206	9,415	1,169
Grand Traverse County, Michigan	77,300	4,978	37,864	1,653	603	39,436	2,501	221
Ingham County, Michigan	241,944	51,103	116,224	24,157	1,583	125,720	24,418	945
Isabella County, Michigan	61,188	18,992	29,698	7,527	1,369	31,490	9,785	311
Jackson County, Michigan	130,811	9,599	66,136	3,154	1,194	64,675	3,825	1,426
Kalamazoo County, Michigan	215,619	33,771	104,729	13,338	2,873	110,890	15,517	2,043
Kent County, Michigan	517,004	41,535	252,374	13,165	4,834	264,630	16,797	6,739
Lapeer County, Michigan	73,592	3,090	37,269	1,328	272	36,323	1,382	108
Lenawee County, Michigan	81,554	5,852	41,092	1,596	1,429	40,462	1,559	1,268
Livingston County, Michigan	156,987	10,766	78,058	4,205	909	78,929	5,009	643
Macomb County, Michigan	720,359	51,801	346,950	17,165	4,983	373,409	24,685	4,968
Marquette County, Michigan	56,328	7,524	28,407	2,800	271	27,921	4,116	337
Midland County, Michigan	68,796	5,033	33,504	1,498	698	35,292	1,577	1,260
Monroe County, Michigan	123,738	6,987	60,911	2,228	552	62,827	3,366	841
Muskegon County, Michigan	141,160	9,096	70,083	2,836	939	71,077	3,891	1,430
Oakland County, Michigan	1,034,965	79,884	501,628	29,156	7,657	533,337	33,243	9,828
Ottawa County, Michigan	228,673	26,615	112,325	9,742	2,346	116,348	11,260	3,267
Saginaw County, Michigan	158,583	12,488	76,037	3,907	586	82,546	7,565	430
St. Clair County, Michigan	132,437	6,821	65,529	2,587	326	66,908	3,347	561
Shiawassee County, Michigan	56,544	3,682	27,961	1,462	180	28,583	1,633	407
Van Buren County, Michigan	60,528	3,250	30,062	965	125	30,466	1,643	517
Washtenaw County, Michigan	311,121	69,734	153,631	33,809	1,587	157,490	32,608	1,730
Wayne County, Michigan	1,409,641	109,809	668,798	38,870	6,642	740,843	54,964	9,333
MINNESOTA								
Anoka County, Minnesota	281,655	18,180	140,164	7,713	1,245	141,491	7,264	1,958
Blue Earth County, Minnesota	56,448	12,699	28,516	5,381	590	27,932	6,417	311
Carver County, Minnesota	79,176	4,786	38,967	1,456	586	40,209	1,865	879
Dakota County, Minnesota	335,743	23,183	163,709	8,997	2,236	172,034	8,167	3,783
Hennepin County, Minnesota	1,019,754	91,716	501,327	33,619	7,663	518,427	40,394	10,040
Olmsted County, Minnesota	123,465	9,762	58,828	2,689	1,138	64,637	4,570	1,365
Ramsey County, Minnesota	440,038	48,900	211,504	11,485	9,918	228,534	16,189	11,308
Rice County, Minnesota	54,056	7,942	27,689	1,221	2,311	26,367	744	3,666
St. Louis County, Minnesota	168,268	18,889	83,744	8,809	1,009	84,524	7,146	1,925
Scott County, Minnesota	111,910	8,105	55,726	3,054	508	56,184	3,358	1,185
Sherburne County, Minnesota	74,077	5,169	38,608	1,865	728	35,469	2,354	222
Stearns County, Minnesota	127,245	16,291	63,744	5,153	2,048	63,501	6,622	2,468
Washington County, Minnesota	204,698	14,446	101,221	4,357	1,868	103,477	5,524	2,697
Wright County, Minnesota	102,977	6,133	51,658	2,361	553	51,319	2,387	832
MISSISSIPPI								
DeSoto County, Mississippi	141,091	8,016	67,452	2,449	452	73,639	4,358	757
Forrest County, Mississippi	60,802	9,333	28,299	3,314	123	32,503	5,031	865
Harrison County, Mississippi	163,431	12,438	78,466	5,474	1,049	84,965	5,530	385
Hinds County, Mississippi	190,781	21,538	86,981	5,568	1,768	103,800	10,510	3,692
Jackson County, Mississippi	115,020	6,401	56,062	2,577	515	58,958	2,980	329
Lauderdale County, Mississippi	60,680	5,064	29,406	1,945	186	31,274	2,905	28
Lee County, Mississippi	66,684	4,098	31,610	801	406	35,074	2,150	741
Madison County, Mississippi	82,929	7,939	39,225	2,787	1,278	43,704	2,556	1,318
Rankin County, Mississippi	122,321	8,376	57,670	2,479	349	64,651	3,311	2,237
MISSOURI								
Boone County, Missouri	147,824	33,429	71,448	14,835	1,112	76,376	16,351	1,131
Buchanan County, Missouri	71,895	4,357	35,397	1,746	99	36,498	2,163	349
Cass County, Missouri	82,606	3,318	40,019	1,188	235	42,587	1,485	410
Christian County, Missouri	68,064	6,232	32,823	2,191	349	35,241	3,071	621
Clay County, Missouri	193,803	15,222	94,476	5,023	2,130	99,327	5,559	2,510
Cole County, Missouri	62,623	3,644	31,660	1,567	47	30,963	1,817	213
Greene County, Missouri	238,627	30,932	115,351	11,510	2,896	123,276	13,076	3,450
Jackson County, Missouri	559,669	36,399	267,550	12,480	2,425	292,119	16,205	5,289
Jasper County, Missouri	95,101	6,948	46,492	2,185	687	48,609	3,552	524
Jefferson County, Missouri	180,876	10,380	90,093	2,776	1,464	90,783	4,606	1,534
Platte County, Missouri	81,327	5,445	39,673	1,699	464	41,654	2,218	1,064
St. Charles County, Missouri	318,534	26,892	154,807	6,038	4,775	163,727	7,660	8,419
St. Francois County, Missouri	55,087	3,023	30,429	1,092	265	24,658	1,461	205
St. Louis County, Missouri	816,535	61,725	381,242	14,353	13,917	435,293	19,429	14,026
St. Louis city, Missouri	257,454	24,927	123,084	4,051	6,519	134,370	7,076	7,281

Table C-3. College Enrollment of the Population, by Selected Counties, 2017—*Continued*

(Number.)

State/County	Total population	Population enrolled in college or graduate school	Male Total population	Male Enrolled in public college or graduate school	Male Enrolled in private college or graduate school	Female Total population	Female Enrolled in public college or graduate school	Female Enrolled in private college or graduate school
MONTANA								
Cascade County, Montana	65,861	3,917	32,918	1,617	333	32,943	1,586	381
Flathead County, Montana	82,311	3,281	40,018	1,481	123	42,293	1,333	344
Gallatin County, Montana	89,326	15,345	46,533	8,294	265	42,793	6,443	343
Lewis and Clark County, Montana	55,565	3,915	26,929	601	1,024	28,636	1,176	1,114
Missoula County, Montana	98,661	12,699	49,027	5,664	1,003	49,634	5,771	261
Yellowstone County, Montana	127,595	6,460	62,592	2,057	652	65,003	2,888	863
NEBRASKA								
Douglas County, Nebraska	440,084	40,749	214,754	13,755	5,419	225,330	13,906	7,669
Lancaster County, Nebraska	253,488	37,320	126,657	16,274	2,235	126,831	14,969	3,842
Sarpy County, Nebraska	140,082	12,040	69,137	4,423	873	70,945	5,211	1,533
NEVADA								
Clark County, Nevada	1,775,740	118,788	881,020	44,093	9,874	894,720	52,015	12,806
Washoe County, Nevada	376,875	33,330	188,385	14,440	1,349	188,490	14,720	2,821
NEW HAMPSHIRE								
Cheshire County, New Hampshire	64,859	8,538	31,095	2,124	1,168	33,764	3,523	1,723
Grafton County, New Hampshire	77,386	9,632	38,056	1,641	2,453	39,330	2,869	2,669
Hillsborough County, New Hampshire	340,709	26,173	168,013	5,833	5,518	172,696	8,006	6,816
Merrimack County, New Hampshire	126,174	8,671	61,422	1,834	1,584	64,752	2,540	2,713
Rockingham County, New Hampshire	258,265	14,960	127,282	3,967	2,615	130,983	5,276	3,102
Strafford County, New Hampshire	109,222	15,744	53,154	6,859	524	56,068	7,375	986
NEW JERSEY								
Atlantic County, New Jersey	222,569	18,370	106,885	6,600	1,458	115,684	8,430	1,882
Bergen County, New Jersey	784,038	62,153	376,351	20,482	11,473	407,687	18,423	11,775
Burlington County, New Jersey	372,319	26,518	182,044	8,945	3,422	190,275	10,245	3,906
Camden County, New Jersey	414,223	31,826	197,262	11,185	3,665	216,961	13,129	3,847
Cape May County, New Jersey	80,131	4,428	38,821	1,684	558	41,310	1,379	807
Cumberland County, New Jersey	122,626	5,798	62,713	1,744	394	59,913	2,982	678
Essex County, New Jersey	649,071	55,560	307,643	18,871	7,158	341,428	20,313	9,218
Gloucester County, New Jersey	239,899	21,332	115,045	7,823	1,705	124,854	9,484	2,320
Hudson County, New Jersey	571,824	50,761	282,652	16,376	8,502	289,172	17,428	8,455
Hunterdon County, New Jersey	105,883	6,847	52,863	1,941	992	53,020	2,398	1,516
Mercer County, New Jersey	309,206	30,987	149,601	7,598	6,422	159,605	9,670	7,297
Middlesex County, New Jersey	692,488	70,880	338,576	27,162	6,248	353,912	30,780	6,690
Monmouth County, New Jersey	518,501	40,353	249,290	11,838	5,240	269,211	16,058	7,217
Morris County, New Jersey	413,841	32,909	201,107	8,567	5,743	212,734	11,135	7,464
Ocean County, New Jersey	478,167	33,806	226,802	7,155	9,351	251,365	11,694	5,606
Passaic County, New Jersey	410,465	36,988	197,084	12,232	5,645	213,381	14,217	4,894
Salem County, New Jersey	51,659	3,008	24,923	851	403	26,736	1,299	455
Somerset County, New Jersey	275,985	17,721	133,664	7,189	2,465	142,321	4,992	3,075
Sussex County, New Jersey	119,737	7,810	59,482	2,673	1,209	60,255	2,533	1,395
Union County, New Jersey	454,837	33,698	219,559	11,680	3,108	235,278	14,391	4,519
Warren County, New Jersey	89,979	5,811	44,077	1,583	568	45,902	2,662	998
NEW MEXICO								
Bernalillo County, New Mexico	552,924	51,673	268,066	20,640	2,180	284,858	23,725	5,128
Doña Ana County, New Mexico	171,099	24,653	84,136	10,968	238	86,963	11,874	1,573
Lea County, New Mexico	51,138	3,222	26,361	1,593	120	24,777	1,457	52
McKinley County, New Mexico	54,857	2,902	25,945	835	0	28,912	1,948	119
Otero County, New Mexico	53,374	3,738	28,593	1,145	591	24,781	1,366	636
Sandoval County, New Mexico	115,149	9,783	55,346	3,744	478	59,803	4,497	1,064
San Juan County, New Mexico	98,608	7,652	47,785	3,218	103	50,823	3,597	734
Santa Fe County, New Mexico	126,394	7,064	61,079	2,406	293	65,315	3,480	885
Valencia County, New Mexico	61,373	3,665	29,981	1,143	165	31,392	2,089	268
NEW YORK								
Albany County, New York	262,034	37,799	126,479	11,850	4,041	135,555	13,677	8,231
Bronx County, New York	1,165,799	105,327	538,317	31,722	14,574	627,482	39,792	19,239
Broome County, New York	162,625	20,647	79,356	10,635	449	83,269	8,780	783
Cattaraugus County, New York	63,103	3,618	31,267	919	989	31,836	710	1,000
Cayuga County, New York	65,604	3,444	33,429	812	430	32,175	1,511	691
Chautauqua County, New York	107,499	7,748	53,087	3,250	225	54,412	3,704	569
Chemung County, New York	70,343	3,611	34,974	655	595	35,369	1,233	1,128
Clinton County, New York	68,765	7,054	35,804	2,611	34	32,961	4,090	319
Dutchess County, New York	250,532	26,787	124,270	6,604	6,027	126,262	6,877	7,279
Erie County, New York	771,041	70,947	369,565	25,031	7,217	401,476	26,653	12,046

Table C-3. College Enrollment of the Population, by Selected Counties, 2017—*Continued*

(Number.)

State/County	Total population	Population enrolled in college or graduate school	Male			Female		
			Total population	Enrolled in public college or graduate school	Enrolled in private college or graduate school	Total population	Enrolled in public college or graduate school	Enrolled in private college or graduate school
NEW YORK—(*Continued*)								
Jefferson County, New York	90,830	5,962	48,237	2,322	441	42,593	2,154	1,045
Kings County, New York	2,133,982	180,326	991,004	51,000	30,252	1,142,978	58,862	40,212
Livingston County, New York	55,060	7,788	27,860	2,898	391	27,200	3,900	599
Madison County, New York	59,499	6,116	29,341	1,127	1,666	30,158	1,647	1,676
Monroe County, New York	618,838	62,031	295,526	12,180	15,903	323,312	16,588	17,360
Nassau County, New York	1,129,254	98,768	542,625	24,698	20,559	586,629	29,952	23,559
New York County, New York	1,459,745	146,880	685,573	19,746	40,321	774,172	31,578	55,235
Niagara County, New York	176,421	10,662	85,389	3,631	2,201	91,032	2,719	2,111
Oneida County, New York	190,216	14,382	94,065	4,930	2,019	96,151	3,953	3,480
Onondaga County, New York	383,661	41,882	183,011	8,145	9,930	200,650	8,956	14,851
Ontario County, New York	92,380	6,920	44,848	1,646	1,647	47,532	1,872	1,755
Orange County, New York	302,135	27,581	150,964	9,957	4,086	151,171	9,163	4,375
Oswego County, New York	98,343	8,912	48,857	3,970	660	49,486	4,108	174
Putnam County, New York	83,475	4,749	41,022	1,495	1,147	42,453	1,070	1,037
Queens County, New York	1,959,335	169,912	938,817	54,065	20,162	1,020,518	67,172	28,513
Rensselaer County, New York	133,900	14,830	65,367	2,588	4,358	68,533	3,261	4,623
Richmond County, New York	393,196	30,547	187,742	7,736	4,194	205,454	12,692	5,925
Rockland County, New York	252,361	23,123	122,042	5,514	5,564	130,319	6,845	5,200
St. Lawrence County, New York	91,683	12,124	46,909	3,621	2,243	44,774	3,763	2,497
Saratoga County, New York	192,098	12,516	93,708	3,482	2,820	98,390	3,503	2,711
Schenectady County, New York	128,366	11,198	61,044	2,351	1,867	67,322	4,473	2,507
Steuben County, New York	79,525	3,302	39,387	928	425	40,138	1,442	507
Suffolk County, New York	1,234,816	100,570	603,153	33,224	13,649	631,663	36,493	17,204
Tompkins County, New York	93,012	27,821	45,710	5,218	8,705	47,302	6,024	7,874
Ulster County, New York	153,537	12,596	75,681	4,700	1,254	77,856	4,890	1,752
Wayne County, New York	74,748	3,733	36,830	1,323	446	37,918	1,187	777
Westchester County, New York	803,210	61,316	383,865	13,764	13,678	419,345	16,781	17,093
NORTH CAROLINA								
Alamance County, North Carolina	131,990	12,553	61,685	2,410	1,658	70,305	5,754	2,731
Brunswick County, North Carolina	113,605	4,004	53,903	1,083	154	59,702	2,560	207
Buncombe County, North Carolina	218,460	14,218	103,536	4,858	991	114,924	6,906	1,463
Burke County, North Carolina	75,495	2,654	38,387	969	544	37,108	648	493
Cabarrus County, North Carolina	162,643	12,627	78,123	5,251	887	84,520	3,974	2,515
Caldwell County, North Carolina	68,600	2,964	33,242	852	363	35,358	1,438	311
Carteret County, North Carolina	58,717	2,937	28,849	1,146	123	29,868	1,274	394
Catawba County, North Carolina	129,335	7,442	62,095	2,292	385	67,240	3,440	1,325
Chatham County, North Carolina	58,500	2,619	28,017	830	58	30,483	921	810
Cleveland County, North Carolina	79,765	5,689	37,839	1,638	237	41,926	2,691	1,123
Craven County, North Carolina	82,637	6,141	41,231	2,500	250	41,406	2,347	1,044
Cumberland County, North Carolina	263,431	28,211	130,912	9,197	3,922	132,519	11,780	3,312
Davidson County, North Carolina	135,222	6,861	65,521	2,022	562	69,701	3,879	398
Durham County, North Carolina	255,780	27,842	120,282	6,730	6,134	135,498	8,360	6,618
Forsyth County, North Carolina	304,184	26,135	142,212	6,863	4,504	161,972	9,241	5,527
Gaston County, North Carolina	179,262	9,289	85,217	3,774	885	94,045	3,635	995
Guilford County, North Carolina	429,893	47,044	200,146	17,320	3,981	229,747	20,397	5,346
Harnett County, North Carolina	102,559	12,356	50,408	2,924	2,677	52,151	4,676	2,079
Henderson County, North Carolina	97,642	5,631	45,929	1,470	608	51,713	2,326	1,227
Iredell County, North Carolina	142,306	8,948	69,534	2,492	751	72,772	4,426	1,279
Johnston County, North Carolina	154,926	10,047	74,859	2,633	723	80,067	5,087	1,604
Lincoln County, North Carolina	68,101	3,152	33,081	1,565	121	35,020	1,191	275
Mecklenburg County, North Carolina	861,629	73,594	408,798	26,946	5,534	452,831	28,825	12,289
Moore County, North Carolina	80,798	5,558	38,353	1,251	203	42,445	2,834	1,270
Nash County, North Carolina	76,867	5,083	36,381	1,458	604	40,486	2,739	282
New Hanover County, North Carolina	191,611	22,180	89,817	9,066	647	101,794	10,976	1,491
Onslow County, North Carolina	153,640	17,192	85,544	8,242	1,137	68,096	6,315	1,498
Orange County, North Carolina	121,085	27,525	56,429	11,001	792	64,656	15,231	501
Pitt County, North Carolina	147,621	33,060	68,873	13,650	138	78,748	18,972	300
Randolph County, North Carolina	117,577	5,682	58,075	1,978	530	59,502	2,564	610
Robeson County, North Carolina	105,093	8,442	50,017	3,382	362	55,076	4,246	452
Rockingham County, North Carolina	75,629	4,258	35,565	1,480	40	40,064	2,250	488
Rowan County, North Carolina	115,051	7,631	56,971	2,166	1,385	58,080	3,102	978
Surry County, North Carolina	59,924	2,938	28,474	1,059	109	31,450	1,649	121
Union County, North Carolina	180,841	11,553	87,752	3,297	1,422	93,089	4,217	2,617
Wake County, North Carolina	857,316	78,705	412,903	32,038	4,067	444,413	35,288	7,312
Wayne County, North Carolina	100,082	7,181	48,094	1,884	875	51,988	3,438	984
Wilson County, North Carolina	66,065	4,687	30,408	768	248	35,657	2,533	1,138

Table C-3. College Enrollment of the Population, by Selected Counties, 2017—*Continued*

(Number.)

State/County	Total population	Population enrolled in college or graduate school	Male Total population	Male Enrolled in public college or graduate school	Male Enrolled in private college or graduate school	Female Total population	Female Enrolled in public college or graduate school	Female Enrolled in private college or graduate school
NORTH DAKOTA								
Burleigh County, North Dakota	75,717	5,936	37,657	1,975	1,010	38,060	1,673	1,278
Cass County, North Dakota	144,164	19,647	73,455	9,910	811	70,709	8,187	739
Grand Forks County, North Dakota	58,203	11,300	30,398	5,593	180	27,805	5,362	165
Ward County, North Dakota	54,815	5,097	28,686	2,062	301	26,129	2,397	337
OHIO								
Allen County, Ohio	83,575	5,326	41,758	1,811	884	41,817	2,082	549
Ashtabula County, Ohio	80,081	3,390	39,767	1,076	231	40,314	1,497	586
Athens County, Ohio	58,700	20,689	29,598	10,108	206	29,102	10,349	26
Butler County, Ohio	306,627	33,948	148,604	14,661	1,349	158,023	15,368	2,570
Clark County, Ohio	109,650	7,443	52,351	2,115	1,296	57,299	1,887	2,145
Clermont County, Ohio	165,165	8,104	80,093	2,495	614	85,072	3,860	1,135
Columbiana County, Ohio	85,778	2,830	42,783	1,155	0	42,995	1,407	268
Cuyahoga County, Ohio	1,033,917	88,776	485,730	25,002	11,793	548,187	33,266	18,715
Delaware County, Ohio	156,382	12,381	76,295	4,184	1,800	80,087	4,169	2,228
Erie County, Ohio	61,998	4,116	29,750	1,599	74	32,248	1,942	501
Fairfield County, Ohio	124,372	7,183	61,001	2,394	482	63,371	3,257	1,050
Franklin County, Ohio	1,036,163	102,943	500,219	35,724	12,243	535,944	41,498	13,478
Geauga County, Ohio	76,608	3,110	37,490	1,025	215	39,118	1,063	807
Greene County, Ohio	138,317	22,547	66,864	8,768	1,813	71,453	8,607	3,359
Hamilton County, Ohio	656,437	56,469	312,976	20,945	5,708	343,461	24,250	5,566
Hancock County, Ohio	61,890	4,349	30,014	663	452	31,876	971	2,263
Jefferson County, Ohio	55,585	3,670	26,474	561	769	29,111	1,075	1,265
Lake County, Ohio	192,713	12,090	92,919	4,274	876	99,794	4,365	2,575
Licking County, Ohio	140,219	8,440	68,722	2,412	1,427	71,497	2,674	1,927
Lorain County, Ohio	252,267	17,597	123,606	4,530	3,629	128,661	6,732	2,706
Lucas County, Ohio	348,439	28,263	167,283	11,634	1,186	181,156	13,209	2,234
Mahoning County, Ohio	192,232	11,448	92,908	4,697	521	99,324	5,640	590
Marion County, Ohio	53,927	3,257	29,083	1,430	20	24,844	1,539	268
Medina County, Ohio	145,377	8,295	70,877	2,232	1,143	74,500	3,736	1,184
Miami County, Ohio	85,329	4,648	41,703	1,297	126	43,626	2,637	588
Montgomery County, Ohio	434,526	40,552	206,790	10,578	10,009	227,736	12,169	7,796
Muskingum County, Ohio	69,773	4,941	33,389	1,267	1,010	36,384	1,872	792
Portage County, Ohio	137,627	20,027	66,792	8,236	696	70,835	9,984	1,111
Richland County, Ohio	99,110	4,545	49,844	970	886	49,266	1,498	1,191
Ross County, Ohio	63,770	2,598	33,752	1,420	163	30,018	896	119
Scioto County, Ohio	62,511	3,150	30,606	1,196	309	31,905	1,445	200
Stark County, Ohio	306,878	21,273	147,924	6,245	3,615	158,954	7,140	4,273
Summit County, Ohio	447,877	34,092	214,995	13,794	2,142	232,882	15,718	2,438
Trumbull County, Ohio	167,064	7,909	81,045	3,040	196	86,019	4,180	493
Warren County, Ohio	182,521	11,367	90,664	3,812	440	91,857	4,800	2,315
Wayne County, Ohio	93,226	6,271	45,735	2,081	1,117	47,491	2,062	1,011
Wood County, Ohio	108,268	17,749	52,857	8,169	156	55,411	9,007	417
OKLAHOMA								
Canadian County, Oklahoma	110,100	9,236	54,071	2,737	1,033	56,029	4,403	1,063
Cleveland County, Oklahoma	229,260	35,661	114,127	16,158	1,419	115,133	16,563	1,521
Comanche County, Oklahoma	97,224	7,356	50,819	2,772	625	46,405	3,587	372
Creek County, Oklahoma	57,556	2,276	28,194	806	45	29,362	1,347	78
Muskogee County, Oklahoma	55,197	2,985	26,403	1,327	186	28,794	1,421	51
Oklahoma County, Oklahoma	615,676	50,286	298,052	19,235	4,661	317,624	19,991	6,399
Payne County, Oklahoma	67,893	22,282	34,424	10,229	250	33,469	11,709	94
Pottawatomie County, Oklahoma	58,069	4,552	27,350	1,068	708	30,719	1,710	1,066
Rogers County, Oklahoma	73,824	4,354	36,673	1,547	426	37,151	2,080	301
Tulsa County, Oklahoma	508,656	37,815	245,056	11,281	6,597	263,600	14,941	4,996
Wagoner County, Oklahoma	62,903	3,649	30,449	1,354	128	32,454	1,918	249
OREGON								
Benton County, Oregon	78,565	23,089	38,799	12,605	195	39,766	9,931	358
Clackamas County, Oregon	339,717	20,508	166,494	7,236	1,876	173,223	8,417	2,979
Deschutes County, Oregon	154,674	6,354	75,114	1,775	518	79,560	3,901	160
Douglas County, Oregon	91,946	3,167	45,027	1,779	257	46,919	984	147
Jackson County, Oregon	179,701	9,308	86,745	3,746	253	92,956	4,559	750
Lane County, Oregon	317,241	33,122	155,379	12,816	431	161,862	18,101	1,774
Linn County, Oregon	101,375	3,418	49,781	1,091	374	51,594	1,682	271
Marion County, Oregon	270,078	17,818	133,789	6,524	1,992	136,289	6,079	3,223
Multnomah County, Oregon	677,356	59,341	332,932	19,999	6,025	344,424	23,037	10,280
Polk County, Oregon	68,280	6,246	34,344	1,537	224	33,936	3,522	963

Table C-3. College Enrollment of the Population, by Selected Counties, 2017—*Continued*

(Number.)

State/County	Total population	Population enrolled in college or graduate school	Male Total population	Male Enrolled in public college or graduate school	Male Enrolled in private college or graduate school	Female Total population	Female Enrolled in public college or graduate school	Female Enrolled in private college or graduate school
OREGON—(*Continued*)								
Umatilla County, Oregon	60,723	3,987	32,294	1,249	91	28,429	2,128	519
Washington County, Oregon	474,799	37,909	232,244	13,066	2,686	242,555	16,523	5,634
Yamhill County, Oregon	86,138	8,124	43,260	1,686	2,225	42,878	1,374	2,839
PENNSYLVANIA								
Adams County, Pennsylvania	85,631	6,732	42,032	845	1,784	43,599	1,847	2,256
Allegheny County, Pennsylvania	1,032,572	87,261	493,895	23,569	16,068	538,677	29,487	18,137
Armstrong County, Pennsylvania	55,304	2,263	27,529	840	155	27,775	692	576
Beaver County, Pennsylvania	139,077	7,566	66,375	2,262	1,157	72,702	3,124	1,023
Berks County, Pennsylvania	340,856	26,485	165,709	6,399	2,718	175,147	11,570	5,798
Blair County, Pennsylvania	102,761	5,767	49,722	1,619	667	53,039	2,338	1,143
Bucks County, Pennsylvania	523,737	32,454	254,741	7,104	6,554	268,996	9,926	8,870
Butler County, Pennsylvania	156,399	10,665	77,264	3,858	836	79,135	5,130	841
Cambria County, Pennsylvania	112,213	7,730	54,567	2,831	1,247	57,646	2,142	1,510
Centre County, Pennsylvania	142,698	40,348	75,720	21,075	1,016	66,978	17,879	378
Chester County, Pennsylvania	422,236	35,090	206,703	10,809	4,334	215,533	13,485	6,462
Clearfield County, Pennsylvania	67,680	1,914	35,223	450	346	32,457	900	218
Columbia County, Pennsylvania	55,987	7,809	26,763	3,013	59	29,224	4,504	233
Crawford County, Pennsylvania	72,121	3,757	35,091	502	1,032	37,030	835	1,388
Cumberland County, Pennsylvania	207,423	18,912	101,762	5,560	2,851	105,661	5,842	4,659
Dauphin County, Pennsylvania	224,386	12,341	107,352	4,091	1,130	117,034	5,503	1,617
Delaware County, Pennsylvania	462,559	42,840	219,748	9,275	9,555	242,811	10,403	13,607
Erie County, Pennsylvania	225,617	21,099	110,852	6,195	4,581	114,765	4,863	5,460
Fayette County, Pennsylvania	110,809	5,113	54,579	1,289	185	56,230	2,815	824
Franklin County, Pennsylvania	126,299	6,439	61,272	1,794	302	65,027	3,017	1,326
Indiana County, Pennsylvania	72,665	8,579	35,564	3,195	135	37,101	4,930	319
Lackawanna County, Pennsylvania	175,415	13,460	83,907	1,470	4,416	91,508	1,863	5,711
Lancaster County, Pennsylvania	435,800	27,050	211,551	7,846	4,968	224,249	9,005	5,231
Lawrence County, Pennsylvania	72,799	4,079	34,844	1,054	675	37,955	1,333	1,017
Lebanon County, Pennsylvania	113,339	5,686	54,763	1,838	943	58,576	1,902	1,003
Lehigh County, Pennsylvania	297,839	21,537	143,915	6,083	3,063	153,924	6,575	5,816
Luzerne County, Pennsylvania	266,430	16,571	130,868	3,864	3,581	135,562	3,893	5,233
Lycoming County, Pennsylvania	94,313	7,464	45,787	3,583	550	48,526	2,030	1,301
Mercer County, Pennsylvania	94,726	5,757	46,103	869	1,878	48,623	1,176	1,834
Monroe County, Pennsylvania	141,713	10,085	69,241	3,967	911	72,472	3,916	1,291
Montgomery County, Pennsylvania	679,570	51,603	326,951	11,351	10,679	352,619	13,108	16,465
Northampton County, Pennsylvania	254,362	23,036	124,137	4,968	5,401	130,225	5,369	7,298
Northumberland County, Pennsylvania	77,532	2,276	38,909	654	80	38,623	927	615
Philadelphia County, Pennsylvania	1,289,114	131,803	599,809	22,578	30,396	689,305	34,862	43,967
Schuylkill County, Pennsylvania	119,830	4,644	61,692	1,445	654	58,138	1,758	787
Somerset County, Pennsylvania	63,536	2,099	33,242	835	407	30,294	744	113
Washington County, Pennsylvania	173,801	10,685	84,540	3,920	1,339	89,261	3,677	1,749
Westmoreland County, Pennsylvania	299,768	17,919	145,152	5,238	2,208	154,616	6,466	4,007
York County, Pennsylvania	364,563	22,774	178,446	6,031	3,901	186,117	7,982	4,860
RHODE ISLAND								
Kent County, Rhode Island	138,673	10,060	65,893	2,595	2,280	72,780	4,019	1,166
Newport County, Rhode Island	72,030	6,152	34,614	1,781	625	37,416	1,608	2,138
Providence County, Rhode Island	528,205	59,157	253,792	12,208	14,800	274,413	14,983	17,166
Washington County, Rhode Island	109,896	15,991	52,619	6,290	764	57,277	7,274	1,663
SOUTH CAROLINA								
Aiken County, South Carolina	137,365	8,812	65,367	2,900	580	71,998	4,416	916
Anderson County, South Carolina	161,465	10,385	77,579	3,655	1,022	83,886	3,633	2,075
Beaufort County, South Carolina	156,374	9,374	75,849	2,936	1,916	80,525	3,101	1,421
Berkeley County, South Carolina	173,818	11,614	85,221	3,362	650	88,597	5,601	2,001
Charleston County, South Carolina	334,482	28,470	160,774	11,817	1,423	173,708	12,957	2,273
Dorchester County, South Carolina	124,694	9,890	60,228	3,926	1,058	64,466	4,269	637
Florence County, South Carolina	111,079	8,231	51,065	2,599	561	60,014	4,396	675
Greenville County, South Carolina	408,717	29,349	196,034	7,778	6,294	212,683	9,006	6,271
Greenwood County, South Carolina	58,394	5,279	26,360	1,156	464	32,034	3,091	568
Horry County, South Carolina	282,816	16,181	134,498	6,228	699	148,318	8,241	1,013
Kershaw County, South Carolina	53,235	3,032	25,387	511	479	27,848	1,691	351
Lancaster County, South Carolina	75,550	3,578	36,142	1,163	88	39,408	2,067	260
Laurens County, South Carolina	54,738	3,190	26,500	877	470	28,238	1,220	623
Lexington County, South Carolina	234,390	12,921	113,063	4,421	988	121,327	6,349	1,163
Orangeburg County, South Carolina	71,971	7,070	32,352	907	1,947	39,619	2,478	1,738

Table C-3. College Enrollment of the Population, by Selected Counties, 2017—*Continued*

(Number.)

State/County	Total population	Population enrolled in college or graduate school	Male Total population	Male Enrolled in public college or graduate school	Male Enrolled in private college or graduate school	Female Total population	Female Enrolled in public college or graduate school	Female Enrolled in private college or graduate school
SOUTH CAROLINA—(*Continued*)								
Pickens County, South Carolina	103,800	17,018	51,275	7,152	821	52,525	7,550	1,495
Richland County, South Carolina	338,226	44,420	162,760	18,609	3,768	175,466	18,746	3,297
Spartanburg County, South Carolina	248,291	19,136	119,020	6,588	1,458	129,271	8,086	3,004
Sumter County, South Carolina	86,032	5,048	41,341	1,869	453	44,691	2,158	568
York County, South Carolina	212,894	14,953	101,427	6,495	385	111,467	7,512	561
SOUTH DAKOTA								
Minnehaha County, South Dakota	147,723	8,880	73,940	2,718	1,281	73,783	2,831	2,050
Pennington County, South Dakota	89,123	6,896	44,772	2,885	868	44,351	2,125	1,018
TENNESSEE								
Anderson County, Tennessee	63,101	2,638	30,362	910	134	32,739	1,343	251
Blount County, Tennessee	108,102	6,166	51,719	2,139	883	56,383	1,823	1,321
Bradley County, Tennessee	86,592	8,743	41,737	2,152	1,325	44,855	2,313	2,953
Davidson County, Tennessee	566,443	55,034	270,600	11,255	12,399	295,843	13,538	17,842
Greene County, Tennessee	58,253	3,444	28,013	933	129	30,240	1,845	537
Hamilton County, Tennessee	298,244	23,074	141,935	7,535	2,097	156,309	11,505	1,937
Knox County, Tennessee	380,914	40,073	182,975	17,350	1,182	197,939	19,016	2,525
Madison County, Tennessee	79,933	7,390	37,378	2,023	1,293	42,555	2,232	1,842
Maury County, Tennessee	74,041	3,871	35,220	1,656	260	38,821	1,693	262
Montgomery County, Tennessee	154,264	17,748	76,666	6,801	1,092	77,598	8,669	1,186
Putnam County, Tennessee	64,050	9,035	31,491	4,350	478	32,559	4,004	203
Rutherford County, Tennessee	251,600	22,327	122,322	10,433	652	129,278	9,395	1,847
Sevier County, Tennessee	81,129	3,441	39,313	1,448	399	41,816	1,422	172
Shelby County, Tennessee	741,676	58,774	346,609	19,770	5,205	395,067	24,982	8,817
Sullivan County, Tennessee	132,381	4,991	63,688	1,977	299	68,693	2,148	567
Sumner County, Tennessee	147,884	8,363	71,353	1,931	1,620	76,531	2,977	1,835
Washington County, Tennessee	107,285	11,775	51,992	4,751	737	55,293	5,937	350
Williamson County, Tennessee	175,514	11,343	84,572	4,337	1,009	90,942	3,974	2,023
Wilson County, Tennessee	109,446	5,250	53,066	1,325	991	56,380	1,998	936
TEXAS								
Angelina County, Texas	69,073	3,732	33,014	1,593	42	36,059	1,822	275
Bell County, Texas	265,256	28,279	130,884	8,578	4,464	134,372	10,947	4,290
Bexar County, Texas	1,537,208	142,946	752,423	53,656	13,332	784,785	56,454	19,504
Bowie County, Texas	75,023	4,452	37,445	1,931	505	37,578	1,463	553
Brazoria County, Texas	282,310	21,043	142,412	8,308	2,487	139,898	9,084	1,164
Brazos County, Texas	183,627	58,578	92,728	29,945	262	90,899	27,731	640
Cameron County, Texas	316,428	24,383	151,732	11,064	363	164,696	12,023	933
Collin County, Texas	760,920	62,229	370,681	27,094	3,654	390,239	27,262	4,219
Comal County, Texas	114,209	6,746	55,697	1,947	631	58,512	3,670	498
Coryell County, Texas	59,973	4,327	29,423	1,728	372	30,550	1,735	492
Dallas County, Texas	2,037,627	155,383	994,738	52,856	15,664	1,042,889	68,905	17,958
Denton County, Texas	662,965	66,921	322,963	26,847	3,557	340,002	33,426	3,091
Ector County, Texas	117,836	7,627	58,841	2,207	417	58,995	4,236	767
Ellis County, Texas	135,260	9,714	66,001	3,174	967	69,259	4,715	858
El Paso County, Texas	648,513	71,333	316,320	31,070	4,965	332,193	30,929	4,369
Fort Bend County, Texas	589,954	54,861	286,397	21,344	5,035	303,557	23,626	4,856
Galveston County, Texas	267,161	20,615	130,728	8,696	875	136,433	10,246	798
Grayson County, Texas	105,150	8,091	51,022	2,139	1,017	54,128	3,852	1,083
Gregg County, Texas	96,397	5,548	46,630	1,984	1,196	49,767	1,724	644
Guadalupe County, Texas	126,007	8,628	61,740	4,226	771	64,267	2,188	1,443
Harris County, Texas	3,604,616	306,037	1,779,535	105,881	24,606	1,825,081	139,241	36,309
Harrison County, Texas	52,437	3,244	25,072	1,601	91	27,365	1,234	318
Hays County, Texas	172,672	31,337	85,834	11,959	1,004	86,838	17,612	762
Henderson County, Texas	66,955	3,044	32,429	1,202	388	34,526	1,312	142
Hidalgo County, Texas	622,991	52,320	300,859	18,634	3,848	322,132	23,793	6,045
Hunt County, Texas	75,087	8,439	36,604	3,772	98	38,483	4,503	66
Jefferson County, Texas	204,488	14,110	104,795	6,151	775	99,693	6,765	419
Johnson County, Texas	131,321	4,992	64,980	1,029	641	66,341	2,607	715
Kaufman County, Texas	94,327	6,042	45,646	1,490	575	48,681	3,215	762
Lubbock County, Texas	243,697	42,475	118,731	19,443	1,704	124,966	19,624	1,704
McLennan County, Texas	200,303	26,795	96,932	6,239	5,578	103,371	7,871	7,107
Midland County, Texas	125,573	6,476	62,805	1,452	1,320	62,768	2,774	930
Montgomery County, Texas	445,963	25,930	219,488	9,033	918	226,475	14,185	1,794
Nacogdoches County, Texas	52,547	9,493	24,408	3,607	67	28,139	5,770	49
Nueces County, Texas	286,873	23,508	140,011	9,356	369	146,862	13,015	768
Parker County, Texas	106,767	7,262	53,291	2,587	531	53,476	3,492	652
Potter County, Texas	92,591	4,989	48,003	1,900	209	44,588	2,801	79

Table C-3. College Enrollment of the Population, by Selected Counties, 2017—*Continued*

(Number.)

State/County	Total population	Population enrolled in college or graduate school	Male			Female		
			Total population	Enrolled in public college or graduate school	Enrolled in private college or graduate school	Total population	Enrolled in public college or graduate school	Enrolled in private college or graduate school
TEXAS—(*Continued*)								
Randall County, Texas	107,652	13,191	52,149	5,377	608	55,503	6,390	816
Rockwall County, Texas	75,858	4,914	36,920	1,710	714	38,938	2,040	450
San Patricio County, Texas	52,469	2,105	26,590	636	116	25,879	1,272	81
Smith County, Texas	181,030	16,060	84,928	7,567	247	96,102	7,886	360
Tarrant County, Texas	1,600,866	132,990	775,272	47,998	11,375	825,594	57,264	16,353
Taylor County, Texas	107,478	10,404	51,917	2,030	2,803	55,561	1,678	3,893
Tom Green County, Texas	94,199	7,793	46,013	2,432	575	48,186	4,209	577
Travis County, Texas	997,377	100,113	502,332	41,883	8,045	495,045	41,893	8,292
Victoria County, Texas	72,196	4,138	35,225	1,440	177	36,971	2,042	479
Webb County, Texas	198,438	17,647	95,768	6,010	1,155	102,670	8,213	2,269
Wichita County, Texas	106,900	10,436	55,020	4,288	718	51,880	4,905	525
Williamson County, Texas	429,532	27,780	208,714	9,369	2,903	220,818	10,781	4,727
Wise County, Texas	52,852	2,754	26,101	1,064	207	26,751	1,259	224
UTAH								
Cache County, Utah	92,788	21,346	46,168	12,237	433	46,620	8,326	350
Davis County, Utah	252,640	21,590	126,047	10,201	2,120	126,593	7,692	1,577
Salt Lake County, Utah	874,112	85,057	436,429	32,491	8,162	437,683	34,449	9,955
Tooele County, Utah	49,107	3,097	24,709	1,382	36	24,398	1,462	217
Utah County, Utah	433,183	74,900	217,263	16,943	21,675	215,920	17,512	18,770
Washington County, Utah	129,256	10,290	63,314	5,428	371	65,942	2,973	1,518
Weber County, Utah	191,715	18,275	95,859	8,342	851	95,856	7,574	1,508
VERMONT								
Chittenden County, Vermont	137,922	20,974	67,014	7,839	2,749	70,908	8,175	2,211
VIRGINIA								
Albemarle County, Virginia	89,890	14,042	42,226	5,035	432	47,664	7,621	954
Arlington County, Virginia	198,136	17,887	97,941	4,748	3,690	100,195	3,744	5,705
Augusta County, Virginia	63,330	2,497	32,581	524	141	30,749	917	915
Bedford County, Virginia	66,022	4,131	32,588	816	566	33,434	2,019	730
Chesterfield County, Virginia	276,669	19,603	130,918	6,276	1,041	145,751	10,819	1,467
Fairfax County, Virginia	925,677	89,058	455,337	36,218	9,185	470,340	33,295	10,360
Fauquier County, Virginia	55,752	3,572	27,114	1,233	136	28,638	1,787	416
Frederick County, Virginia	71,005	4,369	34,887	1,158	815	36,118	1,302	1,094
Hanover County, Virginia	86,837	6,684	42,332	2,573	966	44,505	2,015	1,130
Henrico County, Virginia	265,717	17,078	123,463	5,409	1,366	142,254	7,492	2,811
James City County, Virginia	62,256	4,565	29,311	1,826	349	32,945	2,349	41
Loudoun County, Virginia	303,406	24,193	149,102	8,886	3,564	154,304	9,283	2,460
Montgomery County, Virginia	85,967	30,002	45,322	16,898	540	40,645	12,081	483
Prince William County, Virginia	357,952	33,291	178,069	11,301	3,972	179,883	12,847	5,171
Roanoke County, Virginia	79,577	5,236	37,529	1,673	719	42,048	1,553	1,291
Rockingham County, Virginia	65,977	3,676	32,011	1,117	620	33,966	930	1,009
Spotsylvania County, Virginia	105,915	7,892	51,725	3,354	690	54,190	2,969	879
Stafford County, Virginia	115,635	11,569	57,884	5,142	311	57,751	5,317	799
York County, Virginia	54,453	4,259	26,220	1,567	408	28,233	1,936	348
Alexandria city, Virginia	134,695	11,318	64,237	3,009	2,128	70,458	4,500	1,681
Chesapeake city, Virginia	192,354	17,322	93,053	7,218	1,212	99,301	6,934	1,958
Hampton city, Virginia	111,612	11,874	53,553	2,970	1,327	58,059	3,704	3,873
Lynchburg city, Virginia	67,762	17,436	30,249	1,440	6,382	37,513	1,758	7,856
Newport News city, Virginia	144,054	17,143	68,566	6,275	1,052	75,488	8,828	988
Norfolk city, Virginia	203,169	29,640	106,567	13,143	2,007	96,602	12,416	2,074
Portsmouth city, Virginia	76,080	4,699	35,851	1,187	690	40,229	2,109	713
Richmond city, Virginia	192,231	26,041	89,500	10,544	1,654	102,731	11,986	1,857
Roanoke city, Virginia	81,536	3,700	37,913	779	303	43,623	1,589	1,029
Suffolk city, Virginia	71,818	5,190	34,087	1,787	657	37,731	2,023	723
Virginia Beach city, Virginia	366,353	36,719	178,532	12,000	6,648	187,821	12,605	5,466
WASHINGTON								
Benton County, Washington	154,300	9,004	76,544	3,555	418	77,756	4,396	635
Clallam County, Washington	64,646	3,014	31,043	746	531	33,603	1,392	345
Clark County, Washington	379,737	22,240	186,653	8,552	1,340	193,084	9,781	2,567
Cowlitz County, Washington	86,705	4,616	43,113	1,423	525	43,592	1,909	759
Franklin County, Washington	67,059	5,660	35,240	2,203	89	31,819	3,368	0
Grant County, Washington	71,399	3,320	36,319	863	312	35,080	1,808	337
Grays Harbor County, Washington	60,315	2,324	31,205	970	362	29,110	899	93
Island County, Washington	69,904	4,098	34,310	1,082	136	35,594	2,048	832
King County, Washington	1,812,123	143,489	905,420	53,503	12,454	906,703	61,081	16,451
Kitsap County, Washington	220,799	14,146	112,624	5,952	830	108,175	6,241	1,123

Table C-3. College Enrollment of the Population, by Selected Counties, 2017—*Continued*

(Number.)

			Male			Female		
State/County	Total population	Population enrolled in college or graduate school	Total population	Enrolled in public college or graduate school	Enrolled in private college or graduate school	Total population	Enrolled in public college or graduate school	Enrolled in private college or graduate school
WASHINGTON—*(Continued)*								
Lewis County, Washington	64,390	3,954	31,742	1,266	451	32,648	1,827	410
Pierce County, Washington	703,286	48,110	347,747	18,222	3,889	355,539	19,512	6,487
Skagit County, Washington	102,189	4,655	50,114	1,882	202	52,075	2,231	340
Snohomish County, Washington	649,368	47,267	324,178	18,786	3,769	325,190	19,877	4,835
Spokane County, Washington	412,840	38,590	203,002	12,836	4,941	209,838	14,328	6,485
Thurston County, Washington	229,623	17,428	110,272	6,487	1,597	119,351	6,985	2,359
Whatcom County, Washington	185,502	25,443	91,172	10,915	874	94,330	13,200	454
Yakima County, Washington	187,816	12,109	93,308	4,073	1,354	94,508	4,854	1,828
WEST VIRGINIA								
Berkeley County, West Virginia	92,487	5,667	45,387	1,980	593	47,100	2,535	559
Cabell County, West Virginia	79,083	9,143	38,326	3,403	120	40,757	5,366	254
Kanawha County, West Virginia	152,317	8,531	71,647	1,846	917	80,670	4,990	778
Monongalia County, West Virginia	90,495	21,825	46,647	10,134	714	43,848	10,428	549
Raleigh County, West Virginia	61,835	3,225	31,096	1,154	126	30,739	1,216	729
WISCONSIN								
Brown County, Wisconsin	209,162	15,303	103,203	3,688	2,318	105,959	5,965	3,332
Dane County, Wisconsin	443,773	65,015	219,179	29,942	2,245	224,594	28,720	4,108
Dodge County, Wisconsin	73,475	3,976	38,975	1,566	157	34,500	1,672	581
Eau Claire County, Wisconsin	86,222	13,631	42,013	5,106	212	44,209	7,795	518
Fond du Lac County, Wisconsin	84,492	5,676	41,602	1,617	896	42,890	1,870	1,293
Jefferson County, Wisconsin	70,151	5,617	34,554	2,316	389	35,597	2,140	772
Kenosha County, Wisconsin	136,753	11,740	66,702	4,007	1,296	70,051	5,091	1,346
La Crosse County, Wisconsin	98,790	15,646	47,613	5,717	539	51,177	8,419	971
Manitowoc County, Wisconsin	65,577	3,786	32,250	1,406	250	33,327	1,454	676
Marathon County, Wisconsin	109,921	7,332	54,955	3,116	529	54,966	2,735	952
Milwaukee County, Wisconsin	760,198	67,696	363,006	20,627	10,345	397,192	22,787	13,937
Outagamie County, Wisconsin	149,698	9,761	74,196	3,634	1,114	75,502	3,071	1,942
Ozaukee County, Wisconsin	73,331	5,669	36,096	1,190	1,564	37,235	1,069	1,846
Portage County, Wisconsin	59,455	9,555	29,556	4,169	129	29,899	5,071	186
Racine County, Wisconsin	158,477	8,707	77,181	3,743	736	81,296	3,323	905
Rock County, Wisconsin	130,985	8,424	63,419	2,549	1,081	67,566	3,052	1,742
St. Croix County, Wisconsin	70,367	5,004	34,601	1,775	254	35,766	2,047	928
Sheboygan County, Wisconsin	94,486	5,620	47,582	1,723	1,205	46,904	2,192	500
Walworth County, Wisconsin	85,566	10,064	42,674	4,220	283	42,892	5,007	554
Washington County, Wisconsin	110,823	4,949	56,036	1,117	1,293	54,787	1,557	982
Waukesha County, Wisconsin	330,540	21,157	161,218	6,165	2,792	169,322	7,586	4,614
Winnebago County, Wisconsin	141,073	13,891	71,097	5,254	264	69,976	7,822	551
Wood County, Wisconsin	60,050	2,986	29,348	1,184	64	30,702	1,239	499
WYOMING								
Laramie County, Wyoming	79,157	6,679	40,127	2,512	345	39,030	3,032	790
Natrona County, Wyoming	62,172	4,562	31,507	2,171	34	30,665	2,273	84

Table C-4. Primary and Secondary School Enrollment, by Sex and Selected Counties, 2017

(Number.)

State/County	Population 3 years and over	Male Nursery school, Pre-school	Kindergarten	Grades 1 to 4	Grades 5 to 8	Grades 9 to 12	Female Nursery school, Pre-school	Kindergarten	Grades 1 to 4	Grades 5 to 8	Grades 9 to 12
ALABAMA											
Baldwin County, Alabama	205,713	1,194	1,055	5,431	6,593	6,070	797	1,865	5,383	4,128	5,634
Calhoun County, Alabama	111,814	1,218	723	2,186	3,287	3,259	892	583	2,472	2,738	2,641
Cullman County, Alabama	80,466	443	263	2,185	2,340	1,986	488	523	1,534	2,392	1,792
Elmore County, Alabama	78,905	453	386	1,979	2,703	2,631	402	728	1,252	2,230	2,522
Etowah County, Alabama	100,140	854	419	3,527	2,077	2,634	489	1,056	2,358	2,036	2,763
Houston County, Alabama	100,728	807	740	2,941	2,948	2,875	663	481	3,020	2,435	2,794
Jefferson County, Alabama	634,210	6,703	4,749	14,811	19,507	16,874	5,599	3,578	17,567	15,747	18,775
Lauderdale County, Alabama	89,490	213	365	1,841	1,898	2,721	1,240	709	1,955	1,982	2,490
Lee County, Alabama	155,867	983	1,153	2,937	5,153	3,381	1,283	1,311	4,563	3,157	3,737
Limestone County, Alabama	90,749	541	1,100	2,646	2,520	2,370	487	162	2,044	2,385	2,767
Madison County, Alabama	348,825	2,603	1,789	9,150	9,180	9,949	2,275	2,271	7,095	9,858	9,228
Marshall County, Alabama	92,442	515	960	2,957	2,456	2,442	704	280	2,795	2,962	2,471
Mobile County, Alabama	399,225	3,235	2,714	9,564	11,955	11,318	3,307	1,838	11,107	10,844	11,676
Montgomery County, Alabama	217,268	1,236	1,311	6,090	6,622	5,880	894	808	6,422	5,887	5,897
Morgan County, Alabama	114,575	843	1,105	3,028	3,357	3,082	602	632	2,843	2,681	3,360
Shelby County, Alabama	205,647	1,384	2,044	6,243	6,290	6,605	1,295	1,194	5,090	5,879	6,820
Tuscaloosa County, Alabama	199,826	1,593	884	4,183	4,666	5,215	1,224	790	6,093	3,445	4,469
ALASKA											
Anchorage Municipality, Alaska	281,085	1,412	3,100	7,820	7,209	8,703	2,016	1,763	8,351	6,971	6,815
Fairbanks North Star Borough, Alaska	94,845	233	455	3,637	1,479	3,065	601	1,507	2,073	2,932	1,905
Matanuska-Susitna Borough, Alaska	102,083	324	753	3,250	3,945	3,637	781	605	2,967	3,380	2,892
ARIZONA											
Apache County, Arizona	68,801	322	530	2,339	2,636	2,602	531	808	1,779	2,215	2,775
Cochise County, Arizona	120,103	716	1,227	2,940	2,506	3,168	843	628	3,826	2,088	2,937
Coconino County, Arizona	136,628	781	596	2,141	4,046	4,786	619	556	2,778	3,878	2,530
Maricopa County, Arizona	4,146,200	31,859	25,043	116,767	126,830	123,390	23,707	26,622	109,470	118,585	121,136
Mohave County, Arizona	200,733	1,076	1,152	2,954	4,833	4,319	209	518	3,714	4,885	4,568
Navajo County, Arizona	103,822	820	741	2,998	4,368	3,876	758	278	3,276	4,344	2,869
Pima County, Arizona	990,803	7,394	4,934	27,328	23,133	26,739	6,377	5,436	22,443	25,590	26,171
Pinal County, Arizona	416,521	2,136	2,586	12,308	11,393	12,935	3,037	2,967	10,949	11,185	9,512
Yavapai County, Arizona	222,012	1,242	1,111	4,137	4,874	3,107	1,470	1,093	3,941	3,711	5,298
Yuma County, Arizona	198,929	624	1,091	7,026	5,386	5,752	2,041	1,304	5,049	5,655	6,767
ARKANSAS											
Benton County, Arkansas	255,478	1,298	2,078	7,912	9,627	6,973	1,534	2,092	7,519	8,524	7,327
Craighead County, Arkansas	102,565	1,409	458	3,117	3,772	2,529	1,329	662	2,825	1,993	2,274
Faulkner County, Arkansas	118,985	1,012	1,661	3,621	2,849	2,779	1,154	640	3,667	2,803	3,665
Garland County, Arkansas	95,829	861	642	2,465	1,572	2,459	383	533	2,668	2,615	2,464
Jefferson County, Arkansas	67,021	1,037	400	1,973	1,736	2,633	690	119	1,966	1,509	1,974
Lonoke County, Arkansas	70,249	396	481	2,440	1,694	2,061	863	450	1,730	2,435	2,372
Pulaski County, Arkansas	378,282	3,680	3,313	10,025	9,232	8,847	4,065	2,466	11,395	9,334	9,152
Saline County, Arkansas	116,126	1,198	813	3,309	4,193	3,156	745	1,372	3,010	2,361	2,605
Sebastian County, Arkansas	122,823	808	729	3,982	2,932	4,173	992	1,045	3,373	3,258	3,814
Washington County, Arkansas	222,799	2,741	1,558	6,302	6,947	6,015	1,001	2,330	5,424	5,579	5,108
White County, Arkansas	75,722	413	309	2,496	1,867	2,142	506	456	2,012	2,026	1,709
CALIFORNIA											
Alameda County, California	1,609,612	14,865	9,804	38,439	38,729	37,747	15,131	10,371	35,754	37,989	35,244
Butte County, California	221,940	2,047	1,729	5,520	4,496	4,850	1,335	1,382	5,837	4,120	4,692
Contra Costa County, California	1,111,820	10,989	7,624	29,604	32,200	31,713	8,697	6,723	26,546	31,852	32,549
El Dorado County, California	184,086	1,174	744	5,048	4,036	5,915	1,453	1,087	3,266	4,447	5,793
Fresno County, California	945,650	7,877	8,437	29,896	34,915	31,250	8,378	10,275	29,971	31,351	30,019
Humboldt County, California	131,589	633	898	2,142	2,916	2,847	1,260	904	2,800	2,932	2,239
Imperial County, California	172,861	2,231	1,717	5,436	6,339	7,791	1,086	1,811	5,589	5,221	5,464
Kern County, California	851,029	4,536	9,069	31,254	26,286	30,963	5,227	7,039	28,646	29,947	30,802
Kings County, California	142,909	459	1,015	5,048	5,195	6,727	790	1,156	3,527	4,816	4,208
Los Angeles County, California	9,798,786	81,372	67,922	234,131	252,437	266,448	73,839	63,364	219,505	243,777	258,048
Madera County, California	149,916	1,059	1,610	4,972	5,373	6,882	993	840	5,024	5,484	5,078
Marin County, California	254,264	3,347	1,698	6,157	6,261	6,780	1,758	1,800	6,396	5,380	6,620
Mendocino County, California	84,813	547	362	2,443	2,543	2,067	447	479	1,723	2,398	1,936
Merced County, California	260,778	2,215	2,122	8,839	9,418	11,104	3,817	2,225	8,818	8,597	8,198
Monterey County, California	418,892	3,818	3,361	13,645	12,656	13,722	2,982	4,507	9,987	13,881	13,445
Napa County, California	137,022	1,086	908	2,959	3,864	3,974	634	383	3,198	3,536	3,602
Nevada County, California	97,198	633	789	1,934	2,029	2,203	405	260	1,802	1,755	2,163

Table C-4. Primary and Secondary School Enrollment, by Sex and Selected Counties, 2017—*Continued*

(Number.)

State/County	Population 3 years and over	Male					Female				
		Enrolled in school					Enrolled in school				
		Nursery school, Pre-school	Kindergarten	Grades 1 to 4	Grades 5 to 8	Grades 9 to 12	Nursery school, Pre-school	Kindergarten	Grades 1 to 4	Grades 5 to 8	Grades 9 to 12
CALIFORNIA—*(Continued)*											
Orange County, California	3,082,913	26,120	18,151	74,934	84,894	89,145	26,445	19,089	71,289	78,660	83,596
Placer County, California	374,999	3,582	2,753	9,420	10,895	10,948	3,227	2,686	10,724	8,761	9,198
Riverside County, California	2,330,040	13,635	17,141	70,514	71,002	78,311	14,666	17,472	63,010	70,482	74,179
Sacramento County, California	1,473,384	11,136	10,390	41,611	40,259	43,022	10,272	11,275	38,329	40,344	37,663
San Bernardino County, California .	2,066,841	13,691	15,550	64,842	66,627	69,192	16,195	12,943	58,702	65,793	67,007
San Diego County, California.........	3,214,232	26,530	20,841	74,278	86,107	84,976	26,849	22,971	69,483	80,522	81,433
San Francisco County, California.....	858,658	6,397	3,368	11,930	11,050	13,007	5,605	3,250	10,897	12,007	11,610
San Joaquin County, California	715,868	4,607	6,042	23,943	23,140	26,030	5,991	6,654	21,646	22,493	22,879
San Luis Obispo County, California	276,318	1,740	1,698	5,578	5,703	5,652	2,182	1,003	7,043	5,458	5,478
San Mateo County, California.........	746,061	7,335	6,200	18,454	17,374	18,892	6,619	5,618	17,173	17,689	15,976
Santa Barbara County, California....	430,787	3,628	2,832	10,912	10,970	11,857	2,345	3,177	12,487	9,115	12,156
Santa Clara County, California........	1,870,581	19,247	12,861	45,780	49,780	51,391	17,284	12,299	43,314	48,824	46,055
Santa Cruz County, California.........	268,458	1,579	2,536	5,322	7,576	6,677	1,884	782	5,452	7,188	6,128
Shasta County, California	172,955	1,136	1,013	4,656	4,200	5,214	822	1,106	2,528	4,462	4,968
Solano County, California...............	429,721	3,075	2,844	11,492	11,562	11,732	2,301	3,150	9,876	10,799	11,148
Sonoma County, California.............	489,522	4,104	3,826	10,755	11,355	11,904	2,962	3,128	11,158	10,805	11,778
Stanislaus County, California.........	525,466	5,356	4,099	17,960	16,128	18,286	3,632	3,175	16,241	16,281	16,277
Sutter County, California...............	93,438	1,035	605	2,602	3,315	2,993	656	835	2,078	2,949	2,826
Tulare County, California	442,232	2,128	4,781	15,269	17,527	15,268	2,487	4,033	15,167	15,151	17,874
Ventura County, California..............	823,059	7,279	4,203	23,198	24,064	25,242	7,239	5,088	17,720	24,094	24,547
Yolo County, California..................	211,262	1,380	1,499	5,389	5,364	5,754	1,423	1,716	3,708	6,281	4,905
Yuba County, California.................	73,339	231	309	2,172	3,032	1,893	799	687	3,050	1,456	1,596
COLORADO											
Adams County, Colorado...............	481,170	3,277	4,179	15,411	15,150	16,304	3,432	2,891	17,264	13,802	16,512
Arapahoe County, Colorado...........	619,181	5,788	3,741	16,487	18,368	18,387	4,903	3,617	15,305	18,545	17,693
Boulder County, Colorado	314,162	2,287	2,637	7,013	7,131	7,674	3,094	1,563	7,979	6,885	7,139
Broomfield County, Colorado	66,736	749	512	1,999	2,518	2,031	701	268	1,320	2,234	2,031
Denver County, Colorado	678,332	4,683	4,090	15,776	14,710	14,166	5,835	3,985	15,634	14,342	13,132
Douglas County, Colorado.............	324,148	3,474	1,622	8,750	13,100	12,731	2,823	3,141	7,975	11,250	11,087
El Paso County, Colorado...............	670,451	5,909	4,734	19,117	19,399	19,222	4,295	4,301	17,486	20,782	16,782
Jefferson County, Colorado............	556,328	3,262	3,642	12,535	14,251	14,619	5,489	2,632	12,202	12,726	14,524
Larimer County, Colorado...............	332,109	2,695	2,027	8,126	7,677	8,452	1,293	2,181	7,914	6,494	7,479
Mesa County, Colorado	146,171	963	667	4,281	4,615	3,908	1,311	1,311	2,403	3,026	3,981
Pueblo County, Colorado...............	160,899	889	1,048	4,604	4,336	4,442	1,123	1,069	4,176	4,473	4,254
Weld County, Colorado..................	292,942	2,907	2,354	11,231	7,927	7,684	3,160	2,873	8,354	8,768	6,895
CONNECTICUT											
Fairfield County, Connecticut.........	918,076	8,683	4,609	25,863	26,447	28,575	6,894	7,211	21,903	25,023	27,876
Hartford County, Connecticut.........	868,685	7,182	4,935	20,276	22,804	24,411	6,415	4,134	18,887	22,250	23,942
Litchfield County, Connecticut.......	178,230	1,188	1,062	3,451	4,189	4,851	1,278	436	3,892	3,574	4,196
Middlesex County, Connecticut......	159,438	1,898	501	3,335	3,916	3,900	757	444	2,130	4,951	3,743
New Haven County, Connecticut	833,258	8,007	3,434	19,549	21,242	25,844	4,487	4,461	19,554	18,549	21,820
New London County, Connecticut..	262,269	1,625	1,022	5,777	6,714	7,409	1,874	809	5,506	7,058	6,567
Tolland County, Connecticut.........	147,845	1,157	399	2,336	3,851	3,261	525	1,115	2,602	2,544	4,280
Windham County, Connecticut.......	113,437	935	367	2,535	3,003	3,018	554	216	2,258	2,947	2,190
DELAWARE											
Kent County, Delaware	170,378	1,273	1,681	3,752	5,666	3,769	700	2,017	4,402	3,895	4,437
New Castle County, Delaware.........	541,283	3,997	3,048	15,628	12,797	14,352	5,152	3,092	12,014	15,249	13,499
Sussex County, Delaware...............	217,914	821	1,229	4,260	5,701	4,686	1,593	1,180	4,123	5,649	4,399
DISTRICT OF COLUMBIA											
District of Columbia, District of Columbia...................................	666,887	6,961	4,421	15,206	8,918	11,685	6,158	5,130	12,896	11,557	10,532
FLORIDA											
Alachua County, Florida.................	259,236	2,617	944	4,739	5,635	5,218	2,181	2,548	4,853	3,982	5,364
Bay County, Florida	176,037	1,354	1,382	3,887	4,905	4,695	1,405	714	3,803	5,060	4,134
Brevard County, Florida.................	573,430	4,493	2,129	11,251	14,858	13,147	3,881	2,997	10,925	11,744	15,039
Broward County, Florida................	1,868,637	16,611	12,406	45,130	48,022	50,902	16,319	9,583	43,402	47,136	46,509
Charlotte County, Florida...............	178,561	306	512	2,802	2,264	2,199	589	292	2,621	2,414	2,978
Citrus County, Florida...................	143,413	938	438	2,411	2,337	3,300	84	897	1,503	3,039	2,236
Clay County, Florida	206,948	1,137	1,327	5,778	7,463	7,082	1,644	1,182	5,455	5,751	6,747
Collier County, Florida	363,124	1,464	792	8,004	7,786	6,434	1,227	2,066	7,799	7,119	7,194
Duval County, Florida	898,562	7,734	8,319	23,805	22,171	21,273	6,201	6,012	24,401	20,380	22,296
Escambia County, Florida...............	301,130	2,767	2,135	7,810	6,328	6,056	1,212	1,214	9,067	6,857	6,792

Table C-4. Primary and Secondary School Enrollment, by Sex and Selected Counties, 2017—*Continued*

(Number.)

State/County	Population 3 years and over	Male Nursery school, Pre-school	Male Kindergarten	Male Grades 1 to 4	Male Grades 5 to 8	Male Grades 9 to 12	Female Nursery school, Pre-school	Female Kindergarten	Female Grades 1 to 4	Female Grades 5 to 8	Female Grades 9 to 12
FLORIDA—(*Continued*)											
Hernando County, Florida..............	181,311	91	1,020	4,215	3,960	3,547	805	600	4,409	3,813	4,329
Hillsborough County, Florida.........	1,355,577	11,315	9,624	35,553	35,183	38,281	10,187	7,275	35,961	35,579	34,545
Indian River County, Florida..........	150,471	723	1,500	2,617	3,184	2,887	673	639	2,449	3,532	3,886
Lake County, Florida.....................	338,073	1,369	1,553	8,388	7,779	9,478	1,558	2,027	8,305	6,369	8,055
Lee County, Florida	718,915	4,237	4,754	13,272	16,760	17,033	3,593	2,763	14,142	15,723	16,173
Leon County, Florida.....................	280,632	2,323	607	5,017	8,056	6,487	1,794	1,487	7,079	5,866	5,916
Manatee County, Florida...............	374,557	2,953	1,250	7,719	9,238	8,596	1,363	810	9,522	8,465	8,311
Marion County, Florida..................	344,454	2,495	2,790	7,858	7,502	6,972	1,632	1,337	5,629	9,695	8,829
Martin County, Florida...................	156,198	459	575	3,078	3,552	4,157	1,364	1,491	2,249	2,781	2,780
Miami-Dade County, Florida..........	2,656,689	23,080	14,751	61,433	64,577	67,604	22,747	16,077	60,666	57,630	61,779
Monroe County, Florida.................	75,037	463	237	1,360	1,156	1,149	361	263	1,166	1,099	1,112
Nassau County, Florida.................	80,108	36	870	1,699	1,790	2,350	312	229	2,260	1,868	1,997
Okaloosa County, Florida..............	195,517	2,071	994	5,708	5,206	4,441	1,784	775	6,300	4,302	3,239
Orange County, Florida.................	1,300,782	10,451	9,073	31,933	37,243	35,337	9,133	7,376	34,100	30,425	36,193
Osceola County, Florida................	338,226	2,924	2,740	8,784	11,739	9,694	1,548	2,185	10,252	7,944	12,911
Palm Beach County, Florida..........	1,427,761	13,879	7,918	33,713	31,888	35,856	11,864	8,234	28,950	31,397	32,780
Pasco County, Florida	509,539	3,427	2,901	11,582	14,009	11,284	2,993	3,185	10,654	12,962	11,539
Pinellas County, Florida................	945,526	6,064	4,344	20,325	15,987	19,613	5,629	4,299	17,643	17,285	18,725
Polk County, Florida.....................	662,094	4,230	4,160	16,002	20,565	18,738	2,708	3,567	18,349	16,766	17,900
Putnam County, Florida.................	71,282	489	293	2,249	1,593	1,753	239	352	1,171	2,039	1,960
St. Johns County, Florida..............	235,047	1,667	2,300	5,967	5,273	7,070	1,520	1,334	6,389	5,558	6,519
St. Lucie County, Florida...............	304,995	2,153	1,434	6,425	7,445	7,983	1,989	1,455	6,523	6,299	8,002
Santa Rosa County, Florida	168,473	1,611	773	5,014	4,202	5,074	1,184	636	4,142	4,559	5,411
Sarasota County, Florida..............	409,001	2,435	1,432	6,610	7,890	7,681	1,258	2,108	6,501	6,002	7,267
Seminole County, Florida..............	447,918	4,470	2,750	11,194	10,580	12,397	4,196	2,289	10,504	11,658	12,612
Volusia County, Florida.................	522,502	2,970	2,402	12,406	9,994	12,546	2,465	2,218	10,319	10,055	11,248
GEORGIA											
Barrow County, Georgia	75,859	1,134	477	2,599	2,348	1,824	831	1,000	2,392	2,282	2,314
Bibb County, Georgia....................	145,962	1,268	1,876	4,288	4,167	3,785	1,169	1,611	3,200	4,117	4,090
Bulloch County, Georgia................	73,692	326	198	2,070	2,409	809	226	646	1,091	2,022	2,135
Carroll County, Georgia.................	113,732	1,215	603	3,479	2,854	3,650	518	405	3,018	4,242	3,679
Catoosa County, Georgia..............	65,142	393	430	823	2,638	1,333	310	373	2,260	1,538	2,765
Chatham County, Georgia.............	277,963	2,245	1,102	7,748	6,918	6,440	2,309	1,373	6,402	6,274	7,436
Cherokee County, Georgia............	239,414	1,497	1,074	7,494	8,997	7,753	2,363	1,325	6,008	8,117	7,711
Clarke County, Georgia.................	123,018	628	429	3,295	2,316	2,149	545	359	2,038	2,404	2,823
Clayton County, Georgia...............	271,685	2,119	1,230	9,397	9,872	10,747	2,282	2,073	9,720	8,713	9,092
Cobb County, Georgia	729,494	7,946	4,668	20,926	20,764	21,237	7,978	5,609	19,479	19,639	24,087
Columbia County, Georgia............	146,872	1,640	1,361	3,320	4,785	6,181	1,925	580	3,467	5,471	3,724
Coweta County, Georgia...............	137,424	1,463	1,376	4,498	3,691	3,773	1,102	464	3,435	4,660	4,113
DeKalb County, Georgia	722,294	8,376	6,657	19,067	19,807	17,535	6,757	5,019	19,806	18,344	20,106
Dougherty County, Georgia...........	86,080	901	977	2,524	2,041	3,554	827	625	2,804	1,967	2,454
Douglas County, Georgia..............	139,373	1,253	1,382	3,996	4,541	4,691	2,020	1,150	4,802	3,549	4,524
Fayette County, Georgia	109,495	459	607	3,186	4,123	3,783	1,150	621	2,542	3,392	3,969
Floyd County, Georgia...................	94,254	511	402	2,109	2,363	3,130	377	1,004	2,961	2,727	2,403
Forsyth County, Georgia	219,506	2,253	2,168	7,228	8,407	7,871	2,110	1,426	7,559	7,733	7,567
Fulton County, Georgia.................	1,004,495	10,421	7,460	27,113	26,112	26,896	9,289	5,905	24,715	26,616	27,052
Glynn County, Georgia..................	82,354	541	261	2,531	2,043	2,950	1,325	143	1,874	2,772	1,847
Gwinnett County, Georgia.............	885,716	9,175	8,047	26,530	31,479	31,768	7,991	7,035	30,844	27,136	28,065
Hall County, Georgia	191,436	1,034	1,314	6,254	6,437	6,446	1,144	1,015	5,418	5,509	5,917
Henry County, Georgia..................	219,385	1,714	1,209	5,608	10,305	7,309	1,421	1,062	6,894	6,733	7,369
Houston County, Georgia..............	146,984	1,352	1,029	3,890	5,578	4,452	641	1,139	4,237	4,468	4,925
Jackson County, Georgia..............	65,160	1,016	186	2,185	1,788	1,198	458	104	1,595	2,704	1,899
Lowndes County, Georgia.............	109,845	1,370	461	3,488	2,840	2,809	519	659	2,793	3,042	2,766
Muscogee County, Georgia	186,461	2,105	1,546	5,045	5,335	5,726	1,941	880	5,755	5,146	4,077
Newton County, Georgia	104,391	613	999	3,471	3,139	4,150	581	651	3,361	2,872	4,883
Paulding County, Georgia.............	152,563	1,848	1,017	4,275	4,597	4,505	626	467	4,504	6,542	4,307
Richmond County, Georgia	193,281	1,587	1,090	5,276	4,534	4,895	2,098	1,000	7,034	3,330	5,730
Rockdale County, Georgia............	87,349	389	219	2,719	2,877	3,956	953	1,125	2,462	2,391	2,986
Walton County, Georgia	88,425	796	489	3,871	2,215	2,387	813	398	1,784	3,021	3,102
Whitfield County, Georgia	100,684	639	535	3,455	3,537	2,401	537	533	3,966	2,686	3,717
HAWAII											
Hawaii County, Hawaii..................	192,769	1,369	1,132	4,216	5,553	4,699	1,379	1,578	4,067	4,835	4,022
Honolulu County, Hawaii...............	951,989	8,874	6,481	21,421	23,531	21,814	7,535	5,074	20,472	22,743	20,452
Kauai County, Hawaii....................	69,412	1,061	241	1,939	1,868	1,060	534	716	1,766	1,777	1,897
Maui County, Hawaii	160,861	975	1,190	4,257	3,525	4,149	1,633	591	4,616	3,517	3,516

Table C-4. Primary and Secondary School Enrollment, by Sex and Selected Counties, 2017—*Continued*

(Number.)

		Male					Female				
		Enrolled in school					Enrolled in school				
State/County	Population 3 years and over	Nursery school, Pre-school	Kindergarten	Grades 1 to 4	Grades 5 to 8	Grades 9 to 12	Nursery school, Pre-school	Kindergarten	Grades 1 to 4	Grades 5 to 8	Grades 9 to 12
IDAHO											
Ada County, Idaho	442,687	4,351	3,595	10,984	15,757	12,421	2,834	2,474	11,174	13,218	13,335
Bannock County, Idaho	81,191	701	432	2,530	2,106	2,679	275	108	2,247	2,796	3,242
Bonneville County, Idaho	109,058	1,179	990	4,699	3,699	3,916	1,114	576	3,955	4,014	3,285
Canyon County, Idaho	207,271	1,726	627	7,617	8,405	7,328	789	1,958	4,877	7,831	6,637
Kootenai County, Idaho	151,021	1,370	848	4,223	3,631	4,283	1,307	974	4,338	3,082	3,770
Twin Falls County, Idaho	81,562	603	748	2,333	3,109	2,698	660	92	3,288	2,757	1,958
ILLINOIS											
Adams County, Illinois	63,962	407	1,217	1,582	1,660	1,729	675	504	1,910	857	1,388
Champaign County, Illinois	203,187	1,709	791	4,795	4,581	4,639	1,642	1,855	3,446	4,275	4,162
Cook County, Illinois	5,023,248	47,266	27,723	129,610	129,973	131,983	43,355	28,319	122,388	128,579	130,035
DeKalb County, Illinois	101,418	531	722	2,894	1,516	3,072	1,140	1,036	2,092	2,823	2,387
DuPage County, Illinois	897,295	8,992	4,026	23,120	27,236	28,305	7,177	5,049	23,223	23,997	25,595
Kane County, Illinois	513,310	4,803	3,512	16,082	17,192	19,009	3,800	4,158	13,594	16,451	15,898
Kankakee County, Illinois	105,903	558	970	2,557	3,097	3,712	973	494	2,682	2,922	2,886
Kendall County, Illinois	121,954	1,852	1,556	4,652	4,459	3,519	1,689	906	5,567	3,045	4,918
Lake County, Illinois	679,301	6,788	4,361	19,143	20,845	24,024	5,422	4,096	19,225	20,222	22,027
LaSalle County, Illinois	106,457	943	939	1,994	2,806	3,157	1,033	595	2,622	2,850	3,069
McHenry County, Illinois	300,091	3,535	2,349	7,327	10,035	10,119	2,372	2,004	8,429	7,330	9,898
McLean County, Illinois	166,566	1,163	1,476	3,932	4,361	4,555	1,336	1,331	3,937	4,354	4,057
Macon County, Illinois	102,699	1,348	1,074	2,330	3,248	2,359	730	484	2,329	2,692	2,692
Madison County, Illinois	255,226	1,374	1,201	7,715	6,252	7,682	1,161	999	6,006	7,873	6,115
Peoria County, Illinois	176,276	2,104	628	5,452	5,167	4,712	1,220	832	4,843	4,724	5,193
Rock Island County, Illinois	138,822	755	577	3,501	3,706	3,613	518	774	3,778	3,051	4,241
St. Clair County, Illinois	252,293	2,558	2,338	7,612	6,217	7,513	2,991	1,054	7,285	6,423	7,064
Sangamon County, Illinois	189,645	1,392	1,225	5,269	5,372	5,096	2,300	1,116	4,794	4,756	5,224
Tazewell County, Illinois	129,330	1,699	593	3,318	3,650	3,482	893	1,235	4,065	3,103	3,248
Vermilion County, Illinois	74,961	711	494	2,644	2,258	1,842	470	366	1,783	2,599	1,593
Will County, Illinois	668,679	5,228	3,623	19,886	22,241	22,502	4,438	4,354	17,743	22,208	22,555
Williamson County, Illinois	64,831	367	70	2,246	1,605	1,418	489	249	1,631	1,956	1,305
Winnebago County, Illinois	273,977	2,486	1,773	6,955	7,791	8,452	2,129	1,786	7,162	7,336	8,487
INDIANA											
Allen County, Indiana	358,067	3,419	1,970	10,616	12,193	10,811	3,190	2,595	9,698	10,231	11,081
Boone County, Indiana	63,158	703	352	2,209	1,881	2,503	511	535	1,907	1,958	1,706
Clark County, Indiana	112,597	724	480	2,796	3,246	3,052	1,189	902	2,752	2,482	3,319
Delaware County, Indiana	111,639	554	290	1,956	3,230	1,964	946	360	1,791	2,563	2,217
Elkhart County, Indiana	196,181	1,145	1,353	6,418	7,194	6,604	1,866	1,183	6,639	6,028	5,678
Floyd County, Indiana	74,546	864	517	1,959	2,114	3,562	243	703	1,577	2,042	1,508
Grant County, Indiana	64,586	507	502	1,885	1,497	1,745	539	303	1,549	1,681	1,344
Hamilton County, Indiana	308,978	2,516	2,845	9,901	12,157	10,992	3,246	1,511	9,331	10,344	9,944
Hancock County, Indiana	72,804	590	237	1,225	3,047	2,579	1,116	645	952	2,169	2,116
Hendricks County, Indiana	158,100	1,089	844	4,573	6,097	5,678	1,854	779	4,075	5,982	4,124
Howard County, Indiana	79,322	850	116	1,907	2,680	2,049	903	930	1,977	2,239	2,021
Johnson County, Indiana	147,779	1,506	571	4,538	4,807	3,925	917	1,078	3,923	3,983	4,240
Kosciusko County, Indiana	76,320	500	444	2,229	1,949	2,303	606	330	1,672	1,761	1,775
Lake County, Indiana	468,432	4,368	3,312	11,797	14,018	14,304	3,957	4,161	11,634	13,213	13,352
LaPorte County, Indiana	106,426	658	822	2,310	1,928	3,528	1,002	631	2,316	2,921	2,809
Madison County, Indiana	124,890	1,043	627	3,533	2,989	3,822	473	484	3,067	2,453	3,322
Marion County, Indiana	910,269	7,253	6,212	25,962	24,336	25,610	8,391	7,506	21,536	28,710	23,036
Monroe County, Indiana	142,341	1,059	648	3,167	2,110	3,334	903	684	2,188	3,214	2,059
Porter County, Indiana	163,478	1,385	670	4,753	5,373	5,166	818	2,086	4,215	3,283	4,353
St. Joseph County, Indiana	259,973	2,852	1,349	6,414	7,594	7,753	1,407	2,273	7,223	6,924	6,257
Tippecanoe County, Indiana	183,741	1,089	1,543	4,780	4,043	4,031	1,066	2,183	4,628	3,065	3,823
Vanderburgh County, Indiana	174,424	1,487	1,477	3,962	4,315	3,670	958	668	5,627	3,707	4,431
Vigo County, Indiana	103,749	588	220	2,823	2,369	2,777	753	480	2,084	2,526	2,128
Wayne County, Indiana	63,791	236	393	1,372	2,009	1,737	455	202	1,155	1,849	1,638
IOWA											
Black Hawk County, Iowa	127,703	802	601	3,526	3,610	3,260	681	437	3,799	3,069	2,788
Dallas County, Iowa	83,225	1,285	398	3,056	2,998	3,070	971	688	2,023	3,058	2,441
Dubuque County, Iowa	92,862	957	493	2,424	2,511	2,487	896	654	2,435	2,429	2,503
Johnson County, Iowa	143,644	1,473	829	3,277	3,433	2,937	1,738	830	3,781	2,956	2,244
Linn County, Iowa	214,827	1,274	1,290	5,201	6,844	6,261	1,817	1,443	5,500	6,634	5,652
Polk County, Iowa	460,612	3,906	3,708	12,951	13,569	13,828	4,347	2,999	13,765	12,191	12,923
Pottawattamie County, Iowa	89,415	558	442	2,574	2,818	2,604	563	372	2,843	1,942	2,605
Scott County, Iowa	165,868	1,539	1,404	5,177	4,895	5,170	806	1,186	4,428	5,070	4,643
Story County, Iowa	94,825	566	795	1,542	1,540	1,573	662	448	2,082	1,681	1,547
Woodbury County, Iowa	98,108	581	716	2,692	3,128	2,647	1,076	88	3,132	3,626	2,843

Table C-4. Primary and Secondary School Enrollment, by Sex and Selected Counties, 2017—*Continued*

(Number.)

State/County	Population 3 years and over	Male					Female				
		Enrolled in school					Enrolled in school				
		Nursery school, Pre-school	Kindergarten	Grades 1 to 4	Grades 5 to 8	Grades 9 to 12	Nursery school, Pre-school	Kindergarten	Grades 1 to 4	Grades 5 to 8	Grades 9 to 12
KANSAS											
Butler County, Kansas	64,905	262	460	1,849	2,272	2,348	490	306	1,669	2,308	1,908
Douglas County, Kansas	117,592	909	403	2,080	2,837	2,716	1,156	497	2,907	1,976	2,265
Johnson County, Kansas	568,164	7,365	5,473	16,345	16,616	16,706	5,303	3,885	16,721	15,002	16,311
Leavenworth County, Kansas	78,730	1,646	339	3,143	2,167	2,630	665	456	1,420	2,397	2,122
Riley County, Kansas	70,639	601	256	1,203	973	1,199	323	390	1,502	1,008	1,049
Sedgwick County, Kansas	494,513	6,423	3,337	15,917	13,784	15,038	4,553	3,189	15,646	13,081	16,012
Shawnee County, Kansas	171,706	1,360	1,071	4,978	4,575	5,005	862	1,155	4,930	4,614	4,021
Wyandotte County, Kansas	158,144	1,688	668	5,335	6,022	4,801	2,191	1,881	4,945	5,109	4,216
KENTUCKY											
Boone County, Kentucky	126,036	1,107	1,227	3,791	3,667	4,169	1,167	1,278	4,142	3,526	3,699
Bullitt County, Kentucky	78,020	523	683	1,656	2,270	2,319	145	344	1,616	2,372	2,549
Campbell County, Kentucky	89,431	548	499	1,846	3,011	2,349	555	548	1,722	1,940	2,307
Christian County, Kentucky	66,443	1,132	589	1,974	1,152	1,829	1,035	608	1,397	2,499	1,476
Daviess County, Kentucky	96,173	840	470	2,330	3,523	3,252	823	1,048	1,485	3,697	2,254
Fayette County, Kentucky	310,036	2,934	1,876	8,530	7,050	7,640	1,977	1,248	8,461	6,449	7,294
Hardin County, Kentucky	103,653	700	696	3,588	2,552	2,894	699	409	3,106	2,874	2,512
Jefferson County, Kentucky	744,646	7,013	4,272	19,523	16,345	20,403	5,179	3,179	19,344	18,505	18,690
Kenton County, Kentucky	159,662	1,347	977	4,605	5,311	4,786	1,573	959	5,028	3,593	3,851
Madison County, Kentucky	87,748	957	365	2,041	1,877	1,855	571	86	2,464	1,778	2,188
Oldham County, Kentucky	64,632	807	379	1,800	3,042	2,188	452	291	1,819	2,297	2,770
Warren County, Kentucky	123,630	1,422	432	3,982	2,378	2,004	677	811	3,251	3,909	3,318
LOUISIANA											
Ascension Parish, Louisiana	119,429	1,702	503	4,542	4,786	3,528	1,346	565	5,155	2,709	4,074
Bossier Parish, Louisiana	121,689	644	478	2,694	4,602	2,688	1,067	544	3,468	3,774	2,831
Caddo Parish, Louisiana	236,886	3,025	2,011	6,103	6,921	7,178	2,208	1,456	6,362	6,375	6,556
Calcasieu Parish, Louisiana	193,995	1,723	1,457	5,024	5,541	5,773	1,984	1,647	6,328	4,874	4,511
East Baton Rouge Parish, Louisiana	428,897	3,737	3,085	12,177	10,031	11,950	3,695	1,660	10,833	11,417	11,462
Iberia Parish, Louisiana	69,488	905	360	3,712	1,222	2,525	640	826	1,892	2,919	1,980
Jefferson Parish, Louisiana	422,728	4,396	2,791	11,040	10,108	11,168	4,294	2,544	9,503	10,856	9,625
Lafayette Parish, Louisiana	232,984	2,231	1,378	6,557	6,624	6,485	1,749	2,395	6,839	4,959	6,515
Lafourche Parish, Louisiana	94,025	861	498	3,016	2,248	2,791	263	1,037	1,802	2,788	2,163
Livingston Parish, Louisiana	133,405	745	1,579	4,872	3,429	3,702	1,052	601	3,207	3,424	4,860
Orleans Parish, Louisiana	380,403	4,129	2,069	10,242	7,152	8,027	3,919	2,051	9,336	9,579	7,051
Ouachita Parish, Louisiana	149,554	889	1,088	4,432	4,438	3,869	830	1,024	5,045	3,755	4,141
Rapides Parish, Louisiana	125,831	895	575	4,747	4,088	4,944	985	473	2,858	4,191	3,769
St. Landry Parish, Louisiana	80,852	339	603	3,890	4,147	2,386	99	669	2,369	2,768	2,419
St. Tammany Parish, Louisiana	248,860	2,320	1,333	6,943	8,368	7,030	3,170	1,941	7,349	7,257	6,767
Tangipahoa Parish, Louisiana	127,060	1,688	608	3,583	4,461	3,305	1,629	907	2,381	4,862	2,478
Terrebonne Parish, Louisiana	109,351	1,299	405	2,694	4,113	5,523	851	631	2,800	2,897	3,911
MAINE											
Androscoggin County, Maine	103,000	348	1,148	2,163	2,829	2,268	767	646	1,826	2,917	2,592
Aroostook County, Maine	65,977	283	287	1,727	1,276	1,687	310	183	1,414	1,205	1,915
Cumberland County, Maine	283,697	2,361	1,661	6,035	6,419	7,707	1,586	1,673	5,919	6,026	6,416
Kennebec County, Maine	118,075	423	511	2,494	2,222	3,623	241	383	3,104	2,745	3,120
Penobscot County, Maine	148,079	637	447	3,667	3,067	3,519	823	695	3,090	2,922	2,991
York County, Maine	199,133	1,446	1,295	3,776	5,311	5,076	1,437	864	4,748	3,921	4,121
MARYLAND											
Allegany County, Maryland	69,751	542	284	1,423	1,823	1,720	274	234	1,382	1,648	1,175
Anne Arundel County, Maryland	552,893	5,077	4,424	13,525	14,920	14,119	4,334	2,689	13,192	13,454	15,302
Baltimore County, Maryland	802,664	6,181	3,082	20,614	20,707	20,525	6,043	4,670	18,690	20,399	17,941
Calvert County, Maryland	89,021	424	458	2,444	2,729	2,746	445	689	1,656	2,613	3,357
Carroll County, Maryland	161,811	1,535	1,687	3,654	3,785	4,772	885	1,122	3,444	3,809	5,142
Cecil County, Maryland	100,017	1,078	656	2,686	3,481	3,393	1,049	870	2,559	2,078	2,726
Charles County, Maryland	154,015	1,245	831	3,804	5,456	5,001	1,197	870	3,900	4,439	4,369
Frederick County, Maryland	243,115	2,245	1,674	6,146	7,216	7,110	1,764	1,768	5,354	7,619	7,128
Harford County, Maryland	243,142	2,319	1,317	6,494	5,942	7,527	906	1,181	6,978	5,590	5,998
Howard County, Maryland	309,434	2,813	1,790	9,646	9,464	9,827	4,117	2,222	8,365	8,760	9,006
Montgomery County, Maryland	1,020,685	10,678	5,682	27,816	28,982	31,170	10,973	5,947	26,265	26,824	28,298
Prince George's County, Maryland	877,665	6,487	4,892	23,673	22,605	23,400	6,932	5,744	23,640	21,333	21,163
St. Mary's County, Maryland	109,471	1,145	897	2,905	3,811	2,879	1,431	1,006	3,068	2,293	3,713
Washington County, Maryland	145,817	1,264	589	3,640	4,050	4,547	1,053	695	3,224	3,609	3,634
Wicomico County, Maryland	99,097	288	387	2,887	3,106	2,056	478	886	2,920	2,581	2,428
Baltimore city, Maryland	589,586	4,512	3,599	14,814	13,088	14,134	4,802	3,479	13,657	12,289	13,172

Table C-4. Primary and Secondary School Enrollment, by Sex and Selected Counties, 2017—*Continued*

(Number.)

State/County	Population 3 years and over	Male Nursery school, Pre-school	Male Kindergarten	Male Grades 1 to 4	Male Grades 5 to 8	Male Grades 9 to 12	Female Nursery school, Pre-school	Female Kindergarten	Female Grades 1 to 4	Female Grades 5 to 8	Female Grades 9 to 12
MASSACHUSETTS											
Barnstable County, Massachusetts	208,564	1,224	495	3,362	4,364	5,523	796	776	4,009	3,092	5,810
Berkshire County, Massachusetts ..	123,228	783	344	2,972	2,221	2,696	793	367	1,792	3,791	2,416
Bristol County, Massachusetts	543,954	2,775	2,829	13,281	13,969	14,202	4,977	3,091	11,671	13,579	13,967
Essex County, Massachusetts	760,031	4,711	4,366	17,989	20,102	21,969	6,588	3,603	18,762	17,531	20,558
Franklin County, Massachusetts	68,467	341	129	1,418	1,715	1,658	239	343	1,346	1,244	1,772
Hampden County, Massachusetts ..	454,714	3,326	2,935	10,790	13,097	13,080	3,683	2,201	11,177	11,969	10,442
Hampshire County, Massachusetts	158,610	1,323	445	2,531	2,741	3,506	1,243	330	2,131	3,119	3,026
Middlesex County, Massachusetts .	1,552,118	15,250	8,940	32,343	37,447	41,019	14,594	8,609	33,512	32,892	39,214
Norfolk County, Massachusetts	677,420	6,884	5,871	14,503	17,717	20,498	5,766	3,595	15,177	16,393	20,102
Plymouth County, Massachusetts ..	500,760	4,111	2,640	13,539	14,163	15,278	4,199	3,254	11,740	12,525	14,033
Suffolk County, Massachusetts	771,156	4,863	5,075	15,015	13,903	13,966	4,081	4,611	15,167	13,067	14,854
Worcester County, Massachusetts .	798,692	5,778	3,886	20,663	19,617	23,428	6,538	5,597	16,770	21,201	20,824
MICHIGAN											
Allegan County, Michigan	112,537	971	995	3,260	3,168	3,272	870	1,109	3,354	3,101	2,922
Bay County, Michigan	101,039	330	989	2,572	3,227	2,472	571	574	2,396	1,976	2,319
Berrien County, Michigan	149,527	1,559	1,159	3,948	3,544	4,243	944	393	3,832	4,538	3,803
Calhoun County, Michigan	128,387	807	424	4,161	3,232	4,189	1,234	693	2,961	2,874	3,724
Clinton County, Michigan	74,965	489	379	1,477	2,273	2,206	196	439	1,591	2,613	2,064
Eaton County, Michigan	105,386	818	780	2,535	2,180	3,611	1,172	504	1,844	2,627	3,082
Genesee County, Michigan	393,474	3,314	2,821	8,057	12,861	12,681	3,067	2,463	10,376	10,662	10,911
Grand Traverse County, Michigan ..	89,354	772	742	1,663	2,196	2,736	797	428	2,143	2,209	1,826
Ingham County, Michigan	279,129	1,821	2,352	6,186	6,072	6,083	1,236	1,577	6,132	6,381	6,191
Isabella County, Michigan	69,170	404	473	1,359	1,261	1,390	168	259	1,177	1,354	1,214
Jackson County, Michigan	152,774	1,527	1,571	3,468	3,936	3,796	1,247	645	3,619	4,156	4,101
Kalamazoo County, Michigan	253,649	1,561	1,716	7,391	5,847	6,440	2,549	1,174	5,827	6,457	6,125
Kent County, Michigan	620,905	4,454	5,507	18,742	17,630	17,807	5,071	5,138	17,646	16,178	17,443
Lapeer County, Michigan	85,453	402	479	2,146	2,198	2,779	614	243	2,242	2,040	2,436
Lenawee County, Michigan	95,460	878	660	2,417	2,426	2,889	552	557	2,184	2,010	3,029
Livingston County, Michigan	184,803	1,570	1,324	4,443	5,010	5,740	1,593	807	4,596	4,007	5,237
Macomb County, Michigan	842,020	5,621	4,206	20,586	22,290	23,799	5,753	4,480	17,777	21,852	22,486
Marquette County, Michigan	64,428	292	479	1,237	1,415	1,435	497	194	1,302	1,471	1,510
Midland County, Michigan	80,904	951	532	2,065	2,000	2,477	518	261	1,625	2,286	2,052
Monroe County, Michigan	145,499	1,328	1,208	2,802	4,577	4,533	1,505	923	3,442	3,284	4,011
Muskegon County, Michigan	168,840	684	1,259	4,574	4,585	5,803	1,167	1,256	4,006	3,976	5,243
Oakland County, Michigan	1,207,653	9,842	7,607	28,206	28,880	36,014	9,545	7,041	26,481	31,178	33,778
Ottawa County, Michigan	275,524	2,990	2,789	7,171	7,570	8,919	3,064	1,739	7,273	7,472	7,341
Saginaw County, Michigan	186,042	1,807	1,415	4,080	4,975	4,821	2,037	775	4,298	4,123	5,357
St. Clair County, Michigan	154,504	742	296	3,467	4,691	5,079	1,045	581	4,687	3,557	3,784
Shiawassee County, Michigan	66,484	639	241	1,594	1,897	2,211	285	200	1,508	1,670	2,414
Van Buren County, Michigan	72,767	715	349	2,108	1,991	2,152	330	469	1,963	2,281	2,159
Washtenaw County, Michigan	358,076	3,134	2,357	8,791	7,623	9,032	2,921	2,072	6,371	8,684	7,972
Wayne County, Michigan	1,686,413	11,412	12,690	46,932	46,791	51,141	11,248	9,013	44,650	45,115	48,826
MINNESOTA											
Anoka County, Minnesota	337,746	2,904	2,184	8,787	10,323	10,010	3,006	2,761	10,092	8,319	9,841
Blue Earth County, Minnesota	65,161	518	501	1,148	1,768	1,384	673	195	1,459	1,405	1,184
Carver County, Minnesota	97,556	1,505	761	2,971	2,774	3,342	697	739	3,479	2,812	3,245
Dakota County, Minnesota	405,766	4,037	2,694	11,393	13,517	12,634	2,983	2,792	11,526	11,286	12,105
Hennepin County, Minnesota	1,205,265	11,766	7,667	30,441	29,020	33,565	12,945	7,819	28,650	29,503	28,582
Olmsted County, Minnesota	149,306	1,253	905	4,338	4,366	4,007	1,572	1,135	4,567	3,597	4,202
Ramsey County, Minnesota	524,361	4,212	3,431	13,741	14,747	13,368	4,043	4,162	13,510	14,060	13,485
Rice County, Minnesota	63,452	579	144	1,514	1,534	1,682	461	199	1,678	1,701	1,474
St. Louis County, Minnesota	194,755	1,542	1,479	3,752	5,043	4,714	1,228	848	4,028	4,327	4,978
Scott County, Minnesota	140,279	2,420	1,097	5,061	5,403	4,208	1,218	1,047	3,934	4,955	3,886
Sherburne County, Minnesota	91,104	1,168	786	2,522	2,983	2,725	439	801	2,943	2,507	2,920
Stearns County, Minnesota	152,434	1,373	996	4,240	4,056	3,903	1,210	1,216	2,965	4,923	3,723
Washington County, Minnesota	247,585	1,897	1,326	7,400	6,867	8,539	2,398	1,688	6,852	6,999	8,250
Wright County, Minnesota	128,914	1,635	909	4,761	4,125	4,228	1,055	565	3,939	4,997	4,089
MISSISSIPPI											
DeSoto County, Mississippi	171,408	1,088	1,630	4,874	6,699	5,622	1,770	828	5,413	5,397	5,411
Forrest County, Mississippi	72,586	773	1,088	2,388	1,371	2,358	1,028	462	1,572	1,669	1,569
Harrison County, Mississippi	196,923	1,399	1,311	6,985	4,252	4,952	1,448	1,525	5,534	5,703	4,472
Hinds County, Mississippi	231,770	2,636	2,084	6,582	6,758	6,586	2,546	1,319	7,973	5,871	5,658
Jackson County, Mississippi	137,745	1,225	435	3,259	4,885	4,943	1,172	1,069	2,593	4,528	4,056
Lee County, Mississippi	81,549	735	441	2,034	2,870	2,758	1,074	699	3,050	1,801	1,958
Madison County, Mississippi	101,252	1,817	980	3,285	3,051	3,239	1,086	978	3,288	2,740	2,255
Rankin County, Mississippi	147,077	823	788	4,989	4,019	3,965	1,247	995	3,882	3,639	4,247

Table C-4. Primary and Secondary School Enrollment, by Sex and Selected Counties, 2017—*Continued*

(Number.)

State/County	Population 3 years and over	Male					Female				
		Enrolled in school					Enrolled in school				
		Nursery school, Pre-school	Kindergarten	Grades 1 to 4	Grades 5 to 8	Grades 9 to 12	Nursery school, Pre-school	Kindergarten	Grades 1 to 4	Grades 5 to 8	Grades 9 to 12
MISSOURI											
Boone County, Missouri..............	170,919	1,944	554	4,519	3,836	4,382	1,083	1,136	3,709	2,727	3,391
Buchanan County, Missouri	85,417	1,205	417	2,143	1,645	2,489	704	971	2,274	2,391	2,019
Cape Girardeau County, Missouri...	75,575	243	412	2,364	1,891	1,792	689	341	2,258	1,742	2,032
Cass County, Missouri	100,624	1,400	773	3,663	2,774	3,084	708	455	2,702	3,047	2,601
Christian County, Missouri............	82,091	800	900	1,895	2,776	2,771	884	386	2,214	2,450	2,783
Clay County, Missouri	234,195	1,563	2,362	6,539	6,637	7,089	2,368	1,708	6,668	6,312	6,699
Cole County, Missouri	74,131	367	603	2,010	1,685	2,131	554	253	2,047	1,921	2,191
Franklin County, Missouri	99,997	814	131	2,539	3,401	3,285	931	674	2,438	2,680	2,812
Greene County, Missouri...............	278,558	1,704	2,026	7,027	5,171	7,007	2,204	1,771	6,394	6,322	4,947
Jackson County, Missouri.............	672,910	6,331	3,740	18,702	21,146	15,880	6,086	4,609	18,954	18,228	16,965
Jasper County, Missouri	115,599	980	1,134	3,457	2,571	3,776	440	798	3,295	3,997	2,975
Jefferson County, Missouri	217,030	1,700	833	6,135	7,453	6,952	1,713	1,106	5,078	5,962	5,922
Platte County, Missouri.................	96,765	1,194	256	2,666	2,481	2,931	735	928	2,734	2,445	2,557
St. Charles County, Missouri.........	381,196	3,867	2,380	10,001	11,544	11,844	2,904	3,694	10,128	9,687	10,494
St. Louis County, Missouri............	961,996	10,917	3,893	26,972	25,511	27,827	8,837	5,019	21,032	24,729	27,044
St. Louis city, Missouri	295,432	2,369	1,214	7,445	5,866	6,066	1,448	1,228	6,675	6,646	5,558
MONTANA											
Cascade County, Montana.............	78,562	469	734	2,064	2,020	2,228	328	544	2,101	1,815	1,756
Flathead County, Montana.............	96,937	812	702	2,533	2,071	2,452	499	410	2,159	2,845	2,641
Gallatin County, Montana..............	103,575	1,117	417	1,722	2,597	1,947	812	562	2,591	1,822	2,281
Lewis and Clark County, Montana..	65,156	549	463	1,761	1,685	1,489	779	385	1,740	1,082	1,768
Missoula County, Montana............	113,921	721	1,003	2,317	2,690	1,957	767	186	2,578	3,262	2,344
Yellowstone County, Montana.......	153,987	1,371	1,006	4,119	4,165	3,516	1,061	941	3,977	4,281	3,312
NEBRASKA											
Douglas County, Nebraska	534,519	5,259	4,213	15,274	15,672	14,392	4,267	3,272	13,893	16,022	15,519
Lancaster County, Nebraska..........	302,169	2,213	2,345	8,176	8,076	8,078	2,842	1,880	6,902	8,840	8,035
Sarpy County, Nebraska................	173,335	1,995	1,661	5,651	5,433	5,270	1,954	1,055	5,685	5,454	5,485
NEVADA											
Clark County, Nevada	2,122,526	11,086	14,796	63,632	54,885	58,490	13,369	12,535	55,288	57,817	56,960
Washoe County, Nevada...............	444,542	3,846	3,117	11,666	10,388	12,228	1,921	1,952	10,548	12,660	10,890
NEW HAMPSHIRE											
Cheshire County, New Hampshire..	73,781	935	267	1,986	1,081	1,546	496	102	1,410	1,686	1,507
Grafton County, New Hampshire....	87,318	367	661	1,554	1,877	1,657	470	64	1,593	2,050	1,700
Hillsborough County, New Hampshire	396,808	2,641	2,212	8,470	9,437	11,515	2,739	1,536	7,746	11,601	9,034
Merrimack County, New Hampshire	145,517	1,305	1,143	2,647	3,381	4,854	1,185	1,057	3,323	2,680	3,508
Rockingham County, New Hampshire	298,262	1,746	1,037	6,964	7,215	8,012	1,242	1,898	6,132	6,965	7,603
Strafford County, New Hampshire..	125,105	912	534	2,989	2,687	2,812	701	696	2,474	1,907	2,964
NEW JERSEY											
Atlantic County, New Jersey..........	260,945	2,349	1,486	7,872	5,555	7,437	2,387	1,592	5,933	6,981	7,433
Bergen County, New Jersey...........	919,896	9,266	6,083	22,111	22,982	27,200	7,802	4,575	23,282	22,323	24,337
Burlington County, New Jersey	434,772	4,008	2,128	10,451	12,055	11,803	3,445	2,596	9,825	11,199	12,364
Camden County, New Jersey.........	492,036	5,109	3,668	11,321	13,492	15,674	4,281	2,392	12,510	13,174	12,986
Cape May County, New Jersey	91,238	822	249	1,864	2,265	1,935	941	689	1,106	1,957	1,718
Cumberland County, New Jersey ...	147,249	1,945	970	4,017	4,084	3,934	1,645	1,058	4,717	3,632	3,586
Essex County, New Jersey	778,763	8,449	5,020	23,204	21,379	20,922	9,166	5,090	19,682	21,033	22,003
Gloucester County, New Jersey.....	284,102	2,348	1,962	8,137	8,066	8,228	2,249	1,757	6,642	7,431	8,322
Hudson County, New Jersey	662,341	7,048	3,186	11,996	13,373	12,407	7,373	3,264	15,043	11,678	10,956
Hunterdon County, New Jersey	122,019	1,269	446	2,183	3,619	5,235	975	764	2,682	2,644	4,024
Mercer County, New Jersey...........	361,444	4,160	1,867	8,612	9,901	10,154	2,901	1,912	9,555	8,641	8,017
Middlesex County, New Jersey......	815,849	7,608	6,241	18,855	20,886	22,550	5,923	5,034	19,984	21,752	19,625
Monmouth County, New Jersey	608,446	4,503	4,213	14,684	15,583	21,046	7,060	3,203	14,456	14,826	18,697
Morris County, New Jersey	485,078	3,888	2,864	10,868	13,731	16,099	3,987	2,069	13,347	11,082	13,853
Ocean County, New Jersey............	573,089	6,407	4,260	14,756	16,207	15,392	5,559	4,700	15,330	15,064	14,406
Passaic County, New Jersey..........	490,932	4,839	3,836	14,743	13,766	13,596	4,153	3,186	13,263	13,269	15,035
Salem County, New Jersey............	60,730	295	665	1,738	1,486	1,689	427	460	1,591	1,401	1,467
Somerset County, New Jersey	323,790	2,534	1,313	8,412	10,335	10,581	2,024	1,677	8,540	8,061	9,493
Sussex County, New Jersey	138,020	1,009	499	3,088	3,485	4,607	912	1,149	2,292	3,421	3,678
Union County, New Jersey	542,856	4,896	2,956	15,510	16,249	14,836	5,557	3,673	13,429	15,444	15,201
Warren County, New Jersey	104,366	1,016	927	2,239	2,672	3,454	1,072	741	1,830	2,574	2,960

Table C-4. Primary and Secondary School Enrollment, by Sex and Selected Counties, 2017—*Continued*

(Number.)

State/County	Population 3 years and over	Male					Female				
		Enrolled in school					Enrolled in school				
		Nursery school, Pre-school	Kindergarten	Grades 1 to 4	Grades 5 to 8	Grades 9 to 12	Nursery school, Pre-school	Kindergarten	Grades 1 to 4	Grades 5 to 8	Grades 9 to 12
NEW MEXICO											
Bernalillo County, New Mexico......	651,146	4,399	3,824	16,435	18,138	16,260	4,163	3,882	15,790	18,808	18,667
DoÒa Ana County, New Mexico......	207,652	1,136	1,798	6,557	5,967	7,057	1,412	1,251	7,269	5,952	5,894
McKinley County, New Mexico......	69,332	526	1,011	2,392	2,788	2,512	379	598	2,252	2,687	2,223
Sandoval County, New Mexico......	138,301	842	753	2,930	5,103	3,460	708	971	4,291	3,383	4,225
San Juan County, New Mexico......	121,197	851	640	4,776	3,724	3,609	721	964	3,635	4,231	4,280
Santa Fe County, New Mexico.......	145,009	990	773	3,233	3,188	2,457	862	1,496	3,246	2,438	3,920
NEW YORK											
Albany County, New York..............	299,860	2,595	1,990	5,928	6,271	6,983	1,589	948	6,366	6,939	5,874
Bronx County, New York	1,410,358	13,354	10,443	40,377	45,240	42,462	13,895	9,882	43,012	38,779	39,452
Broome County, New York	187,973	1,147	1,417	4,927	3,781	4,917	1,462	886	3,852	4,548	4,669
Cattaraugus County, New York.......	74,913	417	637	1,893	2,129	2,272	427	396	1,919	2,022	2,019
Cayuga County, New York..............	75,182	382	347	1,941	1,232	2,499	220	238	1,613	1,486	2,538
Chautauqua County, New York......	124,776	618	983	2,435	3,478	2,908	560	752	2,751	3,117	3,118
Chemung County, New York..........	82,661	740	396	2,125	1,775	2,297	951	292	1,686	2,652	2,289
Clinton County, New York..............	78,954	525	495	1,444	1,691	2,287	506	539	2,184	1,249	1,738
Dutchess County, New York..........	287,969	1,708	1,460	4,944	7,791	8,778	1,645	1,462	4,711	7,453	7,196
Erie County, New York...................	894,431	5,706	5,120	20,573	21,418	22,517	6,058	5,508	21,326	17,969	22,912
Jefferson County, New York	107,825	625	981	2,517	2,834	2,362	716	1,036	3,086	1,989	2,531
Kings County, New York.................	2,530,106	24,787	18,837	63,756	68,105	66,604	24,426	15,914	64,615	65,255	62,641
Livingston County, New York	62,108	168	81	1,545	1,145	2,021	179	252	1,107	1,270	1,306
Madison County, New York............	68,975	631	293	1,233	1,434	1,429	432	376	836	1,614	1,962
Monroe County, New York	724,346	4,174	4,997	16,562	18,289	18,914	4,887	4,656	16,984	16,369	17,232
Nassau County, New York..............	1,328,795	13,596	8,189	32,568	32,869	38,987	12,190	8,213	30,915	31,538	36,817
New York County, New York..........	1,613,071	10,771	6,436	22,967	29,788	25,859	12,053	6,436	28,436	22,401	23,508
Niagara County, New York.............	205,140	1,738	1,096	4,183	5,674	5,391	1,488	1,098	4,853	4,077	6,079
Oneida County, New York..............	223,451	1,218	1,237	5,285	5,477	6,349	768	1,837	5,056	4,994	5,370
Onondaga County, New York.........	450,867	2,710	1,667	11,691	11,163	11,396	3,330	2,458	10,518	11,759	10,219
Ontario County, New York	106,465	467	453	1,555	3,368	3,324	546	715	2,467	2,227	3,418
Orange County, New York	367,960	2,582	3,180	10,570	12,734	13,340	2,146	3,136	10,407	10,440	10,896
Oswego County, New York.............	114,777	685	1,033	3,360	2,387	2,884	576	560	2,729	2,634	3,155
Putnam County, New York	96,277	421	214	2,156	2,442	2,942	415	449	1,572	3,508	3,177
Queens County, New York.............	2,271,011	17,559	11,360	54,440	51,731	53,855	15,462	12,732	50,142	48,949	50,896
Rensselaer County, New York	155,854	512	1,381	3,158	4,055	3,797	1,263	604	3,853	3,061	3,944
Richmond County, New York	463,865	2,742	1,750	13,336	12,208	13,096	3,878	2,872	11,549	11,705	12,234
Rockland County, New York	314,658	3,542	3,288	11,683	10,680	10,925	3,254	2,735	9,666	10,226	11,148
St. Lawrence County, New York	106,796	544	464	2,830	2,357	2,123	628	682	2,037	2,349	2,389
Saratoga County, New York...........	223,413	1,440	1,281	5,595	5,292	5,952	2,093	1,203	4,567	5,057	6,695
Schenectady County, New York.....	150,063	1,288	456	3,981	4,700	4,070	1,258	1,048	3,798	3,491	4,325
Steuben County, New York............	93,458	536	653	2,645	2,208	3,086	651	590	2,242	2,389	2,473
Suffolk County, New York..............	1,449,738	11,025	8,176	30,752	41,589	43,723	11,017	8,464	35,470	34,996	39,253
Sullivan County, New York	73,300	354	538	1,550	2,479	2,457	390	231	1,192	1,412	2,305
Tompkins County, New York	102,103	289	266	1,662	2,304	1,644	475	228	1,513	1,408	2,274
Ulster County, New York	174,777	1,001	837	3,560	3,973	3,606	967	490	4,500	3,337	4,051
Warren County, New York	62,576	243	356	1,456	1,146	1,735	349	181	1,374	1,337	1,241
Wayne County, New York..............	87,952	642	598	1,818	2,883	2,342	791	720	1,614	2,832	2,508
Westchester County, New York	949,302	10,400	6,950	23,215	26,719	29,499	9,045	4,939	21,500	25,406	26,539
NORTH CAROLINA											
Alamance County, North Carolina...	157,039	566	1,013	4,730	3,993	3,906	764	1,029	3,805	3,910	4,598
Brunswick County, North Carolina .	127,780	10	497	2,132	2,967	2,479	584	775	2,227	1,733	2,670
Buncombe County, North Carolina .	249,852	1,362	670	6,713	6,059	5,732	1,684	1,032	3,864	4,748	7,166
Cabarrus County, North Carolina....	198,319	1,142	1,205	6,648	6,037	8,080	980	418	5,273	7,445	6,510
Carteret County, North Carolina	67,301	254	191	1,469	2,122	2,222	422	255	1,325	1,364	981
Catawba County, North Carolina....	153,427	1,462	896	4,435	3,755	4,640	1,452	1,124	4,077	3,049	4,418
Cleveland County, North Carolina...	93,818	250	984	2,139	3,018	2,710	124	279	1,113	3,257	3,280
Craven County, North Carolina......	98,764	208	948	2,667	2,912	1,901	828	434	2,715	2,651	3,084
Cumberland County, North Carolina...............................	316,927	1,954	3,486	9,583	8,255	9,440	1,540	2,088	9,063	8,070	9,394
Davidson County, North Carolina ...	161,171	1,669	1,518	4,157	4,102	4,751	1,608	1,265	4,612	3,903	4,140
Durham County, North Carolina	299,323	2,106	1,402	7,206	7,586	8,185	1,944	1,961	6,890	6,655	5,477
Forsyth County, North Carolina	362,699	1,700	3,396	9,976	8,963	10,276	2,147	2,505	10,931	8,108	11,246
Gaston County, North Carolina.......	212,615	1,032	806	6,172	5,633	6,723	1,017	1,045	5,237	6,104	5,508
Guilford County, North Carolina	507,125	3,344	3,133	12,483	14,052	13,302	3,178	3,479	11,083	13,668	13,414
Harnett County, North Carolina	126,579	665	1,124	3,594	4,248	3,965	840	756	3,893	3,418	3,980
Henderson County, North Carolina ..	112,611	755	322	2,782	2,986	3,224	1,156	503	2,732	2,153	2,365
Iredell County, North Carolina	169,980	1,197	716	4,091	5,996	5,442	970	1,015	4,795	4,863	5,199
Johnston County, North Carolina ...	189,910	1,002	1,219	4,500	7,745	5,247	2,321	903	5,625	5,334	6,604

Table C-4. Primary and Secondary School Enrollment, by Sex and Selected Counties, 2017—*Continued*

(Number.)

		Male					Female				
		Enrolled in school					Enrolled in school				
State/County	Population 3 years and over	Nursery school, Pre-school	Kindergarten	Grades 1 to 4	Grades 5 to 8	Grades 9 to 12	Nursery school, Pre-school	Kindergarten	Grades 1 to 4	Grades 5 to 8	Grades 9 to 12
NORTH CAROLINA—*(Continued)*											
Mecklenburg County, North Carolina.................	1,033,886	8,118	7,012	31,626	26,559	26,901	10,987	5,189	28,809	27,548	28,119
Moore County, North Carolina.......	95,118	964	924	2,207	2,189	3,576	853	244	2,016	2,839	2,497
New Hanover County, North Carolina.................	220,166	982	1,113	4,605	5,282	4,181	1,577	2,099	3,596	4,176	5,660
Onslow County, North Carolina......	183,570	1,538	1,054	5,398	4,414	3,772	1,262	1,199	3,413	4,337	5,812
Orange County, North Carolina......	141,214	382	939	4,607	3,208	3,277	1,758	695	2,657	3,838	3,599
Pitt County, North Carolina............	172,382	670	461	4,367	4,953	4,867	927	1,252	4,620	3,981	2,856
Randolph County, North Carolina....	139,311	896	353	3,055	4,820	4,900	803	922	3,457	2,525	3,728
Robeson County, North Carolina....	127,175	648	1,105	4,235	3,465	4,103	1,140	717	3,576	4,228	3,738
Rockingham County, North Carolina.................	89,199	541	720	1,179	2,861	2,258	1,002	229	2,550	2,460	2,304
Rowan County, North Carolina......	136,345	486	957	3,452	4,154	4,164	691	349	4,002	3,348	3,134
Surry County, North Carolina........	70,160	431	580	1,982	1,751	1,674	241	307	1,740	1,709	2,218
Union County, North Carolina........	224,174	1,793	1,987	6,426	7,989	9,315	2,233	1,438	7,991	7,089	8,522
Wake County, North Carolina........	1,033,460	11,056	6,289	31,730	28,137	32,512	6,969	7,262	26,314	30,229	31,289
Wayne County, North Carolina......	119,443	618	968	2,581	3,317	4,176	690	363	2,738	3,640	4,111
Wilson County, North Carolina......	78,845	461	232	2,086	3,092	3,044	496	328	2,912	1,977	2,462
NORTH DAKOTA											
Burleigh County, North Dakota......	90,281	426	704	2,571	1,686	2,431	795	564	2,036	1,516	2,312
Cass County, North Dakota	170,250	1,034	972	4,011	4,731	3,590	495	1,017	5,170	2,643	4,008
Grand Forks County, North Dakota.	67,699	651	162	1,252	1,817	1,213	507	240	2,006	1,200	1,032
Ward County, North Dakota...........	65,463	511	403	1,760	1,767	1,160	297	1,033	1,709	1,815	1,810
OHIO											
Allen County, Ohio.......................	99,821	957	961	2,141	3,258	2,911	773	1,098	2,561	2,923	3,015
Ashtabula County, Ohio................	94,209	537	116	2,846	2,081	3,047	110	531	2,483	2,516	2,817
Belmont County, Ohio	65,972	337	140	991	1,914	2,342	535	384	1,284	1,363	1,984
Butler County, Ohio	365,411	2,711	1,965	11,381	10,093	10,426	2,952	1,674	9,603	10,941	10,031
Clark County, Ohio	130,006	1,181	770	3,653	3,341	3,213	1,049	913	3,112	2,932	3,598
Clermont County, Ohio.................	196,987	1,572	727	5,418	5,780	5,956	2,072	991	4,731	5,542	5,128
Columbiana County, Ohio.............	100,014	633	401	1,915	2,984	2,479	444	627	2,398	2,394	2,295
Cuyahoga County, Ohio................	1,205,463	8,883	7,396	28,551	28,800	33,187	8,537	6,537	26,974	29,862	31,816
Delaware County, Ohio.................	193,921	1,954	1,100	5,847	7,250	6,874	2,566	2,158	5,664	5,479	6,798
Erie County, Ohio	72,051	743	186	2,241	2,293	1,513	677	358	1,101	1,522	1,887
Fairfield County, Ohio..................	149,562	929	592	4,935	3,862	5,876	875	1,003	4,337	3,719	4,281
Franklin County, Ohio..................	1,235,767	10,864	8,044	35,781	30,566	31,648	9,113	8,211	33,230	29,323	32,573
Geauga County, Ohio...................	91,137	471	465	2,179	2,732	2,984	774	569	2,165	3,037	2,291
Greene County, Ohio...................	160,364	1,210	1,701	2,874	4,643	3,776	1,049	834	3,459	3,534	3,470
Hamilton County, Ohio.................	781,746	6,767	5,081	20,189	22,179	19,756	6,073	5,363	20,967	19,116	20,707
Hancock County, Ohio.................	72,259	205	530	2,722	1,502	2,112	327	580	1,301	1,966	1,625
Jefferson County, Ohio................	64,057	289	198	1,289	2,257	1,418	445	194	1,221	1,752	1,442
Lake County, Ohio	223,118	1,848	985	5,330	5,977	6,374	732	1,553	4,081	5,644	7,359
Licking County, Ohio...................	167,557	797	844	3,705	5,226	5,037	1,080	1,518	4,366	4,579	4,675
Lorain County, Ohio....................	296,887	2,602	1,885	6,946	8,229	9,951	1,712	1,136	7,881	7,005	8,307
Lucas County, Ohio.....................	413,887	3,178	3,230	10,887	10,569	14,239	3,040	2,449	11,587	10,468	9,973
Mahoning County, Ohio................	223,036	1,584	696	4,964	6,457	6,422	2,002	1,259	4,715	4,583	6,248
Medina County, Ohio...................	172,163	1,432	1,213	4,595	4,776	4,664	1,540	1,335	3,893	4,917	4,957
Miami County, Ohio.....................	101,606	981	701	2,295	3,527	3,196	1,303	425	2,239	2,880	2,547
Montgomery County, Ohio	512,444	3,633	2,960	14,283	13,550	12,645	3,968	2,264	11,188	13,442	14,075
Muskingum County, Ohio.............	83,428	1,244	745	2,249	2,054	2,120	698	396	2,803	1,739	1,848
Portage County, Ohio..................	157,942	811	969	3,733	3,545	3,982	1,225	1,034	3,348	2,677	4,243
Richland County, Ohio..................	116,850	665	177	2,821	3,372	3,122	636	435	2,451	4,640	2,950
Ross County, Ohio	74,776	608	660	1,994	1,364	2,682	160	235	2,339	1,449	1,758
Scioto County, Ohio	72,979	305	1,148	2,076	1,827	1,910	348	158	1,372	2,458	1,856
Stark County, Ohio......................	361,036	3,348	1,905	8,388	10,171	9,887	2,561	1,787	8,663	9,583	9,026
Summit County, Ohio...................	523,444	4,452	2,817	14,010	12,485	12,716	3,553	2,983	12,584	11,464	13,462
Trumbull County, Ohio	193,113	1,157	555	4,090	5,679	5,499	1,104	1,042	4,615	4,508	4,754
Tuscarawas County, Ohio	89,090	830	387	2,861	2,301	2,319	699	363	2,546	2,419	2,254
Warren County, Ohio....................	219,955	1,866	736	7,853	6,964	7,150	2,131	1,042	6,229	6,851	6,455
Wayne County, Ohio.....................	111,696	1,022	1,508	3,096	2,909	2,010	475	328	2,861	2,804	2,963
Wood County, Ohio	126,389	929	826	3,845	2,965	2,915	793	694	2,766	3,216	2,665
OKLAHOMA											
Canadian County, Oklahoma	134,572	1,013	1,486	3,677	4,818	4,548	1,747	1,615	4,006	3,107	4,180
Cleveland County, Oklahoma.........	270,458	2,269	2,212	6,272	8,578	7,184	1,217	536	6,579	8,328	7,040
Comanche County, Oklahoma	116,331	1,005	524	3,976	2,908	3,257	1,347	724	3,238	3,132	3,088

Table C-4. Primary and Secondary School Enrollment, by Sex and Selected Counties, 2017—*Continued*

(Number.)

		Male					Female				
		Enrolled in school					Enrolled in school				
State/County	Population 3 years and over	Nursery school, Pre-school	Kindergarten	Grades 1 to 4	Grades 5 to 8	Grades 9 to 12	Nursery school, Pre-school	Kindergarten	Grades 1 to 4	Grades 5 to 8	Grades 9 to 12
OKLAHOMA—(*Continued*)											
Creek County, Oklahoma...............	69,011	628	495	1,796	2,122	2,303	451	676	1,811	1,901	1,962
Muskogee County, Oklahoma........	66,358	550	373	2,596	1,644	1,777	621	219	1,624	2,104	2,154
Oklahoma County, Oklahoma........	748,933	7,016	5,700	24,263	21,937	20,444	6,628	4,617	21,090	22,356	20,582
Payne County, Oklahoma	78,204	690	694	1,530	2,138	2,473	362	652	2,126	988	632
Pottawatomie County, Oklahoma ...	69,896	615	521	2,430	1,862	2,212	684	591	2,013	1,722	2,114
Rogers County, Oklahoma..............	88,359	831	507	2,290	2,850	2,817	893	602	2,090	2,730	2,466
Tulsa County, Oklahoma................	618,826	6,185	4,470	19,338	18,977	18,145	6,625	5,376	18,710	16,421	16,408
Wagoner County, Oklahoma..........	76,097	629	457	2,108	2,365	2,596	487	646	2,347	2,238	2,424
OREGON											
Benton County, Oregon	89,190	1,017	160	1,798	1,302	925	600	498	899	2,345	2,830
Clackamas County, Oregon	400,604	4,394	2,669	9,139	11,413	11,762	2,523	2,343	9,169	10,847	11,447
Deschutes County, Oregon............	181,301	972	764	4,063	4,602	4,374	1,210	1,349	2,451	4,177	3,844
Douglas County, Oregon	106,759	1,284	826	2,446	1,822	2,124	960	210	3,002	2,633	2,015
Jackson County, Oregon................	210,100	1,098	903	6,012	5,194	6,182	1,255	1,134	3,962	5,794	4,870
Klamath County, Oregon	64,775	492	197	1,660	1,649	1,527	440	306	1,975	1,206	1,713
Lane County, Oregon.....................	363,677	1,742	825	9,223	7,316	9,675	2,392	1,420	8,024	8,013	7,589
Linn County, Oregon	120,113	404	1,009	3,974	3,140	2,426	363	462	3,107	3,405	3,338
Marion County, Oregon	328,055	1,984	2,530	9,407	11,207	9,562	1,358	2,164	9,744	7,956	9,843
Multnomah County, Oregon	780,549	6,642	3,536	17,897	16,269	17,556	5,801	3,386	18,432	15,140	16,249
Polk County, Oregon	80,458	230	760	1,389	2,439	3,917	342	123	2,653	2,425	2,159
Umatilla County, Oregon	73,168	172	380	2,532	1,839	3,235	365	378	1,591	2,312	2,542
Washington County, Oregon	568,240	5,552	3,775	14,417	16,863	16,923	4,871	3,599	16,153	14,701	14,435
Yamhill County, Oregon.................	102,460	879	1,008	3,429	3,455	2,083	749	361	2,069	2,418	2,614
PENNSYLVANIA											
Adams County, Pennsylvania........	99,337	565	624	2,042	2,740	2,486	402	452	2,267	2,326	2,231
Allegheny County, Pennsylvania.....	1,183,641	9,195	4,981	24,859	28,157	27,251	10,058	5,138	23,449	26,727	24,958
Armstrong County, Pennsylvania...	63,884	351	430	1,284	1,339	1,534	367	267	1,702	1,361	1,513
Beaver County, Pennsylvania........	161,416	1,255	901	3,064	3,694	4,057	1,803	630	4,535	3,278	4,068
Berks County, Pennsylvania	402,315	2,288	1,840	11,044	11,790	12,346	2,224	1,833	10,835	9,557	10,111
Blair County, Pennsylvania............	120,629	1,438	451	2,518	3,226	3,757	1,507	798	2,534	3,036	2,370
Bucks County, Pennsylvania..........	609,646	3,769	3,057	15,139	17,389	17,370	4,954	3,096	13,160	14,727	16,918
Butler County, Pennsylvania..........	181,533	1,370	639	4,369	5,105	5,079	1,644	685	3,773	4,410	4,690
Cambria County, Pennsylvania......	129,467	594	615	2,819	2,760	3,257	1,023	768	2,739	2,893	2,742
Carbon County, Pennsylvania........	62,870	585	287	1,472	1,185	1,802	485	262	1,189	2,158	1,507
Centre County, Pennsylvania.........	158,474	947	1,097	2,270	2,687	3,086	939	407	2,455	3,366	2,273
Chester County, Pennsylvania.......	501,551	4,700	2,857	13,187	15,932	13,687	4,431	2,106	13,510	14,082	14,235
Clearfield County, Pennsylvania.....	77,165	335	386	1,763	1,669	1,773	411	487	1,661	1,484	1,713
Columbia County, Pennsylvania	64,221	109	452	1,084	1,888	1,870	733	293	1,057	1,410	1,147
Crawford County, Pennsylvania.....	83,579	655	598	1,731	2,169	2,252	432	337	2,235	1,607	1,894
Cumberland County, Pennsylvania.	242,615	1,724	2,101	5,981	4,639	5,755	1,500	1,961	6,777	4,851	5,385
Dauphin County, Pennsylvania......	265,394	2,384	1,362	5,880	7,386	6,529	1,017	2,170	5,363	6,402	7,917
Delaware County, Pennsylvania.....	544,830	5,676	2,572	14,563	13,517	15,970	4,166	4,077	11,602	14,272	13,935
Erie County, Pennsylvania	265,699	1,958	1,992	7,392	6,011	6,071	1,864	1,478	6,199	6,654	6,280
Fayette County, Pennsylvania........	127,814	553	268	2,951	3,284	2,924	910	920	2,688	2,924	2,673
Franklin County, Pennsylvania.......	149,541	853	1,296	3,360	4,290	4,809	1,173	599	4,139	3,655	4,681
Indiana County, Pennsylvania........	82,701	393	307	1,685	1,780	1,954	532	232	1,535	2,200	1,473
Lackawanna County, Pennsylvania.	204,859	1,580	890	5,457	5,332	5,254	1,745	1,143	4,696	4,556	4,813
Lancaster County, Pennsylvania.....	520,421	3,776	2,693	13,445	14,782	11,770	2,630	3,560	15,228	12,017	11,267
Lawrence County, Pennsylvania.....	85,051	674	413	1,963	2,119	1,674	558	380	2,067	1,905	2,234
Lebanon County, Pennsylvania	134,504	819	658	4,169	3,524	3,283	619	348	3,228	3,721	3,635
Lehigh County, Pennsylvania	354,125	2,114	2,767	9,017	11,553	10,195	2,567	1,922	7,451	10,263	9,940
Luzerne County, Pennsylvania.......	308,608	2,044	2,047	6,046	7,090	8,105	2,021	1,102	7,540	6,419	7,159
Lycoming County, Pennsylvania.....	110,205	370	212	3,349	2,923	2,420	604	423	2,213	2,554	2,295
Mercer County, Pennsylvania........	108,602	1,033	330	2,822	2,255	3,448	778	532	1,851	2,417	2,955
Monroe County, Pennsylvania.......	164,599	1,325	677	4,050	3,428	4,571	649	905	2,401	4,257	5,354
Montgomery County, Pennsylvania	799,994	8,366	4,135	18,400	22,215	23,870	8,106	3,671	21,092	18,854	20,738
Northampton County, Pennsylvania	295,212	1,852	1,683	7,443	7,258	8,094	1,968	1,156	6,736	7,289	6,718
Northumberland County, Pennsylvania............................	89,154	508	613	2,052	1,994	2,049	275	400	1,495	2,158	1,976
Philadelphia County, Pennsylvania.	1,517,859	14,108	10,400	37,957	37,246	37,235	12,843	10,165	38,571	33,375	33,223
Schuylkill County, Pennsylvania.....	138,618	663	459	3,162	3,281	4,024	670	924	3,166	3,086	3,363
Somerset County, Pennsylvania.....	72,885	226	366	1,688	1,584	2,423	345	666	1,433	1,157	1,722
Washington County, Pennsylvania.	201,626	1,418	1,537	4,101	4,903	5,088	2,316	1,131	4,731	4,244	4,557
Westmoreland County, Pennsylvania............................	343,927	2,199	998	6,824	8,209	8,111	2,802	1,493	7,026	7,921	7,898
York County, Pennsylvania.............	430,681	3,107	2,414	11,291	12,122	11,575	1,966	2,451	10,448	10,477	11,374

Table C-4. Primary and Secondary School Enrollment, by Sex and Selected Counties, 2017—*Continued*

(Number.)

State/County	Population 3 years and over	Male Nursery school, Pre-school	Male Kindergarten	Male Grades 1 to 4	Male Grades 5 to 8	Male Grades 9 to 12	Female Nursery school, Pre-school	Female Kindergarten	Female Grades 1 to 4	Female Grades 5 to 8	Female Grades 9 to 12
RHODE ISLAND											
Kent County, Rhode Island............	158,629	904	542	3,016	4,131	3,375	1,200	671	3,256	3,750	3,283
Newport County, Rhode Island.......	81,405	441	163	1,038	2,407	1,240	421	609	1,562	984	1,614
Providence County, Rhode Island ..	615,056	4,803	2,870	14,961	15,319	15,142	2,616	3,215	15,455	14,336	13,846
Washington County, Rhode Island .	124,045	826	470	2,499	2,658	2,991	752	505	1,869	2,835	3,334
SOUTH CAROLINA											
Aiken County, South Carolina........	163,014	776	1,026	4,262	4,909	3,234	652	1,670	4,086	4,528	2,454
Anderson County, South Carolina ..	191,561	993	1,292	5,344	4,696	5,980	1,658	979	5,300	3,860	5,077
Beaufort County, South Carolina....	179,836	726	813	4,342	4,664	2,558	1,507	586	3,491	4,730	4,044
Berkeley County, South Carolina	208,450	920	989	6,489	5,974	5,785	1,342	1,697	6,540	4,696	6,780
Charleston County, South Carolina.	388,685	2,778	3,187	10,099	6,954	8,123	4,003	2,361	9,246	8,044	7,692
Dorchester County, South Carolina	150,985	1,135	1,232	4,119	5,782	5,465	1,017	1,531	4,243	3,366	4,782
Florence County, South Carolina	133,095	923	1,465	4,234	3,558	3,606	320	712	3,561	3,751	4,090
Greenville County, South Carolina..	486,772	4,021	4,336	14,636	12,192	12,003	2,250	4,290	14,035	11,942	12,169
Greenwood County, South Carolina	68,296	422	1,034	1,741	1,233	1,339	420	452	1,979	1,555	1,849
Horry County, South Carolina	323,835	1,524	1,192	7,465	7,502	6,886	2,084	1,967	5,910	6,969	7,262
Lancaster County, South Carolina ..	89,030	868	554	2,343	1,928	1,405	203	468	3,194	2,417	2,660
Laurens County, South Carolina.....	64,606	606	924	1,633	1,727	1,958	188	488	1,938	1,448	1,605
Lexington County, South Carolina..	280,987	1,721	3,300	7,606	7,393	8,233	2,253	2,054	6,841	9,236	7,000
Orangeburg County, South Carolina...................................	84,775	275	468	2,133	2,708	2,743	47	536	1,870	2,179	2,416
Pickens County, South Carolina	119,773	407	610	3,053	3,775	3,278	525	793	2,112	2,736	2,885
Richland County, South Carolina....	396,318	1,935	3,271	10,473	9,998	8,774	2,509	2,468	8,484	11,306	10,625
Spartanburg County, South Carolina...................................	295,752	1,622	1,748	8,151	9,103	7,323	1,602	2,225	6,737	9,272	7,841
Sumter County, South Carolina.....	103,419	507	629	2,788	3,772	2,934	1,371	1,124	2,479	2,826	3,138
York County, South Carolina	258,170	2,222	1,103	9,013	6,389	7,862	1,412	2,072	6,342	8,363	8,251
SOUTH DAKOTA											
Minnehaha County, South Dakota ..	180,858	1,858	1,768	5,100	5,151	4,642	2,003	1,079	5,874	4,766	4,370
Pennington County, South Dakota .	106,301	975	741	2,345	2,548	3,594	760	922	2,527	2,535	2,608
TENNESSEE											
Anderson County, Tennessee	74,600	1,116	332	1,498	2,180	2,138	258	360	1,303	2,422	2,272
Blount County, Tennessee	126,291	567	852	2,861	2,957	3,011	401	531	3,027	2,699	3,242
Bradley County, Tennessee............	101,768	323	848	2,531	2,539	3,074	536	753	2,615	2,565	2,143
Davidson County, Tennessee.........	662,757	4,403	2,858	17,687	14,794	14,529	5,447	4,813	15,735	14,764	14,743
Hamilton County, Tennessee	349,542	2,553	2,982	9,295	7,882	7,731	2,447	1,476	7,832	9,850	6,259
Knox County, Tennessee	445,981	2,480	3,586	11,659	10,057	11,042	2,428	2,251	9,915	12,217	9,973
Madison County, Tennessee	94,489	645	964	1,578	2,936	2,810	700	222	1,406	3,270	2,960
Maury County, Tennessee	87,953	1,118	465	2,011	3,497	2,301	0	296	1,782	2,273	2,581
Montgomery County, Tennessee	189,870	1,924	1,930	5,337	5,522	5,704	990	1,309	6,514	4,773	4,958
Robertson County, Tennessee........	66,936	166	548	1,769	1,282	2,437	67	487	1,610	1,527	2,620
Rutherford County, Tennessee	304,880	2,517	1,426	9,474	9,849	8,745	2,742	2,466	7,778	8,823	8,494
Sevier County, Tennessee	94,189	466	485	1,808	3,109	2,746	344	770	2,281	1,983	2,154
Shelby County, Tennessee..............	900,669	5,752	6,062	25,393	27,119	24,230	8,036	6,689	25,414	23,496	27,046
Sullivan County, Tennessee............	152,930	846	1,209	3,423	3,250	3,884	952	961	3,360	3,466	3,527
Sumner County, Tennessee	177,113	927	1,352	4,560	5,719	5,117	1,279	1,238	4,487	4,696	4,794
Washington County, Tennessee......	124,175	441	747	2,736	3,039	2,803	682	613	2,226	3,787	2,347
Williamson County, Tennessee......	217,373	2,376	2,706	6,917	6,138	8,105	2,362	1,966	6,215	7,525	7,644
Wilson County, Tennessee	131,987	1,236	1,019	3,114	3,749	4,223	1,244	1,411	3,538	3,895	3,629
TEXAS											
Angelina County, Texas	84,303	550	754	2,704	2,514	2,561	470	449	3,503	2,167	2,496
Bell County, Texas	328,233	2,572	1,902	12,196	10,891	10,017	2,856	2,908	9,149	10,331	9,450
Bexar County, Texas	1,877,138	15,828	15,041	57,806	56,192	57,583	16,459	14,019	56,185	53,763	54,357
Bowie County, Texas	90,946	659	497	3,584	2,305	2,647	1,132	664	1,929	2,988	2,365
Brazoria County, Texas	345,225	3,964	2,126	14,462	8,596	11,388	1,327	2,337	9,313	12,319	9,857
Brazos County, Texas	215,151	2,297	1,166	4,867	5,897	5,328	918	1,237	6,270	4,044	4,875
Cameron County, Texas..................	403,328	4,373	3,515	14,297	14,712	13,941	4,519	3,691	12,876	14,762	15,249
Collin County, Texas.......................	935,668	7,112	5,589	29,638	32,062	33,125	10,195	6,970	29,519	28,736	29,687
Comal County, Texas......................	136,039	836	661	3,847	4,399	4,185	609	605	2,840	4,685	3,176
Coryell County, Texas	72,030	1,201	514	1,980	1,965	1,321	522	67	1,348	2,606	3,183
Dallas County, Texas	2,501,123	22,763	19,647	76,968	79,952	77,060	19,009	16,364	76,263	79,824	73,679
Denton County, Texas.....................	802,984	7,134	5,220	24,703	24,472	25,777	6,757	5,980	23,165	25,137	21,926
Ector County, Texas........................	148,582	1,881	1,757	4,379	5,713	4,294	1,426	1,805	5,499	4,261	5,391
Ellis County, Texas	166,663	1,002	1,229	6,207	5,386	5,733	802	1,748	5,193	4,816	5,258
El Paso County, Texas	798,757	6,192	6,590	25,344	27,892	27,800	4,640	6,127	24,209	26,198	26,742

Table C-4. Primary and Secondary School Enrollment, by Sex and Selected Counties, 2017—*Continued*

(Number.)

| | | Male | | | | | Female | | | | |
| | | Enrolled in school | | | | | Enrolled in school | | | | |
State/County	Population 3 years and over	Nursery school, Pre-school	Kindergarten	Grades 1 to 4	Grades 5 to 8	Grades 9 to 12	Nursery school, Pre-school	Kindergarten	Grades 1 to 4	Grades 5 to 8	Grades 9 to 12
TEXAS—(*Continued*)											
Fort Bend County, Texas..............	733,754	8,158	4,493	22,922	27,519	24,433	6,951	5,499	23,300	26,145	24,749
Galveston County, Texas	321,686	2,373	2,008	12,333	6,953	9,518	2,171	1,074	8,044	10,221	9,877
Grayson County, Texas..................	126,569	1,038	1,087	4,177	3,123	3,438	487	825	3,091	3,880	3,241
Gregg County, Texas	117,343	1,525	487	4,339	3,545	3,183	562	768	4,218	3,243	2,863
Guadalupe County, Texas	153,990	1,153	1,059	4,420	5,018	5,182	1,541	1,092	3,734	4,700	4,562
Harris County, Texas	4,438,062	37,715	33,549	144,092	141,397	141,462	34,143	34,755	137,007	132,557	134,683
Harrison County, Texas	64,254	1,201	75	1,667	2,522	1,942	554	132	866	2,853	2,251
Hays County, Texas	207,926	1,467	896	5,814	5,934	6,144	2,036	1,636	4,453	5,870	4,597
Henderson County, Texas...............	78,165	632	619	2,305	1,337	1,983	517	205	1,427	2,641	1,558
Hidalgo County, Texas...................	812,684	7,155	8,993	31,022	32,801	32,887	9,041	7,217	31,792	28,646	32,083
Hunt County, Texas	90,641	517	686	2,818	2,372	2,260	891	684	2,779	2,749	2,503
Jefferson County, Texas	247,544	1,109	2,631	6,262	6,018	7,331	1,785	2,152	7,696	5,593	5,972
Johnson County, Texas	161,761	662	519	3,752	4,508	3,280	1,019	1,228	3,276	2,601	2,376
Kaufman County, Texas	117,829	1,318	599	4,127	4,074	3,123	1,255	1,067	3,945	3,788	4,698
Lubbock County, Texas	293,390	2,892	1,691	6,384	10,738	8,561	1,892	2,009	7,412	9,312	7,986
McLennan County, Texas	241,514	2,023	2,275	6,502	7,029	6,713	2,190	1,667	6,065	6,384	7,455
Midland County, Texas	157,559	1,514	1,395	5,271	5,799	4,614	1,046	848	5,880	4,792	4,144
Montgomery County, Texas...........	549,009	6,515	4,876	16,199	17,210	19,878	5,782	3,284	18,189	16,287	17,447
Nueces County, Texas....................	347,228	2,157	2,559	11,742	8,931	11,361	2,743	2,389	9,344	11,361	9,334
Orange County, Texas....................	81,626	662	733	2,060	2,796	3,110	863	849	2,661	1,538	2,294
Parker County, Texas	128,717	1,215	886	4,048	3,694	4,307	742	390	3,735	4,013	3,798
Potter County, Texas	114,951	1,168	634	3,675	4,374	3,812	945	660	4,616	2,397	3,585
Randall County, Texas	129,391	932	905	3,536	4,061	4,326	1,220	902	2,957	3,527	3,186
Rockwall County, Texas	93,307	484	578	3,646	2,768	4,770	445	526	3,200	3,175	3,690
Smith County, Texas......................	219,058	1,073	2,535	7,094	5,423	6,239	990	1,726	5,761	7,276	6,775
Tarrant County, Texas....................	1,968,016	20,642	12,693	60,332	66,192	64,058	17,240	14,157	62,253	56,334	61,091
Taylor County, Texas	130,288	855	692	4,055	4,158	3,143	847	830	3,066	4,265	2,785
Tom Green County, Texas	113,613	934	940	2,396	4,001	2,355	664	782	3,884	2,073	3,978
Travis County, Texas......................	1,178,768	11,334	7,959	31,746	31,303	26,601	10,287	6,242	30,614	31,897	27,249
Victoria County, Texas...................	88,627	552	892	2,321	2,854	2,584	557	377	3,414	1,946	2,507
Webb County, Texas......................	259,146	2,727	4,006	9,197	11,529	10,116	1,536	2,845	9,358	10,252	10,198
Wichita County, Texas	127,722	981	1,175	3,800	3,375	2,992	713	1,010	3,291	2,709	3,735
Williamson County, Texas	527,369	5,438	3,306	15,091	18,523	17,972	4,959	3,210	15,701	18,429	16,759
Wise County, Texas.......................	63,756	932	122	1,801	1,853	2,671	387	238	1,528	1,965	1,933
UTAH											
Cache County, Utah.......................	118,200	1,060	698	4,292	4,914	4,818	1,404	1,130	3,735	4,293	4,536
Davis County, Utah........................	329,274	2,513	2,594	13,747	14,754	11,889	3,694	3,751	12,127	12,281	11,131
Salt Lake County, Utah	1,084,107	10,319	9,898	34,041	36,573	35,872	11,359	8,031	35,672	31,678	31,627
Tooele County, Utah......................	64,344	717	370	3,346	2,224	2,656	693	333	2,938	1,980	2,385
Utah County, Utah	573,077	7,256	6,437	22,848	23,080	23,599	6,529	4,673	23,230	22,212	21,003
Washington County, Utah..............	158,697	953	826	6,250	5,429	5,188	1,421	841	5,295	3,508	4,177
Weber County, Utah......................	239,875	2,411	1,741	8,249	8,239	7,994	1,220	1,819	7,908	7,605	8,474
VERMONT											
Chittenden County, Vermont	157,728	1,653	1,455	2,823	3,082	3,378	879	625	2,501	4,127	2,697
VIRGINIA											
Albemarle County, Virginia............	104,492	704	453	3,050	2,462	2,637	658	616	2,382	2,169	2,772
Arlington County, Virginia	227,424	3,003	1,186	5,280	3,883	3,274	2,047	1,239	4,782	4,526	3,948
Bedford County, Virginia	76,136	511	741	1,210	1,703	2,133	442	289	1,810	1,596	1,487
Chesterfield County, Virginia	331,841	2,678	2,962	9,104	8,620	10,468	2,293	1,807	8,207	9,935	10,218
Fairfax County, Virginia	1,105,398	10,145	6,931	27,963	31,891	33,045	11,021	9,108	29,378	27,921	32,535
Fauquier County, Virginia	67,139	405	682	2,217	1,583	2,372	767	543	1,735	1,659	2,192
Frederick County, Virginia	84,187	296	382	1,888	3,052	3,300	821	166	2,877	1,941	2,757
Hanover County, Virginia...............	102,740	907	601	2,848	3,066	3,446	1,119	996	2,033	2,845	2,713
Henrico County, Virginia................	316,188	1,726	1,762	7,441	10,358	8,918	2,510	1,802	8,044	8,929	8,575
James City County, Virginia	73,885	493	433	2,414	2,024	1,336	367	536	1,482	1,701	2,467
Loudoun County, Virginia..............	381,270	4,122	2,762	13,737	13,984	11,744	4,654	3,242	13,623	12,594	12,848
Montgomery County, Virginia.........	94,796	562	423	1,666	1,067	1,832	476	514	1,269	1,536	964
Prince William County, Virginia......	443,383	4,884	2,944	13,044	15,841	14,973	3,523	4,108	13,686	12,014	13,825
Roanoke County, Virginia..............	91,519	968	271	2,140	2,159	2,608	769	623	2,544	1,697	2,499
Rockingham County, Virginia.........	78,073	698	517	2,088	1,876	2,073	735	791	1,329	2,037	2,186
Spotsylvania County, Virginia........	127,605	726	954	3,493	4,348	4,536	613	1,097	2,694	3,923	4,556
Stafford County, Virginia................	140,675	1,093	631	4,334	4,970	5,173	1,199	913	3,687	4,790	5,529
York County, Virginia.....................	65,877	676	579	1,378	2,594	1,462	628	192	2,182	2,362	1,996
Alexandria city, Virginia.................	153,920	999	1,140	2,490	2,708	2,604	1,516	668	2,352	2,609	3,107
Chesapeake city, Virginia...............	231,256	2,212	1,595	7,210	7,327	6,888	1,501	2,372	4,998	7,215	6,219

Table C-4. Primary and Secondary School Enrollment, by Sex and Selected Counties, 2017—*Continued*

(Number.)

| | | Male | | | | | Female | | | | |
| | | Enrolled in school | | | | | Enrolled in school | | | | |
State/County	Population 3 years and over	Nursery school, Pre-school	Kindergarten	Grades 1 to 4	Grades 5 to 8	Grades 9 to 12	Nursery school, Pre-school	Kindergarten	Grades 1 to 4	Grades 5 to 8	Grades 9 to 12
VIRGINIA—(*Continued*)											
Hampton city, Virginia	129,946	994	713	2,875	3,961	4,457	1,008	444	2,562	3,826	2,685
Lynchburg city, Virginia	77,312	501	156	1,937	1,676	1,280	463	427	1,474	1,717	2,661
Newport News city, Virginia	170,921	1,063	1,765	4,425	3,574	4,076	1,825	1,515	5,098	2,802	4,431
Norfolk city, Virginia	236,335	2,131	1,499	5,509	4,619	4,506	1,619	1,061	5,693	4,765	4,060
Portsmouth city, Virginia	90,514	347	461	2,732	2,617	2,146	889	811	2,073	2,554	3,204
Richmond city, Virginia	218,417	1,057	1,532	3,612	4,612	3,375	1,600	805	4,116	4,412	3,796
Roanoke city, Virginia	95,748	1,203	583	1,920	3,110	1,315	279	1,128	2,359	1,845	2,319
Suffolk city, Virginia	86,364	629	370	3,186	2,380	1,860	506	282	2,802	2,380	2,345
Virginia Beach city, Virginia	433,638	3,634	3,069	10,841	12,782	10,606	3,938	3,184	12,180	8,307	10,411
WASHINGTON											
Benton County, Washington	190,291	1,862	2,292	6,594	5,284	7,076	1,332	1,357	7,126	4,692	6,000
Clallam County, Washington	73,185	177	476	1,511	1,499	1,145	362	263	1,870	684	1,504
Clark County, Washington	456,709	2,753	2,849	13,432	14,582	13,521	2,942	2,676	14,551	11,234	13,299
Cowlitz County, Washington	103,558	1,065	562	1,983	3,674	3,225	967	561	2,553	3,323	2,674
Grant County, Washington	91,900	1,544	685	3,973	2,581	3,613	614	920	3,130	3,318	3,004
Grays Harbor County, Washington	70,482	331	407	2,015	1,528	1,991	787	497	1,950	1,323	1,440
Island County, Washington	80,396	738	167	1,812	1,820	1,578	715	535	1,637	1,429	1,172
King County, Washington	2,115,012	18,879	14,520	50,282	47,612	48,228	18,988	14,994	51,108	43,926	45,385
Kitsap County, Washington	258,130	2,051	2,094	6,205	5,044	6,103	2,294	951	5,976	6,276	6,606
Lewis County, Washington	75,695	566	682	1,808	1,876	2,172	391	462	1,668	1,859	1,731
Pierce County, Washington	841,988	6,619	6,328	23,271	21,369	24,288	4,452	4,629	21,773	23,659	21,064
Skagit County, Washington	122,223	1,299	1,110	2,899	2,823	3,123	479	130	3,886	3,518	2,918
Snohomish County, Washington	770,974	6,017	5,319	19,200	20,616	21,138	6,088	4,374	17,603	20,475	20,158
Spokane County, Washington	488,278	4,069	2,577	12,243	13,799	12,435	2,887	3,210	10,761	11,730	12,427
Thurston County, Washington	271,431	1,364	2,484	6,274	7,126	6,487	1,829	894	6,805	6,934	6,800
Whatcom County, Washington	213,868	1,972	849	5,036	5,007	4,489	1,261	501	5,654	4,240	4,884
Yakima County, Washington	238,963	2,004	1,893	7,312	9,682	9,005	1,485	1,459	9,563	8,502	8,226
WEST VIRGINIA											
Berkeley County, West Virginia	111,122	428	678	3,995	2,876	2,939	670	659	2,340	4,099	3,267
Cabell County, West Virginia	91,519	622	501	2,233	2,015	1,137	426	460	2,039	1,785	1,794
Harrison County, West Virginia	66,193	569	323	1,674	1,942	1,716	511	169	1,541	1,991	1,521
Kanawha County, West Virginia	176,690	1,186	1,191	4,797	3,791	3,954	514	1,235	4,450	3,623	4,433
Monongalia County, West Virginia	101,765	1,256	647	1,594	1,896	2,041	364	247	2,316	1,720	1,696
Wood County, West Virginia	82,523	597	1,025	1,000	1,748	1,842	716	268	2,001	2,805	1,933
WISCONSIN											
Brown County, Wisconsin	252,849	1,345	3,013	7,168	6,479	7,528	2,071	2,333	8,143	5,447	6,693
Dane County, Wisconsin	517,752	3,777	3,691	11,462	13,085	12,857	3,868	3,619	11,628	12,193	11,676
Dodge County, Wisconsin	85,710	628	450	2,457	2,110	2,176	587	653	1,482	2,365	2,706
Eau Claire County, Wisconsin	99,693	609	1,229	2,092	2,245	2,310	1,034	381	2,096	2,072	1,817
Fond du Lac County, Wisconsin	99,342	604	795	2,192	2,943	2,676	366	772	2,504	2,514	2,881
Jefferson County, Wisconsin	81,973	487	495	1,854	2,379	2,030	486	294	1,717	2,639	2,050
Kenosha County, Wisconsin	163,430	1,507	1,047	4,354	4,410	4,985	1,162	1,124	4,397	4,186	5,490
La Crosse County, Wisconsin	114,522	436	507	2,721	3,522	2,532	449	244	3,008	2,876	2,451
Manitowoc County, Wisconsin	76,679	318	288	1,536	2,779	1,735	680	157	1,774	2,045	2,258
Marathon County, Wisconsin	131,011	1,581	747	3,391	3,530	3,105	927	821	3,109	3,957	3,263
Milwaukee County, Wisconsin	913,056	5,189	9,565	25,016	27,397	24,290	4,683	9,215	24,698	24,426	25,002
Outagamie County, Wisconsin	178,952	1,588	832	4,925	5,278	4,991	1,827	981	3,786	5,412	4,982
Ozaukee County, Wisconsin	85,574	633	574	1,964	2,372	2,295	447	583	1,718	2,718	2,571
Portage County, Wisconsin	68,056	280	541	1,110	1,719	1,915	438	284	1,128	1,638	1,330
Racine County, Wisconsin	187,963	1,045	1,419	4,713	6,178	4,723	1,335	1,156	4,480	5,445	6,040
Rock County, Wisconsin	156,546	989	1,238	5,266	3,830	4,294	1,450	903	4,280	3,424	5,346
St. Croix County, Wisconsin	85,884	584	559	2,391	3,513	2,799	693	537	2,077	2,884	3,153
Sheboygan County, Wisconsin	111,857	587	857	2,936	3,397	3,413	680	559	3,263	2,927	2,954
Walworth County, Wisconsin	99,587	565	464	1,951	2,911	2,971	802	735	2,467	2,040	1,939
Washington County, Wisconsin	130,607	1,302	792	3,692	3,038	4,239	756	704	3,058	3,545	3,752
Waukesha County, Wisconsin	388,576	2,728	3,644	8,697	10,078	11,302	3,248	2,363	9,853	9,383	10,957
Winnebago County, Wisconsin	164,954	1,028	1,461	3,421	4,082	4,000	1,540	778	3,548	4,103	4,005
Wood County, Wisconsin	70,589	648	243	1,907	1,881	2,015	307	579	1,783	1,467	1,567
WYOMING											
Laramie County, Wyoming	95,257	596	139	3,694	2,277	2,174	461	795	2,196	2,898	1,926
Natrona County, Wyoming	76,370	545	565	1,910	1,973	2,407	485	1,040	1,942	2,191	1,829

NOTES AND DEFINITIONS: COUNTY EDUCATION STATISTICS

Part C presents data items for selected counties, county equivalents, and independent cities. The District of Columbia is included as both a county and a state.

GEOGRAPHIC IDENTIFICATION

A five-digit state and county code is assigned to each entity. The first two digits indicate the state; the remaining three identify the county. Within each state, the counties are numbered in alphabetical order, beginning with 001, with even numbers usually omitted. Independent cities follow the counties and begin with the number 510.

These codes have been established by the U.S. government as Federal Information Processing Standards and are often referred to as "FIPS codes." They are used by U.S. government agencies and many other organizations for data presentation. They are provided in this volume for use in matching the data given here with other data sources in which counties may be identified by FIPS codes.

Not all county equivalents are included in this publication.

County equivalents. In Louisiana, the primary divisions of the state are known as parishes rather than counties. In Alaska, the county equivalents are the organized boroughs, together with the census areas that were developed for general statistical purposes by the state of Alaska and the U.S. Census Bureau.

Several recent changes have occurred in Alaska's county equivalents:

The old Skagway-Hoonah-Angoon Census Area has been divided into the Skagway Municipality and the Hoonah-Angoon Census Area.

A new Prince of Wales-Hyder Census Area was created after part of the old Prince of Wales-Outer Ketchikan Census Area was annexed by the Ketchikan Gateway Borough.

The old Wrangell-Petersburg Census Area was divided into the Wrangell City and Borough and the Petersburg Census Area.

Independent cities. Independent cities are not included in any county; data are presented separately in this volume where available.

Maryland
Baltimore (separate from Baltimore County)

Missouri
St. Louis (separate from St. Louis County)

Nevada
Carson City

Virginia
Alexandria
Bedford
Bristol
Buena Vista
Charlottesville
Chesapeake
Colonial Heights
Covington
Danville
Emporia
Fairfax
Falls Church
Franklin
Fredericksburg
Galax
Hampton
Harrisonburg
Hopewell
Lexington
Lynchburg
Manassas
Manassas Park

Martinsville
Newport News
Norfolk
Norton
Petersburg
Poquoson
Portsmouth
Radford
Richmond
Roanoke
Salem
Staunton
Suffolk
Virginia Beach
Waynesboro
Williamsburg
Winchester

DATA SOURCES AND EXPLANATIONS

The population, characteristics, enrollment, and attainment data in Table C have been compiled from the detailed tables of the American Community Survey (2017 1-year) and can be found on the Census Bureau's website in the "American FactFinder" section.

ACS data are subject to sampling error, which can be especially large in small geographic areas or small population groups. Margins of error can be found on the Census Bureau website.

Table C-1.   Population and Poverty Characteristics, by State and Selected Counties, 2017
Source: U.S. Census Bureau. American Community Survey, 1-Year Estimates.

The population data are Census Bureau estimates of the resident population as of July 1, 2017.

Table C-2. Educational Attainment of the Population, by Selected Counties, 2017
Source: U.S. Census Bureau. American Community Survey, 2017. factfinder2.census.gov.

ACS gathers demographic, social, economic, housing and financial information about the nation's people and communities on a continuous basis, providing the detailed characteristics that have previously come from the sample long form of the decennial census.

People are classified according to the highest degree or level of school completed. The order in which degrees were listed on the questionnaire suggested that doctorate degrees were "higher" than professional school degrees, which were "higher" than master's degrees. The question included instructions for people currently enrolled in school to report the level of the previous grade attended or the highest degree received. Respondents who did not report educational attainment or enrollment level were assigned the attainment of a person of the same age, race, Hispanic or Latino origin, occupation, and sex, where possible, who resided in the same area or nearby. Respondents who filled in more than one box were edited to the highest level or degree reported. The question included a response category that allowed respondents to report completing the 12th grade without receiving a high school diploma. It allowed people who received either a high school diploma or the equivalent, such as those who passed the Test of General Educational Development (G.E.D.) and did not attend college, to be reported as "high school graduate(s)."

High school diploma or less. This category includes all persons who have not received a high school diploma, as well as those high school graduates who never attended college.

High school diploma or more. This category includes people whose highest degree was a high school diploma or its equivalent, people who attended college but did not receive a degree, and people who received a college, university, or professional degree. People who reported completing the 12th grade but not receiving a diploma are not high school graduates.

Bachelor's degree or more. This category includes people whose highest degree was a bachelor's, master's, professional, or doctoral degree. Master's degrees include the traditional M.A. and M.S. degrees and field-specific degrees. Some examples of professional degrees include medicine, dentistry, chiropractic, optometry, osteopathic medicine, pharmacy, podiatry, veterinary medicine, law, and theology. Vocational and technical training, such as barber school training; business, trade, technical, and vocational schools; or other training for a specific trade are specifically excluded.

ACS data are subject to sampling error which can be especially large in small geographic areas or small population groups. Margins of error can be found on the Census Bureau website.

Tables C-3. College Enrollment of the Population, by Selected Counties, 2017 and Table C-4. Primary and Secondary School Enrollment, by Sex and Selected Counties, 2017
Source: U.S. Census Bureau. American Community Survey, 2017. https://factfinder. census.gov.

ACS gathers demographic, social, economic, housing and financial information about the nation's people and communities on a continuous basis, providing the detailed characteristics that have previously come from the sample long form of the decennial census.

People were classified as enrolled in school if they reported attending a "regular" public or private school or college during the three months prior to the interview. The question included instructions to "include only nursery school or preschool, kindergarten, elementary school, and schooling which leads to a high school diploma or a college degree" as regular school or college. Respondents who did not answer the enrollment question were assigned the enrollment status and type of school of a person with the same age, sex, and race/Hispanic or Latino origin whose residence was in the same or a nearby area. All persons 3 years old and over are included.

Public and private schools. Public and private schools include people who attended school during the reference period and who indicated they were enrolled by marking one of the questionnaire categories for either "public school, public college" or "private school, private college." Schools primarily supported and controlled by a federal, state, or local government are defined as public (including tribal schools). Those primarily supported and controlled by religious organizations or other private groups are considered private, as are home schools.

ACS data are subject to sampling error which can be especially large in small geographic areas or small population groups. Margins of error can be found on the Census Bureau website.

INDEX

INDEX